Family Law

P. M. Bromley

M.A. (Oxon.), LL.M. (Manchester)

of the Middle Temple, Barrister;
Professor of Law in the University of Manchester

Sixth Edition

London
Butterworths
1981

ENGLAND: Butterworth & Co (Publishers) Ltd
88 Kingsway, London WC2B 6AB

AUSTRALIA: Butterworth Pty Ltd
271–273 Lane Cove Road, North Ryde, NSW 2113
Also at Melbourne, Brisbane, Adelaide and Perth

CANADA: Butterworth & Co (Canada) Ltd
2265 Midland Avenue, Scarborough, Toronto M1P 4S1

NEW ZEALAND: Butterworths of New Zealand Ltd
33–35 Cumberland Place, Wellington

SOUTH AFRICA: Butterworth & Co (South Africa) (Pty) Ltd
152–154 Gale Street, Durban

USA: Butterworth (Publishers) Inc
10 Tower Office Park, Woburn, Boston Mass 01801

©
Butterworth & Co (Publishers) Ltd
1981

ISBN—Casebound 0 406 56010 2
Limp   0 406 56011 0

Typeset by Colset Pte Ltd, Singapore
Reproduced from copy supplied
printed and bound in Great Britain
by Billing and Sons Limited and Kemp Hall Bindery
Guildford, London, Oxford, Worcester

Preface

The major change that has taken place in family law since the fifth edition of this book was published five years ago is the passing of the Domestic Proceedings and Magistrates' Courts Act 1978. This has radically changed the basis of magistrates' jurisdiction in matrimonial matters and has involved considerable rewriting. Instead of having a chapter devoted entirely to magistrates' orders, I now deal with the relevant law under the appropriate subject headings: maintenance of spouses, personal protection, occupation of the matrimonial home, and custody and maintenance of children. Other changes (less extensive but equally significant) have been brought about by the Domestic Violence and Matrimonial Proceedings Act 1976 and the Housing Act 1980. Consolidating statutes have also involved changes of detail but not of substance: in particular I should mention the Fatal Accidents Act 1976, the Rent Act 1977, the Child Care Act 1980 and the Foster Children Act 1980. For the sake of completeness I have also inserted references to another consolidating measure, the Adoption Act 1976, which cannot come into force until the remaining provisions of the Children Act 1975, which it re-enacts, are themselves brought into effect.

Recent judicial decisions have also led to revision. I feel obliged to draw attention to one matter which has caused me some difficulty: the apparently increasing reluctance of the Court of Appeal to follow its own previous decisions in some branches of family law. A startling example of this may be seen in cases relating to the change of a child's surname. Another—and wider reaching—example is the shift away from the "obvious and gross" test of conduct as affecting financial relief laid down in *Wachtel* v. *Wachtel*. This not only creates problems for the textbook writer but puts practitioners in an extremely difficult position when advising clients.

Changes in social behaviour can be seen in the increasing number of couples living together outside marriage. This has led me to add a new chapter on Extra-Marital Cohabitation—something which, I think, would have occurred to no-one to include in a text book on this subject twenty-five years ago.

It once more gives me great pleasure to express my indebtedness to my friend Mr. F.R. Davies, Senior Lecturer in Law at Brunel University, who has given me great help in preparing the sections dealing with tax. In addition I am extremely grateful to my friends and colleagues, Mr. Martin Davey, Mrs. Brenda Hoggett, and in particular Mrs. Pamela Garlick, all of whom have read at least part of the proofs. They have saved me from many errors:

for those remaining I of course am alone responsible. Finally it is a pleasure to mention all those involved with the publication at Butterworths who have once more shown me their tolerance and unfailing kindness.

I have sought to state the law as it stands on 1st April 1981.

P.M.B.
April 1981

Contents

Chapter 9. Parental Powers and Duties

Chapter 10. Adoption

Chapter 11. Guardianship, Custodianship and Children in the Care of Local Authorities

Part III. Property and Financial Provision

Table of statutes

References in this Table to "Statutes" are to Halsbury's Statutes of England (Third Edition) showing the volume and page at which the annotated text of the Act will be found.

Table of statutes

List of cases

List of cases

Part I

Husband and Wife

(1) MARRIAGE

SUMMARY OF CONTENTS

Chapter 1

Introduction

A. THE SCOPE OF FAMILY LAW

The word "family" is one which it is difficult, if not impossible, to define precisely. In one sense it means all blood relations who are descended from a common ancestor; in another it means all the members of a household, including husband and wife, children, servants and even lodgers. But for the present purpose both these definitions are far too wide. The fact that two persons can claim descent from a common ancestor does not *per se* affect their legal relations at all; it is relevant for only one purpose, that of intestate succession, and even here the remotest relations who can claim are the intestate's grandparents and their issue.[1] Similarly, the legal relationship between the head of a household and his servants and lodgers is essentially contractual and as such lies outside the scope of this book.

For our purpose we may regard the family as a basic social unit which consists normally of a husband and wife and their children. It is not necessary that all of these should be members of the family at the same time. A husband and wife can be considered as constituting a family before the birth of their first child or after all their children have left home to marry and establish families of their own, and some spouses will remain childless throughout their lives. Conversely, some families will consist of a child or children living with only one parent, for example when the other has died or where an unmarried woman is living with her illegitimate children. We must therefore consider the legal effects of two relationships: that of husband and wife and that of parent and child. Further, we must examine three other concepts: adoption, by which a child ceases legally to be a member of one family and becomes a member of another, and guardianship and custodianship, by which one person is placed *in loco parentis* to another, but which do not involve the latter's ceasing to be legally a member of his own family. Many rights and duties which flow from these relationships are personal and not proprietary, but they may affect rights in property as well. It must also be remembered that a number of people cohabit without being married, either from choice or because one or both of them are already married. Although most of the legal consequences of marriage do not attach to such relationships, in some respects the parties' legal position has recently been brought much nearer to that of married couples. Consequently we must examine this too.

---

[1] See *post*, p. 620.

For convenience, therefore, the subject will be broken up into the following four main parts:

Part I. *Husband and Wife.* Here we must consider:

    (1)   The contracting and annulment of marriage and the legal effects of marriage; and

    (2)   The legal consequences of the breakdown of marriage.

Part II. *Parent and Child.* Here we must consider the legal rights and duties flowing from the relationship of parent and child (both legitimate and illegitimate), adoption, guardianship and custodianship.

Part III. *Property and Financial Provision.* Here we must consider those rights in property which are created and affected by membership of the same family, together with the duty to support owed by members of the family to one another.

Part IV. *Cohabitation outside Marriage.* Here we must consider the ways in which cohabitation affects the parties' legal relationship.

Before discussing these problems, however, it will be convenient to consider some other matters, knowledge of which is indispensable to the understanding of much of family law: the courts administering family law, and the concepts of residence and domicile.

B. THE COURTS ADMINISTERING FAMILY LAW

Sometimes a question of family law arises in a case of contract or tort or in a criminal prosecution. For example, it may be necessary to determine whether a woman can claim damages in respect of her husband's death or whether the accused's spouse is a competent or compellable witness. Each of these cases will, of course, be tried in the ordinary civil or criminal courts and no special problem arises. What we are concerned with here are the courts which hear and determine causes raising issues solely of family law, for example the annulment or dissolution of marriage, the custody of children, and financial provision. As one would expect, the High Court has jurisdiction in almost all these matters,[1] but a considerable concurrent jurisdiction has now been given to county courts and magistrates' courts.

The High Court.—The greater part of the jurisdiction of the High Court is derived historically from the ecclesiastical courts. Although they had no power to dissolve a valid marriage, they had exclusive jurisdiction to grant decrees of nullity of marriage, divorce *a mensa et thoro* (equivalent to the modern judicial separation), and restitution of conjugal rights. Obviously this could not long survive the nineteenth century attitude to religious toleration. The Matrimonial Causes Act of 1857 transferred the ecclesiastical jurisdiction in matrimonial causes to a new statutory Divorce Court, which was also empowered to grant divorce by judicial process. In 1875 this jurisdiction was in turn transferred to the High Court and assigned to the Probate,

---

[1] The most noticeable exception is that it has no power to make an affiliation order by which the mother of an illegitimate child can obtain maintenance for the child from the father.

Divorce and Admiralty Division.[1] In addition to the power to make orders relating to financial relief and the custody and education of children by way of ancillary relief in other matrimonial causes, this Division was later given jurisdiction to order financial provision if either spouse was guilty of wilful neglect to provide reasonable maintenance for the other or for the children of the family.

The second principal source of the jurisdiction of the High Court in family matters derives from the Court of Chancery. This court, exercising the prerogative power of the Crown as *parens patriae*, had a general supervisory jurisdiction over minors and, in particular, could make orders with respect to their custody and education, could appoint guardians for them and, by making them wards of court, could exercise a continuing control and supervision of them. This jurisdiction was vested in the Chancery Division when the High Court was created in 1875.[2] In view of this jurisdiction it was natural to add to it the power to make adoption orders when this became possible in 1926.

The Family Division.—The fact that two divisions of the High Court possessed the power to make orders with respect to children was really an historical anomaly. It became a positive embarrassment when the two jurisdictions came into conflict as they could, for example, if an order was sought in divorce proceedings with respect to a child who was already a ward of court. The position was made even more complicated by the fact that custody of a minor could also be claimed in the Queen's Bench Division by habeas corpus. The same confusion is seen if one looks at appeals from magistrates' courts. In proceedings under the Guardianship of Minors Act or the Adoption Act, they went to the Chancery Division; in affiliation proceedings, to the Queen's Bench Division; and in proceedings under the Matrimonial Proceedings (Magistrates' Courts) Act, to the Probate, Divorce and Admiralty Division.

It is obviously desirable to concentrate in one Division jurisdiction to deal with all matters likely to arise when a marriage breaks down. With this object in view, and as a first step perhaps to establishing a new court which could deal with all aspects of family law, section 1 of the Administration of Justice Act 1970 renamed the Probate, Divorce and Admiralty Division as the Family Division of the High Court. All the matters mentioned above, both at first instance and appellate, have been transferred to the Family Division together with a number of other aspects of family law. The complete list of business assigned to the Division will be found in Appendix A, *post*.[3]

County Courts.—The first jurisdiction to deal with family matters vested in county courts was in relation to children, and they were given power to make orders under the Guardianship of Infants Acts in 1886 and to make adoption orders in 1926. Further powers followed, mainly to make orders

---

[1] Supreme Court of Judicature Act 1873, s. 34.

[2] *Ibid.*

[3] Of the other matters formally assigned to the Probate, Divorce and Admiralty Division probate business (other than non-contentious and common form business) is now assigned to the Chancery Division and admiralty and prize cases are assigned to the Queen's Bench Division: Administration of Justice Act 1970, s. 1 (3), (4).

Chap. 1. *Introduction*

with respect to property.[1] But the most important extension of county courts'
jurisdiction was conferred by the Matrimonial Causes Act of 1967. The
enormous increase in the number of divorce petitions during and immediately after the Second World War made it impossible for the High Court
judges in London and on assize to get through the cases themselves. Consequently Divorce Commissioners (who were mainly, but not exclusively,
county court judges) were appointed to try matrimonial causes in London
and certain provincial towns. When it is realised that about two-thirds of
all cases were heard by commissioners and over 90% of all cases were
undefended, it will be appreciated that an enormous number of undefended
petitions were being tried by county court judges. But as they were technically
sitting as a part of the High Court, the proceedings had none of the
advantages of county court proceedings: for example, solicitors could not
settle pleadings and had no right of audience. This anomaly was removed by
the Matrimonial Causes Act 1967, which empowers the Lord Chancellor to
designate any county court as a divorce county court to hear any *undefended*
matrimonial cause.[2] The following are matrimonial causes for this purpose:[3]

> petitions for divorce, nullity, judicial separation and jactitation of
> marriage;
> applications for leave to present a petition for divorce within the first three
> years of the marriage;
> applications for maintenance under section 27 of the Matrimonial Causes
> Act 1973;
> applications to alter maintenance agreements during the lives of both
> parties.

All matrimonial causes must now be commenced in a divorce country
court or in the Divorce Registry in London (which is a county court for this
purpose). If the respondent or any other party enters a defence, the case
must be transferred to the High Court; a county court *may* also order an
undefended case to be transferred if this appears desirable having regard to
all the circumstances including the difficulty or importance of the case or any
issue arising in it. If a defended case subsequently becomes undefended, it
may be transferred back to a county court.[4]

All undefended cases which have not been transferred to the High Court
are now tried in divorce county courts specially designated as courts of trial.[5]

A county court seised of a matrimonial cause may also make any ancillary
order, *i.e.* those orders mentioned in Appendix D, *post*.[6] The fact that an
application for ancillary relief is contested does not make the case a defended
one, but in certain circumstances a county court may order such an application

---

[1] *E.g.*, under s. 17 of the Married Women's Property Act 1882 (*post*, p. 422) and the Matrimonial Homes Act 1967.

[2] Section 1 (1).

[3] Sections 1 (1), 2 and 10 (1); Supreme Court of Judicature (Consolidation) Act 1925, s. 225;
Matrimonial Causes Act 1973, Sched. 2, paras. 1 and 6.

[4] Sections 1 (3), (4) and 4; Matrimonial Causes Rules 1977, rr. 27 and 32.

[5] Section 1 (1).

[6] Section 2. This court may also make an order avoiding or restraining a transaction intended
to defeat a claim for financial relief (*post*, pp. 568-569).

or any application for maintenance to be transferred to the High Court.[1]

Magistrates' Courts.—The oldest jurisdiction possessed by magistrates in the field of family law relates to affiliation orders, by which maintenance for illegitimate children can be obtained from the father. Historically the purpose of such orders was to relieve the poor law authority of the burden of maintaining the child themselves, and this was merely one example of the magistrates' powers to enforce this branch of the law.

Their second head of jurisdiction derives from the administration of the criminal law. Section 4 of the Matrimonial Causes Act of 1878 gave a criminal court, before which a married man had been convicted of an aggravated assault upon his wife, power to make an order that she should no longer be bound to cohabit with him if it felt that her future safety was in peril. The court could also order a husband to pay maintenance to a wife in whose favour such a separation order was made and vest in her the legal custody of any children of the marriage under the age of ten years. In 1886 courts of summary jurisdiction were given a further power to make a maintenance order in favour of a woman whose husband had deserted her and was wilfully refusing or neglecting to maintain her.[2]

Magistrates' domestic jurisdiction was extensively increased in 1895 when they were given much wider powers to make orders on the application of married women. During the next half century a series of Acts, which were collectively known as the Summary Jurisdiction (Separation and Maintenance) Acts 1895 to 1949,[3] gradually extended the grounds on which the wife might apply for an order, enabled the courts to order a married man to pay maintenance in respect of his children, and finally gave a husband a limited power to apply for matrimonial relief himself. The law was again completely overhauled by the Matrimonial Proceedings (Magistrates' Courts) Act of 1960. In particular this Act considerably increased magistrates' powers to make orders with respect to the custody and maintenance of children and also gave them a limited power to compel a wife to contribute towards her husband's maintenance.

The Domestic Proceedings and Magistrates' Courts Act 1978.—The main purpose of earlier Acts was to offer to women of the working and lower middle classes, who could not afford to take proceedings in the High Court, an opportunity to obtain matrimonial orders cheaply and speedily. These advantages, together with the comparative informality and privacy of the proceedings, eventually brought to the courts many women in higher income groups.[4] Furthermore, magistrates can call upon the services of their probation officers to try to bring about a reconciliation, and their attempts are much more likely to be successful than they would be if the parties had

---

[1] Matrimonial Causes Rules 1977, rr. 80, 81, 97 and 99.

[2] Married Woman (Maintenance in Case of Desertion) Act 1886.

[3] These were: the Summary Jurisdiction (Married Women) Act 1895; the Licensing Act 1902, s. 5; the Married Women (Maintenance) Act 1920; the Summary Jurisdiction (Separation and Maintenance) Act 1925; and the Married Women (Maintenance) Act 1949.

[4] This is reflected in the passing of the Maintenance Orders Act 1968 which removed the financial limit formerly set on magistrates' orders and thus enabled them to make appropriate orders for women whose husbands were relatively well off.

reached the divorce court.[1] Nevertheless some stringent criticisms were made
of the operation of the courts and the law they administered.[2] Bearing in
mind that approximately half the complainants in magistrates' courts subsequently obtain a divorce, the emphasis on matrimonial offences and the need
to establish at least one of eight different grounds to obtain a magistrates'
order fitted ill with the new divorce law introduced in 1971. However gross
the husband's conduct had been and whatever the wife's needs were, she was
automatically debarred from obtaining relief for herself if she had committed
a single act of adultery unless the husband had connived at it, condoned it
or conduced to it by his misconduct.[3] This also contrasted oddly with
the practice of the divorce court of ignoring the parties' conduct when
determining the question of financial relief unless it has been "obvious and
gross". These facts, coupled with the relative ease with which it became
possible to obtain a divorce after 1970, doubtless account largely for the
dramatic decline in the number of applications to magistrates' courts in the
last decade.[4]

The Law Commission set up a working party to consider the whole
question of matrimonial proceedings in magistrates' courts, particularly in
the light of the changed divorce law. Their provisional conclusions were
published in 1973,[5] and the Commission's final report followed three years
later.[6] They concluded that "the function of magistrates' courts today was to
provide first aid in a marital casualty clearing station" and set out the
objectives of their jurisdiction as being:[7]

"(a) to deal with family relations during a period of breakdown, which is not
      necessarily permanent or irretrievable—
        (i) by relieving the financial need which such a breakdown can bring to the
             parties,
       (ii) by giving such protection to one or other of the parties as may be
             necessary,
      (iii) by providing for the welfare and support of the children; and
 (b) to preserve the marriage in existence, where possible."

They regarded three principles as fundamental:[8]

"First, that both parties to a marriage should have an absolute obligation to
maintain their dependent children, which should survive irrespective of the way in
which they have behaved towards each other; secondly, that the obligation of each
spouse to maintain the other should be fully reciprocal; and thirdly, that it should

---

[1] See now the Domestic Proceedings and Magistrates' Courts Act 1978, s. 26.
[2] See particularly McGregor, Blom-Cooper and Gibson, *Separated Spouses*, and the Report
of the Committee on One-parent Families (the Finer Report), 1974, Cmnd. 5629.
[3] For details of the law formerly administered in magistrates' courts, see the 5th Ed. of this
book, c. 7.
[4] In 1970 27,905 women applied for orders. The number then declined every year: in 1978
there were 6,851 applicants.
[5] Law Commission's Working Paper No. 53.
[6] Law Com. No. 77 (Report on Matrimonial Proceedings in Magistrates' Courts).
[7] *Ibid.*, paras. 1.11-1.13 and 2.4.
[8] *Ibid.*, paras. 2.5 and 2.14.

be left to the court to determine in particular cases whether an order should be made and for how much in the light of whatever guidelines might be embodied in the law.''

They also concluded that the magistrates' power to order that the complainant should no longer be bound to cohabit with the defendant was of no practical value. It offered no protection to the wife of a violent husband, and they recommended that it should be replaced by a power to make an order forbidding one spouse to use violence against the other and, if necessary, excluding him from the matrimonial home.[1]

These recommendations form the basis of the provisions of the Domestic Proceedings and Magistrates' Courts Act 1978 which came fully into force on 1st February 1981. It remains to be seen what effect the new law will have on the number of applications made to magistrates' courts and whether it will meet the criticisms levelled against the old law.

Other Proceedings in Relation to Children.—Magistrates' jurisdiction in relation to children was further increased in 1925 and 1926, when they were given power to make orders under the Guardianship of Infants Acts and adoption orders respectively.

Domestic Proceedings.—Since 1937 there have been special statutory provisions relating to the constitution and procedure of magistrates' courts when they are hearing "domestic proceedings". These include proceedings under the Domestic Proceedings and Magistrates' Courts Act, the Guardianship of Minors Acts, the Affiliation Proceedings Act, and for adoption orders and custodianship orders under the Children Act 1975.[2] The court must consist of not more than three magistrates (including, so far as is practicable, both a man and a woman) drawn from a special panel.[3] No one may be present in the court except the officers of the court, the parties, their solicitors and counsel, witnesses, other persons directly concerned in the case (such as probation officers), representatives of the press, and any other person whom the court may in its discretion permit to be present.[4] The powers of newspapers to report domestic proceedings are also considerably curtailed.[5]

Proposals for Reform.—This fragmentation of jurisdiction produces some undesirable results. It is not uncommon for a wife to take proceedings in a magistrates' court and then to petition for divorce in a county court, so that two sets of orders in different courts may be in force with respect to the same family. Consequently pressure has been building up for the past few years for the establishment of a unified Family Court (or perhaps, more

---

[1] *Ibid.*, paras. 3.1 *et seq.*

[2] Summary Procedure (Domestic Proceedings) Act 1937. See now the Magistrates' Courts Act 1980, ss. 65-74. For the full definition of "domestic proceedings", see *ibid.*, s. 65. Proceedings for the enforcement of orders and for the variation of periodical payments do not generally come within the definition unless the court otherwise orders.

[3] Magistrates' Courts Act 1980, ss. 66-68. Stipendiary magistrates may sit alone.

[4] *Ibid.*, s. 69.

[5] See *ibid.*, s. 71.

precisely, a unified set of family courts) in which High Court judges, county court judges and lay magistrates would all play a part. This could apply a uniform code of family law and would eliminate the confusion and anomalies caused by the present overlapping and competing jurisdictions. Furthermore, it would have its own welfare staff, which would considerably improve the support given to the parties and the assistance received by the court. Detailed proposals lie outside the scope of this book, but at least the formation of the Family Division of the High Court can be seen as the first step in this direction.[1]

C. RESIDENCE AND DOMICILE

Residence.—Residence is relevant in family law for a number of reasons. For example, persons wishing to marry must normally have banns published in the parish in which each of them resides or give notice to the superintendent registrar of the registration district in which at least one of them resides. Again, a person who is not domiciled in this country may petition for divorce here after one year's habitual residence.

The meaning of the concept was discussed by the Court of Appeal in *Fox* v. *Stirk*.[2] LORD DENNING, M.R., accepted the definition given in the Oxford English Dictionary

"to dwell permanently or for a considerable time, to have one's settled usual abode, to live in or at a particular place".

WIDGERY, L.J., again stressing the need for a degree of permanence, referred to

"the place where a man is based or where he continues to live, the place where he sleeps and shelters and has his home".[3]

It will thus be seen that two elements must be present: physical presence and an intention to remain in the same place for a sufficiently long period to make that presence more than fleeting or transitory. The contrast between the permanent resident and the temporary visitor is an easy one to see; what may be difficult on the facts of a particular case is to decide whether the length of time a person proposes to remain is long enough to give his stay the quality of residence. Obviously there need not be an intention to remain permanently or even indefinitely; perhaps the best test is to ask oneself whether the person can be regarded as being based at the place in question rather than somewhere else.

Just as residence cannot be acquired without a degree of permanence, it will not be lost by a temporary absence.[4] Hence spouses who are normally resident in their matrimonial home will continue to reside there whilst they

---

[1] The most comprehensive proposals yet published are those made in the Report of the Committee on One-parent Families (the Finer Report), Cmnd. 5629, Part 4, Sections 13 and 14, to which attention is particularly drawn. See also Turner, 4 Fam. Law 39; Cretney, *Principles of Family Law*, 3rd Ed., c. 27.

[2] [1970] 2 Q.B. 463; [1970] 3 All E.R. 7, C.A. See also McClean, *The Meaning of Residence*, 11 I.C.L.Q. 1153.

[3] At pp. 477 and 13, respectively.

[4] *Fox* v. *Stirk*, (*supra*), at pp. 475, 12 and 477, 13, respectively.

are physically absent on, say, a month's holiday. Similarly, a person who goes abroad for business reasons but retains a house in this country with the intention of returning whenever he can may still be regarded as resident here.[1] As continuous physical presence is unnecessary, one can have two or more places of residence and can reside in both or all of them or, alternatively, in each of them at different times. In *Fox* v. *Stirk* it was held that students of the University of Bristol who lived in a hall of residence during term time were resident there for the purpose of the Representation of the People Act and thus entitled to be placed on the electoral register. It cannot be doubted that they were also resident at their parents' homes if that was where they spent their vacations.[2]

Habitual Residence.—A concept that is becoming increasingly common as a connecting factor in cases with a foreign element is that of habitual residence. This is due partly to the highly artificial rules that have grown up round the concept of domicile (the traditional connecting factor in English law) and partly to statutory provisions giving effect to international conventions. Unfortunately, there is no authoritative definition of the term. The word "habitual" implies a settled practice[3] and indicates a quality of residence rather than a period of residence,[4] but the period for which a person intends to stay in a country is clearly one of the facts to take into account in deciding whether this residence is habitual. It "must be more than transient or casual; once established, however, it is not necessarily broken by a temporary absence".[5] A month's holiday in a country cannot amount to habitual residence; conversely, a person working in a country where he expects to stay for ten years will be habitually resident there. What is more difficult to predict is whether a person expecting to work there for only, say, six months will be held to be habitually resident in the country whilst he is actually there. One must obviously take into account the duration and continuity of the residence, the intention of the person involved, the residence of the rest of his family, and "other facts of a personal or professional nature which point to durable ties between a person and his residence".[6] The phrase "durable ties" probably sums up the essence of this elusive concept better than anything else.

---

[1] *Sinclair* v. *Sinclair*, [1968] P. 189; [1967] 3 All E.R. 882, C.A. See also *Stransky* v. *Stransky*, [1954] P. 428; [1954] 2 All E.R. 536; *Lewis* v. *Lewis*, [1956] 1 All E.R. 375.

[2] Similarly a person may acquire a residence in this country by residing in a hotel or in a series of hotels or boarding houses: *Re Brauch*, [1978] Ch. 316; [1978] 1 All E.R. 1004, C.A. See also *Levene* v. *I.R.C.*, [1928] A.C. 217, at pp. 223, 232, H.L.; *Morgan* v. *Murch*, [1970] 2 All E.R. 100, 104, C.A.; and *cf. R.* v. *Barnet London Borough Council, ex parte Shah*, [1980] 3 All E.R. 679 (meaning of "ordinary residence").

[3] *Oundjian* v. *Oundjian* (1979), 124 Sol. Jo. 63.

[4] *Cruse* v. *Chittum* [1974] 2 All E.R. 940, 942-943. In this case LANE, J., was of the opinion that habitual residence is equivalent to the residence required for the acquisition of domicile without the necessary *animus*. Whilst a person may clearly be habitually resident in a country without intending to stay there permanently or indefinitely, this dictum is, with respect, unhelpful. If a person has the necessary *animus*, he may acquire a domicile as soon as he sets foot in the country in question: something more than this, however, is necessary before he can be said to be habitually resident.

[5] Law Com. No. 48 (Report on Jurisdiction in Matrimonial Causes), para. 42. In *Oundjian* v. *Oundjian*, (*supra*), the wife was held to have been habitually resident in this country for a year even though she had been physically absent for 149 out of the 365 days.

[6] Law Commission, *loc. cit.* See further Hall, *Habitual Residence Judicially Explained*, 24 I.C.L.Q. 1.

Domicile.—The concept of domicile and the difficulties which it may give rise to are primarily subjects of Private International Law and cannot be dealt with here in any detail. But domicile is of importance for two reasons in family law: first, many problems in family law (such as capacity to marry) are intimately bound up with the law of a man's domicile (or *lex domicilii*) and cannot be resolved without reference to it, and secondly, the domicile of a child under the age of 16 usually depends on that of a parent.

Originally, domicile meant one's personal home. Consequently, it is completely unconnected with nationality. Furthermore, the classical view is that a person can be domiciled only in a place which has a separate legal system; thus a man cannot be domiciled in the United Kingdom but must be domiciled in, say, England or Scotland (which have different legal systems), and he may be domiciled there even though he is not a Citizen of the United Kingdom and Colonies. The reason for this is that many rights and capacities are governed by the *lex domicilii* and hence it is essential that domicile itself be defined by reference to a legal system. In a number of federal countries, however, some legal rules are governed by federal law and some by state or provincial law. In Australia, for example, each state has for the most part its own system of civil law but some matters, like divorce, are the subject of federal law. For such purposes a person can have a domicile in Australia, although for other purposes he will be domiciled in a particular state (or even in some country outside Australia).[1]

This situation apart, however, two principles were early established, the need for which is self-evident. First, every person must have a domicile, and secondly, no person may have more than one domicile at any time. It is largely the necessity of satisfying these two principles that has led to the development of the artificial rules relating to domicile that have been the subject of much criticism.

Dependent Domicile of Children.—Obviously a young child cannot independently acquire a domicile because he will be unable to form the necessary intent. To satisfy the condition that everyone must have a domicile, the principle was established at common law that the domicile of a legitimate child followed his father's and that of an illegitimate child followed his mother's.[2] This domicile of dependence lasted throughout the child's minority. Consequently, if a husband deserted his wife, leaving their minor children with her in England, and emigrated to Victoria, the children would all acquire a domicile there.

Anomalies like this have been reduced by the provisions of the Domicile and Matrimonial Proceedings Act 1973. In the first place, a person is now capable of acquiring an independent domicile when he attains the age of 16 or

---

[1] *E.g.*, a domiciled Englishman arriving in Australia with the intention of settling in the Commonwealth but uncertain in which state he will live, will acquire an Australian domicile for the purpose of divorce but for the purpose of succession will retain his English domicile until he acquires a domicile in a particular state.

[2] *Henderson* v. *Henderson*, [1967] P. 77; [1965] 1 All E.R. 179.

marries under that age.[1] Consequently, in the illustration given above, any child over the age of 16 would now retain his English domicile.

The second change introduced by the Act relates to the dependent domicile of a *legitimate* child whose parents are both alive but are living apart. He will continue to take his father's domicile unless he has a home with his mother and no home with his father, when he will now take his mother's domicile. Once he has acquired his mother's domicile by virtue of this provision, his domicile will continue to be the same as hers provided that he has not since had a home with his father; he will also continue to possess his mother's last domicile after her death if he has not subsequently had a home with his father.[2] Presumably the word "home" refers to the place where the child *normally* resides, so that if he spends 11 months in the year with his mother and one month with his father, this will not be sufficient to give him a home with his father for this purpose. If, however, the time he spends with each is long enough to give him a home with both, the section will not apply and he will continue to take his father's domicile at common law.

The mother's death does not affect her legitimate child's domicile, which will continue to be the same as the father's except in the case noted in the last paragraph. If the father dies, it was held in *Potinger* v. *Wightman*[3] that the child's domicile will *prima facie* change with that of his mother. To this rule GRANT, M.R., himself predicated the possible exception that a mother cannot change her children's domicile fraudulently—in other words if her object in so doing is to obtain an advantage for herself, as it might be if the law of succession were more favourable to her in the country in which she acquires her new domicile of choice. But this rule (even with the exception grafted on it) is not invariable, as is shown by *Re Beaumont*.[4] In this case a widow, whose domicile (like that of her deceased husband) was Scottish, remarried and later moved to London with her second husband, thereby acquiring a dependent domicile in England. She left her minor daughter in Scotland with an aunt who brought her up. It was held that this girl never lost her Scottish domicile. STIRLING, J., held that a widowed mother has the *power* to change her minor children's domicile which the mother had never exercised in this case, as was evidenced by her leaving her daughter in Scotland. This power, he said, must be exercised for the child's welfare, and on this assumption the apparent exception in *Potinger* v. *Wightman* is completely explained.

The domicile of an *illegitimate* child is unaffected by any statutory provision and continues to follow the mother's. An adopted child will acquire by adoption the domicile of his adopter (or his adoptive father in the case of a joint adoption).[5]

After the death of both parents of a legitimate child, both adoptive

---

[1] Section 3. Although a person domiciled in this country cannot marry under the age of 16, one who is lawfully married by his *lex domicilii* under that age can now acquire a separate domicile by English law. Anyone aged between 16 and 18 on 1st January 1974 (when the Act came into operation) could acquire an independent domicile from that date. As the Act is not retrospective, the common law rules will still apply if it is necessary to determine a minor's domicile before 1974.

[2] Section 4. See Palmer, *Domicile of an Infant*, 4 Fam. Law 35.

[3] (1817), 3 Mer. 67.

[4] [1893] 3 Ch. 490.

[5] See *post*, p. 357.

parents, or the mother of an illegitimate child, it is doubtful whether the child's domicile can be changed at all until he acquires the capacity to change it himself.[1]

Domicile of Origin.—In *Henderson* v. *Henderson*[2] SIMON, P., defined a person's domicile of origin as his domicile of dependence at birth. It follows that, generally speaking, a legitimate child's domicile of origin will be that of his father at the time of his birth and an illegitimate child's will be that of his mother.[3] It is submitted that one incidental effect of the Domicile and Matrimonial Proceedings Act 1973 has been to alter this rule in the case of a legitimate child whose parents are separated at the time of his birth. On the assumption that he will have his home with his mother, he will acquire her domicile by virtue of the Act, and it seems absurd to suggest that he momentarily takes his father's domicile as his domicile of origin: this must now be the domicile that his mother has.[4]

If a woman changes her domicile between the death of her husband and the birth of a posthumous child, it is not settled whether the child's domicile of origin is the last domicile of his father or that of his mother at the time of his birth, but most writers assume the latter to be correct.[5]

Domicile of origin is obviously an artificial concept. Its importance lies in the fact that it automatically revives if a person has no other domicile. He must have a domicile somewhere and, if necessary, the domicile of origin is invoked to fill what would otherwise be a vacuum. Suppose, for example, that A has a domicile of origin in Italy and then acquires a domicile of choice in France. He later leaves France with no intention of returning there (thus losing his domicile of choice in that country) and comes to Great Britain but is uncertain whether to settle in England or Scotland. Until he acquires a new domicile of choice in one country or the other, his Italian domicile of origin revives. Again, suppose that B has a domicile of origin in Italy and that his parents later acquire a domicile in South Australia, thus giving him a domicile of dependence there. B is resident in England on his sixteenth birthday: he has no intention of ever living in South Australia (thus losing his domicile there) but proposes to emigrate to New Zealand. He cannot acquire a domicile of choice in that country until he actually takes up residence in it; in the meantime his Italian domicile revives.[6] If A or B has a legitimate child whilst he is here, that child's domicile of origin will then be Italian in each

---

[1] Dicey and Morris, *Conflict of Laws*, 10th Ed., 135-136. Graveson, *Conflict of Laws*, 7th Ed., 210, suggests that a guardian may have power to change it.

[2] [1967] P. 77; [1965] 1 All E.R. 179.

[3] *Udny* v. *Udny* (1869), L.R. 1 Sc. & Div. 441, 457, H.L. It is easy to see that this may give rise to circuity; whether a child is legitimate is a question for his *lex domicilii*, but his domicile may be different according to whether or not he is legitimate: see *post*, pp. 271-272. If an illegitimate child is later legitimated *per subsequens matrimonium*, it is generally assumed, in the absence of authority, that this will not affect his domicile of origin.

[4] *Contra* Cheshire and North, *Private International Law*, 10th Ed., 180.

[5] A foundling is normally presumed to have a domicile of origin in the place where he was found. The Children Act 1975, Sched. 1, para. 3, (prospectively repealed and re-enacted in the Adoption Act 1976, s. 39 (1)) provides that, from the date of an adoption, an adopted child shall be treated as if he had been *born* as the adopters' legitimate child. Although the position is not clear, it is submitted that this should not affect his domicile of origin. *Contra* Dicey and Morris, *op. cit.*, 109.

[6] *Cf. Harrison* v. *Harrison*, [1953] 1 W.L.R. 865.

case: a fact that could conceivably affect his legal capacity in many years' time. It is the artificiality of these technical rules that has led to the movement to get away from domicile as a connecting factor in cases involving a foreign element.

Domicile of Choice.—Anyone over the age of 16 may acquire a domicile of choice.[1] This can only be done *animo et facto*, that is, he must assume residence in the country in question and must have the present intention, formed independently of external pressures, of remaining there permanently. This does not have to be an immutable decision in the sense that, whatever happens in the future, he will not change his mind. But if, when he enters a country, he has the intention of ultimately leaving it on some clearly fore-seen and reasonably anticipated contingency (for example, on retirement), he will lack the intention necessary for the acquisition of a domicile of choice; conversely, if there is only a vague possibility of his doing so or the contingency is so remote that for practical purposes it can be disregarded (for example, his winning a football pool), this will not be inconsistent with such a domicile.[2] Both *animus* and *factum* must be present: a man domiciled and resident in England, who decides to move permanently to Scotland, will not acquire a domicile there until he crosses the Border; conversely, an immigrant who arrives in London, undecided whether to settle in England or Scotland, cannot acquire a domicile in either country until he makes up his mind to stay there.[3]

A domicile of choice is lost by giving up residence in the country and abandoning the intention of residing there permanently. It is not necessary that a person should have the intention of not returning to the country at the moment when he leaves it: it will be sufficient if he leaves first and then decides not to return.[4] What is not clear is whether he must have the intention of never returning or whether it is sufficient that he should not have a definite intention to return. This will be important if he leaves the country uncertain whether he will return or not; if it is necessary to have made a positive decision not to return, he will clearly not lose his domicile of choice; on the other hand, as he lacks a definite intention to return, he would lose it by the latter test. Although there is authority in favour of the latter view,[5] it is submitted that, on principle, he should not lose his domicile of choice unless he has finally abandoned the intention of returning, for "irresolution effects nothing".[6]

---

[1] As may a married person under that age: see *ante*, pp. 10-11. A person suffering from mental disorder will not be able to acquire a domicile of choice if he lacks the power to form the necessary *animus*.

[2] *I.R.C.* v. *Bullock*, [1976] 3 All E.R. 353, C.A.; *Re Fuld*, [1968] P. 675, 684-685; *Buswell* v. *I.R.C.* [1974] 2 All E.R. 520, 526, C.A.; *Re Furse*, [1980] 3 All E.R. 838.

[3] *Cf. Bell* v. *Kennedy* (1868), L.R. 1 Sc. & D. 307, H.L.

[4] *Tee* v. *Tee*, [1973] 3 All E.R. 1105, C.A.

[5] *Re Flynn*, [1968] 1 All E.R. 49, 58; *Qureshi* v. *Qureshi*, [1972] Fam. 173, 191; [1971] 1 All E.R. 325, 328; Dicey and Morris, *op. cit.*, 129.

[6] Cheshire and North, *op. cit.*, 176.

Change of Domicile.—Once it is proved that a person had a particular domicile, this is presumed to continue: in other words, the burden of proving a change of domicile is upon him who asserts it.[1] What is not clear, however, is the standard of proof necessary to rebut this presumption. It has been judicially stated that proof on the balance of probabilities is sufficient,[2] but it is possible that a higher standard is required to displace a domicile of origin in favour of a domicile of choice.[3] Earlier cases suggested that nothing short of proof beyond reasonable doubt would suffice:[4] this has been denied, but "unless the judicial conscience is satisfied by evidence of change, the domicile of origin persists; ... the acquisition of a domicile of choice is a serious matter not to be lightly inferred from slight indications or casual words."[5]

Domicile of Married Women.—At common law a woman automatically acquired her husband's domicile on marriage and retained it throughout her coverture.[6] She was incapable of acquiring a separate domicile even though the spouses separated by agreement[7] or under a decree of judicial separation;[8] similarly, if the husband deserted his wife and acquired a fresh domicile abroad, her domicile still automatically followed his.[9]

Although it is generally desirable that the marriage should be governed by one law and that the spouses should therefore share the same domicile, in a case like the last it was both artificial and unjust to insist that the wife should have thrust upon her a domicile in a country which she had never visited, to which she had no intention of travelling, and with which she had no connection whatsoever. Consequently, section 1 (1) of the Domicile and Matrimonial Proceedings Act 1973 provides that a married woman shall now retain and acquire an independent domicile like any other person of full capacity.[10] Normally, of course, the spouses will have different domiciles only if they have separated: if they are living together, they will still usually have the same domicile because they will share the same residence and the intention of remaining there. There will, however, be some cases where they will have different domiciles even though they are cohabiting, as the following illustrations will show:[11]

---

[1] *Re Fuld, (supra)*, at p. 685; *Re Flynn, (supra)*, at p. 58.

[2] *Per* MEGARRY, J., in *Re Flynn, (supra)*, at p. 58.

[3] See the view of SIMON, P., in *Henderson* v. *Henderson*, [1967] P. 77, 80; [1965] 1 All E.R. 179, 181.

[4] See particularly *Winans* v. *A.-G.*, [1904] A.C. 287, H.L.; *Ramsay* v. *Liverpool Royal Infirmary*, [1930] A.C. 588, H.L.

[5] *Per* SCARMAN, J., in *Re Fuld, (supra)*, at p. 686.

[6] *Harvey* v. *Farnie* (1882), 8 App. Cas. 43, H.L. This would not occur, of course, if the marriage was void; but if it was voidable, the wife retained her husband's domicile until the marriage was annulled: *De Reneville* v. *De Reneville*, [1948] P. 100; [1948] 1 All E.R. 56, C.A.

[7] *Dolphin* v. *Robins* (1859), 7 H.L. Cas. 390, H.L.

[8] *A.-G. for Alberta* v. *Cook*, [1926] A.C. 444, P.C.

[9] *H.* v. *H.*, [1928] P. 206.

[10] See also *Puttick* v. *A.-G.*, [1980] Fam. 1, 16-17; [1979] 3 All E.R. 463, 475-476. The Act came into operation on 1st January 1974. A woman who had her husband's domicile by dependence on that day is to regarded as having retained it (as a domicile of choice if it was not her domicile of origin) until she acquires another: s. 1 (2).

[11] See further Palmer, 123 New L.J. 939, 960; 124 New L.J. 49, 73, 95.

A domiciled Englishwoman marries in England a domiciled Frenchman. She will not be able to acquire his domicile (assuming this is her intention) until she goes to France.

Spouses domiciled in England decide to emigrate to New Zealand. The husband goes first and they agree that the wife will follow in a year's time. He will acquire a domicile in New Zealand when he arrives there but she will retain her English domicile until she joins him.

The spouses have different domiciles of origin. They acquire a joint domicile of choice in a third country but then abandon it without acquiring a fresh domicile of choice. Their different domiciles of origin will revive.

Chapter 2

Marriage

A. THE NATURE OF MARRIAGE

Quite apart from its abstract meaning as the social institution of marriage, "marriage" has two distinct meanings: the ceremony by which a man and woman become husband and wife or the *act of marrying*, and the relationship existing between a husband and his wife or the *state of being married*.[1] This distinction largely corresponds with its dual aspect of contract and status.

Marriage as a Contract.—In English law at least, marriage is an agreement by which a man and woman enter into a certain legal relationship with each other and which creates and imposes mutual rights and duties. Looked at from this point of view, marriage is clearly a contract. It presents similar problems to other contracts—for example, of form and capacity; and like other contracts it may be void or voidable. But it is, of course, quite unlike any commercial contract, and consequently it is *sui generis* in many respects. In particular we may note the following marked dissimilarities.

(1) The law relating to the capacity to marry is quite different from that of any other contract.

(2) A marriage may only be contracted if special formalities are carried out.

(3) The grounds on which a marriage may be void or voidable are for the most part completely different from those on which other contracts may be void or voidable.

(4) Unlike other voidable contracts, a voidable marriage cannot be declared void *ab initio* by repudiation by one of the parties but may be set aside only by a decree of nullity pronounced by a court of competent jurisdiction.

(5) A contract of marriage cannot be discharged by agreement, frustration or breach. Apart from death, it can be terminated only by a formal legal act, usually a decree of dissolution (or divorce) pronounced by a court of competent jurisdiction.

Marriage as creating Status.—This second aspect of marriage is much more important than its first. It creates a status, that is, "the condition of

---

[1] Graveson, *Status in the Common Law*, 80-81. Compare the use of the word "marriage" in the following two sentences: "The marriage took place yesterday between X and Y" and "Their marriage has been dissolved".

belonging to a particular class of persons [*i.e.*, married persons] to whom the law assigns certain peculiar legal capacities or incapacities.''[1]

In the first place, whereas the parties to a commercial agreement may make such terms as they think fit (provided that they do not offend against rules of public policy or statutory prohibition), the spouses' mutual rights and duties are very largely fixed by law and not by agreement. Some of these may be varied by consent; for example, the spouses may release each other from the duty to cohabit. But many may not be altered; thus the wife may not contract out of her power to apply to the court for financial provision in the event of divorce.

Secondly, unlike a commercial contract, which cannot affect the legal position of anyone who is not a party to it, marriage may also affect the rights and duties of third persons. Thus a husband has an action against anyone who by committing a tort against the wife thereby deprives him of her consortium, and it is not open to the tortfeasor to argue that the marriage is *res inter alios acta*.

Definition of Marriage.—The classic definition of marriage in English law is that of LORD PENZANCE in *Hyde* v. *Hyde*:[2]

"I conceive that marriage, as understood in Christendom, may ... be defined as the voluntary union for life of one man and one woman to the exclusion of all others."

It will be seen that this definition involves four conditions.

First, the marriage must be *voluntary*. Thus, as we shall see,[3] it can be annulled if there was no true consent on the part of one of the parties.

Secondly, it must be *for life*. If by marriage "as understood in Christendom" LORD PENZANCE was referring to the view traditionally taken in Western Europe by the Roman Catholic Church and some other denominations, his statement is of course unexceptionable. But it does not mean that by English law marriage is indissoluble: divorce by judicial process had been possible in England for over eight years when *Hyde* v. *Hyde* was decided. The gloss put on the dictum by the Court of Appeal in *Nachimson* v. *Nachimson*[4] —that it must be the parties' intention when they enter into the marriage that it should last for life—is unsatisfactory. If, say, two people enter into a marriage for the sole purpose of enabling a child to be born legitimate, intending never to live together but to obtain a divorce by consent at the earliest opportunity, it cannot be doubted that their union is a marriage by English law. The only interpretation that can be put on LORD PENZANCE'S statement is that the marriage must last for life unless it is previously determined by a decree or some other act of dissolution.[5] If one may draw an analogy (perhaps not very happy) from the law of real property, marriage

---

[1] Allen, *Status and Capacity*, 46 L.Q.R. 277, 288. In this article Sir Carleton Allen critically discusses a number of other definitions of status and analyses this elusive legal concept. See also Graveson, *op. cit.*

[2] (1866), L.R. 1 P. & D. 130, 133. See further *post*, p. 54.

[3] *Post*, pp. 87 *et seq.*

[4] [1930] P. 217, C.A.

[5] *Nachimson* v. *Nachimson*, (supra), at pp. 225, 227 (*per* LORD HANWORTH, M.R.), 235 (*per* LAWRENCE, L.J.), 243-244 (*per* ROMER, L.J.).

must resemble a determinable life interest rather than a term of years absolute.

Thirdly, the union must be *heterosexual*.

Fourthly, it must be *monogamous*. Neither spouse may contract another marriage so long as the original union subsists.

B. AGREEMENTS TO MARRY

A marriage is frequently, although by no means invariably, preceded by an agreement to marry or "engagement". At common law such agreements amounted to contracts provided that there was an intention to enter into legal relations (as there probably would not be in the case of an "unofficial engagement"). Because of their highly personal and non-commercial nature they possessed certain peculiar characteristics, but as a general rule they were governed by the general principles of the law of contract. Consequently if either party withdrew from the engagement without lawful justification, the other could sue for breach of contract. Such actions became rare after the Second World War and were seldom, if ever, brought by men at all—partly no doubt because of the difficulty of proving damage, but probably largely as the result of a change in social views.[1]

The fact that actions for breach of promise of marriage were still occasionally brought raised the question of their utility. If either party to an engagement was convinced that he (or she) ought not to marry the other, it was highly doubtful whether public policy was served by letting the threat of an action push him into a potentially unstable marriage or by penalising him in damages if he resiled. The Law Commission therefore recommended the abolition of these actions[2] and this recommendation was implemented by section 1 of the Law Reform (Miscellaneous Provisions) Act 1970. This provides that no agreement to marry shall take effect as a legally enforceable contract and that no action shall lie in this country for breach of such an agreement, wherever it was made.

Property of Engaged Couples.—The action of breach of promise of marriage might occasionally fulfil a social function by permitting a party to recover expenses which he had incurred in contemplation of the marriage. To take three examples: the woman might have travelled a considerable distance to marry and live in this country; the man might have bought furniture which he no longer needs; both parties might have spent money and labour in securing a mortgage on the proposed matrimonial home, decorating it and carrying out repairs on it. There is now no remedy at all for the first two types of loss. With respect to the third, engaged couples acquiring property for use in their married life together are in a position little different from that of a newly married couple and consequently section 2 (1) of the Law Reform (Miscellaneous Provisions) Act 1970 seeks to give them some protection by enacting:

---

[1] The civil judicial statistics do not disclose how many actions were brought. Nor do we know how far the existence of the action led to settlements out of court.

[2] Law Com. No. 26 (Breach of Promise of Marriage), 1969.

"Where an agreement to marry is terminated, any rule of law relating to the rights of husbands and wives in relation to property in which either or both has or have a beneficial interest ... shall apply, in relation to any property in which either or both of the parties to the agreement had a beneficial interest while the agreement was in force, as it applies in relation to property in which a husband or wife has a beneficial interest."

It therefore follows, for example, that if a man purchases a house in his own name partly with money provided by his fiancée and they enhance its value by doing work on it, the use of her money and her contribution to the improvement of the house will give her the same interest in it as she would have acquired had the parties been married at the time.[1]

In order to bring this sub-section into play it will be seen that there must have been an agreement to marry and at least one of the parties to it must have had an interest in the property whilst the agreement was in force. Now that such agreements are no longer legally enforceable, it is not clear what arrangements are caught by these words: is it sufficient, for example, that there was an "unofficial engagement" between the parties? It is submitted that the correct test is whether the parties had entered into an unconditional agreement to marry: the purpose of the sub-section is to replace an action which lay only when there was a legally enforceable contract; it is only when there was a definite agreement that it can be said to be "in force".[2] The cause of the termination of the agreement to marry is irrelevant: it may be by consent, by repudiation by one of the parties, or by the death of either of them.

It is doubtful whether this sub-section gives the engaged person any advantage that he or she would not otherwise possess. At common law a man who bought property with his own money and had it conveyed into his fiancée's name was presumed to intend to make a gift like a husband who had property conveyed into his wife's name.[3] Similarly, the legal position of a fiancée can scarcely be weaker than that of a mistress, and the courts have now held that the latter, like a wife, may take a beneficial interest in property to the purchase of which she has contributed.[4] What is more important is that, in the case of engaged couples, there is nothing comparable to the power to adjust rights in property that the court has on divorce.[5]

To enable parties to an engagement that has been terminated to settle disputes over property more expeditiously, either of them may now bring summary proceedings under section 17 of the Married Women's Property Act 1882 within three years of the termination of the agreement.[6]

Gifts between Engaged Couples.—At common law a gift made by one party to an engagement to the other in contemplation of marriage could not be rcovered by the donor if he was in breach of contract. This meant, for example, that if the man broke off the engagement without legal

---

[1] For the interests taken by spouses in each other's property, see *post*, pp. 424 *et seq.*
[2] See Law Com. No. 26, para. 44.
[3] *Moate* v. *Moate*, [1948] 2 All E.R. 486. See further *post*, p. 429.
[4] See *post*, p. 654.
[5] See Law Com. No. 26, paras. 35-42; Cretney, 33 M.L.R. 534.
[6] Law Reform (Miscellaneous Provisions) Act 1970, s. 2 (2). See further, *post*, p. 424.

justification, he could not recover the engagement ring, but he could do so if the woman was in breach of contract.[1]

In conformity with the principle that the parties' rights with respect to property should not depend upon their responsibility for the termination of the agreement, section 3 (1) of the Law Reform (Miscellaneous Provisions) Act 1970 now provides:

> "A party to an agreement to marry who makes a gift of property to the other party on the condition (express or implied) that it shall be returned if the agreement is terminated shall not be prevented from recovering the property by reason only of his having terminated the agreement."[2]

Whether a particular gift was made subject to an implied condition that it should be returned if the marriage did not take place must necessarily be a question of fact to be decided in each case. Normally birthday presents and Christmas presents will vest in the donee absolutely, whilst property intended to become a part of the matrimonial home (for example, furniture) will be conditional. It is suggested that the general test to be applied should be: was the gift made to the donee as an individual or solely as the donor's future spouse? If it is in the latter class, it will be regarded as conditional, whereas if it is in the former, it will be regarded as absolute and recoverable only in the same circumstances as any other gift—for example, on the ground that it was induced by fraud or undue influence.

The engagement ring is specifically dealt with by the statute. The gift is presumed to be absolute but this presumption may be rebutted by proving that the ring was given on the condition (express or implied) that it should be returned if the marriage did not take place for any reason.[3] One would have thought that by current social convention an engagement ring was still regarded as a pledge and that the presumption ought to have been the other way. As it is, the ring is likely to be recoverable only in the most exceptional circumstances, for example if it can be shown that it was an heirloom in the man's family.

If a gift in contemplation of marriage is made to one or both of the engaged couple by a third person (as in the case of wedding presents), it is, in the absence of any contrary intention, conditional upon the celebration of the marriage and must therefore be returned if the marriage does not take place for any reason at all.[4] A contrary intention will clearly be shown if the gift is for immediate use before the marriage.

Undue Influence.—It was formerly believed that the fact that an engaged woman would probably place the greatest confidence in her fiancé raised a presumption in equity that he had exercised undue influence over her with

---

[1] *Cohen* v. *Sellar*, [1926] 1 K.B. 536; *Jacobs* v. *Davis*, [1917] 2 K.B. 532. There is no direct authority for the position if the agreement was terminated otherwise than by breach, *e.g.*, by agreement or death. It was generally assumed that the donor (or his personal representatives) could recover conditional gifts: see *Cohen* v. *Sellar*.

[2] This is an unfortunately worded provision. If the man behaved in such a way as to justify the woman in breaking off the engagement, he could not recover conditional gifts at common law. But as it is she who has strictly terminated the agreement, it is arguable that the statute has no application and he still cannot recover the gift: see Cretney, 33 M.L.R. 534.

[3] Law Reform (Miscellaneous Provisions) Act 1970, s. 3 (2). See further Cretney, *loc. cit.*

[4] See *Jeffreys* v. *Luck* (1922), 153 L.T.Jo. 139.

respect to any gift that she made to him or any contract or other transaction that she entered into at his request; consequently if she later sought to set the gift or transaction aside on this ground, the burden immediately shifted to the man to prove that there was in fact no such influence. But the change in relationship between engaged couples during the past century led the Court of Appeal to reconsider the question in *Zamet* v. *Hyman*.[1] All the members of the court were of the opinion that the same rules must be applied today whether it is the man or the woman who secures the benefit. DONOVAN, L.J., said simply that the transaction could be set aside only if the party seeking to do so proved affirmatively that he or she had imposed confidence and trust in the other and that the disposition resulted from the abuse of such confidence and trust.[2] LORD EVERSHED, M.R., (with whose observations DANCKWERTS, L.J., agreed) stated the rule more fully in the following words:[3]

"In any transaction of the kind of a deed or arrangement or settlement ... made between an engaged couple which upon its face appears much more favourable to one party than the other, ... the court may find a fiduciary relationship ... so as to cast an onus on the party benefited of proving that the transaction was completed by the other party only after full, free and informed thought about it."

Thus the majority of the Court of Appeal were of the opinion that once a fiduciary relationship has been established, the burden shifts on to the party who might be expected to have exercised undue influence to prove that he or she did not do so—a burden which can usually be discharged only by showing that the other received genuinely independent advice.[4] In *Zamet* v. *Hyman* a woman aged 71 became engaged to a man aged 79. Both had children by previous marriages and three days before the marriage she executed a deed by which she relinquished all rights she might have on the husband's intestacy and under the Inheritance (Family Provision) Act in consideration of a sum of £600 payable to her out of the husband's estate on his death. Three years later the husband died intestate and left an estate worth about £10,000. In view of the vast discrepancy between the rights that she had relinquished and the sum she had gained and the fact that she had received virtually no legal advice, all the members of the court were of the view that the deed could not stand and that she was not bound by it.

C. THE CONTRACT OF MARRIAGE

In order that a man and woman may become husband and wife, two conditions must be satisfied: first, they must both possess the capacity to contract a marriage, and secondly, they must observe the necessary formalities.

The original view was that the law of marriage in all its aspects was governed by the *lex loci celebrationis* on the ground that those administering the law could not be expected to be familiar with any other rule. But this was

---

[1] [1961] 3 All E.R. 933, C.A.
[2] At p. 942.
[3] At p. 938.
[4] *Cf.* the position where it is alleged that a parent has exercised undue influence over his child: *post*, pp. 574-575.

decisively rejected by the Court of Appeal in 1877 in *Sottomayor* v. *De Barros*.[1] In the words of COTTON L.J.:[2]

> "The law of a country where a marriage is solemnised must alone decide all questions relating to the validity of the ceremony by which the marriage is alleged to have been constituted; but ... personal capacity must depend on the law of the domicile."

The rule may therefore now be stated that, generally speaking, capacity to marry is determined by the parties' *lex domicilii* whilst the formalities to be observed are those required by the *lex loci celebrationis*. Hence if a couple domiciled in England marry in Scotland, they must have capacity by English law and the marriage must be solemnized in a manner recognized by Scots law.

Capacity.—Although it is now settled that capacity to marry is governed by the parties' *lex domicilii*, difficulty arises if they have different domiciles at the time of the marriage or propose to acquire a fresh domicile immediately afterwards. Early cases were ambiguous because only one domicile was in question, and they referred to "the law of the country in which the parties are domiciled at the time of the marriage, and in which the matrimonial residence is contemplated".[3] Where these do not coincide, most authorities accept the "dual domicile test". By this, capacity to marry is governed by the parties' ante-nuptial domicile, and the vital question is: did each have capacity to marry the other by his or her *lex domicilii* at the time of the ceremony?[4] This test has the merit of being relatively easy to apply as one is concerned only with the parties' domicile at a given point in time. On the other hand, it can work arbitrarily. Suppose, for example, that a woman domiciled in England wishes to marry her uncle domiciled in state X, where they intend to live after the marriage. By English law marriage between uncle and niece is forbidden; let us further suppose that it is permitted by the law of X. If they marry in, say, France, the marriage must be void because the woman will still be domiciled in England and therefore lack capacity to marry; if, however, she travels to X and marries her uncle there, she will probably acquire a domicile of choice immediately she sets foot in the country and therefore will have the necessary capacity.

The alternative test can be termed the "intended matrimonial home test" and was thus formulated by its chief English proponent, DR. CHESHIRE:[5]

> "The basic presumption is that capacity to marry is governed by the law of the husband's domicile at the time of the marriage, for normally it is in the country of that domicile that the parties intend to establish their permanent home. This presumption, however, is rebutted if it can be inferred that the parties at the time of the marriage intended to establish their home in a certain country and that they did in fact establish it there within a reasonable time."

---

[1] 3 P.D. 1, C.A.

[2] At p. 5.

[3] *Per* LORD CAMPBELL, L.C., in *Brook* v. *Brook* (1861), 9 H.L. Cas. 193, 207, H.L. See also *Warrender* v. *Warrender* (1835), 2 Cl. & Fin. 488, H.L.

[4] Dicey and Morris, *Conflict of Laws*, 10th Ed., 285 *et seq.*; Morris, *Conflict of Laws*, 2nd Ed., 106 *et seq.*

[5] Cheshire and North, *Private International Law*, 10th Ed., 331.

If one applies this test to the hypothetical facts given above, it will be seen that the marriage will be valid, for the law of state X alone will be relevant.[1] As Dr. CHESHIRE points out, this has much to commend it in principle and on sociological grounds, for if the parties intend to spend their lives in X, it is that state which is primarily interested in their marital relationship, and incapacities imposed by English law have no further relevance.[2] The weakness of the test is that it is contrary to basic principle to permit the parties to be able to change their legal capacity merely by conceiving an intention; furthermore if the parties propose to establish their matrimonial home in a country different from that in which the husband is domiciled at the time of the ceremony, one must wait and see whether they carry out their intention, and the validity of the marriage may be in doubt until they do so. In other cases reference to the husband's *lex domicilii* to the exclusion of the wife's could be justified on the ground that it is more likely that the parties will settle in the country in which he is domiciled.

In more recent cases—all at first instance—where the court has stated the rule unequivocally, the balance of authority is undoubtedly in favour of the dual domicile test. This opinion was most clearly voiced by SIMON, P., in *Padolecchia* v. *Padolecchia*.[3] Two statutory provisions also obviously rest on the assumption that this is the correct test.[4] The intended matrimonial home test is supported by the decision of the Court of Appeal in *De Reneville* v. *De Reneville*,[5] where, however, the court was concerned with the question of jurisdiction to entertain a petition for nullity when the husband was domiciled in France and the marriage was alleged to be voidable because of his inability or wilful refusal to consummate it. It was also applied by CUMMING-BRUCE, J., in *Radwan* v. *Radwan* (*No. 2*).[6] In this case a woman domiciled in England went through a ceremony of marriage at the Egyptian Consulate General in Paris with a man domiciled in Egypt. The parties intended to make their home in Egypt and did so after spending a holiday in France and England. The husband already had a wife living in Egypt and, as

[1] Unless it is void because the parties lack capacity by the *lex loci celebrationis*: see *post*, pp. 26-27.
[2] *Op. cit.*, 332-334. It should be noticed, however, that Dr. Cheshire's views are not shared by Dr. North, the editor of the latest edition: *ibid.*, pp. 338-340. A more elaborate test is proposed by Jaffey, *The Essential Validity of Marriage in the English Conflict of Laws*, 41 M.L.R. 38. He points out that English law would recognise a polygamous marriage which was valid by both parties' *lex domicilii* even though they came to live in England immediately afterwards. He therefore suggests that a marriage should be void on the ground of polygamy or relationship within the prohibited degrees only if it is void by either party's *lex domicilii and* by the law of the country within which they establish a matrimonial home within a reasonable time after the celebration. As the law relating to non-age is designed to protect the immature, he argues that a marriage should be void only if forbidden by the *lex domicilii* of the party under age.
[3] [1968] P. 314, 336; [1967] 3 All E.R. 863, 873, following *Schwebel* v. *Ungar* (1963), 42 D.L.R. (2d) 622; affirmed (1964), 48 D.L.R. (2d) 644. See also *Re Paine*, [1940] Ch. 46; *Pugh* v. *Pugh*, [1951] P. 482; [1951] 2 All E.R. 680; and *cf. Szechter* v. *Szechter*, [1971] P. 286, 295; [1970] 3 All E.R. 905, 913.
[4] Marriage (Enabling) Act 1960, s. 1 (3) (*post*, p. 26); Matrimonial Proceedings (Polygamous Marriages) Act 1972, s. 4 (now repealed and re-enacted in the Matrimonial Causes Act 1973, s. 11 (d)), (*post*, p. 77).
[5] [1948] P. 100; [1948] 1 All E.R. 56, C.A., (*post*, p. 102). See also *Kenward* v. *Kenward*, [1951] P. 124, 144-146; [1950] 2 All E.R. 297, 310-11, C.A. (*per* DENNING, L.J.); *In the Will of Swan* (1871), 2 V.R. 47.
[6] [1973] Fam. 35; [1972] 3 All E.R. 1026.

the presumption that the marriage was formally valid was not rebutted not-withstanding that it was polygamous, it became necessary to decide which test of capacity was to be applied. By the dual domicile test the marriage must be void because the wife, as a domiciled Englishwoman, had no capacity to contract a bigamous marriage; by the intended matrimonial home test, however, it would be valid because there was power to contract such a marriage by Egyptian law. CUMMING-BRUCE, J., held that the marriage was valid and that the wife "had the capacity to enter into a polygamous union by virtue of her pre-nuptial decision to separate herself from the land of her domicile and to make her life with her husband in his country, where the Mohammedan law of polygamous marriage was the normal institution of marriage".[1]

Although the learned judge was careful to limit his decision to the power to enter into a polygamous marriage and expressly declared that he was not concerned with problems of non-age or the prohibited degrees, it is diffi-cult to see why a different rule should apply to the latter. To revert to the hypothetical facts given earlier, CUMMING-BRUCE, J.'s argument would apply with equal force if the impediment by English law had been the fact that the husband was the wife's uncle. Different considerations admittedly might apply in the case of non-age because of the inability of a person under the age of 16 to acquire an independent domicile and the courts' desire to protect parents' rights which might be lost against their will under the intended matri-monial home doctrine.

On the particular facts of the case the application of this test preserved the validity of a marriage which the parties themselves had regarded as valid for over 20 years; it must be remembered, however, that a marriage could be valid by the dual domicile test but void by the law of the intended matri-monial home. The law must be regarded as uncertain until there has been a decision of the Court of Appeal on the matter; in the meantime the balance of authority, the comparative ease of applying the dual domicile test and the social harm and practical inconvenience that might result from applying the intended matrimonial home test if this left the validity of a marriage in doubt all point to the rejection of *Radwan* v. *Radwan* and the adoption of the dual domicile test.[2]

Whichever be the correct test, reference to the *lex domicilii* includes a reference to its relevant conflict of laws rules. In *R. v. Brentwood Superinten-dent Registrar of Marriages, ex parte Arias*[3] an Italian national who was domiciled in Switzerland and who had obtained a divorce in that country wished to marry in England. By Swiss law capacity to marry is governed by the law of the party's nationality and, as Italian law did not recognise the Swiss divorce, he lacked the capacity to marry in Italy and, therefore, in England too.

---

[1] At pp. 54 and 1040, respectively.

[2] As CUMMING-BRUCE, J., himself admitted, the adoption of the intended matrimonial home test would also render s. 11 (d) of the Matrimonial Causes Act 1973 largely otiose (see p. 60, *post*). See further the highly critical note by Karsten, 36 M.L.R. 291, where the writer points out that the decision in *Radwan* v. *Radwan* is scarcely supported by the authorities on which CUMMING-BRUCE, J., relied.

[3] [1968] 2 Q.B. 956; [1968] 3 All E.R. 279.

The actual decision in this case is no longer law. It was regarded as anomalous that we should recognise a divorce but prohibit one of the parties from remarrying, and the opportunity to reverse the decision was taken in section 7 of the Recognition of Divorces and Legal Separations Act 1971, which provides:[1]

> "Where the validity of a divorce obtained in any country is entitled to recognition by virtue of sections 1 to 5 or section 6 (2) of this Act or by virtue of any rule or enactment preserved by section 6 (5) of this Act, neither spouse shall be precluded from remarrying in the United Kingdom on the ground that the validity of the divorce would not be recognised in any other country."

It will be seen that this section has a strictly limited operation. It applies only to remarriage in the United Kingdom; if on otherwise identical facts the parties in *Ex parte Arias* remarried in another country, we should presumably still regard the marriage as void.[2] Furthermore the section operates only if the divorce is recognised by virtue of the Act. We shall examine its scope later,[3] but it should be noted immediately that English decrees are not covered by the Act at all. It seems scarcely credible, however, that we should permit the *lex domicilii* to ignore the effects of an English decree. Suppose, for example, that a married woman, domiciled abroad, obtains a divorce in this country but that this decree is not recognised by her *lex domicilii*. Although she lacks capacity by the law of her own domicile, it is submitted that by English law the decree must be conclusive for all purposes that she is no longer married to her first husband and consequently we should recognise the second marriage as valid wherever it took place.[4] Finally, the Act has no application at all if the question of capacity does not involve the recognition of a previous divorce. Thus if the previous marriage in *Ex parte Arias* had been annulled and not dissolved, we should still have to see whether Italian law recognised the decree of nullity.[5]

Except in *Radwan* v. *Radwan* (*No. 2*) English courts have insisted that, wherever the marriage is celebrated, a person domiciled in this country can contract a valid marriage only so long as he has capacity according to English

---

[1] As amended by the Domicile and Matrimonial Proceedings Act 1973, ss. 2 and 15 (2).

[2] But suppose that the *lex loci celebrationis* had a rule similar to that embodied in s. 7. Would the principle of reciprocity oblige English courts to give effect to it even though this would mean recognising a marriage which is void by the parties' *lex domicilii*?

[3] See *post*, pp. 244 *et seq.*

[4] But in *Breen* v. *Breen*, [1964] P. 144; [1961] 3 All E.R. 225, KARMINSKI, J., would apparently have held a marriage celebrated in Dublin void if the Irish courts had not recognised the validity of a previous English divorce, even though both parties were domiciled in England. See further *post*, p. 27, n. 1.

[5] This point was not taken in *Perrini* v. *Perrini*, [1979] Fam. 84; [1979] 2 All E.R. 323, which is clearly inconsistent with *Ex parte Arias*. It is submitted that the case is nevertheless correctly decided on the facts. The husband's first wife had obtained a decree of nullity in New Jersey. This decree was recognised in England but not in Italy, where the husband was domiciled. The husband then remarried and his second wife later petitioned for a decree of nullity in this country alleging that the marriage was void for bigamy. BAKER, P., dismissed the petition on the ground that by English law the husband was free to marry the petitioner. What, with respect, he should have held is that the marriage was valid because by English law the husband was unmarried and, as the marriage took place in England and the petitioner was domiciled in this country, we should disregard any incapacity imposed by the husband's *lex domicilii* not recognised here. See *infra* and Collier, [1979] C.L.J. 289.

law, and they have consistently declared marriages void where that capacity has been lacking, even though the person concerned would have had capacity by the *lex loci celebrationis*.[1] But they have not applied this principle consistently in the case of a marriage in England of a person domiciled abroad. Where *neither* party is domiciled in England, they will admittedly regard the marriage as void if the parties lacked capacity by their *lex domicilii* even though they would have had capacity had they been domiciled in England; but where one of the parties is domiciled in England, the courts will not take account of any incapacity imposed by the *lex domicilii* of the other party which is not recognised by English law. Hence, if both parties are domiciled in a country where marriage between first cousins is prohibited, such a marriage will be void if celebrated in this country;[2] but if one of them is domiciled in England, the marriage will nevertheless be valid.[3]

This distinction has been judicially justified on the grounds that English courts are bound to protect their own nationals and that "no country is bound to recognise the laws of a foreign state when they work injustice to its own subjects";[4] but the fact that such a marriage may be regarded as void in one country and valid in another is liable to produce greater hardship than it avoids. The social undesirability of producing these so-called limping marriages has been recognised by the departure from the common law rule in the provisions of the Marriage (Enabling) Act 1960. This Act relaxes the stringent rules relating to marriages within the prohibited degrees of affinity by permitting a person to marry certain relations of a former spouse even though the latter is still alive,[5] but it is provided that the Act shall not validate a marriage if *either* party to it is domiciled at the time of the celebration in a country outside Great Britain and the law of that country prohibits the marriage.[6]

There may be two further exceptions to the rule that capacity to marry is a question for the parties' *lex domicilii*. It is possible that their marriage will be

---

[1] *Brook* v. *Brook* (1861), 9 H.L. Cas. 193, H.L. (prohibited degrees of affinity); *Pugh* v. *Pugh*, [1951] P. 482; [1951] 2 All E.R. 680 (nonage); *Sussex Peerage Case* (1844), 11 Cl. & F. 85, H.L. (Royal Marriages Act 1772).

[2] *Sottomayor* v. *De Barros* (1877), 3 P.D. 1, C.A.

[3] *Sottomayor* v. *De Barros* (1879), 5 P.D. 94, approved by the Court of Appeal in *Ogden* v. *Ogden*, [1908] P. 46.

[4] *Per* COTTON, L.J., in *Sottomayor* v. *De Barros* (1877), 3 P.D. at p. 7. But the rule applies to persons *domiciled* in England who may not be British subjects. Nor apparently will an English court reciprocally recognise the validity of a marriage contracted between a domiciled Englishman and a person domiciled in the country where the marriage is solemnized if the former lacks capacity by English law, even though the incapacity is not recognised in that country: *Re Paine*, [1940] Ch. 46. See also Webb, *Some Thoughts on the Place of English Law as* Lex Fori *in English Private International Law*, 10 I.C.L.Q. 818, at pp. 825-829.

[5] See *post*, p. 34.

[6] Section 1 (3). A further attempt to prevent these limping marriages was made by the legislature in the Marriage with Foreigners Act 1906, under which a foreigner marrying a British subject in England and Wales can be required to produce a certificate that there is no impediment to the marriage by foreign law. But the attempt has been wholly ineffective as no Orders in Council have yet been made under the Act. The Law Commission's Working Party rejected the proposal that such certificates should be obligatory on the ground that this would place an undue burden on superintendent registrars: Law Com. No. 53, Annex, para. 57.

void if they lack capacity by the *lex loci celebrationis*.[1] So far as marriages celebrated in England are concerned, we will not permit a polygamous union to be contracted,[2] and it is hardly conceivable that we should permit our marriage laws to be used to enable a marriage to be contracted between persons under the age of 16 or related within the prohibited degrees. This seems to be amply justified on the grounds of public policy. The second possible exception is that English law will disregard any incapacity imposed by the *lex domicilii* if it is penal. It is not clear what incapacities are caught by this rule. It has been held to cover prohibitions against marrying outside one's own caste[3] and against the remarriage of a divorced person;[4] it is submitted that it is really a further example of public policy and would also include prohibitions against marrying persons of a different race and, perhaps, against the marriage of those who have taken vows of celibacy. Clearly, if the marriage was celebrated in England to a person domiciled here, we should disregard the prohibition anyway, and the so called exception may be merely a particular application of the principle we have already discussed. But in *Warter* v. *Warter*[5] HANNEN, P., referred to an incapacity "penal in its character and as such ... inoperative out of the jurisdiction under which it was inflicted". This is wide enough to oblige us to disregard it wherever the marriage was celebrated and whatever was the domicile of the other party. In the absence of any authority it is submitted that on grounds of public policy we should do so unless the marriage was celebrated in the country of the parties' domicile, when it must be void by any test.[6]

Formalities.—English law has rarely departed from the rule that the formal validity of the marriage depends upon the *lex loci celebrationis*. This is so even though persons domiciled in England may deliberately have gone to another country in order to evade the English rules as to formalities. Hence, the courts of this country always recognised the validity of the "Gretna Green" marriages since, until the law was altered by statute in 1939, a valid marriage could be contracted in Scotland *per verba de praesenti* in the presence of a witness, who, at least till a residence requirement was imposed by statute in 1856, was by tradition frequently the blacksmith in the first town over the Border. Similarly, a person resident in England may validly contract a marriage by proxy in a country the law of which permits such marriages,[7]

---

[1] This appears to be the ground on which the marriage would have been held void in *Breen* v. *Breen*, [1964] P. 144; [1961] 3 All E.R. 225. (See *ante*, p. 25, n. 4.) For Commonwealth decisions to the contrary, see *In the will of Swan* (1871), 2 V.R. 47; *Reed* v. *Reed* (1969), 6 D.L.R. (3d) 617; and see Jaffey, 41 M.L.R. 38, 46-47.

[2] See *post*, p. 57.

[3] *Chetti* v. *Chetti*, [1909] P. 67.

[4] *Warter* v. *Warter* (1890), 15 P.D. 152, 155, explaining *Scott* v. *A.-G.* (1886), 11 P.D. 128. But this does not apply if the prohibition is purely suspensive to ensure that the decree is not appealed: *Warter* v. *Warter*.

[5] (1890), 15 P.D. 152, 155.

[6] Dicey and Morris, *op. cit.*, p. 304, suggest that English law might regard the marriage as valid or void according to the view taken by the *lex loci celebrationis*. Whilst it may be illogical to regard as valid a marriage which is void both by the *lex domicilii* and by the *lex loci celebrationis*, it seems equally unacceptable to let another system determine whether English courts are to give effect to a prohibition which offends our ideas of public policy.

[7] *Apt* v. *Apt*, [1948] P. 83; [1947] 2 All E.R. 677, C.A.; *Ponticelli* v. *Ponticelli*, [1958] P. 204; [1958] 1 All E.R. 357.

and if the marriage is initially formally invalid by the *lex loci*, English law will recognise the effect of a local statute retrospectively curing the invalidity.[1] But is should also be borne in mind that a state may recognise the validity of a marriage contracted within its frontiers even though the municipal law as to formalities is not complied with.[2] Conversely, subject to certain very stringent conditions the Foreign Marriage Acts 1892 and 1947 empower a British ambassador or consul or a Governor, High Commissioner or Resident to solemnise a marriage at his official residence provided that he holds a marriage warrant from the Foreign Secretary. At least one of the persons to be married must be a British subject. International comity is preserved and the possibility of limping marriages reduced by the provisions that a marriage must not be celebrated under the Acts unless the authorities of the country in which it takes place will not object to it, insufficient facilities exist for the marriage of the parties by local law, and it will be recognised as a valid marriage by the law of the country to which each party belongs.[3]

Recognition of Common Law Marriages.—Despite the general acceptance of the principle *locus regit actum* it is clear that English law will exceptionally recognise a marriage which is valid at common law even though it is not valid by the *lex loci celebrationis*.

As we shall see,[4] originally at common law no religious ceremony was necessary and the parties could contract a marriage by a declaration that they took each other as husband and wife. Later, however, the rule was modified and a valid marriage could be contracted only in the presence of an episcopally ordained priest. In the type of case we are considering it may not be possible to secure the services of such a person. This occurred in *Wolfenden* v. *Wolfenden*.[5] The marriage had taken place before a minister (not episcopally ordained) at a mission in the Province of Hupeh, China, and by local law it was valid provided that it was valid by English law. Holding that this was a good common law marriage, LORD MERRIMAN, P., expressed the opinion that "in such a territory ... there is ... no obligation that the ceremony shall be performed in the presence of an episcopally ordained

---

[1] *Starkowski* v. *A.-G.*, [1954] A.C. 155; [1953] 2 All E.R. 1272, H.L. *Quaere* whether the retrospective operation would have been recognised if either party had remarried in the meantime. See further Mendes da Costa, *The Formalities of Marriage in the Conflict of Laws*, 7 I.C.L.Q. 217, at pp. 251 *et seq.*; Tolstoy, *The Validation of Void Marriages*, 31 M.L.R. 656.

[2] *Cf. Taczanowska* v. *Taczanowski*, [1957] P. 301; [1957] 2 All E.R. 563, C.A., where the court would apparently have recognised a marriage celebrated in Italy as valid if the parties had complied with the formalities required by Polish law on the ground that it would have been recognised by the Italian conflict of laws. See further, *post*, p. 29. Formerly English law appears to have regarded a marriage celebrated in a foreign embassy in London as valid provided that both (or perhaps one) of the parties were subjects of the ambassador's state: see Cheshire and North, *Private International Law*, 10th Ed., 317. Now that the fiction of extra-territoriality is exploded, it is possible that we might no longer recognise such a marriage unless, perhaps, at least one of the parties was a member of the mission: *cf. Radwan* v. *Radwan*, [1973] Fam. 24; [1972] 3 All E.R. 967.

[3] Does this mean the parties' domicile or nationality? The full conditions are contained in the Foreign Marriage Order, S.I. 1970 No. 1539. For the detailed provisions, see Dicey and Morris, *op. cit.*, 274-276; Cheshire and North, *op. cit.*, 318-319; Graveson, *Conflict of Laws*, 7th Ed., 277-278.

[4] *Post*, pp. 35-36.

[5] [1946] P. 61; [1945] 2 All E.R. 539.

priest''.[1] Similarly in *Penhas* v. *Tan Soo Eng*[2] the Privy Council, following *Wolfenden* v. *Wolfenden*, held that "in a country such as Singapore, where priests are few and there is no true parochial system, where the vast majority are not Christians, it is neither convenient nor necessary'' that a marriage between a Jew and a non-Christian Chinese should be contracted in the presence of a priest. The rule that a priest's presence is necessary probably never applied outside England and Ireland; it certainly does not apply where compliance with it would be impossible, difficult or even inconvenient.

It seems that English law will recognise a common law marriage if no local form exists at all or if it would be impossible or unreasonable to expect the parties to comply with the *lex loci celebrationis* in the circumstances.[3] They would certainly be justified in not observing local formalities if, for example, the ceremony was offensive by English standards or the only form available was a polygamous one. A particular application of the same principle is to be seen in the rule, accepted by our courts, that members of belligerent forces occupying conquered territory cannot be expected to submit to the law of those they have conquered. So far as British forces are concerned, section 2 of the Foreign Marriage Act 1947 permits naval, military and air force chaplains and other persons authorised by the Commanding Officer to solemnize marriages in a foreign territory provided that at least one of the parties is a member of the British forces serving in that territory or is employed there in a capacity defined by Order in Council. The term "foreign territory" excludes any part of the Commonwealth but includes ships in foreign waters.[4] The common law rule, however, applies generally and is certainly not confined to members of the British forces or even to persons domiciled in England. This is clear from a series of cases involving the marriage of members of the Polish forces and Polish civilians in Europe immediately after the Second World War.[5]

The first case we must consider is *Taczanowska* v. *Taczanowski*.[6] In 1946 the husband, who was then a member of the Polish forces in Italy and the wife, who was a civilian refugee, were married in a church in Rome by a Roman Catholic priest. Both parties were Polish nationals and presumably

---

[1] At pp. 66 and 543, respectively.

[2] [1953] A.C. 304, P.C.

[3] A ship is regarded as part of the country whose flag it flies and it is generally accepted that marriages can be conducted on board if the law of the country permits it. Such authority as there is suggests that a marriage can be celebrated on board a ship registered at an English port if it is on the high seas, provided that there is necessity. Whereas necessity could easily arise in the days when ships were at sea for weeks without putting into a port for a period long enough to enable the parties to comply with local law, this is hardly likely to arise today. See Dicey and Morris, *op. cit.*, 271; Cheshire and North, *op. cit.*, 329-330. Graveson, *op. cit.*, 278, takes the view that the marriage would be valid without adding the qualification of necessity.

[4] For further details, see Dicey and Morris, *op. cit.*, 274; Cheshire and North, *op. cit.*, 319-320.

[5] The problem arose particularly with respect to Poles because of the large number of Polish forces and displaced civilians in Central Europe who refused to return to Poland when it became controlled by a communist government after the War. Many subsequently settled in this country and acquired an English domicile.

[6] [1957] P. 301; [1957] 2 All E.R. 563, C.A.; followed in *Merker* v. *Merker*, [1963] P. 283; [1962] 3 All E.R. 928. Contrast *Lazarewicz* v. *Lazarewicz*, [1962] P. 171; [1962] 2 All E.R. 5, where the marriage was held to be void on the ground that the parties had intended, but failed, to comply with the *lex loci celebrationis*.

were domiciled in Poland. The marriage was void by Italian municipal law because they had not complied with Italian civil regulations; by the Italian conflict of laws it would have been valid had they complied with their *lex patriae*, but this did not save the marriage because it was void by Polish law as well. On the wife's petition for nullity on the ground that the marriage was void as formally defective, it was held to be valid as a good common law marriage. As the husband was a member of a conquering army occupying Italy, he could not have been expected to submit to Italian law and consequently the marriage was not void merely because it failed to comply with the *lex loci celebrationis*. The suggestion that, failing the *lex loci*, the *lex domicilii* should be applied (which, as we have seen, would not have saved the marriage) was rejected on the ground that this was relevant only to capacity. The Court of Appeal fell back on the common law as the *lex fori* and upheld the marriage as a good marriage celebrated by the exchange of words before an episcopally ordained priest. This approach is open to the criticism that the application of the *lex fori* makes the validity of the marriage turn upon the accident of the court in which it is put in issue: it is difficult by any process of reasoning to see how a marriage celebrated in Italy between two persons domiciled in Poland can be governed by the English common law. A more acceptable explanation is that put forward by RUSSELL, L.J., in *Preston* v. *Preston*:[1]

> "Once the *lex loci* is rejected, ... it may well leave it open to a court in this country to recognise as a marriage (in the context of the common law marriage) that which by the general law of Christendom was recognised as constituting the basic essence of the marriage contract—the contract *per verba de praesenti* without further formalities."

Taczanowska v. *Taczanowski* was followed by the Court of Appeal in *Preston* v. *Preston*.[2] The facts were identical save that the marriage had taken place in Germany and the court was therefore bound to find the marriage valid. The importance of the case is that it limits the application of *Taczanowska* v. *Taczanowski* to those cases where one party is a member of a foreign occupying force or is "in a foreign country as part of the organisation necessarily or at least commonly set up when there is hostile occupation".[3] Consequently civilians who have no connection with the occupying force cannot maintain that their marriage is valid as a common law marriage and must comply with the *lex loci* even though it might be equally unreasonable to expect them to comply with the law of a country whose nationals had been persecuting and harassing them for the previous six years.[4]

Characterisation.—It is sometimes difficult to decide whether a particular rule should be characterised as relating to capacity (in which case it is governed by the *lex domicilii*) or to formalities (in which case it is governed by

---

[1] [1963] P. 411, 436; [1903] 2 All E.R. 405, 416, C.A. *Quaere* how far the decision was really based on the social necessity of preserving the validity of over 3,000 marriages alleged to have been contracted in similar circumstances?

[2] [1963] P. 411; [1963] 2 All E.R. 405, C.A.

[3] *Per* ORMEROD, L.J., at pp. 427 and 411, respectively.

[4] The earlier decision to the contrary in *Kochanski* v. *Kochanska*, [1958] P. 147; [1957] 3 All E.R. 142, can no longer be regarded as good law.

the *lex loci celebrationis*). The problem arose in *Ogden* v. *Ogden*.[1] A domiciled Frenchman, aged 19, married in England a woman domiciled in this country without obtaining his parents' consent. By French law this meant that he lacked capacity to contract a valid marriage, but by English law parental consent is a question of formality and lack of it will not affect the validity; it therefore became vital to decide which law should govern the question. The Court of Appeal classified parental consent as a part of the ceremony (thus holding the marriage to be valid) apparently on the ground that English law would apply the *lex fori* to characterise a condition in the case of a marriage celebrated in England. It is submitted that the true *ratio* of the case is that we should ignore the effect of lack of parental consent on the husband's capacity as he married a woman domiciled in England in this country;[2] but in any event to fall back on the *lex fori* to characterise the matter is quite indefensible. In order to avoid a limping marriage, one should ask first of all what the relevant law relating to capacity is by the parties' *lex domicilii*; if this regards lack of parental consent as invalidating the marriage, we must accept and apply the rule. One must then ask what the relevant rule relating to formalities is by the *lex loci*. In the *Ogden* v. *Ogden* type of case, where consent is relevant by both systems, the marriage will be void if lack of consent deprives either party of capacity by his *lex domicilii* or if it renders the ceremony a nullity by the *lex loci celebrationis*.

We must now consider in greater detail the relevant English municipal law.

D. CAPACITY TO MARRY

In order that a person domiciled in England should have capacity to contract a valid marriage, the following conditions must be satisfied:

(a) one party must be male and the other female;
(b) neither party must be already married;
(c) both parties must be over the age of 16; and
(d) the parties must not be related within the prohibited degrees of consanguinity or affinity.[3]

Sex.—A new problem, arising out of operations to effect a so-called change of sex, had to be considered by ORMROD, J., in *Corbett* v. *Corbett*.[4]

---

1 [1908] P. 46, C.A., followed in *Lodge* v. *Lodge* (1963), 107 Sol. Jo. 437. In so far as the case also turns on the court's refusal to recognise a French decree of nullity, it is no longer good law: see *post*, p. 105.

2 See *ante*, p. 26.

3 A further prohibition is to be found in the Royal Marriages Act 1772, which was passed to prevent the contracting of highly undesirable marriages by the younger brothers of King George III. It provides that no descendant of King George II (other than the issue of princesses who have married into foreign families) may marry without the previous consent of the Sovereign formally granted under the great seal and declared in Council. Any marriage coming within the Act, consent to which has not been obtained, will be void; but if the descendant in question is over the age of 25 and gives twelve months' notice of the intended marriage to the Privy Council, it may be validly contracted unless both Houses of Parliament have in the meantime expressly declared their disapprobation of it. For a criticism of the Act and a discussion of how far (if at all) it has any force today, see Farran, *The Royal Marriages Act 1772*, 14 M.L.R. 53.

4 [1971] P. 83; [1970] 2 All E.R. 33. For a discussion of the problems involved, see Poulter, *The Definition of Marriage in English Law*, 42 M.L.R. 409, 421-425.

The petitioner in this case was a man; before the marriage the respondent had undergone a surgical operation for the removal of "her" male genital organs and the provision of artificial female organs. After dealing at length with the medical evidence the learned judge (who is also a qualified medical practitioner) came to the conclusion that a person's biological sex is fixed at birth (at the latest) and cannot subsequently be changed by artificial means. That being so, the respondent, who was male at birth, was not a woman and the marriage was therefore void.

In this case the respondent was to be regarded as male by three independent biological criteria: chromosomal, gonadal and genital. There are persons, however, who are male by one test and female by another. ORMROD, J., deliberately left open the question of capacity to marry in such cases but he was inclined to give greater weight to the appearance of the genital organs. It is at least arguable that such persons are neither male nor female and consequently are legally incapable of marrying anyone of either sex.

Monogamy.—As a result of the English view of marriage as a monogamous union, neither party may contract a valid marriage whilst he or she is already married to someone else. If a person has already contracted one marriage, he cannot contract another until the first spouse dies or the first marriage is annulled or dissolved.[1] It follows that a mistaken belief that the first marriage has been terminated, for example, by the death of the spouse, is immaterial: what is relevant is whether it has in fact been terminated. Consequently, the second marriage may be void even though no prosecution for bigamy will lie in respect of it.

Age.—Both by canon law and at common law a valid marriage could be contracted only if both parties had reached the legal age of puberty, *viz.* 14 in the case of a boy and 12 in the case of a girl. If either party was under this age when the marriage was contracted, it could be avoided by either of them when that party reached the age of puberty; but if the marriage was ratified (as it would impliedly be by continued cohabitation), it became irrevocably binding.[2]

It is somewhat surprising that this remained the law until well into the present century. In the words of PEARCE, J.:[3]

> "According to modern thought it is considered socially and morally wrong that persons of an age, at which we now believe them to be immature and provide for their education, should have the stresses, responsibilities and sexual freedom of marriage and the physical strain of childbirth. Child marriages by common consent are believed to be bad for the participants and bad for the institution of marriage."

This change of thought led to the passing of the Age of Marriage Act in 1929. Section 1 (now re-enacted in section 2 of the Marriage Act 1949) effected two changes in the law. First, it was enacted that a valid marriage could not be

---

[1] But this does not apply if the first marriage was *void*: *post*, p. 73.
[2] Co. Litt. 79; Blackstone, *Commentaries*, i, 436.
[3] *Pugh* v. *Pugh*, [1951] P. 482, 492; [1951] 2 All E.R. 680, 687. See further Law Com. No. 33 (Nullity of Marriage), paras. 16-20; Report of the Latey Committee on the Age of Majority, 1967, Cmnd. 3342, paras. 166-177; Cretney, *Principles of Family Law*, 3rd Ed., 42-48.

contracted unless both parties had reached the age of 16, and secondly any marriage to which either party was under this age was made *void* and not voidable as before.

The provision that *both* parties must be over the age of 16 is important when the party under that age is not domiciled in England and has capacity by his or her own *lex domicilii*. This is illustrated by *Pugh* v. *Pugh*.[1] A man over the age of 16 and domiciled in England went through a form of marriage in Austria with a girl aged 15. She was domiciled in Hungary, by the law of which country the marriage was valid. It was nevertheless held that it was void since the man had no capacity by English law to marry her.

Prohibited Degrees.—Most, if not all, civilised states prohibit certain marriages as incestuous. The prohibited relationship may arise from consanguinity (*i.e.*, blood relationship) or from affinity (*i.e.*, relationship by marriage). In the case of consanguinity the prohibition is based on moral and eugenic grounds. Most people view the idea of sexual intercourse (and therefore of marriage) between, say, father and daughter or brother and sister with abhorrence; at the same time, the more closely the parties are related, the greater will be the risk of their children inheriting undesirable genetic characteristics. In the case of affinity, prohibition was orginally based on the theological concept that husband and wife were one flesh, so that marriage with one's sister-in-law was as incestuous as marriage with one's own sister.[2] This view probably commands little support today and justification must now be sought on social and moral grounds. Marriage with close relations of a former spouse might well create intolerable tensions in the family and many might view some unions with repugnance, for example that of a man with his step-daughter.

Before the Reformation English law adopted the canon law of consanguinity and affinity,[3] but one of the results of the break with the Roman Catholic Church was the adoption of a modified table of prohibited degrees. The new law, which was Levitical in origin,[4] was to be found in a series of statutes,[5] but the vague reference in the statute 32 Hen. 8, c. 38, to marriages "prohibited by God's law" left the matter in considerable doubt, and the interpretation of this Act was still the subject of litigation as late as 1861.[6] But there was eventually little doubt that the prohibited degrees were those laid down by Archbishop Parker in 1563 and adopted in 1603 in the ninety-ninth Canon and set out in the Book of Common Prayer.[7]

---

[1] [1951] P. 482; [1951] 2 All E.R. 680.

[2] For the same reason in the Middle Ages extra-marital sexual intercourse created prohibited degrees.

[3] See Pollock and Maitland, *History of English Law*, ii, 383-387. The rules that emerged lacked theological or sociological justification and "are the idle ingenuities of men who are amusing themselves by inventing a game of skill which is to be played with neatly drawn tables of affinity and doggerel hexameters": *ibid.*, 387.

[4] Leviticus 18.

[5] 25 Hen. 8, c. 22, 28 Hen. 8, c. 7, and 32 Hen. 8, c. 38. All three of these statutes were repealed by 1 Ph. & M., c. 8, but 1 Eliz. 1, c. 1, revived 32 Hen. 8, c. 38, and thus by implication so much of the other two as it referred to. See *R.* v. *Chadwick* (1847), 11 Q.B. 173; 2 Cox C.C. 381; *Wing* v. *Taylor* (1861), 2 Sw. & Tr. 278.

[6] *Wing* v. *Taylor*, (*supra*).

[7] *Hill* v. *Good* (1674), Vaugh. 302, 328. But see *R.* v. *Chadwick* (1847), 2 Cox, C.C., at p. 406.

Up till 1835 a marriage within the prohibited degrees was voidable merely, but the Marriage Act of that year made all such marriages void. By the end of the last century wide dissatisfaction was being expressed against the stringent rules relating to affinity, though it was only after bitter controversy that the Deceased Wife's Sister's Marriage Act was passed in 1907 permitting a man to marry his deceased wife's sister, and it was not till 1921 that he was allowed by statute to marry his deceased brother's widow.[1] In 1931 the principle of these two Acts was extended to eight other prohibited degrees of affinity,[2] and the Marriage (Enabling) Act 1960[3] has further relaxed the prohibition by enabling persons to marry within these degrees of affinity if the former marriage has been annulled or dissolved whether or not the previous spouse is still alive.

The degrees of relationship prohibited today are set out in the First Schedule to the Marriage Act of 1949 as later amended (see Appendix B, *post*). The Schedule in fact reproduces Archbishop Parker's Table as qualified by the four Acts passed between 1907 and 1960. It is drawn up in two columns, of which the left and right state the persons with whom a man and a woman respectively may not intermarry. Marriage within these degrees is prohibited at all times and in all circumstances:[4] thus a man may not marry his step-mother even after his father's death. A marriage will be prohibited whether the relationship is traced through the whole blood or the half blood,[5] and, despite the common law rule that a bastard is *filius nullius*, the eugenic basis of the prohibition also brings illegitimate relationships within it.[6] Consequently, a man may marry, for example, neither his half-brother's daughter nor his illegitimate son's widow.[7] On the other hand a degree of affinity can only be created by marriage and not merely by the fact that two persons have had sexual intercourse; thus, whilst a man may not marry his wife's daughter, there is nothing to prevent his marrying the daughter of a woman with whom he has been cohabiting but to whom he had never been married.[8] To annul a marriage on the ground that the husband had on one occasion slept with his wife's mother would involve a return to the chaos of the Middle Ages; but the problem of defining the circumstances in which sexual intercourse should create a prohibited degree of affinity seems the sole justification today for permitting a man to marry a woman with whose mother he has been living and to whom he has been a virtual step-father for years but forbidding him to marry a *de jure* step-daughter whom he might never have met whilst married to her mother.[9]

---

[1] Deceased Brother's Widow's Marriage Act 1921.

[2] Marriage (Prohibited Degrees of Relationship) Act 1931.

[3] Adopting the majority recommendation of the Morton Commission (1956, Cmd. 9678, Part XV). Three members thought that this would be socially undesirable.

[4] Marriage Act 1949, s. 1 (1).

[5] See the definitions of "brother" and "sister" in the Marriage Act 1949, s. 78 (1).

[6] *Haines* v. *Jeffell* (1696), 1 Ld. Raym. 68; *R.* v. *Brighton* (1861), 1 B. & S. 447.

[7] For the effect of adoption orders on the prohibited degrees, see *post*, p. 357.

[8] *Wing* v. *Taylor* (1861), 2 Sw. & Tr. 278.

[9] This difficulty is resolved in some countries (*e.g.* New Zealand) by permitting a prohibition based on affinity to be dispensed with if there are no moral or social reasons for maintaining it: see Bromley and Webb, *Family Law*, 45-47. For a full criticism of the existing English law see Cretney, *op. cit.*, 35-42. The Law Commission see no need for any change: Law Com. No. 33, paras. 49-54.

It should also be observed that the number of persons between whom marriage is forbidden by the Marriage Act is considerably greater than those between whom sexual intercourse is a criminal offence under the Sexual Offences Act 1956,[1] although, of course, all the relationships set out in the latter Act come within the prohibited degrees.

E. FORMALITIES OF MARRIAGE

1. HISTORICAL INTRODUCTION

The history of the English law relating to the formalities of marriage—even the state of the law immediately before the passing of Lord Hardwicke's Act in 1753—is still a matter of considerable doubt.[2] Canon law emphasised the consensual aspect of the contract and before the Council of Trent in 1563 no religious ceremony had to be performed; all that was necessary was a declaration by the parties that they took each other as husband and wife, either *per verba de praesenti* (*e.g.*, "I take you as my wife [or husband]"), in which case the marriage was binding immediately, or *per verba de futuro* (*e.g.*, "I shall take you as my wife [or husband]"), in which case it became binding as soon as it was consummated. But it early became customary for the marriage to be solemnized *in facie ecclesiae* after the publishing of banns (unless this was dispensed with by papal or episcopal licence) and with the consent of the parents of either party who was under the age of 21. The marriage would then be contracted at the church door *per verba de praesenti* in the presence of the priest, after which the parties would go into the church itself for the celebration of the nuptial mass.[3]

It is hardly surprising that the common law favoured the publicity of marriage *in facie ecclesiae*, for upon the existence of the union might depend many property rights and the identity of the heir at law. Consequently, there developed a curious rule that the wife was not dowable unless she was endowed at the church door,[4] and certain other proprietary disabilities may have followed as well.[5] But in the course of time the reason for the common law insistence upon such a marriage was forgotten. Neither the publishing of banns nor the presence of any other witness was any longer considered necessary; the emphasis shifted on to the presence of the priest (or, after the Reformation, a clerk in holy orders), so that eventually the rule was laid

---

[1] Sections 10 and 11.

[2] *Cf.* the conflicting opinions expressed in *R* v. *Millis* (1844), 10 Cl. & F. 534, H.L. See Swinburne, *Spousals*; Jackson, *Formation and Annulment of Marriage*, 2nd Ed., c. 2; Pollock and Maitland, *History of English Law*, ii, 362 *et seq.*; the judgment of SIR W. SCOTT in *Dalrymple* v. *Dalrymple* (1811), 2 Hag. Con. 54; and the opinion of the judges in *Beamish* v. *Beamish* (1861), 9 H.L. Cas. 274, H.L.

[3] The marriage service of the Church of England still preserves this ancient form. The first part of the service takes place in the body of the church and consists of the espousals (in which each party replies "I will") followed by the contracting of the marriage *per verba de praesenti*. This concludes the civil aspect of the marriage: the remainder of the service, which takes place before the Lord's Table, is purely religious in character.

[4] Bracton, f. 303b.

[5] Swinburne, *op. cit.*

down that a valid marriage at common law could be contracted only *per verba de praesenti* exchanged in his presence.[1]

But the old marriage *per verba de praesenti* was not wholly ineffective. Until the middle of the eighteenth century a marriage could be contracted in one of three ways:

(a) *In facie ecclesiae*, after the publishing of banns or upon a licence, before witnesses, and with the consent of the parent or guardian of a party who was a minor. Such a marriage was obviously valid for all purposes.

(b) Clandestinely, *per verba de praesenti* before a clerk in holy orders, but not *in facie ecclesiae*. This, as we have seen, was as valid as if it had been solemnized *in facie ecclesiae*.

(c) *Per verba de praesenti* or *per verba de futuro* with subsequent sexual intercourse, but where the words were not spoken in the presence of an ordained priest or deacon. Whilst such a marriage would no longer produce all the legal effects of coverture at common law, it was nevertheless valid for many purposes. Such a union was indissoluble, so that, if either party to it subsequently married another, the later marriage could be annulled.[2] Moreover, either party could obtain an order from an ecclesiastical court calling upon the other to solemnize the marriage *in facie ecclesiae*.[3]

Lord Hardwicke's Act.—It needs little imagination to picture the social evils which resulted from such a state of law. A person who had believed himself to be validly married for years would suddenly find that his marriage was a nullity because of a previous clandestine or irregular union, the existence of which he had never before suspected. Children would marry without their parents' consent, and if the minor was a girl with a large fortune, the old common law rule that a wife's property vested in her husband on marriage made her a particularly attractive catch. The "Fleet" parsons thrived— profligate clergy who traded in clandestine marriages. By the middle of the eighteenth century matters had come to such a pass that there was a danger in certain sections of society that such marriages would become the rule rather than the exception.

It was to stop these abuses that Lord Hardwicke's Act was passed in 1753. The principle underlying this Act was to secure publicity by enacting that no marriage should be valid unless it was solemnized according to the rites of the Church of England in the parish church of one of the parties in the presence of a clergyman and two other witnesses.[4] Unless a licence had been obtained, banns had to be published in the parish churches of both parties for three Sundays. If either party was under the age of 21, parental consent had to be obtained as well, unless this was impossible to obtain or was unreasonably withheld, in which case the consent of the Lord Chancellor had to be

---

[1] *R.* v. *Millis* (1844), 10 Cl. & F. 534, H.L. There is little doubt that the decision was based on a misunderstanding of the medieval law: Pollock and Maitland, *loc. cit.* During the Commonwealth, marriages could be celebrated before Justices of the Peace: Jackson, *op. cit.*, 59-60.

[2] *Bunting* v. *Lepingwell* (1585), 4 Co. Rep. 29a. This rule was abrogated by 32 Hen. 8, c. 38, in 1540 but revived in 1548 by 2 & 3 Ed. 6, c. 23.

[3] *Bunting* v. *Lepingwell*, (*supra*); *Baxtar* v. *Buckley* (1752), 1 Lee 42.

[4] Marriages according to the usages of the Society of Friends (Quakers) and according to Jewish rites were exempt from the provisions of the Act.

obtained. If these stringent provisions were not observed, the marriage would in the vast majority of cases be void. Furthermore, the Act abolished the jurisdiction of the Ecclesiastical Courts to compel persons to celebrate the marriage *in facie ecclesiae* if they had contracted a marriage *per verba de praesenti* or *per verba de futuro* followed by consummation.

Marriage Act 1823.—Whilst Lord Hardwicke's Act effectively put a stop to clandestine marriages in England, it caused an almost greater social evil. For the new law was so stringent and the consequence of failing to observe it—the avoidance of the marriage—so harsh, that many couples deliberately evaded it by getting married in Scotland. This was particularly the case when one of the parties was a minor and parental consent was withheld; so that the 70 years following the passing of the Act saw an increasing number of "Gretna Green" marriages. It was in an attempt to prevent this that the Legislature in 1823 repealed Lord Hardwicke's Act and replaced it by a new Marriage Act. So far as the positive directions of the earlier Act were concerned, *viz.* the necessity of the solemnization of the marriage in the church of the parish in which one of the parties resided after the publication of banns or the grant of a licence, they were re-enacted with only a few minor alterations of detail; where the new Act differed largely was in the effect of non-compliance with these directions. A marriage was now to be void only if both parties *knowingly and wilfully* intermarried in any other place than the church wherein the banns might be published, or without the due publication of banns or the obtaining of a licence, or if they *knowingly and wilfully* consented to the solemnization of the marriage by a person not in holy orders. In all other cases the marriage was to be valid notwithstanding any breach in the prescribed formalities. But if the marriage of a minor, whose parent or guardian had not given his consent, had been procured by fraud, the Attorney-General, on the relation of the parent of guardian, might sue for the forfeiture of any property acquired as a result of the marriage by the party who had perpetrated the fraud.

This Act remained the principal Act governing the formalities of marriage in England for over 125 years. Naturally, it was greatly amended during that time. Thus, jurisdiction to make an order dispensing with parental consent was extended to county courts and magistrates' courts;[1] and in 1930 it became possible for the parties to be married in a church which was the regular place of worship of one of them even though it was the parish church of neither.[2] But two Acts introduced principles which were so radically different from those of the Acts of 1735 and 1823 that they must be mentioned separately.

Marriage Act 1836.—The principal criticism raised against the two earlier Acts was that they forced Roman Catholics and Protestant dissenters[3] to go through a religious form of marriage which might well be repugnant to them. The growth of religious toleration generally during the early years of the nineteenth century eventually led to the removal of this grievance by the Marriage Act of 1836.

---

[1] Guardianship of Infants Act 1925, s. 9.

[2] Marriage Measure 1930.

[3] Except Quakers who (together with Jews) were still permitted to celebrate their own marriages (see p. 36, n. 4, *ante*).

This Act, together with the Births and Deaths Registration Act which was passed immediately after it, brought into existence the superintendent registrars of births, deaths and marriages, who were empowered to issue certificates to marry as an alternative to the publication of banns or the obtaining of a licence. But the real importance of the Act lay in the fact that it permitted marriages to be solemnized on the authority of a superintendent registrar's certificate (with or without a licence) in other ways than according to the rites of the Church of England. For the first time since the Middle Ages, English law recognised the validity of a marriage, which was purely civil in character and completely divorced from any religious element, by permitting the parties to marry *per verba de praesenti* in the presence of a superintendent registrar and a registrar of marriages and two other witnesses. The Act went even further by permitting places of worship of members of denominations other than the Church of England to be registered for the solemnization of marriages; and it now became lawful for marriages to be celebrated in these "registered buildings" in accordance with whatever religious ceremony the members wished to adopt, provided that at some stage the parties took each other as husband and wife *per verba de praesenti* in the presence of a registrar of marriages and at least two other witnesses.

Marriage Act 1898.—The Act of 1836 had removed the legitimate grievance of Roman Catholics and Protestant dissenters; the remaining disability under which they suffered—the necessity of having a registrar present at a religious ceremony—was removed by the Marriage Act of 1898. This Act permitted the trustees or governing body of a registered building to authorise a person to be present at the solemnization of marriages in that building, and henceforth a marriage could be lawfully solemnized there in the presence of an "authorised person" without a registrar being present at all. Normally, of course, this person would be a minister of the particular denomination, so that the combined effect of the Acts of 1836 and 1898 was to give to the ministers of all religious denominations the power of solemnizing marriages already enjoyed by clergymen of the Church of England.

Marriages Acts 1949-1970.—By 1949 the extremely complicated law relating to the formalities of marriage could be found only by reference to more than 40 statutes, quite apart from the case law which had grown up as the result of their judicial interpretation. The purpose of the Marriage Act of that year was to consolidate these enactments in one Act. As a result, nearly twenty of these statutes were repealed *in toto* and most of the rest were repealed in part. Few changes were made in the substantive law: the only notable exception was that the Attorney-General's power to sue for the forfeiture of property was taken away—a power which the married women's property legislation had, in any case, already made virtually obsolete.
    The Act of 1949 has since been amended in minor details by a series of Acts,[1] one of which deserves special mention. The Acts of 1836 and 1898 had

---

[1] The Marriage Act 1949 (Amendment) Act 1954; the Marriage Acts Amendment Act 1958; the Marriage (Enabling) Act 1960; the Marriage (Wales and Monmouthshire) Act 1962; the Marriage (Registrar General's Licence) Act 1970. These Acts (except for that of 1962) and the Marriage Act 1949 are collectively known as the Marriages Acts 1949-1970.

left those marrying according to the rites of the Church of England one privilege not shared by others: the power to marry in a private building on the authority of a special licence. This has now been extended by the Marriage (Registrar General's Licence) Act 1970, which permits the Registrar General to issue a licence authorising the solemnization of a marriage anywhere if one of the parties is suffering from a serious illness from which he is not expected to recover and cannot be moved to a register office or registered building. A much more important change in the law was the reduction of the age of majority to 18 by the Family Law Reform Act 1969, as a result of which anyone over this age may now marry without the consent of any other person.[1]

In addition to laying down the legal requirements relating to the preliminaries to marriage and the place and method of solemnization, the Marriages Acts also regulate the registration of marriages. The details of the relevant law are far too complex to be considered here,[2] but it must be emphasised that proper registration is of extreme importance not only to the parties themselves but also to others (including government departments) who may wish to have evidence of the marriage.[3]

The above outline will have made it clear that the principles underlying the modern law cannot be understood without a knowledge of their historical origin. The law is now hopelessly out of date: proposals for reform will be considered later.[4]

It will be convenient to consider the modern law under two heads: (a) where the marriage is solemnized according to the rites of the Church of England, and (b) where it is solemnized in some other way. Before doing this, however, we must consider the question of consent to the marriage of a person under the age of 18, and finally it will be necessary to discuss marriages in naval, military and air force chapels.

2. MARRIAGES OF PERSONS UNDER THE AGE OF 18

If either party to the marriage is over the age of 16 but under the age of 18, certain persons are normally required to give their express consent to the marriage or are given a power to dissent from it. The purpose of this provision is, of course, to prevent minors' contracting unwise marriages. Doubtless in 1753 Parliament was primarily concerned to see that property did not get into the hands of undesirable suitors; today its object is to cut down the number of potentially unstable unions.[5] Should the marriage be solemnized without consent, the damage will have been done; consequently lack of consent will normally not make the marriage void.[6]

---

[1] Section 2 (1). This implements the recommendations of the Latey Committee on the Age of Majority, 1967, Cmnd. 3342.

[2] They are contained in Part IV of the Marriage Act 1949 and in the Marriage (Registrar General's Licence) Act 1970, s. 15.

[3] See Law Com. No. 53 (Report on Solemnization of Marriage), Annex, para. 104. See *ibid.*, paras. 105-118 for a critical review of the present law and for suggestions for reform.

[4] *Post*, pp. 51-53.

[5] Report of the Latey Committee, Cmnd. 3342, paras. 135-177; Eekelaar, *Family Security and Family Breakdown*, 63-64; Cretney, *Principles of Family Law*, 3rd Ed., 11-12.

[6] Law Com. No. 53, Annex, para. 49. See *post*, p. 78. But this is not the case if the parent or other person publicly dissents on the publication of banns which will then be void: *post*, p. 79.

Those whose consent is required are the parents or guardians of the minor or the person to whose custody the minor has been committed by a court order: the full details are set out in section 3 and Schedule 2 of the Marriage Act which is reproduced (as later amended) in Appendix C, *post*.[1] It should be noted that no consent is required at all if the minor is a widow or widower.[2] It will also be seen from what follows that, if it is impossible to obtain the necessary consent or, more particularly, if the consent is withheld, the consent of the court may be obtained instead. The "court" for this purpose is the High Court, a county court or a magistrates' court sitting as a "domestic court";[3] in practice, almost all applications are made to a magistrate's court.

Marriages by a Superintendent Registrar's Certificate.—If the parties propose to marry on the authority of a superintendent registrar's certificate (whether by licence or without licence), the necessary consent or consents must be expressly given. If a person's consent cannot be obtained because he is absent or inaccessible or under any disability (*e.g.*, insanity), it is dispensed with entirely if there is any other person whose consent is also required (as will be the case where both parents must consent); where no other person's consent is required, however, either the Registrar General may dispense with the necessity of any consent or the consent of the court must be obtained. Where any person's consent is *refused*, then the consent of the court must be obtained in any case.[4]

Marriages by the Registrar General's Licence.—In this case the position is exactly the same as above except that the consent of a person who is absent, inaccessible or under a disability is never automatically dispensed with. The Registrar General has a discretion to dispense with it in all cases, whether or not there is any other person whose consent is required.[5]

Marriages by a Common Licence.—If the parties propose to marry on the authority of a common licence, the necessary consent or consents must be expressly given, and precisely the same rules apply as in the case of marriages by a superintendent registrar's certificate except that, where the only person whose consent is required is absent, inaccessible or under a disability, the

---

[1] Although the father of an illegitimate child has had a limited power to appoint a testamentary guardian since 1959 (*post*, p. 365), the Schedule of the Marriage Act has not been amended so as to give that guardian any power to assent to or dissent from the child's marriage. Has this anomalous position been produced by an oversight?

[2] Marriage Act 1949, s. 3 (1). If the minor is a ward of court, the court's consent must be obtained in addition to any other consents required by the Marriage Act: *ibid.*, s. 3 (6). See *post*, p. 381.

[3] *Ibid.*, s. 3 (5), as amended by the Family Law Reform Act 1969, s. 2 (2), and the Domestic Proceedings and Magistrates' Courts Act 1978, Sched. 2; Magistrates' Courts Act 1980, s. 65 (1) (c). For the meaning of "domestic court", see *ante*, p. 7. There is no statutory right of appeal from an order of the court giving or withholding consent, so that there is no appeal at all from the decision of a magistrates' court: *Re Queskey*, [1946] Ch. 250; [1946] 1 All E.R. 717. Presumably this also applies in the case of a county court.

[4] Marriage Act 1949, s. 3 (1). Consent once given can be withdrawn at any time before the solemnization: *Hodgkinson* v. *Wilkie* (1795), 1 Hag. Con. 262, 265. *Quaere* whether a superintendent registrar could revoke a certificate on this ground: *cf. post*, p. 46, n. 6.

[5] Marriage (Registrar General's Licence) Act 1970, s. 6.

necessity of obtaining any consent may be dispensed with by the Master of the Faculties and not by the Registrar General.[1]

Marriages after the Publication of Banns.—In this case express consent need not be given but

> "if any person whose consent to the marriage would have been required ... in the case of a marriage intended to be solemnized otherwise than after the publication of the banns, openly and publicly declares or causes to be declared, in the church or chapel in which the banns are published, at the time of the publication, his dissent from the intended marriage, the publication of the banns shall be void."[2]

The Act does not expressly empower the court to consent to the marriage in this case. If the court's consent is obtained, therefore, it is probably necessary for the parties to marry on the authority of a common licence or a superintendent registrar's certificate.[3]

3. MARRIAGES ACCORDING TO THE RITES OF THE CHURCH OF ENGLAND

There are two matters to be considered. First, certain preliminary formalities must be observed: a marriage may be solemnized according to the rites of the Church of England (which includes the Church in Wales)[4] only after the publication of banns or on the authority of a common licence, a special licence or a superintendent registrar's certificate.[5] Secondly, the law relating to the ceremony itself must be discussed.

Publication of Banns.—Since the purpose of publishing banns is to give publicity to the proposed marriage, they must normally be published in the parish church of the parish in which the parties reside, or if, they reside in different parishes, in the parish church of each of the two parishes.[6] But where a party resides in a chapelry (*i.e.*, a district attached to one of certain specified chapels) or in a parish in which the bishop of the diocese has licensed a public chapel or church building for the publication of banns and the solemnization of marriages (as he may do in a remote part of a parish covering a wide area or if the building is shared with other denominations), banns may be published either in that authorised chapel or building or in the parish church,[7] and if he resides in a district in which there is no church or

---

[1] Marriage Act 1949, s. 3 (2).

[2] *Ibid.*, s. 3 (3).

[3] Although it is arguable that, if a person's consent is refused and that of the court is obtained instead, he is no longer "a person whose consent to the marriage would have been required" and therefore any subsequent dissent will be ineffectual.

[4] Marriage Act 1949, ss. 78 (2), 80 (3). A few technical provisions of the Act do not apply in Wales: see *ibid.*, 6th Sched., as amended by the Marriage (Wales and Monmouthshire) Act 1962.

[5] *Ibid.*, s. 5.

[6] *Ibid.*, s. 6 (1). There are special provisions dealing with changes in parish boundaries, the amalgamation of parishes and benefices, and cases where churches are being repaired or rebuilt or have been injured by war damage: *ibid.*, ss. 10, 18, 19 and 23; Pastoral Measure 1968, s. 27. For the meaning of "resides", see *ante*, p. 8.

[7] Marriage Act 1949, s. 6 (1); Sharing of Church Buildings Act 1969, s. 6. See the definition of "authorised chapel" in the Marriage Act 1949, s. 78 (1), and see also *ibid.*, s. 21. For the licensing of chapels, see s. 20.

chapel in which divine service is usually held every Sunday, banns may be published in any adjoining parish or chapelry.[1] Banns may be published in Scotland, Northern Ireland or the Republic of Ireland if either party is residing there,[2] or, provided that both parties are British subjects, in certain other parts of the British Commonwealth.[3] If one of the parties is an officer, seaman or marine on a Royal Naval ship *at sea*, banns may be published on board by the chaplain or, if there is no chaplain, by the captain or other officer in command.[4]

If the parties wish to be married in another church or authorised chapel which is the normal place of worship of either of them,[5] banns must be published there as well as in their parish churches.[6]

Manner of Publication.—Banns must be published on three Sundays during morning service by a clergyman of the Church of England.[7] The form of words is prescribed by the rubric in the Book of Common Prayer.[8]

Names in which Banns should be Published.—Since the purpose of the publication of banns would be defeated if the parties could not be identified, they must be referred to by the names by which they are generally known. This will, of course, usually be their original Christian names and surname, or in the case of a woman who has been previously married, her married surname;[9] but if a person has assumed some other name by which he is generally known, the banns should be published in that name. An example of due publication under an assumed name is to be seen in *Dancer* v. *Dancer*.[10] The wife was the legitimate daughter of Mr. and Mrs. Knight. When she was aged three, her mother went to live with a man called Roberts by whom she had five children. All the children, including the wife, Jessamine, passed as the legitimate children of Roberts and Mrs. Knight (who assumed the name of Roberts) and were known by the name of Roberts; and it was not till she was 17, when Roberts died, that Jessamine discovered that she was not his daughter. She continued to use the name of Roberts, and on the advice of the vicar who published the banns, she was named therein as Jessamine Roberts. It was held that the banns were duly published, for the wife was generally

---

[1] Marriage Act 1949, s. 6 (3). See also s. 6 (2) and the Pastoral Measure 1968, s. 29.

[2] *Ibid.*, s. 13.

[3] Marriage of British Subjects (Facilities) Acts 1915 and 1916. See 17 Halsbury's Statutes (3rd Ed.) 35-38.

[4] Marriage Act 1949, s. 14.

[5] As defined in the Marriage Act 1949, s. 72. The party must be enrolled on the church electoral roll. For marriages in guild churches in the City of London, see the City of London (Guild Churches) Act 1952, s. 22.

[6] Marriage Act 1949, s. 6 (4).

[7] *Ibid.*, ss. 7 and 9. If there is no morning service, banns may be published during the evening service (s. 7 (1)), and a lay reader may publish banns if there is no clergyman officiating (s. 9 (2)). A clergyman is entitled to a week's notice in writing before he publishes banns: s. 8.

[8] "I publish the banns of marriage between *M.* of   and *N.* of   . If any of you know cause or just impediment why these two persons should not be joined together in holy matrimony, ye are to declare it. This is the first [second, *or* third] time of asking."

[9] *Per* Sir R. Phillimore in *Fendall* v. *Goldsmid* (1877), 2 P.D. 263, 264.

[10] [1949] P. 147; [1948] 2 All E.R. 731. See also *R.* v. *Billinghurst* (1814), 3 M. & S. 250. For the converse case of an undue publication under the original surname, see *Tooth* v. *Barrow* (1854), 1 Ecc. & Ad. 371.

known by that name and the purpose of publishing the banns under it was not to conceal her identity but to avoid any concealment.

In all the cases where it has been held that the banns have not been duly published, there has been some fraudulent intention to conceal the party's identity.[1] The reason for the concealment is immaterial: thus it has been held that there was an undue publication where the parties' intention was to conceal the marriage from the man's relations,[2] and where the man was a deserter from the Royal Field Artillery and had assumed a false name to avoid detection and prosecution.[3] A difficult case is *Chipchase* v. *Chipchase*.[4] A woman, whose maiden surname was Matthews, had married in 1915 a man called Leetch. He had deserted her in 1916 and she had not heard of him since. In 1928 she went through a form of marriage with the petitioner after the publication of banns in the name of Matthews, which she had used for some two years before the marriage and by which she was generally known in the district; her reason for having the banns published in this name was not that she was known by it but that it served to conceal, or at least not to emphasise, the fact that she had been married before. HENN COLLINS, J., holding that there had been an undue publication of the banns, said:[5]

"The wife did not conceal her identity from the persons in her parish who knew her by that name, but I think that one of the purposes of the Marriage Act would be defeated if it was open to a person to have banns called in a name by which he was known in the parish when the use of his legal name might lead persons to make uncomfortable inquiries. In my view that is one of the very things against which the Act of Parliament was directed."

In so far as HENN COLLINS, J., held that there must be some intentional concealment before the court will hold that there has not been a due publication, his decision follows the earlier cases. The difficulty is to discover in what name the banns should have been published, for it is submitted that, if she was generally known by the name of Matthews, it would have equally defeated the purposes of the Act to publish the banns under any other name. The common sense answer to this problem is that the banns should have been published under both names in the alternative (*i.e.*, Matthews or Leetch) even though there is no precedent for this.

Common Licences.—Licences dispensing with the necessity of the publication of banns have been granted since the fourteenth century. They are now known as common licences (to distinguish them from special licences granted only by the Archbishop of Canterbury) and may be granted by the bishop of a diocese acting through his chancellor or one of the latter's surrogates.[6]

---

[1] *Chipchase* v. *Chipchase*, [1939] P. 391, 398; [1939] 3 All E.R. 895, 899-900; *Gompertz* v. *Kensit* (1872), L.R. 13 Eq. 369. But if banns are published in a name by which the party is not known at all, there cannot be a due publication even though there is no intention to deceive. See further Jackson, *Formation and Annulment of Marriage*, 2nd Ed., 173-181.

[2] *Tooth* v. *Barrow*, (*supra*).

[3] *Small* v. *Small* (1923), 67 Sol. Jo. 277.

[4] [1942] P. 37; [1941] 2 All E.R. 560.

[5] At pp. 40 and 562, respectively.

[6] Cripps, *Church and Clergy*, 8th Ed., 547-548.

A common licence may be granted for the solemnization of a marriage only in the parish church of the parish, or an authorised chapel in the ecclesiastical district, in which one of the parties has had his or her usual place of residence for fifteen days immediately before the grant of the licence, or in the parish church or authorised chapel which is the usual place of worship of either of the parties.[1] The similarity between the granting of a common licence and the publication of banns is very close: the churches in which the marriage may be solemnized are the same, fifteen days is the period required for the publishing of banns on three successive Sundays, and there appears to be no significant difference between the word "resides" for the purpose of the publication of banns and the phrase "usual place of residence" for the purpose of the granting of a common licence.[2] On the other hand, the residence of the other party is immaterial.

Before a licence may be granted, one of the parties must swear (i) that he or she believes that there is no impediment to the marriage, (ii) that either the residence requirement is satisfied or the church in which the marriage is to take place is the regular place of worship of one of them, and (iii) if either of them is a minor, that all consents required by the Act have been obtained or dispensed with, or that the court has consented to the marriage, or that there is no person whose consent is required.[3]

Any person seeking to prevent the granting of a licence may enter a caveat stating the ground of his objection. In such a case the licence may not be granted until the caveat is withdrawn or the ecclesiastical judge with jurisdiction has decided that it ought not to obstruct the grant.[4] Although a caveat is rarely entered, the power to do so might be exercised, for example, by a parent who fears that his minor child may obtain a licence by falsely swearing that his consent to the marriage had been given.

Special Licences.—A special licence may be granted only by the Archbishop of Canterbury acting through the Master of the Faculties.[5] A special licence differs from any other authorisation to marry according to the rites of the Church of England in that it may permit the parties to marry at any time and in any place;[6] it is, therefore, the only way in which they may marry in a church or chapel in which their banns could not be published or for which a common licence or a superintendent registrar's certificate could not be issued,[7] or in any other building, *e.g.*, a private house or a hospital,

---

[1] Marriage Act 1949, s. 15. If either party resides in a district where there is no church or chapel in which divine service is usually held every Sunday, the licence may authorise the solemnization of the marriage in any adjoining parish or chapelry.

[2] See *ante*, p. 8. But see McClean, *The Meaning of Residence*, 11 I.C.L.Q. 1153.

[3] Marriage Act 1949, s. 16 (1).

[4] Marriage Act 1949, s. 16 (2).

[5] By Roman Catholic canon law the dispensation had to be papal; the power was transferred to the Archbishop of Canterbury by the Ecclesiastical Licences Act 1533. The office of the Master of the Faculties is performed by the Dean of the Arches: Public Worship Regulation Act 1874, s. 7.

[6] Marriage Act 1949, s. 79 (6).

[7] But the marriage *ceremony* may be celebrated there after a marriage in a register office: see *post*, p. 48.

according to the rites of the Church of England. In practice special licences are granted only in exceptional circumstances or grave emergencies.[1]

Superintendent Registrar's Certificates.—A marriage may be solemnized on the authority of a superintendent registrar's certificate in any church or chapel in which banns may be published and which is within the registration district in which either party resides or which is the usual place of worship of either of them.[2] The issue of certificates will be discussed below; it should, however, be observed that a marriage in the Church of England may not be solemnized on the authority of a certificate *by licence*.[3]

The Solemnization of the Marriage.—All marriages according to the rites of the Church of England must be solemnized by a clerk in holy orders of that Church in the presence of at least two other witnesses.[4] Except where the marriage is solemnized on the authority of a special licence, it must also be solemnized between 8 a.m. and 6 p.m.[5] In the case of a marriage after the publication of banns, the marriage may only be solemnized in one of the churches or authorised chapels in which the banns have been published; in the case of a marriage on the authority of a common licence or a superintendent registrar's certificate, it must take place in the church or chapel specified in the licence or certificate.[6] The marriage must also be solemnized within three months of the completion of the publication of the banns, the grant of the licence or the entry of notice in the superintendent registrar's marriage notice book, as the case may be.[7]

4. MARRIAGES SOLEMNIZED OTHERWISE THAN ACCORDING TO THE RITES OF THE CHURCH OF ENGLAND

All marriages other than those celebrated according to the rites of the Church of England may be solemnized only on the authority of a superintendent registrar's certificate, either without a licence or by licence, or on the authority of the Registrar General's licence.[8] The difference between a certificate *simpliciter* and a certificate with a licence corresponds roughly to that between banns and a common licence, in that in the latter case the superintendent registrar is concerned with the residence qualification of one

---

[1] On the average about 250 special licences are granted every year. The cost is £25, which may be waived.

[2] Marriage Act 1949, ss. 17, 34, 35 (3). But the marriage may not be solemnized on the authority of a superintendent registrar's certificate without the minister's consent: *ibid.*, s. 17.

[3] *Ibid.*, s. 26 (2).

[4] *Ibid.*, ss. 22, 25. The precise words of the ceremony need not be spoken by the parties and consent may be given by signs, *e.g.*, in the case of a dumb person: *Harrod* v. *Harrod* (1854), 1 K. & J. 4. The marriage is probably contracted as soon as the parties have taken each other as husband and wife: *Quick* v. *Quick*, [1953] V.L.R. 224.

[5] *Ibid.*, ss. 4, 75 (1) (a).

[6] *Ibid.*, ss. 12 (1), 15, 25 (d).

[7] *Ibid.*, ss. 12 (2), 16 (3), 33.

[8] The Marriage Act does not expressly so enact but this is its obvious intention and must be its effect: see Thompson, 90 L.Q.R. 28, refuting the argument to the contrary put forward by Barton, 89 L.Q.R. 181.

party only and the authorisation to marry may be obtained much more quickly. The Registrar General's licence corresponds to a special licence in that it enables the parties to marry elsewhere than in a building in which they could marry on the authority of a superintendent registrar's certificate. As with marriages in the Church of England, it will be necessary to consider separately the law relating to the preliminary formalities and that relating to the marriage ceremony itself.

Issue of a Superintendent Registrar's Certificate without a Licence.— Notice of the proposed marriage must be given in writing to the superintendent registrar of the registration district in which the parties have resided for at least seven days immediately beforehand, or, if they have resided in different districts, then to the superintendent registrar of each district.[1] The party giving the notice must at the same time make a solemn declaration (i) that he or she believes that there is no impediment to the marriage, (ii) that the residence requirement is satisfied, and (iii) if either of them is a minor, that all consents required by the Act have been obtained or dispensed with, or that the court has consented to the marriage, or that there is no person whose consent is required.[2] The superintendent registrar must then enter the details of the notice in his marriage notice book and display the notice or a copy of it in a conspicuous place in his office for 21 successive days.[3]

As in the case of the granting of a common licence, anyone may enter a caveat against the issue of a certificate. The certificate may not then be issued until either the caveat has been withdrawn or the superintendent registrar or the Registrar General has satisfied himself that it ought not to obstruct the issue of the certificate.[4] Where the objection is that a consent to the marriage of a minor has not been obtained, any person whose consent is required may effectively prevent the marriage by the much simpler means of writing "forbidden" against the entry in the marriage notice book, in which case the certificate may not be issued unless the consent of the court has been obtained.[5]

If no impediment has been shown and the issue of the certificate has not been forbidden, the superintendent registrar must issue it at the end of the 21 days.[6]

As in the case of the publication of banns, a certificate may be issued locally if one of the parties resides in Scotland or Northern Ireland,[7] or,

---

[1] Marriage Act 1949, s. 27 (1). For the matters which the notice must contain, see s. 27 (3). For the meaning of "resides", see *ante*, p. 8.

[2] *Ibid.*, s. 28. *Cf.* the oath required before a common licence may be granted, *ante*, p. 44. The superintendent registrar is entitled to demand written evidence that the consents required have been given if either party is a minor: Family Law Reform Act 1969, s. 2 (3).

[3] *Ibid.*, ss. 27 (4), 31 (1).

[4] *Ibid.*, s. 29. A person entering a caveat frivolously is liable in damages to the person against whose marriage it was entered.

[5] *Ibid.*, s. 30.

[6] *Ibid.*, s. 31 (2). *Quaere* whether he can revoke the certificate before the marriage is solemnized if he discovers some impediment (*e.g.*, that one party is a minor and parental consent has not been given).

[7] *Ibid.*, ss. 37 (as amended by the Marriage (Scotland) Act 1977, Scheds. 2 and 3) and 38. (But not when the other party resides in the Republic of Ireland).

provided that both parties are British subjects, in certain other parts of the British Commonwealth.[1] Similarly, notice of marriage may be given by an officer, seaman or marine borne on the books of one of Her Majesty's ships at sea to the officer commanding the ship, who is empowered to grant a certificate.[2]

Issue of a Superintendent Registrar's Certificate with a Licence.—The law relating to the issue of a certificate with a licence is the same as that relating to the issue of a certificate *simpliciter* except in two important respects. First, notice is to be given to only *one* superintendent registrar—that of the registration district in which *either* party has resided for a period of *fifteen* days immediately beforehand.[3] The residence of the other party is irrelevant provided that it is in England or Wales,[4] and the provisions relating to parties resident in other parts of the United Kingdom and the issue of certificates on board warships do not apply. Secondly, the superintendent registrar is not required to display the notice or a copy of it in his office, but, unless an impediment to the marriage has been shown or the issue of the certificate has been forbidden, he must issue the certificate and licence at any time after the expiration of one whole day after the giving of the notice.[5]

Solemnization of the Marriage.—A marriage on the authority of a superintendent registrar's certificate (whether by licence or without a licence) may be solemnized in a superintendent registrar's office, in a registered building, or according to the usages of the Society of Friends or of the Jews.[6] In any case the marriage must be solemnized within three months of the entry being made in the marriage notice book; and, unless it is a Quaker or Jewish marriage, it must also be solemnized between 8 a.m. and 6 p.m., with open doors and in the presence of at least two witnesses in addition to the superintendent registrar and registrar or, alternatively, the registrar or authorised person.[7]

Marriage in a Register Office.—The parties may marry in the office of the superintendent registrar to whom the notice of the intended marriage was given (or, if notice was given to two superintendent registrars, in the office of either of them), in the presence of the superintendent registrar and also of a registrar of marriages.[8] They must declare that they know of no impediment why they should not be joined in matrimony and then contract the marriage

---

[1] Marriage of British Subjects (Facilities) Acts 1915 and 1916. See 17 Halsbury's Statutes (3rd Ed.) 35-38.
[2] Marriage Act 1949, s. 39.
[3] *Ibid.*, s. 27 (2).
[4] The Act specifically states "whether the persons to be married reside in the same or in different districts" and thus implies that one of these two conditions must be satisfied.
[5] *Ibid.*, s. 32. Hence, if notice is given on Monday, the certificate and licence may be issued on Wednesday.
[6] *Ibid.*, s. 26 (1). For marriages in the Church of England on a certificate without licence, see *ante*, p. 45.
[7] *Ibid.*, ss. 4, 33, 44 (2), 45 (1), 75 (1) (a).
[8] *Ibid.*, ss. 36, 45 (1).

per verba de praesenti.[1] No religious service may be used in a superintendent registrar's office, but, if the parties so wish, the marriage there may be followed by a religious ceremony in a church or chapel. In this case the marriage which is *legally* binding for all purposes is that in the register office.[2] This provision is useful if the parties wish to be married in a private chapel in which banns may not be published (*e.g.*, the chapel of an Oxford or Cambridge college) without being put to the expense of obtaining a special licence or in a non-conformist place of worship which is not a registered building.

Marriage in a Registered Building.—Any building which is certified as a place of religious worship[3] may be registered by the Registrar General for the solemnization of marriages.[4] A superintendent registrar may normally issue a certificate or certificate and licence for the solemnization of a marriage in a registered building only within his own district, or, where the marriage is without a licence and the parties reside in different districts, within the district in which either of them resides.[5] In two cases, however, he may issue a certificate (with or without licence) for the solemnization of a marriage in another district. First, he may do so if there is not in the district in which one of the parties resides a registered building in which marriages are solemnized according to the practices of the religious body to which one of them belongs.[6] Secondly, he may issue a certificate for the solemnization of the marriage in a registered building which is the usual place of worship of one of the parties.[7]

A marriage in a registered building may take place only if there is present a registrar of marriages or an "authorised person".[8] It will be recalled that since the Marriage Act of 1898 the trustees or governing body of a registered building have been empowered to authorise a person to be present at a marriage there and thus dispense with the necessity of having a registrar in attendance.[9] The authorised person will, of course, normally be a minister of

---

[1] Marriage Act 1949, ss. 45 (1), 44 (3). The form of words to be used is: "I call upon these persons here present to witness that I, *AB*, do take thee, *CD*, to be my lawful wedded wife [or husband]." A Welsh form may be used: s. 52. As to marriages of dumb persons, see *Harrod* v. *Harrod*, p. 45, n. 4 *ante*.

[2] *Ibid.*, ss. 45 (2), 46.

[3] Under the Places of Worship Registration Act 1855.

[4] See the Marriage Act 1949, ss. 41 and 42, as amended by the Marriage Acts Amendment Act 1958, s. 1 (1). For church buildings shared by two or more denominations, see the Sharing of Church Buildings Act 1969, s. 6 and Sched. 1.

[5] Marriage Act 1949, ss. 34 and 36. But no marriage may take place in a registered building without the consent of the minister or one of the trustees, owners, deacons or managers: *ibid.*, s. 44 (1).

[6] *Ibid.*, s. 35 (1), as amended by the Marriage Act 1949 (Amendment) Act 1954, s. 2. The registered building in which the superintendent registrar authorises the solemnization of the marriage must be in the registration district nearest to the residence of that party in which there is a registered building where marriages may be so solemnized.

[7] *Ibid.*, s. 35 (2), as amended by the Marriage Act 1949 (Amendment) Act 1954, s. 1.

[8] *Ibid.*, s. 44 (2).

[9] See now the Marriage Act 1949, s. 43, as amended by the Marriage Acts Amendment Act 1958, s. 1 (2); the Sharing of Church Buildings Act 1969, Sched. 1. An authorised person may be present (and thus dispense with the need of having a registrar) at a marriage in any registered building in the same registration district: Marriage Act 1949, s. 44 (2) (b). See also *ibid.*, s. 44 (5).

the particular faith or denomination. The functions of the registrar (or authorised person) are to ensure that certificates (and, if necessary, a licence) have been issued, that the provisions of the Marriage Act relating to the solemnization are complied with, and to register the marriage. The marriage may be in any form provided that, at some stage in the ceremony, a declaration is made similar to that required when the marriage is in a register office, and the parties contract the union *per verba de praesenti*.[1]

Quaker Marriages.—The Act of 1949 preserves the right of the Society of Friends to solemnize marriages according to their own usages. Provided that the rules of the Society permit it, a marriage may be contracted in this way even though one or both parties are not members of the Society.[2]

Jewish Marriages.—The privilege of the Jewish community to celebrate marriages according to their own rites is also preserved. In this case, however, both parties must profess the Jewish religion.[3]

Marriages solemnized on the Authority of the Registrar General's Licence.—The purpose of the Marriage (Registrar General's Licence) Act 1970 is to enable the Registrar General to issue a licence authorising the solemnization of a marriage elsewhere than in a register office or registered building. This is complementary to the Archbishop of Canterbury's power to issue a special licence. But whereas the latter serves two purposes—to enable a person to marry even though he is too ill or infirm to be moved and to permit a wedding to take place for purely social reasons in a church or private chapel where the parties' banns could not be published—the Registrar General's licence is intended to serve only the first. Consequently its issue is subject to two important limitations. In the first place, the Registrar General must be satisfied that one of the parties is seriously ill and not expected to recover and that he cannot be moved to a place where the marriage could be solemnized under the provisions of the Act of 1949. Secondly, no such marriage may be solemnized according to the rites of the Church of England.[4]

No residence qualification is necessary, and notice must be given to the superintendent registrar of the registration district in which it is intended to solemnize the marriage. The party giving the notice must make the same declaration (except as regards the residence qualification) as that required when other notices are given to a superintendent registrar. In addition he must also produce such evidence as the Registrar General may require to

---

[1] Marriage Act 1949, s. 44 (1), (3). A slightly different form of words may be used if the marriage is solemnized in the presence of an authorised person without the presence of a registrar.
[2] *Ibid.*, s. 47. This privilege was first granted by the Marriage (Society of Friends) Act 1860. See the *Marriage Regulations* of the Society of Friends; Jackson, *Formation and Annulment of Marriage*, 2nd Ed., 198-200. The rule that the building in which the marriage is to be solemnized must be within the registration district in which one of the parties resides does not apply to marriages according to the usages of the Society of Friends: s. 35 (4).
[3] Marriage Act 1949, s. 26 (1) (d). Section 35 (4) (see n. 2, *supra*) also applies. See Jackson, *op. cit.*, 200-202.
[4] Marriage (Registrar General's Licence) Act 1970, s. 1. The Registrar General may remit the fee of £15 in whole or in part if he thinks that the payment would cause hardship to the parties: s. 17 (1).

satisfy him (i) that there is no impediment to the marriage, (ii) that all necessary consents have been given if either party is a minor, (iii) that there is a sufficient reason why a licence should be granted, and (iv) that the statutory conditions regarding the health of one party are satisfied and that that person can and does understand the nature and purport of the marriage ceremony.[1] The superintendent registrar must then enter the details in his marriage notice book and inform the Registrar General.[2] As in the case of a superintendent registrar's certificate, a caveat may be entered against the issue of a licence and the marriage may be forbidden by anyone whose consent to the marriage is required and has not been given.[3] If there is no impediment and the Registrar General is satisfied that sufficient grounds exist for the granting of a licence, he must issue it.[4]

The marriage must be solemnized in the place stated in the notice of marriage and within *one* month of the entry in the marriage notice book.[5] It may take the form of a civil ceremony in the presence of the superintendent registrar and a registrar,[6] or it may be according to any form or ceremony the parties choose to adopt (other than the rites of the Church of England) in the presence of a registrar. At least two witnesses must be present, and at some stage the parties must make the same declaration and contract the marriage in the same form of words as would be required at a marriage in a register office.[7]

5. MARRIAGES IN NAVAL, MILITARY, AND AIR FORCE CHAPELS

Part V of the Marriage Act enables certain persons to marry in naval, military and air force chapels certified as such by the Secretary of State for Defence.[8] The purpose of this is to enable members of the Forces to marry in garrison churches, etc. Consequently, in order that a marriage may be solemnized in such a chapel, at least one of the parties must be a serving member or a former regular member of one of the armed forces, or a serving member of one of the women's services, or a daughter of any such person.[9] The privilege has since been extended to members of certain Commonwealth and N.A.T.O. forces and their daughters.[10] If the chapel has been licensed for

---

[1] Marriage (Registrar General's Licence) Act 1970, ss. 2 and 3. In the case of (iv) a registered medical practitioner's certificate is sufficient evidence.

[2] *Ibid.*, ss. 2 (2) and 4.

[3] *Ibid.*, ss. 5 and 7. A caveat may be entered with either the superintendent registrar or the Registrar General; in either case, however, only the Registrar General may decide that it should not obstruct the issue of the licence.

[4] *Ibid.*, s. 7.

[5] *Ibid.*, ss. 8 and 9. The marriage does not necessarily have to take place between 8 a.m. and 6 p.m.: see s. 16 (4).

[6] As in the case of a marriage in a register office, this may be followed by a religious ceremony which will be of no legal effect: *ibid.*, s. 11.

[7] *Ibid.*, s. 10. The provisions relating to the presence of a registrar and two witnesses, the declaration, and the form of words to be used do not apply if the marriage is solemnized according to the usages of the Society of Friends or, if both parties profess the Jewish faith, according to Jewish rites. No clergyman of the Church of England may solemnize the marriage.

[8] Replacing the Marriage (Naval, Military and Air Force Chapels) Act 1932. See also the Defence (Transfer of Functions) Act 1964, s. 1 (2).

[9] For the detailed list, see the Marriage Act 1949, s. 68 and Sched. 3.

[10] Visiting Forces and International Headquarters (Application of Law) Order 1965, arts. 3 and 12 (2) and Sched. 3 (S.I. 1965 No. 1536).

this purpose by the bishop of the diocese, it may be treated as the parish church of the parish in which it is situated, and banns may be published and marriages solemnized in it provided that at least one of the parties resides in that parish.[1] The Registrar General may also register a chapel so as to enable the superintendent registrar of the district in which it stands to issue a certificate to marry in it (either with or without a licence) according to rites other than those of the Church of England.[2] Subject to these limitations and certain other modifications,[3] the same rules apply to marriages in these chapels as to other marriages.

6. RETROSPECTIVE VALIDATION OF MARRIAGES WHICH ARE VOID BECAUSE OF FORMAL DEFECTS

Although, as we shall see later,[4] failure to observe all the formal requirements of English law does not necessarily invalidate the marriage, certain defects in form will have this effect. The complexities of the English law on this subject have in the past led persons who were morally innocent to go through a form of marriage which has subsequently proved to be a legal nullity. Parliament has from time to time intervened to validate these marriages by curing the informality retrospectively.[5] Although the number of cases in which innocent parties contract a marriage that is void because of formal invalidity is not likely to be great today, nevertheless the situation might conceivably arise. Consequently, the Marriages Validity (Provisional Orders) Acts 1905 and 1924 have given the Home Secretary power to make orders for the purpose of curing retrospectively any formal defect in the marriage or of removing any doubt about the validity of a marriage due to informality.[6]

7. PROPOSALS FOR REFORM

It will be seen that the present law relating to the formalities of marriage is still in principle based upon the provisions of Lord Hardwicke's Act of 1753 and the Marriage Act of 1836. It thus reflects the desire to prevent the clandestine marriages which were the disgrace of eighteenth century England. In this respect the law is now hopelessly out of date. Clandestine marriages are no longer the social evil that they were 250 years ago; nor does the modern law effectively prevent them. Provided that both parties are over

---

[1] Marriage Act 1949, s. 69. But the parties may not marry in a chapel solely on the ground that it is the usual place of worship of either of them: see Sched. 4, Part I.

[2] *Ibid.*, s. 70. "Authorised persons" may be appointed by the Secretary of State: Sched. 4, Part IV. It seems that the parties may marry there on the ground that no other registered building is available or that it is the regular place of worship of one of them: *ibid.*, Part III.

[3] See the Marriage Act 1949, Sched. 4, as amended by the Marriage Acts Amendment Act 1958, s. 1 (2).

[4] *Post*, pp. 78-80.

[5] A list of the public general Acts passed for this purpose will be found in 22 Halsbury's Laws of England (4th Ed.), 617. Many private Acts have also been passed.

[6] Orders made under these Acts are subject to special parliamentary procedure under the Statutory Orders (Special Procedure) Acts 1945 and 1965: S.I. 1949 No. 2393. None has been made in recent years: Law Com. No. 53, p. 65, n. 30. There is no power under these Acts to legalise a marriage which is void because of the incapacity of either party.

the age of 18, a marriage can usually be solemnized on a common licence or a superintendent registrar's certificate and licence without the knowledge of the parties' friends and relations. The ease with which people can travel round the country and acquire a new residence makes it virtually impossible for the parents of a determined minor to forbid his marriage before it takes place. Another problem is presented by the speed with which the parties can rush into marriage without giving due thought to the implications of their act. A superintendent registrar's licence may be obtained in 48 hours and a common licence in as many minutes: an extreme case illustrating how a person may be married at literally five minutes' notice may be found in *Cooper v. Crane.*[1]

The law has recently come under a comprehensive review by a Working Party set up by the Law Commission and the Registrar General.[2] They begin by saying:[3]

> "We have assumed that the purpose of a sound marriage law is to ensure that marriages are solemnised only in respect of those who are free to marry and have freely agreed to do so and that the status of those who marry shall be established with certainty so that doubts do not arise, either in the minds of the parties or in the community, about who is married and who is not. To this end it appears to us to be necessary that there should be proper opportunity for the investigation of capacity (and, in the case of minors, parental consent) before the marriage and that the investigation should be carried out, uniformly for parties to all marriages, by persons trained to perform this function. We suggest that the law should guard against clandestine marriages, that there should be proper opportunity for legal impediments to be declared or discovered, that all marriages should be publicly solemnised and that the marriage should be duly recorded in official registers. At the same time we recognise that a marriage ceremony is an important family and social occasion and we feel that unnecessary and irksome restrictions on its celebration should be avoided.
>
> "Moreover, since nearly every person who attains maturity marries at least once and attends numerous marriages of friends and relations and since the marriage creates a status which vitally concerns the public, the law of marriage should be as simple and easily understood as possible."

They conclude that these aims could be achieved only if the superintendent registrar's certificate became the standard legal authorisation to marry.[4] This would ensure that any necessary investigations would be made by an officer trained to conduct them. Furthermore, the abolition of both common licences and superintendent registrar's licences would achieve some measure of publicity of the parties' intention to marry. Both parties should be required to give notice to the superintendent registrar of the district (or districts) in which they have resided for not less than seven days. This would

---

[1] [1891] P. 369. The respondent, who had unknown to the petitioner obtained a licence and arranged the wedding, took her out and, having got her to the church door, threatened to blow his brains out unless she went into the church and married him. It was held that the petitioner had not discharged the burden of proving that her will was overborne and that consequently the marriage was valid.

[2] See Law Com. No. 53 (Solemnisation of Marriage), 1973.

[3] *Ibid.*, Annex, paras. 4-5.

[4] But the Church of England could still retain the publication of banns (or the issue of a licence) as an additional *ecclesiastical* formality if it wished.

mean that each would have to make a declaration about his (or her) own age, status, etc., and might also reduce the chance of a marriage by a person who did not understand the nature of the ceremony or who was under some improper pressure. The risk of minors' marrying without parental consent would be further reduced by requiring the parents to attend the register office in person or to have their signed consent witnessed by a person of standing. There should be a period of fifteen days after notice is given in which an impediment could be disclosed or discovered before the superintendent registrar could issue his certificate. The number of cases in which parties now apply for a common licence or superintendent registrar's licence because of genuine urgency is apparently very small. To meet these the Working Party would empower the Registrar General to reduce the period in appropriate cases: vesting the discretion in him would insulate superintendent registrars from pressure and would also ensure a uniform exercise. They would retain the special licence and the Registrar General's licence to meet the situations they are designed to meet today.

The Working Party made a large number of other proposals, most of which are too detailed to be discussed here. Two should be mentioned, however. First, the person celebrating the marriage should be under a duty to ensure that the parties understand that they are entering into a monogamous marriage and, if their native tongue is not English (or Welsh, where a Welsh form is permitted), that they understand the words used or, if they do not, that they repeat them in a language which they do understand. This is clearly a matter of considerable importance in view of the large number of immigrants now living in this country. Secondly, they drew attention to the defects in the law relating to the persons who are required to consent to the marriage of a minor. At present there are gaps—for example, the Act does not cover the case of parents who have separated by agreement without providing for the custody of their children—and the question of which parent's consent is required may turn on a difficult question of fact and law if it is necessary to decide which of them has deserted the other.

The Working Party probably provides as good a solution to the problems as practical limitations will permit. In the end, nothing will deter a minor determined at all costs to marry in the face of parental opposition or a bigamist determined to go through a ceremony with a woman who is convinced that she is entering into a lawful marriage. Nor perhaps is it realistic to devise a rule which would forbid marriage until the parties had known each other for a minimum period of time:[1] at least the requirement that both parties should give notice would remove the possibility of the facts of *Cooper* v. *Crane* occurring again.[2]

---

[1] The Latey Committee doubted whether the problem was as grave as is commonly supposed and were unanimously opposed to any kind of formal betrothal on the ground that this might encourage potentially unstable marriages rather than the reverse. See Cmnd. 3342, paras. 178-183.

[2] For further criticisms of the existing law, see Cretney, *Principles of Family Law*, 3rd Ed., 11-12 and 25-30; Eekelaar, *Family Security and Family Breakdown*, 69-71. An interesting and instructive comparison may be made with the recommendations of the Kilbrandon Committee dealing with the Scottish law, 1969, Cmnd. 4011.

F. THE RECOGNITION OF FOREIGN MARRIAGES[1]

The rapid development of international communications during the present century has made the question how far English courts will recognise marriages entered into abroad much more burning than it was before. Four questions—selected more or less at random—will indicate the sort of situations in which the problem of recognition will be important.

> The husband, whilst in this country, deserts his wife and leaves her penniless. Can she take proceedings against him for maintenance?
> The husband is killed in this country as a result of another's negligence. Can his wife sue the tortfeasor under the Fatal Accidents Act?
> Can the wife, whilst in this country, claim the benefits of social welfare legislation *qua* wife?
> The husband dies intestate with respect to realty in this country. Can his wife claim it as widow of the intestate?

The Concept of the Christian Marriage.—Our discussion must necessarily begin with an examination of *Hyde* v. *Hyde*.[2] The petitioner, who was originally domiciled in England, embraced the Mormon faith and went out to Utah at a time when polygamy was still being practised by Mormons. He there married the respondent. Some years later he renounced Mormonism and, having returned to England, asked his wife to join him. This she refused to do, and since the excommunication which had followed the petitioner's renunciation left her free to remarry by Mormon law, she went through a form of marriage with the co-respondent. The husband then petitioned for divorce on the ground of the respondent's adultery. LORD PENZANCE held that this marriage was polygamous and therefore not a marriage within the definition cited earlier,[3] and consequently held that he had no jurisdiction to entertain divorce proceedings.

Non-Christian Monogamous Marriages.—Although LORD PENZANCE referred to "marriage as it is understood in Christendom", it must not be supposed that this is synonymous with "a Christian marriage". If the marriage satisfies the four conditions he laid down, it will be recognised by English courts even though neither party professes the Christian faith provided that each had capacity by the relevant *lex domicilii* and they complied with the formalities laid down by the *lex loci celebrationis*.[4]

Most of the cases dealing with the recognition of foreign marriages have in fact been concerned with polygamous unions. It is still an open question how far English courts will recognise monogamous unions which fail to satisfy the other requirements laid down by LORD PENZANCE or which would have been void for some other reason if they had been contracted in England. It is submitted that the proper test to apply is that formulated by SIMON, P., in *Cheni* v. *Cheni*,[5] where he said:

---

[1] See Hartley, *The Policy Basis of the English Conflict of Laws of Marriage*, 35 M.L.R. 571.
[2] (1866), L.R. 1 P. & D. 130. See further *ante*, p. 17.
[3] Page 17.
[4] *Brinkley* v. *A.-G.* (1890), 15 P.D. 76 (marriage between a man domiciled in Ireland and a woman domiciled in Japan before the civil authority in Tokio recognised as a valid marriage). Otherwise all marriages celebrated between Jews would be invalid. For capacity and formal requirements, see *ante*, pp. 21-31.
[5] [1965] P. 85, 98-99; [1962] 3 All E.R. 873, 882-883.

"I believe the true rule to be that the courts of this country will exceptionally refuse to give effect to a capacity or incapacity to marry by the law of the domicile on the ground that to give it recognition and effect would be unconscionable. ...

"What I believe to be the true test [is] whether the marriage is so offensive to the conscience of the English court that it should refuse to recognise and give effect to the proper foreign law. In deciding that question the court will seek to exercise common sense, good manners and a reasonable tolerance."

In that case the court gave recognition to a marriage between an uncle and niece which was valid by the law of the parties' domicile (Egypt) even though it would have been void by English law because they were related within the prohibited degrees.[1] Likewise in *Nachimson* v. *Nachimson*[2] it was held that a marriage celebrated in Russia and intended to be entered into for life came within the *Hyde* v. *Hyde* definition notwithstanding that it could be dissolved by mutual consent declared before a registrar or at the will of either spouse by judicial process. On the other hand it seems inconceivable that English courts would recognise a union between two persons of the same sex; and it is very doubtful whether they would recognise a child marriage, at least unless the parties had ratified it when they were old enough to understand the nature and significance of marriage.

Polygamous Marriages.—For many years after the decision in *Hyde* v. *Hyde* the courts refused to recognise the validity of any marriage which did not satisfy LORD PENZANCE's definition.[3] In practice this meant the refusal to recognise polygamous unions—despite the fact that a large part of the civilised world permits polygamy and that the Judicial Committee of the Privy Council was upholding the validity of such unions on appeal from various courts in the Commonwealth. To fail to recognise a marriage which was valid by a man's *lex domicilii* (which is generally accepted as governing his status) seems the height of absurdity. Moreover, it is clear that LORD PENZANCE himself had intended no such result. At the end of his judgment he said:[4]

"In conformity with these views the Court must reject the prayer for the petition, but ... this decision is confined to that object. This Court [the Divorce Court] does not profess to decide upon the rights of succession or legitimacy which it might be proper to accord to the issue of the polygamous unions, nor upon the rights or obligations in relation to third persons which people living under the sanction of such unions may have created for themselves. *All that is intended to be here decided is that as between each other they are not entitled to the remedies, adjudication, or the relief of the matrimonial law of England.*"

---

[1] But would the court recognise a marriage if we regarded the relationship as criminally incestuous (*e.g.*, between brother and sister)?

[2] [1930] P. 217, C.A. But the court implied that they would not have regarded it as a marriage had it been a mere cloak for casual intercourse, to be dissolved the next day, or if it had conferred no status on the parties (at pp. 233, 244).

[3] See *Re Bethell* (1888), 38 Ch.D. 220, and the remarks of AVORY, J., in *R.* v. *Naguib*, [1917] 1 K.B. 359, 360, C.C.A. *Re Bethell* is an unsatisfactory case because it is not entirely clear what the *ratio decidendi* was. A domiciled Englishman went through a form of marriage with Teepoo, a Baralong girl, according to the custom of the Baralong tribe in Bechuanaland. The Baralongs had no religion and practised polygamy. STIRLING, J., professing to follow *Hyde* v. *Hyde*, held that this marriage was void and that the child born of it was illegitimate.

[4] At p. 138. Italics supplied.

But it was not until 1946 that the decision in *Hyde* v. *Hyde* was put in its proper context by the Court of Appeal in *Baindail* v. *Baindail*,[1] following earlier dicta of LORD MAUGHAM, L.C., in the *Sinha Peerage Case*.[2] In *Baindail* v. *Baindail* a woman domiciled in England went through a ceremony of marriage in England with a Hindu domiciled in India. She later discovered that he already had a wife in India and petitioned for nullity on the ground that the marriage was bigamous and therefore void. The respondent was permitted by his *lex domicilii* to practise polygamy and the first marriage was therefore clearly polygamous. Nevertheless, it was held that, as it was valid by the law of the husband's domicile, it must be recognised as valid here. The petitioner's contention was therefore sound and her marriage void.

During the past thirty years the attitude of the judges towards polygamous marriages has become progressively more liberal. Change has doubtless been hastened by the necessity of doing justice to the large number of immigrants in this country whose marriages are *de jure* polygamous. In 1968 LORD PARKER, C.J., was able to say that a polygamous marriage is now "recognised in this country unless there is some strong reason to the contrary".[3] In 1972 the main disability under which parties to a polygamous marriage still suffered—the inability to obtain any form of matrimonial relief in an English court—was removed by statute,[4] and since then the question whether a particular marriage is monogamous or polygamous has been largely academic. It may, however, still be important for the following reasons.

(1) We shall recognise the validity of a second (or subsequent) marriage during the subsistence of the first only if both (or all) the marriages are polygamous. Suppose that a husband, H, marries successively W[1] and W[2]. If the marriage to W[1] is monogamous, H will be unable to contract any further marriage, so that the marriage to W[2] must be void. If the marriage to W[1] is polygamous but that to W[2] is monogamous, the latter will again be void as in *Baindail* v. *Baindail*,[5] for H, being already married, cannot lawfully contract a monogamous marriage. Only if both are polygamous will we recognise the second one.

(2) If a marriage is polygamous, it will apparently be void if the *lex domicilii* of either party permits him (or her) to contract only a monogamous union.[6]

(3) Certain other problems may arise, particularly if the marriage is *de facto*, and not merely *de jure*, polygamous.

We must therefore examine two questions: what marriages will be regarded

---

[1] [1946] P. 122; [1946] 1 All E.R. 342, C.A. See also *Srini Vasan* v. *Srini Vasan*, [1946] P. 67; [1945] 2 All E.R. 21, where on virtually identical facts BARNARD, J., came to the same decision as the Court of Appeal.

[2] (1939), reported [1946] 1 All E.R. 348, H.L.

[3] *Mohamed* v. *Knott*, [1969] 1 Q.B. 1, 13-14; [1968] 2 All E.R. 563, 567, citing Dicey and Morris, *Conflict of Laws*: see now *ibid.*, 10th Ed., Rule 38. See also *Chaudhry* v. *Chaudhry*, [1976] Fam. 148; [1975] 3 All E.R. 687, (affirmed on other grounds, [1976] Fam. 148; [1976] 1 All E.R. 805, C.A.); *Re Sehota*, [1978] 3 All E.R. 385.

[4] Matrimonial Proceedings (Polygamous Marriages) Act 1972, s. 1. See further *post*, p. 62.

[5] *Supra.*

[6] See *post*, pp. 59-60.

as polygamous, and what disabilities and problems still remain if the union is a polygamous one?

What Marriages are Polygamous?[1]—It should be appreciated at the outset that English law regards a marriage as polygamous if it is possible for either party to take another spouse during its subsistence, whether he does so or not. Consequently, if the parties contract a marriage which is potentially polygamous, the mere fact that they intend to enter into a monogamous union will not without more create a monogamous marriage: their reservations clearly cannot alter the legal effects of their act. This is illustrated by *Sowa* v. *Sowa*.[2] The parties, who were domiciled in Ghana, went through a form of marriage in that country which by tribal custom was potentially polygamous. The husband had previously presented his bride with a ring and a Bible, which symbolised his intention to turn the marriage into a Christian monogamous one, but he took no further steps to implement this. The Court of Appeal held that, as nothing had been done to change the initial character of the marriage, it must still be regarded as polygamous.

Whether a marriage is to be regarded as monogamous or polygamous must be determined in the first place by the *lex loci celebrationis*.[3] If the ceremony is designed to create a monogamous union, the marriage will at its inception be monogamous; conversely, if the ceremony is designed to create a polygamous union, the marriage will at its inception be polygamous. But this does not fix its character for all time: it is certainly possible for a potentially polygamous marriage to become monogamous, and it seems probable that an initially monogamous marriage may become polygamous.

There are a number of examples of a change of the first sort. It is not sufficient that the parties should intend to convert a polygamous marriage into a monogamous one: there must be some other act or event such as the birth of a child,[4] a change of religious faith affecting the parties' legal status,[5] local legislation changing the character of the marriage,[6] or a second

---

[1] The subject of polygamous marriages is dealt with at length in the standard textbooks on Private International Law and in many articles. See particularly Bartholomew, *Recognition of Polygamous Marriages in Canada*, 10. I.C.L.Q. 305; Morris, *The Recognition of Polygamous Marriages in English Law*, 66 Harv. L.R. 961; Mendes Da Costa, *Polygamous Marriages in the Conflict of Laws*, 44 Can. Bar Rev. 293; Hartley, *Polygamy and Social Policy*, 32 M.L.R. 155; 34 M.L.R. 305; Poulter, *Hyde* v. *Hyde—a Reappraisal*, 25 I.C.L.Q. 475; Weston, 28 M.L.R. 484; Jackson, *Formation and Annulment of Marriage*, 2nd Ed., 131-144; Law Com. No. 42 (Report on Polygamous Marriages).

[2] [1961] P. 70; [1961] 1 All E.R. 687, C.A. LORD BROUGHAM'S dictum to the contrary in *Warrender* v. *Warrender* (1835), 2 Cl. & Fin. 488, 535, H.L., can no longer be regarded as good law.

[3] This seems implicit in such cases as *Hyde* v. *Hyde* (1866), L.R. 1 P. & D. 130; *R.* v. *Hammersmith Superintendent Registrar of Marriages, ex parte Mir-Anwaruddin*, [1917] 1 K.B. 634, C.A.; *Sowa* v. *Sowa*, [1961] P. 70; [1961] 1 All E.R. 687, C.A.; *Qureshi* v. *Qureshi*, [1972] Fam. 173; [1971] 1 All E.R. 325. A country, the internal law of which forbids polygamy, may nevertheless recognise the validity of a polygamous marriage celebrated on its soil: *Radwan* v. *Radwan* (*No.* 2), [1973] Fam. 35; [1972] 3 All E.R. 1026.

[4] *Cheni* v. *Cheni*, [1965] P. 85; [1962] 3 All E.R. 873; Higgins, 26 M.L.R. 205.

[5] *Sinha Peerage Case* (1939), [1946] 1 All E.R. 348, H.L. (change of Hindu sect from one practising polygamy to one practising monogamy).

[6] *Parkasho* v. *Singh*, [1968] P. 233; [1967] 1 All E.R. 737 (Indian statute converting polygamous Sikh marriages into monogamous unions); *R.* v. *Sagoo*, [1975] Q.B. 885; [1975] 2 All E.R. 926, C.A. (Kenyan statute to the same effect).

ceremony of marriage designed to create a monogamous union.[1] A more difficult problem arises if the spouses change their domicile. In *Ali* v. *Ali*[2] it was held that the parties' polygamous marriage, which had been contracted when they were domiciled in India and which had remained *de facto* monogamous, was converted into a *de jure* monogamous union when they acquired a domicile in England, as the husband thereby lost the capacity to contract any further marriages so long as the first one was in existence. In that case it was necessary to consider whether the marriage had become monogamous because otherwise the court could not have entertained the proceedings. Now that this rule has been abrogated, however, it is urged that attention should no longer be focused on the character of the union as such but on the real question, *viz.* whether the husband's *lex domicilii* permits him to take further wives. Hence it is submitted that the marriage would not become monogamous if the wife alone acquired a domicile in a country forbidding polygamy, for her unilateral act could not deprive the husband of the capacity he already had to contract further marriages.[3] Again, the acquisition of an English domicile by a man who already had two or more wives could not affect the validity of these marriages. In *Cheni* v. *Cheni*[4] the parties, who were uncle and niece, had contracted a valid marriage in Egypt when they were domiciled in that country. They later acquired a domicile in England and the wife petitioned for a decree of nullity on the ground that they were related within the prohibited degrees of consanguinity. SIMON, P., held that the marriage was still valid. The principle to be deduced is that the acquisition of an English domicile does not affect the validity of a marriage already contracted: it must therefore follow that a man domiciled here can have a plurality of wives. Such a conclusion is startling; but the alternative view, that a change of domicile will automatically render all the marriages void, is wholly unacceptable.

The converse question—whether an initially monogamous marriage may be converted into a polygamous one—is probably less likely to arise but such authority as there is indicates that such a conversion is possible. In *Cheni* v. *Cheni*[5] SIMON, P., said *obiter*: "there are no marriages which are not potentially polygamous, in the sense that they may be rendered so by a change

---

[1] *Ohochuku* v. *Ohochuku*, [1960] 1 All E.R. 253. The parties, who had contracted a potentially polygamous marriage in Nigeria, subsequently went through a second ceremony in England. WRANGHAM, J., held that he could not dissolve the English one. This decision is questionable: as English courts will recognise the first marriage as a marriage, the second ceremony seems to have been of no legal effect at all (see *post*, p. 194, n. 4). See the views of CAIRNS, J., in *Parkasho* v. *Singh*, (*supra*), at pp. 242 and 741, respectively; Mendes Da Costa, 44 Can. Bar Rev. at pp. 310-311; Furmston, 10 I.C.L.Q. 180.

[2] [1968] P. 546; [1966] 1 All E.R. 664. The case is criticised by Eekelaar, 15 I.C.L.Q. 1181, and Tolstoy, *The Conversion of a Polygamous Union into a Monogamous Marriage*, 17 I.C.L.Q. 721, on the ground that, as the *lex loci celebrationis* determines the character of the marriage, a subsequent change of domicile must be irrelevant. It is defended by Morris, 17 I.C.L.Q. 1014, and was followed in *R.* v. *Sagoo*, (*supra*). See also Webb, 12 I.C.L.Q. 672; Cowen, *ibid.*, 1407.

[3] Conversely, if the marriage is polyandrous (by which a woman may take a plurality of husbands), the wife's capacity to contract further marriages would not be affected by the husband's change of domicile.

[4] [1965] P. 85; [1962] 3 All E.R. 873.

[5] [1965] P. 85, 90; [1962] 3 All E.R. 873, 877. See also *Russ* v. *Russ*, [1964] P. 315, 326; [1962] 3 All E.R. 193, 198, C.A., where WILLMER, L.J., referred to a marriage between a man domiciled in Egypt and a woman domiciled in England as potentially polygamous.

of domicile and religion on the part of the spouses'', but he added that it was more reasonable to presume that a polygamous union could be converted into a monogamous one than *vice versa*. This dictum was followed by the Privy Council in *A.-G. of Ceylon* v. *Reid*.[1] The respondent was domiciled in Ceylon and his capacity to marry depended upon his religious faith. Whilst he was a Christian he contracted a monogamous Christian marriage. He was then converted to Mohammedanism and went through a second ceremony of marriage without having the first dissolved. He was later charged with bigamy and the question of law raised by the relevant penal statute was whether the second marriage was valid or void. The Privy Council held that it was valid for, having changed to the Muslim faith, Reid was now permitted to practise polygamy by the law of Ceylon.

This decision is logically unassailable but it raises a number of problems. If the husband alleges that he has acquired the capacity to take further wives as the result of a change of domicile, presumably the fact that the wife has not changed her domicile (if that be the case) will be irrelevant.[2] This raises a much more difficult question: would an English court be prepared to give her an immediate release from the bond if she found her position as the first of two or more wives intolerable? It is submitted that sexual intercourse with one's own wife cannot amount to adultery,[3] and consequently divorce would be possible only if it could be said that the husband's contracting a second marriage was such behaviour on his part that she could not reasonably be expected to live with him. This in turn must depend on whether the court took the view that the basic conditions on which the marriage was contracted were unalterable without the consent of both parties. If a man is free to change his domicile, it is difficult to see why he should not be free to acquire the capacity to contract further marriages, however unfortunate the wife's position might be as a consequence. One feels, however, that no English court would be prepared to leave her without a matrimonial remedy and would almost certainly take the view that the husband could not lawfully bring about such a profound change in the parties' relationship unilaterally. Hence she would be justified in refusing to cohabit with him (with the result that he would be in desertion) and could claim that his behaviour entitled her to a divorce immediately.[4]

Capacity to marry.—It is generally accepted that a polygamous marriage may be contracted only by persons whose *lex domicilii* permits polygamy.[5]

---

[1] [1965] A.C. 720; [1965] 1 All E.R. 812, P.C. Strongly criticised by Koh in 29 M.L.R. 88.

[2] *Cf. Onabrauche* v. *Onabrauche* (1978), 122 Sol. Jo. 210. The parties, who were then both domiciled in Nigeria, contracted a polygamous marriage. After the wife had acquired an English domicile, the husband (who was still domiciled in Nigeria) contracted a second marriage. It was held that the wife could not allege that he had committed adultery.

[3] *Cf. Onabrauche* v. *Onabrauche*, *(supra)*. In *Drammeh* v. *Drammeh* (1970), 78 Ceylon L.W. 55, P.C., it was held that under the law of the Gambia the first wife could petition for divorce on the ground of the husband's adultery with the second wife. It is submitted that this decision should not be followed in this country.

[4] Under s. 1 (2) (b) of the Matrimonial Causes Act 1973: see *post*, p. 199.

[5] *Risk* v. *Risk*, [1950] P. 50, 53; [1950] 2 All E.R. 973, 974. In *Kenward* v. *Kenward*, [1951] P. 124, 144-145; [1950] 2 All E.R. 297, 309-310, C.A., DENNING, L.J., considered that a man, whose *lex domicilii* permitted mónogamy only, could contract a valid polygamous marriage if that was his intention, but there is no authority for this proposition and it does not seem in line with accepted principles: see Morris, 66 Harv. L.R. 984-986.

Hence it is argued that, if a man whose *lex domicilii* forbids polygamy goes through a polygamous form of marriage abroad, the marriage will be void by English law.[1] On the other hand there is no justification for taking this view if the man's *lex domicilii* would recognise it in the circumstances.[2] One cannot draw any distinction between a man and a woman in this respect, and a polygamous marriage contracted by a woman whose *lex domicilii* forbids polygamy would, it is submitted, be equally void.[3] This view admittedly conflicts with the decision in *Radwan* v. *Radwan* (*No. 2*)[4] where CUMMING-BRUCE, J., held that a polygamous marriage would be valid if the parties had capacity to contract it by the law of their intended matrimonial domicile (irrespective of their present domicile), but for reasons already stated the learned judge's conclusions are difficult to accept.[5]

So far as persons domiciled in England are concerned, section 11 (d) of the Matrimonial Causes Act 1973[6] appears to give statutory effect to the rule stated above. This provides that a polygamous marriage entered into outside England and Wales[7] will be void if either party was at the time of the marriage domiciled in England and Wales, even though the marriage was *de facto* monogamous. As CUMMING-BRUCE, J., pointed out in *Radwan* v. *Radwan* (*No. 2*), however, section 14 of the Act[8] expressly preserves the application of foreign law if this is required by the rules of English private international law: consequently, if his view is correct, the law of the intended matrimonial home will still be applied and the marriage can still be valid. With respect to the learned judge, an interpretation of the law that renders section 11 (d) largely otiose is not to be recommended. Leaving this aside, the social justification for the provision is far from clear and produces anomalous results. Suppose that an immigrant coming from state X, the law of which permits polygamy, is resident in England. He goes back to X to marry and then returns to this country. If he is still domiciled in X, his marriage will be valid; on the other hand, if he has acquired an English domicile before his marriage, it will be void. Such a distinction is wholly indefensible. If two people domiciled in England and resident abroad contract a *de facto* monogamous marriage in the local form, which happens to be polygamous, Parliament would have achieved greater justice by enacting that such a marriage should be regarded as *de jure* monogamous rather than void.

On the other hand, however, a person who is permitted to practise polygamy by his *lex domicilii* may lawfully contract a monogamous marriage. This is clear from *R.* v. *Hammersmith Superintendent Registrar of Marriages, ex parte Mir-Anwaruddin*.[9] Mir-Anwaruddin was a Mohammedan

---

[1] *Cf. Re Bethell* (1888), 38 Ch.D. 220. But see Hartley, 32 M.L.R. 158-160.

[2] See James, *Polygamy and Capacity to Marry*, 42 M.L.R. 533, 536.

[3] Morris, *loc. cit.*, 985-988, criticising the opposite view put forward by Beckett, 48 L.Q.R. 360-361. But if the woman goes to a foreign country with the object of marrying and remaining there, she will probably acquire a domicile of choice there as soon as she sets foot in the country and will thus have the necessary capacity at the time of the marriage.

[4] [1973] Fam. 35; [1972] 2 All E.R. 1026.

[5] See *ante*, pp. 23-24.

[6] Re-enacting s. 4 of the Matrimonial Proceedings (Polygamous Marriages) Act 1972.

[7] The reference to marriages contracted outside England and Wales is curious, as no polygamous marriage may be contracted in this country: see *infra*.

[8] Re-enacting s. 4 of the Nullity of Marriage Act 1971.

[9] [1917] 1 K.B. 634, C.A.

domiciled in Madras and by his *lex domicilii* he was permitted to take up to four wives. In 1913 he married X at a register office in England and two years later he executed a declaration of divorcement which by Mohammedan law dissolved his marriage to X by *talak*. He then applied to the Hammersmith Superintendent Registrar for a certificate and licence to marry Y, which the Superintendent Registrar refused to issue on the ground that the *talak* was ineffective to dissolve the first marriage by English law and that Mir-Anwaruddin was therefore still married to X. Mir-Anwaruddin thereupon sued for a writ of mandamus calling on the Superintendent Registrar to issue the certificate and licence. It was never for one moment doubted that Mir-Anwaruddin's marriage to X was valid although he could have contracted other marriages by Indian law, and the sole issue before the court was the validity of the *talak*. This was held to be ineffective[1] and so the mandamus was refused.[2]

As the initial character of the union is determined by the *lex loci celebrationis*, any marriage celebrated in England must be monogamous at its inception.[3] Consequently if a person whose *lex domicilii* permits polygamy has already contracted a valid polygamous marriage abroad, any marriage contracted in this country during the subsistence of the first will be void by English law even though it is valid by the *lex domicilii*.[4]

Problems created by Polygamous Marriages.—Although, as we have seen,[5] polygamous marriages are now generally recognised in this country, we must now consider one or two cases in which difficulty may still arise.[6]

Matrimonial Causes.—*Hyde* v. *Hyde*[7] laid down the rule that matrimonial relief was not open to the parties to a polygamous marriage in this country. This was rigidly enforced for over a century, with the result that English courts would not entertain proceedings for divorce,[8] nullity,[9] or matrimonial relief in a magistrates' court.[10] It will be recalled that this bar operated if the marriage was *de jure* polygamous, even though it was *de facto* monogamous; consequently in recent years a large number of immigrants resident in this country but domiciled in, say, Pakistan or Nigeria found themselves unable

---

[1] See *post*, p. 62.

[2] Logically the difference between the two cases can be defended on the ground that capacity to contract a polygamous marriage (which may remain *de facto* monogamous) must embrace a capacity to contract a monogamous one, whereas the converse is not true. A more realistic justification can be found in the need to give legal protection to women who contract marriages in this country with men whose *lex domicilii* permits polygamy.

[3] See the *Hammersmith Marriage Case*, (*supra*); *Maher* v. *Maher*, [1951] P. 342, 346; [1951] 2 All E.R. 37, 39.

[4] *Baindail* v. *Baindail*, [1946] P. 122; [1946] 1 All E.R. 342, C.A., *ante*, p. 56; *Srini Vasan* v. *Srini Vasan*, [1946] P. 67; [1945] 2 All E.R. 21.

[5] *Ante*, p. 56.

[6] Another point that has been left open in the past is whether parties to a polygamous marriage can be together guilty of conspiracy: *Mawji* v. *R.*, [1957] A.C. 126, 135-136; [1957] 1 All E.R. 385, 387, P.C. There seems to be no reason why they should not be in the same position as parties to a monogamous marriage.

[7] (1866), L.R. 1 P. & D. 130. See *ante*, p. 55.

[8] *Hyde* v. *Hyde* (1866), L.R. 1 P. & D. 130.

[9] *Risk* v. *Risk*, [1951] P. 50; [1950] 2 All E.R. 973.

[10] *Sowa* v. *Sowa*, [1961] P. 80; [1961] 1 All E.R. 687, C.A.

to obtain any form of matrimonial relief here. Thus a wife, deserted by her husband, could obtain maintenance only by applying for supplementary benefit. Such a situation was clearly intolerable and the position was reversed by section 1 of the Matrimonial Proceedings (Polygamous Marriages) Act 1972, which permits a court to grant matrimonial relief or a declaration concerning the validity of the marriage notwithstanding that it is polygamous.[1]

Most of the problems that the working of this Act is likely to produce will probably flow from the difficulty of applying English matrimonial law to parties who have not been fully integrated into English social life. Although no reliable statistics are available, the number of men in this country with two or more wives is believed to be very small; but if one of the parties to a *de facto* polygamous marriage seeks matrimonial relief, the court may find itself in an impossible position. Presumably one wife could not complain of the husband's having sexual intercourse with another wife;[2] would she be justified in leaving the matrimonial home on the ground, for example, that she found it impossible to live with another of her husband's wives? The truth is that English law, designed for monogamous relationships, cannot easily be adapted to deal with polygamous ones; Parliament might have done well to exclude *de facto* polygamous marriages from the Act even though this would have left a small number of spouses unable to obtain any form of matrimonial relief in England even though they were domiciled here.[3]

Recognition of "Polygamous Divorces".—Applying the converse of the rule in *Hyde* v. *Hyde*, SWINFEN EADY, L.J., held in the *Hammersmith Marriage Case*[4] that a monogamous marriage cannot be dissolved by a process devised for polygamous unions. Here a marriage contracted in England was held not to have been dissolved by *talak*, a Mohammedan procedure designed to dissolve a polygamous Mohammedan marriage. In the later case of *Russ* v. *Russ*,[5] however, the Court of Appeal rejected these views as too wide and held that a marriage solemnized in an English register office was validly dissolved by a *talak* pronounced in the presence of the wife and an officer of the Egyptian court and entered on the court records. There now seems to be no reason to assume that an English court will refuse to recognise a divorce on the ground that it is designed to dissolve polygamous unions

---

[1] Now repealed and re-enacted by the Matrimonial Causes Act 1973, s. 47. The Act implemented the recommendations of the Law Commission: Law Com. No. 42 (Report on Polygamous Marriages), 1971. "Matrimonial relief" includes decrees of divorce, nullity, judicial separation, and presumption of death and dissolution of marriage, orders on the ground of wilful neglect to maintain and for the alteration of maintenance agreements, ancillary orders in all such proceedings, and orders under the Domestic Proceedings and Magistrates' Courts Act 1978, s. 47 (2). Proceedings for declaratory judgments could be brought before the Act because they do not affect the parties' status: *Lee* v. *Lau*, [1967] P. 14; [1964] 2 All E.R. 248.

[2] See Law Com. No. 42, para. 50.

[3] This was the reason for Mr. Neil Lawson's dissent from the majority recommendations of the Law Commission: *ibid.*, pp. 46-47.

[4] [1917] 1 K.B. 634, C.A. For the facts, see *ante*, pp. 60-61. See also *Maher* v. *Maher*, [1951] P. 342; [1951] 2 All E.R. 37, disapproved by WILLMER, L.J., in *Russ* v. *Russ*, [1964] P. 315, 328; [1962] 3 All E.R. 193, 200, C.A.

[5] [1964] P. 315; [1962] 3 All E.R. 193, C.A.

even though the marriage was monogamous and the proceedings were extra-judicial.[1]

It must be emphasised, however, that such divorces (like all other foreign divorces) will be recognised only if the parties satisfy the relevant conditions relating to nationality, residence or domicile. In particular, we no longer recognise the validity of any divorce pronounced in the United Kingdom, the Channel Islands or the Isle of Man if it was not obtained in the courts of one of those countries.[2]

Bigamy.—In *R. v. Sagoo*[3] it was stated by the Court of Appeal that a marriage which is to be the foundation for a prosecution for bigamy must be a monogamous one. The critical question, however, is whether the first union is monogamous at the time of the second ceremony. Hence if, as in *R. v. Sagoo*, a man contracts a polygamous marriage with W, which is then converted into a monogamous union by local legislation or the man's changing his domicile, and he later goes through a ceremony of marriage with X, he may be convicted of bigamy. If, however, the first marriage is still polygamous at the time of the second ceremony, he apparently commits no criminal offence even though the second marriage is void, for example because it is contracted in England. This distinction is unwarranted. Difficulty arises because a citizen of the United Kingdom and Colonies may be prosecuted for bigamy even though the second marriage is celebrated abroad, and there is no saving for marriages which are valid by the accused's *lex domicilii*.[4] It is inconceivable, however, that a man would be prosecuted in this country for contracting a lawful second marriage abroad if this is valid by the law of his domicile and the place where it was celebrated.[5] There is no justification whatever for permitting a man who enters into a *void* second marriage to escape conviction for bigamy by pleading that his first marriage was polygamous. The dictum was not essential to the decision in *R. v. Sagoo*, and it is to be hoped that the House of Lords or Parliament will seize an early opportunity of overruling it.[6]

Rights in Property.—Problems with respect to rights in property are likely to arise only if the marriage is *de facto* polygamous. It has been held that one of two widows may apply for an order under the Inheritance (Provision for Family and Dependants) Act 1975:[7] obviously both could apply if necessary.

---

[1] This was the view of SIMON, P., in *Qureshi* v. *Qureshi*, [1972] Fam. 173; [1971] 1 All E.R. 325. See also Swaminathan, *Recognition of Foreign Unilateral Divorces in the English Conflict of Laws*, 28 M.L.R. 540, where a less restricted view is taken of the *Hammersmith Marriage Case*; Hartley, 34 M.L.R. 579.

[2] See further *post*, p. 248.

[3] [1975] Q.B. 885, 889; [1975] 2 All E.R. 926, 929, C.A. The point was left open in *R. v. Naguib*, [1917] 1 K.B. 359, 361, C.C.A., and *Baindail* v. *Baindail*, [1946] P. 122, 130; [1946] 1 All E.R. 342, 347, C.A. See further Bartholomew, *Polygamous Marriages and English Criminal Law*, 17 M.L.R. 344; Polonsky, *Polygamous Marriage—a Bigamist's Charter*, [1971] Crim. L.R. 401; Pearl, [1976] C.L.J. 48; Morse, 25 I.C.L.Q. 229.

[4] Offences against the Person Act 1861, s. 57; British Nationality Act 1948, s. 3 (1).

[5] Dicey and Morris, *Conflict of Laws*, 10th Ed., 321.

[6] The dictum fails to comply with the Court of Appeal's own view that the rules relating to the recognition of the status created by marriage should be the same in criminal law and family law: [1975] Q.B. 885, 890; [1975] 2 All E.R. 926, 930.

[7] *Re Sehota*, [1978] 3 All E.R. 385.

There seems to be no reason why two or more wives should not have a right to occupy the matrimonial home under the Matrimonial Homes Act; similarly two widows who have been living together require the same protection against eviction from the former matrimonial home as one does, and it is submitted that a statutory tenancy should vest in them as joint tenants under the Rent Act after the husband's death. Intestate succession presents a more complicated problem: do both widows take £40,000 (or £85,000) each or as joint tenants or tenants in common? In fairness to other beneficiaries, they should not take more than the statutory sum in total, and it seems more just to divide this between them equally as tenants in common.[1]

Legitimacy of the Issue of a Polygamous Union.—Since legitimacy is primarily a question for the child's *lex domicilii*,[2] the real test to be applied here is not whether English law will recognise the validity of his parents' marriage, but whether the *lex domicilii* will regard the issue of it as legitimate. This may still be important in determining whether the child may take a gift under an English will or settlement in favour of the children of one of his parents.

The Privy Council has held that the offspring of a polygamous marriage are children for the purpose of the former English Statute of Distributions,[3] and there is little doubt that English courts will follow suit. But it seems that to inherit an entailed interest a child must be legitimate within the narrowest common law sense of the term and so the child of a polygamous marriage cannot be an heir.[4]

Social Welfare Legislation.—Refusal to allow benefit to a woman who had been married under a system allowing polygamy resulted in legislation to define the position of spouses in such cases. Under existing regulations a polygamous marriage is to be treated as valid for the purpose of the Social Security Act 1975 at any time while it is monogamous in fact.[5]

The reason for this provision is that contributions and benefits are calculated on the assumption that a man has only one wife at a time.[6] On the other hand, a man cannot be permitted to throw the burden of supporting his wife or wives on the taxpayer merely because his marriage is polygamous and consequently he is bound to support them for the purpose of the Supplementary Benefits Act even though the unions are *de facto* polygamous.[7]

---

[1] The personal chattels would have to be divided equally between them too.

[2] See *post*, pp. 270-272.

[3] *Bamgbose* v. *Daniel*, [1955] A.C. 107; [1954] 3 All E.R. 263, P.C. See further Falconbridge, *Legitimacy or Legitimation and Succession in the Conflict of Laws*, 27 Can. Bar Rev. 1163, 1183 *et seq*.

[4] The point was left open by LORD MAUGHAM, L.C., in the *Sinha Peerage Case*, [1946] 1 All E.R. 348, 349, H.L. The reason is apparently that otherwise there might be a conflict between the older son of a later marriage and the younger son of an earlier marriage. This is hardly convincing.

[5] Social Security Act 1975, s. 162 (b); Social Security and Family Allowances (Polygamous Marriages) Regulations, S.I. 1975 No. 561. See Pearl, [1978-79] J.S.W.L. 24.

[6] Similarly for the purposes of income tax a husband cannot claim personal relief in respect of either (or any) wife if his marriages are *de facto* polygamous: *Nabi* v. *Heaton* (1981), 125 Sol. Jo. 204.

[7] *Din* v. *National Assistance Board*, [1967] 2 Q.B. 213; [1967] 1 All E.R. 750. For the Supplementary Benefits Act, see *post*, pp. 495-497.

G. PRESUMPTION OF MARRIAGE

It has long been established law that, if a man and woman cohabit and hold themselves out as husband and wife, this in itself raises a presumption that they are legally married.[1] Consequently, if the marriage is challenged, the burden lies upon those challenging it to prove that there was in fact no marriage and not upon those alleging it to prove that it has been solemnized. This may be important, for example, if the parties have been married abroad and have no written or other evidence of the solemnization, or if the validity of the marriage is called into question indirectly when the parties can no longer give evidence, as it may be if the legitimacy of their children is put in issue after their deaths.

A closer examination will show that there are really two presumptions: first, that at some time or other the parties went through a valid form of marriage, and, secondly, that, when they did so, they both had the capacity to marry. This distinction is important when the standard of proof necessary to rebut the presumption is considered.

Presumption of Formal Validity.—The presumption that the parties went through a valid form of marriage may always be rebutted, of course, by proving that they never contracted any marriage at all, and although this will usually be difficult to do by direct evidence, it may be possible to do so by inference.[2] Even if it is not disputed that the parties went through a form of marriage, it may still be alleged that owing to some formal defect the ceremony was a legal nullity. But in this case *omnia praesumuntur rite esse acta*, and the generally accepted view is that the presumption will not be rebutted unless the evidence to the contrary satisfies one beyond reasonable doubt that there has been no valid marriage.[3] The number of cases in which this has been done is in fact extremely small.

Presumption of Capacity.—In *Tweney* v. *Tweney*[4] PILCHER, J., said:

"The petitioner's marriage to the present respondent being unexceptionable in form and duly consummated remains a good marriage until *some* evidence is adduced that the marriage was, *in fact*, a nullity."

This raises the question: what evidence will suffice for this purpose? Although this point still has to be decided, it is tentatively submitted on the present state of the authorities that, if any evidence is adduced showing that either of the parties lacked capacity, the presumption in favour of the validity of the marriage disappears and the question has to be decided on the balance of probability in the light of all the available evidence. It will usually be easy

---

[1] But in a prosecution for bigamy the presumption of the prisoner's innocence outweighs the presumption of marriage to be drawn from cohabitation and the marriage must be strictly proved by the prosecution: see Smith and Hogan, *Criminal Law*, 4th Ed., 676.

[2] As in *Re Bradshaw*, [1938] 4 All E.R. 143, where the presumption was rebutted by evidence that the parties had subsequently intermarried.

[3] See *Mahadervan* v. *Mahadervan*, [1964] P. 233, 246; [1962] 3 All E.R. 1108, 1117, and the cases there cited, particularly *Hill* v. *Hill*, [1959] 1 All E.R. 281, 285, P.C.; *Piers* v. *Piers* (1849), 2 H.L. Cas. 331, H.L., at pp. 362, 370. But in *Re Taylor*, [1961] 1 All E.R. 55, 63, C.A., HARMAN, L.J., was of the opinion that the evidence in rebuttal should be *firm and clear*.

[4] [1946] P. 180, 182; [1946] 1 All E.R. 564, 565. (Italics supplied.)

to determine whether either party was at the time of the marriage under the age of 16 or whether they are within the prohibited degrees of consanguinity or affinity; difficulty may arise when one of the parties has been previously married and it is alleged that this earlier marriage was still subsisting when the later union was contracted. The common problem is therefore this: A marries X and they later separate; A then marries Y without having the former marriage dissolved and not knowing whether X is still alive. Is the marriage between A and Y to be presumed to be valid?[1]

Whether X was still alive at the time of A's marriage to Y is a question of fact.[2] If X was suffering from a fatal disease when A last heard of him, he may be presumed to have died within a relatively short time; the converse is true if X was a young person in good health. The presumption that the second marriage was valid was rebutted in *Re Peete*.[3] W had separated from her first husband some time before 1916. In that year she was told by his sister that he had been killed in an explosion in a factory where he was employed but that she (the sister) had been unable to identify his body. In 1919 W went through a form of marriage with H. In an application under the Inheritance (Family Provision) Act by W as H's widow, it was held that she could not succeed. Although there was an initial presumption that the marriage between H and W was valid, there was some evidence that she had not at that time the capacity to marry him, *viz.* the existence of the previous marriage. The sister's statement that the first husband had been killed was clearly inadmissible as it was hearsay; hence W had remarried only four years after last seeing her first husband and there was no admissible evidence to rebut the presumption that he was still alive after that short period.

If X has been absent for seven years or more and has not been heard of during that time, this may of itself raise a presumption of law that he is dead provided that certain conditions are satisfied. The nature of this presumption was thus stated by SACHS, J., in *Chard* v. *Chard*:[4]

"Where ... there is no acceptable affirmative evidence that he was alive at some time during a continuous period of seven years or more, then if it can be proved first, that there are persons who would be likely to have heard of him over that period, secondly, that those persons have not heard of him, and thirdly, that all due inquiries have been made appropriate to the circumstances, [X] will be presumed to have died at some time within that period."

If any of these conditions is missing, the presumption cannot be invoked. In *Chard* v. *Chard* the husband went through a form of marriage with the respondent 16 years after last seeing his first wife. He had spent almost the whole of that time in prison, and there was some evidence that his first wife

---

[1] The question in dispute may be alternatively whether a previous marriage was validly dissolved: *Gatty* v. *A.-G.*, [1951] P. 444.

[2] *Chard* v. *Chard*, [1956] P. 259; [1955] 3 All E.R. 721.

[3] [1952] 2 All E.R. 599. *Cf. MacDarmaid* v. *A.-G.*, [1950] P. 218; [1950] 1 All E.R. 497 (first wife presumed to be still alive after three years).

[4] [1956] P. 259, 272; [1955] 3 All E.R. 721, 728; criticised by Nokes in 19 M.L.R. 208. See also Treitel, *Presumption of Death*, 17 M.L.R. 530. The first spouse was presumed to be dead in the following cases: *Tweney* v. *Tweney*, [1946] P. 180; [1946] 1 All E.R. 564 (12 years' absence during which exhaustive enquiries had been made); *Re Watkins*, [1953] 2 All E.R. 1113 (25 years' absence); *Bullock* v. *Bullock*, [1960] 2 All E.R. 307 (14 years' absence during which police had sought husband).

had also contracted a bigamous marriage. That being so, the husband was not likely to have heard of her during the intervening period and so the first of the three conditions was not satisfied. Hence no presumption was raised that the first wife was dead at the end of the 16 years, and as she would be only 44 years old at the time of the second marriage, the court inferred that she was still alive and granted a decree of nullity in respect of the second marriage. Again, in *Bradshaw* v. *Bradshaw*[1] it was inferred that the first husband was still alive after 19 years' absence. In this case the presumption could not be invoked because the third condition was not satisfied, as the wife had failed to make obvious enquiries about her husband (who, when she last saw him, was a regular soldier) from his Corps records.

These cases were distinguished in *Taylor* v. *Taylor*,[2] where the question in issue was whether a *previous* marriage was to be presumed to have been valid. W went through a form of marriage with G. She later left him and, having discovered facts which led her to conclude that this marriage was void because G was already married to another woman, she went through a form of marriage with H whilst G was still alive. H then petitioned for a decree of nullity on the ground that his marriage to W was void as she had been married to G when it was celebrated. These facts gave rise to conflicting presumptions and CAIRNS, J., resolved the problem by "leaning towards the preservation of existing unions" rather than "towards the avoiding of existing unions in favour of doubtful earlier and, to all intents and purposes, dead ones."[3] He accordingly held that the presumption that W was validly married to H was not rebutted. It may be doubted, however, whether he was justified in coming to this conclusion. Had the sole question in issue been the validity of W's marriage to G, the court must have pronounced in its favour in the absence of any evidence to rebut the presumption. The facts indicated that the marriage to H was presumptively void and there was no evidence to rebut this presumption either. However practically convenient this decision may be, it seems to be logically unsupportable.[4]

H. JACTITATION OF MARRIAGE AND DECLARATORY JUDGMENTS

Jactitation of Marriage.—The decree of jactitation is a curious survival which is seldom sought today. The petitioner alleges that the respondent is not married to the petitioner but is wrongfully boasting or asserting that he or she is the petitioner's spouse. As an alternative to proving the marriage or denying the assertions, the respondent may raise as a defence the fact that the petitioner had authorised him or her to make the representations; and it seems that if the petitioner once gives an authorisation of this sort, he will be debarred from subsequently asking for the decree even though he has

---

[1] [1956] P. 274, n.

[2] [1967] P. 25; [1965] 1 All E.R. 872.

[3] At pp. 39 and 881, respectively.

[4] W could easily have petitioned for a decree of nullity with respect to her first marriage, and the hardship worked in *Re Peete* (*ante*, p. 66) was much greater. It is also submitted that CAIRNS, J., applied the wrong standard of proof by requiring decisive evidence to rebut the presumption of capacity.

withdrawn the authority.[1] The decree, if granted, is in the form of an injunction restraining the respondent from making any further claims to be married to the petitioner. The decree may still be of use today in order to prevent a presumption of marriage being raised, although, of course, it was of much greater importance before Lord Hardwicke's Act put a stop to clandestine marriages.[2]

Declaratory Judgments.—A spouse may petition for a declaration that his marriage was a valid one under the provisions of section 45 of the Matrimonial Causes Act 1973.[3] Such a judgment will bind the Crown and any other person joined as a respondent. In addition, the Court of Appeal held in *Har-Shefi* v. *Har-Shefi*[4] that the court has a general power to make an order declaratory of the parties' marital status without giving any other relief. This has introduced a new class of proceedings into the Family Division, but the tendency in recent cases has been to limit their scope and to restrict them to situations where no other relief is available.[5] Thus, the court has refused to make a declaration that a marriage was validly contracted (for which the proceedings mentioned above are available)[6] or that it was void (when the proper procedure is to petition for a decree of nullity).[7] Declaratory judgments are usually sought to determine whether or not a marriage is still subsisting as this is the only means of testing whether English courts will recognise the validity of a foreign decree of divorce or nullity.[8]

Jurisdiction to make Declaratory Orders.—In *Garthwaite* v. *Garthwaite*[9] the Court of Appeal held that it had no jurisdiction to declare that a marriage, celebrated in England, was still subsisting when neither party was domiciled or resident in this country. Unfortunately, the court did not state clearly what the basis of jurisdiction is. Undoubtedly it exists if the petitioner is domiciled here,[10] and it may be safely asserted that this will also be true if the respondent alone is domiciled in this country on the ground that an English court must always be able to adjudicate on the status of a person domiciled here. Jurisdiction can also be assumed if both parties are resident

---

[1] *Hawke* v. *Corri* (1820), 2 Hag. Con. 280; *Thompson* v. *Rourke*, [1893] P. 11; *ibid.*, 70, C.A.

[2] Jurisdiction is vested in the High Court, and county courts can hear *undefended* petitions: Matrimonial Causes Act 1967, s. 1 (see *ante*, p. 4). A decree of jactitation is a judgment *in personam* only and therefore binds only the parties and their privies: *R.* v. *Kingston* (1776), 20 State Tr. 355, 573, H.L. The Law Commission are provisionally of the opinion that jactitation proceedings should be abolished as they no longer fulfil any purpose: Working Paper No. 34.

[3] See *post*, pp. 274–275.

[4] [1953] P. 161; [1953] 1 All E.R. 783, C.A. The power is exercisable under R.S.C. O. 15, r. 16.

[5] See *Verwaeke* v. *Smith*, [1981] 1 All E.R. 55, C.A.

[6] *Collett* v. *Collett*, [1968] P. 482; [1967] 2 All E.R. 426. But this would not apply if the court would not have jurisdiction under s. 45 (*e.g.* because the petitioner was not domiciled in this country).

[7] *Kassim* v. *Kassim*, [1962] P. 224; [1962] 3 All E.R. 426.

[8] As in *Har-Shefi* v. *Har-Shefi*, (*supra*). But ORMROD, J., has questioned whether the provisions of the Supreme Court of Judicature (Consolidation) Act 1925, s. 21 (b) do not prevent the court from declaring a marriage valid (as distinct from annulled or dissolved) under O. 15, r. 16: *Aldrich* v. *A.-G.*, [1968] P. 281, 293; [1968] 1 All E.R. 345, 350.

[9] [1964] P. 356; [1964] 2 All E.R. 233, C.A. Criticised by Hooper in 14 I.C.L.Q. 264. See generally North, *Declaratory Judgments in the Divorce Court*, 14 I.C.L.Q. 579.

[10] *Har-Shefi* v. *Har-Shefi*, (*supra*).

in this country on the ground that this was the basis of the ecclesiastical courts' jurisdiction which the High Court now exercises.[1] If the petitioner also seeks some other form of matrimonial relief (for example, divorce) which the court has jurisdiction to grant, it can make a declaration with respect to the validity and subsistence of the marriage because it must resolve this issue before adjudicating on the main one. In *Lepre* v. *Lepre*[2] the husband had obtained a decree of nullity in Malta. The wife then brought proceedings in England for a declaration that this decree would not be recognized in this country and also for a decree of divorce. SIMON, P., held that, as he had jurisdiction to entertain the divorce proceedings, he must be able to make the declaration sought, for he could not pronounce the divorce without first ascertaining whether there was a subsisting marriage to dissolve.[3]

---

[1] *Qureshi* v. *Qureshi*, [1972] Fam. 173, 194; [1971] 1 All E.R. 325, 340. Residence of the respondent alone is probably sufficient, for the petitioner *ipso facto* submits to the jurisdiction by invoking it: *cf. Sim* v. *Sim*, [1944] P. 87; [1944] 2 All E.R. 344.

[2] [1965] P. 52; [1963] 2 All E.R. 49.

[3] For a review of the present law and suggestions for reform, see the Law Commission's Working Paper No. 48 (Declarations in Family Matters), 1973. The Commission's provisional view is that English courts should have jurisdiction to make a declaration of validity of marriage or validity of a foreign decree of divorce or nullity if either party is domiciled in this country or has been habitually resident here for one year: *ibid.*, para. 48. (This would bring jurisdiction into line with that in other matrimonial causes.)

Chapter 3

Void and Voidable Marriages

A. INTRODUCTORY

The view of the Roman Catholic Church that marriage is a sacrament inevitably meant that the law relating to marriage would become a part of the canon law, over which the ecclesiastical courts successfully claimed exclusive jurisdiction.[1] This had the most profound effect on subsequent legal developments. Not only were these courts the only tribunals competent to declare whether the parties were validly married, but the Roman Catholic doctrine of the indissolubility of marriage became a tenet of English law.

Whilst this doctrine precluded the courts from granting decrees of divorce, it did not stop them from declaring that, although the parties had gone through a ceremony of marriage, some impediment prevented their acquiring the status of husband and wife. Clearly there was no valid marriage if either of the spouses was already married to somebody else, if they were related within the prohibited degrees, or if one of them did not fully consent to the solemnization. Furthermore, a marriage was not regarded as consummated until the parties had become one flesh by sexual intercourse; consequently, if either of them was impotent, he or she was regarded as lacking capacity to contract the union, which could therefore be annulled. The same principles were applied by the English ecclesiastical courts after the breach with Rome in the sixteenth century. Such marriages were said to be void for, although the parties by going through a ceremony had apparently contracted a marriage, the result of the impediment was that there was never a marriage either in fact or in law. Consequently, the marriage could be formally annulled by a decree of an ecclesiastical court and, even without such a decree, either party was free to contract another union (unless he or she was already married to somebody else). As the marriage was a complete nullity, its validity could also be put in issue by any other person with an interest in so doing, even after the death of one or both of the parties to it. So, for example, after the death of a tenant in fee simple his brother might claim his estate on the ground that the tenant's marriage was void, with the result that his children, being illegitimate, could not inherit and his "widow", never having been married, could not claim dower.

Void and Voidable Marriages.—By the beginning of the seventeenth century, however, the royal courts were obviously becoming concerned at the

---

[1] Pollock and Maitland, *History of English Law*, ii, 364-366.

3. ESTOPPEL

Once one of the grounds considered above has been established, the court is usually bound to find in favour of the party alleging that the marriage is void, whether he is petitioning for nullity or the question of the validity of the marriage has arisen in some other proceedings. It now seems clear, however, that in certain circumstances a party will be estopped from asserting the invalidity of the marriage even though he could prove that it is void. Two illustrations will indicate the sort of problem that can arise. If a married man goes through a form of marriage with a woman after representing to her that he is a bachelor or a widower and then leaves her unsupported, may he raise the nullity of this marriage as a defence to any action brought by her for maintenance? Alternatively, if previous matrimonial proceedings have been brought between the same parties on the assumption that the marriage is valid, may either subsequently petition for nullity or put the validity of the marriage in issue in later proceedings?

It is submitted that a distinction must be drawn between estoppel by conduct and estoppel *per rem judicatam* for this purpose. In the former case the better view seems to be that the parties by their own conduct cannot prevent the court from enquiring into the real state of affairs and declaring what their true status is. In *Miles* v. *Chilton*,[1] where the husband petitioned for nullity on the ground that the wife was already married at the time of the ceremony in question, DR. LUSHINGTON held that the wife's averment that the husband had deceived her into believing that she had already been divorced by her first husband was no answer to the petition. The position with respect to estoppel *per rem judicatam* is more complicated. Decrees of nullity, divorce and judicial separation are all judgments *in rem* and bind not only the parties but the whole world. Hence nobody can assert the validity of a marriage after a decree of nullity has been pronounced or deny its validity after a decree of judicial separation.[2] If a petition for nullity, divorce or judicial separation is dismissed, this will create an estoppel *inter partes* only. If, for example, H unsuccessfully petitions for a decree of nullity on the ground that the other party to the marriage, W, was married to another man at the time of the ceremony, neither H nor W can now assert that the marriage is void for this reason, although a third person who was not a party to the proceedings or privy to them could still do so.[3] If the outcome of any other proceedings between the parties in the High Court rests on the validity of their marriage, this will presumably also create an estoppel *inter partes*, so that neither of them could assert that the marriage was void if, for example, successful

---

[1] (1849), 1 Rob. Eccl. 684. The contrary view stated *obiter* by the Divisional Court in *Bullock* v. *Bullock*, [1960] 2 All E.R. 307, at pp. 309 and 313, does not seem to be supported by the authorities there cited.

[2] See Tolstoy, *Marriage by Estoppel*, 84 L.Q.R. 245, and the authorities there cited, particularly *Woodland* v. *Woodland*, [1928] P. 169.

[3] The problem arose in an acute form in *Wilkins* v. *Wilkins*, [1896] P. 108, C.A. On the wife's petition for divorce the respondent husband's answer had been that the marriage was void because the wife's first husband was alive at the time of his marriage to the petitioner. This fact was expressly found against him. The first husband later returned to England and the second husband then petitioned for nullity. It was held that the first judgment estopped him from doing so, but the Court of Appeal solved the problem by giving him leave to apply for a new trial on that issue.

proceedings for maintenance had been previously brought under section 27 of the Matrimonial Causes Act.[1] It has been held that proceedings before magistrates cannot create an estoppel in the High Court[2] or, presumably, in a county court. Although non-matrimonial proceedings in a county court have been held to create an estoppel in a magistrates' court, it has been stated obiter that they cannot bind the High Court in matrimonial proceedings.[3]

When questions of status are involved, estoppel inevitably creates difficulties. There may be little justification for permitting either party to assert the invalidity of a marriage when he or she has already had an opportunity of doing so but, as PHILLIMORE, J., said in *Hayward* v. *Hayward*,[4] public policy demands that, when status is in issue, the courts should declare the truth unencumbered by technical rules. At the moment a man may be validly married to one woman but estopped from denying that he is also married to a second: a result no less absurd than the fact that a stranger may be able to show that a marriage is void whilst, as between themselves, the parties are prevented from doing so.

In all the cases cited the marriages in question were alleged to be void. It is arguable that exactly the same principles applied if the marriage was voidable so long as annulment had retrospective effect. But now that such a marriage is treated as having existed up to the decree absolute, there is no longer anything inconsistent in an earlier decision based on the assumption that the marriage is valid and a later decree declaring the marriage to be voidable. If, say, the wife obtains a decree of judicial separation during the first three years of marriage, this should not *as such* preclude the husband from subsequently petitioning for a decree of nullity on the ground that she was at the time of the marriage pregnant by another man. His failure to cross-petition for nullity when she petitioned for judicial separation might amount to such conduct on his part as to lead her reasonably to believe that he would not seek a decree of nullity, but this would enable her to raise a statutory bar and not an estoppel. The former would succeed only if the husband knew at the time of the earlier proceedings that it was open to him to have the marriage annulled and if it would be unjust to the wife to grant the decree.[5] Estoppel, if it were relevant, would operate automatically: it is submitted that it cannot apply at all.

---

[1] See *post*, p. 515.

[2] *Hayward* v. *Hayward*, [1961] P. 152, 161; [1961] 1 All E.R. 236, 243.

[3] *Whittaker* v. *Whittaker*, [1939] 3 All E.R. 833, 837. Presumably undefended matrimonial proceedings in a county court will raise an estoppel in all courts; they have been held to create an estoppel in non-matrimonial proceedings in the High Court: *Razelos* v. *Razelos*, [1969] 3 All E.R. 929.

[4] [1961] P. 152, 158-159; [1961] 1 All E.R. 236, 241-242; approved *obiter* in *Rowe* v. *Rowe*, [1980] Fam. 47 at pp. 53 and 58; [1979] 2 All E.R. 1123, at pp. 1127 and 1131, C.A. It is submitted, however, that the learned judge did not sufficiently differentiate between estoppels *per rem judicatam* and estoppels *in pais*. In *Taylor* v. *Taylor*, [1967] P. 25, 29; [1965] 1 All E.R. 872, 875, it was conceded that no estoppel of any kind would bind the court but the point was not argued.

[5] See *post*, pp. 93-96.

C. VOIDABLE MARRIAGES

1. GROUNDS ON WHICH A MARRIAGE WILL BE VOIDABLE

The six grounds on which a marriage celebrated after 31st July 1971 will be voidable are now set out in section 12 of the Matrimonial Causes Act 1973.[1] Five of these grounds are, with two slight modifications, the same as those which existed before 1st August 1971. The modifications are relevant, however, in only one case (which will be noted), because petitions on the other ground are now barred by effluxion of time. The remaining ground—lack of consent—probably made the marriage void before that date, although this is a matter of some doubt.[2] If this was the effect of lack of consent, marriages affected by it and celebrated before 1st August 1971 will, of course, still be void.

Two of the grounds, inability to consummate the marriage and wilful refusal to do so, are so closely related that it will be convenient to deal with them together. We shall then consider the other four grounds in turn.

The Unconsummated Marriage.—Even in canon law a marriage was not always finally and irrevocably indissoluble if it had not been consummated by the sexual act. If at the time of the ceremony either spouse was incapable of consummating it, he or she was regarded as lacking the physical capacity (as distinct from the legal capacity) to contract a valid marriage and the union could therefore be annulled. If, on the other hand, the marriage remained unconsummated because of one party's refusal to have sexual intercourse, canon law offered no relief because the ground of complaint was conduct following the ceremony.[3] Despite this, decrees were probably in fact given in some cases in reliance on the presumption that, if the marriage had not been consummated after three years' cohabitation through no fault of the petitioner, the respondent must be impotent.[4] The law was put on a more rational footing by the Matrimonial Causes Act 1937, which enacted that a marriage should be voidable if it had not been consummated owing to the respondent's wilful refusal to do so. This was frequently criticised because it offended against the principle that an impediment avoiding a marriage should exist at the time of the ceremony. The Law Commission, however, recommended that it should remain a ground for nullity; the most cogent reason they advanced was that the petitioner is often uncertain whether failure to consummate is due to the respondent's impotence or wilful refusal and in practice will then plead both grounds in the alternative.[5] Only the legal or theological purist will object to the principle's giving way to practical

---

[1] Re-enacting the Nullity of Marriage Act 1971, s. 2, which came into force on 1st August 1971.

[2] For a full discussion of the problem, see the fourth edition of this book, at pp. 79-83.

[3] *Napier* v. *Napier*, [1915] P. 184, C.A.

[4] *G.* v. *M.* (1885), 10 App. Cas. 171, H.L., at pp. 189-190, 198-199. *Cf. S.* v. *S.* (*orse W.*), [1963] P. 162, 171; [1962] 2 All E.R. 816, 818-819, C.A. The petitioner did not have to rely on this presumption and could always allege impotence during the first three years of the marriage.

[5] Thus in the five years 1973-1977 of all petitions alleging impotence and wilful refusal 23% alleged impotence alone, 55% alleged wilful refusal alone, and 22% alleged both in the alternative. No separate figures for the last category have been published since 1977.

expediency.[1] But it must be admitted that there is something highly artificial about the whole concept. The petitioner's real complaint is that he (or she) is being deprived of normal sexual relations because of the respondent's impotence or conduct. If intercourse takes place once (perhaps after great delay and difficulty), the petitioner's power to petition for nullity goes and his sole remedy lies in divorce if the respondent is unable or unwilling to have further sexual relations. In the case of impotence, this could mean having to wait for five years' separation if the respondent refuses to consent to a decree.

It must be emphasised that non-consummation *as such* does not make a marriage voidable. There are two separate grounds on which a party may petition: that the marriage has not been consummated owing to the incapacity of either party to consummate it or that it has not been consummated owing to the respondent's wilful refusal to do so.[2] Clearly, it would be wholly unjust to permit the petitioner to rely on his own wilful refusal.

Meaning of Consummation.—A marriage is said to be consummated as soon as the parties have sexual intercourse after the solemnization.[3] The distinction between the act of intercourse and the possibility of that act resulting in the birth of a child must be kept clear: once the parties have had intercourse the marriage is consummated even though one or both are sterile.[4] If this were not so, the marriage could never be consummated if, for example, the wife were beyond the age of child bearing. Conversely, if the spouses have not had intercourse, the birth of a child as the result of fecundation *ab extra* or artificial insemination will not amount to consummation.[5]

In order to amount to consummation, the intercourse must, in the words of Dr. Lushington in *D——E* v. *A——G*[6] be "ordinary and complete, and not partial and imperfect". Hence, as in *D——E* v. *A——G*, there will be no consummation if the husband does not achieve full penetration in the normal sense. The necessity of complete intercourse has raised difficulties where the spouses use some form of contraception. In 1945 the Court of Appeal held in *Cowen* v. *Cowen*[7] that there had been no consummation where the husband had invariably either worn a contraceptive sheath or practised *coitus interruptus*,[8] but two years later the House of Lords in *Baxter* v. *Baxter*[9] overruled at least the first part of the decision in *Cowen* v. *Cowen* by holding that the marriage had been consummated notwithstanding the husband's use of a sheath. As Lord Jowitt, L.C., pointed out, the possibility of conception is irrelevant to the question of consummation and when Parliament passed

---

[1] But see Cretney, *Principles of Family Law*, 3rd Ed., 54-57.

[2] See now the Matrimonial Causes Act 1973, s. 12 (a), (b).

[3] Not *before* the solemnization. Hence the marriage is not automatically consummated by reason of the fact that the parties have had pre-marital intercourse: *cf. Dredge* v. *Dredge*, [1947] 1 All E.R. 29.

[4] *D——E* v. *A——G* (1845), 1 Rob. Eccl. 279; *Baxter* v. *Baxter*, [1948] A.C. 274; [1947] 2 All E.R. 886, H.L.

[5] *Cf. Clarke* v. *Clarke*, [1943] 2 All E.R. 540; *L.* v. *L.*, [1949] P. 211; [1949] 1 All E.R. 141.

[6] (1845), 1 Rob. Eccl. 279, 298.

[7] [1946] P. 36; [1945] 2 All E.R. 197, C.A.

[8] *I.e.*, deliberate withdrawal before ejaculation.

[9] [1948] A.C. 274; [1947] 2 All E.R. 886, H.L.

the Matrimonial Causes Act in 1937 (the statute on which the petition was based) it was common knowledge that many people, especially young married couples, used contraceptives and that in common parlance this would amount to consummation.[1] The decision in *Baxter* v. *Baxter* obviously applies if either party uses any form of mechanical or chemical contraception, but the House of Lords deliberately 'left open the question whether *coitus interruptus* would amount to consummation.[2] There have been three reported cases at first instance since *Baxter* v. *Baxter*, in one of which it was held that it did not,[3] and in the other two that it did and that since *Baxter* v. *Baxter* neither branch of the decision of *Cowen* v. *Cowen* could any longer be regarded as good law.[4] In the last of these, *Cackett* v. *Cackett*,[5] HODSON, J., in holding that the marriage was consummated by *coitus interruptus*, stated that the court would be driven into an impossible position if it tried further to define what normal sexual intercourse was.[6] It has since been held that a marriage is consummated even though the husband is physically incapable of ejaculation after penetration,[7] but not if he is incapable of sustaining an erection for more than a very short period of time after penetration.[8] Perhaps inevitably the courts have tended to concentrate on the husband's role during intercourse,[9] and on the authority of these cases it is suggested that the marriage is consummated as soon as the husband achieves full penetration (unless this is only transient) and that ejaculation is irrelevant.

Inability to Consummate.—A marriage is voidable if it has not been consummated owing to the incapacity of either party to consummate it.[10]

Inability to consummate may be due to physiological or psychological causes and may be either general or merely *quoad* the particular spouse. It will be seen that the statute re-enacts the common law rule that a petitioner may show that the marriage has not been consummated because of either spouse's incapacity and may therefore petition in reliance on his own impotence.[11] This follows from the premise that one of the objects in giving relief when the marriage cannot be consummated is to prevent the formation of an adulterous union[12] and the recognition of the fact that a spouse may be

---

[1] At pp. 286 and 290, 890 and 892, respectively.
[2] At pp. 283 and 888, respectively.
[3] *Grimes* v. *Grimes*, [1948] P. 323; [1948] 2 All E.R. 147.
[4] *White* v. *White*, [1948] P. 330; [1948] 2 All E.R. 151; *Cackett* v. *Cackett*, [1950] P. 253; [1950] 1 All E.R. 677.
[5] [1950] P. 253; [1950] 1 All E.R. 677.
[6] At pp. 258-9 and 680, respectively.
[7] *R.* v. *R.*, [1952] 1 All E.R. 1194.
[8] *W. (otherwise K.)* v. *W.*, [1967] 3 All E.R. 178 n.
[9] Thus there can be consummation even though the wife's vagina has been artificially extended (or, perhaps, wholly constructed): *S.* v. *S.* (*otherwise W.*) (*No. 2*), [1963] P. 37; [1962] 3 All E.R. 55, C.A. But she must be biologically female to begin with: *Corbett* v. *Corbett*, [1971] P. 83; [1970] 2 All E.R. 33.
[10] Matrimonial Causes Act 1973, s. 12 (a).
[11] This rule was finally established in *Harthan* v. *Harthan*, [1949] P. 115; [1948] 2 All E.R. 639, C.A.
[12] See *D——E* v. *A——G* (1845), 1 Rob. Eccl. 279, 299.

impotent *quoad* the other but be perfectly capable of having normal sexual intercourse with others.[1]

At common law it was said that relief would be granted only if the impotence was incurable and the term "incapacity" presumably still imports this element. In this context, however, "incurable" has received a very extended meaning and it will be considered incurable not only if it is wholly incapable of any remedy but also if it can be cured only by an operation attended by danger or, in any event, if it is improbable that the operation will be successful or the party refuses to undergo it. But where the petitioner relies upon his own impotence, it is submitted that the court might well take the view that he should not be allowed to complain of the situation if the impediment could be removed without danger to himself.[3]

The petitioner's knowledge of the *respondent's* impotence before marriage is not necessarily a bar to the petition,[4] although if he knew that impotence was a ground for nullity, his marrying the respondent in the circumstances might amount to such conduct as would entitle the latter to invoke the statutory bar that has replaced approbation.[5] But if the petitioner relied upon *his own* impotence, he failed at common law if he was aware of it beforehand and deceived the respondent, who could then plead the *suppressio veri* as a bar, or apparently in any case if at the time of the marriage he knew that the respondent was also impotent.[6] It is not clear whether these restrictions survive under the Act. If they are regarded as bars, they appear to have been swept away along with all the other common law bars;[7] it is possible to argue, however, that the absence of these conditions was a prerequisite to the petitioner's being able to bring proceedings at common law,[8] in which case they will have survived. The balance of authorities indicates that the latter view is correct.

At common law impotence was a ground for avoiding the marriage only if it existed at the time of the solemnization and there was still no practical possibility of the marriage being consummated at the date of the hearing.[9]

---

[1] See *C. v. C.*, [1921] P. 399. Hence if each is impotent *quoad* the other, either may petition: *G. v. G.*, [1912] P. 173.

[2] *S. v. S. (orse C.)*, [1956] P. 1, 11; [1954] 3 All E.R. 736, 741; *M. v. M.*, [1957] P. 139; [1956] 3 All E.R. 769. *Cf. L. v. L.* (1882), 7 P.D. 16; *G. v. G.* (1908), 25 T.L.R. 328.

[3] A wilful refusal to take treatment in such a case might amount to wilful refusal to consummate the marriage: *S. v. S. (orse C.)*, [1956] P. at pp. 15-16; [1954] 3 All E.R. at pp. 743-744.

[4] *Nash* v. *Nash*, [1940] P. 60, 64-65; [1940] 1 All E.R. 206, 209; *J. v. J.*, [1947] P. 158, 163; [1947] 2 All E.R. 43, 44, C.A., (overruled on another point by *Baxter* v. *Baxter*, *(ante)*).

[5] See *post*, p. 94.

[6] *Harthan* v. *Harthan*, [1949] P. 115, 129; [1948] 2 All E.R. 639, 644, C.A. In the latter case therefore he should petition on the ground of the respondent's impotence for the knowledge will not necessarily bar him. See Bevan, *Limitations on the Right of an Impotent Spouse to Petition for Nullity*, 76 L.Q.R. 267.

[7] By the Nullity of Marriage Act 1971, s. 3 (4). See *post*, p. 93.

[8] See the cases cited in Jackson, *Formation and Annulment of Marriage*, 2nd Ed., 352-354; Bevan, *loc. cit.*

[9] *Napier* v. *Napier*, [1915] P. 184, C.A.; *S. v. S. (orse W.)*, [1963] P. 162; [1962] 2 All E.R. 816, C.A., approving *S. v. S. (orse C.)*, [1956] P. 1; [1954] 3 All E.R. 736. For if the party is cured or curable at the time of the hearing, he or she could not have been incurably incapable at the time of the solemnization. In Scotland, it has been held that the party must have been incurable at all times since the solemnization: *M.* v. *W.*, 1966 S.L.T. 25. This is a logical extension of the rule.

Consequently, if a party was capable of having sexual intercourse at the time of the ceremony but became impotent before the marriage was consummated (for example, as the result of an injury), it is highly doubtful whether a petition for nullity could have succeeded. The Act, however, makes no reference to incapacity at the time of the marriage and it therefore seems that a petition would now succeed in these circumstances.

Wilful Refusal to Consummate. —A marriage will be voidable if it has not been consummated owing to the *respondent's* wilful refusal to do so.[1] (As the petitioner is complaining of marital misconduct, he may not of course rely on his own refusal.) Wilful refusal connotes "a settled and definite decision come to without just excuse", and the whole history of the marriage must be looked at.[2] Thus in *Kaur* v. *Singh*[3] the parties, who were both Sikhs, married in a register office on the understanding that they should not cohabit until they had gone through a religious ceremony of marriage in a Sikh temple, and it was held that in the circumstances the husband's refusal without excuse to make arrangements for such a ceremony amounted to wilful refusal to consummate the marriage.

Refusal to have intercourse in any form will clearly come within the statute, and so may wilful refusal to take treatment (attended by no danger) to remove a physical or psychological impediment to consummation.[4] As we have seen, there will not be a wilful refusal to consummate if one spouse insists upon the use of contraceptives or, probably, of *coitus interruptus*. But *Baxter* v. *Baxter*[5] has raised a difficulty which cannot be easily solved. Suppose the marriage is never consummated because the husband, H, refuses to use a contraceptive and the wife, W, refuses to let him have intercourse unless he does. It is difficult to see how either of them can be said to have refused to consummate, for W has been prepared to do so within the meaning given to the term by *Baxter* v. *Baxter*, and H has expressed his willingness to have intercourse in the natural way.

Once the marriage has been consummated, it will not be voidable if one spouse subsequently refuses to continue to have intercourse. In such a case, as in the case of the use of contraceptives or the practice of *coitus interruptus* against the other spouse's will, the latter's only remedy lies in divorce.

Lack of Consent. —Section 12 (c) of the Matrimonial Causes Act 1973 provides that a marriage shall be voidable if either party did not validly consent to it, whether in consequence of duress, mistake, unsoundness of mind or otherwise. Marriage is a contract and consequently absence of consent will

---

[1] Matrimonial Causes Act 1973, s. 12 (b), re-enacting provisions going back to the Matrimonial Causes Act 1937.

[2] *Per* LORD JOWITT, L.C., in *Horton* v. *Horton*, [1947] 2 All E.R. 871, 874, H.L. He left open the question whether the petitioner could succeed if he had originally refused to consummate but then changed his mind by which time the respondent had changed her mind and refused to let the petitioner have intercourse. *Cf. Potter* v. *Potter* (1975), 5 Fam. Law 161, C.A. (husband's refusal due to loss of sexual ardour for wife in similar circumstances not wilful).

[3] [1972] 1 All E.R. 292, C.A., following *Jodla* v. *Jodla*, [1960] 1 All E.R. 625. *Cf. Boggins* v. *Boggins*, [1966] C.L.Y. 4041 (husband who deserted wife before consummating marriage held to have wilfully refused to do so).

[4] *S.* v. *S. (orse C.)*, [1956] P. 1, 15-16; [1954] 3 All E.R. 736, 743-744.

[5] *Ante*, p. 84. For a contrary view, see Gower, *Baxter* v. *Baxter in Perspective*, 11 M.L.R. 176, particularly at 186-187.

invalidate the ceremony. But a contract of marriage is not quite on the same footing as other contracts in this respect because some facts which may vitiate a commercial contract (for example, fraud) did not affect a marriage at all at common law and the Act does not appear to have extended the grounds on which it can be annulled.

As has already been pointed out, lack of consent probably made the marriage void at common law.[1] The reason for making such a marriage voidable is that the parties themselves may wish to ratify it when true consent can be given and consequently third parties should not be able to impeach it.[2]

It will be seen that the petitioner may rely on the fact that the respondent did not consent to the marriage even though the petitioner himself was responsible for this state of affairs, for example by inducing a mistake or uttering threats. Whilst this logically followed when lack of consent made the marriage void, it may leave a respondent who wishes to adopt the marriage with a legitimate sense of grievance in such circumstances. Nevertheless, he will have no defence to the petition unless he can plead one of the statutory bars.[3]

We must now consider what facts will be regarded in law as vitiating consent.

Unsoundness of Mind.—This will affect a marriage if, as a consequence, at the time of the ceremony either party was unable to understand the nature of the contract he was entering into. There is a presumption that he was capable of doing so and the burden of proof therefore lies upon the party impeaching the validity of the marriage.[4] The test to be applied was thus formulated by SINGLETON, L.J., in *In the Estate of Park*:[5]

> "Was the [person] ... capable of understanding the nature of the contract into which he was entering, or was his mental condition such that he was incapable of understanding it? To ascertain the nature of the contract of marriage a man must be mentally capable of appreciating that it involves the responsibilities normally attaching to marriage. Without that degree of mentality, it cannot be said that he understands the nature of the contract."

Drunkenness and the Effect of Drugs.—In the absence of any binding English authority, it is submitted that the effect of drunkenness and drugs will be the same as that of unsoundness of mind. Consequently the marriage will be voidable if, as a result of either, one of the parties was incapable of understanding the nature of the contract into which he was entering.[6]

---

[1] In which case a marriage affected by lack of consent will still be void if it was contracted before 1st August 1971.

[2] See Law Com. No. 33, paras. 11-15.

[3] See *post*, pp. 94-95.

[4] *Harrod* v. *Harrod* (1854), 1 K. & J. 4, 9. But if the person is proved to have been generally insane, there will be a presumption that he was insane at the time of the marriage and the burden of proof will consequently shift on to the party seeking to uphold its validity: *Turner* v. *Meyers* (1808), 1 Hag. Con. 414, 417.

[5] [1954] P. 112, 127; [1953] 2 All E.R. 1411, 1430, C.A. *Cf.* KARMINSKI, J. (in the Div. Court), at pp. 99 and 414; BIRKETT, L.J., at pp. 134-135 and 1434; HODSON, L.J., at pp. 137 and 1436-1437 respectively; *Hunter* v. *Edney* (1881), 10 P.D. 93, 95; *Durham* v. *Durham* (1885), 10 P.D. 80, 82.

[6] *Cf. Legey* v. *O'Brien* (1834), Milw. 325; *Sullivan* v. *Sullivan* (1818), 2 Hag. Con. 238, 246 (*per* SIR W. SCOTT).

Mistake.—A mistake will affect the marriage in two cases only. First, a mistake as to the identity of the other contracting party will make the marriage voidable if this results in one party's failing to marry the individual whom he or she intends to marry. In the New Zealand case of *C.* v. *C.*[1] W married H in the erroneous belief that he was a well known boxer called Miller. It was held that the marriage was not invalidated by the mistake because she married the very individual she meant to marry. Secondly, the marriage will be voidable if one of the parties is mistaken as to the nature of the ceremony and does not appreciate that he is contracting a marriage. In *Valier* v. *Valier*[2] the husband, who was an Italian and whose knowledge of the English language was poor, was taken to a register office by the wife and there went through the usual form of marriage. He did not understand what was happening at the time, the parties never cohabited and the marriage was never consummated. It was held that he was entitled to a decree of nullity.

But if each party appreciates that he is going through a form of marriage with the other, no other type of mistake apparently can affect the contract.[3] Thus, it has been held that the marriage will not be invalidated by a mistake as to the monogamous or polygamous nature of the union,[4] the other party's fortune,[5] the woman's chastity,[6] or the recognition of the union by the religious denomination of the parties.[7]

Fraud and Misrepresentation.—Unlike the case of a commercial contract, neither a fraudulent nor an innocent misrepresentation will of itself affect the validity of a marriage.[8] But if the misrepresentation induces an operative mistake (*e.g.*, as to the nature of the ceremony), the marriage will be made voidable by the latter.[9]

Fear and Duress.—If, owing to fear or threats, one of the parties is induced to enter into a marriage which, in the absence of compulsion, he would never have contracted, the marriage will be voidable. The fear may be due to a number of causes. In *Buckland* v. *Buckland*,[10] for example, the petitioner, a youth aged 20 resident in Malta, was groundlessly charged with

---

1 [1942] N.Z.L.R. 356. But if A becomes engaged to B, whom she has never seen before, by correspondence, and C successfully personates B at the wedding, the marriage would be voidable because A intends to marry B and nobody else: *ibid.*, p. 359. It would be void if the personation invalidated the publication of banns: see *ante*, p. 42.

2 (1925), 133 L.T. 830. See also *Ford* v. *Stier*, [1896] P. 1, and *Kelly* v. *Kelly* (1932), 49 T.L.R. 99 (mistaken belief that ceremony was formal betrothal); *Mehta* v. *Mehta*, [1945] 2 All E.R. 690 (mistaken belief that Hindu marriage ceremony was ceremony of religious conversion).

3 *Moss* v. *Moss*, [1897] P. 263, 271-273; *Kenward* v. *Kenward*, [1950] P. 71, 79; [1949] 2 All E.R. 959, 963; (*per* HODSON, J.); [1951] P. 124, 133-134; [1950] 2 All E.R. 297, 302, C.A. (*per* EVERSHED, M.R.).

4 *Kassim* v. *Kassim*, [1962] P. 224; [1962] 3 All E.R. 426.

5 *Wakefield* v. *Mackay* (1807), 1 Hag. Con. 394, 398.

6 Even though she is pregnant *per alium: Moss* v. *Moss*, (*supra*).

7 *Ussher* v. *Ussher*, [1912] 2 I.R. 445.

8 *Swift* v. *Kelly* (1835), 3 Knapp 257, 293, P.C.; *Moss* v. *Moss*, (*supra*), at p. 266.

9 *Moss* v. *Moss*, (*supra*), at pp. 268-269.

10 [1968] P. 296; [1967] 2 All E.R. 300. See also *Scott* v. *Sebright* (1886), 12 P.D. 21 (threats to make petitioner bankrupt, to denounce her and finally to shoot her); *Griffith* v. *Griffith*, [1944] I.R. 35 (fear of prosecution for unlawful carnal knowledge); Poulter, *The Definition of Marriage in English Law*, 42 M.L.R. 409, 410-418. All the earlier cases are collected and exhaustively discussed by Manchester, *Marriage or Prison: the Case of the Reluctant Bridegroom*, 29 M.L.R. 622.

defiling the respondent, a girl of 15. Although he protested his innocence, he
was twice advised that he stood no chance of an acquittal but would probably
be sent to prison for a period of up to two years unless he married her. He did
so and it was held that he was entitled to a decree of nullity. Nor it is necessary
that the fear should have been inspired by any acts on the other party's part.
In *Szechter* v. *Szechter*[1] the petitioner was a Polish national who had been
arrested by the security police in Warsaw. After 14 months' interrogation and
detention in appalling conditions she was sentenced to three years' imprisonment for "anti-state activities". Her health, which had always been poor,
deteriorated rapidly and she came to the conclusion that she would not
survive the sentence; if she did come out of prison alive, she believed that she
was likely to be re-arrested and in any case would be unable to get any job
other than one of a menial nature. The respondent was a distinguished Polish
historian of Jewish origin whose presence in Poland was something of an
embarrassment to the authorities and whom they were prepared to allow to
emigrate. In order to effect the petitioner's release he divorced his wife and
went through a ceremony of marriage with the petitioner in prison. The
scheme was successful, and eventually all the parties reached England, where
the petitioner brought proceedings for nullity so that the respondent and his
first wife could remarry. SIMON, P., held that the marriage was voidable
applying the following test:[2]

> "It is, in my view, insufficient to invalidate an otherwise good marriage that a party
> has entered into it in order to escape from a disagreeable situation, such as penury
> or social degradation. In order for the impediment of duress to vitiate an otherwise
> valid marriage, it must, in my judgment, be proved that the will of one of the parties
> thereto has been overborne by genuine and reasonably held fear caused by threat of
> immediate danger (for which the party is not himself responsible), to life, limb or
> liberty, so that the constraint destroys the reality of consent to ordinary wedlock."

Whether there was present a sufficient degree of fear to vitiate the party's
consent is clearly a question of fact, and if he happens to be more susceptible
to the pressure brought to bear on him than another might be, the marriage
may still be annulled even though a person of ordinary courage and resilience
would not have yielded to it.[3] It may be doubted, however, whether the three
limitations which SIMON, P., placed upon the operation of duress as a ground
for nullity are desirable or supported by earlier authorities. First, it does not
seem necessary that there should be a threat of immediate danger to "life,
limb or liberty". Admittedly most of the cases reported come into this category, but why, for example, should a threat of financial or social ruin not be
sufficient if it affects the party's conduct?[4] Secondly, if the condition that the

---

[1] [1971] P. 286; [1970] 3 All E.R. 905. See also *H.* v. *H.*, [1954] P. 258; [1953] 2 All E.R. 1229
(marriage contracted in Budapest to enable woman to escape from Hungary where she was likely
to be sent to prison or concentration camp); *Parojcic* v. *Parojcic*, [1959] 1 All E.R. 1 (fear
imposed by petitioner's father).

[2] At pp. 297-298 and 915, respectively, cited with apparent approval in *Singh* v. *Singh*, [1971]
P. 226, 231; [1971] 2 All E.R. 828, 831, C.A.

[3] *Scott* v. *Sebright* (1886), 12 P.D. 21, 24; *Cooper* v. *Crane*, [1891] P. 369, 376.

[4] The respondent's threats to see that bankruptcy proceedings were taken against the
petitioner and to "accuse her to her mother and in every drawing-room in London of having
been seduced by him" were apparently regarded as grounds (along with a threat to shoot her) for
annulling the marriage in *Scott* v. *Sebright*, (*supra*). See also Davies, *Duress and Nullity of
Marriage*, 88 L.Q.R. 549, at p. 552; Pearl, [1971] C.L.J. 206; Bates, 130 New L.J. 1035, and the
Australian cases there cited.

fear must be reasonably held means that the marriage will be voidable only if
a reasonable person, placed in the position of the petitioner, would have
concluded that the threats would have been implemented if the marriage had
not taken place, it is directly contrary to the view stated earlier by Butt, J., in
Scott v. *Sebright*[1] and it is submitted that the latter is to be preferred. If a
person is in a mental state in which he is no longer capable of offering
resistance to threats, it seems immaterial that it would be obvious to a reasonable person, similarly placed, that the other has no intention of carrying them
out at all.[2] Thirdly, although Scarman, J.'s decision in *Buckland* v. *Buckland*
is clear authority for the proposition that the fear must arise from some
external circumstances for which the party is not himself responsible, it is
doubtful whether this rule is correctly expressed. In that case the petitioner
succeeded because his fear arose from the false charge preferred against him;
presumably he would have failed had he actually been guilty of defiling the
respondent. Originally it was said that the fear must be unjustly imposed;[3]
and whilst it could not be justly imposed if the party was not responsible for
the events which had given rise to the threat, it does not follow that it will be
justly imposed if he was responsible. If a man is threatened with affiliation
proceedings unless he marries the woman allegedly carrying his child, it seems
proper that he should be able to petition for nullity if he is not the father but
that he should not be able to do so if the child is his. If, however, the woman's
father threatens to shoot him if he does not marry her or, to take a different
situation, if an employer threatens to prosecute a clerk for theft if he does not
marry his daughter, one feels that the marriage should be voidable in both
cases whether or not the man in question is responsible for the pregnancy or
has committed the theft. The distinction is that it is reasonable to face a man
with the choice between marriage and affiliation proceedings but not to face
him with the choice between marriage and death or prosecution for theft. It is
therefore submitted that the only limitation on duress or fear as a ground for
nullity is that a marriage will not be voidable if the fear is justly imposed in the
sense that the party is responsible for the state of affairs which has given rise
to the threat and it is reasonable to face him with the choice between marriage
and the implementation of the threat.[4]

"Sham Marriages".—The question has been canvassed whether a "sham
marriage"—that is, where the parties go through the form of marriage purely
for the purpose of representing themselves as married to the outside world

---

[1] (1886), 12 P.D. 21, 24. But Simon, P.'s views are supported by *Buckland* v. *Buckland*,
[1968] P. 296, 301; [1967] 2 All E.R. 300, 302 (*per* Scarman, J.) and *H.* v. *H.*, [1954] P. 258,
269; [1953] 2 All E.R. 1229, 1234 (*per* Karminski, J.).
[2] This is the view of the Law Commission in Law Com. No. 33, at p. 27. Professor Davies,
loc. cit., suggests that the rule that the fear must be reasonably entertained applies only when it is
imposed by someone other than the respondent or his agent. This is ingenious but it is not the
basis of any reported case and could work injustice. In *Parojcic* v. *Parojcic*, (*supra*), for
example, the petitioner entered into the marriage because her father threatened to send her back
to Jugoslavia if she did not do so; why should she be tied to the marriage if a reasonable woman
in her position would have realised that he had no intention of implementing his threat?
[3] *Griffith* v. *Griffith*, [1944] I.R. 35, 43-44.
[4] See also Law Com. No. 33, paras. 63-66 (to which Scarman, J., as chairman, was a party);
Davies, *loc. cit.*

with no intention of cohabiting—is to be regarded in law as a nullity. This problem may become more important in these days of political, racial and religious persecution and restricted immigration when, for example, a woman who is a citizen of state X may go through a form of marriage with a citizen of state Y merely in order to escape from X or to enter Y on the strength of her husband's nationality or passport.

The question had to be decided by COLLINGWOOD, J., in *Silver* v. *Silver*.[1] In this case the wife, who was a German subject, had gone through a form of marriage with the respondent, who was a British subject, in order to be able to enter England and remain here. The spouses separated immediately after their arrival in this country, never cohabited, and in fact met only twice in the next 29 years, when the wife commenced nullity proceedings as she wanted to marry another man. COLLINGWOOD, J., decided that, as they had entered into the marriage contract with the intention of becoming man and wife, in the absence of duress the marriage was perfectly valid and could not be affected by any mental reservations. This is in keeping with earlier decisions and dicta,[2] and it would be difficult to defend any other view.

Mental Disorder.—A marriage is voidable if, at the time of the ceremony, *either party*, though capable of giving a valid consent, was suffering (whether continuously or intermittently) from mental disorder within the meaning of the Mental Health Act 1959 of such a kind or to such an extent as to be unfitted for marriage.[3] "Unfitted for marriage" in this context has been defined as "incapable of carrying out the ordinary duties and obligations of marriage".[4]

This must be distinguished from a ground for nullity that we have already considered: mental illness producing lack of consent. In the case of mental disorder it is presumed that the party was capable of giving a valid consent to the marriage but that the general state of his mental health at the time of the ceremony was such that it is right that the marriage should be annulled. It will be observed that the petitioner does not have to rely on the respondent's mental disorder but may rely on his own. This is necessary to enable a party to withdraw from a marriage if he entered into it in ignorance of the existence or extent of his illness or the effect which it would have upon his married life.

Venereal Disease.—A marriage is voidable if at the time of the ceremony *the respondent* was suffering from venereal disease in a communicable form.[5]

Pregnancy *per alium.* —A husband may petition for nullity if at the time of the marriage *the respondent wife* was pregnant by someone other than himself.[6]

---

[1] [1955] 2 All E.R. 614, followed in *Puttick* v. *A.-G.*, [1980] Fam. 1; [1979] 3 All E.R. 463.

[2] See *Bell* v. *Graham* (1859), 13 Moo. P.C.C. 242, P.C.; *Kelly* v. *Kelly* (1932), 49 T.L.R. 99, 101; *H.* v. *H.*, [1954] P. 258, 269; [1953] 2 All E.R. 1229, 1234. See also Rogers, *Sham Marriages*, 4 Fam. Law 4.

[3] Matrimonial Causes Act 1973, s. 12 (d). This ground and the next two go back to the Matrimonial Causes Act 1937. For the meaning of "mental disorder", see the Mental Health Act 1959, s. 4.

[4] *Bennett* v. *Bennett*, [1969] 1 All E.R. 539.

[5] Matrimonial Causes Act 1973, s. 12 (e).

[6] *Ibid.*, s. 12 (f).

2. BARS TO RELIEF

As in the case of any other voidable contract, at common law a party to a voidable marriage might effectively put it out of his own power to obtain a decree of nullity by his own conduct. In addition to specific limitations attached to the statutory grounds for nullity, there were two bars of general application: approbation and collusion. We shall consider the nature of approbation shortly; the essence of collusion was that the initiation or conduct of the suit had been in some measure procured or determined by an agreement or bargain between the parties, and the reason that it was a bar was that the existence of such an agreement raised doubts whether the decree would be granted on the merits at all. This did not prevent the presentation of a false case in an undefended suit, however, and withholding a decree for collusion was open to the objection that it implied that "the sanctity of marriage is maintained by insisting that people should remain married as a punishment for their misbehaviour".[1] Consequently on the recommendation of the Law Commission collusion was abolished as a bar by the Nullity of Marriage Act 1971 and all the others were replaced by statutory bars which are now the only ones applicable. There are three.[2]

Petitioner's Conduct.—Section 13 (1) of the Matrimonial Causes Act 1973 provides:

"The court shall not ... grant a decree of nullity on the ground that the marriage is voidable if the respondent satisfies the court—
(a) that the petitioner, with knowledge that it was open to him to have the marriage avoided, so conducted himself in relation to the respondent as to lead the respondent reasonably to believe that he would not seek to do so; and
(b) that it would be unjust to the respondent to grant the decree."

This replaces the former bar of approbation (or lack of sincerity, as it was called in the older cases). The principle underlying this bar was thus summarised by LORD WATSON.[3]

"In a suit for nullity of marriage there may be facts and circumstances proved which so plainly imply, on the part of the complaining spouse, a recognition of the existence and validity of the marriage, as to render it most inequitable and contrary to public policy that he or she should be permitted to go on to challenge it with effect."

It is clear that the same principle underlies the statutory bar and consequently much of the old law remains unaltered although there have been some changes in detail and some doubts have been resolved. Before we examine the question of the petitioner's conduct in more detail, however, three preliminary points must be made. First, the court will be bound to apply the bar only if the respondent satisfies it that the statutory conditions are fulfilled. Not only does this mean that the burden of proof is on the respondent, but if he

---

[1] Law Com. No. 33, para. 37.
[2] Nullity of Marriage Act 1971, ss. 3 and 6 (1); Matrimonial Causes Act 1973, s. 13. These provisions implement the recommendations of the Law Commission: Law Com. No. 33, paras. 36-45 and 76-86.
[3] *G.* v. *M.* (1885), 10 App. Cas. 171, 197-198, H.L.

chooses not to raise the bar at all, the court must grant a decree if a ground
has been made out even if it is clear from the facts that these conditions are
fulfilled.[1] Secondly, no conduct on the petitioner's part can raise the bar
unless he knew at the time that it was open to him to have the marriage
avoided. This means that he must have been aware not only of the facts upon
which the petition is based (for example, that he is not the father of the
child that the respondent was carrying at the time of the marriage) but also
that these facts would entitle him to petition for a decree of nullity. Any
act or omission when he was ignorant of either of these matters must be
disregarded.[2] Thirdly, only conduct in relation to the petitioner can act as a
bar.

Positive Acts.—It is clear that any positive act by the petitioner may raise
the bar if a reasonable person in the respondent's position would have
concluded that the petitioner intended to treat the marriage as valid and the
respondent in fact drew this conclusion. An example of this is to be seen in *D.*
v. *D.*[3] The parties adopted two children at a time when the husband knew that
he could have the marriage annulled because of his wife's wilful refusal to
consummate it. He later brought nullity proceedings. It was held that by
agreeing to the adoption he had so conducted himself in relation to the wife as
to lead her to believe that he would not seek to do so. *But Petition granted on 2nd limb*

In some cases spouses may well resort to adoption or artificial insemination if one of them is impotent so that a child cannot be conceived in the
normal way, and the same principle will apply. If by consenting to the act the
petitioner admits that the marriage is never likely to be consummated and
also implies that any child which may be conceived will be born into a normal
family where the husband and wife are validly married, the respondent may
well infer that he will not thereafter petition for nullity. Nor can it make any
difference if the petitioner gives consent in the hope that the adoption or birth
of the child will remove a psychological impediment. If he has made the
position clear to the respondent, he will still be able to petition if his purpose
fails and the marriage remains unconsummated because nothing he has done
will have led the respondent to believe that he will not seek to have the
marriage annulled. But he may not later rely on a mental reservation "locked
in his bosom and not declared" to the respondent if the reasonable conclusion from his acts and declared intentions is that he is waiving his power to
bring proceedings.[4]

In some circumstances the mere fact that the petitioner has married the
respondent at all may reasonably lead the latter to believe that the former will
not subsequently petition for nullity. If a man marries a woman knowing that
one of them is impotent or suffering from mental disorder and knowing also
that this is a ground for nullity, she may reasonably conclude that he intends
to treat the marriage as valid and thus raise the marriage itself as a bar if he
does petition. For the same reason a party who has deprived the other of the

---

[1] This point was not taken in *D.* v. *D.*, [1979] Fam. 70; [1979] 3 All E.R. 337, where the wife,
having raised the defence, then elected not to pursue it. DUNN, J., however, held that in such
circumstances it could not be said to be unjust to grant the decree.
[2] This re-enacts the common law rule: see *G.* v. *M.*, (*supra*), at p. 186.
[3] [1979] Fam. 70; [1979] 3 All E.R. 337.
[4] *Cf. W.* v. *W.*, [1952] P. 152, 168; [1952] 1 All E.R. 858, 866, C.A.

power of consenting freely to the marriage by inducing a mistake or uttering threats may not be able to petition. A similar case arises if the parties entered into an agreement before marriage that they would not have sexual inter- course. Although this is regarded as contrary to public policy and is therefore not binding on them,[1] it may preclude either of them from obtaining a decree of nullity if the marriage is in fact never consummated and the agreement led the respondent to believe that the petitioner would not bring proceedings.[2] If one of the parties is old, infirm or seriously crippled, the marriage may well have been on this understanding, express or implied. *A fortiori* an agreement between the spouses that the petitioner will not institute proceedings for nullity will be a good defence to a petition.[3]

Although estoppel in the strict sense of the term cannot apply if the marriage is voidable, a party who brings other matrimonial proceedings with the knowledge that it is open to him to have the marriage annulled may thereby bar himself from petitioning for nullity later if the other spouse draws the conclusion that he does not intend to do so. Thus a wife who knows that her marriage is voidable because of her husband's impotence may lose her power to petition for nullity if she brings proceedings for an order in a magistrates' court based on his desertion.[4] Her husband might likewise lose his power to petition if he took part in the proceedings without indicating that he reserved the right to have the marriage avoided later.

Delay.—Just as some active step on the petitioner's part may bar him from bringing proceedings for nullity, delay in bringing them may equally bar him if he knows that it is open to him to have the marriage avoided and the delay has led the respondent reasonably to believe that he does not intend to do so. Obviously this will depend *inter alia* on the length of the delay and whether the petitioner has made it reasonably clear that he intends to bring proceedings, or at least may do so at a not too remote time in the future. The question must be one of fact: did the petitioner lull the respondent into a false sense of security or a false belief that he would not petition?

Injustice of Decree.—As we have seen, it is not sufficient that the petitioner has led the respondent to believe that he will not seek to have the marriage avoided, the latter must also show that it would be unjust to him (or her) to grant the decree. As in the case of divorce, justice will rarely be served by refusing to set aside a marriage that is already dead, particularly when the petitioner will usually be able to obtain a divorce after five years' separation; but there will undoubtedly be some cases when it would be manifestly unjust to grant a decree against an unwilling respondent. For example, a respondent in the position of the wife in *D.* v. *D.*[5] might satisfy the court that it would be

---

[1] *Cf. Brodie* v. *Brodie*, [1917] P. 271 (*post*, p. 171, n. 2).

[2] *Cf. Morgan* v. *Morgan*, [1959] P. 92; [1959] 1 All E.R. 539; *Scott* v. *Scott*, [1959] P. 103 n.; [1959] 1 All E.R. 531.

[3] *Cf. Aldridge* v. *Aldridge* (1888), 13 P.D. 210.

[4] *Cf. Tindall* v. *Tindall*, [1953] P. 63; [1953] 1 All E.R. 139, C.A. Similarly, a wife might bar herself if she continued to accept income from a trust in the wife's favour in a marriage settlement.

[5] For the facts see *ante*, p. 94. In this case it was held not to be unjust to grant the decree because the respondent did not pursue the defence.

unjust to her to annul the marriage because she would be left with two adopted children. The defence is perhaps most likely to succeed if the petitioner relies on his own impotence (or mental disorder) for consideration must necessarily be given to the respondent's attitude and reaction to a situation for which he is in no way responsible.[1] Among the matters which the court should take into account in deciding whether to grant a decree are the length of time the marriage has lasted, the existence of any children of the family, any religious or other personal objections that the respondent has to the decree, and the financial loss that he (or she) might suffer as a result of nullity (for example, the loss of pension rights or Social Security benefits).

Lapse of Time.—In all cases except those based on impotence or wilful refusal to consummate, a decree of nullity must be refused if the proceedings were not instituted within three years of the date of the marriage.[2] This is independent of the bar last considered, and even if the petition is brought within three years, the respondent may still raise the petitioner's delay or other conduct as a bar if it reasonably led him to conclude that the petitioner would not seek to have the marriage annulled. The reason for this further bar is to ensure that the validity of the marriage is not left in doubt for too long: consequently there is no power to extend the period even though the petitioner was unaware of the facts or that they made the marriage voidable. This may well work injustice, however. If, for example, the husband does not discover for more than three years that he is not the father of the child which his wife was carrying at the time of the marriage, he cannot claim any matrimonial relief at all as he cannot base a petition for divorce on her pre-marital sexual intercourse.[3]

Lapse of time is not a bar in the case of inability or wilful refusal to consummate the marriage because the petitioner may properly try to overcome the impediment or aversion for a longer period than three years.[4]

Petitioner's Knowledge.—If the petition is based on the respondent's venereal disease or pregnancy *per alium*, the decree must be refused unless the court was satisfied that the petitioner was ignorant of the facts alleged at the time of the marriage.[5] This bar applies to no other ground although, as we have seen, the fact that the petitioner knew of its existence and knew that it

---

[1] *Cf. Pettit* v. *Pettit*, [1963] P. 177; [1962] 3 All E.R. 37, C.A., in which, under the old law of approbation, the court refused to grant a decree to a husband, who petitioned on the ground of his own impotence more than 20 years after the marriage and after the birth of a child as the result of *fecundatio ab extra*, because it would have been inequitable to do so. Passingham, *Matrimonial Causes*, 3rd Ed., 71, regards the decision as still binding (which means that the husband still could not petition in such circumstances even though he was ignorant that his own impotence was a ground for nullity). But this is inconsistent with the provisions of s. 3 of the Nullity of Marriage Act 1971 (*ante*, p. 93) and with the decision in *D.* v. *D.* (*ante*, p. 94).

[2] Matrimonial Causes Act 1973, s. 13 (2).

[3] See *post*, pp. 203 and 219-220. The Law Commission have suggested that the court should have a power to extend the time limit if the petitioner is suffering from mental incapacity: see their Working Paper No. 76, Part III. *M L F P A (9 P 4 D P)*

[4] See Law Com. No. 33, paras. 79-85. Until 1971 there was a bar of one year in the case of petitions based on mental disorder, venereal disease and pregnancy *per alium*. The provisions of the Matrimonial Causes Act implement the recommendations of the Law Commission.

[5] Matrimonial Causes Act 1973, s. 13 (3). This replaces similar legislation going back to the Matrimonial Causes Act 1937.

was a ground for nullity might enable the respondent to argue that he was led to believe that the petitioner did not intend to have the marriage annulled.

3. EFFECT OF DECREE

Although a decree has always been necessary to annul a voidable marriage, at common law (as in the case of a void marriage) it pronounced the marriage "to have been and to be absolutely null and void to all intents and purposes in the law whatsoever". The consequence was that before the decree the parties were regarded as husband and wife both in law and in fact but after the decree absolute they were deemed in law never to have been married at all. The logical application of this anomalous doctrine produced some startling results. The children of a voidable marriage were automatically bastardised by the decree; the trusts under a marriage settlement all failed and the interest of the person entitled before the solemnization of the marriage revived; and if a widow remarried and the second marriage was annulled, she reverted to the status of her first husband's widow and could therefore claim an annuity payable to her *dum vidua*.[1] Some of these anomalies were swept away by statute—for example, children of a voidable marriage retained their legitimacy[2]—and after the Second World War there was an increasing tendency for the judges to regard decrees of nullity in respect of voidable marriages more like decrees of divorce.[3] This doctrine was never consistently applied, however, and by 1971 it was becoming increasingly difficult to predict in any given case whether the court would apply the strict logic of the old common law principle or follow the more realistic approach of some of the more recent cases.

The Nullity of Marriage Act sought to sweep away the remaining anomalies and to clarify the law. It is now provided:[4]

"A decree of nullity granted after 31st July 1971 in respect of a voidable marriage shall operate to annul the marriage only as respects any time after the decree has been made absolute, and the marriage shall, notwithstanding the decree, be treated as if it had existed up to that time."

Unfortunately the effect of this obscurely worded section is far from clear. It leaves no doubt that the parties must now be regarded as having been married throughout the whole period between the celebration of a voidable marriage and the decree absolute. Two examples will illustrate the operation of this part of the provision:

---

[1] *Re Wombwell's Settlement*, [1922] 2 Ch. 298 (marriage settlement); *Re D'Altroy's Will Trusts*, [1968] 1 All E.R. 181 (widow's annuity). See also *Newbould* v. *A.-G.* [1931] P. 75, and *Re Rodwell*, [1970] Ch. 726; [1969] 3 All E.R. 1363 (parties regarded as never having been married).

[2] See *post*, pp. 267-268.

[3] *R.* v. *Algar*, [1954] 1 Q.B. 279; [1953] 2 All E.R. 1381, C.C.A. (wife remained incompetent to give evidence against husband); *Wiggins* v. *Wiggins*, [1958] 1 All E.R. 555 (second marriage contracted during subsistence of voidable marriage remained void notwithstanding annulment of the first).

[4] Matrimonial Causes Act 1973, s. 16, re-enacting the Nullity of Marriage Act 1971, s. 5, and implementing the recommendations of the Law Commission: Law Com. No. 33, paras. 21-22 and 25. *Quaere* whether this provision also applies to foreign decrees. On principle it should not do so: see Graveson, *Conflict of Laws*, 7th Ed., 345; North, *The Private International Law of Matrimonial Causes*, 267.

If H marries W, then marries X, and then obtains a decree of nullity of the first marriage on the ground of W's impotence, the marriage to X will still be void because H was married to W when he contracted it.

If a pension is payable to W, the widow of A, until she remarries and she then contracts a voidable marriage with H which is later annulled, she cannot reclaim her pension because she is still regarded as having remarried.[1]

What is not clear is the effect of the decree on the parties' status after it has been made absolute. The Act expressly states that it shall operate to *annul* the marriage, not to terminate it. This implies that the effect is different from that of a decree of dissolution and it is arguable that the parties revert to their previous status. Thus in the second example given above W would once more be regarded as the widow of A even though she is also regarded as having been married to H; consequently although she could not claim a pension payable until remarriage, she could claim it if it were payable during her widowhood. It is difficult to believe that Parliament really intended such a Gilbertian situation and, despite the infelicitous wording of the Act, it is submitted that the consequences of the annulment of a voidable marriage must be the same as those of the dissolution of a valid one.

The section has effect only if the decree absolute was granted on or after 1 August 1971 (when the Nullity of Marriage Act came into operation). In the case of a decree pronounced before this date it may still be necessary to consider the law as it was before the Act was passed.[2] In this connection it should particularly be noted that concluded transactions would never be reopened—a rule that will be of equal importance whenever the decree was pronounced if, contrary to the above submission, the parties still revert to their previous status. Before the marriage was annulled money might have been paid and property distributed on the assumption (valid at the time) that the parties to the marriage were husband and wife. To attempt to set these transactions aside might not only produce chaos but also work substantial injustice, so that the rule was evolved that "transactions which have been concluded, things which have been done, during the period [of the voidable marriage] on the footing of the existence of that status, cannot be undone or reopened".[3] Thus, in *Re Eaves*[4] property was bequeathed to the testator's son subject to a life interest in favour of the plaintiff so long as she remained the testator's widow. Six years after the testator's death the widow remarried, and on the eve of her second marriage she permitted the son to sell the property and to use the proceeds for his own purposes on the assumption that her own interest would cease. The second marriage was subsequently annulled on the grounds of the husband's impotence, and the widow then claimed a life interest in the proceeds of the sale. It was held that she must fail, for the sale was a concluded transaction carried out on the footing that the second marriage was valid.

---

[1] *Cf.* decision R(G) 1/73 of the National Insurance Tribunal, where it was held that a widow's pension, which is not payable for any period after the widow's remarriage, could not be claimed again in such circumstances.

[2] See the 4th Edition of this book, pp. 69-71.

[3] *Per* CLAUSON, L.J., in *Re Eaves*, [1940] Ch. 109, 117; [1939] 4 All E.R. 260, C.A.

[4] [1940] Ch. 109; [1939] 4 All E.R. 260, C.A., following *Dodworth* v. *Dale*, [1936] 2 K.B. 503. This case is complicated by the fact that the widow, having acquiesced in the sale of the property, could not be permitted in equity to go back on the transaction.

What "transactions and things" are included in this category are not clear, but it is submitted that any out and out payment of money (whether capital or income) or assignment of property would come within the exception.

D. NULLITY IN THE CONFLICT OF LAWS

This subject is a difficult one which still wants final settlement by the House of Lords or legislation in some important respects. Three problems have to be considered:

(1) In what circumstances does an English court have jurisdiction if the case contains a foreign element?
(2) Given that the court has jurisdiction, is it to apply English law or the law of some other country?
(3) In what circumstances will an English court recognise the validity of a decree of nullity pronounced by a foreign court?

1. JURISDICTION OF ENGLISH COURTS

Before 1974 an English court had jurisdiction to pronounce a decree if one of the parties was domiciled in this country on the principle that it could always adjudicate on the status of a person domiciled within the jurisdiction.[1] It also had jurisdiction if both parties were resident in this country because this was the basis of the ecclesiastical courts' jurisdiction which divorce courts now exercise.[2] If the marriage was void, a petition could also be brought if the marriage had been celebrated in England.[3] Additional jurisdiction to pronounce a decree on the wife's petition had been conferred by statute in two cases: (a) if the husband had deserted the wife or had been deported and had been domiciled in England immediately before the desertion or deportation, and (b) if the wife had been ordinarily resident in England for three years before the commencement of the proceedings.[4]

---

[1] *De Reneville* v. *De Reneville*, [1948] P. 100; [1948] 1 All E.R. 56, C.A. There is no English authority to support the proposition that the court had jurisdiction if the respondent alone was domiciled here, but this was generally accepted to be the position.

[2] *Ramsay-Fairfax* v. *Ramsay-Fairfax*, [1956] P. 115; [1955] 3 All E.R. 695, C.A. In fact residence of the respondent alone was apparently sufficient, for the petitioner *ipso facto* submitted to the jurisdiction by invoking it: *Magnier* v. *Magnier* (1968), 112 Sol. Jo. 233. But residence of the petitioner alone would not suffice, for in the absence of statutory authority a respondent who was neither domiciled nor resident in this country and whose marriage had not been celebrated here could not be compelled to appear in an English court to answer a petition which might affect his status: *De Reneville* v. *De Reneville*, (*supra*).

[3] *Simonin* v. *Mallac* (1860), 2 Sw. & Tr. 67; *Padolecchia* v. *Padolecchia*, [1968] P. 314; [1968] 3 All E.R. 863. This did not apply if the marriage was voidable: *Ross Smith* v. *Ross Smith*, [1963] A.C. 280; [1962] 1 All E.R. 344, H.L.

[4] (a) was originally enacted by the Matrimonial Causes Act 1937. It was particularly important when the marriage was alleged to be voidable when the wife's domicile would automatically be the same as the husband's. (b) was originally enacted by the Law Reform (Miscellaneous Provisions) Act 1949 following a large number of marriages contracted between English women and foreign servicemen during the Second World War. Both were re-enacted in s. 46 of the Matrimonial Causes Act 1973, now repealed by the Domicile and Matrimonial Proceedings Act 1973, Sched. 6.

These rules produced some anomalous results. The fact that a void marriage had been celebrated here sufficed to give the court jurisdiction when the parties had only a slight connection with this country;[1] the statutory bases applied only if the wife petitioned; and it is obviously desirable to have a uniform set of rules applying to both nullity and divorce so that, if necessary, a cross-petition may be brought and all litigation relating to the marriage may be disposed of at the same time. This last consideration formed the basis of the recommendations made by the Law Commission in 1972[2] which were implemented by the Domicile and Matrimonial Proceedings Act 1973. By section 5 (3) of that Act the court has jurisdiction in nullity proceedings instituted on or after 1st January 1974 if (and only if) either of the parties to the marriage:

"(a) is domiciled in England and Wales on the date when the proceedings are begun; or
(b) was habitually resident there throughout the period of one year ending with that date: or
(c) died before that date and either
    (i) was at death domiciled in England and Wales, or
    (ii) had been habitually resident there throughout the period of one year ending with the date of death."[3]

It will be seen that the same rules now apply whether the marriage is alleged to be void or voidable and that it is immaterial whether the party domiciled or resident here is petitioner or respondent.

The court also has jurisdiction if proceedings for divorce, nullity or judicial separation, over which it has jurisdiction, have already begun, even though it would no longer have jurisdiction when the nullity petition is presented.[4] The operation of this provision can be illustrated by the following hypothetical facts. A wife petitions for divorce and the sole ground on which the court could assume jurisdiction is that she is habitually resident in this country. She then ceases to be resident here. The husband can cross-petition for nullity whilst the divorce proceedings are pending even though he could no longer have brought proceedings if the wife had not previously petitioned herself.

Stays.—It is obvious that other matrimonial proceedings between the parties could be brought in another country whilst nullity proceedings are pending here: for example, whilst a wife is petitioning for nullity in this country, her husband might bring proceedings for divorce elsewhere. To prevent embarrassment, the court has a discretionary power to stay nullity proceedings here if before the beginning of the trial it appears that any proceedings in respect of the marriage or capable of affecting its validity or

---

[1] *Cf. Padolecchia* v. *Padolecchia*, (*supra*), where the petitioner, who was domiciled in Italy, went through a ceremony of marriage with the respondent, who was domiciled in Denmark, whilst on a short visit to England.

[2] Law Com. No. 48 (Report on Jurisdiction in Matrimonial Causes).

[3] Para. (c) presupposes that the court has jurisdiction to pronounce a decree of nullity after the death of one or both parties and will therefore apply only if the marriage is void: see *ante*, p. 75.

[4] Domicile and Matrimonial Proceedings Act 1973, s. 5 (5).

subsistence are continuing in any country outside England or Wales. The law relating to the facts to be taken into account in deciding whether to exercise the discretion, the removal of stays and their effect on ancillary orders is the same as in divorce, and in view of the comparative rarity of petitions for nullity, these matters will be considered when we deal with dissolution.[1]

There are no obligatory stays in nullity proceedings as there are in divorce.[2]

2. CHOICE OF LAW

In nullity suits the petitioner will normally plead facts which, he alleges, prevented a valid marriage from being contracted at the time of the ceremony.[3] It follows that the existence and consequences of a defect should be determined by reference to the *lex loci celebrationis* or the parties' *lex domicilii* at that time, and if the marriage was solemnized abroad and neither party was then domiciled in this country, English law cannot be applicable. It is, however, difficult to extract the relevant principles from the decided cases because in some the distinction between jurisdiction and choice of law has apparently been overlooked whilst in others it seems to have been assumed without question that English law applied. This assumption may have been due to the petitioner's failure to adduce evidence of the relevant foreign law. The rule that the court will apply English law in these circumstances is reasonable in a contested action for damages when either party can be expected to plead foreign law if it is to his advantage; it is urged that it should not be applied in a nullity suit, however, because it may enable the parties to obtain matrimonial relief to which they are not entitled. In such cases the court should always be satisfied that it has before it sufficient evidence of the law applicable.[4]

What follows, therefore, is to a certain extent speculative. The present state of the law is even more uncertain because there has been no reported case on this subject since it became possible for a wife to acquire an independent domicile. At common law a woman whose marriage was voidable necessarily had the same domicile as her husband until the marriage was annulled, with the result that the courts probably placed more emphasis upon the consequences of the alleged defect under his *lex domicilii* than under hers. There is now no justification for this approach.

Formal Defects.—It seems indisputable that questions of formal invalidity (and its consequences) must normally be referred to the *lex loci*

---

[1] See *post*, p. 242.

[2] The reason is that a conflict has always been possible between different jurisdictions in the United Kingdom and in practice this did not give rise to any problems. If the other proceedings are for divorce or judicial separation, the nullity suit should always be disposed of first. See Law Com. No. 48, para. 88.

[3] But in the case of wilful refusal to consummate the marriage, the petitioner is relying on facts which have occurred since the celebration. Other legal systems may have similar grounds.

[4] Lack of sufficient evidence of foreign law would seem to be a proper reason for the court's seeking the assistance of the Queen's Proctor under ss. 8 (1) (a) and 15 of the Matrimonial Causes Act 1973: see *post*, p. 194, n. 3. For the application of English law in the absence of evidence of foreign law, see Dicey and Morris, *Conflict of Laws*, 10th Ed., 1216.

celebrationis by which they are governed. In exceptional cases it may be necessary to test the validity of the marriage by reference to the provisions of the Foreign Marriage Acts or the rules relating to the recognition of common law marriages.[1]

Lack of Capacity.—If the marriage is void or voidable as a consequence of either party's lack of capacity by his or her *lex domicilii* at the time of the marriage, we must in principle apply that law and treat the marriage as void or voidable in this country.[2] There seems little doubt that the courts would follow this rule if the impediment were a legal one—for example, bigamy or relationship within the prohibited degrees—and they should also follow it if the impediment is physical—for example, impotence.

Lack of Consent.—In *Szechter* v. *Szechter*[3] SIMON, P., held that the reality of a party's consent (as distinct from the form in which it is expressed) is a matter of essential validity and must therefore be governed by the parties' *lex domicilii*. In that case both parties were domiciled in Poland at the time of the ceremony and consequently Polish law clearly applied; if they have different domiciles, it is submitted that, as in the case of capacity, the validity of the marriage must be tested by reference to each. In the words of SIMON, P., "no marriage is valid if by the law of *either party's* domicile one party does not consent to marry the other".[4]

Other Grounds for Nullity.—The position becomes more obscure if some other ground for nullity is relied on. This is particularly true in the case of wilful refusal to consummate the marriage because the petitioner is relying on facts which have occurred since the ceremony and which by the *lex domicilii* of one of the parties may not affect the validity of the marriage at all. The problem has arisen in two cases. In the first, *De Reneville* v. *De Reneville*,[5] the husband was domiciled in France but the wife had been domiciled in England before the marriage, which had taken place in France. The parties lived together in France and the French Congo until the wife left the husband, returned to England and petitioned here for a decree on the ground of the husband's inability or wilful refusal to consummate the marriage. The Court of Appeal held that the validity of the marriage must be determined by French law either as the law of the husband's domicile at the time of the marriage or as the law of their intended matrimonial domicile. In the second case, *Ponticelli* v. *Ponticelli*,[6] the husband, who was at all material times domiciled in England and had married in Italy a woman domiciled in that

---

[1] See *ante*, pp. 28-30.

[2] Unless the courts apply the law of the intended matrimonial home. See *ante*, pp. 22-27.

[3] [1971] P. 286; [1970] 3 All E.R. 905. For the facts, see *ante*, p. 90. In *H.* v. *H.*, [1954] P. 258; [1953] 2 All E.R. 1229, the marriage took place in Hungary, where the wife was presumably domiciled. The husband's domicile was not stated. It was agreed that the case was governed by either English or Hungarian law, but as both were the same on the point in issue, it was unnecessary to decide which applied. In *Buckland* v. *Buckland*, [1968] P. 296; [1967] 2 All E.R. 300, no reference was made to Maltese law at all. (For the facts, see *ante*, pp. 89-90.)

[4] *Szechter* v. *Szechter*, (*supra*), at pp. 294-295 and 912, respectively. Italics supplied.

[5] [1948] P. 100; [1948] 1 All E.R. 56, C.A.

[6] [1958] P. 204; [1958] 1 All E.R. 357.

country, petitioned here for a decree on the ground of the wife's refusal to consummate the marriage. The choice lay between applying English law (by which the marriage was voidable) or Italian law (which probably afforded no remedy in the circumstances). SACHS, J., held that he should apply the former as the husband's *lex domicilii* or (should that be wrong) as the *lex fori* or the law of the intended matrimonial domicile.

It is submitted that in any case the *lex fori* is irrelevant and is to be avoided as it makes the outcome of the proceedings depend on the country in which the petitioner brings them. In both *De Reneville* v. *De Reneville* and *Ponticelli* v. *Ponticelli* the husband's domicile was the same throughout as the intended matrimonial domicile and so it was not necessary for the court to choose between them. Support for applying the law of the parties' actual domicile is to be found in the judgment of SIMON, P., in *Szechter* v. *Szechter*,[1] where he referred to

> "... the old distinction between, on the one hand, 'forms and ceremonies', the validity of which is referable to the *lex loci contractus*, and, on the other hand, 'essential validity', by which is meant ... all requirements for a valid marriage other than those relating to forms and ceremonies, for the validity of which reference is made to the *lex domicilii* of the parties."

Unfortunately, it is not clear from this passage whether it is necessary to refer to the parties' *lex domicilii* at the time of the ceremony or at the time of the proceedings. As wilful refusal to consummate resembles a ground for divorce rather than a fact which invalidates the marriage at the time of the ceremony, it is tempting to apply the law of the parties' domicile at the time of the proceedings, but this should be resisted for the following reasons. First, the context indicates that SIMON, P., was referring to their domicile at the time of the marriage;[2] secondly, however anomalous wilful refusal to consummate may be as a ground for nullity, consistency requires the application of the same rule in all cases of nullity, and the other grounds demand the application of the relevant law at the time of the marriage; thirdly, wilful refusal and impotence are frequently alleged as grounds for nullity in the alternative, and it would be undesirable to have to apply one law when dealing with one ground and a different law when dealing with the other.

Parties having Different Domiciles.—A further problem arises if the parties have different domiciles at the time of the marriage, the consequences of which have been little explored in either judicial decisions or textbooks. Suppose, for example, that at the time of the ceremony one of the parties is domiciled in England and the other is domiciled in state X. If it is subsequently alleged that the marriage is invalid for some reason other than a formal defect, the consequences of the alleged invalidity may be quite different in English law and the law of X. Which is to be applied? If one disregards the references to the *lex fori* and to the law of the intended matrimonial home, the cases all indicate that it is to the husband's *lex*

---

[1] [1971] P. 286, 295; [1970] 3 All E.R. 905, 912.

[2] At pp. 295 and 913, respectively, he said: "Both [parties] were domiciled in Poland at the time of the ceremony ... It is therefore for Polish law to answer whether ... the marriage was valid by reason of duress".

domicilii alone that reference must be made.[1] The uniform application of this rule, however, produces some remarkable results. If a woman domiciled in England is compelled to go through the ceremony under duress imposed by the husband, can it seriously be argued that an English court will refuse to grant her a decree of nullity on the ground that duress does not affect the validity of the marriage by the law of his domicile?

At the outset it may safely be said that, if the result of the defect is to make the marriage void by either legal system, it must be regarded as void by both: a marriage cannot be partly void and partly valid. If a man domiciled in England marries his first cousin domiciled in a state which forbids such unions, we must regard it as void.[2] The difficult problems arise if the marriage is valid by one system and voidable by the other or, alternatively, voidable at the suit of either party by one system and voidable at the suit of only one of them by the other. In the absence of any decision given after full argument on the point, it is submitted that the court should apply the *lex domicilii* of the petitioner as the party seeking relief.[3] Two illustrations are given to support this thesis.

(a) The wife, W, refuses to consummate the marriage. If the husband, H, is domiciled in England, he can petition for nullity, as in *Ponticelli* v. *Ponticelli*. But if he is domiciled in state X, by the law of which wilful refusal does not affect the marriage, he ought not to be able to petition here relying solely on the accident that his wife's *lex domicilii* would afford him relief which his own *lex domicilii* withholds.

(b) W is impotent. If she is domiciled in England, she can petition for nullity relying on her own impotence. But if the law of her domicile affords relief only to the spouse capable of consummating the marriage, there is no logical reason why she should be able to rely on H's *lex domicilii* with which she has no other connection.[4]

It will be seen that, if this argument is correct, an English court would have to be prepared to grant a decree on a ground wholly unknown to English law if the facts invalidated the marriage by the petitioner's *lex domicilii*—for example, a mistake as to the other spouse's qualities. Although there is no authority on the point, there seems to be no reason why it should not do so unless the foreign law offends against our own concepts of morality or public policy.[5]

---

[1] *De Reneville* v. *De Reneville* and *Ponticelli* v. *Ponticelli*, (*ante*). But on the question of consent, see *ante*, p. 102.

[2] Unless the marriage was celebrated in England, when it will be valid: see *ante*, p. 26.

[3] *Cf.* Jaffey, *The Essential Validity of Marriage in the English Conflict of Laws*, 41 M.L.R. 38, 47-49; Bishop, *Choice of Law for Impotence and Wilful Refusal*, 41 M.L.R. 512.

[4] Alternatively, could it be argued that, if the respondent is domiciled in this country, English law should be applied on the ground that an English court will apply English law in litigation involving its own domiciliaries? This may be illogical but *cf.* the courts' refusal to recognise an incapacity to marry imposed by one party's *lex domicilii* if the other is domiciled in England and the marriage is celebrated in this country (*ante*, p. 26).

[5] This is the view of Cheshire and North, *Private International Law*, 10th Ed., 405; North, *The Private International Law of Matrimonial Causes*, 130.

3. RECOGNITION OF FOREIGN DECREES[1]

In the past English courts have recognised decrees of nullity pronounced by the courts of the country in which both parties were domiciled,[2] both parties were resident,[3] and in which a void marriage had been celebrated.[4] It will be noticed that in all these cases an English court would have had jurisdiction *mutatis mutandis* before the law was changed by statute.[5] In *Travers* v. *Holley*[6] it was laid down that an English court would recognise a decree of divorce pronounced by a foreign court provided that the basis of jurisdiction corresponded with a basis of jurisdiction accepted by an English court, and there is express authority for applying the same rule to nullity.[7] Hence, although *Travers* v. *Holley* no longer applies in divorce since the passing of the Recognition of Divorces and Legal Separations Act 1971, it is submitted that it should continue to apply in all cases of nullity.[8]

As in the case of divorce, an English court will also recognise a decree pronounced in a third country which is recognised by the court of both parties' domicile.[9]

Two doubts remain. The first arises from the change in the law relating to the jurisdiction of English courts brought about by the Domicile and Matrimonial Proceedings Act 1973. If we apply the doctrine of reciprocity strictly, we should no longer recognise a decree if the sole connection with the country in which it was granted is that a void marriage was celebrated there. Conversely, we should now recognise it if one party had been habitually resident there for a year previously. But if the decree was pronounced before 1974, shall we still recognise it if the jurisdiction was based on the celebration of the marriage or refuse to recognise it if only the petitioner was resident there? A similar problem arose in *Indyka* v. *Indyka*,[10] where the House of Lords had to consider the effect of a change in the law of jurisdiction on the recognition of a foreign decree of divorce. In this case W obtained a decree of divorce in Czechoslovakia. Ten years later her former husband, H, married R. The question in issue was the validity of this second marriage, which in turn depended on the validity of the Czech divorce. At the time it was pronounced, an English court would not have had jurisdiction *mutatis mutandis*, although it would have had jurisdiction at the time of H's remarriage. The House of Lords in effect took the view that, as the question

---

1 North, *op. cit.*, c. 12.

2 *Salvesen* v. *Administrator of Austrian Property*, [1927] A.C. 641, H.L. In *Lepre* v. *Lepre*, [1965] P. 52; [1963] 2 All E.R. 49, SIMON, P., would have been prepared to recognise a decree if, contrary to the facts, only the petitioner had been domiciled in the country in question.

3 The alternative ground of recognition in *Corbett* v. *Corbett*, [1957] 1 All E.R. 621.

4 *Corbett* v. *Corbett*, (*supra*); *Merker* v. *Merker*, [1963] P. 283; [1962] 3 All E.R. 928.

5 See *ante*, p. 99.

6 [1953] P. 246; [1953] 2 All E.R. 794, C.A. See *post*, p. 244, n. 2.

7 *Merker* v. *Merker*, (*supra*), at pp. 296 and 935, respectively; *Lepre* v. *Lepre*, (*supra*), at pp. 61 and 56, respectively; *Perrini* v. *Perrini*, [1979] Fam. 84; [1979] 2 All E.R. 323.

8 The principle of reciprocity was not followed in the earlier case of *Chapelle* v. *Chapelle*, [1950] P. 134; [1950] 1 All E.R. 236, on the ground that one of the parties was domiciled in England, but it is submitted that this case cannot stand with other authorities. For a detailed criticism, see Cross in 3 I.C.L.Q. 247.

9 *Abate* v. *Cauvin*, [1961] P. 29; [1961] 1 All E.R. 569. Presumably we should also give effect to a decree if the parties were domiciled in different countries both of which recognised it. *Quaere* if it is recognised by only one party's *lex domicilii*. *Cf. post*, p. 247.

10 [1969] 1 A.C. 33; [1967] 2 All E.R. 689, H.L.

before them was whether H was capable of marrying R, they should consider what jurisdiction English courts had when he remarried and not what jurisdiction they had had ten years earlier. But it is difficult to see how a change in the law of jurisdiction can retrospectively affect the law of recognition. The Lords' decision was dictated not by logic but by a desire to limit the number of limping marriages, and it is impossible to predict how it will be applied when the change has cut down the basis of jurisdiction in one direction whilst extending it in another.

The second doubt arises from the much wider additional basis for recognition of divorce decrees that all five members of the House of Lords adopted in *Indyka* v. *Indyka*, namely that we should recognise a decree if there was a real and substantial connection between one of the parties and the country in which the decree was granted.[1] Does that principle also apply to the recognition of nullity decrees? There will admittedly be few cases of a real and substantial connection with a county in which neither party is domiciled or resident, but this could conceivably occur. As the principle underlying the decision in *Indyka* v. *Indyka* is aimed at reducing the number of limping marriages by giving effect to a decree granted in a country with which at least one of the parties is closely connect, it is submitted that it should be extended as far as possible, and it has in fact been applied to a decree of nullity in two cases at first instance.[2]

In any case, an English court will not recognise the validity of a foreign decree which has been obtained by collusion or fraud[3] or which offends against English ideas of substantial justice. Originally recognition was refused on the latter ground only if there was some procedural shortcoming as a result of which, for example, the respondent had been unable to defend the proceedings. We should also presumably refuse to recognise a decree obtained by duress. In *Formosa* v. *Formosa*,[4] however, the Court of Appeal apparently took the view that they would not recognise a decree when they considered that the substantive law applied produced a result contrary to natural justice. In that case the husband, whose domicile of origin was Maltese, acquired a domicile of choice in England and married the wife who was also domiciled here, in an English register office. He subsequently re-acquired a Maltese domicile and a Maltese court annulled the marriage on the ground that, as the husband was a Roman Catholic, he could marry only in a Roman Catholic church. The Court of Appeal refused to recognise the decree. Although the judgment of the Maltese court is indefensible, the

---

[1] In *Indyka* v. *Indyka* it was the petitioning wife who had the real and substantial connection with Czechoslovakia. The principle was later extended in *Blair* v. *Blair*, [1968] 3 All E.R. 639 (petitioning husband), and *Mayfield* v. *Mayfield*, [1969] P. 119; [1969] 2 All E.R. 219 (respondent wife). It cannot now be doubted that it must apply to either spouse, whether petitioner or respondent.

[2] *Law* v. *Gustin*, [1976] Fam. 155; [1976] 1 All E.R. 113; *Perrini* v. *Perrini*, [1979] Fam. 84; [1979] 2 All E.R. 323, approved in *Verwaeke* v. *Smith*, [1981] 1 All E.R. 55, 88, C.A.

[3] *Salvesen* v. *Administrator of Austrian Property*, [1927] A.C. 641, at pp. 663, 671-672, H.L. *Casey* v. *Casey*, [1949] P. 420, 433; [1949] 2 All E.R. 110, 117, C.A.

[4] [1963] P. 259; [1962] 3 All E.R. 419, C.A. The case is strongly criticised by Lewis in 12 I.C.L.Q. 298 and by Blom-Cooper in 26 M.L.R. 94 but was followed in *Lepre* v. *Lepre*, [1965] P. 52; [1963] 2 All E.R. 49.

decision of the Court of Appeal goes against the principle that an English court will not enquire into the substantive merits of a decree pronounced by a competent court abroad. The case stands alone and it remains to be seen whether it will be followed in other fields or, ultimately, accepted by the House of Lords.

Chapter 4

The Effects of Marriage

A. INTRODUCTORY

The principal effect of marriage at common law was that for many purposes it fused the legal personalities of husband and wife into one. The clearest exposition of this doctrine of unity of husband and wife is probably that of BLACKSTONE, who said:[1]

"By marriage, the husband and wife are one person in law; that is, the very being or legal existence of the woman is suspended during the marriage, or at least is incorporated and consolidated into that of the husband; under whose wing, protection, and *cover*, she performs everything; and is therefore called in our law-French a *feme-covert, femina viro co-operta*; is said to be *covert-baron*, or under the protection and influence of her husband, her *baron*, or lord; and her condition during marriage is called her *coverture*. Upon this principle of a union of person in husband and wife, depend almost all the legal rights, duties, and disabilities, that either of them acquire by the marriage."

The principle was enunciated in the *Dialogus de Scaccario* in the twelfth century and has been repeated by every leading common law writer since.[2] But it may be doubted whether this doctrine was ever a firmly established rule of the common law. One or two examples will suffice to show that it was but imperfectly applied. Thus it operated to prevent any action at common law between the spouses, but if a tort was committed either by or against a married woman both she and her husband were correctly joined as co-defendants or co-plaintiffs to the action, and notwithstanding the maxim *actio personalis moritur cum persona*, if the husband predeceased the wife, she could still be sued or sue in person. A woman on marriage *ipso facto* acquired her husband's domicile but not his nationality. Similar inconsistencies were to be found in the law relating to the interest taken by a husband in his wife's property. He acquired an absolute interest in her chattels, a similar interest in her choses in action but only provided that they were reduced into possession, a power to dispose of her leasehold interests during his lifetime but no power to dispose of them by will, and no more than an interest for his life in her inheritable estates of freehold. It is difficult to see on what single principle the common law could logically arrive at all these conclusions.

---

[1] *Commentaries,* i, 442.
[2] See Williams, *Legal Unity of Husband and Wife*, 10 M.L.R. 16, at pp. 16-18, and the exhaustive judgment of OLIVER, J., in *Midland Bank Trust Co., Ltd.* v. *Green (No. 3)*, [1979] Ch. 496; [1979] 2 All E.R. 193.

Neither equity nor the ecclesiastical law accepted this doctrine of unity of personality, and both gave married women access to their courts and even permitted actions between spouses. But it was not until 1870 that the Married Women's Property Act of that year gave a wife an extremely limited right to maintain an action in her own name in the courts of common law.[1] Whilst a series of statutes extending over 65 years and culminating in the Law Reform (Married Women and Tortfeasors) Act of 1935 have to a very large extent put a married woman in the same legal position as her unmarried sister, it would be dangerous to assume that they have abolished the common law doctrine in its entirety. These statutes have been typical of so much English legislative reform in that they have created extensive exceptions to the old rules without striking at the root of the trouble by abolishing outright the fundamental principle on which the anomalies are based. Time and again the courts have reiterated that these Acts have not given a wife the legal status of a feme sole except in certain clearly defined and limited fields, and even these exceptions have been construed, if not narrowly, at least inconsistently. In only one case, *Rees* v. *Hughes*,[2] does there appear to have been a departure from the strict wording of the statutes with a bold application of the maxim *cessante ratione legis cessat ipsa lex*, and even here the Court of Appeal did no more than hold that a husband is no longer under a legal duty to bury his deceased wife at his own expense if her estate is large enough to enable her personal representatives to do so themselves. As Lush puts it:[3]

> "It is untraversable that a married woman's position in law is anomalous and enigmatic. ...
> The rule of unity ... still prevails as a rule in those matters wherein it was established at common law and has not been abrogated by statute. The rule at the present day lifts its head hydra-like and is on occasions applied with surprising results."

These changes have of course affected the spouses' rights and obligations *vis-à-vis* third persons. For example, a married woman now has a capacity to enter into contracts which she lacked at common law and her husband is no longer liable for torts committed by her. But, what is of much greater importance, their rights and obligations towards each other have also been fundamentally altered. As we shall see, during the past century the wife's position has steadily changed from something in many respects inferior to that of a servant (who could at least quit her master's service by giving notice) to that of the joint, co-equal head of the family. Consequently in this chapter we shall first discuss the right to consortium and the corresponding duty to cohabit that each spouse owes to the other. We shall then consider how far marriage affects rights and duties in contract and tort both as between the spouses themselves and between the spouses and third persons. Finally we shall examine two matters of public law: the problems created by

---

[1] But a woman judicially separated from her husband could sue and be sued as if she were a feme sole by the Matrimonial Causes Act 1857, s. 26.

[2] [1946] K.B. 517; [1946] 2 All E.R. 47, C.A.

[3] *Husband and Wife*, 4th Ed., pp. 21 and 58. See generally the whole of the first chapter of that work; Williams, *Legal Unity of Husband and Wife*, 10 M.L.R. 16; Kahn-Freund, *Inconsistencies and Injustices in the Law of Husband and Wife*, 15 M.L.R. 133, 16 M.L.R. 34, 148; *A Century of Family Law* (ed. Graveson and Crane).

the relationship of husband and wife in the criminal law and its relevance in the law of nationality. The effect of the relationship on rights in property and the duty of support will be considered in later chapters.[1]

B. THE RIGHT TO CONSORTIUM

1. THE NATURE OF CONSORTIUM

Mutual Duty to Cohabit.—Consortium means living together as husband and wife with all the incidents that flow from that relationship. At one time it would have been said that the husband had the right to his wife's consortium whilst the latter had not so much a reciprocal right to her husband's consortium as a correlative duty to give him her society and her services—a view which was not entirely obsolete in the middle of the nineteenth century.[2] A clear illustration of the wife's legal subjection to her husband can be seen in the old common law rule that a woman who murdered her husband was guilty of petit treason, like the vassal who slew his lord or the servant who slew his master.[3] In BACONS's *Abridgement* in 1736 it was stated that a husband might beat his wife (but not in a violent or cruel manner) and confine her.[4] Whether he ever had a legal power to administer corporal punishment is open to some doubt: HALE denied that he had,[5] although BLACKSTONE maintained that, whilst the practice had become obsolete in polite society, "the lower rank of people, who were always fond of the old common law, still claim and exert their ancient privilege".[6] In any event, this is no longer law, and it would be no defence today to a husband prosecuted for assaulting his wife that he was doing no more than administering reasonable chastisement.[7]

But the husband's right to enforce consortium by confining her remained longer in doubt. In 1852 the Court of Queen's Bench held that they would not force a wife to return to her husband against her will by enabling him to obtain custody of her by habeas corpus.[8] But this decision did not determine whether he could enforce his right extra-judicially by lawfully confining her once she was in his house. More than a century earlier the Court of King's Bench had held that he was entitled to restrain her only in order to protect his property or his honour, for example if she squandered his wealth or went "into lewd company",[9] but in 1840 COLERIDGE, J., denied that there was any such limitation on the husband's powers.[10] It was eventually not until the Legislature had accorded to a married woman a measure of financial

---

[1] See *post*, chapters 13 and 14.

[2] See the judgment of COLERIDGE, J., in *Re Cochrane* (1840), 8 Dowl. 630.

[3] The distinction between petit treason and murder was abolished in 1828 by 9 Geo. 4, c. 31, s. 2.

[4] Tit. Baron and Feme (B).

[5] *Lord Leigh's Case* (1674), 3 Keble 433, where he said that *castigatio* meant no more than admonition and confinement.

[6] *Commentaries*, i, 445.

[7] *R. v. Jackson*, [1891] 1 Q.B. 671, at pp. 679, 682, C.A.

[8] *R. v. Leggatt* (1852), 18 Q.B. 781.

[9] *R. v. Lister* (1721), 1 Str. 478. *Cf.* Viner's *Abridgement*, Tit. Baron and Feme, V a, 11.

[10] *Re Cochrane, supra.* See Lush, *Husband and Wife*, 4th Ed., 24 *et seq.*

independence of her husband by the Married Women's Property Act of 1882[1] that it was finally established that she had a similar right to her personal liberty by the decision of the Court of Appeal in *R.* v. *Jackson* in 1891.[2] In that case the wife had gone to live with relations whilst her husband was absent in New Zealand. After his return she refused to live with him again and failed to comply with a decree for restitution of conjugal rights. Consequently he arranged with two men that they should seize her as she came out of church one Sunday afternoon, and she was then put into a carriage and taken to her husband's residence, where she was allowed complete freedom of the house but was not permitted to leave the building. She then applied for a writ of habeas corpus and it was unanimously held by the Court of Appeal that it was no defence that the husband was merely confining her in order to enforce his right to her consortium. So ended the husband's right to treat his wife as he would a recalcitrant animal. In the words of McCardie, J.:[3]

"From the date of their decision the shackles of servitude fell from the limbs of married women and they were free to come and go at their own will."

In *R.* v. *Jackson* both Lord Halsbury, L.C., and Lord Esher, M.R., left open the question whether a husband might not still be entitled to restrain his wife to protect his honour, for example if she was in the very act of eloping,[4] but there can be no doubt that today even this conduct would not justify his using force to restrain her. This was certainly the view of the Court of Appeal in *R.* v. *Reid*,[5] where it was held that a husband who steals, carries away or secretes his wife against her will is guilty of the common law offence of kidnapping her. As Cairns, L.J., said in delivering the judgment of the court:[6]

"The notion that a husband can, without incurring punishment, treat his wife, whether she be a separated wife or otherwise, with any kind of hostile force is obsolete."

But it is important to remember that these cases have in no way altered the law relating to a husband's right to his wife's consortium; they merely decided that he is not entitled to resort to extra-judicial methods to enforce it. Hence it was still possible even forty years ago to speak of the husband as the head of the family. But the movement for the equality of the rights of the sexes, which had begun in the middle of the nineteenth century and which had gained renewed impetus by women's work in the First World War, was now to be felt in the home. The victory gained in the field of public law in the Sex Disqualification (Removal) Act of 1919 was carried into the field of private law. In 1923 Parliament equated the rights of the spouses to petition for divorce;[7] in 1925 it established the principle that they have equal rights with respect to their children;[8] and in 1967 it gave each of them the power to apply for an

---

[1] *Post*, p. 416.
[2] [1891] 1 Q.B. 671, C.A.
[3] *Place* v. *Searle*, [1932] 2 K.B. 497, 500-501.
[4] At pp. 679-680 and 683, respectively.
[5] [1973] Q.B. 299; [1972] 2 All E.R. 1350, C.A.; Hall, [1972A] C.L.J. 220.
[6] At pp. 303 and 1353, respectively.
[7] *Post*, p. 188.
[8] *Post*, p. 285.

order regulating their rights to occupy the matrimonial home.[1] All these changes reflect the modern view that the wife is no longer the weaker partner subservient to the stronger but that both spouses are the joint, co-equal heads of the family. This, it is submitted, is also the position today as regards consortium, so that it can be said: "It seems to be clear that at the present day a husband has a right to the consortium of his wife, and the wife to the consortium of her husband",[2] and these rights must now be regarded as exactly reciprocal.

It follows, of course, that a wife has no greater right to force herself upon her husband than he has to compel her to cohabit with him. In *Nanda* v. *Nanda*[3] a wife, whose husband had deserted her, installed herself against his will in the flat in which he was living with another woman and their two children. It was held that she had no right to trespass on her husband's property which had never been the matrimonial home and that he was entitled to an injunction to restrain her from doing so again in the future.

The Incidents of Consortium.—As has already been stated, consortium primarily means living together as husband and wife. Normally this will involve sharing the common matrimonial home, but this is not absolutely essential. It may be possible for the spouses to cohabit only from time to time, as where the husband has to spend long periods away from home for reasons of business or where he is a member of the armed forces and consequently can live with his wife only when he is on leave.[4] So long as both spouses retain the intention of cohabiting whenever possible, the consortium is regarded as continuous and will come to an end only if one or both of them lose this intention.[5]

Consortium, then, connotes as far as possible the sharing of a common home and a common domestic life. It is difficult to go beyond this and to define with more precision the duties which the spouses owe to each other: this is, after all, a matter of common knowledge rather than a subject for legal analysis. The incidents of consortium are capable of considerable variation and clearly will depend upon such factors as the age, health, social position and financial circumstances of the spouses. In many families the husband's duties will be largely conditioned by the fact that he is the bread-winner; the wife will then usually be primarily responsible for the running of the home, a duty which may take the form of supervising domestic staff or of doing the household "chores" herself, such as cooking, cleaning, mending and looking after the children; but today in very many cases (particularly where both spouses are working) these tasks are shared by both. Juris-prudentially, in a sense consortium resembles ownership, for husband and

---

[1] *Post*, p. 458.

[2] *Per* SCRUTTON, L.J., in *Place* v. *Searle*, [1932] 2 K.B. 497, 512, C.A.

[3] [1968] P. 351; [1967] 3 All E.R. 401. The wife's position was, if anything, strengthened by her having obtained a decree for restitution of conjugal rights but this gave her no right to insist on cohabitation. Decrees for restitution of conjugal rights have now been abolished: see *post*, p. 121.

[4] *Cf. Huxtable* v. *Huxtable* (1899), 68 L.J.P. 83 (both spouses domestic servants residing with different families).

[5] *R.* v. *Creamer*, [1919] 1 K.B. 564, C.C.A.; *Santos* v. *Santos*, [1972] Fam. 247; [1972] 2 All E.R. 889, C.A. See further *post*, p. 226.

wife enjoy "a bundle of rights some hardly capable of precise definition".[1] Nevertheless it may be worth while to examine in a little more detail one or two of these rights which have been directly or indirectly the subject of judicial decision.

The Wife's Use of her Husband's Name.—By custom, on marriage a wife assumes her husband's surname and, if he is a peer, his title and rank. She is entitled to retain his name after the marriage has been terminated either by death or by divorce, and a man has no such property in his name as to entitle him to sue for an injunction to prevent his divorced wife from using it unless, at any rate, she is doing so for the purpose of defrauding him or some other right of his is being invaded.[2] If she is still holding herself out as his wife, he may of course restrain her from doing so by jactitation proceedings.[3]

The Matrimonial Home.—As we have already seen, it is the duty of the spouses to live together as far as their circumstances will permit. But differences may arise between them as to where the matrimonial home is to be. In accordance with the view that the husband was the head of the household, the earlier opinion was that he had the right to determine this and a judicial dictum to this effect is to be found as late as 1940.[4] Today, however, this, like other domestic matters of common concern, is something in which both spouses have a right to be heard and which they must settle by agreement—a view most clearly voiced by DENNING, L.J., in *Dunn* v. *Dunn*.[5] Such an agreement may be entered into before marriage[6] or after it, and will remain in force until a change of circumstances (for example, a change in the spouses' financial position or health or business interests) makes it necessary or desirable for them to change their home and thus come to a fresh agreement.

Where the spouses find it impossible to come to an agreement, it seems imperative that one of them should have a casting vote in order to resolve the deadlock. As a matter of law neither of them has an absolute right in this respect against the other and all the circumstances must be taken into consideration. This means that in a large number of cases the husband will be entitled to the last word for the simple reason that he will be the breadwinner and must be able to live near his place of work,[7] but it is easy to conceive of cases where the wife's considerations will come first—for example, where she

---

[1] *Per* LORD REID in *Best* v. *Samuel Fox & Co., Ltd.,* [1952] A.C. 716, 736; [1952] 2 All E.R. 394, 401, H.L.

[2] *Cowley* v. *Cowley,* [1900] P. 305, C.A.; affirmed, [1901] A.C. 450, H.L. *Cf. Du Boulay* v. *Du Boulay* (1869), L.R. 2 P.C. 430, 441, P.C. Thus, if she holds herself out as his wife after he has remarried, she may be guilty of libel or slander if the reasonable inference is that he is not legally married to his second wife.

[3] See *ante*, p. 67.

[4] *Mansey* v. *Mansey,* [1940] P. 139, 140; [1940] 2 All E.R. 424, 426. See also *King* v. *King,* [1942] P. 1, 8; [1941] 2 All E.R. 103, 110.

[5] [1949] P. 98, 103; [1948] 2 All E.R. 822, 823, C.A.. See also *McGowan* v. *McGowan,* [1948] 2 All E.R. 1032, 1035; *Walter* v. *Walter* (1949), 65 T.L.R. 680; *Hosegood* v. *Hosegood* (1950), 66 T.L.R. (Part 1) 735, 739, C.A.

[6] *King* v. *King, (supra). Cf. G.* v. *G.,* [1930] P. 72.

[7] *Per* DENNING, L.J., in *Dunn* v. *Dunn, (supra),* at pp. 103 and 823, respectively. *Cf.* HODSON, L.J., in *W.* v. *W. (No. 2),* [1954] P. 486, 515; [1954] 2 All E.R. 829, 840, C.A.

is working and the husband is not.[1] Moreover, whatever arrangements the husband proposes must be reasonable from the wife's point of view; he cannot, for example, insist upon her living with his mother when the two women obviously will not be able to share the same house.[2] Similarly, if business requirements make it necessary for one spouse to move, the other will not be bound to go too if, say, the proposed removal would be liable to impair the latter's health or would be contrary to his or her own business interests.[3]

The practical importance of the question of the right to choose the matrimonial home lies in the fact that where the spouses separate as a result of their inability to agree on where the home is to be, it is the spouse who is acting unreasonably who will be in desertion. Where both act unreasonably (or, at least, where it cannot be said that either clearly has right upon his side), it would seem that neither can allege that the other is in desertion.[4]

Sexual Intercourse.—We have already seen that each spouse owes the other a duty to consummate the marriage and that (with certain exceptions) the incapacity of either or the wilful refusal of the respondent to do so will entitle the petitioner to a decree of nullity.[5] This mutual right to intercourse continues after the marriage has been consummated provided that it is reasonably exercised; but one spouse is not bound to submit to the demands of the other if they are inordinate, perverted or otherwise unreasonable, or in any case if they are likely to lead to a breakdown in health.[6] Similarly a husband is not entitled to insist upon using contraceptives or practising *coitus interruptus* against the wife's will if it is unreasonable to deprive her of the opportunity of bearing children.

If one spouse insists upon intercourse in such circumstances or wilfully refuses to have intercourse at all, the other will be entitled to withdraw from cohabitation without being in desertion and may charge the guilty party with constructive desertion. A course of conduct of this sort would also enable the spouse suffering as a consequence to establish such behaviour that he (or she) could not reasonably be expected to live with the other for the purpose of divorce and proceedings under the Domestic Proceedings and Magistrates' Courts Act.[7] Supervening impotence, on the other hand, like any other deterioration in a spouse's health, would not on principle appear to be a ground for any sort of matrimonial relief at all.[8]

The old common law rule is that by marriage a wife consents to intercourse with her husband and thus confers on him a privilege which she is not entitled

---

[1] As in *King* v. *King*, (*supra*).

[2] *Millichamp* v. *Millichamp* (1931), 146 L.T. 96; *Munro* v. *Munro*, [1950] 1 All E.R. 832, C.A. Contrast *Jackson* v. *Jackson* (1932), 146 L.T. 406.

[3] See *Walter* v. *Walter* (1949), 65 T.L.R. 680 (*post*, p. 220).

[4] *Post*, p. 221.

[5] *Ante*, pp. 83-87.

[6] Either because of the state of the spouse's health or because of the manner in which the other insists upon intercourse (*e.g., coitus interruptus*). Similarly, a husband may not insist upon intercourse if he knows himself to be suffering from a venereal disease: *Foster* v. *Foster*, [1921] P. 438, C.A.

[7] See *post*, pp. 202-203 (behaviour) and 216 (desertion).

[8] But see *post*, pp. 205 and 216.

to withdraw whenever she pleases.[1] From this it must follow that as a general rule a husband cannot be guilty as a principal of rape on his own wife.[2] Today, however, most people would doubtless find abhorrent the idea that a man could with impunity use force to compel his wife to have intercourse with him against her will. This has been reflected in judicial attempts to limit the application of the common law rule. In *R.* v. *Clarke*[3] BYRNE, J., held that a husband could be guilty of rape if the wife had obtained a judicial separation, because this relieves her of the duty of cohabiting and thus of having sexual intercourse with him. This principle also applies if the wife has obtained an injunction forbidding the husband to molest her or a magistrates' order forbidding him to use violence against her: both are inconsistent with continued consent to sexual intercourse.[4] It was extended in *R.* v. *O'Brien*[5] to the case where a decree nisi of divorce had been obtained, for the marriage is *de facto* dead (even though legally it is still alive) and consequently the wife's consent must be regarded as revoked. In *R.* v. *Miller*[6] LYNSKEY, J., stated *obiter* that a husband could also be guilty of raping his wife if the spouses had entered into a separation agreement, at any rate if it contained a non-molestation clause. He declined to extend the exception further, however, and directed the jury that they must acquit a husband of rape who had had intercourse with his wife against her will when they were living apart, even though she had in fact already filed a petition for divorce. On the present state of the authorities, therefore, it would seem that before the husband can be guilty of raping his wife either they must have agreed to live apart or a court order must have been made. This is clearly anomalous and the Court of Appeal has left open the question whether it would still uphold *R.* v. *Miller*.[7]

LYNSKEY, J., nevertheless did ameliorate the position by holding that, following *R.* v. *Jackson*,[8] a husband cannot insist upon his right to have intercourse by force and that he could therefore in the circumstances be convicted of an assault on his wife, even though he used no more force than was necessary to effect his aims. It is difficult to see logically how this can be, for if the wife is deemed to have given an implied consent to intercourse, she ought also to be considered to have given an implied consent to any acts connected therewith, and her consent should clearly be a defence to the charge of assault.[9] But even though logically unsupportable, the decision is clearly consonant with changed social views.[10]

---

1 *R.* v. *Clarence* (1888), 22 Q.B.D. 23, at pp. 53-54; *R.* v. *Clarke*, [1949] 2 All E.R. 448.

2 1 Hale P.C. 629; *R.* v. *Miller*, [1954] 2 Q.B. 282; [1954] 2 All E.R. 529. But he may be guilty of aiding or abetting: *Lord Audley's Case* (1631), 3 St. Tr. 401, H.L.; *R.* v. *Leak*, [1976] Q.B. 217; [1975] 2 All E.R. 1059, C.A.

3 [1949] 2 All E.R. 448.

4 *R.* v. *Steele* [1976] 65 Cr. App. R. 22, C.A. (husband, who had given an undertaking to court not to molest wife, guilty of rape).

5 [1974] 3 All E.R. 663. This must equally apply to a decree nisi of nullity if the marriage is voidable. If it is void, there is no marriage and therefore the "husband" has no defence at all.

6 [1954] 2 Q.B. 282; [1954] 2 All E.R. 529.

7 *R.* v. *Reid*, [1973] Q.B. 299, 302; [1972] 2 All E.R. 1350, 1352, C.A.

8 [1891] 1 Q.B. 671, C.A. (*ante*, p. 111).

9 He would of course clearly be guilty of assault if he used more force than was necessary (*e.g.*, by knocking her partly unconscious).

10 See further the Criminal Law Revision Committee's Working Paper on Sexual Offences, paras. 28-43.

Marital Confidences.—Referring to the relationship of husband and wife, UNGOED-THOMAS, J., said in *Argyll* v. *Argyll*:[1]

"There could hardly be anything more intimate or confidential than is involved in that relationship, or than in the mutual trust and confidences which are shared between husband and wife. The confidential nature of the relationship is of its very essence and so obviously and necessarily implicit in it that there is no need for it to be expressed."

But if the marriage breaks down, bitterness and vindictiveness may lead one spouse to seek to break these confidences. Does the law offer the other any remedy in such circumstances?

In *Argyll* v. *Argyll* it was held that it did. Some two years after divorcing the plaintiff on the ground of her adultery, the defendant wrote a series of articles for a newspaper some of which contained information relating to the plaintiff's "private life, personal affairs and private conduct, communicated to the defendant in confidence during the subsistence of the marriage". UNGOED-THOMAS, J., held that equity's general jurisdiction to restrain breach of confidence was sufficiently wide to enable him to grant an injunction to prevent the defendant from divulging these secrets and the newspaper from publishing them. The protection apparently extends only to confidential communications[2] and clearly the court will have to decide in each case whether the publication of the material in question will work the very mischief which the law seeks to prevent.

It is also probable that equity will assist the plaintiff only if he or she comes to the court with clean hands. An attempt was made to raise this defence in the *Argyll* case on the grounds that the plaintiff had herself published articles disclosing matrimonial secrets and that her own view of marriage, as exemplified by her adultery, could only be described as immoral. It failed, however, first because the defendant proposed to disclose much more intimate confidences so that his breaches would have been "of an altogether different order of perfidy", and secondly because, however reprehensible the plaintiff's own adultery may have been, her subsequent conduct could only undermine confidence for the future and not retrospectively release the defendant from his duty to keep confidences already disclosed.

It is obvious, however, that two rules of public policy may come into conflict. Whilst on the one hand the law should protect marital confidences, on the other hand it is a fundamental principle that in any legal proceedings, civil or criminal, no relevant evidence should be excluded if it will help the court or the jury to arrive at the truth. If a person accused of a criminal offence has confessed his guilt to his wife, the prosecution may wish to call the wife to give evidence of the confession; similarly a statement made by a party in civil proceedings may be helpful to his adversary. A compromise must be effected and it will be convenient at this stage to consider how far the relationship of husband and wife affects the law of evidence generally.

Evidence in Civil Proceedings.—At common law neither the parties nor their spouses were competent witnesses in civil proceedings. The reason for excluding the testimony of the latter does not appear to have been based upon

---

[1] [1967] Ch. 302, 322; [1965] 1 All E.R. 611, 619.
[2] At pp. 330 and 625, respectively.

the fiction of unity but partly upon the fact that their evidence might be untrustworthy, partly on the wish to protect marital confidences, and partly upon the undesirability of having a witness giving evidence against his or her spouse and the consequent unfairness of permitting him or her to give evidence for the spouse. The rule was abolished with respect to the parties themselves by the Evidence Act 1851 and with respect to their spouses by the Evidence Amendment Act 1853,[1] so that now they are competent and compellable witnesses for any party to the action.

The Common Law Commissioners, on whose recommendation the Act of 1853 had been passed, had further advised that communications between spouses (which would now really for the first time become admissible) should nevertheless be privileged because, as they said, "so much of the happiness of human life may fairly be said to depend on the inviolability of domestic confidence". Accordingly section 3 of the Act of 1853 provided:

> "No husband shall be compellable to disclose any communication made to him by his wife during the marriage, and no wife shall be compellable to disclose any communication made to her by her husband during the marriage."

This is a curious piece of legislation because it gave the privilege to the spouse *to whom* the statement was made and not to the maker of it. Hence, if the statement in question was made by the husband to his wife, *he* might be compelled to disclose it although his wife might not; but if she waived her privilege he had no power to prevent her from breaking his confidence. This was illogical and indefensible and for these reasons the privilege was abolished and section 3 repealed by the Civil Evidence Act 1968.[2] It will thus be seen that *in civil proceedings* the principle that relevant evidence should not be excluded has been allowed to oust completely the principle that marital confidences should be protected.

A married witness may, however, claim certain other privileges. The rule that a witness may not be compelled to answer any question or produce any document that tends to expose him to criminal proceedings has now been extended to questions and documents that might incriminate his or her spouse.[3] Furthermore no statement made by either spouse to the other or to a third person *with a view to effecting a reconciliation* may be put in evidence without the consent of the spouse who made it. The reason for this is, of course, that it is more important that spouses should be reconciled than divorced and complete frankness will not be obtained if the parties have at the back of their minds the fear that whatever is said may be given in evidence in matrimonial proceedings if the attempt at reconciliation fails.[4]

---

[1] Section 1. But they were not competent to give evidence in proceedings instituted in consequence of adultery until the Evidence Further Amendment Act 1869 and (subject to certain exceptions) could not be compelled to answer any question tending to show they were guilty of adultery until the Civil Evidence Act 1968, s. 16 (5).

[2] Section 16 (3), implementing the recommendations of the Law Reform Committee contained in their 16th Report, Cmnd. 3472. The Committee was of the opinion that the judge's discretion to exclude evidence gave sufficient protection: see paras. 42-43.

[3] Civil Evidence Act 1968, s. 14.

[4] *Theodoropoulas* v. *Theodoropoulas*, [1964] P. 311; [1963] 2 All E.R. 772, and the cases there cited; *Pais* v. *Pais*, [1971] P. 119; [1970] 3 All E.R. 491. It is immaterial whether the intiative was taken by one of the spouses or by a third person: *Henley* v. *Henley*, [1955] P. 202; [1955] 1 All E.R. 590, n. See also the Domestic Proceedings and Magistrates' Courts Act 1978, s. 12 (7).

Evidence in Criminal Proceedings.—Until the passing of the Criminal Evidence Act in 1898, the accused could not give evidence in criminal proceedings except in a few isolated cases where there were statutory provisions to the contrary. It is not surprising that generally speaking the accused's spouse was equally incompetent, for if it was considered contrary to public policy that a witness should give evidence either for or against his or her spouse in civil proceedings, *a fortiori* this would not be permissible in a criminal cause. To this rule there is one exception at common law, *viz.* that a spouse is a competent witness for the prosecution if the accused is charged with committing a crime of personal violence against him or her[1] or perhaps of any crime affecting the witness's liberty or health:[2] otherwise it would frequently be impossible to prove the offence. In *Hoskyn* v. *Metropolitan Police Comr.*[3] the majority of the House of Lords held that he is not compellable, principally on the ground that it would be repugnant to force one spouse to give evidence against the other unwillingly and thus perhaps destroy the marriage. Consequently all the cases coming within the common law exception now appear to be caught by the second exception created by the Theft Act[4] and the common law rule is no longer of any practical significance.

The Criminal Evidence Act 1898 has made the accused's spouse a competent witness subject to two limitations. First, the spouse may not be called except upon the application of the accused.[5] Secondly, the privilege formerly accorded to matrimonial communications by the Evidence Amendment Act in civil proceedings was extended to criminal proceedings.[6] This provision is still in force. It means that if a married man charged with, say, burglary calls his wife as a witness and she is asked in cross-examination whether her husband has confessed his guilt to her, it is she alone who decides whether or not to preserve his confidence. This rule, which prevents the accused from controlling whether statements made by him to his spouse

---

[1] This includes any form of violence, *e.g.*, causing grievous bodily harm (*R.* v. *Lapworth*, [1931] 1 K.B. 117, C.C.A.), rape (*Lord Audley's Case* (1631), 3 St. Tr. 401, H.L.), sodomy (*R.* v. *Blanchard*, [1952] 1 All E.R. 114).

[2] *Per* PICKFORD and AVORY, JJ., in *D.P.P.* v. *Blady*, [1912] 2 K.B. 89, at pp. 90, 91. Some of the older authorities suggest that the spouse is competent only if the prosecution could not otherwise prove the offence but this limitation does not seem to be accepted today and in any case would be difficult to apply. In *R.* v. *Verolla*, [1963] 1 Q.B. 285; [1962] 2 All E.R. 426, STEVENSON, J., admitted the evidence of a wife whose husband was charged with attempting to poison her, preferring these dicta to the decision in *R.* v. *Yeo*, [1951] 1 All E.R. 864, n., where GORMAN, J., refused to admit the evidence of a wife whose husband was charged with sending her a letter threatening to murder her. *Cf. R.* v. *Deacon*, [1973] 2 All E.R. 1145, C.A. (wife competent to give evidence on charge of attempting to murder her). The cases are distinguishable on the ground that the same rule should apply to an attempt as to a completed offence but not to a mere threat. The spouse may also be a competent witness for the Crown on a charge of treason, but there is no authority.

[3] [1979] A.C. 474; [1978] 2 All E.R. 136, H.L. For the counter-arguments, see the dissenting speech of LORD EDMUND-DAVIES.

[4] See *post*, p. 119.

[5] Section 1 (c). By analogy with *Leach* v. *R., (infra)*, this does not make the spouse *compellable* on the accused's application, but there is no direct authority. Mere silence by the defence when the spouse is called by the prosecution does not amount to an application and the evidence is inadmissible: *R.* v. *Deacon, (supra)*.

[6] Section 1 (d).

should be disclosed or withheld, is even more illogical in criminal proceedings than it was in civil proceedings. It also illustrates the principle that such protection as exists is purely statutory and that no privilege attaches to the communication as such. Consequently the prosecution may always put the statement in evidence if they can prove it without calling the accused or the spouse. This occurred in *Rumping* v. *D.P.P.*[1] The police intercepted a letter written by the accused, who was charged with murder, to his wife and containing a virtual confession of guilt. It was held by the House of Lords that it had been properly admitted as evidence.

The principle that a spouse should not give evidence against the accused has been further eroded by statute. In certain specified crimes (mainly of a sexual nature or against children) the wife or husband of the accused is a competent (but not compellable)[2] witness for the prosecution or the defence without the accused's consent.[3] Two further exceptions were introduced by the Theft Act 1968. First, a person is a competent witness for the prosecution in any proceedings *brought by that person* against his or her spouse.[4] The witness is probably compellable,[5] but the point will be academic in most cases as he is not likely to refuse to give evidence in proceedings instituted by himself unless there has been a reconciliation in the meantime. Secondly, anyone is now competent (but not compellable) to give evidence for the prosecution or for the defence in any proceedings not brought by him or her in which his or her spouse is charged with any offence with reference to that person or that person's property.[6] The latter provision is vague and obscure. Offences "with reference to the witness's property" presumably include such crimes as theft, obtaining property by deception, burglary and criminal damage. It is not at all clear, however, what is meant by an offence "with reference to that person". This expression presumably covers any conduct on the accused's part which affects or threatens the witness physically and must therefore include not only any crime involving assault or false imprisonment but also such offences as sending written threats to murder her (or him), supplying her with the means of procuring her own abortion, and living on her immoral earnings. But the only reported case in which the scope of the sub-section has been considered indicates that it is much wider than this. In *R.* v. *Noble*[7] the Court of Appeal held that it made a husband a competent witness against his wife, who was prosecuted for forging his signature as guarantor of a loan to her, on the ground that the signature, if genuine, would have affected his obligations. The court, however, was clearly

---

[1] [1964] A.C. 814; [1962] 3 All E.R. 256, H.L. The only protection given to the accused is the general discretion vested in the court to exclude prejudicial evidence improperly obtained.

[2] *Leach* v. *R.*, [1912] A.C. 305, H.L.

[3] Criminal Evidence Act 1898, s. 4 and Sched. (as amended); Sexual Offences Act 1956, s. 39; Protection of Children Act 1978, s. 2 (1) (which also confers on the witness the privilege not to disclose communications made during the marriage). For a full list of the offences to which this provision applies (including those added by later statutes), see Phipson, *Evidence*, 12th Ed., 606.

[4] Section 30 (2).

[5] Contrast the wording of this sub-section with that of s. 30 (3) which specifically provides that the spouse shall not be compellable.

[6] Section 30 (3).

[7] [1974] 2 All E.R. 811, C.A.

unwilling to lay down any general test to determine whether an offence came within the provision. If the correct inference is that it enables a spouse to give evidence whenever the accused's alleged acts affected the witness's rights or liabilities or, alternatively, sought or purported to do so, its ambit is clearly very wide indeed.[1]

In only the last of the three statutory exceptions just mentioned is the witness specifically given the statutory privilege to decline to disclose any communication made by the accused during the marriage.

If a spouse is incompetent to give evidence against the accused, the incompetence continues in respect of matters which occurred during the marriage after a decree of divorce or after a decree of nullity where the marriage was voidable.[2]

2. LOSS OF THE RIGHT TO CONSORTIUM

The right to consortium can be lost, broadly speaking, in four ways.

First, if the spouses agree to live apart, the agreement divests each of them of the right to the other's consortium. But once the agreement comes to an end, the right will revive. Hence if, say, the husband entirely repudiates his obligations under the agreement, the wife will be entitled to treat it as at an end and, if she does so, may demand that the husband should resume cohabitation. Separation agreements will be treated more fully in the next chapter.

Secondly, a decree of judicial separation relieves the spouse obtaining the order from the duty of cohabiting with the other, so that, as long as the order is in force, the right to consortium ceases to exist. This topic will be discussed in greater detail in chapter 6. Although an order excluding one spouse from the matrimonial home does not specifically suspend the right to consortium, its practical effect is of course the same.[3]

Thirdly, although a marriage is not legally terminated until a decree of divorce (or of nullity in the case of a voidable marriage) is made absolute, the duty to cohabit will come to an end once the decree nisi is pronounced.[4] At this stage the marriage is dead in fact and clearly neither party can now call on the other to cohabit.

Finally, matrimonial misconduct will also deprive the spouse mis-

---

[1] It would clearly include the offence of persistently refusing or neglecting to maintain the witness: see *post*, p. 496, n. 4. One test that might be applied is whether it is necessary to name the accused's spouse in the indictment or information. A further exception to the general rule is provided by s. 1 of the Evidence Act 1877, under which the accused's spouse is a compellable witness for the Crown or the accused in certain cases relating to public highways and proceedings instituted for the purpose of trying or enforcing a civil right.

[2] *R.* v. *Algar,* [1954] 1 Q.B. 279; [1953] 2 All E.R. 1381, C.C.A.; Matrimonial Causes Act 1973, s. 16. If the marriage is *void*, of course, either party to it may give evidence against the other: *R.* v. *Young and Muezzell* (1851), 5 Cox C.C. 296. Judicial separation does not affect the rules relating to marital incompetence: *Moss* v. *Moss*, [1963] 2 Q.B. 799; [1963] 2 All E.R. 829. For criticisms of the existing law and proposals for reform which would greatly extend the admissibility of spouses' evidence, see the Eleventh Report of the Criminal Law Revision Committee, 1972, Cmnd. 4991, paras. 153-187.

[3] See further *post*, pp. 459 *et seq.*

[4] Only on this assumption could the husband be legally capable of raping his wife: see *R.* v. *O'Brien*, [1974] 3 All E.R. 663 (*ante*, p. 115).

conducting himself of the right to the other's consortium. Clearly this term is sufficiently wide to include any conduct which would afford a defence to a charge of desertion brought against the other spouse: it would obviously be absurd to say in the same breath that the latter owes a duty to cohabit and yet is not in desertion if he breaks off cohabitation.[1] It must not be forgotten that this duty is mutual, and, as JEUNE, P., put it:[2]

> "Neither party to a marriage can, I think, insist on cohabitation unless she or he is willing to perform a marital duty inseparable from it."

Moreover, it would seem that a matrimonial offence committed by one spouse will deprive him of the right to the other's consortium whatever be the other's own conduct. Hence, a husband is not bound to cohabit with his wife if she has committed adultery, even though he has committed adultery too.[3]

3. BREACH OF THE DUTY TO COHABIT

Although the right to consortium has been likened to the rights attached to ownership, in one important respect this analogy breaks down, for as between the spouses the duty to cohabit is legally completely unenforceable. The doctrine of unity of personality prevented either spouse from suing the other at common law, and consequently the only remedy that a deserted spouse had was to petition for a decree for restitution of conjugal rights. Petitions were originally brought in the ecclesiastical courts; they were transferred to the Divorce Court in 1858 and finally to the High Court in 1875. The decree called upon a spouse in desertion to resume cohabitation with the petitioner. If it was disobeyed, the respondent could originally be excommunicated, but the power to excommunicate on this ground was abolished by statute in 1813 and was replaced by a power to commit for contempt.[4] This was in turn abolished by the Matrimonial Causes Act of 1884, after which there was no direct sanction for failure to comply with the decree at all. The Act of 1884 compensated for this by enacting that disobedience to a decree for restitution should give the other spouse an immediate right to petition for judicial separation or, until 1923 in the case of a wife, for divorce if the husband had also committed adultery. For many years petitions were still brought by wives who wanted to take advantage of the court's power to make ancillary orders, particularly orders for maintenance, but the need to use this machinery was largely removed by the Law Reform (Miscellaneous Provisions) Act 1949, which gave them power to petition for maintenance in the High Court without bringing any other proceedings. The decree for restitution had obviously become a complete anomaly and it was eventually abolished by section 20 of the Matrimonial Proceedings and Property Act 1970.[5]

---

[1] For good cause for separation, see *post*, pp. 215-216.
[2] *Synge* v. *Synge*, [1900] P. 180, 195.
[3] *Brooking-Phillips* v. *Brooking-Phillips*, [1913] P. 80, C.A.
[4] Ecclesiastical Courts Act 1813.
[5] During the years 1965-1969 there were on the average 29 petitions for restitution a year and nine decrees. The courts still give *indirect* support to the right to consortium, *e.g.* by declaring void any condition attached to a bequest providing an incentive for the beneficiary to live apart from his or her spouse or to obtain a divorce: see *Re Johnson's Will Trusts*, [1967] Ch. 387; [1967] 1 All E.R. 553, and the cases there cited.

Although the duty to cohabit is not specifically enforceable, a breach of it may lead to other consequences. If there is a total breach, the spouse in default will be in desertion, and this will in turn enable the other to petition for divorce or judicial separation at the end of two years or to make an application immediately for an order under the Domestic Proceedings and Magistrates' Courts Act. If there is only a partial breach of the mutual duties that the spouses owe each other, this may in itself give the innocent party the right to petition for divorce, judicial separation or nullity if it is sufficiently serious (for example, behaviour such that the other spouse cannot reasonably be expected to live with him or wilful refusal to consummate the marriage). If the conduct is something less than this, it may nevertheless still entitle the other to break off cohabitation completely without being in desertion (or even so as to put the defaulting spouse in constructive desertion) if it is such as to make married life together virtually impossible.[1]

C. PHYSICAL PROTECTION OF A SPOUSE

The legal machinery available when one spouse (usually the wife) is physically ill-treated or molested by the other received scant attention until recent years. With respect to past acts the victim has of course the usual legal remedies and may bring an action for damages in tort for battery or a criminal prosecution for assault. In practical terms, however, these are frequently of little value: the husband will normally not be worth suing, and the police are notoriously loth to intervene in domestic quarrels because the wife may refuse to give evidence if they prosecute the husband.[2] A more urgent problem is what steps the wife (or husband) may take to prevent further violence or annoyance in the future. Publicity given to the problem of violence in the family[3] and the concern of a number of Members of Parliament led to the establishment of a Select Committee which heavily critized the effectiveness of the existing remedies and made a number of proposals for reform.[4] For the most part these have not been implemented, but one of the most important of the recommendations has been embodied in the provisions of the Domestic Violence and Matrimonial Proceedings Act of 1976.

Injunctions in other Proceedings.—If other proceedings are pending between the spouses (whether in the High Court or a county court), the most effective way of obtaining protection for a wife will usually be by seeking an injunction restraining her husband from molesting her. The court has a general power to grant an injunction in any case or matter before it, and in a case of urgency the petitioner may apply for such relief before presenting the

---

[1] See *post*, pp. 215-220.

[2] For a discussion of the effectiveness of police intervention, see Maidment, [1980] J.S.W.L. 26. The victim also has a limited right to apply for compensation from the Criminal Injuries Compensation Board.

[3] See, for example, *Violence in the Family* (ed. Borland); Pizzey, *Scream Quietly or the Neighbours will Hear*. For a comprehensive discussion of the whole problem see Freeman, *Violence in the Family*.

[4] See the Report of the Select Committee on Violence in Marriage, H.C. 553 (1974-75). See also Maidment, *Law's Response to Marital Violence*, 26 I.C.L.Q. 403.

petition.[1] The injunction must "bear some sensible relationship to the cause of action".[2] Consequently, a court could properly order one spouse not to molest the other in proceedings for divorce or judicial separation because the decree, if granted, would terminate the petitioner's duty to cohabit with the respondent; on the other hand, it would not do so if the petitioner was bringing proceedings for financial provision under section 27 of the Matrimonial Causes Act 1973.[3] The order, once made, can remain in force after the final decree has been pronounced,[4] but there is some doubt about the extent of the court's powers after a decree absolute of divorce or nullity or a decree of judicial separation. So long as ancillary proceedings are pending, the court may still be regarded as seised of the cause and may therefore grant an injunction provided that it has some connection with the ancillary relief sought. Thus, as molestation of the wife will usually affect the children living with her, an injunction prohibiting molestation of her could be granted if there were in existence an application or order relating to them.[5] This would not apply, however, if the only outstanding matter was the wife's application for periodical payments. In such a case—and *a fortiori* if there are no ancillary proceedings at all—the court is no longer seised of any relevant matter and consequently appears to have lost its power to grant an injunction. Nevertheless the contrary view has been taken in cases at first instance and an injunction granted after the final decree.[6] Whilst this is practically expedient and obviates the necessity of commencing fresh proceedings, it is difficult to support the decisions in logic.[7]

The Domestic Violence and Matrimonial Proceedings Act 1976.—It was the inadequacy of these remedies (at least if no other matrimonial proceedings were on foot) that led to the passing of the Domestic Violence and Matrimonial Proceedings Act. Section 1 gives a county court power to grant

---

[1] Supreme Court of Judicature (Consolidation) Act 1925, s. 45; County Courts Act 1959, s. 74, as amended by the Administration of Justice Act 1969, s. 6; R.S.C., O. 29, r. 1; C.C.R., O. 13, r. 8. If proceedings have not begun, the court will put the petitioner on terms providing for the presentation of the petition within a given time. An injunction may also be sought in proceedings for leave to present a petition for divorce within the first three years of the marriage: *McGibbon* v. *McGibbon*, [1973] Fam. 170; [1973] 2 All E.R. 836.

[2] *Per* FINER, J., in *McGibbon* v. *McGibbon*, (*supra*), at pp. 173 and 838, respectively. Consequently it is doubtful whether the court can grant an injunction relating to the occupation of property on an application for leave to present a petition for divorce within the first three years of the marriage: *ibid*.

[3] *Des Salles d'Epinoix* v. *Des Salles d'Epinoix*, [1967] 2 All E.R. 539, C.A.

[4] *Robinson* v. *Robinson*, [1965] P. 39; [1963] 3 All E.R. 813. *Cf. Vaughan* v. *Vaughan*, [1973] 3 All E.R. 449, C.A.

[5] In this connection it should be remembered that orders relating to custody and care and control are made "from time to time" and therefore will remain in force until the child's eighteenth birthday.

[6] *Ruddell* v. *Ruddell* (1967), 111 Sol. Jo. 497; *Beasley* v. *Beasley*, [1969] 1 W.L.R. 226 (decree absolute of divorce); *Montgomery* v. *Montgomery*, [1965] P. 46; [1964] 2 All E.R. 22 (judicial separation). The last two cases professed to follow *Robinson* v. *Robinson*, (*supra*), where, however, the court was still seised of the matter because the decree nisi of divorce had not been made absolute.

[7] Could it be seriously argued that the wife could return to the court 20 or 30 years after the decree? If not, where can one draw the line? The view stated here is supported by an unreported decision that an injunction cannot be granted if the petition has been dismissed: *Pickering* v. *Pickering*, (1959) C.A., cited in Rayden, *Divorce*, 13th Ed., 956.

an injunction on the application of either party to a marriage whether or not the applicant seeks any other relief. An injunction granted under this section may contain one or more of the following:

    (a) a provision restraining the other party to the marriage from molesting the applicant;

    (b) a provision restraining him from molesting a child living with the applicant;

    (c) a provision excluding him from the whole or any part of the matrimonial home or from a specified area in which the matrimonial home is included;

    (d) a provision requiring him to permit the applicant to enter and remain in the matrimonial home or any part of it.[1]

Two of these provisions require special comment. The word "molest" has a wide meaning and includes pestering, causing trouble, vexing, annoying and putting to inconvenience.[2] Clearly it will cover any form of assault and physical interference; it will also extend to such activities as lying in wait for the other party, following her about, repeated telephoning, sending threatening letters or any other form of harassment. Secondly, a spouse may be restrained from molesting *any* child living with the applicant. The Act does not define "child", and the term probably includes anyone under the age of 18;[3] he obviously does not have to be a child of both spouses or even of either of them. What is less certain is whether the provision extends to an adult who is a child (in the sense of a son or daughter) of the applicant or, perhaps, of the defendant. If, say, the husband is assaulting or pestering his 20 year old daughter, she needs the same protection as her younger sister, and it would be regrettable if the Act were to be interpreted narrowly so as to prevent the court from affording it to her.

This section confers jurisdiction only on county courts. The practice of the High Court, however, has been similarly changed and it may now grant an injunction containing any of the provisions mentioned above even though no other relief is sought.[4] But, like section 1 of the Act, this applies only to a party to a marriage. Hence a divorced wife may take advantage of neither: she must still seek such ancillary relief as is available to her in divorce proceedings.[5]

Exercise of the Power to grant an Injunction.—Failure to comply with an injunction may result in the committal of the spouse in default. Consequently the power to make an order (whether exercised under the Act or by way of ancillary relief in other proceedings) should be exercised only in really serious cases. Moreover the court is not prepared to grant relief of this sort if the applicant has it in his or her power to avoid the molestation. Thus an injunction has been refused when the spouses were living under the same roof

---

    [1] Section 1 (1). This section also applies to a man and woman living with each other as husband and wife: see *post*, p. 652. Presumably, if the spouses are already living apart, the "matrimonial home" is the home in which they last lived together. See Freeman, 127 New L.J. 159.

    [2] See *Vaughan* v. *Vaughan*, [1973] 3 All E.R. 449, C.A.

    [3] *Cf.* the definition of "child" for the purpose of the Children Act 1975: *ibid.*, s. 107 (1).

    [4] R.S.C., 0. 90, r. 17. The decision in *Crutcher* v. *Crutcher* (1978), *Times*, 18th July, seems inconsistent with this new rule.

    [5] Unless the former spouses are living together as husband and wife. See n. 1, *supra*.

and the husband (who was seeking it) could afford to move elsewhere.[1]

Injunctions relating to the occupation of the matrimonial home will be dealt with later.[2] Injunctions restraining a spouse from coming within a specified distance of the matrimonial home are rare although not entirely unheard of; in practice they will be granted in cases where this is the only way of giving effective protection to the applicant or child.[3]

Enforcement of Injunctions.—The usual means of enforcing an injunction is by applying to the court to have the party in default committed to prison for contempt.[4] This will normally take a number of days and in the meantime the wife may be at the mercy of a violent husband. Consequently section 2 of the Domestic Violence and Matrimonial Proceedings Act 1976 affords what may prove to be a much more effective weapon. If a judge grants an injunction restraining the applicant's spouse from using violence against the applicant or a child living with the applicant or excluding the spouse from the matrimonial home or a specified area in which the home is included, he may attach to it a power of arrest. It should be noted that this power exists whenever such an injunction is granted and is not confined to those granted under section 1 of the Act.[5] The detailed provisions, too, are different from those of section 1: section 2 refers to injunctions restraining violence (and not to other forms of molestation) and apparently does not apply to an injunction excluding the spouse from part only of the matrimonial home. Furthermore, the court may attach a power of arrest only if it is satisfied that the defendant has caused actual bodily harm to the applicant or the child, as the case may be, and is likely to do so again. Actual bodily harm is not confined to physical assault but includes "any hurt or injury calculated to interfere with the health or comfort" of another: hence it will be sufficient if the defendant's conduct causes nervous shock or any other injury to the other's state of mind.[6]

If a power of arrest is attached to an injunction, any constable may arrest the defendant if he has reasonable cause for suspecting that he is in breach of any provision mentioned in the last paragraph. This gives immediate protection to the spouse obtaining the injunction because he (or, as will most often be the case, she) may invoke the assistance of the police without having to take proceedings to have the defendant committed.[7] For this reason the power should be exercised sparingly and only in exceptional circumstances.[8] Once arrested, the defendant must be brought before a judge within 24 hours (disregarding Sundays, Christmas Day and Good Friday) but may not be released within that time except on a judge's direction.[9]

---

[1] *Freedman* v. *Freedman*, [1967] 2 All E.R. 680.

[2] See *post*, pp. 459-465.

[3] *E.g.*, if the spouse repeatedly follows the applicant about.

[4] The other method is by a writ of sequestration.

[5] *Lewis* v. *Lewis*, [1978] Fam. 60; [1978] 1 All E.R. 729, C.A.

[6] See *R.* v. *Miller*, [1954] 2 Q.B. 282, 292; [1954] 2 All E.R. 529, 534 (*per* LYNSKEY, J.).

[7] She is further helped by the requirement that, if a power of arrest has been attached, a copy of the injunction must be delivered to the officer in charge of the police station for her address: R.S.C., O. 90, r. 17; C.C.R., O. 46, r. 28.

[8] *Lewis* v. *Lewis*, (*supra*).

[9] Section 2 (3)-(5), as amended by the Domestic Proceedings and Magistrates' Courts Act 1978, Sched. 2. A power of arrest should not normally be attached for more than three months because experience has shown that it rarely has to be exercised after this lapse of time: *Practice Note*, [1981] 1 All E.R. 224.

Proceedings in Magistrates' Courts.—It has always been possible for either spouse to seek an order from a magistrates' court requiring the other to enter into a recognisance to be of good behaviour towards the complainant. If the other spouse fails to comply with the order, he may then be committed to prison for a period not exceeding six months or until he does comply.[1] Clearly this procedure is of limited value, particularly when compared with the summary power of arrest that can now be attached to an injunction. As we have already seen,[2] the power formerly possessed by magistrates to make a separation order was abolished on the recommendation of the Law Commission who proposed that it should be replaced by a power to make an order forbidding either spouse to use violence against the other or a child and, if necessary, excluding him from the matrimonial home. They considered that such proceedings would not be made redundant by the powers given to county courts by the Domestic Violence and Matrimonial Proceedings Act but would complement them by affording summary, local and inexpensive relief.[3] Their proposals are now substantially embodied in the provisions of sections 16, 17 and 18 of the Domestic Proceedings and Magistrates' Courts Act 1978.

Orders for Personal Protection.—On the application of either party to a marriage, a magistrates' court may now make an order that the other spouse shall not use or threaten to use violence against the person of the applicant or the person of a child of the family. The court must be satisfied that the respondent has already used or threatened to use such violence and that the order is necessary for the protection of the applicant or a child. In addition it may include a further provision that the respondent shall not incite or assist any other person to use or threaten to use violence; this power may prove very valuable when it is believed that a husband might instigate a friend or relation to use violence.[4]

Only a party to a marriage may apply for an order: these proceedings are not available to a divorced person or (unlike those under section 1 of the Domestic Violence and Matrimonial Proceedings Act 1976) to a man or woman cohabiting outside marriage. A comparison of the two sections will show that magistrates' powers are more limited in three other respects. First, even though they are convinced that there is a real danger that the respondent will use violence, they cannot make an order, for example, if he has used violence against another person but has not done so or threatened to do so against the applicant or a child of the family. Secondly, the order may only prohibit violence *against the person*: magistrates have no power to forbid the respondent from carrying out psychological warfare on

---

[1] Magistrates' Courts Act 1980, s. 115. The defendant may also be required to find sureties. See Parker, 9 Fam. Law 76.

[2] *Ante*, p. 7.

[3] Law Com. No. 77 (Report on Matrimonial Proceedings in Magistrates' Courts), paras. 3.15-3.17.

[4] Section 16 (1), (2), (10). The court has jurisdiction whether or not the application is coupled with an application for any other order under the Act.

the applicant or a child or from indulging in any other form of molestation.[1] Thirdly, the order may relate only to the applicant or a child *of the family*: on the other hand, the child need not be living with the applicant and may apparently be of any age.[2]

Magistrates have also been given a power to exclude a spouse from the matrimonial home and they may make an order requiring the respondent to leave the home, prohibiting him from entering it, and requiring him to permit the applicant to enter and remain there. In order to ensure that the power will be exercised only where there is substantial evidence that the respondent is likely to resort to violence, much more stringent conditions must be fulfilled. The court must be satisfied, first, that the applicant or a child of the family is in danger of being physically injured by the respondent (or would be in such danger if they were to enter the matrimonial home)[3] and, secondly, that the respondent

(a) has already used violence against the person of the applicant or a child of the family; or
(b) has threatened to do so and has actually used violence against another person; or
(c) has threatened to do so in contravention of an order previously made under this section.[4]

If it is essential that the application should be heard without delay, some of the requirements relating to the constitution of domestic courts may be waived.[5] If there is imminent danger of physical injury to the applicant or a child of the family, a single justice has a peremptory power to make an order forbidding the respondent to use violence (but not an order excluding him from the matrimonial home) known as an expedited order, which may not remain in force for more than 28 days (although a further expedited order may then be made).[6] Subject to this, magistrates have an unlimited power to determine the length of time for which an order shall remain in force and to attach such exceptions or conditions as they think fit.[7] Either spouse may apply to have any order varied or revoked.[8]

---

[1] The Law Commission justified this on the ground that allegations of psychological damage might involve the difficult task of assessing expert evidence given by psychiatrists. This overlooks the fact that the applicant would probably be advised not to commence proceedings in a magistrates' court if such evidence was likely to be adduced and that in any case magistrates had been trying cases of mental cruelty since 1895.

[2] For the meaning of "child of the family", see *post*, p. 304.

[3] It need not be an *immediate* danger: *McCartney* v. *McCartney*, [1981] 1 All E.R. 597.

[4] Section 16 (3), (4). An order has no further effect on any estate or interest in the matrimonial home possessed by the respondent or any other person: s. 17 (4). See further pp. 459-465, *post*.

[5] See s. 16 (5).

[6] In particular an order may be made even though no summons has been served on the respondent: *i.e.*, this is akin to an *ex parte* injunction. An expedited order will also come to an end if the hearing of the complaint begins within 28 days. See ss. 16 (6)-(8) and 17 (3).

[7] Section 16 (9).

[8] Section 17 (1). The High Court or a divorce county court may direct that the order shall cease to have effect in any subsequent matrimonial proceedings. If either spouse applies for an order relating to the occupation of the matrimonial home (or former matrimonial home) under s. 1 (2) of the Matrimonial Homes Act 1967 or s. 4 of the Domestic Violence and Matrimonial Proceedings Act 1976, the court hearing that application may discharge an order relating to the occupation of the home made under the Domestic Proceedings and Magistrates Courts Act: *ibid.*, s. 28.

Enforcement of Orders.—Like judges under the Domestic Violence and Matrimonial Proceedings Act magistrates may attach a power of arrest to an order, but the details differ considerably. Magistrates may do this only if the order forbids the respondent to use violence against the person of the applicant or a child of the family or to enter the matrimonial home, and the court must be satisfied that the respondent has already physically injured one of them and is likely to do so again. As in the case of a power of arrest attached to an injunction, a constable may arrest anyone whom he has reasonable cause for suspecting of being in breach of such an order and must then bring him before a magistrate within 24 hours (excluding Sundays, Christmas Day and Good Friday).[1] It will therefore be seen that a constable cannot exercise this power if he has reason to believe that the respondent has merely threatened to use violence (but has not actually used it) or is refusing to leave the matrimonial home or to permit the applicant to enter it.

If no power of arrest is attached, an applicant may apply for a warrant for the arrest of a respondent alleged to have disobeyed an order.[2] A person guilty of disobedience may be fined up to £1,000 or committed to prison for not more than two months for each breach.[3]

D. REMEDIES FOR INTERFERENCE WITH THE RIGHT TO CONSORTIUM

1. DAMAGES FOR LOSS OF CONSORTIUM AND SERVICES

At common law a husband had a writ of ravishment or trespass *vi et armis de uxore rapta et abducta*, under which he could obtain damages against a defendant who had taken away his wife, but this action is now completely obsolete. It was replaced by the much wider action for damages for enticement which emerged in the middle of the eighteenth century and which was available to both spouses.[4] The husband had two further remedies: an action for damages for harbouring his wife[5] and an action for damages for adultery. The latter began as the common law action for criminal conversation (or crim. con.) by which the husband could obtain compensation for the loss of his wife's comfort and society as the result of the adulterer's wrongful act. Crim. con. was abolished by the Matrimonial Causes Act of 1857 and was replaced by a statutory claim for damages in the divorce court which was almost always made on a petition for divorce. The reason that neither of these remedies was available to the wife was that they were based upon the quasi-proprietary interest which the husband had in his wife and her services at common law.

---

[1] Section 18 (1)-(3).

[2] Section 18 (4), (5). The effect (probably unintended) of these provisions is that a respondent who disobeys an order by *threatening* to use violence or by refusing to leave the matrimonial home or to permit the applicant to enter it may be arrested on a warrant if no power of arrest is attached but may not be arrested at all if one is attached.

[3] Magistrates' Courts Act 1980, s. 63.

[4] The earliest reported case seems to be *Winsmore* v. *Greenbank* (1745), Willes 577. It was established that the wife could sue in *Gray* v. *Gee* (1923), 39 T.L.R. 429.

[5] This was probably obsolete before it was formally abolished: see the judgment of DEVLIN, J., in *Winchester* v. *Fleming*, [1958] 1 Q.B. 259; [1957] 3 All E.R. 711.

The common law actions were brought very rarely and even the claim for damages for adultery was becoming uncommon. It was anomalous that the matter should be confined to the husband, and it was doubtful whether it was any longer socially desirable to give either spouse a remedy if the loss of the other's consortium was due to the latter's voluntary act, even though the defendant had induced or encouraged it. Consequently the Law Reform (Miscellaneous Provisions) Act of 1970 abolished actions for enticement and harbouring and the right to claim damages for adultery.[1] This means that the plaintiff now has an action for damages for loss of consortium only if this was due to the defendant's breach of contract or tort.

Loss of Consortium due to Breach of Contract.—If as a result of a breach of a contractual duty owed by the defendant to the plaintiff the latter loses the consortium of his spouse, he may recover for this loss by way of damages for breach of contract provided that it was likely to result from the breach and therefore not too remote. Thus in *Jackson* v. *Watson & Sons*,[2] where the plaintiff's wife died from food poisoning as a result of eating salmon which the defendant had sold to the plaintiff, the Court of Appeal held that he could recover for the loss of his wife's services.

Loss of Consortium due to the Defendant's Tort.—Loss of consortium due to the defendant's tortious act may arise in one of two ways.

First, it may be the result of a tort committed against the plaintiff himself. In *Oakley* v. *Walker*[3] the plaintiff's wife left him because of a change in his personality due to an accident caused by the defendant's negligence. It was held that, as this was a foreseeable consequence of the latter's act, the plaintiff could recover for his loss.

Secondly, if a husband loses his wife's consortium as a result of a tort committed against *her*, he has a separate cause of action against the tortfeasor for loss of consortium. Thus, if as a result of X's negligence W (a married woman) is injured and has to spend a considerable time in hospital, X may be sued not only by W for her personal injuries but also by her husband for the loss of her consortium. This cause of action is entirely independent of the wife's; hence it was held in *Mallett* v. *Dunn*[4] that although the wife's claim for personal injuries had to be reduced because of her own contributory negligence, her husband's claim was not liable to be reduced at all and he could recover in full. Presumably, however, the husband could recover nothing if the wife's claim were barred completely, as it would be, for example, if the injury had been entirely due to her own negligence.

Action for Loss of Consortium by the Wife.—This last cause of action—that resting on loss of consortium due to a tort committed against the plaintiff's wife—is really an anomalous survival of the old common law concept that the husband's interest in the wife is quasi-proprietary, and in

---

[1] Sections 4 and 5 (a) and (c). This implements the recommendation of the Law Commission: Law Com. No. 25, paras. 99-102.

[2] [1909] 2 K.B. 193, C.A.

[3] (1977), 121 Sol. Jo. 619. *Cf. Lynch* v. *Knight* (1861), 9 H.L. Cas. 577, H.L.; *Lampert* v. *Eastern National Omnibus Co., Ltd.*, [1954] 2 All E.R. 719.

[4] [1949] 2 K.B. 180; [1949] 1 All E.R. 973.

Best v. *Samuel Fox & Co., Ltd.*[1] the House of Lords refused to extend it so as to give the wife a similar cause of action. In that case the plaintiff's husband had been rendered impotent as a result of the defendant's negligence and she sued the defendant for the loss which she suffered as a consequence of being no longer able to enjoy normal sexual relations with her husband. The House unanimously held that no action of this sort would lie at the suit of the wife and expressed the view that if the rights of the spouses should be equalised in this respect, this should be done by abolishing the husband's right by legislation and not by extending the anomaly further. This clearly precludes the wife from suing for loss of consortium occasioned by a tort committed against her husband; what is not now clear is whether she may sue if the loss is due to a tort committed against herself or to a breach of a contractual duty owed to her. LORD GODDARD's speech (in which LORD OAKSEY and LORD REID concurred on this point) is sufficiently wide to preclude any action by a wife for loss of consortium,[2] but it must be borne in mind that loss of consortium due to a tort committed against the husband was the sole question before the House and LORD PORTER and LORD MORTON were clearly considering this point only.[3] In the earlier case of *Lynch* v. *Knight*[4] the House of Lords was divided on this matter; but it is submitted that on principle the wife should be able to recover provided that the loss is not too remote a consequence of the tort or breach of contract, since she can establish an independent cause of action.[5] This was the view of HILBERY, J., in the later case of *Lampert* v. *Eastern National Omnibus Co., Ltd.*,[6] where he held that the plaintiff, who had been badly disfigured in an accident for which the defendant's servant was partly to blame, could have recovered for the loss of her husband's consortium had she been able to prove that the disfigurement was the cause of his leaving her.[7]

Impairment of Consortium.—In *Best* v. *Fox*[8] the House of Lords left open the further question whether an action can ever lie for the impairment, as distinct from the complete loss, of consortium. LORD GODDARD took the view that consortium is an indivisible abstraction and that consequently no action will lie for its mere impairment—an opinion with which LORD PORTER was inclined to agree.[9] LORD REID (with whom LORD OAKSEY concurred) maintained that since consortium is a bundle of rights, a husband could recover if any of these rights were interfered with, even though he was only in part deprived of his wife's comfort and society.[10] LORD GODDARD's and LORD

---

[1] [1952] A.C. 716; [1952] 2 All E.R. 394, H.L. See Fridman, *Consortium as an "Interest" in the Law of Torts*, 32 Can. Bar Rev. 1065.

[2] At pp. 732-733 and 399, respectively.

[3] At pp. 726, 735 and 395, 400, respectively.

[4] (1861), 9 H.L. Cas. 577, H.L.

[5] But if the tort is not actionable *per se* and the *only* damage which the wife can show is the loss of her husband's consortium *quaere* whether she can succeed.

[6] [1954] 2 All E.R. 719. See Fridman, *loc. cit.*

[7] In fact she failed because the spouses had been getting on badly together for a long time and the husband had merely used his wife's disfigurement as an excuse for leaving her.

[8] [1952] A.C. 716; [1952] 2 All E.R. 394, H.L. See further 18 M.L.R. 514.

[9] At pp. 733-734, 728 and 399-400, 396, respectively. This was the ratio of the decision of the Court of Appeal in this case: [1951] 2 K.B. 639; [1951] 2 All E.R. 116.

[10] At pp. 736 and 401, respectively. LORD MORTON expressed no opinion on this aspect of the case.

PORTER'S objection to giving damages for the impairment of consortium is based upon the fact that in truth the husband's claim is always for the expenses occasioned by the medical attention required by his wife and by the loss of her services—in other words that he is claiming for pecuniary loss rather than for any personal injury. But expenses due to the impairment of consortium could be quite high, for example if the husband had to hire a nurse or domestic help, and consequently it is submitted that the action should lie. This argument prevailed in *Lawrence* v. *Biddle.*[1]

Effect of the Spouse's Death.—Since the decision of LORD ELLENBOROUGH, C.J., in *Baker* v. *Bolton*[2] it has been the accepted rule in tort that "in a civil court the death of a human being could not be complained of as an injury". In that case the stage coach in which the plaintiff and his wife were travelling overturned owing to the defendant's negligence, and the wife died a month later in hospital. It was held that the plaintiff could recover for the loss of his wife's consortium only until the time of her death, from which of course it follows that if the wife dies instantaneously no action will lie at common law for the loss of her consortium at all. In such a case the spouse's sole remedy is that afforded by the Fatal Accidents Act.[3]

In *Jackson* v. *Watson & Sons*,[4] however, the Court of Appeal held that the rule in *Baker* v. *Bolton* has no application where the cause of action is contractual, and consequently permitted the plaintiff to recover for the loss of his wife's consortium due to her death as a result of eating defective salmon sold to him by the defendant. The absurdity of this distinction can be demonstrated by the fact that the plaintiff would have had no remedy (other than that provided by the Fatal Accidents Act) if the defendant had sold the tin of salmon to the plaintiff's wife instead of to the plaintiff, for in that case there would have been no privity of contract between the parties.

Measures of Damages.[5]—The commonest head of damages is for medical and nursing expenses[6] and for the pecuniary loss of the wife's services, for example the cost of providing a housekeeper to look after the husband and children whilst the wife is in hospital. Although it seems that compensation can be recovered for loss of companionship, damages are usually low.[7] In particular, the husband cannot claim *as such* for loss of earnings occasioned by the injury to his wife;[8] if, for example, he and his wife were professional

---

[1] [1966] 2 Q.B. 504; [1966] 1 All E.R. 575, followed in *Cutts* v. *Chumley*, [1967] 2 All E.R. 89. See also *Hare* v. *British Transport Commission*, [1956] 1 All E.R. 578. Damages for impairment of consortium have also been awarded by the High Court of Australia (*Toohey* v. *Hollier* (1955), 92 C.L.R. 618) but refused by the Supreme Court of Ireland (*Spaight* v. *Dundon*, [1961] I.R. 201). See further Milner, *Injuries to Consortium in Modern Anglo-American Law*, 7 I.C.L.Q. 417. For a full criticism of the law relating to loss of consortium and services, see Williams, *Some Reforms in the Law of Tort*, 24 M.L.R. 101.

[2] (1808), 1 Camp 493. The principle was affirmed by the House of Lords in *Admiralty Comrs.* v. *S.S. Amerika*, [1917] A.C. 38.

[3] See *post*, pp. 134 *et seq.*

[4] [1909] 2 K.B. 193, C.A. See *ante*, p. 129.

[5] See Street, *Principles of the Law of Damages*, 227-235.

[6] Unless, of course, the wife has already recovered them.

[7] *Sellars* v. *Best*, [1954] 2 All E.R. 389 (£100). *Ladd* v. *Jones*, [1975] R.T.R. 67 (£150).

[8] *Kirkham* v. *Boughey*, [1958] 2 Q.B. 338; [1957] 3 All E.R. 153. *Cf.* the analogous rule under the Fatal Accidents Act, *post*, p. 136.

entertainers and as a result of her incapacity he could earn less than half the
sum they jointly earned, he would have no claim for his loss any more than he
could claim for injury to any other business partner. But there appear to be at
least three cases in which loss of earnings may be claimed. First, if the loss
arises directly and peculiarly out of the loss of consortium, the husband may
recover for it. This occurred in *Behrens* v. *Bertram Mills Circus, Ltd.*,[1] where
it was held that the plaintiff, a midget who earned his living by appearing with
his wife (another midget) in exhibitions in funfairs and who stayed at home
whilst his wife was incapacitated as a result of an accident for which the
defendants were liable, could recover for his loss of earnings, as he was peculiarly dependent on his wife in that he could not easily mix with persons of a
normal stature and that it was not reasonable to expect him to go on tour
alone in his caravan and look after himself. Secondly, if the husband loses his
earnings in order to be with his wife and thus speeds her recovery, he may
recover for this loss if his action is a proper step taken to mitigate the damage
sustained by the loss of consortium.[2] Thirdly, if, as a result of the injury she
has suffered, the wife has to live away from her home and the husband's
usual place of work and the latter elects not to be deprived of her consortium
but to forgo his earnings instead, it would seem that he can claim for this loss
instead of claiming for loss of consortium. Thus in *McNeill* v. *Johnstone*[3] the
husband, who was an officer in the United States Air Force stationed at Mar-
gate, took unpaid leave to be near his wife who was in hospital at Swindon,
and DEVLIN, J., held that he could recover such part of his loss of earnings
and his expenses as were attributable to his preserving his consortium.

Damages Recoverable by the Injured Spouse.—The law relating to
damages for loss of consortium is uncertain, inconsistent and anomalous. A
much more rational approach to the problem of compensating a spouse for
the loss he or she suffers as the result of a tort committed against the other is
to be found in the decision of the Court of Appeal in *Cunningham* v.
Harrison.[4] This must be read with the judgment of a different division of the
court in *Donnelly* v. *Joyce*[5] delivered on the following day, which deals with
the allied question of compensating parents for loss suffered as a result of the
defendant's tortiously injuring their child. In *Cunningham* v. *Harrison* the
plaintiff was permanently paralysed in a road accident caused by the
defendant's negligence. His wife looked after him at home for 15 months
until her own death just before the trial. She devoted the whole of her day to
him and normally had to get up in the night as well. On legal advice he entered
into an agreement with her to pay her £2,000 a year for nursing him and then
claimed compensation for this from the defendant. It was held that he could

---

[1] [1957] 2 Q.B. 1; [1957] 1 All E.R. 583.
[2] *Kirkham* v. *Boughey*, (*supra*). Hence the loss is not recoverable if the sole justification for
the husband's action is the comfort or pleasure that it gives to the wife: *ibid.*, pp. 343 and 157,
respectively.
[3] [1958] 3 All E.R. 16. *Quaere* whether he can recover the full loss of his earnings if this sum is
greater than that at which the court would assess the loss of consortium.
[4] [1973] Q.B. 942; [1973] 3 All E.R. 463, C.A.
[5] [1974] Q.B. 454; [1973] 3 All E.R. 475, C.A. Followed in *Taylor* v. *Bristol Omnibus Co.,
Ltd.*, [1975] 2 All E.R. 1107, C.A., and *Daly* v. *General Steam Navigation Co., Ltd.*, [1980] 3 All
E.R. 696, C.A. (wife entitled to recover part-time earnings lost by husband because of need to
assist her in the home). For loss of services of a child, see further *post*, pp. 329-332.

properly recover the value of the additional services rendered to him as a part of *his* damages: it is not necessary to create a legal obligation to pay the wife by entering into a contract with her.[1] In the second case of *Donnelly* v. *Joyce* the plaintiff, aged six years, sustained serious injuries to his leg as the result of the defendant's negligence. He was in hospital for three months and then had to attend daily as an out-patient. The leg required special bathing and dressing twice a day and consequently his mother gave up her job in order to be able to take him to hospital and to carry out the necessary treatment. As in the earlier case it was held that the child could recover the mother's loss of earnings as part of *his* damages.

The basis of the decision in *Donnelly* v. *Joyce* was explained by MEGAW, L.J., in the following words (which apply equally to the facts of *Cunningham* v. *Harrison*):[2]

> "The plaintiff's loss ... is not the expenditure of money ... to pay for the nursing attention. His loss is the existence of the need ... for those nursing services, the value of which for the purpose of damages—for the purpose of the ascertainment of the amount of his loss—is the proper and reasonable cost of supplying those needs."

If professional services are hired, the measure of damages will be their cost; if the services are rendered by a spouse or parent who is not working, the damages should be the same for this as what it would cost to obtain them outside. If this is so, there seems no reason for limiting the damages to the actual loss of earnings if, as in *Donnelly* v. *Joyce*, a member of the family gives up work to provide them.[3]

It was also held in *Donnelly* v. *Joyce* that the plaintiff could recover for the value of goods which had to be specially provided (in this case socks and boots) even though his parents had paid for them. In an appropriate case it is submitted that he could also recover for, say, structural alterations to the parents' (or spouse's) house to accommodate a wheelchair or even the cost of moving house if this was reasonable and necessary in the circumstances.

In *Cunningham* v. *Harrison* it was suggested that the plaintiff held any damages recovered under this head on trust for the spouse who had rendered the services.[4] This is difficult to reconcile with the ratio decidendi of *Donnelly* v. *Joyce*: if the plaintiff is recovering for his own loss and does not have to show any legal or moral obligation to reimburse the person who has provided the services or goods, the latter has no apparent claim for their value even though the sums involved are large. The use of the trust would clearly avoid hardship if he refused to pay over any part of the compensation he had received for their provision.

It will be appreciated that, if the husband is the injured spouse, any claim for compensation for the wife's services will have to be made by him because she has no independent action for loss of his consortium. If the wife is injured, however, it will be more advantageous for the husband to sue

---

[1] Assuming that this agreement did create a legal obligation. Was there a genuine intention to enter into legal relations?

[2] At pp. 462 and 480, respectively.

[3] *Cf. Taylor* v. *Bristol Omnibus Co., Ltd.*, (*supra*), at p. 1112. If the loss of earnings exceeded the cost of hiring professional services, the plaintiff should not be able to recover more than the latter on the general principle of having to mitigate his loss.

[4] *Per* LORD DENNING, M.R., at pp. 952 and 469, respectively.

independently if she has been guilty of contributory negligence because this will not reduce his damages.[1]

Proposals for Reform.—Insofar as the present law of damages for loss of consortium is based upon the common law view that a husband's interest in his wife's services and consortium is quasi-proprietary, it is clearly anachronistic and there is no justification today for refusing the wife compensation in her own right for any financial loss she suffers as a result of a tort committed against her husband. Consequently the Law Reform Committee would equate the rights of the spouses and propose that "where a husband or a wife is tortiously injured, the other spouse should be able to recover reasonable medical and nursing expenses and all other costs properly incurred in consequence of the injury, such as reasonable visits to hospital and the reasonable cost of providing domestic help to replace the injured partner". Such a claim would include any loss of earnings reasonably incurred by any action taken in consequence of the injury.[2] The Law Commission have similarly recommended the abolition of actions for loss of services and consortium and would replace them by a claim for compensation for financial loss suffered by the plaintiff as a result of a tort committed to a third person. This would include reasonable expenses incurred on behalf of the person injured and, provided that the plaintiff was a dependant of the victim for the purpose of the Fatal Accidents Act, the loss of the value of services rendered by him.[3]

The Royal Commission on Civil Liability and Compensation for Personal Injury (the Pearson Commission) likewise recommended the abolition of these actions. Their preference, however, was to apply the principle of *Donnelly* v. *Joyce*. In their opinion this would give an adequate remedy: if the person injured recovered damages for loss of amenities (including the ability to look after his or her spouse) and for the value of the services which had to be rendered to him as the result of his injury, the Commission saw no need for a separate action by the spouse.[4] They would, however, leave the plaintiff free to use the damages recovered as he thought fit and would not impress any trust on them in favour of a spouse who had been put to any expense.

2. THE FATAL ACCIDENTS ACT

The rule in *Baker* v. *Bolton*[5] gave rise to the cynical maxim that it was cheaper to kill than to maim. The consequences of the fact that the dependants of a person who had been killed as the result of the negligence of another might be left penniless without recourse against the tortfeasor

---

[1] See *ante*, p. 129; *Wattson* v. *Port of London Authority*, [1969] 1 Lloyd's Rep. 95; Carr, 37 M.L.R. 341; Jolowicz, [1974] C.L.J. 40; Wharam, 121 New L.J. 786.

[2] Eleventh Report (Loss of Services, etc.), 1963, Cmnd. 2017. In the analogous case of an employer's right to recover expenses incurred in consequence of a tortious injury inflicted on his employee, they recommend that the amount recoverable should be reduced in proportion to the latter's contributory negligence (para. 10). Presumably the same principle should be applied in the case of a spouse's claim.

[3] Law Com. No. 56, Report on Personal Injury Litigation—Assessment of Damages, paras. 115-161.

[4] Cmnd. 7054, 1978, paras. 343-351 and 445-447.

[5] *Ante*, p. 131.

became much more serious with the introduction of heavy machinery and the invention of the railway in the early nineteenth century. Parliament eventually intervened to ameliorate the position by passing in 1846 the Fatal Accidents Act (commonly called Lord Campbell's Act). This Act was extensively amended during the next 100 years, and all the relevant statutes were repealed and their provisions consolidated in the Fatal Accidents Act 1976.

The Act of 1846 introduced an action which is "new in its species, new in its quality, new in its principle, in every way new",[1] for it permitted a claim to be made on behalf of certain dependants of any person who had been killed as the result of the defendant's wrongful act, neglect or default. The damages must accordingly be assessed in accordance with the financial loss suffered by the dependants as a result of the death.

For whose Benefit the Action will lie.—The action will not lie on behalf of everyone who was dependent on the deceased but only on behalf of persons standing in the following relationships to him or her: wife, husband, parent, grandparent, child, grandchild, brother, sister, uncle, aunt and the issue of a brother, sister, uncle and aunt.[2] An adopted person is to be treated as the child of his adopter or adopters;[3] and (subject to this) any relationship by affinity is to be treated as a relationship by consanguinity,[4] any relationship of the half blood as a relationship of the whole blood, the stepchild of any person as his child, and an illegitimate person as the legitimate child of his mother and reputed father.[5]

The claimant must also have suffered some pecuniary loss as a result of the death, and no action will lie in the absence of any such loss.[6] Hence, if the wife had parted from her husband before his death, she can claim nothing under the Act if she could have obtained no maintenance from him and there was no reasonable or substantial expectation of their resuming cohabitation.[7] On the other hand, she has a claim if she was being supported by him under a court order. Nor can she recover anything if the sole support she had from him came from the proceeds of his criminal activities for *ex turpi causa non oritur actio*.[8] Where the claimant has been wholly or partly dependent on the deceased before his death, pecuniary loss is obviously easy to prove, as, for

---

[1] *Per* LORD BLACKBURN in *Seward* v. *"Vera Cruz"* (1884), 10 App. Cas. 59, 70-71, H.L.

[2] Fatal Accidents Act 1976, s. 1 (2), (3), (4). A posthumous child (and presumably any other child *en ventre sa mère* at the date of the death) may claim: *The George and Richard* (1871), L.R. 3 A. & E. 466. A divorced spouse is not a dependant: *Payne-Collins* v. *Taylor Woodrow Construction, Ltd.*, [1975] Q.B. 300; [1975] 1 All E.R. 898. The Law Commission and the Pearson Commission recommend that he or she should be included amongst the category of dependants along with *de facto* adopted children: Law Com. No. 56, paras. 257-260; Cmnd. 7054, paras. 401-404.

[3] Children Act 1975, Sched. 1, para. 3 (prospectively repealed and re-enacted in the Adoption Act 1976, s. 39). See *post*, p. 357.

[4] There is an ambiguity here. A man may clearly claim on the death of, *e.g.*, his wife's father. He may presumably claim on the death, *e.g.*, of his sister's husband. May this process be extended to include relationships traced through two (or even more) marriages? *E.g.*, may a man claim on the death of his wife's sister's husband?

[5] Can a person claim on the death, *e.g.*, of his stepparent's natural parent and can an illegitimate person claim on the death, *e.g.*, of his mother's parent?

[6] *Duckworth* v. *Johnson* (1859), 4 H. & N. 653.

[7] *Davies* v. *Taylor*, [1974] A.C. 207; [1972] 3 All E.R. 836, H.L. A mere speculative possibility of a reconciliation is not enough.

[8] *Burns* v. *Edman*, [1970] 2 Q.B. 541; [1970] 1 All E.R. 886.

example, in the case of a wife who has been supported by her husband, a child supported by his parent, or an old person supported by his adult child. Benefits received in kind are also sufficient, provided that they are capable of being assessed. Thus, a husband has an interest in the domestic services performed in the house by his wife,[1] and it has been held that an action will lie by parents in respect of the death of a son who had from time to time given them presents of food as well as small sums of money[2] and of a son who had gratuitously performed services for which they were paid.[3]

Even though the deceased had made no contribution to the claimant's support before his death, an action will lie under the Fatal Accidents Act provided that the latter had a reasonable expectation of pecuniary advantage in the future, had the other survived. This is particularly important in the case of a child who could have looked to the deceased to pay for his education or, conversely, in the case of a parent who had reasonable hopes of being supported by his child in his old age.[4] In cases such as these the court must assess the chance that the dependant would have received some financial benefit from the deceased had he lived and then scale down the award proportionately. In *Wathen* v. *Vernon*[5] an action was brought in respect of the death of a boy aged 17. His father had had a stroke and the Court of Appeal estimated that, if the father were disabled or died as the result of another stroke (of which there was a chance of about one in six), the son would have given his mother financial help for about five years, after which time he would probably have married. In the circumstances they awarded £500, which was described as little more than a nominal amount and all of which was to go to the mother. But if there is no more than a "mere speculative possibility of benefit"[6] or a "bare chance of receiving some slight pecuniary help",[7] no action is maintainable at all. In *Barnett* v. *Cohen*[8] a father brought an action under the Act in respect of the death of his four-year-old son. The boy had been very bright and the plaintiff had had hopes of ultimately sending him to a university. In view of the fact that the son, who could not have been expected to contribute anything to his father's income for at least twelve years, would all that time have been subject to all the risks of illness, disease, accident and death, and that the father might not have lived so long because of the poor state of his own health, it was held that the chance of financial benefit to the father, had the son not been killed, was too remote and that the action must fail.

Furthermore, the financial benefit which the claimant has lost as a result of the death must derive from the relationship and must not be a mere business loss. In *Burgess* v. *Florence Nightingale Hospital for Gentlewomen*[9]

---

[1] *Berry* v. *Humm & Co.*, [1915] 1 K.B. 627.
[2] *Dalton* v. *South Eastern Rly Co.* (1858), 4 C.B.N.S. 296.
[3] *Franklin* v. *South Eastern Rly Co.* (1858), 3 H. & N. 211.
[4] *Taff Vale Rly Co.* v. *Jenkins*, [1913] A.C. 1, H.L.; *Kandalla* v. *British Airways Board*, [1980] 1 All E.R. 341.
[5] [1970] R.T.R. 471, C.A. See also *Davies* v. *Taylor*, [1974] A.C., at pp. 212, 219, 220, 223; [1972] 3 All E.R., at pp. 838, 843-844, 845, 847; Fleming, [1973] C.L.J. 17.
[6] *Per* McCARDIE, J., in *Barnett* v. *Cohen*, [1921] 2 K.B. 461, 471.
[7] *Per* STEPHEN, J., in *Stimpson* v. *Wood* (1888), 57 L.J.Q.B. 484, 486.
[8] [1921] 2 K.B. 461. *Cf. Burns* v. *Edman*, (*supra*) (possibility of deceased husband's reforming and taking up honest work too remote).
[9] [1955] 1 Q.B. 349; [1955] 1 All E.R. 511.

the plaintiff and his wife had been professional dancing partners who, as a team, had earned more than twice the husband could expect to earn with any other partner. They had shared their income and also their expenses which, in view of the fact that they could live together in hotels, etc., were less than twice the husband's individual expenses. In a claim under the Act as a result of the wife's death, it was held that the plaintiff could recover nothing for his loss of income, for this benefit arose from a business partnership to which their relationship of husband and wife was, as it were, incidental; but that he could recover for the loss due to the increased expenses for this arose immediately from the fact that they were husband and wife. As the Court of Appeal pointed out in *Malyon* v. *Plummer*,[1] however, the matter must be viewed realistically, and if a benefit was in fact derived from the relationship, its loss will be recoverable even though it appears at first sight to be a business loss. In that case the plaintiff's husband had turned his business into a private company; he held 999 shares and the plaintiff held the remaining share. The spouses were both directors, but it was essentially a one-man business under the husband's control. The wife worked casually and intermittently in the office, and although she was paid sums varying from £600 to £800 a year as a director, the actual value of her services (which the husband would otherwise have had to pay someone else to carry out) was assessed at £200 a year. The husband was killed as a result of the defendant's negligence and the wife's attempts to keep the business going were unsuccessful. In an action under the Fatal Accidents Act it was held that, as her directorship and the fact that her earnings were grossly in excess of their value were really due to the relationship of husband and wife and not to a business relationship, she was entitled to recover compensation for her loss based upon the difference between her actual earnings and the value of the work she had put in.

The action must be brought by the personal representatives on behalf of the dependants,[2] but if there are no personal representatives or the personal representatives do not commence proceedings under the Act within six months of the death, the action may be brought by any one or more of the dependants themselves.[3] Only one action may be brought, so that if any dependant is not included as a claimant, he has no remedy under the Act at all.[4]

Against whom the Action may be brought.—An action under the Fatal Accidents Act will lie against any person whom the deceased could himself

---

[1] [1964] 1 Q.B. 330; [1963] 2 All E.R. 344, C.A. *Cf. Saikaley* v. *Pelletier* (1966), 57 D.L.R. (2d) 394 (damages recovered for loss of mother who lived with son and daughter-in-law and did housework in return for board, lodging and pocket money). Cases like *Franklin* v. *South Eastern Rey. Co. (ante)* are clearly distinguishable, for there the deceased gave his services free as a result of the relationship between himself and the plaintiff.

[2] Hence personal representatives have no power to compromise the claim of any dependant unless the latter is *sui juris* and agrees to the compromise: *Jeffrey* v. *Kent C.C.*, [1958] 3 All E.R. 155.

[3] Fatal Accidents Act 1976, s. 2. If no personal representatives have been appointed, the dependants may sue in their own name even within the first six months: *Holleran* v. *Bagnell* (1879), L.R. 4 Ir. 740.

[4] *Ibid.*, s. 2 (3). But if a dependant has been improperly excluded, he may have a remedy against the personal representatives or other plaintiffs: *per* LORD ATKIN in *Avery* v. *London and North Eastern Rly Co.*, [1938] A.C. 606, 613; [1938] 2 All E.R. 592, 595, H.L.

have sued in respect of the injury causing death had he not died.[1] The crucial test is therefore: could the deceased have maintained an action against the defendant at the date of his death? Hence no action will lie if the latter could have raised the defence of *volenti non fit injuria*,[2] if the deceased had already sued for his own injuries,[3] if he had received during his lifetime compensation in full satisfaction[4] or, generally, if his own claim was statute barred.[5]

It is doubtful whether any action can be brought under the Crown Proceedings Act against the Crown for damages under the Fatal Accidents Act.[6]

Assessment of Damages.[7]—Damages are to be measured solely by reference to the material loss which the dependants have suffered as a result of the death, except that they may also be awarded in respect of funeral expenses if these have been incurred by any party for whose benefit the action is brought.[8] Hence, no damages may be recovered for wounded feelings, mental suffering or loss of love or a happy home.[9]

---

[1] *Ibid.*, s. 2 (1), (5). This is so whether the original cause of action was tortious or contractual: *Grein* v. *Imperial Airways, Ltd.*, [1937] 1 K.B. 50, at pp. 71, 88; [1936] 2 All E.R. 1258, at pp. 1275, 1287.

[2] *Senior* v. *Ward* (1859), 1 E. & E. 385. *Cf. Haigh* v. *Royal Mail Steam Packet Co., Ltd.* (1883), 52 L.J.Q.B. 640, C.A. (no liability under the Act when the deceased had wholly contracted out of liability).

[3] Somewhat surprisingly, LORD DENNING, M.R., and JAMES, L.J., did not firmly state this to be the law in *McCann* v. *Sheppard*, [1973] 2 All E.R. 881, at pp. 885 and 892, C.A. But there can be no doubt of the accuracy of the statement because the deceased could not have maintained a second action. In *Murray* v. *Shuter*, [1972] Lloyd's Rep. 6, C.A., the court permitted an action brought by a man whose expectation of life was less than a year to be stood out so that his dependants could bring an action under the Fatal Accidents Act later if necessary.

[4] *Read* v. *Great Eastern Rly. Co.* (1868), L.R. 3 Q.B. 555.

[5] Limitation Act 1980, s. 12 (1). If the deceased's own claim was not statute barred at the time of his death, an action under the Fatal Accidents Act must be brought within whichever of the following periods elapses later (unless it is barred by some other statute): three years of the death or three years of the dependant's knowledge (a) that the injury to the deceased was significant (*i.e.*, sufficiently serious to justify the institution of proceedings against a defendant who admitted liability and was able to satisfy a judgment) and (b) that it was attributable to the act or omission of an identified defendant or an identified person for whose acts the defendant was liable: *ibid.*, ss. 12 (2) and 14. The knowledge of one dependant does not affect the claim of any other: *ibid.*, s. 13. The court may allow an action to be brought notwithstanding that the deceased's claim was barred at his death or that the limitation periods imposed by s. 12 (2) have expired if this would be equitable having regard to the degree to which allowing or disallowing the claim would prejudice the defendant or the dependants respectively: *ibid.*, s. 33 *q.v.* for the facts to be taken into account. If death results from a collision at sea, any action against the *other* vessel is normally barred after two years: Maritime Conventions Act 1911, s. 8; *The Alnwick*, [1965] P. 357; [1965] 2 All E.R. 569, C.A.; *The Niceto de Larrinaga*, [1966] P. 80; [1965] 2 All E.R. 930.

[6] See Street, *Torts*, 6th Ed., 416.

[7] See generally Kemp and Kemp, *Quantum of Damages*, 4th Ed., vol. 1, part 3; McGregor, *Damages*, 14th Ed., paras. 1274 *et seq.*; Street, *Principles of the Law of Damages*, particularly pp. 148-166 and 179-183; Ogus, *Law of Damages*, 264-278.

[8] Fatal Accidents Act 1976, s. 3 (3). Funeral expenses may be recovered even though the claimant cannot prove financial dependency, but in any case they must be reasonable: *Stanton* v. *Ewart F. Youldon, Ltd.*, [1960] 1 All E.R. 429; *Hart* v. *Griffith-Jones*, [1948] 2 All E.R. 729 (claim for embalming body of child allowed, but not £225 for a monument to place over the grave).

[9] *Blake* v. *Midland Rly. Co.* (1852), 18 Q.B. 93.

In order to arrive at the correct sum to award by way of damages, the court must first assess the dependency, that is the annual benefit which the dependant or dependants would have received from the deceased. There must then be applied to the dependency the appropriate multiplier based upon the number of years for which the dependency was likely to have continued if the deceased had not been killed. Finally, there must be deducted from the sum so obtained any financial benefit accruing to the dependant as a result of the death. So if the court assesses the dependency at £1,000 a year and applies a multiplier of twelve, the damages will *prima facie* be £12,000. But if the deceased's estate valued at £2,000 (of which the dependant would not otherwise have had the enjoyment) passes to him, this must be deducted so as to give a final award of £10,000.[1]

In some abnormal cases, however, it may be necessary to take other financial losses into account and, for example, to give the dependants compensation for the value of a lump sum or gift of which the death has deprived them. In *Davies* v. *Whiteways Cyder Co., Ltd.*[2] the deceased had made a number of substantial gifts to his wife and son. Under the law as it then stood, no estate duty would have been payable had he survived for seven years after making the gifts; as the result of his premature death, however, an additional £17,000 duty became payable. It was held that this sum (less £500 to take account of the fact that he might have died before the end of the seven years from other causes) was recoverable under the Fatal Accidents Act as a financial loss suffered by the widow and son as a direct result of the death.

The Dependency.—The normal way of calculating the dependency is to assess the deceased's probable earnings had he remained alive and the benefit which the dependants were likely to have received from them. Often this must obviously be a matter of speculation. "In most cases the most reliable guide as to what would happen in the future if the deceased had lived is what did in fact happen when he was alive."[3] It is obviously easier to make an estimate of the dependants' loss between the date of death and the date of the trial. Evidence can be given of what the deceased's salary would have been had he stayed in the same job and allowance made for any chance of promotion:[4] his gross salary over this period can then be calculated and the dependency assessed.[5] With respect to the potential loss after the trial, the court starts with the salary the deceased would probably have been receiving at that time and applies the multiplier to this. Again, account must be taken of any chances of promotion but not of the consequences of inflation in the future:

---

[1] See generally LORD WRIGHT in *Davies* v. *Powell Duffryn Associated Collieries, Ltd.*, [1942] A.C. 601, 617; [1942] 1 All E.R. 657, 665, H.L.; LORD DIPLOCK in *Malyon* v. *Plummer*, [1964] 1 Q.B. 330, 349-350; [1963] 2 All E.R. 344, 353, C.A., and *Mallett* v. *McMonagle*, [1970] A.C. 166, 176-178; [1969] 2 All E.R. 178, 191, H.L.; LORD MORRIS and LORD PEARSON in *Taylor* v. *O'Connor*, [1971] A.C. 115, at pp. 131-132 and 141-142; [1970] 1 All E.R. 365, at pp. 370 and 377-378, H.L.

[2] [1975] Q.B. 262; [1974] 3 All E.R. 168.

[3] *Per* DIPLOCK, L.J., in *Malyon* v. *Plummer*, at pp. 349 and 353, respectively.

[4] *Cf. Young* v. *Percival*, [1974] 3 All E.R. 677, C.A. (although the judgment must now be read in the light of *Cookson* v. *Knowles*, [1979] A.C. 556; [1978] 2 All E.R. 604, H.L.).

[5] *Cookson* v. *Knowles*, (*supra*).

the latter are too speculative and a sound investment of the damages awarded can largely offset its effect provided at least that the resultant income would not attract tax at a high rate.[1] In calculating the dependency the court must try to estimate what part of any additional income would probably have been used for the benefit of the dependants and what part for the deceased himself: only the former, of course, will amount to a loss to the dependants which can be taken into account in determining the damages to which they are entitled.[2] Similarly the dependency will be increased if a widow has to stop work or take a less well paid job as the result of her husband's death.[3]

It must also be realised that the dependency need not have been a benefit in cash: the value of services in kind must also be assessed. Hence, in the case of the death of a wife, the husband may claim for the loss of her services less the cost of maintaining her.[4] He may also recover compensation for the loss of her care and attention, although the damages awarded under this head are likely to be small.[5] It may be more difficult to arrive at a figure to represent her value as a mother. No compensation may be given to the children for the loss of her love and affection, but the view today is that her personal attention to their upbringing can never be wholly replaced by the services of another and that this has a financial value for the loss of which damages can be awarded.[6] In *Mehmet* v. *Perry*[7] the plaintiff gave up work after his wife's death in order to look after their two children who suffered from a rare blood disorder and required constant medical care. It was held that his conduct was reasonable in the circumstances and that he could accordingly claim for his loss of earnings in full under the Act.

Usually it is unnecessary to decide what part of the deceased's earnings were used for the benefit of each dependant because the dependants together constitute one family unit and the total sum to be awarded, once it has been assessed, can then be apportioned amongst them.[8] This method cannot be used, however, when they do not all live in one family: if, for example, a man maintaining his wife and children in the matrimonial home and his widowed mother in a house of her own, the latter's dependency (together with a completely different multiplier) will have to be assessed quite separately. The

---

[1] *Cookson* v. *Knowles*, (*supra*). See Davies and Russell, 42 M.L.R. 98.

[2] Similarly, if the deceased had been saving part of his income, the court must assess what part of the savings would have been used for the benefit of the dependants and compensate them for this loss: *Gavin* v. *Wilmot Breeden, Ltd.*, [1973] 3 All E.R. 935, C.A.

[3] *Cookson* v. *Knowles*, [1977] Q.B. 913; [1977] 2 All E.R. 820, C.A. (This point was not taken on appeal to the House of Lords, *supra*.)

[4] *Berry* v. *Humm & Co.*, [1915] 1 K.B. 627, 630. *Cf. Burgess* v. *Florence Nightingale Hospital for Gentlewomen*, [1955] 1 Q.B. 349; [1955] 1 All E.R. 511 (increase in husband's expenses due to wife's death); *Peacock* v. *Amusement Equipment Co., Ltd.*, [1954] 2 All E.R. 123 (loss of house in which dependant had been living with the deceased. Overruled on another point, [1954] 2 Q.B. 347; [1954] 2 All E.R. 689, C.A.).

[5] *Mehmet* v. *Perry*, [1977] 2 All E.R. 529 (£1,000 awarded).

[6] See *Regan* v. *Williamson*, [1976] 2 All E.R. 241; *Mehmet* v. *Perry*, (*supra*); *Hay* v. *Hughes*, [1975] Q.B. 790, 802-803; [1975] 1 All E.R. 257, 261, C.A.; *K.* v. *J.M.P. Co., Ltd.*, [1976] Q.B. 85, 96-97; [1975] 1 All E.R. 1030, 1038, C.A.

[7] [1977] 2 All E.R. 529.

[8] See *post*, p. 147.

same problem arose in *K*. v. *J.M.P. Co., Ltd.*[1] At his death the deceased was living with a woman to whom he was not married (and who was therefore not a dependant) and their three illegitimate children. He was the sole wage earner and his income was used to house, clothe and feed the family as a whole and to pay for their annual holiday to Ireland. In assessing the children's dependency there had to be deducted the amount spent by the deceased on himself and on his own holidays together with the cost of his and the mother's food and clothes. The Court of Appeal, however, refused to apportion the cost of fuel, rent, television or the washing machine between the mother and the children: all were used by them jointly and it would have been unrealistic not to regard their full value as a benefit to the children.[2] Nor would they leave out of account the cost of her holidays because depriving her of them would inevitably have had the effect of depriving the children of theirs too and so would have constituted a pecuniary loss to them: if it is impossible to maintain the children's standard of life without maintaining their mother's as well, the compensation that the defendant pays them must include a sum to cover the latter.

The Multiplier.—It is perhaps even more difficult to arrive at the correct multiplier. Essentially this represents the number of years for which the dependency was likely to have continued if the deceased had not been killed. It must be calculated from the date of the death, and the period before the date of the trial is then substracted to determine what multiplier is to be applied to calculate future loss.[3] It is therefore frequently appropriate to start with the deceased's estimated working life; it must be remembered, however, that the dependency of a child will normally cease when he starts earning his own living[4] and, conversely, a rich man can be expected to use his savings to provide for his family after his retirement and his death so that the basic figure is his widow's expectation of life.[5] The estimated duration of the dependency must now be reduced to take account of various contingencies, for example the possibility that the deceased might have died prematurely in any event (particularly if his expectation of life was not great),[6] that the dependant might die prematurely (again with specific reference to the

---

[1] [1976] Q.B. 85; [1975] 1 All E.R. 1030, C.A. See also *Dodds* v. *Dodds*, [1978] Q.B. 543; [1978] 2 All E.R. 539 (mother unable to recover because she was the tortfeasor who caused the father's death). If the parents of illegitimate children were not living together, the value of the dependency would be the amount of an affiliation order or of other financial help that the mother was likely to have got from the father had he lived.

[2] *Cf. Hay* v. *Hughes*, (*supra*), at pp. 812 and 270, respectively: "The children have lost the enjoyment of a home, not of a fraction of a home" (*per* BUCKLEY, L.J.).

[3] *Cookson* v. *Knowles*, (*supra*).

[4] Or marries in the case of a daughter: see *Rawlinson* v. *Babcock and Wilcox, Ltd.*, [1966] 3 All E.R. 882; *Dodds* v. *Dodds*, (*supra*). In the case of a young child it will be frequently difficult to tell whether he is likely to become a wage earner at 16 or carry on with full time education after that time. If a man is survived by a widow and children, the problem is less because the widow's dependency will continue after the children leave home and she could expect more money for herself once they have done so, but it will be critical if he leaves children but no widow: see *K*. v. *J.M.P. Co., Ltd.*, (*supra*), and *cf. Hay* v. *Hughes*, (*supra*).

[5] *Taylor* v. *O'Connor*, [1971] A.C. 115; [1970] 1 All E.R. 365, H.L.

[6] *Hall* v. *Wilson*, [1939] 4 All E.R. 85. But see *Bishop* v. *Cunard White Star Co., Ltd.*, [1950] P. 240, 248; [1950] 2 All E.R. 22, 26.

particular dependant's expectation of life)[1] or that, if the marriage was unstable, it might have broken down.[2] Similarly, damages will be less in the case of the death of a son than that of a husband because a child is under no legal obligation to support his parents and, had he married, he might well have cut down the sum he was prepared to pay his mother or father.[3]

On the same principle the sum awarded to a widow used to be less if it was probable that she might remarry. The necessity of assessing her prospects, however, was offensive to some judges and members of the public alike, and consequently in assessing damages *payable to a widow* in respect of the death of her husband neither her remarriage nor the prospects of her remarriage are now to be taken into account.[4] Whilst this relieves judges and litigants of embarrassment, there is no doubt that it will appear unjust to some defendants, who will in effect find themselves giving a wedding present to the woman's second husband, and it will "in many cases inevitably introduce an element of unreality to the assessment of real loss to the widow".[5] Furthermore, the words italicised above must mean that these matters will still have to be taken into account in assessing damages payable to a widower or a child.[6]

The multiplier must be further reduced to take account of the fact that the dependant is receiving a lump sum now representing annual payments in the future. As the House of Lords pointed out in *Taylor* v. *O'Connor*,[7] the dependant is expected to invest the damages prudently and to live on both income and capital; if one merely multiplied the dependency by the number of years it was likely to have lasted (reduced to take account of contingencies), no account would be taken of the income which this capital sum would produce.[8] Similarly, if the award is large (as it was in that case),

---

[1] *Williamson* v. *John I. Thornycroft & Co., Ltd.*, [1940] 2 K.B. 658; [1940] 4 All E.R. 61, C.A. If the dependent dies before judgment the element of doubt disappears and the damages may be assessed more accurately: *ibid.* See also *Whittome* v. *Coates*, [1965] 3 All E.R. 268, C.A.

[2] *Gadsby* v. *Hodkinson* (1966), 110 Sol. Jo. 834, C.A.

[3] *Dolbey* v. *Goodwin*, [1955] 2 All E.R. 166, C.A.

[4] Fatal Accidents Act 1975, s. 3 (2) (re-enacting the Law Reform (Miscellaneous Provisions) Act 1971, s. 4 (1)).

[5] *Per* CUMMING-BRUCE, J., in *Howitt* v. *Heads*, [1973] Q.B. 64, 70; [1972] 1 All E.R. 491, 495. See also the Pearson Report, Cmnd. 7054, paras. 409-416.

[6] *Thompson* v. *Price*, [1973] Q.B. 838; [1973] 2 All E.R. 846; *Regan* v. *Williamson*, [1976] 2 All E.R. 241. See further *post*, p. 145. The Law Commission recommended that remarriage and prospects of remarriage be disregarded in all cases: Law Com. No. 56, paras. 251-252.

[7] [1971] A.C. 115; [1970] 1 All E.R. 365, H.L.

[8] The following example given by LORD PEARSON in *Taylor* v. *O'Connor*, (*supra*), at pp. 144 and 379, respectively, may make the point clearer. Suppose £45,000 is invested at 3% and it is required to give an annual sum of £3,750.

	CAPITAL £	ANNUAL SUM TO BE PROVIDED £	INCOME AT 3% £	WITHDRAWN FROM CAPITAL £
	45,000 2,400	3,750	1,350	2,400
After 1 year	42,600 2,472	3,750	1,278	2,472
After 2 years	40,128 2,546	3,750	1,204	2,546
After 3 years	37,582	3,750	1,127	2,623

The fund will be completely exhausted after 15 years.

account must also be taken of the incidence of income tax and either the multiplier or the dependency must be increased to give the dependant the same net sum as she would have received had the deceased still been alive.[1] It is submitted that the question that ought to be asked is this: if the dependency is £x and its probable duration, reduced to take account of contingencies, is *y* years, what sum, invested at current rates of interest, will enable the dependant, using both capital and income, to receive £x a year net for *y* years? The sum is not difficult to calculate and ought to give a reasonably accurate assessment of the damages to be awarded; it seems, however, as though it does not commend itself to the judges who prefer to trust their own and practitioners' experience to give the correct multiplier.[2]

Benefit Accruing to the Dependant.—The principle that the purpose of the Fatal Accidents Act is to compensate the dependants for their financial loss has been applied in a series of cases which have established the rule that any claim must be reduced by the amount of any gain which accrues to a dependant as a direct result of the death. Thus, a dependant must bring into account any part of the deceased's estate which devolves on him or her (including any damages awarded to the personal representatives under the Law Reform (Miscellaneous Provisions) Act 1934 for personal injuries to the deceased and for loss of his expectation of life),[3] if this represents a gain which would not have accrued but for the death.[4]

To this general rule, however, there are a number of exceptions, some of which are more apparent than real. In the first place if the estate includes property of which the dependant would have had the use had the deceased remained alive, this is clearly not a financial advantage resulting from the

---

[1] *Taylor* v. *O'Connor*, (*supra*); *Cookson* v. *Knowles*, [1979] A.C. 556, 577-578; [1978] 2 All E.R. 604, 616, H.L. It must be assumed that income tax will remain at its present rate. But the House of Lords refused (without giving reasons) to take into account the fact that the dependant's private income might mean that she will be paying tax on the income at a much higher rate: see *Taylor* v. *O'Connor*, *per* LORD REID at pp. 129 and 368 and LORD DILHORNE at pp. 139 and 376, respectively. This seems arbitrary and unsatisfactory.

[2] In *Taylor* v. *O'Connor*, (*supra*), both LORD GUEST (at pp. 135 and 373) and LORD PEARSON (at pp. 140 and 377, respectively) deprecated the use of actuarial tables as giving a false appearance of accuracy and increasing the length and expense of trials. This is a surprising attitude and the current practice produces many inaccuracies: see Street, *op. cit.*, c. 5; Prevett, *Actuarial Assessment of Damages*, 35 M.L.R. 140. Eighteen years' purchase appears to be the most that the courts have sanctioned.

[3] *Davies* v. *Powell Duffryn Associated Collieries, Ltd.*, [1942] A.C. 601; [1942] 1 All E.R. 657, H.L. But this does not include any damages awarded to the estate for loss of earnings before death because this represents belated payment of a sum which would have been used for the dependant's benefit: *Murray* v. *Shuter*, [1976] Q.B. 972; [1975] 3 All E.R. 375, C.A. Nor does it include damages awarded for loss of or damage to property of which the dependant would have had the use had the deceased not been killed, on the principle exemplified in *Heatley* v. *Steel Co. of Wales, Ltd.*, (*infra*): *Bishop* v. *Cunard White Star Co., Ltd.*, [1950] P. 240, 248; [1950] 2 All E.R. 22, 26. It is usually better to claim the damages under the Fatal Accidents Act, for they do not then attract capital transfer tax and they cannot be taken by the deceased's creditors if the estate is insolvent: see *Hutchinson* v. *London and North Eastern Rly. Co.*, [1942] 1 K.B. 481, 491, C.A. But if the deceased was young, it may be more advantageous to claim damages under the 1934 Act: see *Gammell* v. *Wilson*, [1981] 1 All E.R. 578, H.L. The Law Commission recommend the abolition of this rule: Law Com. No. 56, paras. 254-256.

[4] *E.g.*, investments, for the dependants' interest in them is increased by the amount by which their present value exceeds the interest in expectancy: *Bishop* v. *Cunard White Star Co., Ltd.*, (*supra*), pp. 248 and 26, respectively.

death, and so the value does not have to be taken into account. Thus in *Heatley* v. *Steel Company of Wales, Ltd.*[1] the plaintiff's husband, in respect of whose death the action was brought, had died intestate, with the result that the beneficial interest in the matrimonial home, which was valued at £750, passed to the plaintiff. It was held that her claim under the Fatal Accidents Act was not to be reduced by this £750, for the net gain to her was nothing, as she still had to have a roof over her head.[2] Similarly, it follows from the principle that the dependants are entitled to be put back in the financial position they were in when the deceased was alive that if, say, a widow decides to go out to work after her husband's death, she does not have to bring her earnings into account.[3]

A further apparent exception arises when the gain to the dependant is not a benefit which could have been claimed as of right but is a gratuitous payment or transfer of property due to the charity or generosity of another. It has been held that a payment out of a fund launched to help the dependants of the victims of a railway disaster does not diminish a claim under the Act, for otherwise the generosity of the subscribers would merely benefit the defendant by reducing his liability and the springs of charity in the future might well dry up.[4] This is obviously a policy decision, but it exemplifies a wider principle formulated by SOMERVELL, L.J., in *Peacock* v. *Amusement Equipment Co., Ltd.*,[5] where he pointed out that the benefit must be brought into account only if there was some probability or reasonable expectation of it at the time of the death. In that case the plaintiff's wife had left all her property in her will to her two children by a former husband. The children later paid to the plaintiff a sum representing one-third of the value of the estate and it was held that this sum did not have to be brought into account in assessing the plaintiff's damages in an action under the Fatal Accidents Act as it was paid solely as the result of the step-children's generosity and was not a benefit of which the plaintiff had any expectation when his wife died. Although it is difficult to reconcile the cases and to extract a definite rule, it is clear that the courts are becoming increasingly loth to make deductions for purely voluntary benefits. In *Hay* v. *Hughes*,[6] for example, the Court of Appeal refused to take into account the fact that after the death of both parents in a road accident two small children went to live with their maternal grandmother who was bringing them up: this was an act of generosity on her

---

[1] [1953] 1 All E.R. 489, C.A. *Cf. Daniels* v. *Jones*, [1961] 3 All E.R. 24, C.A.

[2] But if, contrary to obvious facts, it would seem that the dependant has lost nothing financially by the death, arithmetic must give way to common sense: *Daniels* v. *Jones*, (*supra*). *Cf. Kassam* v. *Kampala Aerated Water Co., Ltd.*, [1965] 2 All E.R. 875, P.C.

[3] *Buckley* v. *John Allen & Ford* (*Oxford*), *Ltd.*, [1967] 2 Q.B. 637; [1967] 1 All E.R. 539 (no deduction made for rent received by widow from letting rooms in the former matrimonial home); *Cf. Howitt* v. *Heads*, [1973] Q.B. 64; [1972] 1 All E.R. 491 (widow's potential earning capacity ignored). The point was left open by the Court of Appeal in *Cookson* v. *Knowles*, [1977] Q.B. 913; [1977] 2 All E.R. 820 and was not mentioned on appeal to the House of Lords.

[4] *Redpath* v. *Belfast and County Down Rly.*, [1947] N.I. 167. *Cf. Baker* v. *Dalgleish Steam Shipping Co.*, [1922] 1 K.B. 361, at pp. 369, 380, C.A. *Bowskill* v. *Dawson*, [1955] 1 Q.B. 13, at pp. 24, 26; [1954] 2 All E.R. 649, at pp. 655, 656, C.A.

[5] [1954] 2 Q.B. 347, 353; [1954] 2 All E.R. 689, 692, C.A. See also *Green* v. *Russell*, [1959] 1 Q.B. 28, 39-40; [1958] 3 All E.R. 44, 47-48; *Voller* v. *Dairy Produce Packers, Ltd.*, [1962] 3 All E.R. 938; *Moore* v. *Babcock & Wilcox, Ltd.*, [1966] 3 All E.R. 882; *Hay* v. *Hughes*, [1975] Q.B. 790; [1975] 1 All E.R. 257, C.A.

[6] [1975] Q.B. 790; [1975] 1 All E.R. 257, C.A.

part and there was no reasonable expectation before the parents' death that she would act as she did.

Somewhat anomalously, in claims made on behalf of children the courts have made deductions for the fact that their widowed mother has remarried and their step-father treats them as though they were his own children. In this connection it must be borne in mind that a man may now be made liable to maintain his wife's children by a former marriage if they are members of the family;[1] consequently, it was held in *Reincke* v. *Gray*[2] that if the second husband is a man whose financial position is such that he can reasonably be expected to provide for the children as well as their own father would have done, they will not be able to recover for any financial loss after their mother's remarriage for they will have suffered none. This overlooks the fact that, if the second marriage comes under strain or the husband's financial position deteriorates, he is less likely to offer help to his step-children than their own father would have done. The rule came under attack in *Hay* v. *Hughes* but it requires a decision of the House of Lords to upset it. There was more justification for it when the mother's own claim was reduced or even extinguished by her remarriage, but now that that event is to be ignored in assessing her damages, the children's position has become even more anomalous. This is illustrated by *Thompson* v. *Price*.[3] The deceased left a widow and a son aged 18 months. The widow remarried before the action and her second husband accepted the boy as a child of the family and thus became legally liable for his support. The parties agreed the dependency of £12 a week, of which £9 was apportioned to the widow and £3 to the son. BOREHAM, J., held that her remarriage must still reduce the sum payable to the child but that, as the cost of his maintenance would fall on her, this should form part of her damages and therefore was not reducible. Whilst this approach neatly overcomes some of the difficulties, it is hard to justify it logically. The damages apportioned to the child should strictly include all the financial loss that he suffers as a result of the death and not merely the sum over and above his keep which he might have expected to receive if his father had not been killed.[4]

On the face of it the decision in *Thompson* v. *Price* undermines the principle that a judge shall not be required to estimate a widow's prospects of remarriage if there are dependent children. It must be borne in mind, however, that in this case (as in *Reincke* v. *Gray*) the mother had actually remarried. Any change in the children's financial position will depend on three things: her remarriage, her second husband's treating them as children of the family, and his financial position. It could be argued, therefore, that this depends on so many contingencies that they should be entirely ignored if the widow has not already married. At least this will relieve the trial judge of having to assess her prospects of doing so.

---

[1] See *post*, pp. 584 *et seq*.
[2] [1964] 2 All E.R. 687, C.A.
[3] [1973] Q.B. 838; [1973] 2 All E.R. 846.
[4] This may demonstrated by assuming that the widow had died (not as the result of any tortious act) before trial. The damages awarded to the children would obviously have to include a sum in respect of their future maintenance.

If the second husband is financially worse off than the first, or if in any case his income is low so that he could not be expected to fulfil the obligations of a father and maintain the children to the same extent, they will clearly be entitled to recover for their loss under the Fatal Accidents Act.[1]

This rule as a whole may well be regarded as an unwarranted judicial fetter upon the operation of the Act which serves no one but the tortfeasor. Its application was most hurtful to the dependants of a breadwinner who had had the foresight to take out a substantial insurance policy upon his own life or whose employer had provided for the payment of a pension to his widow and children. The position in this respect has been considerably improved by the provision that in assessing damages under the Fatal Accidents Act no account shall be taken of any insurance money,[2] benefit under the Social Security Act,[3] payment by a friendly society or a trade union for the relief or maintenance of dependants, pension,[4] or gratuity which has been or will be or may be paid as a result of the death.[5] Although the term "gratuity" is not defined, it is submitted that it probably does not include all gratuitous payments but, like the other payments specified, presupposes an existing relationship between the payer and the deceased.

In view of the cases and statutory provisions mentioned, it may be asked how much is left of the rule that a dependant must bring into account any benefits accruing to him as a result of the death. It clearly still applies to any part of the deceased's estate devolving on him if this represents a real gain; it apparently still applies in an attenuated form to the benefit derived by dependent children from their widowed mother's remarriage. It is highly doubtful in the present climate of judicial opinion whether it will be extended to cover any other cases.

Contributory Negligence.—If the death was caused partly by the deceased's contributory negligence, the damages recoverable under the Fatal Accidents Act must be reduced in proportion to the deceased's share of the responsibility for the damage causing his death.[6] Although the point is not free from doubt, if the death was caused partly by the fault of one of the dependants, his damages will be proportionately reduced.[7] This might occur,

---

[1] *Mead* v. *Clarke Chapman & Co., Ltd.*, [1956] 1 All E.R. 44, C.A. This case was decided before a step-father was placed under a statutory duty to maintain his step-children but it was distinguished on both grounds in *Reincke* v. *Gray*, (*supra*).

[2] Including a return of premiums. The money need not necessarily be paid or payable to the dependant or the deceased's personal representatives: see *Malyon* v. *Plummer*, [1964] 1 Q.B. 330; [1963] 2 All E.R. 344, C.A., (*ante*, p. 137), where it was held that insurance money paid to a company on the death of a director which benefited his widow by increasing the value of her shares was to be left out of account. As a result of this provision, a dependant may finish up financially better off than he would have been if the deceased had not been killed: *Humphry* v. *Ward Engineering Services, Ltd.* (1975), 119 Sol. Jo. 461.

[3] These include industrial death benefits, widow's allowances and pensions, and guardian's allowances. But supplementary benefit received in consequence of the death must be brought into account: *Mehmet* v. *Perry*, [1977] 2 All E.R. 529.

[4] Including a return of contributions and any payment of a lump sum in respect of employment.

[5] Fatal Accidents Act 1976, s. 4 (re-enacting the Fatal Accidents Act 1959, s. 2).

[6] *Ibid.*, s. 5.

[7] So held in Northern Ireland: *Mulholland* v. *McCrea*, [1961] N.I. 135. See Winfield and Jolowicz, *Tort*, 11th Ed., 544; Williams, *Joint Torts and Contributory Negligence*, 443-444.

for example, if a husband was a passenger in a car driven by his wife and was killed as the result of the combined negligence of the wife and a third person. If the dependant was the sole cause of the death, he should be able to recover nothing. The negligence of one dependant will not affect the claim of another, however. Consequently, in the example given above, a child who was also a passenger in the car would be able to recover in full for the death.[1]

Apportionment.—The court must apportion the damages amongst the claimants if there are more than one.[2] The normal practice today is for the court first to assess the total sum to be awarded and then to apportion it rather than to assess each dependant's claim and then to aggregate these amounts.[3] This simplifies procedure and rests upon the assumption that apportionment is of only minor importance because the damages will be used to maintain the family however they are apportioned; hence if the dependants are the widow and children of the deceased, the bulk of the damages will be given to the widow as she can be expected to use them to maintain her children.[4] But this is not an invariable rule and the court will make a genuine apportionment if failure to do so might prejudice the claimant. In *Moore* v. *Babcock and Wilcox, Ltd.*[5] the deceased left two dependants, his widow and a daughter. The widow died before the action came to trial. Had the bulk of the sum payable in respect of loss before the widow's death been paid to her estate, it would have received nothing because the sum was less than that awarded for loss of the deceased's expectation of life which had to be brought into account. CHAPMAN, J., therefore made a genuine apportionment and gave five-sevenths to the widow and two-sevenths to the daughter.

3. THE CARRIAGE BY RAILWAY ACT 1972

The Carriage by Railway Act 1972 was passed to give effect to the Additional Convention to the International Convention concerning the Carriage of Passengers and Luggage by Rail to which the United Kingdom is a party. Under the Convention (which is now in force and is set out in the Schedule to the Act)[6] a railway is liable for damage resulting from death or personal injury to a passenger caused by an accident arising out of the operation of the railway whilst the passenger is in, entering, or alighting from a train. It is not liable if the accident was due to circumstances not connected with the operation of the railway or to a third person's act provided that, in each case, the railway was not negligent. Liability is also reduced or extinguished by the passenger's own contributory negligence or wrongful act. The railway is vicariously liable for the acts of its servants unless they are rendering services at the request of a passenger which the railway is under no obligation to perform, and any term in the contract of carriage exempting it

---

[1] *Dodds* v. *Dodds*, [1978] Q.B. 543; [1978] 2 All E.R. 539.
[2] Fatal Accidents Act 1976, s. 3 (1).
[3] See *Jeffrey* v. *Kent County Council*, [1958] 3 All E.R. 155, 157.
[4] See the Report of the Committee on Funds in Court, 1959, Cmnd. 818, para. 15.
[5] [1966] 3 All E.R. 882.
[6] Minor amendments have been made by the Carriage by Railway (Revision of Conventions) Order, S.I. 1974 No. 1250.

from liability or limiting the amount of compensation recoverable is void.[1] The Act applies to carriage by rail in this country and to international journeys; in either case an action can be brought only against the responsible railway and in the country in which the accident occurred.[2] Certain obligatory procedural steps must be taken.[3]

In the case of a fatal accident persons "towards whom [the deceased] had, or would have had in the future, a legally enforceable duty to maintain [and who] are deprived of their support" may be indemnified for their loss.[4] Obviously this would include, for example, a divorced wife who had obtained an order for financial support against the deceased although she could not maintain an action under the Fatal Accidents Act.[5] But it is not clear under which law the duty to maintain must exist and whether the person in question must be able to enforce it himself. Suppose, for example, that under the law of state X an adult child is bound to support an infirm parent, could the latter maintain an action for the death of the child in this country under the Act if he were domiciled or normally resident in X or a national of that country? A further problem arises if the duty to maintain is enforceable only through a state agency. The Act gives no indication of the answers to these questions and an English court may feel compelled to apply English law as the *lex fori* in which case the parent could not sue under the Act. The matter is of some importance because no action may be brought under the Fatal Accidents Act for the benefit of anyone with a right of action under the Carriage by Railway Act (although an action may still be brought under the former Act by a person who had no legally enforceable right to be maintained by the deceased).[6] Furthermore, the limitation periods under the two Acts are different: actions under the Carriage by Railway Act must normally be brought within five years of the accident or three years of the death (whichever period is the shorter).[7]

4. THE CARRIAGE BY AIR ACT 1961

In the case of injury or death of a passenger on an aircraft, the application of the common law rules and the provisions of the Fatal Accidents Act are modified by the Carriage by Air Act 1961.[8] The carrier's liability is absolute unless he proves that he and his servants or agents have taken all necessary

---

[1] Carriage by Railway Act 1972, Sched., Part I, Arts. 2, 10 and 11.

[2] *Ibid.*, Arts. 14 and 15.

[3] *Ibid.*, Arts. 13 and 16.

[4] *Ibid.*, Art. 3. A claim will also lie for any necessary expenses following on the death, in particular the cost of transporting the body and burial or cremation. No deduction is to be made for the matters mentioned in s. 4 of the Fatal Accident Act 1976 (see *ante*, p. 146): this implies that other benefits must be brought into account as under the Fatal Accidents Act.

[5] The words "would have had in the future a duty to maintain" are apt to cover claims by a person unborn at the time of the death.

[6] *Ibid.*, s. 3 and Sched., Part I, Art. 3, para. 2.

[7] *Ibid.*, Art. 17. The period may be extended in certain circumstances. For the limitation period under the Fatal Accidents Act, see *ante*, p. 138, n. 3.

[8] This Act gives effect to the Warsaw Convention as amended at the Hague in 1955. Further amendments made in 1975 are incorporated in the Carriage by Air and Road Act 1979, which is not yet fully in force. The Convention applies only to contracts of international carriage by air, but s. 10 (1) of the Act and the Carriage by Air Act (Applications of Provisions) Order, S.I. 1967 No. 480, extend it to non-international carriage.

measures to avoid the damage or that it was impossible for them to take such measures;[1] but if the negligence of the person injured or killed contributed to the damage, the damages awarded are reduced in proportion to the passenger's share in the responsibility.[2]

The Carriage by Air Act imposes two limitations upon causes of action arising out of personal injuries. In the first place, the action must be brought within two years.[3] Secondly, the carrier's liability is limited to 250,000 francs unless the contract of carriage fixes a higher maximum sum.[4] Any provision in a contract of carriage relieving the carrier of liability or fixing a lower limit than 250,000 francs is void.[5] But there is no limit to the carrier's liability at all if the damage resulted from an act or omission of the carrier (or, provided that they were acting within the scope of their employment, of his servants or agents) done either with intent to cause damage or recklessly with knowledge that damage would probably result.[6]

E. CONTRACT

The Law until 1935.—At common law a married woman possessed no contractual capacity whatever and could therefore make a binding agreement neither with her husband nor with any other person.[7] This rule did not apply to a woman whose husband had abjured the realm or been transported,[8] but subject to this exception neither she nor her husband could sue or be sued on any contract made by her (except as his agent), even though she was living apart from him by agreement with separate maintenance[9] or (save by custom in the City of London)[10] engaging in trade on her own account.[11] Moreover the marriage automatically vested in the husband the benefit of all contracts

---

[1] Carriage by Air Act 1961, 1st Sched., Arts. 17 and 20.

[2] *Ibid.*, s. 6 and 1st Sched., Art. 21.

[3] *Ibid.*, 1st Sched., Art. 29.

[4] *Ibid.*, s. 4 and 1st Sched., Art. 22 (1). The sterling equivalent is £10,246: Carriage by Air (Sterling Equivalents) Order, S.I. 1979 No. 765. Under the 1979 Act the amount will be 16,600 (and eventually 100,000) special drawing rights as defined by the International Monetary Fund: *ibid.*, s. 4 (1) and Sched. 1, Art. 22.

[5] *Ibid.*, 1st Sched., Art. 23.

[6] *Ibid.*, 1st Sched., Art. 25. This provision will disappear when the 1979 Act comes into force. If an action is brought against the carrier's servant or agent, he has the same protection as the carrier if he was acting within the scope of his employment: Art. 25A; Carriage by Air (Supplementary Provisions) Act 1962.

[7] See further Morrison in *A Century of Family Law*, chap. 6. Even if she expressly contracted as a feme sole, she was not estopped from pleading her coverture for capacity cannot be created by estoppel: *Cannam* v. *Farmer* (1849), 3 Exch. 698. But an executed contract seems to have been valid for the purpose of transferring property: *Dalton* v. *Midland Counties Rly Co.* (1853), 13 C.B. 474.

[8] *Carrol* v. *Blencow* (1801), 4 Esp. 27. Otherwise she would have been wholly unable to provide herself with necessaries, as no tradesman would accept her husband's credit in such circumstances.

[9] *Lean* v. *Schutz* (1778), 2 W.Bl. 1195; *Marshall* v. *Rutton* (1800), 8 Term Rep. 545. An attempt to introduce a contrary rule in *Corbett* v. *Poelnitz* (1785), 1 Term Rep. 5, was apparently abortive. Whether the same rule applied if the husband was a foreigner residing abroad is doubtful: see *De Gaillon* v. *L'Aigle* (1798), 1 B. & P. 357; *Williamson* v. *Dawes* (1832), 9 Bing. 292; *Stretton* v. *Busnach* (1834), 1 Bing. N.C. 139.

[10] See *La Vie* v. *Phillips* (1765), 3 Burr. 1776.

[11] *Clayton* v. *Adams* (1796), 6 Term Rep. 604.

already made by the wife and both spouses were liable during coverture to be sued on them;[1] but if the husband died before the wife and a contract made by her before marriage was still executory, she and not her husband's personal representatives could sue and be sued on it. Any ante-nuptial contract made between the spouses themselves was automatically discharged by the marriage.

Equity did not take the same strict view of a married woman's incapacity as the common law. Hence if a wife had separate property in equity, she could effectively bind this by contract, although she could not render herself *personally* liable on any agreement.[2]

Nineteenth Century Legislation.—The first statutory inroad on this principle was made by the Matrimonial Causes Act 1857, which provided that so long as a decree of judicial separation was in force, a married woman should be considered as a feme sole for the purpose, *inter alia*, of the making and enforcement of contracts.[3] But the first exception of general application was made by the Married Women's Property Act of 1870, which made the first statutory extension to the equitable concept of separate property by enacting that a married woman's wages and earnings should be regarded as her separate property and giving her a power to maintain an action to recover them in her own name.[4] This Act also abolished the common law rule that a husband should be liable for his wife's ante-nuptial contracts,[5] a provision which worked extreme injustice on her creditors for, since her property continued to a very large extent to vest in her husband on marriage, there was frequently nothing on which they could levy execution. The absurdity of this position which gave the husband the best of both worlds[6] was recognised by the Legislature in the Married Women's Property Act (1870) Amendment Act 1874, which repealed the relevant part of the Act of 1870 but limited the husband's liability for his wife's ante-nuptial contracts to the extent of the value of her property which vested in him *jure mariti*.

The Married Women's Property Act of 1882 extended the principle of statutory separate property by enacting that all property belonging to a woman who married after 1882 should remain her separate property and that any property acquired by a wife after that date (whether she was married before or after the commencement of the Act) should similarly remain her separate property.[7] Furthermore this Act (as amended by the Married Women's Property Act 1893) gave her full contractual capacity and enacted that every contract entered into by her otherwise than as an agent should be deemed to be a contract with respect to her separate property and bind it. But it must be remembered that these Acts did no more than extend the existing

---

[1] Judgment was entered against both and consequently both became personally liable to satisfy it. Hence before the Debtors Act 1869 the wife could be taken in execution under a *ca. sa.* and held in prison till the debt was paid, although it was the practice to discharge her if she had no separate property: *Edwards* v. *Martyn* (1851), 17 Q.B. 693.

[2] See further Pollock, *Contracts*, 20th Ed., 557-561.

[3] S. 26. Later legislation has made this exception unnecessary.

[4] Ss. 1 and 11. See further *post*, p. 415.

[5] S. 12.

[6] And also had the effect of making it difficult for an engaged woman to obtain credit.

[7] See further *post*, p. 416.

principles of equity; hence a married woman's contract bound only her estate and the Act did not make her personally liable. Consequently she could still not be committed under a judgment summons[1] or be made bankrupt if she failed to satisfy a judgment debt.[2]

The Act of 1882 retained the principle of the Act of 1874 by enacting that a husband should be liable for his wife's ante-nuptial debts and contracts only to the extent of property belonging to her which he acquired or to which he became entitled.[3]

The Modern Law.—The modern position is to be found in the Law Reform (Married Women and Tortfeasors) Act of 1935. This Act abolished the concept of the separate estate and enabled a married woman to hold and dispose of property in all respects as if she were a feme sole.[4] As regards her power to contract, section 1 provides that she shall be capable of rendering herself and being rendered liable in respect of any contract, debt or obligation, and of suing and being sued in contract, and also that she shall be subject to the law relating to bankruptcy and the enforcement of judgments and orders as if she were a feme sole.

It is thus obvious that she now has full power to enter into a contract either with a stranger or with her own husband.[5] But the law relating to the contracts between spouses is subject to one important qualification. Whilst an agreement between them will clearly be enforceable if it represents a business arrangement, the courts are not prepared to interfere in the running of the home by giving legal effect to the sort of arrangements that spouses living together make every day in order to regularise their domestic affairs. The leading case in this field is still that of *Balfour* v. *Balfour*[6] where the Court of Appeal held that an agreement, under which the husband, who was about to go abroad, promised to pay the wife £30 a month in consideration of her not looking to him for further maintenance, was unenforceable because there was no intention to enter into legal relations. If the spouses are cohabiting when they enter into the agreement, there is a presumption that they do not intend to be legally bound.[7] Although public policy obviously demands that the courts should not be compelled to adjudicate on matters of domestic convenience, this principle can work injustice in the situation of which *Balfour* v. *Balfour* itself is typical, where the spouses subsequently

---

[1] *Scott* v. *Morley* (1887), 20 Q.B.D. 120, C.A. But she was still personally liable on her ante-nuptial contracts: *ibid.*, p. 125.

[2] *Ex parte Jones* (1879), 12 Ch.D. 484, C.A. She was, however, expressly made subject to the bankruptcy laws if she was carrying on a trade separately from her husband: Married Women's Property Act 1882, s. 1 (5). If her separate property was subject to a restraint on anticipation, only income due at the time the contract was made could be seized: Married Women's Property Act 1893, s. 1; *Wood* v. *Lewis*, [1914] 3 K.B. 73, C.A.

[3] S. 14.

[4] See further *post*, p. 417.

[5] She had power to contract with her husband under the Act of 1882: *Butler* v. *Butler* (1885), 14 Q.B.D. 831 (WILLS, J.); affirmed, 16 Q.B.D. 374, C.A.

[6] [1919] 2 K.B. 571, C.A. See also *Spellman* v. *Spellman*, [1961] 2 All E.R. 498, C.A. (agreement as to ownership of car unenforceable).

[7] This appears to be the view of the majority of the Court of Appeal in *Gould* v. *Gould*, [1970] 1 Q.B. 275; [1969] 3 All E.R. 728. An agreement made when the spouses "were not living together in amity" was held to be legally binding in *Re Windle*, [1975] 3 All E.R. 987.

separate and the wife takes no steps to obtain a maintenance order in reliance on her husband's promise to make her periodical payments. Consequently its application should be strictly limited. The presumption does not operate if the parties have separated or are at arm's length and about to separate: in these circumstances their intention becomes a question of fact to be inferred from all the evidence.[1] In most cases of this sort, where the agreement relates to financial arrangements, it will be almost impossible to conclude that they did not intend to be legally bound by the terms.

The Act of 1935 has entirely abolished the husband's liability for his wife's contracts entered into before marriage, since he now acquires no property out of which he can meet her debts.[2] The only problem that remains is whether marriage automatically discharges executory contracts already entered into between the spouses, since the old common law rule has never been expressly abolished. In *Butler* v. *Bulter*[3] WILLS, J., held that under the Act of 1882 the common law position still obtained. His interpretation of the relevant sections seems to be very narrow, and in any event the unambiguous wording of the 1935 Act suggests that today the spouses may mutually enforce any ante-nuptial contract notwithstanding the marriage.[4] Thus, if a man and woman enter into articles of partnership, it is submitted that the contract will subsist even though they later intermarry. But just as some agreements entered into by the spouses after marriage will be unenforceable because there is no intention to create legal relations, contracts of the same nature entered into beforehand may well be discharged on marriage by a tacit agreement because it cannot be the parties' intention that the obligations created by them should any longer be enforceable by the courts.

The Wife as her Husband's Agent.—At common law a married woman could always act as an agent since the latter does not require to have any contractual capacity. The fact that the agent happens to be the principal's spouse is clearly immaterial if the other party to the contract relies upon an express authorisation or a presumed authority arising from a business relationship or a ratification by the principal of the other's acts.[5] But the relationship of husband and wife presents two particular problems: the wife's presumed agency arising from cohabitation and a particular example of agency by holding out.[6]

Presumption of Agency from Cohabitation.—If a married woman is cohabiting with her husband, there is a presumption that she has his authority

---

[1] In *Merritt* v. *Merritt*, [1970] 2 All E.R. 760, C.A., LORD DENNING, M.R., was of the opinion that there was a presumption that they intend to be bound; WIDGERY, L.J., went no further than saying that there was no presumption that they did not intend to be bound; KARMINSKI, L.J., regarded the question simply as one of fact.

[2] S. 3.

[3] *Ante*. There was no appeal against this part of the decision and the Court of Appeal expressed no opinion on it.

[4] See Chitty, *Contracts*, 24th Ed., i, 244; Kahn-Freund, 15 M.L.R. 138-140. The Court of Appeal upheld the validity of such a contract in *Re Kendrew*, [1953] 1 All E.R. 551, C.A.; [1953] Ch. 291, but the point was not argued and the contract was made in contemplation of marriage.

[5] As in *West* v. *Wheeler* (1849), 2 Car. & Kir. 714.

[6] Until 1970 the wife also had an agency of necessity: see *post*, p. 484.

to pledge his credit for necessary goods and services which belong to those departments of the household which are normally under her control.[1] Coming within this category are such contracts as those for the purchase of food, clothing for the wife and children, domestic utensils and small articles of furniture, contracts for the hire of domestic servants, contracts for repairs and probably also contracts for the education of children.

This presumption was obviously of much greater importance in times when a married woman had no contractual capacity than it is today; for as she is the person who normally makes such contracts, tradesmen would have had no remedy at all had she not been acting as her husband's agent. As it was, they had a *prima facie* cause of action against him if the goods supplied were necessaries. Today it may still be necessary to rely on the presumption if the wife has no property and is therefore not worth suing. In other cases the question will be whether the tradesman can properly hold the husband or the wife liable for the price of the goods (or services) supplied, for the husband cannot be made liable if the tradesman has given credit exclusively to the wife and has treated her throughout as the principal.[2] If he has in fact supplied the goods on the husband's credit, he may still rely on the presumption that the wife had her husband's authority to pledge it, and if the husband rebuts this, the wife will then be personally liable on her implied warranty of authority to bind him.[3]

The burden of proving that the goods (or services) supplied were necessaries is on the plaintiff.[4] The term "necessaries" in this context bears the same meaning as it does in other branches of the law of contract, that is, goods (or services) which are suitable to the wife's condition of life and to her actual requirements at the time they are sold and delivered (or rendered).[5] Hence articles of mere luxury can never be necessaries. If the goods (or services) could be classed as necessary but are of an expensive variety, for example an expensive dress, they can be necessaries only if they are not extravagant when tested against the husband's ostensible standard of living and that which he permitted his wife to adopt;[6] and if they were extravagant

---

[1] *Debenham* v. *Mellon* (1880), 6 App. Cas. 24, H.L.; *Phillipson* v. *Hayter* (1870), L.R. 6 C.P. 38. *Cf. Gregory* v. *Parker* (1808), 1 Camp. 394 (acknowledgement by the wife of a debt incurred by her in purchasing goods deemed to be an acknowledgement by the husband's agent for the purpose of the Statute of Limitations). In *Debenham* v. *Mellon*, where the spouses lived in an hotel as manager and manageress, LORD SELBORNE, L.C., expressed doubts whether there was a sufficient matrimonial establishment to raise the presumption at all (at p. 33). *Sed quaere?* There is no presumption of authority after the spouses have separated and an actual authority must then be proved: *Wallis* v. *Biddick* (1873), 22 W.R. 76.

[2] *Miss Gray, Ltd.* v. *Cathcart* (1922), 38 T.L.R. 562; *Callot* v. *Nash* (1923), 39 T.L.R. 292.

[3] For an agent's warranty of authority, see Bowstead, *Agency*, 14th Ed., 95-99; Fridman, *Agency*, 4th Ed., 183 *et seq.*; Hanbury, *Agency*, 2nd Ed., 144 *et seq.* The fact that the goods are supplied on the order of a wife cohabiting with her husband raises no presumption of joint liability: *Morel Bros. & Co., Ltd.* v. *Westmorland*, [1904] A.C. 11, H.L. If a tradesman signs judgment against the wife, this amounts to an election to treat her as personally liable: *ibid.*; contrast *C. Christopher (Hove), Ltd.* v. *Williams*, [1936] 3 All E.R. 68, C.A. (obtaining liberty to sign judgment against her not such a conclusive election).

[4] *Callot* v. *Nash*, (*supra*).

[5] *Cf.* the Sale of Goods Act 1979, s. 3 (3), and see Cheshire and Fifoot, *Contract*, 9th Ed., 402-404.

[6] *Morgan* v. *Chetwynd* (1865), 4 F. & F. 451; *Phillipson* v. *Hayter* (1870), L.R. 6 C.P. 38; *Seymour* v. *Kingscote* (1922), 38 T.L.R. 586.

by this test[1] or if the wife is already adequately supplied with goods of this kind,[2] the action against the husband must fail.

As McCardie, J., emphasised in *Miss Gray, Ltd.* v. *Cathcart*,[3] this presumption is rebuttable. In addition to proving that the contract was not one for necessaries or of a sort which one could expect the husband to have given his wife authority to make, the husband may rebut it in any one of three different ways:

(1) By showing that he had already forbidden the plaintiff to give the wife credit.[4]

(2) By proving that he had forbidden his wife to pledge his credit. After considerable judicial controversy it was finally settled by the House of Lords in *Debenham* v. *Mellon*[5] that such a prohibition is effective even though the plaintiff was unaware of it, although of course in such a case the husband may be liable by holding out.[6]

(3) By showing that the wife had an adequate allowance out of which she could herself have paid for the goods or services.[7] In fact the payment of a *fixed* sum (whether it is adequate or not) will usually carry with it an implied prohibition against pledging the husband's credit further and thus defeat the plaintiff.[8] Whether the presumption is raised if the wife has an adequate income of her own, so that she has no need to rely on her husband for money to buy necessaries, is more doubtful; in the absence of an agreement between the spouses that the wife alone shall be liable for necessaries bought by herself (which will of course have the effect of an implied prohibition),[9] the question must be regarded as an open one, but it would probably be more in keeping with modern social opinion to hold that the wife was contracting as principal, at least if the goods were for her own use.[10]

Agency by Estoppel. —If a husband has in the past paid for goods supplied by his wife in such circumstances as to lead the tradesman with whom she has been dealing to conclude that he has given her an authority to buy goods on his credit, he will then be estopped from denying that she had any such authority and will consequently be liable for any further goods sold to her by

---

[1] *Miss Gray, Ltd.* v. *Cathcart*, (*infra*).

[2] *Reneaux* v. *Teakle* (1853), 8 Ex. 680; *Miss Gray, Ltd.* v. *Cathcart*, (*infra*).

[3] (1922), 38 T.L.R. 562.

[4] *Miss Gray, Ltd.* v. *Cathcart*, (*supra*).

[5] (1880), 6 App. Cas. 24, H.L., following *Jolly* v. *Rees* (1864), 15 C.B.N.S. 628.

[6] See *infra*.

[7] Even though the plaintiff was unaware of this: *Morel Bros. & Co., Ltd.* v. *Westmorland*, [1904] A.C. 11, H.L.; *Slater* v. *Parker* (1908), 24 T.L.R. 621.

[8] *Remmington* v. *Broadwood* (1902), 18 T.L.R. 270, C.A.; *Miss Gray, Ltd.* v. *Cathcart*, (*supra*). The question whether a mere agreement to pay a fixed allowance would have the same effect was left open in *Remmington* v. *Broadwood*. If the husband opens an account on which he permits the wife to draw, this will not amount to an implied prohibition against pledging his credit if the arrangement is merely for his own convenience: *Goodyear* v. *Part* (1897), 13 T.L.R. 395.

[9] See *Seymour* v. *Kingscote* (1922), 38 T.L.R. 586, at pp. 587-588.

[10] Her income was stated to be immaterial in *Callot* v. *Nash* (1923), 39 T.L.R. 292, 293, and *Seymour* v. *Kingscote*, (*supra*), at p. 587. In *Biberfeld* v. *Berens*, [1952] 2 Q.B. 770, 782; [1952] 2 All E.R. 237, 243, C.A., these dicta were criticised by Denning, L.J., but that case was concerned with the wife's agency of necessity (based on the husband's duty to maintain her) where the principle involved was essentially different.

that particular tradesman.[1] The importance of this rule lies in the fact that the husband's merely forbidding his wife to pledge his credit will not relieve him of liability for debts contracted by her if he has held her out in the past to have such an authority and does not inform those tradesmen with whom she has been dealing that it has been revoked.[2] Consequently his inserting a disclaimer in a newspaper will be insufficient for this purpose unless he can discharge the difficult burden of proving that the plaintiff in fact read the statement: the obvious step to take is to send a private notification to the tradesmen concerned.

What will amount to a sufficient holding out for this purpose must necessarily depend upon the facts of each case. Repeated paying of bills will doubtless create an estoppel, as may taking an active part in selecting the goods and directing the performance of the contract.[3] But a husband does not hold out his wife as having authority to pledge his credit merely by accompanying her when she shops,[4] or by giving her a cheque to pay her debts;[5] nor does his having paid for goods delivered to the matrimonial home in the past make him liable to pay for those subsequently ordered by his wife to be sent elsewhere.[6]

Presumably the general law of agency will apply in the case of contracts made by the wife after the husband's death or bankruptcy, so that in the former case his personal representatives will not be estopped from denying the wife's power to render the estate liable,[7] and in the latter the trustee in bankruptcy will be able to disclaim any contract made by the wife after the date of the receiving order or of any available act of bankruptcy[8] of which the tradesman had notice. Whilst the general rule is that an agency is terminated by the principal's insanity (whether or not the agent or person dealing with him was aware of this fact), it was held by the Court of Appeal in *Drew* v. *Nunn*[9] that a husband who had held out his wife as having his authority remained liable to a tradesman who had supplied her with goods in ignorance of his insanity.

---

[1] *Drew* v. *Nunn* (1879), 4 Q.B.D. 661, C.A.; *Filmer* v. *Lynn* (1835), 1 Har. & W. 59.

[2] See *Debenham* v. *Mellon* (1880), 6 App. Cas. 24, H.L., at pp. 34, 36-37. Similarly he may be estopped from denying her authority even after they have ceased to live together: *Wallis* v. *Biddick* (1873), 22 W.R. 76, 77.

[3] *Jetley* v. *Hill* (1884), Cab. & El. 239 (contract for the supply of furniture and for the decoration of the matrimonial home).

[4] *Seymour* v. *Kingscote* (1922), 38 T.L.R. 586, 588; *Callott* v. *Nash* (1923), 39 T.L.R. 292, 294.

[5] *Durrant* v. *Holdsworth* (1886), 2 T.L.R. 763.

[6] *Swan & Edgar, Ltd.* v. *Mathieson* (1910), 103 L.T. 832. Similarly a man may be liable by estoppel for the contracts of a woman with whom he has been living but to whom he is not married if he has held her out as having his authority: contrast *Ryan* v. *Sams* (1848), 12 Q.B. 460, with *Gomme* v. *Franklin* (1859), 1 F. & F. 465.

[7] *Cf. Blades* v. *Free* (1829), 9 B. & C. 167.

[8] *I.e.*, any act of brankruptcy committed within the three months preceding the presentation of the petition for the receiving order: see Bowstead, *Agency*, 14th Ed., 429-432.

[9] (1879), 4 Q.B.D. 661, C.A. Hanbury, *Agency*, 2nd Ed., 37, submits that this result, though practically convenient, is inconsistent; Powell, *Agency*, 2nd Ed., 403-404, doubts the correctness of the case but admits that sometimes it may work justice.

F. TORTS

The fiction of legal unity produced two separate rules in tort:

(1) If a tort was committed by or against a married woman, her husband had to be joined as a party to the action and failure to do so could be pleaded in abatement.

(2) No liability in tort could arise between spouses and no action in tort could be brought by either of them against the other.

We must now consider how far these rules still apply.

Torts committed against the Wife.—At common law the husband had to be joined as a party to any action brought by the wife in respect of any tort committed against her, whether before or after the marriage, on the general principle that he was entitled to reduce her choses in action into possession. But in one sense the right remained hers rather than his, for, if she died, the maxim *actio personalis moritur cum persona* applied to prevent him from continuing with the action, but if the husband died, the cause of action survived to the widow. The necessity of joining the husband as a co-plaintiff was abolished by the Married Women's Property Act of 1882 and she may now retain any damages recovered as her own property.[1]

Torts committed by the Wife.—At common law the position where the wife was the tortfeasor was very similar to that where she was the person injured. Her husband had to be joined as a co-defendant in any action brought in respect of a tort committed by her either before or after the marriage;[2] if she died before judgment, the action abated, but if the husband died or the marriage was dissolved, the action survived against her alone.[3] As in the case of contract, the Married Women's Property Acts of 1874 and 1882 limited the husband's liability for her ante-nuptial torts to the extent of her property which he acquired or became entitled to,[4] but, whilst the latter Act made the wife personally liable for all her torts, neither Act affected his liability for torts committed by her during coverture.[5] The retention of the common law rule may have been justified in 1882, because few married women then would have had any property on which a successful plaintiff could execute judgment, but the passage of years rendered absurd the anomaly that the husband could be sued for her torts although he acquired none of her property *jure mariti*.[6] This was eventually removed by the Law Reform (Married Women and Tortfeasors) Act 1935, which has abolished his

---

[1] See now the Law Reform (Married Women and Tortfeasors) Act 1935, s. 1 (c). A married woman was first given the power to maintain an action in her own name to recover her separate property by the Married Women's Property Act 1870, s. 11.

[2] But the husband was not liable for a tort committed by his wife *during coverture* where the cause of action was substantially contractual: *Liverpool Adelphi Loan Association* v. *Fairhurst* (1854), 9 Ex. 422; *Edwards* v. *Porter*, [1925] A.C. 1, H.L. (obtaining loans by fraud). *Cf.* the law relating to minors' liability in tort.

[3] *Capel* v. *Powell* (1864), 17 C.B.N.S. 743.

[4] See *ante*, pp. 150-151. His liability for ante-nuptial torts was not affected by the Act of 1870 at all.

[5] *Edwards* v. *Porter*, (*supra*).

[6] See the observations of SWIFT, J., in *Newton* v. *Hardy* (1933), 149 L.T. 165, 168 (an enticement case and therefore more absurd than most).

liability *as husband* for all her torts whenever committed.[1] But he may of course still be vicariously liable on other grounds, for example because he has authorised the commission of the particular act or because his wife was his servant acting in the course of her employment.

Actions between Spouses.—Until 1857 there was no exception at all to the common law rule that neither spouse could sue the other in tort. The Matrimonial Causes Act of that year permitted either to bring an action against the other if a judicial separation was in force,[2] and after the passing of the Married Women's Property Act of 1870 a wife could maintain an action to recover her separate property against anyone (including her own husband).[3] This principle—that normally the only action in tort that either spouse could bring against the other was by the wife for the protection and security of her own property—produced both anomalies and injustice. It was anomalous that a husband could not sue his wife for damage to his property, however maliciously caused, or that, even though the spouses were living at arm's length, one could slander the other with impunity. It was unjust that third parties' rights could be affected if the tortfeasor and his victim happened to be married to each other. For example, if the driver of a motor car negligently injured his wife, his insurance company was relieved from its duty to compensate her, for the husband was under no liability; for the same reason, if the wife was injured as the result of the combined negligence of her husband and a third person, the latter had to bear the whole loss and could claim no contribution from the other.[4]

This situation has been remedied by section 1 of the Law Reform (Husband and Wife) Act 1962,[5] which provides that each spouse shall have the same right of action against the other in tort as though they were not married. This applies equally to an action brought after the marriage has been dissolved (or presumably annulled) in respect of a tort committed during matrimony,[6] but in one respect the law here is different, for if the action is brought during the subsistence of the marriage, the court has a discretion to stay the action in two cases. First, it may do so if it appears that no substantial benefit would accrue to either party from the continuation of the proceedings. This is designed to prevent trivial actions brought in bitterness to air matrimonial grievances;[7] consequently it is not contemplated that the power would be exercised if the parties were no longer living together as an economic unit and the damage was real, or if the spouse was a purely

---

[1] S. 3.

[2] S. 26. The common law rule was reintroduced (probably unintentionally) by the Law Reform (Married Women and Tortfeasors) Act 1935, which repealed the relevant part of the Supreme Court of Judicature (Consolidation) Act 1925, s. 194, which had replaced the Matrimonial Causes Act 1857, s. 26.

[3] S. 11. Re-enacted in principle by the Married Women's Property Act 1882, s. 12, and the Law Reform (Married Women and Tortfeasors) Act 1935, s. 1.

[4] *Drinkwater* v. *Kimber*, [1952] 2 Q.B. 281; [1952] 1 All E.R. 701, C.A. But a master was vicariously liable if a servant in the course of employment tortiously injured his or her spouse: *Broom* v. *Morgan*, [1953] 1 Q.B. 597; [1953] 1 All E.R. 849, C.A.

[5] Passed as a result of the Ninth Report of the Law Reform Committee, 1961, Cmnd. 1268. See Stone, 24 M.L.R. 481; Kahn-Freund, 25 M.L.R. 695.

[6] S. 3 (3).

[7] See Cmnd. 1268, paras. 10-13.

nominal defendant and the real purpose of the action was to recover damages from a source outside the family. Such would be the case, for example, if the driver of a car wished to claim an indemnity from his insurance company.[1] Secondly, the court may stay the action if it relates to property and the questions in issue could more conveniently be disposed of by an application under section 17 of the Married Women's Property Act 1882. As we shall see,[2] the court has much more extensive powers under that section than it has in a common law action in tort. Consequently if the case raises complex questions of the spouses' rights in matrimonial assets or if a just solution is likely to demand an order for the sale or division of property, it is submitted that it should be dealt with under section 17.[3] On the other hand, if there is no dispute over title and damages or an injunction is the appropriate remedy, the case should proceed as an action in tort.

It must be remembered that, quite apart from the provisions of section 17 of the Married Women's Property Act, other proceedings are also open to a husband or wife in respect of a tortious act committed by the other. In practice these are most important in the case of molestation and interference with the right to occupy the matrimonial home and are considered more fully elsewhere in this book.[4]

Some Miscellaneous Rules.—Whatever the theoretical basis of the old law may have been, any peculiar privileges or liabilities that still exist can be justified only on the grounds of public policy and not by reference to the doctrine of unity. This is illustrated by two cases in libel. In *Wenman* v. *Ash*[5] it was held that the publication by the defendant to the plaintiff's spouse of a statement defamatory of the plaintiff is actionable. In *Wennhak* v. *Morgan*[6] on the other hand communication by one spouse to the other of a statement defamatory of a third person was held not to constitute a publication of that statement for the purpose of the law of libel and slander.[7] The second case reflects the principle that communications between spouses should be privileged; in *Wenman* v. *Ash*, however, there was no reason why the normal rule should not apply: indeed publication of a defamatory statement to the spouse of the person defamed may do him a greater injury than publication to a stranger.

---

[1] For presumably the court would look at all the facts and not stay the action merely because no substantial benefit would arise from the defendant's satisfying the judgment. But suppose the wife were to be injured by her husband and a third person and the latter were to claim contribution from the husband who was not insured. Could the husband then argue that an action between the spouses would have been stayed on the ground that no substantial benefit would accrue to either of them and that consequently he cannot be made to contribute because he is not a person "who would if sued have been liable for the damage" for the purpose of the Law Reform (Married Women and Tortfeasors) Act 1935, s. 6 (1)?

[2] *Post*, pp. 422-424.

[3] See Cmnd. 1268, para. 14. In an action for damages the court may exercise any power that it has under s. 17 or direct that any question should be dealt with under that section: Law Reform (Husband and Wife) Act 1962, s. 1 (2).

[4] See *ante*, pp. 122-128 (molestation), and *post*, p. 459 (occupation of the matrimonial home).

[5] (1853), 13 C.B. 836.

[6] (1888), 20 Q.B.D. 635.

[7] HUDDLESTON, B., and MANISTY, J., both agreed that publication was precluded by the doctrine of unity. MANISTY, J., alone rested his decision on the further ground of public policy.

This approach formed the basis of the judgment of OLIVER, J., in *Midland Bank Trustee Co., Ltd.* v. *Green (No. 3)*.[1] As the doctrine of unity apparently prevented the spouses from being prosecuted alone for a criminal conspiracy,[2] it was widely believed that they could not be sued alone for the tort of conspiracy (although of course it was accepted that they could both be sued for conspiring together with a third person). OLIVER, J., in holding that they can be sued together, refused to apply "the primitive and inaccurate maxim that spouses are one person"[3] and concluded that there was no overriding principle of public policy protecting them from liability for injury which, acting in concert, they inflicted on the defendant. It is to be hoped that the doctrine of unity has now been finally laid to rest in this branch of the law and that public policy will not be invoked to give spouses an immunity which they should not enjoy.

G. CRIMINAL LAW

The doctrine of unity has never applied generally in the criminal law so as to make a husband vicariously liable for his wife's crimes or to prevent either of them from being liable in most cases for a crime committed against the other. But it has made a number of periodical and inconsistent appearances which must be considered *seriatim*.

Marital Coercion.—There was a rule of common law that if a married woman committed certain offences in the presence of her husband, this raised a presumption (which was rebuttable)[4] that she had committed the crime under his coercion and consequently he and not she was *prima facie* liable to be convicted. Both the origin[5] and the extent of this rule are uncertain, but it seems to have applied to all misdemeanours[6] and most felonies, but not to grave felonies such as murder or to treason.[7] It had in any event become anomalous by the twentieth century and it was finally abolished by section 47 of the Criminal Justice Act of 1925 which replaced it by the following statutory defence:

> "On a charge against a wife for any offence other than treason or murder it shall be a good defence to prove that the offence was committed in the presence of, and under the coercion of, the husband."

It will be observed that this section effects two changes in the law. First, the burden of proof is now upon the wife to prove the coercion; secondly, it would seem to apply to all offences, both indictable and summary, except for the two named. It is not clear, however, what is meant by "coercion" in this

---

[1] [1979] Ch. 496; [1979] 2 All E.R. 193.

[2] See *post*, p. 160.

[3] At pp. 525 and 218, respectively.

[4] *R.* v. *Smith* (1916), 12 Cr. App. Rep. 42, C.C.A.; *R.* v. *Torpey* (1871), 12 Cox C.C. 45.

[5] Stephen saw in it à method of circumventing the rule that a woman could not plead benefit of clergy: *History of Criminal Law*, ii, 105. Turner thought it more likely that it orignated at a time when the wife was considered to have no will of her own and was entirely *sub virga viri sui*: Kenny, *Criminal Law*, 19th Ed., 69.

[6] *R.* v. *Torpey*, (*supra*). *R.* v. *Smith*, (*supra*), was also a case of a misdemeanour. For the contrary view, see *R.* v. *Cruse* (1838), 8 C. & P. 541.

[7] Kenny, *op. cit.*, 68.

context. It presumably means something more than a threat of physical violence, which is a defence available to anyone charged with a criminal offence except murder and, perhaps, treason. It will probably be sufficient for the wife to show that her will was overborne either by her husband's conduct (for example, a threat to keep her or their children short of money) or merely by his dominating personality.[1]

Impeding a Spouse's Arrest.—The generally accepted view is that at common law a wife could not become an accessory after the fact to her husband's felony or a principal to his treason by receiving him, because she was bound in law to do so.[2] The offence of being an accessory after the fact to a felony has now been abolished,[3] but by section 4 of the Criminal Law Act 1967 it is now an offence for any person, knowing or believing that another has committed an arrestable offence, to do any act with intent to impede his arrest or prosecution without lawful authority or reasonable excuse. It is arguable that the old law relating to accessories survives to give a wife a lawful authority for harbouring her husband or, alternatively, that either spouse must now have a reasonable excuse for harbouring the other by virtue of their marital relationship. But even under the old law the courts were apparently reluctant to permit the wife to raise the defence and they are probably even less likely to let either spouse do so under the new statutory provision.[4]

Conspiracy.—It is now provided by statute that a husband and wife may not be convicted of conspiring together, and it is generally believed that this was the position at common law.[5] But this does not prevent them from both being convicted of conspiring with a third person.

Theft.—Under the doctrine of unity husband and wife were deemed to have unity of possession so that neither could be guilty of stealing the other's property. But once the concept of separate property had been extended by the Married Women's Property Act of 1882, it is obvious that the fiction once more worked an anomaly. Accordingly the Act modified the rule by

---

[1] See further Williams, *Criminal Law: The General Part*, 2nd Ed., s. 249; Smith and Hogan, *Criminal Law*, 4th Ed., 207-209; Edwards, *Compulsion, Coercion and Criminal Responsibility*, 14 M.L.R. 297.

[2] But in *R.* v. *Holley*, [1963] 1 All E.R. 106, C.C.A., the Court of Criminal Appeal were of the opinion that the rule was merely a particular application of the rule of marital coercion and had therefore been abolished by the Criminal Justice Act, 1925, s. 47, (*supra*), in the absence of actual coercion. *Sed quaere?* In *R.* v. *Holley* the actual decision was that, if a wife assisted her husband and another together, she might be an accessory after the fact to the *latter's* felony. It was also formerly said that a wife could not be an accessory after the fact by concealing a felon jointly with her husband. Curiously enough, the husband was not bound to shelter his wife and might therefore by so doing become an accessory after the fact to her felony.

[3] By s. 1 of the Criminal Law Act 1967 which abolished the distinction between felonies and misdemeanours and enacted that the law relating to misdemeanours should apply to all indictable offences.

[4] See *R.* v. *Holley*, (*supra*). In any event the offence may be prosecuted only with the consent of the Director of Public Prosecutions: Criminal Law Act 1967, s. 4 (4).

[5] Criminal Law Act 1977, s. 2 (2) (a); *Mawji* v. *R.*, [1957] A.C. 126; [1957] 1 All E.R. 385, P.C. But see Williams, *Legal Unity of Husband and Wife*, 10 M.L.R. 20-24. Either spouse may be convicted of inciting the other to commit a crime.

providing, broadly speaking, that either could be guilty of stealing the other's property if they were not living together.[1] This effected a compromise between the rule of public policy which militates against criminal proceedings being instituted by one spouse against the other and the desirability of protecting interests in property by the sanctions of the criminal law.

These provisions have been repealed by the Theft Act 1968 which has produced a different sort of compromise. For the purposes of that Act and the Theft Act 1978 a husband and wife are to be regarded as separate persons and each can now be convicted of theft of the other's property, obtaining it by deception and so forth.[2] But neither the spouse nor a third person may institute proceedings against anyone for any offence of stealing or doing unlawful damage to property which at the time belongs to his or her spouse, or for any attempt, incitement or conspiracy to commit such an offence, without the consent of the Director of Public Prosecutions. There are two exceptions to this rule. The Director's consent is not required, first, if at the time of the offence the accused and his or her spouse were not bound to cohabit by virtue of a judicial decree or order[3] or, secondly if the accused is charged with committing the offence jointly with the spouse. It is not immediately obvious what sort of situation the second exception contemplates. In as much as it envisages one spouse stealing his or her own property, it would presumably apply, if say, the wife pawned property belonging to her and the spouses then jointly took it back without the pawnbroker's consent.[4]

Institution of Proceedings.—Save in the cases just noticed either spouse now has the same power to institute criminal proceedings against the other as though they were not married.[5]

H. NATIONALITY AND RIGHT OF ABODE IN THE UNITED KINGDOM

Nationality.—Strangely enough, the doctrine of unity had no application at common law with respect to nationality. A foreign woman did not acquire British nationality by marrying a British subject, and a woman who was a British subject did not lose her status by marrying a foreigner.[6] This rule was completely reversed by legislation during the nineteenth century,[7] but the

---

[1] Married Women's Property Act 1882, s. 12, later replaced by the Larceny Act 1916, s. 36.

[2] Theft Act 1968, s. 30 (1); Theft Act 1978, s. 5 (2). Either of them can also be guilty of the theft of property belonging to them both jointly.

[3] This includes an injunction restraining one spouse from molesting the other and debarring him from the matrimonial home: *Woodley* v. *Woodley*, [1978] Crim. L.R. 629.

[4] Theft Act 1968, s. 30 (4). The difficulty inherent in this interpretation of the proviso is that for the purpose of the Theft Act the property would be regarded as belonging to the pawnbroker. See further Smith, *Law of Theft*, 4th Ed., paras. 461-465. An offence of theft would include robbery. The sub-section does not prevent the arrest of the thief except by his or her spouse or on an information laid by the spouse.

[5] Theft Act 1968, s. 30 (2).

[6] Jones, *British Nationality*, 72; Parry, *British Nationality*, 36. But see Baty, *The Nationality of a Married Woman at Common Law*, 52 L.Q.R. 247.

[7] Aliens Act 1844, s. 16; Naturalization Act 1870, s. 10 (1).

swing back of the pendulum can be seen in a series of statutes passed between 1914 and 1933.[1]

The change in status of married women is now reflected in the provisions of the British Nationality Act of 1948, which is peculiar in that it shows a break from the nineteenth century position by reverting to the original common law. Since 1949 a woman who is not already a citizen of the United Kingdom and Colonies does not become such a citizen by marrying a man who possesses citizenship, nor does a woman who is a citizen of the United Kingdom and Colonies lose her citizenship by marrying an alien.[2] But a woman who marries a citizen of the United Kingdom and Colonies is entitled to acquire such citizenship by registration,[3] and a woman who becomes a subject of her husband's state on marriage may, like anyone else possessing dual nationality, divest herself of citizenship of the United Kingdom and Colonies by a declaration of renunciation.[4]

Right of Abode in the United Kingdom.[5]—The problems presented by the large-scale immigration of Commonwealth citizens into this country during the past 25 years has led to legislation restricting the right of abode in the United Kingdom, and citizens of the United Kingdom and Colonies no longer have an automatic right to enter and stay in this country. The new law is to be found in the Immigration Act 1971. It is too complex to be set out in detail here but, broadly speaking, a person will be patrial (that is, he or she will have a right of abode and be free to enter, live in, and leave the United Kingdom without let or hindrance) only if he (or she) satisfies one of the following conditions:[6]

---

[1] Status of Aliens Act 1914, s. 10; British Nationality and Status of Aliens Act 1918, s. 2 (5); British Nationality and Status of Aliens Act 1933, s. 1 (1). These Acts provided that a British woman marrying a foreigner should not lose her British nationality if she did not acquire that of her husband, that the status of the wife of a man who acquired or lost British nationality after the marriage should not automatically follow that of her husband but that she should be given the option of doing likewise, and that a woman who was a British subject at birth should be entitled to resume British nationality if the state of which her husband was a subject was at war with this country.

[2] Whilst the Act preserved the British nationality of women who had acquired it by marriage before 1949, it revested it in those who had lost it by marriage to an alien under the old law: ss. 12 (5) and 14.

[3] Unless she has formerly renounced or been deprived of citizenship, in which case the registration requires the approval of the Home Secretary: s. 6 (2), (3). Registration may also be refused on the ground of public policy: *R.* v. *Secretary of State for the Home Department, ex parte Puttick*, [1981] 1 All E.R. 776 (registration properly refused when the marriage had been contracted by committing a criminal offence: for the facts, see further *post*, p. 275). Similar provisions apply to a woman who marries a British subject without citizenship: British Nationality Act 1965, ss. 1-3. For a further case where a woman may rely on her husband's "qualifying connection" with the United Kingdom and Colonies or a protected state, see the British Nationality Act 1964, s. 1.

[4] S. 19. The Home Secretary may withhold the registration of a declaration during wartime.

[5] See Grant and Constable, 125 New L.J. 897, 917.

[6] Immigration Act 1971, ss. 1 (1) and 2. "Parent" includes the mother (and therefore, by implication, not the father) of an illegitimate child. "Registration" does not include registration by virtue of marriage to a citizen of the United Kingdom and Colonies unless the marriage took place before the passing of the Act (28th October 1971). There are special provisions relating to entry from the Channel Islands, the Isle of Man and the Republic of Ireland: see ss. 1 (3) and 9 and Sched. 4.

(a) If he is a citizen of the United Kingdom and Colonies
  (i) By virtue of his birth, adoption, naturalisation or registration in the United Kingdom, the Channel Islands or the Isle of Man; *or*
  (ii) Who was born to or adopted by a parent who was at the time of the birth or adoption a citizen of the United Kingdom and Colonies either by virtue of the conditions set out above or because he was himself born to or adopted by a parent who satisfied these conditions; *or*
  (iii) Who has at any time been ordinarily resident in the United Kingdom without being subject to any restriction under the immigration laws on the period for which he might remain here and had at that time (and while a citizen of the United Kingdom and Colonies) been ordinarily resident here for at least five years.
(b) If he is a Commonwealth citizen born to or legally adopted by a parent who at the time of the birth or adoption was a citizen of the United Kingdom and Colonies by birth.

Citizens of the Republic of Ireland are generally exempt from immigration control and certain restrictions do not apply to E.E.C. nationals, but except for them, women who can claim to be patrial by virtue of their marriage, and one or two other special cases,[1] all other persons (whether they be citizens of the United Kingdom and Colonies, other Commonwealth citizens, or foreign nationals) may enter this country and stay here only if they are permitted to do so under the Immigration Rules made by the Home Secretary.[2] Permission may be unconditional or, if the individual is here for a particular purpose (for example, as a student or to take up employment), it may be given for a limited period of time and made subject to other conditions such as registration with the police.[3]

The question of the right of abode is of particular importance in family law because it may be valueless to an individual if his family has no right to live here too. The only person on whom the Act itself confers any rights by virtue of the fact that another member of the family is patrial is a wife. A woman will have a right of abode if she is a Commonwealth citizen and is, or at any time has been, the wife of a man who satisfies the conditions set out in the last paragraph.[4] It will be seen that this provision reflects the old principle that marriage may extend to a wife a right possessed by a husband but will not confer on him any right possessed by her. Husbands and other members of the family of a person admitted into the United Kingdom or already resident here may enter the country and stay here only so long as they satisfy the conditions set out in the Immigration Rules.

If a man has been given permission to live in this country for a limited period (for example, to work or study here), his wife and children under the age of 18 will be given permission to stay for the same period.[5] If he is settled in the United Kingdom (that is, ordinarily resident here without having

---

[1] See *ibid.*, ss. 8 and 9 and Sched. 4.
[2] The current rules are to be found in H.C. 394 (1979-1980). See Hartley, 43 M.L.R. 440.
[3] Immigration Act 1971, ss. 1 (2), (4), (5) and 3.
[4] *Ibid.*, s. 2 (1); *R.* v. *Secretary of State for the Home Department, ex parte Phansopkar,* [1976] Q.B. 606; [1975] 3 All E.R. 497, C.A. This presumably includes both or all wives if the marriage is polygamous. Even if she is not a citizen of the United Kingdom and Colonies, her marriage will entitle her to acquire citizenship (and thus patriality) by registration.
[5] H.C. 394 (1979-1980), paras. 25 and 40. They will not be permitted to enter this country unless they have previously obtained entry clearance.

entered or remained in breach of the immigration laws and without any restriction on the period for which he may remain) or is admitted for settlement, his wife will also be admitted.[1] The position of the husband of a woman in this position is much more complex. After considerable pressure the rules were altered in 1974 to give husbands the same rights of entry as wives, but in 1980 these were considerably restricted because it was believed that some men (particularly from India) were obtaining entry into this country by the device of the arranged marriage to women whom they had never seen. Now a husband will be refused entry clearance by the British authorities in the country from which he is emigrating (without which he cannot enter the United Kingdom at all) if the marriage was entered into primarily to secure admission to this country, or if one spouse no longer has any intention of living permanently with the other, or if the spouses have never met. In addition, he will be given clearance only if his wife is a citizen of the United Kingdom and Colonies and either she or one of her parents was born in this country. If he is given entry clearance, he will be admitted for 12 months in the first instance; at the end of this period he will be given indefinite leave to remain subject to certain restrictions relating *inter alia* to the *bona fides* and continuation of the marriage.[2]

Unmarried children under the age of 18 will be admitted (a) if both parents are settled here or are admitted for settlement, (b) if one parent only is settled or admitted for settlement and either he (or she) has had sole responsibility for the child's upbringing or the other parent is dead, or (c) if the Home Secretary has authorised admission because the circumstances make exclusion undesirable.[3] Special consideration may be given to fully dependent unmarried daughters between the ages of 18 and 21 if they formed part of the family unit overseas and have no relatives to turn to in their own country. Subject to certain other restrictions, dependent parents and grandparents over the age of 65 and, in exceptional compassionate circumstances, other children, parents, grandparents, brothers, sisters, uncles and aunts may be allowed to enter if the person to whom they stand in that relationship is settled here.[4]

A woman intending to marry a man settled here will be admitted for three months in the first instance; if the marriage takes place within that period, the limitation will be removed. A man intending to marry a woman settled here will be given entry clearance if *mutatis mutandis* he satisfies the same conditions as a husband seeking entry. He too will be admitted for three months in the first instance; if the marriage takes place within this period,

---

[1] *Ibid.*, para. 44. A woman living in permanent association with a man may also be admitted subject to certain restrictions: para. 45. (There is no comparable rule relating to men living in permanent association with women who are settled.) Dependants (in whatever category they fall) will be admitted only if the settled person is able and willing to maintain and accommodate them: para. 42.

[2] *Ibid.*, paras. 50-51 and 116-117.

[3] *E.g.*, because the other spouse is physically or mentally incapable of looking after the child. "Children" includes illegitimate children, stepchildren (provided that the natural parent is dead) and adopted children (provided that the adoption is not one of convenience to facilitate the child's admission into the United Kingdom).

[4] *Ibid.*, paras. 46-49. If E.E.C. nationals enter the country to take or seek employment, to set up business or to work as self-employed persons, leave to enter will be given to their spouses, their children under the age of 21 (or over that age if they are dependent), and their dependent parents, grandparents and grandchildren: *ibid.*, paras. 62-63.

leave will be extended for 12 months and finally all restrictions will be removed if he satisfies the conditions laid down with respect to other husbands.[1]

If a non-patrial is deported, his or her minor children and, if the person deported is a man, his wife and her minor children are liable to be deported too.[2] In deciding whether to order the deportation of members of the family, the Home Secretary will take into account such matters as their length of residence in this country, their ties with the United Kingdom, and whether they can be maintained without recourse to public funds. The Home Secretary will not normally order the deportation of a wife and her children living with her if she is settled here herself or if she has been living apart from her husband, or the deportation of a child if he is nearly 18, if he has left home and is financially independent, or if he is married.

British Nationality Bill.—The law relating to citizenship will be fundamentally changed if the provisions of the British Nationality Bill, introduced in 1981, receive the royal assent.[3] Its main purpose is to replace citizenship of the United Kingdom and Colonies by three separate concepts: British citizenship, citizenship of British Dependent Territories and British Overseas citizenship. The significance of this from the point of view of family law is that only those possessing British citizenship will have the right of abode and the concept of patriality will disappear.

Virtually all existing citizens of the United Kingdom and Colonies with the right of abode will become British citizens. Subject to transitional provisions, a person born in the United Kingdom in the future will become a British citizen only if one of his parents[4] is a British citizen or is settled in the United Kingdom, that is ordinarily resident here without any restriction under the immigration laws on the period of time for which he may remain. (Under pressure the Government has accepted an amendment under which other children born here will be able to be registered as British citizens after ten years' residence.) A woman marrying a British citizen will no longer be entitled to be registered as one herself, but the wife or husband of a British citizen will be able to apply for naturalisation after three years' residence in this country. This will mean, of course, that acquisition of citizenship will become a matter of discretion, not right, and the applicant will have to satisfy the Home Office that she (or he) is of good character and has a sufficient knowledge of English or Welsh.

No further change is contemplated in the conditions in the Immigration Rules permitting persons who are not British citizens to enter this country and remain here.

---

[1] *Ibid.*, paras. 52-55 and 114-117. Similar provisions apply to persons admitted in a temporary capacity who then marry a man or woman settled here.

[2] Immigration Act 1971, ss. 3 (5) and 5.

[3] Implementing the proposals set out in the White Paper on British Nationality Law, Cmnd. 7987. It should not be assumed that all these provisions will receive the royal assent in their present form as they have been subjected to heavy criticism both in and out of Parliament. For further proposals, see *post*, p. 334.

[4] An illegitimate child will be a British citizen only if his mother satisfies these conditions. A child adopted by a British citizen will automatically acquire British citizenship.

Part I

Husband and Wife

(2) BREAKDOWN OF MARRIAGE

SUMMARY OF CONTENTS

The breakdown of marriage is not synonymous with divorce. A marriage can be said to have broken down when the spouses stop living with each other as husband and wife. This will occur if one deserts the other, if they separate by agreement, if one of them obtains a judicial separation releasing him or her from the duty of cohabiting with the other, or if the marriage is brought to an end by a decree of divorce. The significance of this order is that, with each step, the chance of reconciliation becomes more remote.[1]

Desertion will be dealt with in Chapter 7 as one of the facts on which a spouse may petition for divorce. The other matters—separation agreements, judicial separation and the dissolution of marriage—will form the subject matter of the three chapters in this second half of Part 1.

---

1 "The divorce rate does not measure the number of marriages which actually break down but only the number of factually separated spouses who acquire licences to marry again": Finer Report, Cmnd. 5629, para. 3.35. On the subject of breakdown of marriage generally, see *ibid.*, paras. 3.26 *et seq*.

Chapter 5

Separation Agreements

A. INTRODUCTORY

The essence of a separation agreement is that the husband and wife agree to live separate and apart—*i.e.*, each releases the other from his or her duty to cohabit. It is usual for a separation agreement to contain provisions for the maintenance of the wife and children, but this of course is not always true; conversely, it is possible for an agreement to be framed placing the husband under a duty to maintain his wife whilst they are living separately without, however, binding the spouses to live apart.[1] Basically, of course, all such agreements are governed by the general law of contract.

Form.—Provided that each party gives consideration, an agreement will be perfectly valid as a parol contract and consequently may be entered into orally or even by conduct. This is almost invariably the case in the simplest type of separation agreement, and each party gives consideration by forgoing his or her right to the other's consortium.[2] But clearly the agreement will be much more complicated if the spouses wish to agree upon such matters as the maintenance of the wife and children, the custody of the children, and the division and use of the property constituting the matrimonial home. In such a case it will usually be reduced into writing and, by tradition, frequently will be embodied in a deed. Where a deed is intended to be executed, the parties usually enter into a binding preliminary agreement known as "articles of separation".

Owing to a married woman's inability to contract with her husband at common law, it was formerly necessary to join trustees as parties to a separation deed to enter into covenants on the wife's behalf and thus provide consideration for the husband's covenants. The Married Women's Property Act of 1882, by giving the wife full contractual capacity, has made trustees for this purpose redundant;[3] but they are still necessary where it is proposed that the husband should secure the wife's maintenance by settling property for this purpose.

Legality of Separation Agreements.—Up till the middle of the last century there was considerable doubt whether any separation agreement was valid, on the ground that such agreements tended to undermine the social structure

---

[1] So that one of them may be in desertion: see *post*, p. 212, n. 1. If the parties are cohabiting and the maintenance agreement is no more than a domestic arrangement, it will usually not be enforceable: see *ante*, p. 151.

[2] *Cf. Re Weston*, [1900] 2 Ch. 164. See Lush, *Husband and Wife,* 4th Ed., 465-469.

[3] *McGregor* v. *McGregor* (1888), 21 Q.B.D. 424, C.A.; *Sweet* v. *Sweet*, [1895] 1 Q.B. 12.

170

of the state and were therefore contrary to public policy. By adopting this attitude the courts were merely closing their eyes to common practice and refusing to accept the fact that, when a marriage has clearly broken down and there is virtually no immediate possibility of the parties' continuing to live together in amity, it is better for all concerned and for society as a whole that they should be able to settle their differences out of court than that their matrimonial quarrels should be dragged into the open. This view eventually prevailed, and in 1848 the House of Lords held in *Wilson* v. *Wilson*[1] that there was nothing *per se* illegal in an agreement for an *immediate* separation.

In *Wilson* v. *Wilson* the House of Lords was concerned only with the position where the marriage has already broken down. But where spouses who are living together enter into an agreement regulating their legal rights in case they should separate in the future, the agreement is still contrary to public policy and void.[2] To this rule, however, there is one exception. If spouses, who are living apart, negotiate a reconciliation which contains provisions regulating their position if their attempt to live together again should prove to be unsuccessful, it is obvious that they are more likely to resume cohabitation than they would be if their future rights were left entirely in the air. Consequently, since such an agreement tends to promote the spouses' cohabiting rather than the reverse, it was held in *Re Meyrick's Settlement*[3] that it would not be void, even though it envisaged a separation in the future, and consequently would be legally enforceable if they in fact did separate again.

A separation agreement may of course be illegal for other reasons, for example if the parties' purpose is to promote the commission of adultery.[4]

Void and Voidable Agreements.—A separation agreement may be void or voidable for the same reason as any other contract. Thus it may be void on the grounds of mistake. A particular application of this rule to separation agreements is to be seen in *Galloway* v. *Galloway*,[5] where it was held that a separation deed entered into on the assumption that the parties were validly married, when in fact the marriage was (unknown to either party) bigamous, was itself void for mistake. Similarly, the agreement may be voidable for fraudulent[6] or innocent misrepresentation or for undue influence.[7]

---

[1] (1848), 1 H.L Cas. 538, H.L.

[2] *Hindley* v. *Westmeath* (1827), 6 B. & C. 200; *Westmeath* v.*Westmeath* (1830), 1 Dow & Cl. 519, H.L; distinguished in *Wilson* v. *Wilson*, (*supra*), at p. 573. *A fortiori* an ante-nuptial agreement that the parties will not cohabit after marriage is void: *Brodie* v. *Brodie*, [1917] P. 271.

[3] [1921] 1 Ch. 311; following *MacMahon* v. *MacMahon*, [1913] 1 I.R. 428. Followed in *Lurie* v. *Lurie*, [1938] 3 All E.R. 156.

[4] *Fearon* v. *Aylesford* (1884), 14 Q.B.D. 792, 808, C.A.

[5] (1914), 30 T.L.R. 531; followed in *Law* v. *Harragin* (1917), 33 T.L.R. 381. In *Butcher* v. *Vale* (1819), 8 T.L.R. 93, where the parties were aware of the fact that the wife's first husband might still be alive and that their own marriage might be void but "took their chance", it was held that the agreement was valid.

[6] *E.g.*, if one party induces the other to enter into the contract without having any intention of fulfilling the terms himself: *Crabb* v. *Crabb* (1868), L.R. 1 P. & D. 601, 604 (*per* LORD PENZANCE).

[7] *Cf. post,* p. 212. In *Evans* v. *Carrington* (1860), 2 De G. F. & J. 481, 491-492, LORD CAMPBELL, L.C., suggested that the wife's undisclosed adultery might be a ground for avoiding a separation agreement because the husband's promise to pay maintenance would be given for no consideration as he would be under no obligation to maintain her. *Sed quaere*? It does not seem to be a contract *uberrimae fidei: cf. Wales* v. *Wadham*, [1977] 2 All E.R. 125.

B. COMMON TERMS IN AGREEMENTS

As has already been stated, separation agreements may vary from simple oral agreements to live apart to somewhat complex deeds. It is therefore impossible to intimate what a standard form of agreement will contain; but the following are some of the terms which will appear in many agreements.

Agreement to live apart.—This is the basic term in all separation agreements by which each spouse is released from the duty of cohabiting with the other.

Non-molestation Clause.—It is frequently a term that neither spouse will "molest, annoy or interfere with the other". In order to amount to molestation, there must be some act done by the spouse or on his or her authority; the nature of the act was thus described by BRETT, M.R., in *Fearon* v. *Aylesford*[1] (where it was alleged that the wife had failed to observe a covenant not to molest her husband):

> "I am of the opinion that the act done by the wife or by her authority must be an act which is done with intent to annoy, and does in fact annoy; or which is in fact an annoyance; or, to put the latter proposition into another shape, that it must be an act done by her with a knowledge that what she is so doing must of itself without more annoy her husband, or annoy a husband with ordinary and reasonable feeling."

In *Fearon* v. *Aylesford* the spouses entered into a separation agreement in which the wife covenanted not to molest her husband. She later lived in adultery with the Marquis of Blandford and as a result of this adulterous intercourse a child was born which Lord Aylesford alleged was being held out as his son.[2] It was held that the wife's committing adultery could not amount to a molestation of her husband, for that act would be committed, not to annoy him, but to gratify the wife or her paramour; consequently the birth of the child, which was the natural result of the adultery, could no more amount to a molestation than the act which had caused it. On the other hand her holding the child out as the legitimate child of her husband would clearly amount to molestation by this definition; but the action failed on this head too, as there was no evidence that the statements to this effect, which had been made by the wife's servant, had ever been authorised by the wife.

Similarly a spouse's subsequently petitioning for divorce will not amount to a breach of a non-molestation clause if he does so to secure his own release from the marriage, although it clearly will amount to molestation if his purpose is purely to annoy the respondent.[3]

Maintenance of Wife.—The usual form of maintenance clause provides that the husband shall make periodical payments to the wife or to an agent on

---

[1] (1884), 14 Q.B.D. 792, 801-802, C.A. See also *Besant* v. *Wood* (1879), 12 Ch.D. 605, and *cf. Vaughan* v. *Vaughan*, [1973] 3 All E.R. 449, C.A.

[2] See further the *Aylesford Peerage Case* (1885), 11 App. Cas. 1, H.L.

[3] *Hunt* v. *Hunt*, [1897] 2 Q.B. 547, C.A. Similarly if he or she petitions for judicial separation: *Thomas* v. *Everard* (1861), 6 H. & N. 448; or commences proceedings for separation or maintenance in a magistrates' court: *Welch* v. *Welch* (1916), 85 L.J.P. 188, C.A.

her behalf. Where it is desired to secure payment, capital will normally be transferred to trustees on trust to pay the wife's maintenance out of the income.

Great care should be taken to define precisely the extent of the husband's liability, for a number of cases have held that the husband's covenant may be construed as independent of the agreement to separate *stricto sensu*. If his obligation is coterminous with the spouses' living apart by consent, then it will clearly cease if they resume cohabitation, live apart under a court order, or if the marriage is annulled, dissolved or terminated by the husband's death.[1] But if the covenant is independent in the sense that it can be construed as a separate undertaking to pay the wife, the obligation may continue notwithstanding the occurrence of any of these events. Little help can be obtained from the cases, for each must depend upon the interpretation of the agreement in question; but it has been held that the liability may continue after the parties have resumed cohabitation[2], after divorce[3] and after a decree of nullity where the marriage was voidable.[4] The modern tendency is to regard the provision as one to last for the wife's life,[5] and it has been held that such a covenant may be enforced against the husband's executors if he predeceases her.[6]

Sums which were perfectly reasonable when they were agreed may become wholly unreasonable in the light of subsequent events, for example a change in the financial position of one of the spouses. If one of them refused to renegotiate the terms, at common law the other was saddled with the original agreement and had no legal remedy. To overcome this difficulty he or she now has a power in certain circumstances to apply to the court to alter the agreement. This provision will be considered fully later in the general context of financial provision for the spouses.[7]

Dum Casta **Clause.**—The fact that the husband may remain liable on his covenant to maintain the wife whatever may happen in the future means that it is prudent to limit his obligation "so long as the wife shall lead a chaste life",[8] so that he will no longer remain under any contractual duty to maintain her should she subsequently commit adultery. Although a *dum casta* clause is usually inserted in a formal separation agreement—in fact precisely because it is usually inserted—the Court of Appeal held in *Fearon* v.

---

[1] As in *Covell* v. *Sweetland*, [1968] 2 All E.R. 1016 (divorce). If this is the true construction of the agreement, the husband's obligation will never arise if the parties never separate at all: *Bindley* v. *Mulloney* (1869), L.R. 7 Eq. 343.

[2] *Negus* v. *Forster* (1882), 46 L.T. 675, C.A.

[3] *May* v. *May*, [1929] 2 K.B. 386, C.A.; *Charlesworth* v. *Holt* (1873), L.R. 9 Exch. 38.

[4] *Adams* v. *Adams*, [1941] 1 K.B. 536; [1941] 1 All E.R. 334, C.A.; *Fowke* v. *Fowke*, [1938] Ch. 774. But this is not necessarily so if the decree is for the annulment of a *void* marriage: see *ante*, p. 171.

[5] *Re Lidington*, [1940] Ch. 927, 934; [1940] 3 All E.R. 600, 603.

[6] *Kirk* v. *Eustace*, [1937] A.C. 491; [1937] 2 All E.R. 715, H.L.; *cf. Re Lidington*, (*supra*). Contrast *Langstone* v. *Hayes*, [1946] K.B. 109; [1946] 1 All E.R. 114, C.A.

[7] See *post*, pp. 492-495.

[8] "*Dum casta vixerit.*"

Ayslesford[1] that such a clause will not be implied if it is not expressly included.[2]

Wife's Indemnity and Covenant not to sue for Maintenance.—If the agreement is in writing, it will usually be a "maintenance agreement" for the purpose of section 34 of the Matrimonial Causes Act 1973 and any clause purporting to restrict either party's right to apply to any court for an order containing financial arrangements will be void.[3] This, however, does not avoid any other financial arrangements contained in the agreement. Some agreements still include a covenant by the wife to indemnify her husband against all debts which she may contract after the separation. Such a clause now seems to have little effect unless the husband is bound by a contract made by her because he is estopped from denying that she has his authority to pledge his credit.[4]

Agreement not to bring Matrimonial Proceedings.—The spouses sometimes agree that neither of them shall base a petition for divorce (or other matrimonial proceedings) on conduct that has occurred in the past. This is frequently referred to as a *Rose* v. *Rose* clause (from the name of the leading case on this subject in the Court of Appeal).[5] Thus if they agree that the wife shall not rely on the husband's previous adultery in any future matrimonial proceedings between them, she could not allege its commission in any petition for divorce or judicial separation or in any proceedings in a magistrates' court.

A *Rose* v. *Rose* clause will not be implied into a separation agreement and must be expressly included.[6] Furthermore, it will always be strictly construed; consequently a promise not to base a petition for judicial separation upon past offences will not prevent the petitioner's seeking a divorce in reliance upon them.[7] Nor will a party be bound by the clause if the agreement as a whole falls, for example if it is voidable or illegal or if it is discharged.[8]

Custody and Maintenance of Children.—At common law any agreement by which a parent divested himself of the custody of his children was considered to be contrary to public policy and therefore void. So far as separation agreements are concerned, however, the position is now governed by section 1 (2) of the Guardianship Act 1973, which enacts that a spouse may give up in whole or in part his or her rights and authority in relation to the

[1] (1884), 14 Q.B.D. 792, C.A. For the facts, see *ante*, p. 172.

[2] But if it were deliberately omitted in order to give the wife a licence to commit adultery, the whole agreement might be contrary to public policy and therefore void: *ibid.*, at p. 808 (*per* COTTON, L.J.). It may be possible to imply a *dum casta* clause from a recital: *Crouch* v. *Crouch*, [1912] 1 K.B. 378.

[3] Matrimonial Causes Act 1973, s. 34 (1). See further *post*, pp. 491-492.

[4] For agency by estoppel, see *ante*, pp. 154-155.

[5] *Rose* v. *Rose* (1883), 8 P.D. 98, C.A., following the decision of the House of Lords in *Rowley* v. *Rowley* (1866), L.R. 1 Sc. & Div. 63.

[6] *Letbe* v. *Letbe* (1928), 140 L.T. 199.

[7] *Goldblum* v. *Goldblum*, [1939] P. 107; [1938] 4 All E.R. 477, C.A.

[8] *Newsome* v. *Newsome* (1871), L.R. 2 P. & D. 306 (wife, who was to be bound only if husband "remained true to her", not bound when he later committed adultery); *Balcombe* v. *Balcombe*, [1908] P. 176 (wife not bound after discharge of agreement by husband's repudiation).

custody or upbringing of a minor and the administration of his property in a separation agreement, but that no court shall enforce any such provision if it is of the opinion that it is not for the child's benefit.[1]

If one spouse is given actual custody of the children, it is usual to provide that the other shall have access to them and also, if relevant, that the latter shall pay periodical sums by way of maintenance for them. In consideration of this, the spouse with custody frequently undertakes to be fully liable for educating and maintaining them. As much care must be taken in framing this covenant as in framing the husband's covenant to maintain the wife, as otherwise the covenantor may find himself liable on his covenant notwithstanding a subsequent resumption of cohabitation or even after the children attain their majority.[2]

As in the case of maintenance of the wife, either spouse may now apply to the court to alter any term relating to financial provision for children in certain circumstances.[3]

Agreements relating to Property.—The spouses may obviously wish to come to an agreement with respect to the property which formed their matrimonial home or with respect to their interests in other property. Clauses giving effect to their wishes must necessarily vary considerably from one agreement to another.

C. EFFECTS OF THE AGREEMENT

The principal effect of a separation agreement, as has already been pointed out, is to release each spouse from the duty of cohabiting with the other. This will prevent either side from alleging that the other is in desertion.[4] Apart from the general duty placed on both parties to perform and observe their respective covenants, the agreement may have other effects: for example, a husband who has sexual intercourse with his wife without her consent may be guilty of rape, at least if the agreement contains a non-molestation clause.[5]

D. DISCHARGE OF AGREEMENTS

From what has been said about its effects, it will be seen that it may be vital to determine whether an agreement once entered into is still in force. For example, if the agreement is discharged, desertion may commence,[6] the husband may cease to be liable on the contract to maintain his wife and children, and agreements relating to property may similarly be terminated. Basically, of course, the discharge of separation agreements is governed by the law relating to the discharge of contracts generally.

---

[1] See *post*, p. 288.

[2] As in *De Crespigny* v. *De Crespigny* (1853), 9 Exch. 192.

[3] See *post*, pp. 492-495.

[4] See *post*, pp.211-212.

[5] *Per* LYNSKEY, J., in *R.* v. *Miller*, [1954] 2 Q.B. 282, 290; [1954] 2 All E.R. 529, 533. See further, *ante*, p. 115.

[6] See *post*, pp. 212-213.

Discharge by Agreement.—The agreement may be effectively discharged in accordance with its terms. Thus, in *Newsome* v. *Newsome*,[1] where the wife promised to be bound only if her husband "remained true to her", it was held that his subsequently committing adultery terminated the agreement. Similarly, it may be discharged by a later independent agreement between the parties.[2]

Resumption of Cohabitation.—Whether a resumption of cohabitation will amount to a consent to terminate an agreement so as to discharge it automatically is a matter of some doubt. It is submitted, however, that much of the difficulty has been caused by a failure to distinguish between two separate questions. It is obvious that an agreement to separate *stricto sensu* must be discharged on the parties' resuming cohabitation; the problem that has always arisen is whether, if the spouses then separate again, the husband remains liable on the covenant in the original agreement to maintain his wife and children or whether the parties are still bound by terms in that agreement relating to the division and use of their property.[3] If those covenants are to remain in force only so long as the spouses are living apart, their resuming cohabitation will have discharged them; on the other hand, if the husband has independently created a trust in favour of the wife and children or covenanted to pay his wife an annuity for the rest of her life, his liability will remain notwithstanding their having lived together again.[4] The question is therefore one of construction in each individual case and little help can be obtained by applying a decision on the wording of one deed to the entirely different wording of another. LORD ELDON'S dictum that there is a presumption that all obligations cease on a resumption of cohabitation[5] has been followed, doubted and criticised, and the whole question has been fully discussed by the Court of Appeal in *Negus* v. *Forster*[6] and *Nicol* v. *Nicol*.[7] But, as BOWEN and FRY, L.JJ., pointed out in the latter case, the question in the end is always that of giving effect to the parties' intention to be inferred from the agreement itself.[8]

Discharge by Breach.—A repudiation of the agreement by one of the spouses will clearly give the other the right to treat it as discharged if he wishes to do so. In this respect these agreements differ from commercial contracts, for, as GREENE, M.R., stated when delivering the judgement of the Court of Appeal in *Pardy* v. *Pardy*,[9] the innocent party is not bound to inform the spouse in breach that he has accepted the repudiation: it is sufficient if there is

---

[1] (1871), L.R. 2 P. & D. 306.

[2] But if the deed has created a *trust* in favour of the children, this cannot be discharged by an agreement between the spouses.

[3] As in *Nicol* v. *Nicol* (1886), 31 Ch. D. 524, C.A.

[4] This distinction was drawn in *Ruffles* v. *Alston* (1875), L.R. 19 Eq. 539, and *Negus* v. *Forster* (1882), 46 L.T. 675, C.A. See also Lush, *Husband and Wife*, 4th Ed., 438-444. In any event resumption of cohabitation will not *per se* destroy a cause of action already vested in the wife, so that she will still be able to sue for arrears of maintenance which had accrued before the reconciliation: *Macan* v. *Macan* (1900), 70 L.J.K.B. 90.

[5] *Bateman* v. *Ross* (1813), 1 Dow 235, 245, H.L.

[6] (1882), 46 L.T. 675, C.A.

[7] (1886), 31 Ch. D. 524, C.A.

[8] At pp. 529, 530. See also Lush, *loc. cit*.

[9] [1939] P. 288, 305-307; [1939] 3 All E.R. 779, 784-786, C.A.

other evidence that he has not insisted upon the performance of the terms but has treated the agreement as a dead letter. As neither party regards it as still in force, neither can rely on it to justify the continued separation.

Whether there has been a repudiation is purely a question of fact. Mere failure on the husband's part to pay maintenance to his wife will not *per se* amount to a repudiation[1] although failure to do so for a long time might well be construed as such,[2] as would non-payment coupled with some other act implying an intention not to be bound by the agreement.[3]

There may also be a breach by failure to perform or observe some other covenant. In order that the other party may lawfully treat himself as discharged, there must be a substantial breach: a trivial breach will clearly not suffice for this purpose.[4] It may in fact be doubted whether a breach of one covenant will ever entitle a party to repudiate liability on another. In *Fearon* v. *Aylesford*[5] BRETT, M.R., stated that a husband's covenant to pay maintenance and a wife's covenant not to molest her husband were not interdependent, so that she would still be able to enforce her husband's obligation even if she had failed to observe her own. For this reason a prudent draftsman will make the covenants expressly interdependent.

Subsequent Matrimonial Proceedings.—The problem here, it is submitted, is the same as that presented by resumption of cohabitation. The agreement to separate *stricto sensu* must necessarily be discharged by a decree of nullity, divorce or judicial separation, for in each case the decree removes the duty to cohabit; it then becomes a question of construction whether such covenants as the husband's covenant to maintain the wife and children remain alive. In *May* v. *May*[6] the Court of Appeal held that divorce does not automatically terminate such an obligation, and in *Adams* v. *Adams*[7] extended this principle to nullity where the marriage is voidable. But, as we have already seen,[8] this rule does not apply to a decree where the marriage is void, for normally the agreement will have been entered into under a mistake as to the subsistence of the marriage. These decisions are less likely to work hardship than might at first be supposed in view of the courts' powers to vary maintenance agreements and post-nuptial settlements.[9]

---

[1] For it may not be a *wilful* breach: *Clark* v. *Clark (No. 2)*, [1939] P. 257; [1939] 2 All E.R. 392.

[2] *Pardy* v. *Pardy*, [1939] P. 288; [1939] 3 All E.R. 779, C.A.

[3] *Waller* v. *Waller* (1910), 26 T.L.R. 223; *Kennedy* v. *Kennedy*, [1907] P. 49; *Balcombe* v. *Balcombe*, [1908] P. 176 (emigration to America).

[4] *Besant* v. *Wood* (1879), 12 Ch. D. 605 (husband's attempt to stop wife from using her married name in contravention of non-molestation clause); *Kunski* v. *Kunski* (1898), 68 L.J.P. 18 (husband's delay in paying maintenance for four days). In neither case was there a sufficiently serious breach to entitle the wife to treat the agreement as discharged. In *Morrall* v. *Morrall* (1881), 6 P.D. 98, it was held that the husband's committing incestuous adultery was such conduct as to entitle the wife to repudiate the deed, but it is not clear what covenant was alleged to have been broken.

[5] (1884), 14 Q.B.D. 792, 800, C.A. See futher, *ante*, p. 172.

[6] [1929] 2 K.B. 386, C.A. The Court followed *Charlesworth* v. *Holt* (1873) L.R. 9 Ex. 38, not so much because they thought it correctly decided as because it had stood unquestioned and acted on for over 50 years. See also *Gandy* v. *Gandy* (1882), 7 P.D. 168, C.A. (judicial separation).

[7] [1941] 1 K.B. 536; [1941] 1 All E.R. 334, C.A. The position must now be the same as on divorce: see the Matrimonial Causes Act 1973, s. 16 (*ante*, p. 97).

[8] *Ante*, p. 171.

[9] See *post*, pp. 492 (maintenance agreements) and 535 (post-nuptial settlements).

In *Hyman* v. *Hyman*[1] it was sought to prove that the contract was frustrated by the decree. The spouses entered into a separation agreement in 1919 and after the Matrimonial Causes Act of 1923 came into force the wife obtained a divorce on the ground of her husband's adultery. The latter's argument that the contract was frustrated by the change of law in 1923, which extended the wife's power to petition for divorce, was rejected at any rate by LORD ATKIN, who held that since divorce was possible in 1919 the extension of the grounds on which it could be obtained was not so unforeseen as to discharge the agreement automatically.[2] Whilst admittedly LORD BUCKMASTER'S speech seems more in keeping with the view that the contract was frustrated,[3] LORD MERRIMAN, P., has since held that the doctrine of frustration has no application at all where the basis of a separation agreement has been changed by an alteration in the law.[4] Indeed, if the premise be correct that the question is entirely one of construction, each case must be decided purely upon the wording of the particular agreement.

Husband's Bankruptcy.—As sums payable to the wife in the future under a separation agreement are provable in the husband's bankruptcy, no action will lie against him on the covenant in respect of them.[5] Consequently, since this effectively terminates his liability and thus destroys the basis of the agreement, the wife is entitled to treat the whole contract as discharged.[6]

E. REMEDIES FOR BREACH OF AGREEMENT

Damages.—Common law damages may always be obtained for breach of the agreement. Whilst this is the obvious remedy for arrears of maintenance, damages may be awarded for failure to perform and observe other covenants as well.[7]

Specific Performance.—Specific performance may be sought in two cases. First, either party refusing to execute a deed of separation may be ordered to do so in accordance with the terms of separation articles to which he is a party,[8] and secondly, if the agreement includes a contract to create a trust, the husband (or other settlor) may be ordered to transfer property or funds to the trustees in accordance with the terms of his promise.[9] In neither

---

[1] [1929] A.C. 601, H.L.

[2] At pp. 627-628.

[3] At pp. 623-624; he did not decide the point directly. No other member of the House considered it.

[4] *H*—— v. *H*——, [1938] 3 All E.R. 415.

[5] *Victor* v. *Victor*, [1912] 1 K.B. 247, C.A. This is so even though there is a *dum casta* clause or the wife's right is determinable in other circumstances: *Ex parte Neal* (1880), 14 Ch. D. 579, C.A.

[6] *McQuiban* v. *McQuiban*, [1913] P. 208.

[7] *Fearon* v. *Aylesford* (1884), 14 Q.B.D. 792, C.A. (wife's failure to observe non-molestation clause).

[8] *Wilson* v. *Wilson* (1848), 1 H.L. Cas. 538, H.L.; *Hart* v. *Hart* (1881), 18 Ch. D. 670. Specific performance will not be ordered if the articles are in any way contrary to public policy (see *ante*, p. 171): *Vansittart* v. *Vansittart* (1858), 2 De G. & J. 249.

[9] *Lurie* v. *Lurie*, [1938] 3 All E.R. 156.

case, of course, will an action lie if there is no consideration even though the agreement is under seal.[1]

Injunction.—An injunction may be granted to prevent the breach of a negative covenant, for example the breach of a non-molestation clause.[2] It will similarly be granted to restrain a party from instituting legal proceedings if he has expressly undertaken not to do so.[3]

---

[1] *Wilson* v. *Wilson, (supra)*.

[2] *Sanders* v. *Rodway* (1852), 16 Beav. 207.

[3] *Besant* v. *Wood* (1879), 12 Ch. D. 605. But once a High Court action has been commenced, no injunction will lie to restrain its further prosecution: Supreme Court of Judicature (Consolidation) Act 1925, s. 41.

Chapter 6

Judicial Separation

The decree of judicial separation is a creature of statute and was first introduced by the Matrimonial Causes Act of 1857 to replace the old ecclesiastical decree of divorce *a mensa et thoro* which that Act abolished. Like the old decree, its prime purpose is to relieve the petitioner from the duty of cohabiting with the respondent. During the past decade there has been a steady but remarkable increase in the number of petitions for judicial separation presented each year—from 211 in 1971 to 3,650 in 1979.[1] These figures should be compared with the drop in the number of applications for magistrates' orders during the same period;[2] the two trends may not be unconnected. In the absence of any reliable evidence, the most probable explanation for the increase is that the court now has the same powers to make orders for financial relief on judicial separation as it has on divorce and that most petitioners wish to invoke these powers but for some reason cannot or do not wish to petition for divorce. In some cases this will be due to religious conviction or to the fact that divorce is unobtainable because the parties have not been married for three years. There may also be some petitioners who still hope for an ultimate reconciliation but by obtaining a decree of judicial separation they obtain an immediate remedy and at the same time leave the way open for divorce on the ground on which the decree has been granted if these hopes are not fulfilled.[3]

Jurisdiction.—The Act of 1857 vested the power of granting decrees of judicial separation in the Divorce Court, from which it was transferred in 1875 to the High Court. If the petition is undefended, the decree is now granted under special procedure in a divorce county court.[4]

Jurisdiction was originally based on the parties' residence (the basis of jurisdiction in the ecclesiastical courts) or domicile in this country. When proposing changes in the law relating to jurisdiction in divorce, however, the

---

[1] *I.e.*, there has been a seventeenfold increase. In the same period the number of petitions for divorce increased by 50%. Over 92% of the petitions for judicial separation were brought by wives; 75% of all petitions were based on the respondent's behaviour, and fewer than 3% were based on desertion or separation (when the parties would have had to have been married for at least two years). The number of decrees pronounced amounted to only 45% of the number of petitions.

[2] See *ante*, p. 6, n. 4.

[3] See *post*, p. 193. These conclusions are reached by Mrs. P. A. Garlick after (unpublished) research for the Law Commission.

[4] Matrimonial Causes Act 1967, s. 1; Matrimonial Causes Rules, 1977, r. 33 (3). For special procedure, see *post*, pp. 239-241.

Law Commission pointed out that judicial separation declares the parties' marital status, affects their mutual obligations, and enables the court to make the same orders in relation to financial provision and the children of the family as it can make on divorce. They therefore recommended that jurisdiction to pronounce both decrees should be the same.[1] Effect was given to these proposals in the Domicile and Matrimonial Proceedings Act 1973, and the court now has jurisdiction to entertain a petition for judicial separation if (and only if) (a) either of the parties is domiciled in England or Wales when the proceedings are begun or has been habitually resident there throughout the period of one year ending with that date, or (b) proceedings for divorce, nullity or judicial separation, over which the court has jurisdiction, have already begun.[2] The latter provision means, for example, that if a husband brings a petition for divorce, which the court has jurisdiction to hear solely by virtue of his habitual residence in England, and he then ceases to be resident here, the wife can cross-petition for judicial separation notwithstanding that at the time of her cross-petition neither of the spouses is domiciled or resident in this country. There are no obligatory stays in proceedings for judicial separation (as there are in divorce), but the law relating to discretionary stays, their removal and their effect on ancillary orders is exactly the same as in divorce.[3] The court should usually stay a petition for judicial separation if proceedings for nullity or divorce are being brought elsewhere so that the question of the validity or subsistence of the marriage may be determined first.

Choice of Law.—The Act does not provide for the choice of the substantive law to be applied. In the past it was always assumed that English law would be applied and this is undoubtedly still true.[4]

Grounds for Judicial Separation.—A decree of divorce *a mensa et thoro* could be pronounced on the grounds of the respondent's adultery or cruelty or, if the wife were the petitioner, on the grounds that the husband had committed (or possibly attempted to commit) rape or an unnatural offence. The Matrimonial Causes Act of 1857 preserved all these as grounds for judicial separation, and over the years were added the respondent's desertion,[5] failure to comply with a decree for restitution of conjugal rights[6] and incurable insanity.[7]

It will be seen that under the old law the main grounds for a judicial separation were the same as the grounds for divorce. Given that the law of divorce was based essentially on the commission of a matrimonial offence by the respondent, this is not surprising. There is, however, another good reason

---

[1] Law Com. No. 48 (Report on Jurisdiction in Matrimonial Causes), paras. 63-66. For jurisdiction in divorce, see *post*, p. 241.

[2] S. 5 (2), (5). This change deprives spouses of a remedy which they formerly had if both are resident in this country but neither satisfies the statutory requirements. See Hartley and Karsten, 37 M.L.R. 179, at p. 184.

[3] See *post*, pp. 242-243.

[4] See Law Com. No. 48, para. 105.

[5] For two years under the Matrimonial Causes Act 1857; for three years under the Matrimonial Causes Act 1937.

[6] Matrimonial Causes Act 1884.

[7] Matrimonial Causes Act 1937.

for keeping the grounds the same. For spouses who have a conscientious objection to divorce a decree of judicial separation may mark the *de facto* end of the marriage, and it is arguable that they should be able to obtain a decree only in similar circumstances to those who wish to bring their marriage to a *de jure* end by a decree of divorce. This principle was adopted by the Divorce Reform Act 1969. All the former grounds for a decree of judicial separation were abolished and it is now provided that the five facts on which a petitioner can rely to establish irretrievable breakdown of the marriage as the ground for divorce shall be *grounds* for judicial separation.[1] As these are much more important in connection with divorce, we shall defer a detailed consideration of them until we deal with that subject.[2]

As the decree does not dissolve the marriage bond but can in fact be rescinded, the court is not concerned with whether or not the marriage has irretrievably broken down; if any of the grounds is made out, the court must grant a decree provided that the provisions of section 41 of the Matrimonial Causes Act 1973 (relating to the welfare of children) are complied with.[3] Furthermore, sections 5 and 10 of that Act do not apply to judicial separation:[4] they are both inappropriate because the decree is not irreversible and does not affect the parties' status. On the other hand, the provisions in the Act relating to reconciliation do apply; and the court may adjourn the proceedings, the petitioner's solicitor must provide his certificate, and periods of cohabitation not exceeding six months may be ignored just as in proceedings for divorce.[5]

Unlike a divorce, a petition for judicial separation may be presented within the first three years of the marriage without the leave of the court.

The Decree and its Effects.—Since a decree of judicial separation effects no change of status and may in certain circumstances subsequently be discharged, it is not made in two stages like a decree of divorce or nullity but takes effect immediately it is pronounced.

The principal effect of the decree is that it relieves the petitioner from the duty of cohabiting with the respondent.[6] This means that so long as it is in force neither spouse can be in desertion,[7] and also that a husband who has intercourse with his wife against her will may be guilty of rape.[8] In addition the court has power to make a number of orders relating to the custody and welfare of the children of the family and to financial relief.[9] The decree will also affect the devolution of a spouse's property if he or she dies intestate.[10]

---

[1] See now the Matrimonial Causes Act 1973, s. 17 (1).

[2] *Post*, pp. 194 *et seq.*

[3] See *post*, pp. 308-310. But if one party petitions for divorce and the other petitions for judicial separation, the court should not grant the latter if it pronounces a decree nisi of divorce: *Lawry* v. *Lawry*, [1967] 2 All E.R. 1131, C.A.

[4] These permit a respondent in certain circumstances to oppose a decree nisi of divorce on the ground of hardship, to have a decree nisi rescinded if his consent was obtained by a misrepresentation, or to delay its being made absolute pending suitable financial provision. See *post*, pp. 227 and 230-236.

[5] See *post*, pp. 228-230.

[6] Matrimonial Causes Act 1973, s. 18 (1).

[7] *Post*, pp. 213-214.

[8] *R.* v. *Clarke*, [1949] 2 All E.R. 448. See *ante*, p. 115.

[9] See *post*, pp. 307 (children), and 525 and 589 (financial relief).

[10] See *post*, p. 619.

But it must be remembered that for all other purposes the spouses remain husband and wife; neither of them is at liberty to remarry, for example, and such of the common law disabilities arising from coverture as remain will continue in force.[1]

Discharge of Decrees.—The ground on which either party is most likely to apply for the discharge of a decree of judicial separation is that the spouses have resumed cohabitation. The court clearly has power to order a discharge in such circumstances[2] and there is at least one dictum that the decree will be automatically discharged in such a case.[3] In addition there is probably a residual power to rescind the decree whenever common sense and justice demand it, at least provided both spouses consent.[4]

Recognition of Foreign Decrees.—The question of the recognition of foreign decrees is now governed by statute. Following the recommendations of the Law Commission and the Scottish Law Commission,[5] the Recognition of Divorces and Legal Separations Act 1971 gives effect in a somewhat modified form to the Hague Convention of 1968 on this subject.[6] With the two exceptions noted below the law relating to the recognition of legal separations is now the same as that relating to the recognition of divorces. In view of the much greater practical importance of the latter subject, the detailed provisions of the Act will be considered when we deal with divorce: the position with respect to foreign separations may be discovered by substituting "legal separation" for "divorce" throughout that discussion.[7]

Decrees of judicial separation (like decrees of divorce) pronounced in the British Isles before 1st January 1972 will still be recognised only if they were recognised at common law.[8] A decree was recognised if both parties were domiciled in the territory in which it was obtained:[9] it would probably also be recognised if both were resident there, if their common *lex domicilii* recognised it, or if either of them had a real and substantial connection with the country in question, but authority on these points is lacking. The second difference between decrees of judicial separation and divorce in this respect is that the provisions of section 16 of the Domicile and Matrimonial Proceedings Act 1973 (which precludes the recognition of certain divorces when the proceedings have not been instituted in a court of law) do not apply to legal separations. The reason is that, as the parties are still married to each

---

[1] *Cf. Moss* v. *Moss*, [1963] 2 Q.B. 799; [1963] 2 All E.R. 829 (one spouse remains incompetent to give evidence on the prosecution of the other).

[2] *Oram* v. *Oram* (1923), 129 L.T. 159.

[3] *Per* A. L. SMITH, J., in *Haddon* v. *Haddon* (1887), 18 Q.B.D. 778, 782-783. The correctness of this decision is of vital importance if it is alleged that desertion has started to run after a resumption of cohabitation following a decree.

[4] See *Schlesinger* v. *Schlesinger* (1966), *Times*, 22nd June, where a decree was discharged to enable the wife (who was not domiciled in this country) to obtain a divorce in South Africa.

[5] Law Com. No. 43.

[6] The Act has been amended in detail by the Domicile and Matrimonial Proceedings Acts 1973.

[7] See *post*, pp. 243-251.

[8] Recognition of Divorces and Legal Separations Act 1971, ss. 1 and 10 (4); Domicile and Matrimonial Proceedings Act 1973, s. 15 (2).

[9] *Tursi* v. *Tursi*, [1958] P. 54; [1957] 2 All E.R. 828.

other, the wife remains able to apply for financial provision in an English court.

The Act nowhere defines a legal separation. When referring solely to decrees pronounced in the British Isles[1] it uses the term "judicial separation", so that one may safely assume that a legal separation is a decree that has the same effect, in other words a decree which releases the petitioner from the duty of cohabiting with the respondent. It is very doubtful whether English courts would give any effect at all to a decree which released the spouses from some of the duties of cohabitation but not from them all.

Nor does the Act define the purposes for which a foreign decree will be effective. Some years earlier this had to be considered in *Tursi* v. *Tursi*.[2] The husband, who was domiciled in Italy, deserted the wife in 1942. Four years later she obtained a decree of *separazione legale* in Italy on the ground of his desertion and cruelty. This decree relieved the spouses from the duty of cohabiting and was thus similar to the English decree of judicial separation. In 1949 the wife came to England and eventually petitioned for divorce on the ground of her husband's desertion. SACHS, J., held that the existence of the Italian decree prevented the husband from being in desertion after it had been pronounced, but as it was comparable to an English decree of judicial separation, the marriage could be dissolved on the ground that the respondent had been in desertion for a continuous period of three years immediately preceding the institution of the proceedings in Italy.[3]

This decision was limited to the effect of a foreign decree upon subsequent proceedings for divorce, and SACHS, J., deliberately left open the question how far it would affect other matters.[4] It is submitted that an English court should give effect to a foreign decree or order in so far as it terminates the duty to cohabit (so that, for example, a husband could be guilty of raping his wife), and there is no reason in principle why it should not be held to be capable of varying rights in property.[5]

---

[1] *E.g.*, in s.1.

[2] [1958] P. 54; [1957] 2 All E.R. 828.

[3] See the Matrimonial Causes Act 1973, s. 4 (3), *post*, p. 214. (The period of desertion required is now two years.)

[4] At pp. 70 and 837, respectively.

[5] Some further problems are discussed by Spiro, *Foreign Judicial Separation*, 6 I.C.L.Q. 392.

Chapter 7

The Termination of Marriage

In English law a valid marriage may be terminated only by the death of one of the parties or by a decree of dissolution or divorce pronounced by a court of competent jurisdiction.

A. DEATH AND PRESUMPTION OF DEATH

Death.—The death of either party *ipso facto* brings the marriage to an end.

Decree of Presumption of Death and Dissolution of Marriage.—Before 1938 the disappearance of one of the spouses presented an insurmountable difficulty. If H's wife, W, disappeared in such circumstances as to lead to the reasonable inference that she was dead (although her death could not be proved), H could remarry without committing the crime of bigamy and his second marriage would be *presumptively* valid. But if it were later proved that W was in fact alive when H remarried, then, of course, the second marriage would be *conclusively* void with all the legal consequences that that entailed. In order to meet this situation, section 19 of the Matrimonial Causes Act 1973 permits the High Court to make a decree of presumption of death and of dissolution of the marriage if it is satisfied that there are reasonable grounds for supposing that the petitioner's spouse is dead.[1] The general presumption of death which may be raised by seven years' absence is specifically applied to these proceedings by the provision that

"...the fact that for a period of seven years or more the other party to the marriage has been continually absent from the petitioner and the petitioner has no reason to believe that the other party has been living within that time shall be evidence that the other party is dead until the contrary is proved."[2]

The petitioner is not bound to rely on this period of absence. The court may accept any satisfactory evidence from which it may be presumed that the spouse is dead:[3] the inference to be drawn from the seven years' absence is of particular importance when there is no evidence at all of what has happened since. It will be observed that the statutory presumption is different from that which arises at common law after seven years' absence. What is important

---

[1] The power was originally given by the Matrimonial Causes Act 1937.
[2] Matrimonial Causes Act 1973, s. 19 (3).
[3] *E.g.*, the otherwise inexplicable disappearance of an explorer.

185

under the statute is the petitioner's belief. The provision was analysed by
SACHS, J., in *Thompson* v. *Thompson*,[1] where he held that nothing must have
happened during the period of seven years from which the petitioner, as a
reasonable person, would conclude that the other spouse was still alive.
Although the point was left open in *Thompson* v. *Thompson*,[2] the court is
hardly likely to accept that the belief is reasonably held unless the petitioner
has made all appropriate enquiries. The jurisdiction is discretionary; consequently, even if the petitioner can claim the benefit of the presumption, the
court will not pronounce a decree, contrary to the justice of the case, where
there is a probability that the other party is still alive. This might occur, for
example, if an explorer had announced his intention of spending more than
seven years in a country with which communication is impracticable.[3]

A decree nisi must be rescinded if the other spouse is found to be still alive.[4]
Once it has been made absolute, however, it dissolves the marriage irrevocably even though the other subsequently reappears.[5]

As in the case of divorce, the court has jurisdiction if the petitioner is
domiciled in England when the proceedings are begun or has been habitually
resident here throughout the period of one year ending with that date.[6]

Now that a spouse may seek a divorce after five years' separation,
proceedings for presumption of death and dissolution are obviously of less
importance than they were formerly. In some cases, of course, he might
succeed in reliance on five years' separation although he would certainly fail
if he asked the court to presume that the other spouse was dead. On the other
hand, he will have to petition for presumption of death if he wishes to have
the marriage dissolved within five years of the other's disappearance or of his
own decision to bring consortium to an end.

B. DIVORCE

1. HISTORICAL INTRODUCTION[7]

We have already seen that the doctrine of the indissolubility of marriage
was accepted by the English ecclesiastical courts after the Reformation, so

---

[1] [1956] P. 414; [1956] 1 All E.R. 603. A pure speculation is insufficient. The petitioner must
give evidence: *Parkinson* v. *Parkinson*,[1939] P. 346; [1939] 3 All E.R. 108. (It was also held in
this case that the fact that the spouses parted under a separation agreement is no bar to the
proceedings.) For the common law presumption, see *ante*, p. 66.

[2] At pp. 421 and 605, respectively.

[3] *Thompson* v. *Thompson*, (*supra*), at pp. 424-425 and 608, respectively.

[4] *Manser* v. *Manser*, [1940] P. 224; [1940] 4 All E.R. 238. Presumably the decree would also
have to be rescinded if the petitioner relied on the presumption and it was proved that the other
spouse had been alive at some time during the previous seven years, even though it was not
known whether he was still alive.

[5] But in that case the court has power to make orders for financial relief: *Deacock* v.
Deacock, [1958] P. 230; [1958] 2 All E.R. 633, C.A. The Court of Appeal was unimpressed by
the argument that the Matrimonial Causes Act draws a distinction between these proceedings
and divorce and empowers the court to order financial relief only on divorce.

[6] Domicile and Matrimonial Proceedings Act 1973, s. 5 (4), implementing the recommendations of the Law Commission: Law Com. No. 48 (Report on Jurisdiction in Matrimonial
Causes), paras. 71-74.

[7] For an eminently readable brief account of the history of divorce, see the Report of the
Committee on One-parent Families, Cmnd. 5629, Part 4, Sections 2 and 3.

that these courts had no power to pronounce a decree of divorce *a vinculo matrimonii* which would permit the parties to remarry.[1] In addition to decrees of nullity and jactitation of marriage, they could pronounce decrees of restitution of conjugal rights and divorce *a mensa et thoro*. The former called on a deserting spouse to resume cohabitation with the petitioner, and the latter (which was granted on the grounds of adultery, cruelty or the commission of an unnatural offence) relieved the petitioner from the duty of cohabiting with the respondent without severing the marriage tie.[2] The only way in which an aggrieved party could obtain a divorce *a vinculo matrimonii* was by Act of Parliament, the expense of which was sufficient to put relief beyond the hope of most. In addition, by the end of the eighteenth century, the practice of the House of Lords was to give a reading to a bill introduced on behalf of the husband only on the ground of adultery and then only after he had obtained a divorce *a mensa et thoro* in an ecclesiastical court and had successfully sued the adulterer for damages in the old common law action of criminal conversation. Adultery alone would not suffice in the case of a bill presented on behalf of the wife, who had to show that the adultery was aggravated (for example, bigamous or incestuous) or that her husband had committed an unnatural offence.[3]

Matrimonial Causes Act 1857.—This Act was passed to give effect to the report of a royal commission which had been appointed in 1850 to enquire into the law relating to matrimonial offences. In addition to vesting the existing jurisdiction of the ecclesiastical courts in a new statutory Divorce Court (from which it was transferred to the High Court in 1875)[4] the Act for the first time in English law permitted divorce *a vinculo matrimonii* by judicial process. The term "divorce" was henceforth confined to this decree, whilst that of divorce *a mensa et thoro* was renamed "judicial separation". But the distinction between the position of the husband and that of the wife was retained, for a husband could petition for divorce on the ground of adultery alone (provided that he joined the alleged adulterer as a co-respondent instead of suing him at common law in criminal conversation), whilst a wife had to prove either adultery coupled with incest, bigamy, cruelty or two years' desertion, or , alternatively, rape or an unnatural offence.[5]

It will be seen that all the Act did was to change the process by which a divorce was obtained from a legislative one to a judicial one: adultery remained the one matrimonial offence which was regarded as sufficiently heinous to justify the dissolution of the marriage bond. Here, too, one sees reflected the mid-Victorian attitude to sexual morality: whilst one act of adultery by a wife was considered unforgivable and gave the husband the power to petition for divorce without more, she could not even rely on a series

---

[1] *Ante*, p. 70.

[2] Readers unfamiliar with ecclesiastical reports before 1858 are warned of the confusing terminology. The word "divorce" *simpliciter* almost always means divorce *a mensa et thoro*; if "divorce *a vinculo matrimonii*" is used, it always means nullity.

[3] There were on the average fewer than two divorces by statute a year on the husband's petition and only a total of four on the wife's petition. See generally Jackson, *Formation and Annulment of Marriage*, 2nd Ed., 27-40, and the authorities there cited.

[4] By the Judicature Acts of 1873 and 1875.

[5] Matrimonial Causes Act 1857, s. 27.

of associations by him unless the adultery was "aggravated".[1] The principle that divorce was a remedy for a matrimonial wrong was further applied in provisions absolutely precluding the court from pronouncing a decree if the petitioner had been guilty of connivance or condonation of if the parties had entered into a collusive agreement concerning the prosecution of the suit. The court was also given a discretionary power to refuse a decree in certain circumstances, in particular if. the petitioner had himself been guilty of adultery.[2]

Extension of the Grounds for Divorce.—The law remained in this state until 1923, when the Matrimonial Causes Act of that year put the husband and wife in the same position by permitting the latter to petition on the grounds of adultery *simpliciter*.[3] A. P. Herbert's Matrimonial Causes Act of 1937 further extended the grounds for divorce by permitting either spouse to base his or her petition on the other's cruelty, desertion for three years, or (subject to certain other conditions) supervening incurable insanity.[4] This last provision shows an important departure from the principles underlying the law of divorce, for whereas before 1938 it had always been necessary for the petitioner to show that the respondent had committed a matrimonial offence, a petition based upon the respondent's insanity disclosed a state of affairs in no way due to his fault which nevertheless made it socially undesirable that the petitioner should still be tied to the respondent by marriage.

The Movement for Reform.—The enormous social changes following the Second World War led to much public discussion of the whole basis of the law of divorce and a radical reappraisal of the principles underlying it. There had been a vast increase in the number of divorces,[5] and although this must in some measure reflect an increase in the number of marriages that had broken down, other factors came into play. Legal aid had opened the doors of the divorce court to many who could not previously have afforded it; the attitude of society towards divorced spouses (particularly "guilty" spouses) had

---

[1] One reason for the distinction was the fear that the wife might try to palm illegitimate children upon the husband. If the wife left the husband in consequence of his adultery, this would put him in constructive desertion, so that in theory the effect of the legislation was merely to delay the wife's remedy for two years. In practice, however, she would usually not be able to afford to do so; the only way in which she could obtain maintenance from him by a court order was by obtaining a judicial separation based on his adultery, which would automatically prevent desertion from running.

[2] Matrimonial Causes Act 1857, ss. 30 and 31.

[3] Matrimonial Causes Act 1923, s. 1. It did not strictly equate the spouses' rights for the wife could still petition on the grounds of the husband's rape or unnatural offence, while there was no corresponding basis for the husband's petition.

[4] Matrimonial Causes Act 1937, ss. 2 and 3. This Act very largely gave effect to the recommendations of the majority of the members of a Royal Commission appointed in 1909 (the Gorell Commission, Cd. 6478). For a lively account of the history of the passage of this bill through Parliament, see Sir Alan Herbert's *The Ayes have it* (1937).

[5] In 1938 (following A.P. Herbert's Act) there were 9,970 petitions; the figure rose steadily during and immediately after the Second World War reaching a peak in 1947 with 47,041. Following the introduction of legal aid, the figure rose from 29,096 in 1950 to 37,637 in 1951. After another decline the figures have risen steadily since 1959. In 1970 (the last year before the Divorce Reform Act came into force) there were 70,575 petitions; in 1979 there were 162,867.

changed; and many religious bodies were taking a far less rigid attitude.[1] More than 90% of all petitions were undefended and some of these undoubtedly amounted to divorce by consent. The law could be abused by the husband's providing his wife with evidence of adultery committed on one occasion in a hotel bedroom.[2] In other cases both spouses were guilty and cross-petitions were launched purely to give the parties an advantage when it came to the question of financial provision.

Consequently the idea that the purpose of divorce was to provide a remedy available only to the "innocent" spouse for a matrimonial wrong committed by the other seemed to many to be a singularly outdated concept which obscured the true social function of divorce. Essentially this exists to enable the spouses to enter into a fresh legal union if they wish to do so. At the same time the court must give such protection as it can to the children of the family affected by the breakdown and adjust financial and property rights in view of the possibility of remarriage. There should also be machinery to facilitate a reconciliation if there is still any possibility of this being successful.[3] Hence, it was argued, divorce should be available to either spouse when the marriage has irretrievably broken down: to insist on the commission of a matrimonial offence lays stress upon the symptoms of breakdown rather than on the breakdown itself. The introduction of this principle would have the effect of reducing the number of stable illicit unions where there was no foreseeable chance of the parties being able to marry or of their children being legitimated because the spouse of one of them refused to release his or her partner on account of moral scruple, financial advantage or vindictiveness. Some people, on the other hand, regarded the idea as fundamentally unjust in that it would enable a party to take advantage of his own wrong and obtain a divorce against the will of an innocent spouse, who might have a conscientious objection to divorce, and that a wife in particular might suffer serious financial hardship as a consequence of the decree.

In 1951 a Royal Commission (the Morton Commission) was appointed to enquire into the law of England and Scotland concerning marriage and divorce. Its report was published in 1956.[4] Of the nineteen members only one was in favour of totally scrapping the matrimonial offence as the basis of our divorce law, but nine of the rest would have introduced the breakdown of the marriage as evidenced by separation for seven years as an alternative ground. But apart from one unsuccessful attempt to change the law in a private member's bill in the House of Commons,[5] little was done until two major publications appeared in 1966. In the first, *Putting Asunder*, a group appointed by the Archbishop of Canterbury to consider the law of divorce in contemporary society came down in favour of the breakdown theory. Logically they argued that this must be the sole ground of divorce and that possible abuse must be guarded against by a judicial inquest in each case.

---

[1] The courts also took a less restrictive attitude by widening the concept of cruelty.

[2] The judges have always viewed such evidence with suspicion but there can be no doubt that many such "arranged" petitions were successful.

[3] See Law Commission, *Reform of the Grounds of Divorce: the Field of Choice*, Cmnd. 3123, paras. 13 *et seq*.

[4] Cmd. 9678.

[5] Introduced by Mr. LEO ABSE, M.P. By withdrawing the controversial clauses, he enabled the rest of the bill to get on the statute book as the Matrimonial Causes Act of 1963.

They further recommended that a decree should be refused if it would be unjust because of the petitioner's conduct or because the financial provision proposed was inadequate. *Putting Asunder* was referred to the Law Commission who in turn reported in *Reform of the Ground of Divorce: the Field of Choice*.[1] They concluded that the Archbishop's group's proposals were impracticable and put forward a number of possible alternatives based on the fundamental assumption that the aims of a good divorce law are "to buttress, rather than undermine, the stability of marriage, and when, regrettably, a marriage has irretrievably broken down, to enable the empty legal shell to be destroyed with the maximum fairness and the minimum bitterness, distress and humiliation". Their own preference was for introducing as an additional ground for divorce the breakdown of the marriage as evidenced by a period of separation which should be shorter if the respondent consented than if he did not.

The Divorce Reform Act.—The consequence was the passing of the Divorce Reform Act in 1969. It represented a compromise between the views put forward by the Archbishop's group and the Law Commission. All the old grounds for divorce were abolished and replaced by one ground, that the marriage has irretrievably broken down. This, however, may be established only by proof of one or more of five facts set out in the Act. Three of these are akin to, but not identical with, the old grounds of adultery, cruelty and desertion, and therefore impute fault to the respondent. The other two are periods of separation: two years if the respondent consents to the granting of the decree and five years if he does not. The old bars to divorce, both absolute (like the petitioner's connivance and condonation) and discretionary (like the petitioner's own adultery), were abolished, but various safeguards are to be found to give financial protection to the respondent if the petitioner relies on a period of separation. In all such cases the respondent may apply for the decree not to be made absolute until adequate financial provision is made for him, and in the case of five years' separation the respondent may oppose the grant of a decree nisi on the ground that divorce will result in grave financial or other hardship to him (or her). Other provisions are designed to encourage reconciliation and to ensure that spouses are not prejudiced if their attempts are unsuccessful.

Because of the fears expressed that parties (particularly wives) divorced against their will could well suffer financial hardship, the Act did not come into force until 1st January 1971. This enabled Parliament to pass the Matrimonial Proceedings and Property Act of 1970, which reformed the whole law relating to the powers of the High Court and divorce county courts to grant financial relief for the protection of the spouses and the children of the family.[2]

---

[1] Cmnd. 3123. See further MacKenna, *Divorce by Consent and Divorce for Breakdown of Marriage*, 30 M.L.R. 121; Kahn-Freund, 30 M.L.R. 180.

[2] For a critical examination of the provisions of the Divorce Reform Act 1969, see Passingham, *The Divorce Reform Act 1969*; Levin, 33 M.L.R. 632; Freeman, *The Search for a Rational Divorce Law*, Current Legal Problems 1971, 178. For comparison with other legislation in the Commonwealth, see Selby, *The Development of Divorce Law in Australia*, 29 M.L.R. 473; Holden, *Divorce in the Commonwealth*, 20 I.C.L.Q. 58.

The Matrimonial Causes Act 1973.—By 1972 the law relating to matrimonial causes administered in the High Court and divorce county courts was to be found mainly in the two Acts mentioned in the last paragraph together with the Matrimonial Causes Act 1965 and the Nullity of Marriage Act 1971. On the recommendation of the Law Commission,[1] the whole lot was brought together in one Act, the Matrimonial Causes Act of 1973. This repealed the Divorce Reform Act and the Nullity of Marriage Act in their entirety, together with most of the provisions of the Matrimonial Causes Act 1965 and the Matrimonial Proceedings and Property Act[2] and isolated sections of ten other Acts. It is essentially a consolidating statute and made only minor changes in the existing law.

2. PETITIONS AND DECREES

Petitions.—All proceedings must now be begun in a divorce county court. County courts have jurisdiction to try *undefended* petitions.[3]

Petitions during the First Three Years of Marriage.—When the grounds for divorce were extended in 1937, a counterbalancing restriction was placed upon the presentation of a petition during the first three years of the marriage.[4] No petition may be presented during this period, partly to prevent persons from rushing into irresponsible or trial marriages and partly to prevent them from rushing out of marriage again without at least having some time to try to make a success of it. But in case an arbitrary application of this rule should work injustice to some petitioners, the court has power to give leave to present a petition before the expiration of the period if "the case is one of exceptional hardship suffered by the petitioner or of exceptional depravity on the part of the respondent".[5] The courts have declined to fetter their discretion by laying down any general rules for its exercise,[6] but it should be noticed that the hardship or depravity must be exceptional, so the mere fact that the respondent has committed adultery or behaved in such a way that the petitioner cannot reasonably be expected to live with him (which the Act itself envisages) cannot *per se* be a ground for giving leave. Typical of the facts on the basis of which the courts have granted leave are serious

---

[1] Law Com. No. 51.

[2] Some sections had to be kept alive because they affect other branches of the law (*e.g.*, matrimonial property).

[3] Matrimonial Causes Act 1967, s. 1. See *ante*, p. 4. For criticisms of the existing procedure, see Mortlock, *The Inside of Divorce; Elston, Fuller and Murch, Judicial Hearings of Undefended Divorce Petitions*, 38 M.L.R. 609.

[4] See now the Matrimonial Causes Act 1973, s. 3. But a petitioner may always base a petition upon any matter that occurred during the first three years of the marriage: s. 3 (4).

[5] *Ibid.*, s. 3 (2). The case cannot be tried twice. Hence the court must decide whether the allegations, *if true*, amount to exceptional hardship or depravity; it may also take into account the facts disclosed in the petition and any other evidence available at this stage: *W*. v. *W*., [1967] P. 291; [1966] 2 All E.R. 889; *C*. v. *C*., [1967] P. 298; [1967] 1 All E.R. 928. If leave is given but it appears to the court at the hearing that it was obtained by the petitioner's misrepresentation or concealment of the nature of the case, the court may either dismiss the petition or grant a decree nisi on condition that it is not made absolute until three years from the date of the marriage: Matrimonial Causes Act 1973, s. 3 (3); *Stroud* v. *Stroud*, [1963] 3 All E.R. 539.

[6] See *Fisher* v. *Fisher*, [1948] P. 263, C.A.

cruelty coupled with physical injury, sexual perversion, desertion of the petitioner within three months of the marriage due to the respondent's homosexuality, and conduct leading to nervous breakdown or other serious illness.[1]

Exceptional depravity will probably be rarely relied on today.[2] When considering whether the case is one of exceptional hardship, one must consider what effect the facts have had on the particular petitioner, and it is irrelevant that a reasonable person might have been expected to react differently in the circumstances.[3] It is sufficient if the consequences are more extensive and more serious than one would normally expect, and it is not necessary to show that they are quite abnormal.[4] There may be exceptional hardship even though the situation has been brought about by external events[5] or by the petitioner himself. Thus in *W.* v. *W.*[6] it was held that the fact that the wife was pregnant by another man whom she wished to marry was relevant but in the circumstances was not sufficient to entitle her to petition immediately because the child could be legitimated after its birth; the position might well have been different, however, if worrying about the situation had brought the wife to the verge of a nervous breakdown.

By speaking of "exceptional hardship suffered by the petitioner", the Act implies that he must have suffered it in the past or at least be suffering it at the present. Judicial opinion has been divided on the question whether account may be taken of the probability of his suffering it in the future if leave to present the petition immediately is not given,[7] but the courts now appear to do so.[8] It is submitted that this is a much more important matter than the hardship suffered in the past and clearly should be taken into account.

In deciding whether to exercise its discretion in the petitioner's favour once a case of exceptional hardship or depravity has been made out, the court must have regard in particular to the interests of the children of the family and the probability of a reconciliation between the spouses if leave is not given.[9] If leave is refused, this will not prevent the petitioner from subsequently basing a petition on any matter that occurred during the first three years of the marriage.[10]

---

[1] See the judgment of DENNING, L.J., in *Bowman* v. *Bowman*, [1949] P. 353, 356-357; [1949] 2 All E.R. 127, 128-129, C.A.; *Hillier* v. *Hillier*, [1958] P. 186; [1958] 2 All E.R. 261, C.A.; *C.* v. *C.*, [1980] Fam. 23; [1979] 1 All E.R. 556, C.A.; *Woolf* v. *Woolf* (1978), 9 Fam. Law 216, C.A. For a useful review of the cases, see Ingman, 9 Fam. Law 165, and the Law Commission's Working Paper No. 76, paras. 17-22.

[2] *C.* v. *C.*, [1980] Fam. 23; [1979] 1 All E.R. 556, C.A.

[3] *Hillier* v. *Hillier*, (*supra*), at pp. 190 and 263, respectively; *W* v. *W.*, [1967] P. 291, 297; [1966] 2 All E.R. 889, 893.

[4] *Woolf* v. *Woolf*, (*supra*).

[5] *Sanders* v. *Sanders* (1967), 111 Sol. Jo. 618, C.A. (petitioner's mental state).

[6] [1967] P. 291; [1966] 2 All E.R. 889.

[7] *Hillier* v. *Hillier*, (*supra*); *Brewer* v. *Brewer*, [1964] 1 All E.R. 539, C.A.

[8] *C.* v. *C.*, (*supra*), at pp. 28 and 560, respectively. *Cf. W.* v. *W.*, (*supra*).

[9] Matrimonial Causes Act, 1973, s. 3 (2); *C.* v. *C.*, (*supra*). For the meaning of "child of the family", see *post*, p. 304. The court can refer suitable cases to the court welfare officer: see *Practice Direction*, [1971] 1 All E.R. 894; *S.* v. *S.*, [1968] P. 185, 188-189; [1967] 3 All E.R. 139, 141. During the years 1969-1977 the number of applications for leave to present petitions rose from 498 to 1599 a year: it fell slightly in 1978 and 1979. It is believed that leave is refused in only about 5% of cases: see the Law Commission's Working Paper No. 76, para. 40.

[10] *Ibid.*, s. 3(4).

The Law Commission have recently questioned whether the restriction in its present form serves any useful social purpose.[1] So far from enabling the empty legal shell to be destroyed with the minimum bitterness, the need to categorize details of the respondent's behaviour is likely to exacerbate the relationship between the parties. In Scotland the absence of any comparable restriction does not lead to a rush to the divorce court within the first three years of marriage,[2] and now that irretrievable breakdown of the marriage is the only ground for divorce, it seems illogical to withhold a decree simply because this has occurred within the statutory period. The latter argument would be more impressive if the finding of irretrievable breakdown was based on more than a presumption from the existence of one of the five facts set out in the Matrimonial Causes Act; consequently one of the possible alternative possibilities canvassed by the Commission is the retention of a restriction with a power to permit a petition to be presented within the period if the court is in fact satisfied that the marriage has broken down irretrievably. Other possibilities are the complete removal of any bar and the introduction of a shorter period with no discretion to permit divorce within it at all. The last of these seems the least satisfactory of all for it would undoubtedly work severe hardship in those cases where the respondent's conduct has been the worst.

Divorce after previous Proceedings.—One of the provisions of the Matrimonial Causes Act of 1973 was designed to help the possibility of reconciliation without slamming the door to divorce if the attempt failed. If a husband, say, commits adultery or deserts his wife, she may wish for some form of matrimonial relief less than divorce in the hope of a reconciliation; on the other hand, there would be a danger that, if this hope were not fulfilled, she might later be unable to obtain a divorce because of the difficulty of proving the alleged offence or, in the case of desertion, because she had consented to the separation by obtaining a judicial separation or separation order. Consequently, it is now provided that on a petition for divorce the court *may* treat any previous decree of judicial separation or any order made in domestic proceedings in a magistrates' court as sufficient evidence of the ground on which it was granted provided that the petitioner gives evidence in the later divorce proceedings.[3] The special application of these provisions when the petition is based upon desertion will be considered below.[4]

---

[1] Working Paper No. 76 (Time Restrictions on Presentation of Divorce and Nullity Petitions), 1980.

[2] *Ibid.*, paras. 42-44. See also paras. 48-49.

[3] See now Matrimonial Causes Act 1973, s. 4, as amended by the Domestic Proceedings and Magistrates' Courts Act 1978, Sched. 2. But the court is not bound to treat the previous finding as conclusive. If previous proceedings have been brought in the High Court, the parties are generally bound by any findings of facts in issue *provided that they have been the subject of investigation and adjudication.* This applies in any subsequent proceedings in the High Court or in an inferior court, but proceedings in a magistrates' court will apparently not estop a party from alleging or denying the same facts later in the High Court. A divorce county court is now presumably in the same position as the High Court. Nor does an estoppel bind the court, which is under a statutory duty to investigate the facts alleged by each party. See *ante*, pp. 81-82, and *Thoday* v. *Thoday*, [1964] P. 181; [1964] 1 All E.R. 341, C.A., and the cases there cited.

[4] *Post*, p. 214.

The Decree and its Effects.—The decree is made in two stages: the decree nisi, followed by the decree absolute. Subject to the provisions of section 41 of the Matrimonial Causes Act 1973, when the welfare of children is involved,[1] the petitioner may apply for the decree to be made absolute at any time after the expiration of six weeks from the granting of the decree nisi unless the court fixes a shorter time in the particular case; if the petitioner fails to apply for a decree absolute, the respondent may make the application at any time after the expiration of three months from the earliest date on which the petitioner could have applied.[2] The purpose of the delay is to enable the Queen's Proctor or anyone else to intervene to show cause why the decree should not be made absolute.[3]

Whether the decree is one of divorce or presumption of death and dissolution, the marriage ceases as soon as the decree is made absolute[4] and either spouse is then free to remarry.[5] The decree nisi does not have this effect, and if either party remarries before it is made absolute, the second marriage will be void. If the decree absolute is void (as it will be if no order relating to the children of the family has been made under section 41 of the Matrimonial Causes Act[6]) or is rescinded (which it may be if it is obtained contrary to the rules of substantial justice or of the requirements of the Act[7]), the second marriage will thereby automatically become void *ab initio*.[8]

C. THE GROUND FOR DIVORCE

By section 1 (1) of the Matrimonial Causes Act 1973 there is only one ground for divorce, that the marriage has broken down irretrievably.

---

[1] See *post*, pp. 308-310.

[2] Matrimonial Causes Act 1973, ss. 1 (5) and 9 (2); Matrimonial Causes (Decree Absolute) General Order 1972. It should rarely be necessary for the court to reduce the period: *Practice Note* (*Divorce: Decree Absolute*), [1972] 3 All E.R. 416. This is particularly true if the petition is based on two or five years' separation because the respondent may then lose the financial protection afforded by s. 10 of the Matrimonial Causes Act 1973 (see *post*, pp. 227 and 235), as happened in *Dryden* v. *Dryden*, [1973] Fam. 217; [1973] 3 All E.R. 526. For a case where the period was reduced, see *Torok* v. *Torok*, [1973] 3 All E.R. 101 (decree expedited to prevent a Hungarian court from dissolving the marriage, which would have left the wife with no effective claim for financial provision).

[3] Interventions by the Queen's Proctor are now very rare. During the years 1972-1975 (the last year for which statistics were published) there were only eight a year on the average. The Queen's Proctor's assistance may be invoked by the court itself, *e.g.* if an undefended suit presents a difficult point of law which counsel briefed by him can then argue. See the Matrimonial Causes Act 1973, ss. 8 and 9 (1), and the Report of the Morton Commission, Cmd. 9678, paras. 947-968.

[4] The decree dissolves the marriage *status* and not the marriage *ceremony*: *Thynne* v. *Thynne*, [1955] P. 272; [1955] 3 All E.R. 129, C.A. In this case the parties, who had already been married secretly, went through a second form of marriage which was therefore a nullity. In the wife's petition for divorce and the decrees made thereon the particulars of the *second* ceremony were inserted. It was held that the decree nisi and the decree absolute could be amended so as to make it clear that the parties' marriage had been dissolved.

[5] A decree nisi must not be made absolute if an appeal is pending: *Lloyd-Davies* v. *Lloyd-Davies*, [1947] P. 53; [1947] 1 All E.R. 161, C.A. No clergyman of the Church of England or of the Church in Wales can be compelled to marry any divorced person during the lifetime of his or her former spouse or to permit his church or chapel to be used for the solemnization of such a marriage: Matrimonial Causes Act 1965, s. 8 (2).

[6] See *post*, pp. 309-310.

[7] See Rayden, *Divorce*, 13th Ed., 636-637.

[8] *Rogers* v. *Rogers*, [1962] C.L.Y. 1045.

Irretrievable breakdown, however, may be established only by proving one of the five facts set out in section 1 (2). If none of these is made out, the court may not pronounce a decree even though it is convinced that the marriage is at an end.[1] If any one of the facts is proved, the court must pronounce a decree nisi (subject to one exception)[2] unless it is satisfied that the marriage has not broken down irretrievably.[3] Hence proof of any of the facts raises a presumption of breakdown.[4] Although it is the duty of the court "to inquire, so far as it reasonably can, into the facts alleged" by both parties,[5] in practical terms the burden on the petitioner is solely to establish one of the facts and it is for the respondent in a defended suit to show, if he wishes, that the marriage has not broken down irretrievably. The petitioner's assertions, though clearly highly relevant, cannot be conclusive,[6] but there can be very few cases indeed where there is still any chance of a reconciliation by the time the case has got as far as the hearing.[7]

We must now examine the five facts set out in the Act.

1. THE RESPONDENT'S ADULTERY

The first fact on which the petitioner may rely is that the respondent has committed adultery and that the petitioner finds it intolerable to live with him.[8] It will be seen that there are two limbs. Adultery by itself is no longer sufficient: Parliament has accepted that infidelity may be a symptom of breakdown rather than a cause of it and that an isolated act of adultery may not even be a symptom.

Adultery.—Adultery may be defined as sexual intercourse between two persons of whom one or both are married but who are not married to each other.[9]

---

[1] As in *Richards* v. *Richards*, [1972] 3 All E.R. 695 (*post*, p. 205).

[2] *I.e.*, grave hardship to the respondent if the petitioner relies on five years' separation: see *post*, pp. 230-235.

[3] Matrimonial Causes Act 1973, s. 1 (4).

[4] But even when the petitioner relies on a fact imputing misconduct to the respondent, this need not have been the cause of the breakdown: *Stevens* v. *Stevens*, [1979] 1 W.L.R. 885.

[5] Matrimonial Causes Act 1973, s. 1 (3).

[6] *Ash* v. *Ash*, [1972] Fam. 135, 141; [1972] 1 All E.R. 582, 586; *Katz* v. *Katz*, [1972] 3 All E.R. 219, 223. But if the decree is granted under the special procedure (as will usually be the case), the petitioner's assertions will in fact be conclusive: See *post*, pp. 240-241.

[7] It must be shown that the marriage has irretrievably broken down at the date of the hearing (and not at the date of the petition). Any other interpretation of the Act would make nonsense of the provisions empowering the court to adjourn the proceedings to enable the parties to attempt a reconciliation (see *post*, p. 228): *Pheasant* v. *Pheasant*, [1972] Fam. 202, 206; [1972] 1 All E.R. 587, 589.

[8] Matrimonial Causes Act 1973, s. 1 (2) (a). It will be observed that, unlike previous statutes, the Act does not require the adultery to have been committed since the celebration of the marriage. It is inconceivable, however, that the courts will construe this as enabling a petitioner to rely on pre-marital adultery (to which he could have been a party). *Cf.* the rule that pre-marital conduct cannot justify desertion, *post*, p. 216.

[9] Unless the court otherwise orders, any person still alive with whom it is alleged that the respondent has committed adultery must be joined as a party to the proceedings: Matrimonial Causes Act 1973, s. 49; Matrimonial Causes Rules 1977, r. 13. A finding of adultery in matrimonial proceedings in the High Court or a county court is *prima facie* evidence (which may be rebutted) of its commission in any subsequent civil proceedings: Civil Evidence Act 1968, s. 12. Hence if H obtains a decree of divorce alleging W's adultery with X, X's wife could use this as evidence of X's adultery if she were to bring divorce proceedings.

Nature of the Act.—There need not be full penetration to constitute adultery,[1] but, as the Court of Appeal held in *Dennis* v. *Dennis*,[2] there must be some penetration of the female by the male organ, although, as in the case of rape, any degree of penetration, however slight, will suffice. Hence it seems that a woman who has herself artificially inseminated with another man's seed does not thereby commit adultery.[3]

Act must be Voluntary.—In order to be guilty of adultery, a person must have had sexual intercourse voluntarily.[4] Hence if a married woman is raped, she does not commit adultery.[5] The principle applies equally if a woman's consent is negatived by force or fear; a more difficult problem arises if either party alleges that his act was not voluntary because he was suffering from mental disorder at the time that he committed it. The moral turpitude of a person who commits a matrimonial offence resulted in a tendency to regard adultery and cruelty as similar in character to criminal offences and therefore to apply the *M'Naghten* rules to them.[6] Consequently insanity was held to be a defence if the party alleged to have committed adultery was so insane as not to know the nature and quality of his act, or, if he did, that he did not know that what he was doing was wrong in the sense of morally blameworthy or culpable.[7] Although it was subsequently held that insanity is not necessarily a defence to a charge of cruelty,[8] it is submitted that it should remain so in the case of adultery, at least if its effect was that the party could not be said to have consented to the act at all. The effect of drink or drugs raises a much more difficult question. It has been held that a wife is not guilty of adultery if she has consented to the act because of drink taken in excusable circumstances:[9] what circumstances, however, will be considered excusable? The House of Lords has laid down the principle that self-induced intoxication is no defence to a criminal charge when no special intent has to be proved, because there is no justification for giving a person in this position a protection that he would otherwise not have.[10] It is submitted that this should apply

---

[1] *Rutherford* v. *Richardson*, [1923] A.C. 1, H.L.; *Thompson* v. *Thompson*, [1938] P. 162; [1938] 2 All E.R. 727; *Sapsford* v. *Sapsford*, [1954] P. 394; [1954] 2 All E.R. 373.

[2] [1955] P. 153; [1955] 2 All E.R. 51, C.A.

[3] Artificial insemination has been held not to amount to adultery in Scotland: *Maclennan* v. *Maclennan*, 1958 S.L.T. 12. See also Bartholomew, *Legal Implications of Artificial Insemination*, 21 M.L.R. 236, at pp. 251 *et seq.* For the contrary view see Tallin, *Artificial Insemination*, 34 Can. Bar Rev. 1, 166, where a number of problems arising out of this practice are discussed. But she might be guilty of "unreasonable behaviour" or constructive desertion if she were inseminated without her husband's consent.

[4] *Clarkson* v. *Clarkson* (1930), 143 L.T. 775. *Cf. N.* v. *N.* (1963), 107 Sol. Jo. 1025.

[5] *Clarkson* v. *Clarkson*, (*supra*). The fact that the man would not be guilty of a criminal offence because he believed that the woman was consenting is irrelevant, but as the question whether or not she consented is peculiarly within her knowledge, the burden of proving lack of consent is on her: *Redpath* v. *Redpath*, [1950] 1 All E.R. 600, C.A.

[6] *R.* v. *M'Naghten* (1843), 10 Cl. & F. 200, H.L. See Smith and Hogan, *Criminal Law*, 4th Ed., 162 *et seq.*

[7] *Yarrow* v. *Yarrow*, [1892] P. 92; *Hanbury* v. *Hanbury* (1892), 8 T.L.R. 559, C.A.; *S.* v. *S.*, [1962] P. 133; [1961] 3 All E.R. 133.

[8] *Williams* v. *Williams*, [1964] A.C. 698; [1963] 2 All E.R. 994, H.L.

[9] *Goshawk* v. *Goshawk* (1965), 109 Sol. Jo. 290.

[10] *R.* v. *Majewski*, [1977] A.C. 443; [1976] 2 All E.R. 142, H.L. Thus self-induced intoxication would be a defence to murder if the accused was incapable of forming an intent to kill or to do grievous bodily harm but it would be no defence to manslaughter where malice aforethought does not have to be established.

to adultery for the same reason; consequently, a wife should be excused, for example, if unknown to her her drinks had been "laced" but not if she was entirely responsible for her own situation.[1]

Standard of Proof.—There has been considerable judicial controversy over the standard of proof required when there is an allegation of adultery. As the proceedings are civil, one would expect it to be sufficient to show that the party was guilty on the balance of probabilities; confusion has arisen because of the tendency (seen above in connection with insanity) to treat adultery as akin to a criminal offence and therefore to require proof beyond reasonable doubt. In *Blyth* v. *Blyth*[2] the House of Lords were divided in their *obiter* views about the correct test. Two years later the Court of Appeal in *Bastable* v. *Bastable*[3] took up an intermediate position and said that the law requires a high standard of proof or "a degree of probability . . . commensurate with the occasion": a direction which, it is respectfully submitted, is vague and unhelpful. The problem has been further complicated by the rule at common law that the presumption of legitimacy could be rebutted only by evidence putting the matter beyond reasonable doubt; if a husband's evidence of his wife's adultery was the birth of a child of which he alleged he could not be the father, the courts declined to be forced into a position in which they might have to hold that the wife had committed adultery but that the child was legitimate.[4] But now that the Family Law Reform Act 1969 provides that the presumption of legitimacy may be rebutted on the balance of probabilities,[5] the courts must surely accept the same standard of proof of adultery: otherwise, in the situation outlined above, they might have to hold that the wife had not committed adultery but that the child was illegitimate—an even more absurd situation than the opposite.

Intolerability.—Whether or not the petitioner finds it intolerable to live with the respondent is clearly a question of fact and the test is subjective: did *this* petitioner find it intolerable to live with *this* respondent?[6] If the court is satisfied of this, it is quite irrelevant that the petitioner's attitude is wholly unreasonable, but he may be required to give some explanation or justification for his attitude so that its genuineness may be tested.[7]

It will be observed that the Act does not require there to be any causal connection between the two limbs. After some initial doubts, when it was suggested that the petitioner should be able to allege that he found it intolerable to live with the respondent only if this was in consequence of the

---

[1] In any case, even though force, fraud, insanity, etc., will exculpate one party, the party acting voluntarily will be guilty of adultery: see *Barnett* v. *Barnett*, [1957] P. 78; [1957] 1 All E.R. 388; *S.* v. *S.*, (*supra.*) See further Fridman, *Mental Incompetency*, 80 L.Q.R. 84, pp. 96-98.

[2] [1966] A.C. 643; [1966] 1 All E.R. 524, H.L.

[3] [1968] 3 All E.R. 701, 704, C.A.

[4] *F.* v. *F.*, [1968] P. 506; [1968] 1 All E.R. 242, following dicta in *Preston-Jones* v. *Preston-Jones*; [1951] A.C. 391; [1951] 1 All E.R. 124, H.L., where the same situation had arisen.

[5] See *post*, p. 259.

[6] *Goodrich* v. *Goodrich*, [1971] 2 All E.R. 1340, 1342; *Pheasant* v. *Pheasant*, [1972] Fam. 202, 207; [1972] 1 All E.R. 587, 590.

[7] *Goodrich* v. *Goodrich*, (*supra*), at p. 1342; *Roper* v. *Roper*, [1972] 3 All E.R. 668, 670; *Cleary* v. *Cleary*, [1974] 1 All E.R. 498, at pp. 501 and 503, C.A.

adultery, the Court of Appeal held in *Cleary* v. *Cleary*[1] that the statute must be interpreted literally and that the petitioner may therefore rely not only on the adultery but also on any other matter to show that further cohabitation would be intolerable to him. In that case the husband took the wife back after she had committed adultery, but she continued to correspond with the man in question, went out at night and finally left him to live with her mother. The husband stated in evidence that he could no longer live with her because "there was no future for the marriage at all". The court held that he had established irretrievable breakdown of the marriage notwithstanding that he found life with her intolerable not on account of her adultery but on account of her subsequent conduct. In other cases a decree has been granted when the petitioner found life with the respondent intolerable because of the latter's refusal to consider a reconciliation[2] and because of his treatment of the parties' children.[3]

Cleary v. *Cleary* has not passed without judicial criticism[4] and it may yet be overruled by the House of Lords. It is difficult to reconcile this interpretation with the provision that cohabitation for a period not exceeding six months after the petitioner discovers the respondent's adultery shall be disregarded in determining whether he finds it intolerable to live with the respondent,[5] which implies that it must be the discovery of the adultery that makes cohabitation intolerable. More substantial criticism may be levelled against it when one considers some of the anomalies that it produces. If the petitioner finds life with the respondent intolerable because of the latter's personal habits, it is not immediately apparent why the commission of adultery (which may be purely fortuitous) should forthwith give him the power to petition for divorce. Nor, indeed, need the petitioner find it intolerable to live with the respondent because of the latter's conduct at all. If the reason is that he has fallen in love with another woman, there is no logical reason why he should not establish irretrievable breakdown of his marriage.[6] *Cleary* v. *Cleary* also opens the door to divorce based on adultery at which the petitioner has connived. He clearly could not be heard to say that he found life with the respondent intolerable because of such an act, but if he finds it intolerable for some other reason, the express abolition of all the old bars indicates that he could now obtain a divorce by persuading the respondent to commit adultery. One feels that the judges would hesitate to assist him in achieving this end, but it is difficult to see how they could avoid doing so unless they fell back on the general principle of *volenti non fit injuria* and refused to let him base a petition on an act which he had brought about himself.

---

[1] [1974] 1 All E.R. 498, C.A. See Rudd, 5 Fam. Law 176.

[2] *Goodrich* v. *Goodrich*, (*supra*).

[3] *Carr* v. *Carr*, [1974] 1 All E.R. 1193, C.A.

[4] See *Carr* v. *Carr*, (*supra*). For a contrary view, see Eekelaar, 90 L.Q.R. 292.

[5] Matrimonial Causes Act 1973, s. 2 (2). See *post*, p. 229.

[6] This runs counter to the view expressed by LORD DENNING, M.R., in *Cleary* v. *Cleary*, (*supra*), at p. 76, where he denied that the petitioner would be able to show irretrievable breakdown in these circumstances. The inference from this *obiter dictum* is that he can say that he finds life with the respondent intolerable only if this is the result of the latter's own conduct. *Sed quaere*? Now that the Court of Appeal has adopted the literal interpretation of the Act, no further gloss should be put on it.

2. THE RESPONDENT'S BEHAVIOUR

The petitioner may establish that the marriage has irretrievably broken down by showing that the respondent has behaved in such a way that the petitioner cannot reasonably be expected to live with him.[1]

It is unfortunate that this is frequently abbreviated to "unreasonable behaviour". This suggests that all one has to look at is the quality of the respondent's behaviour, whereas in fact what is important is the effect of that conduct upon the petitioner.

Nature of the Test to be applied.—In order to understand the difficulties that this fact has given rise to, it is first necessary to say something of the grounds for divorce under the old law which it has replaced.[2]

The first of these is constructive desertion. This is still a fact upon which a petitioner may rely but, as we shall see, it now serves little purpose.[3] The essence of desertion is the respondent's unjustifiable withdrawal from cohabitation and one of the most important elements in it is the spouses' conduct. If one of them (say, the husband) treats the other so badly that she leaves, the latter will not be in desertion because she will be justified in going; the husband for his part will be regarded as having brought cohabitation to an end by driving the wife out and will himself be in constructive desertion. In order to bring about this state of affairs the husband's conduct must "amount to such a grave and weighty matter as renders the continuance of the matrimonial cohabitation virtually impossible".[4] The similarity between conduct of this sort and behaviour such that the petitioner cannot reasonably be expected to live with the respondent is immediately apparent.

The second of the old grounds is cruelty. This was a ground for divorce *a mensa et thoro* in ecclesiastical law and remained a ground for judicial separation until 1970. It was also a ground for divorce until that year and for relief in a magistrates' court until the Domestic Proceedings and Magistrates' Courts Act 1978 came into force. As the law developed, it became necessary to prove two things in order to establish a charge of cruelty: that the respondent had been guilty of "reprehensible conduct or departure from the normal standards of conjugal kindness"[5] and that this had caused actual or apprehended injury to the petitioner's health.[6] Eventually the courts adopted the same test to determine whether conduct was sufficiently reprehensible to found a charge of cruelty as they adopted to determine whether it would found a charge of constructive desertion. In each case it had to be "grave and weighty", and if it was not sufficiently grave and weighty to constitute cruelty, it could not be relied on to justify withdrawal from cohabitation or to constitute constructive desertion.[7] It has never been suggested that injury to health is a necessary ingredient of "unreasonable behaviour", although

---

[1] Matrimonial Causes Act 1973, s. 1 (2) (b).

[2] It has also replaced the ground of commission of an unnatural offence by the husband.

[3] *Post*, p. 219.

[4] See *post*, pp. 215-219.

[5] *Per* LORD PEARCE in *Gollins* v. *Gollins*, [1964] A.C. 644, 695; [1963] 2 All E.R. 966, 992, H.L.

[6] *Russell* v. *Russell*, [1897] A.C. 395, H.L.

[7] *Young* v. *Young*, [1964] P. 152; [1962] 3 All E.R. 120; *Ogden* v. *Ogden*, [1969] 3 All E.R. 1055, C.A.

obviously the petitioner's case will be strengthened if her health has suffered as a result of the respondent's conduct. On the other hand, the relationship between cruelty and constructive desertion and the nature of the test that was applied in cruelty suggest a close link between the old offence and the new fact.

Whether the respondent's behaviour has been such that the petitioner can no longer reasonably be expected[1] to live with him is essentially a question of fact. It is neither desirable nor possible to categorise conduct as guilty or blameless in the abstract. But one point must be stressed at the outset. As we have seen, the question whether the petitioner finds it intolerable to live with the respondent must be answered subjectively: whether his attitude is reasonable is irrelevant. In dealing with behaviour, however, the question is whether the petitioner can *reasonably* be expected to live with the respondent and it is for the court, and not the petitioner, to answer it[2] The test is thus objective, but this is not the same as asking whether a hypothetical reasonable spouse in the petitioner's position would continue to live with the respondent. The court must have regard to the personalities of the individuals before it, however far these may be removed from some theoretical norm, and it must assess the impact of the respondent's conduct on the particular petitioner in the light of the whole history of the marriage and their relationship. In the words of Dunn, J., in *Livingstone-Stallard* v. *Livingstone-Stallard*:[3]

> "Would any right-thinking person come to the conclusion that *this* husband has behaved in such a way that *this* wife cannot reasonably be expected to live with him, taking into account the whole of the circumstances and the characters and personalities of the parties?"

This was spelled out rather more fully by Bagnall, J., in *Ash* v. *Ash*:[4]

> "I have to consider not only the behaviour of the respondent . . . but the character, personality, disposition and behaviour of the petitioner. The general question may be expanded thus: can this petitioner, with his or her character and personality, with his or her faults and other attributes, good and bad, and having regard to his or her behaviour during the marriage, reasonably be expected to live with this respondent?"

Consequently the respondent's behaviour must be looked at not in isolation but in relation to all the relevant circumstances.

Respondent's Conduct.—Clearly one must start by looking at the respondent's conduct. A conscious attempt on the part of the judges to get away from the old concept of the matrimonial offence has produced some hesitation about the correct legal test to be applied. It has already been

---

[1] *I.e.*, required: *Pheasant* v. *Pheasant*, [1972] Fam. 202, 207; [1972] 1 All E.R. 587, 590. The word "expected" is not used in an anticipatory sense.

[2] See *Ash* v. *Ash*, [1972] Fam. 135, 139-140; [1972] 1 All E.R. 582, 585; *Pheasant* v. *Pheasant*, (*supra*), at pp. 207-208 and 590, respectively; *Katz* v. *Katz*, [1972] 3 All E.R. 219, 223; *Richards* v. *Richards*, [1972] 3 All E.R. 695, 699; *Thurlow* v. *Thurlow*, [1976] Fam. 32, 46; [1975] 2 All E.R. 979, 988; *O'Neill* v. *O'Neill*, [1975] 3 All E.R. 289, 292, C.A.

[3] [1974] Fam. 47, 54; [1974] 2 All E.R. 766, 771; adopted by Roskill, L.J., in *O'Neill* v. *O'Neill*, (*supra*), at p. 295. Italics supplied. See also *Ash* v. *Ash*, (*supra*), at pp. 140 and 585, respectively.

[4] [1972] Fam. 135, 140; [1972] 1 All E.R. 582, 585.

pointed out, however, that there can be no sensible difference between the behaviour in question and conduct which would justify the petitioner in leaving the respondent and so provide a defence to a charge of desertion. It certainly cannot be less grave and weighty than this: otherwise, as ORMROD, J., indicated in *Pheasant* v. *Pheasant*,[1] a petitioner, who would be in desertion if he left the respondent, would nevertheless be able to obtain a divorce. In his view:[2]

> "The test to be applied . . . is closely similar to, but not necessarily identical with, that which was formerly used in relation to constructive desertion. I would not wish to see carried over into the new law all the technicalities which accumulated round the idea of constructive desertion but rather to use the broader approach indicated by PEARCE, J., in *Lissack* v. *Lissack*[3] and consider whether it is reasonable to expect this petitioner to put up with the behaviour of this respondent, bearing in mind the characters and difficulties of each of them, trying to be fair to both of them, and expecting neither heroic virtue nor selfless abnegation from either."

This test has subsequently been adopted by BAKER, P., in *Katz* v. *Katz*[4] and by REES, J., in *Richards* v. *Richards*[5] and its appropriateness has been doubted in only one reported case. In *Livingstone-Stallard* v. *Livingstone-Stallard*[6] DUNN, J., after admitting that he had previously followed ORMROD, J.'s reasoning in *Pheasant* v. *Pheasant*, nevertheless questioned whether it was helpful to import notions of constructive desertion into this new fact or to analyse the degree of gravity of conduct required to enable a petitioner to succeed under it. With respect to the learned judge, however, it is impossible to fault ORMROD, J.'s argument; moreover, to apply DUNN, J.'s alternative test,[7] a right-thinking person would conclude that the petitioner could not be expected to live with the respondent only if the latter's behaviour had been such as to make married life together impossible in the circumstances. There must be some guideline to enable practitioners to advise prospective petitioners and to ensure uniformity of judicial decisions, and if the yardstick of "grave and weighty conduct" is abandoned, it is not easy to see what could replace it.[8]

An examination of the facts of reported cases also indicates that the courts are granting relief only in circumstances where they would be prepared to say that the respondent's conduct would support a charge of constructive desertion. For example, a wife has obtained a decree against a husband who has treated her with violence,[9] who persisted in a course of conduct designed to drive her from the matrimonial home,[10] whose domineering manner led him to belittle her and level abuse and unwarranted criticism at her,[11] and who

---

[1] [1972] Fam. 202, 208; [1972] 1 All E.R. 587, 591. *Cf. Stringfellow* v. *Stringfellow, post*, p. 202.

[2] At pp. 208 and 591, respectively.

[3] [1951] P. 1; [1950] 2 All E.R. 233.

[4] [1972] 3 All E.R. 219, 223.

[5] [1972] 3 All E.R. 695, 699.

[6] [1974] Fam. 47, 54; [1974] 2 All E.R. 766, 771.

[7] See *ante*, p. 200.

[8] See Hall, [1974] C.L.J. 219.

[9] *Ash* v. *Ash*, (*supra*).

[10] *Stevens* v. *Stevens*, [1979] 1 W.L.R. 885.

[11] *Livingstone-Stallard* v. *Livingstone-Stallard*, (*supra*).

made the matrimonial home virtually uninhabitable for months by carrying out building operations (which he was not qualified to do) as well as quite unjustifiably alleging that the two children of the marriage were not his.[1] Similarly, a husband has successfully relied on his wife's association with another man stopping short of adultery.[2] From this it follows that the petitioner could complain of the respondent's adultery under this head without also having to show that he found life with the other intolerable, although he could scarcely do so if he had connived at the adultery in question or there was some other conduct on his part (for example, his own adulterous association) which might lead the court to conclude that he could reasonably be expected to live with the respondent notwithstanding the latter's adultery.[3]

On the other side of the line, in *Pheasant* v. *Pheasant*, ORMROD, J., dismissed the petition of a husband whose sole charge against the wife was that she was unable to give him the demonstrative affection for which he craved whereas, as the learned judge found, she had given him all the affection she could and nothing in her behaviour could be regarded as a breach of any of the obligations of marriage. Similarly in *Stringfellow* v. *Stringfellow*[4] the Court of Appeal held that simple desertion on the part of the respondent cannot found a petition based on this fact. The reason given was that any other conclusion would make the third fact on which a petitioner can rely—two years' desertion—wholly redundant. An equally valid argument would be that, as a petitioner is bound to accept an offer to resume cohabitation made by a deserting spouse,[5] desertion alone cannot possibly justify a claim that he cannot reasonably be expected to live with the respondent.

Given that the behaviour is sufficiently serious, it can take a variety of forms. It must be stressed, however, that it implies some form of conduct and not merely a state of mind. As BAKER, P., put it in *Katz* v. *Katz*:[6]

> "Behaviour is something more than a mere state of affairs or a state of mind, such as for example a repugnance to sexual intercourse, or a feeling that the wife is not reciprocating the husband's love, or not being as demonstrative as he thinks she should be. Behaviour in this context is action or conduct by one which affects the other. Such conduct may either take the form of acts or omissions or may be a course of conduct, and, in my view, it must have some reference to the marriage."

To take examples of positive acts from the old law of cruelty, behaviour could consist of sexual perversion and homosexual activities,[7] persistent drunkenness, addiction to gambling, commission of criminal offences

---

[1] *O'Neill* v. *O'Neill*, [1975] 3 All E.R. 289, C.A.

[2] *Wachtel* v. *Wachtel* (1972), *Times*, 1st August.

[3] *Cf. Poon* v. *Tan* (1973), 4 Fam. Law 160, C.A. (bigamy). The significance of this will be appreciated more fully when we consider the consequences of cohabitation for more than six months after the discovery of the adultery (*post*, pp. 229-230). See Levin, 33 M.L.R. 632, 640-641.

[4] [1976] 2 All E.R. 539, C.A. Contrast *Shears* v. *Shears* (1972), 117 Sol. Jo. 33, where a decree was granted to a husband whose wife had obtained an injuction ordering him to leave the matrimonial home on grounds which subsequently proved to be baseless and then persistently and unreasonably refused him access to their children. Her conduct would have justified him in leaving her, however anxious she might have been to resume cohabitation later.

[5] See *post*, p. 223.

[6] [1972] 3 All E.R. 219, 223.

[7] *Arthur* v. *Arthur* (1964), 108 Sol. Jo. 317, C.A. (husband respondent); *Coffer* v. *Coffer* (1964), 108 Sol. Jo. 465 (wife respondent).

(particularly of a sexual character),[1] threats, insults, nagging, persistent dishonesty causing embarrassment,[2] maliciously taking matrimonial proceedings,[3] and obsessional conduct of various kinds.[4] It is equally clear that behaviour may be negative. In practice it may be more difficult for a petition to succeed in reliance on negative behaviour because a spouse may often be expected to tolerate more in the way of inactivity than of violent conduct,[5] but neglect, indifference, meanness and failure to provide maintenance have all been held to constitute cruelty in the past.[6] But when the petitioner is relying on an omission, it is submitted that it must be wilful: it is difficult to see how an involuntary failure to act can ever amount to "behaviour". This has caused difficulty in the past when the basic trouble between the spouses has been sexual. As BAKER, P., pointed out in the passage quoted above, repugnance to sexual intercourse is not behaviour; but refusal of intercourse clearly will be if it is wilful.[7] It has been held, however, that a wife could not rely on this fact when she had been made unhappy by infrequent and unsatisfactory intercourse due to the husband's low sexual drive;[8] *a fortiori* involuntary abstinence due to supervening impotence cannot be behaviour on the part of a spouse who may be desperately anxious to have normal sexual relations.

Obviously the whole history of the marriage must be looked at: the cumulative effect of a series of acts might well amount to behaviour which the petitioner could not reasonably be expected to put up with, even though each of them taken separately might be too trivial.[9] Conduct which has occurred since cohabitation came to an end may also be relied on, for example assaults or pestering telephone calls.[10] On the other hand, by analogy with the law of desertion, the petitioner probably cannot complain of the respondent's behaviour before the marriage.[11]

The Respondent's Knowledge, Belief, Motive and Intention.—In 1963 the House of Lords decisively rejected the view that cruelty necessarily connotes any intention on the respondent's part and they held that, if his conduct could

[1] *H* v. *H.* (1964), 108 Sol. Jo. 544. Contrast *Boushall* v. *Boushall* (1964), *Times*, 7th November.

[2] *Stanwick* v. *Stanwick*, [1971] P. 124; [1970] 3 All E.R. 938, C.A.

[3] *Buxton* v. *Buxton*, [1967] P. 48; [1965] 3 All E.R. 150.

[4] *Williams* v. *Williams*, [1964] A.C. 698; [1963] 2 All E.R. 994, H.L. (constant accusations of infidelity and searching for wife's lovers); *Howell* v. *Howell* (1964), *Times*, 10th June (obsessional cleaning of house all night); *Crump* v. *Crump*, [1965] 2 All E.R. 980 (ritual wiping of everything to kill "cancer germs").

[5] *Per* REES, J., in *Thurlow* v. *Thurlow*, [1976] Fam. 32, 46; [1975] 2 All E.R. 979, 988.

[6] *Gollins* v. *Gollins*, [1964] A.C. 644; [1963] 2 All E.R. 966, H.L.

[7] *Sheldon* v. *Sheldon*, [1966] P. 62; [1966] 2 All E.R. 257, C.A. (cruelty).

[8] *Dowden* v. *Dowden* (1977), 8 Fam. Law 106, C.A. Cf. *B.(L.)* v. *B.(R.)*, [1965] 3 All E.R. 263, C.A.; *P.* v. *P.*, [1964] 3 All E.R. 919. But in *P. (D.)* v. *P.(J.)*, [1965] 2 All E.R. 456, it was held that a wife was guilty of cruelty by refusing to have intercourse even though this was due to an invincible fear of conception and childbirth. By approving these decisions, the Court of Appeal in *Sheldon* v. *Sheldon*, (*supra*), apeared to be demanding different standards of sexual participation from husbands and wives. This appears to be quite out of keeping with modern views of the spouses' roles in the sexual side of their marriage, and *Dowden* v. *Dowden* should be applied whichever spouse is the petitioner.

[9] *Stevens* v. *Stevens*, [1979] 1 W.L.R. 885. As HENN COLLINS, J., put it in relation to cruelty, "Dropping water wears the stone": *Atkins* v. *Atkins*, [1942] 2 All E.R. 637, 638.

[10] Cf. *Britt* v. *Britt*, [1955] 3 All E.R. 769, C.A. (cruelty).

[11] See *post*, pp. 219-220.

fairly be called cruel, it does not matter whether it springs from a desire to hurt or from selfishness or sheer indifference.[1] Obviously this principle must apply even more strongly to the new fact of behaviour. But this does not mean that the state of the respondent's mind will be irrelevant in every case. Admittedly it is likely to be so when the effect of his conduct on the petitioner is physical. If a husband makes a savage attack on his wife, his motive is immaterial. But even here his knowledge of the probable consequences of his acts could be decisive. If he buys a cat as a pet, for example, this will not normally be behaviour on his part which will enable the wife to allege that she cannot reasonably be expected to live with him, but she might be able to do so if he knows that she is made physically ill by cats and *a fortiori* if he introduces it into the house with the intention of injuring her health. If the effect of the respondent's conduct is psychological, however, these matters will frequently be important, particularly if the petitioner's complaint is that she has been neglected, and in doubtful cases they will be decisive. In the words of LORD PEARCE:[2]

> "Whereas a blow speaks for itself, insults, humiliations, meannesses, impositions, deprivations, and the like may need the interpretation of underlying intention for an assessment of their fullest significance."

One may adapt the illustration that he drew in his speech in *Gollins* v. *Gollins*,[3] where he contrasted the situation of two wives taken seriously ill abroad and left there by their husbands who return to England. The first is a woman who is timorous, unable to speak the language, left without adequate nursing arrangements or money and the reason for the husband's return is that he wishes to watch a football match; the second wife has a more robust and independent nature, a knowledge of the language, a less severe illness and more adequate nursing arrangements and her husband has a more cogent reason for returning. The husband's behaviour in the first case is clearly such that the wife cannot be expected to live with him; that in the second *prima facie* is not but would be if he deliberately intended to hurt. Indeed such an intention must always entitle the other spouse to petition if it is sufficiently grave and weighty.

Effect of the Respondent's Mental Illness.—In *Williams* v. *Williams*[4] the House of Lords laid down the rule that the respondent's mental illness was not necessarily a defence to a charge of cruelty but was one of the matters to be taken into account along with the parties' temperaments and other circumstances. The tendency has been to follow that case when dealing with the respondent's behaviour under the new law. In *Katz* v. *Katz*[5] and *Richards* v. *Richards*[6] BAKER, P., and REES, J., independently adapted the test propounded by LORD REID in the following words:[7]

---

[1] *Gollins* v. *Gollins*, (supra).

[2] *Gollins* v. *Gollins*, (supra), at pp. 690 and 989, respectively.

[3] [1964] A.C. 644, 693; [1963] 2 All E.R. 966, 990-991, H.L.

[4] [1964] A.C. 698, particularly at pp. 731 and 762; [1963] 2 All E.R. 994, particularly at pp. 1009 and 1029, H.L.

[5] [1972] 3 All E.R. 219, 224.

[6] [1972] 3 All E.R. 695, 700. See also *Thurlow* v. *Thurlow*, [1976] Fam. 32, 44; [1975] 2 All E.R. 979, 987.

[7] At pp. 723 and 1004, respectively.

"In my judgment, decree should be pronounced against such an abnormal person...simply because the facts are such that, after making all allowances for his disabilities and for the temperaments of both parties, it must be held that the character and gravity of his behaviour was such that the petitioner cannot reasonably be expected to live with him."

A wife may reasonably be expected to nurse a sick husband and to tolerate some degree of abnormal behaviour on his part: the question in each case is whether this particular husband's conduct has become so abnormal that she can no longer reasonably be expected to live with him. Thus in *Richards* v. *Richards* the petition was dismissed when the wife's only substantial complaint was that the husband, whose illness made him moody and taciturn and caused him to disturb his wife at night when he got up because of insomnia, had on one occasion lost his temper and struck her on the head four or five times without causing any injury. In *Katz* v. *Katz*, however, the wife was granted a decree where the husband, who was a manic depressive and had spent some time in a mental hospital, constantly made her feel small before visitors, called her a slut before their children, and produced in her such a severe state of anxiety that she made a determined attempt to commit suicide.

The later decision of REES, J., in *Thurlow* v. *Thurlow*,[1] however, appears to have gone much further. As a result of mental disease the wife became progressively less able to perform any domestic duties. She threw things at her mother-in-law (with whom their circumstances obliged the spouses to live), burnt articles on the electric heater and wandered into the street, causing her husband stress and worry. Eventually she became bedridden and incontinent and was admitted to hospital when her husband could no longer cope with the situation. There was no reasonable hope that her condition would improve and the husband petitioned for divorce alleging that her behaviour was such that he could no longer reasonably be expected to live with her. REES, J., granted him a decree.

The learned judge stated explicitly that, if the behaviour in question stems from misfortune, such as mental or physical illness or an accident, the court must take full account of all the obligations of the married state including the normal duty to accept and share the burdens imposed by the respondent's ill-health. But it must also consider the length of time the petitioner has had to bear them, the effect upon his health and his capacity to bear the stresses imposed, and in the end must decide whether he can fairly be required to live with the respondent.[2] This, however, overlooks the real problem: how far can one regard as "behaviour" conduct over which the respondent has no control? There can be no doubt that acts can amount to behaviour if they are genuinely voluntary even though they are the consequences of derangement like the wife's throwing things and wandering in the street in *Thurlow* v. *Thurlow*. To take an extreme case, a wife could not reasonably be expected to live with a husband who attacked her with a knife in the insane belief that she was about to murder him. But could the same be said if he struck her during an epileptic fit or was found in the street whilst sleepwalking? These cannot be regarded as his acts at all. The same principle applies if the alleged behaviour is negative in nature. Although REES, J., left the point open, a person

---

1 [1976] Fam. 32; [1975] 2 All E.R. 979. See Hall, [1975] C.L.J. 207.
2 At pp. 44 and 987, respectively.

who is rendered permanently comatose or turned into a "human vegetable" as the result of a road accident cannot be said to be "behaving" in any sense of the word. Why should the result be legally different if he is gradually reduced to this state as a result of mental deterioration?[1] No social purpose would be served in keeping the marriage alive in cases like *Thurlow* v. *Thurlow* and it is urged that the petitioner should be granted a decree whenever possible, but once the respondent ceases to have any control whatever over his conduct, the courts are compelled to withhold relief because he is not "behaving". It is for Parliament, not the judges, to amend the Act.[2]

The Petitioner's Health, Temperament and Conduct.—Although it has been repeatedly said that the judges are no longer required to pass judgment on the parties but merely to consider the impact of the respondent's conduct on the petitioner, it is obvious that the latter's temperament and behaviour cannot be ignored. The court must consider the particular petitioner's capacity to endure the respondent's behaviour and how far that capacity was or ought to have been known to the respondent. Thus, if a wife is pregnant or in a poor state of health, she is entitled to more considerate treatment from her husband.[3] Conversely, acts which appear on the face to be unpardonable may in the particular circumstances be, if not justified, at least excused by the petitioner's own conduct and the amount of provocation she offered to the respondent. In *Ash* v. *Ash*[4] BAGNALL, J., concluded that a violent petitioner can be expected to live with a violent respondent, a taciturn and morose petitioner can be expected to live with a taciturn and morose respondent, and so forth. Within limits this statement is obviously true; on the other hand, there must come a time when, for example, each is treating the other with such exceptional violence that neither can reasonably be expected to live with the other. The petitioner's acquiescence in the respondent's behaviour in the past will also be relevant in determining whether he can reasonably be expected to live with the latter in the future. In *Archard* v. *Archard*[5] both parties were devout Roman Catholics at the time of their marriage. The wife was later advised on medical grounds that she should not conceive for another two years and, having lost her faith, insisted on the use of contraceptives. The husband was then told by his priest that he should stop sleeping with his wife and his resulting dilemma caused great unhappiness to both spouses. WRANGHAM, J., held that in the circumstances there was a conflict of two reasonable attitudes and that the wife had failed to establish behaviour on the part of her husband such that she could not reasonably be expected to live with him. Having entered into marriage on the understanding that they

---

[1] In *Smith* v. *Smith* (1973), 118 Sol. Jo. 184, a decree was refused when the wife's inertia and cabbage-like existence was due solely to presenile dementia: her actions were involuntary and "her mind did not go with her body". This followed *Priday* v. *Priday*, [1970] 3 All E.R. 554, where CUMMING-BRUCE, J., held that such a person could no more be regarded as cruel than one who had been physically paralysed by a stroke, even though the petitioner was worn down as a result. In *Thurlow* v. *Thurlow* REES, J., expressly disagreed with *Smith* v. *Smith* and distinguished *Priday* v. *Priday* on the ground that it was dealing solely with cruelty (at pp. 43-44 and 986, respectively).

[2] But see Eekelaar, 92 L.Q.R. 10.

[3] *Cf. Lauder* v. *Lauder*, [1949] P. 277; [1949] 1 All E.R. 76, C.A., (cruelty).

[4] [1972] Fam. 135, 140; [1972] 1 All E.R. 582, 585-586.

[5] (1972), *Times*, 19th April.

would not use artificial means of birth control because of the husband's religious beliefs, the wife could not complain if he refused to change his views. Equally, it is submitted, he could not have complained at his wife's refusal to have intercourse in view of her medical condition.

In any event, submission to behaviour must be voluntary if it is to be called acquiescence, and if the petitioner has virtually no option but to submit, he will not be precluded from petitioning in reliance on these acts.[1] Again, as we shall see later, no account may be taken of the fact that the parties have lived with each other for a period or periods not exceeding six months since the occurrence of the final incident relied on. If the petitioner has lived with the respondent for a longer period, this must necessarily be strong evidence to negative an allegation that he or she cannot reasonably be expected to do so. It is not conclusive, however, and will not stand in the way of a decree if it can be explained away on other grounds.[2]

Probability of Recurrence of Behaviour.—A question that could be important in some cases is whether the petitioner is entitled to obtain a decree in reliance on the respondent's behaviour if there is no probability that it will recur. This might occur, for example, if it has been the result of mental illness that is now cured. It is submitted that the answer must depend on all the facts and, in particular, on the nature of the conduct which has occurred. If, say, the respondent has committed savage physical attacks on the petitioner, it might be unreasonable to expect her to resume cohabitation with him in any circumstances, and as the Act provides that the petitioner must establish that the respondent *has behaved* in such a way that she *cannot* reasonably be expected to live with him, the fact is made out. If, on the other hand, less serious conduct has had a milder effect (for example, if constant nagging in the home has caused the petitioner to become depressed), the court might well conclude that she cannot say that she cannot reasonably be expected to live with him once the cause of the conduct has been removed.

3. THE RESPONDENT'S DESERTION

The petitioner may show that the marriage has irretrievably broken down by proving that the respondent has deserted the petitioner for a continuous period of at least two years immediately preceding the presentation of the petition.[3]

Desertion consists of the unjustifiable withdrawal from cohabitation without the consent of the other spouse and with the intention of remaining separated permanently. It therefore follows that four elements must be present before desertion can be proved:

(a) The *de facto* separation of the spouses;
(b) The *animus deserendi*—*i.e.*, the intention on the part of the spouse in desertion to remain separated permanently;

---

[1] *Cf. Meacher* v. *Meacher*, [1964] P. 216; [1946] 2 All E.R. 307, C.A. (wife obtained decree on ground of cruelty based on husband's assaulting her for visiting her sister notwithstanding that she could have avoided assaults by giving in to his unreasonable demands); *T.* v. *T.*, [1964] P. 85; [1963] 2 All E.R. 746, C.A., (submission to sodomy).

[2] See *post*, p. 230.

[3] Matrimonial Causes Act 1973, s. 1 (2) (c).

(c) The absence of consent on the part of the deserted spouse; and

(d) The absence of any reasonable cause for withdrawing from cohabitation on the part of the deserting spouse.

These four conditions will shortly be considered in turn.

It must not be thought that it is the party who takes the physical step of leaving the matrimonial home or otherwise withdrawing from cohabitation who is necessarily the deserting spouse. In cases of simple desertion this is so, but where one spouse virtually drives the other from the home or behaves in such a way that the latter can no longer reasonably be expected to live with him or her, then it may be the spouse remaining in the matrimonial home and not the spouse who departs from it who is in desertion. Such a case is known as "constructive desertion" and will have to be considered separately.

Desertion for Two Years.—The requirement that the respondent must have deserted the petitioner for a continuous period immediately preceding the presentation of the petition means that, subject to a statutory exception which will be mentioned later,[1] two or more periods cannot be added together so as to give a period of two years in the aggregate. Consequently if, say, a husband deserts his wife for a year, resumes cohabitation for a period of eight months and then deserts her again, the two years' period must be calculated from the date on which he left her for the second time.[2] Moreover the desertion must still be running when the proceedings are commenced. A rigid application of this principle might work hardship if the petitioner had previously obtained a judicial separation and consequently, as we shall see, an exception has also been provided to this rule too.[3]

Separation.—There can be no desertion unless there is a *de facto* separation between the spouses. It is not sufficient for this purpose that one of them has abandoned some of the obligations of matrimony or refused to perform isolated duties (*e. g.*, refused to have sexual intercourse);[4] there must be a rejection of all the obligations of marriage,[5] in other words, there must be a complete cessation of cohabitation.

This state of affairs, of course, is normally brought about by one spouse's leaving the matrimonial home, so that they are no longer living under the same roof. In such a case, there is clearly a sufficient separation. But it may be impossible for the spouse wishing to leave to find accommodation elsewhere, and the situation may arise where the spouses continue to live under the same roof but where one shuts himself off from the other so that they are living as two units rather than one. Although there is a presumption that in such a case there is no *de facto* separation sufficient to constitute desertion,[6]

---

[1] See *post*, p. 230.

[2] In *Warr* v. *Warr*, [1975] Fam. 25; [1975] 1 All E.R. 85, it was held that, as two whole years must elapse, a petition presented on the second anniversary of the separation was presented a day too soon and must be dismissed. But, as the judgment indicates, the authorities are not in agreement.

[3] See *post*, p. 214.

[4] *Weatherley* v. *Weatherley*, [1947] A.C. 628; [1947] 1 All E.R. 563, H.L.

[5] Per EVERSHED, M.R., in *Perry* v. *Perry*, [1952] P. 203, 215; [1952] 1 All E.R. 1076, 1082, C.A.

[6] *Bull* v. *Bull*, [1953] P. 224, at pp. 226, 228; [1953] 2 All E.R. 601, at pp. 602, 603, C.A.

this is rebuttable, for, in the oft cited words of LORD MERRIVALE, P., "desertion is not the withdrawal from a place, but from a state of things".[1] Hence, if there has been a total cessation of cohabitation, there can be desertion just as effectively as if the husband and wife were living in two separate houses.

The correct test to be applied in such a case is: Are the spouses living as two households or as one?[2] This must be very strictly construed: cohabitation must have entirely ceased and therefore there cannot be desertion if any matrimonial services are performed even though these are isolated and intermittent.[3] Each case must turn upon its own facts, and the line separating the two types of cases is a fine one as can be seen by contrasting two leading cases. In *Naylor* v. *Naylor*[4] the husband returned home after cross-petitions for divorce had both been dismissed. A quarrel took place during which the wife indicated that she had no further intention of being a wife to him by removing her wedding ring, which she never wore again. From that time on the wife performed no marital duties, the husband stopped giving her house-keeping money and, although they continued to reside under the same roof, they lived separately without any communal or family life. The Divisional Court held that in the circumstances there was a sufficient separation to sustain a finding by magistrates that the wife was in desertion. In *Hopes* v. *Hopes*[5] sexual intercourse had ceased and the husband had withdrawn to a separate bedroom because the nature of his work necessitated his getting up (and therefore going to bed) early and he objected to his wife's going to bed at a normal time after he had retired. After this their relationship deteriorated. The wife objected to her husband's going out at night and abused his friends; quarrels were frequent and the husband often retired to his bedroom for the sake of peace. The wife did no mending or washing for him and never cooked separate meals for him, but he had most meals in common with the rest of the family in their dining-room, and when he was not in his bedroom he shared the rest of the house with his wife and daughters. The Court of Appeal held that here there was not sufficient separation to amount to desertion. In this case the husband had for the most part shared a common table and to some extent a common life with the rest of the family so that to an outsider the situation would not have appeared abnormal. To call this desertion would, as BUCKNILL, L.J., pointed out, give that term a very artificial meaning. It will be seen, therefore, that all matrimonial services and any form of common life must entirely cease.

Since all that must be proved is the *factum* of separation, it is irrelevant for this purpose that the spouses are forced to live apart and therefore could not

---

[1] *Pulford* v. *Pulford*, [1923] P. 18, 21. *Cf.* the meaning of "living apart", *post*, pp. 225-226.

[2] *Hopes* v. *Hopes*, [1949] P. 227, at pp. 231, 236; [1948] 2 All E.R. 920, at pp. 922, 925, C.A.; *Bull* v. *Bull*, (*supra*), at pp. 226, 230 and 602, 604, respectively; *Walker* v. *Walker*, [1952] 2 All E.R. 138, C.A.; *Baker* v. *Baker*, [1952] 2 All E.R. 248, C.A.

[3] But the mere fact that the husband pays his wife maintenance will not prevent there being a *de facto* separation: *Smith* v. *Smith*, [1940] P. 49; [1939] 4 All E.R. 533.

[4] [1962] P. 253; [1961] 2 All E.R. 129, where the earlier cases are fully examined.

[5] [1949] P. 227; [1948] 2 All E.R. 920, C.A. *Cf. Littlewood* v. *Littlewood*, [1943] P. 11; [1942] 2 All E.R. 515; *Le Brocq* v. *Le Brocq*, [1964] 3 All E.R. 464, C.A.

live together even had they wished to do so. Thus, in *Beeken* v. *Beeken*[1] the husband and wife, who were resident in China, were taken prisoners by the Japanese and interned in a camp where they shared a room. The wife formed an attachment to another man and refused to permit her husband to have sexual intercourse or to perform any wifely services for him, and eventually in December, 1942, said that she would do no more for him unless he promised to commence divorce proceedings on his release—an undertaking which the husband refused to give. In the following June they moved to separate camps, and in March, 1944, the wife visited the husband and reaffirmed her intention of marrying the other man. After their release the wife refused to return to her husband, who presented a petition for divorce on the ground of her desertion in July, 1947. It was held by the Court of Appeal that desertion had commenced in March, 1944, at the latest, even though at that time the wife could not have rejoined her husband had she wanted to do so.

The converse question was also raised in *Beeken* v. *Beeken*, *viz.* whether there can be desertion if the parties are forced to live together but where they would have lived apart had they been free to do so. On the facts it did not have to be answered; should the problem arise again, one must ask whether they are living as two households. If this is possible in such circumstances, the fact that they are obliged to share living accommodation to a certain extent should not prove fatal.[2]

The *Animus Deserendi.* —Even though there is a *de facto* separation, there will be no desertion unless the guilty spouse has the intention of remaining permanently separated from the other. Clearly there will be no question of desertion if one spouse is temporarily absent on holiday or for reasons of business or health;[3] nor *prima facie* will there be desertion if the absence is involuntary, for example owing to service in the armed forces or imprisonment. But in these cases there will be desertion if the intention can be specifically proved; thus, in *Beeken* v. *Beeken*[4] the wife's *animus* was shown by her statement that she wished to marry another man and to have nothing more to do with her husband.

Normally the *animus deserendi* will be present when one spouse leaves the other, so that the desertion will commence immediately there is a *de facto* separation. But if, when the original separation took place, the parties intended to return to each other, and one of them later resolves not to resume cohabitation, desertion begins as soon as the *animus* is formed.[5]

If the party alleged to be in desertion suffers from mental illness, it is a question of fact whether he is capable of forming the necessary *animus*. In

---

[1] [1948] P. 302, C.A.

[2] *Cf.* LORD MERRIMAN, P., in *Everitt* v. *Everitt*, [1949] P. 374, 387-388; [1949] 1 All E.R. 908, 917-918, C.A.; *Adeoso* v. *Adeoso*, [1981] 1 All E.R. 107, C.A.

[3] See *G.* v. *G.*, [1964] P. 133; [1964] 1 All E.R. 129. For the facts, see *post*, p. 216.

[4] *Supra. Cf. Drew* v. *Drew* (1888), 13 P.D. 97 (husband in desertion although serving a sentence of penal servitude). Contrast *Townsend* v. *Townsend* (1873), L.R. 3 P. & D. 129 (husband in prison—no *animus deserendi*).

[5] *Pulford* v. *Pulford*, [1923] P. 18; *Pardy* v. *Pardy*, [1939] P. 288; [1939] 3 All E.R. 779, C.A. There can be desertion even though the parties have never cohabited at all: *De Laubenque* v. *De Laubenque*, [1899] P. 42; *Shaw* v. *Shaw*, [1939] P. 269; [1939] 2 All E.R. 381.

Perry v. *Perry*[1] the wife left her husband because she suffered from the insane delusion (quite unfounded in reason) that he was trying to murder her. LLOYD-JONES, J., held that her conduct must be judged as though her belief was true and in these circumstances it was clear that there could be no desertion because she believed that she had good cause for leaving her husband.[2] Again, if a party already in desertion develops mental illness, the desertion will continue only if it can be proved that he retains the *animus deserendi*,[3] and consequently the petitioner's power to obtain a divorce alleging this fact would go. This might work a double hardship if the evidence indicates that the respondent would have remained in desertion had he not become ill, because he might also lack the capacity to consent to a divorce after two years' separation. Hence the Matrimonial Causes Act expressly provides that the court may treat the desertion as continuing in such circumstances.[4]

Lack of Consent.—Desertion is a matrimonial offence; consequently if one spouse agrees to the other's departing, he cannot then complain of it: there can be no desertion if the separation is by consent.[5] But "consent" in this context must be construed strictly. In the words of BUCKLEY, L.J., in *Harriman* v. *Harriman*:[6]

"Desertion does not necessarily involve that the wife desires her husband to remain with her. She may be thankful that he has gone, but he may nevertheless have deserted her."

There must be many cases of deserted spouses who have been thankful to see the other go. The real test is whether the separation is really due to the conduct of the deserting spouse (in which case there can be desertion even though the other is glad to see the back of him) or to the other's consent to a permanent separation. The same principle can be extended to a resumption of cohabitation in an attempt to effect a reconciliation following a period of desertion. If the spouses then live apart again after agreeing that the attempt has been unsuccessful, it does not follow that this will necessarily be a separation by consent. The law seeks to facilitate reconciliation, and in these circumstances it would be much more realistic to regard the desertion as starting again.[7]

Whether or not consent to the separation in this sense has been given is, of course, a question of fact. It may be expressly given as a simple licence to go

---

[1] [1963] 3 All E.R. 766. *Cf. Brannan* v. *Brannan*, [1973] Fam. 120; [1973] 1 All E.R. 38. Contrast *Kaczmarz* v. *Kaczmarz*, [1967] 1 All E.R. 416 (wife, who believed husband to be guilty of grave sin—apparently by having sexual intercourse with her—not amounting to a matrimonial offence, held to be in desertion when she refused to cohabit with him as a consequence).

[2] For good cause for separation, see *post*, pp. 215 *et seq*.

[3] *Crowther* v. *Crowther*, [1951] A.C. 723; [1951] 1 All E.R. 1131, H.L.

[4] Matrimonial Causes Act 1973, s. 2 (4). This sub-section comes into play only if desertion has already begun: it has no application to cases like *Perry* v. *Perry*.

[5] *Pardy* v. *Pardy*, [1939] P. 288; [1939] 3 All E.R. 779, C.A.

[6] [1909] P. 123, 148, C.A. See also *Kinnane* v. *Kinnane*, [1954] P. 41; [1953] 2 All E.R. 1144, and *cf. Beigan* v. *Beigan*, [1956] P. 313; [1956] 2 All E.R. 630, C.A.; *Pizey* v. *Pizey*, [1961] P. 101; [1961] 2 All E.R. 658, C.A.

[7] *Cf. Morgan* v. *Morgan* (1973), 117 Sol. Jo. 223.

or be embodied in a separation agreement;[1] alternatively, it may be implied by the party's conduct. For example, in *Joseph* v. *Joseph*[2] the wife obtained a *get* which by Jewish law effects a divorce; although this would not dissolve the marriage by English law, nevertheless it was held by the Court of Appeal that the wife had thereby shown her consent to living apart from her husband and could therefore no longer assert that he was in desertion.

But in any event, of course, the consent, to be effective, must have been freely given, and what at first sight appears to be a clear consent may, in all the circumstances of the case, prove to be nothing of the sort. Thus, it has been held that a wife, who had been virtually forced by her husband to sign a separation agreement, with no legal advice and under great mental stress because she thought that this would be the only means of obtaining maintenance from him, had not genuinely consented to living apart from him.[3]

If the consent to the separation is withdrawn, desertion will automatically begin provided that the other conditions are all satisfied.[4] It is necessary, however, to draw a distinction between different types of consensual separation. In the first place, the parties might intend originally that it should be purely temporary. This could be for a given period of time (for example, a fortnight's holiday or a business trip); alternatively, it could depend on the happening of some future event or the fulfilment of a condition (for example, the husband's obtaining a suitable job near the matrimonial home). The consent will cease to be effective at the end of the period or on the satisfaction of the condition, and if the other spouse then unjustifiably refuses to resume cohabitation, he will be in desertion.[5] If in the meantime one spouse decides not to return to the other at all, desertion will begin to run as soon as the latter becomes aware of the *animus deserendi*; if he is unaware of it, there can be no desertion because the separation will still be with his consent.[6]

A separation which is not intended to be purely temporary may be of one of two kinds: it can be either for the parties' joint lives or until one of them asks the other to resume cohabitation. If it is not clear into which category a particular agreement falls, the court must try to infer the parties' intention from the terms of the agreement and the circumstances of their parting. In

---

[1] Where it is alleged that the consent has been embodied in a separation agreement, it is a question of construction whether the agreement binds the parties to live apart. Thus, in *Crabtree* v. *Crabtree*, [1953] 2 All E.R. 56, C.A., it was held that a husband's promise to pay his wife £2 a week "if they shall so long live separate and apart from each other" did not amount to a consent by the wife to his leaving her, for the words merely defined the duration of the husband's financial liability; a similar conclusion was reached in *Bosley* v. *Bosley*, [1958] 2 All E.R. 167, C.A. See further Blom-Cooper, *Separation Agreements and Grounds for Divorce*, 19 M.L.R. 638, where Australian and New Zealand cases are also discussed.

[2] [1953] 2 All E.R. 710, C.A. Distinguished on the facts in *Corbett* v. *Corbett*, [1957] 1 All E.R. 621.

[3] *Holroyd* v. *Holroyd* (1920), 36 T.L.R. 479.

[4] *Pardy* v. *Pardy*, [1939] P. 288, 303; [1939] 3 All E.R. 779, 783, C.A. The burden of proof is on the spouse alleging that the other is in desertion: *Pizey* v. *Pizey*, [1961] P. 101, 110; [1961] 2 All E.R. 658, 664, C.A.

[5] *Shaw* v. *Shaw*, [1939] P. 269; [1939] 2 All E.R. 381 (separation until the husband was earning enough to set up a home for himself and his wife).

[6] *Nutley* v. *Nutley*, [1970] 1 All E.R. 410, C.A.

recent years the courts have leaned against finding that the parties intended to separate for their joint lives. In the words of PEARCE, L.J., in *Bosley* v. *Bosley*:[1]

> "Often in the rather haphazard parting of husband and wife, the fact of a mutual agreement to separate has to be deduced from things done and things said in emotion and temper. The court should, I think, be slow to decide that there is imported a term that the separation shall be for ever and that there shall be no opportunity for any unilateral change of mind, no right ever to ask the other party to return to cohabitation."

If the separation is for an indefinite period and not for the parties' lives, either of them can resile and if the other unjustifiably rejects an offer to resume cohabitation, he will be in desertion. But there must be a genuine offer and not merely an exploratory approach or preliminary enquiry. If the party making the offer has been guilty of conduct in the past which would have justified the other in leaving, he must also give a credible assurance that it will not be repeated in the future; and in any event there must be no unreasonable conditions attached.[2] But the spouse to whom it is addressed is bound to consider the offer, and as the Court of Apeal held in *Gallagher* v. *Gallagher*,[3] if he fails to do so and rejects it out of hand, he will be in desertion whether it is reasonable or not.

If the agreement is intended to last for ever, it will normally be terminated (like any other contract) only by the consent of both spouses or by a breach by one accepted by the other as terminating his own obligations. In *Pardy* v. *Pardy*[4] the parties had entered into such an agreement under which the husband had covenanted to pay the wife 25/- a week. He paid these sums for twelve weeks and thereafter paid small sums from time to time. For more than three years before the wife presented her petition the husband had paid her nothing at all. The wife never made any attempt to enforce the deed. It was held that in the circumstances the parties had regarded the agreement as a dead letter for over three years and it was therefore incorrect to say that they were any longer living apart by consent. As in the case of commercial contracts, the repudiation of one term may be a repudiation of the whole agreement if the term is fundamental and goes to the root of the contract; but (unlike the case of a commercial contract) there is no need for the other party to inform the party in breach that he elects to treat himself as discharged: it is sufficient if he makes no attempt to insist upon performance and is in fact willing to resume cohabitation.[5]

Effect of other Matrimonial Proceedings.—The majority of the Court of Appeal held in *Harriman v. Harriman*[6] that, if the deserted spouse obtained a

---

[1] [1958] 2 All E.R. 167, 173, C.A.; followed in *Hall* v. *Hall*, [1960] 1 All E.R. 91.

[2] *Fraser* v. *Fraser*, [1969] 3 All E.R. 654. *Cf.* the position when a spouse in desertion asks the other to resume cohabitation, *post*, pp. 223-224.

[3] [1965] 2 All E.R. 967, C.A.

[4] [1939] P. 288; [1939] 3 All E.R. 779, C.A. *Cf. Papadopoulos* v. *Papadopoulos*, [1936] P. 108.

[5] But if the party not in breach enforces the agreement and so refuses to accept the repudiation, desertion will not begin: *Clark* v. *Clark (No. 2)*, [1939] P. 257; [1939] 2 All E.R. 392 (wife's suing on husband's covenant to pay maintenance). See further *ante*, pp. 176-177.

[6] [1909] P. 123, C.A.

judicial separation, he could not then allege that the other was still in desertion: the decree showed a desire on the petitioner's part not to have the respondent back and, by relieving the former of the duty of cohabiting with the latter, effectively put it out of the power of the deserting spouse to return. This also applied if the deserted spouse obtained a magistrates' order containing a non-cohabitation clause because this had the same effect as a judicial separation.[1] It could also be argued that this rule would operate if a spouse obtained an injunction or order excluding the other from the matrimonial home for again this would prevent the excluded spouse from resuming cohabitation.

It will thus be seen that, by obtaining short-term relief, a spouse might effectively lose the power to obtain a divorce in reliance on desertion. The hardship that might otherwise result has been mitigated by two statutory provisions. First, if a decree of judicial separation is in force, a spouse petitioning for divorce may rely on the fact that the respondent had been in desertion for a continuous period of two years immediately preceding the institution of the earlier proceedings provided that the decree has been in force continuously and that the parties have not resumed cohabitation since it was granted.[2] This provision also applies to orders containing a non-cohabitation clause made under the Matrimonial Proceedings (Magistrates' Courts) Act 1960; moreover if a petition for divorce is presented after 31st January 1981 and such an order was in force on that date, the court may treat any period during which the clause was included in the order as a period during which the respondent was in desertion.[3] Secondly, to ensure that the same principle will apply to exclusion orders, the court may also treat the respondent as having been in desertion during any period in which there was in force (a) an injunction excluding him from the matrimonial home, (b) an order made under section 1 of the Matrimonial Homes Act 1967 or section 4 of the Domestic Violence and Matrimonial Proceedings Act 1976 prohibiting him from occupying the matrimonial home (or former matrimonial home), or (c) an order made under section 16 of the Domestic Proceedings and Magistrates' Courts Act 1978 requiring him to leave the matrimonial home or prohibiting him from entering it.[4] Presumably in all these cases the court may regard the respondent as in desertion only if it is satisfied that the other constituent elements of the offence are present and could not do so, for example, if the spouses had cohabited or the respondent lacked the necessary *animus*. In practice, the provision relating to injunctions and exclusion orders is likely to be relied on comparatively rarely because the respondent's conduct which led to the making of the order will usually be such that the petitioner cannot

---

[1] *Harriman* v. *Harriman*, (*supra*); *Robinson* v. *Robinson*, [1919] P. 352.

[2] Matrimonial Causes Act 1973, s. 4 (3).

[3] *Ibid.*, s. 4 (5) (added by the Domestic Proceedings and Magistrates' Courts Act 1978, s. 62). Provided that the petition was presented after 31st January 1981, it does not matter whether the period in question was before or after that date. Note that this provision does not apply to petitions for judicial separation.

[4] *Ibid.*, s. 4 (4) (added by the Domestic Proceedings and Magistrates's Courts Act 1978, s. 62). For injunctions and exclusion orders, see *ante*, pp. 122-128, and *post*, p. 459. Note that this subsection does not apply in the case of an order made under s. 1 of the Matrimonial Homes Act 1976 suspending or restricting the respondent's right of occupation. It does, however, apply to petitions for judicial separation.

reasonably be expected to live with him and will thus itself provide the ground for divorce.

Once a decree of judicial separation (or a magistrates' separation order) is discharged, desertion can of course begin to run in any event.[1]

Want of Reasonable Cause.—If one spouse has a reasonable cause or excuse for leaving the other, then there will be no unjustifiable separation and consequently he will not be in desertion. Whether a particular excuse is sufficient in law is often a question of great difficulty, but it should be noted at the outset that it may be due either to the other spouse's misconduct or to circumstances (for example, illness) connected with the spouse who would otherwise be in desertion.[2]

The Petitioner's Behaviour.—It has always been recognised that one spouse's adultery will justify the other in breaking off cohabitation unless the latter has put it out of his own power to complain of it by having conduced to it, connived at it or condoned it.[3] This, however, is only a particular example of a general rule, that one spouse's conduct may be such that the other is justified in breaking off cohabitation and, if he does so, he will not be in desertion. The test to determine whether the conduct has reached this pitch has been formulated in various ways. The best known and most frequently cited is that of LORD PENZANCE who said that the conduct must be "grave and weighty";[4] this was expanded by SIMON, P., to conduct amounting to "such a grave and weighty matter as renders the continuance of the matrimonial cohabitation virtually impossible".[5] On the other hand it has been said that "the ordinary wear and tear of conjugal life does not in itself suffice".[6]

It will be recalled that the same test of "grave and weighty conduct" was also applied in cruelty and, it is submitted, must now be applied to determine whether the respondent has behaved in such a way that the petitioner cannot reasonably be expected to live with him.[7] Hence the same matters must be borne in mind including the parties' temperaments, the circumstances surrounding the conduct complained of, and the whole history of the marriage. Thus it has been held that, although the separation cannot be justified by want of attention or affection alone,[8] it may be by the fact that

---

[1] But not automatically: see *Gatward* v. *Gatward*, [1942] P. 97, 99; [1942] 1 All E.R. 477, 478.

[2] See Irvine, *"Reasonable Cause" and "Reasonable Excuse" as Justification for Separation*, 30 M.L.R. 659.

[3] *Callister* v. *Callister*, [1947] W.N. 221, C.A. (conduct conducing to adultery); *Wells* v. *Wells*, [1954] 3 All E.R. 491, C.A. (condonation). For a full account of the law relating to connivance, condonation and conduct conducing to adultery (which is now of virtually no relevance), see the 5th Edition of this book, at pp. 216-229.

[4] *Yeatman* v. *Yeatman* (1868), L.R. 1 P. & D. 489, 494.

[5] *Young* v. *Young*, [1964] P. 152, 158; [1962] 3 All E.R. 120,124. *Cf. Dyson* v. *Dyson*, [1954] P. 198, 206; [1953] 2 All E.R. 1511, 1514; and *Oldroyd* v. *Oldroyd*, [1896] P. 175, 184 ("practically impossible for the spouses to live properly together").

[6] *Per* ASQUITH, L.J., in *Buchler* v. *Buchler*, [1947] P. 25, 45-46; [1947] 1 All E.R. 319, 326, C.A.

[7] See *ante*, pp. 199-206.

[8] *Buchler* v. *Buchler*, (*supra*). Similarly, if a wife tells her husband that she has fallen in love with another man and begs the husband to help her to put an end to the situation, he should do so and, in the absence of adultery, he will have no defence to a charge of desertion if he leaves her: *Forbes* v. *Forbes*, [1954] 3 All E.R. 461, 467-468.

the other spouse is overbearing and domineering and always insists on having his own way.[1] Unfounded allegations of adultery may well justify one spouse in leaving the other,[2] as will charges of homosexuality.[3] Similarly, a wife's prodigality has been held to be a good cause for her husband's refusing to take her back when it reached such a pitch that his business partners warned him that he would have to leave the firm if she rejoined him.[4]

One spouse's conduct may entitle the other to withdraw from cohabitation even though it is not culpable. For example, physical or mental illness will justify separation if it is likely to jeopardize the other's health or safety. An extension of the same principle is to be seen in *G.* v. *G.*[5] where the husband developed a mental illness which led him to frighten his children. It was held that the wife was entitled to remain apart from him so long as was necessary for the children's sake. The older cases indicate that, where no blame can be imputed to either spouse, the only justification for the separation that can be raised is the protection of the spouse leaving or of their children. Thus, to take one example, a wilful and inexcusable refusal to have sexual intercourse or insistence on *coitus interruptus* has been held to be a good cause for separation;[6] on the other hand, where a wife's refusal to permit her husband to have intercourse was due to invincible repugnance beyond her control, it was held that her husband was in desertion when he left her.[7] It is clearly impossible to reconcile this rule with recent developments in the law relating to the respondent's behaviour. If, for example, the husband can argue that the wife's "negative behaviour" over which she has no control is such that he cannot reasonably be expected to live with her,[8] she obviously cannot be heard to say that he is in desertion if he leaves her as a result. An acceptance of the former view must necessarily involve a modification of the law relating to desertion.

It must be stressed that no conduct can be regarded as a good cause for separation unless it in fact led to it. Hence, if a wife leaves her husband after he has committed adultery, she will none the less be in desertion if she did not know of his offence or was indifferent to it and intended to leave anyway.[9] Furthermore, as in the case of constructive desertion,[10] the other spouse's conduct presumably cannot be a good cause for separation unless it occurred during the marriage. If this is so, discovery after marriage of the other spouse's pre-marital activities can never be a defence to desertion.

---

[1] *Timmins* v. *Timmins*, [1953] 2 All E.R. 187, C.A. *Cf. Devi* v. *Gaddu* (1974), 118 Sol. Jo. 579 (conduct of other members of the family living with spouses).

[2] *Marsden* v. *Marsden*, [1968] P. 544; [1967] 1 All E.R. 967.

[3] *Russell* v. *Russell*, [1895] P. 315, C.A.

[4] *G.* v. *G.*, [1930] P. 72.

[5] [1964] P. 133; [1964] 1 All E.R. 129.

[6] *Slon* v. *Slon*, [1969] P. 122; [1969] 1 All E.R. 759, C.A.; *Hutchinson* v. *Hutchinson*, [1963] 1 All E.R. 1; *Rice* v. *Raynold-Spring-Rice*, [1948] 1 All E.R. 188.

[7] *Beevor* v. *Beevor*, [1945] 2 All E.R. 200. *Cf. Chapper* v. *Chapper* (1966), *Times*, 25th May (husband aged 60 held to be in desertion when he left wife aged 57 because her desire for sexual intercourse had "faded with the years").

[8] See *ante*, pp. 205-206.

[9] *Herod* v. *Herod*, [1939] P. 11; [1938] 3 All E.R. 722; *Day* v. *Day*, [1957] P. 202; [1957] 1 All E.R. 848. But there is a presumption that the offence has induced the defendant to leave the complainant, so that the burden of proving ignorance or indifference is on the latter: *Earnshaw* v. *Earnshaw*, [1939] 2 All E.R. 698, C.A.

[10] See *post*, pp. 219-220.

The Respondent's Circumstances. —The most obvious example of his own circumstances on which a spouse might rely to justify a separation is an enforced absence due to illness or business. In such cases it will almost always be temporary and for this reason could not amount to desertion. If he is advised to remain away from the other for good medical reason, it would seem on principle that he ought to be able to defeat a charge of desertion on the further ground that he has good cause for remaining apart, even though the separation may be for ever. This reasoning, however, does not seem to have commended itself to the Court of Appeal in *Lilley* v. *Lilley.*[1] Owing to mental illness the wife developed an invincible and apparently incurable repugnance to her husband. After being discharged from a mental hospital, she refused to return to him and made it clear that she never would do so. This was a rational decision in the sense that she was capable of forming an *animus deserendi* and the Court of Appeal accordingly held that she was in desertion. But this entirely overlooks the possible adverse effect of a return upon her mental health. Furthermore, had her illness been curable, her present intention never to return would presumably not have put her in desertion because she would have lost the *animus* on recovering her health; why, then, should the incurable nature of the disease make any difference? The injustice of branding such a spouse as a deserter is manifest, and the case was applied with obvious reluctance in *Tickle* v. *Tickle,*[2] where a Divisional Court was compelled to hold a mentally ill husband to be in desertion in similar circumstances even though the medical evidence indicated that a return to his wife would almost certainly result in his having to go back to hospital.

Reasonable Belief in Grounds for Separation. —It has been held in a series of cases going back to *Ousey* v. *Ousey*[3] in 1874 that if one spouse has a reasonable belief that he has good cause for leaving the other based upon the other's own conduct, then he is entitled to break off cohabitation and will not be in desertion even though the belief is a mistaken one. In *Ousey* v. *Ousey* the husband was held not to be in desertion when he left his wife whom he thought either unable or unwilling to consummate the marriage. In *Glenister* v. *Glenister*[4] the same principle was applied where the husband, who was in the Forces and who believed himself to have been infected with gonorrhea by his wife on a previous occasion, returned home on leave at night to find three men in the house with his wife (one of whom, in fact, was in her bedroom) and was refused admission to the house till the following morning, although he had no positive proof of adultery.

But, as in these two cases, the belief must be based upon the other spouse's conduct and not upon circumstantial evidence: in other words the cause of separation must still be the other spouse's own acts. These cases illustrate an exception to the general rule that an unlawful act cannot be justified by a mistaken belief, however reasonably held, and it would clearly be unjust to the deserted spouse if the exception were extended to cases where that spouse

---

[1] [1960] P. 169; [1959] 3 All E.R. 283, C.A.

[2] [1968] 2 All E.R. 154.

[3] (1874), L.R. 3 P. & D. 223. See Bevan, *Belief in the other Spouse's Adultery*, 73 L.Q.R. 225.

[4] [1945] P. 30; [1945] 1 All E.R. 513.

had in no way contributed to the mistake. Thus in *Elliott* v. *Elliott*[1] it was held that a husband had no good cause for living apart from his wife when he had been told by his mother that the wife had committed adultery. Similarly he will not be justified in living apart if the conduct on which the belief in adultery is based was originally brought about or procured by himself any more than he could justify the separation by proof of the commission of adultery at which he had connived.[2]

The belief must be entertained reasonably and in good faith, and whether or not it is reasonable is to be determined objectively.[3] A spouse entertaining a mere suspicion, not based on evidence pointing to adultery, must give the other an opportunity of giving an explanation and, if he withdraws from cohabitation before doing so, he will himself be in desertion.[4] *A fortiori* one spouse will have no grounds for leaving the other if the latter produces a reasonable and innocent explanation of his or her conduct;[5] and if the spouse who has left ceases to have reasonable cause for believing that the other has committed an offence, he must resume cohabitation and will himself be in desertion if he fails to do so.[6] Hence he may not set up a reasonable belief in the commission of a matrimonial offence after he has unsuccessfully sought matrimonial relief based upon that very offence. In *Allen* v. *Allen*[7] the husband left the wife because he believed that she had committed adultery. He subsequently petitioned for divorce on this ground and his petition was dismissed. It was held by the Court of Appeal that, although he was not in desertion before the termination of the divorce proceedings, it was no longer open to him to plead that he had good reason for living apart from his wife even though his suspicions had not in fact been allayed.

Constructive Desertion.—As has already been stated, it is not necessarily the spouse who takes the physical step of leaving the matrimonial home who will be in desertion. At least as early as 1864 it was recognised that where one spouse behaves in such a way that the other is virtually compelled to leave, the former may be in law the deserter.[8] In such a case the spouse who intends to bring cohabitation to an end or whose conduct causes the separation is said to be in constructive desertion.

The most obvious example of constructive desertion (although in fact the least frequent) is that of the husband who physically evicts his wife or bars the doors of the matrimonial home against her. Similarly, a spouse who virtually orders the other to leave will be in desertion if the circumstances reasonably

---

[1] [1956] P. 160; [1956] 1 All E.R. 122, C.A. See also *Wood* v. *Wood*, [1947] P. 103; [1947] 2 All E.R. 95; *Beer* v. *Beer*, [1948] P. 10; [1947] 2 All E.R. 711.

[2] *Hartley* v. *Hartley*, [1955] 1 All E.R. 625.

[3] *Cox* v. *Cox*, [1958] 1 All E.R. 569. In this case the court doubted whether a mistaken belief in anything other than the commission of adultery would justify a separation (at p. 573). This overlooks the facts of *Ousey* v. *Ousey*. (*supra*). The belief may also be a good defence even though it is based on insane delusions: see *ante*, pp. 210-211.

[4] *Marsden* v. *Marsden*, [1968] P. 544; [1967] 1 All E.R. 967.

[5] *Beer* v. *Beer*, (*supra*), at pp. 14 and 713, respectively.

[6] *Forbes* v. *Forbes*, [1954] 3 All E.R. 461, where DAVIES, J., pointed out (at p. 466) that failure to bring proceedings based on adultery may raise doubts whether the belief is reasonably held.

[7] [1951] 1 All E.R. 724, C.A.; followed in *Bright* v. *Bright*, [1954] P. 270; [1953] 2 All E.R. 939; *West* v. *West*, [1954] P. 444; [1954] 2 All E.R. 505, C.A.

[8] *Graves* v. *Graves* (1864), 3 Sw. & Tr. 350.

lead the other to believe that the command was meant and he acts upon it.[1] In
these cases it will be observed that the same four elements are present as in
simple desertion: there is a *de facto* separation, the eviction shows an *animus
deserendi*, the facts negative any consent on the part of the spouse evicted,
and there will be no desertion if the evictor had good cause for barring the
other from the matrimonial home.

It is not necessary, however, for there to be an actual eviction or order to
leave. Other conduct, which need not in itself amount to a matrimonial
offence, can be sufficient to justify one spouse in leaving, thus putting the
other in constructive desertion. If a domineering and bullying husband treats
his wife in such a way that married life with him becomes impossible and she
leaves, he has just as effectively brought cohabitation to an end as if he had
physically evicted her. Similarly, if the wife refuses to let the husband into the
matrimonial home because of his conduct, he will be the deserter.[2] Whether
his conduct is serious enough to justify her in breaking off cohabitation raises
precisely the same issue of fact as simple desertion: if it is sufficiently grave
and weighty to make married life impossible, she will not be in simple
desertion and she can rely on it to build up a case of constructive desertion.[3] It
has already been argued that the same test must be used to determine whether
the respondent's behaviour has been such that the petitioner cannot reasonably be expected to live with him.[4] If this argument is correct, two results
follow. First, a spouse petitioning for divorce will rarely, if ever, need to rely
on constructive desertion because she can base her petition on the respondent's behaviour alone. Secondly, if the respondent successfully defends a
petition based on "unreasonable behaviour" by showing that he has not
behaved in such a way that the petitioner cannot reasonably be expected to
live with him, the latter cannot subsequently rely on the same conduct in a
petition based on constructive desertion, for she will be estopped from alleging that it is sufficiently grave and weighty.[5]

Two further points in connection with the respondent's conduct should be
mentioned. If it does not of itself justify the petitioner in leaving, she cannot
put the other in constructive desertion by presenting him with an ultimatum.[6]
Furthermore the conduct complained of must have taken place during the

---

[1] *Dunn* v. *Dunn*, [1967] P. 217; [1965] 1 All E.R. 1043. The complaining spouse must have
left in consequence of the order and not of his or her own free will: *Charter* v. *Charter* (1901),
84 L.T. 272. *Cf. Buchler* v. *Buchler*, [1947] P. 25; [1947] 1 All E.R. 319, C.A., and see Irvine, 29
M.L.R. 438. In *Jones* v. *Jones*, [1952] 2 T.L.R. 225, C.A., it was held that the wife was in constructive desertion when the justices who had heard her complaint told the husband that he
would have to leave the matrimonial home (which was the wife's property) within seven days,
since in so doing they were acting not judicially but at the wife's instigation.

[2] *W.* v. *W.* (*No. 2*), [1962] P. 49; [1961] 2 All E.R. 626.

[3] *Buchler* v. *Buchler*, (*supra*); *Hall* v. *Hall*, [1962] 3 All E.R. 518, C.A.; *Saunders* v.
Saunders, [1965] P. 449; [1965] 1 All E.R. 838. The principle of *Ousey* v. *Ousey* has also been
applied to constructive desertion: *Baker* v. *Baker*, [1954] P. 33; [1953] 2 All E.R. 1199; *Forbes* v.
Forbes, [1954] 3 All E.R. 461. See further Bevan in 73 L.Q.R. 249 *et seq.*

[4] *Ante*, pp. 201-202.

[5] *Cf.* the rule that an unsuccessful case of cruelty could not succeed as a case of constructive
desertion: *Ogden* v. *Ogden*, [1969] 3 All E.R. 1055, C.A., and the cases there cited. Nor could the
unsuccessful petitioner himself justify any further separation by pleading the same facts:
Thoday v. *Thoday*, [1964] P. 181; [1964] 1 All E.R. 341, C.A.

[6] *Buchler* v. *Buchler*, (*supra*), at pp. 44-45 and 325, respectively; *Bartholomew* v.
Bartholomew, [1952] 2 All E.R. 1035, C.A.

marriage. In *Sullivan* v. *Sullivan*[1] a husband left his wife immediately after discovering that she was pregnant *per alium* at the time of the marriage but failed to take any steps to have the marriage annulled. He later petitioned for divorce on the ground of his wife's desertion. The Court of Appeal held that he must fail because he was in fact complaining of her physical state at the time of the marriage: the conduct which had given rise to it had occurred beforehand. This decision is regrettable because it implies that a husband who leaves his wife in such circumstances is in desertion himself and he has no immediate remedy if he does not discover the facts within three years (as might happen if he thought he was the father himself). A more desirable solution would have been to hold that pre-marital conduct can give rise to constructive desertion if (as in this case) it is bound to have an effect on the parties' relationship after marriage.

As in the case of simple desertion there must have been a *de facto* separation for a period of at least two years preceding the presentation of the petition without the petitioner's consent. Similarly, earlier cases on constructive desertion emphasised the need to prove that the respondent intended to bring cohabitation to an end permanently. But to speak of an *animus deserendi* in this context is highly artificial for most spouses in this position will be too occupied with their own ends to formulate any real intention at all. Consequently a series of cases in the 1960's laid down the principle that there would be sufficient *animus* if, to cite the words of DIPLOCK, L.J., in *Hall* v. *Hall*, "*this* [respondent] must have known that *this* [petitioner] would in all probability not continue to endure his conduct if he persisted in it".[2] In most cases, of course, this will present no problem for knowledge will of necessity be imputed to him, but even if it cannot be, for example because of his mental illness, the petitioner will usually still be able to base a petition on the respondent's behaviour.

Mutual Desertion.—A question that has been canvassed is whether it is possible for both spouses to be in desertion simultaneously. The problem arises when one spouse is obliged to go away for reasons of business or health and the other cannot or will not go too. This happened in *Walter* v. *Walter*,[3] where the husband and wife were both working in different parts of London. The husband moved to be nearer his place of work and the wife remained in the former matrimonial home to be near hers. Neither consented to the separation. It was held by WILLMER, J., that in such circumstances neither of them could succeed on petitions based upon desertion because neither could prove that the separation was due to the other's fault.

---

[1] [1970] 2 All E.R. 168, C.A.

[2] [1962] 3 All E.R. 518, 527, C.A. (husband's persistent drunkenness held capable of amounting to constructive desertion). See also *Gollins* v. *Gollins*, [1964] A.C. 644, 666; [1963] 2 All E.R. 966, 974, H.L. (*per* LORD REID); *Saunders* v. *Saunders*, [1965] P. 499, 504; [1965] 1 All E.R. 838, 841 (*per* SIMON, P.) (constructive desertion by husband who failed to give wife proper help in their shop). For a fuller discussion of the problem of the *animus deserendi* in constructive desertion, see the 5th Edition of this book at pp. 206-208; Bates, *Animus Deserendi in Constructive Desertion*, 33 M.L.R. 144.

[3] (1949), 65 T.L.R. 680. For choice of the matrimonial home, see *ante*, pp. 113-114.

This decision has been criticised by LORD DENNING who has expressed the obiter view that in such a case both spouses are in desertion.[1] But this opinion can itself be attacked on two grounds. It has been suggested that each spouse has a duty to compromise in such circumstances:[2] in that case, if either rejects a genuine and reasonable compromise put forward by the other, he will be in desertion. But if neither will even propose a compromise or no reasonable compromise is possible in the circumstances, it seems contrary to principle to permit either to allege that the other is in desertion, because neither could show that the other has brought about the separation. Secondly, it has been doubted whether mutual desertion is legally possible.[3] It is submitted, however, that there is no logical basis for this view, even if the facts which could give rise to it are not likely to occur very often. Suppose that a husband, whilst in hospital, decides not to return to his wife and, on his discharge, does not go back to the matrimonial home. His wife in the meantime has decided to leave him and, unbeknown to him, has already gone to live elsewhere. There is a *de facto* separation, each has the *animus deserendi*, each has acted in ignorance of the other's decision and therefore cannot have consented to his or her withdrawal from separation; consequently if neither has any justification for his action, both have satisfied all the conditions for simple desertion.[4] If both have a reasonable cause for leaving (in other words, each drives the other away), there could apparently be mutual constructive desertion in the sort of situation outlined above (although this is likely to occur even more rarely). It remains to be seen, however, whether the courts will accept this argument.

Termination of Desertion.—As the petitioner must show that the desertion has been continuous for a period of two years, its termination is of the same importance as its commencement. All four conditions must be present in order to constitute the offence, so that desertion will terminate if any one or more of these conditions cease to be satisfied.

Resumption of Cohabitation.—If the spouses resume cohabitation, there will then be no *de facto* separation and therefore no desertion. Just as

---

[1] *Hosegood* v. *Hosegood* (1950), 66. T.L.R. (pt. 1) 735, 740, C.A.; *Beigan* v. *Beigan*, [1956] P. 313, 320; [1956] 2 All E.R. 630, 632, C.A.

[2] Irvine, *Mutual Desertion*, 30 M.L.R. 46.

[3] *Simpson* v. *Simpson*, [1951] P. 320, 330; [1951] 1 All E.R. 955, 960 (*per* LORD MERRIMAN, P.); *Lang* v. *Lang* (1953), *Times*, 7th July (*per* JENKINS and HODSON, L. JJ.); *Crossley* v. *Crossley* (1962), 106 Sol. Jo. 223 (*per* SIMON, P.). In *Price* v. *Price*, [1970] 2 All E.R. 497, C.A., DAVIES, L.J., left the question open (at p. 498) and SACHS, L.J., was inclined to follow the dicta in *Lang* v. *Lang* (at p. 501).

[4] See DENNING, L.J., in *Beigan* v. *Beigan*, (*supra*); Irvine, *loc. cit*. On similar facts to these WRANGHAM, J., found both spouses in desertion in *Price* v. *Price*, [1968] 3 All E.R. 543, but this was reversed by the Court of Appeal (*supra*) on the further ground that the wife, having discovered that her husband had gone elsewhere, never put her plan into effect and consequently the husband alone was in desertion. This seems to lay undue weight on the question of which of them took the technical step of leaving the home and, insofar as the wife would have left herself if the husband had come back, makes desertion turn on a question of luck (which it ought not to do). If, as PHILLIMORE, L.J., stated at p. 502, it is necessary for a party, having formed the intention to desert, to leave the other *in pursuance of it*, the case is inconsistent with the earlier decision of the Court of Appeal in *Pardy* v. *Pardy, ante*, p. 213. See Irvine, 34 M.L.R. 194.

desertion is "the withdrawal from a state of things", so, in the words of LORD MERRIMAN, P., in *Mummery* v. *Mummery*:[1]

> "A resumption of cohabitation must mean resuming a state of things, that is to say, setting up a matrimonial home together, and that involves a bilateral intention on the part of both spouses so to do."

A number of points emerge from this.

Normally cohabitation will be resumed by the spouses' living together again in the matrimonial home, but where owing to force of circumstances there is no home, cohabitation may be resumed elsewhere provided that the intention is there. Thus, in *Abercrombie* v. *Abercrombie*[2] the husband was a doctor who had held a number of appointments as a *locum tenens* and, before the spouses separated, they had no settled home. They eventually spent a weekend together in a hotel on what they hoped would be their second honeymoon, but again separated on discovering that they probably could not live happily together again. It was held that since they had spent the weekend together with the intention of starting life together again, there was in the circumstances a resumption of cohabitation.

Conversely, whilst there will be a presumption that cohabitation has been resumed if the spouses start residing under the same roof again,[3] this can be rebutted if it can be shown that there was no intention to live together as husband and wife. In *Bartram* v. *Bartram*[4] the husband went to live with his mother for business reasons and his wife refused to join him because she wanted nothing more to do with him and thus put herself in desertion. Later the husband sold the matrimonial home in the hope of forcing his wife to return to him. She eventually did go to his mother's house because she had nowhere else to live, but she refused to sleep with him, performed no wifely duties for him and generally treated him like a lodger whom she disliked, although she was obliged to share the common meals with him. In these circumstances it was held by the Court of Appeal that there was no true reconciliation and no bilateral intention to set up home again together and therefore she remained in desertion.

Although sexual intercourse between the parties may be evidence of their intending to resume cohabitation and, if they have no home in which they can live together, may in fact amount to resumption of cohabitation,[5] it will not bring desertion to an end if there is no bilateral intention of starting life together again, even though it takes place on a number of occasions.[6] In *Mummery* v. *Mummery*[7] the spouses had separated in consequence of the husband's introducing another woman into the matrimonial home. On his return from Dunkirk in 1940, he called upon the wife and spent the night with

---

[1] [1942] P. 107, 110; [1942] 1 All E.R. 553, 555.

[2] [1943] 2 All E.R. 465. See also *Lowry* v. *Lowry*, [1952] P. 252; [1952] 2 All E.R. 61.

[3] *Watson* v. *Tuckwell* (1947), 63 T.L.R. 634; *Bull* v. *Bull*, [1953] P. 224; [1953] 2 All E.R. 601, C.A.

[4] [1950] P. 1; [1949] 2 All E.R. 270, C.A.; *Watson* v. *Tuckwell*, (*supra*). Contrast *Bull* v. *Bull*, (*supra*).

[5] *Eaves* v. *Eaves*, [1939] P. 361; [1939] 2 All E.R. 789.

[6] *Perry* v. *Perry*, [1952] P. 203; [1952] 1 All E.R. 1076, C.A. (where a child was born as the result of the intercourse); *Lynch* v. *Lynch*, [1966] N.I. 41. But there may be intercourse so regular and frequent as to compel a finding of resumption of cohabitation: *Marczuk* v. *Marczuk*, [1956] P. 217, 236; [1955] 3 All E.R. 758, 768.

[7] [1942] P. 107; [1942] 1 All E.R. 553.

her, having sexual intercourse. The wife consented to his doing so in the hope of effecting a reconciliation. The husband left her again on the following day and it then became clear that he had never intended to resume cohabitation with her. It was held that the intention on the wife's part alone was not enough to bring the husband's desertion to an end.

At common law if one spouse, knowing that the other has committed a matrimonial offence, resumes cohabitation, he will be presumed to have condoned the offence and thus cannot complain of it again in the future. It is, of course, the resumption of cohabitation which will bring desertion to an end, but condonation is still relevant because the spouse who has condoned the other's conduct may not rely on it to justify any subsequent separation.[1] Thus, suppose that a wife leaves her husband because of his ill-treatment of her; she will not be in desertion because she has good cause for living apart. The spouses later resume cohabitation but the wife then leaves for a second time, not because of his conduct but because of her own dissatisfaction with the marriage. She cannot now allege that his ill-treatment entitles her to live apart from him: she has condoned it and is therefore in desertion herself.[2]

Loss of Animus Deserendi.—Desertion will similarly come to an end if the party in desertion loses the *animus deserendi*. But it is not sufficient in this case for him mentally to resolve to return to the other spouse; he must communicate his intention by offering to return.[3] In the case of simple desertion all that is necessary is for the guilty spouse to make the offer. His motive for doing so is irrelevant: the fact that the offeror may formerly have brought unsuccessful divorce proceedings or admittedly hates the offeree and wishes to return merely to obtain maintenance or a roof over her head may be evidence that the offer is not genuine, but, if it is, the other is bound to accept it.[4] If he fails to do so, he himself will be in desertion and "the tables are turned".[5]

But if the deserting spouse has been guilty of behaviour which entitles the other to stay away, a simple offer to return need not necessarily be accepted. If he has been guilty of adultery, the innocent spouse is never bound to take him back;[6] in other cases the offending spouse must give the other a credible assurance that the conduct complained of will not be repeated in the future. The amends that the guilty spouse must make is a question of degree;

---

[1] *Cf. Howard* v. *Howard*, [1956] P. 65; [1962] 2 All E.R. 539; *France* v. *France*, [1969] P. 46; [1969] 2 All E.R. 870, C.A.; *Pizey* v. *Pizey*, [1961] P. 101; [1961] 2 All E.R. 658, C.A.

[2] Conduct may be condoned by sexual intercourse without a resumption of cohabitation; in the wife's case she must intend to forgive her husband: *Henderson* v. *Henderson*, [1944] A.C. 49; [1944] 1 All E.R. 44, H.L.; *Morley* v. *Morley*, [1961] 1 All E.R. 428. For a full discussion of the subject, see the 5th Edition of this book at pp. 221-229.

[3] *Williams* v. *Williams*, [1939] P. 365, 369; [1939] 3 All E.R. 825, 828, C.A.

[4] *Dyson* v. *Dyson*, [1954] P. 198; [1953] 2 All E.R. 1511; *Price* v. *Price*, [1951] P. 413; [1951] 2 All E.R. 580 n.; *Irvin* v. *Irvin*, [1968] 1 All E.R. 271.

[5] *Pratt* v. *Pratt*, [1939] A.C. 417; [1939] 3 All E.R. 437, H.L.; *Thomas* v. *Thomas*, [1946] 1 All E.R. 170; *Everitt* v. *Everitt*, [1949] P. 374; [1949] 1 All E.R. 908, C.A.

[6] *Everitt* v. *Everitt*, (*supra*), at pp. 381-386 and 913-916, respectively. This applies equally if the innocent spouse has reasonable grounds for believing that the other has committed adultery even though he has not in fact done so: *Everitt* v. *Everitt*, at pp. 379-381 and 911-913, respectively.

obviously the more reprehensible his conduct has been in the past, the stronger must his assurances be for the future, and some conduct may be so gross that the innocent spouse is not bound to accept the offer at all.[1]

In either case the offer must be genuine in the sense that the spouse making it must be prepared to implement it if it is accepted. Where there is real doubt about this, the correct way of resolving it may be by accepting the offer,[2] but this is not necessary if the evidence clearly points to the contrary. Thus in *Dunn* v. *Dunn*[3] it was held that a husband was entitled to reject an offer made by his wife (who had previously ordered him to leave the matrimonial home) in view of the fact that she had ordered him out before, had refused to let him have a key to the house, was bringing unjustified charges of cruelty against him, and had sent the invitation, couched in affectionate terms, by registered post. Moreover, a spouse is bound only to accept an offer to resume cohabitation in the full sense of the word and not, for example, on condition that the parties no longer have sexual intercourse.[4] Similarly, an offer with unreasonable conditions attached need not be accepted. In *Barrett* v. *Barrett*[5] the wife deserted her husband in 1941, taking with her the three daughters of the marriage (whose ages ranged from 17 to 19), and went to live in another part of London. The husband asked her to return but refused to have the daughters back. The wife declined to go back without them. On the husband's petition for divorce on the ground of his wife's desertion, it was held that the wife was entitled to remain apart from him, for there had been nothing in his daughters' conduct to justify him in refusing to have them back, and it was not unreasonable of the mother to decline to leave them to fend for themselves in view of their ages and the conditions obtaining in London during the air raids of 1941.[6]

Supervening Consent.—If the deserted spouse subsequently consents to living apart, the desertion will automatically come to an end.[7] Whether or not

---

[1] *Edwards* v. *Edwards*, [1948] P. 268, 272; [1948] 1 All E.R. 157, 160. See also *Thomas* v. *Thomas*, [1924] P. 194, C.A.; *Theobald* v. *Theobald*, [1962] 2 All E.R. 863. Tiley, *Desertion and the Bona Fide Offer to Return*, 83 L.Q.R. 89, argues forcefully that, even though the innocent spouse can never be bound to accept an offer to resume cohabitation made by a spouse who has committed adultery, this will nevertheless terminate the offeror's desertion if it is made in good faith. The logic of this is unassailable if one assumes that the *animus deserendi* must always be present in the subjective sense. But the cases all indicate that the criterion for the *continuation* of desertion is whether the deserted spouse is justified in refusing to resume cohabitation: see Irvine, 83 L.Q.R. 338; 29 M.L.R. 331.

[2] *Dunn* v. *Dunn*, [1967] P. 217, at pp. 226, 228-229; [1956] 1 All E.R. 1043, at pp. 1048, 1049.

[3] [1967] P. 217; [1965] 1 All E.R. 1043. See also *Thomas* v. *Thomas*, [1924] P. 194, C.A.; *W.* v. *W. (No. 2)*, [1954] P. 486; [1954] 2 All E.R. 829, C.A.

[4] *Hutchinson* v. *Hutchinson*, [1963] 1 All E.R. 1.

[5] [1948] P. 277, C.A. *Cf. Fletcher* v. *Fletcher*, [1945] 1 All E.R. 582, where it was held that a wife was not bound to accept her husband's invitation to join him in a community devoted to service in retreat and believing in the communal ownership of property.

[6] Except where the spouse alleged to be in desertion becomes insane (see *ante*, p. 211), he is presumed to retain the *animus*, so that the burden is upon him to prove that desertion has come to an end: *Bowron* v. *Bowron*, [1925] P. 187, 195, C.A.; *W.* v. *W. (No. 2)*, (*supra*), at pp. 502 and 832-833, respectively; *Coulter* v. *Coulter*, [1962] N.I. 145.

[7] Desertion is presumed to continue, so that the complainant does not have to show that he was at all times ready and willing to take the defendant back: *Sifton* v. *Sifton*, [1939] P. 221; [1939] 1 All E.R. 109.

he has done so is purely a question of fact: clearly a spouse can no longer allege that the other is in desertion if he obtains a judicial separation or enters into a separation agreement.

Good Cause for Separation Supervening.—If the deserted spouse commits some act which would justify the other in refusing to live with him any longer, the desertion will come to an end unless it can be shown that this act did not alter the other's intention to live apart. *Prima facie*, therefore, the desertion will cease, and the burden is upon the spouse originally deserted to prove that his conduct did not affect the other's mind.[1] Thus, in *Richards* v. *Richards*[2] the wife committed adultery two years after her husband had deserted her, and it was held that this brought the existing desertion to an end, because she failed to show that her act had not impeded any possible reconciliation. Conversely, as in *Brewer* v. *Brewer*,[3] even if the deserted spouse communicates to the other the clear intention of not having him or her back, this will not bring the desertion to an end if the evidence shows that this did not effectively prevent the deserter from taking steps to bring about a reconciliation.

4. TWO YEARS' SEPARATION

The petitioner may establish that the marriage has broken down irretrievably by showing that the spouses have lived apart for a continuous period of at least two years immediately preceding the presentation of the petition *and* that the respondent consents to the decree being granted.[4] This was one of the most controversial provisions of the Divorce Reform Act because it introduced, albeit to a limited extent, divorce by consent.

Living Apart.—The Matrimonial Causes Act provides that spouses are to be treated as living apart unless they are living with each other in the same household.[5] On this base the courts have built up two principles. First, if the spouses are living under the same roof, they can be regarded as living apart only if they are living in two households: in other words there must be the same degree of separation as is necessary to constitute desertion.[6] Hence they will not be living apart if they share their meals and living accommodation,

---

[1] *Herod* v. *Herod*, [1939] P. 11; [1938] 3 All E.R. 722. Obviously it cannot affect the other's intention if he is unaware of the commission of the act: *cf. ante*, p. 216.

[2] [1952] P. 307; [1952] 1 All E.R. 1384, C.A.

[3] [1962] P. 69; [1961] 3 All E.R. 957, C.A. See also *Bevan* v. *Bevan*, [1955] 3 All E.R. 332; *Church* v. *Church*, [1952] P. 313; [1952] 2 All E.R. 441 (subsequent adultery); *Pardy* v. *Pardy*, [1939] P. 288; [1939] 3 All E.R. 779, C.A. (subsequent adultery of which the respondent was unaware). But if the deserted spouse communicates his or her intention of not taking the other back at or near the beginning of the separation, this may be evidence of consensual separation and thus negative desertion: *per* HOLROYD PEARCE, L.J., in *Brewer* v. *Brewer* at pp. 89 and 967, respectively.

[4] Matrimonial Causes Act 1973, s. 1 (2) (d).

[5] *Ibid.*, s. 2 (6).

[6] *Mouncer* v. *Mouncer*, [1972] 1 All E.R. 289. See *ante*, pp. 208-209.

even though they sleep in separate rooms, no longer have sexual intercourse and largely live their own lives.[1] Conversely, they will be treated as still living apart if the wife, having left her husband for another man, subsequently takes him in as a lodger because he is ill and has nowhere else to go.[2]

But even if the spouses are physically separated, it does not follow that they are living apart for the purpose of the Act. The second principle, formulated by the Court of Appeal in *Santos* v. *Santos*,[3] is that they will not be so treated unless consortium has come to an end. So long as both spouses intend to share a home when circumstances permit them to do so, consortium is regarded as continuing;[4] consequently before they can be said to be living apart, one of them at least must regard the marriage as finished. If they agree to separate or one deserts the other, it will be obvious to both that consortium is at an end; if the separation is temporary or enforced (for example, because of a business trip or treatment in hospital), consortium will usually continue, but it will come to an end if either spouse decides not to return to the other. In the latter case the Court of Appeal in *Santos* v. *Santos* further held that it is not necessary for that spouse to communicate his or her decision to the other and the statutory period can begin to run immediately. Suppose, for example, that a husband is serving a long term of imprisonment and his wife stands by him and regularly visits him; one of them resolves not to live with the other again but says nothing and the visits continue as before. Two years after making this decision he (or she) may petition for divorce with the other's consent. At first sight this seems surprising,[5] but in fact it accords with the policy of the Act. The period of separation is designed to provide evidence that the marriage has broken down irretrievably and this of itself justifies a restrictive interpretation of the words "living apart" by requiring evidence that consortium was at an end during the whole of the period. Otherwise the following sort of situation could arise: a husband, who has been abroad for more than two years, has a bitter quarrel with his wife on his first day home and so much heat is engendered that they agree to a divorce forthwith although neither up to that time had considered the marriage to be on the rocks. It cannot have been the intention of Parliament to permit divorce by consent in a case like this; some sort of cooling-off period is not only desirable but essential. Given this policy, however, the fact that one spouse has regarded the marriage as dead for at least two years must normally be pretty clear evidence that it has broken down irretrievably whether or not the

---

[1] *Mouncer* v. *Mouncer*, (*supra*). *Cf. Hopes* v. *Hopes*, (*ante*, p. 209).

[2] *Fuller* v. *Fuller*, [1973] 2 All E.R. 650, C.A. *Cf. Bartram* v. *Bartram*, (*ante*, p. 222). Would the parties be regarded as living apart if the husband never moved out but merely changed places with the lodger? They would no more be living with each other than the spouses in *Fuller* v. *Fuller*, but the courts may be less ready to infer that separation has begun than to hold that, once begun, it is continuing.

[3] [1972] Fam. 247; [1972] 2 All E.R. 246, C.A. See Bromley, 88 L.Q.R. 328. The decision is in line with the interpretation of similar statutory provisions in other common law jurisdictions within the Comonwealth: see particularly *Sullivan* v. *Sullivan*, [1958] N.Z.L.R. 912.

[4] See *ante*, p. 112.

[5] It may seem even more surprising that at the end of five years he could launch divorce proceedings without the other's consent: see *post*, p. 228.

other knew of this.[1] Despite the suggestion[2] that it must be the petitioner who has formed the intention to break off consortium, it is submitted that it should be sufficient to show that either of them did so. The evidence that the marriage has broken down is equally strong in either case, and such a limitation would give a wholly unwarranted advantage to the spouse who made the decision not to return.

Respondent's Consent.—The respondent must affirmatively consent to the decree: it is not sufficient that he does not oppose it.[3] It follows that a petitioner cannot seek a decree relying on this fact if the respondent cannot be found or cannot give a valid consent because of mental illness. The mental capacity required to give a consent to the dissolution of a marriage is the same as that required for its formation: did the respondent understand the nature and consequences of what he was doing?[4] He must be given such information as will enable him to understand the effect of a decree being granted.[5] He may withdraw his consent at any time before a decree nisi is pronounced, and if he does so (or does not give his consent in the first place) and two years' separation is the only fact alleged by the petitioner, the proceedings must be stayed.[6]

After decree nisi the respondent has only a qualified power to withdraw his consent and to attempt to prevent the decree being made absolute. If the court grants a decree solely on the fact of two years' separation coupled with the respondent's consent, the latter may apply to have the decree nisi rescinded on the ground that the petitioner misled him (whether intentionally or unintentionally) about any matter which he took into account in deciding to give his consent.[7] The court is not bound to rescind the decree; presumably it will order a rescission only if the respondent has been seriously misled. A change of mind after the decree has been made absolute will, of course, be too late.

---

[1] Presumably one spouse need not have categorically decided never to resume cohabitation. If the parties agree that, if they live apart for a period, they may be able to live together again amicably in the future but their expectations are not fulfilled, the total time for which they have been separated ought to indicate whether or not the marriage has broken down irretrievably and therefore should count towards the statutory period: see *Macrae* v. *Macrae* (1967), 9 F.L.R. 441, 464.

[2] Made *obiter* in *Beales* v. *Beales*, [1972] Fam. 210, 218; [1972] 2 All E.R. 667, 671, allegedly following *Santos* v. *Santos*. See further Bromley, *loc. cit.*

[3] *McG.* v. *R.*, [1972] 1 All E.R. 362. The usual way of proving consent is by producing the completed acknowledgment of service stating that the respondent consents to the decree, which must be signed by him personally: see Matrimonial Causes Rules 1977, r. 16 (1) and Form 6.

[4] *Mason* v. *Mason*, [1972] Fam. 302; [1972] 3 All E.R. 315.

[5] Matrimonial Causes Act 1973, s. 2 (7). This is printed on the Notice of Proceedings served on the respondent: Matrimonial Causes Rules 1977, Form 5.

[6] Matrimonial Causes Rules 1977, r. 16 (2). In *Beales* v. *Beales*, (*supra*), at pp. 222 and 674, respectively, BAKER, P., left open the question whether a respondent could ever be estopped from withdrawing a consent once given if the petitioner had acted on it to her detriment, for example by vacating the matrimonial home. With respect to the learned President, this cannot be a true case of estoppel because the representation would be to future conduct; nor could it be a form of quasi-estoppel because the petitioner is not using it as a shield. The real question must be whether a respondent can bind himself by contract not to withdraw his consent. Insofar as the Act implies that the respondent must be a consenting party at the time of the trial, it is submitted that his consent cannot be made irrevocable by being given under seal or for valuable consideration.

[7] Matrimonial Causes Act 1973, s. 10 (1). The matters on which a respondent is most likely to be misled are those relating to financial provisions.

5. FIVE YEARS' SEPARATION

The last fact on which a petitioner may rely is that the spouses have lived apart for a continuous period of at least five years immediately preceding the presentation of the petition.[1] This provision is even more controversial than the last because it enables the marriage to be dissolved against the will of a spouse who has committed no matrimonial offence and who has not been responsible for the breakdown of the marriage. On the one hand it was hailed as a measure that would bring relief to hundreds of couples who would otherwise live in stable illicit unions unable to marry because one or both of them could not secure release from another union; on the other hand it was castigated as a "Casanova's charter".

This fact is identical with the last except that the period of separation is five years and the respondent's consent is not required. It will thus be seen that a decree could be granted even though the respondent is hopelessly insane. If five years' separation is established, a decree can still be refused if it would cause the respondent grave financial or other hardship.[2]

D. DIVORCE: RECONCILIATION AND PROTECTION OF THE RESPONDENT AND CHILDREN

1. RECONCILIATION

The emphasis of the whole of the Divorce Reform Act is on irretrievable breakdown and thus on the possibility of reconciliation. A number of provisions in the Matrimonial Causes Act are designed to promote this.[3]

Adjournment of Proceedings.—If at any stage it appears that there is a reasonable possibility of a reconciliation between the spouses, the court may adjourn the proceedings for such period as it thinks fit to enable attempts at reconciliation to be made.[4] Once the case has come to trial, it is of course highly improbable that they will be successful save in the most exceptional circumstances.[5] What is much more likely is that some form of *conciliation* may enable the parties to agree to a solution to at least some of the matters in dispute between them, such as the custody of the children or the financial provision to be made. Even if it fails to do this, it should identify the issues on which they remain seriously at variance and on which therefore they will require the adjudication of the court. Consequently a procedure has been evolved by which the court may refer a case to the court welfare officer not only when it considers that there is a reasonable possibility of a reconciliation but also if there are ancillary proceedings in which it appears that conciliation might serve a useful purpose.[6]

---

[1] Matrimonial Causes Act 1973, s. 1 (2) (e).
[2] See *post*, pp. 230-235.
[3] For a critical appraisal of these provisions, see Griew, *Marital Reconciliation—Context and Meanings*, [1972A] C.L.J. 294.
[4] *Ibid.*, s. 6 (2).
[5] See Griew, *loc. cit.*, 308-310.
[6] For the details, see *Practice Direction*, [1971] 1 All E.R. 894.

Solicitor's Certificate.—If the petitioner instructs a solicitor to act for him, the latter is required to certify whether or not he has discussed with the petitioner the possibility of a reconciliation and given him the names and addresses of persons qualified to help effect a reconciliation between estranged spouses. The object of this provision is "to ensure that parties know where to seek guidance when there is a sincere desire for a reconciliation, and it is important that reference to a marriage guidance counsellor or a probation officer should not be regarded as a formal step which must be taken in all cases irrespective of whether or not there is any prospect of reconciliation".[1] If there has been no discussion, the court may feel bound in some cases to exercise its power to adjourn the proceedings to see whether a reconciliation can be effected, but it will not do so if it is satisfied from the evidence that reconciliation is out of the question.[2]

It is doubtful whether this provision achieves anything of value. Most solicitors will presumably discuss the prospects of reconciliation with their clients before launching divorce proceedings anyway; others may still treat the certificate as a formality unlikely to lead to any real attempt to resume married life. In many cases the estrangement will probably be too deep by the time either spouse seeks legal advice for there to be any real chance of their coming together again.[3]

Cohabitation.—Certain provisions of the Matrimonial Causes Act are designed to enable the spouses to try to effect a reconciliation by resuming cohabitation for a limited period without prejudicing their right to petition for divorce if the attempt fails.

Adultery.—If the parties live with each other in the same household for any period or periods not exceeding six months in all after the petitioner discovered that the respondent had committed adultery, their living together for this time is to be disregarded in determining whether the petitioner finds it intolerable to live with the respondent. But if they live with each other for more than six months, the petitioner cannot rely on the adultery at all.[4] "Living with each other in the same household" has the same meaning as it has in relation to two or five years' separation as a fact establishing irretrievable breakdown of the marriage,[5] so that time will not run against the petitioner if the spouses are living under the same roof as two separate

---

[1] Matrimonial Causes Act 1973, s. 6 (1). See *Practice Direction*, [1972] 3 All E.R. 768; Griew, *loc. cit.*, 307-308.

[2] *Goodrich* v. *Goodrich*, [1971] 2 All E.R. 1340.

[3] But undoubtedly much more could be done in appropriate cases as experience in other jurisdictions in the Commonwealth and the U.S.A. shows. See Eekelaar, *Family Law and Social Policy*, 144-151. For a highly critical but valuable and constructive analysis of the position see Manchester and Whetton, *Marital Conciliation in England and Wales*, 23 I.C.L.Q. 339.

[4] Matrimonial Causes Act 1973, s. 2 (1), (2), (6). This includes cohabitation after decree nisi which will bar the grant of a decree absolute: *Biggs* v. *Biggs*, [1977] Fam. 1; [1977] 1 All E.R. 20. The fact that the parties have lived with each other for more than six months will not stop the petitioner from relying on further adultery committed since they separated even though this is a continuation of the same adulterous association: *Carr* v. *Carr*, [1974] 1 All E.R. 1193, C.A. It is highly doubtful whether the period is long enough to effect a reconciliation in many cases or whether the attempt is likely to be successful if the petitioner has to keep his eye on the calendar: see Griew, *loc. cit.*, 313-314.

[5] See *ante*, pp. 225-226.

households. Conversely, if they are living apart but both treat the marriage as still on foot notwithstanding the adultery, they will be regarded as living with each other for this purpose.

Respondent's Behaviour.—A similar rule applies if the petitioner relies on the respondent's behaviour. If the parties have lived with each other in the same household for a period or periods not exceeding six months in all after the date of the final incident relied on by the petitioner, this is to be disregarded in determining whether he can reasonably be expected to live with the respondent.[1] But in this case the Act does not expressly state what the position is to be if they cohabit for more than six months. This is obviously strong evidence that the the petitioner can be expected to live with the other spouse, but the deliberate omission of any express enactment (as appears in the case of adultery) indicates that it is not to be conclusive. In most cases it will be difficult for the court to resist the inference that the petitioner can be expected to live with the respondent or even that the marriage has not irretrievably broken down,[2] but it may do so if the petitioner can show some other reason for his or her actions, for example if he or she cohabited for the protection of the children or because there was nowhere else to live.[3]

Desertion and Separation.—In determining whether the period of two years' desertion or two or five years' separation has been continuous, the court must similarly disregard any period or periods not exceeding six months in all in which the parties have lived together in the same household. In these cases, however, the periods of cohabitation must be ignored in calculating the length of time the parties have been apart.[4] Hence if the husband leaves his wife, they then live together for four months, and he then leaves her again, she will not be able to petition for divorce alleging desertion or separation until two years and four months have elapsed from his first leaving her. This is the only exception to the rule that two or more periods of desertion or separation cannot be added together to give a period of two or five years in the aggregate.

2. PROTECTION OF THE RESPONDENT

Two provisions of the Matrimonial Causes Act are designed to give protection to the respondent when the petitioner relies on two or five years' separation—in other words when the petition does not disclose any fault or breach of matrimonial obligation on the respondent's part.

Hardship to the Respondent.—If the petitioner relies on *five years'* separation, section 5 of the Act permits the respondent to oppose the grant of a decree nisi on the ground that the dissolution of the marriage will result in grave financial or other hardship to him *and* that it would in all the circumstances be wrong to dissolve the marriage. If the court finds that the petitioner has established five years' separation and makes no such finding as

[1] Matrimonial Causes Act 1973, s. 2 (3), (6).
[2] *Katz* v. *Katz*, [1972] 3 All E.R. 219, 224.
[3] *Bradley* v. *Bradley*, [1973] 3 All E.R. 750, C.A.
[4] Matrimonial Causes Act 1973, s. 2 (5), (6). It is doubtful whether the period is long enough: *cf.* p. 229, n. 4, *ante.*

to any other fact from which irretrievable breakdown of the marriage could be inferred, it must dismiss the petition if it is satisfied that the respondent's allegations are true.

In the vast majority of cases the wife is much more likely to suffer hardship, particularly financial hardship, from the granting of a decree than the husband.[1] Consequently in the following discussion it will be assumed that the wife is resisting the husband's petition. It must be remembered, however, that precisely the same principles will apply if the respondent is the husband.

The hardship must result from the dissolution of the marriage: it is not enough for the respondent to show that hardship would result if the divorce were based on five years' separation. In *Grenfell* v. *Grenfell*[2] the wife presented a petition for divorce based on her husband's behaviour. He cross-petitioned on the basis of five years' separation, and in her reply the wife pleaded that, as she was a practising member of the Greek Orthodox Church, her conscience would be affronted if the marriage were to be dissolved "otherwise than on grounds of substance". It was held that, as she was seeking a divorce herself, she could not argue that she would suffer hardship if the marriage were dissolved and so her reply was struck out. Furthermore, the hardship must be the result of dissolution and not of the breakdown of the marriage.[3] Hence the fact that the husband will be supporting two families will be irrelevant if he is already living with the woman he wishes to marry and has children by her. Whether it be financial or other hardship, it must also be grave.[4] Whether or not there would be grave hardship must be considered "subjectively in relation to the particular marriage and the circumstances in which the parties lived while it subsisted",[5] but what matters is not whether the respondent feels that she would suffer (which she would in most cases) but whether sensible people knowing all the facts would think so.[6] It has been said that one must look at the situation through the eyes of the respondent and then judge the reality of the apprehension.[7] It would clearly be wrong to deprive the petitioner of relief because of the respondent's ill-founded fears, and the objective test of whether the reasonable man would agree that the particular wife would suffer grave hardship must be the only one that the court can apply.

Divorce will frequently cause financial hardship to a wife (particularly if she has children), but the courts are slow to find that this will be grave. Hardship includes the loss of the chance of acquiring any benefit which the

---

[1] In every reported case in which grave hardship has been alleged the wife has been the respondent.

[2] [1978] Fam. 128; [1978] 1 All E.R. 561, C.A.

[3] *Talbot* v. *Talbot* (1971), 115 Sol. Jo. 870.

[4] "Grave" qualifies both "financial" and "other hardship": *Rukat* v. *Rukat*, [1975] Fam. 63; [1975] 1 All E.R. 343, C.A.

[5] *Per* DUNN, J., in *Talbot* v. *Talbot*, (*supra*), cited with apparent approval by KARMINSKI, L.J., in *Mathias* v. *Mathias*, [1972] Fam. 287, 299; [1972] 3 All E.R. 1, 6, C.A.

[6] *Per* LAWTON, L.J., in *Rukat* v. *Rukat*, (*supra*) at pp. 73 and 351, respectively. To quote his homely example: "The rich gourmet who because of financial stringency has to drink vin ordinaire with his grouse may well think that he is suffering hardship; but sensible people would say he was not."

[7] *Per* OMROD, L.J., *ibid.*, at pp. 75 and 353, respectively. *Cf.* the view of MEGAW, L.J., at pp. 72 and 350, respectively. But how does one judge the reality of an apprehension that one will damned in the next world if one dies divorced?

respondent might acquire if the marriage were not dissolved.[1] We have already seen that, if the husband has already set.up another home, divorce will not make the slightest difference to his current financial obligations and therefore could not cause the wife any further hardship.[2] Likewise, the potential loss of rights on the husband's intestacy will usually be immaterial because he will presumably be advised to make a will in favour of other beneficiaries: whether the marriage is dissolved or not, the wife will have a claim under the Inheritance (Provision for Family and Dependants) Act 1975.[3] In practice grave hardship will be due to one (or both) of two causes. First, the wife will no longer be able to claim Social Security benefits (such as a widow's pension and a retirement pension) by virtue of her husband's contributions. This does not apply if she is over the age of 60 at the time of the divorce because she will then be entitled to benefits as though her husband had died,[4] but in other cases the Court of Appeal in *Reiterbund* v. *Reiterbund*[5] laid down the principle that the court must not ignore the claims she has to supplementary benefit. There is no stigma attached to its receipt and it can make no difference to the wife which public fund the money comes from. If, therefore, the amount she would receive from supplementary benefit is not substantially less than what she would receive from the contributory benefit, she will suffer no hardship as a result of the divorce. If, on the other hand, she is likely to be earning a wage after her husband's death or retirement, she might receive considerably more from the contributory benefit because her earnings might not reduce it to the same extent as they would reduce the sum she received by way of supplementary benefit. Each case must turn on its own facts: in *Reiterbund* v. *Reiterbund* the wife could not rely on the potential loss of a widow's pension as grave financial hardship because she was likely to remain incapable of earning her own living and would therefore still be partially dependent on supplementary benefit whether she received a widow's pension or not.

The other likely cause of grave financial hardship will be the potential loss of pension rights (other than those payable under the Social Security Act) accruing to an employee's widow. It will be necessary to make a reasonable assessment of the possible loss and the wife will not be able to argue that this amounts to grave financial hardship if it is too remote a contingency. In this connection it must be remembered that some funds are held on discretionary trusts under which the trustees may pay a pension to a woman with whom the husband has been living to the exclusion of his widow. Similarly, a middle-aged wife is more likely to be affected than a young one, and it will be unusual for a young, able-bodied wife, capable of earning her own living, to be able to

---

[1] Matrimonial Causes Act 1973, s. 5 (3).

[2] This means that the husband will suffer if he and the other woman are not prepared to live with each other unless they marry, because divorce will affect his obligations.

[3] See *post*, pp. 623 *et seq.*. It is equally irrelevant for the wife to complain that the amount being paid by the husband under an existing order is too little; this has nothing to do with the consequences of dissolution and the wife's remedy is to apply for a variation of the order: *Dorrell* v. *Dorrell*, [1972] 3 All E.R. 343, 347.

[4] See the Social Security (Widow's Benefit and Retirement Pensions) Regulations, S.I. 1979 No. 642, regs. 8 and 12.

[5] [1975] Fam. 99; [1975] 1 All E.R. 280, C.A.; affirming the judgment of FINER, J., [1974] 2 All E.R. 455; Bissett-Johnson and Pollard, 38 M.L.R. 449; Lowe, 6 Fam. Law 24, 59; Snaith, 126 New L.J. 341.

make out a case of grave financial hardship.[1] Although it has been held that the loss can be offset if the husband purchases an annuity or secures the payment of premiums of an insurance policy of equal value,[2] this may be worth little in days of inflation, particularly if the pension is "index-linked" and so subject to periodical revision as the cost of living goes up. The courts are obviously loth to keep alive a marriage that has irretrievably broken down and in *Le Marchant* v. *Le Marchant*[3] the Court of Appeal held that the husband's offer to transfer the matrimonial home (worth about £5,000) to the wife, to pay her a further £5,000 on his retirement and to take out an insurance on his own life for £5,000, which would be payable to her if she survived him, offset an index-linked widow's pension then worth £1,300 a year. One wonders what the real value of this settlement will be in the future. It is clear, however, that a husband will be at a disadvantage if he has neither the capital nor the income to offer some real compensation to his wife: in *Julian* v. *Julian*,[4] for example, the difference between a pension of £790 a year (which the respondent could claim as the petitioner's widow) and an annuity of £215 a year (which was all the husband could afford to purchase) was held to be so great as to cause the wife grave financial hardship, and the petition was dismissed.

The position of the children may also be relevant in determining whether the respondent would suffer financial hardship. In *Lee* v. *Lee*[5] the wife needed accommodation to look after her son who was then in hospital but who would require constant attention during the day time on his discharge. As the husband's proposal to sell the matrimonial home and give her half the proceeds of sale would not have enabled her to buy a flat for this purpose, the petition was dismissed.[6]

The Court of Appeal has refused to define what "other grave hardship" could comprise,[7] but in all the cases reported up to now the respondent has alleged that the divorce would be anathema to her on religious grounds or would result in social ostracism.[8] In most of them the wife has come from overseas and has sought to have the petition dismissed because of the effect that a divorce would have on her standing amongst her own community. A

---

[1] *Per* STEPHENSON, L.J., in *Mathias* v. *Mathias*, (*supra*), at pp. 301-302 and 8, respectively.

[2] *Parker* v. *Parker*, [1972] Fam. 116; [1972] 1 All E.R. 410. *Cf. post*, pp. 553-554.

[3] [1977] 3 All E.R. 610, C.A.

[4] (1972), 116 Sol. Jo 763. *Cf. Brickell* v. *Brickell*, [1974] Fam. 31; [1973] 3 All E.R. 508, C.A. (potential loss of pension of £232 a year, grave financial hardship). See further Vickers, 123 New L.J. 240.

[5] (1973), 117 Sol. Jo. 616. (On appeal a decree was granted because regrettably the son had died in the meantime: 5 Fam. Law 48, C.A.)

[6] Obviously in many cases the wife's allegation will involve a detailed examination of the parties' financial position before decree nisi, thus anticipating the similar enquiry that will have to be made in chambers if the decree is granted and the wife claims financial relief (as she presumably will). Consequently the judge should reserve this question to himself to avoid unnecessary waste of time and costs. If the petitioner has misled the respondent about his financial position or about the terms he proposes for her provision, with the result that the respondent has consented to the petition which she would otherwise have opposed, she may have the decree nisi rescinded: *Parkes* v. *Parkes*, [1971] 3 All E.R. 870, C.A. *Quaere* whether she could still do so if the decree has already been made absolute: presumably this would be in the court's discretion. See generally Cretney, 122 New L.J. 48.

[7] *Banik* v. *Banik*, [1973] 3 All E.R. 45, 48, C.A.

[8] *Cf.* the opinion of ORMROD, L.J., in *Rukat* v. *Rukat*, [1975] Fam. 63, 75; [1975] 1 All E.R. 343, 352, C.A.

typical example is to be found in *Banik* v. *Banik*,[1] where the wife was a Hindu
still living in India. It was held by the Court of Appeal that it was not
sufficient that the divorce would cause her distress and unhappiness or that
she personally would regard it as immoral or contrary to the rules of her
community; she must establish that shame, disgrace or degradation would
fall on her. Whether this would amount to grave hardship if it were
established is a question of fact and degree: the defence has not been successful in any reported case.

Even if the respondent does prove that the decree would cause her grave
hardship, the court must still pronounce a decree unless it is also of the
opinion that it would be wrong to do so. The use of "wrong" in this context is
unusual and its meaning is ambiguous and obscure; in *Brickell* v. *Brickell*[2]
DAVIES, L.J., was of the opinion that it meant "unjust or not right in all the
circumstances of the case". The court must take into account specifically the
conduct and interests of the parties and the interests of any children[3] and
other persons concerned (for example, the person whom the petitioner wishes
to marry),[4] and in the end will have to balance those interests against the
hardship that a divorce would cause the respondent.[5] The latter's age,
earning capacity and prospects of remarriage and the length of time that the
parties have cohabited are all highly relevant, and in practice the courts are
not likely to refuse a decree if the wife is young, healthy and capable of
earning her own living or if the marriage has lasted for only a short time or
has been dead for many years.[6] The respondent's conduct may likewise be a
vital fact, and in *Brickell* v. *Brickell* a decree was pronounced against a wife
who had deserted her husband and broken up his business by her conduct
even though the potential loss of a pension caused her grave financial hardship. Although the children's interests must be considered, the Court of
Appeal in *Mathias* v. *Mathias*[7] apparently paid no regard to the wife's argument that the husband's remarriage (which would be possible only if he were
granted a divorce) could cause financial hardship to their child. The
husband's father had left half his residuary estate (which was worth £20,000)
to the husband's legitimate children in equal shares, and by remarriage the

---

[1] [1973] 3 All E.R. 45, C.A. The court remitted the case for rehearing and a decree was later
pronounced because the wife's statement that she would become a social outcast could be discounted and it would not be wrong to dissolve the marriage: 117 Sol. Jo. 874. See also *Parghi* v.
Parghi (1973), 117 Sol. Jo. 582 (Hindu wife resident in Bombay); *Rukat* v. *Rukat*, (*supra*)
(Roman Catholic wife with family in Sicily).

[2] [1974] Fam. 31, 37; [1973] 3 All E.R. 508, 511, C.A.

[3] This could include children who would be legitimated if the petitioner remarried.

[4] Matrimonial Causes Act 1973, s. 5 (2). "Children" includes children over the age of 18:
Allan v. *Allan* (1973), 4 Fam. Law 83.

[5] See *Rukat* v. *Rukat*, (*supra*), at pp. 75 and 352, respectively. In *Mathias* v. *Mathias*, [1972]
Fam. 287, 299; [1972] 3 All E.R. 1, 7, C.A., KARMINSKI, L.J., adopted the words of DUNN, J., in
Talbot v. *Talbot* (1971), 115 Sol. Jo. 870, that "regard had to be had to the circumstances of the
persons involved, including the children, and also to the balance which had to be maintained
between upholding the sanctity of marriage and the desirability of ending 'empty' ties". The
reference to upholding the sanctity of marriage seems scarcely relevant to a case where *ex
hypothesi* the marriage has irretrievably broken down.

[6] *Mathias* v. *Mathias*, (*supra*), at pp. 301-302 and 8, respectively; *Rukat* v. *Rukat*, (*supra*), at
pp. 76 and 353, respectively.

[7] [1972] Fam. 287; [1972] 3 All E.R. 1, C.A. It was further held that the potential loss of state
and army pensions was not grave financial hardship to a wife of 32 and that it would be wrong
not to dissolve the marriage when the parties had cohabited for less than three years out of ten.

husband might have further legitimate children and thus reduce the existing child's interest. No reason was given for disregarding this: but it is submitted that it would have been unjust to the petitioner to keep the marriage on foot merely to prevent the birth of further legitimate children.

Financial Protection for the Respondent.—If a decree nisi is pronounced based solely on *two or five years' separation*, the respondent may apply for the decree not to be made absolute unless the court is satisfied (a) that the petitioner should not be required to make financial provision for the respondent *or* (b) that the financial provision made by the petitioner for the respondent is reasonable and fair or the best that can be made in the circumstances. If the court is not so satisfied, it *must* withhold the decree.[1]

It should be noticed that the latter condition is satisfied only if the provision is *made*; it is not sufficient for the petitioner to make proposals which would be satisfactory if they were carried out. Thus, if the court approves the payment of a lump sum, the decree should not be made absolute until the sum is actually paid in order to prevent the petitioner from frustrating the purpose of the provision by obtaining his decree and then failing to carry out his undertaking.[2]

This provision is designed to afford further protection to the respondent by giving her another weapon that can be used against the petitioner. The threat to delay the latter's remarriage by holding up the decree absolute may be perfectly proper if the petitioner is deliberately evading his financial responsibilities, but obviously it can be abused. Consequently, even though the court finds that the petitioner has not made such financial provision as he should have made, it may nevertheless make the decree absolute if it appears that there are circumstances making it desirable that this should not be delayed *and* the court has obtained a satisfactory undertaking from the petitioner that he will make such financial provision for the respondent as the court may approve.[3] This does not mean that the court can accept a blanket undertaking which would leave the petitioner ignorant of what he is to do and the respondent ignorant of what she is to get. The petitioner must give an outline of what he proposes and the court should not make the decree absolute unless it is satisfied that these proposals are reasonable and fair or the best that can be made.[4]

In deciding what financial provision (if any) the respondent ought to make for the petitioner, the Act requires the court to consider all the circumstances including specifically the age, health, conduct, earning capacity, financial resources and financial obligations of each of the spouses, and also the probable financial position of the respondent if the marriage is dissolved and the petitioner dies first.[5] Generally speaking, the court should take into account the same matters as it considers when assessing financial provision.[6]

---

[1] Matrimonial Causes Act 1973, s. 10 (2), (3). Failure to comply with this provision makes the decree absolute voidable, not void: *Wright* v. *Wright*, [1976] Fam. 114; [1976] 1 All E.R. 796.

[2] *Wilson* v. *Wilson*, [1973] 2 All E.R. 17, C.A. This would apply equally to the transfer or settlement of property and to securing periodical payments. How can it apply to unsecured periodical payments, which create a continuing obligation? Is it necessary to obtain a court order before the decree is made absolute?

[3] Matrimonial Causes Act 1973, s. 10 (4).

[4] *Grigson* v. *Grigson*, [1974] 1 All E.R. 478, C.A.

[5] Matrimonial Causes Act 1973, s. 10 (3).

[6] *Lombardi* v. *Lombardi*, [1973] 3 All E.R. 625, 629, C.A. See *post*, pp. 547-558.

Thus in *Krystman* v. *Krystman*[1] it was held that the petitioner should not be required to make any provision for his wife when the parties had cohabited for only a fortnight at the beginning of the marriage, which had taken place 26 years before, and the wife (whose income exceeded the husband's) had previously made no financial claim on him at all.

A comparison of this provision with that contained in section 5 shows three important differences between them. First, it applies to both two and five years' separation whilst section 5 applies only to five years' separation. In practice, however, it is unlikely that a respondent will invoke this provision in the case of two years' separation because she (or he) will consent to the decree only if she is satisfied that she will receive the best financial provision possible in the circumstances and, if she has been misled, she can apply to have the decree nisi rescinded.[2] Secondly, section 5 applies to grave financial or other hardship (and is therefore not confined to financial matters) whilst the provision we have just considered refers at the highest to reasonable and fair financial provision. Finally, reflecting the second point of difference, it merely enables the respondent to delay the decree absolute, whilst section 5 enables him to oppose the making of the decree nisi *in limine* and is therefore a much more powerful weapon.

3. PROTECTION OF CHILDREN

As we shall see,[3] the court may not pronounce a decree absolute unless it has made an order with reference to the arrangements for the welfare of the children of the family. This differs from the protection given to the respondent just considered in that the latter applies only if the petitioner relies on two or five years' separation and the respondent specifically invokes the relevant provision, whereas the court is required to make an order with respect to children in all cases and the decree absolute will be void if it fails to do so.

E. THE WORKING OF THE NEW DIVORCE LAW IN PRACTICE[4]

The chief criticism that can be made against the new divorce law is that it is a compromise between the old law based on matrimonial fault and the new concept of irretrievable breakdown which perpetuates many of the defects of the former without necessarily producing the advantages of the latter. The necessity of establishing one of the five facts set out in section 1 (2) of the Matrimonial Causes Act is largely designed to ensure that the technically "innocent" spouse shall not be divorced against his will until the parties have been separated for five years. This has produced the inevitable consequence

---

[1] [1973] 3 All E.R. 247, C.A. See further *post*, p. 552.

[2] See Passingham, *Law and Practice in Matrimonial Causes*, 3rd Ed., 53. For rescission of decree nisi, see *ante*, p. 227.

[3] *Post*, pp. 308-310.

[4] A considerable amount has been written on this subject. Attention is particularly drawn to Mortlock, *The Inside of Divorce;* Eekelaar, *Family Security and Family Breakdown*, 230-249, and *The Place of Divorce in Family Law's New Role*, 38 M.L.R. 241; Finlay, *Reluctant but Inevitable: the Retreat of Matrimonial Fault*, *ibid.*, 153, and the other authorities there cited; Elston, Fuller and Murch, *Judicial Hearings of Undefended Divorce Petitions*, 38 M.L.R. 609 (an informative study of petitioners' attitudes); Murch, *The Role of Solicitors in Divorce Proceedings*, 40 M.L.R. 625, 41 M.L.R. 25.

that, however the Act is worded, practitioners still tend to think in terms of five grounds for divorce. Furthermore, it is no credit to a legal system, which makes irretrievable breakdown the sole ground for divorce, that judges are compelled to dismiss a petition because none of the facts has been established even though they are satisfied that the marriage has broken down irretrievably.

One of the advantages of adopting the irretrievable breakdown theory is that the decree merely recites a state of affairs without attributing blame or passing any sort of moral judgment, and one would hope that the bitterness might be taken out of some of the proceedings if one party were not to be labelled as technically innocent and the other as technically guilty when in many cases the conduct of both has contributed to the collapse of their marriage. But this is precisely what the court still has to do if any of the first three facts is alleged. The position is exacerbated if the petitioner wants a divorce (or is prepared to accede to the respondent's request for one) without having to wait for two years' separation, because she is then compelled to rely on the respondent's adultery or behaviour and is thus forced to establish a breach of the latter's matrimonial obligations. If she alleges that the respondent is in desertion or has behaved in such a way that she cannot reasonably be expected to live with him, the court must still make a value judgment about the parties' conduct towards each other. Irretrievable breakdown based on separation is also open to criticism. If a period of two years is long enough to indicate that the marriage has broken down if the respondent consents to the divorce, it must logically be long enough even if he does not consent. If the spouses are living apart and one of them wishes to be released, sooner or later the other is going to be divorced whether she (or he) likes it or not, unless she can establish that this would cause her grave hardship; what the existing law does is to enable her to hold up the other's chance of remarriage for a further period of three years whether for reasons of conscience or out of vindictiveness. It is difficult to see what social purpose this serves. Furthermore, the provisions designed to protect the respondent from grave hardship and to ensure that she receives reasonable financial protection may be used as a form of blackmail against a relatively wealthy husband who may agree to make much more liberal financial provision for his wife than a court would order.[1]

---

[1] To these criticisms Finlay, *loc. cit.*, would add another: that the courts have been guilty of excessive legalism in interpreting the definition of the five facts. The following analysis of the 162,867 petitions filed in 1979 may be of some interest. The numbers based on each fact (excluding 5 based on presumption of death) were:

    (a) adultery, 44,092;
    (b) respondent's behaviour, 60,846;
    (c) desertion, 4,449;
        two or all of the above, 1,431;
    (d) two years' separation, 38,714;
    (e) five years' separation, 12,957;
        consent and five years' separation, 50; other combinations, 323.

From this it will be seen that in 68% of the cases the petitioner was alleging fault but in 65% the spouses need not have been separated for two years. What is noticeable is that the number of petitions based on two years' separation was over nine times as many as the number based on desertion. This suggests that many cases which could have proceeded on the latter fact were proceeding on the former. Another remarkable fact is the increase in the number of petitions based on the respondent's behaviour: 38% compared with 18.5% in 1971.

Over 90% of petitions under the old law were undefended. In many other cases cross-petitions were filed: in other words, both spouses were anxious to have the marriage dissolved but each wished the other to appear as the guilty party on the record. The usual reason for this was that a guilty wife was in a worse position than a technically innocent one when it came to the question of the award of maintenance. Now that the innocence or guilt of the parties will no longer affect the award of financial relief and their conduct will be taken into consideration only if it is "obvious and gross",[1] there is less incentive to oppose the making of a decree. This means that the two vital issues between the spouses will usually be the welfare of the children and financial relief, and the parties and their advisers should make every attempt to come to an acceptable agreement out of court.[2] The Matrimonial Causes Act contemplates a procedure by which the parties (or either of them) may refer an agreement to the court so as to obtain the judge's view as to its reasonableness.[3] It has been judicially stated, however, that, if the spouses have reached an agreement with the assistance of their legal advisers, it will rarely be necessary or desirable to incur the expense involved in referring it to a judge,[4] and it is significant that the current Matrimonial Causes Rules make no provision for this procedure at all.

There is no doubt that the new law has gone a long way to achieve its object of enabling "the empty legal shell to be destroyed with the minimum bitterness, distress and humiliation". In 1979 about 1% of petitions were defended but in the majority of these cases a decree was granted to the respondent on a cross-petition. There are a number of reasons for this. Some parties still consider that a stigma attaches to divorce, at least so far as the "guilty" spouse is concerned, and consequently will try to avoid having this label attached to them.[5] If the petitioner pleads that the respondent has been guilty of gross misconduct and the latter does not defend, he may find himself faced with an estoppel in ancillary proceedings relating to financial provision.[6] Whatever may be the respondent's motive, defended proceedings will generally still be attended by the bitterness, distress and even humiliation that the Law Commission deplored. For this reason, if the respondent admits the petitioner's

---

[1] See *post*, p. 555.

[2] An agreement "subject to the approval of the court" constitutes a binding contract from which neither party can resile unless and until the court disapproves: *Smallman* v. *Smallman*, [1972] Fam. 25; [1971] 3 All E.R. 717, C.A. See further *post*, pp. 539-541.

[3] S. 7. This replaces legislation going back to 1963. Relevant rules were in existence until January 1974.

[4] See *Practice Direction*, [1972] 3 All E.R. 704, and *cf. Beales* v. *Beales*, [1972] Fam. 210, 220-221; [1972] 2 All E.R. 667, 673-674. But the parties may still wish to refer some agreements, *e.g.* those relating to children, when the petitioner wishes to rely on two years' separation and the respondent will consent only on the terms agreed. There is apparently now no means by which a reference can be made. But see the judgment of ORMROD, L.J., in *Brockwell* v. *Brockwell* (1975), 6 Fam. Law 46, C.A.

[5] The courts have recognised the legitimacy of this attitude by permitting a respondent to file an answer out of time when the petition is based on the respondent's behaviour and the latter wishes to cross-petition for divorce based on the petitioner's own adultery, but not when it is based on five years' separation: *Rogers* v. *Rogers*, [1974] 2 All E.R. 361, C.A.; *Collins* v. *Collins*, [1972] 2 All E.R. 658, C.A.

[6] See *post*, pp. 557-558. Quite apart from the question of estoppel, it may be necessary for the court to have a clear picture of the cause of the breakdown when dealing with ancillary matters: *Mustafa* v. *Mustafa*, [1975] 3 All E.R. 355.

allegations (thus admitting that a ground for divorce has been made out), the court will not normally permit him to cross-petition for the purpose of obtaining a decree on allegations made against the petitioner.[1] A further attempt to reduce the number of defended causes has been the introduction of a compulsory "pre-trial review" in all such cases proceeding in the Principal Registry in London. This procedure had already been adopted in some district registries and the experience there indicates that "under the registrar's guidance the parties are often able to compose their differences or to drop unsubstantial charges and defences and to concentrate on the main issues in dispute". As a consequence many cases become undefended and the parties agree to consent orders relating to financial provision and to custody of, and access to, children.[2]

Following the argument advanced above, it is suggested that after two years' separation either spouse should be able to petition for divorce without the other's consent. This would make two years' desertion redundant as a fact evidencing irretrievable breakdown and would replace the last three facts now to be found in section 1 (2) of the Matrimonial Causes Act.[3] It is also submitted that, if adultery does not constitute such behaviour on the respondent's part that the petitioner can no longer be expected to live with him, it should not be a fact on which the petitioner should be able to rely at all, and consequently the first fact could be swept away. It is probably still desirable to retain the possibility of divorce before the parties have been separated for two years: a wife may not be able to afford to live apart from her husband, there may be some cases where one spouse's conduct has been so gross that the other ought to be able to get a divorce forthwith, and if one of them has established a stable union with another person, little point will be served in keeping the existing marriage alive until the statutory period has run out.[4] In the last case logic dictates that the "guilty" spouse ought to be able to petition himself, but many people would probably find wholly unacceptable a suggestion which would enable a husband to petition for divorce immediately after leaving his wife for another woman. Consequently, it would be necessary either to retain the existing fact based on the respondent's behaviour or to introduce some other provision permitting an "innocent" spouse to petition within the first two years of separation in certain specified circumstances.[5]

The Special Procedure.—In almost every undefended case a decree was granted following the uncontested evidence of the petitioner and any other witness necessary to support his case. Appearance in court led to anxiety for

---

[1] *Grenfell* v. *Grenfell*, [1978] Fam. 128; [1978] 1 All E.R. 561, C.A.

[2] *Practice Direction*, [1979] 1 All E.R. 112.

[3] It would probably be necessary to retain the respondent's power to oppose a decree on the ground that it would cause her grave financial hardship but to add a proviso that this should not apply if her own conduct had been responsible for the breakdown of the marriage. This would involve an enquiry into the cause of the breakdown in some cases but the number would probably be small.

[4] But under new legislation in Australia the sole ground for divorce is now irretrievable breakdown of the marriage evidenced by one year's separation.

[5] *E.g.*, exceptional hardship to the petitioner or exceptional depravity on the part of the respondent. *Cf.* the existing law relating to divorce within the first three years of marriage, *ante*, pp. 191-192.

the petitioner and to costs which, whether borne by the parties or by the legal aid fund, were not insignificant. It also involved a great deal of judicial time. Consequently in 1973 there was introduced a "special procedure" to dispense with the need to give evidence in court if the case was not defended. Originally it applied only to petitions based on two years' separation; in 1975 it was extended to all undefended petitions except those based on the respondent's behaviour or where there were children of the family to whom section 41 of the Matrimonial Causes Act applied.[1] These limitations were removed in 1977 and now all undefended petitions for divorce or judicial separation are dealt with under this procedure. At the same time legal aid ceased to be available to virtually all petitioners in undefended proceedings for divorce and judicial separation, although it can still be obtained to make or oppose an application for financial relief or custody of, or access to, children.[2] This means that the petitioner must now file the petition and take all further steps himself or pay a solicitor to do it out of his own pocket. If, however, his disposable capital and income do not exceed the sums fixed by the relevant Regulations, he may apply for legal advice under the Green Form scheme to which, depending on his income, he may have to contribute part of the cost.[3] Under this scheme a solicitor may give advice on drafting the petition and taking procedural steps; if the petitioner is not in receipt of advice, the court staff will give assistance.

If the respondent does not defend the petition, the petitioner must swear and file an affidavit in support of the petition. If the registrar is satisfied that the petitioner has proved his case and is entitled to a decree, he makes and files a certificate to this effect and a day is fixed on which the judge will pronounce the decree nisi in open court. It is not necessary for either party to be present when this is done.[4]

Whilst the special procedure has certainly reduced costs, strain on the petitioner and the time spent by judges on undefended cases, its results have not been entirely beneficial. Whereas judges would permit the amendment of a petition which was technically defective at the trial without the need to reserve it if the respondent would not be prejudiced, registrars inevitably reject all defective documents with resultant delay.[5] Judges have virtually lost all control over undefended divorce petitions decrees, which are in effect obtained by an administrative process. The provisions relating to reconciliation are now completely meaningless.[6] Despite earlier warnings by the Court of Appeal that the court should not necessarily accept the petitioner's assertions,[7] there is no alternative to doing so, and the court certainly cannot

---

[1] For s. 41, see *post*, pp. 308-310.

[2] Legal Aid (Matrimonial Proceedings) Regulations 1977. See further Passingham, *Law and Practice in Matrimonial Causes*, 3rd Ed., 340-341.

[3] For details, see Passingham, *op. cit.*, 330-333.

[4] Matrimonial Causes Rules 1977, rr. 33 (3) and 48 and Forms 7 (a)-(e); *Practice Direction*, [1977] 1 All E.R. 845. The same procedure applies *mutatis mutandis* if the case goes undefended on a cross-petition contained in the respondent's answer; if the petition is based on two years' separation, the respondent must give notice that he consents to the decree. Once the registrar has made his certificate, the decree nisi must be pronounced unless the respondent obtains leave to have the certificate set aside: this will be granted only if the justice of the case requires that he be given leave to defend. See *Day* v. *Day*, [1980] Fam. 29; [1979] 2 All E.R. 187, C.A.

[5] See Westcott, 8 Fam. Law 209.

[6] See *ante*, p. 228.

[7] See *ante*, p. 195.

enquire into the facts alleged by the petitioner as the Matrimonial Causes Act requires it to do.[1] The special procedure in fact "makes the complexity of the substantive law ... seem unnecessary and irrelevant".[2] Although it is impossible to test the hypothesis, one cannot help suspecting that a number of decrees are granted on grounds that are legally insufficient and there is indeed little to stop a petitioner prepared to commit a flagrant act of perjury from obtaining a decree based on desertion or separation long before the relevant period of separation has elapsed. It is obvious that not only the substantive law but also the whole basis of divorce procedure needs immediate review.[3]

F. DIVORCE IN THE CONFLICT OF LAWS

1. JURISDICTION OF ENGLISH COURTS

Jurisdiction was originally based solely on domicile and a court could pronounce a decree only if the husband (and therefore the wife) was domiciled in England when the petition was presented.[4] Had domicile retained its original meaning of a person's home, this might have been a satisfactory principle; but the technical meaning that it acquired produced many anomalies. One of the most glaring flowed from the wife's inability to acquire a separate domicile, so that, even though she had always been resident in this country, she could not obtain relief here if her husband was domiciled abroad. Two statutory bases of jurisdiction were introduced to meet this case, and a wife was able to petition (a) if her husband had deserted her or had been deported and had been domiciled in England immediately before the desertion or deportation, or (b) if she had been ordinarily resident in this country for three years immediately preceding the presentation of the petition and her husband was not domiciled in any other part of the United Kingdom or in the Channel Islands or the Isle of Man.[5]

Nevertheless hardship remained. A man habitually resident in this country but domiciled abroad could never obtain a divorce here. A woman in this position could do so if she could bring herself within one of the statutory exceptions, and it was anomalous that she alone could rely on three years' residence here. If the parties were British subjects domiciled in a country which based its divorce jurisdiction on nationality, they could get a divorce in neither country. Consequently the Law Commission recommended that jurisdiction should be extended to enable either spouse to petition if he or she had been habitually resident in this country for a year.[6] This recommendation (together with a modification of the original principle necessitated by the wife's ability to acquire a separate domicile) was implemented by the Domicile and Matrimonial Proceedings Act 1973, which also swept away the former statutory bases of jurisdiction.

---

[1] Section 1 (4).

[2] Cretney, *Principles of Family Law*, 3rd Ed., 163.

[3] See Eekelaar, *Family Law and Social Policy*, 151-156; Davis and Murch, 7 Fam. Law 71.

[4] *Le Mesurier* v. *Le Mesurier*, [1895] A.C. 517, P.C.

[5] The first exception was introduced by the Matrimonial Causes Act 1937, s. 13, and the second by the Law Reform (Miscellaneous Provisions) Act 1949, s. 1.

[6] Law Com. No. 48 (Report on Jurisdiction in Matrimonial Causes), 1972.

Jurisdiction.—The court now has jurisdiction if (and only if) either of the parties (a) is domiciled in England and Wales on the date when the proceedings are begun *or* (b) was habitually resident here throughout the period of one year ending with that date.[1] In addition, once proceedings for divorce, nullity or judicial separation, over which the court has jurisdiction, are pending, it may entertain other proceedings with respect to the marriage falling into any of these three categories even though it would not otherwise have jurisdiction when the second proceedings were begun.[2] Suppose, for example, that a wife petitions for judicial separation and that the only fact giving the court jurisdiction is that she has been habitually resident here for a year. She then ceases to be resident in this country and the husband cross-petitions for divorce. The court will have jurisdiction to hear the divorce petition even though neither party is then domiciled or resident in this country.

Discretionary Stays.—One of the consequences of this increased jurisdiction is the greater likelihood that other matrimonial proceedings will be brought simultaneously in another country. If, for example, the husband starts divorce proceedings elsewhere, the wife may be tempted to petition in this country in the belief that she is likely to obtain better financial provision. To prevent the embarrassment that might ensue, the court has a discretionary power to stay any matrimonial proceedings in this country if before the beginning of the trial it appears that any proceedings in respect of the marriage in question or capable of affecting its validity or subsistence are continuing in any country outside England or Wales. The court may order a stay only if the balance of fairness is such that it is appropriate that the other proceedings should be disposed of first, and in deciding this the court must have regard to all relevant facts including the convenience of the parties and witnesses and any delay or expense that might otherwise result. It should also consider the question of custody and the need to grant financial relief for a spouse or children resident in England.[3] The court may act on its own initiative: to ensure that it has before it all the necessary information the petitioner and, if the respondent cross-petitions, the respondent are bound to furnish particulars of all such proceedings that they know to be pending: if they fail to do so, the court may order a stay even after the trial has begun.[4]

Obligatory Stays.—Because of their proximity, conflicts between jurisdictions within the British Isles are likely to occur more often and to be more embarrassing than conflicts with other countries. Factors other than the country with which the marriage is most closely connected will not affect the court's judgment in deciding in which jurisdiction the proceedings should be permitted to continue, and clear rules are desirable for the guidance of the parties' advisers and to ensure uniform decisions within the United Kingdom. Consequently if proceedings for divorce or nullity (which may have the effect of altering the parties' status) are also being brought in Scotland, Northern Ireland, the Channel Islands or the Isle of Man, the court is *bound* to order a stay on the application of either of the parties provided that, to ensure that

---

[1] Domicile and Matrimonial Proceedings Act 1973, s. 5 (2).

[2] *Ibid.*, s. 5 (5).

[3] *Shemshadfard* v. *Shemshadfard*, [1981] 1 All E.R. 726; *Mytton* v. *Mytton* (1977), 7 Fam. Law 244.

[4] Domicile and Matrimonial Proceedings Act 1973, s. 5 (6) and Sched. 1, paras. 7 and 9.

proceedings are continued in the appropriate jurisdiction, three further conditions are also satisfied: (i) the parties must have resided together since the celebration of the marriage; (ii) the place where they last resided together (or where they were residing together when the English proceedings were begun) must have been in the other jurisdiction; and (iii) one of the parties must have been habitually resident in the other jurisdiction throughout the year ending with the date on which they last resided together.[1]

Removal of Stay.—Once the court has made an order staying proceedings (whether discretionary or obligatory), it may remove the stay on the application of either party if the proceedings in the other country have been concluded or stayed or if a party to those proceedings has been guilty of unreasonable delay in prosecuting them.[2]

Ancillary Orders.—If the court orders a stay on the ground that proceedings are being brought outside the British Isles, it has a complete discretion with respect to ancillary orders. When the proceedings are being brought in Scotland, Northern Ireland, the Channel Islands or the Isle of Man, however, detailed rules are laid down to ensure that all matters are dealt with by the same court. Essentially no ancillary orders may be made and any order already made will cease to have effect three months after a stay (discretionary or obligatory) is imposed unless an order is necessary because a matter needs to be dealt with urgently. If the other court makes an order for periodical payments for a spouse or child or for the custody or education of a child, the English court has no further power at all to make an order dealing with the same matters and any such order already made will cease to have effect.[3]

Choice of Law.—Strangely enough, the Act does not expressly provide rules for the choice of law to be applied. In the case of the former statutory exceptions it was assumed that this was to be English law even though this was not the parties' *lex domicilii*,[4] and this principle was confirmed by later legislation.[5] It is generally accepted that this rule still applies:[6] any other would produce insuperable difficulties if the parties were domiciled in different countries or if their *lex domicilii* did not permit divorce at all.

2. RECOGNITION OF FOREIGN DECREES

Following the principle that jurisdiction in divorce was based on domicile, English courts originally recognised a decree only if it was obtained in the country in which the parties were domiciled[7] or if it was obtained elsewhere

---

[1] *Ibid.*, Sched. 1, para. 8.

[2] *Ibid.*, Sched. 1, para. 10. An obligatory stay, once removed, cannot be reimposed.

[3] *Ibid.*, Sched. 1, para. 11. Nor may the court make an order for the payment of a lump sum to a child if the other court has made an order for periodical payments for the child.

[4] *Zanelli* v. *Zanelli* (1948), 64 T.L.R. 556, C.A.

[5] See the Matrimonial Causes Act 1950, s. 18 (3), and subsequent legislation re-enacting it.

[6] Dicey and Morris, *Conflict of Laws*, 10th Ed., 337; Cheshire and North, *Private International Law*, 10th Ed., 364-366; Law Com. No. 48, paras. 103-108.

[7] *Harvey* v. *Farnie* (1882), 8 App. Cas. 43, H.L.

but recognised by their *lex domicilii*.[1] These rules were regrettably narrow because many foreign countries have other bases for jurisdiction, for example nationality. Nevertheless no other decrees were recognised until after the Second World War, when the courts indicated that they were prepared to take a much more liberal attitude. First, they held that a divorce would be recognised if the facts were such that *mutatis mutandis* an English court would have assumed jurisdiction.[2] Secondly, the much wider principle was established that we should recognise a foreign decree whenever there was a real and substantial connection between either party and the country in which the decree was obtained.[3]

In order to reduce the number of limping marriages, it is obviously essential that as many countries as possible should apply the same rules of recognition (which should ideally correspond with uniform rules of jurisdiction). For this purpose, a Convention on the Recognition of Divorces and Legal Separations was signed at the Hague in 1968, and the recommendations of the Law Commission and the Scottish Law Commission that effect should be given to the Convention in a somewhat modified form[4] were implemented in the Recognition of Divorces and Legal Separations Act 1971. The Act came into force on 1st January 1972 and has since been amended by the Domicile and Matrimonial Proceedings Act 1973.[5]

British Divorces.—An English court is now bound to recognise a decree of divorce granted under the law of any other part of the British Isles, that is Scotland, Northern Ireland, the Channel Islands and the Isle of Man.[6] It will be observed that the decree must be granted *under the law of* the jurisdiction in question, hence it must be obtained by proceedings in a court of law.[7] This provision applies only to divorces granted after the Act came into force, but in such cases the jurisdiction of the court cannot now be questioned. If the decree was pronounced before the Act came into force, we shall recognise it only if the common law rules relating to recognition are satisfied. As will be seen below, foreign divorces are now recognised whenever they were granted. The Law Commission justified this on the ground that it would be capricious and anomalous to recognise a decree pronounced after the Act came into

---

[1] *Armitage* v. *A.-G.*, [1906] P. 135, approved in *Indyka* v. *Indyka*, [1969] 1 A.C. 33; [1967] 2 All E.R. 689, H.L. There were also some statutory grounds for recognition, *e.g.* those contained in the Colonial and Other Territories (Divorce Jurisdiction) Acts 1926-1950.

[2] *Travers* v. *Holley*, [1953] P. 246; [1953] 2 All E.R. 794, C.A., approved in *Indyka* v. *Indyka*, (*supra*). The court would have been prepared to recognise a decree granted by a New South Wales court to a wife whose husband had lost his New South Wales domicile after deserting her. *Cf.* the former English basis of jurisdiction (*ante*, p. 241).

[3] *Indyka* v. *Indyka*, (*supra*). See further, *ante*, p. 106.

[4] Cmnd. 4542 (1970).

[5] For the sake of brevity these two Acts will be referred to as the 1971 and the 1973 Act respectively. See generally, Dicey and Morris, *op. cit.*, 338-366; Cheshire and North, *op. cit.*, 366-389; Karsten, 35 M.L.R. 299; Polonsky, 22 I.C.L.Q. 343; North, *Private International Law of Matrimonial Causes*, cc. 10 and 11, and *Recognition of Extra-judicial Divorces*, 91 L.Q.R. 36; Jaffey, *ibid.*, 320; Maidment, *Legal Effect of Religious Divorces*, 37 M.L.R. 611.

[6] 1971 Act, s. 1 (as amended by the 1973 Act, s. 15) and s. 10 (2).

[7] *Cf.* s. 16 of the 1973 Act, *post*.

force but not one pronounced beforehand;[1] it is not clear why this argument does not apply equally to British divorces.

Overseas Divorces.—An "overseas divorce" is defined as one obtained by judicial or other proceedings in any country outside the British Isles (as defined above) and effective under the law of that country.[2] It will be seen that this definition involves three elements, each of which presents difficulties.

(1) It must be obtained by *judicial or other proceedings*. The meaning of this phrase had to be considered by the House of Lords in *Quazi* v. *Quazi*.[3] The husband pronounced a talaq in Pakistan, of which state he and the wife were both nationals. The talaq was a threefold pronouncement of divorce made in writing before two witnesses which in pure Muslim law would in itself dissolve the marriage. A Pakistani statute, however, required the husband to give notice of it to the Chairman of a local administrative body and provided that it should not take effect until 90 days after this had been done. The husband duly gave notice and the Chairman then took certain prescribed steps to bring about a reconciliation. The House of Lords held unanimously that, as the talaq was ineffective unless notice was given, the talaq and the notice together constituted "proceedings" for the purpose of the Act.

It is clear that the proceedings do not have to be judicial or quasi-judicial, but apart from this it is difficult to spell out any general test. LORD FRASER was of the opinion that the acts relied on must be officially recognised and have some regular definite form but that "anything that can properly be regarded as proceedings will qualify so long as it is legally effective".[4] LORD SCARMAN'S test was even wider: he considered that we should recognise "any act or acts, officially recognised as leading to divorce in the country where the divorce was obtained, and which itself is recognised by the law of the country as an effective divorce".[5] These views suggest that the proceedings do not have to be taken before any particular body or officer and that, provided the steps follow some officially recognised form, they can be taken in private. This is of some importance, because in some Muslim states the pronouncing of talaq without more will still effect an immediate divorce. The view that this would constitute proceedings is strengthened by section 6 of the Act.[6] This preserves the common law rule that an English court will recognise a foreign decree if it is obtained under or recognised by the spouses' *lex domicilii* and requires that the parties must have been domiciled in the country in question "at the time of the institution of proceedings". As purely informal divorces were recognised at common law,[7] this suggests that the word should be given the widest possible interpretation. Moreover, section 16 of the 1973 Act precludes the court from recognising a divorce obtained by "any proceeding" in the British Isles unless it is instituted in a court of law. LORD FRASER was of the opinion in *Quazi* v. *Quazi* that there was no significant

[1] Cmnd. 4542, paras. 45-50.
[2] 1971 Act, s. 2.
[3] [1980] A.C. 744; [1979] 3 All E.R. 897, H.L; Karsten, 43 M.L.R. 202. For a discussion of the difficulties raised by this case, see Sylvester, *The Islamic Talaq*, [1980] J.S.W.L. 282.
[4] At pp. 814 and 908, respectively.
[5] At pp. 824 and 916, respectively. VISCOUNT DILHORNE agreed with LORD SCARMAN'S speech.
[6] As substituted by s. 2 of the 1973 Act. See *post*, p. 247.
[7] *Lee* v. *Lau*, [1967] P. 14; [1964] 2 All E.R. 248 (divorce by agreement).

difference between the words "proceedings" and "proceeding";[1] as the purpose of the section is to protect women domiciled abroad but resident in this country,[2] both words should include informal divorces to avoid the anomaly of giving the wife protection if a talaq was attended by some formality but none if it was not.

(2) The divorce must be obtained in a country outside the British Isles. Hence a divorce obtained in a religious court in England could not be an "overseas divorce". A problem arises if different steps in the proceedings are taken in different countries. Suppose, for example, that a husband executes a written talaq in England and that it is served on his wife in an Asiatic Muslim state. Is the divorce obtained where the document is executed or where it is received? It is submitted that the answer must depend upon the place in which the document is effective. Hence if the marriage is dissolved immediately the talaq is executed, the divorce will be obtained in England; but if dissolution is conditional on its receipt, the divorce will be obtained wherever it is delivered to the wife.[3]

(3) The divorce must be effective under the law of the country where it is obtained. Suppose a national of state X, resident in state Y, obtains a divorce in a court of his own religious sect situated in Y and that this takes effect under the law of X. At first sight it might seem that it is effective under the law of X and not Y and consequently is not an overseas divorce for the purpose of the Act. On the other hand, if the conflict rules of Y recognise it as valid, it is arguable that it is effective under the law of Y.[4] This wider interpretation is to be preferred because the alternative would leave the parties free to marry by their *lex patriae* and the law of the country in which they reside but not by English law. The point, however, must be regarded as doubtful.

An overseas divorce will be recognised in this country if, at the date of the institution of the proceedings, either spouse was habitually resident in the country in which it was obtained or was a national of that country.[5] If a country comprises territories with different legal systems (such as the U.S.A.), each territory is to be regarded as a separate country for the purpose of residence.[6] Furthermore, if a country bases jurisdiction on domicile, a

---

[1] At pp. 818 and 911, respectively. But he declined to express an opinion as to whether a bare talaq would be recognised under the Act (at pp. 817 and 911, respectively). In *Sharif* v. *Sharif* (1980), 10 Fam. Law 216, WOOD, J., was apparently of the opinion that it would not be.

[2] See *post*, pp. 247-248.

[3] In *R.* v. *Registrar General of Births, Deaths and Marriages, Ex parte Minhas*, [1977] Q.B. 1; [1976] 2 All E.R. 246, the facts were identical to those in *Quazi* v. *Quazi* except that the talaq was pronounced in England. A Divisional Court held that the "proceedings" were the writing of the talaq and doubted whether serving the notice on the Chairman of the administrative body or sending a copy of the document to the wife were "proceedings" at all. *Sed quaere* as the talaq would have been ineffective without them. The Court evidently misunderstood the Pakistani statute: see *Quazi* v. *Quazi*, at pp. 816 and 910, respectively (*per* LORD FRASER).

[4] See North *op. cit.*, 230-232; 91 L.Q.R. 54-55.

[5] 1971 Act, s. 3 (1). For nationality in the case of British colonies and dependencies, see *ibid.*, s. 10 (3). If there are cross-proceedings, the validity of a divorce obtained either in the original proceedings or in the cross-proceedings will be recognised if the provisions relating to habitual residence or nationality were satisfied at the time of the institution of either the original proceedings or the cross-proceedings: s. 4 (1).

[6] *Ibid.*, s. 3 (3). *Quaere* whether in such a case we shall recognise a decree on the ground that a spouse was a national of the state unless the law of divorce is uniform within the federation (as it is, for example, in Australia). See Dicey and Morris, *op. cit.*, 349-351; Morris, *Recognition of American Divorces in England*, 24 I.C.L.Q. 635; North, *op. cit.*, 173-175.

person is to be regarded as habitually resident there if he is domiciled there *within the meaning of that law.*[1] This may lead to anomalies. If the law of a country provides that jurisdiction is to be based on domicile and that a person is deemed to be domiciled in the country if he satisfies some nominal condition such as six weeks' residence, English courts will apparently be compelled to recognise a divorce right outside the spirit of the Convention.

Any finding of fact made in the foreign proceedings on the basis of which jurisdiction was assumed (including any finding relating to either spouse's habitual residence, domicile or nationality) is conclusive evidence of that fact if both spouses took part in the proceedings. In other cases it is sufficient evidence unless the contrary is proved.[2]

In some countries (for example, in Scandinavia) it is possible for a legal separation to be converted into a divorce after a lapse of time. If this is done and we recognise the separation under the rules just discussed, we must also recognise the divorce as well.[3]

Recognition based on Domicile.—The Act of 1971 preserved the common law rule that we should recognise a divorce if it was obtained under or recognised by the spouses' *lex domicilii*. This had to be modified when it became possible for a wife to have a different domicile from her husband. Now a divorce obtained outside the British Isles will be recognised if any of the following four conditions is satisfied:

(a) if at the material time both spouses were domiciled in the country in which it was obtained; or

(b) if it was recognised as valid by the law of the spouses' common domicile; or

(c) if at the material time one of the spouses was domiciled in the country in which it was obtained and it was recognised as valid under the other's *lex domicilii*; or

(d) if neither of them was domiciled there at the material time but it was recognised as valid under the *lex domicilii* of each.[4]

In each of the above cases the word "domicile" is used in its English sense and "the material time" is the time when the proceedings were instituted.[5]

None of the provisions discussed affected the validity of extra-judicial divorces obtained in the British Isles. These, of course, would not be valid by the municipal law of the country in question but would still be recognised as valid if they were recognised by the spouses' *lex domicilii*. This meant, for example, that a talaq pronounced in England could validly dissolve the marriage of spouses domiciled in Pakistan.[6] The consequences of this could be disastrous to the wife, for such divorces frequently make no financial provision for her and she would no longer be able to invoke the jurisdiction of

---

[1] *Ibid.*, s. 3 (2).

[2] *Ibid.*, s. 5. A spouse who has appeared in the proceedings is to be treated as having taken part in them.

[3] *Ibid.*, s. 4 (2).

[4] *Ibid.*, s. 6, as substituted by s. 2 of the 1973 Act.

[5] This implies that the divorce must have been obtained by "proceedings", which must have the same meaning as it has in s. 2: see *ante*, p. 245.

[6] As in *Qureshi* v. *Qureshi*, [1972] Fam. 173; [1971] 1 All E.R. 325.

an English court to do so.[1] Consequently section 16 of the Domicile and
Matrimonial Proceedings Act 1973 now imposes two limitations on the
application of the rules relating to recognition of divorces obtained after
1973. First, no proceeding[2] in any part of the British Isles will be regarded as
validly dissolving a marriage unless it is instituted in the courts of law of one
of those countries. Hence a talaq obtained here will no longer be recognised
for any purpose. Secondly, if a divorce is obtained in a country outside the
British Isles otherwise than by a proceeding instituted in a court of law, it will
not be recognised here if both parties have been habitually resident in the
United Kingdom throughout the period of one year immediately preceding
the institution of the proceeding unless it can be recognised as an "overseas
divorce" in the sense defined in the Act.[3] The purpose of this provision is to
prevent a spouse resident here from getting round the restriction on the
recognition of extra-judicial divorces obtained in this country by taking a day
trip abroad. But whereas no extra-judicial divorce obtained in the British
Isles will be recognised, those obtained abroad will be caught by the
prohibition only if they are not "overseas divorces" and in addition *both*
spouses have been habitually resident in the United Kingdom for a year.
Thus, if both parties are Pakistani nationals, domiciled in Pakistan, who
have been resident in this country for 13 months, we should not recognise a
written talaq delivered in England or France, even though it has the effect of
dissolving the marriage by Pakistani law; but we should recognise it if the
proceeding took place in Pakistan because it would be effective under the law
of the country in which it was obtained and of which the parties were both
nationals.[4]

Exclusion of other Grounds for Recognition.—A divorce may also be
recognised by virtue of any other statute,[5] but with this exception no divorce
obtained outside the British Isles will now be recognised in this country unless
one of the conditions set out above is satisfied.[6] Unlike the case of British
divorces, these rules apply whether the divorce was obtained before or after
the Act of 1971 came into force, but to prevent hardship two cases had to be
excluded: the provisions of the Act do not affect any property rights to which
any person became entitled before 1972 or apply if the question of the validity
of the divorce had been decided by any competent court in the British Isles
before that date.[7]

Dissolution by means other than Proceedings.—The provisions of the Act
refer only to divorces obtained by "proceedings". This raises the question

---

[1] *Turczak* v. *Turczak*, [1970] P. 198; [1969] 2 All E.R. 317.

[2] On the question of "proceeding", see *ante*, pp. 245-246. These provisions will give rise to
difficulty if one of the spouses later remarries, because by his *lex domicilii* (which will recognise
the divorce) he will have capacity to do so. Must we then regard him as having two wives? See
North, 91 L.Q.R. 45-46.

[3] See *ante*, p. 245.

[4] It might be possible for the husband to get round this restriction by obtaining a proxy
divorce in Pakistan: Pearl, [1978-79] J.S.W.L. 24, 32.

[5] *E.g.*, the Colonial and Other Territories (Divorce Jurisdiction) Acts 1926-50. See Dicey and
Morris, *op. cit.*, 352-353.

[6] 1971 Act, s. 6 (5), as substituted by the 1973 Act, s. 2.

[7] 1971 Act, s. 10 (4).

whether English law will now recognise the dissolution of a marriage by other means and, if so, in what circumstances recognition will be accorded. The Court of Appeal had to face this problem in *Viswalingham* v. *Viswalingham*.[1] The parties were domiciled in Malaysia; at the time of the marriage the husband was Hindu by religion and the wife was a Christian. Unknown to the wife (who was living in England) the husband embraced the Muslim faith which by Malaysian law automatically terminated his marriage. The Court held that, as the Act did not apply, we should recognise the dissolution at common law if it was effected under the law of the parties' common domicile. Presumably if they had different domiciles, it would have to be recognized by the *lex domicilii* of each. This principle, however, is subject to the proviso that we shall not recognise the dissolution if to do so would offend against our notion of substantial justice. In this case the very rigid interpretation in Malaysia of the relevant Muslim law coupled with the fact that the husband kept the wife in ignorance of his conversion for a year and so prevented her from obtaining legal advice was regarded as so alien to our own concepts that recognition was refused.

Exceptions from the General Rule.—The Act specifies three circumstances in which recognition shall or may be refused even though the conditions set out above have been satisfied.

In the first place, no divorce is to be recognised in this country if by English law the marriage was void.[2] This provision is mandatory and applies whether the divorce was obtained in some other part of the British Isles or abroad.

Secondly, recognition *may* be refused if the divorce was obtained outside the British Isles by one spouse

"(i) without such steps having been taken for giving notice of the proceedings to the other spouse as, having regard to the nature of the proceedings and all the circumstances, should reasonably have been taken; *or*

(ii) without the other spouse having been given (for any reason other than lack of notice) such opportunity to take part in the proceedings as, having regard to the matters aforesaid, he should reasonably have been given."[3]

It will be observed that this applies only to divorces obtained abroad[4] and the court is given a discretion to refuse recognition. If the foreign court had followed its own procedural rules relating to waiver of notice or substituted service, failure to give notice to the other spouse would not invalidate the proceedings in the eyes of an English court at common law unless the party obtaining the divorce had fraudulently misled the court or the rules themselves offended our ideas of natural justice.[5] Whilst recognition will still doubtless be refused in such cases, there is a growing tendency to compare the

---

[1] (1979), 123 Sol. Jo. 604, C.A. This report is brief and the comments in the text are based on the full transcript of the judgment. See also Palmer, [1980] J.S.W.L. 175.

[2] 1971 Act, s. 8 (1). "English law" includes the relevant rules of private international law.

[3] *Ibid.*, s. 8 (2) (a).

[4] In the case of a divorce obtained in another part of the British Isles the party's remedy is to have the decree set aside by the court that pronounced it or to appeal from the decision. The Law Commission thought that it would be objectionable to allow another court in the British Isles to refuse to recognise it: Cmnd. 4542, p. 43.

[5] *Igra* v. *Igra*, [1951] P. 404; *Macalpine* v. *Macalpine*, [1958] P. 35; [1957] 3 All E.R. 134; *Hornett* v. *Hornett*, [1971] P. 255; [1971] 1 All E.R. 98.

procedural rules applied by the foreign court with those applied in this country and to withhold recognition if the foreign rules are unreasonable by this standard. This can be seen in two recent cases. In *Newmarch* v. *Newmarch*[1] the husband was granted a decree in New South Wales on the ground of the desertion of his wife, who was resident in England. The suit was undefended because, despite repeated requests, her Australian solicitors had failed to file an answer. REES, J., held that, had this occurred in this country, a court would have set the decree aside and consequently, applying the same test, she could not be said to have had a reasonable opportunity to take part in the proceedings. In *Joyce* v. *Joyce*[2] LANE, J., refused to recognize a decree pronounced in Quebec on the husband's petition. The wife, who was unable to obtain legal aid, had taken every step to inform the husband's legal advisers and the court that she wished to defend the proceedings, but the court was not informed of this or of the fact that the husband had been found guilty of adultery and desertion in magistrates' proceedings here. On the other hand, if the divorce is by a unilateral act, it is unlikely that an English court would refuse to recognise it solely on the ground that the other party was given no notice of it or was able to take no part in the proceedings, because even with such notice, he could not have prevented the marriage from being dissolved.

Thirdly, the court *may* refuse to recognise a divorce obtained outside the British Isles if its recognition would be manifestly contrary to public policy.[3] Again, it will be seen that this applies only to foreign divorces and that the court is given a discretion. At common law this power was exercised sparingly and only if the divorce would be offensive to the conscience of the English court,[4] for example where the petitioner committed perjury in order to lead the foreign court to believe that it had jurisdiction,[5] or where fear for her safety compelled a woman to obtain a divorce against her Jewish husband in Nazi Germany.[6] The courts will probably continue to refuse recognition in the same circumstances, as is shown by *Kendall* v. *Kendall*[7] (the only reported case in which the statutory provision has been considered). The decree had been obtained in Bolivia on the wife's application but without her knowledge and against her will. She spoke little Spanish and had been fraudulently led to sign a power of attorney authorising lawyers to act on her behalf and in her absence. It is hardly surprising that the court refused to recognise the decree. What is less clear is whether the courts will now follow the precedent set in the case of nullity and refuse to recognise a foreign decree on the ground that they regard the substantive law applied as manifestly contrary to public policy.[8] In the past they have declined to do this, and whilst there may be cases where the

---

[1] [1978] Fam. 79; [1978] 1 All E.R. 1.

[2] [1979] Fam. 93; [1979] 2 All E.R. 156. See also *Sharif* v. *Sharif* (1980), 10 Fam. Law 216.

[3] 1971 Act, s. 8 (2) (b). The word "manifestly" adds nothing to our concept of public policy: *Sharif* v. *Sharif*, (*supra*).

[4] *Qureshi* v. *Qureshi*, [1972] Fam. 173, at pp. 199 and 201; [1971] 1 All E.R. 325, at pp. 345 and 346.

[5] *Middleton* v. *Middleton*, [1967] P. 62; [1966] 1 All E.R. 168.

[6] *Meyer* v. *Meyer*, [1971] P. 298; [1971] 1 All E.R. 378. After the Second World War the parties resumed cohabitation in England. See Hartley, 34 M.L.R. 455.

[7] [1977] Fam. 208; [1977] 3 All E.R. 471. It was assumed that the wife could not have challenged the decree under the second exception because on the face of it she had obtained the decree. Could it not be argued, however, that in reality the husband had obtained it by fraud?

[8] See *ante*, pp. 106-107.

foreign law is so removed from accepted norms as to shock the conscience of the court, this is likely to occur only in the most exceptional circumstances.[1]

In all these cases it will be seen that the court has a discretion to refuse recognition: it is not bound to do so even though one of the statutory conditions is satisfied. It is hardly likely to recognise a decree if this would be manifestly contrary to public policy: in other cases all the circumstances must be taken into account including particularly the probable outcome of the proceedings if the party had had an opportunity of taking part in them, that party's legitimate objectives and the extent to which these can be achieved if the divorce is recognised, and the likely consequences to the spouses and the children of the family if it is not.[2] In *Newmarch* v. *Newmarch*[3] the wife's chief concern was to secure financial provision for herself, which she could do in other proceedings already before the court; in addition she would not have been able to defend the Australian proceedings effectively and the husband could have obtained a decree on the ground of the parties' separation irrespective of fault. In these circumstances the decree was recognised notwithstanding that the wife had not been given a reasonable opportunity to take part in the proceedings. One can imagine other cases where more hardship might be caused by recognising the decree than by refusing to do so: for example, if the party who has a legitimate complaint against the way in which the foreign proceedings have been conducted has remarried on the assumption that it is valid or if one party has led the other to believe that he will not challenge it.

Finally, it should be noted that, even if the court is bound to recognise a decree and to regard the marriage as dissolved, it is not bound to recognise any finding of fault made in the proceedings or any ancillary order.[4]

However welcome the extended rules relating to recognition may be in reducing the number of limping marriages, they can present one real difficulty. A man domiciled and resident in England, who is not a British subject, may obtain a divorce under his *lex patriae*, and if this makes inadequate financial provision for his wife, there are no proceedings she can take here to remedy the situation. As we recognise that she is no longer a married woman, she cannot take proceedings to obtain maintenance from her former husband in this country and she has lost the protection she might have had if the divorce had been obtained in England. This state of affairs is becoming more common and accounts for much of the litigation started by wives anxious to avoid the consequences of recognition.[5] This calls for an immediate change in the law to enable a party whose marriage has been dissolved abroad to take advantage of the provisions relating to financial relief contained in the Matrimonial Causes Act 1973: a reform now advocated by the Law Commission.[6]

---

1 *Cf. Viswalingham* v. *Viswalingham, ante,* p. 249.
2 *Newmarch* v. *Newmarch, (supra).* See also *Joyce* v. *Joyce, (supra).*
3 [1978] Fam. 79; [1978] 1 All E.R. 1.
4 1971 Act, s. 8 (3).
5 See *Turczak* v. *Turczak,* [1970] P. 198; [1969] 2 All E.R. 317 (although the ground on which the decree was recognised is not clear from the report); *Quazi* v. *Quazi,* [1980] A.C. 744; [1979] 3 All E.R. 897, H.L. *Cf.* the haste to obtain a decree absolute and so avoid this situation in *Torok* v. *Torok,* [1973] 3 All E.R. 101. See Pearl, [1974] C.L.J. 77; Wade, 23 I.C.L.Q. 461.
6 Law Com. Working Paper No. 77 (Financial Relief after Foreign Divorce). See also *Quazi* v. *Quazi, (supra),* at pp. 819 and 912 (*per* LORD SCARMAN) and 810 and 904, respectively (*per* VISCOUNT DILHORNE).

Part II

Parent and Child

SUMMARY OF CONTENTS

Chapter 8
Legitimacy

Despite recent legislation which has tended in many respects to assimilate the legal position of an illegitimate person to that of a legitimate one, the legal relationship between a child and his parents still depends in part upon whether or not he is legitimate. Consequently, the discussion of that part of family law dealing with the relationship of parent and child must necessarily begin with a discussion of the meaning of legitimacy.

It seems impossible to define legitimacy as an abstract concept without reference to a particular legal system. Nevertheless most systems of jurisprudence have drawn a distinction between the legal position of a child born of a legally recognised union and that of a child born of an illicit union or as the result of a casual act of intercourse.[1] Common law, like Roman law and the modern systems based upon it,[2] adhered rigidly to the rule that no child could be legitimate unless it was either born or conceived in wedlock. But it has, of course, always been possible for the legislature to legitimate a person illegitimate at common law. Occasionally a special Act has been passed for that purpose, although there have been no instances of an Act of this sort in modern times. There are, however, three statutory provisions in force today of general application, which modify the common law rules. First, the children of a void marriage may now be legitimate in certain circumstances notwithstanding that their parents have not been married at all. Secondly, the effect of section 16 of the Matrimonial Causes Act 1973 is to preserve the legitimacy of the children of parties to a voidable marriage which is subsequently annulled, despite the rule at common law that, once a voidable marriage had been annulled, it was deemed never to have been contracted at all. Thirdly, a person born illegitimate may now be legitimated if his parents subsequently intermarry. We must, therefore, consider first the position at common law and then the effect of these three statutory provisions.

[1] New Zealand law now draws no distinction between the legal relationship of a child and its parents whether or not the latter have been married: Bromley and Webb, *Family Law*, 429-439. Soviet law, which in 1918 abolished the distinction between legitimate and illegitimate children, nevertheless found it necessary for certain purposes in 1944 to draw a distinction between those born to parents who had registered their marriage and others. Hence, as one writer has observed, "children born outside a registered marriage after July 8, 1944, are comparable to illegitimate children in other countries, even if such terminology is not used": Gsovski, *Soviet Civil Law*, vol. 1, pp. 111, 121-122. See also Lapenna, *The Illegitimate Child in Soviet Law*, 25 I.C.L.Q. 156. For the proposal to abolish the distinction in English law, see *post*, pp. 273-274.

[2] But this is not the only criterion accepted in Western Europe. See further, Wolff, *Private International Law*, 2nd Ed., 385, and the *American Restatement of the Conflict of Laws*, s. 137 and Comment, where it is pointed out that in some legal systems a person may be the legitimate child of one parent but not of the other.

A. LEGITIMACY AT COMMON LAW

A child is legitimate at common law if his parents were married at the time of his conception or at the time of his birth.[1] Although in most cases he will be both conceived and born in wedlock, this need not necessarily be true.

(1) He will be legitimate if his parents were married at the time of his conception, even though the marriage was terminated before his birth. Consequently, a posthumous child will be legitimate, as will be one whose parents' marriage was terminated by divorce between the time of his conception and his birth.[2]

(2) He will be legitimate if his parents were married when he was born even though he must have been conceived before their marriage.[3]

(3) Although there is no authority on this point, there may be one case where he will be legitimate although his parents were married neither when he was conceived nor when he was born. If he is conceived as the result of pre-marital intercourse and his parents then marry but his father dies before his birth, he will presumably be legitimate. Had the father survived, the child would certainly have been legitimate, and, as we have seen, the common law does not bastardise a child merely because he is born posthumously.

It is thus obvious that legitimacy is basically a question of fact. Whether or not a person is legitimate can only be determined by reference to the following questions:

(1) Who was his mother? Normally, this question presents no difficulties, because the fact of birth and identity can be established by the evidence of the doctor or other persons present at the birth. But it is not unknown for mothers to be given the wrong children in maternity hospitals and there have been cases where parents have attempted to pass off a supposititious child as their own, usually in order to defraud others who would be entitled to property in default of children of the marriage.[4]

(2) Who was his father? This can never be established by direct evidence: paternity can normally be inferred only from the fact that the alleged father had sexual intercourse with the mother about the time when the child must have been conceived. Consequently, if two men had intercourse with her during the relevant period, it may be impossible to prove affirmatively which is the father.[6] Moreover, the fact that intercourse took place can in most cases

---

[1] Blackstone's *Commentaries*, i, 446, 454-457. For a full account of the common law relating to legitimacy and a detailed examination of the cases before 1836, see Nicolas, *Adulterine Bastardy*.

[2] *Knowles* v. *Knowles*, [1962] P. 161; [1962] 1 All E.R. 659.

[3] Co. Litt. 244a; Blackstone's *Commentaries*, i, 454. See also Nicolas, *op. cit.*, and the cases cited *post*, p. 257.

[4] *E.g.*, *Slingsby* v. *A.-G.* (1916), 33 T.L.R. 120, H.L., where the wife deceived her own husband. *Cf.* the popular belief, current at the time, that the son born to James II's consort was smuggled into the queen's room in a warming-pan in order to prevent the descent of the Crown to James's Protestant daughters.

[5] The significance of this will be seen more clearly when we consider the rebuttal of the common law presumption of legitimacy (*post*, pp. 261-265) and the establishment of the paternity of an illegitimate child where the mother is seeking an affiliation order (*post*, p. 598).

be proved only by the evidence of the parties themselves or circumstantially from their conduct and the opportunities which were presented to them.

(3) Were the father and mother legally married at the relevant time? The problems presented here have already been considered.[1]

Presumption of Legitimacy.—The impossibility of proving affirmatively the paternity of a child led at least as early as the twelfth century to the adoption of the civil law maxim '*Pater est quem nuptiae demonstrant*', that is, the presumption that, if a child is born to a married woman, her husband is to be deemed to be its father until the contrary is proved.[2] This means that if it is alleged that it is not legitimate, the burden of rebutting the presumption is immediately cast upon the party alleging the illegitimacy. This presumption will still apply even though the child is born so soon after the marriage that it must have been conceived beforehand, for, in the words of LORD CAIRNS, L.C., in *Gardner* v. *Gardner*[3] (adopting the judgment of LORD GIFFORD in the same case in the Court of Session):

> "Where a man marries a woman who is in a state of pregnancy, the presumption of paternity from that mere fact is very strong.... Still further where the pregnancy is far advanced, obvious to the eye, or actually confessed or announced ... to the intended husband, a presumption is reared up which, according to universal feeling, and giving due weight to what may be called the ordinary instincts of humanity, it will be very difficult indeed to overcome."

But if the husband was ignorant of the wife's pregnancy when he married her, the presumption may be rebutted by other evidence. Thus, in the *Poulett Peerage Case*[4] the wife was three months pregnant at the time of the marriage. Two months later the husband separated from her on the ground that she was pregnant by another man. He had deposed that he had not had sexual intercourse with her before the marriage and that he had never acknowledged the child as his. Evidence was also given that the wife had told a friend that another man was the father of the child. It was held that the presumption of the child's legitimacy was rebutted.

The presumption applies equally in the case of a posthumous child if it is born within the normal period of gestation after the husband's death.[5] Difficulty arises, however, if the birth takes place an abnormally long time afterwards. In *Preston-Jones* v. *Preston-Jones*[6] the House of Lords were agreed that the court could take judicial notice of the fact that there is a normal period of gestation (although the period is variously given as 270 to 280 days or as nine months),[7] but LORD MACDERMOTT added that judicial notice must also be taken of the fact that the normal period is not always followed and that the actual period in a given case may be considerably longer

---

[1] *Ante*, ch. 2.

[2] Glanvil, book 7, ch. 12. See also Bracton, fol. 6; Co. Litt. 373; Blackstone's *Commentaries*, i, 457; Nicolas, *op. cit.*

[3] (1877), 2 App. Cas. 723, 729, H.L. See also *R.* v. *Luffe* (1807), 8 East 193; *Anon.* v. *Anon.* (1856), 23 Beav. 273; *Turnock* v. *Turnock* (1867), 36 L.J.P. & M. 85.

[4] [1903] A.C. 395, H.L.

[5] *Re Heath,* [1945] Ch. 417, 421-422, *per* COHEN, J.

[6] [1951] A.C. 391; [1951] 1 All E.R. 124, H.L. See further, *post,* p. 260.

[7] *Per* LORD SIMONDS at pp. 401 and 127, LORD MORTON at pp. 413 and 136, LORD MACDERMOTT at pp. 419 and 139-140, respectively.

or shorter. It would seem, however, that the longer the period deviates from the normal, the more easily will the presumption be rebutted, until there comes a time when it is not raised at all, although it is extremely difficult to say where the line is to be drawn.[1]

It seems that the presumption applies equally in the case of a child born after a decree of divorce. In *Knowles* v. *Knowles*[2] the facts were such that the child could have been conceived before or after the decree absolute. WRANGHAM, J., held that the presumption of legitimacy operated in favour of presuming that conception took place whilst the marriage was still subsisting and that the husband was the father although, as he pointed out, in such circumstances it may be rebutted much more easily.

If the child must have been conceived during the subsistence of a marriage, which has since been terminated by the first husband's death or divorce, and the mother has remarried before its birth, two conflicting presumptions arise. But in the absence of evidence to the contrary, it is submitted that it ought to be presumed that the mother has not committed adultery, so that there should still be a presumption that the child is the legitimate issue of the first husband.[3]

There is one case where it is presumed that a child born to a married woman is illegitimate. This occurs when the child must have been conceived at a time when the husband and wife were living apart under a decree of judicial separation, for in such circumstances it is presumed that they have observed the decree and have not had intercourse.[4] But this reasoning has no application if they had separated voluntarily, and consequently a child conceived in such circumstances will be presumptively legitimate even though the husband and wife had entered into a separation agreement.[5]

Former proceedings may also raise an estoppel as to paternity. For example if the issue of the legitimacy of a child has been determined in divorce proceedings, the finding will bind the spouses *as between themselves*, but it cannot bind either of them as against a third person nor can it bind the child or any other person who was not a party to the proceedings.[6] Two statutory provisions should also be noted. If a man has been adjudged to be the putative father of a child *in affiliation proceedings*, this is to be accepted

---

[1] See *ibid.*, pp. 402, 403, 407, 413-414 and pp. 128, 129, 130, 132, 135-136, respectively.

[2] [1962] P. 161; [1962] 1 All E.R. 659. *Cf. Re Leman's Will Trusts* (1945), 115 L.J.Ch. 89. It is submitted that the dictum to the contrary in *Re Bromage*, [1935] Ch. 605, 609, cannot be supported.

[3] See *Re Overbury*, [1955] Ch. 122; [1954] 3 All E.R. 308, where HARMAN, J., found in favour of the first husband's paternity on the facts.

[4] *Hetherington* v. *Hetherington* (1887), 12 P.D. 112; *Ettenfield* v. *Ettenfield*, [1940] P. 96, 110; [1940] 1 All E.R. 293, 301, C.A. The reason is hardly satisfactory because the decree relieves the petitioner from the duty of cohabiting with the respondent; it does not forbid cohabitation, let alone sexual intercourse. The same rule applied to magistrates' separation orders when they had power to make them, but the presumption of legitimacy would not be displaced if there was in force a maintenance order but no separation order: *Bowen* v. *Norman*, [1938] 1 K.B. 689; [1938] 2 All E.R. 776.

[5] *Ettenfield* v. *Ettenfield*, (*supra*). But the presumption may be rebutted more easily: *Knowles* v. *Knowles*, [1962] P. 161, 168; [1962] 1 All E.R. 659, 661.

[6] *B.* v. *A.-G.*, [1965] P. 278; [1965] 1 All E.R. 62. But the husband's failure to deny that a child is a child of the family in undefended proceedings will not raise an estoppel because to permit it to do so might invite unnecessary litigation: *Rowe* v. *Rowe*, [1980] Fam. 47; [1979] 2 All E.R. 1123, C.A.

as proof of his paternity in any other *civil* proceedings, whether or not he is a party to them, until the contrary is shown.[1] Secondly, the entry of a man's name as that of the father on the registration of a child's birth will be *prima facie* evidence of paternity;[2] if the child is illegitimate, however, this can be done only with his consent unless an affiliation order has been made against him.

Rebutting the Presumption.—The presumption of legitimacy is strictly twofold:

(1) that the husband and wife had sexual intercourse; and
(2) that the child is the issue of that intercourse.

It therefore follows that it may be rebutted either by showing that the spouses could not or did not have intercourse or by establishing by medical or other evidence that, in any event, the husband could not be the father of the child in question.

Standard of Proof.—At common law the generally accepted view was that the presumption could be rebutted only by evidence indicating beyond reasonable doubt that the child was illegitimate. This was due to the serious legal incapacities and social disadvantages attached to bastardy. Now that the position of the illegitimate child has been so much improved both legally and socially, it would be anomalous to retain the common law rule as an exception to the general standard of proof in civil cases. Consequently section 26 of the Family Law Reform Act 1969 now enacts that in any civil proceedings any presumption of legitimacy or illegitimacy may be rebutted by evidence which indicates the contrary on the balance of probabilities.[3]

Rebutting the Presumption of Access.—That the former presumption can be rebutted has been accepted since at least the thirteenth century.[4] The classic statement of the law is to be found in the opinion of the judges given to the House of Lords in the *Banbury Peerage Case* in 1811,[5] where they stated in substance that the presumption of legitimacy can be rebutted only by proof of the husband's impotence or of the fact that intercourse did not take place between the husband and wife at such time that the child could be the issue of it.[6]

---

[1] Civil Evidence Act 1968, s. 12.

[2] *Brierley* v. *Brierley*, [1918] P. 257. For registration of an illegitimate child's birth, see *post*, p. 319.

[3] This implements the recommendations of the Law Commission: see Law Com. No. 16, Blood Tests and the Proof of Paternity in Civil Proceedings, para. 15. In criminal proceedings apparently the presumption must still be rebutted by evidence placing the matter beyond reasonable doubt. Can therefore a man be convicted of incest with a girl who is presumed to be his daughter but whom he would not be compelled to maintain in civil proceedings?

[4] Bracton, fol. 6 and fol. 63. See also Co. Litt. 244a; Nicolas, *Adulterine Bastardy*, 249 *et seq.*

[5] 1 Sim. & St. 153, H.L. For a full account of the case, see Nicolas, *op. cit.*, 291 *et seq.*

[6] For some exceptional rules of evidence applicable to issues of legitimacy, see textbooks on the law of evidence. The common law rule that neither spouse could give evidence of non-access which would tend to bastardise the wife's children (the so-called rule in *Russell* v. *Russell*, [1924] A.C. 687, H.L.) was abrogated by the Law Reform (Miscellaneous Provisions) Act 1949, s. 7; see now the Matrimonial Causes Act 1973, s. 48 (1).

If it can be shown that, at the time when the child must have been conceived, the husband was either permanently impotent (at least *quoad* the wife) or temporarily impotent (whether from illness or any other cause), this will generally suffice to prove that he cannot be the child's father.[1] But it must be remembered that, even though the husband could not have had intercourse, the wife might nevertheless have become pregnant as a result of fecundation *ab extra*[2] or of artificial insemination with her husband's seed.[3] Although this problem has not yet been considered by any English court, it is tentatively suggested that once it has been established that the wife could not have conceived as a result of intercourse in the usual way, this would be sufficient to shift on to the party seeking to establish the child's legitimacy the burden of showing that in the special cicumstances the husband could in fact be the father.

The presumption of legitimacy can also be rebutted by showing that the husband could not have had intercourse with his wife because of his absence at the relevant time. This will be easy to prove if, for example, he was abroad for the whole period during which the child must have been conceived; in other cases the court must decide on the balance of probability whether the spouses met in such circumstances as to afford them the opportunity of having sexual intercourse. In practice more difficult problems arise when the husband has been absent for a relatively short time and it is sought to establish the child's illegitimacy by showing that it must have been conceived during that period. It will be seen that the problem is basically the same as that which occurs when a child is born to a widow an abnormally long time after her husband's death, and the conclusions to be drawn from *Preston-Jones* v. *Preston-Jones*[4] apply equally to the present problem. In that case the husband did not have access to his wife for a period of 360 days to 186 days before the child's birth, and it was held that the evidence adduced was sufficient to rebut the presumption that he was the father.

Even though sexual intercourse was not impossible owing to the husband's absence, the presumption of legitimacy can still be rebutted if it can be shown that intercourse was so unlikely that it can be concluded on the balance of probability that it did not take place. If the spouses shared the same bed, it would seem to be almost impossible to prove that they did not have intercourse unless the husband is impotent.[5] If they were together in the same house, it will still be very difficult to rebut the presumption, unless it can be shown by other persons present that they were never alone together or that their relationship was such that it is improbable that they had intercourse in the circumstances.[6] If the husband and wife merely continue to live in the same town or district, the presumption can obviously be rebutted more easily than if they have in fact met in the same house.[7]

---

[1] *Banbury Peerage*, (ante).

[2] As in *Clarke* v. *Clarke*, [1943] 2 All E.R. 540.

[3] As in *R.E.L.* v. *E.L.*, [1949] P. 211; [1949] 1 All E.R. 141.

[4] [1951] A.C. 391; [1951] 1 All E.R. 124, H.L. See *ante*, p. 257.

[5] See *Cotton* v. *Cotton*, [1954] P. 305, [1954] 2 All E.R. 105, C.A. But the presumption was rebutted in such circumstances in *Smith* v. *May* (1969), 113 Sol. Jo. 1000.

[6] See, *e.g.*, the *Aylesford Peerage Case* (1885), 11 App. Cas. 1, H.L.

[7] See *Sibbet* v. *Ainsley* (1860), 3 L.T. 583. The fact that the spouses never met openly is strong evidence of their not having met secretly either: *Atchley* v. *Sprigg* (1864), 33 L.J.Ch. 345.

Despite some doubts expressed in earlier cases,[1] it has been clear since the decision of the House of Lords in *Morris* v. *Davies*[2] in 1837 that, in order to rebut the presumption that intercourse took place, evidence may be given not only of circumstances existing at the time of the conception and birth but also of relevant facts both preceding and following these. Clearly, the conduct of the spouses towards each other as well as statements made by them are highly relevant if they point to their not having had intercourse for some time.[3] Similarly, the wife's concealing her pregnancy from her husband and his relations or the family doctor, and *a fortiori* concealment of the birth, indicate not only that the wife does not believe that the child is her husband's but also that she knows that he will inevitably draw the same conclusion.[4] The parties' conduct towards the child after its birth is equally relevant; and if the putative father recognises the child as his, either directly[5] or inferentially, for example by permitting his name to be registered as that of the father,[6] by having the child brought up by his own parents,[7] or by paying for medical attention at the birth and for nursing and education afterwards,[8] that is strong evidence that the husband could not have been the father.

Rebutting the Second Presumption.—It will be seen that the *Banbury Peerage Case* and all the other cases cited above have dealt only with the rebuttal of the first presumption, *viz.* that the husband and wife did not in fact have sexual intercourse. It now remains to consider in what circumstances, if intercourse did take place or must be presumed to have taken place, it is possible to rebut the second presumption, *viz.* that the child must be the issue of that intercourse. The problem is this: if at the time when a child, C, must have been conceived, his mother, M, was having intercourse with her husband, H, and with another man, X, what evidence can be led to show that it is more probable that X is C's father than H?

The fact that the wife committed adultery cannot *per se* rebut the presumption, because this merely shows that either H or X could be the father.[9] But if H is shown to be sterile, this must be conclusive. In the past the courts were slow to admit evidence suggesting that C had inherited some physical characteristic from X and must therefore be his child and on a number of occasions excluded evidence of facial resemblance on the ground

---

[1] *E.g.*, by LORD ELDON, L.C., in *Head* v. *Head* (1823), Turn. & R. 138, 141.

[2] (1837), 5 Cl. & F. 163, H.L.

[3] *Per* LORD LANGDALE, M.R., in *Hargrave* v. *Hargrave* (1846), 9 Beav. 552, 555-556.

[4] *Morris* v. *Davies*, (*supra*); *Bosvile* v. *A.-G.* (1887), 12 P.D. 177; *Burnaby* v. *Baillie* (1889), 42 Ch.D. 282.

[5] *Atchley* v. *Sprigg*, (*supra*); *Hawes* v. *Draeger* (1883), 23 Ch.D. 173.

[6] Births and Deaths Registration Act 1953, s. 34.

[7] *Morris* v. *Davies*, (*supra*); *Re Bromage*, [1935] Ch. 605; *Re Heath*, [1945] Ch. 417.

[8] *Aylesford Peerage Case* (1885), 11 App. Cas. 1, H.L.; *Burnaby* v. *Baillie*, (*supra*); *Re Heath*, (*supra*).

[9] It was formerly held that this was so even though the husband invariably used a contraceptive (*Francis* v. *Francis*, [1960] P. 17; [1959] 3 All E.R. 206) but this might now rebut the presumption on the balance of probability if the other man did not use one. Similarly, if the presumption is raised by the wife's pregnancy at the time of the marriage, it cannot be rebutted merely by showing that she had intercourse with another man before her marriage: *Gardner* v. *Gardner* (1887), 2 App. Cas. 723, H.L.

that it was too vague.[1] This is obviously a matter of degree, however; it would clearly be wrong to exclude such evidence in all cases (particularly in view of the changed standard of proof) and it was admitted in *C. v. C.*[2] in 1972. In many cases little weight should be attached to it, but in others it should put the matter well beyond the balance of probabilities. Other evidence—for example that of race—is much more cogent. If M and H are both white, X is a negro, and C is coloured, it cannot be doubted that C must be X's child.[3]

Blood Tests.—Much more reliable evidence is produced by blood tests. These may be of use in a number of different circumstances. The husband may try to rely on the birth of the child to prove the wife's adultery and consequently may want the blood test as evidence on which he can obtain a divorce. Alternatively, the question may be whether the child is a child of the family for the purpose of orders relating to custody, financial provision, etc. In this type of case the husband is usually trying to prove that he is under no obligation to support the child, but if it is clear that either he or a particular individual must be the father, each is sometimes prepared to assume parental obligations if his paternity can be established. Blood tests may also be useful to establish paternity if the child is admittedly illegitimate, for example in affiliation proceedings, where the mother is seeking maintenance from the man alleged to be the child's father, or if the illegitimate person himself is laying claim to property as another's child.

Certain characteristics of a person's blood are inherited. It therefore follows that, if the mother's blood does not possess a characteristic possessed by the child's, he must have inherited it from his father. If the blood of both men who might be the father possesses this characteristic, a blood test cannot establish from which of them the child inherited it, but if the blood of one of them does not possess it, he must be the child of the other. From this it will be seen that, although blood tests cannot be used to show *conclusively* that a particular man must be the child's father, they may prove that he cannot be. In some cases, however, the statistical chance of another man's blood possessing unusual characteristics shared by that of the child and the man tested may be so slight as to establish the latter's paternity on the balance of probabilities. Obviously tests must be carried out on both the child's and the alleged father's blood; in most cases these will be inconclusive unless the mother's blood is tested as well.[4]

This presents a grave difficulty. If all the adult parties and the person with the custody of the child (if it is still of tender years) agree, there is no problem. But as the tests can only prove that a given man could not be the father, a wife might well object to submitting herself and the child to them. This is

---

[1] *Slingsby* v. *A.-G.* (1916), 33 T.L.R. 120, at pp. 122, 123, H.L.; *Plowes* v. *Bossey* (1862), 31 L.J.Ch. 681, 683.

[2] [1972] 3 All E.R. 577.

[3] Such evidence was apparently admissible even before the standard of proof was changed; *Slingsby* v. *A.-G.*, (*supra*), at p. 122.

[4] See Taylor, *Medical Jurisprudence*, 12th Ed., vol. 2, pp. 46-50; Gradwohl, *Legal Medicine*, 3rd Ed., ch. 11; Race and Sanger, *Blood Groups in Man*, 6th Ed., particularly ch. 25; Law Com. No. 16, *Blood Tests and the Proof of Paternity in Civil Proceedings*. For the problems raised by artificial insemination, see Tallin, *Artificial Insemination*, 34 Can. Bar Rev. 166 *et seq.*

understandable: why should she provide a piece of evidence which might establish her adultery and leave the child unsupported, when it could never affirmatively help her case? Moreover, if a paternity issue is ordered to be tried or the child is made a ward of court, he will usually be separately represented, and his guardian *ad litem* might well object to a blood test for the same reason.[1]

The common law position was eventually settled by the House of Lords in *S. v. S.; W. v. Official Solicitor.*[2] There is no power to order a blood test of an adult against his will, for this is a battery which, however trivial, no court may authorise.[3] For the same reason, as the power to consent to a surgical operation on a young child lies in the parent with legal custody, the court probably cannot order a child's blood to be tested without the consent of the parent or of the child himself if he is old enough to understand the nature of the operation.[4] But if the parent (or child) consents to the test, the court will override any objection on the part of the guardian *ad litem*, the other spouse or any other interested person, unless it can be shown that the test would be against the child's interest.

Defects in the law were pointed out by the Law Commission in their Report on Blood Tests and the Proof of Paternity in Civil Proceedings[5] and their recommendations were implemented by Part III of the Family Law Reform Act 1969. By section 20 (1) any court may direct blood tests to be used in any *civil* proceedings in which the paternity of any person is in issue. The purpose of the test must be to ascertain whether *a party to the proceedings* is or is not excluded from being the father of the person in question and consequently no order may be made, for example, in administration proceedings if the question is whether a claimant is the child of a deceased person, information about whose blood happened to be available. The court may direct that blood samples shall be taken from the person whose legitimacy is in issue, his mother and any *party* alleged to be his father. "Party" in this context presumably means a party to the proceedings; this means that if it is agreed that either the mother's husband or a given man, X, must be the child's father and it is desired to have X's blood tested to see whether he can be excluded, a direction to this effect could be given only if X were joined as a party. In divorce proceedings he will normally be a co-respondent, and the High Court and county courts have a general power to direct that a person, from whom it is desired that a sample should be taken, should be joined as a party.[6] But there is no way in which he can be made a party to proceedings brought in a magistrates' court under the Guardianship of Minors Act or the Domestic Proceedings and Magistrates' Courts Act 1978.

---

[1] If the Official Solicitor is appointed guardian *ad litem* in a matrimonial cause, a *Practice Direction*, [1968] 3 All E.R. 607, forbids anyone from having the child medically examined with a view to providing evidence without giving the Official Solicitor notice, so that he can consider whether to oppose a blood test. But if the child's blood is tested in defiance of this ban, the evidence is probably admissible, whatever penalties the party might incur: *S. v. S.*, [1972] A.C. 24, 44; [1970] 3 All E.R. 107, 112, H.L.

[2] [1972] A.C. 24; [1970] 3 All E.R. 107, H.L.

[3] *W. v. W. (No. 4)*, [1964] P. 67; [1963] 2 All E.R. 841, C.A. See also *S. v. S.*, (*supra*), at pp. 43 and 111 (*per* Lord Reid) and 57 and 123, respectively (*per* Lord Hodson).

[4] *S. v. S.*, (*supra*), at pp. 44 and 112, respectively (*per* Lord Reid).

[5] 1968, Law Com. No. 16.

[6] R.S.C. O. 112, r. 4; C.C.R. O. 46, r. 23 (3).

There is no compulsion attached to the direction. Except in the case of a person suffering from mental disorder, blood samples may not be taken without the consent of the person himself if he is over the age of 16 or of the person having care and control of him if he is under that age.[1] But the court may draw such inferences as appear proper from a person's failure to give consent or to take steps to give effect to the direction, and if he is a party claiming relief in reliance on the presumption of legitimacy, the court may dismiss his claim even though there is no evidence to rebut the presumption.[2] The last provision would apply, for example, to a wife claiming maintenance for a child which she alleges is her husband's who refuses to have herself and the child tested, or to a former ward of court claiming maintenance for himself who refuses to be tested when it is alleged that he is illegitimate. To bar the claimant from relief in such circumstances appears on the face of it to be reasonable: the difficulty is that an adverse inference drawn against an adult party might also be adverse to the child. It is questionable whether the Act was right to give a court power to refuse to make an order for mainten- ance because the mother declines to submit to a blood test when it could have made submission compulsory; what one must guard against is drawing the wholly illogical and unjustified conclusion that the child must be illegitimate.

A written report of the result of the tests is admissible.[3] It must state whether the party is excluded from being the father and, if not, the value of the results in determining whether he is the father.[4]

It will be seen that these provisions in no way inhibit the giving of evidence: if all the parties agree, they do not have to obtain the court's consent before having a test carried out. What the Act does is to give the court a discretion to direct a test if they do not agree. In *S.* v. *S.* the House of Lords indicated that the discretion will have to be judicially exercised, but they refused to lay down any guidelines. So far as blood tests of children are concerned, it is submitted that the courts should continue to follow *S.* v. *S.* itself. All the members of the House were of the opinion that a test should usually be ordered; but the court has a duty to protect a child and the general rule would be displaced if the test "would be against the child's interests",[5] if "having regard to the facts and circumstances of a particular case, an infant's interests are such that their protection necessitates the withholding from a court of evidence which may be very material"[6] or if "it would be unjust to order a test for a collateral reason to assist a litigant in his or her claim".[7] Neither the social stigma nor the legal disabilities attached to illegitimacy are as great as they used to be, and the House of Lords refused to accept that the mere fact that a test could establish conclusively that the child was illegitimate was sufficiently against its interest to withhold consent even though, as in *W.* v. *Official Solicitor*,

---

[1] S. 21. For persons suffering from mental disorder, see s. 21 (4).
[2] S. 23.
[3] S. 20 (2). It should rarely be necessary to call persons conducting tests to give oral evidence. For evidence and the procedure to be adopted generally, see ss. 20 and 22, the Blood Tests (Evidence of Paternity) Regulations 1971 and the Magistrates' Courts (Blood Tests) Rules 1971. See also Vickers, 122 New L.J. 209.
[4] *I.e.*, presumably, the statistical chances of his being the father.
[5] *Per* LORD REID, [1972] A.C. at p. 45; [1970] 3 All E.R. at p. 113.
[6] *Per* LORD MORRIS, at pp. 53 and 120, respectively.
[7] *Per* LORD HODSON, at pp. 58 and 124, respectively.

this would leave it with no known father at all. This danger is far outweighed by the demands of public policy that all relevant evidence should be made available. Furthermore the suppression of evidence would not encourage the mother's husband, whose suspicions would be unallayed, to accept the child as his, whereas he might be prepared to do so if a test did not exclude his paternity; and the child itself in later life might resent the fact that a full investigation was not conducted at the time. It will usually be in the child's interest—as well as in the public interest—that the truth should out,[1] and in divorce proceedings, at least, a direction is usually given.[2]

As the Court of Appeal stressed in *Re J.S.*,[3] however, a paternity issue should be pursued only if it has a material bearing on some other issue which has to be tried, and a blood test should be directed only when this condition is satisfied. In that case the mother of a child, who was admittedly illegitimate, lived with X. Either X or Y could have been the child's father. Y made the child a ward of court and sought to establish paternity in the hope of gaining access. The court refused to let him pursue the paternity issue because he would not be granted access in any event and it was not in the child's interest to disturb his relationship with X.

Similarly there is little doubt that a court would refuse to direct a test if the husband sought it solely in the hope of acquiring evidence of his wife's adultery. What is less clear is how the courts will exercise their discretion in the sort of situation exemplified by *B. v. B. and E.*[4] The mother did not suggest that the child was illegitimate until, three years after its birth, she left her husband to live with the co-respondent who she then alleged was the father. The husband, who wished to retain custody of the child, refused to submit to a blood test and insisted on standing on the presumption of legitimacy. It was held that in the circumstances he was acting reasonably and no adverse conclusions could be drawn from his refusal; that being so, no order would be made with respect to the child. But this overlooks the vital point that, if the evidence of blood groups was neutral, the presumption of legitimacy would prevail; if it proved that the co-respondent and not the husband must be the father, why should the latter be able to take advantage of a legal presumption designed to protect a child in the days when this sort of evidence was unheard of?[5]

Artificial Insemination.—The increase in the practice of artificial insemination in recent years has highlighted the legal consequences of the birth of a child conceived in this way. If the husband is fertile but conception following normal sexual intercourse is difficult or impossible (as it would be, for example, if the husband was impotent), the wife may undergo artificial insemination with the husband's own semen (A.I.H.). In certain circumstances, however, a woman may wish to have a child as the result of artificial

---

[1] *S. v. S.*, (*supra*), at pp. 45 and 113 (*per* LORD REID), pp. 55-56 and 122 (*per* LORD MORRIS), pp. 59 and 124, respectively (*per* LORD HODSON).

[2] *Practice Direction (Paternity: Guardian ad litem)*, [1975] 1 All E.R. 223, *q.v.* for the circumstances in which a guardian *ad litem* should be appointed for the child.

[3] [1981] Fam. 22; [1980] 1 All E.R. 1061, C.A.

[4] [1969] 3 All E.R. 1106, C.A.

[5] For further discussion of the problems presented by blood tests, see Hayes, *The Use of Blood Tests in the Pursuit of Truth*, 87 L.Q.R. 86; Hall, [1971] C.L.J. 34.

insemination by the semen of a donor other than the husband (A.I.D.). This could occur, for example, if the husband was sterile or sub-fertile or if he was the possible carrier of an inheritable disease and the spouses preferred to have a child which was at least biologically the wife's.

A child born as the result of A.I.H. will, of course, be the spouses' legitimate child just as though he had been conceived in the normal way. Conversely, a child conceived by A.I.D. must be illegitimate as he would have been if the wife had committed adultery with the donor. Whereas, however, the adulterine child will frequently be rejected by the husband, both spouses will usually wish to treat a child born of A.I.D. as though he were the husband's.[1] In some cases there may be genuine doubt about paternity, but even if it is established that the husband cannot be the father, this will make little difference to the legal relationship between him and the child because his treating the child as his own will make the latter a child of the family.[2] Good clinical practice requires the doctor carrying out the insemination not to divulge the identity of the donor and the mother to each other, so that there is virtually no risk of legal claims arising between the donor and the child;[3] problems may arise, however, in relation to claims to property from or through the spouses. The child is entitled to no part of the husband's estate if the latter dies intestate,[4] nor can he claim if any of his mother's relations dies intestate or if property is held on trust for the husband's children or the wife's legitimate children. If he makes such a claim and the spouses know that the husband is not the father, they must either connive at the deception or be forced to disclose facts which they wish to keep secret; if paternity is in doubt, litigation may well arise long after the spouses' death.

It is not surprising that pressure has been mounted to change the law so that a child born as the result of A.I.D. would be deemed to be the legitimate child of the husband. The principal objection to this is that it could legalise a deception on third persons. There can be little doubt that such deception is being practised at the moment and the only alternative proposed, that of adoption before the child's birth, would be artificial, inappropriate and unnecessarily expensive. No ready solution can be put forward which will both satisfy the spouses and protect the interests of third parties and in 1979 the Law Commission sought views as to how the difficulties could best be met.[5]

B. LEGITIMACY OF CHILDREN OF VOID MARRIAGES

Since a void marriage is not a marriage either in fact or in law, the children of such a marriage were necessarily illegitimate at common law. Many legal systems recognise the legitimacy of children of putative marriages, that is,

---

[1] They may even register the husband as the father. If the husband is known not to be the father, the person registering the birth will commit an offence under the Perjury Act 1911, s. 4.

[2] Unless the spouses were to separate before the child's birth. See *post*, p. 304.

[3] But sometimes the donor's identity is known to the mother. Does he realise that if, for example, he dies intestate, the child may be entitled to a part or the whole of his estate?

[4] Although he would have a claim to provision under the Inheritance (Provision for Family and Dependants) Act 1975 as a child of the family. See *post*, p. 625.

[5] Law Commission's Working Paper No. 74 (Family Law: Illegitimacy), Part X. For earlier views on the problem see the Report of the Departmental Committee on Human Artificial Insemination, 1960, Cmnd. 1105; Tallin, *Artificial Insemination*, 34 Can. Bar Rev. 166.

those void marriages to which one or both parties were unaware of the invalidity. This avoids working an injustice on the children and the Morton Commission on Marriage and Divorce recommended the adoption in England of a rule that has always been a part of the common law of Scotland.[1] Effect was given to this recommendation in section 2 of the Legitimacy Act of 1959, which has now been replaced by section 1 (1) of the Legitimacy Act 1976. This provides:

> "The child of a void marriage, whenever born, shall ... be treated as the legitimate child of his parents if at the time of the act of intercourse resulting in the birth (or at the time of the celebration of the marriage if later) both or either of the parties reasonably believed that the marriage was valid."

As this provision determines status, it is expressly enacted that it shall apply only if the child's father was domiciled in England at the time of the child's birth or, if he died before the birth, immediately before his death.[2] The Act seems to lay the burden of proof upon the person asserting the legitimacy, a burden which it may well be extremely difficult to discharge. Bearing in mind that the question may arise in relation to the devolution of property upon death, it is easy to see that one or both parties to the marriage may already be dead and the evidence that can be adduced may well be purely circumstantial. If the marriage preceded the conception, the precise time at which it is necessary to prove that the belief was held may also be uncertain. Furthermore, it is not clear what *reasonable* belief means in this context. Presumably the test is an objective one; in other words, the belief must be one that a reasonable man would have held in the circumstances[3] and it is arguable that a mistake of law cannot be reasonably held in this sense so as to create a putative marriage which is void, say, because the parties were ignorant of the law relating to the prohibited degrees of consanguinity or affinity.[4]

C. LEGITIMACY OF CHILDREN OF VOIDABLE MARRIAGES

At common law a decree of nullity, where the marriage was voidable, had retrospective effect and automatically bastardised the issue of the marriage.[5] When the grounds for nullity were extended by the Matrimonial Causes Act 1937, it was appreciated that this rule might work hardship in those cases where the marriage was annulled because the respondent was of unsound

---

[1] Cmd. 9678, paras. 1184-1186.

[2] Legitimacy Act 1976, s. 1 (2). Cf. the provisions relating to *legitimatio per subsequens matrimonium, post*, p. 269.

[3] *Hawkins* v. *A.-G.*, [1966] 1 All E.R. 392, 397. See Samuels, 29 M.L.R. 559.

[4] This appears to be the law in Scotland; see Walton, *Husband and Wife*, 3rd Ed., 233-234. Insofar as s. 1 could affect the succession to any dignity or title of honour or of any property settled so as to devolve therewith, it does not apply to children born before 29th October 1959 (when the 1959 Act came into force); nor does it affect any rights under the intestacy of a person dying before that date, the operation or construction of any disposition coming into operation before that date, or the succession to the throne: Legitimacy Act 1976, Sched. 1, paras. 3, 4 (1) and 5. "Disposition" includes the conferring of a power of appointment and the creation of an entailed interest: *ibid.*, s. 10 (1), (4). For other problems, see Bevan, *Children*, 246-248.

[5] See *ante*, p. 97.

mind or epileptic or was suffering from a venereal disease in a communicable form, since the wife might conceive before the petitioner discovered the existence of the impediment. Consequently, this Act expressly provided that in these two cases any child born of the marriage should be legitimate notwithstanding the annulment of the marriage.[1] Where the respondent was pregnant by a man other than the petitioner, the question of the legitimacy of the child did not arise, and apparently the legislature did not foresee that any child would be born if the marriage had not been consummated. This proved to be untrue, however, for children were born as a result of pre-marital inter-course,[2] of fecundation *ab extra*[3] and of artificial insemination.[4]

This anomaly was removed by section 4 (1) of the Law Reform (Miscellaneous Provisions) Act 1949, which provided that *any* child who would have been the legitimate child of the parties to a voidable marriage had it not been annulled should be deemed to be their legitimate child. The same result is now reached by section 16 of the Matrimonial Causes Act 1973 which, by enacting that a voidable marriage shall be treated as if it had existed up to the date of the decree absolute, must necessarily preserve the legitimacy of any child born or conceived between the date of the marriage and the date of the decree as well as any child legitimated by the marriage.[5]

The Law Reform Act of 1949 did not have retrospective effect. Consequently, except in those cases provided for in section 7 (2) of the Matrimonial Causes Act 1937, the children of voidable marriages annulled before 16th December 1949, remain illegitimate.[6]

D. LEGITIMATION

Canon law adopted the Roman law rule that a bastard would become legitimate if his parents subsequently intermarried, provided that they had been free to marry each other at the time of the child's birth. But the importance of establishing the identity of the heir at law, to whom descended the valuable private rights and important public duties of the ownership of an inheritable estate of freehold land in the Middle Ages, led the common law to reject this doctrine of *legitimatio per subsequens matrimonium*, and an attempt to introduce it by the Statute of Merton in 1235 was successfully resisted by the temporal peers.[7] Consequently, no form of legitimation was

---

[1] S. 7 (2).

[2] As in *Dredge* v. *Dredge*, [1947] 1 All E.R. 29.

[3] As in *Clarke* v. *Clarke*, [1943] 2 All E.R. 540.

[4] As in *R.E.L.* v. *E.L.*, [1949] P. 211; [1949] 1 All E.R. 141.

[5] For s. 16, see *ante*, p. 97. The section will not legitimate a child who never was legitimate (*e.g.*, because the husband was not the father): *Re Adams*, [1951] Ch. 716; [1951] 1 All E.R. 1037. *Quaere* whether the section operates if the parties are not domiciled in England and the decree bastardises the child by the *lex domicilii*. The wording suggests that it will continue to be regarded as legitimate in this country.

[6] *Re Adams*, (*supra*).

[7] But under the curious doctrine of *bastard eigne* and *mulier puisne*, if the parents of an illegitimate child (the *bastard eigne*) married and had a legitimate child (the *mulier puisne*) and the bastard entered on the father's freehold land after his death and himself died seised so that it descended to his (the bastard's) issue, this gave the bastard's heirs an indefeasible right to the land and the rights of the *mulier puisne* and all other heirs were completely barred: Jackson, *Formation and Annulment of Marriage*, 2nd Ed., 46-48, and the authorities there cited.

recognised by English municipal law until the passing of the Legitimacy Act in 1926, by which time the property legislation of 1925 had rendered it almost wholly unnecessary to establish the identity of the heir save in the case of the descent of an unbarred entailed interest.

Conditions under which an Illegitimate Person will be Legitimated.—The Legitimacy Act of 1926 provided that a child should be legitimated by the subsequent marriage of his parents (or on 1st January 1927, if they had married before that date). But it also adopted the Canon Law rule that legitimation was impossible if either parent was married to any other person at the time of the child's birth.[1] This did not necessarily prevent the legitimation of an adulterine bastard, for even though he was conceived whilst one of his parents was married, he could still be legitimated if this marriage was terminated before his birth, and in many cases decrees of divorce were expedited for this reason. Consequently the Legitimacy Act of 1959 extended these provisions to children born when either or both of their parents were married. They too would now be legitimated by their parent's marriage to each other (or on 29th October 1959, if they had married before that date).[2]

The Acts of 1926 and 1959 have now been repealed and their provisions re-enacted in the Legitimacy Act 1976. Section 2 provides:

"... where the parents of an illegitimate person marry one another, the marriage shall, if the father of the illegitimate person is at the date of the marriage domiciled in England and Wales, render that person, if living, legitimate from the date of the marriage."

It will be observed that a person will be legitimated by the operation of this section only if his *father* was domiciled in England and Wales *at the time of the marriage.* The reason for this provision is that a legitimate child's status is determined by the law of his father's domicile: hence the mother's domicile is quite irrelevant for this purpose. Moreover, since it is the marriage that legitimates him, it is the father's English domicile at this time that is important.

Whether or not the child is the issue of the husband is of course a question of fact. That the parties married at all in the circumstances affords some slight evidence that the husband is the father of the wife's illegitimate child,[3] but normally the only evidence available will be the husband's recognition of his paternity, whether before or after the marriage. In the words of JAMES, L.J., delivering the opinion of the Judicial Committee of the Privy Council in *La Cloche* v. *La Cloche*:[4]

"The principle ... is, that where a man marries a woman who has had an illegitimate child, whether that child is thenceforth to be considered the legitimate child of the man must depend on the only evidence which can generally be given of it; that is to say the man's recognition of his paternity—if that is sufficiently and abundantly proved, it does not signify in what particular manner that recognition is effected."

---

[1] S. 1 (2).
[2] S. 1.
[3] See *Battle* v. *A.-G.*, [1949] P. 358. But contrast *James* v. *McLennan*, 1971 S.L.T. 162, H.L. The existence of an affiliation order against the husband is *prima facie* evidence of his paternity: Civil Evidence Act 1968, s. 12 (*ante*, pp. 258-259).
[4] (1872), L.R. 4 P.C. 325, 333, P.C. See also *Battle* v. *A.-G.*, (*supra*).

In this case ample evidence of such recognition was to be found in the husband's declarations at the time of the marriage, in letters to the child in which he called him "son", and in a deed executed by the husband in which he referred to the child's son as his own grandson.

Two further matters should be noted. First, legitimation does not have retrospective effect, so that no one can be legitimated unless he is still alive when his parents marry (or, if they were married before the date on which the Act by virtue of which he was legitimated came into force, on that date).[1] Secondly, the fact that an adopted child is to be regarded as the child of the adoptive parent and of no other person does not prevent an illegitimate child from being legitimated if he has been adopted *solely* by one of his parents who then marries the other parent.[2]

Effects of Legitimation.—It is expressly provided that a legitimated person shall have the same rights and obligations in respect of the maintenance and support of himself and other persons as if he had been born legitimate, and any legal claim for damages, compensation, allowances, etc., that could be made by or in respect of a legitimate person, can now be made by or in respect of one legitimated.[3] Similarly, for the purpose of determining whether he is a citizen of the United Kingdom and Colonies, he is to be treated as being born legitimate on the date of his parents' marriage.[4] Subject to what will be said later with respect to rights in property[5] a legitimated person is, after his legitimation, in exactly the same position as if he had been born legitimate. In the words of ROMER, J.:[6]

> "Legitimacy is a question of status. ... This status of legitimacy can be obtained by being born legitimate or by being legitimated by virtue of the provision of the Act. The plaintiff had attained that status, and it is an irrelevant consideration whether she attained it in one way or the other."

E. LEGITIMACY AND LEGITIMATION BY FOREIGN LAW

Legitimacy at Birth.—Although very real doubts on the question are still entertained, the most widely held view today is that, if a child is the legitimate child of his parents by the law of their domicile at his birth, English law will recognise that status for all purposes save that of succession to an unbarred entail.[7] Thus in *Re Bischoffsheim*,[8] where the question was whether a child

---

[1] Legitimacy Act 1926, s. 1 (1); Legitimacy Act 1959, s. 1 (2); Legitimacy Act 1976, Sched. 1, para. 1. But if the parents had married before the relevant Act came into force, the children could be legitimated on that date, even though one or both *parents* had already died: *Re Lowe*, [1929] 2 Ch. 210.

[2] Legitimacy Act 1976, s. 4. For the effect of adoption, see *post*, pp. 357-358.

[3] Legitimacy Act 1976, s. 8.

[4] British Nationality Act 1948, s. 23.

[5] See *post*, pp. 578-580 and 621.

[6] *Re Lowe*, [1929] 2 Ch. 210, 212-213. See also *C. v. C.*, [1948] P. 19; [1947] 2 All E.R. 50.

[7] For a discussion of this topic generally and the difficulties arising, see Dicey and Morris, *Conflict of Laws*, 10th Ed., 456 *et seq.*; Cheshire and North, *Private International Law*, 10th Ed., 440 *et seq.*; Graveson, *Conflict of Laws*, 7th Ed., 361 *et seq.*; Falconbridge, *Legitimacy or Legitimation in the Conflict of Laws*, 27 Can. Bar Rev. 1163.

[8] [1948] Ch. 79; [1947] 2 All E.R. 830, following *Re Goodman's Trusts* (1881), 17 Ch.D. 266, C.A. See also *Bamgbose* v. *Daniel*, [1955] A.C. 107; [1954] 3 All E.R. 263, P.C.

born of parents domiciled in New York could take an interest in a legacy in favour of his mother's children contained in an English will, it was held that for the purpose of construing the will the term "children" must mean legitimate children as a rule of English law but to determine whether or not the claimant was legitimate reference must be made to the law of New York. In the words of ROMER, J.:[1]

> "Where the succession to personal property depends on the legitimacy of the claimant, the status of legitimacy conferred on him by his domicile of origin (*i.e.*, the domicile of his parents at his birth) will be recognised by our courts; and if that legitimacy be established, the validity of his parents' marriage should not be entertained as a relevant subject for investigation."

These last words are apparently in conflict with the decision of the House of Lords in *Shaw* v. *Gould*,[2] but ROMER, J., distinguished this case on the ground that it dealt with the exceptional question of the heir. If this view is correct, it follows that the question of legitimacy is to be determined solely by reference to the parties' domicile. If they both have the same domicile, the answer can be easily ascertained; but if they have different domiciles, a further problem arises. If the child is legitimate, his domicile of origin is that of his father; but if he is illegitimate, his domicile is that of his mother.[3] Consequently, in order to determine the child's domicile, it is apparently first necessary to determine his legitimacy, which in turn depends on the domicile. There are two possible solutions to this problem. One is to concede that a child will be legitimate only if he has this status by the law of the domiciles of both parents;[4] the other is to hold that, if there is a conflict, he will be legitimate if he is legitimate by his father's *lex domicilii*.[5] The former has the advantage of not leaving the matter in doubt; the latter, however, is to be preferred because it would bring the recognition of legitimacy into line with the recognition of legitimation (where English law has always concentrated solely on the effect of a subsequent marriage in the father's *lex domicilii*) and also with our own law relating to the legitimacy of children of void marriages.[6] In the only recent reported case raising the problem, *Hashmi* v.

---

[1] At pp. 92 and 836, respectively.

[2] (1868), L.R. 3 H.L. 55, H.L. In this case the child's father, who was domiciled in Scotland, had married the mother after she had obtained a divorce from her first husband, who was domiciled in England, in a Scottish court. As the court had no jurisdiction, the House of Lords, on appeal from an English court, took the view that the mother was still married to her first husband and that the child was *therefore* illegitimate.

[3] See *ante* p. 12.

[4] Supported by Dicey and Morris, *op. cit.*, 457 *et seq. Shaw* v. *Gould*, (*supra*), could be further distinguished on the ground that by English law the mother was still married to her first husband and therefore still domiciled in England, by the law of which country the child must necessarily be illegitimate. A further argument that, where the child is claiming under an English deed or will, he must as a matter of construction be legitimate according to the rules of English law (see LORD CHELMSFORD in *Shaw* v. *Gould*, (*supra*), at p. 80, and BENNETT, J., in *Re Paine*, [1940] Ch. 46) was demolished by ROMER, J., in *Re Bischoffsheim* at pp. 86-87 and pp. 833-834, respectively, where he pointed out that the sole question of construction was that by English law children meant legitimate children and that it did not follow that this meant children legitimate according to the narrow test of English law.

[5] Supported by Cheshire and North, *op. cit.*, 447-450, and Graveson, *op. cit.*, 364.

[6] See *ante*, p. 267.

Hashmi,[1] the court took the view that the children were legitimate because they were legitimate by their father's *lex domicilii*, but it does not appear to have considered the question of their status under their mother's *lex domicilii* or the view that they would be legitimate only if they had this status by the law of both parents' domiciles. Consequently the question must still be regarded as an open one.

Legitimation *per subsequens Matrimonium*. —The common law would recognise legitimation *per subsequens matrimonium* by foreign law only if the father was domiciled in a country recognising legitimation both at the time of the child's birth and at the time of the marriage.[2] Consequently, if the father had no such domicile when the child was born, English law would not recognise the legitimation, whatever the father's domicile was when he married. Now, however, section 3 of the Legitimacy Act 1976 provides that a person shall be regarded as legitimated for the purpose of English law if the father was domiciled in a country recognising legitimation *per subsequens matrimonium* at the time of the marriage, even though his *lex domicilii* at the time of the birth did not recognise the doctrine.[3]

But in certain cases the common law rule may still be relevant. A person whose parents married before 1st January 1926 (or, if either of them was married to a third person at the time of the child's birth, before 29th October 1959) will not be recognized as legitimated by statute until the date on which the relevant Act came into force.[4] In order to establish a claim to property, however, it may be necessary to prove that he was legitimated before this date,[5] and he may still succeed if the common law conditions are satisfied.

Legitimation otherwise than by subsequent Marriage.—Where the legitimation is by some other act (for example, the parents' recognition), the Legitimacy Act has no application at all. Hence it will be recognised here only if the common law rules are satisfied—that is, the father must be domiciled in a country, the law of which accepts the validity of the legitimation, both at the time of the child's birth and at the time of the performance of the act effecting the legitimation.[6]

---

[1] [1972] Fam. 36; [1971] 3 All E.R. 1235. Goldberg and Lowe resolve the problem by arguing that the child will take the father's domicile if we recognise the validity of the parents' marriage and the mother's domicile if we do not: 35 M.L.R. 431. Although this neatly reconciles *Re Bischoffsheim* with *Shaw* v. *Gould*, there is no direct authority for it and it is inconsistent with *Hashmi* v. *Hashmi*, where the marriage was void by English law.

[2] *Re Grove* (1888), 40 Ch.D. 216, C.A. See further, Dicey and Morris, *op. cit.*, 472 *et seq.*; Cheshire and North, *op. cit.*, 451 *et seq.*; Graveson, *op. cit.*, 369 *et seq.*; Mann, *Legitimation and Adoption in Private International Law*, 57 L.Q.R. 112; Falconbridge, *loc. cit.*

[3] Re-enacting s. 8 of the Legitimacy Act 1926.

[4] Legitimacy Act 1926, s. 8; Legitimacy Act 1976, Sched. 1, para. 1. Although there is no direct authority, it seems that the legitimation of a person, either of whose parents was married at the time of his birth, could not be recognized by statute before the passing of the Legitimacy Act of 1959: see the Legitimacy Act 1926, s. 1 (2), and *cf. ante*, p. 269.

[5] *E.g.*, to establish seniority. See *post*, p. 579.

[6] *Re Luck's Settlement Trusts*, [1940] Ch. 864; [1940] 3 All E.R. 307, C.A. (criticised by Mann, *loc. cit.*, at pp. 118 *et seq.*). *Quaere* whether the father's *lex domicilii* must permit legitimation *by the particular means*. *E.g.*, if the father is domiciled in England at the child's birth and then, following a change of domicile, legitimates him by recognition, would we now recognise the legitimation?

F. PROPOSALS FOR REFORM

Recent years have seen considerable changes in the attitude of society towards the concept of legitimacy. Less rigid attitudes towards cohabitation outside marriage have necessarily produced less rigid attitudes towards the offspring of such unions. Over and above this we have become more compassionate in this respect and no longer consider that the sins of the fathers should be visited on their children. This is illustrated by a Council of Europe Convention signed in 1975, which aims to assimilate the status of children born out of wedlock with that of those born in wedlock. As a consequence of these and other pressures the Law Commission set up a Working Party in 1976 which resulted in the publication of a Working Paper on Illegitimacy in 1979.[1]

Much of the present English law reflects the attitudes of an earlier age and is designed to deal with the unwanted issue of a casual relationship rather than with the children of a previously stable union which has broken down.[2] Change is therefore essential. The Law Commission see two possible solutions: abolition of the adverse consequences of illegitimacy and abolition of the concept of illegitimacy altogether. They have provisionally come down in favour of the latter, principally on the ground that changing the child's status could help to lessen social prejudices. They argue:[3]

"Changes in the law ... can at least remove the *additional* hardship of attaching an opprobrious description to him. Mere tinkering with the law would disguise the fact that a new principle has been established: indeed, it would tend to suggest that there is still some justification for the old discriminatory attitudes. That is an impression which we are anxious the law should not give."

Such a change would of course immediately give children who are at present illegitimate the same rights as others, for example full rights of succession on the intestacy of a relative. It would also give both parents equal rights and duties. Thus, a father would have the same right to custody and guardianship whether he had been married to the mother or not; similarly he would have the right to withhold his consent to the adoption or marriage of a minor. Both parents could also be made to contribute towards the child's maintenance under the Guardianship of Minors Act and affiliation proceedings would disappear. But it must be realised that a father's rights and obligations would be no greater than those now enjoyed by or imposed on the fathers of legitimate children. In the event of a dispute over custody, for example, the court would give first and paramount consideration to the welfare of the child, and it would not normally give the father custody if he had never lived with the mother and child or shown any interest in its welfare. Likewise his consent to the child's adoption or marriage could be dispensed with as it can be now in the case of a legitimate child.

In one respect the position of a child born to an unmarried woman would still be different from that of one born to a married woman. The present

---

[1] Working Paper No. 74.
[2] In 1976 half of the illegitimate births were registered on the joint application of both parents, which may give some idea of the number born to parents living together: *ibid.*, para. 3.3.
[3] *Ibid.*, para. 3.15.

presumption of legitimacy is, of course, really a presumption of paternity applied when the mother is married. The Law Commission feel that this should be preserved but could not be applied to cohabitation generally because of the impossibility of formulating with precision the circumstances in which the presumption would arise. In many cases, of course, it would not be difficult to draw an inference from the facts. Evidence of paternity could still be provided by the man's permitting his name to be registered as that of the father; in other cases a court order would be necessary. This could be made in other proceedings (for example, for custody, access or maintenance) or in proceedings for a declaration of paternity brought by the child himself.[1]

The other consequences of adopting these proposals are too extensive to set out here and reference must be made to the Working Paper. The principle of abolishing the concept of legitimacy is not novel; in New Zealand, for example, the relationship between a person and his father and mother is now the same whether or not his parents have ever been married to each other.[2] It is not yet known whether the Law Commission will modify their recommendations in the light of reaction to their Working Paper: these have not been received without criticism.[3]

G. DECLARATIONS OF LEGITIMACY

As may have already been gathered from what has been said above, the question of a person's legitimacy may be put in issue in a number of ways. This will occur, for example, if he claims an interest in property or if in divorce proceedings the husband relies upon the fact of his birth as evidence of his mother's adultery. Normally, however, any judicial decision will be a judgment *in personam* and consequently will bind only the parties to it and their privies, that is, persons claiming through them. The desirability of some sort of procedure to enable a disputed question of legitimacy to be settled once for all led to the passing in 1858 of the Legitimacy Declaration Act, now repealed and substantially re-enacted in section 45 of the Matrimonial Causes Act 1973. Under the provisions of this section, any person may petition for a decree that he is legitimate or that he or his parents or grandparents are or were validly married. But no petition will lie unless:

   (a) the petitioner is a British subject or his right to be deemed a British subject depends wholly or in part on his legitimacy or the validity of any marriage; *and*
   (b) *either* he is domiciled in England or Northern Ireland *or* he claims any real or personal estate situate in England.[4]

No provisions exist to enable a petitioner to obtain a declaration of legitimacy of anyone other than himself,[5] nor is there any power to declare

---

[1] *Ibid.*, Part IX.
[2] The law was changed in 1970: Bromley and Webb, *Family Law*, 429-439. But an "ex-nuptial" child may find it more difficult to establish a claim in some cases: *ibid.*, 732 *et seq.*
[3] See *e.g.* Hayes, 43 M.L.R. 299; Deech, 10 Fam. Law 101.
[4] S. 45 (1). It will be observed that neither domicile nor the situation of property in Scotland will entitle a person to petition; domicile in Northern Ireland will give the court jurisdiction, but the situation of property there will not. The proceedings must be brought in the High Court.
[5] *Aldrich* v. *A.-G.*, [1968] P. 281; [1968] 1 All E.R. 345.

anyone illegitimate[1] or to make a declaration of paternity of an illegitimate child.[2]

It will be inferred from condition (a) set out above that one of the objects of this piece of legislation is to enable a person to establish not only his legitimacy but also his right to be treated as a British subject. It is accordingly expressly provided that any person who satisfies condition (b) may petition for a decree to this effect even though his legitimacy is not in issue.[3]

The possibility of a person's legitimation coming into question has been provided for in section 45 (2), which enacts that, where any person claims that he or his parents or any remoter ancestor[4] has been legitimated by virtue of the Legitimacy Act or that his legitimation has been recognised under section 3 of the Act, he may petition for a decree to this effect.[5]

The Attorney-General must be joined as a respondent to any petition.[6] The court may make such decree as it thinks just;[7] in *Puttick* v. *A.-G.*[8] BAKER, P., refused to make any decree at all when the petitioner (better known as Astrid Proll) had entered this country on a forged passport to evade prosecution in Germany, had comitted perjury to obtain a superintendent registrar's certificate and licence, and had shown a general disregard for the law of this country. It is not clear, however, what purpose withholding the decree really served. Granted that the petitioner was validly married, the fact that she had achieved her aim by illegal means seems to be irrelevant; it is not really sensible to compel her to re-litigate this matter whenever the question is raised.

A declaration made on a petition brought under this section binds all persons given notice of the proceedings or made parties (including the Crown) and anyone claiming through them, unless the decree was obtained by fraud or collusion.[9] In order to ensure that the petitioner's legitimacy cannot be questioned in any other proceedings, it is clearly imperative to join as a party anyone who, as a result of possible claims to property, might attempt to dispute it later.[10]

---

[1] *B.* v. *A.-G.*, [1966] 2 All E.R. 145.

[2] *Re J.S.*, [1981] Fam. 22; [1980] 1 All E.R. 1061, C.A.

[3] S. 45 (4).

[4] *I.e.*, lineal ancestor. The expression does not therefore include an uncle: *Knowles* v. *A.-G.*, [1951] P. 54; [1950] 2 All E.R. 6.

[5] Proceedings under this subsection may be brought in the High Court or in a county court: s. 45 (2), (3).

[6] S. 45 (6).

[7] S. 45 (5).

[8] [1980] Fam. 1; [1979] 3 All E.R. 463. The peition was dismissed on the further ground that the petitioner was not domiciled in England.

[9] S. 45 (5); *Ampthill Peerage Case*, [1977] A.C. 547; [1976] 2 All E.R. 411, H.L.

[10] The court may order interested persons to be given notice of the proceedings and they may then become parties and oppose the application: s. 45 (7). For criticisms of the existing law and proposals for reform, see the Law Commission's Working Paper No. 48 (Declarations in Family Matters), 1973.

Chapter 9
Parental Powers and Duties

A. THE SCOPE OF PARENTAL POWERS AND DUTIES

Common Law.—Common law recognised the natural duties of protecting and maintaining one's legitimate minor children, and although the machinery for enforcing these duties was almost wholly ineffectual, nevertheless they could properly be regarded as unenforceable legal obligations. Moreover, it is obvious that, at any rate in early law, these duties could be performed only if the parent actually had the custody of the child, and in many cases the father would be the only member of the family who would be physically capable of carrying them out. Consequently it is not surprising to discover that his duty to protect carried with it the correlative right to the custody of all minor children and that this right was absolute even against the mother except in the rare cases where the father's conduct was such as gravely to imperil the children's life, health or morals. Admittedly, on the father's death the mother became entitled to the custody of her children until they came of age, but under the Tenures Abolition Act of 1660 the father could defeat this right too by appointing a testamentary guardian.

Custody carried with it many rights and powers in addition to care and control. A father was entitled to the services of his children in his custody and to correct them by administering reasonable corporal punishment. He alone might determine the form of their religious and secular education. Whilst his powers were never as wide as those of the *paterfamilias* in Roman law, the same fundamental approach is apparent. Physical control represented the kernel of his rights; without it the others could not be enforced, and the procedural machinery of the common law was such that only this right could be specifically enforced by the writ of habeas corpus.

Equity.—The jurisdiction of equity to intervene between parent and child is derived from the prerogative power of the Crown as *parens patriae* to interfere to protect any person within the jurisdiction not fully *sui juris*. This power was naturally exercised by the Lord Chancellor, and although it fell into abeyance when the Court of Wards was set up in 1540, successive Chancellors began to use their powers more and more extensively when this court was abolished in 1660.[1] From the Court of Chancery the jurisdiction passed to the High Court under the Judicature Acts of 1873 and 1875.

---

[1] Holdsworth, *History of English Law*, vi, 648. The Court of Wards was set up by 32 Hen. 8, c. 46, and abolished by the Tenures Abolition Act 1660.

Whilst equity left untouched the common law duties of parents, its attitude towards the exercise of their rights underwent a fundamental change during the nineteenth century.[1] Earlier cases indicated that effect would always be given to the father's legal rights unless he had forfeited them by his immoral or cruel conduct or was seeking to enforce them capriciously or arbitrarily. As COTTON, L.J., said in *Re Agar-Ellis*:[2]

> "This Court holds this principle—that when, by birth, a child is subject to a father, it is for the general interest of families, and for the general interest of children, and really for the interest of the particular infant, that the Court should not, except in very extreme cases, interfere with the discretion of the father, but leave to him the responsibility of exercising that power which nature has given him by the birth of the child."

On the other hand there was a growing view, which ultimately prevailed, that the welfare of the child was the first consideration and equity would not hesitate to deprive a father of his rights if it would clearly be contrary to the child's best interests to give effect to them. In the words of LORD ESHER, M.R., in *R.* v. *Gyngall*:[3]

> "The Court is placed in a position by reason of the prerogative of the Crown to act as supreme parent of the child, and must exercise that jurisdiction in the manner in which a wise, affectionate, and careful parent would act for the welfare of the child. The natural parent in the particular case may be affectionate, and may be intending to act for the child's good, but may be unwise, and may not be doing what a wise, affectionate, and careful parent would do. The Court may say in such a case that, although they can find no misconduct on the part of the parent, they will not permit that to be done with the child which a wise, affectionate, and careful parent would not do. The court must, of course, be very cautious in regard to the circumstances under which they will interfere with the parental right. ... The Court must exercise this jurisdiction with great care, and can only act when it is shown that either the conduct of the parent, or the description of person he is, or the position in which he is placed, is such as to render it not merely better, but—I will not say 'essential', but—clearly right for the welfare of the child in some very serious and important respect that the parent's rights should be suspended or superseded; but ... where it is so shown, the Court will exercise its jurisdiction accordingly."

A further advantage that equity had over the common law was that its procedure was much better adapted to deal with disputes concerning children. Common law, limited as it was to the issue of a writ of habeas corpus, could only enforce the right to physical control; equity, on the other hand, acts *in personam*, so that it could not only make orders concerning, for example, the child's education, but also effectively ensure that they were carried out. A further step that could be taken was to have the child made a ward of court. This procedure had a number of advantages. Not only could the person to whom care and control was given always turn to the court for advice, but the ward remained under the permanent control of the court during minority, so that any dereliction of duty on the part of the former and any interference with the latter were punishable as a contempt of court.

---

[1] See Hall, *The Waning of Parental Rights*, [1972 B] C.L.J. 248.

[2] (1883), 24 Ch.D. 317, 334, C.A.

[3] [1893] 2 Q.B. 232, 241-242, C.A. See also *Re O'Hara*, [1900] 2 I.R. 232; *Official Solicitor* v. *K.*, [1965] A.C. 201; [1963] 3 All E.R. 191, H.L.

Furthermore, the court could give care and control of the child to its own parent, which meant that the child would remain in the latter's possession whilst the court could ensure that the parental powers were exercised in its best interests.

As in other fields, equity ensured that where its own rules were in conflict with those of common law, the former should prevail. It would not only grant an injunction to restrain a person from applying for a writ of habeas corpus to obtain the custody of a child[1] but would also prevent a person who had already obtained the writ from interfering with the child if this was not in its interests.[2] As in the case of other conflicts between law and equity, the Judicature Act of 1873 expressly provided that the rules of equity relating to the custody and education of minors should prevail over those of common law.[3]

Illegitimate Children.—Up to now we have been considering the legal position of legitimate children and their parents. The position of illegitimate children was quite different, for at common law a bastard was *filius nullius* and consequently none of the legal powers and duties which flowed from the relationship of parent and legitimate child was accorded to him or his parents.[4] During the past century, however, there has been a considerable reduction in the legal disabilities attached to bastardy, reflecting a similar change in the illegitimate child's position in society generally. The judges have tended more and more to give legal effect to the natural powers and duties which the relationship creates—a tendency which can also be seen in recent legislation—so that today the sins of the parents are no longer so rigorously visited upon their illegitimate children and the legal position of the latter has been greatly assimilated to that of their legitimate brothers.[5] This is more noticeable in the case of proprietary rights;[6] so far as the personal powers and duties of a parent are concerned, in the absence of an order of the court to the contrary these are vested in the mother of an illegitimate child to the exclusion of the father, even though the latter's paternity is not in dispute. Consequently she alone can exercise *vis à vis* her illegitimate children those powers which in the case of legitimate children are vested today in both parents.[7]

Statutes.—In addition to those statutes which have given the Divorce Court power to make orders relating to the custody, education and maintenance of the children of the marriage in matrimonial causes, a mass of legislation has been passed during the past 100 years affecting parental powers and duties. At least six distinct principles can be seen.

---

[1] *Per* LINDLEY, L.J., in *R.* v. *Barnado, Jones's Case*, [1891] 1 Q.B. 194, 210, C.A.

[2] *Andrews* v. *Salt* (1873), 8 Ch. App. 622.

[3] See now the Supreme Court of Judicature (Consolidation) Act 1925, s. 44.

[4] Blackstone, *Commentaries*, i, 458-459.

[5] For the change in approach to the construction of statutes permitting the word "child" to include an illegitimate child if the object of the statute so requires, see *Minister of Home Affairs* v. *Fisher*, [1980] A.C. 319; [1979] 3 All E.R. 21, P.C. For the proposal to abolish the concept of legitimacy altogether, see *ante*, pp. 273-274.

[6] See *post*, pp. 577 and 621-622.

[7] See now the Children Act 1975, s. 85 (7).

(1) Statutory effect has now been given to the rule that in every case involving the custody or upbringing of a child "the court shall regard the welfare of the minor as the first and paramount consideration".

(2) Not only were the common law duties of a parent to protect and maintain his children wholly inadequate to ensure that they grew up fit to take their place as members of the complex industrial society which evolved in the nineteenth century, but the unenforceable nature of these duties led to scandalous cruelty, abandonment and depravity. A number of statutes have been passed, therefore, to prevent physical cruelty and neglect and to provide for children's moral and mental welfare as well. For example, an obligation is now laid on parents to ensure that their children receive adequate secular education, and a parent may in certain circumstances be deprived of the custody of a child who is in need of care or control.

(3) The same development that can be seen in all other branches of family law—the evolution of the wife from a subordinate member of her husband's household to the joint, co-equal head of the family—is most noticeable here. Whereas at common law her husband could deprive her of the care even of her young baby and could completely disregard all her wishes, her powers are now in every respect the same as his.

(4) Whilst a century ago disputes concerning the custody and maintenance of children could be resolved only in the Court of Chancery or in one of the superior courts of common law, jurisdiction has now been given to county courts and magistrates' courts.

(5) Local authorities—that is to say, non-metropolitan county, metropolitan district and London borough councils—have been made increasingly responsible for the welfare of children who may be in special need of protection. In particular they are bound to care for those whose parents or guardians are dead or unable or unwilling to look after them, to supervise the arrangements made for foster-children and to maintain an adoption service.

(6) At common law a person attained his majority at the age of 21. Now, under section 1 of the Family Law Reform Act 1969, he attains it on his eighteenth birthday. Consequently all parental powers over him cease when he reaches that age and all orders in relation to him (except with respect to financial provision) come to an end.

Principles underlying the Modern Law.—The key-note of the law relating to the exercise of parental rights and powers as it had developed by the middle of the present century is to be found in section 1 of the Guardianship of Minors Act 1971 which provides:[1]

"Where in any proceedings before any court ...
   (a) the legal custody or upbringing of a minor; or
   (b) the administration of any property belonging to or held on trust for a minor, or the application of the income thereof,

---

[1] Re-enacting s. 1 of the Guardianship of Infants Act 1925 and as subsequently amended by the Guardianship Act 1973, Sched. 3, and the Domestic Proceedings and Magistrates' Courts Act 1978, s. 36 (1). See also s. 15 of the last named Act and *cf.* the Children and Young Persons Act 1933, s. 44 (1), *post*, pp. 390–391. In proceedings for custody or access brought under s. 9 (1) of the Guardianship of Minors Act 1971, the court is required to have regard not only to the welfare of the child but also to the parent's conduct and wishes; in practice this does not seem to alter the courts' approach to the problem. See further Lowe and White, *Wards of Court*, 1-5-131.

is in question, the court, in deciding that question, shall regard the welfare of the minor as the first and paramount consideration, and shall not take into consideration whether from any other point of view the claim of the father in respect of such legal custody, upbringing, administration or application is superior to that of the mother, or the claim of the mother is superior to that of the father.''

It is immediately apparent that, in the strict jurisprudential sense, it is no longer correct to speak of a parent's *rights*.[1] Neither father nor mother has an absolute claim to control any aspect of the child's conduct because, whatever his or her wishes may be, the court may refuse to implement them if it considers that this will not be in the interests of the child's welfare. In some cases too the legal authority is no longer vested in the parent as such but in the person with *de facto* control. Even parental powers (for example, to consent to a child's marriage or adoption) are qualified in the sense that a refusal to exercise them does not amount to an absolute veto, because in certain circumstances the consent may be dispensed with. It might be more accurate today to speak of the qualified authority of a parent. Nevertheless judges and Parliament alike continue to use the words "rights" and "powers" to signify this authority, with the result that the meaning of a statute is not always plain.[2] An opportunity to remedy the situation was lost and the confused terminology perpetuated in section 85 (1) of the Children Act 1975 which provides:[3]

"In this Act, unless the context otherwise requires, 'the parental rights and duties' means as respects a particular child (whether legitimate or not), all the rights and duties which by law the mother and father have in relation to a legitimate child and his property; and references to a parental right or duty shall be construed accordingly and shall include a right of access and any other element included in a right or duty."

It is clear that the word "right" in this context means the qualified authority referred to above and not a right in the strict sense. This point must be borne in mind in any discussion of the legal relationship of parent and child.

A further point to be noted about section 1 of the Guardianship of Minors Act is that it applies only if proceedings are brought before any court: in the absence of an order vesting custody (or any other aspect of parental authority) in the mother, it does not affect the common law rule that in the case of legitimate children powers are vested exclusively in the father. This was usually only of academic importance because the right to exercise them normally becomes important only when the marriage breaks down and custody and other matters in relation to the child will become the subject of a court order. In any case the parent's last resort would be to a court which would then be bound by the section. But occasionally the old rule had a surprising habit of obtruding itself, for example in the Foreign Office's refusal to issue a passport to a minor without his father's authority or the view taken by some voluntary bodies with whom a child had been left by his mother that they were bound to return him to the father even though they did

---

[1] For exceptionally penetrating and valuable analyses, see Eekelaar, *What are Parental Rights?*, 89 L.Q.R. 210, and Hall, *loc. cit.*

[2] See Eekelaar, *loc. cit.*, pp. 211-212.

[3] This definition will also apply for the purpose of any statutes passed subsequently: Interpretation Act 1978, Sched. 1 and Sched. 2, para. 4. See further Bevan and Parry, *Children Act*, 105-111.

not believe this to be in the child's best interest.[1] The law has now been modified by two important enactments. The first, section 1 (1) of the Guardianship Act 1973, sought to cure the defect just mentioned and provides:[2]

> "In relation to the legal custody or upbringing of a minor, and in relation to the administration of any property belonging to or held in trust for a minor or the application of income of any such property, a mother shall have the same rights and authority as the laws allows to a father, and the rights and authority of mother and father shall be equal and shall be exercisable by either without the other.'

It must be emphasised that this applies only to legitimate children; in the absence of any court order parental rights and duties still vest exclusively in the mother of an illegitimate child.[3] But it must now be read in conjunction with the following provision contained in section 85 (3) of the Children Act 1975:

> "Where two or more persons have a parental right or duty jointly, any one of them may exercise or perform it in any manner without the other or others if the other or, as the case may be, one or more of the others have not signified disapproval of its exercise or performance in that manner."

It will be seen that this provision is very much wider than the last because it applies not merely to parents but to *all* persons who have a parental right or duty jointly. Hence it applies, for example, to guardians, a guardian and a surviving parent, and (when the relevant sections of the Children Act 1975 come into force) custodians.[4] But perhaps the most important and surprising aspect of it is that neither parent (or other person with parental rights) is under any obligation to inform the other of the proposed exercise of authority, so that the latter will not necessarily have the opportunity of voicing his disapproval. It is important that either should have the power to act in an emergency (for example, to consent to immediate surgical or medical treatment) and it is convenient to enable them to act independently over trivial matters. The consent of both is still required for some important matters by particular statutes, for example the marriage or adoption of a minor. What is astonishing is that a father, say, can take advantage of his wife's temporary absence to change the child's school or to consent to a major surgical operation where there is no need of an immediate decision.[5] The old legal exercise of powers by the father is in danger of being replaced by an arbitrary exercise by either parent, and one must question whether the new law is basically any more just than the old.

Although either parent's power to signify disapproval may at first sight appear to be capable of causing serious difficulties, in practice they are likely

---

[1] This point appears to have been overlooked by ORMROD and CUMMING-BRUCE, L.JJ., in *Dipper* v. *Dipper*, [1980] 2 All E.R. 722, at pp. 731 and 733, C.A.

[2] As amended by the Domestic Proceedings and Magistrates' Courts Act 1978, s. 36 (2).

[3] Guardianship Act 1973, s. 1 (7); Children Act 1975, s. 85 (7).

[4] Maidment argues that the sub-section does not apply as between father and mother because s. 1 (1) of the Guardianship Act gives them equal but separate rights: 126 New L.J. 1024. Despite the infelicity of wording, it would be surprising if the courts were to limit its application in this way.

[5] If the other parent has signified disapproval but a third person (*e.g.*, a surgeon) is unaware of this, may he act on the assumption that the parent exercising the power is legally entitled to do so? Presumably he must be able to act; any other solution would create impossible difficulties for him.

to be no more serious than those that arose before the Guardianship Act was passed. Differences of opinion about, say, a child's education are hardly likely to occur more frequently as a consequence of the new legislation. If the parents disagree on any question affecting the child's welfare, the Guardianship Act enables either of them to apply to the court for directions and the court may make such order regarding the matters in difference as it thinks proper.[1] Any order may be subsequently varied or discharged on the application of either parent or any guardian or other person having custody of the child.[2] This has produced a welcome simplification of procedure; before the Act the only way in which such disputes could have been resolved was by one parent's seeking custody or having the child made a ward of court. The same courts have jurisdiction as under the Guardianship of Minors Act.[3] One of the purposes of the Act is to enable parents living together to obtain the assistance of the court; consequently there is no power in these proceedings to make an order relating to custody or access.[4]

One of the parental powers, that of consenting to a child's marriage, has already been considered.[5] Those of consenting to a child's being adopted or freed for adoption, of appointing a testamentary guardian, and of consenting to an application for a custodianship order will be dealt with in the next two chapters. The parent's duty to maintain a child will be considered in chapter 16. We shall now consider the remaining legal aspects of the relationship of parent and child.

B. CUSTODY, AND CARE AND CONTROL

1. INTRODUCTORY

Meaning of Custody.—Because of the way in which the law has evolved, custody has developed two meanings. As we have already seen, in the earlier law only a person with *de facto* care and control of a child could exercise the other rights which were attached *de jure* to the guardianship of a parent or other person. As a result there was a tendency to use the word "custody" sometimes to designate all these rights and sometimes to designate only care and control. In *Hewer* v. *Bryant*[6] SACHS, L.J., emphasised this dual aspect of the meaning of custody in the following words:

"In its wider meaning the word 'custody' is used as if it were almost the equivalent of 'guardianship' in the fullest sense. ... Adapting the convenient phraseology of counsel, such guardianship embraces a 'bundle of rights' or to be more exact a 'bundle of powers', which continue until a male attains [18] or a female infant marries. These include the power to control education, the choice of religion, and the administration of the infant's property. They include entitlement to veto the

---

[1] S. 1 (3). *Cf.* the power given to magistrate's courts to adjudicate between two persons who have a parental right or duty jointly by virtue of an order made under the Domestic Proceedings and Magistrates' Courts Act 1978: *post*, p. 305.

[2] S. 1 (5). A variation or discharge may be made after the death of either parent.

[3] S. 1 (6). Appeals lie in the same way. For proceedings under the Guardianship of Minors Act, see *post*, pp. 302-304.

[4] S. 1 (4).

[5] *Ante*, pp. 39-41.

[6] [1970] 1 Q.B. 357, 373; [1969] 3 All E.R. 578, 585, C.A. See Maidment, *The Fragmentation of Parental Rights*, [1981] C.L.J. 135; Hall, *loc. cit.*

issue of a passport and to withhold consent to marriage. They include also both the personal power physically to control the infant until the years of discretion and the right ... to apply to the courts to exercise the powers of the Crown as *parens patriae*. It is thus clear that somewhat confusingly one of the powers conferred by custody in its wide meaning is custody in its limited meaning, namely such personal power of physical control as a parent or guardian may have.''

Similarly, as KARMINSKI, L.J., pointed out in the same case,[1] ''physical possession is only one aspect of custody''. In LORD DENNING, M.R.'s words (as usual vivid and realistic),[2]

''[custody] is a dwindling right which the courts will hesitate to enforce against the wishes of the child, and the more so the older he is. It starts with a right of control and ends with little more than advice.''

The Children Act 1975 has tried to rationalise the position by enacting that for the purpose of that Act and of any Act passed after it *legal custody* means:

''so much of the parental rights and duties as relate to the person of the child (including the place and manner in which his time is spent)''.[3]

This is contrasted with *actual custody* which means the actual possession of the child's person, whether or not that possession is shared with anyone else.[4] This narrow sense of the word is sometimes denoted by the words ''care and control'' or ''possession''.

As custody is a separable concept, the rights inherent in it may be split. Clearly if a child's parents are living apart, only one of them can have actual custody. If, say, the court gives this to the mother but all the other parental rights to both of them jointly, the father will have an equal right to decide on the child's education. Similarly, if a child is made a ward of court, care and control must necessarily be given to an individual but the other rights of custody will remain in the court.

Common Law.—At common law the father was entitled to the legal custody of his legitimate children until they reached the age of 21.[5] His rights might be lost, however, if to enforce them would probably lead to the physical or moral harm of the child[6] or if his claim was not made *bona fide*.[7] After his death, the mother was entitled to the legal custody of her minor

---

[1] At pp. 376 and 588, respectively.

[2] At pp. 369 and 582, respectively.

[3] S. 86; Interpretation Act 1978, Sched. 1 and Sched. 2, para. 4. In the Guardianship of Minors Act 1971 and the Guardianship Act 1973 the word ''custody'' has similarly been replaced by ''legal custody'' with the same meaning: Domestic Proceedings and Magistrates' Courts Act 1978, s. 36. ''Legal custody'' thus means so much of the rights and duties which by law the mother and father have in relation to the person of a legitimate child even though the particular child is illegitimate (see *ante*, p. 280). S. 86 further provides that a person shall not be entitled to effect or arrange the child's emigration by virtue of his having legal custody unless he is the child's parent or guardian.

[4] Children Act 1975, s. 87 (1); Domestic Proceedings and Magistrates' Courts Act 1978, ss. 36 (1) (c) (amending s. 20 (2) of the Guardianship of Minors Act 1971) and 88 (1). *Cf.* the definition of the person with whom a child has his home, *post*, p. 347.

[5] *Thomasset* v. *Thomasset*, [1894] P. 295, C.A.; *Re Agar-Ellis* (1883), 24 Ch.D. 317, C.A.

[6] *E.g.* apprehension of cruelty or grossly immoral or profligate conduct: *Re Andrews* (1873), L.R. 8 Q.B. 153, 158.

[7] *E.g.*, if his purpose was to hand the child over to another: *cf. Re Turner* (1872), 41 L.J.Q.B. 142.

children for nurture,[1] but even this right was superseded after 1660 if the father appointed a testamentary guardian under the provisions of the Tenures Abolition Act.[2] Common law accorded no other right to the mother as such, and so absolute against her were the father's rights that he could lawfully claim from her the possession even of a child at the breast.[3]

Equity.—As the passages cited from *Re Agar-Ellis* and *R*. v. *Gyngall* will already have shown,[4] equity *prima facie* gave effect to the father's right to the custody of his children, but would deprive him of it if their welfare so demanded. Although originally equity interfered with the father's rights hardly less readily than the common law, by the end of the nineteenth century it would do so if there was any threat of physical or moral harm to the child; and if a father once abandoned or abdicated his right, he would not be allowed to reassert it arbitrarily if this would be contrary to the child's interests.[5]

Even before the Judicature Acts of 1873 and 1875 the common law courts recognised the superiority of the jurisdiction of the Court of Chancery to this extent, that, if proceedings were pending in the latter court, an application for habeas corpus would be stayed until the decision of Chancery was known.[6] Since the rules of equity are now bound to prevail, the circumstances in which common law would refuse a father custody are now of historical interest only.

Statutory Provisions relating to Claims for Custody.—Since the middle of the nineteenth century Parliament has intervened in a series of statutes, the effect of which has been to whittle down the father's rights further and also to give the mother positive rights to custody which even equity did not accord to her. The history of this change in attitude can best be seen by a brief examination of the principal provisions of each statute.

Talfourd's Act 1839.—This Act,[7] although now repealed, marks a decisive point in the history of family law, for it empowered the Court of Chancery to give the mother custody of her children until they reached the age of seven and access to them until they came of age. But the Act specifically provided that no order was to be made if the mother had been guilty of adultery.

Custody of Infants Act 1873.—This extended the principle of Talfourd's Act by empowering the court to give the mother custody until the child reached the age of 16. It did not, however, repeat the proviso relating to her adultery. Section 2 introduced a further reform, which had long been overdue, by enacting that agreements as to custody or control in separation deeds (which had formerly been void as contrary to public policy) should be enforceable so long as they were for the child's benefit.[8]

---

[1] *R*. v. *Clarke* (1857), 7 E. & B. 186, 200.
[2] See *post*, p. 365.
[3] *R*. v. *De Manneville* (1804), 5 East 221.
[4] *Ante*, p. 277.
[5] See *Re O'Hara*, [1900] 2 I.R. 232, 240-241; *Re Fynn* (1848), 2 De G. & Sm. 457, 474-475.
[6] *Wellesley* v. *Duke of Beaufort* (1827), 2 Russ. 1, 25-26; *R*. v. *Isley* (1836), 5 Ad. & El. 441.
[7] 2 & 3 Vict., c. 54.
[8] See further, *post*, p. 288.

Guardianship of Infants Act 1886.—This further extended the provisions of the earlier Acts by empowering the court to give the mother custody of her children until they reached the age of 21. Furthermore the father was now stopped from defeating the mother's rights after his death by appointing a testamentary guardian, for it was enacted that the mother was to act jointly with any guardian so appointed, and for the first time she herself was given limited powers to appoint testamentary guardians.

Custody of Children Act 1891.—This Act was passed as the direct result of a number of cases in which parents had succeeded in recovering from Dr. Barnardo children whom they had placed in his now famous "homes" or whom they had abandoned and he had taken in. It provides that if a parent has abandoned or deserted his (or her) child, the burden shall shift to him to prove that he is fit to have custody of the child claimed[1] and that the court may refuse to give him possession of the child altogether.[2] Moreover, if at the time of the parent's application for custody the child is being brought up by another person, the court may now, upon awarding custody to the parent, order him to pay the whole or part of the costs incurred in bringing it up.[3]

Guardianship of Infants Act 1925.—This Act gave statutory effect to the rule that in any dispute relating to a child the court must regard its welfare as the first and paramount consideration. It also enacted that in any proceedings before any court neither the father nor the mother should from any other point of view be regarded as having a claim superior to the other[4] and gave to the mother the same right to appoint testamentary guardians as the father.[5] Jurisdiction to make orders relating to custody, etc., which had formerly been exercisable only by the High Court and (since 1886) by county courts was extended (subject to certain limitations) to magistrates' courts.[6]

Guardianship of Minors Act 1971.—This Act repealed the Guardianship of Infants Acts 1886 and 1925 and consolidated their provisions into one Act. It made no changes to the substantive law.

Guardianship Act 1973.—This completed the process of assimilating the parents' legal position by providing that in relation to the custody of a child the mother should have the same rights and authority as the father.[7]

Illegitimate Children.—Up to now we have been considering the position with respect to legitimate children (including, of course, legitimated children). The father has never been able to claim custody of an illegitimate child at

---

[1] See further, *post*, p. 291.

[2] S. 1.

[3] S. 2. The same applies if the application is made by any other person entitled to the custody of the child or legally liable to maintain it: s. 5. Such an order should not be made if it will prejudice the child by reducing the parent's ability to provide for it: *Re O'Hara*, [1900] 2 I.R. 232, 244-245.

[4] For the wording of s. 1 (now s. 1 of the Guardianship of Minors Act 1971), see *ante*, pp. 279-280.

[5] See *post*, p. 365.

[6] See *post*, p. 302.

[7] S. 1 (1). See *ante*, p. 281.

common law or in equity, and originally the mother had no claim either.[1] But in *R.* v. *Nash*[2] in 1883 JESSEL, M.R., formulated the rule that the law will give effect to the natural rights created by the relationship and eight years later in the leading case of *Barnardo* v. *McHugh*[3] the same view was expressed in the Court of Appeal and the House of Lords. This total reversal of the original position provides an outstanding example of the ability of the common law to adapt itself to meet changing social views, and the principle that the mother *prima facie* has the exclusive claim to custody has now been put beyond doubt by statute.[4] In addition, the father may also claim custody of an illegitimate child by bringing proceedings under the Guardianship of Minors Act.[5]

Unborn Children.—It has been argued[6] that a father might have a claim to custody of his unborn child which would enable him, for example, to seek an injunction to prevent the mother from having an abortion. This view has been untenable since the decision of BAKER, P., in *Paton* v. *British Pregnancy Advisory Service Trustees*,[7] when he refused to grant such an injunction. He expressed strong *obiter* doubts whether a court would interfere even though the medical practitioners involved had not acted in good faith in issuing the certificate required by the Abortion Act 1967 and there was an obvious attempt to commit a crime: it is not for the civil courts to interfere with the exercise of doctors' discretion under the Act. Even if the abortion were *ex facie* illegal, it is submitted that the father still could not obtain an injunction to prevent the commission of the proposed criminal act once it is accepted that he has no right which would be affected.[8] It is believed that any attempt to make the child a ward of court would similarly fail, for it is not a legal person. If this were not so, the consequences would be bizarre involving, for example, such further claims as a power to apply for an injunction restraining a pregnant woman from leaving the country on the ground that she would be taking the child out of the jurisdiction. If it is desirable that the father's consent should be obtained (or, at least, that his wishes should be taken into account), this should be made explicit by Act of Parliament and not left to the judges to achieve by a very dubious extension of the law of custody.[9]

Loss of Custody.—A parent's right to custody can be terminated or suspended in at least four ways.

First, custody has always automatically ceased when the child attained his majority. At common law this occurred at the age of 21, but by statute a child

---

[1] See *Re Lloyd* (1841), 3 Man. & G. 547.

[2] 10 Q.B.D. 454, C.A.

[3] [1891] A.C. 388, H.L.; *sub nom. R.* v. *Barnardo, Jones's Case*, [1891] 1 Q.B. 194, Q.B.D. and C.A.

[4] Children Act 1975, s. 85 (7).

[5] Guardianship of Minors Act 1971, ss. 9 (1) and 14 (1), replacing the Legitimacy Act 1959, s. 3. See *post*, p. 302.

[6] O'Neil and Watson, *The Father and the Unborn Child*, 38 M.L.R. 174.

[7] [1979] Q.B. 276; [1978] 2 All E.R. 987. See further Kennedy, 42 M.L.R. 324; Phillips, 95 L.Q.R. 332; Lowe, 96 L.Q.R. 29.

[8] *Cf. Gouriet* v. *Union of Post Office Workers*, [1978] A.C. 435; [1977] 3 All E.R. 70, H.L. But see Kennedy, *loc. cit.*

[9] Under the existing law the father's view may be of considerable importance in deciding whether to terminate a pregnancy because of the risk of injury to the health of the mother or existing children of her family: Bevan, *Children*, 182.

now comes of age on his eighteenth birthday and any existing order relating to custody will cease to have effect when he reaches that age.[1]

Secondly, there are a number of dicta that the right to custody of a minor daughter ceases if she marries.[2] This is apparently equally true of a son.[3]

Thirdly, the right is suspended whilst the child is serving in the armed forces, although it will automatically revive when the service ceases.[4] Although the point has never been decided, it is suggested that the right to custody will also be suspended if the child is engaged on a similar form of service, for example, in the Merchant Navy.

Finally, as the outline of the relevant statutory provisions will have indicated,[5] a parent may lose custody as the result of a court order. Similarly, if a child is made a ward of court, all the rights of custody vest in the court. In certain circumstances a local authority may assume parental rights[6] and a parent is effectively deprived of custody if a care order[7] or an order under the Mental Health Act 1959 is made in respect of a child.

Custody on the Death of either Parent.—The growth of the concept of equality of parents' rights and powers with respect to their children is reflected in the provisions of section 3 of the Guardianship of Minors Act 1971, which enacts that on the death of either parent the survivor shall be guardian of their legitimate minor children together with any guardian appointed by the other. If the deceased parent has appointed no guardian, or if the guardian or guardians so appointed refuse to act, the court may, if it thinks fit, appoint one to act with the survivor,[8] but this power should be exercised only if the court thinks it will be for the benefit of the infant to have both persons acting jointly and not purely in order to secure some collateral purpose, for example to enable the person appointed to obtain custody.[9] It is very rarely exercised in practice, so that on the death of one parent the other will become solely entitled to custody if the deceased appointed no testamentary guardian.

The father of an illegitimate child can claim its custody as of right after the mother's death only if an order under the Guardianship of Minors Act is in force granting him legal custody. If it is, he will continue to be entitled to the child's custody along with any guardian appointed by the mother.[10] If an affiliation order is in force under which payments are to be made to the mother and she dies (or becomes of unsound mind or is sent to prison),

---

[1] Family Law Reform Act 1969, ss. 1 (1) and 9 and Sched. 3, para. 3.

[2] See, *e.g.*, the judgment of SACHS, L.J., in *Hewer* v. *Bryant*, cited *ante*, p. 282.

[3] See *R.* v. *Wilmington* (1822), 5 B. & Ald. 525, 526; *Lough* v. *Ward*, [1945] 2 All E.R. 338, 348.

[4] *R.* v. *Rotherfield Greys* (1832), 1 B. & C. 345, 349-350.

[5] See *ante*, pp. 284-285.

[6] See *post*, p. 397.

[7] See *post*, p. 393. See also the Sexual Offences Act 1956, s. 38, as substituted by the Guardianship Act 1973, Sched. 1 (loss of custody on conviction of incest or attempted incest).

[8] Guardianship of Minors Act 1971, s. 3. This power is exercisable by the High Court, a county court or a magistrates' court: *ibid.*, s. 15, as amended by the Domestic Proceedings and Magistrates' Courts Act 1978, s. 38(1). The power to act jointly with guardians appointed by the father was first conferred on the mother by s. 2 of the Guardianship of Infants Act 1886.

[9] *Re H.*, [1959] 3 All E.R. 746. The proper procedure to obtain custody (or any other order) in such a case is to apply to have the child made a ward of court.

[10] Guardianship of Minors Act 1971, s. 14 (3). For custody orders, see *post*, p. 302.

magistrates may appoint some other person to have the custody of the child and receive payments under the order.[1]

Agreements as to Custody.—As in the case of all agreements which tend to curtail a parent's rights or to destroy the unity of the family, any agreement by which a parent purports to assign the custody of his minor child to another is contrary to public policy at common law and therefore void.[2] This principle has now been given statutory authority.[3] In one respect its application could be unsatisfactory, for if a husband and wife agree to separate they will naturally usually wish to come to some arrangement about the custody and care of their children and their inability to do so might well lead to unnecessary litigation. Consequently they were given a power to do so by section 2 of the Custody of Infants Act 1873, which has now been repealed and replaced by section 1 (2) of the Guardianship Act 1973. This provides that[4]

> "... an agreement made between husband and wife which is to operate only during their separation while married may, in relation to a child of theirs, provide for either of them to [give up in whole or in part the rights and authority referred to in section 1 (1) of this Act]; but no such agreement ... shall be enforced by any court if the court is of the opinion that it will not be for the benefit of the child to give effect to it."

It will be observed that the agreement will be preserved only if it is to operate during their separation *while married*: as we shall see, custody after divorce is a question for the divorce court. The proviso that it is not to be enforced if it is not for the child's benefit is, of course, in keeping with other statutory provisions relating to custody.

Access.—The object of access is to enable the parent and child to keep in touch with each other by allowing periodical visits at specified times—for example, between stated hours each Saturday or Sunday—or holidays for longer periods (sometimes referred to as "staying access"). It may be granted to either or both of the parents (including the parents of an illegitimate child) under the Guardianship of Minors Act[5] or to a parent (or a spouse if he is not a parent) under the Domestic Proceedings and Magistrates' Courts Act.[6] A grandparent (including the grandparent of an illegitimate child) may now apply for access if an order is in force under either of these Acts or, in any case, if one or both of the child's parents are dead: all these, of course, are circumstances which might lead to loss of contact between one or both pairs of grandparents and their grandchildren.[7] The court also has a power to grant

---

[1] Affiliation Proceedings Act 1957, s. 5 (4). For penalties for misconduct by such a guardian, see *ibid.*, s. 11. The order may be subsequently revoked and another guardian appointed.

[2] *Vansittart* v. *Vansittart* (1858), 2 De G. & J. 249; *Walrond* v. *Walrond* (1858), John. 18; *Humphrys* v. *Polak*, [1901] 2 K.B. 385, C.A. (illegitimate child).

[3] Guardianship Act 1973, s. 1 (2); Children Act 1975, s. 85 (2). For criticisms of this rule, see Law Com. Working Paper No. 74 (Illegitimacy), paras. 4.21-4.23.

[4] For the rights and authority referred to in s. 1 (1), see *ante*, p. 281.

[5] Ss. 9 (1) and 14 (1).

[6] S. 8 (2) (b). On the ordinary canons of construction this would not include the parent of an illegitimate child.

[7] Domestic Proceedings and Magistrates' Courts Act 1978, ss. 14 and 40 (adding a new s. 14A to the Guardianship of Minors Act). This provision was not among the Law

access to anyone under the Matrimonial Causes Act[1] and clearly has such a power under its inherent jurisdiction if the child is made a ward of court. In most cases, at least in the divorce court, it is usual for the court to order "reasonable access" and to leave the parties to make their own arrangements.[2]

As it is normally the basic right of both parent and child to have each other's companionship, it is only in the most exceptional circumstances that the court will sever the link between them by denying the parent access altogether.[3] Consequently the fact that a mother has neglected her children in the past and abandoned them with their father on the breakdown of the marriage has been held to be insufficient reason for refusing her access to them.[4] In at least one reported case the same principle has been applied in the case of an illegitimate child and access was granted to the father even though he had never lived with the child.[5] If actual custody is given to a third person (or if a custodianship order is made or the child is placed in the care of the local authority), access will usually be given to both parents. In an appropriate case the High Court or a county court can make an order giving access abroad provided that it is satisfied that the child will be returned to this country.[6]

The welfare of the child must remain the paramount consideration, and today access tends to be regarded as the right of the child rather than of the parent. Consequently it will be refused if the parent is not a fit and proper person to see the child at all.[7] The same approach is to be seen in *B. v. B.*,[8] where the Court of Appeal regretfully denied access to the father of a 16 year old boy who had developed such hostility to him that it might have been harmful to force them to meet. Account must also be taken of the effect that access may have upon the parent with actual custody: if it will adversely affect his relationship with the child, it will not be in the latter's interest to grant it.[9] Again, it may not be for the child's welfare to permit a parent to see it alone, for example if he is likely to kidnap it. In such a case "supervised

---

Commission's recommendations but was added in the House of Commons. It is regrettable that it does not extend to other relations (*e.g.*, an uncle or aunt) to whom the child might wish to have access. *Quaere* whether it applies if the grandparent's own child (*i.e.* the child's own parent) is illegitimate: normally relationships cannot be traced through illegitimate persons.

[1] Ss. 42 (1) and 52 (1) (definition of "custody").

[2] *Cf.* Eekelaar and Clive, *Custody after Divorce*, para. 13.30. It has been held that the court should not leave access to be determined by a welfare officer: *Mnguni* v. *Mnguni* (1979), 123 Sol. Jo. 859, C.A.; *Orford* v. *Orford* (1979), 10 Fam. Law 114, C.A. But in *V.-P.* v. *V.-P.* (1978), 10 Fam. Law 20, C.A., the court ordered that the father should have access when the supervising officer thought it right. Presumably the degree of control exercised by the officer when a supervision order is in force justifies leaving the discretion to him; otherwise the cases are inconsistent.

[3] But Eekelaar and Clive found that in over 30% of the cases they examined the parent who did not have actual custody was not exercising access at the time of the petition even though he had previously been given it by a magistrates' court: *op. cit.*, paras. 2.5-2.6 and Tables 12-16.

[4] *S.* v. *S.*, [1962] 2 All E.R. 1, C.A.

[5] *S.* v. *O.* (1977), 8 Fam. Law 11. Contrast *M.* v. *J.* (1977), *ibid.* 12.

[6] *Re F.*, [1973] Fam. 198; [1973] 3 All E.R. 493. It is doubtful whether a magistrates' court can make such an order because of its limited powers of enforcing it should the child not be returned.

[7] *C.* v. *C.* (1971), 115 Sol. Jo. 467 (mother suffering from manic depressive psychosis).

[8] [1971] 3 All E.R. 682, C.A. *Cf. M.* v. *M.*, [1973] 2 All E.R. 81.

[9] *M.* v. *J.*, (*supra*).

access'' may be granted, when the parent will be allowed to meet the child in the presence of a neutral third person or a welfare officer.[1] Similarly, if other considerations lead the court to conclude that it is in the child's interests to permit the parent with custody to take it abroad permanently, he will be allowed to do so even though this will effectively deprive the other parent of access altogether.[2]

Control of Child.—There can be no doubt that, if a child is made a ward of court, the court can impose conditions to control the way in which a person exercises care and control. The High Court must have the same powers in whatever way the proceedings were begun and a divorce county court presumably has similar powers under the Matrimonial Causes Act.[3] But they must be used sparingly and with common sense and conditions should never be attached which will interfere unduly with the discretion of the person with actual custody. In *Bell* v. *Bell*,[4] for example, a judge giving custody of children aged four and two to the mother imposed conditions that, until they reached the age of six, they were to be in bed by 6.30 p.m. and that, if the mother went out after that hour, they were to be left with the father, his mother or some other person approved by him. The Court of Appeal held that these requirements were far too onerous and too difficult to enforce and therefore deleted them. Whilst it might be reasonable to stipulate, for example, that the child should not be brought into contact with a named person (such as the father's mistress) or that a mother with care and control should not take full-time employment, it was quite unreasonable to control her leisure in this way.

It is very doubtful if a county court has powers to attach conditions of this sort in any other proceedings or if a magistrates' court has them at all. The only way in which a similar fetter could be imposed would be by leaving some parental rights and duties with the parent deprived of actual custody so that he could continue to exercise some control over the child's upbringing. Obviously, however, this device is of limited value.

2. DISPUTES OVER CUSTODY AND CARE AND CONTROL

General Principles.—A dispute over legal or actual custody may take one of two forms: it may be a dispute between the father and the mother, or it may be a dispute between one parent and a stranger, for example a testamentary guardian appointed by the other parent or a person who has obtained *de facto* control of the child either with the parent's consent or as a result of his having abandoned it.

As the House of Lords held in *J.* v. *C.*,[5] the principle laid down in section 1 of the Guardianship of Minors Act 1971, that the welfare of the child is to

---

[1] See *Practice Direction*, [1980] 1 All E.R. 1040.

[2] *Nash* v. *Nash*, [1973] 2 All E.R. 704, C.A. *Cf. P.(L.M.)* v. *P.(G.E.)*, [1970] 3 All E.R. 659, C.A. See generally Manchester, 123 New L.J. 738.

[3] The power of a county court judge to impose conditions does not appear to have been questioned in *Bell* v. *Bell*, (*infra*).

[4] (1980), 10 Fam. Law 117, C.A.

[5] [1970] A.C. 668; [1969] 1 All E.R. 788, H.L., at pp. 697 and 809 (*per* Lord Guest), 709-710 and 820 (*per* Lord MacDermott), 724 and 832 (*per* Lord Upjohn), 727 and 835 (*per* Lord Donovan).

be regarded as the first and paramount consideration, applies equally whether the dispute is between the parents or between one or both parents and a stranger. In the latter case, however, the wishes of an unimpeachable parent stand high among the remaining considerations: "they can be capable of ministering to the total welfare of the child in a special way, and must therefore preponderate in many cases".[1] But there is no presumption that the natural parents should have custody; in the words of LORD MACDERMOTT,[2]

> "... when all the relevant facts, relationships, claims and wishes of parents, risks, choices and other circumstances are taken into account and weighed, the course to be followed will be that which is most in the interests of the child's welfare as that term has now to be understood".

The court did not give effect to this relationship in *J.* v. *C.* The parents of the child were Spanish nationals resident in Spain, but the child, who was then aged ten years, had spent the whole of his life except for eighteen months with foster parents in England. He had been brought up as an English boy, spoke little Spanish and scarcely knew his natural parents. The House of Lords refused to interfere with the order of the trial judge who left custody, care and control with the foster parents and refused to give it to the natural parents on the ground that they "would be quite unable to cope with the problems of adjustment or with consequential maladjustment and suffering and that the father's character would inflame the difficulties" if the boy were to go to live with them in Spain.

The one statutory exception to this rule is to be found in section 3 of the Custody of Children Act 1891. This provides that where a parent has abandoned or deserted his child or allowed it to be brought up by, and at the expense of, another person, school, institution or local authority, in such circumstances as to show that he was unmindful of his parental duties, no order is to be made giving him the custody of the child unless he proves that he is a fit person to have it. But in order to bring this section into play the parent's conduct must show some degree of moral turpitude: if he relinquishes control temporarily because this is the best that he can do for the child in the circumstances, the court ought not on this ground alone to deprive him of custody.[3] In practice this section is rarely invoked.

Power of Appellate Courts.—It will be seen that the court must always be guided by the interests of the child and, as the House of Lords emphasised in *J.* v. *C.*,[4] a court of first instance has a discretion with which no appellate court will interfere unless it is satisfied that the lower court has clearly acted on the wrong principles. Thus an appeal will lie if the court of trial acted under a misapprehension of fact, or gave weight to irrelevant or unproved matters, or failed to take relevant matters into account.[5] An appellate court

---

[1] *Per* LORD MACDERMOTT, at pp. 715 and 824, respectively.

[2] *Ibid.*, at pp. 710-711 and 821, respectively. See also pp. 714, 715, 724 and 823, 824, 832, respectively.

[3] See *Re O'Hara*, [1900] 2 I.R. 232, at pp. 238, 243, 251; *Re Carroll*, [1931] 1 K.B. 317, 360-363, C.A.; *R.* v. *Bolton Union* (1892), 36 Sol. Jo. 255.

[4] [1970] A.C. 668; [1969] 1 All E.R. 788, H.L.

[5] *B. (B.)* v. *B. (M.)*, [1969] P. 103, 115; [1969] 1 All E.R. 891, 901.

may also act on admissible evidence which was not before the judge.[1] On the other hand, it is not entitled to allow an appeal and substitute its own discretion merely because it would have come to a different conclusion on the evidence. Difficulty arises because in some cases appellate courts are so convinced that the lower court exercised its discretion wrongly that they will reverse the decision even though the latter purported to apply the right principles in reaching it.[2] On hearing an appeal, a court is apparently entitled to consider the relative weight which the lower court attached to the various facts which it had to take into account and to conclude that the court acted on the wrong principles if it disagrees with the weighting.[3]

If an appellate court is satisfied that the order appealed was wrong, it may substitute a fresh order. If it is unsure what order should be made, the case should be remitted for further consideration.[4].

If the effect of an order is that the child is likely to be removed from the jurisdiction, the court making it should always place a stay on it if an appeal is pending in case the appellate court reverses the order and the child is not returned.[5] The appalling consequences of failing to grant a stay are to be seen in the Desramault case, which dragged on in England, France and Switzerland for over two years.[6]

Nature of the Proceedings.—The fact that the inherent jurisdiction of the High Court is derived from the Crown's prerogative powers as *parens patriae* invests the proceedings with a somewhat unusual character. Inasmuch as there is a justiciable issue between the parties, the court is clearly exercising a judicial function, but as its first duty is to protect the child irrespective of the parents' wishes, its jurisdiction is also administrative. The House of Lords concluded in *Official Solicitor* v. *K.*[7] that this entitled it to depart from the normal rules of evidence if this is necessary in the child's interest. It has always been accepted that the judge is entitled to see the child and each of the parents in private:[8] in *Official Solicitor* v. *K.* it was held that he may receive a confidential report from the child's guardian *ad litem* without disclosing it to the parties if he considers that disclosure would be detrimental to the child. This is an extreme step which should be taken only in the most exceptional circumstances for, once evidence is withheld, justice is not seen to be done, the losing party will leave the court with a sense of grievance, and the proper preparation of an appeal becomes impossible. The last point (and to a less extent the other two) can be met by showing the evidence to the parties' legal advisers if they are prepared not to divulge it to the parties themselves.

---

[1] *B.* v. *W.*, [1979] 3 All E.R. 83, H.L.

[2] *Re O.*, [1971] Ch. 748; [1971] 2 All E.R. 744, C.A.

[3] *Re F.*, [1976] 1 All E.R. 417, C.A.; *Re K*, [1977] Fam. 179, 183-184; [1977] 1 All E.R. 647, 649, C.A.; *B.* v. *W.*, (*supra*). See also Pace, 3 Fam. Law 27.

[4] *Per* LORD SCARMAN in *B.* v. *W.*, (*supra*), at pp. 95-96.

[5] *Smith* v. *Smith* (1971), 115 Sol. Jo. 444, C.A.

[6] See *Re Desramault* (1971), *Times*, 11th February.

[7] [1965] A.C. 201; [1963] 3 All E.R. 191, H.L. Contrast *B.* v. *W.*, (*supra*), where on the facts it was held that the Court of Appeal had not been justified in relying on the contents of a document not disclosed to the appellant.

[8] But the judge should not promise not to disclose what is said to him because of the difficulty this would cause in the event of an appeal: *H.* v. *H.*, [1974] 1 All E.R. 1145, C.A. Magistrates have no power to see children privately: *Re W.* (1980), 10 Fam. Law 120.

Official Solicitor v. *K*. was concerned with the High Court's exercise of its inherent jurisdiction. It is submitted that the same principle should apply to all proceedings relating to custody in the High Court: it would be regrettable if the court's power to receive or withhold evidence should turn upon the technical nature of the proceedings, and it should be able to exercise an inherent power even though the particular jurisdiction is statutory.[1] But as no other courts can claim the prerogative powers of the Crown, it is very doubtful whether they can receive evidence which is not available to all the parties unless they agree.[2]

A further consequence of the administrative nature of the proceedings is that, if the court is of the opinion that the nature of the case is such that the child ought to be separately represented, it can of its own motion ask the Official Solicitor (or any other suitable person) to act as the child's guardian *ad litem*. This power is limited to the High Court and divorce county courts.[3] One situation in which it may be highly desirable to appoint a guardian *ad litem* should be noted. The reception of medical evidence—and particularly of psychiatric evidence—is becoming much more common and there is a danger that a doctor who is consulted and called by one side only may be, at least subconsciously, biased in favour of that party. It is highly desirable, therefore, that a pediatrician or psychiatrist should be consulted jointly by both parents or, if they cannot agree to do so, that a guardian *ad litem* should be appointed so that he can take the necessary steps.[4]

3. FACTS TO BE TAKEN INTO ACCOUNT IN RESOLVING QUESTIONS OF CUSTODY
AND CARE AND CONTROL

It must be borne in mind at the outset that the court has to consider two questions: Who is to have legal custody and who is to have actual custody? "Split orders" under which the parent deprived of actual custody retains some or all of the remaining parental rights have always been possible in the divorce court. It was formerly considered proper to give such rights to a wholly unimpeachable parent on the ground that he should not be deprived of a voice in the child's future even though its welfare demanded that care and control should be given to the other.[5] Until fairly recently, however, it was rare to permit the latter to retain those rights as well because of the practical difficulties that would arise in the event of disagreement between the parents. The difficulties facing a parent who had possession of the child but none of the other attributes of legal custody were equally real, however, and consequently it became increasingly common to leave the remaining parental rights with both parties whenever there was a reasonable prospect that they

---

[1] It is submitted that *Fowler* v. *Fowler*, [1963] P. 311; [1963] 1 All E.R. 119, C.A., to the contrary is no longer of authority on this point as it followed the decision of the Court of Appeal reversed by the House of Lords in *Official Solicitor* v. *K*.

[2] This might be a ground on which a divorce county court should be asked to transfer an application for custody to the High Court.

[3] Under the inherent jurisdiction and Matrimonial Causes Rules 1977, r. 115. Magistrates' courts have a limited power to appoint a guardian *ad litem* in certain proceedings: see *post*, p. 393, n. 3, and p. 398, n. 4. On the question of separate representation generally, see Levin, 5 Fam. Law 129.

[4] *B. (M.)* v. *B. (R.)*, [1968] 3 All E.R. 170, C.A.

[5] *Wakeham* v. *Wakeham*, [1954] 1 All E.R. 434, C.A.

would co-operate. In *Jussa* v. *Jussa*,[1] for example, the father of three children, aged seven, five and two, was an Indian Muslim, and the mother was an English Christian. The father conceded that the mother should have care and control of them but sought to retain the remaining parental rights. Each of them agreed that the other was an admirable parent and each obviously had much to offer to children of mixed blood and culture. As there appeared to be every reason to suppose that they would be able to co-operate with each other in the interests of the children, legal custody was given to them both. In fact such an order is unnecessary because if the court does no more than order actual custody to one parent, the remaining parental rights will automatically remain in them both by virtue of section 1 of the Guardianship Act 1973.[2] In practice, however, the difficulties of leaving any rights in a parent who does not have actual custody usually appear to be too great, and at least in divorce proceedings joint orders are rare.[3]

The undesirability of depriving a person with care and control of the other attributes of legal custody is reflected in the provisions of the Guardianship of Minors Act and the Domestic Proceedings and Magistrates' Courts Act. If in proceedings brought under either Act legal custody is given to one parent (or any other person), the court may order that the other may retain such of the other parental rights (other than actual custody) as may be specified. If such an order is made, the rights and duties retained are exercisable jointly.[4] It will be seen from this that the party given care and control cannot be deprived of legal custody in these proceedings; if the other is given, say, the right to determine the child's education, the parent with possession will be able to exercise this right herself (or himself) unless the other signifies his disapproval.[5]

Welfare of the Child.—As we have already seen, this is the first and paramount consideration in determining any question relating to its custody and upbringing.[6] In the words of Lord MacDermott in *J*. v. *C*.:[7]

> "[These words] must mean more than that the child's welfare is to be treated as the top item in a list of items relevant to the matter in question. I think they connote a process whereby, when all the relevant facts, relationships, claims and wishes of parents, risks, choices and other circumstances are taken into account and weighed, the course to be followed will be that which is most in the interests of the child's welfare as that term has now to be understood. That is the first consideration because it is of first importance and the paramount consideration because it rules upon or determines the course to be followed."

---

[1] [1972] 2 All E.R. 600.

[2] See *ante*, p. 281.

[3] Eekelaar and Clive, *Custody after Divorce*, found that joint orders were made in only 3.4% of the cases examined, to which must be added 8.8% where no order was made: paras. 13.16-13.17 and Table 34.

[4] Domestic Proceedings and Magistrates' Courts Act 1978, ss. 8 (4) and 37 (adding a new s. 11A to the Guardianship of Minors Act 1971).

[5] See *ante*, p. 281.

[6] *Ante*, pp. 279-280.

[7] [1970] A.C. 668, 710; [1969] 1 All E.R. 788, 820-821, H.L. See also *Re K.*, [1977] Fam. 179; [1977] 1 All E.R. 647, C.A.; *S.(B.D.)* v. *S. (D.J.)*, [1977] Fam. 109; [1977] 1 All E.R. 656, C.A.

In deciding what order will be in the best interests of the child, a number of facts must be borne in mind. In any given case some of these are bound to weigh more heavily in favour of one parent or claimant and others will weigh more heavily in favour of the other. The court must then reach the best decision it can on all the evidence; as MEGARRY, J., pointed out in *Re F.*,[1] one cannot solve the problem arithmetically or quantitatively by using some sort of "points system".

Retention of the Existing Position.—Much more is now known about the effects of a change of care and control on a child's development and his future mental and physical health. Whereas Victorian judges dismissed a child's grief at being parted from the person with whom he had been living as transitory, it is now established that the result may well be highly detrimental if not disastrous. When there is a grave danger of this sort, the court must try at all costs to avoid a change.[2] At least in divorce cases the retention of the existing position appears to be the paramount consideration and the divorce itself affects actual custody in only a tiny fraction of cases.[3]

Personality and Character of the Claimants.—Obviously these are amongst the most important matters to be taken into consideration. To take an extreme case, the court must avoid making an order which is likely to lead to physical ill-treatment of the child. Similarly, although there is a dearth of modern authority, the child must not be exposed to the danger of moral corruption by example or encouragement.[4] Even if there is no suggestion of harm from either parent, the court must always consider which of them is likely to be the better parent and, if they are divorced and propose to remarry, which of their partners will probably make the better parent substitute.[5]

Whenever there is a contest over care and control, particularly of a young child, the court should see the parents to assess what effect each is likely to have on the child if awarded possession of it.[6]

Medical Evidence.—Medical evidence may be of vital importance, for example, in estimating the effect which living with a particular parent may have on the child. Although it will rarely be decisive, it may be of great weight in a particular case.

Sex and Age of Children.—Common sense dictates that normally the mother should have the care and control of young[7] or sickly children

---

[1] [1969] 2 Ch. 238, 241; [1969] 2 All E.R. 766, 768.

[2] *Cf.* the observations of CROSS, J., in *Re W.*, [1965] 3 All E.R. 231, 249, and see Michaels, *The Dangers of a Change of Parentage in Custody and Adoption Cases*, 83 L.Q.R. 547.

[3] In less than 1% of the cases studied by Eekelaar and Clive: *op. cit.*, paras. 13.14 and 13.29.

[4] See *Wellesley* v. *Duke of Beaufort* (1827), 2 Russ. 1 (drunkenness, profligacy and the use of obscene and profane language); *Re Besant* (1879), 11 Ch.D. 508, C.A. (publication of obscene libel).

[5] *Re F.*, *(supra)*. Similarly if a parent is cohabiting outside marriage.

[6] *H.* v. *H. and C.*, [1969] 1 All E.R. 262, C.A. Similarly the court should see either party's fresh partner: *S.* v. *S.* (1972), 117 Sol. Jo. 34. The resolution of issues of custody purely on affidavit evidence was also deprecated in *W.* v. *W.* (1971), 115 Sol. Jo. 367, C.A.

[7] See *Re B.*, [1962] 1 All E.R. 872, C.A. Contrast *H.* v. *H. and C.*, [1969] 1 All E.R. 262, C.A., where custody and care and control of a child aged three were refused to the mother who had left the child with her husband and had not seen him for 20 months.

(particularly little girls)[1] or those who for some other reason especially need a mother's care. In recent years courts have tended to take the view that, other things being equal, it may be better for an older boy to have the influence of his father.[2]

Against this, it should be borne in mind that it is generally desirable to keep brothers and sisters together and not to split the family up more than is necessary. But this will not usually be decisive, particularly if staying access to both parents will mean that the children will meet frequently during the holidays.[3] In *Re O.*[4] an Englishwoman who had married a Sudanese brought the son and daughter of the marriage back to this country. It was held that the boy, who was aged six or seven, should go back to the Sudan with his father where he would eventually succeed to his business, whilst the girl, who was a year or so younger, should stay in this country with her mother apparently on the ground that the future prospects of a girl of mixed parentage was better here.

Education.—The problem of care and control may go hand in hand with that of education, particularly of religious education. It is inconceivable that a parent will be refused custody today on the ground of atheism, as Shelley was,[5] and in the case of a very young child (or probably with any child of no fixed religious beliefs) the question of religious upbringing will probably have little bearing on the issue of care and control.[6] Occasionally, however, the limitations imposed by a particular sect on the child's activities may be relevant. Thus the fact that membership of the Exclusive Brethren would deprive the child of normal social contacts and limit his opportunities for further education has influenced the court in its decision to vest custody in the parent who does not profess these views.[7] On the other hand, if the child has already had religious instruction, the continuation of his education will be of vital importance if a break in it would produce emotional disturbance.[8]

During the nineteenth century, when religious passions tended to run higher than they do now, the courts were loth to give custody to a person whose beliefs differed from those of the child on the ground that this might drive a wedge between parent and child or, alternatively, because of the fear of proselytism.[9] Today custody or care and control may be given to a person who does not share the child's beliefs on his undertaking that his religious education will be continued. In *Re E.*[10] a Roman Catholic mother had placed her illegitimate son for adoption after formally abdicating her right to choose

---

[1] *Re F.*, [1969] 2 Ch. 238, 243; [1969] 2 All E.R. 766, 769.

[2] But there is no principle to this effect: *Re C. (A.)*, [1970] 1 All E.R. 309, C.A.

[3] *Re P.*, [1967] 2 All E.R. 229 (where separation was described on the facts as the least bad course); *Re B.* (1966), *Times*, 5th April, C.A.

[4] [1962] 2 All E.R. 10, C.A.

[5] *Shelley* v. *Westbrooke* (1817), Jac. 266 n.

[6] *Cf. Re C. (M.A.)*, [1966] 1 All E.R. 838, at pp. 856 and 864-865, C.A.

[7] *Hewison* v. *Hewison* (1977), 7 Fam. Law 207, C.A. See Bradney, 9 Fam. Law 139. Contrast *Re H.* (1980), *Times*, 19th June.

[8] This certainly influenced WILLMER, L.J., considerably in *Re M.*, [1967] 3 All E.R. 1071, 1074, C.A.

[9] See the pithy comment of LORD ESHER, M.R., in *R.* v. *Barnardo, Jones's Case*, [1891] 1 Q.B. 194, 205, C.A., where referring to habeas corpus proceedings, he said, "It is a dispute not over the body, but over the soul of the child."

[10] [1963] 3 All E.R. 874. Contrast *Roughley* v. *Roughley* (1973), 4 Fam. Law 91, C.A.

the boy's religious education. She later changed her mind and the application for an adoption order failed as the court held that her consent had not been unreasonably withheld. The applicants, who were Jewish but practised no religion, then took proceedings to have the child made a ward of court and asked for care and control. The mother opposed this, not because she wanted to have custody herself but because she wished to hand the boy over to a religious society for adoption. This would have been extremely difficult to effect in view of the child's age and the fact that he was of mixed English, Cuban and Chinese blood. In these exceptional circumstances the court declined to restore him to his mother but gave care and control to the applicants on their undertaking to have him brought up in the Roman Catholic faith.

Accommodation and Material Advantages.—The fact that one claimant to custody or care and control is in a position to give the child a better start in life than another does not give him a prior claim. It is the happiness of the child, not its material prospects, with which the court is concerned, and any other rule would automatically put a poor parent at a disadvantage. Obviously, however, a party's financial position cannot be ignored entirely: for example, if he is so poor that he cannot even provide a home for his children, this in itself might be enough to refuse him actual custody.[1] Even in a less extreme case a parent who can offer a child good accommodation must, other things being equal, have the edge over one who cannot.[2] But again the quality of the home life that the child will have must not be measured in purely material terms: the amount of time and energy that a parent can devote to its care and upbringing is of considerable importance. This may mean that a mother who can spend the whole of her time with her children will necessarily have an advantage over a father who will be out at work all day, whatever alternative arrangements he can make to have them looked after.[3]

Stability of Home Life.—The fact that the child has lived for some time with one parent may in itself be a good reason for not moving him: it is important that he should have as stable a home life as possible. Similarly, the court should try to avoid imposing yet another move on a child who has already been moved about a great deal. For these reasons, as well as that of discouraging parents from taking the law into their own hands, the courts have always set their faces against kidnapping. Consequently, if, say, a child is in the mother's care and the father takes it away against her will, the proper course will usually be to restore it to her forthwith in the absence of any evidence that this is likely to harm the child.[4]

The Child's Wishes.—If the child is old enough to express its own wishes, the court will consider them, not so that it can give effect to those wishes but to be the better able to judge what is for its welfare. But it must be

[1] *Re Story*, [1916] 2 I.R. 328, 345-346.
[2] *Re F.*, [1969] 2 Ch. 238; [1969] 2 All E.R. 766.
[3] See *Re K.*, [1977] Fam. 179; [1977] 1 All E.R. 647, C.A.; *S. v. S.*, [1977] Fam. 109; [1977] 1 All E.R. 656, C.A.
[4] *G. v. G.* (1975), 6 Fam. Law 43, C.A. *Quaere* whether courts will now be more anxious to consider the case on its merits: *cf. post*, p. 379.

remembered that the child may have been coached by one parent and that sometimes the child's own wishes are so contrary to its long-term interests that the court may feel justified in disregarding them altogether.[1]

The Parties' Conduct.—During the nineteenth century it was the practice of the Divorce Court not to give care and control to a mother who had been guilty of adultery[2] and it was not until the turn of the century that the courts were prepared to concede that this should not automatically deprive her of her rights.[3] Today, however, it is clear that, in making an order in relation to a child, the court is not concerned with punishing any adult for his conduct.[4] Even as late as 1962 the Court of Appeal was of the opinion that, however rare it was for one spouse to be solely responsible for the breakdown of the marriage, when this occured the "unimpeachable" parent's wishes must be given special consideration.[5] In *S.* v. *S.*,[6] however, the Court held that its earlier decisions were inconsistent with the later decision of the House of Lords in *J.* v. *C.*,[7] and that, if the welfare of the child so demands, care and control at least must be left with the "guilty" party, however unjust the other will believe the decision to be.[8]

The parties' conduct in the past may, however, be relevant as throwing light on their probable behaviour as parents in the future.[9] If one of them has abandoned or deserted the child, this in itself may indicate that he is unfit to have care and control and should be refused it for this reason.[10] Similarly, a parent who permits another to bring up his child cannot be allowed arbitrarily to put an end to this arrangement if to do so would be injurious to the child.[11] Parental conduct might also tip the balance if the child's welfare would be served equally by giving custody to either of them.[12]

The court will obviously not accede to a claim for possession of a child if it is not made *bona fide*—for example, if the claimant's purpose is to deliver the child to another.

Removing the Child from the Jurisdiction.—There is an obvious danger that, if a child is removed from the jurisdiction by a parent (or any other person) with actual custody or access, he will not be brought back, with the result that the other parent will not be able to exercise his rights. In an attempt to avoid this situation, a court making an order (including an interim order)

---

[1] *Re. S.*, [1967] 1 All E.R. 202, 210; *Doncheff* v. *Doncheff* (1978), 8 Fam. Law 205, C.A.

[2] See, e.g., *Clout* v. *Clout* (1861), 2 Sw. & Tr. 391. *Cf.* the provisions of Talfourd's Act, *ante*, p. 284. But custody was not refused to an adulterous father in the absence of some further factor likely to lead to the child's corruption.

[3] *Re A. and B.*, [1897] 1 Ch. 786, C.A.

[4] *Re L.*, [1974] 1 All E.R. 913, 926, C.A.

[5] *Re L.*, [1962] 3 All E.R. 1, C.A.

[6] [1977] Fam. 109; [1977] 1 All E.R. 656, C.A.; followed in *Re. K.*, [1977] Fam. 179; [1977] 1 All E.R. 647, C.A. See Hall, [1977] C.L.J. 252.

[7] [1970] A.C. 668; [1969] 1 All E.R. 788, H.L. See *ante*, p. 290.

[8] As in *Re K.*, (*supra*), where the father (a clergyman) was prepared to go to any lengths to effect a reconciliation with his wife and to avoid the children being brought up in a house in which she would be living in adultery with her lover. See further Berkovits, 10 Fam. Law 164.

[9] *Re F.*, (*supra*), at pp. 243 and 769-770, respectively.

[10] *Cf.* the Custody of Children Act 1891, s. 1.

[11] *Re Mathieson* (1918), 87 L.J. Ch. 445, C.A.

[12] *Re F.*, (*supra*), at pp. 241 and 768, respectively. See Hoggett, 121 Sol. Jo. 469.

for legal custody under the Guardianship of Minors Act or the Domestic Proceedings and Magistrates' Courts Act may forbid the removal of the child from the jurisdiction.[1] Furthermore, any order relating to custody or care and control in proceedings for divorce, nullity or judicial separation must provide that the child shall not be removed from England and Wales without the leave of the court except on such terms as may be specified.[2] In most cases, of course, it is highly improbable that any attempt would be made to kidnap the child and there can be no real objection to his being taken to, say, Scotland or France for a short holiday. Consequently an order in the divorce court commonly provides that either parent may remove the child from the jurisdiction if he gives a written undertaking to return him and the other parent consents in writing.[3]

On the other hand, a proposal to remove a child from the country permanently by a parent intending to live abroad might well meet with strenuous opposition. At one time the court would not normally permit a child to be removed out of its jurisdiction; now, however, it will do so if the child's welfare so demands even though this will deprive the other parent of all future contact with him. This matter may be of particular importance if one of the parents is an immigrant who decides to return to his native country. If the child was born in England, the court must take into account the psychological damage that might be done by removing him to a country where his native language is not spoken, where he will be divorced from the social customs and contacts to which he is used, and where his education may be adversely affected.[4] Hence the court will be slow to make an order which would have the effect of sending a child brought up in this country to an alien community, even though this is the country of his parents' origin.[5] If, on the other hand, one parent intends to live in a foreign country in which the child was brought up, it may be better to give care and control to that parent if there is a chance that the other will then go and live there too, for a local court may be able to make an order which will enable the child to keep in contact with them both.[6]

Proceedings to prevent the Removal of the Child.—Before any order relating to legal or actual custody is made, a parent fearing that a child is about to be taken out of the country may apply for an injunction to prevent this in any proceedings pending in the High Court or a county court.[7] Failure to comply with such an injunction, like failure to observe any restriction contained in an order made by these courts or to comply with an undertaking

---

[1] Domestic Proceedings and Magistrates' Courts Act 1978, ss. 34 and 39 (adding a new s. 13A to the Guardianship of Minors Act 1971).

[2] Matrimonial Causes Rules 1977, r. 94.

[3] See Rayden, *Divorce*, 13th Ed., 3996.

[4] *Re L.*, [1974] 1 All E.R. 913, 925-926, C.A.

[5] Such orders were refused in *Re E.O.* (1973), *Times*, 16th February, C.A. (Nigeria); *Re O.* (1973), *Times*, 27th February, C.A. (Ghana); *Re N.* (1975), 5 Fam. Law 186, C.A. (Zambia). An order was made in *Au* v. *Au* (1980), 10 Fam. Law 116, C.A. (Hong Kong).

[6] *Cf. Re T.*, [1968] Ch. 740; [1968] 3 All E.R. 411, C.A.

[7] An injunction may be granted even before the proceedings are commenced on the applicant's undertaking to bring them within a specified time: *Re N.*, [1967] Ch. 512; [1967] 1 All E.R. 161; *L.* v. *L.*, [1969] P. 25; [1969] 1 All E.R. 852. *Cf. ante*, pp. 122-123.

given to them, will amount to a contempt of court. This may be of little help if the parent has no intention of returning to England and in any event does not apply to orders made by magistrates' courts. In such cases the claimant may be put to great expense and inconvenience in bringing proceedings in the country where the child happens to be. Consequently, once an order has been made, the Home Office will give all the help it can either by refusing to issue a passport for the child on the application of the other parent or by keeping a special watch at ports and airports to prevent his embarkation.[1]

Foreign Orders.—Since the jurisdiction of equity in suits involving children is based upon the Crown's prerogative as *parens patriae*, all minors within the jurisdiction are entitled to the same protection even though they are neither domiciled in this country nor even British subjects. In all cases the welfare of the infant must be the court's first consideration, and consequently, although an English court must take an order for custody made by a foreign court into consideration, it will give effect to it only if this would be for the child's benefit. This is clear from the decision of the Privy Council in *McKee* v. *McKee*[2] following the earlier English case of *Re B's Settlement*.[3] The husband and wife, who were both United States citizens, had been divorced in 1942, and a Californian court, which had jurisdiction, ultimately gave the mother the custody of the child of the marriage, a boy born in 1940. At the same time the court affirmed an agreement previously entered into between the parties that neither of them should remove the child from the United States without the written permission of the other. In contravention of this order, the father took the boy to Canada in 1946. The mother then instituted habeas corpus proceedings in Ontario and the trial judge awarded custody to the father. On appeal the Privy Council affirmed this order. Two years had elapsed between the making of the two orders and in this time the child had developed rapidly and the father's circumstances had undergone a considerable change. Taking all things into consideration, there was no reason for interfering with the trial judge's exercise of discretion.[4]

4. METHODS BY WHICH DISPUTES OVER CUSTODY AND CARE AND CONTROL MAY BE RESOLVED

Preliminary Observations.—It was always a rule of common law that the parent's right to custody would not be enforced against the child's will once the latter had reached the so-called age of discretion. This was fixed at 14 in the case of a boy and 16 in the case of a girl and, because of the difficulties

---

[1] For details, see *Practice Note*, [1963] 3 All E.R. 66, and *Practice Direction*, [1973] 3 All E.R. 194; Law Com. Working Paper No. 68 (Custody of Children), paras. 117-138; Lowe and White, *Wards of Court*, 330-333. A caveat against the issue of a passport will be ineffective if the child already has a passport or is on the other parent's passport and the "stop-list" procedure is likely to be effective only if the Home Office is given an indication of the date and place of embarkation and the probable destination.

[2] [1951] A.C. 352; [1951] 1 All E.R. 942, P.C.

[3] [1940] Ch. 54. See also *Re Kernot*, [1965] Ch. 217; [1964] 3 All E.R. 339. For criticisms of the present state of the law relating to possible conflict of orders made by different courts in the United Kingdom, see the Report of the Committee on Conflicts of Jurisdiction affecting Children (1959, Cmnd. 842); Law Com. Working Paper No. 68 (Custody of Children).

[4] See further *post*, pp. 376-379.

which might otherwise ensue, the same age applied in all cases and no allowance was made for the precocity of the individual child.[1] This rule has since been adopted by equity and in the Divorce Court.[2] It must not be supposed, however, that it would be applied arbitrarily today in exceptional cases, for example if the child in question were mentally retarded.[3]

Writ of Habeas Corpus.—The writ of habeas corpus, which may be used by anyone to regain his liberty if he is unlawfully detained against his will, may also be used by anyone claiming the custody of a child who has not yet reached the age of discretion. Before that age the child cannot in law exercise any choice in the matter, for to permit him to do so "would only expose him to danger and seductions",[4] and consequently he is deemed to be at liberty when he is in the custody of the person with the right to it.[5] It is therefore extremely doubtful whether this remedy is available at all once the child has reached the age of discretion.[6] In any event the view has been expressed that this procedure is no longer the most appropriate and that claims to custody in the Family Division should be dealt with, if necessary, under the wardship jurisdiction.[7]

Wardship of Court.—If a parent wishes to invoke the jurisdiction of the Family Division of the High Court without taking other matrimonial proceedings, the simplest procedure is to make an application under the Guardianship of Minors Act.[8] If a stranger, who is not the child's guardian, wishes to obtain care and control, he should start proceedings to have the child made a ward of court. Any interested person may do this but he naturally runs the risk of having to pay costs if he is unsuccessful.[9] An application may also be made by a parent to have the child made a ward of court, a procedure which has the advantage that either parent may be given care and control whilst the exercise of his parental rights will remain under the supervision of the court.[10]

---

[1] *R.* v. *Howes* (1860), 3 E. & E. 332; *Ex parte Barford* (1860), 8 Cox C.C. 405. In the case of a daughter this age was apparently fixed by reference to the statute 4 & 5 Ph. & M., c. 8, s. 3 (which has now been repealed and re-enacted in the Sexual Offences Act 1956, s. 20, *post*, p. 327); in the case of a boy the age of 14 was presumably taken as being the age at which guardianship for nurture ceased at common law. In Scots law a child ceases to be a pupil and becomes a minor at these ages: Walker, *Principles of Scottish Private Law*, 261.

[2] *Re Agar-Ellis* (1883), 24 Ch.D. 317, C.A.; *Thomasset* v. *Thomasset*, [1894] P. 295, C.A.; *Hall* v. *Hall* (1945), 175 L.T. 355, C.A.

[3] *Cf. Thomasset* v. *Thomasset*, (*supra*); *Stark* v. *Stark*, [1910] P. 190, C.A.; *Hall* v. *Hall*, (*supra*).

[4] *Per* LORD DENMAN, C.J., in *R.* v. *Greenhill* (1836), 4 Ad. & El. 624, 640.

[5] *R.* v. *Greenhill*, (*supra*); *R.* v. *Clarke* (1857), 7 E. & B. 186, 193-194; *Barnardo* v. *McHugh*, [1891] A.C. 388, H.L. (illegitimate child). The writ will lie only against the person with actual control of the child at the time and not against one who once had it but has now lost it: *Barnardo* v. *Ford, Gossage's Case*, [1892] A.C. 326, H.L. Unlike cases where the writ is sought to obtain release from an unlawful detention, *either* party may appeal from an order granting or refusing it: *Barnardo* v. *McHugh*.

[6] But see *Lough* v. *Ward*, [1945] 2 All E.R. 338, 348 (although this may be due to a misreading of the judgments in *Re Agar-Ellis, supra*); *R.* v. *Lewis* (1893), 9 T.L.R. 226, 227.

[7] *Re K.* (1978), 122 Sol. Jo. 626.

[8] *Infra.*

[9] *Re McGrath*, [1893] 1 Ch. 143, 146-147, C.A.

[10] See further, *post*, pp. 374 *et seq.*

Injunctions.—An injunction may also be obtained to restrain the defendant from interfering with the plaintiff's right to custody. This was granted in *Lough* v. *Ward*[1] where the plaintiff's daughter was over the age of 16. It will thus be seen that the court may grant an injunction even though it would not positively enforce the right to custody by ordering the child to return to its parents.

Guardianship of Minors Act.—Either parent (including the mother or father of an illegitimate child) may apply for an order under the Guardianship of Minors Act.[2] Such an order may be made by the High Court, a county court or a magistrates' court.[3] The court may vest legal custody in one parent exclusively, in which case he alone will have actual custody; it may also order that the other parent retain such other parental rights and duties as may be specified, when they will be shared by both parents jointly.[4] It may also make an order for access by either parent or a grandparent.[5] There is a general power to postpone the operation of the order or any provision in it for a period of time or until the occurrence of a specified event.[6] It may be proper to exercise this if the effect of the order is to transfer actual custody of the child from one parent to the other and the former intends to appeal or the latter wants time to make preparations to receive the child.[7]

As the law now stands, the court may give custody to a third person, but when the provisions of the Children Act 1975 relating to custodianship come into force, this power will be abolished and replaced by one to make a custodianship order in favour of anyone other than one of the parents.[8]

---

[1] [1945] 2 All E.R. 338. The application for the injunction was coupled with an action for damages for enticement. Although enticement is no longer a tort (see *post*, p. 329), an injunction can clearly still be granted to protect the parent's right to custody.

[2] Guardianship of Minors Act 1971, ss. 9 (1) and 14 (1).

[3] *Ibid.*, s. 15 as amended by the Guardianship Act 1973, Sched. 2, and the Domestic Proceedings and Magistrates' Courts Act, ss. 38 (1) and 47 (1). A county court has jurisdiction only if the respondent or respondents are resident in England or a summons can be served on them in this country. A magistrates' court has jurisdiction (i) if all the parties reside in England, (ii) if the defendant resides here and the applicant resides in Scotland or Northern Ireland, or (iii) if one parent and the child reside in England and the other parent resides in any other part of the United Kingdom. A magistrates' court must refuse to make an order if it considers the matter would be more conveniently dealt with by the High Court and no appeal will lie from such a refusal: *ibid.*, s. 16 (4), as amended by the Children Act 1975, Sched. 3, para. 75 (3) (b). For appeals and transfer of cases to the High Court, see *ibid.*, s. 16, as amended by the Domestic Proceedings and Magistrates' Courts Act 1978, s. 48.

[4] *Ibid.*, s. 11A (1) (added by the Domestic Proceedings and Magistrates' Courts Act 1978, s. 37).

[5] *Ibid.*, ss. 9 (1) and 14A (added by the Domestic Proceedings and Magistrates' Courts Act 1978, s. 40); *Re W. (J.C.)*, [1964] Ch. 202; [1963] 3 All E.R. 459, C.A.; *Jussa* v. *Jussa*, [1972] 2 All E.R. 600. In *Re H.* (1977), 121 Sol. Jo. 253, it was held that the court may make an order for access in favour of any other person; applying the principle *expressio unius exclusio alterius*, this is difficult to justify.

[6] *Ibid.*, s. 11A (2) (added by the Domestic Proceedings and Magistrates' Courts Act 1978, s. 37).

[7] See Law Com. No. 77 (Report on Matrimonial Proceedings in Magistrates' Courts), paras. 5.39-5.47. For stays pending appeal, see *Wyatt* v. *Wyatt* (1976), 6 Fam. Law 106, C.A.

[8] Guardianship of Minors Act 1971, s. 9, as amended by the Guardianship Act 1973, Sched. 2, and the Children Act 1975, Sched. 3, para. 75; Children Act 1975, s. 37 (3), (4). See further *post*, p. 384. In contrast to applications for custodianship under the Children Act, the child will not be required to have had his home with the custodian for any period of time beforehand.

Any order in favour of a parent may be varied or discharged on the application of either parent or, after a parent's death, by a guardian.[1] On hearing such an application, the court has greater latitude in admitting evidence which could have been adduced when the original order was made, for in custody disputes no relevant fact should be excluded.[2] The order will automatically terminate when the child reaches the age of 18.[3] .

Two further powers possessed by the court must be noted. First, if it appears that there are exceptional circumstances making it desirable that the child should be under the supervision of an independent person, the court may make a supervision order, placing him under the supervision of a local authority or probation officer. This may be desirable if a social worker has already been working with the child or another member of the family, or if there is a danger of harm to the child if it is not supervised. A supervision order may be varied or discharged at any time on the application of either parent, the child's guardian, or the probation officer or local authority having supervision. In any event, it will cease to have effect when the child reaches the age of 18.[4] Secondly, if there are exceptional circumstances making it impracticable or undesirable for a child under the age of 17 to be entrusted to either parent, it may be committed to the care of a local authority. It may be essential to exercise this power if there is a real possibility of harm if the child is left with either parent and there is no question of making a custodianship order. A care order may be varied or discharged on the application of the same persons as a supervision order; otherwise it will remain in force until the child reaches the age of 18 notwithstanding any claim by a parent or any other person.[5]

An order in favour of one of the parents may be made even though they are living with each other in the same household—a provision which is designed to ensure that, if the children are living with one of them at the time of the application, the other may remain with them till the determination of the case. But the order will cease to have effect if they continue to live with each other, or subsequently resume living with each other, for a continuous period of six months. The court has a discretion to determine whether a supervision order or a care order is to operate and remain in force in such circumstances.[6]

---

[1] Guardianship of Minors Act 1971, s. 9 (4). A grandparent may also apply for a variation of an order for acess in his favour: s. 14A (5).

[2] *Per* JENKINS, J., in *Re Wakeman*, [1947] Ch. 607, 613-614; [1947] 2 All E.R. 74, 78; *B.(B.)* v. *B. (M.)*, [1970] P. 103, 114; [1969] 1 All E.R. 891, 900.

[3] Guardianship of Minors Act 1971, s. 11A (3) (added by the Domestic Proceedings and Magistrates' Courts Act 1978, s. 37).

[4] Guardianship Act 1973, ss. 2 (2) and 3, as amended by the Domestic Proceedings and Magistrates' Courts Act 1978, s. 38 (2), (3) and Sched. 3, and the Children Act 1975, Sched. 3. See further Hoggett, *Parents and Children*, 53-55.

[5] *Ibid.*, ss. 2 (2) (b) and 4, as amended by the Children Act 1975, Sched. 3, and the Domestic Proceedings and Magistrates' Courts Act 1978, s. 38 (4) and Sched. 2. The local authority is the non-metropolitan county, metropolitan district or London borough in which the child is resident: *ibid.*, ss. 2 (8) and 4 (1).For the powers and duties of local authorities with respect to children in care, see *post*, p. 400. It should be noted that, if the child is placed in care in proceedings brought under the Guardianship of Minors Act, the Home Secretary may not authorise the child's emigration and, if the order is made by the High Court, the exercise of all powers is subject to any directions given by the court: Guardianship Act 1973, s. 4 (4).

[6] Guardianship Act 1973. s. 5A (added by the Domestic Proceedings and Magistrates' Courts Act 1978, s. 46). For the meaning of "living together in the same household", see *ante*, p. 225. For further discussion of the effects of continued cohabitation, see *post*, p. 306. An application under the Guardianship of Minors Act is unlikely in these circumstances.

At any time before the final adjudication the court may make an interim
order for the payment of maintenance for the child and, if there are special
circumstances justifying this, for custody and access. A magistrates' court
has similar powers if it refuses to make an order on the ground that the case
would be more conveniently dealt with by the High Court. An interim order
may not remain in force for more than three months or such shorter period as
the court specifies but it may be extended for not more than a further three
months. In any event it will cease to have effect when the court makes a final
order or dismisses the application.[1]

Failure to comply with an order for custody or access made in the High
Court or a county court is punishable with committal or sequestration until
the child is handed over to the person in question.[2] If the order is made in a
magistrates' court, the party refusing to carry it out may be ordered to pay a
sum not exceeding £1,000 or, alternatively, £50 for every day that he is in
default up to a maximum of £1,000, or he may be committed to custody until
he has complied with the order or for a period of two months whichever be
the shorter.[3]

Domestic Proceedings and Magistrates' Courts Act.—Magistrates' courts
have extensive jurisdiction to make orders with respect to any children of the
family under the age of 18 on hearing an application under Part I of this Act.

Child of the Family.—The definition of "child of the family" is now the
same in both this Act and the Matrimonial Causes Act 1973.[4] The term
comprises any child (including an illegitimate child) of both parties or
adopted by both parties and any other child who has been treated by both
parties as a child of their family other than a child who is being boarded out
with them by a local authority or voluntary organisation.[5]

Whether a child has been so treated is clearly a question of fact. Common
sense excludes some children, for example young lodgers, au pair girls, and
relations who are being looked after during their parents' temporary absence.
In other cases the payment of maintenance by the child's natural parents may
indicate that he has not become a member of the foster parents' family,
although this is obviously not decisive.[6] On the other hand, the fact that the
husband mistakenly believed the wife's illegitimate child to be his own will

---

[1] Guardianship Act 1973, ss. 2 (4)-(5E) and 5, as amended by the Domestic Proceedings and
Magistrates' Courts Act 1978, s. 45 and Scheds. 2 and 3. For the power to call for welfare
reports, see *ibid.*, s. 6, as amended by the Children Act 1975, s. 90 and Sched. 3, para. 81.

[2] R.S.C. O. 45, r. 5; County Court Rules, O. 25, r. 67.

[3] Guardianship of Minors Act 1971, s. 13 (1); Magistrates' Courts Act 1980, s. 63; *Re K.*,
[1977] 2 All E.R. 737. For the power to restrain the removal of a child from the jurisdiction, see
ante, pp. 298-300.

[4] Readers are warned that the definition under the Matrimonial Proceedings (Magistrates'
Courts) Act 1960, although superficially similar, was significantly different.

[5] Domestic Proceedings and Magistrates' Courts Act 1978, s. 88 (1); Children Act 1975,
Sched. 1, para. 3; Adoption Act 1976, s. 39 (1). A child could be illegitimate if he was born
before his parents' marriage and was not legitimated under his father's *lex domicilii*.

[6] See Law Com. No. 25 (Report on Financial Provision in Matrimonial Proceedings), paras.
23-32.

not prevent him from being a child of the family if the husband treated him as such.[1]

There are two sets of circumstances in which it may be legally impossible for a child to be treated as a child of the family. First, there must be a family of which the child may be treated as a member; consequently a child may not become a child of the family once the unit has been broken up by the spouses' separation. If, for example, the wife has an illegitimate child after the husband has left her but he agrees to treat it as his own, it is not a child of the family for the purpose of the two Acts.[2] Secondly, there is authority for the proposition that a child cannot be treated as a child of the family before it is born. In *A.* v. *A.*[3] the husband had married the wife knowing her to be pregnant and believing himself to be the father. Six days after the marriage the wife left him. When the child was born five months later, it was obviously not the husband's child but the daughter of a Pakistani with whom the mother had also had intercourse before the marriage. The only evidence that the husband had treated the child as his own was the fact that he had married the mother, but BAGNALL, J., held that treatment involved behaviour towards a person who must be in existence. This seems an extremely narrow interpretation of the Act engendered by the learned judge's desire to avoid hardship to the husband;[4] in other cases it could have the effect of working hardship on the wife and child, for it would prevent the court from making an order even though he knew all along that he was not the father. For these reasons it is urged that it should not be followed.

Orders that may be made.—Either spouse may apply for an order under section 1, 6 or 7 of the Act. The grounds for applications are much more important in connection with claims for maintenance and will be considered in detail when that subject is dealt with.[5] The court hearing an application may order the legal custody of any child of the family under the age of 18 to be given to either spouse or, if the child is not the child of them both, to a parent. It may also make an order for access in favour of either spouse or a parent or grandparent of the child. It may not give legal custody to more than one person, but it may direct that a party to the marriage shall retain such parental rights and duties as it may specify, in which case he or she will have those rights and duties jointly with the person given legal custody.[6] If they disagree about the child's welfare, either of them may apply to the court for its direction.[7] If the court is of opinion that legal custody ought to be given to some other person, it will be able to direct that he shall be treated as an

---

[1] *W. (R.J.)* v. *W. (S.J.),* [1972] Fam. 152; [1971] 3 All E.R. 303. *Cf.* the Matrimonial Causes Act 1973, s. 25 (3) (b) (*post*, pp. 590-591), and the Domestic Proceedings and Magistrates' Courts Act 1978, s. 3 (3) (b) (*post*, p. 587).

[2] *Re M.* (1980), 10 Fam. Law 184, C.A. *Cf. B.* v. *B. and F.*, [1969] P. 37; [1968] 3 All E.R. 232 (decided under the different definition contained in the Matrimonial Proceedings (Magistrates' Courts) Act 1960).

[3] [1974] Fam. 6; [1974] 1 All E.R. 755.

[4] Hardship need not follow because one of the facts that the court must take into consideration in deciding whether to make an order against a husband is whether he knew that the child was not his: see *post*, pp. 587 and 590-591.

[5] See *post*, pp. 498 *et seq.*

[6] Domestic Proceedings and Magistrates' Courts Act 1978, ss. 8 (2), (4) and 14.

[7] *Ibid.*, s. 13. Directions may be varied or revoked: s. 13 (2).

applicant for a custodianship order when the relevant sections of the Children Act 1975 come into force.[1]

As under the Guardianship of Minors Act, if a custody order is made, the court may further order the child to be placed under the supervision of a probation officer or the local authority if there are exceptional circumstances making this desirable.[2] Similarly, if there are exceptional circumstances making it impracticable or undesirable to entrust a child under the age of 17 to any individual, the court may commit the care of it to the local authority.[3] Both orders may remain in force until the child reaches the age of 18.[4]

The court has a general power to postpone the operation of an order for custody or access as it has under the Guardianship of Minors Act.[5] An order may be made even though the spouses are living with each other in the same household; this may be important if they are about to separate or if the court feels that a supervision order or a care order should be made as a matter of urgency. If the spouses continue to live with each other for a continuous period exceeding six months or, whether they are living together at the time or not, they subsequently resume living with each other for such a period, this will indicate that the reconciliation is likely to be permanent. There will therefore be no further use for an order giving the actual custody of the child to one of them and it will automatically cease to have effect. This argument, however, does not necessarily apply if legal custody is given to a parent who is not one of the spouses or if the court makes a supervision order or a care order. In these cases, therefore, the order will continue to have effect unless the court otherwise orders.[6]

The need to consider the welfare of the child means that the court is bound to consider what orders (if any) it should make in relation to children of the family irrespective of the spouses' own wishes and it may call upon a probation officer or the Director of Social Services of the local authority to make such reports as it considers necessary.[7] In order to protect the child and to avoid further proceedings, it must also consider how its powers should be exercised and may make an order for custody and access even though no ground for complaint is made out and an application for maintenance is dismissed.[8] The court's powers are, however, circumscribed in two respects. It may make no order at all if there is already in force an order in respect of the child's custody made by a court in England and Wales, and it may not make an order for access, a supervision order or a care order if the child is already in the care of a local authority.[9]

---

[1] Domestic Proceedings and Magistrates' Courts Act 1978, s. 8 (3). See further, *post*, p. 384.

[2] *Ibid.*, s. 9.

[3] *Ibid.*, s. 10. For the meaning of "local authority", see *ante*, p. 303, n. 5.

[4] *Ibid.*, ss. 9 (3) and 10 (6).

[5] *Ibid.*, s. 8 (6). See further *ante*, p. 302.

[6] *Ibid.*, s. 25 (1), (2). *Cf. post*, p. 508.

[7] *Ibid.*, s. 12 (3)-(7), (9). Notice of the proceedings must be given to a parent who is not a spouse (except the father of an illegitimate child against whom no affiliation order has been made) and the parent (including the father of an illegitimate child in any case) is entitled to appear and be represented: s. 12 (1), (2).

[8] *Ibid.*, s. 8 (1). If the court makes no order with respect to a child of the family but makes some other order under ss. 2, 6 or 7, either spouse may subsequently apply for an order in relation to the child: s. 21 (2).

[9] *Ibid.*, ss. 8 (7), 9 (4), 10 (8) and 14 (2). Nor may the court make an order for access if it makes a care order itself: ss. 10 (9) and 14 (2). But it can make an order with respect to custody

Interim Orders.—If there are special circumstances making it desirable to do so, the court may make an interim order for legal custody and access at any time before the final adjudication. It has a similar power if it refuses to make an order on the ground that the case would be more conveniently dealt with by the High Court. Interim orders may remain in force for the same periods as interim orders made under the Guardianship of Minors Act.[1]

Variation and Revocation of Orders.—Either spouse, or the parent of a child if he is not one of the spouses, may apply to have any order varied or revoked. The probation officer or local authority supervising the child may similarly apply to have a supervision order varied or revoked and the local authority may apply for the revocation of a care order. On hearing such an application the court has all the powers that it has on hearing the original application and consequently it could, for example, make a supervision order on hearing an application to vary an order for custody.[2] The rules relating to the admissibility of evidence available when the original order was made probably apply to applications to vary and revoke orders in relation to children made under the Domestic Proceedings and Magistrates' Courts Act as they do under the Guardianship of Minors Act.[3]

All orders automatically cease to have effect when the child reaches the age of 18.[4]

Enforcement of Orders.—Orders may be enforced in the same way as orders made by magistrates' courts under the Guardianship of Minors Act.[5]

Custody of Children in Matrimonial Causes.—The court[6] may make an order for the custody of any child of the family under the age of 18 in proceedings for divorce, nullity and judicial separation and also in proceedings brought under section 27 of the Matrimonial Causes Act 1973 on the ground of failure to provide reasonable maintenance.[7] The definition of "child of the family" is the same as that contained in the Domestic Proceedings and Magistrates' Courts Act 1978.[8]

Orders that may be made.—In the case of divorce, nullity and judicial separation, the court may make an order for custody and access in respect of

---

even though the child is in care: see *M.* v. *Humberside County Council,* [1979] Fam. 114, 119; [1979] 2 All E.R. 744, 748.

[1] Domestic Proceedings and Magistrates' Courts Act 1978, s. 19 (1), (5)-(9). The court may postpone the operation of an interim order (s. 19 (4)) and vary or revoke it (s. 21 (3)).

[2] *Ibid.*, ss. 14 (3) and 21. A care order may be revoked and not varied. A grandparent with access may also apply for variation of access: s. 14 (3) (a).

[3] See *ante*, p. 303.

[4] *Ibid.*, ss. 8 (5), 9 (3), 10 (6) and 14 (2).

[5] See *ante*, p. 304. See also the Domestic Proceedings and Magistrates' Courts Act 1978, s. 33. For the power to restrain the removal of a child from the jurisdiction, see *ante*, pp. 298-299.

[6] *I.e.* the court (High Court or county court) in which the matrimonial cause is proceeding. A county court judge may transfer an application for custody to the High Court if this seems desirable and in certain circumstances he must do so: Matrimonial Causes Act 1967, s. 2; Matrimonial Causes Rules 1977, rr. 80, 81 and 97.

[7] For proceedings under section 27, see *post*, p. 515.

[8] Matrimonial Causes Act 1973, s. 52 (1). See *ante*, pp. 304-305.

any child of the family under the age of 18 before, on or after the final decree. Alternatively, it may direct the child to be made a ward of court. The court may also make an order if the petition is dismissed.[1] In the case of proceedings under section 27, the court may make an order for custody only if it makes an order for financial provision and the custody order will remain in force only so long as the order for financial provision is in force and the child is under the age of 18.[2] In either case the court is not limited to giving custody or care and control to one of the spouses and may commit them to a third person. It may make a "split order" giving legal custody to one person and care and control to another.[3]

As in the case of proceedings under the Guardianship of Minors Act, if the court commits the care of the child to any person, it may order it to be placed under the supervision of a welfare officer or the local authority if there are exceptional circumstances making this desirable.[4] Similarly, if there are exceptional circumstances making it impracticable or undesirable to entrust a child under the age of 17 to any individual, the court may commit it to the care of a local authority.[5] Unless previously discharged, a care order remains in force until the child reaches the age of 18, but a supervision order automatically ceases to have effect if the order relating to care and control comes to an end.[6]

The parents and guardians of children of the family who are not the children of both spouses are protected by the provision that no order is to affect the rights over a child of any person (other than a party to the marriage) unless the child is the child of one of the parties (or a child adopted by one of them) and the person concerned has been made a party to the proceedings.[7]

Withholding of Decrees.—It is a notorious and lamentable fact that the persons most likely to suffer when a marriage breaks down are the children. As a means of ensuring that proper arangements have been made for them, the court must withhold a decree unless the provisions of section 41 of the Matrimonial Causes Act are complied with. These apply to any child of the family who is (i) under the age of 16 or (ii) under the age of 18 and in receipt of

---

[1] Matrimonial Causes Act 1973, ss. 42 (1) and 52 (1) (definition of "custody"). In the case of an order made on the dismissal of the petition, it must be made forthwith or within a reasonable time after the dismissal. The reason for dismissal is immaterial: *P. (L.E.)* v. *P. (J.M.)*, [1971] P. 318; [1971] 2 All E.R. 728 (marriage already dissolved abroad). The court may make an order with respect to a child born after the final decree: *Knowles* v. *Knowles*, [1962] P. 161; [1962] 1 All E.R. 659.

[2] *Ibid.*, s. 42 (2).

[3] See *Wakeham* v. *Wakeham*, [1954] 1 All E.R. 434, C.A., *ante*, p. 294. For the uncertain nature of these orders, see Cretney, *Principles of Family Law*, 3rd Ed., 439. For the removal of a child from the jurisdiction, see *ante*, pp. 298-300.

[4] Matrimonial Causes Act 1973, s. 44, as amended by the Children Act 1975, Sched. 3. Supervision orders were made in 3.5% of the cases examined in Eekelaar and Clive, *Custody after Divorce*, para. 13.15.

[5] *Ibid.*, s. 43. Care orders were made in only 0.4% of the cases examined by Eekelaar and Clive: *op. cit.*, Table 34. Whilst a care order is in force, neither a parent nor any other person may claim the child. For the powers and duties of local authorities with respect to children in care, see *post*, p. 400. If a care order is made in proceedings brought under the Matrimonial Causes Act, the Home Secretary may not authorise the child's emigration and the exercise of all powers is subject to any directions given by the court: *ibid.*, s. 43 (5).

[6] *Ibid.*, ss. 43 (4) and 44 (1). Hence if the proceedings were brought under s. 27, a supervision order (but not a care order) will terminate if the order for financial provision comes to an end.

[7] *Ibid.*, s. 42 (5).

instruction at an educational establishment or undergoing training for a trade, profession or vocation (whether or not he is also in-gainful employment), or (iii) any other child of the family if the court so directs on the ground that special circumstances make this desirable in the child's interests. The last limb enables the court to ensure that provision is made for, say, a mentally or physically handicapped child over 16 or a child over 18 who is still receiving education or training.

The court may not pronounce a decree absolute of divorce or nullity or a decree of judicial separation unless it has by order declared that it is satisfied:

(a) that there are no such children; *or*
(b) that the only children to whom the section applies are those named in the order and that
   (i) arrangements for their welfare have been made and are satisfactory or the best that can be devised in the circumstances; *or*
   (ii) it is impracticable for the party or parties appearing before the court to make any such arrangements; *or*
(c) that there are circumstances making it desirable that the decree should be made absolute (or granted) without delay notwithstanding that there are or may be children of the family to whom the section applies and the court cannot make a declaration in accordance with (b) above.

In the case of (c) the court must not make the declaration unless it obtains a satisfactory undertaking from either or both of the parties to bring the question of the arrangements before the court within a specified time. "Welfare" includes custody, education and financial provision. ~ s 41 (6)

Too rigid an application of these provisions could obviously work hardship in many cases. Any arrangements proposed can be satisfactory only if they are reasonably permanent,[1] so that any dispute over custody would have to be resolved before the court could make a declaration. Again, where a child is to live may depend on one party's remarriage or the financial provision to be ordered at a later stage and a minute examination of the spouses' income and assets could cause intolerable delays. Consequently the statutory requirements must be interpreted sensibly. If the parties can agree on the provision to be made for a child, the court is not required to make a detailed enquiry into the terms proposed unless it has reason to believe that the sum is inadequate or that a significantly better order could be obtained, and it is immaterial whether the money will come from a parent, a third person or supplementary benefit.[2] If there is a contest over custody which is likely to be resolved within a short period, the judge can defer making an order under section 41. In other cases "the primary purpose of [the section] is to ensure that the judge is seised of the question of the interests of the children",[3] and the proper procedure will be to make one of the orders set out in paragraphs (b) and (c) and give directions for a further hearing.[4]

Any decree absolute of divorce or nullity or decree of judicial separation s 41(3) made in the absence of such a declaration will be void. Consequently if a

---

[1] *McKernan* v. *McKernan* (1970), 114 Sol. Jo. 284.
[2] *Cook* v. *Cook*, [1978] 3 All E.R. 1009, C.A.
[3] *Per* ORMROD , L.J., in *A.* v. *A.*, [1979] 2 All E.R. 493, 496, C.A.
[4] *A.* v. *A.*, (*supra*).

party remarries on the faith of such a decree absolute of divorce, the second marriage will itself be void. But if the declaration is made, no one may challenge the validity of the decree on the ground that the conditions prescribed were not fulfilled.[1]

It is very doubtful how far the object of these provisions is achieved in practice.[2] The petitioner is bound to state what arrangements are proposed for all the relevant children, on which the respondent may file a written statement of his views if he wishes.[3] If the decree is pronounced under the special procedure (as it will be in the vast majority of cases), the registrar fixes an appointment for consideration of the arrangements by the judge unless the court thinks this inappropriate in the particular circumstances:[4] what is not known is when the appointment is in fact dispensed with and how often judges have an opportunity of discussing the arrangements with the parties. The evidence indicates that in over 90 per cent of all cases the proposal is that the existing arrangements should continue and that the court expresses satisfaction with them.[5] Before expressing satisfaction or making an order the court may call for a welfare officer's report: obviously it is more likely to do so if the proceedings are contested. In exceptional cases it may order the child to be separately represented and appoint the Official Solicitor or any other person willing to act as guardian *ad litem*.[6]

Variation and Discharge of Orders.—All orders relating to custody, care, access, and supervision are made "from time to time" and may be varied, suspended, revived and discharged.[7] They all automatically come to an end on the child's eighteenth birthday.

Declaration of Unfitness.—The court may include in a decree absolute of divorce or a decree of judicial separation a declaration that either party is unfit to have the custody of the children of the family. This means that, if he (or she) is a parent of any child of the family, he is not entitled as of right to the custody or guardianship of it on the death of the other parent.[8] If he then seeks custody, the burden is on him to prove that his conduct has so changed that he is now a fit and proper person to have it.[9] Consequently the court will

---

[1] Matrimonial Causes Act 1973, s. 41 (3).

[2] The best analysis of the operation of the law in practice is to be found in Eekelaar and Clive, *Custody after Divorce.* For a less extensive study, see Maidment, 6 Fam. Law 195, 236. A valuable study was carried out earlier by J.C. Hall: Law Com. Working Paper No. 15. See also Davis and Murch, 7 Fam. Law 71.

[3] Matrimonial Causes Rules 1977, rr. 8 (2) and 50 and Form 4.

[4] *Ibid.*, r. 48 (4).

[5] Eekelaar and Clive, *op. cit.*, c. 3; Maidment, *loc. cit.* Eekelaar and Clive question whether the best use is being made of welfare services: paras. 13.25-13.27.

[6] Matrimonial Causes Rules 1977, rr. 95 and 115. See Hoggett, *Parents and Children*, 62-64; Graham Hall, 7 Fam. Law 101; Maidment, *ibid.* 246. If custody is contested, *quaere* whether evidence which could have been adduced at the trial may be given to controvert express findings; the point was left open by SALMON and FENTON ATKINSON, L.JJ., in *F.* v. *F.*, [1968] 2 All E.R. 946, 950, C.A. Evidence may be adduced if it has become available only since the trial or if it relates to matters not then in issue.

[7] Matrimonial Causes Act 1973, ss. 42 (6), (7), 43 (7) and 44 (5).

[8] *Ibid.*, s. 42 (3), (4); *Buckley* v. *Buckley*, [1977] 3 All E.R. 544.

[9] *Webley* v. *Webley* (1891), 64 L.T. 839; *S.* v. *S.*, [1949] P. 269; [1949] 1 All E.R. 285 n.

not cast such a stigma upon a parent unless a very strong case is made out against him.[1] It has been made where the husband has been guilty of ill-treating his children[2] and where he has forced his wife to submit to grossly depraved and perverted sexual practices;[3] on the other hand it has been refused where the grounds upon which it was sought were that he had committed adultery and failed to support his children for ten years.[4]

Concurrent Orders.—It is obvious that the various proceedings open to parents may produce a clash in jurisdiction. One spouse may be taking proceedings in one court whilst the other is taking proceedings in another, or an application may be made in one court whilst an order in respect of the same child is still in force in another.[5]

If the High Court is already seised of the matter, the accepted view is that no other court should interfere.[6] The converse case, where proceedings are brought in the High Court when another order is already is force, presents more problems. In matrimonial proceedings (for example, divorce) the High Court will make an order with respect to custody and access notwithstanding the existence of a magistrates' order because of the desirability of dealing with all the questions relating to the family together.[7] If wardship proceedings are brought, STAMP, J., held in *Re P.*[8] that, although he undoubtedly had jurisdiction to hear the case, he should exercise it only in exceptional circumstances. This could be done if, for example, the case showed special complexity,[9] if the jurisdiction of the High Court were more extensive, efficacious or convenient, or if it were necessary to supplement the magistrates' jurisdiction by giving relief which they had no power to give. Thus in *Re H.(G.J.)*[10] the same judge continued the wardship of a child and issued an injunction prohibiting the father from taking it out of the jurisdiction as a means of giving effect to a magistrates' order awarding custody to the mother. *Obiter* doubts were cast on this principle by DUNN, J., in *Re D.*,[11] but it is submitted that it is a sound one. Parties should be discouraged from instituting a second set of proceedings and, whenever possible, they should apply to the magistrates for a variation or discharge of their order or appeal against it.

---

[1] *Per* JEUNE, J., in *Woolnoth* v. *Woolnoth* (1902), 86 L.T. 598, 599.

[2] *Webley* v. *Webley, (supra).*

[3] *S.* v. *S.*, *(supra)*. See also *Hitchings* v. *Hitchings* (1892), 67 L.T. 530.

[4] *Woolnoth* v. *Woolnoth, (supra).*

[5] Before the creation of the Family Division there could also be a conflict of jurisdiction between the Chancery and Probate Divisions of the High Court (*e.g.*, if one of the parents of a ward of court took divorce proceedings).

[6] *R.* v. *Middlesex Justices; ex parte Bond*, [1933] 2 K.B. 1, C.A. But if magistrates are already hearing a summons when divorce proceedings are commenced, they can properly make an order to prevent the delay which would otherwise occur: *per* ORMROD, L.J., in *F.* v. *F.* (1976), 6 Fam. Law 208, C.A.

[7] *Re D.*, [1973] Fam. 179, 193; [1973] 2 All E.R. 993, 1005-1006. Presumably this practice also applies if matrimonial proceedings are brought in a county court.

[8] [1967] 2 All E.R. 229.

[9] See *Re P. (A.J.)*, [1968] 1 W.L.R. 1976, and *cf. Re D.*, *(supra)*.

[10] [1966] 1 All E.R. 952.

[11] [1977] Fam. 158, 163; [1977] 3 All E.R. 481, 485. See Lowe and White, *Wards of Court*, 222-229.

In which court a parent chooses to seek an order is a question of practical expediency. If proceedings are pending in the divorce court or in a magistrates' court under the Domestic Proceedings and Magistrates' Courts Act, it is clearly best that all matters relating to the family should be dealt with together in the same court. If no other proceedings are pending (as may be the case if the applicant has no ground for taking them), he will normally choose to proceed in a county court or magistrates' court under the Guardianship of Minors Act unless he makes the child a ward of court in order to obtain a comprehensive order relating to other aspects of the child's upbringing or to invoke the High Court's power to make supplementary orders.[1]

C. SECULAR AND RELIGIOUS EDUCATION

1. PARENTS' DUTY TO SECURE THE EDUCATION OF THEIR CHILDREN[2]

Although common law and equity both recognised the parents' moral and social duty to give their children an education suitable to their station, neither system provided the legal means for enforcing it.[3] It was not till 1870 that Parliament took steps to see that a sufficient number of public elementary schools should be built, and finally, in the Elementary Education Act of 1876, placed all parents under a duty to ensure that their children should receive "efficient elementary instruction in reading, writing and arithmetic". Now, under the Education Act of 1944, the parent of every child between the ages of five and sixteen[4] must ensure that he receives "efficient full-time education suitable to his age, ability and aptitude either by regular attendance at school or otherwise".[5] Parents who fail to perform this duty or whose children fail to attend school regularly are liable to be prosecuted and the local education authority can take care proceedings with respect to the child.[6]

Parents have never been under any legal duty to provide their children with religious education. In the past courts have put pressure on them indirectly to do so (for example, by refusing custody to an atheistic parent), but in view of the attitude towards the absence of religious belief which society takes today, it is doubtful whether this policy is now pursued.

---

[1] *Cf. T.* v. *T.*, [1968] 3 All E.R. 321.

[2] See Bevan, *Children*, 432-444.

[3] *Hodges* v. *Hodges* (1796), Peake, Add. Cas. 79.

[4] If the child's sixteenth birthday falls between 1st September and 31st January, inclusive, he remains of compulsory school age until the end of the spring term; in other cases until the end of May: Education Act 1962, s. 9; Education (School-leaving Dates) Act 1976, s. 1.

[5] Education Act 1944, ss. 35 and 36; Raising of the School Leaving Age Order 1972, S.I. 1972 No. 444. If the child is living with both parents, the statutory duty is cast on both of them: *Plunkett* v. *Alker*, [1954] 1 Q.B. 420; [1954] 1 All E.R. 396.

[6] *Ibid.*, ss. 37, 39, 40 and 40A, as amended by the Education (Miscellaneous Provisions) Acts 1948 and 1953 and the Children and Young Persons Acts 1963 and 1969. For care proceedings, see *post*, pp. 390-394; Bevan, *op.cit.*, 438-439.

2. PARENTS' POWER TO DETERMINE THEIR CHILDREN'S RELIGIOUS AND SECULAR EDUCATION

Problems of secular and religious education almost invariably go together. Disputes over religious education usually arise out of "mixed" marriages or, more rarely, out of one parent's changing his religious belief after the marriage. Disputes over secular education reflect the same problem because they usually arise out of one parent's desire to have the child educated at a school under the direction of a particular religious sect or order, and there are few reported cases in which the dispute has been over two types of secular education *simpliciter*. The following discussion will therefore be confined to the determination of religious education; but it should be remembered that disputes over secular education will be resolved according to the same principles and that in all cases the court's first consideration must be for the welfare of the child.

In strict legal theory a minor cannot choose his own religion and certainly cannot determine what form of education he is to have.[1] Subject to certain exceptions, both at common law and in equity the father had the absolute right to determine the form of his legitimate minor children's education and his wishes had to be respected after his death.[2] After the passing of the Guardianship of Infants Act in 1886, however, the courts began to pay more attention to the welfare of the child than to the father's wishes,[3] and the Guardianship of Infants Act of 1925 went further by making it obligatory for the court to put the child's welfare first.[4] The Guardianship Act of 1973 has now given the mother powers equal to those of the father in this respect,[5] and today the court must consider both parents' wishes unless they are displaced by considerations of the child's welfare.

The power to choose the type of education that an illegitimate child should have and the religious belief in which it should be brought up is vested *prima facie* in the mother.[6]

Even if the court refuses to enforce a parent's right to the custody or care and control of a child, it has power to make an order to secure that his wishes with respect to its religious upbringing shall be observed.[7] Similarly a local authority is not to cause a child who is in their care under a care order or over whom they have assumed parental rights to be brought up in any religious creed other than that in which he would otherwise have been brought up.[8]

Disputes over Religious Education.—The change of emphasis from the almost absolute enforcement of the parent's right to choose his children's religion (which was forfeited in far fewer circumstances than his right to

---

[1] *Re Carroll*, [1931] 1 K.B. 317, 336, C.A. *Cf. Re May*, [1917] 2 Ch. 126.

[2] *Andrews* v. *Salt* (1873), 8 Ch. App. 622.

[3] See the remarks of VISCOUNT CAVE in *Ward* v. *Laverty*, [1925] A.C. 101, 108, H.L.; *J.* v. *C.*, [1970] A.C. 668; [1969] 1 All E.R. 788, H.L.

[4] *Re Collins*, [1950] Ch. 498; [1950] 1 All E.R. 1057, C.A.

[5] See *ante*, p. 281.

[6] Children Act 1975, s. 85 (7) (*ante*, p. 281). The principle was laid down in *Re Carroll*, (*supra*).

[7] Custody of Children Act 1891, s. 4. This does not apply if the parent has for any reason lost the right to determine the child's religious education (*vide infra*). In any case the making of the order is permissive not obligatory.

[8] Child Care Act 1980, ss. 4 (3) and 10 (3).

custody) to the paramount consideration of the child's welfare has been so much more marked than in the case of his rights to custody that many cases decided before 1925 are no longer of any real authority. Nevertheless some are still of help in illustrating the principles which the court will bear in mind in solving disputes of this kind.

No Bias in Favour of any one Faith.—The courts will never attempt to adjudicate between the merits of different faiths, whether they be different sects of the Christian church or non-Christian religions[1] although, as we have seen,[2] the social and other consequences of bringing a child up in a particular faith may be relevant in deciding who is to have custody. It is very doubtful whether the courts still favour some form of religious instruction to none at all.[3]

Child with Fixed Beliefs.—If the child is old enough to have developed fixed religious convictions of its own, the court will never attempt to disturb them. This is illustrated by *Stourton* v. *Stourton*.[4] A boy aged ten (who appears to have been unusually precocious) had been brought up for the previous five or six years as a member of the Church of England. His father had been a Roman Catholic and the boy himself had been baptised according to the rites of that Church. Proceedings were then taken to have him made a ward of court and directions were sought with respect to his religious education. The Court of Appeal in Chancery was of the opinion that it was now too late to change his Anglican beliefs. In the words of KNIGHT BRUCE, L.J.:[5]

> "He spoke ... in a manner convincing me that the Protestant seed sown in his mind has taken such hold, that if we are to suppose it to contain tares, they cannot be gathered up without great danger of rooting up also the wheat with them. Upon much consideration, I am of the opinion that the child's tranquillity and health, his temporal happiness and, if that can exist apart from his spiritual welfare, his spiritual welfare also, are too likely now to suffer importantly from an endeavour at effacing his Protestant impressions, not to render any such attempt unsafe and improper."

But the principle of *Stourton* v. *Stourton* will be applied only when a change of religious education is fraught with such consequences. When there is no such danger, the court will not let the child determine its own education against the express wishes of those who have a right to determine it themselves, and no encouragement to begin proselytising will be given to those who have the custody of a child of tender years. In *Hawksworth* v. *Hawksworth*[6] the Court of Appeal in Chancery issued a warning against

---

[1] *Re Carroll*, [1931] 1 K.B. 317, at pp. 323, 336, 347, 353, C.A. This view has been expressed in many other cases.

[2] *Ante*, p. 296.

[3] See *H.*v. *H.* (1975), 119 Sol. Jo. 590 (custody of boy aged five given to agnostic mother and not to father who was practising Muslim).

[4] (1857), 8 De G. M. & G. 760. See also *Ward*v. *Laverty*, [1925] A.C. 101, H.L.; *Re Newton*, [1896] 1 Ch. 740, C.A.; *Re Meades* (1871), I.R. 5 Eq. 98.

[5] At pp. 767-768. The fact that it is *per se* irrelevant that the child has already been baptised or otherwise initiated in a different religion is further illustrated by *D'Alton* v. *D'Alton* (1878), 4 P.D. 87.

[6] (1871), 6 Ch. App. 539. See also *Davis* v. *Davis* (1862), 10 W.R. 245.

extending *Stourton* v. *Stourton* and ordered that a girl aged eight, who was being brought up as a Protestant, should be brought up as a Roman Catholic in accordance with her father's wishes, as she had not yet formed such definite opinions that to change them would work to her prejudice.

As in the case of disputed custody, the court will interview the child in suitable cases, not in order to give effect to its wishes but to discover whether its opinions are so set as to make a change of education dangerous.[1]

Religion and Custody.—It has already been pointed out that problems of actual custody and religious upbringing may go hand in hand.[2] In cases of this sort, if the child is too young to have developed any fixed religious convictions, the court will generally consider the question of custody first and let that solve the question of religious education. It will also try to secure that all the children are brought up in the same religion in order to avoid creating a division of faiths in the same family.[3]

Parents' Acquiescence in a Particular Education.—Before 1926 there were many cases in which the father's acquiescence in his children's being brought up in a different religion from his own was treated as an "abdication" of his right so as to disentitle him from later insisting on their being educated in his own faith. In most of these cases the court would have refused to enforce his right on the further ground that the child had already acquired fixed ideas of its own, but this was not always so, as is shown by *Hill* v. *Hill*.[4] A Roman Catholic father had agreed that his daughters should be brought up as Protestants, had permitted his wife (who was a Protestant) to have them both baptised as Protestants and to appoint a Protestant governess for them, and had himself attempted to give them no religious instruction at all. In his will he nevertheless appointed a Roman Catholic to act with his wife as guardian and directed that the children should be brought up in the Roman Catholic faith. Although the elder girl was aged only seven at the time of the suit, the court held that the father had waived his right to determine their religious education and directed that they should be brought up as Protestants.

Today one parent's acquiescence in the other's bringing a child up in a different religion may still be important in resolving a question of religious education when the child is too young to have fixed opinions of its own and no dispute over custody arises. The observation of LINDLEY, L.J., in *Re McGrath*[5] that, where the father is indifferent and his children are in fact being brought up in a particular religion, it is not in their interest to change it, is no less true now than it was in 1893.

Agreements relating to Education and Religion.—Like agreements relating to custody, agreements as to religious and secular education are contrary to public policy and therefore void. The parent is given the right to determine his children's education for their benefit and not his own, and

[1] *Stourton* v. *Stourton*, (*ante*), at p. 772.
[2] *Ante*, pp. 296-297.
[3] *Re Clarke* (1882), 21 Ch. D. 817; *Re Newton*, [1896] 1 Ch. 740, C.A.; *Ward* v. *Laverty*, [1925] A.C. 101, H.L. For a case in which this was not done, see *Re W.*, [1907] 2 Ch. 557, C.A.
[4] (1862), 31 L.J.Ch. 505.
[5] [1893] 1 Ch. 143, 151, C.A.

consequently he cannot divest himself of it.[1] This is particularly important because of the practice of some churches of insisting in the case of "mixed" marriages that the parents should give an undertaking to have all the children brought up in that particular faith. Such a promise, however, might be evidence of the promisor's having abdicated his right to choose his children's religion[2] and consequently the court might give effect to the marital agreement on this ground. As in the case of custody, an undertaking relating to secular or religious education contained in a separation agreement may be enforced provided it is for the child's benefit.[3]

Means of determining Disputes.—As a parent with custody has the power to determine a child's education, any court with jurisdiction to do so may effectively direct what education the child shall have by making a custody order. Either parent of a legitimate child may also apply to the court for an order under section 1 of the Guardianship Act 1973.[4] It is more usual, however, for directions for education to be made by the Family Division under its inherent jurisdiction if the child is made a ward of court. On divorce, nullity and judicial separation, the court is expressly empowered to make orders with respect to the education of a child of the family,[5] but there is no power to make such an order in proceedings under section 27 of the Matrimonial Causes Act.

D. MISCELLANEOUS PARENTAL RIGHTS AND POWERS

Punishment.—A parent may lawfully inflict moderate and reasonable corporal punishment for the purpose of correcting a child or punishing an offence.[6] Whether or not the punishment is reasonable must depend upon all the facts of the case, and in particular the age and strength of the child and the nature and degree of the punishment. If it goes beyond what is reasonable, it is unlawful and would therefore render the parent criminally liable for assault.[7] Only a parent or person *in loco parentis* has this right and it has been held to be unlawful for an elder brother to administer corporal punishment where both sons were living with their father and consequently the elder could not be considered as being *in loco parentis* to the younger.[8]

Consent of Medical Treatment.—Section 8 of the Family Law Reform Act 1969 now provides that a minor over the age of 16 may effectively consent to any surgical, medical or dental treatment without his parent's or guardian's

---

[1] *Andrews* v. *Salt* (1873), 8 Ch. App. 622, 636-637; *Re Agar-Ellis* (1878), 10 Ch. D. 49, at pp. 60, 71, C.A.; Children Act 1975, s. 85 (2).

[2] *Per* MELLISH , L.J., in *Andrews* v. *Salt*, (*supra*), at p. 637.

[3] Guardianship Act 1973, s. 1 (2). See *ante*, p. 288.

[4] See *ante*, p. 282.

[5] Matrimonial Causes Act 1973, s. 42 (1). Such orders may always be varied from time to time: s. 42 (6).

[6] *R* v. *Hopley* (1860), 2 F. & F. 202; *R.* v. *Woods* (1921), 85 J.P. 272.

[7] *R.* v. *Derriviere* (1969), 53 Cr. App. Rep. 637, C.A. If the child died, the parent could be guilty of manslaughter or even murder: see *post*, pp. 320-321.

[8] *R.* v. *Woods*, (*supra*). For the power of school authorities to inflict corporal punishment, see Street, *Torts*, 6th Ed., 87-88; Bevan, *Children*, 211-212.

concurrence. Strangely enough, however, there is no firm authority laying down whose consent is necessary for treatment of a child under this age. Normally, of course, the question will be academic because no legal consequences are likely to flow from giving the treatment: in any case if the treatment were necessary to preserve the child's life, the person giving it could plead necessity. Serious problems could arise, however, if the consent of either parent or child was withheld or not sought and the treatment was not essential for the child, however desirable it might be for him or for somebody else. This might occur, for example, if a surgeon were asked to perform an abortion on a girl aged 15 or wished to transplant a young child's kidney to a twin. If he failed to obtain legally effective consent, he could lay himself open to an action for battery by the child or loss of services by the parent[1] or a prosecution for one of the graver forms of assault.

If the child is old enough to understand the nature of the treatment or operation in question and the risks which he may run from it, it is submitted that it his consent that is needed. If he gives it, his parent ought not to be able to sue for loss of services[2] and the medical practitioner should have an absolute defence to a charge of assault; if he withholds it, the latter seems to have no defence to an action for battery brought by the child. In the absence of authority, however, it must be conceded that the doctor would be prudent to take no action without the consent of both except in cases of emergency where treatment is necessary in the patient's interest. Even then, if time permits, it might be wise to obtain further protection by taking care proceedings or having the child made a ward of court: the local authority or court would then be guided by what is in the best interests of the child in deciding whether the treatment should be given. If the child is too young to be able to give his consent, there can be no real doubt that his parent's consent must be effective to give the doctor protection, unless the treatment is clearly contrary to the child's interests. As LORD HODSON has said, "a parent is not guilty of assault if he physically interferes with his child … for therapeutic reasons".[3] Whether this would apply if the operation were necessary in somebody else's interest (for example, the kidney transplant mentioned above) is much more controversial. In such a case someone has to take the decision whether or not the operation is to take place and the best person to take it is the parent, properly guided by medical advice. If a reasonable parent, weighing the risks to the donor against the advantage to the other, would give his consent, all concerned should be given legal protection.[4]

Further difficulty arises if the treatment is not necessary for the cure of an existing disease but will have lasting and irreversible results. Even though the parent agrees to it, it will be open to anyone else to ward the child when the court may forbid the treatment if it considers that it will not be for the child's welfare. In *Re D.*[5] a gynaecologist intended permanently to sterilize a

---

[1] See *post*, pp. 329-332.

[2] See *post*, p. 331.

[3] *S. v. S.*, [1972] A.C. 24, 57; [1970] 3 All E.R. 107, 123.

[4] For a discussion of the problem generally, see Skegg, *Consent to Medical Procedures on Minors*, 36 M.L.R. 370, and *Justification for Medical Procedures performed without Consent*, 90 L.Q.R. 512, at 519-523; Foulkes, 120 New L.J. 194; Bevan, *Children*, p. 25, n. 16.

[5] [1976] Fam. 185; [1976] 1 All E.R. 326. For wardship proceedings, see *post*, pp. 374 *et seq*. See also Bissett-Johnson and Everton, 126 New L.J. 104.

mentally handicapped girl aged eleven (with her parent's consent) to prevent
the possibility of her having children in the future. An educational psy-
chologist concerned with the case then made the child a ward of court. As
HEILBRON, J., came to the conclusion that there was no foreseeable risk of an
unwanted pregnancy and that the girl would have sufficient understanding to
be able to make up her own mind on the matter when she was older, she
ordered that the operation should not take place.

Child's Services.—Both parents of a legitimate child and the mother of an
illegitimate child are entitled to the domestic services of their children under
the age of 18 actually living with them as part of their family. The legal
enforcement of this right is of course impossible; its significance lies in the
fact that it provides the parent with his only common law remedy against a
stranger for interference with parental rights.[1]

Child's Name.—By convention a legitimate child takes his father's
surname. A child of tender years has no power to change his name,[2] but both
parents acting in agreement can apparently do so and, after the death of
either, the survivor probably has a similar power provided that any other
guardian concurs. In practice difficulty arises if a mother with actual custody
of the child remarries (or takes the surname of the man with whom she is
living) and wishes the child to take her own new surname.

At common law the fact that the mother was given custody by a court
order did not entitle her to change the child's name unilaterally because this
would have infringed the residual rights of the father as natural guardian.
Nor could the father do so because this would have affected the rights of the
mother as custodian.[3] Now that the Guardianship Act has given the mother
the same rights and authority as the father, the same result must follow if sole
custody is given to the father. Furthermore, as both parties have always had
to agree to any change and the purpose of the rule is to try to strengthen the
links between them and the child, it is submitted that the statutory power
given to each parent to exercise parental authority without the positive assent
of the other[4] should not apply in this situation. So far as proceedings for
divorce, nullity and judicial separation are concerned, any order giving a
parent custody or care and control must now provide that no step shall be
taken to change the child's name without the consent of the other parent or
the leave of a judge.[5]

In any case, if either parent (or anyone else) tries to change the child's surname without the other's concurrence, the latter may apply for an injunction
to restrain him. As in all other disputes involving children, the court must be

---

[1] See *post*, pp. 329 *et seq.*

[2] *Re T.*, [1963] Ch. 238, 241; [1962] 3 All E.R. 970, 971. It is very doubtful whether any minor
has such a power even though he is no longer of tender years.

[3] *Re T.*, (*supra*); *Y.* v. *Y.*, [1973] Fam. 147; [1973] 2 All E.R. 574.

[4] See *ante*, p. 281.

[5] Matrimonial Causes Rules 1977, r. 92 (8). The court making the order may direct
otherwise. The execution and enrolment of a deed poll merely provide evidence of the
executant's intention to be known by a different name and have no other legal significance. For
the conditions to be satisfied if a parent wishes to enrol a deed poll relating to the change of a
child's name, see the Enrolment of Deeds (Change of Name) Regulations 1949, r. 8, as amended
by the Enrolment of Deeds (Change of Name) (Amendment) Regulations 1969; *Practice
Direction*, [1977] 3 All E.R. 451.

guided by what is in the child's best interest. There is no doubt, however, that the cases show two marked differences of approach. The earlier view was that a change of name was an important matter which should be permitted only when the child's welfare demanded that this step be taken.[1] Later cases, on the other hand, suggested that it was relatively unimportant and that fathers were tending to lay too much emphasis on it when the purpose was to avoid embarrassment and there was no intention of destroying their links with their children.[2] The most recent case in the Court of Appeal, *W.* v. *A.*,[3] recognizing this irreconcilable difference, has come down decisively in favour of the original view.

In many cases the mother's motive in wishing to change the child's name will probably be mixed. She may wish to disguise the fact that she has already had an unsuccessful marriage; vindictiveness may lead her to try to cut the father out of the child's life altogether; she may feel that the child will be better intergrated into the new family if it bears the same name as herself, her new husband and any other children. When considering the child's welfare, the first of these considerations will normally be irrelevant. The second will be justified only if this is desirable for some other reason, for example if the name had notorious associations owing to the father's conduct. The third is obviously laudable but against it must be weighed the need to try to keep an association between the child and its father and the fact that the change of name may itself weaken such links as there are. All the facts must be taken into account, including the embarrassment that the child itself may suffer if it bears a different name from the other members of the family, the stability of the mother's new marriage, and the child's need to be satisfied about its own background. In *W.* v. *A.* the Court of Appeal refused to reverse a decision declining to permit a change of name even though the child was emigrating to Australia with his mother and stepfather; if this case is to be followed, it may prove to be more difficult to obtain a judge's leave than it has been in the past unless, perhaps, the father has disappeared from the scene entirely. It is ironic that a mother who changes the child's name unlawfully may thereby gain an advantage because, if it has been used for some time, it may not be in the child's interest to change it back again.[4]

An illegitimate child normally takes his mother's surname, but he may, of course, be known by his father's. So far as registration of the birth is concerned, the father's name may be entered only at the joint request of both parents or at the request of the mother alone provided that she produces a statutory declaration made by the man acknowledging himself to be the father or a certified copy of an affiliation order naming him as the putative father. If she relies on an affiliation order, the child himself must also consent if he is over the age of 16.[5] If the birth of an illegitimate child has been registered with no father named, it may be re-registered showing the father's name if one of these conditions is satisfied.[6]

[1] *Re T.*, (*supra*); *Y.*v. *Y.*, (*supra*); *Re W.G.*, (1976), 6 Fam. Law 210, C.A.

[2] *R.* v. *R.*, [1978] 2 All E.R. 33, C.A.; *D.* v. *B.*, [1979] Fam. 38; [1979] 1 All E.R. 92, C.A.

[3] [1981] Fam. 14; [1981] 1 All E.R. 100, C.A., following *L.* v. *F.* (1978), *Times*, 1st August. *Quaere* whether the mother may initially register the child in a name different from the husband's. She should be able to do so only in the same circumstances as she can change it, but see 97 L.Q.R. 197.

[4] As in *Y.*v. *Y.*, (*supra*).

[5] Births and Deaths Registration Act 1953, s. 10, as amended by the Family Law Reform Act 1969, s. 27 (1), and the Children Act 1975, s. 93 (1).

[6] Births and Deaths Registration Act 1953, s. 10A, added by the Children Act 1975, s. 93 (2).

E. PROTECTION

1. PHYSICAL PROTECTION

The common law duty to afford physical protection to a child is partly a reflection of the obvious natural duty, but it is also an example of the general proposition that if anyone willingly undertakes to look after another who is incapable of looking after himself, there is a duty to perform that task properly. Consequently the duty does not necessarily last till the child comes of age: it would be absurd, for example, to say that a crippled mother is under any duty to protect a healthy son aged 17. Thus in *R. v. Shepherd*,[1] where a girl aged 18, who normally lived away in service but returned home from time to time, died there in childbirth, it was held that her mother was under no duty to send for a midwife because the girl was beyond the age of childhood and was entirely emancipated. Conversely the duty to afford physical protection may continue after the child comes of age if he is unable to look after himself owing to some physical or mental disability.[2] Moreover, since the obligation arises out of the assumption of responsibility for protection, a similar duty may be owed to a step-child or foster child.[3] Whether or not the duty exists in any given case, therefore, is a question of fact depending upon the necessity of protection and the assumption of responsibility.[4]

Death of the Child.—In accordance with the general principles of the law relating to homicide, if a child's death is caused or accelerated by a breach of this duty to protect, the parent (or any other person owing the duty) may be guilty of manslaughter. There is a difference in this respect between an act of commission and an omission. In the former case it is sufficient to establish an unlawful act and thus a parent will be guilty of manslaughter if he beats a child so severely that it dies.[5] In the case of omission, however, the Court of Appeal, expressing its distaste for constructive manslaughter, held in *R. v. Lowe*[6] that the parent will not be guilty unless he has shown a degree of negligence amounting to recklessness. It must be proved, therefore, that he was indifferent to an obvious risk of injury to the child's health, welfare or safety or that he actually foresaw the risk but determined to run it.[7] In that case the father, whose intelligence was below average, failed to ensure that the child received proper medical attention with the result that it died. The jury expressly found that he had not been reckless and the Court of Appeal accordingly quashed a conviction for manslaughter.[8]

---

[1] (1862), Le. & Ca. 147. (The age of majority was then 21.)

[2] *R. v. Chattaway* (1922), 17 Cr. App. Rep. 7, C.C.A. (starvation of a helpless daughter aged 25).

[3] *R. v. Bubb* (1850), 4 Cox C.C. 455; *R. v. Gibbins and Proctor* (1918), 13 Cr. App. Rep. 134, C.C.A.

[4] *Cf.* the Children Act 1975, s. 87 (2).

[5] *R. v. Griffin* (1869), 11 Cox C.C. 402.

[6] [1973] Q.B. 702; [1973] 1 All E.R. 805, C.A.

[7] *Cf. R. v. Stone*, [1977] Q.B. 354; [1977] 2 All E.R. 341, C.A.

[8] For cases where parents have been found guilty of manslaughter by neglect, see *R. v. Walters* (1841), Car. & M. 164 (exposure); *R.v. Bubb*, (*supra*) (failure to provide food and clothing); *R. v. Downes* (1875), 1 Q.B.D. 25 (failure to call in medical advice).

If the parent's act or omission is intended to cause the child's death (for example by intentional starvation) then he or she will be guilty of murder, and the same is true if the conduct is so intrinsically likely to do so that a jury can infer that the death must have been contemplated.[1]

Where Death does not ensue.—A parent will be criminally liable for assault if he inflicts physical injury on a child or puts it in fear that he will do so. The Offences against the Person Act 1861 has also created the specific statutory offence of an aggravated assault upon a boy under the age of 14 or upon any female, as well as the more serious offence of unlawfully and maliciously wounding or inflicting grievous bodily harm.[2]

But where the breach of parental duty takes the form of neglect, abandonment or some other omission, the common law criminal sanctions are wholly inadequate to ensure the child's protection. In *R.* v. *Friend*[3] the judges gave it as their opinion that it is an indictable misdemeanour at common law for a person under a duty to provide for an infant of tender years to neglect to do so and thereby injure its health. Few indictments appear to have been preferred, and in any case no offence was committed unless the child's health actually suffered as a result. It was not till 1889 that Parliament passed the first Prevention of Cruelty to, and Protection of, Children Act.[4] The principles underlying this Act were considerably extended by later statutes, and the modern law is largely contained in the Children and Young Persons Acts 1933 to 1969.[5]

By far the most important provision is to be found in section 1 of the Children and Young Persons Act of 1933, which enacts:

> "If any person who has attained the age of sixteen years and has the custody, charge, or care of any child or young person under that age, wilfully assaults, ill-treats, neglects, abandons, or exposes him,[6] or causes him to be assaulted, ill-treated, neglected, abandoned, or exposed, in a manner likely to cause him unnecessary suffering or injury to health (including injury to or loss of sight, or hearing, or limb, or organ of the body, and any mental derangement), that person shall be guilty of [an offence] ..."[7]

---

[1] *R.* v. *Walters*, (*supra*); *R.* v. *Bubb*, (*supra*); *R.* v. *Handley* (1874), 13 Cox C.C. 79; *R.* v. *Gibbins and Proctor*, (*supra*).

[2] Ss. 20 and 43. For criminal assault generally; see Smith and Hogan, *Criminal Law*, 4th Ed., c. 12.

[3] (1802), Russ. & Ry. 20. See also *R.* v. *Hogan* (1851), 2 Den. 277.

[4] Earlier statutory intervention (more limited in its scope) is to be seen in the Poor Law Amendment Act 1868, s. 37.

[5] Children and Young Persons Act 1933; Children and Young Persons (Amendment) Act 1952; Children and Young Persons Act 1963; Children and Young Persons Act 1969.

[6] These terms are not mutually exclusive. Hence conduct may amount to ill-treatment even though it also constitutes an assault or neglect: *R.* v. *Hayles*, [1969] 1 Q.B. 364; [1969] 1 All E.R. 347, C.A.

[7] The phrase "in a manner likely to cause ... injury to health" governs the whole of the preceding phrase "wilfully assaults ... abandoned, or exposed": *R.* v. *Hatton*, [1925] 2 K.B. 322, C.C.A. This section has virtually superseded the Offences against the Person Act 1861, s. 27, which relates to the abandonment and exposure of children under two years of age. The maximum punishment is a fine and two years' imprisonment. See further Bevan, *Children*, 188-200.

By section 17 of the Act the following are liable under section 1:[1]

The parent[2] or legal guardian of the child;
Any person legally liable to maintain him;
Any person to whose charge the child is committed by anyone having custody of
   him;
Any person having actual possession or control of him.

This wording is extremely wide and would cover, for example, a school teacher and anyone over the age of 16 years acting as a baby sitter.

It will be seen that the object of the Act is to make criminal any wilful course of conduct likely to cause physical or mental injury to the child. The Act itself specifies that neglect shall include failure to provide adequate food, clothing, medical aid[3] or lodging or, if the parent or guardian is unable to provide any of them, failing to take steps to procure them through the Department of Health and Social Security.[4] But clearly many other types of cruelty and neglect are covered, such as beating a child, locking it up alone, leaving it in an otherwise deserted house or shutting it out in inclement weather, if such acts are likely to cause the child concerned suffering or ill-health. A person will be liable, however, only if his act is *wilful*: hence he must either know that his conduct might cause suffering etc. or not care whether this results or not.[5] Consequently an ignorant parent who does not know that the child's health is at risk will not be guilty of an offence if he fails to summon medical aid even though a reasonable person would be aware of this fact; if he does know this, however, he will presumably be guilty even though he has some religious or other reason for refusing to provide assistance.[6]

Parents (and others having the care or custody of children) may also be criminally liable for causing the death of a child under the age of three by overlying it in bed whilst drunk,[7] for allowing a child under the age of 12 to be in a room containing an unguarded fire or other heating appliance with the result that the child is killed or seriously injured,[8] or for permitting children under the age of 16 (subject to certain exceptions) to take part in or train for dangerous performances.[9]

---

[1] The Act says "presumed to be liable", but the presumption is apparently irrebuttable: *Brooks* v. *Blount*, [1923] 1 K.B. 257.

[2] This does not include the father of an illegitimate child who has not obtained an order for custody. He will not be liable, therefore, unless he is legally liable to maintain the child or has actual possession or control of it: *Butler* v. *Gregory* (1902), 18 T.L.R. 370; *Liverpool S.P.C.C.* v. *Jones*, [1914] 3 K.B. 813.

[3] Unreasonable refusal to permit a surgical operation may amount to wilful neglect: *Oakey* v. *Jackson*, [1914] 1 K.B. 216.

[4] Children and Young Persons Act 1933, s. 1 (2) (a).

[5] *R.* v. *Sheppard*, [1980] 3 All E.R. 899, H.L.

[6] As in *R.* v. *Senior*, [1899] 1 Q.B. 283 (religious objection to calling in medical aid), which appears to have been approved on its facts in *R.* v. *Sheppard*, (*supra*).

[7] Children and Young Persons Act 1933, s. 1 (2) (b).

[8] *Ibid.*, s. 11, as amended by the Children and Young Persons (Amendment) Act 1952, s. 8.

[9] *Ibid.*, ss. 23 and 24; Children and Young Persons Act 1963, s. 41 and Scheds. 3 and 5. The punishments vary for each offence: the maximum is five years' imprisonment and a fine.

Orders forbidding Molestation and Violence.—If other proceedings (for example, for divorce) are pending between the spouses, the court has a general power to intervene to protect the interests of the children.[1] It may therefore grant an injunction against either party to restrain him or her from molesting any child of the family or, probably, any other child living with the applicant. As we have already seen, section 1 of the Domestic Violence and Matrimonial Proceedings Act 1976 now enables a county court to grant an injuction containing *inter alia* a provision restraining the respondent from molesting any child living with the applicant even though no other relief is sought. This provision applies to spouses and to unmarried persons living together as husband and wife alike and the practice of the High Court has been altered so as to enable it to make a similar order.[2] Similarly, under section 16 of the Domestic Proceedings and Magistrates' Courts Act 1978 a spouse may apply to a magistrates' court for an order forbidding the other spouse from using or threatening to use violence against the person of any child of the family or from inciting or assisting any other person to do so.[3] In appropriate cases the respondent may also be excluded from the whole or part of the matrimonial home.[4]

2. MORAL PROTECTION

Although a parent might be refused the custody of his child on the ground that he was not taking adequate steps to secure its moral welfare, there was no positive method of ensuring that he did so either at common law or in equity. But just as Parliament has intervened to enforce the parent's duty to afford physical protection to his child, it has cast on him the obligation to afford moral protection as well. An attempt has been made to prevent the acquisition of sexually depraved habits by making it an offence for a parent to cause or encourage the seduction or prostitution of his daughter under the age of 16, or to permit a child between the ages of four and 16 to be in a brothel.[5] Similarly it is an offence to allow a child under the age of 16 to beg,[6] and penalties are imposed upon parents who permit children to take part in entertainments or to go abroad for the purpose of performing for profit except under stringent conditions.[7]

3. CIVIL LIABILITY

Up to now only the criminal sanctions for a breach of the duty to protect have been discussed. These are clearly the more important because, quite apart from the unlikelihood of litigation between parent and child, cruelty and neglect are on the whole more rife amongst poorer families. It remains to consider, however, whether any civil action will lie. The liability of a parent may be relevant if he is insured (as in the case of a car driver) or if another

---

[1] *Stewart* v. *Stewart*, [1973] Fam. 21; [1973] 1 All E.R. 31; *Phillips* v. *Phillips*, [1973] 2 All E.R. 423, C.A.

[2] See *ante*, pp. 123-125.

[3] See *ante*, pp. 126-128.

[4] *Stewart* v. *Stewart*, (*supra*); *Phillips* v. *Phillips*, (*supra*). See further *post*, pp. 462-465.

[5] Sexual Offences Act 1956, s. 28; Children and Young Persons Act 1933, s. 3. These provisions also apply to anyone having the custody, charge or care of the child.

[6] Children and Young Persons Act 1933, s. 4.

[7] *Ibid.*, s. 25; Children and Young Persons Act 1963, ss. 37-40 and 42.

defendant wishes to join the parent as a third party (for example, if the driver of a car which has injured the child wishes to claim contribution from a parent who has let him stray on the road). It is also conceivable that a child might sue his own parent if the natural ties which would normally prevent his doing so have been severed by the breaking up of the family as a whole.

It seems clear that the only possible action (apart from assault) is a common law action for damages for negligence. The child must therefore prove that he has been injured as a result of his parent's breach of duty to take care to avoid such acts or omissions as are foreseeably likely to injure him.

Independent Duty of Care.—Where a duty of care exists independently so that, had the injured person been a stranger, he could have recovered from the tortfeasor, the relationship of parent and child should not *ipso facto* bar the action. An obvious example would occur if a child, who is a passenger in his father's car, is injured as a result of the latter's negligent driving. The only possible defence—that it is contrary to public policy to permit a child to sue his own parent—does not seem to have been raised in the past.[1]

No independent Duty.—Where there is no independent duty, so that the child has to rely solely on the common law duty to protect owed to him by his parent or other person having charge of him, the position is less clear. Suppose a parent negligently lets a young child run on to a road with the result that he is injured by a passing vehicle; can the child recover damages for his injury from the parent? It is submitted that he can and the existence of such liability was recognised by the New Zealand Court of Appeal in *McCallion* v. *Dodd*.[2] In that case parents alighted from a bus at night with their two children and started to walk along the road in the dark. The mother, who was deaf and, as the father knew, was not wearing her hearing aid, took the plaintiff, aged four, by the hand and the father carried the baby in his arms. A car driven by the defendant hit the mother and the plaintiff, killing the mother and severely injuring the boy. The plaintiff sued the defendant in negligence and the defendant claimed contribution from the father on the ground that he had also broken a duty of care owed to the plaintiff. The jury found that the defendant had been negligent and also found that the father had been negligent in permitting the boy to walk in the road on the wrong side and in the path of oncoming traffic. They assessed the father's contribution at 20% and this was upheld by the Court of Appeal. All three members of the court took the view that, even though the boy was under the immediate control of his mother, the father continued to be under a special duty because of her deafness. It should be noticed, however, that they did not agree on the extent of the duty. TURNER and McCARTHY, JJ., were both of the opinion that no duty of care was set up purely by the relationship of parent and child but that it arose from the fact that the father had taken the boy on to the road,[3] although admittedly the relationship is evidence of the fact that the parent has undertaken the duty to supervise and control the child's conduct.[4]

---

[1] *Ash* v. *Ash* (1698), Comb. 357 (daughter's suing mother for assault). Such an action will lie in Scotland (*Young* v. *Rankin*, 1934 S.C. 499), Canada, Australia and New Zealand: see the cases cited in *McCallion* v. *Dodd*, [1966] N.Z.L.R. 710, 728.

[2] [1966] N.Z.L.R. 710. See Mathieson, 30 M.L.R. 96.

[3] At pp. 725 and 728.

[4] *Per* McCARTHY, J., at p. 729.

NORTH, P., however, took the view that, although a stranger would be liable in negligence only if he had assumed or accepted the care of the child, parents "at all times *while present* are under a legal duty to exercise reasonable care to protect their children from foreseeable dangers" and that duty cannot be shed by a parent who is present.[1] In most cases it will make little difference which view is correct but the wider rule formulated by NORTH, P., is to be preferred. Indeed, it is submitted that it should be even more broadly based. If a parent leaves a child in the care of one known to be unreliable and the child comes to harm as the result of the latter's irresponsibility, the parent should be civilly liable.

All the members of the court in *McCallion* v. *Dodd* were agreed that the doctrine of identification could not apply and that there was no question of the plaintiff's damages being reduced as the result of the father's negligence. Here they followed *Oliver* v. *Birmingham and Midland Omnibus Co., Ltd.*[2] The plaintiff, aged four, was crossing a road with his grandfather, who was holding his hand, when an omnibus bore down on them. The grandfather let go of the plaintiff's hand and jumped to safety; the plaintiff was struck by the omnibus owing to the driver's negligence and was injured. It was held that his action for damages against the omnibus company was not affected by his grandfather's contributory negligence.

F. PARENTS' LIABILITY FOR CHILDREN'S ACTS

Contracts.—A parent will never be liable as such for any contract made by his child.[3] But he may of course be liable on the ordinary principles of agency if he has authorised the child to make the contract or, in the case of unauthorised contracts, by estoppel or ratification.[4]

Torts.—As in the case of contracts, a parent will not be liable as such for his child's torts. But he may be liable on some other ground, for example if he has authorised the commission of the tort or if the child is for this purpose his servant. If the child commits a tort whilst running an errand for his parent, the latter may be liable as the master *quoad hoc.*[5]

A parent may also be personally liable if he himself has been negligent in affording the child an opportunity of injuring another. This is a particular application of the tort of negligence, and the test is therefore: did the parent by his act or omission cause or permit his child to do an act which was foreseeably likely to harm the person injured and against which a reasonably prudent parent would have guarded? If so, he will be liable. This is illustrated by *Newton* v. *Edgerley*.[6] The defendant, a farmer, permitted his twelve year

---

[1] At p. 721. (Italics supplied.)
[2] [1933] 1 K.B. 35.
[3] *Mortimore* v. *Wright* (1840), 6 M. & W. 482.
[4] See generally works on the law of contract and on agency.
[5] For liability for servants' torts generally, see works on the law of tort.
[6] [1959] 3 All E.R. 337. See also *Bebee* v. *Sales* (1916), 32 T.L.R. 413.

old son to have possession of a shotgun. He instructed the boy in the use of it but forbade him to take it off the farm or to use it when other children were near and therefore did not instruct him how to handle it when others were present. Ultimately the boy disobeyed his father and took the gun to a wood with other boys (including the plaintiff). Whilst they were walking in single file the gun, which was loaded and cocked, went off as the result of interference by another boy and the plantiff was injured. It was held that the defendant was personally liable in negligence for he ought to have foreseen that his son would succumb to temptation and consequently should either have forbidden him to use the gun at all or have instructed him how to handle it in the presence of others.

But the parent will not be liable if he could not reasonably have foreseen that the child's act would injure the plaintiff or if he took all precautions that a reasonably prudent parent would have taken. In *Donaldson* v. *McNiven*[1] the defendant had let his son aged 13 buy an airgun. He forbade him to fire it outside the house and the boy gave his word that he would not do so. He always fired it in a cellar under the house until one day he took it outside, fired it and in so doing put out the plaintiff's eye. It was held that the father was not liable, for he had taken all reasonable precautions to ensure that the gun was fired in a safe place and no damage would have resulted but for the son's disobedience, unfaithfulness and folly which the defendant could not reasonably have foreseen.

Although these cases both deal with a parent's liability for permitting his child to have a dangerous toy or weapon, there is no reason why it should be restricted to this field. Thus if a parent (or other adult) in charge of a young child on a busy road negligently lets it run out into the traffic with the result that the driver of a car, in swerving to avoid the child, injures himself or another, the parent must on principle be liable for the damage.[2]

Crimes.—At common law a parent was not liable for his child's crimes unless he himself was guilty of aiding and abetting. But the fact that a child's criminal propensities may be due to bad home influences or a lack of parental supervision has now been recognised by statute. If a court imposes a fine or costs or makes a compensation order for the commission of an offence by a child under the age of 17, it may order that these be paid by the child's parent or guardian unless the latter cannot be found or the court is satisfied that he has not conduced to the commission of the offence by neglecting to exercise due care or control of the child.[3]

---

[1] [1952] 2 All E.R. 691, C.A. See also *Gorely* v. *Codd*, [1966] 3 All E.R. 891.

[2] *Cf. Carmarthenshire County Council* v. *Lewis*, [1955] A.C. 549; [1955] 1 All E.R. 565, H.L., where a school authority was liable in similar circumstances for negligently letting a child run out of the school premises on to a road with the result that a lorry driver was killed. See further Waller, *Visiting the Sins of the Children*, 4 Melbourne U.L.R. 17.

[3] Children and Young Persons Act 1933, s. 55; Children and Young Persons Act 1969, s. 3 (6) and Scheds. 5 and 6; Administration of Justice Act 1970, Sched. 11; Criminal Justice Act 1972, Sched. 5. The court *must* exercise this power if the child is under 14. For the problems that have arisen in relation to children in the care of a local authority, see Hoggett, 118 Sol. Jo. 722; *Lincoln Corporation* v. *Parker*, [1974] 2 All E.R. 949; *Somerset County Council* v. *Kingscott*, [1975] 1 All E.R. 326; *Leicestershire County Council* v. *Cross*, [1976] 2 All E.R. 491. See also the Criminal Law Act 1977, s. 36 (liability of parent or guardian for unpaid fine). For the court's power to require a parent to enter into recognisances to exercise care and control of the child, see *post*, p. 392.

G. LIABILITY FOR INTERFERENCE WITH PARENTS' AND CHILDREN'S RIGHTS

1. CRIMINAL LIABILITY

Although the contrary view was once held,[1] there is apparently no common law offence of taking a child against its parents' will.[2] A number of statutory offences have been created, however. They are now principally contained in section 56 of the Offences against the Person Act 1861 and sections 19 to 21 of the Sexual Offences Act 1956 (which repealed and consolidated earlier legislation on the subject).[3] Three distinct cases must be considered.

Children under the age of 14 years.—It is an offence by force or fraud to lead, take away, decoy, entice away, or detain any child under the age of 14 with intent to deprive its parent, guardian, or other person having lawful care or charge of it, of its possession, or to harbour a child knowing it to have been obtained in this way.[4] The offence may be committed in respect of a child of either sex, and there need be no intention to deprive the parent or other person of custody permanently.[5] Either force or fraud[6] must be used, and therefore it will not be an offence to *persuade* a boy under the age of 14 to leave his parents. The statute specifically provides that neither the mother, the father of an illegitimate child nor any person claiming a right to possession of the child can be prosecuted for getting possession of it or for taking it out of the possession of anyone with lawful charge of it.[7]

Girls under the age of 16 years.—It is an offence for a person acting without lawful authority or excuse to take an unmarried girl under the age of 16 out of the possession[8] of her parent or other person having the lawful care or charge of her against his will.[9] Unlike the offence just considered, this can be committed only in respect of a girl and neither force nor fraud is

---

[1] 1 East, *Pleas of the Crown*, 429-430.

[2] *R. v. Hale*, [1974] Q.B. 819; [1974] 1 All E.R. 1107.

[3] See also the Child Care Act 1980, ss. 13 and 16 (4), which make it an offence knowingly to compel, persuade, incite or assist a child in the care of a local authority to become or continue to be absent. The Criminal Law Revision Committee propose that the first two offences mentioned below should be replaced by new offences of abduction and, in certain circumstances, aggravated abduction of a child under the age of 14: see their 14th Report, Offences against the Person, 1980, Cmnd. 7844, paras. 239-249.

[4] Offences against the Person Act 1861, s. 56. (Maximum punishment: 7 years' imprisonment.) "Detain" connotes keeping in confinement or custody and not merely harbouring: *R. v. Pryce*, [1972] Crim. L.R. 307.

[5] *R. v. Powell* (1914), 24 Cox C.C. 229.

[6] The fraud may be perpetrated on the child, parent or, apparently, anyone else: *R. v. Bellis* (1893), 17 Cox C.C. 660.

[7] But he can apparently be prosecuted for detaining it: Smith and Hogan, *Criminal Law*, 4th Ed., 387. The defence is personal; consequently another may be convicted of aiding and abetting the mother, etc.: *R. v. Austin*, [1981] 1 All E.R. 374, C.A.

[8] Therefore taking a girl for a walk will not constitute an offence under this section: *R. v. Jones*, [1973] Crim. L.R. 621.

[9] Sexual Offences Act 1956, s. 20. (Maximum punishment: 2 years' imprisonment.) The importance of this provision has been considerably lessened since the Criminal Law Amendment Act 1885 made it an offence to have unlawful sexual intercourse with a girl under the age of 16.

necessary:[1] mere persuasion to leave home is sufficient. If she leaves without any persuasion or force on the part of the accused, no offence is committed, even though he subsequently acquiesces in her suggestion that they should stay together and takes no steps to send her home; but if he takes the active step of suggesting that she should leave her parents, he will be liable.[2] Since the object of the section is to protect the parents' rights, the consent of the girl is irrelevant.[3]

As in the case of children under the age of 14, a person may be guilty even though he did not intend to deprive the parent of custody permanently. The offence is committed once the accused puts the girl in a situation which is inconsistent with her parent's custody of her. In *R.v. Timmins*[4] it was held that there was a sufficient taking where the accused took a girl to London for three days for the purpose of sleeping with her and at the end of that time told her to return to her father. On the other hand, a mere temporary absence will not suffice if it is not inconsistent with the relationship of parent and daughter.

The accused will have a good defence if he neither knew nor ought to have known that the girl was in anyone's custody, for then there will be no *mens rea* at all.[5] But if he knows that he is interfering with parental rights, it will be no defence that he thought that the girl was over the age of 16.[6] Similarly it will be a good defence that the accused honestly believed that he had a right to the girl's custody;[7] but no other motives, for example religious or philanthropic, will excuse his conduct.[8]

Girls under the age of 18 years and Defective Girls.—It is an offence to abduct any unmarried girl under the age of 18 years or a girl or woman of any age who is a defective with the intention in either case that she should have unlawful sexual intercourse.[9] The offence is the same as in the case of a girl under the age of 16 except that the prosecution must also prove the accused's intent.[10] It is also a defence that the accused had reasonable cause to believe

---

[1] But taking a girl by either of these means will of course amount to the commission of the offence: *R. v. Hopkins* (1842), Car. & M. 254, where the accused fraudulently induced the parent to let him take the girl away.

[2] *R. v. Jarvis* (1903), 20 Cox C.C. 249; *R. v. Olifier* (1866), 10 Cox C.C. 402. But it is to be inferred from the earlier cases that if the accused and the girl leave her house together, he will be liable whoever made the suggestion: *R. v. Robins* (1844), 1 Car. & Kir. 456; *R. v. Biswell* (1847), 2 Cox C.C. 279.

[3] *R. v. Manktelow* (1853), 6 Cox C.C. 143. But see Eekelaar, 89 L.Q.R. at p. 215. The parent's having previously permitted the girl to lead an immoral life may be evidence that her leaving was not against his will: *R. v. Primelt* (1858), 1 F. & F. 50; *R. v. Frazer and Norman* (1861), 8 Cox C.C. 446.

[4] (1860), 8 Cox C.C. 401.

[5] *R. v. Hibbert* (1869), L.R. 1 C.C.R. 184. But the number of cases today where the accused would not have constructive knowledge must be negligible.

[6] *R. v. Prince* (1875), L.R. 2 C.C.R. 154.

[7] *R. v. Tinkler* (1859), 1 F. & F. 513.

[8] *R. v. Booth* (1872), 12 Cox C.C. 231.

[9] Sexual Offences Act 1956, ss. 19 and 21. (The maximum punishment in either case is 2 years' imprisonment.) "Unlawful" sexual intercourse means intercourse outside the marriage bond: *R. v. Chapman*, [1959] 1 Q.B. 100; [1958] 3 All E.R. 143, C.C.A. Hence no offence will be committed if the accused takes the girl away from her parents with the honest and *bona fide* intention of marrying her.

[10] *R. v. Henkers* (1886), 16 Cox C.C. 257.

that the girl was over the age of 18 or that he had no reason to suspect her of being a defective as the case may be.

2. DAMAGES FOR LOSS OF SERVICES

At common law one could obtain damages for the abduction of one's heir. But the action did not extend to the abduction of other children,[1] and although it has never been formally abolished, it is now completely obsolete.[2] This meant that there was no civil remedy for interference with parental rights—a gap which the common law judges filled at the latest in 1653 by adapting the existing action which a master had for the loss of his servant's services and permitting a parent to sue alleging as special damage the loss of his child's services.[3] It thus became an actionable tort to do any act which wrongfully deprives a parent of his child's services. This is an independent cause of action vested in the parent. If the loss was due to a tort committed against the child, he too would have a cause of action, but in the commoner examples of loss of services—enticement (where the child went voluntarily with the defendant) or seduction (where the loss was due to a daughter's pregnancy and childbirth as a consequence of sexual intercourse with the defendant)—the child clearly could not sue at all.

Actions were rare and it was coming to be considered an anomaly that the child's voluntary act could give rise to an action by the parent. Consequently section 5 of the Law Reform (Miscellaneous Provisions) Act 1970 now provides that no action shall lie for loss of services due to rape, seduction, enticement or harbouring.[4] This limits the action to loss of services resulting from the commission of a tort against the child, and even this will not lie if the tort consisted of battery involving rape. One sees the connection between rape and seduction but it is anomalous that a parent may sue a man who negligently knocks his daughter down but not one who deliberately rapes her.[5]

By analogy with the law relating to a husband's claim for the loss of his wife's consortium, a parent could also claim damages for loss of a child's services if this was the result of a breach of contract made with the parent himself. The damage must not, of course, be too remote; but a father could obviously recover if he bought poisoned food and the child became ill as the result of eating it.[6]

Although the real cause of action is interference with parental rights, its theoretical basis is still loss of services, and accordingly the plaintiff must show that the child performed some service for him.[7] This may of course be a

---

[1] *Barham* v. *Dennis* (1600), Cro. Eliz. 770.

[2] HOLROYD, J., thought it was still extant in 1825: *Hall* v. *Hollander* (1825), 4 B. & C. 660, 662, but there seems to have been no attempt to bring such an action for over 300 years.

[3] *Norton* v. *Jason* (1653), Sty. 398. See Holdsworth, *History of English Law*, viii, 427-429; Pollock, *Torts*, 15th Ed., 167 *et seq.*; Winfield, *Tort*, 8th Ed., 528.

[4] Following the recommendations of the Law Commission (Working Paper No. 19).

[5] But he can presumably sue if he can prove that the loss of services was due to another tort committed at the same time as the rape, *e.g.* a blow knocking the girl unconscious beforehand.

[6] *Cf. Jackson* v. *Watson & Sons, ante,* p. 129, *q.v.* for loss of wife's consortium due to breach of contract.

[7] See the cases cited in the following footnotes, and in particular *Hall* v. *Hollander, (supra)*; *Grinnell* v. *Wells* (1844), 7 Man. & G. 1033; *Evans* v. *Walton* (1867), L.R. 2 C.P. 615.

contractual service (although it rarely will be); in almost every case the parent will rely on domestic services rendered at home which may be real but may be purely nominal such as making tea.[1] If the child is over the age of 18, the burden is on the plaintiff to prove that some sort of service was in fact performed, but if the child is still a minor, the mere fact that he is living in the parent's family is sufficient to raise a presumption of service which need not therefore be specifically proved.[2]

But the necessity of showing loss of services means that there will be two cases where the parent cannot sue at all. First, no action will lie if the child is too young to render any services, as happened in *Hall* v. *Hollander*,[3] where it was held that no action for loss of services could be brought by the father of a boy aged two whom the defendant had injured by running him down with his carriage. Secondly, no loss of service can be proved if the child owes a contractual service to another and as a result is no longer living with the parent.[4] The law on the latter point is not entirely clear but is now of little practical importance because the difficulties almost always arose when a daughter was living with another family as a domestic servant: a situation which now rarely arises.

Illogicality was caused by the courts' having caught at straws to give the parent a remedy where perhaps in strict legal theory he should have none. A further example of the same kind is seen in the development of the concept of constructive service. In *Terry* v. *Hutchinson*[5] the plaintiff's daughter had been employed by a milliner in Deal who dismissed her. On her way home to Canterbury she was seduced by the defendant in a railway carriage. The Court of Queen's Bench held that the father could recover damages for the seduction for, since the girl was a minor, his right to her services revived as soon as she left the milliner's service with the intention of returning home, and there was an immediate constructive service even though he had not yet exercised his right. This decision might still be relevant if the child in question were living away from home in lodgings or a flat of its own. There will clearly be no *de facto* service and so no action will lie if the child is over the age of 18. But if the child is still a minor, it could be argued by analogy with *Terry* v. *Hutchinson* that there is a constructive service because the child is serving no other master at the time, and in view of the court's evident desire to give the parent a remedy whenever possible the argument might well succeed.

It was formerly held that, if the parents are living together, a legitimate child's services are owed exclusively to the father as head of the family and consequently the mother has no cause of action for loss of them.[6] But now that the Guardianship Act has given the mother the same rights with respect to the child as the father,[7] both parents must be able to maintain an action.

---

[1] *Per* ABBOTT, C.J., in *Carr* v. *Clarke* (1818), 2 Chit. 260, 261.

[2] *Peters* v. *Jones*, [1914] 2 K.B. 781, 784.

[3] (1825), 4 B. & C. 660.

[4] For the problems arising when the child is at home during holidays or free time, see *Hedges* v. *Tagg* (1872), L.R. 7 Exch. 283; *Dent* v. *Maguire*, [1917] 2 I.R. 59. A parent can sue with respect to a child *living at home* even though he is contractually employed by another during working hours: *Ogden* v. *Lancashire* (1866), 15 W.R. 158. Nor does a temporary absence from home prevent the action from lying: *Griffiths* v. *Teetgen* (1854), 15 C.B. 344.

[5] (1868), L.R. 3 Q.B. 599.

[6] *Beetham* v. *James*, [1937] 1 K.B. 527; [1937] 1 All E.R. 580; following *Hamilton* v. *Long*, [1903] 2 I.R. 407, affirmed, [1905] 2 I.R. 552, and *Peters* v. *Jones*, [1914] 2 K.B. 781.

[7] See *ante*, p. 281.

An illegitimate child's services will normally be owed to the mother but apparently these are owed to the father as well if he is living with the mother.[1]

As in the case of a husband's action for the loss of his wife's consortium or services,[2] no damages may be claimed for the loss of services caused by the child's death as a result of the defendant's tortious act.[3] But again this rule will not apply where the parent sues for breach of contract. Hence we once more have the anomalous rule that if, say, the child is killed whilst riding on an omnibus owing to the driver's negligence, the father could recover for loss of services if he had bought the tickets for them both, but he could not do so if the child were travelling alone and contracted on its own behalf. Where the defendant's tort results in death, the parent's remedy (if he has one at all) will exist under the Fatal Accidents Act.[4]

It has never been decided how far the defendant may raise against the parent any defence that he could raise in an action brought against him by the child. Since the parent's cause of action is independent, it would seem on principle that the defences ought to be independent too. Hospitals certainly take this view; although a child over the age of 16 now has a statutory power to consent to any medical, surgical or dental treatment without his parent's concurrence, medical authorities still insist on obtaining the parent's consent to an operation on a child under that age.[5] On the other hand it is absurd to suppose that a participant in a boxing match could be liable to his opponent's parent for an injury caused to his child on the ground that, unknown to the first person, the parent had forbidden the other to take part in it, if a claim brought by the child himself would be defeated by the application of the maxim *Volenti non fit injuria*. A child's contributory negligence should not affect the parent's claim,[6] but if the court were to hold that this was the sole cause of the damage so that the child could recover nothing, it would seem that the parent's claim should be dismissed as well on the ground that the contributory negligence has made the damage too remote.

A much more rational solution to the problem of compensating parents for the loss they suffer as the result of a tort committed against their child is to be found in the decision of the Court of Appeal in *Donnelly* v. *Joyce*,[7] where it was held that the child could recover the value of nursing services rendered by his mother and goods specially provided by his parents as a part of his own damages. The decision and its implications have already been considered:[8] it has obviously gone a long way to resolve the complications and anomalies arising from the fact that English law has never recognised an action for loss of parental rights as such but has had to adapt another action which has filled the gap imperfectly. Whilst it is founded upon a fiction, the trouble is that

---

[1] *Beetham* v. *James*, (*supra*), at pp. 532-533 and 584, respectively.

[2] See *ante*, p. 131.

[3] *Clark* v. *London General Omnibus Co., Ltd.*, [1906] 2 K.B. 648, C.A.; following *Osborn* v. *Gillett* (1873), L.R. 8 Exch. 88.

[4] See *ante*, pp. 134-149.

[5] See *ante*, p. 317.

[6] *Cf.* a husband's claim for loss of his wife's consortium and services, *ante*, p. 129.

[7] [1974] Q.B. 454; [1973] 3 All E.R. 475, C.A.; followed in *Taylor* v. *Bristol Omnibus Co., Ltd.*, [1975] 2 All E.R. 1107, C.A. See Carr, 37 M.L.R. 341; Wharam, 121 New L.J. 786.

[8] See *ante*, pp. 132-134.

"for that fiction there must be some foundation, however slender, in fact".[1] Consequently both the Law Reform Committee and the Law Commission have recommended that the action for loss of services should be abolished and that instead a father or mother (or, alternatively, the victim himself) should be able to recover financial loss suffered as the result of a tortious injury inflicted on a dependent child. This would include, for example, medical and nursing expenses, the cost of visiting the child in hospital or elsewhere, and any consequential loss of earnings.[2]

3. THE FATAL ACCIDENTS ACT

We have already seen that parents and children come within the category of dependants for the purposes of the Fatal Accidents Act, so that either may sue any person who has unlawfully caused the death of the other for compensation for pecuniary loss resulting from the death.[3]

H. NATIONALITY AND RIGHT OF ABODE IN THE UNITED KINGDOM

Nationality.—As citizenship of the United Kingdom and Colonies is acquired almost wholly by operation of law, it cannot strictly be considered a question of parental rights and duties. But since in certain circumstances a person may be a citizen of the United Kingdom and Colonies solely by virtue of his father's possessing such citizenship, the subject will be dealt with here for the sake of completeness.

At common law British nationality was acquired at birth by those born within British territory and only in very limited circumstances (for example in the case of children of a British ambassador) by those born outside it.[4] Legislation during the eighteenth century conferred the status of a British subject on anyone born abroad whose father or paternal grandfather was a natural-born British subject.[5] The Naturalization Act of 1870 extended British nationality to the children of naturalized subjects provided that they resided in this country during their minority,[6] and the same Act also provided that, if his parents lost British nationality by naturalization in a foreign country, a minor residing in that country would also lose his British

---

[1] *Per* KELLY, C.B., in *Hedges* v. *Tagg* (1872), L.R. 7 Exch. 283, 285. For early calls for reform, see notes to the reports of *Speight* v. *Oliviera* (1819), 2 Stark. 493, 496, and *Grinnell* v. *Wells* (1844), 7 Man. & G. 1033, 1044.

[2] Eleventh Report of the Law Reform Committee (Loss of Services, etc.), 1963, Cmnd. 2017, paras. 20-23; Law Com. No. 56, Report on Personal Injury Litigation—Assessment of Damages, paras. 115-121. The Pearson Commission on Civil Liability and Compensation for Personal Injury similarly recommended its abolition: Cmnd. 7054, paras. 445-447.

[3] See *ante*, pp. 134 *et seq.*

[4] Jones, *British Nationality*, (1947 Ed.), 34 *et seq.*

[5] Foreign Protestants (Naturalization) Act 1708; British Nationality Acts 1730 and 1772. See Jones, *op cit.*, 69-72. Another remarkable example of nationality by descent is to be found in the provisions of 4 Anne, c. 16, 1705 (now repealed), under which all the issue of Princess Sophia, the mother of King George 1, other than Roman Catholics, who were born before 1949, are British subjects: *A.-G.* v. *Prince Ernest Augustus of Hanover*, [1957] A.C. 436; [1957] 1 All E.R. 49, H.L.

[6] S. 10 (5). See Jones, *op. cit.*, 101-103.

nationality.[1] These rules were considerably modified by the British Nationality and Status of Aliens Acts 1914 to 1943 and again underwent complete revision in the British Nationality Act of 1948 which created the new status of citizen of the United Kingdom and Colonies.

This Act retains the common law rule by enacting that almost all children born within the United Kingdom and Colonies shall be citizens thereof.[2] In addition, anyone born outside the United Kingdom and Colonies will be a citizen thereof by descent, if at the time of his birth[3] his father is a citizen of the United Kingdom and Colonies otherwise than by descent or, alternatively, if his father is a citizen by descent and one of the following conditions is also satisfied:

(a) the child or his father was born in a place where the Crown lawfully had jurisdiction over British subjects; or
(b) the birth is registered within a year at a United Kingdom consulate; or
(c) the father at the time of the birth is in Crown service under the United Kingdom government; or
(d) the child is born in a Commonwealth country but does not become a citizen of that country at birth.[4]

It will thus be seen that, unless one of these conditions is satisfied, citizenship will be conferred only on the first generation born abroad and not on two generations as it was under the earlier Acts.

None of the provisions relating to citizenship by descent can apply to an illegitimate child for, as *filius nullius*, he can claim no legal status through his father. One further rule should be noted which applies to any child, legitimate or illegitimate. If he is and always has been stateless, he is entitled to be registered as a citizen of the United Kingdom and Colonies if his mother was a citizen thereof at the time of his birth.[5]

If changes currently proposed by the Home Office are implemented, the law outlined here will be altered in two respects. First, it will be possible to claim British citizenship by descent through either parent: this means that an illegitimate child will be able to claim citizenship through his mother. Secondly, save in exceptional circumstances only one generation will be able to claim citizenship by descent and not two, as at present.[6]

Naturalization of a parent no longer *ipso facto* confers citizenship on his minor children if they reside in this country (as happened under the Act of 1870) or if their names are included in his certificate of naturalization (as was the position under the Act of 1914). But the Home Secretary has a

---

[1] S. 10 (3).

[2] For the exceptions, see the British Nationality Act 1948, s. 4; Parry, *British Nationality*, 121-128; Jones, *British Nationality Law*, Revised Ed., 154-156.

[3] Or, in the case of a posthumous child, at the time of the father's death: British Nationality Act 1948, s. 24.

[4] *Ibid.*, s. 5. See Parry, *op. cit.*, 129-140; Jones, *op. cit.*, Revised Ed., 156-160. For the somewhat wider application of these provisions to a person who would otherwise be stateless, see the British Nationality (No. 2) Act 1964, ss. 1-3, and the British Nationality Act 1965, s. 4.

[5] British Nationality (No. 2) Act 1964, s. 1. For stateless children born within the United Kingdom and Colonies, see *ibid.*, s. 2.

[6] See Cmnd. 7987, *British Nationality—Outline of Proposed Legislation*.

discretionary power on their parents' application to register any such children as citizens of the United Kingdom and Colonies.[1]

Right of Abode in the United Kingdom.—As we have already seen, the right of abode in this country of a citizen of the United Kingdom and Colonies may depend upon the fact that one of his parents or grandparents was born, adopted, naturalised or registered in this country. The claim of a non-patrial child to enter the United Kingdom and to stay here with one or both of his parents depends on whether he satisfies the conditions laid down in the Immigration Rules, which have already been discussed.[2]

British Nationality Bill.—The changes relating to the acquisition of British citizenship by birth in this country proposed in the British Nationality Bill have already been noted[3]. In addition, it is proposed that, in future, the son or daughter of a British citizen born abroad will be able to claim British citizenship by descent only if at the time of his or her birth a parent was a British citizen by virtue of birth in the United Kingdom or was in Crown service or in some other service designated as closely associated with the activities of the British Government. This means that the number of cases of descent for two generations will be reduced. On the other hand, a legitimate or legitimated child will be able to claim citizenship by descent if *either* parent satisfies one of these conditions (and not the father only as at present): an illegitimate child will be able to do so if his mother satisfies it.

---

[1] Under the provisions of s. 7 (1) of the British Nationality Act 1948. If a person has dual nationality, he may renounce citizenship of the United Kingdom and Colonies by declaration after he comes of age: s. 19. A minor who lost British nationality by reason of his parents' naturalization in a foreign country before 1949 may obtain citizenship of the United Kingdom and Colonies by making a declaration to that effect within twelve months of coming of age (or such longer period of time as the Home Secretary shall allow): s. 16. See also the British Nationality Act 1964, s. 1 (resumption of citizenship after renunciation).

[2] See *ante*, pp. 162-165.

[3] See *ante*, p. 165.

Chapter 10

Adoption

In the last chapter we were primarily concerned with the exercise of powers and duties by the parents themselves. In this chapter and the next we shall consider the provisions that the law makes for children who are orphaned or whose parents are unable or unwilling to bring them up. These provisions take various forms. The child may be adopted, which severs the legal ties between it and its natural parents and places it in the position of the legitimate child of its adoptive parents. A parent may appoint a guardian to act after his death or the court may appoint guardians or custodians. These have custody of their wards and the children to whom they are custodian, but their appointment does not affect the devolution of property or destroy the remaining legal ties between the child and its parents. In certain circumstances a child may be taken into care by a local authority. Finally, it may be placed with foster parents who exercise care and control on behalf of the parent or local authority but do not have the remaining rights and powers attached to custody.

In this chapter we shall discuss adoption.

A. INTRODUCTORY

In common parlance the term "adoption" is frequently used in a sense much wider than its strict legal one. If a child's parents die or abandon it and it is brought up by someone else, the latter is often said to have adopted the child, particularly if he is a stranger in blood. This relationship is described as foster parenthood in this book, and its legal results will be discussed later.[1] One of the disadvantages of mere *de facto* control is that, since the relationship is one which is strictly not recognised by the law at all, the legal position of the person assuming control is precarious. One of the gravest threats is that the child's parents or legally appointed guardians may try at any time to assert their legal powers, and although their claim may well be defeated on the grounds that it will not be in the interests of the child to be torn away from those who have brought it up,[2] the latter may nevertheless live in real fear of losing the child. When the relevant sections of the Children Act came into force, it will be possible for people in this position to have themselves

---

[1] *Post*, pp. 361-363.
[2] See also the provisions of the Custody of Children Act 1891, *ante*, p. 285.

appointed custodians of the child and thus give some legal authority to the situation. But their relationship to the child in cases such as these often resembles that of parent rather than custodian, and there were no means either at common law or in equity of creating a legal relationship in any way equivalent to that of parent and legitimate child. The view taken by English law that a parent's rights over his child were inalienable meant that it could recognise no change of status comparable to the *adoptio* or *adrogatio* of Roman law. Consequently, spouses who were probably childless and anxious to bring up another's child as their own hesitated to do so, and the child was in turn deprived of the opportunity of a normal home life and remained in the orphanage or some other institution.

The result was a demand for reform which led eventually to the passing of the Adoption of Children Act in 1926.[1] The provisions of this Act were revolutionary, for, subject to certain limitations, it permitted anyone wishing to bring up somebody else's child as his own to apply for an adoption order from a court of competent jurisdiction, the effect of which, if it was granted, was to break entirely the legal relationship between the child and its natural parents and to vest the parental rights and duties relating to it in the adopters.[2] The result, in brief, is that the adopters for all legal purposes step into the shoes of the child's natural parents; by its "parents" in other words are now meant not its natural parents but its adoptive parents.

The relationship between the parties is thus distinguishable from that of parent and legitimate child, parent and illegitimate child, and guardian (or custodian) and ward. It resembles most closely the first, for, although there need be no blood relationship between the parties, the legal consequences are almost the same. It differs most markedly from the second for the law still does not always give effect to the natural rights and duties which the blood relationship creates: adoption in fact creates virtually the converse situation. It resembles the third in that the adoptive parents, like guardians and custodians, stand *in loco parentis* to the child to whom they are not necessarily related in blood, but differs from it in that the relationship of guardian (or custodian) and ward does not make the latter a member of the former's family for the purposes, for example, of the devolution and acquisition of property.

Children Act 1975.—The Act of 1926 was extensively amended in the light of subsequent experience and criticisms, and all earlier legislation was repealed and the law consolidated by the Adoption Act of 1958. Dissatisfaction with various aspects of the law and procedure led to the appointment of a Departmental Committee in 1969 whose report (the Houghton (or Stockdale) Report) was published in 1972.[3] Most of their recommendations (some of them in a modified form) were implemented by the Children Act 1975. Because these involve extensive administrative reorganisation and considerable expenditure of public money, it will be some time before most of the

---

[1] Passed following the Report of the Committee on Child Adoption, Cmd. 1254 (1921) and two Reports of the Child Adoption Committee, Cmd. 2401 and 2469 (1925).

[2] See now the Children Act 1975, s. 8 (1).

[3] Cmnd. 5107. The original chairman was Sir William Houghton; after his death the chair was taken by Judge Stockdale. On the report generally see Stockdale, 3 Fam. Law 15; Samuels, 36 M.L.R. 278.

provisions of the Act come into force.[1] In the following discussion, therefore, it will be necessary to consider both the existing law and the changes that will be made when the relevant parts of the Act are brought into operation.

Adoption Act 1976.—All the statutory provisions relating to adoption (including the sections of the Children Act not yet in force) have now been consolidated in the Adoption Act 1976. This Act is not yet in force either and presumably will not be brought into force until the relevant sections of the Children Act come into effect. It prospectively repeals the existing legislation and for ease of reference the corresponding section numbers will be printed in the footnotes.[2]

The Adoption Service.—Until recent years the majority of adoption orders were made in respect of illegitimate children who were placed for adoption very shortly after birth. Today, however, it is apparent that many unmarried mothers (even excluding those living in stable unions) are keeping their children, and the majority of adoptions are by one of the parents and her or his spouse.[3] If it is desired to have a child adopted by strangers, arrangments are usually made by an adoption society or a local authority. At present, there is nothing to stop parents from making arrangements with the proposed adopters personally or through a private individual (for example, a doctor or minister of religion) but this is to be discouraged for two reasons. In the first place adoption societies and local authorities have experienced case workers who can do much more than an inexperienced individual to ensure that the adoption is likely to be a success. They will interview the applicants and form a reliable judgment of their suitability to act as adoptive parents and will also try as far as possible to match the child and the adopters. Secondly, provided that the natural parents are prepared to consent to the procedure (which in practice they normally will), the identity of the applicants can be withheld from them. This will prevent any attempt by the parents to get in touch with the child later, which might destroy the security which adoption is designed to give to the child and adopters alike.[4]

The first object of the Children Act is to provide a comprehensive adoption service (to be called "the Adoption Service") through the agency of local authorities, that is, non-metropolitan counties, metropolitan districts and London boroughs.[5] The Act of 1958 had already placed on them responsibility for supervising arrangements for adoption and securing the wellbeing

---

[1] The provisions not yet in force will come into force on such date or dates as the Home Secretary shall appoint: s. 108 (2).

[2] These will be printed in square brackets preceded by the words "1976 Act".

[3] The total number of children adopted in any one year reached a peak of 24,859 in 1968. Since then the number has fallen steadily and in 1979 there were only 10,870. In 1968 22% of children adopted were legitimate; in 1979 the figure was 42%. In 1968 one of the adopters was a parent in 74% of the orders made in respect of legitimate children and in 23% of the orders made in respect of illegitimate children; in 1979 the figures were 83% and 43% respectively. A parent was an applicant in 34% of all cases in 1968; by 1979 the figure had risen to 60%.

[4] Anonymity is preserved by referring to the proceedings throughout by a serial number. This may raise difficult problems if the parent withdraws consent to the adoption and the application is contested: *Re M.*, [1973] Q.B. 108; [1972] 3 All E.R. 321, C.A. Contrast the *child's* eventual right to discover his parent's identity: *post*, pp. 352-353.

[5] S. 107 (1). [1976 Act, s. 72 (1).]

of children awaiting adoption, and when the relevant sections of the Children
Act come into force, each authority will be under a duty to establish and
maintain a service to meet the needs of children who have been or may be
adopted, the parents and guardians of such children, and persons who have
adopted or may adopt a child. The authority must provide certain facilities[1]
in conjunction with its other relevant social services or secure their provision
by adoption societies approved by the Department of Health and Social
Security after satisfying what will doubtless be very rigorous conditions to
ensure that they can make an effective contribution to the adoption service.[2]

A further object of the Children Act is to prevent children being placed for
adoption by private persons (or "third parties", as they are often called). At
present the law is primarily concerned to protect the child by preventing
commercial trafficking in adoption which could easily result from the fact
that the number of people wishing to adopt children always far exceeds the
number of children being placed. It is illegal for any body of persons to make
arrangements for an adoption unless it is an adoption agency, that is, a local
authority or an approved adoption society, but this does not prevent an individual from doing so.[3] The Children Act attempts to stamp out third party
adoptions altogether by making it illegal (in a section not yet in force) for
anyone other than an adoption agency to place a child or make any other
arrangements for an adoption unless the proposed adopter is a relative of the
child or is acting in pursuance of a High Court order.[4] Further protection is
given by provisions in the Act of 1958 which forbid the giving or receiving of
any payment or reward in consideration of an adoption[5] and prohibit any
advertisement indicating that a parent or guardian wishes to have a child
adopted, that a person wishes to adopt a child or that anyone except an

---

[1] Ss. 1 and 2. [1976 Act, ss. 1 and 2.] The facilities include the provision of temporary board
and lodging for pregnant women, mothers and children; arrangements for assessing children and
prospective adopters and for placing children for adoption; and counselling for persons with
problems relating to adoption.

[2] Ss. 4-7; Child Care Act 1980, s. 76. Approval must be renewed every three years and may
be withdrawn if the society ceases to make an effective contribution to the adoption service. For
other detailed provisions, see the Adoption Act 1958, ss. 32 and 33, as amended by the Children
Act 1975, Sched. 3 and Sched. 4, Part VII. [1976 Act, ss. 3-5 and 8-10.] At present societies are
registered with local authorities: see Adoption Act 1958, ss. 30-33. The reasons for transferring
the power of approval to the Department are to ensure uniformity of standards and to prevent
local authorities having to exercise control over bodies with whom they are required to work: see
Cmnd. 5107, paras. 51-60. For the duties of adoption agencies, see the Adoption Agencies
Regulations 1976.

[3] Adoption Act 1958, s. 29. At present the Act refers to a registered adoption society.

[4] Children Act 1975, s. 28, amending s. 29 of the Adoption Act 1958. [1976 Act, s. 11.]
"Relative" is defined as grandparent, brother, sister, uncle or aunt, whether of the full blood, of
the half blood or by affinity, and, in the case of an illegitimate child, its natural father and any
person who would be a relative if it were the legitimate child of its father and mother: Adoption
Act 1958, s. 57 (1). [1976 Act, s. 72 (1).]

[5] Adoption Act 1958, s. 50, as amended by the Children Act 1975, Sched. 3. But an adoption
agency may be paid reasonable expenses and the court to which an application for an adoption
order is made may authorise payments or rewards: s. 50 (3) and (3A) (added by the Criminal
Law Act 1977, Sched. 12). [1976 Act, s. 57, as amended by the 1977 Act.] In some cases suitable
adopters may fail to apply for an order because they cannot afford to adopt a child unless an
allowance is paid. For an experimental period of seven years the Secretary of State will be able to
authorise the payment of allowances: Children Act 1975, s. 32. See Cmnd. 5107, paras. 93-94.

adoption agency is willing to make arrangements for its adoption.[1] Furthermore, except under the authority of an order of the court, it is forbidden to take or send a minor who is a British subject to any place outside the United Kingdom, Channel Islands or the Isle of Man with a view to his adoption by any person who is not his parent, guardian or relative.[2]

B. THE MAKING OF ADOPTION ORDERS

The overriding principle is now embodied in section 3 of the Children Act 1975,[3] which is already in force and which provides:

> "In reaching any decision relating to the adoption of a child, a court or adoption agency shall have regard to all the circumstances, first consideration being given to the need to safeguard and promote the welfare of the child throughout his childhood; and shall so far as practicable ascertain the wishes and feelings of the child regarding the decision and give due consideration to them, having regard to his age and understanding."

This must be contrasted with the wording of section 1 of the Guardianship of Minors Act 1971 which requires the court to regard a minor's welfare as the first *and paramount* consideration in deciding any question relating to his custody or upbringing. The effect of the omission of the words italicised in the 1975 Act is not entirely clear: it probably means that the child's welfare is to be considered of the first importance but is not necessarily to rule upon or determine the course to be followed.[4]

Who may be adopted.—An adoption order may be made only in respect of a person who is under the age of 18 and has never been married. A child who has been adopted before may be readopted.[5]

Who may apply for an Adoption Order.—As adoption creates the legal relationship of parent and legitimate child between the adopter and the adopted child, an order may not be made upon the application of more than one person unless the applicants are married to each other, in which case they may apply for an order jointly.[6] Alternatively, it may be made on the application of one person alone. Adoption agencies almost invariably place a

---

[1] Adoption Act 1958, s. 51, as amended by the Children Act 1975, Sched. 3. [1976 Act, s. 58.]

[2] *Ibid.*, s. 52, as amended by the Children Act 1975, Sched. 3 and Sched. 4, Part I. [1976 Act, s. 56.] This includes any step in a process the ultimate purpose of which is adoption: *Re M.*, [1973] Fam. 66; [1973] 1 All E.R. 852. A British subject includes a citizen of the Republic of Ireland: s. 57 (3). For the meaning of relative, see *ante*, p. 338, n. 4; for orders in relation to children to be adopted abroad, see *post*, p. 354. This does not apply in the case of a child emigrating under the authority of the Home Secretary (see *post*, p. 400, n.7): Child Care Act 1980, s. 24 (5).

[3] [1976 Act, s. 6.]

[4] *Per* CUMMING-BRUCE, J., in *Re B.*, [1976] Fam. 161, 166; [1976] 3 All E.R. 124, 128 (overruled in *Re P.*, [1977] Fam. 25; [1977] 1 All E.R. 182, C.A., on other grounds). For s. 1 of the Guardianship of Minors Act, see *ante*, pp. 279-280.

[5] Children Act 1975, ss. 8 (5), (8) and 107 (1) (definition of "child"). [1976 Act, ss. 12 (5), (7) and 72 (1).] The child's domicile does not affect jurisdiction: *Re B.*, [1968] Ch. 204; [1967] 3 All E.R. 629. But see *post*, p. 350, n. 5.

[6] If joint applicants are not in fact married to each other, the order is voidable and not void: *Re F.*, [1977] Fam. 165; [1977] 2 All E.R. 777, C.A.

child with a married couple so that it will be brought up in a "normal" family with two parents; consequently a sole applicant is likely to be the mother of an illegitimate child or a relative. In the case of a joint application both spouses must be over the age of 21 and, unless the application is for a convention adoption order, one of them must be domiciled in a part of the United Kingdom, the Channel Islands or the Isle of Man. An adoption may be made on the application of one person only if he is over 21 and (unless the application is for a convention adoption order) domiciled in one of the countries mentioned above.[1] In addition, an adoption may not be made on the sole application of a married person unless his spouse cannot be found or is by reason of ill health, whether physical or mental, incapable of making an application for an adoption order[2] or, alternatively, if the spouses have separated and are living apart and the separation is likely to be permanent.[3] This of course is designed to avoid the highly artificial situation of a child being adopted by one of two married persons living together, the other of whom refuses to apply for an order.

Agreement to the Making of an Order.—Since the effect of an adoption order is to destroy the legal relationship existing between the child and its natural parents, the Act provides that no order may be made unless each parent or guardian of the child agrees freely and unconditionally with full understanding of what the making of the order involves.[4] In the case of a child who has been adopted previously, its "parents" are its adoptive parents under the first order. In the case of an illegitimate child the mother's consent will always be required[5] but that of the father will be required only if he has been granted custody by virtue of an order under the Guardianship of Minors Act.[6] If he does not have custody, he has no rights which the adoption order will extinguish and consequently there is nothing to rebut the presumption that the term "parent" does not include the father of a bastard.[7] He is entitled to be heard, however, if he is contributing to the child's maintenance

---

[1] Children Act 1975, ss. 10 (1), (2) and 11 (1), (2). [1976 Act, ss. 14 (1), (2) and 15 (1), (2).] Before the Children Act came into force, a sole applicant and at least one of joint applicants had to be aged 25 unless he or she was a parent or relative of the child. The Houghton Committee recommended the introduction of a uniform age because there was some evidence that the minimum age of 25 was preventing some suitable couples from adopting and a minimum age of 21 would give an opportunity of testing the strength of a teenage marriage: Cmnd. 5107, paras. 70-78. For convention orders, see *post*, pp. 355-356.

[2] What does this provision contemplate? It is easy to see that a person's mental health may be such that he is incapable of making an application but difficult to see how his physical health can have this effect. Does it envisage a spouse whose health is such that no court would make an order? If so, this might in any case lead the court to conclude that the applicant's home is such that it would not be for the child's benefit to make an order in his favour.

[3] Children Act 1975, s. 11 (1) (b). [1976 Act, s. 15 (1) (b).]

[4] *Ibid.*, s. 12 (1). [1976 Act, s. 16 (1) (b) (i).] In the case of a ward of court the consent of the court must also be obtained: *F. v. S.*, [1973] Fam. 203; [1973] 1 All E.R. 722, C.A.

[5] *Cf. Re M.*, [1955] 2 Q.B. 479; [1955] 2 All E.R. 911, C.A.; *Watson* v. *Nikolaisen*, [1955] 2 Q.B. 286; [1955] 2 All E.R. 427.

[6] Children Act 1975, s. 107 (1) (definition of "guardian"). [1976 Act, s. 72 (1).]

[7] *Re M.*, (*supra*). Contrast the court's reluctance to sever the link between the legitimate child and its father: see Eekelaar, 38 M.L.R. 335, and the cases there cited, particularly *Re E. (P.)*, [1969] 1 All E.R. 323, C.A.

under any order or agreement;[1] in other cases the court may permit him to be heard and will normally do so if he is showing parental concern about the child's future. If, contrary to the mother's wishes, he does not want the child to be adopted, he may try to prevent it by applying for custody.[2] In such a case the real question is whether the court should award custody to him or make the adoption order, and in order to arrive at a proper conclusion and enable all parties to be heard, the court should hear both applications at the same time and not give judgment on one until it has heard the other.[3] As in other cases involving custody, the problem must be resolved by reference to what is best for the child's welfare. In such circumstances the tie of blood cannot, of course, be ignored, and in *Re C. (M.A.)*[4] the Court of Appeal upheld a decision in which custody had been given to the father (who was married and could offer the child a good home) even though the applicants for an adoption order had had care and possession of it for 15 months. Two members of the court went so far as to say that adoption is a second best step which should not be taken when a real parent wants the child and can make suitable arrangements for it, but these dicta are in direct conflict with the earlier decisions of the Court of Appeal in *Re Adoption Application 41/61*[5] and *Re O.*[6] and cannot be regarded as a correct statement of the law. The true position, as was emphasised in the two earlier cases, is that the father is entitled to special consideration but no more, and if the welfare of the child demands it, an adoption order will be made.[7]

Dispensing with Agreement.—As the purpose of requiring the agreement of parents and guardians is to ensure that their rights are not arbitrarily destroyed, it follows that it is not required if the person concerned has not performed his natural or legal duties or is incapable of giving his consent or is acting unreasonably. Consequently, the court may dispense with agreement in the following circumstances.[8]

(1) If the parent or guardian cannot be found[9] or is incapable of giving his agreement.[10]

(2) If he is withholding his agreement unreasonably. This in practice is the commonest ground for applying to the court to dispense with agreement and gives rise to most difficulty. Whether or not agreement is unreasonably withheld is a question of fact in each case. Although some earlier cases

---

[1] Adoption (High Court) Rules 1976, r. 18 (e); Adoption (County Court) Rules 1976, r. 4 (2) (e); Magistrates' Courts (Adoption) Rules 1976, r. 4 (1) (d).

[2] Under the Guardianship of Minors Act 1971, ss. 9 (1) and 14 (1) (see *ante*, p. 302).

[3] *Re O.*, [1965] Ch. 23; [1964] 1 All E.R. 786, C.A. Steps should be taken to prevent the putative father from discovering the adopters' identity if necessary: *Re O.; Re Adoption Application 41/61 (No. 2)*, [1964] Ch. 48; [1963] 2 All E.R. 1082. The same procedure must be followed if the child is a ward of court.

[4] [1966] 1 All E.R. 838, C.A.

[5] [1963] Ch. 315; [1962] 3 All E.R. 553, C.A.

[6] [1965] Ch. 23; [1964] 1 All E.R. 786, C.A.

[7] As in *Re Adoption Application 41/61 (No. 2)*, (*supra*), and *Re O.*, (*supra*).

[8] Children Act 1975, s. 12. [1976 Act, s. 16.] This is permissive and the court must consider whether or not to exercise its discretion in any given case: *Re C.S.C.*, [1960] 1 All E.R. 711, 714.

[9] *I.e.*, cannot be found by taking all reasonable and proper steps: *Re F. (R.)*, [1970] 1 Q.B. 385; [1969] 3 All E.R. 1101, C.A.

[10] This covers the case of a person whose whereabouts is known but with whom it is impossible to communicate: *Re R.*, [1966] 3 All E.R. 613 (impossible to communicate with parents in a country under totalitarian government for political reasons).

stressed that, before a parent could be deprived of his rights, the court must be satisfied that he had in some way been culpable, this approach was firmly rejected by the House of Lords in *Re W*.[1] All members of the House agreed that the test is objective: would a reasonable parent, placed in the situation of the particular parent, withhold agreement? Obviously unreasonableness can include culpability; it can also include callous indifference and "(when carried to excess) sentimentality, romanticism, bigotry, wild prejudice, caprice, fatuousness or excessive lack of common sense".[2] In many cases it will be easy to say whether, looked at objectively, the parent is acting reasonably or not, but in others one reasonable parent might withhold his agreement whilst another might not do so. In the latter type of case the court must respect the particular parent's decision to refuse to agree and must not substitute its own view. As LORD HAILSHAM, L.C., said:[3]

> "The question in any given case is whether a parental veto comes within the band of possible reasonable decisions and not whether it is right or mistaken. Not every reasonable exercise of judgment is right, and not every mistaken exercise of judgment is unreasonable."

Prima facie it must always be reasonable for a parent to withhold agreement in view of the consequences of the making of an order, and it will be exceptional for a court to dispense with it.[4] All the facts must be looked at, but obviously the reasonable parent will give the greatest weight to the child's welfare.[5] Although it is not necessary to show a prognosis of lasting damage if an order is not made, there must be some really serious factor justifying the use of the guillotine:[6] it was said in *Re W*. that agreement may be dispensed with if the parent has ignored or disregarded some *appreciable* ill or risk or some *substantial* benefit likely to be avoided or to accrue if the child were adopted.[7]

A reasonable parent must clearly take account of financial and educational prospects, but of much greater importance, of course, is the child's future happiness and the stability of its home life.[8] Strictly speaking, section 3 of the Children Act has no bearing on the question whether agreement has been unreasonably withheld because it requires the court, not the parent, to give first consideration to the child's welfare:[9] none the less there is no doubt that the courts are paying much more attention to it. Although little weight should be given to the parent's vacillation under stress or to the pain that the loss of the child will inevitably cause the applicants,[10] it must be appreciated

---

[1] [1971] A.C. 682; [1971] 2 All E.R. 49, H.L.

[2] *Per* LORD HAILSHAM, L.C., at pp. 700 and 56, respectively.

[3] At pp. 700 and 56, respectively.

[4] *Per* LORD HAILSHAM, L.C., at pp. 699 and 55, LORD HODSON at pp. 718 and 72.

[5] See *Re D.*, [1977] A.C. 602, at pp. 633 and 638; [1977] 1 All E.R. 145, at pp. 156 and 161, H.L.

[6] *Per* CUMMING-BRUCE, J., in *Re B.*, [1975] Fam. 127, 143; [1975] 2 All E.R. 449, 462, cited with approval in *Re D.*, (*supra*), at pp. 632 and 644 and 155 and 166, respectively.

[7] *Re W.*, (*supra*), *per* LORD HAILSHAM, L.C., at pp. 700 and 56, LORD MACDERMOTT at pp. 709 and 64.

[8] *Cf. Re F.*, [1970] 1 All E.R. 344, at pp. 347 and 349, C.A., where it was stated obiter that the court could dispense with the agreement of a father who had strangled the child's mother even though he was found guilty of manslaughter on the ground of diminished responsibility. (See further *post*, p. 368.)

[9] *Re P.*, [1977] Fam. 25; [1977] 1 All E.R. 182, C.A. For a criticism of this view, see Bevan and Parry, *Children Act*, 29; Freeman, 127 New L.J. 679.

[10] *Per* LORD HAILSHAM, L.C., in *Re W.* (*supra*), at pp. 700 and 56-57, respectively.

that to tear the child away from those whom it has come to regard as its parents may have disastrous consequences. This in itself may force the reasonable parent to agree to the adoption; and the longer the child has been with the applicants, the greater is the danger to be guarded against. Once a parent has given his agreement and the child has been placed with the applicants, time, so to speak, begins to run against the parent and it becomes progressively more difficult for him to show that a change of mind is reasonable.[1] In *Re W*. the child, who was illegitimate, had been with the applicants for 18 months and had settled down well with them. The mother (who later withdrew her agreement) already had two other illegitimate children; there was a grave risk of more (which would reduce her prospects of marriage); there was no man in the household; and it was doubtful whether she had the capacity to bring up three children. In these circumstances the House of Lords held that there was ample evidence to support the county court judge's finding that the mother was unreasonably withholding her agreement.[2]

On the other hand, the court is much less likely to dispense with agreement if the child will remain with the applicants in any event and the sole purpose of the application is to cut the parent out of the child's life altogether. This happened in *Re B*.,[3] where the parents had been divorced and the mother and her second husband wished to adopt the child and bring it up as their own to the total exclusion of the father. As the court pointed out, it will rarely be in the child's interests to sever all links with a parent in this way, and as the father's wish to retain them was honest and the welfare of the child did not point decisively to the need for adoption, the order made by a magistrates' court was quashed. This case should be contrasted with *Re D*.,[4] where the father was a practising homosexual who had lived with a series of young men. His wife had divorced him and remarried and the child of the marriage, a boy aged seven, was living with her and her second husband who now wished to adopt him. If the father were to continue to have access, the boy was inevitably going to come into contact with other men of his own proclivities sooner or later. The county court judge hearing the case had concluded: "A reasonable man would say 'I must protect my boy even if it means parting from him for ever so that he can be free from this danger.' . . . The father has

---

[1] *Re H*., [1977] 2 All E.R. 339, 340, C.A. Consequently the court should defer the question of dispensing with agreement until it has decided the application on its merits because it must consider the merits when deciding whether to dispense with agreement: *Re B*., [1975] Fam. 127, 137; [1975] 2 All E.R. 449, 457.

[2] See also *O'Connor* v. *A. and B*., [1971] 2 All E.R. 1230, H.L. (agreement of both natural parents dispensed with, notwithstanding that they were married to each other and could offer child a home, because of their instability and the disruptive effect of transfer of possession on child who had lived with applicants for three years); *Re R*., [1973] 3 All E.R. 88, C.A. (agreement of mother dispensed with because she had little love for child who was likely to be in care if returned to her); *Re P*., [1977] Fam. 25; [1977] 1 All E.R. 182, C.A. (agreement of unmarried mother aged 16 living with no man in household dispensed with).

[3] [1975] Fam. 127; [1975] 2 All E.R. 449. Contrast *Re S*. (1978), 9 Fam. Law 88, C.A. (father's agreement dispensed with when his sole contact with child was for a few minutes when it was three weeks old). The question of access should be dealt with in divorce proceedings: see now the Children Act 1975, s. 10 (3), *post*, p. 351.

[4] [1977] A.C. 602; [1977] 1 All E.R. 145, H.L. See Bissett-Johnson, 41 M.L.R. 96. Insofar as the decision turns upon the fact that no appeal would lie from a county court on a question of fact in adoption proceedings, this is no longer the law since the Children Act 1975, Sched. 3, para. 41, was brought into operation.

nothing to offer his son at any time in the future.'' In view of this finding, the House of Lords held that he had correctly come to the conclusion that the father was withholding his agreement unreasonably. It must be emphasized, however, that each case will turn on its own facts: the parent's homosexuality will not of itself mean that his refusal to agree to his child's adoption will be unreasonable if this presents no danger to the child.[1]

(3) If the parent or guardian has persistently failed without reasonable cause to discharge the parental duties in relation to the child. This does not merely include the legal obligations towards the child (for example, to maintain it) but also the natural and moral duty to show affection, care and interest.[2] But the failure must be culpable and "of such gravity, so complete, so convincingly proved that there can be no advantage to the child in keeping continuous contact with the natural parent who has so abrogated his duties that he for his part should be deprived of his own child against his wishes".[3] Thus, in *Re D.*[4] the court refused to dispense with the agreement of the father of a legitimate child solely on the ground that he had failed to provide for her or to see her for a year. As Baker, P., pointed out, when a marriage breaks down, the husband will often withdraw or drift apart from the family temporarily, particularly when, as in that case, he is living with another woman.

(4) If the parent or guardian has abandoned or neglected the child.[5]

(5) If he has persistently ill-treated the child.

(6) If he has seriously ill-treated the child and (whether because of the ill-treatment or for some other reason) the rehabilitation of the child within his household is unlikely.[6]

Agreement to the making of an adoption order may be given before or at the time of the hearing; in the former event, documentary evidence of the giving of consent is admissible, except that, if the person giving the consent is the child's mother, the document cannot be admitted unless the child was at least six weeks old when it was executed and it is also attested by a justice of the peace, a county court officer empowered to take affidavits or a magistrates' clerk.[7] The agreement must be operative when the order is made,

---

[1] See *ibid.*, at pp. 629, 640, 641-642 and 647, and 153, 162, 163 and 168, respectively. An appellate court should not interfere with the exercise of discretion by a court of first instance unless there is an error of law, a conclusion based on inadmissible evidence or so little regard to the witnesses and their demeanour that the appellate court is in as good a position as the trial judge to form an opinion: *Re W.*, (*supra*), at pp. 700 and 56, respectively; *O'Connor* v. *A. and B.*, (*supra*), at p. 1239; *Re D.*, (*supra*). See further Michaels, *The Dangers of a Change of Parentage in Custody and Adoption Cases*, 83 L.Q.R. 547, particularly at pp. 560 *et seq.*; Blom-Cooper, *Adoption Applications and Parental Responsibility*, 20 M.L.R. 473; 34 M.L.R. 681; Prime, 116 Sol. Jo. 751, 774.

[2] *Re P.*, [1962] 3 All E.R. 789; *Re B.*, [1968] Ch. 204; [1967] 3 All E.R. 629.

[3] *Per* Baker, P., in *Re D.*, [1973] Fam. 209, 214; [1973] 3 All E.R. 1001, 1005.

[4] [1973] Fam. 209; [1973] 3 All E.R. 1001.

[5] "Abandoned" and "neglected" connote conduct which would render the parent or guardian liable to criminal proceedings under the Children and Young Persons Act 1933, s. 1 (*ante*, p. 321): *Watson* v. *Nikolaisen*, [1955] 2 Q.B. 286; [1955] 2 All E.R. 427; *Re W.* (unreported), cited in *Re P.*, [1962] 3 All E.R. 789, 793.

[6] *I.e.*, if the ill-treatment is serious, it does not have to be persistent. Rehabilitation may be unlikely because, *e.g.*, the child is in care or the parent is in prison.

[7] Adoption Act 1958, s. 6; Children Act 1975, s. 12 (4). The last condition is clearly designed to prevent the mother from being persuaded to give her consent before she has recovered from

however, and consequently any agreement previously given may be withdrawn at any time before that.[1]

Freeing Child for Adoption.[2]—One of the main weaknesses of the present
law is that, until an adoption order is actually made, the applicant cannot be
sure that a parent who has given his or her consent will not withdraw it.
Although this rarely happens in practice, it is a source of fear to many
applicants. To overcome this difficulty, the Children Act (in sections which
are not yet in force) will enable a court to make an order freeing the child for
adoption.[3] Only an adoption agency may apply for an order, and as it will
enable an adoption to be made without the further consent of the child's
parents and guardians, it may not be made unless the latter freely, and with
full understanding of what is involved, agree generally and unconditionally
to the child's being adopted or their agreement is dispensed with on one of the
grounds enabling the court to dispense with it when making an adoption
order.[4] The court must also be satisfied in the case of an illegitimate child that
the putative father does not intend to apply for custody (when his agreement
to adoption would be necessary) or, if he were to do so, that his application
would be likely to be unsuccessful.

The effect of an order freeing a child for adoption is to vest the parental
rights and duties in the adoption agency.[5] So long as the order is in force, the
parent or guardian cannot veto any proposed adoption. Unless he makes a
declaration that he prefers not to be involved in future questions concerning
the adoption of the child, the agency must inform him at the end of twelve
months whether the child has been adopted or placed for adoption and must
thereafter give him notice whenever the child is placed or ceases to have its
home with a person with whom it has been placed, until an adoption order is
made. Once this initial period of twelve months has elapsed, the parent or
guardian may apply for the order to be revoked provided that the child has
not been adopted and does not have his home with a person with whom he has
been placed for adoption. In deciding whether to revoke the order, the court
must have regard to the principle embodied in section 3 of the Act.[6] If the
order is revoked, parental rights and duties revest in the person or persons in
whom they were vested before the order freeing the child for adoption was
made;[7] if it is not revoked, the agency ceases to be under any obligation to

---

the child's birth. When s. 20 of the Children Act 1975 comes into force, written consent will be
witnessed by a "reporting officer". See also *ibid.*, s. 102. [1976 Act, ss. 16 (4), 61 and 65.]

[1] *Re F.*, [1957] 1 All E.R. 819; *Re K.*, [1953] 1 Q.B. 117; [1952] 2 All E.R. 877, C.A.

[2] See Bevan and Parry, *Children Act* 1975, c. 5.

[3] Ss. 14-16, implementing recommendations of the Houghton Committee. See Cmnd. 5107,
paras. 173-186. [1976 Act, ss. 18-20.]

[4] But at least one parent or guardian must consent to the making of the *application* unless the
child is in the care of the agency. The mother's agreement is ineffective if given within six weeks
of the child's birth. Agreement cannot be dispensed with unless the child has been placed for
adoption or the court is satisfied that it is likely that it will be.

[5] The rights and duties may be transferred to another adoption agency by a court order:
Children Act 1975, s. 23. [1976 Act, s. 21.]

[6] See *ante*, p. 339. The adoption agency must not place the child for adoption pending the
hearing of the application.

[7] If they were then vested in a local authority or voluntary organisation, they will vest in the
individuals in whom they were vested before being vested in that body. Any duty to make
payments arising by virtue of an agreement or order also revives.

give notice of the child's progress and the parent or guardian making the application cannot make a further application for its revocation without the leave of the court.

Procedure for the Making of Adoption Orders.—Before a court can make an adoption order, a number of preliminary conditions must be satisfied.

Actual Custody of the Child.—In order to ensure as far as possible that the adopters are suitable people to bring the child up, he must have been continuously in their actual custody for at least three consecutive months preceding the making of the order and after he reached the age of six weeks. The Adoption Act originally required the child to have been in the applicants' care and possession, but this term was replaced by "actual custody" by the Children Act 1975.[1] There was formerly some doubt whether the applicants could be said to have care and possession if they parted with the child for even one night;[2] it is believed, however, that the change of wording has confirmed the decision of BUCKLEY, J., in *Re B.*[3] where he applied the test: was the applicant throughout the period in effective control of the child's life and was that control of a kind and exercised in a way which was quasi-parental? In that case the applicant was a nurse who wished to adopt her own illegitimate son aged two years. She was employed in a hospital and because of night duties she left the boy with neighbours with whom he spent on the average four days and five nights a week. As they acted in accordance with the mother's wishes and directions and were really in a similar position to the child's nurse, BUCKLEY, J., concluded that care and control were exercised on the applicant's behalf and therefore vicariously by her, and he held that he had jurisdiction to make the order. Scottish cases have held that there is continuous care and possession notwithstanding that the child was in hospital for a part of the time,[4] or that she was a probationer nurse in a hospital and returned to the applicant's home only at the weekends and on holiday.[5] Obviously there is a danger that the purpose of the Act could be defeated; if, for example, the child spent the whole of the time in hospital or at a boarding school, there would be no opportunity of seeing whether he was likely to settle down in his new home. In the absence of any other evidence, the court could refuse to make an order in such a case on the ground that it was not satisfied that it would be for the child's welfare.

If the applicants are normally resident in England, the custody will usually be in this country, but it is submitted that this does not prevent them from taking the child out of the jurisdiction, say, for a holiday or for reasons of

---

[1] Adoption Act 1958, s. 3 (1); Children Act 1975, Sched. 3, para. 21 (4).

[2] See *Re C.S.C.*, [1960] 1 All E.R. 711.

[3] [1964] Ch. 1, 7; [1963] 3 All E.R. 125, 129. *Cf. Re A.*, [1963] 1 All E.R. 531, 535, where CROSS, J., speaking of a case where the child was aged 20, said that it was artificial to talk of care and possession in such circumstances but stressed that the applicants must be *in loco parentis* to him.

[4] *Re G., Petitioner*, 1955 S.L.T. (Sh. Ct.) 27.

[5] *Re A., Petitioners*, 1953 S.L.T. (Sh. Ct.) 45. In *Re A., Petitioners*, 1958 S.L.T. (Sh. Ct.) 61, it was held "with difficulty and hesitation" that the child was in the care and possession of both applicants when he lived with the wife, and the husband, a soldier, was away on service. A child in the armed forces cannot be in the care and possession of the applicants: *Re M., Petitioner*, 1953 S.C. 227.

health.[1] If they are not normally resident in England or Scotland, however, the position is more complicated. If there is only one applicant, the above provisions must be complied with. If the spouses apply jointly, they satisfy the statutory conditions if they both have actual custody for three months although, if the child is above school age (in which case no notice has to be given to the local authority),[2] this need not be in Great Britain at all.[3] This might be impossible, however, if one of them has to return to their normal place of residence; consequently the Act specifically provides as an alternative that it is sufficient if the child has been in the actual custody of one of them during the previous three months provided that the applicants have lived together in Great Britain for at least one of those months.[4]

The Children Act will preserve this principle if one of the applicants (or the sole applicant) is a parent, step-parent or relative of the child or if the child was placed with the applicants by an adoption agency. In such cases the child must have had his home with the applicants or one of them for the 13 weeks preceding the making of the order and the child must be at least 19 weeks old.[5] A child is to be regarded as having his home with the person who, disregarding absence of the child at a hospital or boarding school and any other temporary absence, has actual custody of him.[6] The possibility that the whole period could be spent away from the applicants' home is guarded against by the further provision that the agency placing the child or, if it was not placed by an agency, the local authority, must have sufficient opportunities to see the child with the applicant or, in the case of a joint application, both applicants together in the home environment.[7] As a further discouragement to third party placements and to deter parents from evading the prohibition of them by ostensibly placing the child with foster parents who would then apply for an adoption, the court will not be able to make an order in other cases unless the child has had his home with one of the applicants for the whole of the preceding twelve months.[8]

Once an application for an order has been made, no parent or guardian who has agreed to the adoption nor any adoption society or local authority who has arranged it can demand the return of the child from the applicant

---

[1] In *Re W.*, [1962] Ch. 918, 925; [1962] 2 All E.R. 875, 878, WILBERFORCE, J., said *obiter* that there *must* be custody in England or Scotland. In *Re M.*, [1973] Fam. 66, 70; [1973] 1 All E.R. 852, 855, BRANDON, J., interpreted this decision as imposing no such restriction. Whilst it is difficult to agree with the learned judge's views, this approach is clearly preferable and should be followed.

[2] See *infra*.

[3] *Re W.*, (*supra*). Presumably this would also apply if the applicant was the child's parent as no notice has to be given in that case either.

[4] Adoption Act 1958, s. 12 (3); *Re W.*, (*supra*). "Living together" has the usual wide meaning given to consortium (see *ante*, p. 112) and the spouses need not have resided in the same house continuously for a month: *Re M.*, [1965] Ch. 203; [1964] 2 All E.R. 1017. In *Re W.* WILBERFORCE, J., stated that the care and possession must be exercised in Great Britain. But see *Re M.*, (*supra*).

[5] Children Act 1975, s. 9 (1). [1976 Act, s. 13 (1).] This also applies if the child was placed by order of the High Court. For the meaning of "relative", see *ante*, p. 338, n. 4.

[6] Ibid., s. 87 (3).

[7] *Ibid.*, s. 9 (3). [1976 Act, s. 13 (3).] The wording is regrettably vague. Presumably the agency or authority must have sufficient opportunity to see whether the proposed adoption is likely to be for the child's welfare. "Home environment" sounds like a piece of jargon meaning no more than "home".

[8] *Ibid.*, s. 9 (2). [1976 Act, s. 13 (2).] See Cmnd. 5107, paras. 81-91.

without the leave of the court.[1] When it becomes possible to make an order
freeing a child for adoption, the same restriction will apply to any parent or
guardian who has not agreed to the order being made whilst an application
for such an order is pending.[2] Much greater protection is given to applicants
with whom the child has had his home *for five years*, because *no one* is
entitled to remove the child from his custody after he has made an application
for an adoption order or for three months after he has given notice to the
local authority of his intention to do so.[3] This provision is designed
particularly to protect foster parents wishing to adopt because, as the law
now stands, there is a danger that a parent may seek repossession of the child
to prevent adoption and a local authority is consequently inhibited from
broaching the subject of adoption of children in their care even though this is
in the child's interest.[4]

Notice to Local Authority.—If the child is below the upper limit of the
compulsory school age, no adoption order may be made unless the applicant
has given to the local authority within whose area he has his home three
months' notice in writing of his intention to apply for the order. This
provision does not apply if the applicant (or one of the applicants) is the
child's parent.[5]

The purpose of the notice is to ensure the proper supervision of children
placed for adoption. As soon as it is given, the child becomes a "protected
child" for the purpose of Part IV of the Adoption Act—a term which, until
the relevant provisions of the Children Act come into force, will also cover
most children below the upper limit of the compulsory school age placed for
adoption by virtue of an arrangement made by someone other than a parent
or guardian.[6] The authority's chief duty is to see that the child is visited from
time to time, to satisfy themselves as to its well-being, and to give any advice
about its care and maintenance.[7] They may prohibit a person from taking the
care and possession of a protected child if this would appear to be detrimental
to the child unless an adoption society or local authority took part in the

---

[1] Adoption Act 1958, ss. 34 (as substituted by the Children Act 1975, s. 29) and 35 (1) (b),
(2). [1976 Act, ss. 27 and 30 (1) (b), (2).]

[2] *Ibid.*, s. 34, as substituted. [1976 Act, s. 27.]

[3] *Ibid.*, s. 34A, added by the Children Act 1975, s. 29, and amended by the Domestic Proceedings and Magistrates' Courts Act 1978, Sched. 2. For the return of children taken away in
breach of ss. 34 and 34A, see the Children Act 1975, s. 30. [1976 Act, ss. 28 (as amended by
ibid.) and 29.]

[4] See Cmnd. 5107, paras. 139-147 and 161-164. The Houghton Committee abandoned their
original proposal that after five years foster parents should be able to apply for an adoption
order with the agreement of the local authority (but without the parents' agreement) because this
might have led foster parents to weaken links between parent and child, caused anxiety to
parents, and inhibited them from placing children in care as a consequence. See further Bevan
and Parry, *Children Act* 1975, 69-74.

[5] Adoption Act 1958, s. 3 (2), as amended by S.I. 1976 No. 1744. "Home" is not defined;
presumably it is the place where the applicant normally resides or where joint applicants have
their matrimonial home. If one or both of the applicants have not had their home in Great
Britain, notice may be given by either of them: *ibid.*, s. 12 (3).

[6] *Ibid.*, s. 37, as amended by the Children and Young Persons Act 1969, s. 52 (4), and
prospectively by the Children Act 1975, Sched. 3, para. 31, and Sched. 4, Part XI, *q.v.* for the
exceptions. [1976 Act, s. 32.]

[7] *Ibid.*, ss. 38 and 39. [1976 Act, s. 33.] The Secretary of State may also authorise an
inspection: Child Care Act 1980, ss. 74 and 75.

arrangements,[1] and a magistrates' court can order the removal of a protected child from unsuitable surroundings.[2]

If the child has been placed for adoption by an adoption society, it will be seen that two social workers (one appointed by the society and one by the local authority) will become involved with each adoption. This not only leads to unnecessary duplication of work but also bewilders many applicants. The child does not need the protection afforded by this procedure in such cases and there will be even less justification for it when the new co-ordinated adoption service is set up. Consequently, when section 18 of the Children Act[3] comes into force, it will be necessary to give three months' notice to the local authority only when the child was not placed by an adoption agency.

Guardian ad litem.—The court must appoint a guardian *ad litem* to safeguard the child's interests.[4] His duties are extensive and are laid down in the Adoption Rules; they may be broadly classified under four heads. First, he must interview the applicants and get from them all relevant information about their home conditions, means and health. They are bound to provide a medical certificate that they are physically, mentally and emotionally suitable to adopt a child; unless one of the applicants is a parent or relative of the child, they must also name a referee whom the guardian *ad litem* must also interview. Secondly, he must find out all relevant information about the child. A medical report must be submitted, and the guardian *ad litem* must interview the natural parents and anyone who has taken part in arranging the adoption and must obtain a report from the local authority and adoption society. If the child is old enough to understand the nature of an adoption order, he must also find out whether the child wishes to be adopted. Thirdly, he must make sure that any agreement to the making of the order has been freely given. Finally, he must make a confidential report to the court. This report may not be seen by any party to the proceedings except with the leave of the court:[5] this procedure is objectionable in that an unsuccessful applicant cannot controvert any statement of fact;[6] on the other hand the guardian *ad litem* might well be inhibited and the value of his report correspondingly reduced if he knew that others might read it.

---

[1] Adoption Act 1958, s. 41. An appeal lies to a juvenile court: s. 42. This provision will be repealed when third party placements are prohibited.

[2] *Ibid.*, s. 43. [1976 Act, s. 34.] A single justice may act in an emergency. The local authority may receive such a child into their care under s. 2 of the Child Care Act 1980 (see *post*, p. 395).

[3] [1976 Act, s. 22.]

[4] Adoption Act 1958, s. 9 (7). The guardian *ad litem* is usually the Official Solicitor (in the High Court) or the director of Social Services of the local authority or a probation officer (in other courts). No one who has taken part in the arrangements for the adoption or who represents a society or authority which has done so may be the guardian *ad litem*.

[5] *Re P.A.*, [1971] 3 All E.R. 522, C.A. LORD DENNING, M.R., (with whom the other members of the court agreed) relied on the decision in *Official Solicitor* v. *K.*, (*ante*, p. 292). Whereas there is undoubtedly an inherent jurisdiction in the High Court to treat the report as confidential, it is questionable whether this extends to other courts. DONOVAN, L.J., left the point open in *Re G. (T.J.)*, [1963] 2 Q.B. 73, 97; [1963] 1 All E.R. 20, 29, C.A. (decided before *Official Solicitor* v. *K.*).

[6] Consequently he should be informed of facts which he might wish to controvert unless this would clearly conflict with the child's wellbeing. The difficulties can be overcome in part by disclosing sections of the report or permitting the parties' legal advisers to read it. See *Re M.*, [1973] Q.B. 108; [1972] 3 All E.R. 321, C.A.

Just as social workers appointed by an adoption society and a local authority frequently duplicate each other's work, the guardian *ad litem* may also do no more than make the same enquiries as the others have already made. Provided that the initial case work has been done carefully, it will rarely be necessary to have the child's interest further protected by a guardian *ad litem* unless perhaps there is a conflict between the adopters or the adoption agency on the one hand and the parents on the other. Consequently by section 20 of the Children Act (which is not yet in force) a guardian is to be appointed only in the circumstances to be prescribed by the Adoption Rules.[1] It will then become the duty of the adoption agency (or local authority if the child has not been placed by an agency) to conduct the necessary enquiries and to submit a report to the court.[2]

Functions of the Court.—An adoption order (or an order freeing a child for adoption) may be made by the High Court, a county court or a magistrates' court.[3]

The court must be satisfied of three things: that every parent or guardian of the child freely, and with full understanding of what is involved, agrees unconditionally to the making of the order (unless his agreement has been dispensed with); that no unauthorised payments or rewards for the adoption have been made or agreed upon; and that the order, if made, will be for the child's welfare.[4] It will obviously have to rely very heavily (although by no means exclusively) on the report of the guardian *ad litem* or, under the Children Act, of the adoption agency or local authority.

The main benefit that the child is likely to receive is the substitution of statutory parents, who can show real care and affection, for those who are unable or unwilling to perform their parental duties. But "welfare" is a sufficiently wide term to include material benefit as well,[5] and consequently the court may properly make an order for a mother to adopt her own illegitimate child as this will go a long way to remove the social stigma and

---

[1] Cmnd. 5107, paras. 244-256. [1976 Act, s. 65.] The Secretary of State may establish a panel of persons from whom guardians *ad litem* and reporting officers may be drawn: Children Act 1975, s. 103.

[2] Children Act 1975, ss. 18 (2), (3) and 22 (3). [1976 Act, ss. 22 (2), (3) and 23.]

[3] Children Act 1975, ss. 21 (as amended by the Domestic Proceedings and Magistrates' Courts Act 1978, s. 73) and 100. [1976 Act, ss. 62 and 64 (as amended).] Over 80% of all orders are made by county courts; the number made in the High Court is very small (52 out of 10,870 in 1979). If an order relating to custody has already been made in matrimonial proceedings, magistrates' courts have jurisdiction if the custody order is first discharged but normally it will be preferable to bring the application for adoption before the High Court or county court, as the case may be: *Re B.*, [1975] Fam. 127; [1975] 2 All E.R. 449. A magistrates' court must refuse to make an order if it considers that the matter would be more conveniently dealt with by the High Court, and the High Court can order the transfer to itself of a case pending in a county court: Children Act 1975, s. 101 (1), (3), as amended by the Domestic Proceedings and Magistrates' Courts Act 1978, Sched. 2. Only the High Court has jurisdiction if the child is not in Great Britain when the application is made: *ibid.*, s. 100 (4). [1976 Act, ss. 62 (3) and 63.]

[4] Children Act 1975, ss. 3, 12 (1) and 22 (5). [1976 Act, ss. 6, 16 (1) and 24 (2).]

[5] *Re A.*, [1963] 1 All E.R. 531, 534. If the child has a substantial connection with a foreign country (for example, if he is domiciled there or is a foreign national), one of the matters to be taken into account in deciding whether the order will be for his benefit is whether it will be recognised in that country: *Re B.*, [1968] Ch. 204; [1967] 3 All E.R. 629.

remaining legal disabilities of illegitimacy.[1] Conversely, adoption by one parent and that parent's spouse or by some other relative may act to the child's detriment because it distorts true relationships; what is more important is that severing the legal link between parent and child will not usually be for the latter's benefit because it will cut the former out of the child's life altogether. An attempt in *Re J.*[2] to preserve the link by imposing a condition that the father should have access when an illegitimate child was adopted by its mother and her husband is obviously unsatisfactory because of the confusion and distress this may well cause the child.[3] Adoption by parents and step-parents has been made much more difficult by the Children Act. The court is now precluded from making an order on the sole application of one parent unless the other is dead or cannot be found or there is some other reason justifying his or her exclusion.[4] If the sole applicant is a step-parent of a legitimate child or if a joint application is made by one parent and a step-parent, the court is bound to dismiss the application if it considers that the matter would be better dealt with under the court's power to make orders in relation to children of the family in matrimonial proceedings.[5] When the relevant section comes into force, the court will be able to direct in all cases that any application shall be treated as an application for a custodianship order if it considers that the child's welfare would not be better safeguarded by the making of an adoption order and a custodianship order would be appropriate.[6] The welfare of the child must remain the first consideration; it seems probable, however, that adoptions by parents and close relatives will become much rarer in the future except possibly where the other parent has virtually disappeared from the scene[7] or where for some other reason (for example, his way of life) it is desirable to shut him out altogether.

---

[1] *Re D.*, [1959] 1 Q.B. 229; [1958] 3 All E.R. 716, C.A.

[2] [1973] Fam. 106; [1973] 2 All E.R. 410, followed in *Re S.*, [1976] Fam. 1; [1975] 1 All E.R. 109, C.A. *Re J.* was exceptional in that the court gave effect to an agreement arrived at between the parties as the only means of preventing lengthy litigation which would have embittered relations between them. See generally Maidment, *Access and Family Adoptions*, 40 M.L.R. 293. For criticism of adoption by parents generally, see *Re D.*, [1973] Fam. 209, 216; [1973] 3 All E.R. 1001, 1007 (*per* BAKER, P.); the Houghton Report, Cmnd. 5107, c. 5; Hoggett, 117 Sol. Jo. 606.

[3] If the child is adopted by strangers, it will normally be undesirable for it to have further contact with its parents: *Re B. (M.F.)*, [1972] 1 All E.R. 898, C.A.

[4] Children Act 1975, s. 11 (3). [1976 Act, s. 15 (3).] See further Bevan and Parry, *Children Act* 1975, 53-58. At first sight this does not appear to apply to the father of an illegitimate child who is *prima facie* not a parent for the purpose of the Act, but see Bevan and Parry, *op. cit.*, 54.

[5] *Ibid.*, ss. 10 (3) and 11 (4). [1976 Act, ss. 14 (3) and 15 (4).] See *Re S.*, [1977] Fam. 173; [1977] 3 All E.R. 671, C.A. Mother and step-father were permitted to adopt a child in *Re S.* (1979), 9 Fam. Law 88, C.A. (father had seen it for only a few minutes when it was three weeks old) and *Re D.* (1980), 10 Fam. Law 246, C.A. (father had disappeared from scene and applicants proposing to emigrate). See further Hopkins and Benson, 128 New L.J. 339.

[6] *Ibid.*, s. 37. The court *must* make such a direction if the conditions are satisfied and the applicant is a relative (as defined *ante*, p. 338, n. 4) or step-parent; in other cases it has a discretion. It may make a custodianship order even though the child has not had its home with the applicant for the period laid down by s. 33 (*post*, pp. 383-385), but custodianship cannot be given to a parent (who may apply for custody if he wishes) and this provision does not apply to an application by a step-parent if the child has been named in an order made under s. 41 of the Matrimonial Causes Act 1973 (see *ante*, pp. 308-309), when the matter will have to be dealt with under the powers given to the court by that Act.

[7] *Cf. Re D.* (1980), *Times*, 17th June, C.A.

In any case, there must be a genuine intention that the applicants should stand *in loco parentis* to the child and in *Re A*.[1] Cross, J., refused to make an order for what he described as an accommodation adoption of a French boy aged 20, which was sought purely in order to give him the advantage of British nationality.

The court may impose any terms and conditions it thinks fit in the order.[2] In the past the most common condition related to religious education, because a parent was entitled to stipulate that the child should be brought up in a particular faith in giving his consent to the adoption. This could be contrary to the best interests of the child if there were a shortage of adopters of the particular persuasion.[3] Consequently this power was taken away by the Children Act, although an adoption agency is still bound to have regard so far as is practicable to the parent's wishes when placing a child.[4] In any event conditions attached to an order are usually unenforceable because the Act provides no sanction if they are not observed. Normally the court will rely on the good faith of the adopters: if this is felt to be insufficient in a given case, they can be required to give an undertaking to the court that they will fulfil any terms laid down. In the event of non-compliance, the undertaking can then be enforced by committal proceedings or the child can be made a ward of court and the court asked to enforce the conditions.[5]

Registration of Adoptions.—The Registrar General keeps a separate register of adoptions. Records are also kept enabling connections between entries in this register and the register of births to be traced, but these records may be searched only with the leave of the court.[6] There is one exception to this rule: any person over the age of 18 who has been adopted may now obtain a copy of his birth certificate which means that he may be able to trace his natural parents.[7] It is a matter for debate how far this change in the law was desirable. A person seeking this information often needs more help in dealing with problems of identity than mere knowledge of the facts recorded in the register can be expected to afford him.[8] At the same time his mother may have

---

[1] [1963] 1 All E.R. 531. Distinguished in *Re R.*, [1966] 3 All E.R. 613, where the child was also aged 20 and desired to acquire British nationality, on the ground that there was also a genuine desire that he should become a member of the applicant's family. (Until 1969 an adoption order could be made if the child was under 21.)

[2] Children Act 1975, s. 8 (7). [1976 Act, s. 12 (6).]

[3] See Cmnd. 5107, paras. 228-229.

[4] Children Act 1975, s. 13. [1976 Act, s. 7.]

[5] See *Re J.*, (*supra*). Proceedings will usually have to be brought by the adoption agency. There is evidence of an increasing tendency to impose conditions to enable the child to preserve its identity: see Freeman, *Child Law at the Crossroads*, Current Legal Problems 1974, at pp. 195-196.

[6] Adoption Act 1958, ss. 20, 21 and 24. [1976 Act, s. 50 and Sched. 1.] The court for this purpose means the court making the adoption order, the High Court or the Westminster County Court. A search might be ordered, for example, if the child was entitled to a gift under a disposition taking effect before the adoption order but not vesting until after it had been made.

[7] *Ibid.*, s. 20A, added by the Children Act 1975, s. 26. [1976 Act, s. 51.] An adopted person under the age of 18 intending to marry in England or Wales may obtain information indicating whether or not the parties are likely to be related within the prohibited degrees.

[8] See Cmnd. 5107, paras. 295-305. Consequently counselling services are available for persons seeking this information and, if they were adopted before 12th November 1975 (the date on which the Children Act was passed), they are bound to have an interview with a counsellor before the Registrar General will give the information. See further Bevan and Parry, *Children Act 1975*, 94-98.

been prepared to have him adopted on the assurance (properly given at the time) that her identity would never be divulged: it requires little imagination to picture the shattering effect that a successful attempt to find her could have on her and her present family.

Interim Orders.—Instead of making the order applied for, the court may make an interim order to last for not more than two years, the effect of which is to give the custody of the child to the applicant subject to any conditions imposed by the court as regards its maintenance, education and the supervision of its welfare.[1] The purpose of an interim order is to enable the adopters to act for a probationary period, and it is thus a useful compromise when the court is genuinely unable to make up its mind whether the applicants will make good adopters. It has also been used when the court was uncertain whether the child should be adopted or go to live with a parent,[2] although it must be rarely desirable for interim orders to be made in such circumstances because of the uncertainty which they produce. A court has jurisdiction to make an interim order only if it has jurisdiction to make an adoption order.

Refusal to make an Order.—If the court refuses to make any order at all (or if at any stage the application is withdrawn) and the child was placed for adoption by an adoption society or local authority, it must be returned to that body within seven days.[3] There is no statutory obligation to return the child in other cases.[4] The reason for the difference is this: in the first case the body concerned must obviously try to find other suitable applicants, whereas in the second there may be good reasons for permitting the applicants to retain care and control even though an adoption order has not been made. This might occur, for example, if the court had to refuse to make the order because the child's mother withdrew her agreement; if she wishes to recover care and control it is for her to bring the necessary proceedings, the outcome of which must depend primarily on what is in the child's best interests.[5]

The court has a power to make a supervision order or a care order on refusing to make an adoption order if there are exceptional circumstances making either order desirable. If it makes a care order, it may also order either parent (other than the father of an illegitimate child) to make periodical payments towards the child's maintenance. The effect of these orders is the same as that of similar orders made under the Guardianship of Minors Act.[6]

---

[1] Adoption Act 1958, s. 8., Children Act 1975, s. 19. [1976 Act, s. 25.] The period laid down in the original order may be extended provided that the total period is not greater than two years.

[2] *S.* v. *Huddersfield B.C.*, [1975] Fam. 113; [1974] 3 All E.R. 296, C.A.

[3] Adoption Act 1958, s. 35. This also applies if an interim order expires without a full order being made. The court may order a stay for not more than six weeks: *ibid.*, s. 35 (5A) (added by the Children Act 1975, s. 31). This power might be exercised *e.g.* if unsuccessful applicants wished to appeal. If they wished to retain care and control, they could make the child a ward of court, although their chances of success might be slim if the court hearing the adoption application had refused to make a custodianship order in their favour. [1976 Act, s. 30.]

[4] Unless the child is in the care of a local authority and the authority demands its return: Adoption Act 1958, s. 36 (1). [1976 Act, s. 31 (1).]

[5] See *ante*, pp. 290 *et seq.*

[6] Children Act 1975, s. 17, as amended by the Domestic Proceedings and Magistrates' Courts Act 1978, s. 72. [1976 Act, s. 26, as amended by *ibid.*] See further *ante*, p. 303.

If the application is refused, the applicants may normally make a further application only if the court is satisfied that, because of a change of circumstances or for some other reason, this is proper.[1]

Adoption of Children Abroad.—Since 1959 the High Court and county courts have had a power that they did not possess before, that of making a provisional adoption order.[2] The purpose of such an order is to enable a person who is not domiciled in any part of the British Isles (and in whose favour therefore a full adoption order cannot be made) to remove a minor out of the country to obtain an adoption order under his *lex domicilii*. The court has jurisdiction to make such an order only if it would have had jurisdiction to make a full order had the applicant possessed the relevant domicile.[3] A provisional order authorises the applicant to remove the child out of the country for the purpose of his adoption elsewhere and in the meantime gives the legal custody of it to the applicant pending the adoption. Such an order has all the effects of a full order save that it will not affect any devolution of property and will not affect the child's citizenship.

Under the Children Act the term "provisional order" will disappear but the court will retain the power to make an order vesting parental rights and duties in a person who is not domiciled in England or Scotland and who intends to adopt the child under his *lex domicilii*. Most of the remaining provisions of the Act will apply except that the court will have no power to make an interim order or an order freeing the child for adoption.[4]

Revocation of Adoption Orders.—It is specifically provided that an adoption order may be revoked if an illegitimate person, who has been adopted by his mother or father alone, is subsequently legitimated by his parents' marriage so that he may have the advantage of being treated as the legitimate child of both parents.[5] There is no further provision for revoking an order although an appeal will, of course, lie from the making of an order (as it will from a refusal to make one).[6]

---

[1] Children Act 1975, s. 22 (4). [1976 Act, s. 24 (1).]

[2] Adoption Act 1958, s. 53. Formerly a magistrate's licence had to be obtained.

[3] But the child must have been in the actual custody of the applicant continuously for *six* months since the former was six weeks old and before the date of the order and *six* months' notice must have been given to the local authority: s. 53 (5). In the case of joint applicants not resident in Great Britain, it is sufficient if the child has been in the actual custody of one of them for six months provided that the applicants have lived together for at least one of the previous *three* months: *Re M.*, [1965] Ch. 203; [1964] 2 All E.R. 1017.

[4] Children Act 1975, s. 25. [1976 Act, s. 55.] If the applicant is a parent, step-parent or relative of the child or if the child was placed for adoption by an adoption agency, the child must be 32 weeks old and have had its home with one of the applicants for the preceding 26 weeks.

[5] Adoption Act 1958, s. 26. The order may be revoked by the court that made it on the application of any of the parties concerned. An order may also be revoked if a child previously adopted by both parents was legitimated by the Legitimacy Act 1959 (*ante*, p. 269): Adoption Act 1960, s. 1 (1). [1976 Act, s. 52.]

[6] In the case of an appeal from a magistrates' court, to the High Court (Children Act 1975, s. 101 (2)); in other cases to the Court of Appeal. [1976 Act, s. 63 (2).] An order made by a county court or by a magistrates' court may be quashed by *certiorari*. On the question of revocation, see *Skinner* v. *Carter*, [1948] Ch. 387, at pp. 389, 395 and 397; [1948] 1 All E.R. 917, at pp. 920 and 921, C.A. For the bringing of wardship proceedings to undo the effect of an adoption in most exceptional circumstances, see *Re O.*, [1978] Fam. 196; [1978] 2 All E.R. 27,

C. CONVENTION ADOPTION ORDERS

Whereas the traditional basis of jurisdiction to make adoption orders in English law is the applicants' domicile, in many foreign systems it is the parties' nationality. This has naturally caused difficulties in cases with a foreign element (for example, where the applicants are British subjects domiciled abroad) and the desire to produce a uniform law of jurisdiction and recognition led to the Hague Convention on the adoption of children in 1965.[1] The terms of the convention were embodied in the Adoption Act of 1968 and so far as they relate to jurisdiction to make orders are now contained in section 24 of the Children Act 1975.[2] As it will be seen, the essential connecting links are the nationality and residence of the parties.

It will be convenient at the outset to define some of the technical terms used in the Acts. An adoption order made under section 24 is known as a *Convention adoption order.* A *Convention country* is any country outside British territory designated by the Secretary of State as a country in which the Convention is in force.[3] *British territory* means the United Kingdom, the Channel Islands, the Isle of Man and a colony, being a country designated for this purpose or, if no country is designated, any of those countries. A *United Kingdom national* is a citizen of the United Kingdom and Colonies satisfying such conditions as the Secretary of State may specify.[4] If a United Kingdom national is also a national of another state, he is to be regarded as a United Kingdom national only; in other cases of dual nationality, the person in question is to be treated as a national of the country with which he is most closely connected unless one only of the countries is a convention country, in which case he is to be treated as a national of that country. A stateless person is to be regarded as a national of the country in which he habitually resides.[5]

Only the High Court has power to make a convention adoption order.[6] Subject to what is said below, the same law and procedure apply to applications for convention orders as to applications for other orders.

Who may be adopted.—An adoption order may be made only in respect of a person who (i) is under the age of 18; (ii) has not been married; (iii) is a national of the United Kingdom or a Convention country; and (iv) habitually resides in British territory or a Convention country.[7]

Who may apply for an Order.—A sole applicant must either (a) habitually reside in Great Britain *and* be a national of the United Kingdom or a Convention country, or (b) habitually reside in British territory or a Convention country *and* be a United Kingdom national. A joint application

---

C.A. ("which should never be cited as a precedent for anything", *per* ORMROD, L.J., at pp. 205 and 28, respectively).

[1] Cmnd. 2613.

[2] [1976 Act, s. 17.]

[3] At present only Austria and Switzerland have been so designated: S.I. 1978 No. 1431.

[4] Children Act 1975, s. 107 (1). [1976 Act, s. 72 (1).] For details, see the Convention Adoption (Miscellaneous Provisions) Order, S.I. 1978 No. 1432. To qualify as a United Kingdom national one must have a right of abode.

[5] *Ibid.*, s. 24 (9); Adoption Act 1968, s. 9. [1976 Act, s. 70.]

[6] Children Act 1975, s. 100 (2), (5). [1976 Act, s. 62 (4).]

[7] *Ibid.*, ss. 24 (2) and 107 (1). [1976 Act, ss. 12 (5), 17 (2) and 72 (1).]

may be made by a husband and wife, in which case both must satisfy either
condition (a) or condition (b). No order may be made on the sole application
of a married person except in the cases applicable to other adoptions set out in
the Children Act.[1]

Consents and Consultations.—If the child is not a United Kingdom
national, no order may be made unless the provisions relating to "consents
and consultations" of the internal law of the country of which he is a national
are complied with. This does not, however, apply to consents by members of
the applicant's family or to consultations between them and the applicant. If
the child is a United Kingdom national, the law relating to the consent of
parents and guardians is the same as it is on other applications for adoption
orders. If consent may be dispensed with under the relevant law, the body
empowered to do this is the High Court in the case of any application made in
England, whatever the child's nationality.[2]

Restrictions on the making of Orders.—In two cases the court has no
power to make a convention order at all:

(1) If the applicant or applicants are not United Kingdom nationals and
the order is prohibited by the internal law of the country of which they are
nationals.[3] Such a prohibition might relate, for example, to the relative ages
of the child and the applicants or their blood relationship.

(2) If the applicant or applicants and the child are all United Kingdom
nationals living in British territory.[4] The purpose here is clearly to restrict the
operation of section 24 to adoptions with a foreign element. It will be seen
that there is a gap, however, for if the above conditions are satisfied and the
applicants are not domiciled in any part of the British Isles, there is no jurisdiction to make an order at all.

Annulment of Orders.—There is a power to annul Convention adoption
orders which does not apply to other orders. Provided that either the child or
the adopters reside in Great Britain, the High Court may annul an order on
the ground that the adoption was prohibited by the internal law of the
country of which the adopters were nationals or that it contravened provisions relating to consents of the internal law of the country of which the child
was a national.[5] As in the case of other orders, a Convention adoption order
may also be revoked if the child was adopted by his father or mother and has
subsequently been legitimated by their marriage.

---

[1] *Ibid.*, s. 24 (4), (5). [1976 Act, s. 17 (4), (5).] For sole applications by married persons, see
ante, p. 340.

[2] *Ibid.*, s. 24 (6), (7), (9); Adoption Act 1968, s. 10 (1). [1976 Act, ss. 17 (6), (7) and 71.]

[3] *Ibid.*, s. 24 (4), (5), (8). [1976 Act, s. 17 (4), (5), (8).]

[4] *Ibid.*, s. 24 (3). [1976 Act, s. 17 (3).] For other difficulties, see McClean and Patchett,
English Jurisdiction in Adoption, 19 I.C.L.Q. 1; Blom, *The Adoption Act* 1968 *and the Conflict
of Laws*, 22 I.C.L.Q. 109.

[5] *Ibid.*, s. 24 (8A), added by the Domestic Proceedings and Magistrates' Courts Act 1978,
s. 74 (1). [1976 Act, s. 53 (1), as amended by *ibid.*, s. 74 (2).] This sub-section (which applies to
Convention adoption orders provisions already applicable to certain overseas adoptions and set
out *post*, pp. 358-359) also enables a Convention adoption order to be annulled on the ground
that it could have been impugned on any other ground under English law. The order would then
presumably be a nullity anyway.

D. THE LEGAL CONSEQUENCES OF THE MAKING OF AN ADOPTION ORDER

Rights and Duties with respect to the Child's Person.—As has already been pointed out, the effect of an adoption order is to establish the legal relationship of parent and legitimate child between the adopter and adopted child. This has two aspects: the legal rights and duties flowing from the relationship between the child and his natural parents or guardians automatically cease and these rights and duties then vest in the adoptive parent or parents as though the child had been born to him or them in lawful wedlock. Paragraph 3 of Schedule 1 of the Children Act 1975 enacts in general terms:[1]

"(1) An adopted child shall be treated in law—
    (a) where the adopters are a married couple, as if he had been born as a child of the marriage (whether or not he was in fact born after the marriage was solemnized);
    (b) in any other case, as if he had been born to the adopter in wedlock (but not as a child of any actual marriage of the adopter).
(2) An adopted child shall be treated in law as if he were not the child of any person other than the adopters or adopter.
(3) It is hereby declared that this paragraph prevents an adopted child from being illegitimate."

It is expressly provided that adoption will extinguish any existing parental right or duty vested in a parent or guardian (other than one of the adopters) or in any other person by virtue of a court order and any duty to make payments for the child's maintenance by virtue of an order or agreement unless the agreement constitutes a trust or expressly provides to the contrary.[2] Similarly, it is enacted that adoption automatically discharges a care order made under the Children and Young Persons Act 1969[3] and a resolution under section 3 of the Child Care Act 1980 vesting parental rights in a local authority.[4]

One or two other matters are expressly dealt with by the Act. So far as marriage is concerned, an adopted child and its adoptive parent are deemed to come within the prohibited degrees of consanguinity, so that they may not intermarry.[5] Adoption, however, does not prevent a marriage between the child and its adoptive sister (or brother) or with any other adoptive relative. Conversely, as the modern law bears some relation to genetics, the child may not marry any person who would have come within the prohibited degrees if no adoption had been made.[6] A child who is not a citizen of the United Kingdom and Colonies will acquire such citizenship on adoption if his adoptive parent possesses it.[7] On the other hand, an adopted child may

---

1 [1976 Act, s. 39.]
2 Children Act 1975, s. 8 (2), (3), (4). [1976 Act, s. 12 (2), (3), (4).]
3 Children and Young Persons Act 1969, s. 21A, added by the Children Act 1975, Sched. 3, para. 70.
4 Child Care Act 1980, s. 5 (2) (a).
5 Children Act 1975, Sched. 3, para. 8 (amending the Marriage Act 1949, Sched. 1). This continues to apply if a subsequent adoption order is made, and the child may not marry a former adoptive parent.
6 Children Act 1975, Sched. 1, para. 7 (1). [1976 Act, s. 47 (1).] Nor does adoption affect the law relating to incest.
7 Adoption Act 1958, s. 19; Adoption Act 1968, s. 9 (5). [1976 Act, s. 40.] In the case of a joint adoption, the child will acquire citizenship of the United Kingdom and Colonies if the male adopter possesses such citizenship.

continue to claim a pension which was being paid to him or for his benefit at the time of the adoption as though no order had been made,[1] and adoption does not affect the descent of any peerage or dignity or title of honour.[2] Nor will adoption of an illegitimate child by a natural parent as *sole* adoptive parent prevent his legitimation if the adopter later marries the other parent.[3]

For the purposes of all other statutes an adopted child is to be regarded as the child of his adopter or adopters, whenever the statute was passed and the adoption took place.[4] So, for example, an adopted child may claim under the Fatal Accidents Act as a dependant of his adoptive parent or other adoptive relative.

An adopted child's right to claim property under any disposition or on an intestacy will be dealt with when we consider children's rights to claim property generally.[5]

E. FOREIGN ADOPTION ORDERS

Since 1950 children adopted in Scotland have been in precisely the same position as those adopted in England for the purposes of English law. Since 1964 this has also been true of children adopted in Northern Ireland, the Isle of Man and the Channel Islands.[6]

A much wider extension has been made by the Adoption Act of 1968, under which the Secretary of State can specify by order that any class or classes of adoption made outside Great Britain (whether or not in a convention country) shall be "overseas adoptions". These have the same effect as English orders except that they do not automatically confer citizenship of the United Kingdom and Colonies on a child adopted by a person possessing such citizenship.[7] English courts will normally have to recognise any decision of the appropriate authority in a Convention country or specified country making, confirming or terminating a Convention adoption or an adoption made in a specified country,[8] but in certain cases they may annul such an adoption or declare it invalid. Provided that either the adopters or the child

---

[1] Children Act 1975, Sched. 1, para. 8. For the effect of adoption on certain policies of insurance, see *ibid.*, para. 11. [1976 Act, ss. 48 and 49.]

[2] *Ibid.*, para. 10. [1976 Act, s. 44 (1).]

[3] Legitimacy Act 1976, s. 4. See *ante*, p. 270.

[4] Children Act 1975, Sched. 1, para. 3 (4), (5). This does not affect things done or events occurring before 1st January 1976, which will be governed by the law in force on that date: *ibid.*, para. 3 (6). For the effect of adoption on some technical provisions of the Social Security Act 1975, see *ibid.*, para. 7 (3)-(5). [1976 Act, ss. 39 (5), (6) and 47 (3)-(5).]

[5] See *post*, pp. 580-581 and 621.

[6] See now the Children Act 1975, Sched. 1, para. 1 (2) (c). [1976 Act, s. 38 (1) (c). See also s. 59 (2), (3).]

[7] Adoption Act 1968, s. 4 (3); Children Act 1975, Sched. 1, paras. 1 (2) (d) and 7 (2). [1976 Act, ss. 38 (1) (d), 47 (2) and 72 (2).] Adoptions already specified as overseas adoptions include those made in most parts of the British Commonwealth, Western Europe, South Africa, the U.S.A. and Israel provided that they take effect under the law in force in the country in question (other than customary law or common law): Adoption (Designation of Overseas Adoptions) Order, S.I. 1973 No. 19. See Kerse, 117 Sol. Jo. 314.

[8] Adoption Act 1968, ss. 5 and 6 (5). For the meaning of "Convention", "Convention country" and other technical terms see *ante*, p. 355. A "specified country" is a British territory outside Great Britain designated for this purpose and a Convention adoption is an overseas adoption designated as an adoption regulated by the Convention: s. 5 (2) and 11 (1). [1976 Act, ss. 53 (5), 59 (1) and 72 (1), (2).] Northern Ireland has been designated as a specified

adopted resides in Great Britain, the High Court may annul or revoke an order if (i) the adoption was prohibited by the internal law of the country of which the adopters were nationals; (ii) it contravened provisions relating to consents of the internal law of the country of which the child was a national; (iii) it could have been impugned on any other ground under the law of the country where the adoption was made; *or* (iv) the child was adopted by his father or mother alone and has subsequently been legitimated by his parents' marriage. Irrespective of the parties' residence, the High Court may also order that *any* adoption made overseas shall cease to be valid in this country on the ground that it is contrary to public policy or that the authority making it lacked jurisdiction; and *any* court may decide on either of the last two grounds that the adoption shall be treated as invalid for the purpose of the proceedings before it.[1] This means that if, for example, a claim under the Inheritance (Provision for Family and Dependants) Act were brought in a county court on behalf of a child adopted overseas, the court could declare the adoption invalid on the ground that the authority making it had lacked jurisdiction, but this decision would not affect the outcome of any other proceedings which depended on the child's adoption.

A foreign adoption may also be recognised at common law, even though it is not an "overseas adoption" in the technical sense used above, in which case it will have the same effect as an overseas adoption.[2] The difficulty is that there is little authority indicating the circumstances in which an adoption will be recognised, and such authority as there is relates solely to the capacity of a child adopted abroad to claim rights in property under English law. In the past it was arguable that an adoption might be recognised for this purpose and not for others (for example, to enable the child to claim damages as a dependant under the Fatal Accidents Acts), but the express wording of the Children Act 1975 must mean that the same test will now have to be applied in all cases.

The leading case is the decision of the Court of Appeal in *Re Valentine's Settlement*.[3] By a deed executed in 1946 the settlor had settled a fund on her son's children. The son and his wife had adopted two children in 1939 and 1944. At all relevants times they had been domiciled and resident in Southern Rhodesia and both adoption orders had been made by a court in the Union of South Africa where the children were resident. The question was whether the children could claim under the settlement. LORD DENNING, M.R., held that the English courts would recognise a foreign order only if the court making it assumed a jurisdiction on the same ground as English courts:[4] in other words,

---

country and Convention adoptions are the same as those specified in n. 7. *supra*: S.I. 1978 No. 1432.

1 Adoption Act 1968, ss. 6, 7 and 9 (3). [1976 Act, ss. 53, 54 and 70 (3).]

2 Children Act 1975, Sched. 1, paras. 1 (2) (e) and 7 (2). [1976 Act, ss. 38 (1) (e) and 47 (2).] This applies only from 1st January 1976 and does not entitle the child to claim any property rights under an instrument made *inter vivos* or under the will or intestacy of a person dying before that date. For claims to property before 1976, see the fourth edition of this book, pp. 467-469. There is no authority on the effect of such orders in other cases before 1976.

3 [1965] Ch. 831; [1965] 2 All E.R. 226, C.A.

4 *Cf.* the recognition of foreign divorces (*ante*, pp. 243-244). See also *Re Wilson*, [1954] Ch. 773; [1954] 1 All E.R. 997, where VAISEY, J., held that a child could not claim on the intestacy of an adoptive parent, domiciled in England, who had obtained an adoption order in Montreal, even though this was valid by Quebec law.

the adopters must be domiciled in that country and, as the law then stood, the child would have to be ordinarily resident there. As the first condition was not satisfied, the orders in this case would not be recognised here. DANCKWERTS, L.J., held that, as status is governed by the *lex domicilii*, it is sufficient if the adopters are domiciled in the country where the order is made, and consequently in his opinion also these orders could not be recognised. SALMON, L.J., dissenting, held that English courts should always recognise an order if the court making it had jurisdiction over the child in question (as it obviously had in this case) provided that the principles applied by the court are basically the same as those applied in England and the same safeguards exist to ensure that the order will be for the benefit of the child. It is to be regretted that this view was not generally accepted. If spouses domiciled in England but ordinarily resident abroad adopt a child in the country where they are resident, it seems absurd that English courts will not recognise this adoption, for the only way in which a valid adoption can now be made is for the parties to go to the expense of applying for an order under the English Act.

As the law now stands, however, we can say with certainty that at common law a foreign adoption will be recognised only if the adopters were domiciled in the country in which it was made. In addition, by analogy with the common law rules relating to recognition of foreign divorces, we should also recognise an adoption effected elsewhere if it would be recognised by the adopters' *lex domicilii*.[1] But even if we accept that the order was made in a country which had jurisdiction, a further question remains: will we recognise an adoption if its effect by local law is markedly different from the effect of an adoption in English law? The earlier case of *Re Marshall*,[2] where a child adopted in British Columbia was held to be unable to claim as his adoptive mother's child under an English will because he could not do so under the law of British Columbia, indicates that a foreign adoption will be recognised at common law only if its effects are substantially the same as an English adoption. It is submitted that the case should no longer be followed insofar as it implies that rights of succession under the foreign law should be identical with those under English law, because this seems to be in direct conflict with the express wording of the Children Act; on the other hand, it is in the highest degree unlikely that we should recognise a foreign order which does not place the adopter *in loco parentis* to the person adopted. Hence we should probably not regard as a valid adoption for any purpose in English law an order by which a man adopts his wife or (as happened in the case of the author, Somerset Maugham) a French order by which a man of 82 adopted another man of 57 in order to give a financial advantage to the latter.[3]

---

[1] See *ante*, pp. 243-244. LORD DENNING, M.R.'s views are even more surprising in view of his strictures on the artificiality of the concept of domicile in the comparable jurisdiction relating to wards of court: *Re P. (G.E.)*, [1965] Ch. 568; [1964] 3 All E.R. 977, C.A.

[2] [1957] Ch. 507; [1957] 3 All E.R. 172, C.A. See also the extra-judicial views of SCARMAN, L.J., *English Law and Foreign Adoptions*, 11 I.C.L.Q. 635.

[3] See Dicey and Morris, *Conflict of Laws*, 10th Ed., 502-503, and the cases cited *ibid.*, n. 63. In fact the adoption was rescinded in the *Maugham* case because the adopter was a British subject: *ibid.*

Chapter 11

Guardianship, Custodianship and Children in the Care of Local Authorities

A. GUARDIANSHIP

1. INTRODUCTORY

Strictly speaking, the term "guardian" includes a parent, for parents are regarded at common law as the natural guardians of their children and now by statute after the death of one parent the survivor is the guardian of their minor children either alone or jointly with any testamentary guardian appointed by the other.[1] But in common parlance the concepts of parent and guardian are quite distinct, for the rights and duties of the former arise automatically and naturally on the birth of the child, whilst the latter voluntarily places himself *in loco parentis* to his ward and his rights and duties flow immediately from this act.[2] It is in this latter sense—that of the person who places himself *in loco parentis* to his ward, as distinct from the natural parent—that the word will be used in this chapter.

Foster Parents.[3]—A guardian must be also distinguished from a foster parent, who has *de facto* control and custody of a child without being its legal guardian. If a parent is dead or is unfit to exercise his parental rights and duties, it is clearly essential that they should be exercisable by somebody else standing *in loco parentis* to a child; but by English law they will not vest in a guardian unless he has been appointed in one of a number of recognised ways, for example by a court order or by the will of a deceased parent. In a large number of cases, of course, this never happens; and if both parents die, a child's grandparents or other near relations will assume *de facto* control of the child without taking steps to have themselves appointed legal guardians at all. The position of such people, like all those who assume legal rights and powers without a good title, is precarious. Both at common law and under the Children and Young Persons Act 1933 there will be a duty to afford

---

[1] Guardianship of Minors Act 1971, s. 3. *Ante*, p. 287.
[2] Many Acts of Parliament draw a similar distinction. *E.g.*, the Children Act 1975, s. 12, requires the agreement of each parent or guardian to the making of an adoption order.
[3] See Bevan, *Children*, 375-385.

protection.[1] Although there is no common law duty to maintain the child, the person with control will be criminally liable under the Children and Young Persons Act 1933 if he wilfully fails to provide it with adequate food, clothing, medical aid or lodging.[2] Similarly, the Education Act 1944 places him under a duty to see that the child receives full-time education.[3] So long as no one else claims the care and control of the child, the person who actually has it will be clearly entitled to retain it; if this is disputed, the court must be guided by the child's welfare in determining in whose favour to make an order.[4] It seems that a person standing *in loco parentis* to a child may sue for damages for loss of services provided that actual services were being rendered to him by the child;[5] but whether he can recover possession itself by habeas corpus proceedings is much more doubtful.[6] The point appears never to have been decided, and it would clearly be more advisable for him to have the child made a ward of court and ask the court for care and control.

Anyone (other than a relative,[7] guardian or custodian) who undertakes the care and maintenance of a child (whether for reward or not) is now subject to the provisions of the Foster Children Act 1980. Their purpose is to ensure that the child is visited periodically by officers of the Social Services Department of the local non-metropolitan county, metropolitan district or London borough council who must satisfy themselves of his well-being and give any necessary advice to the foster parent.[8] These provisions apply only to children below the upper limit of compulsory school age,[9] but if they apply to a child when he reaches that age they will continue to apply until he attains the age of 18 provided that he continues to reside with the same foster parent.[10] The Act does not apply if he resides in the same premises as a parent, guardian or adult relative, or, broadly speaking, whilst he is in the care of a local authority, or in a school in which he is receiving full-time education,[11] hospital, nursing home or other institution maintained by a local or public authority, or whilst he is in the care of anyone by virtue of a supervision order, for in all these cases proper supervision will be effected by the body or authorities concerned.[12] Nor is it intended to control purely temporary arrangements frequently entered into during parents' absence, and consequently the Act does not apply if the person in question does not intend to undertake the child's care and maintenance for more than 27 days (six days if he is a

---

[1] *Ante*, pp. 320 *et seq.*
[2] Ss. 1 (2) (a) and 17. See *ante*, p. 322.
[3] Ss. 36 and 114.
[4] Guardianship of Minors Act 1971, s. 1.
[5] *Irwin* v. *Dearman* (1809), 11 East 23; *Peters* v. *Jones*, [1914] 2 K.B. 781.
[6] No objection on this point was raised in *Re Kerr* (1889), 24 L.R. Ir. 59.
[7] "Relative" has the same meaning as it has in the Adoption Act 1958; see *ante*, p. 338, n. 4.
[8] Ss. 3 and 22. *Cf.* the provisions of the Nurseries and Child-Minders Regulation Act 1948, which places local authorities under a duty to control nurseries and arrangements for looking after children under five years of age for reward: Bevan, *op. cit.*, 391-395.
[9] See *ante*, p. 312.
[10] Ss. 1 and 18.
[11] Except for certain schools during school holidays: s. 17.
[12] For details, see s. 2.

"regular foster parent") and does not in fact do so.[1] As these provisions are complementary to those relating to protected children under the Adoption Act, they do not apply to such children either.[2]

Anyone proposing to maintain a foster child must give notice to the local authority.[3] The authority may empower its officers to inspect premises in which foster children are being kept and may also impose conditions *inter alia* upon the number, age and sex of the children that may reside there and the accommodation, equipment and medical arrangements to be provided for them. It may completely forbid a person to keep foster children (or a particular child) or to use premises for that purpose.[4] An appeal from the authority's ruling may be made to a juvenile court, which may also order the removal of any foster children if the foster parent is unfit to have the care of them or has failed to comply with requirements laid down by the authority.[5] Certain persons, whose previous history or connections indicate that they are not fit to have the care of foster children, are forbidden to maintain foster children unless they first obtain the local authority's written consent.[6] There are also restrictions on advertisements for foster parents and children.[7]

Fostering also occurs when a child in the care of a local authority or in the charge of a voluntary organisation is boarded out. As we have seen, the provisions of the Foster Children Act 1980 do not apply to such foster parents; their selection and supervision are largely governed by the Boarding Out of Children Regulations 1955. We shall consider the problems that can arise when the authority or organisation wishes to remove the child against the foster parent's will when we discuss children in care.[8]

Guardians.—Once a guardian is lawfully appointed, most of the rights and duties which a parent has with respect to his legitimate children vest in him. The close similarity between the position of a parent and a guardian naturally gave the Crown as *parens patriae* the power to intervene, if necessary, to protect the ward, and after the abolition of the Court of Wards in 1660 the Court of Chancery assumed a general supervisory jurisdiction over guardians.[9] From 1875 this jurisdiction was exercised by the Chancery Division of the High Court, from which it has now been transferred to the Family Division. In addition, jurisdiction was given to county courts in guardianship matters by the Guardianship of Infants Act of 1886, and to magistrates' courts by the Guardianship of Infants Act of 1925. Magistrates'

---

[1] S. 2 (3), *q.v.* for the definition of regular foster parent. [F.C.A., s. 2 (3).]

[2] S. 2 (6). For protected children, see *ante*, p. 348.

[3] S. 5. Regulations may be made requiring parents to give notice as well: s. 4.

[4] Ss. 8-10. See also s. 13. The Home Secretary also has power to authorise an inspection: Child Care Act 1980, ss. 74 and 75.

[5] Ss. 11 and 12. A further appeal lies to the Crown Court: s. 14.

[6] For details, see s. 7. Failure to comply with the requirements of the Act renders the foster parent liable to six months' imprisonment and a fine of £400: s. 16.

[7] S. 15.

[8] See *post*, pp. 402-403. See generally Bevan, *op. cit.*, 385-390.

[9] Holdsworth, *History of English Law*, v, 315; vi, 648-650.

courts, however, have no power to entertain any application involving the administration or application of any property belonging to or held in trust for a minor or the income thereof.[1]

In view of the intervention of equity, it is hardly surprising to see a marked similarity between the office of guardian and that of trustee. As regards the ward's property, the guardian is a trustee in every respect, with precisely the same powers and duties as the trustee has over any other trust property; and as a trustee he is bound to account to his beneficiary, the ward, when his guardianship comes to an end. But whereas a trustee has no personal rights and duties with respect to his beneficiary, these are today the guardian's chief responsibility. But the similarity between the two offices can be seen here too. As in the case of a trustee, no one may be appointed a guardian against his will, but once he has accepted the office he cannot resign it by his unilateral act. The nature of the office was thus described by ROMILLY, M.R.:[2]

> "The relation of guardian and ward is strictly that of trustee and *cestui que trust*. I look on it as a peculiar relation of trusteeship. ... A guardian is not only trustee of the property, as in an ordinary case of trustee, but he is also the guardian of the person of the infant, with many duties to perform such as to see to his education and maintenance. ... Of all the property which he gets into his possession in the character of guardian, he is trustee for the benefit of the infant ward."

These two different duties of guardians—the protection of the person and the protection of the property of the ward—may in fact be vested in two entirely different sets of people: guardians of the person, with no right to control the ward's property, and guardians of the estate, with no right to control the ward's person.[3] The property legislation of 1925 has virtually rendered the latter type of guardianship obsolete, for now in almost every case property, in which a minor has an interest, will be vested in trustees; and although the guardians may be appointed the trustees for this purpose, it will be in the latter capacity and not in the former that they will control the property.

2. APPOINTMENT OF GUARDIANS

At common law the feudal overlord automatically became the guardian of an infant tenant by knight service or grand serjeanty, and since the guardian was entitled to the profits of the ward's estate, this right was extremely valuable to the Crown and the mesne lords. Wardship was never an incident of tenure by petit serjeanty or socage, and consequently, after the abolition of knight service and the incidents of tenure by grand serjeanty in 1660, guardianship assumed its modern characteristic of an office of trust and responsibility rather than that of a valuable piece of property.[4] Accordingly, the Tenures Abolition Act for the first time gave a parent the power to

---

[1] Guardianship of Minors Act 1971, s. 15 (2), as amended by the Domestic Proceedings and Magistrates' Courts Act 1978, s. 38 (1).

[2] *Mathew* v. *Brise* (1851), 14 Beav. 341, 345.

[3] *Rimington* v. *Hartley* (1880), 14 Ch. D. 630, 632. If there is no separate guardian of a minor's estate, a guardian appointed by a deceased parent or by the court under the Guardianship of Minors Act 1971 has all the rights, powers and duties of a guardian of the estate in addition to being guardian of the person: Guardianship Act 1973, s. 7.

[4] See Holdsworth, *History of English Law*, iii, 512-513; Simpson, *Introduction to the History of the Land Law*, 17-19.

appoint a testamentary guardian for his minor children—a power which was later extended by the Guardianship of Infants Acts of 1886 and 1925.

Once equity had established its right to supervise guardians and wards, it followed as a corollary that the Court of Chancery had the power to appoint guardians. In addition, there still exist some customary rights to guardianship, *e.g.*, that of the City of London over orphans of deceased freemen;[1] and an infant apparently has a power to appoint a guardian for himself, although the powers of such a guardian never seem to have been defined.[2] In practice, guardians are always appointed either by a parent or by the court, and it is with these two modes of appointment that we shall now deal in greater detail.[3]

Testamentary Guardians.—Section 8 of the Tenures Abolition Act 1660 empowered a father by deed or will to appoint a guardian or guardians of his legitimate children, who were under the age of 21 and unmarried on the father's death, until they respectively reached their majority or for any less time. As the mother had no right as such to the custody of her children at common law, it is hardly surprising that no power of appointing testamentary guardians was given to her. Section 3 of the Guardianship of Infants Act of 1886 gave her a limited power to do so, but her nominees could only act after the death of both parents (when they would act jointly with any guardian appointed by the father) or, if the father survived her, jointly with him if the court considered that he was unfit to be the sole guardian. It was not until 1925 that the mother was given equal rights with the father in this respect. Now both the father and the mother may by deed or will appoint one or more guardians for their legitimate children.[4]

The Tenures Abolition Act gave the father no power to appoint a testamentary guardian for his illegitimate children,[5] but in *Re A*.[6] BENNETT, J., held that the Guardianship of Infants Act of 1925 had given such a power to the mother. The Schedule to that Act[7] provided that after the death of the mother of an illegitimate minor, the guardian appointed by her must consent to the child's marriage and thus impliedly gave her the power to appoint a testamentary guardian. A more limited power was given to the father by the Legitimacy Act 1959; now he may appoint a testamentary guardian provided that an order made under the Guardianship of Minors Act giving him legal custody of the child is in force at the time of his death.[8]

The power to appoint a testamentary guardian is clearly one of the "rights and duties which by law the mother and father have in relation to a child" and consequently appears to be an incident of legal custody, at least for the

---

[1] Comyns' *Digest*, Gardian (G). See also Simpson, *Infants*, 4th Ed., p. 162.

[2] *Re Brown's Will* (1881), 18 Ch. D. 61, C.A., at pp. 65, 67, 72.

[3] For a full list of the various types of guardian, see Simpson, *Infants*, pp. 149 *et seq*.

[4] Guardianship of Minors Act 1971, s. 4. The Act states that they may appoint "any person to be guardian", but s. 3 assumes that there may be more than one so appointed. If the court appoints another to act as guardian with the surviving parent under s. 3 (see *ante*, p. 287), that person shall continue to act after the death of the surviving parent together with any testamentary guardians appointed by the latter: s. 4 (6).

[5] *Sleeman* v. *Wilson* (1871), L.R. 13 Eq. 36.

[6] (1940), 164 L.T. 230.

[7] Now repealed and re-enacted in the Marriage Act 1949, Sched. 2 (see Appendix C, *post*).

[8] See now the Guardianship of Minors Act 1971, s. 14 (3). For custody orders, see *ante*, p. 302.

purpose of the Children Act 1975 and any subsequent Act.[1] Hence it is arguable that a parent deprived of custody loses the power to appoint a guardian. It is submitted, however, that the courts should be slow to reach such a conclusion and, as the Guardianship of Minors Act is silent on the point and gives the power to the father and mother in general terms, it should survive.[2] The position is even more obscure if a resolution is in force under section 3 of the Child Care Act 1980 which has the effect of vesting *all* parental rights and duties in the authority except the right to consent to adoption; the point is largely academic, however, as the guardian could not claim custody so long as the resolution was in force.[3]

The reduction in the age of majority means that no guardian may now be appointed for any child (legitimate or illegitimate) over the age of 18.[4]

Although a deed is usually irrevocable, a deed appointing a guardian is a "testamentary instrument in the form of a deed",[5] and consequently an appointment by deed is revoked by a subsequent appointment by will.[6] Although the point has never been decided, an appointment by deed may presumably be similarly revoked by a later deed; but in view of the wording of section 20 of the Wills Act 1837, it would appear that an appointment by will cannot be revoked by a subsequent appointment by deed.[7] Since a minor has no power to make a will unless he is a soldier or airman on active service or a sailor at sea,[8] it will be seen that the only way in which a minor, who does not come within this category, can appoint a guardian for his own children is by deed.

Whether the appointment will be effective if the child, in respect of whom it is made, is married when the testator dies is doubtful. Section 8 of the Tenures Abolition Act (now repealed) expressly excluded this case, but the Guardianship of Minors Act imposes no such limitation. On the other hand, a guardian is rarely, if ever, appointed by the court for a married infant, and, even assuming the power to make a testamentary appointment in such a case, the court might well remove a testamentary guardian who attempted to interfere with a married ward.

Presumably the parents' power is no less than the father's power was under the Tenures Abolition Act. Under that Act the appointment could be during the child's minority or for any less period, and could take effect immediately or in the future. Hence an appointment "of X till the child reaches the age of 16 and then of Y" ought still to be valid. Moreover, it was held in *In the Goods of Parnell*[9] that under the earlier Act a father could give

---

[1] See *ante*, p. 283.

[2] As in most cases the person with custody would probably object to the appointment of the guardian, the court might direct that the latter should not act: see *infra*.

[3] See further *post*, pp. 398-399; Thomson, 90 L.Q.R. 311.

[4] Family Law Reform Act 1969, s. 1.

[5] *Per* LORD ELDON, L.C., in *Ex parte Ilchester* (1803), 7 Ves. 348, 367.

[6] *Shaftsbury* v. *Hannam* (1677), Cas. *temp*. Finch 323.

[7] Unless it is made in contemplation of marriage, a will is revoked by the subsequent marriage of the testator (Wills Act 1837, s. 18; Law of Property Act 1925, s. 177). But this probably does not apply to the appointment of a guardian by *deed*, in which case the appointment will include the guardianship of the children of a subsequent marriage as well: *Ex parte Ilchester*, (*supra*).

[8] Wills Act 1837, s. 11; Wills (Soldiers and Sailors) Act 1918, ss. 4, 5 (2); Family Law Reform Act 1969, s. 3 (1). For the persons included in this exception, see Mellows, *Succession*, 3rd Ed., 95-99.

[9] (1872), L.R. 2 P. & D. 379. But in the absence of any express power a testamentary guardian may not assign his office: *Mellish* v. *De Costa* (1737), 2 Atk. 14.

another the power to appoint a guardian. A testator appointed X and Y to be the guardians of his daughter and on the death of either of them he gave the survivor power to appoint another in the place of the deceased. X subsequently died and Y by deed appointed Z to be joint guardian with himself. It was held by LORD PENZANCE that Z's appointment was valid.

If they accept the office, testamentary guardians act jointly with the surviving parent unless the latter objects.[1] In the event of such an objection, or if the guardian considers the parent unfit to have the custody of the child, the guardian may apply to the court[2] which must then decide whether either the parent or guardian is to act to the exclusion of the other or whether they are to act jointly.[3] The child's welfare must of course be the court's chief concern, and it is hardly likely that it will be in his best interest to have them acting together in such circumstances. If the court orders that the testamentary guardian is to be the sole guardian, it may make such order as it thinks fit as to the legal custody of the child. If it gives custody to a guardian, it may provide that the surviving parent shall retain jointly with him such parental rights and duties (other than actual custody) as it shall specify. It may also give the parent or a grandparent access to the child.[4]

If both parents appoint testamentary guardians, all the guardians so appointed, who are willing to act, do so jointly after the death of the surviving parent.[5]

Guardians appointed by the Court.—The High Court now has the inherent jurisdiction formerly possessed by the Court of Chancery to appoint guardians.[6] In addition a statutory power to appoint guardians is conferred in two cases on the High Court, county courts and magistrates' courts by the Guardianship of Minors Act. If a deceased parent has appointed no testamentary guardian, or if the guardian or guardians so appointed refuse to act, the court may, if it thinks fit, appoint one to act with the survivor.[7] A similar power exists if there is no parent, guardian or other person having parental rights with respect to the child.[8] A guardian can probably be appointed even though the child is married but there is no precedent for such an appointment

---

[1] Guardianship of Minors Act 1971, s. 4 (3).
[2] *I.e.*, the High Court, a county court or a magistrates' court.
[3] Guardianship of Minors Act 1971, s. 4 (4).
[4] *Ibid.*, ss. 10, 11A (1) (added by the Domestic Proceedings and Magistrates' Courts Act 1978, s. 37) and 14A (2) (added by *ibid.*, s. 40). The operation of the order may be postponed and it may be varied or discharged at any time. It will automatically terminate when the child reaches the age of 18: *ibid.*, ss. 10 (2) and 11A (2), (3). For criticisms of the present law and suggestions for reform, see Law Com. Working Paper No. 74 (Illegitimacy), paras. 4.15-4.17.
[5] *Ibid.*, s. 4 (5).
[6] *Quaere* whether this can be exercised only if the child is made a ward of court.
[7] Guardianship of Minors Act 1971, s. 3. See *ante*, p. 287.
[8] *Ibid.*, s. 5 (1). A person can have parental rights only if he has the same legal rights as a parent and consequently they must have been vested in him, *e.g.*, by a court order. Hence a stepparent has no such rights even though he may have obligations if the child is a child of the family: *Re N.*, [1974] Fam. 40; [1974] 1 All E.R. 126. See Bevan, [1974] C.L.J. 74. The court may exercise this power even though a local authority has assumed parental rights by resolution under s. 3 of the Child Care Act 1980 (see *post*, p. 397), in which case the resolution will cease to have effect: Child Care Act 1980, s. 5 (2) (c). In practice there are few applications under this subsection, for a near relative usually takes *de facto* control of the child without troubling to obtain an order. For the duties of local authorities when there is no one to take care of the child, see *post*, p. 395.

and the court would probably be slow to act in such a case.[1]

In determining whom to appoint as guardians

"the Court, according to its ordinary practice, gives a preference to the nearest blood relations, and does not appoint strangers when fit persons are to be found among the relations".[2]

But this preference may be displaced by a number of other factors. Personal unfitness will certainly exclude anybody, the ward's religious education will be taken into account whenever it is relevant,[3] and due attention will be paid to a deceased parent's wishes even though the latter has not availed himself of the power of appointing a testamentary guardian.[4] But both the parent's and the nearest relatives' wishes will be ignored if this is necessary in the interests of the child. In *Re F.*[5] the father of a girl only a few months old had strangled his wife, the girl's mother, and had been convicted of manslaughter on the ground of diminished responsibility. He wanted the girl to be brought up by his brother and sister-in-law (who lived in the same neighbourhood) and obviously had some hope of making contact with her again in the future. The child was then made a ward of court. The Court of Appeal had no doubt that it was highly desirable that her connection with her father (and therefore his family) and the neighbourhood should be completely severed and therefore gave care and control to the mother's cousin and her husband who had taken care of the child, were prepared to move away and hoped to adopt her.

Foreign Guardians.—Although in *Johnstone* v. *Beattie*[6] and *Stuart* v. *Bute*[7] the House of Lords laid down the rule that, even if a guardian has been validly appointed by a foreign court, the High Court is not precluded from appointing another guardian in this country, subsequent cases have shown that a foreign guardian's rights may be enforced here provided, at any rate, that they do not conflict with our ideas of public policy. It is obviously desirable that a child should not have one set of guardians in one country and another elsewhere, and guardianship being a question of status, the proper law to apply is obviously that of the child's domicile:[8] it is only where the protection of the child requires the courts of this country to interfere that the rights of a guardian validly appointed in another country should not be recognised here. Clearly, if a foreign guardian comes within the jurisdiction, he can apply to be appointed guardian here; and even if he does not do so his rights over the ward's person and property may be enforced.[9] There is also

---

[1] There is also a statutory power to appoint a guardian if a parent or guardian is convicted of incest or attempted incest with the child: see *ante*, p. 287, n. 7.

[2] *Per* CHITTY, J., in *Re Nevin*, [1891] 2 Ch. 299, 303. An appellate court will not interfere with the discretion of the judge at first instance except for very strong reasons: *Re Kaye* (1866), 1 Ch. App. 387.

[3] See *ante*, pp. 296-297.

[4] *Re Kaye*, (*supra*).

[5] [1970] 1 All E.R. 344, C.A.

[6] (1843), 10 Cl. & F. 42, H.L.

[7] (1861), 9 H.L. Cas. 440, H.L.

[8] Although in *Re P. (G.E.)*, [1965] Ch. 568; [1964] 3 All E.R. 977, C.A., the Court of Appeal preferred the test of ordinary residence as more realistic.

[9] *Nugent* v. *Vetzera* (1866), L.R. 2 Eq. 704; *Monaco* v. *Monaco* (1937), 157 L.T. 231. For the circumstances in which the court will order the child to be returned to another country without considering the merits of the application, see *post*, pp. 377-379.

authority for the proposition that a foreign guardian can give a valid receipt for income out of a trust fund in which the ward has a beneficial interest, although the court again has a discretion in the matter and may, for example, withhold payment until it is satisfied that the sums paid will be used for the ward's benefit.[1]

3. GUARDIANS' RIGHTS AND DUTIES WITH RESPECT TO THE PERSON OF THE WARD

A guardian has custody of his ward and therefore, broadly speaking, has the same rights and duties with respect to his person as a parent has with respect to his legitimate child. These may therefore be considered very briefly and the chief differences between the two noted.

Physical and Moral Protection.—A duty to protect the ward at common law will clearly arise once the guardian assumes responsibility for doing so.[2] The Children and Young Persons Act 1933 specifically renders a guardian criminally liable for breach of the various duties imposed by the Act to ensure the physical and moral protection of children.[3]

Maintenance.—As we have already seen, a guardian will be criminally liable under section 1 of the Children and Young Persons Act 1933 if he wilfully fails to provide his ward with adequate food, clothing, medical aid or lodging.[4]

If the guardian is acting jointly with the surviving parent or an order has been made that he shall act to the exclusion of the surviving parent, the latter may be ordered to make periodical payments or a lump sum payment (or both) either to the guardian for the benefit of the ward or to the ward himself.[5] Moreover, if the ward is a beneficiary under a trust, the settlor may have authorised the trustees to pay the guardian income or capital for the maintenance or advancement of the ward. Even if he has not done so, the High Court may order income and, in certain circumstances, capital to be used for these purposes, and the Trustee Act 1925 has given trustees wide powers of the same nature.[6] But a guardian may not otherwise recoup himself out of the ward's property.[7]

---

[1] *Re Chatard's Settlement*, [1899] 1 Ch. 712. See also *Re Brown's Trust* (1865), 12 L.T. 488; *Mackie* v. *Darling* (1871), L.R. 12 Eq. 319.

[2] See *ante*, p. 320.

[3] S. 17. See *ante*, p. 322.

[4] *Ante*, p. 322.

[5] Guardianship of Minors Act 1971, ss. 10 (1) (b), (2) and 11 (b), (c), as amended by the Domestic Proceedings and Magistrates' Courts Act 1978, s. 41 (3), (4). "Parent" includes the father of an illegitimate child who has obtained a custody order: s. 14 (3). These powers are exercisable by the High Court, county courts and magistrates' courts but the last named may not make an order for the payment of a lump sum exceeding £500. For payment to the child himself, see *post*, p. 586. Orders for periodical payments may remain in force after the ward reaches the age of 17 in the same circumstances as those made under the Domestic Proceedings and Magistrates' Courts Act (see *post*, p. 586). For the principles to be applied in assessing an order and the court's powers on variation, see *post*, pp. 586-589. See generally ss. 12-12C of the Guardianship of Minors Act 1971, as amended and added by the Domestic Proceedings and Magistrates' Courts Act 1978, ss. 42 and 43.

[6] Ss. 31-33 and 53. See Pettit, *Equity*, 4th Ed., 355-365. The guardian may also be entitled to a guardian's allowance under the Social Security Act 1975: see *post*, p. 584.

[7] *Cf. Walker* v. *Wetherell* (1801), 6 Ves. 473.

Actual Custody.—Where there is only one guardian, he will *prima facie* have the right to the actual custody of his ward, a right which he may enforce by habeas corpus[1] or alternatively by proceedings in the Chancery Division, in which case the child may have to be made a ward of court.[2] Where there are more guardians than one, however, this *prima facie* rule cannot operate: in fact when a guardian is acting with a surviving parent, it will obviously usually be the latter who will be entitled to actual custody. Moreover, a parent appointing a guardian may direct that someone other than the guardian should have actual custody, in which case, although the person nominated will clearly have no absolute right to have the testator's wishes carried out, the court will give effect to them unless it is contrary to the ward's welfare, whilst leaving the guardian with the remaining parental rights and duties.[3]

But, of course, as in the case of a claim by a parent, the court's first concern must be for the ward's welfare. The same facts must be borne in mind in each case: the ward's religion, family ties, and, if he is old enough to exercise a choice, his own wishes, are clearly as important in one type of dispute as in the other.

Education.—A guardian is under the same statutory duty as a parent to ensure that his ward receives an efficient full-time education.[4] But so far as the choice of secular and religious education is concerned, the guardian's position is radically different from the parent's, for his duty is to see that the ward has a secular education befitting his position and expectations and is brought up in the faith in which he would have been brought up had his parents still been alive. Formerly, of course, this meant that, if the child was legitimate, the father's wishes had to be implemented, but today the guardian must observe the mother's wishes as much as the father's.[5] These may be deduced either directly or inferentially from the parents' own acts, for example, by express directions, by their having children brought up in a particular faith during their lifetime, or by the appointment of testamentary guardians professing a particular creed;[6] if there is no other guide, then it is presumed that parents wish to have their children brought up in the same religion as they themselves practised.[7]

But, as in the case of disputes between parents over the religious upbringing of their children, the final choice of a ward's religious education must depend upon what is best for its own welfare and the same factors must be borne in mind in each case. If the father's and mother's wishes were not the

---

[1] *R.* v. *Isley* (1836), 5 Ad. & El. 441. But see *ante*, p. 301.

[2] Since the application would have to be made under the inherent jurisdiction of the court and not under any statutory power. The court may award custody to a guardian living abroad if this would be for the child's benefit: *Ex parte Nickells* (1891), 7 T.L.R. 498.

[3] *Knott* v. *Cottee* (1847), 2 Ph. 192.

[4] Education Act 1944, ss. 36, 114.

[5] As their right to determine their children's faith is now equal: see *ante*, p. 313. *Cf. Re Collins*, [1950] Ch. 498; [1950] 1 All E.R. 1057, C.A.

[6] See *Re Nevin*, [1891] 2 Ch. 299, C.A.; *Hill* v. *Hill* (1862), 31 L.J. Ch. 505; *Andrews* v. *Salt* (1873), 8 Ch. App. 622; *Re McGrath*, [1893] 1 Ch. 143, C.A.

[7] *Re McGrath*, (*supra*), at p. 148; *Hawksworth* v. *Hawksworth* (1871), 6 Ch. App. 539; *Re Scanlan* (1888), 40 Ch.D. 200, 213; *F.* v. *F.*, [1902] 1 Ch. 688, 689. Would the court now implement a direction by the parent that the child should be brought up as an atheist?

same, the same test must be applied as is applied during their lifetime, and the court will not order a ward to be educated in its parents' religion if it has already developed firm convictions of its own and has reached an age when it would be dangerous to attempt to effect a change.[1] Less attention will be paid to a parent's wishes after his death than during his life, because he could not possibly have foreseen all the circumstances which might subsequently arise,[2] and if a guardian is acting jointly with a surviving parent, much greater attention will normally be paid to the latter's wishes.[3]

Ward's Marriage and Adoption.—The guardian's consent is required for the marriage of a ward over the age of 16,[4] and he must agree to the ward's adoption.[5]

Guardian's Liability for his Ward's Acts.—A guardian's liability for his ward's acts are precisely the same as a parent's, for in both cases he will be liable if he has authorised or ratified the act and he will also be liable for a tort if it has been occasioned by his own negligence in failing to avert its commission.[6] The provisions empowering a court to order a parent to pay any fine, compensation or costs imposed in respect of an offence committed by a child under the age of 17 apply equally to guardians.[7]

Liability for interfering with Guardian's Rights.—Criminal liability will be incurred for taking a ward under the age of 14 or a female ward over that age out of the custody of his or her guardian in the same circumstances as it will for taking a child out of the custody of its parents.[8] As regards civil liability, no action will lie at the suit of a guardian as such[9] under the Fatal Accidents Act; but it would seem that, as a person with *de facto* control of a child can apparently sue for loss of its services,[10] *a fortiori* a guardian can do so provided the ward was in fact rendering services to him. There is no authority on the question of a guardian's ability to sue in reliance upon a constructive service: whether the courts would be prepared to extend the parent's right to a guardian is highly doubtful.

Disputes between Guardians.—In *Gilbert* v. *Schwenck*[11] PLATT, B., delivering the judgment of the Court of Exchequer, laid down the rule that one of two joint guardians cannot act in defiance of the other and that each has an equal power. Machinery for solving disputes is provided by section 7 of the

---

[1] *Stourton* v. *Stourton* (1857), 8 De G. M. & G. 760; *Re W.*, [1907] 2 Ch. 557, C.A.; *Ward* v. *Laverty*, [1925] A.C. 101, H.L.

[2] *Re Meades* (1871), I.R. 5 Eq. 98, 112.

[3] See Eekelaar, 89 L.Q.R. at p. 234.

[4] Marriage Act 1949, Sched. 2 (see Appendix C, *post*). The Act has not been amended to require the consent of a guardian appointed by the father of an illegitimate child. For the position if the guardian's consent cannot be obtained or is refused, see *ante*, pp. 39-41.

[5] Or his agreement must be dispensed with: see *ante*, pp. 341-344.

[6] See *ante*, pp. 325-326.

[7] See *ante*, p. 326.

[8] See *ante*, pp. 327-329.

[9] But he might be able to sue, *e.g.*, as a grandparent or other relation. For the Fatal Accidents Act, see *ante*, pp. 134 *et seq.*

[10] *Ante*, p. 362.

[11] (1845), 14 M. & W. 488, 493.

Guardianship of Minors Act 1971, which gives any of them the power to apply to the High Court, county court or a magistrates' court, which may then make such order as it thinks proper.[1]

4. GUARDIANS' RIGHTS AND DUTIES WITH RESPECT TO THE PROPERTY OF THE WARD

We have already seen that a guardian will become a trustee of any of his ward's property of which he possesses himself, but that modern legislation has greatly reduced the importance of guardianship of the estate by virtually ensuring that almost all a minor's property will be held by trustees. If trustees pay the income to the guardian for the maintenance of the ward under any express or statutory powers, they will be discharged by the guardian's receipt.[2]

On the termination of the guardianship the guardian must account to the ward for all property that has come into his hands.[3] As a result of the doctrine of undue influence, however, the court may order the account to be re-opened if it is accepted and the guardian released by the former ward immediately after the latter comes of age.[4]

Undue Influence.—The office of a guardian is so confidential and the opportunities that he has to influence his ward so great that equity will assume that, in any transaction between the parties from which the guardian reaps an advantage, he has exercised undue influence over the other. The attitude of the courts was thus summarised by LORD BROUGHAM, L.C., in *Hunter* v. *Atkins:*[5]

> "There are certain relations known to the law, as attorney, guardian, trustee; if a person standing in these relations to client, ward, or *cestui que trust*, takes a gift or makes a bargain, the proof lies upon him, that he has dealt with the other party ... exactly as a stranger would have done, taking no advantage of his influence or knowledge, putting the other party on his guard, bringing everything to his knowledge which he himself knew. In short, the rule rightly considered is, that the person standing in such relation must, before he can take a gift, or even enter into a transaction, place himself in exactly the same position as a stranger would have been in, so that he may gain no advantage whatever from his relation to the other party, beyond what may be the natural and unavoidable consequence of kindness arising out of that relation."

It will, of course, be difficult for the guardian to prove that he exercised no influence over his ward; virtually the only way of doing so is to show that the latter received genuinely independent advice. If the guardian fails to

---

[1] If one of the guardians is the child's surviving parent to whom the court does not give legal custody, the court may grant him or her access and any parental rights and duties other than actual custody: Guardianship of Minors Act 1971, ss. 11 (a) and 11A (added by the Domestic Proceedings and Magistrates' Courts Act 1978, s. 37).

[2] *Re Long,* [1901] W.N. 166. But one guardian is not discharged by payment to a co-guardian: *Re Evans* (1884), 26 Ch. D. 58, C.A.

[3] It will be presumed that money paid to a guardian for maintenance has been properly so used unless the contrary is clearly shown, when the guardian will have to account for all sums so received: *Re Evans, (supra); Macrae* v. *Harness* (1910), 103 L.T. 629. On the question of periods of limitation, see *Mathew* v. *Brise* (1851), 14 Beav. 341.

[4] *Steadman* v. *Palling* (1746), 3 Atk. 423.

[5] (1834), 3 My. & K. 113, 135. See also LORD LYNDHURST, L.C., in *Archer* v. *Hudson* (1846), 15 L.J. Ch. 211.

discharge the burden cast upon him, the ward may have the gift or contract set aside and demand to be put back in the position he was in before he entered into the transaction, and he may also recover any property passed from anyone into whose hands it has come except a *bona fide* purchaser for value without notice of the way in which the property was originally obtained.

Moreover, it is absurd to consider that any influence which the guardian may have over his ward will automatically come to an end as soon as the relationship of guardian and ward ceases, and consequently the doctrine will also apply for some time after the ward comes of age. It is, of course, impossible to draw any hard and fast line at any point of time, and whether the presumption will be raised in any given case must depend upon its particular facts. An illustrative case is *Maitland v. Irving*.[1] The defendants agreed to sell their business to Maclean who was unable to raise the money but who told them that he would obtain a guarantee from the plaintiff who had property, who was his niece, and who had been his ward until she had come of age some 18 months previously. He then induced her to draw a cheque for £3,000 in favour of the defendants which he transferred to them. It was held that the plaintiff was not liable to the defendants because she had been induced to act as a result of the influence which Maclean had over her and, since he had told the defendants of the relationship between himself and the plaintiff, they had sufficient notice of her right in equity to have the transaction set aside.

5. TERMINATION OF GUARDIANSHIP

Death, Majority or Marriage of the Ward.—The guardian's duties will clearly cease if the ward dies: they automatically determine when he comes of age. Whether the guardian's powers cease if the ward marries before he or she reaches the age of 18 is doubtful. It seems to have been accepted in the past that they came to an end on the marriage of a girl but not of a boy,[2] but this cannot now be accepted with any certainty. The Tenures Abolition Act gave a parent no power to appoint a guardian for a married child but did not state that the guardianship would terminate if the ward subsequently married, and the Guardianship of Minors Act does not impose any limitations of this sort at all.[3] In any event, as the guardian must consent to the marriage, it is highly unlikely that the court will permit him to interfere with a married ward.

Death of the Guardian.—If one guardian dies leaving others in office, the survivors continue to act.[4] Although a deceased guardian's personal

---

[1] (1846), 15 Sim. 437. See also *Maitland v. Backhouse* (1848), 16 Sim. 58; *Archer v. Hudson*, (*supra*). Cf. the re-opening of an account presented immediately after the ward comes of age, *ante*, and the presumption of undue influence exercised by a parent over his child, *post*, pp. 574-575.

[2] See the views of LORD HARDWICKE, L.C., in *Mendes v. Mendes* (1748), 1 Ves. Sen. 89.

[3] It does not seem to have been suggested in *Eyre v. Shaftesbury* (1725), 2 P. Wms. 103, that the guardianship of Eyre, C.B., was determined on his ward's marriage, nor does wardship of court cease on marriage (see *post*, p. 380).

[4] Children Act 1975, s. 85 (4). In equity this rule applied only to testamentary guardians; the death of one joint guardian appointed by the court determined the authority of all: *Eyre v. Shaftesbury*, (*supra*), at p. 107; *Bradshaw v. Bradshaw* (1826), 1 Russ. 528.

representatives will have no rights or duties with respect to the person of the ward, the estate will be liable for any breach of trust committed by the guardian in his dealings with the ward's property.

Discharge and Removal of a Guardian by the Court.—Like a trustee, a guardian once having accepted the office cannot resign it at will,[1] and although in some earlier cases the court did not look favourably upon a guardian's request to be discharged, the modern view is that, if he is unwilling to act, it will be in the ward's interest that he should be replaced.[2]

But the court's jurisdiction is not confined to those cases where the guardian wishes to be released and the High Court has power to remove a guardian whenever the welfare of the ward so demands.[3] This may be due to the actual or threatened misconduct of the guardian (for the court will attempt to avert a possible danger to the ward rather than wait for it to happen),[4] to the abandonment of his rights for such a length of time that it would not be in the ward's interest to permit him to reassert them,[5] or merely to a change of circumstances which render it for some reason better for the ward to have a new guardian and which do not necessarily cast any reflection on the existing guardian's integrity at all.[6]

B. WARDS OF COURT[7]

Historically the jurisdiction to make a child a ward of court goes back to the Crown's rights over infant tenants in chief in chivalry and its prerogative powers as *parens patriae*. Wardship of court differs from other forms of wardship in one important respect: if a child is made a ward of court, custody in the sense of the sum of parental rights and powers will vest in the court. Care and control must of course be given to an individual but he will be more in the nature of an agent of the court, responsible solely for the day to day supervision of the ward. Two consequences flow from the fact that the residuum of powers remains in the court. First, the person with care of the child must keep the court informed of the progress of the ward and may always turn to the court for guidance and assistance. All major decisions, for example those relating to control, access, education and marriage, must be

---

[1] *Spencer* v. *Chesterfield* (1752), Amb. 146.

[2] Contrast the view taken by LORD HARDWICKE, L.C., in *Spencer* v. *Chesterfield*, (*supra*), with that of ROMILLY, M.R., in *Kay* v. *Johnston* (1856), 21 Beav. 536, at p. 539.

[3] *Re McGrath*, [1893] 1 Ch. 143, 147-148, C.A.; *Re X.*, [1899] 1 Ch. 526, 531, C.A.; Guardianship of Minors Act 1971, ss. 6 and 17 (1). In *Smith* v. *Bate* (1784), 2 Dick. 631, a guardian was removed on the grounds of bankruptcy; whilst this might still be a reason for removing him if he held a large amount of the ward's property, there seems to be no reason for removing him from the guardianship of the person if no moral slur is cast on him.

[4] *Beaufort* v. *Berty* (1721), 1 P. Wms. 703, 704-705; *Re X.*, (*supra*), at p. 531.

[5] *Andrews* v. *Salt* (1873), 8 Ch. App. 622.

[6] *Re X.*, (*supra*), at pp. 535-536; *F.* v. *F.*, [1902] 1 Ch. 688, where a guardian who had become a Roman Catholic was removed although she had made no attempt to influence her ward, a Protestant.

[7] For a detailed analysis of the whole subject, see Lowe and White, *Wards of Court*. The only other authoritative account of the working of this jurisdiction (by a judge of the Chancery Division) is that of Cross, *Wardship of Court*, 83 L.Q.R. 201.

made by the court itself. Secondly, any wilful interference with the ward or the guardian will amount to a contempt of court. Older authorities indicated that this rule applied even though the person interfering was unaware that the child was a ward of court, although his ignorance might well excuse him in the sense that the court would not punish him.[1] There are, however, some modern *dicta*, albeit *obiter*, that a contempt cannot be committed without guilty knowledge or intent.[2] Similarly, the ward himself may be committed for contempt if he wilfully refuses to obey the court's directions.[3]

In practice children are made wards of court in two sorts of situation. First of all there are cases where orders relating to custody are sought in the Family Division but no other matrimonial proceedings are pending so that the court cannot exercise its jurisdiction under the Matrimonial Causes Act. This might occur if a comprehensive order was required or if the case raised some particular difficulty (for example, the existence of a foreign order) so that it was inappropriate to take advantage of the statutory jurisdiction under the Guardianship of Minors Act. Alternatively this procedure would have to be used if someone other than a parent wished to invoke the jurisdiction of the court on the ground, for example, that neither parent was fit to have custody, although a strong *prima facie* case will have to be made out before a child is removed from its natural or adoptive parents.[4] One advantage of making a child a ward of court in these circumstances is that the father or mother may be given care and control of it, whilst the exercise of his or her parental rights will be constantly subject to the supervision of the court. The effect is to give the maximum control over, and protection to, the ward and to leave the minimum discretion to the parent, and consequently this procedure should usually be adopted only when this balance is desirable. An example of such a case is *Re D.*,[5] where a third person warded a girl aged eleven in a successful attempt to prevent her from being permanently sterilized even though her mother had consented to the operation.

In the second type of case the child is made a ward of court for her (or his) own protection, for example to prevent her associating with undesirable companions or contracting a marriage opposed by the parents. This type of ward is almost always a girl nearing the age of majority and, whereas in the first sort of case the parents will often be opposed to each other, in the "teenage wardship" the parents will be acting together but in open conflict with the child.[6] Consequently the court will consider only the point at issue and will not interfere with other matters, such as education and maintenance, which remain in the parents' hands.[7]

It will be apparent from the second type of case described in the last paragraph that in wardship proceedings the court may forbid someone other

---

[1] *Re H.'s Settlement*, [1909] 2 Ch. 260.

[2] *Re F.*, [1977] Fam. 58; [1977] 1 All E.R. 114, C.A., particularly *per* LORD DENNING, M.R., at pp. 89-90 and 122-123, respectively; Lowe and White, *op. cit.*, 141.

[3] *Re H.'s Settlement*, (*supra*).

[4] See *Re O.*, [1978] Fam. 196; [1978] 2 All E.R. 27, C.A. A local authority may similarly take wardship proceedings if there are no grounds for taking care proceedings: *Re D.*, [1977] Fam. 158; [1977] 3 All E.R. 481.

[5] [1976] Fam. 185; [1976] 1 All E.R. 326. See further *ante*, pp. 317-318.

[6] See Lowe and White, *op. cit.*, 201-205; Cross, *loc. cit.*, pp. 209-211.

[7] For the help that can be obtained in finding a missing ward, see *Practice Note (Disclosure of Addresses)*, [1973] 1 All E.R. 61; Lowe and White, *op. cit.*, 325-333.

than the ward from doing that which he might otherwise lawfully do. Jurisdiction to make orders for the ward's protection is in theory unlimited and consequently must be exercised with great care when the rights of third persons are liable to be seriously infringed. The court has to balance the interests of the child against those of others who would be affected by any order, and in practice it is extremely rare to restrain anyone but a person who would come into personal contact with the ward. An attempt to obtain an order that would have gone right outside the conventional limits of the jurisdiction failed in *Re X*.[1] The defendants were the author and publishers of a book which included passages describing the depraved sexual activities and sordid conduct of the deceased father of a girl of 14. She was described as sensitive, highly strung and emotionally vulnerable, and the discovery of the sort of person her father had been was likely to be psychologically damaging to her. Her stepfather therefore made her a ward of court and sought an injunction to restrain the defendants from including the offending passages in the book when it was published. The Court of Appeal refused to make the order. The judgments indicate that the court will rarely, if ever, permit the interests of the child to prevail over the wider interests of the freedom of publication. Although the case is clearly not an authority for such a wide proposition, it is submitted that, once one moves outside the circle of the ward's family and acquaintances, the fact that the person likely to be injured by another's conduct is a minor is no justification for using wardship proceedings to obtain an injunction that could not be obtained were he over 18. The publication of the fact that a 15 year old girl has had an abortion or the unwarranted expulsion of a child from school in breach of contract with a parent may be highly damaging, but if the law of tort or contract affords no remedy by way of injunction, it should not be possible to obtain one in the Family Division. As LORD DENNING, M.R., has pointed out, wardship confers no privileges over and above those possessed by other minors who are not wards of court.[2]

A problem arises if the purpose of making the child a ward of court is to obtain an order relating to some matter, the power to determine which has been vested by statute in some other body. This could occur, for example, if the child were in the care of a local authority. The latter's discretion cannot usually be fettered by warding the child, and consequently the court will entertain the proceedings only in exceptional circumstances, for otherwise the court and the body, both acting in good faith, might reach opposing decisions.[3]

Jurisdiction to make a Child a Ward of Court.—Since the jurisdiction is based upon the necessity of protecting the child, any minor actually in England may be warded even though he is neither domiciled here nor a British

---

1 [1975] Fam. 47; [1975] 1 All E.R. 697, C.A.

2 *Re F.*, [1977] Fam. 58, 86; [1977] 1 All E.R. 114, 120, C.A. It is a contempt of court knowingly to publish information about wardship proceedings heard in private, including details of evidence, reports, etc., before the court: *Re F.*; Lowe and White, *op. cit.*, 77-80, 145-151. Hence it may be a question of chance whether a statement may be published.

3 See *post*, pp. 402-404. Similarly the discretion vested in an immigration officer to refuse a child admission into the country cannot be called in question by warding the child: *Re A.*, [1968] Ch. 643; [1968] 2 All E.R. 145, C.A.

subject. Thus in *Re D.*[1] a German Jewish refugee who had been brought to this country in 1939 was made a ward of court even though he was not a British subject and had no property within the jurisdiction. But clearly this should be done only in the most exceptional circumstances if the child is here only temporarily, for example for educational purposes or on holiday.[2] Conversely, the court has jurisdiction if the child is a British subject even though he is not resident in England at all, because he continues to be entitled to the protection of the Crown as *parens patriae* wherever he may happen to be.[3] In *Re P. (G.E.)*[4] the Court of Appeal went further and held that there is jurisdiction to make an order in respect of an alien who is ordinarily resident here even though he is not in the country when the application is made. In that case the stateless parents of a child who was almost seven years old when the proceedings were commenced had left Egypt following the Suez crisis and had come to England. They later separated and agreed that the boy should live with his mother but spend every weekend with his father. One Saturday the father, having obtained a British travel document, flew to Israel with the son. On the mother's application to have the boy made a ward of court it was held that the court had jurisdiction as the son's ordinary residence was in England with his mother, and the father, having agreed to this, could not change it without the mother's consent or acquiescence. This conclusion was fortified by the fact that the father still held the travel document, which entitled him to return to England, and had entered Israel on only a temporary visa and also that justice demands that a parent left in this country should have a remedy here when the other has spirited the child out of the jurisdiction by force, deception or fraud.

But it does not follow that the court is bound to continue the wardship even though it has jurisdiction. It will always be slow to do so if the child is not in the country, particularly if proceedings are also being taken elsewhere and the other court is the *forum conveniens*.[5] Nor will it make an order if there are no means of enforcing it and no probability that it will be obeyed or if it would be contrary to the law of the state where the child is.[6]

"Kidnapping" Cases.—Speedy international transport has given rise to a number of "kidnapping" cases in which a parent, who has failed to obtain custody in another country, has brought the child to England in the hope of being successful here. Naturally the court will do its utmost to discourage this practice. Consequently the principle was laid down in *Re H.*[7] that it may

---

[1] [1943] Ch. 305; [1943] 2 All E.R. 411. See also *Johnstone* v. *Beattie* (1843), 10 Cl. & F. 42, H.L.

[2] *Per* LORD CAMPBELL, L.C., in *Stuart* v. *Bute* (1861), 9 H.L. Cas. 440, 464-465, H.L.; *per* PEARSON, L.J., in *Re P. (G.E.)*, [1965] Ch. 568, 588; [1964] 3 All E.R. 977, 983-984, C.A.

[3] *Hope* v. *Hope* (1854), 4 De G. M. & G. 328. See also *Re Willoughby* (1885), 30 Ch. D. 324, C.A. In *Re P. (G.E.)*, (*supra*), RUSSELL, L.J., was prepared to extend the jurisdiction to the case of a stateless person travelling abroad on a British travel document or *a fortiori* an alien holding a British passport (at pp. 595 and 988, respectively).

[4] [1965] Ch. 568; [1964] 3 All E.R. 977, C.A. See Webb in 14 I.C.L.Q. 663.

[5] *Re S. (M.)*, [1971] 1 All E.R. 459, 462 (proceedings pending in Scotland where the child was domiciled and resident).

[6] *Hope* v. *Hope*, (*supra*), at pp. 347-348; *Dawson* v. *Jay* (1854), 3 De G. M. & G. 764, 772.

[7] [1965] 3 All E.R. 906; affirmed, [1966] 1 All E.R. 886, C.A. A similar conclusion was reached in *Re G.*, [1969] 2 All E.R. 1135, where the child was ordered to be returned to Scotland.

order the child to be sent back to the country where the original order was made without considering the merits of the case at all, provided that it is satisfied that this can be done without fear of immediate harm. As CROSS, J., pointed out, this procedure is consonant with the general principles of comity and is called for if the foreign court is the *forum conveniens*: if the case were delayed for an enquiry as to the merits, the child would begin to acquire roots in this country which it might not be in his interest to sever, with resulting injustice to the wronged parent. In that case a New York court had given the custody of two boys to their mother with liberal access to the father. It had further ordered that the children should not be removed from the jurisdiction without the father's written consent. In breach of this order and in contempt of the New York court the mother brought her sons to England where she intended to settle permanently. The children were then made wards of court. The Court of Appeal affirmed the decision of CROSS, J., that this was a case where the court should do no more than order the children to be sent back to New York where the question of their future custody could be considered on its merits. A number of considerations led them to this conclusion: this was a serious example of "kidnapping"; the father and both children were American citizens so that an American court was the *forum conveniens*; an enquiry on the merits of the parents' claims (which might have resulted in the court's giving custody to the father in the U.S.A.) would have led to great delay during which time the children would have settled down in England; and there was no evidence that sending them back with their father would cause them any harm.

In *Re E. (D.)*[1] CROSS, J., went so far as to say that, where there is a foreign order, the proper course is to send the child back unless there are compelling reasons to the contrary. There were such compelling reasons in that case. The parents of a baby girl were divorced in New Mexico. Custody was originally given to the mother, but this was later varied in favour of the father with whom the girl lived until, nearly four years later, he was killed in a motor accident. The father, who was convinced that his wife was wholly unfit to have custody, had previously indicated that in the event of his death he wished his sister, Mrs. Z who lived in England, to have custody. Immediately after the father's death, the child's paternal grandfather took her from the hospital where she was being treated and handed her over to Mrs. Z with an assurance that there was no legal objection to her being taken to England. In the meantime the mother had obtained an injunction from the New Mexico court prohibiting the child from being removed from the U.S.A. and giving her temporary custody, but Mrs. Z and the girl had left the country before the injunction could be served. The mother later came to England and Mrs. Z made the child a ward of court. It was held that she should stay in this country with Mrs. Z. The latter had acted more or less innocently, she had believed the mother was unfit to have custody, she had become a second mother to her niece, who had no other home, and—the critical consideration—the court felt that it would be disastrous for the child to remove her and send her back to the U.S.A. An even stronger case is that of *Re C.*[2] Three children, all under

---

[1] [1967] Ch. 287, 301; [1967] 1 All E.R. 329, 338; affirmed, [1967] Ch. 761; [1967] 2 All E.R. 881, C.A. *Cf. Re T.A.* (1972), 116 Sol. Jo. 78 (children hostile to father in Malta).
[2] [1978] Fam. 105; [1978] 2 All E.R. 230, C.A.

the age of ten, lived with their mother and her second husband in California. After the mother's death the stepfather obtained an interim order for custody in California, but the children's father flew them to England, where he proposed that they should be brought up by him and his second wife. As the children had settled down reasonably well in this country, there was no female relation of the stepfather's able to look after them in America and, most importantly, the welfare report to the Californian court indicated that that court would itself give custody to the father, the court refused to make a peremptory order for the children's return but directed that they should remain wards of court in the care and control of the father.

But there is no doubt that this principle has been modified in recent cases. The older the child is and the longer the order has been in force, the weaker becomes the presumption that the child should be sent back.[1] In *Re A*.[2] the Court of Appeal held that the principle does not apply at all if the child was originally brought to this country not by stealth but with the agreement of both parties and *a fortiori* if, as in that case, one parent is normally resident here, the other has the means of coming to this country, the parties are probably domiciled here and matrimonial proceedings are about to be launched here. Two more recent decisions of the Court of Appeal indicate a much more radical departure from the views expressed earlier. In *Re L*.[3] it was stressed that the welfare of the child must determine whether the case is to be heard on its merits and from this it was concluded in *Re C*.[4] that the judge at first instance had erred in concluding that he should make a peremptory order for the children's return unless he was satisfied that this involved some obvious moral or physical danger. One of two inferences can be drawn from these cases. One is that, if a peremptory order is sought in a kidnapping case, the judge may make it if he is satisfied that it is for the child's welfare: in other words, the burden is now on the party applying for the order to satisfy the court that this is the correct course. The other is that the courts are becoming increasingly reluctant to make peremptory orders and are now much readier to consider the merits. It is not easy to reconcile these authorities and only an authoritative ruling of the House of Lords can clarify the position. At the moment the Court of Appeal appears more inclined to consider the merits, but it should be remembered that CROSS, J.'s views are as valid now as they were when he stated them 15 years ago.

Procedure to make a Child a Ward of Court.[5]—Until 1949 a child automatically became a ward of court in a number of cases, for example on a petition to appoint a guardian or on payment into court under the Trustee Act of a fund belonging to him or, in fact, upon any application made to the court

---

[1] *Re T.*, [1969] 3 All E.R. 998 (principle not applied when boy in question was aged 16 and the order was 12 years old).

[2] [1970] Ch. 665; [1970] 3 All E.R. 184, C.A.

[3] [1974] 1 All E.R. 913, C.A. It seems to have been overlooked that what was said was that, *if the court embarks on an investigation and considers the merits*, it must apply the same principles in kidnapping cases as in all others and that the parent's conduct is merely one of the matters to be taken into account.

[4] [1978] Fam. 105; [1978] 2 All E.R. 230, C.A. For the facts, see *supra*. See further Lowe and White, *op. cit.*, 343-349.

[5] See Lowe and White, *op. cit.*, c. 4.

on his behalf.[1] But now section 9 of the Law Reform (Miscellaneous Provisions) Act 1949, has enacted that a child shall be made a ward of court only by virtue of an order to that effect made by the court. Immediately an application for an order is made, the child becomes a ward of court; but he ceases to be one unless an appointment to hear the summons is obtained within 21 days or if the court refuses to make the order.[2]

Even though the child does not become a ward until a summons is issued, in an emergency the court may make an order on the applicant's undertaking to start proceedings at the earliest possible opportunity.[3] This might be necessary, for example, if one parent was threatening to remove the child from the jurisdiction before the other could take the appropriate procedural steps. If the court could not act in such a case there would be no means of preventing irreparable damage.

A divorce court may also direct proceedings to be taken to have the children of the marriage made wards of court in any proceedings for divorce, nullity or judicial separation, either before, by or after the final decree.[4] This power is rarely exercised but is useful if the court feels that the continuous supervision that this will produce is necessary for the child's welfare.

The child can always be ordered to be separately represented and the Official Solicitor then usually acts as guardian *ad litem*. If the dispute is between a "teenage" child and its parents, separate representation is always ordered; but if it is between the parents themselves or others claiming custody, this will be done only if the case presents particular difficulty or for some other reason it is desirable for the court to have the benefit of an independent opinion.[5] The court may also call for a report from a welfare officer.[6]

The court may at any time order that a child shall cease to be a ward of court.[7] If this is not done, the court's jurisdiction ceases immediately the ward reaches the age of 18, but it does not cease on the ward's marriage.[8]

Supervision by the Court.—Apart from the fact that discretion will have to be exercised by the court and not by the guardian, the principles to be applied when the ward is under the supervision of a testamentary guardian or guardian appointed by the court are equally applicable when he is a ward of court. Thus the court must make all necessary orders relating to care and

---

[1] See Simpson, *Infants*, 4th Ed., 165.

[2] Law Reform (Miscellaneous Provisions) Act 1949, s. 9 (2); R.S.C. O. 90, rr. 3 and 4. The applicant must state his relationship to the child, and if the application appears to be an abuse of process, the summons may be dismissed forthwith: *Practice Direction*, [1967] 1 All E.R. 828 (made following *Re Dunhill* (1967), 111 Sol. Jo. 113, where a nightclub owner made a girl a ward of court as a piece of advertisement).

[3] *Re N.*, [1967] Ch. 512; [1967] 1 All E.R. 161. See also *L. v. L.*, [1969] P. 25; [1969] 1 All E.R. 852; and *cf. ante*, pp. 122-123. Insofar as the earlier decision of *Re E.*, [1956] Ch. 23; [1955] 3 All E.R. 174, indicates a contrary view, it is submitted that it is not good law.

[4] Matrimonial Causes Act 1973, s. 42 (1).

[5] For a valuable account of the role and work of the Official Solicitor, see Lowe and White, *op. cit.*, c. 8, and an article by the present holder of the office in 2 Adoption and Fostering 30.

[6] See Lowe and White, *op. cit.*, c. 9.

[7] Law Reform (Miscellaneous Provisions) Act 1949, s. 9 (3).

[8] *Cf. Re Elwes* (1958), *Times*, 30th July.

control, access, education, medical treatment, and so forth. Six points call for special comment.

Care and Supervision.—Section 7 of the Family Law Reform Act 1969 has given two new powers to the court, both of which can be exercised only if there are exceptional circumstances making this desirable. If it is impracticable or undesirable to leave the ward in the care of either parent or a third person, he may be committed to the care of a local authority. Alternatively, he may be placed under the supervision of a welfare officer or a local authority. It will be seen that this brings the powers of the Family Division in wardship proceedings into line with its powers under the Guardianship of Minors Act and the Matrimonial Causes Act.[1]

Medical Evidence and Treatment.—If psychiatric evidence is desired, a psychiatrist should not be appointed without the court's approval. If both sides agree on the necessity for an examination and on the name of the psychiatrist, the court will normally follow their wishes. In the event of a disagreement, the Official Solicitor should be asked to act as guardian *ad litem* (if he has not been appointed already) and he can then decide (subject to the court's direction) whether an examination is necessary. This procedure has the advantage that the psychiatrist will not be the witness of either of the parties in dispute[2] and that the Official Solicitor can obtain a second opinion if necessary.[3]

Clearly it must be possible for the person with care and control to authorise medical and surgical treatment in the ordinary course of events. It is doubtful, however, how far he is entitled to permit the ward to undergo non-therapeutic surgery (for example, sterilization or the donation of an organ) without the court's consent. Although a child over the age of 16 may consent to treatment without his parent's or guardian's consent,[4] even this may not justify his action without the court's approval if he has been warded; indeed he might be made a ward of court to prevent him undergoing the treatment in question.[5] It would certainly be prudent to refer the matter to the court before taking any irrevocable step.

Maintenance.—Formerly the court could not order maintenance to be paid for a ward of court unless there was some fund out of which sums could be paid for his benefit. Now, however, the court can order either parent of a *legitimate* child who is a ward of court to make periodical payments to the other or to a third person who has care and control of the child.[6]

Marriage of Ward of Court.—The court's consent must be obtained to the marriage of its ward[7] and the consent will be withheld if the court is of the

---

[1] See *ante*, pp. 303 and 308.

[2] See *ante*, p. 293; Lowe and White, *op. cit.*, 64-65, 74-75.

[3] See the views of CROSS, J., in *Re S.*, [1967] 1 All E.R. 202, 209, approved and followed in *Re R. (P.M.)*, [1968] 1 All E.R. 691, 693, and *B. (M.) v. B. (R.)*, [1968] 3 All E.R. 170, 174, C.A.

[4] See *ante*, p. 316.

[5] *Cf. Re D.*, [1976] Fam. 185; [1976] 1 All E.R. 326; *ante*, p. 317. See Lowe and White, *op. cit.*, 76-77, 108-109.

[6] See *post*, p. 594.

[7] *Re H.'s Settlement*, [1909] 2 Ch. 260; Marriage Act 1949, s. 3 (6).

opinion that the proposed match would be unsuitable. It is a contempt for a ward to marry (or even to attempt to marry)[1] without this consent, for which not only the parties but also anyone else who has knowingly brought about the marriage or taken any active part in its celebration[2] may be punished.

Adoption of Ward of Court.—In addition to the need for parental agreement, the court must give leave before proceedings may be commenced to adopt a ward of court. Somewhat anomalously, the Court of Appeal has held that all the court must do before giving leave is to satisfy itself that the proceedings are likely to succeed: it need not be satisfied that adoption will be in the ward's best interest.[3]

Removal of a Ward of Court from the Jurisdiction.—The danger that, if a ward left the jurisdiction, the court might lose complete control of him because it had no means of securing his return, led to the formulation of the rule that a ward of court would never be permitted to leave England. Thus, in 1801, LORD ELDON, L.C., stated that the court would never make an order for taking a ward out of the jurisdiction and he refused the guardian permission to take his ward to his own house in Scotland.[4] But by the middle of the last century the courts were coming round to the view that a ward might be taken out, at least temporarily, if sufficient reason were shown, for example for the sake of his health or to rejoin his family, provided that his return could be ensured if the court demanded it.[5] This wider rule was gradually extended and by the end of the century it was accepted that an application should be granted whenever it was shown to be for the ward's benefit.[6] It must now be extremely common for wards to be taken abroad for holidays and the court may give general leave for temporary visits abroad if the other party does not object.[7] Only in the most exceptional circumstances would the court refuse to permit a ward to be taken out of the jurisdiction permanently if its welfare so demanded. The person most likely to oppose the application is one of the parents if the proposal is that the child should emigrate with the other; in such circumstances the court must take into account the same facts as it would if this situation arose after a divorce.[8]

C. CUSTODIANSHIP

As we have seen, a guardian, whether appointed by a deceased parent or by the court, stands *in loco parentis* to his ward only after the death of the ward's parent. As the law now stands, there is no other way by which legal

---

[1] *Warter* v. *Yorke* (1815), 19 Ves. 451, 453. (In this case the marriage was void but nevertheless was held to be a contempt.)

[2] *E.g.*, the parties' parents or the officiating clergyman: *Warter* v. *Yorke*, (*supra*).

[3] *F.* v. *S.*, [1973] Fam. 203; [1973] 1 All E.R. 722, C.A. Criticised by Lowe and White, *op. cit.*, 252-253.

[4] *Mountstuart* v. *Mountstuart* (1801), 6 Ves. 363.

[5] See *Campbell* v. *Mackay* (1837), 2 My. & Cr. 31, and *Dawson* v. *Jay* (1854), 3 De G. M. & G. 764.

[6] See *Re Callaghan* (1884), 28 Ch. D. 186, 189, C.A.

[7] See *Practice Note* (*Wardship: Visit Abroad*), [1973] 2 All E.R. 512.

[8] See also *Re Benner*, [1951] W.N. 436; *Re O.*, [1962] 2 All E.R. 10, C.A. The court would usually deward the child if it was going abroad permanently.

custody of a minor can be given to a third person (other than a step-parent who has treated him as a child of the family) except in proceedings under the Matrimonial Causes Act.[1] One solution is for the person wishing to secure custody to apply to adopt the child, but this may not be for the latter's welfare if the applicant is a relative (because family relationships may become distorted) or if the parent is still anxious to keep in touch with the child, however unlikely it is that he will ever be in a position to exercise care and control. It is also possible to make the child a ward of court and then seek care and control, but the proceedings lack the convenience and relative cheapness of an application to a magistrates' court or even a county court.[2] This gap in the law is a source of particular hardship to foster parents whose position is always precarious and who may have had the care and control of a child for years with no hope of being able to adopt it or obtain legal custody. Consequently the Houghton Committee recommended that in appropriate cases the court should have power to vest custody in someone other than the parent.[3] This recommendation has been implemented by the Children Act of 1975 in provisions (not yet in force) which will enable the court to make a custodianship order.

Who may apply for an Order.—The Children Act specifies three categories of persons qualified to apply for an order. They are:[4]

(a) a relative or step-parent of the child[5]—
  (i) who applies with the consent of a person having legal custody of the child, and
  (ii) with whom the child has had his home for the three months preceding the making of the application;
(b) any person—
  (i) who applies with the consent of a person having legal custody of the child, and
  (ii) with whom the child has had his home for a period or periods before the making of the application which amount to at least twelve months and include the three months preceding the making of the application;
(c) any person with whom the child has had his home for a period or periods before the making of the application which amount to at least three years and include the three months preceding the making of the application.

The reason that the child must have had his home with the applicant for the previous three months is to enable the local authority to ensure that he is

---

[1] At present there is also a power to order custody to a third person if one of the parents takes proceedings under the Guardianship of Minors Act. This will be abolished when the provisions in the Children Act relating to custodianship are brought into force. See *ante*, p. 302.

[2] An applicant may still have to ward the child if he is not qualified to apply for custodianship, and a parent opposed to custodianship may ward the child as a counter-measure. See further Lowe and White, *op. cit.*, 243-249.

[3] Cmnd. 5107, c. 6.

[4] S. 33 (3). For the meaning of "had his home", see *ante*, p. 347.

[5] "Relative" has the same meaning as in the Adoption Act 1958: s. 107 (1). See *ante*, p. 338, n. 4. As there is nothing to rebut the presumption that "parent" does not include the father of an illegitimate child, the father's wife is presumably not a step-parent. The mother's husband presumably is.

likely to settle down there. The consent of a person with legal custody is required in the first two cases because of the fear that the whole system of fostering might be jeopardised if foster parents could automatically destroy the parents' rights by applying for an order: this can be done only if there is a long term fostering which has lasted for at least three years.[1] There is no such danger if no one has legal custody of the child, if the applicant has legal custody himself, or if the person with custody cannot be found, and consequently in these cases the requirement relating to consent does not apply.[2]

An application may be made by one or more persons.[3] Although a joint application will usually be made by a husband and wife, it is not necessary for joint applicants to be married to each other. Hence, for example, two sisters could apply for an order together. The child must be in England or Wales when the application is made, but neither the applicant's domicile nor his residence is relevant.[4]

Two classes of person may not apply even though they come within the categories set out above. Neither the mother nor the father of the child may do so:[5] if they do not already have custody, they must obtain it in one of the ways already open to them. Nor may a step-parent apply for an order if the child was named as a child of the family in previous proceedings for divorce or nullity in an order under section 41 of the Matrimonial Causes Act 1973 unless the parent other than the one married to the applicant has died or cannot be found.[6] In this case jurisdiction to make orders relating to custody must remain in the divorce court already seised of the matter.

Two special cases must be mentioned. A court hearing an application for custody by a parent under the Guardianship of Minors Acts or an application by a spouse under the Domestic Proceedings and Magistrates' Courts Act may make a custodianship order in favour of a third person if it is of the opinion that this would be for the child's welfare. A custodianship order may also be made in favour of the applicant or applicants for an adoption order if the court is satisfied that the child's welfare would not be better safeguarded and promoted by making an adoption order and that it would be appropriate to make a custodianship order. In the last case the child must be free for adoption or the agreement of each parent or guardian to adoption must have been given or dispensed with, but with this exception a court may make a custodianship order in any of these proceedings even though the requirements

---

[1] The reference to *a* person in paras. (a) and (b) implies that, if two persons have legal custody (*e.g.*, both parents), it will be sufficient if only one consents. The wishes of both parents must be taken into account before an order is made. The Secretary of State may by order substitute a different period for the period of three years: Children Act 1975, s. 33 (7).

[2] Children Act 1975, s. 33 (6). The reference to *the* person with custody implies there is only one.

[3] S. 33 (1).

[4] S. 33 (1). See also s. 46. The applicant will normally have to be resident within this country as he has to give notice to the local authority in whose area the child resides and the child must have his home with him: see *infra*.

[5] S. 33 (4). This includes the father of an illegitimate child.

[6] S. 33 (5), (8). For s. 41, see *ante*, pp. 308-310. This does not apply if the court declared that there were circumstances making it desirable that the decree should be granted without delay notwithstanding that the requirements of the section had not been complied with and it has since been determined that the child was not a child of the family.

relating to consent and the minimum period of time during which the child must have had his home with the applicant are not satisfied.[1]

Procedure.—A custodianship order may be made by the High Court, a county court or a magistrates' court.[2] Within seven days of making the application the applicant must give notice to the local authority in whose area the child resides, and an officer of the local authority must then make a report to the court. This must deal with all matters relating to the child's welfare, his wishes and feelings in the matter (having regard to his age and understanding), the applicant's means and suitability (including relevant information about other members of his household), the wishes and means of the child's mother and father, and any other matters which may be prescribed.[3] The court may independently request the local authority or a probation officer to make a report on any specific matter.[4]

As soon as an application has been made, nobody (including a local authority in whose care the child is) may remove him from the custody of any applicant with whom he has had his home for a period or periods totalling at least three years, without the consent of the applicant or the leave of the court.[5] This protects the applicant who might otherwise be inhibited from applying for an order if it was likely to result in the removal of the child.

In deciding whether to make a custodianship order the court must give first and paramount consideration to the welfare of the child. It has the same power to make an interim order, a supervision order and an order committing the child to the care of a local authority as it has on an application by a parent under the Guardianship of Minors Act.[6]

Effect of Custodianship Order.[7]—So long as a custodianship order is in force, the legal custody of the child is vested in the custodian or custodians and the right of any other person to legal custody is suspended. This does not

---

[1] Children Act 1975, s. 37; Domestic Proceedings and Magistrates' Courts Act 1978, ss. 8 (3) and 69. If the order is made in proceedings brought under either of the Acts named, its operation (or the operation of any of its provisions) may be deferred. In adoption proceedings the court *must* direct the application to be treated as one for a custodianship order if the conditions are satisfied and the applicant or one of the applicants is a relative or the spouse of the child's father or mother; if neither applicant is a relative or step-parent, the court *may* do so. See *ante*, pp. 302, 305-306 and 351. A custodianship order cannot be made if the applicant for an adoption order comes within either of the classes mentioned in the last paragraph.

[2] Ss. 33 (1) and 100 (1), (2), (7), (8). The High Court may order a case pending in a county court to be removed to the High Court and a magistrates' court must refuse to make any order if it considers that the case would be more conveniently dealt with by the High Court: s. 101.

[3] S. 40. The period of seven days may be extended by the court or the local authority. See further Bevan and Parry, *Children Act* 1975, 135-138. As in other cases relating to the welfare of children, local authorities are non-metropolitan counties, metropolitan districts and London boroughs: s. 107 (1).

[4] S. 39.

[5] S. 41. The Secretary of State may by order substitute a different period for three years: *cf.* p. 384, n. 1, *ante*. If the child is in care but has not had his home with the applicant for three years, the local authority can still lawfully remove him even though the parents consent to the making of the order; this is clearly necessary to protect the child in some cases. For the return of a child taken away in breach of these provisions, see s. 42.

[6] S. 34 (5), as substituted by the Domestic Proceedings and Magistrates' Courts Act 1978, s. 64. See *ante*, pp. 303-304.

[7] See Bevan and Parry, *op. cit.*, 111-114; Eekelaar, *Children in Care and the Children Act* 1975, 40 M.L.R. 121, at pp. 137-139.

apply if the person who already has custody is the child's parent and the order is made in favour of that parent's spouse: in that case the spouses will have custody jointly.[1] It must not be assumed, however, that a custodian's position is identical with a parent's. Certain powers are by statute given to a parent or guardian alone and will not be transferred to a custodian, for example the power to consent to marriage, to agree to adoption, and to appoint a guardian.[2] So if a minor child wishes to contract a marriage of which the custodian approves but to which the minor's parent will not give his consent, the consent of the court must be obtained. Conversely, if the parent consents but the custodian does not, the only way in which the latter could attempt to prevent the wedding is by making the child a ward of court. Again, legal custody comprises only those parental rights and duties which relate to the person of the child, so that a custodian cannot administer the child's property.

The court may include in the order a provision giving access to the child's mother, father or grandparent or to any other person who has treated him as a child of the family.[3] It may also make an order forbidding the removal of the child from the jurisdiction without the leave of the court.[4]

If two joint custodians (or the parent of a child and his or her spouse who has obtained a custodianship order) cannot agree on the exercise of any parental right or the performance of any duty, either of them may apply to the court which may make such order regarding its exercise or performance as it thinks fit.[5]

Maintenance.—Although there are likely to be few cases where it will be appropriate to order a parent to contribute to the child's maintenance when a custodianship order is in force, it may be reasonable to do so if, for example, the parent has the means to pay and wishes to have access.[6] Consequently the court may order periodical payments or a lump sum payment to be made by either or both of the parents (other than the father of an illegitimate child) or by a person who has treated it as a child of the family. The amount that can be ordered by way of periodical payments is unlimited, but a magistrates' court may not order a lump sum payment exceeding £500. Payment may be made either to the custodian for the child's benefit or to the child himself; a lump sum may be payable by instalments and periodical payments may be made to begin at a future date and may not last for a longer time than they could under the Domestic Proceedings and Magistrates' Courts Act. In general terms the court must have regard to the same matters as it would under that Act (insofar as they are relevant) in determining what order to make.[7]

---

[1] S. 44. For the enforcement of orders made by magistrates' courts, see s. 43.

[2] But on the question of appointment of a guardian, see Bevan and Parry, *op. cit.*, 112-113, where the authors appear to have overlooked the statutory source of the power.

[3] S. 34 (1) (a), (2) (as substituted). An order for access may be made at any time whilst the custodianship order is in force.

[4] S. 43A (added by the Domestic Proceedings and Magistrates' Courts Act 1978, s. 70).

[5] S. 38.

[6] See Cmnd. 5107, para. 130.

[7] S. 34 (as substituted) and ss. 34A, 34B and 35A (added by the Domestic Proceedings and Magistrates' Courts Act 1978, ss. 65 and 67). For orders under the 1978 Act and the matters to be taken into account, see *post*, pp. 586-588. The Secretary of State has power to increase the maximum lump sum that may be awarded. An order may be made when the custodianship order

If the custodian wishes to obtain maintenance from the putative father of an illegitimate child and no affiliation order is in force, he must take proceedings under the Affiliation Proceedings Act. It will be immaterial that the mother is not a "single woman", and in place of the time limits imposed if the mother is the applicant, proceedings must be brought within three years of the making of the custodianship order. No application at all may be made if the custodian is married to the mother: in this case she alone can bring proceedings.[1] The court may also vary or discharge any order (including an affiliation order) made in any other proceedings requiring the child's father or mother to contribute towards its maintenance and, specifically, may vary it by substituting the custodian as the person to whom the contributions should be made.[2] Orders are enforceable in the same way as other orders for periodical payments made by the court in question.[3]

As persons with whom children are boarded out by local authorities are paid, they might be unable to afford to apply for custodianship if this were to entail the loss of the allowance. Consequently local authorities are empowered to make contributions to custodians towards the cost of the accommodation and maintenance of children in appropriate cases except when the custodian is the husband or wife of the child's parent.[4]

Variation and Revocation of Orders.—The court may revoke a custodianship order on the application of the custodian, the child's mother, father or guardian, or a local authority.[5] The reason that the last named may apply is that many children with respect to whom custodianship orders may be made will previously have been in care and it may be necessary for the authority to seek another care order if the child becomes difficult.[6] In order to prevent undue harassment of the custodian by a parent, no one may reapply for a revocation after a previous unsuccessful application without the leave of the court.[7] Unless the court otherwise orders, revocation revives the right of the person or persons who would have been entitled to legal custody had the order not been made;[8] consequently before revoking the order the court must ascertain who those persons are and may request the local authority or a probation officer to make a report on the desirability of returning the child to them.[9] If the child would be in the custody of no one at all or if it is undesirable to return him to the person who would have custody, the court must commit him to the care of the local authority; in other cases it

---

is made or at any time while it is in force. An interim order may be made for not more than three months in the first instance but may be extended for not more than a further period of three months.

[1] S. 45. In other respects the procedure is the same; hence if the mother gives evidence, it must be corroborated. For affiliation proceedings generally, see *post*, pp. 595 *et seq*.

[2] Children Act 1975, s. 34 (1) (d), (e) (as substituted).

[3] This includes the power to register the order in another court: see s. 43 (3) and Sched. 3, paras. 10, 11 and 73 (2).

[4] S. 34 (6) (as substituted). Presumably it could make payments to the wife of the father of an illegitimate child: *cf.* p. 383, n. 5, *ante*.

[5] S. 35 (1).

[6] See Cmnd. 5107, para. 133.

[7] S. 35 (2). Normally this will be given only if there has been a change of circumstances.

[8] S. 44 (1).

[9] S. 36 (1), (4), (7).

may make an order placing the child under the supervision of a local authority or a probation officer if its welfare so requires.[1]

An order relating to access may be varied or revoked on the application of the custodian or the person in whose favour it was made.[2] Either the custodian or the person against whom the order was made may apply for the variation or revocation of an order for periodical payments, as may the child himself if he is over the age of 16.[3] There is a general power to suspend such orders and to revive orders which have been suspended, and if the order ceased to have effect not earlier than the child's sixteenth birthday and not later than his eighteenth, he may apply to have it revived himself so long as he is under the age of 21.[4] On varying an order the court may require a lump sum payment to be made by either parent (other than the father of an illegitimate child) or any person who has treated the child as a child of his family.[5] If a lump sum is payable by instalments, the court may vary the number and amount of the instalments and the date on which they are to be paid, but it may not alter the total sum.[6]

Orders relating to access and periodical payments cease to have effect if the custodianship order is revoked except that, if the child is then committed to the care of a local authority, the court may order either parent (other than the father of an illegitimate child) to make periodical payments. If these are made payable to the authority, they cannot be made to last longer than the period for which the child is in care; if they are made payable to the child himself, they may last for the same time as if the order had been made when the custodianship order was made.[7]

A custodianship order automatically comes to an end when the child reaches the age of 18[8] and probably also if he marries under that age.[9]

Position of Custodians.—The nature of custodianship may be seen more clearly by comparing the position of a custodian with that of others with a similar role. He is most nearly akin to a person (other than a parent) who is given custody of a child when proceedings are brought under the Matrimonial Causes Act. Each will be entitled to legal custody so long as the order

---

[1] S. 36 (2), (3), (6). If the child is committed to the care of a local authority, the court may require his parents (other than the father of an illegitimate child) to make periodical payments to the local authority or to the child: s. 36 (5)-(5C), as substituted and added by the Domestic Proceedings and Magistrates' Courts Act 1978, s. 68.

[2] S. 35 (3), (4) (as amended by the Domestic Proceedings and Magistrates' Courts Act 1978, s. 66).

[3] S. 35 (3)-(4A), (8), (9) (as amended).

[4] S. 35 (7), (10) (as amended). If the child is over the age of 18, he can apply for the order to be revived only if one of the conditions enabling the court to continue an order after his eighteenth birthday is in force (see *post*, p. 586).

[5] S. 35A (3), (4), (6) (added by the Domestic Proceedings and Magistrates' Courts Act 1978, s. 67). A magistrates' court may not order the payment of a lump sum exceeding £500.

[6] S. 35A (5) (as added).

[7] Ss. 35 (5) and 36 (5)-(5C) (added by the Domestic Proceedings and Magistrates' Courts Act 1978, s. 68). It will be seen that no order can be made against a person (other than a parent) who has treated the child as a member of his family.

[8] S. 35 (6) (as amended).

[9] Bevan and Parry, *op. cit.*, 132-133. Curiously, the Act makes no provision for legal custody on the death of a sole custodian. Does this also revive the rights of those who would be entitled to it had no order been made? See *ibid.*, 133.

is in force and the parents' rights will be suspended.[1] We have already noted that the essence of guardianship is that the guardian should act only after a parent's death: he is also distinguishable from the custodian in that he can (and usually will) be appointed not by the court but by the parent himself. Furthermore, whilst a custodian will have actual custody of the child, this will not normally be vested in a guardian because the ward will usually be living with the surviving parent. Guardians and persons given custody under the Matrimonial Causes Act have three other points in common which differentiate them from custodians: they have power to deal with the child's property; it is not necessary for him to have had his home with the guardian or person given custody for any minimum period of time before an order is made; and the local authority has no power to intervene at a later stage and seek the dismissal of the guardian or revocation of the custody order. For this reason a person qualified to apply for guardianship (for example, a relative or friend with whom the child is living after both parents' death) would be well advised to do so rather than to apply for custodianship. Custodians differ most markedly from adoptive parents, for adoption not only completely destroys all the legal ties between the child and its natural parents but also puts the former in the position of the adopters' legitimate child for the purpose of claims to property. Nor can an adoption order be revoked.

D. CHILDREN IN THE CARE OF LOCAL AUTHORITIES[2]

Since the end of the Second World War the policy of successive administrations has been to increase the responsibility of local authorities for the provision of welfare services. For this purpose local authorities are non-metropolitan counties, metropolitan districts and London boroughs,[3] and by the Local Authority Social Services Act of 1970 they are required to set up a single social services committee responsible for all the services. The day to day running of the authority's social services is under the control of the Director of Social Services.[4]

So far as children are concerned, the authority's first duty is to give advice, guidance and assistance in order to prevent a child having to be received into care or brought before a juvenile court. In addition to working with voluntary organisations, the authority may give assistance in kind and, in exceptional cases, in cash.[5] Other duties, which we have already considered,

---

[1] But the custodian's rights and duties relate only to the child's person whilst those given custody under the Matrimonial Causes Act apparently have power to administer the child's property as well.

[2] Most of the relevant law is contained in the Child Care Act 1980. This consolidates provisions formerly contained in the Children and Young Persons Acts 1933, 1963 and 1969 and the Children Act 1948 and 1975 *inter alia*. See generally Maidment, *The Fragmentation of Parental Rights and Children in Care*, [1981] J.S.W.L. 21.

[3] Child Care Act 1980, s. 87 (1).

[4] Local Authority Social Services Act 1970, s. 6.

[5] Child Care Act 1980, s. 1; *R.* v. *Local Commissioner for Administration, ex parte Bradford City Council*, [1979] Q.B. 287, 317-318; [1979] 2 All E.R. 881, 902, C.A. The authority has similar powers with respect to a person under the age of 21 formerly in their care: *ibid.*, s. 29. *Cf.* their duty of after-care under ss. 28 and 69. For their powers to contribute towards the maintenance, education and training of such children, see *ibid.*, s. 27. Voluntary organisations would include such bodies as a Family Service Unit, the Family Welfare Association and the W.R.V.S.

are the supervision of the welfare of foster-children[1] and children who are the subject of supervision orders,[2] the establishment and maintenance of an adoption service (including the duty to investigate and make a report to the court if an application is made for the adoption of a child who has not been placed by an adoption agency),[3] and the duty to make a report to the court on an application for a custodianship order.[4]

A further and extremely important function of local authorities is to look after children in their care. Children may come into care as the result of an order made under the Guardianship of Minors Act,[5] the Matrimonial Causes Act[6] or the Domestic Proceedings and Magistrates' Courts Act,[7] and in proceedings for adoption,[8] wardship[9] or custodianship.[10] These have already been dealt with elsewhere in this book; what we must now discuss is the further power to make a care order in care proceedings and in criminal proceedings. We must then consider the reception of children into care under the provisions of the Child Care Act 1980 and finally discuss the duties and powers of authorities with respect to all children in their care.

1. CARE ORDERS

Care Proceedings.[11]—Early legislation dealt with three distinct types of children: juvenile offenders, children in need of care and protection, and children beyond parental control. It is obvious that the last two categories overlap, and it has long been recognised that juvenile delinquency may well be the result of home surroundings.[12] The law relating to all three has therefore gradually been assimilated. It was radically altered by the Children and Young Persons Act 1969, the main purpose of which was to give effect to the White Paper "Children in Trouble".[13] The main statutory provisions are now to be found in the Children and Young Persons Acts 1933 to 1969:[14] the basic principle underlying them is thus stated in section 44 (1) of the Act of 1933:

"Every court in dealing with a child or young person who is brought before it ... shall have regard to the welfare of the child or young person and shall in a proper

---

[1] See *ante*, pp. 362-363.
[2] See *ante*, pp. 303, 306, 308, 353, 381, 385 and 388.
[3] See *ante*, pp. 337 and 350.
[4] See *ante*, p. 385.
[5] See *ante*, p. 303.
[6] See *ante*, p. 308.
[7] See *ante*, p. 306.
[8] See *ante*, p. 353.
[9] See *ante*, p. 381.
[10] See *ante*, pp. 385 and 387.
[11] Bevan, *Children*, 19-31, 50-55, 71-74, 78-85, 91.
[12] *Cf.* the Infant Felons Act of 1840 which enabled the court to assign the custody of an infant convicted of felony to anyone willing to take charge of him if this would be for his benefit.
[13] 1968, Cmnd. 3601. For a critical review of the provisions of the Act, see Stone, *Children without a Satisfactory Home*, 33 M.L.R. 649, and of its working, see Hoggett, 117 Sol. Jo. 3, 27; 11th Report from the Expenditure Committee, H.C. 534-I (1974-1975).
[14] Children and Young Persons Act 1933; Children and Young Persons (Amendment) Act 1952; Children and Young Persons Act 1963; Children and Young Persons Act 1969. For the sake of brevity, these will be referred to as the 1933 Act, etc.

case take steps for removing him from undesirable surroundings, and for securing that proper provision is made for his education and training.''

Under the 1969 Act care proceedings have replaced proceedings for bringing a child under the age of 17[1] before the court as being in need of care, protection or control, and they will eventually partly replace criminal proceedings as well. A local authority is under a duty to investigate if they believe that there are grounds for bringing care proceedings and to bring them if necessary;[2] care proceedings may also be brought by a constable or other authorised person or by an officer of an authorised society (such as the N.S.P.C.C.), who must first give notice to the local authority.[3] In some cases the child's parent or guardian may himself want proceedings to be taken (for example if the child is beyond control). He may ask the local authority to take them, and if the authority refuses to do so or takes no action within 28 days, the parent or guardian may then apply to the juvenile court which, after investigating the facts, may order the authority to bring the child before it.[4]

A juvenile court before which the child is brought may make an order only provided that at least one of seven specified conditions is satisfied and also that, in any case, the child is in need of care or control which he is unlikely to receive unless an order is made.[5] The seven conditions are:

(a) The child's proper development is being avoidably prevented or neglected or his health is being avoidably impaired or neglected or he is being ill-treated.

(b) Condition (a) will probably be satisfied having regard to the fact that the court or another court has found that it is or was satisfied in the case of another child who is or was a member of the same household.[6]

(c) Condition (a) will probably be satisfied having regard to the fact that a person who has been convicted of one or more specified offences is or may become a member of the same household.[7]

(d) The child is exposed to moral danger. Problems may arise in the case of immigrants and foreigners resident in this country, for the principle was

---

[1] The Children and Young Persons Acts differentiate between a child under the age of 14 and a young person between 14 and 17. The word "child" is used in the text to include both.

[2] 1969 Act, s. 2 (1), (2).

[3] *Ibid.*, ss. 1 (1), (6) and 2 (3).

[4] 1963 Act, s. 3, as amended by the 1969 Act, Sched. 5. This procedure is designed to avoid parent and child confronting each other in the same proceedings.

[5] 1969 Act, s. 1 (2), as amended by the Children Act 1975, Sched. 3, para. 67. "Care" includes protection and guidance and "control" includes discipline: 1969 Act, s. 70 (1). See *Re S.*, [1978] Q.B. 120; [1977] 3 All E.R. 582, C.A. (failure to send child to school because of implacable objection to comprehensive education in itself showed child to be in need of care). Insofar as the conditions are set out in the present tense (*e.g.* "development *is being* prevented") they refer to a present state of affairs and not one that may arise in the future, however likely this may be: *Essex County Council* v. *T.L.R.* (1978), 9 Fam. Law 15. If none of the conditions is satisfied, a local authority can seek a care order by making the child a ward of court: *Re D.*, [1977] Fam. 158; [1977] 3 All E.R. 481.

[6] The court may find that the condition is satisfied with respect to child A in proceedings taken in respect of child B: *Surrey County Council* v. *S.*, [1974] Q.B. 124; [1973] 3 All E.R. 1074, C.A., where no proceedings had been taken in respect of child A who was now dead.

[7] Added by the Children Act 1975, (*supra*). The offences are set out in Sched. 1 of the 1933 Act (as amended) and comprise offences against children and sexual offences. For the complete list, see Clarke Hall and Morrison, *Children*, 9th Ed., 287-289.

laid down in *Mohamed* v. *Knott*[1] that account must be taken of their background and customs in deciding whether a child is exposed to moral danger. In that case it was held that a Nigerian girl aged 13 was not exposed to moral danger merely because she was having sexual intercourse with a man aged 26 to whom she was validly married by Nigerian law. The difficulty facing the courts now is to decide what standards of morality they are to apply if they depart from those traditionally adopted in this country. Would the decision in *Mohamed* v. *Knott* have been the same, for example, if the girl had been aged 10 or if the union had been incestuous? Sooner or later the courts will have to determine at what point an immigrant community must be compelled to abandon family laws and customs which are not only different from English ones but which *mutatis mutandis* would be regarded in this country as contrary to public policy or even criminal.

(e) He is beyond the control of his parent or guardian.

(f) He is of compulsory school age and is not receiving efficient full-time education suitable to his age, ability and aptitude.[2]

(g) He is guilty of an offence other than homicide. The proceedings may be brought only by a local authority or a constable and the court can make an order only if it would have found the child guilty had he been prosecuted. This means that this condition can never be satisfied if the child is under the age of ten.[3] Furthermore the child is entitled, for example, to plead autrefois acquit or convict (including the fact that the same offence has been considered in previous care proceedings) or that the six months' limitation period has expired in the case of a summary offence.[4]

The court has no jurisdiction to entertain care proceedings if the child is over the age of 16 and is or has been married.[5] If he is under the age of five, the court may permit proceedings to be taken even though he is not in court, provided that his parent or guardian has been given notice of the proceedings or is in court.[6]

Orders that may be made.—If the court finds that the above conditions are satisfied, it may make one of the following orders.[7]

(a) An order requiring the child's parent or guardian to enter into a recognisance to take proper care of him and exercise proper control over him.[8]

---

[1] [1969] 1 Q.B. 1; [1968] 2 All E.R. 563. See Karsten, 32 M.L.R. 212; Deech, 123 New L.J. 110.

[2] In this case proceedings may be brought only by the local education authority: 1969 Act, s. 2 (8). See further *ante*, p. 312.

[3] Because he is legally incapable of committing a crime: 1933 Act, s. 50, as amended by the 1963 Act, s. 16 (1).

[4] 1969 Act, s. 3.

[5] *Ibid.*, s. 1 (5) (c).

[6] *Ibid.*, s. 2 (9).

[7] *Ibid.*, s. 1 (3). See Bevan, *op. cit.*, 94–110. If a child is found guilty of an indictable offence, the court may also order the payment of compensation for loss of property or damage to it: *ibid.*, s. 3 (6). See further *ante*, p. 326.

[8] An order may be made only with the parent's or guardian's consent and must not be for an amount exceeding £200 or for a period of more than three years or extending beyond the child's eighteenth birthday (whichever is the shorter): *ibid.*, s. 2 (13), as amended by the Criminal Law Act 1977, s. 58 (2).

(b) A *supervision order* placing the child under the supervision of the local authority or a probation officer.[1] There are elaborate provisions in the 1969 Act laying down the directions that a supervision order may contain relating to residence, medical treatment for mental illness (including treatment as an in-patient), and what the White Paper termed "intermediate treatment" such as residence away from home for not more than 90 days and participation in specified activities. Supervision orders and their directions may be varied, replaced by care orders, or discharged; they may not last for more than three years (or any shorter period specified in the individual order) and must terminate on the supervised person's eighteenth birthday if this occurs earlier.[2]

(c) A *care order* committing the child to the care of a local authority. Unless the order is varied, it remains in force until the age of 18 or, if he has already reached the age of 16 when it is made, the age of 19. There are powers to extend all orders to the age of 19 if this is in the child's interest or the public interest in view of his mental condition or behaviour, and if he is over the age of 15, the local authority may apply to a juvenile court to have him sent to a borstal institution if his behaviour is detrimental to other persons accommodated in a community home. Either the authority or the child may apply to have the order discharged, in which case the court has a discretion to replace it by a supervision order.[3] It will also automatically come to an end if the child is adopted or freed for adoption or if an order is made permitting him to be taken outside the British Isles for the purpose of adoption abroad. Interim orders may also be made for a period not exceeding 28 days.[4]

The authority is bound to keep the child in their care so long as the order is in force notwithstanding any claim by the parent or guardian[5] and by section 10 (2) of the Child Care Act 1980

> "A local authority shall ... have the same powers and duties with respect to a person in their care by virtue of a care order ... as his parent or guardian would have apart from the order ... and may ... restrict his liberty to such extent as the authority consider appropriate.

The authority must not cause him to be brought up in any religious creed other than that in which he would have been brought up apart from the order, nor may it agree to his adoption. In certain circumstances it must appoint a

---

[1] Children and Young Persons Act 1969, s. 11. If the child is under the age of 13, a probation officer may be appointed only if he has already worked with the family and the local authority so requests: *ibid.*, s. 13 (2), as amended by the Powers of Criminal Courts Act 1973, Sched. 5; S.I. 1973 No. 485 and 1974 No. 1083.

[2] See generally *ibid.*, ss. 11-19, as amended by the Children Act 1975, Sched. 3, para. 68, and the Criminal Law Act 1977, ss. 37 and 58 (5) and Scheds. 12 and 13. Variations and discharge are dealt with in ss. 15 and 16.

[3] A parent may bring an appeal or proceedings for the variation of an order in the name of the child when the discharge or variation of the order may not be for the child's welfare. Hence the court may order that the parent is not to be regarded as representing the child and in certain circumstances may appoint a guardian *ad litem; ibid.*: ss. 32A and 32B, added by the Children Act 1975, s. 64, following the Maria Colwell case. See Bevan and Parry, *Children Act* 1975, c. 12; Hayes, 8 Fam. Law 91; Kent [1978-79] J.S.W.L. 399.

[4] See generally *ibid.*, ss. 20-24 and 31, as amended by the Children Act 1975, Sched. 3, paras. 69 and 70.

[5] Child Care Act 1980, s. 10 (1).

visitor for him if he is not visited by his parent or guardian or communication with them is infrequent.[1]

(d) A *hospital order* under the Mental Health Act 1959 directing him to be detained in a mental hospital if he is found to be suffering from certain types of mental disease.

(e) A *guardianship order* under the Mental Health Act 1959 placing him under the guardianship of a local social services authority or other approved person in similar circumstances.[2]

The court may make a care order and a hospital order simultaneously, but apart from this not more than one order may be made.[3] If the court is not in a position to decide what order to make, it may make an interim care order.[4] If care proceedings are brought in respect of a child *over the age of 14 found guilty of an offence*, the court may, if he consents, order him to enter into a recognisance to keep the peace or to be of good behaviour instead of making any of the above orders.[5]

Detention in a Place of Safety.[6]—In cases of urgency there is a more peremptory power to take children out of their parents' or guardians' control. This can be exercised only in certain specified circumstances: for example, if he is being assaulted, ill-treated or neglected, if certain offences have been committed in respect of him, or if any of conditions (a) to (f) set out above in relation to care proceedings is satisfied. In such a case a court or magistrate may authorise or order a child under the age of 17 to be taken to a place of safety, and in certain circumstances a constable may take a child there without any previous authorisation.[7] The authorisation or order must state a period of time not exceeding 28 days in which care proceedings must be brought unless the child has been previously released or received into the care of a local authority; if he is taken to a place of safety otherwise than on such an authorisation or order or if he has taken refuge there himself, the period is eight days.[8]

Criminal Proceedings.—A child under the age of ten cannot be guilty of a criminal offence at all.[9] Under the 1969 Act the Home Secretary has power to

---

[1] Child Care Act 1980, ss. 10 (3) and 11.

[2] For the circumstances in which hospital and guardianship orders can be made and the effects of such orders, see the Mental Health Act 1959, ss. 60 and 63.

[3] 1969 Act, s. 1 (4).

[4] *Ibid.*, ss. 2 (10) and 20 (1).

[5] *Ibid.*, s. 3 (7), as amended by the Criminal Law Act 1977, s. 58 (3). The recognisance must not be for an amount exceeding £50 or for a period of more than a year.

[6] Bevan, *op. cit.*, 55-59.

[7] See 1933 Act, s. 40; 1969 Act, s. 28; Adoption Act 1958 s. 43 (prospectively repealed and re-enacted in the Adoption Act 1976, s. 34); Foster Children Act 1980, s. 12; *R.* v. *Lincoln (Kesteven) County Justice,* [1976] Q.B. 957; [1976] 1 All E.R. 490. As the order is designed to give immediate protection to the child, it may be made even though he is a ward of court: *Re B.* (1979), 124 Sol. Jo. 81. A "place of safety" means a community home, police station, hospital, surgery, or other suitable place the occupier of which is willing to receive a child temporarily: 1933 Act, s. 107 (1), as amended by the 1969 Act, Sched. 5.

[8] 1963 Act, s. 23; 1969 Act, s. 28 and Scheds. 5 and 6.

[9] 1933 Act, s. 50, as amended by the 1963 Act, s. 16 (1). But the fact that he has committed the offence may be evidence that some other condition has been fulfilled enabling care proceedings to be taken in respect of him.

make an order providing that a person who has reached that age but has not reached the age stated in the order (which must not exceed 14) shall not be *charged* with a criminal offence.[1] The Act also imposes restrictions on bringing criminal proceedings against a child aged between 14 and 17, but the relevant section has not yet been brought into operation.[2]

If follows that, unless and until these provisions become operative, there are two ways of proceeding against a child between the ages of ten and 17 who has committed a criminal offence: either (as before) he may be charged in a juvenile court or care proceedings may be brought in respect of him. If criminal proceedings are taken and he is found guilty, various orders can be made; in particular a care order may be made if the offence is punishable with imprisonment if committed by an adult.[3]

2. RECEPTION OF CHILDREN INTO CARE

By section 2 of the Child Care Act 1980, a local authority is under a duty to receive a child under the age of 17 into care if it appears

"(a) that he has neither parent nor guardian, or has been and remains abandoned by his parents or guardian, or is lost; *or*
(b) that his parents or guardian are, for the time being or permanently, prevented by reason of mental or bodily disease or infirmity or other incapacity or any other circumstances from providing for his proper accommodation, maintenance and upbringing; *and*,
(c) in either case, that the intervention of the local authority is necessary in the interests of the welfare of the child."[4]

The authority must endeavour to secure that care is taken of the child by a parent, guardian, relative or friend if this is consistent with his welfare,[5] but if necessary, they may keep him in their care until he reaches the age of 18.[6]

It is important to realise that in many cases a parent voluntarily relinquishes care because of illness or some other cause which temporarily leaves her (or him) incapable of looking after the child. Once the position has changed, she will wish to regain actual custody, and there is a danger that, if the authority were able to put too many obstacles in the way of her doing so, she would be tempted to make other arrangements (which might well be unsuitable) to have the child looked after by somebody else. Consequently the authority has no power under section 2 to keep a child in care if any parent or guardian desires to take over his care.[7] It is easy to see, however, that the immediate removal of the child may not be in his interest in some cases. The

---

[1] 1969 Act, ss. 4 and 34. The consent of both Houses of Parliament is needed to raise the age above 12: s. 34 (7).

[2] See 1969 Act, s. 5; Bevan, *op. cit.*, 31-33.

[3] 1969 Act, ss. 7 (7) and 34 (1) (c). See generally Bevan, *op. cit.*, 111-138.

[4] Bevan, *op. cit.*, 144-145, points out that, if the section is construed narrowly, there is no power to receive a child into care if one parent comes within para. (a) and the other comes within para. (b) (e.g. if one parent abandons him and the other is prevented from providing for his proper accommodation). This cannot have been the intention of Parliament.

[5] Child Care Act, 1980, s. 2 (3). The parent or guardian may apparently take over the care of the child by ensuring that he is accommodated and maintained by someone else: *Re A.B.*, [1954] 2 Q.B. 385; [1954] 2 All E.R. 287.

[6] *Ibid.*, s. 2 (2).

[7] *Ibid.*, s. 2 (3).

parent may still be incapacitated from providing for him properly; similarly, if he has been in care and living with the same foster parents for a long period, wrenching him away from those whom he may regard with much greater affection than his natural parents may do untold psychological damage. The latter situation is now guarded against by section 13 (2) of the Child Care Act which makes it a criminal offence for a parent or guardian to take away a child who has been in care for the preceding six months without the authority's consent unless he gives 28 days' notice of his intention of doing so.[1] This period will not only prevent impulsive and temporary removal but will also enable the authority to let the child get to know its natural parents again if this is the appropriate course.

This still leaves unanswered the question what action the authority is to take if it is satisfied that returning the child will not be for its welfare at all, for example if it fears that it may be physically ill-treated. The problem was considered by the House of Lords in *Lewisham London Borough Council* v. *Lewisham Juvenile Court Justices*.[2] A mother voluntarily placed her illegitimate son, then aged 18 months, in the care of the appellant authority. Nine months later she gave a month's notice of her desire to take over his care. The authority then passed a resolution under section 2 of the Children Act (which is now re-enacted in section 3 of the Child Care Act and which will be discussed below) and the question for the House was whether they had power to do so. They unanimously held that, once a child had been received into care under section 2, it remained in the authority's care until delivered up to the parent or until the parent removed it, notwithstanding the parent's expressing a desire to take it back. It is implicit in all the speeches that, if section 13 (2) applies, the authority may lawfully keep the child for the statutory period of 28 days, but subject to this section 2 gives it no residual discretion to keep the child. It is said that there is no mandatory obligation cast on the authority to return it:[3] this means that if the authority has 28 day's grace, it will be able to pass a resolution under section 3 and in other cases it may still have time to do so before the parent tries to take actual possession. But if it does not do so, it will generally speaking have no defence to the parent's claim. There are apparently some exceptional cases in which a court may not order the authority to return the child: the Court of Appeal has refused to make such an order when the child was only a month short of her eighteenth birthday[4] and has suggested that it would not force the authority to embark on litigation against its will to recover the child from foster parents or anyone else who refused to deliver it up.[5] A much more important exception was mentioned by members of the House of Lords in the *Lewisham* case: a court should not order the child to be returned pending an application to

---

[1] Experience may indicate that the periods of six months and 28 days are not the right ones. Consequently the Secretary of State may by order substitute different periods. A similar provision applies to children in voluntary homes or boarded out by voluntary organisations, even though they are not in the care of a local authority. See *ibid.*, ss. 13 (2), (5) and 63.

[2] [1980] A.C. 273; [1979] 2 All E.R. 297, H.L. See Thomson, 96 L.Q.R. 25; Hoggett, 43 M.L.R. 69; Freeman, 129 New L.J. 648.

[3] At pp. 283 and 301 (*per* VISCOUNT DILHORNE); 302 and 315 (*per* LORD KEITH).

[4] *Krishnan* v. *Sutton London Borough Council*, [1970] Ch. 181; [1969] 3 All E.R. 1367, C.A.

[5] *Bawden* v. *Bawden*, [1979] Q.B. 419; [1978] 3 All E.R. 1216, C.A.

make it a ward of court.[1] If, therefore, the authority does not have time to pass a section 3 resolution or lacks a ground on which to do so, its proper course is to ward the child immediately if it wishes to prevent the parent from obtaining possession of it.[2]

Assumption of Parental Rights and Duties.—Section 3 of the Child Care Act provides local authorities with a speedy means of assuming parental rights and duties over a child against its parent's will. They can be exercised only if the child is in care *under section 2*: the significance of *Lewisham London Borough Council* v. *Lewisham Juvenile Court Justices*[3] in this connection is that care under this section continues so long as the child is still physically under the control of the authority even though the mother has expressed a desire to take over care herself. In addition, at least one of the following eight conditions must be satisfied. (In each of them the term "parent" excludes the father of an illegitimate child but includes any person to whom custody of the child has been given by a court order and, except in (a), a guardian or custodian.)[4]

(a) The child's parents are dead and he has no guardian or custodian.

(b) A parent of the child has abandoned him. If that person's whereabouts have remained unknown for 12 months after the child was received into care, he will be deemed to have abandoned him.[5]

(c) A parent of the child suffers from some permanent disability rendering him incapable of caring for him.

(d) A parent of the child suffers from a mental disorder within the meaning of the Mental Health Act 1959 which renders him unfit to have the care of him. This is complementary to (c): the disorder need not be permanent or render the parent incapable of looking after the child.

(e) A parent of the child is of such habits or mode of life as to be unfit to have the care of him.

(f) A parent of the child has so consistently failed without reasonable cause to discharge the obligations of a parent as to be unfit to have the care of him. The wording of this provision was analysed by a Divisional Court in *M.* v. *Wigan Metropolitan Borough Council*,[6] where it was held that, as in the case of the similar provision in the Adoption Act, "the obligations of a parent" include moral as well as legal duties and that the failure must be culpable. Whether it was without reasonable cause must be tested objectively: it must result from the voluntary behaviour of the parent in question and not, for example, from some physical disability or mental disorder. The word "consistently" does not necessarily imply a failure over

---

[1] *Cf.* pp. 291 and 306 (*per* LORD SALMON); 302 and 315 (*per* LORD KEITH).

[2] See further *post*, p. 404.

[3] [1980] A.C. 273; [1979] 2 All E.R. 297, H.L. See *supra*.

[4] Child Care Act 1980, ss. 3 (10), 8 (2) and 87 (1).

[5] *Ibid.*, s. 3 (8). "Abandoned" probably has the same meaning as it has in relation to adoption: *Wheatley* v. *Waltham Forest London Borough Council*, [1980] A.C. 311; [1979] 2 All E.R. 289. See *ante*, p. 344, n. 5.

[6] [1980] Fam. 36; [1979] 2 All E.R. 958. Followed in *O'Dare A i* v. *South Glamorgan County Council* (1980), 10 Fam. Law 215, C.A. An unexplained failure to visit the child over a long period of time is evidence of consistent failure: *W.* v. *Sunderland Borough Council*, [1980] 2 All E.R. 514, 517. See also *Wheatley* v. *Waltham Forest London Borough Council*, (*supra*). For the provision in the Adoption Act, see *ante*, p. 344.

the whole or even the greater part of the child's life; in this context it "comtemplates behaviour over a period which has constantly adhered to the pattern of which complaint is made".[1]

(g) A resolution under one of the conditions (b) to (f) above is in force in relation to one parent of the child who is, or is likely to become, a member of the household comprising the child and his other parent. This provision (which is new) is not easy to understand. Suppose that a mother becomes mentally ill so that she is incapable of looking after the child and is also likely to harm it. The child is received into care under section 1 of the Act and the authority passes a resolution under (d) above. Although, as we shall see, this vests the mother's parental rights in the authority, there is nothing to prevent the father from claiming the child back. If his claim were successful and he were living with the mother, the child would find himself living with her again. The condition under discussion therefore is presumably designed to enable the authority to divest the father of his rights too. The difficulty arises from the fact that it appears to be satisfied only if the child is *already* living with the father because he could not otherwise be a member of the household comprising the father. One suspects that the object of the provision would have been achieved if the condition had required that the child was likely to become a member of the household comprising the mother, but it is quite impossible to interpret it in this way.

(h) Throughout the period of three years preceding the passing of the resolution the child has been in the care of a local authority under section 2 of the Act or partly in the care of a local authority and partly in the care of a voluntary organisation.[2] This provision (which is also new) supplements that which requires the parent to give the local authority 28 days' notice before removing a child who has been in care for six months and gives even greater protection against the arbitrary removal of a child after a long period of care or fostering.

To assume parental rights and duties, the authority must pass a resolution to this effect. They must immediately give notice to the parent whose rights and duties vest in them by virtue of the resolution if his whereabouts are known and he has not consented in writing to its being passed. He has then a month in which he may object to it; if he does so, the resolution will lapse 14 days after the service of notice of objection unless in the meantime the authority makes a complaint to a juvenile court. The court may then order that the resolution shall remain in force if it is satisfied that the grounds on which the authority purported to pass it were made out, that there are still grounds at the time of the hearing on which a resolution could be founded,[3] and that it is in the child's interest to keep the resolution alive.[4]

The effect of the resolution is to vest in the authority the parental rights and duties with respect to the child except the right to agree or consent to the

---

[1] *Per* SHELDON, J., at pp. 45 and 963, respectively.

[2] *I.e.* a body (other than a public or local authority) the activities of which are not carried on for profit: Child Care Act 1980, s. 87 (1). The Secretary of State may by order substitute a different period for that of three years: *ibid.*, s. 3 (9).

[3] Note that they need not be the same grounds.

[4] *Ibid.*, s. 3 (2)-(7). The court may appoint a guardian *ad litem* for the child and an appeal lies from the making of an order to the High Court: *ibid.*, ss. 6 and 7.

making of an adoption order, an order authorising adoption abroad or an order freeing the child for adoption. If the rights and duties were vested in the parent on whose account the resolution was passed jointly with another person, they shall be vested in the local authority jointly with that other person.[1] Unfortunately, the section does not define the phrase "on whose account the resolution was passed". Presumably if the authority based the resolution on any of the conditions (b) to (f) above, it will divest only the parent named of his rights and duties (that is, the parent who has abandoned the child, etc.); in case (g) it will divest the other parent of them; and in cases (a) and (h) it will divest all parents, guardians and custodians of them.

This may well cause difficulty. Suppose, for example, that a husband has to go abroad and leaves his wife with their legitimate child. The wife then deserts her husband and abandons the child with respect to whom the local authority assumes parental rights and duties. It would be monstrous if, on the father's return, he were to find that his rights had been entirely superseded; on the other hand, the authority may take the view that his situation leaves him wholly incapable of looking after the child. If they refuse to hand the child back, the father's only remedy is to seek actual custody[2] when the court would be guided by the interests of the child's welfare in deciding what order to make. Even greater difficulty is likely to arise if the father accepts that the child must physically stay where he is but cannot agree with the authority on matters relating to day to day care, for example schooling or access, because the court is loth to interfere with the exercise of a discretion vested in a local authority by statute. This point has arisen in connection with an authority's assumption of parental rights and duties in respect of an illegitimate child. In *R.* v. *Oxford Justices, ex parte H.*[3] it was held that, as the father is not a parent for the purpose of the Children Act, the resolution cannot affect his right to claim custody of the child under the Guardianship of Minors Act; but the court has declined to interfere with the authority's refusal to permit him access, apparently on the ground that this must be left to the discretion of the authority.[4]

The resolution may remain in force until the child reaches the age of 18, but the local authority may rescind it at any time if this would be for his

---

[1] Child Care Act 1980, s. 3 (1), (10). For the meaning of parental rights and duties, see *ante*, p. 280. On the face of it, this includes the power to consent to the marriage of a child over the age of 16. But as the Children Act 1975 (which amended the provisions of the Children Act 1948 now contained in the Child Care Act 1980) amended the Marriage Act in other respects and did not provide for the local authority to give its consent, it seems that this power remains with the parent. Bevan and Parry, *Children Act* 1975, 155, argue that the section could give the local authority an interest in the estate of the child if it died. It would be surprising if a court were to interpret "rights in relation to the child's property" in this way: what the Administration of Estates Act 1925, s. 47, does is to give a beneficial interest to named persons. See Thomson, 90 L.Q.R. 310; Maidment, [1981] J.S.W.L. at pp. 30-34. The authority may not cause the child to be brought up in any religious creed other than that in which he would have been brought up but for the resolution, and existing supervision and probation orders are unaffected: Child Care Act 1980, ss. 4 (3) and 8 (1).

[2] Under the Guardianship of Minors Act or in wardship proceedings.

[3] [1975] Q.B. 1; [1974] 2 All E.R. 356.

[4] *Re K.*, [1972] 3 All E.R. 769. It is not easy to see how this case was distinguished in *R.* v. *Oxford Justices*, (*supra*). See further Bevan and Parry, *op. cit.*, 156-157; Eekelaar, *Children in Care and the Children Act* 1975, 40 M.L.R. 121 at 132-134.

benefit and a juvenile court may also determine it on the application of any person who would otherwise be entitled to parental rights. It will also cease to have effect if the child is adopted or freed for adoption, if an order is made vesting parental rights in a person wishing to adopt the child abroad, or if a guardian is appointed for him.[1]

Children in Care of Voluntary Organisations. —If a child is in the care of a voluntary organisation, the local authority has a similar power to vest parental rights and duties in the organisation at the latter's request.[2] One of the conditions set out in section 3 of the Child Care Act must be fulfilled and the authority must be satisfied that the resolution is necessary in the interests of the child's welfare. The same procedure relating to the giving of notice, the lodging of an objection and the making of a complaint to a juvenile court applies.[3] A resolution has the same consequences as one passed under section 3 except that the parental rights and duties will vest in the organisation, and it will cease to have effect in the same circumstances.[4] The local authority may also terminate it if the child's welfare so requires by passing a further resolution that the parental rights and duties shall vest in the authority itself. Notice of this second resolution must be given to the organisation and to every parent, guardian and custodian whose whereabouts is known.[5]

3. POWERS AND DUTIES OF LOCAL AUTHORITIES[6]

By whatever means the child has come into care, the authority must give first consideration to the need to safeguard and promote his welfare throughout his childhood and, so far as practicable, they must ascertain his wishes and feelings and give due consideration to them having regard to his age and understanding. They must provide accommodation and maintenance for him either by boarding him out with foster parents or by maintaining him in a community home or a voluntary home. They may also permit him to be under the charge and control of a parent, guardian, relative or friend and may regulate access by them. But if the child was committed to their care by the High Court in any proceedings or by a county court in matrimonial proceedings, the exercise of their powers is subject to the overriding control of the court making the order.[7]

---

[1] Child Care Act 1980, s. 5. For liability for taking the child away and similar offences, see *ibid.*, s. 13.

[2] The power exists only if the organisation is a body corporate (because otherwise there would be no legal person in whom the rights and duties could be vested). The child must be living in a voluntary home or boarded out by the organisation: *ibid.*, s. 64 (1), (5).

[3] *Ibid.*, ss. 64 (1), (4) and 67.

[4] *Ibid.*, s. 64 (2), (3), (6), (7).

[5] *Ibid.*, ss. 65 and 66. Any person deprived of parental rights and duties may appeal to a juvenile court on the ground that the resolution should not have been passed or that it is in the child's interests that it should be determined: *ibid.*, s. 67 (2)-(4). The use of the word "appeal" is unusual: could more than one such application be made?

[6] Bevan, *op. cit.*, 156-174; Maidment, [1981] J.S.W.L. 21.

[7] Child Care Act 1980, ss. 18 and 21; Matrimonial Causes Act 1973, s. 43 (1), (5); Guardianship Act 1973, s. 4 (4); Family Law Reform Act 1969, s. 7 (2), (3); Children Act 1975, ss. 17 (3) (prospectively repealed and re-enacted in the Adoption Act 1976, s. 26 (3)) and 36 (6); Domestic

Community homes, which are planned by local authorities on a regional basis, have not only replaced approved schools, remand homes, and probation homes and hostels but have also superseded children's homes and hostels. This means that a number of different types of community home must be provided and, in the case of children in respect of whom a care order has been made, the local authority, and not the court, has become the classifying authority to determine what type of home an individual child is to be sent to.[1]

Maintenance.—If the child is in care by virtue of a care order (other than an interim order made under the Children and Young Persons Act 1969) or has been received into care under section 2 of the Child Care Act 1980, his mother and (if he is legitimate) his father are under a duty to contribute to his maintenance until he reaches the age of 16. Once the child has reached this age, he is liable to contribute to his own maintenance if he is engaged in remunerative full-time work.[2] The amount of contribution is to be fixed by agreement between the contributory and the authority or, if they cannot agree, by the court in proceedings for a contribution order.[3] If no contribution order is in force, the authority may apply for an arrears order requiring the contributory to pay such weekly sums as the court thinks fit which must not, in the aggregate, exceed what he should have paid for the child's maintenance during the previous three months.[4]

If the child is committed to the care of a local authority in matrimonial, custody or wardship proceedings, the court has a power to order either or both parents (other than the father of an illegitimate child), or a spouse in respect of whose marriage the child is a child of the family, to make payments towards his maintenance.[5]

Proceedings and Magistrates' Courts Act 1978, s. 10 (4); *Re Y.*, [1976] Fam. 126; [1975] 3 All E.R. 348. The authority may depart from the basic principle if this is necessary to protect the public. Shortage of accommodation has forced many authorities to permit children to remain with unsuitable parents. For the difficulties that this gives rise to, see Hoggett, 117 Sol. Jo. 3, 27. For the powers of the Home Secretary to authorise the emigration of a child received into care under the Children Act or under a care order, see the Child Care Act 1980, s. 24. The child must consent if he is of an age to be able to do so and, whenever possible, his parents or guardians must be consulted.

[1] See the Child Care Act 1980, ss. 31-44. For the arrest of absconders and the prosecution of those aiding and abetting them, see *ibid.*, ss. 15 and 16.

[2] *Ibid.*, s. 45. For the liability of the father of an illegitimate child, see *post*, pp. 600-601. No contribution is payable so long as the child is permitted to be under the control of a parent, guardian, relative, friend or applicant for an adoption order. A child over 16 in care by virtue of an order made under the Domestic Proceedings and Magistrates' Courts Act 1978 is also liable to contribute to his own maintenance: *ibid.*, s. 10 (4) (b).

[3] Child Care Act 1980, ss. 46 and 47. The amount proposed by the local authority or ordered by the court must not exceed the amount which the authority would normally be prepared to pay if the child were boarded out. A person ordered to make a contribution may appeal to the Crown Court: *ibid.*, s. 52. Contribution orders may be varied, suspended, revived and discharged, and are enforceable in the same way as an affiliation order (see *post*, pp. 511-515). See the Child Care Act 1980, s. 48; Magistrates' Courts Act 1980, s. 60; Adoption Act 1958, s. 36 (2) (prospectively repealed and re-enacted in the Adoption Act 1976, s. 31 (3)).

[4] *Ibid.*, s. 51. Arrears orders are treated as contribution orders and are enforceable in the same way.

[5] See *ante*, p. 388, n. 1 (revocation of custodianship order) and *post*, pp. 585 (matrimonial proceedings in magistrates' courts), 590, n. 2 (Matrimonial Causes Act), 593 (Guardianship of Minors Act) and 594, n. 4 (wards of court).

Disputes over Care and Control.[1]—If the child is in care by virtue of a court order, he continues in care notwithstanding any claim by a parent or any other person.[2] But attempts have been made to invoke the prerogative jurisdiction of the court, particularly after the child has been received into care under the Act. Three distinct persons may have an interest in his custody, care and control: his parents or guardian, the authority itself, and the foster-parents with whom he is boarded out. The authority may wish to terminate the arrangement with foster-parents who are unwilling to return the child; alternatively, his natural parents or guardian may wish to resume care and control, which the authority or foster-parents (or both) are anxious to retain, or to have access to the child against their wishes.

As between the authority and foster-parents the latter are usually bound to return the child whenever the former demands it and the authority may recover custody from them.[3] In *Re M.*,[4] where the authority had assumed parental rights and duties under section 3 of the Child Care Act, and in *Re T. (A.J.J.)*,[5] where the child was subject to what is now a care order, the foster-parents tried to tie the authority's hands by making the child a ward of court. In both cases the Court of Appeal held that the court's prerogative jurisdiction is not entirely superseded by the statute so that wardship proceedings may still be brought even though the child is in the care of a local authority.[6] Although the welfare of the child must always be the paramount consideration, the court will not exercise control over those matters in respect of which the Act has given the authority a discretion unless the latter has acted with impropriety or in breach or disregard of its statutory duties or the evidence suggests that for some other reason its action cannot be supported.[7] As the sole question in each case related to the child's care and control which lay exclusively within the authority's discretion and no attack had been made on the propriety of its actions, the court refused to intervene, thus leaving the authority free to regain the child from the foster-parents.

Basically the same principle applies if the contest is between the parents and the authority or if a party relies on the statutory (as distinct from the inherent) jurisdiction of the court. In *Re W.*[8] for example, the local authority in whose care two children had been placed under a care order decided in the children's interest to deny further visits to them by their mother. She thereupon warded them with a view to obtaining access. In the absence of any

---

[1] See Lowe and White, *Wards of Court*, c. 11.

[2] Matrimonial Causes Act 1973, s. 43 (3); Family Law Reform Act 1969, s. 7 (3); Guardianship Act 1973, s. 4 (5); Children Act 1975, ss. 17 (3) (prospectively repealed and re-enacted in the Adoption Act 1976, s. 26 (3)) and 36 (6); Domestic Proceedings and Magistrates' Courts Act 1978, s. 10 (5); Child Care Act 1980, s. 10 (1).

[3] *Re A.B.*, [1954] 2 Q.B. 385; [1954] 2 All E.R. 287. The agreement which foster parents are required to sign under the Boarding-out of Children Regulations 1955 includes an undertaking to permit the authority to remove the child.

[4] [1961] Ch. 328; [1961] 1 All E.R. 788, C.A. Followed in *Re Baker*, [1962] Ch. 210; [1961] 3 All E.R. 276 C.A.; *Re K.*, [1972] 3 All E.R. 769 (proceedings brought by parent seeking access).

[5] [1970] Ch. 688; [1970] 2 All E.R. 865, C.A.

[6] A divorce court has the same powers: *E.* v. *E.* (1979), 9 Fam. Law 185, C.A.

[7] *E.g.*, if those responsible for the resolution recalling the child have been motivated by malice or personal hostility towards the foster-parents. A flagrant disregard of the child's welfare would be a disregard of the authority's duty, but where it is a matter of discretion, the court will not substitute its own for the authority's: *Re C. (A.)*, [1966] 1 All E.R. 560.

[8] [1980] Fam. 60; [1979] 3 All E.R. 154, C.A. See also *Re D.F.* (1977), 76 L.G.R. 133.

evidence that the authority had acted with impropriety, the Court of Appeal refused to interfere with the exercise of a discretion relating to children in their care. Similarly in *H.* v. *H.*[1] WRANGHAM, J., dismissed an application by a wife in divorce proceedings for an order that her son, with respect to whom a care order had been made, should live with foster parents selected by her. On the other hand, whatever the basis of the jurisdiction, the court will always intervene at the instance of a parent or any other interested party if there has been a breach of duty by the authority. Furthermore, even though the authority has acted with perfect propriety, there are signs that the courts are now more inclined to assume jurisdiction if the purpose of the application is to obtain custody of the child (and thus effectively discharge the order altogether) as distinct from controlling the authority's exercise of discretion with respect to a child which will remain in their care.[2] They may intervene more readily if the child has been placed in care following care proceedings brought under the Children and Young Persons Act 1969 because there is no statutory appeal to the High Court in such a case: the ground for intervention becomes even stronger if the child has been guilty of no criminal offence. As BAKER, P., warned in *M.* v. *Humberside County Council*,[3] however, the court must be slow to interfere with an order properly made by another court and should act only in exceptional circumstances. One of the few cases in which the court has done so is *Re H.*[4] A child had been placed in care following the infliction of physical injury by one of the parents, who were Pakistanis. They now wished to return to Pakistan with the child, but the authority opposed any move to return it to them on the ground that this would expose it to the risk of further injury. Any application by the child to have the order discharged would probably have failed because the court hearing the application would not have been satisfied that it would receive the care and control it required. The Court of Appeal upheld the view of the trial judge that the risk of psychological damage to the child if it were not returned exceeded the risk of physical damage if it were and, in these very unusual circumstances, ordered that wardship should be continued and that the parents should be given leave to take the child back to Pakistan.

The court will also intervene if the facts indicate that the authority acted *ultra vires* or failed to follow the proper procedure. In *Re L. (A.C.)*[5] a local authority passed a resolution under section 3 of the Child Care Act. Owing to a procedural muddle the child's mother was told that she need not make a formal objection to the resolution, as a result of which she lost her right of having the case heard by a juvenile court. She then warded the child. In view of the doubts about the validity of the proceedings and the fact that the

[1] [1973] Fam. 62; [1973] 1 All E.R. 801. Distinguish the position where the court itself commits the care of the child to the local authority in matrimonial proceedings: the authority then remains subject to the overriding control of the court (see *ante*, p. 400).

[2] *Cf. Re D.F.*, (*supra*); *Re D.* (1978), 76 L.G.R. 653.

[3] [1979] Fam. 114; [1979] 2 All E.R. 744. The court refused to intervene in that case even though the proceedings had gone no further than the making of an interim care order. See also Kent, 8 Fam. Law 124; V. Bevan, 9 Fam. Law 170.

[4] [1978] Fam. 65; [1978] 2 All E.R. 903, C.A. The High Court might also assume jurisdiction if the case involved a large body of evidence or conflicting views of experts. An interim adoption order may also be made even though this will deprive the authority of parental rights and duties: *S.* v. *Huddersfield Borough Council*, [1975] Fam. 113; [1974] 3 All E.R. 296, C.A.

[5] [1971] 3 All E.R. 743. See also *Re D* (*supra*); Cretney, 116 Sol. Jo. 282, 284.

relevant committee of the local authority had been insufficiently informed about the mother's capacity to care for the child, the wardship was continued and the case was considered on its merits.

The assistance of the court can always be invoked to supplement the authority's statutory powers and duties. In *Re B.* [1] a care order had been made with respect to a girl aged two because of the severe ill-treatment she had received at the hands of her step-father. Her grandmother made her a ward of court in an attempt to gain care and control. Although the grandmother's application was dismissed, LANE, J., continued the wardship at the request of the local authority concerned so that, if necessary, they could apply for an injunction to restrain the step-father from seeing the child and take committal proceedings if he failed to observe it. A similar need to seek the court's help may arise if a parent or guardian demands the return of a child received into care under section 2 of the Child Care Act and the authority is unable to pass a resolution under section 3. As it has no residual discretion to retain the child, [2] the court's jurisdiction may be invoked not only by the authority [3] but also by the foster-parents. In *Re S.* [4] a local authority wished to return a boy, whom they had received into care under section 2 of the Act, to his mother and therefore demanded his return from the foster-parents with whom he had been boarded out. The foster-parents, believing that the boy's welfare demanded that he should remain with them, made him a ward of court. The authority contended that they were bound to return the child and that the court should therefore make no order as in *Re M.* It was held, however, that the court must consider the question of care and control on its merits. *Re M.* (which was a case under section 3) was distinguished on the ground that, when a child is in care under section 2, the authority's interest is purely transient and consequently the court must have jurisdiction because otherwise an arbitrary re-assumption of control by the parent might imperil the child's well-being. [5] In any case it is submitted that if the contest is solely between the authority and the foster-parents, the principles laid down in *Re M.* and *Re T. (A.J.J.)* will apply and the court will not normally interfere; where, however, the problem has arisen because of the parent's desire to resume care and control, the court's jurisdiction may be invoked by anyone, including the foster-parents, even though the authority does not support them. [6]

---

[1] [1975] Fam. 36; [1974] 3 All E.R. 915. See also *Re C.B.*, [1981] 1 All E.R. 16, C.A.; Re C. (1979), 10 Fam. Law 84, C.A. (child warded on authority's application after magistrates' refusal to make care order).

[2] See *ante*, pp. 396-397.

[3] *Re R. (K.)*, [1964] Ch. 455; [1963] 3 All E.R. 337; *Re G.*, [1963] 3 All E.R. 370.

[4] [1965] 1 All E.R. 865, C.A.

[5] The distinction between the local authority's position under ss. 2 and 3 was also emphasised in *Re T. (A.J.J.)*, (*supra*).

[6] See further Lasok, 120 New L.J. 817; Cretney, 33 M.L.R. 696; Davies, *The Tug of War Cases*, 36 M.L.R. 245.

Part III

Property and Financial Provision

SUMMARY OF CONTENTS

Chapter 12

The Economic Aspects of Family Law

In this Part we shall be concerned with property and maintenance. Broadly speaking these two subjects reflect the difference between capital and income and between them they compose the economic aspects of family law.

The rights in property which we must examine are of course only those which concern members of the family as such and they are essentially of two different sorts. First we must consider ownership and title, in other words the question: to whom does a particular piece of property belong? Secondly we must consider rights of possession, occupation and use, in other words the question: what rights does one member of the family have in property belonging to another? These two problems are particularly relevant in connection with the matrimonial home. Beneficial ownership will not only *prima facie* give the spouse in whom it is vested the right to occupy as owner but will also determine who is entitled to the proceeds if the house is sold; but if, say, the house and furniture belong exclusively to the husband, the further problem arises: what rights, if any, has the wife to occupy the house and use the furniture even against his wishes? The same problems can arise, although to a much more limited extent, between parent and child. It will, therefore, be necessary to consider first the rights in property created and affected by the relationship of husband and wife and the spouses' duty to maintain each other and, secondly, the rights in property created and affected by the relationship of parent and child and the former's duty to maintain the latter.

Husband and Wife.—So long as the family is a going concern, rights in property and rights to maintenance are of largely academic interest. If the spouses are living together in the matrimonial home, it is of no practical consequence whether it belongs to one or both of them or, if one is the owner, what legal right the other has to be there. Again, if both spouses have an income, it does not matter at this stage whether the husband accepts the sole responsibility for supporting the family and lets the wife do what she likes with her own money or whether the wife uses her own income to pay the household bills and leaves the husband to use his to pay off the mortgage on the house, plough it back into his business or invest it and save for their future enjoyment or their children's education. The need for precise definition and formulation of these rights normally arises in one of three situations.

The commonest—and that which most frequently gives rise to litiga-tion—occurs when the marriage breaks down during the parties' lifetime. If the husband has deserted his wife and children, it may be a matter of prime importance to her to know whether she can stay in the former matrimonial home; if the house is to be sold, probably for much more than they paid for it, both spouses may lay claim to the proceeds of sale. Maintenance will be of equal or greater importance to most wives in this position because their earning capacity, which may be less than their husband's in any case, will probably be reduced by their having to look after the children. Again some spouses—husbands as well as wives—who are incapable of self-support as a result of age, infirmity or disability may well have been completely dependent on the other. As the breakdown of the marriage usually produces two families instead of one, it almost always involves a reduction in the standard of living of at least one of the spouses; the question that has to be settled is how this reduction is to be borne.[1]

Secondly, these rights may become relevant on the death of one of the spouses. A dispute may arise between the survivor and the other's personal representatives over the ownership of a particular piece of property, or the former may claim that the property in question was beneficially vested in both spouses jointly and so does not form part of the other's estate. Alternatively a survivor, left completely unsupported as a result of the other's testamentary dispositions, may wish to claim maintenance from the estate. This is most likely to occur if the marriage broke down before the death and the deceased deliberately cut the other out of his will or left the whole estate to the woman or man with whom he or she was living at death. A similar problem can arise if the deceased has been married twice and leaves the bulk of his estate to the children by his first marriage who, resentful of their stepmother, refuse to make her an adequate allowance. More rarely, an unreasonable or eccentric testator may leave his or her spouse nothing as the result of groundless suspicion or an obsessional interest in the objects of a particular charity.

Finally, the same problems arise if one spouse becomes insolvent. The following are the sort of questions which then become vital. Does a particular piece of property belong to the insolvent spouse (in which case it will now vest in the trustee in bankruptcy) or the solvent one? Does the insolvent spouse's obligation to maintain his family take priority over his trade debts? Can a spouse with a maintenance order claim in the other's bankruptcy? There is, of course, a danger that the spouses might conspire to defeat creditors by vesting all their property in one (usually the wife) and leaving the other to take all the commercial risks which may result in bankruptcy, and consequently, as we shall see,[2] certain transactions which prejudice creditors may be set aside. As a general rule a spouse's claim to maintenance is subordinated to the claims of the other's creditors so that, for example, arrears under a main-tenance order are not provable in bankruptcy.[3] This is a question of social

---

[1] For the help that a wife seeking to obtain or enforce an order for maintenance for herself or her children can request from certain government departments in tracing her husband see *Practice Note* (*Disclosure of Addresses*), [1973] 1 All E.R. 61.

[2] *Post*, pp. 433-437.

[3] See *post*, pp. 512, n. 1 and 566, and also pp. 467-468 (occupation of the matrimonial home).

policy and has been justified on the ground that, marriage being a partnership, neither partner should be permitted to claim against the other until all
the partner's debts are paid.[1] This argument unfortunately confuses the
social partnership of marriage with a commercial partnership between
persons carrying on a business in common with a view to profit and is, to say
the least, unconvincing.

Parent and Child.—Spouses' rights become confused because property is
frequently bought for their common use: both may have contributed, directly
or indirectly, to the price and little or no thought is given to the question of
ownership at the time of purchase. These complications do not often occur in
the case of parent and child and consequently this relationship rarely affects
rights in property.[2] Like the spouses' duty to maintain each other, the
parents' duty to maintain their children is normally of no practical
importance so long as the whole family is living together. The question of its
enforcement will usually arise if the marriage breaks down, and may also
arise if a deceased parent's will or the rules of intestate succession leave a
child without support (as might happen, for example, if the surviving spouse
refused to accept responsibility for the other's children by a previous
marriage). But it should be appreciated that the obligation to maintain can
also be relevant in other circumstances. Even though the husband and wife
are still cohabiting, their children may be living not with them but with
relations or foster parents who may seek a contribution towards their maintenance. Conversely, a woman who is bringing up her illegitimate child may
wish to claim maintenance for it from the father even though she has never
lived with him and has no right to maintenance for herself.

The Interrelationship of Property and Maintenance.—It is obvious that
rights in property and rights to maintenance are inevitably interrelated. For
example, a deserted or divorced wife who owns or remains in occupation of
the former matrimonial home is in a better financial position than one who
does not and who will therefore require a lump sum payment to enable her to
buy a house or flat or periodical payments to enable her to lease one. Again,
income from investments or a settlement may provide adequate maintenance. Consequently, if a court is to be able to ensure that proper financial
provision is made for the members of the family on the breakdown of the
marriage, it must have power to deal with capital as well as income—in other
words, to order the transfer and settlement of property and the variation of
settlements as well as the payment of money.

It is proposed to consider these subjects in the following order:

Rights in property created and affected by the relationship of husband and
    wife;
Financial support for the spouses during marriage;
Financial relief for the spouses on divorce, nullity or judicial separation;
Rights in property affected by the relationship of parent and child and
    financial provision for children;
Property and financial provision on the death of a member of the family.

---

[1] Law Com. No. 25, para. 78.
[2] See *post*, p. 572.

Chapter 13

Rights in Property Created and Affected by the Relationship of Husband and Wife

A. HISTORICAL INTRODUCTION

During the last century legislation has considerably simplified the law of property as it is affected by the relationship of husband and wife. But since this branch of the law shows the development of the status of the wife from a subservient member of the family to the co-equal head of it more clearly than any other (except possibly the parents' rights with respect to their children), we shall start with a brief historical conspectus of the effects of coverture upon rights in property.[1]

1. COMMON LAW

Freeholds.—The highly technical nature of the common law relating to real property is well reflected in the effects which coverture produced.

The Husband's Interest in his Wife's Freeholds.—It was not unnatural that the medieval law should look to the husband rather than to the wife for the performance of the feudal dues which arose from freehold tenure. By marriage a husband gained seisin of all freehold lands which his wife held at the time of the marriage or acquired during coverture and was entitled to the rents and profits of them. If he predeceased the wife, she immediately resumed the right to all her freeholds; if she predeceased him, her estates of inheritance descended to her heir subject to the husband's right to retain seisin as tenant by the curtesy of England. This arose if the husband had issue born alive by the wife which was *capable* of inheriting her freeholds,[2] in which case he was entitled as tenant by the curtesy to an estate for his life in all her freeholds of inheritance to which on her death she was entitled in possession otherwise than as a joint tenant.

---

[1] For further details and authorities reference must be made to the editions of standard works on real and personal property and equity published during the nineteenth and early twentieth centuries. The classic exposition of the common law position is to be found in Blackstone's *Commentaries*, vol. ii. See also Dicey, *Law and Opinion*, 2nd Ed., 371-395.

[2] Hence if the wife were tenant in tail female, the birth of a son would not give the husband curtesy. Once the child was born alive, it was immaterial that it did not survive. See further Farrer, *Tenant by the Curtesy of England*, 43 L.Q.R. 87.

The wife had no power to dispose of her realty at all during marriage,[1] and the husband alone could not dispose of it for more than his own interest. But together they could dispose of the whole estate. This was done by both spouses' levying a fine, when the court would examine the wife separately in order to ensure that her consent had been freely given. After the Fines and Recoveries Act 1833 the disposition was effected by deed which had to be separately acknowledged by the wife before a judge or commissioners who still had to examine her.[2]

The Wife's Interest in her Husband's Freeholds.—During marriage the wife took no interest in her husband's realty at all, but, if she survived him, she became entitled by virtue of her dower to an estate for life in a third of all her husband's freeholds of inheritance of which he had been seised in possession (otherwise than as a joint tenant) *at any time during marriage* provided that she *could* have borne a child capable of inheriting, whether such a child was ever born or not.[3] Since dower created a legal estate, it attached even though the husband alienated the land, and it could be barred only by the wife's levying a fine. The practical inconvenience of this is obvious, so much so that the Statute of Uses enacted that dower could be barred by making a jointure in favour of the wife[4] and conveyancers went to great lengths to ensure that a husband should never be solely seised of an estate of inheritance in possession.[5] These difficulties were eventually obviated by the Dower Act of 1833, which provided that dower should not attach to any land which the husband disposed of during his lifetime or by will and that the wife's right to dower out of his estates of inheritance in respect of which he died intestate should be barred if he made a declaration to this effect by deed or will. As a *quid pro quo* the Act gave the wife dower in her husband's equitable freeholds in respect of which he died intestate, if he had not barred her right by declaration.

Tenancy by Entireties.—The doctrine of unity of legal personality produced another striking consequence in the law of property.[6] If land were granted to a husband and wife and their heirs, they were said to take by entireties and received an interest which could not be turned into a tenancy in

---

[1] But even at common law she could exercise a power of appointment given to her without her husband's concurrence.

[2] The necessity of acknowledgment was abolished by the Law of Property Act 1925, s. 167.

[3] Hence if land were limited to H and the heirs of his body by his wife W, and after W's death H married X, X could not claim dower in the land since no child of hers could ever succeed to the tail special.

[4] If the jointure was settled before marriage, the dower was barred absolutely; if it was settled after marriage, the wife could elect between her jointure and her dower.

[5] The usual way of doing this was to vest a life estate in the husband until forfeiture, with remainder to trustees for the rest of the husband's life, with remainder to the husband's heirs. Although the trustees' estate would rarely vest in possession, it was a vested remainder and therefore prevented the husband's life estate from merging with his fee simple in remainder.

[6] Another consequence was that at common law there could be no conveyance between spouses. After the passing of the Statute of Uses in 1535, this difficulty was overcome by a grant to feoffees to the use of the other spouse.

common by severance. Hence, unless they disposed of the estate during marriage, the survivor was bound to take the whole. Similarly, if land were granted in fee simple to a husband, his wife and a third person, the spouses were regarded as one person and consequently they were entitled to only one half of the rents and profits and the third person was entitled to the other half.

Copyholds.—As a general rule the law relating to copyholds was the same as that relating to freeholds. But the husband did not take as tenant by the curtesy unless there was a custom of the manor to that effect, and a widow's interest in her deceased husband's copyhold land was known as her free-bench. The exact nature of this varied from place to place and sometimes gave her an interest in the whole of her husband's copyholds and sometimes only in a third. But it usually attached only to that land which he had neither devised nor alienated in his lifetime and consequently did not give rise to the same difficulties as dower. Freebench was unaffected by the Dower Act.

Leaseholds.—The wife's leaseholds belonged to the husband during coverture and he therefore had the absolute power to dispose of them *inter vivos*. If the wife predeceased him, he took the whole of the balance of the term *jure mariti*; but if he predeceased the wife, her leaseholds automatically reverted to her and the husband had no power to dispose of them by will.

Pure Personalty.—All choses in possession belonging to the wife at the time of the marriage or acquired by her during coverture vested absolutely in the husband who therefore had the power to dispose of them *inter vivos* or by will. Even if he died intestate during the wife's life, they did not revert to her. The only exception to this rule applied to the wife's paraphernalia, that is those articles of apparel and personal ornament which were suitable to her rank and degree. Whilst the husband could dispose of these during his life-time and the wife could alienate them neither *inter vivos* nor by will during coverture, nevertheless the husband could not deprive her of them by bequest and on his death they became her property and did not form a part of his estate.[1]

The wife's choses in action belonged to the husband if he reduced them into possession or obtained judgment in respect of them during coverture. If he died before this was done, the right of action survived to the wife; if she predeceased him, he could sue by taking out letters of administration.[2] It follows that if the chose in action was reversionary, the husband would not be entitled to it if he died before it fell into possession leaving his wife surviving him.

Fraud on the Husband's Marital Rights.—A contract to marry clearly gave the husband an expectant interest in all his wife's property—an interest in return for which he would of course on marriage be liable to maintain her and would be saddled with the liability for all her ante-nuptial torts and

---

[1] Unless the husband's estate was insolvent, in which case his creditors could take the wife's paraphernalia in satisfaction but not her necessary clothing.
[2] See *ante*, pp. 149-150 and 156.

contracts.[1] Consequently the rule developed that any disposition made by an engaged woman without her fiancé's consent was voidable by him as a fraud on his marital rights. Since it was voidable only, it could not be set aside against a *bona fide* purchaser for value without notice of the engagement.

2. EQUITY

As a general rule equity followed the law. Thus the husband had the same rights over his wife's equitable freeholds and leaseholds and her equitable interests in pure personalty and the same power to dispose of them (subject to her concurrence in the case of her freeholds) as he had in respect of her legal estates and interests.[2] In only one case was there a marked difference: whilst the husband was entitled to a life interest in his deceased wife's equitable freeholds as tenant by the curtesy, the wife was not entitled to dower in her deceased husband's equitable freeholds until the passing of the Dower Act in 1833.[3]

The Wife's Equity to a Settlement.—The husband's right to his wife's equitable interests in property was indefeasible once he had got posession of it, as would be the case, for example, if a trustee paid over the trust fund or an executor paid over a legacy. But if the husband was obliged to invoke the aid of Chancery to obtain the property, the court applied the maxim "He who seeks equity must do equity" and, if the property was such that the husband would have an absolute power to dispose of it, it would lend him its assistance only on condition that he settled an adequate part of it on his wife and children for their maintenance.[4] This "equity to a settlement" was personal to the wife and she could compromise her claim to it, but once the order had been made, it took priority over any assignment made by the husband and the claims of his creditors. In order to prevent the husband and trustee from acting together so as to defeat the wife's equity, it was eventually held that she might bring an action herself to enforce her right before the fund was paid over.

Assignment of Choses in Action.—In equity the husband alone had the right to assign any chose in action, legal or equitable, vested in the wife, subject to her equity to a settlement. But, as we have already seen, his interest in her reversionary choses in action was contingent, and consequently, since she had no power to assign, it was impossible for the spouses even jointly to make an absolute assignment of such an interest. This difficulty was removed in 1857 by Malins' Act[5] which enabled her by a deed acknowledged under the Fines and Recoveries Act[6] to concur in any disposition of a future interest in personalty to which she should be entitled under any instrument (other than

---

[1] See *ante*, pp. 150 and 156.

[2] A power of appointment given to a married woman could be exercised without her husband's concurrence.

[3] But then only if he died intestate with respect to them and had not barred her dower: see *ante*, p. 411.

[4] Usually he would be ordered to settle half his interest, but this would clearly depend upon the wife's financial circumstances and on occasion the husband was ordered to settle the whole fund. The husband took the reversionary interest.

[5] The Married Women's Reversionary Interests Act 1857.

[6] See *ante*, p. 411.

her marriage settlement) made after 1857 unless it were subject to a restraint upon anticipation. The Act also permitted her in the same way to release and extinguish her equity to a settlement out of personalty in possession.

The Wife's Separate Estate.—But by far the most important contribution of equity to the law relating to a married woman's property was the development of the concept of the separate estate. By the end of the sixteenth century[1] it was established that if property was conveyed to trustees *to the separate use* of a married woman, she retained in equity the same right of holding and disposing of it as if she were a feme sole.[2] This applied whether the interest was in realty or personalty and whether it was in possession or reversion. She could therefore dispose of it *inter vivos* or by will and, like any other beneficiary of full age who was absolutely entitled, she could call upon her trustees to convey the legal estate. Only if she died intestate in respect of her separate estate did the husband obtain the same interest that he would have had in her equitable property had it not been settled to her separate use. Moreover it was finally held that not even the interposition of trustees was necessary, and if property were conveyed, devised or bequeathed to a married woman to her separate use so that the legal estate vested in the husband *jure mariti*, he was deemed in equity to hold it on trust for her and he acquired no greater interest in it than he would have done if it had been conveyed to trustees on similar terms.[3]

The Restraint upon Anticipation.—Whilst separate estate in equity did much to mitigate the harshness of the common law rule, there was still one situation which it did not meet. For there was nothing to prevent a married woman from assigning her beneficial interest to her husband and thus vesting in him the interest which the separate use had sought to keep out of his hands, and the temptation presented to a grasping, spendthrift or insolvent husband was great. To circumvent this, equity developed about 1800 a second concept, complementary to the first, that of the restraint upon anticipation.[4] This could be imposed only if property was conveyed, devised or bequeathed to a woman's separate use, and, once it attached, it prevented her from anticipating and dealing with any income until it actually fell due. A restraint could be and usually was attached to the *corpus* too, in which case the whole fund became completely inalienable during marriage.

A restraint on anticipation could even be attached to the separate property of an unmarried woman. In this case she could deal with the property as if there were no restraint and could also totally remove the restraint by executing a deed poll to this effect. A woman to whose separate property a restraint had been attached before or during marriage could do the same after the marriage was terminated by her husband's death or by divorce. But in the absence of any such deed, as soon as she married or re-married, the restraint

---

[1] See Holdsworth, *History of English Law*, v, 310-315.

[2] If property were settled on an unmarried woman to her separate use, it also remained her separate estate after marriage. Hence, if an engaged woman settled her property on herself to her separate use without her fiancé's concurrence, he could have the settlement set aside as a fraud on his marital rights: see *ante*, pp. 412-413.

[3] For the wife's power to bind her separate estate by contract, see *ante*, p. 150.

[4] See Hart, *The Origin of the Restraint upon Anticipation*, 40 L.Q.R. 221.

became operative as regards any property not alienated whilst she was a feme sole.

The restraint on anticipation was designed to protect not only the wife but also the members of her family who would be entitled to the property on her death.[1] Whilst it effectively kept the property out of the hands of the husband and his creditors, it had one obvious drawback. There might be a number of occasions on which it might be in the wife's interest to deal with property subject to a restraint, but nothing short of a private Act of Parliament could remove it. It was in order to overcome this difficulty that the Conveyancing Act 1881 gave the court power to bind her interest in such property provided that this was for her benefit.[2] But the court could only render a specific disposition binding and it had no general power to remove the restraint altogether.

3. MODERN LEGISLATION

By the middle of the nineteenth century it was clear that the old rules would have to be reformed. More and more women were earning incomes of their own, either in trade, or on the stage or by writing, and there were a number of scandalous cases of husbands' impounding their wives' earnings for the benefit of their own creditors or even mistresses. No relief could be obtained by the woman whose husband deserted her and took all her property with him. The separate use and restraint upon anticipation were clumsy creatures and were in practice unlikely to affect the property of any but the daughters of the rich who would have carefully drawn marriage settlements and would be the beneficiaries under complicated wills. Agitation for reform was discernible in many quarters and eventually produced a series of Acts of ever wider scope.[3]

The Matrimonial Causes Act 1857.—So far as married women's property was concerned, this Act sought to remedy two existing defects in the law only. First, so long as a judicial separation was in force, the wife was now to be deemed to be a feme sole with respect to any property which she should acquire and thus for the first time in the history of English law she had the sole power to dispose of a legal interest either *inter vivos* or by will.[4] If the parties resumed cohabitation, all property so acquired was to be held for her separate use. Secondly, if a wife were deserted, she might obtain a protection order which would have the effect of protecting from seizure by her husband and his creditors any property and earnings to which she became entitled after the desertion and of vesting them in her as if she were a feme sole.[5]

The Married Women's Property Act 1870.—As originally conceived, this Act was to anticipate the much wider provisions of the Act of 1882. But the

---

[1] Kahn-Freund in *Matrimonial Property Law* (ed. Friedmann), 274. For the position in equity generally, see Dicey, *Law and Opinion*, 2nd Ed., 375-382.

[2] S. 39, subsequently replaced by the Conveyancing Act 1911, s. 7, and the Law of Property Act 1925, s. 169.

[3] See Dicey, *op. cit.*, 382-395.

[4] S. 25.

[5] S. 21.

Bill was so cut down in Parliament that in its final form the Act presented no more than a series of exceptions to the common law rule by providing that in a number of specified cases property acquired by the wife (for example, her earnings, deposits in savings banks, stocks and shares, and in very limited circumstances property devolving upon her on an intestacy) should be deemed to be held for her separate use. Moreover certain provisions applied only to women marrying after the passing of the Act. The whole Act was repealed by the Married Women's Property Act of 1882, but it remains of historical importance in that it gave a statutory extension to the existing equitable concept of the separate estate: the device that was later to be used in the Act of 1882.[1]

The Married Women's Property Act 1882.—Historically this Act is the most important of the whole series. It was of universal application, although it did not affect any rights which had vested by marriage before 1883. It provided that any woman marrying after 1882 should be entitled to retain all property owned by her at the time of the marriage as her separate property and that, whenever she was married, any property acquired by a married woman after 1882 should be held by her in the same way.[2] It also enacted that

"A married woman shall ... be capable of acquiring, holding, and disposing by will or otherwise, of any real or personal property as her separate property, in the same manner as if she were a feme sole, without the intervention of any trustee".[3]

It further provided that the law relating to restraint upon anticipation should remain unaffected.[4]

The sweeping nature of these changes is obvious. It now became impossible for a married man to acquire any further interest in his wife's property *jure mariti* by operation of law. It immediately rendered obsolete the doctrine of fraud upon a husband's marital rights. Henceforth a widower could claim an interest in his deceased's wife's property acquired after 1882 only if she died intestate with respect to it. The necessity of both spouses' joining in a conveyance of the wife's realty and the provisions of Malins' Act became obsolescent. But in one sense the changes were even more fundamental than these, for whilst the statute adapted the equitable concept of separate property,[5] it went further by vesting in the wife the *legal* interest in her property. The detailed provisions of the Act are too complex to be considered here,[6] but subject to the restraint on anticipation a married woman's capacity to hold and dispose of property was very nearly the same as that of a feme sole.

[1] For the effect of the Act of 1870 on spouses' liability in contract and tort and the modification of these provisions by the Married Women's Property Act (1870) Amendment Act 1874, see *ante*, pp. 150 and 156.

[2] Ss. 2 and 5.

[3] S. 1 (1).

[4] S. 19.

[5] Hence, for example, a married woman still could not be made bankrupt unless she came within the express provisions of s.1 (5) by carrying on a trade separately from her husband: see *ante*, p. 151.

[6] Amongst them are spouses' liability in contract (see *ante*, p. 150), tort (*ante*, p. 156) and criminal law (*ante*, p. 160), claims in bankruptcy (*post*, p. 437), policies of insurance in favour of a spouse or children (*post*, p. 438), and disputes over property arising between spouses (*post*, pp. 422-424).

The Married Women's Property Acts 1884, 1893, 1907 and 1908.—These four Acts effected no change of principle but were passed to clear up a number of difficulties and ambiguities in the Act of 1882 and to fill one or two gaps which this Act had left.

The Property Legislation of 1925.—This legislation only incidentally affected rights in property of spouses as such. Its most important effect in this field lay in the changed rules of succession on an intestacy;[1] in particular dower and freebench[2] were abolished and the husband's right to his wife's freeholds as tenant by the curtesy is now limited to the case where she is a tenant in tail and has not barred the entail by deed or will.[3] Tenancy by entireties has also been abolished, so that a grant to a husband, his wife and a third person will now give each of them a third interest in the property.[4]

The Law Reform (Married Women and Tortfeasors) Act 1935.—By 1935 almost all married women's property was owned by them as their separate property. To speak of "separate property" therefore was becoming something of an anomaly, since married women in almost all cases had the same capacity to hold and dispose of it as a man or a feme sole. This was eventually recognised by Parliament in the Law Reform (Married Women and Tortfeasors) Act of that year which abolished the concept of the separate estate and gave to the wife the same rights and powers as were already possessed by other adults of full capacity. It provided:[5]

"... A married woman shall be capable of acquiring, holding, and disposing of, any property ... in all respects as if she were a feme sole.
... All property which—
(a) immediately before the passing of this Act was the separate property of a married woman or held for her separate use in equity; *or*
(b) belongs at the time of her marriage to a woman married after the passing of this Act; *or*
(c) after the passing of this Act is acquired by or devolves upon a married woman, shall belong to her in all respects as if she were a feme sole and may be disposed of accordingly."

The Act did not affect any rights in property which had accrued as the result of a marriage before 1883[6] nor did it touch any existing restraint on anticipation.[7] But it sounded the death knell of the latter, for it rendered void any attempted imposition of a restraint on anticipation in any instrument

---

[1] See *post*, pp. 616 *et seq*.
[2] Copyhold tenure was emancipated and converted into freehold tenure by the Law of Property Act 1922.
[3] Administration of Estates Act 1925, s. 45. Although this section does not apply to entailed interests, the Act repealed the Dower Act which gave the wife the right to dower in her husband's equitable freeholds. It thus entirely abolished dower, as a fee tail can now exist only as an equitable interest. There may also be curtesy in certain circumstances of the wife's determinable fee simple: Farrer, *Tenant by the Curtesy of England*, 43 L.Q.R. 87, at pp. 100-102.
[4] Law of Property Act 1925, s. 37. After 1882 the spouses could sever their half share as *between themselves* they took as ordinary joint tenants.
[5] Ss. 1 (a) and 2 (1).
[6] S. 4 (1) (a).
[7] S. 2 (1).

executed after 1935 and in the will of any person dying after 1945, even though it was executed before 1936.[1]

The Married Women (Restraint upon Anticipation) Act 1949.—Although after 1945 restraint upon anticipation was bound to disappear in the course of time, the Act of 1935 did not affect the validity of restraints already imposed. Whilst in 1882 it was apparently still necessary to protect a married woman's property in this way, the restraint could no longer be justified in the middle of the present century, when it served no further purpose but merely acted as an undue fetter on the wife's powers of alienation. Although the court could sanction individual dispositions if these were for her benefit,[2] the only way in which a restraint could be wholly removed was by a private Act of Parliament. It was the presentation of a bill for this purpose that ultimately led to the passing of the Married Women (Restraint upon Anticipation) Act in 1949, which removed all restraints whenever imposed and thus rendered the property to which they were attached freely alienable.

B. THE MODERN LAW[3]

1. GENERAL PRINCIPLES

The Effect of the Married Women's Property Acts.—By extending the equitable principle of the separate estate, the Married Women's Property Acts replaced the total incapacity of a married woman to hold property at common law by a rigid doctrine of separate property. In the well known words of Dicey,[4] "the rules of equity, framed for the daughters of the rich, have at last been extended to the daughters of the poor". But, as Professor Kahn-Freund has shown,[5] the effects of the Acts were much wider than this. Spouses' property may be broadly divided into two types: that intended for common use and consumption in the matrimonial home and that intended for personal use and enjoyment. The latter is often in the form of investments or derived from the interest on investments, and it is obvious that, whilst in a poor family almost the whole of the property will fall into the first category, the richer the spouses the greater fraction of their property will fall into the second. Before 1883 the matrimonial home and its contents would almost invariably be vested in the husband to the exclusion of the wife, and the latter's separate property did little more than protect her investments. But, impelled by a movement which was ultimately to secure the almost complete legal equality of the sexes, Parliament extended the doctrine of separation to property forming the matrimonial home as well—a situation which the equitable concept was never intended to cover and with which it was ill adapted to deal.

---

[1] S. 2 (2), (3).

[2] See *ante*, p. 415. If the restraint were attached to land, the woman could sell the land under the provisions of the Settled Land Act, but the restraint continued to attach to the capital.

[3] See generally Miller, *Family Property and Financial Provision*; Lesser, *The Acquisition of Inter Vivos Matrimonial Property Rights in English Law*, 23 U. of Toronto L.J. 148.

[4] *Law and Opinion*, 2nd Ed., 395.

[5] In *Matrimonial Property Law* (ed. Friedmann), 267 *et seq*. See also his article, *Recent Legislation on Matrimonial Property*, 33 M.L.R. 601.

This was inevitably bound to produce difficulties. But so long as the husband remained the bread winner, they were not acute, as it could still be argued that he retained the ownership of property bought out of his earnings. But during the Second World War most married women were wage earners as well, and what before 1939 had been something of an exception has now become the usual situation in most families, at least during the early years of married life. To apply the strict doctrine of separate property to matrimonial assets in such circumstances is manifestly absurd. As a result, judges have sought to adapt the principle by regarding both the spouses as having an interest in the matrimonial home in many cases, even though the legal estate is vested solely in the husband. Legislation has also been passed to overcome some difficulties, particularly with respect to the occupation of the matrimonial home.

Doctrines effecting such radical changes are bound to bristle with difficulties. Marked differences of opinion amongst the judges have been reflected in confusing and sometimes contradictory decisions, and whilst clear patterns seem to emerge from time to time, they are liable to be suddenly obscured by a new case out of line with recent trends. In practice the most difficult problems arise when the marriage breaks down in the parties' lifetime, and whenever possible the parties should rely on the wide powers now possessed by the court to make orders for the transfer and settlement of property on divorce, nullity and judicial separation which largely remove the need to make an enquiry into the precise interest that each spouse has in the matrimonial home or other asset.[1] It should not be thought, however, that the question of ownership is now merely academic. It may still be more valuable for a wife to show that she has a half interest in the matrimonial home than to rely on, say, the third share that the court might otherwise award her. Furthermore, if a dispute arises between one spouse and the other's creditors or personal representatives, the court's discretionary powers cannot be invoked at all.

The real trouble is that, except for family provision on death, such legislation as there has been during this century has sought to deal with isolated problems, and we need to complete the statutory overhaul of the whole field of matrimonial property law. Solutions adopted by other legal systems include community of property (under which the property belonging to both spouses is administered by the husband and divided between them or their personal representatives when the marriage comes to an end), community of gains (which limits community to property acquired during the marriage otherwise than by gift or inheritance), and deferred community (under which each spouse remains free to acquire and dispose of his or her own property but at the end of the marriage any net gain or surplus is divided equally between them). English courts already have a wide discretion to adjust rights by ordering the transfer and settlement of property following divorce, nullity and judicial separation. There are also extensive powers to order provision for members of the family and other dependants out of the estate of a deceased person. Bearing these points in mind, the Law Commission has concluded that it is not necessary to introduce any form of community of

---

[1] See *Kowalczuk* v. *Kowalczuk*, [1973] 2 All E.R. 1042, 1045, C.A.; *Griffiths* v. *Griffiths*, [1974] 1 All E.R. 932, 941, C.A. For the court's powers, see *post*, pp. 534-535.

property in this country: most remaining hardship would be avoided if the spouses were co-owners of the matrimonial home, which is the most substantial asset in the majority of families. As it is, well over a half of all married couples who own their own homes own them jointly:[1] the Commission has recommended that this principle should be extended by statute to other spouses.[2]

Essentially, what is envisaged is that husband and wife should be statutory co-owners of any property used as their matrimonial home. This would apply whether the estate or interest was freehold or leasehold, legal or equitable. It would have to be a beneficial and absolute interest in possession and not, for example, a life interest or one held by one of the spouses as a trustee. Once the statutory co-ownership arose, the parties would hold as beneficial joint tenants but would be able to sever their tenancy in the normal way. A number of exceptions are contemplated: the most important relate to homes which are expressly conveyed to both spouses, property acquired before or on marriage which the owner declares in writing is not to be the subject of statutory co-ownership, gifts with respect to which the donor, settlor or testator makes a similar declaration, and property which the spouses agree shall be owned by them both as tenants in common in specified shares or by one of them alone. Once the statutory trust was attached to the land, it could not be disposed of unless both spouses consented; in the event of disagreement, the court would have power to dispense with consent. In order to protect the spouse whose name would not appear on the title, she (or he) would be able to register her interest as a new Class G land charge. If the charge were registered, the spouse's interest would not be overreached unless the purchaser paid the price to two or more trustees in the usual way; if it were not registered, he would take free of the interest even though he had actual notice of it.

Although the matrimonial home will usually be the most substantial asset owned by the spouses, many are likely to have a number of valuable chattels as well, for example a car, washing machine, freezer or stereo equipment. If the wife is not working, the beneficial ownership of the goods will usually be in the husband alone, so that he may lawfully dispose of them without the wife's consent. It will be seen that, if he deserts the wife, taking goods of this

---

[1] See Todd and Jones, *Matrimonial Property* (H.M.S.O.). Joint ownership is becoming much more popular than this figure suggests because the proportion of spouses buying a house in the decade 1962-71 and having it conveyed into joint names rose from 47% to 74%.

[2] Law Com. No. 86 (Third Report on Family Property). See also Law Commission Working Paper No. 42 and Law Com. No. 52 (First Report on Family Property); Report of the Morton Commission, Cmd. 9678, Part IX; Simon, *With all my Worldly Goods* ... (published by the Holdsworth Club of the University of Birmingham); Nevitt and Levin, *Social Policy and the Matrimonial Home*, 36 M.L.R. 345; Baxter, 37 M.L.R. 175; Kahn-Freund, *Matrimonial Property—Where do we go from here*? (Joseph Unger Memorial Lecture); Freeman, *Towards a Rational Reconstruction of Family Property Law*, Current Legal Problems 1972, 84. For further criticisms particularly with respect to rented accommodation (including lettings by local authorities), see the Finer Report, Cmnd. 5629, Part 6. For discussion of some foreign systems, comparison with which is interesting and profitable, see *Matrimonial Property Law* (ed. Friedmann); Milner, *A Homestead Act for England*, 22 M.L.R. 458; Tarlo, *Possession of the Matrimonial Home in Australia*, 22 M.L.R. 479; Górecki, *Matrimonial Property in Poland*, 26 M.L.R. 156; Pedersen, *Matrimonial Property Law in Denmark*, 28 M.L.R. 137; Johnson, *Matrimonial Property in Soviet Law*, 16 I.C.L.Q. 1106; Eekelaar, *Family Security and Family Breakdown*, 98 *et seq.*

sort with him and leaving her with the children, the latter will suffer as well as the wife. The Law Commission rejected the possibility of introducing compulsory co-ownership of goods, partly because the value of used goods is usually so much less than that of new goods that compensation in the form of half the actual value of the goods lost would not enable her to replace them. Instead they have proposed that either spouse should be able to apply for an order concerning the use and enjoyment of "household goods" owned by either or both of them and in the possession or control of either of them. "Household goods" are defined as "any goods, including a vehicle, which are or were available for use and enjoyment in or in connection with any home which the parties to the marriage have at any time during the marriage occupied as their matrimonial home". In deciding whether to make such an order, the court should be guided particularly by the extent to which the applicant needed them to meet the normal requirements of her daily life and family responsibilities. If the other spouse contravened an order, he would be subject to the usual penalties for disobeying an order of the court; in addition, if he disposed of the goods, the court could order him (and the person receiving them if he were aware of the order) to pay the applicant such sum as it thought fair and reasonable by way of compensation. It would also be able to order the husband to make compensation in appropriate cases with respect to goods disposed of even though a use and enjoyment order was not in force. The scheme would extend to caravans and houseboats; the principal goods excepted from these proposals are goods in which third parties have an interest, including goods subject to hire, hire-purchase and conditional sale agreements.[1]

These proposals represent a compromise between the present English system of separate property and a comprehensive adoption of community. Whatever merits they may possess, they have not obtained universal support. A bill to establish statutory co-ownership of the matrimonial home was introduced in the House of Lords at the beginning of 1980 but it was made clear that Government time would not be made available for it. There is no doubt that any future bill is likely to meet serious opposition and it may well be some considerable time before even this degree of reform reaches the statute book.[2]

Issues between the Spouses.—Two questions arise here: in whom are the legal and equitable interests in the property vested and what rights short of ownership may one spouse have in the property of the other? So long as they are living amicably together, these questions never have to be answered, and they become vital only if the marriage breaks down. This adds considerably to the difficulty, for the parties rarely contemplate the collapse of the marriage when they acquire property, and their respective rights in it are never discussed, let alone defined. Hence the courts are faced with the problem of having to impute to them an intention which they never possessed at all.[3]

---

[1] See Law. Com. No. 86, Book Three.
[2] See Hansard, H.L., 12th February 1980; Murphy and Rawlings, 10 Fam. Law 136.
[3] *Cf. Re Rogers' Question*, [1948] 1 All E.R. 328, C.A.; *Cobb* v. *Cobb*, [1955] 2 All E.R. 696, 699, C.A.

There are three different ways of solving disputes open to the spouses.

Action for Damages in Tort.—As we have already seen,[1] either spouse may now protect his or her interests in property by suing the other in tort, for example in trespass or conversion. Either may also bring an action against the other for the recovery of land. In this connection it should be remembered that if the spouses are jointly in possession of property or are jointly entitled to possession, one may be liable in trespass if he or she completely ousts the other or in conversion if he or she completely destroys the property.[2]

It will be recalled that the court may stay the action if the questions in issue could be disposed of more conveniently by an application under section 17 of the Married Women's Property Act 1882.[3]

Proceedings for an Injunction.—Either spouse may obtain an injunction to prevent the other from committing a continuing or threatened wrong against the plaintiff's property.[4] In practice this remedy is most frequently sought when the wife is trying to exclude the husband from entering the matrimonial home, and the particular problems that arise here will be dealt with later.[5]

Proceedings under Section 17 *of the Married Women's Property Act* 1882.—This section[6] provides that "in any question between husband and wife as to the title to or possession of property"[7] either of them may apply for an order to the High Court or a county court and the judge "may make such order with respect to the property in dispute ... as he thinks fit".[8] These proceedings are of course usually invoked when the marriage has broken down. Disputes over rights in property may still be going on after the

---

[1] *Ante*, p. 157.

[2] Torts (Interference with Goods) Act 1977, s. 10; Salmond, *Torts*, 16th Ed., 47, 111-112.

[3] *Ante*, p. 158. For proceedings under s. 17, see *infra*.

[4] This may be done by bringing an action in tort under the Law Reform (Husband and Wife) Act 1962, in proceedings under the Domestic Violence and Matrimonial Proceedings Act 1976, or by way of ancilliary relief in other matrimonial proceedings.

[5] *Post*, pp. 459 *et seq*.

[6] Replacing and extending the Married Women's Property Act 1870, s. 9. The section has been amended by the Law Reform (Husband and Wife) Act 1962, Sched., (repealing s. 23 of the Act of 1882) and the Statute Law (Repeals) Act 1969, Sched, Part III, which have taken away the power of a deceased wife's personal representatives and of banks, companies and other bodies to take proceedings under s. 17.

[7] Including choses in action (*Spellman* v. *Spellman*, [1961] 2 All E.R. 498, 501, C.A.) and property of which the claimant is a bare trustee and in which he has no beneficial interest at all (*Re Knight's Question*, [1959] Ch. 381; [1958] 1 All E.R. 812). If there is no question as to title or possession but one spouse is, *e.g.*, seeking to enforce a trust for sale against the other, proceedings under s. 17 are inappropriate and the same proceedings should be taken as would be taken between strangers: *Rawlings* v. *Rawlings*, [1964] P. 398; [1964] 2 All E.R. 804, C.A.

[8] Proceedings in the High Court are now assigned to the Family Division. The county court has jurisdiction whatever the value of the property, but if this exceeds the normal statutory maximum of the court's jurisdiction, the defendant may have the case transferred to the High Court: s. 17. As far as possible, applications under s. 17, the Matrimonial Homes Act (*post*, p. 458) and for financial relief under the Matrimonial Causes Act (*post*, ch. 15) should be heard by the same tribunal, because the same evidence is often relevant in two or more applications and the outcome of one set of proceedings may affect another. There would also be a common appeal to the same tribunal. See *Practice Note (Matrimonial Property: Related Applications)*, [1971] 1 All E.R. 895.

marriage has been legally terminated, and consequently section 17 has now been extended to enable former spouses to make an application for a period of three years after a decree absolute of divorce or nullity.[1] Similarly, engaged couples may well buy furniture and start to buy a house in contemplation of their marriage, and this may give them rights in property which are virtually indistinguishable from those acquired by married couples. The abolition of actions for damages for breach of promise of marriage deprived them of the means of recovering the expenses they had lost if the marriage did not take place. Consequently the summary procedure of section 17 has now been made available to the parties to an agreement to marry which has been terminated as well. An application must relate to property in which either or both of them had an interest while the agreeement was in force and must be brought within three years of the termination of the agreement.[2]

It will be seen that the court has jurisdiction to determine questions of title and possession. In order that it may do this, it was formerly held that there must be in existence specific property or a specific fund with respect to which the order might be made and that if the property or fund had ceased to exist, there was no power to make what would be in effect an order for damages for trespass, conversion or debt.[3] This clearly worked injustice if the defendant had already disposed of the property or fund in question; this has been remedied by section 7 of the Matrimonial Causes (Property and Maintenance) Act 1958, which has given the court power in such a case either to order the defendant to pay to the plaintiff such sum of money as represents the latter's interest in the property or fund or to make an order with respect to any other property which now represents the whole or part of the original.[4]

For some years there was considerable judicial controversy over the width of the powers which the wording of the section gave to the judges. It was, however, finally settled by the House of Lords in *Pettitt* v. *Pettitt*[5] that the court has no jurisdiction under this section to vary existing titles and no wider power to transfer or create interests in property than it would have in any other type of proceedings. At the most it has, in the words of LORD DIPLOCK, "a wide discretion as to the enforcement of the proprietary or possessory rights of one spouse in any property against the other".[6] Furthermore, the fact that the marriage has broken down, the circumstances of the breakdown and the conduct of the parties cannot affect title in the absence of an agreement between the spouses and are therefore all irrelevant to the outcome of proceedings brought under section 17.[7] But there are clearly two types of case in which the court will still have a wide discretion. In the first place, the

---

[1] Matrimonial Proceedings and Property Act 1970, s. 39.

[2] Law Reform (Miscellaneous Provisions) Act 1970, s. 2 (2). For the abolition of actions for breach of promise, see *ante*, p. 18, and also see generally Law Com. No. 26 (Breach of Promise of Marriage).

[3] *Tunstall* v. *Tunstall*, [1953] 2 All E.R. 310, C.A.

[4] But a specific property or fund must have been in existence originally and proceedings cannot be brought under s. 17 for the recovery of a debt: *Crystall* v. *Crystall*, [1963] 2 All E.R. 330, C.A. The Limitation Act has been held not to apply to such proceedings and consequently an order may be made even though the property was disposed of more than six years earlier: *Spoor* v. *Spoor*, [1966] 3 All E.R. 120.

[5] [1970] A.C. 777; [1969] 2 All E.R. 385, H.L.

[6] At pp. 820 and 411, respectively.

[7] *Pettitt* v. *Pettitt*, (*supra*).

spouses' rights may not be precisely defined: for example, they may both have contributed to the purchase of the matrimonial home, so that they both have a beneficial interest in it, but there may be no agreement over the size of their shares. In such a case the court can usually ensure that justice is done by ordering the interest to be divided in such proportions as it thinks fit. Secondly, by using its powers to make different types of orders, the court may effectively control the way in which the property is used without departing from the principle that it cannot alter the title. Thus it may order a spouse to give up possession of a house, to deliver up chattels, to transfer shares and other choses in action or to pay over a specific fund, and it may even forbid him to dispossess the other spouse or to deal with the property in any way inconsistent with the other's rights.[1] Similarly the court may order the property to be sold and direct how the proceeds of sale are to be divided[2] or, if both spouses have an interest, it may order one of them to transfer his or her share to the other on the latter's paying the value of the property transferred.[3]

Issues between one of the Spouses and a Stranger.—The question to be considered here is how far rights in property created or affected by marriage can be enforced by one of the spouses against a third person. The latter may claim in one of a number of capacities, for example as a purchaser for value from the other spouse, as the other's creditor or trustee in bankruptcy, or as a beneficiary entitled to a deceased spouse's estate. It is essential to decide first what rights the claiming spouse has against the other spouse and then how far these rights are enforceable against the third person. This will depend upon the application of general principles of the law of property and in particular the nature of the latter's title. If he is, say, the husband's donee, the wife may enforce against him all those rights (other than purely personal rights) which she would have against her husband; if he is a purchaser of a legal estate or interest for value, he will take the property subject to the wife's legal rights but will not be bound by her equitable interests if he purchased in good faith and without notice of them.

2. PROPERTY ACQUIRED BY THE SPOUSES

Property owned by the Spouses at the Time of the Marriage.—Presumptively marriage will not affect the ownership of property vested in either of the spouses at the time. This will also be true of property which is used by them jointly in the matrimonial home (for example, furniture) in the absence of an express gift of a joint interest in law or in equity.[4]

---

[1] As in *Lee* v. *Lee*, [1952] 2 Q.B. 489 n.; [1952] 1 All E.R. 1299, C.A. In *Re Bettinson's Question*, [1956] Ch. 67; [1955] 3 All E.R. 296, it was held that an order could be made with respect to property which was subject to the doctrine of community of property under the law of the parties' domicile (California).

[2] Matrimonial Causes (Property and Maintenance) Act 1958, s. 7 (7).

[3] *Bothe* v. *Amos*, [1976] Fam. 46; [1975] 2 All E.R. 321, C.A.

[4] Since the cases indicate that a joint interest will not be created unless both have contributed in some way to the purchase, in which case they will probably already own the property jointly before marriage: see *post*, p. 446. For the effect of the subsequent acquisition of

Income.—The income of either spouse, whether from earnings or from investments, will *prima facie* remain his or her own property.[1] But where the spouses pool their incomes and place them into a common fund, it seems that they both acquire a joint interest in the whole fund.

This occurred in *Jones* v. *Maynard*.[2] In 1941 the husband, who was about to go abroad with the R.A.F., authorised his wife to draw on his bank account, which was thereafter treated as a joint account. Into this account were paid dividends on both the husband's and the wife's investments, the husband's pay and allowances and rent from the matrimonial home which was their joint property and which had been let during the War. The husband's contributions were greater than the wife's; the spouses had never agreed on what their rights in this fund were to be, but they regarded it as their joint savings to be invested from time to time. The husband withdrew money on a number of occasions and invested it in his own name, and finally, after the spouses had separated in 1946, he closed the account altogether. The marriage was later dissolved and the plaintiff sued her former husband for a half share in the account as it stood on the day it was closed and in the investments which he had previously purchased out of it. VAISEY, J., held that the claim must succeed. He said:[3]

> "In my judgment, when there is a joint account between husband and wife, a common pool into which they put all their resources, it is not consistent with that conception that the account should thereafter ... be picked apart, and divided up proportionately to the respective contributions of husband and wife, the husband being credited with the whole of his earnings and the wife with the whole of her dividends. I do not believe that, when once the joint pool has been formed, it ought to be, and can be, dissected in any such manner. In my view a husband's earnings or salary, when the spouses have a common purse and pool their resources, are earnings made on behalf of both; and the idea that years afterwards the contents of the pool can be dissected by taking an elaborate account as to how much was paid in by the husband or the wife is quite inconsistent with the original fundamental idea of a joint purse or common pool.
>
> "In my view the money which goes into the pool becomes joint property. The husband, if he wants a suit of clothes, draws a cheque to pay for it. The wife, if she wants any housekeeping money, draws a cheque, and there is no disagreement about it."

What, then, constitutes a "common purse"? It would seem on principle to be essential that there must be a fund intended for the use of both spouses from which either may withdraw money and this will normally take the form of a joint bank account. Where they both contribute to this fund, as in *Jones* v. *Maynard*, it is submitted that this intention will be imputed to the parties in

---

an English domicile by parties whose original *lex domicilii* imposed on them the doctrine of community of property, see *De Nicols* v. *Curlier*, [1900] A.C. 21, H.L.; for the converse case of the parties' acquiring a foreign domicile after the marriage, see *Re Egerton's Will Trusts*, [1956] Ch. 593; [1956] 2 All E.R. 817. See also Stone, *The Matrimonial Domicile and the Property Relations of Married Persons*, 6 I.C.L.Q. 28; Goldberg, *The Assignment of Property on Marriage*, 19 I.C.L.Q. 557.

[1] *Cf. Dixon* v. *Dixon* (1878), 9 Ch.D. 587 (stock settled to the wife's separate use); *Barrack* v. *M'Culloch* (1856), 3 K. & J. 110 (rents from houses settled to the wife's separate use); *Heseltine* v. *Heseltine*, [1971] 1 All E.R. 952 (income from wife's investments). For criticisms of the existing law and proposals for reform, see Deech, 123 New L.J. 1107.

[2] [1951] Ch. 572; [1951] 1 All E.R. 802.

[3] At pp. 575 and 803, respectively.

the absence of any other agreement; where, however, the fund is derived from the income of one spouse alone, it is a question of fact whether this is to remain his or her exclusive property or whether there is an intention to establish a common fund. If the wife is the sole contributor to a joint account, she will *prima facie* take the whole beneficial interest.[1] On the other hand, if the husband is the sole contributor, the presumption of advancement will operate so as *prima facie* to give her an interest;[2] but this will be rebutted if, for example, it can be shown that the power to draw on the account was given for the husband's convenience by enabling the wife to draw cheques for the payment of housekeeping expenses.[3] Even though the beneficial interest in a joint account is initially vested in one spouse alone, his or her intention may change and it may be converted into a joint interest.[4] The courts will doubtless tend to find a joint beneficial interest today much more readily than they did in the past.

If either spouse withdraws money from the common purse, property bought with it will *prima facie* belong solely to that spouse and not to both jointly. Where the property is for personal use (for example, clothes), this presumption will not normally be rebuttable; in the case of investments it could be rebutted if it were clear that they were still intended to represent the original fund. In *Re Bishop*[5] large sums had been withdrawn by both spouses to purchase investments in their separate names. In many cases blocks of shares were bought and half put in one name and the other half put in the other; other money was spent in taking up shares offered to the husband by virtue of rights which he possessed as an existing shareholder in the companies concerned. In these circumstances STAMP, J., had no difficulty in holding that the presumption could not be rebutted and that the spouse in whose name the shares had been purchased was entitled to the whole beneficial interest in them. He distinguished *Jones* v. *Maynard* where VAISEY, J., had held that the husband was to be regarded as trustee for them both of investments which he had purchased, for in that case they had agreed that when there had been a sufficient accumulation the money should be invested and that that was to be their savings.

Like any other joint interest the balance of the fund will accrue to the survivor on the death of either spouse as it did in *Re Bishop*. It can of course be severed by agreement or assignment in the lifetime of both; in such a case or where, as in *Jones* v. *Maynard*, the marriage breaks down and the court is asked to effect a partition, then, as we have seen from the passage of

---

[1] *Heseltine* v. *Heseltine*, (*supra*) (houses purchased by husband out of joint account provided by wife's money held to belong to her absolutely). Contrast *Boydell* v. *Gillespie* (1970), 210 Estates Gazette 1505 (wife's directing that property bought with her money should be conveyed into names of both spouses jointly held to give both an interest in it).

[2] *Re Figgis*, [1969] 1 Ch. 123; [1968] 1 All E.R. 999. Although the effect of these presumptions is considerably weaker today than it used to be (see *post*, p. 429), they will still operate in a case like *Re Figgis* where both parties are dead and there is virtually no direct evidence of the parties' intentions at all.

[3] *Marshal* v. *Crutwell* (1875), L.R. 20 Eq. 328; *Hoddinott* v. *Hoddinott*, [1949] 2 K.B. 406, 413, C.A.; *Harrods, Ltd.* v. *Tester*, [1937] 2 All E.R. 236, C.A. (where the whole of the balance of a bank account opened by the husband in the wife's name was held to belong to the husband).

[4] *Re Figgis*, (*supra*), at pp. 145 and 1011, respectively.

[5] [1965] Ch. 450; [1965] 1 All E.R. 249.

VAISEY, J.'s judgment quoted above, the spouses will hold the balance of the fund as tenants in common in equal shares.[1]

Allowances for Housekeeping and Maintenance.—This question is obviously closely allied to the last and originally the same principles were applied. Hence it was consistently held that if a husband supplied his wife with a housekeeping allowance out of his own income, any balance and any property bought with the allowance *prima facie* remained his property.[2] This might well work an injustice for it took no account of the fact that any savings from the housekeeping money were as much due to the wife's skill and economy as a housewife as to her husband's earning capacity.[3] It was to remedy his that the Married Women's Property Act 1964 was passed. Section 1 provides:

"If any question arises as to the right of a husband or wife to money derived from any allowance made by the husband for the expenses of the matrimonial home or for similar purposes, or to any property acquired out of such money, the money or property shall, in the absence of any agreement between them to the contrary, be treated as belonging to the husband and wife in equal shares."

In the first place it should be noted that the Act applies only if the allowance is provided by the husband; it does not apply to the case where the wife goes out to work to support a husband who does the housekeeping. In such a case the allowance and any property bought with it presumably remain the wife's.[4] Secondly, it is not clear what the phrase "expenses of the matrimonial home or similar purposes" covers. If, for example, a husband gives his wife money to pay off instalments of the mortgage on the matrimonial home, she may well be regarded as no more than his agent and thus acquire no interest in the house; but if he gives her a housekeeping allowance out of which it is intended that she should pay the instalments, it has been suggested that the effect of the section is to give her a half share in the fraction represented by each payment.[5] In the absence of any binding authority the words "expenses of the matrimonial home" seem more apt to describe money spent in running it than in acquiring it.

If the allowance is made for this purpose, the rule applies not only to the money but also to any property bought with it. Hence, if the wife were to buy furniture with the housekeeping savings, this would presumably belong to her and her husband equally. This can be rebutted by proof of an express agreement between the spouses; what is not clear is whether the courts will be prepared to spell out an implied agreement when the circumstances demand

[1] *Cf. post*, p. 450.

[2] *Blackwell* v. *Blackwell*, [1943] 2 All E.R. 579, C.A.: *Hoddinott* v. *Hoddinott*, [1949] 2 K.B. 406, C.A.

[3] See the judgments of DENNING, L.J., in *Hoddinott* v. *Hoddinott*, *(supra)*, at p. 416, and *Rimmer* v. *Rimmer*, [1953] 1 Q.B. 63, 74; [1952] 2 All E.R. 863, 868-869, C.A.

[4] Earlier cases indicate that if the wife gives money to her husband for use in the home, she is deemed to give it to him as head of the family and the money therefore becomes his: see *e.g.*, *Edward* v. *Cheyne* (*No.* 2) (1888), 13 App. Cas. 385, H.L.: *Re Young* (1913), 29 T.L.R. 319 (where the presumption was rebutted on the facts). But it is very doubtful whether the courts would take such a view today. The Morton Commission recommended that the allowance should belong to both spouses equally, whichever of them provided it: Cmd. 9678, para. 701.

[5] See the conflicting views in *Tymoszczuk* v. *Tymoszczuk* (1964), 108 Sol. Jo. 676, and *Re Johns' Assignment Trusts*, [1970] 2 All E.R. 210, 213.

it. If the wife uses part of the allowance to buy clothes for herself, it seems absurd that a half share of them should belong to the husband; can it not be argued that there must be a tacit agreement that the whole should belong to the wife?[1]

Two further weaknesses may be seen in the Act. First, the money or property is to be treated as belonging to the spouses in equal shares. Consequently on the death of one the whole beneficial interest will not automatically pass to the survivor (as it does in the case of the "common purse")[2] but half will go to the personal representatives of the other. It is highly doubtful whether this is what the spouses will want or expect. In their desire to remedy the injustice caused by earlier cases where the marriage had broken down, the promoters of the Bill apparently overlooked the obvious fact that most marriages survive and that, whilst a joint interest can always be severed by the unilateral act of one party, it requires the conscious act of both to turn a tenancy in common into a joint tenancy. Neither this rule nor its consequences will be known to the vast majority of spouses and it is not inconceivable that a half share of furniture will inadvertently pass under a residuary bequest. Secondly, it is not clear whether the Act is to have retrospective effect. As there is no clear intention to affect vested rights, it is submitted that money and property belonging to the husband when the Act came into force[3] should remain his. Obviously in the course of time it will be forgotten when particular pieces of property were bought and it will become impossible to divide the balance of the fund into that which was provided before the operative date and that which was provided afterwards, so that the courts will probably be forced to hold that the Act does have retrospective effect. This can potentially work as much injustice as it avoids.

Property purchased by one Spouse.—Any property purchased by one spouse with his or her own money will presumptively belong exclusively to the purchaser. Property bought out of money coming from the "common purse" will also presumptively belong to the purchaser except for investments representing joint savings which will remain part of the spouses' joint property.[4]

But this presumption is obviously rebuttable. Thus property bought by one spouse as a gift for the other will become the donee's. Hence if a husband buys clothes for his wife or gives her money to buy them for herself, they become her property,[5] and the same rule will *prima facie* apply in any other case where goods are bought for the other's personal use.[6]

---

[1] Perhaps a more difficult case would arise if the wife bought herself an expensive piece of jewellery. In the case of a "common purse" contributed to by both the property would belong to the wife exclusively: see *ante*, p. 426.

[2] See *ante*, p. 426.

[3] 25th March 1964. This view seems to have commended itself to GOFF, J., in *Re Johns' Assignment Trusts*, (*supra*), at p. 213. The opposite view was taken by Master JACOB in *Tymoszczuk* v. *Tymoszczuk*, (*supra*), on the ground that the Act creates a presumption and therefore changes adjective law. For further difficulties that may arise, see Stone, 27 M.L.R. 576.

[4] See *ante*, p. 426.

[5] *Masson, Templier & Co.* v. *De Fries*, [1909] 2 K.B. 831, C.A. Contrast *Rondeau, Le Grand & Co.* v. *Marks*, [1918] 1 K.B. 75, C.A., where it had been agreed that they should remain the husband's property.

[6] *Re Whittaker* (1882), 21 Ch. D. 657 (piano).

Difficulties can arise if one spouse's money is used to buy property which is conveyed into the other's name or into joint names or, alternatively, if both spouses' money is used to buy property which is conveyed into the name of only one of them. The classic way of solving the problem is by applying two maxims of equity. If the wife alone provides the purchase money, there is a resulting trust in her favour and the husband (or the spouses jointly if the legal estate is vested in both) is presumed to hold the property on trust for her absolutely. On the other hand, if the husband provides the purchase money and has the property put into his wife's name or into joint names, he is presumed to intend a gift to his wife, and the presumption of advancement operates to give her *prima facie* the sole or a joint beneficial interest.[1] Precisely the same rules operate if both provide the money. If the property is conveyed into the husband's name alone, he will hold it on trust for them both and each will be entitled to a share proportionate to the contribution.[2] If the property is conveyed into the wife's name alone, the husband will be presumed to have made a gift of the whole of the property to her. These presumptions have always been rebuttable by evidence that the wife intended a gift in the first case or that the husband intended to keep the beneficial interest in the second.[3] But as the members of the House of Lords agreed in *Pettitt* v. *Pettitt*,[4] they are much less strong today because some explanation of the parties' conduct will usually be available unless they are both dead. LORD DIPLOCK went so far as to question whether they were still valid at all. As he observed, they are no more than a judicial inference of what the spouses' intention most probably was, drawn in cases relating to the propertied classes of the nineteenth and early twentieth century among whom marriage settlements were common and where the wife rarely contributed to the family income by her earnings. As such, they have little significance today when the parties may be legally aided, the wife is working, and their biggest asset, the matrimonial home, is being purchased by means of a mortgage.[5] The

---

[1] *Mercier* v. *Mercier*, [1903] 2 Ch. 98, C.A. (presumption of resulting trust for wife); *Silver* v. *Silver*, [1958] 1 All E.R. 523, C.A. (presumption of advancement). Hence if the husband had property conveyed to both spouses and a stranger, all three would hold on trust for the husband and wife jointly: *Re Eykyn's Trusts* (1877), 6 Ch. D. 115. There is a presumption of advancement even though the marriage is *voidable*: *Dunbar* v. *Dunbar*, [1909] 2 Ch. 639; but not if the husband knows it to be *void*, for then there is to his knowledge no duty to maintain: *Soar* v. *Foster* (1858), 4 K. & J. 152. *Quaere* if he does not know it is void. The presumption of advancement is also raised if a man has property conveyed into his fiancée's name: *Moate* v. *Moate*, [1948] 2 All E.R. 486.

[2] This could be relevant *e.g.* if furniture or a car were bought by the husband on hire purchase and both spouses contributed to the payment of the instalments. See Law Com. Working Paper No. 42, pp. 131-134.

[3] The husband may not rebut the presumption by adducing evidence of his own fraudulent or unlawful intention: *Re Emery's Investment Trusts*, [1959] Ch. 410; [1959] 1 All E.R. 577 (evasion of tax in the U.S.A.); *Tinker* v. *Tinker*, [1970] P. 136; [1970] 1 All E.R. 540, C.A. (defrauding creditors). Contrast *Griffiths* v. *Griffiths*, [1973] 3 All E.R. 1155; affirmed on this point, [1974] 1 All E.R. 932, C.A. (fraudulent statements made after acquisition of interest held not to prevent husband's claiming it).

[4] [1970] A.C. 777; [1969] 2 All E.R. 385, H.L.; at pp. 793 and 389 (*per* LORD REID); 811 and 404 (*per* LORD HODSON); 814-815 and 406-407 (*per* LORD UPJOHN); 824 and 414 (*per* LORD DIPLOCK).

[5] At pp. 823-824 and 414, respectively. See also LORD DENNING, M.R., in *Falconer* v. *Falconer*, [1970] 3 All E.R. 449, 452, C.A.

particular application of this problem to the purchase of the matrimonial home will be considered later.[1]

Gifts to Spouses.—Whether a gift belongs to one spouse alone or to both of them is a question of the donor's intention. In the case of wedding presents it is reasonable to assume in the absence of any evidence to the contrary that the husband's friends and relations intended to make the gift to him and the wife's to her. There is no rule of law to this effect, however, and the court, exercising its discretion under section 17 of the Married Women's Property Act, may order the presents to be divided equally between them both.[2]

3. TRANSACTIONS BETWEEN HUSBAND AND WIFE

Gifts between Spouses.—With the exceptions discussed below in the case of chattels, gifts between husband and wife are subject to the general law. In particular it should be noted that there is no presumption that either party has exercised undue influence over the other.[3] This is somewhat surprising when one bears in mind the special treatment that equity accorded to married women in the past and the fact that spouses rarely take independent legal advice unless they are already at arm's length. It is probably fair to say, however, that the courts will look with particular care at any transaction entered into at the time of the breakdown of the marriage when both spouses are likely to be in an emotional state.[4] If its effect is to give one of them a considerable financial advantage with no counter-balancing advantage to the other, it will be set aside if the transferor is relatively poor and ignorant of the effects of property transactions in general and of the transaction in question in particular, and has neither received independent advice nor been urged to seek it.[5]

One recent decision of the Court of Appeal, however, deserves special mention because it has apparently extended the concept of the resulting trust in a surprising and quite unprecedented way. In *Heseltine* v. *Heseltine*[6] the wife, who was considerably richer than her husband, transferred to him two sums of £20,000 each. She did this at his request in order to reduce the amount of estate duty that would be payable if she predeceased him. Later she gave him another £20,000 so that he would have sufficient assets to qualify as an underwriter at Lloyd's. At the time the marriage appeared to be perfectly happy, but the husband subsequently left the wife for another woman and she brought proceedings under section 17 of the Married Women's Property Act to recover *inter alia* the £60,000 transferred. The Court of Appeal held that she had not intended that these sums should be an

---

[1] *Post*, p. 445.

[2] *Samson* v. *Samson*, [1960] 1 All E.R. 653, C.A. Contrast *Kelner* v. *Kelner*, [1939] P. 411; [1939] 3 All E.R. 957 (£1,000 deposited by the wife's father at the time of the marriage in a joint bank account in both spouses' names ordered to be divided equally between them).

[3] *Howes* v. *Bishop*, [1909] 2 K.B. 390, C.A.; *MacKenzie* v. *Royal Bank of Canada*, [1934] A.C. 468, P.C. Contrast *Bank of Montreal* v. *Stuart*, [1911] A.C. 120, P.C., where undue influence was in fact exercised.

[4] *Backhouse* v. *Backhouse*, [1978] 1 All E.R. 1158, 1166.

[5] *Backhouse* v. *Backhouse*, (*supra*), following *Cresswell* v. *Potter*, [1978] 1 W.L.R. 255. See Smith, 123 Sol. Jo. 193.

[6] [1971] 1 All E.R. 952, C.A. See Lloyd, 121 New L.J. 157; Cretney, 115 Sol. Jo. 614.

outright gift to the husband but that he should hold them for the benefit of
the family as a whole. Consequently he was a trustee of the money and,
having left the family, he was bound to return them to her.

The case bristles with difficulties. The majority of the court[1] seem to have
imputed to the parties an intention which they never had. Furthermore a trust
"for the benefit of the family" is so vague as to be virtually void for
uncertainty; in any case it is not clear why it entitled the wife to the whole
beneficial interest when the husband left. The court was clearly influenced by
a desire to protect the wife after the breakdown of the marriage due to the
husband's desertion and therefore took into account the husband's conduct,
a matter which cannot affect title. What they succeeded in doing was to make
an order under section 17 of the Married Women's Property Act which in
strict law they would have had power to make only under the Matrimonial
Causes Act if the wife had petitioned for divorce or judicial separation. They
doubtless did justice: the real difficulty is to see how far this doctrine can be
extended and to reconcile it with contrary dicta in the House of Lords.[2]

Transactions involving Land.—The relationship of husband and wife
would seem to affect such transactions in only one particular. An oral
contract for the sale or other disposition of land or any interest in land will
usually be wholly unenforceable, for if one spouse goes into or remains in
possession of the other's land, this could normally be explained on the
ground that he is there with the other's leave as spouse and consequently
would not indicate the existence of any contract between them so as to
amount to an act of part performance.[3]

Transactions involving Chattels Personal.—A sale of goods by one spouse
to the other normally creates no difficulty, as property usually passes
independently of delivery.[4] But gifts, which will be the usual transactions
between spouses, raise more complicated problems.[5] In order to perfect a gift
of a chattel there must be an intention on the part of the donor to pass
property to the donee and, in addition, either a deed executed by the former
or a delivery of the chattel to the latter. Gifts by deed will be rare between
spouses but, when they do occur, will again present no difficulties since the
intention can be inferred from the execution of the deed. But a spouse who
alleges that the other has effected a gift by delivery has to surmount two
obstacles. First, since spouses frequently use each other's property, an
intention to make a gift cannot readily be inferred from permission to use the
chattel in question, and consequently the burden of proof upon a spouse
alleging a gift will probably be higher than upon a stranger.[6] Secondly, it may
be wellnigh impossible in many cases to prove delivery. Where the goods are

[1] MEGAW, L.J., reached the same conclusion on the ground that the wife did not intend a gift.
[2] In *Pettitt* v. *Pettitt*, where it was emphatically stated that the parties' conduct is irrelevant in
proceedings under s. 17; see *ante*, p. 423. The decision is also objectionable on the ground that
the wife was using proceedings under s. 17 to recover a debt: see *ante*, p. 423, n. 4.
[3] *Steadman* v. *Steadman*, [1976] A.C. 536; [1974] 2 All E.R. 977, H.L.
[4] Sale of Goods Act 1979, ss. 17 and 18.
[5] See Thornely, *Transfer of Choses in Possession between Members of a common Household*, 11 C.L.J. 355; Diamond, 27 M.L.R. 357.
[6] *Cf. Bashall* v. *Bashall* (1894), 11 T.L.R. 152, C.A.

intended for the exclusive use of the donee (for example, clothes or jewellery), delivery will normally take place at the time the gift is made by a physical handing over and taking; but if the goods in question have already been used by both spouses in the home and will continue to be used in this way (for example, articles of furniture), there is not likely to be any apparent change of possession. There may indeed be an effective symbolic delivery of one chattel as representing the whole but spouses are hardly likely to carry out such an artificial act, the significance of which will not occur to them.[1] Where the possession of goods could be in one of two people (as will happen in the case of furniture used by both spouses in the matrimonial home), it is presumed to be in the owner, so that if ownership is changed by a sale or deed of gift, the buyer or donee will be presumed to have taken possession as soon as the transaction is complete;[2] but this presumption cannot apply in the case of a gift by delivery since the delivery must be proved before a change in ownership can be established.[3] English courts have always been slow to infer a delivery of a chattel from one spouse to the other, doubtless because of the danger that they may fraudulently allege a prior gift of the husband's goods to the wife in order to keep them out of the hands of the former's creditors. An example of this reluctance can be seen in *Re Cole*.[4] In this case the husband completely furnished a new house before his wife set foot in it. When she arrived, he put his hands over her eyes, took her into the first room, uncovered her eyes and said "Look". She then went into all the other rooms and handled various articles; at the end the husband said to her: "It's all yours". The furniture nevertheless remained insured in his name. He subsequently became bankrupt and the question arose whether the trustee or wife was entitled to the goods in question. It was held that she had failed to establish an effective delivery and consequently the gift to her was never perfected. In the circumstances it would always seem wisest for a gift of goods used by both spouses to be made by means of a deed.[5]

Two statutory provisions should also be noticed. Under section 10 of the Married Women's Property Act 1882, a gift made by a husband to his wife may be avoided by his creditors if the property continues to be "in the order and disposition or reputed ownership of the husband". The Court of Appeal in *French* v. *Gething*[6] has in effect rendered this section inapplicable to goods in the matrimonial home by holding that the maxim "possession follows title" puts the goods outside the order and disposition or reputed ownership of the husband once the property has changed hands by the execution of a deed or by delivery;[7] but it will presumably apply to goods on, say, the

---

[1] *Lock* v. *Heath* (1892), 8 T.L.R. 295 (husband held to have given all his furniture to wife by symbolic delivery of chair); Thornely, *loc. cit.*, 357-358. For an effective constructive delivery by a father to his daughter, see *Kilpin* v. *Ratley*, [1892] 1 Q.B. 582.

[2] *Ramsay* v. *Margrett*, [1894] 2 Q.B. 18, C.A.; *French* v. *Gething*, [1922] 1 K.B. 236, C.A.

[3] *Hislop* v. *Hislop*, [1950] W.N. 124, C.A.

[4] [1964] Ch. 175; [1963] 3 All E.R. 433, C.A. Would the court have arrived at the same decision if, say, after the husband's death the question had arisen whether the goods belonged to the wife or to his personal representatives? See also *Bashall* v. *Bashall*, (*supra*); *Valier* v. *Wright & Bull, Ltd.* (1917), 33 T.L.R. 366.

[5] A similar difficulty would arise if one spouse pledged goods with the other. A mortgage would not create this problem, but it would have to comply with the Bills of Sales Acts: see Thornely, *loc. cit.*, 373-374.

[6] [1922] 1 K.B. 236, C.A.

[7] This assumes, of course, that the delivery can be proved.

husband's business premises of which the wife is never in apparent possession at all.[1] Secondly, a bill of sale will be void against the transferor's creditors with respect to goods in his possession or apparent possession seven days after the bill is executed, unless the bill is registered or the transferee obtains possession of the goods before the transferor becomes bankrupt or assigns his property for the benefit of his creditors generally or before an execution creditor levies execution.[2] A bill of sale is defined to include a number of documents by which property is transferred in goods capable of transfer by delivery.[3] But with respect to furniture and other goods used by both spouses in the matrimonial home and transferred by one of them to the other, *French* v. *Gething* has made the provisions of the Bills of Sale Act as inapplicable as those of section 10 of the Married Women's Property Act, since the goods will be in the actual possession of the transferee and not in the apparent possession of the transferor.[4]

Improvements to Property.—If one spouse makes a substantial contribution to the improvement of any property in which the other has a beneficial interest, he (or she) is to be regarded as having thereby acquired an interest or a greater interest, as the case may be, in the property in question.[5] This provision is of particular importance in relation to the matrimonial home and will be considered in detail later.[6]

Voidable Transactions.—It is easy to see how transactions between husband and wife might be used as a means of defrauding creditors. To a man who is on the verge of bankruptcy or who is about to engage in a hazardous business operation there is a great temptation to settle the bulk of his property on trust for his wife and children and thus keep it out of the hands of his creditors and at the same time ensure that his family will be provided for. In a number of statutory provisions Parliament has sought to protect the creditors of the rogue who incidentally benefits his family whilst not prejudicing the members of the family of a man who settles property in good faith and then runs into financial difficulties.

Section 172 *of the Law of Property Act* 1925.—This section[7] enacts that every conveyance[8] of property made with intent to defraud creditors shall be voidable at the instance of anyone thereby prejudiced. But this does not apply

---

[1] BANKES, L.J., suggested in *French* v. *Gething*, at p. 244, that the operation of the Act might be limited to cases where the spouses were living on premises where the husband was carrying on business.

[2] Bills of Sale Act 1878, s. 8.

[3] *Ibid.*, s. 4, *q.v.*

[4] For the Act to apply the goods must in effect remain in the transferor's sole possession or apparent sole possession or be in premises solely occupied by him or be solely used or enjoyed by him: *Koppel* v. *Koppel*, [1966] 2 All E.R. 187, C.A. See also *Ramsay* v. *Margrett*, (*ante*), and contrast *Hislop* v. *Hislop*, (*ante*). But the Act would apply in the case of a sale of goods if the property was not to pass immediately and the buyer's title depended on a written contract: Thornely, *loc. cit.*, 371.

[5] Matrimonial Proceedings and Property Act 1970, s. 37.

[6] See *post*, p. 453.

[7] Replacing (with amendments) 13 Eliz. 1, c. 5.

[8] This includes any assurance of property or any interest in property by any instrument except a will: Law of Property Act 1925, s. 205 (1) (ii).

to disentailing assurances (which are therefore valid even though executed to defraud creditors) or any conveyance made in good faith for valuable or good consideration to any person not having notice of the intent to defraud at the time of the conveyance.[1]

The purpose of this section is to avoid transactions made by the debtor with the intent of depriving his creditors of timely recourse against property which would otherwise be applicable for their benefit.[2] This could take the form of disposing of property which would otherwise be available to satisfy a judgment debt or of dealing with property that has been charged in such a way as to deprive the creditor of the value of his security. There must be an intent to defraud, which implies some element of dishonesty or sharp practice.[3] The intent may be inferred from the circumstances in which the disposition was made, for example from the fact that the consideration given for the transfer is appreciably less than the value of the property, from the settlor's being about to engage in a hazardous business undertaking[4] or from the fact that this would be the natural and probable consequence of the transaction;[5] but it is a question of fact to be determined in each case and the inference may be rebutted by other evidence.[6]

The conveyance may be set aside by any person prejudiced by it. He must have an enforceable debt at the time when he seeks to have it rescinded;[7] normally he will also have to have been a creditor when it was made, but it has been held that, if the conveyance is made to defraud possible future creditors, it may be set aside by them even though they had no claim against the settlor at the time it was executed.[8] Since the transaction is voidable and not void, it may not be set aside as against a *bona fide* purchaser for value from the original transferee, provided that the purchaser himself had no notice of the intent to defraud.[9]

Section 42 of the Bankruptcy Act 1914.—The provisions of this section are designed to give even wider protection to a settlor's creditors. No intent to defraud them need be proved, but whereas any creditor prejudiced may have a settlement set aside under section 172 of the Law of Property Act,

---

[1] Presumably constructive notice will deprive the transferee of protection: *Lloyds Bank, Ltd.* v. *Marcan*, [1973] 2 All E.R. 359, 369. It is not clear whether it is sufficient if he takes in good faith or whether the transferor must act in good faith: *ibid.*, p. 369. In accordance with the general principle that a *bona fide* purchaser will be protected if the transaction is voidable, the former interpretation is to be preferred; the latter would also make redundant the requirement that the transferor must have a fraudulent intent, because he could not act in good faith if he had one. But see Langstaff, *The Cheat's Charter?*, 91 L.Q.R. 86; Elkan, *ibid.*, 317.

[2] *Lloyds Bank, Ltd.* v. *Marcan*, (*supra*), at p. 367.

[3] *Lloyds Bank, Ltd.* v. *Marcan*, [1973] 2 All E.R. 359, 367; affirmed, [1973] 3 All E.R. 754, C.A. A husband sought to deprive the plaintiffs of the right to take vacant possession of land mortgaged to them by leasing it to his wife: the lease was set aside.

[4] *Mackay* v. *Douglas* (1872), L.R. 14 Eq. 106; *Re Butterworth; ex parte Russell* (1882), 19 Ch.D. 588, C.A.

[5] *Freeman* v. *Pope* (1870), 5 Ch. App. 538.

[6] *Re Wise; ex parte Mercer* (1886), 17 Q.B.D. 290, C.A.

[7] *Re Maddever* (1884), 27 Ch.D. 523, C.A., in which it was held that a specialty creditor could set the conveyance aside ten years after it had been executed and that the doctrine of laches has no application to actions brought under s. 172. But see *Cadogan* v. *Cadogan*, [1977] 3 All E.R. 831, C.A., where it was stated that the category of person who might apply might be wider.

[8] *Mackay* v. *Douglas*, (*supra*).

[9] *Harrods, Ltd.* v. *Stanton*, [1923] 1 K.B. 516.

section 42 of the Bankruptcy Act applies only if the settlor has been adjudicated bankrupt.

Under sub-section (1) a settlement of property is voidable by the settlor's, trustee in bankruptcy for a period of ten years after the date of the settlement. The two most important transactions excluded from the operation of this sub-section are settlements made before and in consideration of marriage[1] and settlements made in good faith and for valuable consideration;[2] on the other hand, the fact that a settlement or transfer of property was made in order to comply with an order for financial provision on divorce, nullity or judicial separation made under section 24 of the Matrimonial Causes Act 1973 will not prevent it from being a voidable settlement for this purpose.[3]

The term "settlement" for the purpose of this sub-section includes any conveyance or transfer of property.[4] Hence the husband's trustee in bankruptcy can recover jewellery which the husband has given to his wife as a present[5] and shares which he has settled for her benefit.[6] But the settlor must intend the property to be preserved and consequently a gift of money to be spent at the time is not a settlement for this purpose.[7] The sub-section "is clearly framed to prevent properties from being put into the hands of relatives to the disadvantage of creditors"[8] and the courts will pay more attention to the substance of a transaction than to its form. The purchaser must provide a *quid pro quo* in the commercial sense,[9] and consequently if a husband transfers to his wife the equity of redemption in the matrimonial home, the mere fact that she assumes liability to repay the mortgage does not make her a purchaser for value if the equity is of value.[10]

Any transaction which is a settlement for the purpose of section 42 (1) can always be set aside by the trustee in bankruptcy if the settlor becomes bankrupt within a period of two years after its execution. If it was made more than two years but less than ten years before the bankruptcy, the Act strikes a compromise between the competing claims of the beneficiaries and the creditors by providing that the settlement cannot be avoided if the beneficiaries can prove that at the time of making it the settlor was able to pay all his debts without the aid of the property settled and that his interest passed to the trustees of the settlement or to the beneficiaries at the time of its execution.[11] In neither case, however, can the trustee recover property which has come

---

[1] *I.e.*, made with a view to encouraging or facilitating the marriage and conditioned to take effect only on its celebration: *Re Densham*, [1975] 3 All E.R. 726, 734.

[2] Any settlement made on or for the settlor's wife or children of property which has accrued to the settlor after marriage in right of his wife is also excluded, but this is now of little practical importance.

[3] Matrimonial Causes Act 1973, s. 39.

[4] Bankruptcy Act 1914, s. 42 (4).

[5] *Re Vansittart; ex parte Brown*, [1893] 1 Q.B. 181.

[6] *Re Ashcroft; ex parte Todd* (1887), 19 Q.B.D. 186, C.A.

[7] *Re Player; ex parte Harvey* (1885), 15 Q.B.D. 682.

[8] *Per* STAMP, J., in *Re A Debtor*, [1965] 3 All E.R. 453, 457.

[9] *Re Windle*, [1975] 3 All E.R. 987, 994; *Re Densham*, (*supra*).

[10] *Re Windle*, (*supra*); *Re A Debtor*, (*supra*).

[11] Bankruptcy Act 1914, s. 42 (1); *Re Lowndes; ex parte Trustee* (1887), 18 Q.B.D. 677. The bankruptcy relates back and is deemed to commence on the commission of the act of bankruptcy on which the receiving order was made or on the commission of any earlier act of bankruptcy occurring not more than three months before the bankruptcy petition was presented: Bankruptcy Act 1914, s. 37 (1).

into the hands of a *bona fide* purchaser for value without notice of an act of bankruptcy on the part of the settlor, for until the trustee actually has the transfer set aside the beneficiaries have a voidable title which will be cured by the subsequent sale.[1]

Ante-nuptial settlements and settlements executed in pursuance of an ante-nuptial agreement are dealt with in sub-sections (2) and (3). These apply to

> "any covenant or contract made by [the settlor] in consideration of his or her marriage, either for the future payment of money for the benefit of the settlor's wife or husband, or children, or for the future settlement on or for the settlor's wife or husband or children, of property, wherein the settlor had not at the date of the marriage any estate or interest, whether vested or contingent, in possession or remainder,[2] and not being money or property in right of the settlor's wife or husband."

Two situations must be considered. First, if the covenant has not been executed by the payment of the money or the transfer of the property at the date of the commencement of the bankruptcy, it may be avoided by the trustee in bankruptcy and the sole remedy of the beneficiaries entitled under the covenant or contract is to claim in the settlor's bankruptcy. In that case, however, they will be entitled to nothing until all other creditors for valuable consideration in money or money's worth have been paid in full. Secondly, once the covenant or contract has been executed, any payment of money (other than the payment of premiums on a policy of life assurance) or transfer of property made in pursuance of it may be avoided by the trustee in bankruptcy. The payee or transferee may prove for the sum or value of the property which he has lost but again he will be postponed to all creditors for valuable consideration in money or money's worth. But the trustee's power to avoid an executed payment or transfer is limited in two important respects. First, he will lose his right altogether if the payee or transferee can prove:

> "(a) that the payment or transfer was made more than two years before the date of the commencement of the bankruptcy; *or*
> (b) that at the date of the payment or transfer the settlor was able to pay all his debts without the aid of the money so paid or the property so transferred; *or*
> (c) that the payment or transfer was made in pursuance of a covenant or contract to pay or transfer money or property expected to come to the settlor from or on the death of a particular person named in the covenant or contract and was made within three months after the money or property came into the possession or under the control of the settlor."

It will be seen that this protects the beneficiaries whose interests cannot be upset at an indefinite time after their interest vested and who will take their benefit in full if the settlor was not insolvent at the time of the payment or transfer; it also protects a third person providing money or property to be settled, as this cannot be touched by the creditors provided that the conditions in (c) above are satisfied. Secondly, as under sub-section (1), the trustee may not recover property which has come into the hands of a *bona*

---

[1] *Re Hart; ex parte Green*, [1912] 3 K.B. 6, C.A. (notwithstanding that the Act states that the transaction shall be *void* against the trustee in bankruptcy).

[2] The clause "wherein the settlor . . . in possession or remainder" governs only "property" and not "money": *Re Cumming and West*, [1929] 1 Ch. 534. "Property" in s. 42 does not include property over which the settlor merely has a power of appointment: *Re Mathieson*, [1927] 1 Ch. 283, C.A.

fide purchaser for value without notice of an act of bankruptcy on the part of the settlor.

Money lent by one Spouse to the Other.—A loan by one spouse to the other usually raises no presumption of a gift by way of advancement, so that the lender will be able to recover the sum lent in the absence of evidence that a gift was intended.[1] This same principle has been applied to other transactions of a similar nature, for example the guarantee of the other's credit[2] and the fulfilling of the other's legal obligations;[3] in each case the spouse making the payment is *prima facie* entitled to recover it from the other.

But if one spouse becomes bankrupt, the other is a deferred creditor in respect of any money or other estate lent or entrusted to the bankrupt *for the purpose of his or her trade or business* and may not claim for such loans until all other creditors for valuable consideration have been paid in full,[4] which in practice will mean that trade loans of this sort will rarely be repaid if the borrower becomes bankrupt. But the section has been strictly construed. Thus it has been held that a wife who has lent money to a firm in which her husband is a partner may prove against the joint estate as an ordinary creditor[5] and that a wife, who has given security to a bank for advances to her husband for the purpose of his trade and then redeemed her security by paying off the loan, is subrogated to the rights of the lender and may therefore prove in her husband's bankruptcy on the same footing as other creditors.[6] Similarly if the original loan is discharged and replaced by an obligation of a different kind, this is not a loan for the purpose of trade or business and is therefore not caught by the section.[7]

4. CONTRACTS OF INSURANCE

Insurable Interests.—Because of the relationship of husband and wife and their mutual rights and duties, each has an insurable interest in the life of the

---

[1] *Hall* v. *Hall*, [1911] 1 Ch. 487 (mortgage of the wife's property to secure a loan to the husband). Contrast *Paget* v. *Paget*, [1898] 1 Ch. 470, C.A., where the facts indicated that a gift was intended. See further George, *Disputes over the Matrimonial Home*, 16 Conv. 27, 31-33.

[2] *Re Salisbury-Jones*, [1938] 3 All E.R. 459; *Anson* v. *Anson*, [1953] 1 Q.B. 636; [1953] 1 All E.R. 867.

[3] *Outram* v. *Hyde* (1875), 24 W.R. 268 (husband's discharging incumbrance on wife's realty); *Re McKerrell*, [1912] 2 Ch. 648 (wife's paying money due from husband on insurance policy). But if the husband purchases realty in the wife's name (thus raising a presumption of advancement) and raises the purchase money by a mortgage, sums paid on the mortgage will likewise be construed as a gift: *Moate* v. *Moate*, [1948] 2 All E.R. 486; *cf. Silver* v. *Silver*, [1958] 1 All E.R. 523, C.A.

[4] Bankruptcy Act 1914, s. 36 (replacing and extending the Married Women's Property Act 1882, s. 3); *Re Clark*, [1898] 2 Q.B. 330, C.A. Consequently the lender cannot exercise a right of retainer in respect of such a debt as personal representative of the borrower: *Re Patten*, [1936] Ch. 735; [1936] 2 All E.R. 1119. But *quaere* whether *all* such lenders are not in the same position: *Re Meade*, [1951] Ch. 774; [1951] 2 All E.R. 168.

[5] *Re Tuff* (1887), 19 Q.B.D. 88.

[6] *Re Cronmire*, [1901] 1 Q.B. 480, C.A.

[7] *Re Slade*, [1921] 1 Ch. 160, where the original loan was replaced by a bond to pay the lender £40 *per annum* for life and it was held that the wife *as annuitant* could prove in competition with other creditors. But the conversion of the original debt into a judgment debt does not substantially change its character and the creditor is therefore still deferred: *Re Lupkovics*, [1954] 2 All E.R. 125.

other. This means that if, say, a husband insures his wife's life up to any amount, he may recover the sum due on her death without proving any financial loss at all.[1] Each may also apparently insure any of the other's property which forms a part of the matrimonial home, as the use which he or she enjoys is sufficient to create an insurable interest.[2]

Life Assurance Policies in favour of the Spouse or Children of the Assured.—By section 11 of the Married Women's Property Act 1882, if either spouse effects a policy of assurance on his or her own life[3] expressed to be for the benefit of the assured's spouse or any or all of his or her own children[4] (or for the benefit of both the spouse and children), this creates a trust in favour of those persons. This has two important results. First, in the absence of privity of contract between the objects and the insurance company, the former would not normally be able to sue on the policy.[5] Secondly, the objects as beneficiaries under a trust are entitled to the whole of the sum assured notwithstanding the bankruptcy of the assured or the insolvency of his estate. In only one case will his or her creditors have any claim on the policy, for the Act specifically provides that if the policy was effected to defraud them, they shall be entitled to receive out of the money payable under the policy a sum equal to the premiums so paid.[6]

If the policy is taken out in favour of a *named* spouse or children, they take an immediate vested interest in equity. Thus in *Cousins* v. *Sun Life Assurance Society*,[7] where the policy was issued for the benefit of Lilian Cousins, the assured's wife, who predeceased the life assured, it was held that the husband held the policy on trust for her personal representatives. But where the beneficiaries are merely designated as the husband, wife or children of the assured without being specifically named, this is construed as referring to those who fall into this category at the moment when the trust falls in, *i.e.*, at the assured's death, and before that time the spouse and existing children have only a contingent interest dependent upon their surviving the assured. In *Re Browne's Policy*[8] H, who was then married to W, took out a policy on his own life for the benefit of his wife and children. W predeceased H, who then

---

[1] *Reed* v. *Royal Exchange Assurance Co.* (1795), Peake, Add. Cas. 70.; *Griffiths* v. *Fleming*, [1909] 1 K.B. 805, C.A.; Married Women's Property Act 1882, s. 11. Otherwise the policy would be void under the Life Assurance Act 1774. For joint policies taken out on both lives to be paid to the survivor on the death of either, see *Griffiths* v. *Fleming*.

[2] *Goulstone* v. *Royal Insurance Co.* (1858), 1 F. & F. 276.

[3] This includes a policy providing for payment on death or disablement as the result of an accident provided that the sum is in fact paid on death (*Re Gladitz*, [1937] 3 All E.R. 173) and an endowment policy payable on the earlier death of the assured (*Re Ioakimidis' Policy Trusts*, [1925] Ch. 403).

[4] This includes adopted children and, in the case of policies effected after 1969, illegitimate children: Children Act 1975, Sched. 1, para. 3 (prospectively repealed and re-enacted in the Adoption Act 1976, s. 39 (1)); Family Law Reform Act 1969, s. 19 (1), (3).

[5] *Cleaver* v. *Mutual Reserve Fund Life Association*, [1892] 1 Q.B. 147, at pp. 152, 157, 160, C.A.

[6] S. 11. This is particularly important in the case of a single premium policy.

[7] [1933] Ch. 126, C.A. See also *Re Smith's Estate*, [1937] Ch. 636; [1937] 3 All E.R. 472. If there are more beneficiaries than one, they take a joint interest: *Re Seyton* (1887), 34 Ch.D. 511. But the interest may of course be made expressly conditional upon the beneficiary's surviving the assured, in which case the former will have only a contingent interest during the assured's life: *Re Fleetwood's Policy*, [1926] Ch. 48.

[8] [1903] 1 Ch. 188. See also *Re Parker's Policies*, [1906] 1 Ch. 526; *Re Seyton*, (*supra*).

married X. H was survived by X, five children of his first marriage and one child of his second. It was held that X and the six surviving children took a joint interest in the insurance money. If all the objects fail, there will be a resulting trust in favour of the assured's estate.[1]

Unless other trustees are appointed, the assured holds the policy as trustee, and as such must exercise options and otherwise deal with it in the way most favourable to the beneficiaries.[2] Similarly, after the death of a named object with a vested interest, the assured is presumed to continue to pay premiums to preserve the property for those entitled to the deceased beneficiary's estate and consequently may recover premiums paid after the death from the deceased's personal representatives.[3]

5. INCOME TAX

Husband's Liability to pay Wife's Tax.—If the spouses are living together and have not elected to be separately taxed, the wife's income is deemed to be that of her husband for the purpose of tax and he is therefore assessed in respect of it.[4] For this purpose they are regarded as living together unless they are separated under a court order or a deed of separation or are in fact separated in such circumstances that the separation is likely to be permanent.[5]

A married man's personal relief is greater than that of a single person but is less than twice that sum; on the other hand if the wife has an earned income, additional personal relief is given.[6] Consequently the spouses' tax position under aggregation will be better than it would be under separate taxation if the wife has no income at all or only a small income (particularly if it is earned): the details will obviously change with every change in rates of tax and allowances. The larger the wife's income, the worse their position will become, for their combined income may come into a higher band than either would if taken separately.

The husband is also liable to pay the whole of the tax on their combined incomes unless separate assessment has been claimed. Should he fail to do so, however, the wife is bound to pay the tax on her own income as though a separate assessment had been made.[7] These rules not only produce the result that it may be "cheaper to live in sin than to marry" (which is scarcely socially desirable) but also give considerable advantages to the Crown which seem to rest on suppositions about the husband's right to the wife's income which

---

[1] *Re Collier*, [1930] 2 Ch. 37. *Cf. Cleaver* v. *Mutual Reserve Fund Life Association*, (*supra*).
[2] *Re Equitable Life Assurance Society of the United States* (1911), 27 T.L.R. 213.
[3] *Re Smith's Estate*, (*supra*). For a fuller discussion of the operation of the section and criticisms of the existing law, see Finlay, *"Family" Life Insurance Problems*, 2 M.L.R. 266.
[4] Income and Corporation Taxes Act 1970, s. 37. For exceptions, see *ibid.*, ss. 226 (8) and 414 (1). But this gives the husband no interest in the wife's income: *Murphy* v. *Ingram*, [1974] Ch. 363; [1974] 2 All E.R. 187, C.A. Consequently he must pay over to her any repayment of tax arising from her financial affairs: *Re Cameron*, [1967] Ch. 1; [1965] 3 All E.R. 474. For the circumstances in which repayment is made to the wife herself, see the Finance Act 1978, s. 22.
[5] Income and Corporation Taxes Act 1970, s. 42 (1). If one spouse is resident in the U.K. and the other is not or is absent, they are also regarded as separated but this will not increase the total amount of tax payable: *ibid.*, s. 42 (2).
[6] *Ibid.*, s. 8.
[7] *Ibid.*, s. 40. For separate assessment, see *infra*.

have not been true since the passing of the Married Women's Property Act of 1870.

Aggregation does not begin until 6th April following the marriage. During the financial year in which the parties marry they are assessed and taxed separately. The husband is entitled to a personal allowance as a married man for that part of the year during which he was married.[1] His wife is assessable as though she were unmarried and she may claim a full year's allowances as a single person.[2]

Separate Assessment.—Either spouse may claim to be separately assessed for income tax. Separate assessment makes no difference to the total amount of tax which the spouses together have to pay but this sum is apportioned between them according to their respective incomes, reliefs and allowances and the wife is solely legally liable for the payment of her own part to the exclusion of her husband.[3]

Separate Taxation of Wife's Earnings.—A fundamental modification of the basic principle underlying the taxation of spouses' income was introduced in the Finance Act of 1971, which has partly reduced the disadvantageous consequences of aggregation. Now, if a husband and wife are living together and they jointly so elect, the wife's earned income may be separately taxed. Unlike separate assessment, this will affect the total amount of tax payable. Each will be entitled to the personal relief to which he or she would have been entitled as a single person, but certain other reliefs will be lost and any loss sustained in the wife's trade cannot be deducted from the income on which the husband is taxed and *vice versa*. In certain circumstances, therefore, spouses will still be better off under aggregation. It must be emphasised that this applies only to the wife's *earned* income: the husband remains liable to be taxed on his wife's unearned income.[4]

Effect of Death, Separation, Divorce and Nullity.[5]—If the spouses are living together and the wife dies, the husband remains liable to pay tax in respect of her income up to the date of her death and may claim a full year's allowances as a married man. If the husband dies, his personal representatives are liable to pay tax on both spouses' incomes up to the date of the death and may claim a full year's allowances as for a married man; the widow is liable to pay tax on that part of her own income which has accrued since the death but may claim a full year's allowances as a single woman.[6]

---

[1] Income and Corporation Taxes Act 1970, s. 8 (3), as amended by the Finance Act 1970, s. 14 (1) (a) (iv). If the marriage takes place on 6th April, aggregation begins at once.

[2] Finance Act 1976, s. 36. But the husband cannot claim the wife's earned income relief.

[3] Income and Corporation Taxes Act 1970, ss. 38 and 39.

[4] Finance Act 1971, s. 23 and Sched. 4. See Lowe, *Family Taxation*, 116 Sol. Jo 343.

[5] See Adams, *Taxation Problems arising on Marriage Breakdown*, Current Legal Problems 1974, 122.

[6] See *Palmer* v. *Cattermole*, [1937] 2 K.B. 581; [1937] 2 All E.R. 667. The widow is also entitled to a widow's bereavement allowance: Finance Act 1980, s. 23. For the power of a widower to disclaim liability for his deceased's wife's tax, see the Income and Corporation Taxes Act 1970, s. 41.

If the spouses separate in the sense in which this word is used in the Income and Corporation Taxes Act,[1] they are thereafter treated as single persons for income tax purposes. They are assessed separately, given the allowances and reliefs appropriate to single persons and are liable for the payment of tax in respect of their own incomes only.[2] For the financial year in which they separate the husband is liable to pay tax on both incomes up to the date of separation and may claim a full year's allowances as a married man; the wife is liable for the payment of tax on her own income after that date but may claim a full year's allowances as a single person. Divorce and nullity will normally be preceded by a separation for the purposes of the Act; if they are not, however, exactly the same principles apply if the marriage is dissolved or a voidable marriage is annulled as apply in the case of separation. If the marriage is void, the spouses are of course treated as single persons throughout.

If after separation the husband pays maintenance to his wife or former wife in pursuance of an agreement imposing a legal obligation, he is entitled to deduct income tax at the basic rate before payment and then to pay her only the balance.[3] If the wife is not liable to tax or is entitled to reliefs not already given, she may then claim a refund of the whole or part of the tax already paid. Conversely, it must be borne in mind that the payments, grossed up at the basic rate, form part of her total income and consequently may make her liable to pay tax at a higher rate if her income is large enough.[4] Likewise, if the husband pays the wife maintenance for the children (whether by agreement or under a court order), this becomes her income and will be taxed accordingly unless the agreement constitutes her a trustee for the children.[5]

C. THE MATRIMONIAL HOME

We have already seen that the main problem that still has to be solved in English matrimonial property law is the adaptation to modern conditions of the doctrine of separate estate introduced by the Married Women's Property Act of 1882. It is when the property in question constitutes a "family asset"—that is to say the matrimonial home and its contents—that the problem becomes most acute, for the spouses do not regard the house and furniture as belonging to either of them exclusively but, at least in a loose sense, to both of them together. There are of course two distinct problems— that of ownership and title and that of occupation and use. The first is

---

[1] See *supra*.

[2] Since they do not come within the provisions of the Income and Corporation Taxes Act 1970, s. 37. But a husband will still be entitled to a married man's allowance if he is wholly maintaining his wife by voluntary contributions: *ibid.*, s. 8 (1) (a) (ii).

[3] Income and Corporation Taxes Act 1970, ss. 52 and 53. Thus if the husband is paying tax at the basic rate of 30% and covenants to pay the wife £1,000 a year, he will first deduct £300 and pay her the balance of £700. He is not liable to higher or additional rate tax on the amount paid.

[4] But maintenance payments are not investment income so as to attract additional rates: Finance Act 1974, s. 15, as amended by the Finance Act 1978, s. 21.

[5] This will rarely be the case unless the wife is expressly made a trustee. If there is a trust and the husband is the father of the children and they are unmarried and under 18, the income is deemed still to be his: *ibid.*, s. 437, as amended by the Finance Act 1971, s. 16; Lowe, *loc. cit.* For the position with regard to maintenance *orders* , see *post*, p. 530.

concerned with the question, in whom are the legal and equitable interests in the property vested? The second is concerned with the question, what rights of occupation and use does one spouse have in property beneficially owned by the other? They will be considered in that order.

An engaged couple may well begin to buy furniture and purchase their proposed matrimonial home before they marry and in this respect their position may be little different from that of a newly married couple. Consequently, if an agreement to marry is terminated, the principles relating to the rights of husbands and wives to property have now been extended by statute to property in which either or both of the parties to the agreement had a beneficial interest whilst the agreement was in force.[1]

1. OWNERSHIP

Earlier cases followed the general rule that property purchased by one spouse with his or her own money presumptively belonged to that spouse to the exclusion of the other. Hence if the house was bought out of the husband's earnings (which would usually be the case) the whole beneficial interest vested in him;[2] if he had it conveyed into his wife's name, the presumption of advancement operated to give the whole interest to her.[3] This rule will still obviously apply to property purchased before the parties became engaged; if, for example, the spouses set up home in a house already owned by the husband, the wife will acquire no interest in it in the absence of any express agreement.[4]

In recent years, however, the whole position has had to be re-examined. The wife is now frequently a wage earner making a contribution to the common expenses of buying and running the home and justice demands that, even though property is purchased in the husband's name, she should be given some credit for her help. The position has been further complicated by the steady increase in the value of most houses during the past 25 years. Suppose, for example, that a house was bought in 1960 for £4,000, to which the wife contributed £1,000, and that it has recently been sold for £20,000. Assuming that her contribution gives the wife some interest in the property, it is vital to determine whether she can merely recover her £1,000, or a quarter of the present value (which will give her £5,000), or some other fraction of the price at which it was sold. A further difficulty has arisen because some judges (notably LORD DENNING) have been prepared to go much further than others in giving credit to the wife for her services in kind as a housekeeper or for the use of her own income or savings in such a way as to enable her husband to use his for the purchase of a house, and this in turn led to a tendency to divide the proceeds of sale equally between the spouses whenever it could be said

---

[1] Law Reform (Miscellaneous Provisions) Act 1970, s. 2 (1). See further *ante*, pp. 18-19.

[2] *Re Sims' Question*, [1946] 2 All E.R. 138. Consequently rent received from a lodger was held to belong exclusively to the husband: *Montgomery* v. *Blows*, [1916] 1 K.B. 899, C.A.

[3] *Moate* v. *Moate*, [1948] 2 All E.R. 486; George, *Disputes over the Matrimonial Home*, 16 Conv. 27.

[4] *Cf. Kowalczuk* v. *Kowalczuk*, [1973] 2 All E.R. 1042, C.A. A legal estate would have to be conveyed by deed and an equitable interest in writing: Law of Property Act 1925, ss. 52 (1), 53 (1) (c). Any contract or declaration of trust would have to be evidenced in writing: *ibid.*, ss. 40, 53 (1) (b).

that they both contributed to its purchase. Some principles have now been settled by the decisions of the House of Lords in *Pettitt* v. *Pettitt*[1] and *Gissing* v. *Gissing*,[2] but many problems still remain unsolved and some later cases appear irreconcilable not only with the majority views expressed in the House of Lords but also with one another. The extent to which the judges can adapt legal rules to meet changed social and economic circumstances is necessarily limited and the difficulties will remain until the position is changed by statute.[3]

Nevertheless two fundamental rules can be stated immediately. It is clear from *Pettitt* v. *Pettitt* that English law knows of no community of property nor of any special rules of law applicable to family assets.[4] Consequently if one spouse buys property for their common use—whether it is a house, furniture or a car—this cannot *per se* give the other any proprietary interest. From this it must follow, as was stated in *Gissing* v. *Gissing*,[5] that if one spouse seeks to establish a beneficial interest in property, the legal title to which is vested in the other, he or she can do so only by proving that the legal owner holds the property on trust for the claimant. If it becomes necessary to determine the spouses' interests on the breakdown of the marriage, the courts are faced with a problem which is logically insoluble, for the ownership of property depends upon the purchaser's intention at the time it is bought and spouses buying a house and furniture will rarely contemplate the termination of the marriage except by death. Hence in many cases the court is bound to attribute to them an intention that they clearly never had. As in other branches of English law where a person's intention is of vital importance, in the absence of direct evidence the court must infer what it was from his conduct at the time. As the majority of the House of Lords held in *Pettitt* v. *Pettitt*,[6] if the spouses did not apply their minds at all to the question of how the beneficial interest in a particular piece of property should be held when it was bought, the court cannot give effect to an agreement which they never entered into even though it is satisfied that they would have made it had they thought about it. In other words, it can impute to them an intention which they probably never had but it cannot impute to them an agreement which they clearly did not make. This nicety reflects ingrained principles of English law, but its application here is unfortunate because the opposite rule would have been much more likely to work justice. The court's function was thus summed up by EVERSHED, M.R., in *Re Rogers' Question*:[7]

---

[1] [1970] A.C. 777; [1969] 2 All E.R. 385, H.L.

[2] [1971] A.C. 886; [1970] 2 All E.R. 780, H.L.

[3] For the recommendations of the Law Commission, see *ante*, pp. 419-420. See further Miller, *Family Assets*, 86 L.Q.R. 98 (written after *Pettitt* v. *Pettitt* but before *Gissing* v. *Gissing*); Lesser, *The Acquisition of Inter Vivos Matrimonial Property Rights in English Law*, 23 U. of Toronto L.J. 148; Zuckerman, *Ownership of the Matrimonial Home*, 94 L.Q.R. 26; Tiley, [1969] C.L.J. 191 and [1970] C.L.J. 210; Jones, [1969] C.L.J. 196; Earnshaw, 122 New L.J. 146.

[4] At pp. 800-801 and 395 (*per* LORD MORRIS), 810 and 403 (*per* LORD HODSON), and 817 and 409 (*per* LORD UPJOHN).

[5] At pp. 896 and 782 (*per* LORD REID), 900 and 785 (*per* LORD DILHORNE), and 904-905 and 789 (*per* LORD DIPLOCK).

[6] At pp. 804 and 398 (*per* LORD MORRIS), 810 and 403 (*per* LORD HODSON), and 816 and 408 (*per* LORD UPJOHN).

[7] [1948] 1 All E.R. 328, C.A.

"What the judge must try to do ... is ... to conclude what at the time was in the parties' minds and then to make an order which, in the changed conditions, now fairly gives effect in law to what the parties, in the judge's finding, must be taken to have intended at the time of the transaction itself."

One must start with the conveyance and *prima facie* give effect to its wording. As the Court of Appeal held in *Leake* v. *Bruzzi*,[1] if this expressly declares in whom not only the legal title but also the beneficial interests are to vest, it will be conclusive in the absence of fraud or mistake. Hence, if as is common, the matrimonial home is conveyed to both spouses on express trust for sale for themselves as joint tenants in equity, it will be very exceptional for either to be able to claim that this gives each anything other than a joint interest in the proceeds of sale or, on severance, an equal half share. If the beneficial interests are not declared, *prima facie* they will follow the legal title; consequently a conveyance to both spouses jointly at law will presumptively give them a joint interest in equity, and a conveyance to the husband alone on the face of it gives the wife no interest at all. But provided at any rate that the equitable interests are not spelled out, this presumption can be rebutted by showing that the spouses had a different common intention, and if this indicates, for example, that when the husband purchased the house in his own name, they intended to take a joint interest, he will hold the legal estate on trust for them both jointly in equity. The problem is therefore: what evidence will suffice to show a contrary intention?

The basic equitable principles were extensively reviewed by BAGNALL, J., in *Cowcher* v. *Cowcher*.[2] Clearly proof of an express agreement may be relied on to determine their interests—indeed this is the best possible evidence of their common intention[3]—but, as BAGNALL, J., pointed out, it is essential in this connection to distinguish between agreements producing express trusts and those producing resulting or constructive trusts. An express trust is intentionally created by the settlor and in the case of land must either be evidenced in writing[4] or be constituted by a contract of which equity will grant specific performance. A resulting trust, as we have already seen, can arise if property is conveyed to one party but another has provided the whole or part of the consideration, and it does not need to be evidenced in writing. If the parties agree the interest that each is to take irrespective of their contributions, this will create an express trust. Hence if the agreement refers to the matrimonial home (and therefore amounts to a declaration of trust respecting an interest in land), the wife can claim nothing if it is not evidenced in writing and she has provided no consideration because, as a volunteer, she cannot obtain specific performance. If, however, she provides consideration, equity will not let the husband benefit by going back on the agreement under which he was given the money. Consequently, as in *Re Densham*[5], the wife will be able to claim

---

[1] [1974] 2 All E.R. 1196, C.A., following RUSSELL, L.J., in *Wilson* v. *Wilson*, [1963] 2 All E.R. 447, 453, C.A. See also LORD UPJOHN in *Pettitt* v. *Pettitt*, (*supra*), at pp. 813 and 405, respectively; Miller, *Conveyances and Beneficial Interests*, 34 Conv. 156.

[2] [1972] 1 All E.R. 943, approved in *Re Nicholson*, [1974] 2 All E.R. 386, 390. See Levin, 35 M.L.R. 547.

[3] But it must be possible to infer the existence of an agreement from the evidence. The court may not impute to the parties an agreement they never made at all; see *supra*.

[4] Law of Property Act 1925, s. 53 (1) (b).

[5] [1975] 3 All E.R. 726 (use of wife's savings).

the share agreed even though there is no written evidence. Similarly, if the agreement relates solely to the amount that each is to provide towards the price, it will define what they can claim under a resulting trust and will be enforceable even though not evidenced in writing. Again, if the parties agree that property is to be owned jointly but it is conveyed to one (say, the husband) only, he will be a constructive trustee of one half of it for the other if the latter has acted on the agreement to her detriment. Consequently she can enforce the trust, for equity will not permit the statute to be used as an engine of fraud when it would be inequitable to keep the property and repudiate the agreement.[1] There is no doubt that the courts look very liberally on informal agreements made by the parties, as can be seen from the facts of *Re Nicholson*.[2] The spouses bought a house for £900 in 1938. The wife contributed £75 towards the deposit and the husband contributed £15. The house was conveyed into the husband's name and he was responsible for paying almost all the mortgage instalments for the next five years. At the time of the purchase the wife knew that her husband's aunt intended to leave her a substantial legacy and she told her husband that she would pay off the mortgage when she got the money. This she did when the old lady died in 1943. In these circumstances, PENNYCUICK, V.-C., held that, although the agreement was informal and related to a legacy which the wife might never receive, it was sufficient to give her an equal half share in the proceeds of sale of the house.

The more usual way of raising a resulting trust is to show that the party claiming the beneficial interest has made an actual contribution (as distinct from an agreement to contribute) to the purchase of property conveyed in the other's name. In these circumstances the presumptions of advancement and a resulting trust may come into play if there is no other evidence but, as we have already seen,[3] these are of considerably less importance today than they used to be. LORD UPJOHN has said:[4]

"In the absence of all evidence, if a husband puts property into his wife's name he intends it to be a gift to her, but if he puts it into joint names then .... the presumption is the same as a joint beneficial tenancy. If a wife puts property into her husband's name it may be that in the absence of all other evidence he is a trustee for her, but in practice there will in almost every case be some explanation (however slight) of this (today) rather unusual course. If a wife puts property into their joint names I would myself think that a joint beneficial tenancy was intended, for I can see no other reason for it."[5]

In practice, however, the problem is usually the converse of those discussed here, for one party (in most cases the wife) alleges that both have contributed but that the conveyance has been taken in the other's name. In a

---

[1] *Re Densham*, (*supra*). This point was not mentioned by BAGNALL, J., in *Cowcher* v. *Cowcher*, (*supra*). See Webb, 92 L.Q.R. 489.

[2] [1974] 2 All E.R. 386.

[3] *Ante*, p. 429. See also Earnshaw, 121 New L.J. 96, 120.

[4] *Pettitt* v. *Pettitt*, [1970] A.C. 777, 815; [1969] 2 All E.R. 385, 407, H.L. *Cf. Boydell* v. *Gillespie* (1970), 210 Estates Gazette 1505 (conveyance into both names jointly held to give both a beneficial interest even though wife provided whole of purchase money).

[5] But see *Grzeczkowski* v. *Jedynska* (1971), 115 Sol. Jo. 126, where property purchased with the wife's money but conveyed into joint names to satisfy the building society's requirements was held to belong beneficially to the wife alone.

series of cases decided between 1950 and 1969 the Court of Appeal had in effect established the rule that if both spouses had made a contribution to the purchase (whether directly or indirectly), this gave both an interest in the property bought and presumptively they would take equal shares in the proceeds of sale. But this has now been limited by the decisions of the House of Lords in *Pettitt* v. *Pettitt* and, particularly, *Gissing* v. *Gissing*.

There is no doubt that a *direct cash contribution* to the purchase will be regarded as sufficient evidence of the spouses' common intention that the party making it should take a beneficial interest so as to turn the other into a trustee provided, at least, that it is substantial. It may be to the price as a whole (if the house is purchased for cash outright), to the deposit, to mortgage repayments, or even to legal charges. This principle, which had been followed in a number of cases in the Court of Appeal,[1] seems implicit in all the speeches in *Gissing* v. *Gissing* and was spelt out by Lord Dilhorne and Lord Diplock.[2] The position with respect to *indirect contributions* has always been less certain. The problem arises, for example, if both spouses are working and they agree that the easiest way to manage is for the husband to pay the instalments due on the mortgage and for the wife to pay the household bills. Is it then to be said that, because the payment of the price of the house came exclusively from the husband's earnings, he has the sole beneficial interest? It is submitted that such an approach is fundamentally wrong, for the truth of the matter is that both are contributing to the total cost of the home in the way that happens to be most convenient at the time and title to property (which may be of considerable value) ought not to depend on the accident of temporary convenience, particularly when the parties have given no thought to the possible legal consequences of their agreement. This was certainly the view of Denning, L.J., in *Fribance* v. *Fribance*[3] where he said:

> "In the present case it so happened that the wife went out to work and used her earnings to help run the household and buy the children's clothes, whilst the husband saved. It might very well have been the other way round ... The title to the family assets does not depend on the mere chance of which way round it was. It does not depend on how they happened to allocate their earnings and their expenditure. The whole of their resources were expended for their joint benefit ... and the product should belong to them jointly. It belongs to them in equal shares."

After initial hesitation[4] the Court of Appeal followed Lord Denning's lead and held that the wife acquired an interest in the matrimonial home purchased in her husband's name when she augmented the family's income by going out to work,[5] by giving unpaid help in the husband's greengrocery business (and thus saving the wages he would have had to pay to an assistant)[6] and by going into partnership with the husband.[7]

Gissing v. *Gissing* has left the law in an uncertain state. Lord Reid could see no good reason for the distinction between direct and indirect

---

[1] See, *e.g., Rimmer* v. *Rimmer*, [1953] 1 Q.B. 63; [1952] 2 All E.R. 863, C.A. (deposit and mortgage repayments); *Ulrich* v. *Ulrich*, [1968] 1 All E.R. 67, C.A. (deposit and charges).
[2] [1971] A.C. at pp. 900 and 907, respectively; [1970] 2 All E.R. at pp. 786 and 791-792.
[3] [1957] 1 All E.R. 357, 360, C.A.
[4] See *Allen* v. *Allen*, [1961] 3 All E.R. 385, C.A.
[5] *Ulrich* v. *Ulrich*, (*supra*); *Chapman* v. *Chapman*, [1969] 3 All E.R. 476, C.A.
[6] *Nixon* v. *Nixon*, [1969] 3 All E.R. 1133, C.A.
[7] *Muetzel* v. *Muetzel*, [1970] 1 All E.R. 443, C.A.

contributions and thought that in many cases it would be unworkable.[1] On the other hand, LORD DILHORNE said that "proof of expenditure for the benefit of the family by one spouse will not of itself suffice to show any such common intention as to the ownership of the matrimonial home".[2] LORD PEARSON stated:[3]

> "Contributions are not limited to those made directly in part payment of the price of the property or to those made at the time when the property is conveyed into the name of one of the spouses. For instance there can be a contribution if by arrangement between the spouses one of them by payment of the household expenses enables the other to pay the mortgage instalments."

LORD DIPLOCK was more specific. He pointed out that, if the wife had made an initial contribution to the deposit or legal charges which indicated that she was to take some interest in the property, the court should also take account of her contributions to the mortgage instalments, even though these were indirect, because this would be consistent with both spouses' intention that her payment of other household expenses would release the husband's money to pay off the mortgage and would thus be her contribution to the purchase of the home. But, he added, if the wife has made no initial contribution to the purchase, no direct contribution to the repayment of the mortgage, and "no adjustment to her contribution to other expenses of the household which it can be inferred was referable to the acquisition of the house", she cannot claim an interest in it "merely because she continued to contribute out of her own earnings or private income to other expenses of the household".[4]

It will be seen that the majority of the House were of the opinion that a wife can claim an interest in the house as a result of indirect contributions in certain circumstances. It seems that she must show that this was referable to the acquisition of the house in the sense that it freed the husband's own money and thus enabled him to use it to pay the deposit, legal charges or mortgage instalments. An even narrower interpretation may be put on LORD PEARSON'S and LORD DIPLOCK'S words and it may be necessary for the wife to prove an arrangement that she should continue to work or use her own income for this purpose. Unfortunately later decisions of the Court of Appeal lack consistency and make it impossible to see which of the conflicting (and in places imprecise) views expressed by the members of the House of Lords should be followed. In *Falconer* v. *Falconer*[5] LORD DENNING, M.R., was of the opinion that *Gissing* v. *Gissing* enabled the court to draw the inference of a trust whenever both spouses had made a contribution to the price, even though this was indirect, "as where both go out to work, and one pays the housekeeping and the other the mortgage instalments. It does not matter which way round it is. It does not matter who pays what". A year later he reiterated these words in *Hargrave* v. *Newton*[6] but at the same time

---

[1] [1971] A.C. 886, 896; [1970] 2 All E.R. 780, 782, H.L.

[2] At pp. 901 and 786, respectively.

[3] At pp. 903 and 788, respectively.

[4] At pp. 907-910 and 792-793, respectively.

[5] [1970] 3 All E.R. 449, 452, C.A. The other members of the court did not comment on this point. *Cf. Davis* v. *Vale*, [1971] 2 All E.R. 1021, 1025-1026, C.A.; *Peck* v. *Sheridan* (1971), 115 Sol. Jo. 709, C.A.

[6] [1971] 3 All E.R. 866, 869, C.A. The other members of the court agreed with the judgment.

appeared to be modifying his view slightly by speaking of the wife's relieving the husband of other expenses "so that he would not have been able to meet the mortgage instalments or the loan without her help". In the latest case of *Hazell* v. *Hazell*,[1] however, he again took up his original position. He said that he hoped less would be heard of the phrase "referable to the acquisition of the house" in the future and added:

> "It is sufficient if the contributions made by the wife are such as to relieve the husband from expenditure which he would otherwise have had to bear. By so doing the wife helps him indirectly with the mortgage instalments because he has more money in his pocket with which to pay them. It may be that he does not strictly need her help—he may have enough money of his own without it—but, if he accepts it (and thus is enabled to save more of his own money), she becomes entitled to a share."

Similarly, the wife's giving substantial unpaid help in the husband's fruit, vegetable and fish business for 30 years has been held to give her an interest in the property that he bought with the profits.[2] This principle will not apply, however, if the wife was paid for her services as they cannot then be regarded as a contribution to the family finances.[3]

With the authorities in such confusion, it is impossible to state with confidence what the present law is. There is no doubt that, under the leadership of LORD DENNING, the Court of Appeal would allow any substantial indirect contribution to give the wife an interest in the matrimonial home. It is equally clear, however, that this approach is in conflict with the views of the majority of the House of Lords in *Gissing* v. *Gissing* by which, in the end, the Court of Appeal will have to be bound. In most cases the solution preferred by the Court of Appeal will be fairer for the reasons constantly advanced by the Master of the Rolls. On the other hand, once the principle of "referability" is abandoned, the wife ought to be able to claim a share in any property purchased by the husband and the position would become impossible.[4] There can be few fields in which the wish of the Court of Appeal to avoid what it considers to be the undesirable consequences of a decision of the House of Lords has led to such uncertainty in the law.

The authorities are even more difficult to reconcile in those cases where the contributions actually made by the parties differ substantially from those they agreed to make. Suppose, for example, that H buys a house for £8,000 of which W provides £4,000 and H raises the balance on mortgage. W later has a windfall and pays off the last £2,000. BAGNALL, J.'s view in *Cowcher* v. *Cowcher*[5] was that the parties' shares were fixed at the time of the purchase and could be varied only by agreement, which would have to be evidenced in writing. This means that *prima facie* the wife would be entitled to half the proceeds of sale and would be subrogated to the rights of the mortgagor with respect to the further £2,000. Thus she could claim only this sum in addition

---

[1] [1972] 1 All E.R. 923, 926, C.A. The other members of the court again agreed.

[2] *Re Cummins*, [1972] Ch. 62; [1971] 3 All E.R. 782, C.A.

[3] *Simon* v. *Simon* (1971), 115 Sol. Jo. 673, C.A. (wife's paid work in husband's bakery not such as to give her share of house bought out of profits); *Heyland* v. *Heyland* (1972), *Times*, 25th January (wife received salary and husband supported her illegitimate children as a *quid pro quo*).

[4] See Eekelaar, 88 L.Q.R. 333.

[5] [1972] 1 All E.R. 943. See *ante*, p. 444.

and not a further quarter of the proceeds of sale (which might be much greater). This is inconsistent with the decision of the Court of Appeal in *Hargrave* v. *Newton*.[1] The husband bought the matrimonial home for £4,375 with money lent to him by his employers. The wife went out to work to help the family finances and her contribution increased substantially when, two years later, she found a large sum of money stolen by the Great Train Robbers and was given a reward of some £5,000. On these facts the Court of Appeal held that by her indirect contributions she was entitled to half the proceeds of sale of the house. On the other hand, in *Kowalczuk* v. *Kowalczuk*,[2] where the husband had bought the house before the parties ever contemplated marriage, it was held that the wife's indirect contributions to the family budget gave her no interest in it at all. The conclusion is that, if the parties together embark upon the purchase of a house with a common intention *at the time it is bought* that they should both contribute towards discharging the purchase price, this will raise a resulting trust in the wife's favour and the precise size of her interest will depend upon the sums she actually contributes at the time of the purchase or later. The parties can be regarded as having agreed to contribute what they can: a solution much fairer than the narrower principle of equity enunciated by BAGNALL, J.[3]

In any event, the contribution must be a substantial one, and a spouse will not be able to claim any interest in the house by virtue of an insignificant contribution or the purchase of other property, for example furniture. In *Gissing* v. *Gissing* the husband had bought a house for £2,695, partly out of his own savings, partly by a loan and partly by a mortgage. The wife spent £220 on furniture and equipment and on relaying the lawn. The House of Lords had no difficulty in holding on these facts that she had made no substantial contribution, direct or indirect, *to the purchase of the house* and that she took no interest in it.

It should also be appreciated that the contribution may be by labour rather than in cash. In *Smith* v. *Baker*[4] a husband and wife built a bungalow themselves, and the wife gave up a job that brought her in about £10 a week to do so. This was regarded as a contribution in money's worth and it is submitted that the decision is unaffected by *Gissing* v. *Gissing*.

If the purchase money (or part of it) comes from a "common purse" in which the spouses have a joint interest, a house bought as the matrimonial home for their common use will presumably be intended by both of them to represent the original fund. In the absence of any evidence in rebuttal, therefore, this must give them both an interest in the property bought even though the conveyance is taken in the name of one only.[5]

The principle that a trustee must not take advantage of his position to make a personal profit for himself[6] applies equally when one spouse holds the matrimonial home or other property on trust for the other. In *Protheroe* v. *Protheroe*[7] the husband purchased the leasehold of the matrimonial home

---

[1] [1971] 3 All E.R. 866, C.A.

[2] [1973] 2 All E.R. 1042, C.A.

[3] See also Sexton, 122 New L.J. 357.

[4] [1970] 2 All E.R. 826, C.A.

[5] For the "common purse", see ante, p.425.

[6] *I.e.* the rule in *Keech* v. *Sandford* (1726), 2 Eq. Cas. Abr. 741.

[7] [1968] 1 All E.R. 1111, C.A. For a criticism of the case, see Cretney, *The Rationale of Keech* v. *Sandford*, 33 Conv. 161.

which he held for himself and his wife in equal shares. He later purchased the freehold reversion and it was held that he held this on the same trusts subject to his right to be repaid the price and legal costs incurred.

α

Division of Proceeds.—Up to now we have been considering the circumstances in which a spouse may take a beneficial interest in the matrimonial home even though the legal estate is vested in the other. Where the beneficial title is vested in one of them only, the position on sale is simple. If, say, the husband holds the legal fee simple on trust for the wife alone, she has the equitable fee simple and after the sale of the house is absolutely entitled to the proceeds. But if it was the spouses' common intention that both should take a beneficial interest, a further question is raised. If the marriage breaks down and the property has to be sold, how are the proceeds to be divided?

The question can be readily answered if the parties agreed on the interests that they should take or the contribution that each should make, because the court must give effect to the trust thereby created and divide the proceeds in the proportions agreed.[1] If it was their intention that both should take an interest but there was no clear indication that this should be a tenancy in common in identifiable shares, there developed an increasing tendency to order a division in equal shares. But this received a decided check in *Gissing* v. *Gissing*.[2] Both LORD REID and LORD PEARSON were of the opinion that the maxim "Equality is equity" had been applied too widely in this type of case. The approach most likely to be followed in the future is that indicated by LORD REID and LORD DIPLOCK.[3] If each spouse's contribution has been in cash, then in the absence of any agreement between them, the inference is that the proceeds of sale should be divided in proportion to their contributions. This will be easily calculable if there has been one lump sum payment or regular payments (*e.g.* of mortgage instalments) over a period of time. But the calculation will become more difficult if the payments have been erratic, so that in many cases the division will have to be a rough and ready one.[4] Eventually one reaches the point where the spouses' financial affairs have become so inextricably entangled that "an equitable knife must be used to sever the Gordian knot" and an equal division will be the only possible solution.[5] Again, if the wife, having made a direct cash contribution, makes further payments, the inference is that the spouses intended that she should

---

[1] If they agreed to take a beneficial joint interest, this can be severed so as to produce a tenancy in common in equal shares: see the judgment of RUSSELL, L.J., in *Bedson* v. *Bedson*, [1965] 2 Q.B. 666, 689; [1965] 3 All E.R. 307, 318, C. A. LORD DENNING, M.R.'s view that neither can sever without the other's consent (at pp. 678 and 311, respectively) seems wholly without foundation: see RUSSELL, L.J., *ibid.*, at pp. 690 and 319, respectively; *Re Draper's Conveyance*, [1969] 1 Ch. 486; [1967] 3 All E.R. 853; *Cowcher* v. *Cowcher*, [1972] 1 All E.R. 943, 949; Saunders and McGregor, *Disposal of Equitable Interest in Joint Tenancy*, 37 Conv. 270; R.E.M. in 82 L.Q.R. 29.

[2] [1971] A.C. 886; [1970] 2 All E.R. 780, H.L.

[3] [1971] A.C. at pp. 897 and 907-909; [1970] 2 All E.R. at pp. 782-783 and 791-793, respectively.

[4] One must also take into account the obligations undertaken by each, for example to repay money lent to provide the deposit: *Earley* v. *Earley* (1975), 119 Sol. Jo. 658, C.A.

[5] See LORD UPJOHN in *National Provincial Bank, Ltd.* v. *Ainsworth*, [1965] A.C. 1175, 1236; [1965] 2 All E.R. 472, 487, H.L.; LORD MORRIS in *Pettitt* v. *Pettitt*, [1970] A.C. 777, 804; [1969] 2 All E.R. 385, 397, H.L.; LORD HODSON, *ibid.*, at pp. 810 and 403, respectively.

take more than the proportion represented by her initial contribution and that the interest should be quantified when the total amount contributed by each was known. Obviously the problem becomes much more difficult if the contribution has been indirect and an equal division may be the only possible way of dealing fairly with both parties. In many cases (particularly if the house is bought in the early days of the marriage) the wife's earning capacity (and consequently her ability to make direct or indirect contributions to the purchase) will drop if she has children, and in this sort of situation the court may well infer that their intention was that each should contribute what he or she could afford from time to time but that the beneficial interest should be held in equal shares.

Some cases decided by the Court of Appeal before *Gissing* v. *Gissing* would obviously still be decided in the same way today. In *Re Rogers' Question,*[1] where the wife had paid £100 in cash towards the price of £1,000 and had made it clear that this was the limit of her contribution, the court divided the proceeds in the ratio of nine to one. In *Rimmer* v. *Rimmer,*[2] where both contributed directly and indirectly what they conceived to be their share towards the purchase over a number of years, the court ordered an equal division. Again, an adjustment has been made to take account of unequal contributions or other financial advantages.[3] But many other decisions doubtless gave rise to the strictures in *Gissing* v. *Gissing* on the too ready resort to equal division and can no longer be regarded as any sort of precedent at all.

As the parties' rights must be determined by reference to their common intention when the property was purchased, no account may be taken of the responsibility for the breakdown of the marriage.[4] This may become relevant, however, in settling accounts of payments made after the parties have separated. There can be no further presumption of a gift from one party to the other, so the general rule is that, if both spouses have a beneficial interest in the property, all income and disbursements must be shared. If, for example, each is entitled to half the proceeds of sale and the wife leaves voluntarily, she must account to the husband for her share of the mortgage instalments and other outgoings disbursed by him after her departure.[5] But if she was driven out by her husband's conduct, he must bear the whole cost. He cannot be allowed to take advantage of his own wrong and he also has the advantage of living rent free whilst the wife will have to pay for other accommodation.[6] The same principle has been applied where the spouses jointly own a business and the wife brings the partnership to an end by

---

[1] [1948] 1 All E.R. 328, C.A.

[2] [1953] 1 Q.B. 63; [1952] 2 All E.R. 863, C.A. See also *Smith* v. *Baker,* [1970] 2 All E.R. 826, C.A.

[3] See *Nixon* v. *Nixon,* [1969] 3 All E.R. 1133, C.A.; *Muetzel* v. *Muetzel,* [1970] 1 All E.R. 443, C.A. See also *Falconer* v. *Falconer,* [1970] 3 All E.R. 449, C.A. (decided after *Gissing* v. *Gissing*) where the wife recovered the value of the site but the value of the building on it was divided equally between the spouses.

[4] *Hickson* v. *Hickson,* [1953] 1 Q.B. 420; [1953] 1 All E.R. 382, C.A.; *Wilson* v. *Wilson,* [1963] 2 All E.R. 447, 454, C.A.

[5] *Wilson* v. *Wilson,* (*supra*); *Davis* v. *Vale,* [1971] 2 All E.R. 1021, C.A.; *Cracknell* v. *Cracknell,* [1971] P. 356; [1971] 3 All E.R. 552, C.A.

[6] *Falconer* v. *Falconer,* [1970] 3 All E.R. 449, C.A., as explained in *Cracknell* v. *Cracknell,* (*supra*). Cf. *Shinh* v. *Shinh,* [1977] 1 All E.R. 97.

walking out on her husband. The assets and goodwill must be assessed at that
date, and the husband alone will be entitled to any subsequent increase in
their value.[1] The result is that the court may find itself involved in allegations
of misconduct when determining questions of contribution. This is regrettable when the general move is away from the courts' making judgments
about the parties' conduct in matrimonial proceedings, and there is some
indication that they will try to avoid doing so and leave each of the spouses to
bear his or her aliquot part except in the most exceptional circumstances. In
Leake v. *Bruzzi*[2] the wife left the matrimonial home, which was expressly
held on trust for both spouses jointly, and later obtained a divorce alleging
that her husband's conduct had been such that she could not reasonably be
expected to live with him. Armed with this decree, she then argued that she
should not have to contribute anything towards the mortgage instalments
(amounting to some £900) which the husband had paid since she left him.
Nevertheless she was ordered to repay half the sum in question insofar as it
represented the repayment of capital and therefore increased the value of her
share: the husband was left to bear the whole cost of repaying interest as the
equivalent of paying rent for the use and occupation of the premises. This
represents a compromise between the parties' competing claims and obviates
the need for a lengthy investigation into the cause of the breakdown of the
marriage. If, however, one spouse has been forced out by the other's
"obvious and gross" conduct, it is arguable that, by analogy with the
principles applied to orders for financial provision in matrimonial causes, the
courts will continue to make the spouse at fault bear the whole cost of the outgoings.[3]

Improvements to the Matrimonial Home.—The value of the matrimonial
home may be considerably enhanced after its purchase by extension,
improvement or other work done on it. Suppose that the beneficial title is
vested in one spouse exclusively but the other contributes to the improvement
by cash payments or by doing some of the work himself; will this give him any
interest in the property? This is the question that had to be answered in *Pettitt*
v. *Pettitt*.[4] The husband alleged that as a result of doing work on the
matrimonial home (which had been purchased by the wife out of her own
money) he had increased its value by over £1,000. Most of the work had
consisted of redecorating the bungalow in question, but he had also made the
garden, built a wall and patio, and done other jobs outside. All the members
of the House were agreed that he could claim nothing, on the ground that he
could acquire no interest by doing work of an ephemeral nature or "do-it-
yourself" jobs which any husband could be expected to do in his leisure
hours. They were, however, divided on the question whether, in the absence
of an agreement, one spouse could acquire an interest in the other's property
by doing work of a more substantial nature on it.

---

[1] *Bothe* v. *Amos*, [1976] Fam. 46; [1975] 2 All E.R. 321, C.A.
[2] [1974] 2 All E.R. 1196, C.A., followed in *Suttill* v. *Graham*, [1977] 3 All E.R. 1117,.C.A.
[3] See Denyer, 128 New L.J. 828. For "obvious and gross" conduct, see *post*, p. 555.
[4] [1970] A.C. 777; [1969] 2 All E.R. 385, H.L.

As a consequence the law was made more certain by section 37 of the Matrimonial Proceedings and Property Act 1970.[1] This provides:

"...where a husband or wife contributes in money or money's worth to the improvement of real or personal property in which or in the proceeds of sale of which either or both of them has or have a beneficial interest, the husband or wife so contributing shall, if the contribution is of a substantial nature and subject to any agreement to the contrary express or implied, be treated as having then acquired by virtue of his or her contribution a share or an enlarged share, as the case may be, in that beneficial interest. . . ."

It will be observed that this section (which refers to any property and is not limited to improvements to the matrimonial home) applies whether the contribution is in money or money's worth: in other words, it does not matter whether the spouse does the job himself or pays a contractor to do it. In the latter case, however, he must show that his contribution is identifiable with the improvement in question: a general contribution to the family's finances (like an indirect contribution to the price) will give him an interest in the home only if it is referable to the improvement.[2]

It will be seen that there are two limitations on the operation of the section. First, it will apply only if the contribution is of a substantial nature. Whether any particular improvement is sufficiently substantial to bring it within the ambit of the section is, of course, a question of fact, but it seems clear that the sort of work done by the husband in *Pettitt* v. *Pettitt* will still not give him any interest in the matrimonial home. In *Re Nicholson*,[3] for example, the installation of central heating for £189 in premises worth £6,000 was regarded as a substantial contribution, but the purchase of a gasfire worth less than £23 was not. Secondly, the section applies "subject to any agreement between the spouses to the contrary express or implied", so that if they agreed that the improvements should confer no interest on the party making them, this will be conclusive.

Section 37 applies in any proceedings including, for example, litigation between one spouse and a stranger claiming through the other. If the parties agreed on the size of the interest which the improvements were to confer on the spouse making them, the court must give effect to the agreement; in other cases it has power to make such order as appears just in all the circumstances. Normally this should reflect the amount by which the value of the property was increased at the time; if, for example, the wife puts the value of the husband's house up from £4,000 to £5,000, she should obtain one-fifth of the price when it is sold. The section also applies if both spouses have a beneficial interest in the property before the improvements are made: hence if in the above example the spouses were tenants in common of the house in equal shares when the wife made the improvements, she should now obtain three-fifths of the price.[4]

---

[1] Enacted on the recommendation of the Law Commission: see Law Com. No. 25, paras. 56-58 and pp. 102-105. For difficulties arising under the section, see Oerton, 120 New L.J. 1008.

[2] *Harnett* v. *Harnett*, [1973] Fam. 156, 167; [1973] 2 All E.R. 593, 603, *per* BAGNALL, J. (The question did not arise on appeal: [1974] 1 All E.R. 764, C.A.) For contributions referable to the purchase, see *ante*, p. 447.

[3] [1974] 2 All E.R. 386.

[4] *Re Nicholson*, (*supra*).

Sale of the Property.—If the legal estate is vested in one spouse only but both have a beneficial interest, the equitable joint tenancy or tenancy in common should take effect behind a trust for sale.[1] Consequently the legal owner should appoint another trustee (who would normally be the other spouse) and the trustees must consider the wishes of both beneficial owners before dealing with the property.[2] In many cases this will not be done, however, and a purchaser will take a legal estate from one spouse alone. The question then arises whether he takes it free from the other spouse's beneficial interest or subject to it. This will be of the utmost importance, for example, if the legal estate is vested in the husband alone and he mortgages it without the knowledge or consent of the wife. If the mortgagee later has to take steps to realize his security, will the wife be able to enforce her rights against him?

If the legal estate is registered under the Land Registration Act 1925, the position has been put beyond doubt by the decision of the House of Lords in *Williams and Glyn's Bank, Ltd.* v. *Boland.*[3] The husband was registered as the sole proprietor of the legal estate of the matrimonial home, but the wife had contributed a substantial sum towards the purchase and was admittedly an equitable tenant in common to the extent of her contribution. The husband later executed a legal mortgage to the appellant bank which made no enquiries of the wife. When the husband failed to pay the sum secured, the bank started proceedings for possession of the house with a view to selling it under their powers as mortgagees. The wife resisted the action on the ground that her interest took priority over the bank's. It was conceded that her claim was good only if she could establish an overriding interest as a person in actual occupation of the land with an interest "for the time being subsisting in reference thereto".[4] The House of Lords held that her physical presence in the house coupled with the right to exclude all others without a similar right clearly gave her actual occupation, and the fact that her husband (the owner of the legal estate) was also in actual occupation could not affect this. Furthermore, although the land was held on trust for sale, the wife had an interest subsisting in reference to the land itself: to hold that she had no more than an interest in the proceeds of sale of a house to the purchase of which she had contributed as a matrimonial home for herself and her husband would be highly artificial. It therefore followed that her claim succeeded.

If the land is unregistered, the position is more complex. As payment to a single trustee will not overreach the wife's equitable interest,[5] anyone dealing with the land will probably be protected only by the general equitable doctrine that a *bona fide* purchaser of a legal estate for value will take it free of any equitable interest of which he does not have actual or constructive notice.[6] Hence if he takes an *equitable* interest (for example, if a bank takes an equitable charge from the husband), the wife must have priority. A

---

[1] Law of Property Act 1925, ss. 34 and 36; Settled Land Act 1925, s. 36 (4).
[2] Law of Property Act 1925, ss. 26 (3) and 27 (2); Trustee Act 1925, ss. 14 (2) and 36 (6). See *Waller* v. *Waller*, [1967] 1 All E.R. 305; *Taylor* v. *Taylor*, [1968] 1 All E.R. 843, 846-847, C.A.
[3] [1980] 2 All E.R. 408, H.L.; Freeman, 43 M.L.R. 692.
[4] Land Registration Act 1925, s. 70 (1) (g).
[5] Law of Property Act 1925, ss. 2 (2) and 27.
[6] See Megarry and Wade, *Real Property*, 4th Ed., 122; Rudden, *The Wife the Husband and the Conveyancer*, 27 Conv. 51; Garner, *A Single Trustee for Sale*, 33 Conv. 240.

purchaser of a *legal* estate will normally have constructive notice of the rights of any person in occupation of the land: this raises the question whether the fact that the wife is residing in the house will itself be sufficient notice of her interest to give her priority over the purchaser. In *Caunce* v. *Caunce*[1] STAMP, J., held that it will not do so for her presence is not inconsistent with the husband's being the sole beneficial owner, but this case was doubted, although not expressly overruled, in *Williams and Glyn's Bank, Ltd.* v. *Boland*.[2] One of the principal objections to holding that the wife's occupation gives the purchaser constructive notice of her rights is that this compels him to make distasteful and embarrassing enquiries. In an earlier case dealing with the so-called "deserted wife's equity", UPJOHN, J., refusing to cast upon a prospective purchaser or mortgagee the duty to enquire whether the owner of the property in question had deserted his wife, said:[3]

> "If the law were otherwise it would mean that every intending purchaser or lender must inquire into the relationship of husband and wife and inquire into matters which are no concern of his and will bring thousands of business transactions into the area of domestic life and ties. That could not be right."

This applies with equal force to the problem we are considering here. The House of Lords, however, was obviously more concerned to protect the wife than the purchaser. In the words of LORD WILBERFORCE:[4]

> "The extension of the risk area follows necessarily from the extension, beyond the paterfamilias, of rights of ownership, itself following from the diffusion of property and earning capacity. What is involved is a departure from an easy-going practice of dispensing with enquiries as to occupation beyond that of the vendor and accepting the risks of doing so. To substitute for this a practice of more careful enquiry as to the fact of occupation, and if necessary, as to the rights of occupiers cannot, in my view of the matter, be considered as unacceptable except at the price of overlooking the widespread development of shared interests of ownership."

Although he was speaking only of conveyancing practice when the land is registered, precisely the same principle applies to unregistered land, and it is submitted that, if an intending purchaser fails to make proper enquiries of a wife in occupation, the interest he acquires will necessarily be subject to hers. *A fortiori* this must be so if the spouses have separated and she is living in the house alone. It does not follow, however, that she will be able to remain in occupation indefinitely. In many cases the husband will be insolvent and the court may enforce a sale and leave her to claim her share of the proceeds.[5]

Death of one of the Spouses.—A further problem arises if the marriage ends not by breakdown during the parties' lifetime but by the death of one of them. If both have a beneficial interest in the house, it may be vital to decide whether they hold as joint tenants or tenants in common, for the whole

---

[1] [1969] 1 All E.R. 722.

[2] At pp. 413 (*per* LORD WILBERFORCE, with whom three other members of the House agreed) and 418 (*per* LORD SCARMAN).

[3] *Westminster Bank, Ltd.* v. *Lee,* [1956] Ch. 7, 22; [1955] 2 All E.R. 883, 889. For the deserted wife's equity, see *post,* p. 466.

[4] *Williams and Glyn's Bank, Ltd.* v. *Boland,* (*supra*), at pp. 415-416.

[5] See *post,* p. 465.

interest in a joint tenancy will pass to the survivor *jure accrescendi* if it has not been severed during the lifetime of both whilst an undivided share will form a part of the deceased's estate.

If the beneficial interests have been spelled out in the conveyance, effect will obviously be given to them. In other cases where the beneficial interest would have been divided equally between the spouses during their lifetime, the tendency is to hold that they were tenants in common in equity.[1] There are some dicta that suggest that, if the court would order an unequal division *inter vivos*, the spouses hold the property as joint tenants in unequal shares,[2] but it is submitted that this offends against fundamental principles of our land law. The unilateral severance of a joint tenancy has always produced equal undivided shares;[3] conversely in the absence of other evidence equity has always regarded an unequal contribution towards the purchase money as producing a tenancy in common.[4] If we accept the principle that the matrimonial home is governed by the same rules as other property—as we are bound to do since the decision in *Gissing* v. *Gissing*[5]—facts producing an unequal division *inter vivos* must necessarily create a tenancy in common and consequently the property will not pass to the survivor by operation of law but will become part of the other's estate.

2. OCCUPATION

Right to occupy the Matrimonial Home.—We must now consider what rights the spouses have to occupy the matrimonial home and to use the furniture in it. *Prima facie* each has a right to the other's consortium, and as this will be normally enjoyed in the matrimonial home, each will have a right to use the house and its furniture in whichever of them the legal or equitable title is vested.[6] Obviously, however, their precise rights will depend in the first place on who owns the property in question.

If the matrimonial home is vested in both spouses as joint tenants in law and equity, *prima facie* both will be entitled to remain in occupation of it as beneficial owners. If the legal and equitable title is vested in the husand exclusively, the wife can claim a right of occupation at common law not only by virtue of her right to her husband's consortium but also by virtue of her right to be maintained by him. Generally speaking, these rights are co-extensive, and the husband's duty to provide his wife with maintenance is primarily

---

[1] See *Re Cummins*, [1972] Ch. 62; [1971] 3 All E.R. 782, C.A.; *Re Nicholson*, [1974] 2 All E.R. 386. *Quaere* whether the parties would not have wished and expected the *jus accrescendi* to operate.

[2] *E.g.* by LORD DENNING, M.R., in *Bedson* v. *Bedson*, [1965] 2 Q.B. 666, 681-682; [1965] 3 All E.R. 307, 314, C.A.; *Nixon* v. *Nixon*, [1969] 3 All E.R. 1133, 1137, C.A.; *Muetzel* v. *Muetzel*, [1970] 1 All E.R. 443, 445, C.A.

[3] *Cf.* the judgment of RUSSELL, L.J., in *Bedson* v. *Bedson*, (*supra*), at pp. 689 and 318, respectively; BAGNALL, J., in *Cowcher* v. *Cowcher*, [1972] 1 All E.R. 943, 949; Megarry and Wade, *Law of Real Property*, 4th Ed., 494.

[4] *Lake* v. *Craddock* (1733), 3 P. Wms. 158.

[5] [1971] A.C. 886; [1970] 2 All E.R. 780, H.L. See *ante*, p. 443.

[6] See *National Provincial Bank, Ltd.* v. *Ainsworth*, [1965] A.C. 1175; [1965] 2 All E.R. 472, H.L.

discharged by his providing her with a home.[1] Consequently, even though he deserts her and she ceases to enjoy his consortium, she will normally be entitled to remain in the matrimonial home. At common law she forfeited her right to his consortium and maintenance if she committed a matrimonial offence;[2] although by statute she may now claim maintenance in such circumstances, the loss of her right to consortium presumably still deprives her of the right to stay in the matrimonial home. In any case her right to her husband's consortium does not entitle her to occupy any other property belonging to him and he may obtain an injunction restraining her from entering it even though he has no justification for his refusal to cohabit.[3]

If the legal and equitable interests are vested solely in the wife, her duty to cohabit with her husband will normally mean that he will have a right to the use and occupation of the matrimonial home.[4] If he has forfeited the right to her consortium by his own conduct, the position is the same *mutatis mutandis* as when the property is vested solely in the husband.[5]

If the marriage breaks down, the exact nature of these rights and the extent to which they can be enforced may become of the utmost importance. The wife may wish to exclude the husband from the matrimonial home because his ill-treatment of her or their children makes it impossible for her to live with him any longer. If the husband has left, he may wish to realise his capital and so will need to get the wife out of the house in order to be able to sell it with vacant possession. If he succeeds in selling it over her head (or if he mortgages the house and fails to pay the mortgage instalments so that the mortgagee wishes to exercise his power of selling the property), the question will arise whether the wife has any right to remain in occupation against the purchaser or mortgagee. If she is a beneficial owner, she can of course continue to exercise such rights of occupation as her ownership gives her, but it is obvious that the common law rights of a non-owner, being no more than personal claims against the other spouse, are precarious in the extreme. It was in order to strengthen them that the Matrimonial Homes Act was passed in 1967, following the decision of the House of Lords in *National Provincial*

---

[1] See *post*, p. 483. She also has a right, within reason, to invite guests into the home: *Jolliffe* v. *Willmett & Co.*, [1971] 1 All E.R. 478, 483 (no right to authorise entry of enquiry agent seeking evidence of husband's adultery 13 years after wife had left home). *Quaere* whether the husband may forbid her to do so.

[2] See *post*, p. 484.

[3] *Nanda* v. *Nanda*, [1968] P. 351; [1967] 3 All E.R. 401, *ante*, p. 112. If the husband still has a beneficial interest in the matrimonial home and the wife stays in possession of it with his consent or by virtue of her right *qua* wife to stay there, he retains sufficient beneficial occupation to make him (and not her) liable for the payment of rates provided that he is using the house as a means of discharging his obligation to maintain her: *Malden and Coombe Corporation* v. *Bennett*, [1963] 2 All E.R. 527; *Des Salles d'Epinoix* v. *Kensington and Chelsea Royal London Borough Council*, [1970] 1 All E.R. 18; *Brown* v. *Oxford City Council*,[1979] Q.B. 607; [1978] 3 All E.R. 1113. This right must terminate on divorce but the former husband may then remain the rateable occupier if her occupation is the means by which he discharges his duty to provide a home for his children: *Routhan* v. *Arun District Council* (1980), 10 Fam. Law 218; *Mourton* v. *Hounslow London Borough*, [1970] 2 Q.B. 362; [1970] 2 All E.R. 564. See Miller, *Expenses of the Matrimonial Home*, 35 Conv. 332, at pp. 333-338.

[4] *Shipman* v. *Shipman*, [1924] 2 Ch. 140, 146, C.A. This right extends to the husband's visitors as well (*Jolliffe* v. *Willmett & Co., supra*) but not to one entering the house on the husband's authority for the purpose of annoying the wife: *Weldon* v. *De Bathe* (1884), 14 Q.B.D. 339, C.A.

[5] *Shipman* v. *Shipman*, (*supra*).

Bank, Ltd. v. *Ainsworth*[1] which considerably cut down the rights of a deserted wife.

Matrimonial Homes Act 1967.—The original purpose of the Act was to give greater protection to a spouse who could not claim any proprietary interest to occupy the matrimonial home, but it became apparent that its effect was to place such a spouse in a better position than one who had such an interest. Whereas the former could invoke the provisions of the Act, the latter was left to pursue such remedies as he (or, more often, she) was afforded at common law or by some other statute. Consequently it has been extensively amended, particularly by the Domestic Violence and Matrimonial Proceedings Act of 1976, and its provisions now cover the rights of occupation of all spouses.

"Where one spouse is entitled to occupy a dwellinghouse by virtue of any estate or interest or contract or by virtue of any enactment giving him or her the right to remain in occupation, and the other spouse is not so entitled", the Act gives the latter rights of occupation.[2] It will be seen that these provisions apply, for example, if one spouse is a statutory tenant under the Rent Act or a secure tenant under the Housing Act 1980 (because he will be entitled to occupy the house by virtue of a statute) or if he goes into possession as a licensee[3] or under a contract to take a lease or to purchase the freehold. If the husband is a lessee or his right is contractual, however, the wife's position is necessarily more precarious because if the husband's own breach of contract entitles the legal owner to treat himself as discharged (for example, by failing to pay rent or the purchase money), the wife's statutory right will automatically be terminated. Formerly there was a difficulty if the house had been conveyed into the husband's name but the wife could claim an interest in equity because she had contributed to the purchase money. This was sufficient to take her right of occupation outside the Act so that it could not be registered; on the other hand, her interest would not appear on the title and consequently she lost the protection she could otherwise have had against a purchaser from the husband. To solve this problem it is now provided that a spouse who has an equitable interest in a dwellinghouse or in the proceeds of sale may nevertheless have a statutory right of occupation provided that he or she has no legal estate in the land either solely or jointly.[4]

If a spouse with rights of occupation is in actual occupation of the dwellinghouse, he (or she) has a right not to be evicted or excluded from any part of it except by a court order; if he is out of occupation, he has a right to apply for an order permitting him to enter and occupy.[5] So long as the rights of occupation are in existence, either spouse may apply to the court for an order declaring, enforcing, restricting or terminating them.[6] The term "dwellinghouse" includes any building or part of a building occupied as a

---

[1] [1965] A.C. 1175; [1965] 2 All E.R. 472, H.L. See further *post*, p. 466.

[2] S. 1 (1).

[3] As in *Hardwick* v. *Johnson*, [1978] 2 All E.R. 935, C.A., where, however, the wife was joint licensee and therefore had a right to possession under her contract and not under the Act.

[4] S. 1 (9), added by the Matrimonial Proceedings and Property Act 1970, s. 38. See further Law Com. No. 25, para. 59.

[5] S. 1 (1).

[6] S. 1 (2).

dwelling together with any yard, garden, garage or outhouse. The Act does not apply, however, to any house which has never been the spouses' matrimonial home; consequently, although the wife is protected if she has been constructively deserted, she has no right to occupy premises into which the husband has moved after leaving her.[1]

The spouse's rights of occupation under the Act are obviously purely personal. Common sense dictates that he should be able to invite guests to come into the house (or the part of it of which he is in occupation) and to stay there for a reasonable period of time. The requirement of the Act that the court should have regard to the needs of the children in determining any application also indicates that he may have his children to live there.[2] It is very doubtful, however, whether his right extends to permitting him to take in lodgers or guests for a long period.

The rights continue only so long as the marriage subsists and will come to an end on the other spouse's death or on the dissolution or annulment of the marriage. But in the event of a matrimonial dispute or estrangement the court may order that the rights shall continue after the marriage has been terminated (whether by death or a court order).[3]

Exclusion of Spouse.—It is obvious that if, say, a husband is physically assaulting his wife or children, her right to occupy the matrimonial home will of itself be valueless, for she will not be able to enjoy it in any real sense so long as he is there too. We must therefore now consider the means by which one spouse can seek an order excluding the other from the home and the circumstances in which the court will make it.

Matrimonial Homes Act 1967.—The Act gives the court a power to make orders restricting the rights of occupation of *all* spouses, whether they are proprietary or statutory. So long as one of them has statutory rights of occupation, either of them may apply for an order prohibiting, suspending or restricting the exercise of the other's right to occupy the dwellinghouse or requiring the other to permit the applicant to exercise his own right.[4] Furthermore, if *both* spouses are entitled to occupy a dwellinghouse by virtue of a legal estate vested in them jointly or by virtue of a contract or any enactment, either of them may apply for a similar order. In the latter case, as both have a right to occupy, no rights of occupation can arise under the Act, but as in the case of the statutory rights, the parties must have or have had their matrimonial home in the house in question and the court may make orders only with respect to the exercise of the right to occupy it during the subsistence of

---

[1] S. 1 (7) and (8). *Cf. Collins* v. *Collins* (1973), 4 Fam. Law 133, C.A. (separate flat in house owned by wife not part of the matrimonial home).

[2] But see the doubts expressed by MEGARRY, J., in *Wroth* v. *Tyler*, [1974] Ch. 30, at pp. 45 and 52; [1973] 1 All E.R. 897, at pp. 908 and 915.

[3] Ss. 1 (8) and 2 (2). It is not clear what is meant by the expressions "matrimonial dispute or estrangement"; presumably they cover litigation and separation. See further generally Crane, *The Matrimonial Homes Act* 1967, 32 Conv. 85, 33 Conv. 148; Stone, 31 M.L.R. 305; Kahn-Freund, *Recent Legislation on Matrimonial Property*, 33 M.L.R. 601, particularly at pp. 609 *et seq.* For changes proposed by the Law Commission, see Law Com. No. 86, Book Two.

[4] S. 1 (2), as amended by the Domestic Violence and Matrimonial Proceedings Act 1976, s. 3.

the marriage.[1] Jurisdiction to make orders is vested in the High Court or a county court.[2] The court may make such order as it thinks just and reasonable and may terminate either spouse's rights entirely or limit them to certain parts of the house; in particular it may exclude him or her from any part of it used wholly or mainly for the other's trade, business or profession. Hence, if the husband is a medical practitioner, the wife might be forbidden to enter his surgery or use his garage: the court would have power to make such an order whether the legal estate was vested exclusively in the husband or the wife or vested in them both jointly. The court may also order a spouse occupying the house or any part of it by virtue of these provisions to pay the other an occupation rent and may impose on either of them obligations to repair and maintain the house and to pay other outgoings (for example, rates or mortgage repayments). Orders may be for a limited period of time, and the court may make an interim order to last, say, until the hearing of divorce proceedings or until the wife finds suitable alternative accomodation.[3]

Injunctions.—A divorce court has jurisdiction to grant an injunction excluding either spouse from the matrimonial home in any proceedings for divorce, nullity or judicial separation. It may do so as soon as the petition has been presented or even, in a case of urgency, before this step has been taken.[4] After a decree nisi has been pronounced, the court should usually deal with the ownership and occupation of the matrimonial home under its extensive powers to make property adjustment orders, and the parties' common law rights will cease to be of importance.[5] If the court's jurisdiction is not invoked, however, it must be remembered that, once the marriage has been dissolved or annulled, the wife's right to her husband's consortium and maintenance go and consequently, as the Court of Appeal held in *Vaughan* v. *Vaughan*,[6] in the absence of any agreement to the contrary, she normally ceases to have any right at all to remain in the former matrimonial home if it is the husband's property. Similarly, he will no longer be entitled to stay in her house.[7] But if there are children of the family, proceedings relating to their care and custody may be brought at any time during their minority, and if it is necessary to exclude a spouse from the matrimonial home for their protection, the court has jurisdiction to order him to quit even though he is the sole owner and no other proceedings relating to the property are pending.[8]

The High Court or a county court also has power to make an order in relation to the matrimonial home under section 17 of the Married Women's

---

[1] Domestic Violence and Matrimonial Proceedings Act 1976, s. 4.

[2] Matrimonial Homes Act 1967, s. 1 (6).

[3] *Ibid.*, s. 1 (3), (4); Domestic Violence and Matrimonial Proceedings Act 1976, s. 4 (2); *Baynham* v. *Baynham*, [1969] 1 All E.R. 305, C.A.

[4] *Semble* it has no jurisdiction on an application for leave to present a petition for divorce within the first three years of the marriage or in proceedings for financial provision under s. 27 of the Matrimonial Causes Act 1973. See further *ante*, pp. 122-123.

[5] See *post*, pp. 558 *et seq.*

[6] [1953] 1 Q.B. 762; [1953] 1 All E.R. 209, C.A. If the wife is in possession in pursuance of an agreement, the contract might be altered under the provisions of s. 35 of the Matrimonial Causes Act 1973: see *post*, p. 492.

[7] *Morris* v. *Tarrant*, [1971] 2 Q.B. 143; [1971] 2 All E.R. 920. Nor will either party have any further right of occupation under the Matrimonial Homes Act 1967 unless the court has made an order that it shall continue: see *ante*, p. 459.

[8] *Stewart* v. *Stewart*, [1973] Fam. 21; [1973] 1 All E.R. 31.

Property Act 1882.[1] In addition, whether or not the applicant seeks any other relief and whether or not there is any fear of violence, section 1 of the Domestic Violence and Matrimonial Proceedings Act 1976 now gives a county court jurisdiction to grant an injunction excluding a party to a marriage from the whole or any part of the matrimonial home or from a specified area in which the matrimonial home is situated and requiring him to permit the applicant to enter and remain in the matrimonial home or any part of it. Rules of Court give the High Court similar powers.[2] Only a spouse may bring such proceedings; hence they are not available to a divorced person after decree absolute.

Breach of an injunction can be enforced in the usual way by committal for contempt. In addition, if the judge granting it is satisfied that the respondent has caused actual bodily harm to the applicant or a child living with the applicant and is likely to do again, he may attach a power of arrest to an injunction excluding the respondent from the matrimonial home or any area in which it is situated. It will be observed that a power of arrest cannot be attached if the injunction excludes the respondent from part only of the matrimonial home or simply requires him to permit the applicant to enter and remain in it. Normally it will be attached only if the court also grants an injunction restraining the respondent from using violence against the applicant or a child. The effect of attaching a power of arrest has already been discussed: in particular it should be noted that this may be done whenever an injunction containing the provisions mentioned is granted and is not confined to injunctions granted under the Domestic Violence and Matrimonial Proceedings Act.[3]

Magistrates' Orders.—It will be recalled that section 16 of the Domestic Proceedings and Magistrates' Courts Act 1978 enables a magistrates' court to make an order requiring a party to a marriage to leave the matrimonial home, prohibiting him from entering it and requiring him to permit the applicant to enter and remain there. Unlike the analogous power in the High Court or a county court, however, stringent conditions must be fulfilled before the power can be exercised. Provided that the court is satisfied that the respondent has already physically injured the applicant or a child of the family and considers that he is likely to do so again, it may attach a power of arrest to an order forbidding him to enter the matrimonial home. The relevant details have already been discussed.[4]

It will be seen that in many cases a spouse wishing to obtain an order excluding the other from the matrimonial home may seek it in a variety of ways. If other matrimonial proceedings are on foot, it will clearly be advantageous to have one court dealing with all aspects of the spouses' relationship and consequently the applicant should apply to the divorce court for an injunction. If no matrimonial proceedings are pending and the requisite conditions are satisfied, a spouse may prefer the relatively cheap and speedy procedure of the magistrates' court to proceedings in the High Court or a county court, particularly if she (or he) is also applying for an order forbidding the respondent from using violence. If these conditions are not satisfied, an applicant wishing to obtain an injunction containing provisions

---

[1] See *ante*, p. 422.

[2] R.S.C. 0. 90, r. 17; *Spindlow* v. *Spindlow*, [1979] Fam. 52; [1979] 1 All E.R. 169, C.A. See further *ante*, pp. 123-125.

[3] See *ante*, p. 125.

[4] See *ante*, p. 127.

relating to both molestation and exclusion from the home would usually be advised to proceed under the Domestic Violence and Matrimonial Proceedings Act. It should be borne in mind, however, that proceedings under this Act (and presumably those under the Domestic Proceedings and Magistrates' Courts Act) are intended to provide a short term remedy and consequently the injunction should last only so long as is reasonable to enable the applicant to find alternative accommodation or to take other proceedings. In most cases a period of three months should suffice in the first instance, although it will of course be open to the applicant to apply for an extension or to the respondent to apply for a discharge.[1] If the only order sought relates to the matrimonial home, a spouse should normally go under the Matrimonial Homes Act in order to take advantage of the extensive powers that it gives the court to make orders ancillary to occupation, for example relating to the payment of an occupation rent and outgoings.

Circumstances in which a Spouse will be excluded.—Whatever proceedings are taken and in whatever court a remedy is sought, the effect of the order will be the same, and consequently the court should clearly exercise its discretion in the same way. In practice few orders appear to be made limiting a spouse to part of the matrimonial home, presumably because few couples live in a house big enough to divide in such a way as to provide an effective solution to their matrimonial differences. In the past courts have been slow to make "a drastic order" depriving either spouse of the use of the home entirely.[2] They were even more reluctant to exclude an owner from his or her own property,[3] and earlier cases indicated that they would order a spouse to leave the premises only if the position had become impossible or intolerable. But the judicial view now is that an order will be made whenever the only fair, just, reasonable and practicable solution is to give one of them exclusive possession.[4] Mere tension, unpleasantness and inconvenience are not enough; on the other hand, it is not necessary to prove physical assault.[5] If the wife has a good reason for leaving her husband, *prima facie* she needs the protection of the court.[6] It is essential to think in terms of homes, especially for the children, and their health and welfare will always be a paramount consideration. In many cases the need to leave them in the matrimonial home, so that they will have a roof over their heads, will be conclusive, and if they and the spouse with actual custody of them cannot continue to live there with the other spouse, the latter must go[7] Consequently, if there is a dispute over custody, it may be necessary to resolve this before making a final decision about occupation of the home.[8]

---

[1] *Hopper* v. *Hopper*, [1979] 1 All E.R. 181, C.A.; *Practice Direction*, [1978] 2 All E.R. 1056.

[2] *Hall* v. *Hall*, [1971] 1 All E.R. 762, C.A.; Prichard, [1973] C.L.J. 227. See generally Hoggett, 118 Sol. Jo. 470.

[3] *Cf. Pekesin* v. *Pekesin* (1978), 8 Fam. Law 244, C.A. (husband excluded from council house which had been transferred from the wife's tenancy to joint tenancy on marriage).

[4] *Walker* v. *Walker*, [1978] 3 All E.R. 141, C.A.

[5] *Hall* v. *Hall*, (*supra*); *Phillips* v. *Phillips*, [1973] 2 All E.R. 423, C.A.

[6] *Bassett* v. *Bassett*, [1975] Fam. 76, 83; [1975] 1 All E.R. 513, 518, C.A.

[7] *Spindlow* v. *Spindlow*, [1979] Fam. 52; [1979] 1 All E.R. 169, C.A.; *Gurasz* v. *Gurasz*, [1970] P. 11; [1969] 3 All E.R. 822, C.A. *Cf. Rennick* v. *Rennick*, [1978] 1 All E.R. 817, C.A.; *Re V.* (1979), 123 Sol. Jo. 201; *Beard* v. *Beard*, [1981] 1 All E.R. 783, C.A. (divorced wife excluded from her own home to enable former husband to live there with children as an emergency measure); Matrimonial Homes Act 1967, s. 1 (3).

[8] *Smith* v. *Smith* (1979), 10 Fam. Law 50, C.A.

In the end the court must balance the hardship that one spouse would suffer if he were evicted against the hardship that the other would suffer if he were permitted to remain. The health, behaviour and financial position of each spouse are clearly relevant, and it is important not to overlook the difficulty that a husband may face in finding alternative accommodation.[1] The court must also consider the state of the marriage. If a reconciliation is still on the cards, the court should be slow to prevent it by keeping the spouses apart; but if the marriage has broken down completely, the hardship may be considerably less on the spouse required to leave because sooner or later one of them will have to go in any event.[2] The way in which the courts weigh the various facts may seen in *Bassett* v. *Bassett*.[3] The spouses, who had a baby aged 18 months, lived in a two-roomed flat where they were joined by the husband's son by his first marriage, then aged 15. This caused a great deal of overcrowding and eventually the wife, who accused the husband of drunkenness and violence, left him to live with her parents in even more grossly overcrowded conditions. She returned to her husband for a couple of months but eventually left him again; she then petitioned for divorce, alleging that his behaviour had been such that she could not reasonably be expected to live with him, and applied for an injunction to exclude him from the matrimonial home so that she could return to it. The husband denied her allegations but offered no other explanation of why she had left him. The Court of Appeal took the view that the position was intolerable and that, if the husband were to continue to live in their small flat, the only way in which the wife could keep out of his way would be to leave the home altogether. There was no evidence that he would experience difficulty in finding other accommodation and, balancing the hardships likely to be suffered by both, the wife had greater need of the home than the husband. He was accordingly ordered to leave it.

Even though the position has not become intolerable, the court will protect a wife who has not forfeited her right to live in the matrimonial home if her husband unlawfully tries to evict her or to deal with the property in a way which might prejudice her right of occupation (or even declines to give an undertaking not to do so). Consequently, she may obtain an injunction forbidding him to perform the threatened act until he provides her with suitable alternative accommodation or at least reasonable financial provision.[4] Similarly, if other matrimonial proceedings are pending, an injunction will be granted excluding the husband whenever the court considers that the wife is entitled to remain in the matrimonial home until the hearing of the petition and that she will not be able to do so if he is there.[5] Conversely, an order may

---

[1] *Cf. Thompson* v. *Thompson*, [1976] Fam. 25; [1975] 2 All E.R. 208, C.A.

[2] *Bassett* v. *Bassett*, (*supra*), at pp. 82-83 and 517, respectively.

[3] [1975] Fam. 76; [1975] 1 All E.R. 513, C.A. See also *Phillips* v. *Phillips*, (*supra*) (husband ordered to leave home where his presence was turning his wife and son into psychiatric invalids). Contrast *Hall* v. *Hall*, (*supra*) (order refused when all wife proved was tension and unhappiness).

[4] *Halden* v. *Halden*, [1966] 3 All E.R. 412, C.A., following *Lee* v. *Lee*, [1952] 2 Q.B. 489 n. [1952] 1 All E.R. 1299. *Cf. Pinckney* v. *Pinckney*, [1966] 1 All E.R. 121 n. (husband ordered to remove mistress whom he had installed in the matrimonial home).

[5] *Jones* v. *Jones*, [1971] 2 All E.R. 737, C.A. (husband ordered to leave house with his mistress whom he had installed there). *Secus* if the wife will ultimately have to surrender possession to the husband whatever the outcome of the proceedings: *Murcutt* v. *Murcutt*, [1952] P. 266; [1952] 2 All E.R. 427. See also *Boyt* v. *Boyt*, [1948] 2 All E.R. 436, C.A.: *Pinckney* v. *Pinckney*, (*supra*).

be obtained solely to protect the proprietary rights of the owner if the other spouse has forfeited his right to consortium (and thus to occupy the home) and his continued presence is diminishing the value of the property, provided that no other facts (such as the position of the children) have to be considered.[1]

If both spouses have a beneficial interest in the matrimonial home, the position is further complicated because, whether they are joint tenants or tenants in common in equity, the property will be held on a statutory trust for sale. This is subject to an implied power to postpone the sale and both spouses, as trustees, must concur in the sale. If they cannot agree, either of them may call for an order that the trusts be executed, when the court may make such order as it thinks fit.[2] So long as the marriage is a going concern and the house is being used as the matrimonial home, a sale will not be ordered because this would defeat the purpose of the trust. If the marriage breaks down, the courts much prefer to use their wide powers under the Matrimonial Causes Act because they can then make a fair order after taking all relevant facts into account.[3] This can be done, however, only if one spouse petitions for divorce, nullity or judicial separation; if there is no likelihood of this in the immediate future, the court will implement the trust for sale if it is reasonable and equitable to do so to enable both parties to realize their capital.[4] Even then it is important to bear in mind that the prime object of the trust is to provide a home: all the circumstances must be taken into account and a postponement may be justified, for example, if this is necessary in the interests of the children,[5] if one of the spouses needs time to find other accommodation,[6] or if there is a reasonable chance of a reconciliation. The court will also be less ready to force a deserted spouse to leave the house, but it will do so if it would be inequitable in the circumstances to compel the other to keep his or her capital locked up.[7] There may be other cases where it would

---

[1] *Shipman* v. *Shipman*, (*supra*); *Symonds* v. *Hallett* (1883), 24 Ch. D. 346, C.A. *Cf. Wood* v. *Wood* (1871), 19 W.R. 1049. See George, *Disputes over the Matrimonial Home*, 16 Conv. 27. In *Des Salles d'Epinoix* v. *Des Salles d'Epinoix*, [1967] 2 All E.R. 539, 544, C.A., WILLMER, L.J., stated that the court would not grant an injunction restraining the wife from locking the husband out of the matrimonial home of which they were joint lessees because this was not necessary to protect his person or such right of property as he had in the house. *Sed quaere*?

[2] Law of Property Act 1925, ss. 25, 30 and 34-36; *Rawlings* v. *Rawlings*, [1964] P. 398; [1964] 2 All E.R. 804, C.A.; *Waller* v. *Waller*, [1967] 1 All E.R. 305.

[3] *Williams* v. *Williams*, [1976] Ch. 278; [1977] 1 All E.R. 28, C.A.; *Fielding* v. *Fielding*, [1978] 1 All E.R. 267, C.A.

[4] *Jackson* v. *Jackson*, [1971] 3 All E.R. 774, C.A.; *Bigg* v. *Bigg* (1975), 6 Fam. Law 56, C.A.; Miller, *Trusts for Sale and the Matrimonial Home*, 36 Conv. 99, and *Sale of the Matrimonial Home*, [1978] Conv. 301; Saunders and McGregor, *Disposal of Equitable Interest in Joint Tenancy*, 37 Conv. 270.

[5] See *Burke* v. *Burke*, [1974] 2 All E.R. 944, C.A. *Cf. Re Evers' Trust*, [1980] 3 All E.R. 399, C.A.

[6] *Mayes* v. *Mayes* (1969), 210 Estates Gazette 935 (husband temporarily unemployed and therefore finding it difficult to raise mortgage to buy another flat). In *Re Johns' Assignment Trusts*, [1970] 2 All E.R. 210, it was suggested that the spouses, who were trustees for sale, might let the house to the husband who was still living there.

[7] *Jackson* v. *Jackson*, (*supra*). But in many cases it will be fairer to give the deserting spouse a charge on the house equal to the value of his share and leave the other to pay interest on it (which will be equivalent to rent) until the court orders the charge to be enforced: *Danchevsky* v. *Danchevsky*, [1975] Fam. 17, 20; [1974] 3 All E.R. 934, 936, C.A.

be unjust to order an immediate sale: thus in *Bedson* v. *Bedson*[1] the court refused to do so where the wife was in desertion and the property in question (a draper's shop with a flat over it) had been bought out of the husband's savings and was his sole livelihood.

Bankrupt Spouse.—If the matrimonial home forms a part of the assets of a bankrupt spouse, the trustee in bankruptcy will normally wish to sell it so as to increase the sum available to the creditors. If the bankrupt (who, for the sake of example, will be assumed to be the husband) is the sole owner, his creditors' interests take priority over the wife's right of occupation and consequently she cannot take any steps to prevent the sale.[2] If both spouses have a beneficial interest in the property, only the bankrupt's part will vest in the trustee; hence if the wife will not join in the sale, the trustee must apply for a court order. The court has a discretion to refuse to make the order and will seek to avoid a sale if possible, for example by permitting the wife to buy the husband's share.[3] If this cannot be done, it will weigh the conflicting claims of the wife (who will still want a roof over her head) and the creditors (who may be able to realise the husband's part share only by selling the whole with vacant possession). It will order a sale much more readily if the marriage has broken down so that the purpose of the trust has come to an end.[4] The welfare of the children must also be taken into account, and if it is imperative that they should stay in the matrimonial home, this may be a valid reason for postponing the sale at least until suitable alternative accommodation can be found for them.[5] When the equities are equal, the claims of the creditors will prevail, but the court will not order the spouses to surrender possession until they have had reasonable time to make other arrangements.[6]

Furniture.—The only reported case dealing solely with the spouses' rights with respect to the furniture—*W.* v. *W.*[7]—indicates that the courts will not protect the wife's right to use it as fully as they will protect her right to remain in the matrimonial home. The furniture (the ownership of which was not in dispute) belonged partly to the husband and partly to the wife. After the husband had left the wife, he claimed his portion of the goods, which included a table and chairs and the matrimonial bed. It was held that the court's discretion under section 17 of the Married Women's Property Act will not necessarily be exercised in the same way with respect to the furniture as it will with respect to the house itself, and that in this case the husband should

[1] [1965] 2 Q.B. 666; [1965] 3 All E.R. 307, C.A. See also *Hayward* v. *Hayward* (1974), 237 Estates Gazette 577; Samuels, 110 Sol. Jo. 5.
[2] *Cf. Re Solomon*, [1967] Ch. 573; [1966] 3 All E.R. 255. The statutory right of occupation under the Matrimonial Homes Act is void against the owner's trustee in bankruptcy; see *post*, p. 467. The trustee has a similar claim to the furniture owned by the bankrupt, who is entitled to retain tools, wearing apparel and bedding for himself, his wife and children only up to a value of £20: Bankruptcy Act 1914, s. 38 (2).
[3] She might be able to raise the money by mortgaging the whole property.
[4] *Re Solomon, (supra)*.
[5] As in *Re Holliday*, [1980] 3 All E.R. 385, C.A. (sale postponed until children aged 17). Contrast *Re Bailey*, [1977] 2 All E.R. 26.
[6] *Re Turner*, [1975] 1 All E.R. 5; *Re McCarthy*, [1975] 2 All E.R. 857. But immediate possession might be given to the trustee *e.g.* if the spouses were being obstructive; *Re McCarthy*, at p. 859. See further Palley, *Wives, Creditors and the Matrimonial Home*, 20 N.I.L.Q. 132; Miller, 119 Sol. Jo. 582.
[7] [1951] 2 T.L.R. 1135.

be entitled to take his own property because the wife could be expected to replace it in the course of time. But DEVLIN, J., stated that he would not have been prepared to make this order if the husband had been acting vindictively or, in any case, if the wife would have been left with nothing but bare boards. If she has not forfeited the right to be maintained, she must be left with the means of subsistence; it then becomes a question of fact in each case where the line is to be drawn.

The Spouses' Rights against Third Persons.—Up to now we have been considering the spouses' rights *inter se*. A series of cases from 1952 had gone much further by laying down the rule that a deserted wife could enforce her right to remain in the matrimonial home (of which her husband was the beneficial owner) not only against him but also against anyone claiming through him other than a *bona fide* purchaser for value of a legal or equitable estate or interest without notice of her claim. The validity of this so-called "deserted wife's equity" was eventually considered by the House of Lords in *National Provincial Bank, Ltd.* v. *Ainsworth*.[1] The husband had deserted his wife (the respondent) and left her and their children in the matrimonial home. He then conveyed the house to a company in which he had a controlling interest and which in turn charged it to the appellant bank to secure a loan. This was not repaid and the bank, as mortgagee, claimed possession of the property charged. The wife set up her "deserted wife's equity" but it was unanimously held that her defence must fail. The only case in which the wife's equity will avail her is where the sale by the husband is a completely sham transaction designed to enable him to obtain possession. Four of the members of the House of Lords in *Ainsworth's* case[2] considered that the earlier case of *Ferris* v. *Weaven*[3] could still be justified on its special facts. In that case the husband, having deserted his wife and left her in the matrimonial home, sold the house to the plaintiff, his brother-in-law, for the sum of £30 which was never paid. The sole purpose of this conveyance was to enable the husband, who could not personally have obtained possession in the circumstances, to do so through the purchaser. It was held that the plaintiff could have no greater right than the husband and his claim must fail. The decision may still be of importance if the wife has not registered her right of occupation under the Matrimonial Homes Act,[4] although in many cases she could have the sale set aside as a transaction intended to defeat her claim for financial relief.[5]

---

[1] [1965] A.C. 1175; [1965] 2 All E.R. 472, H.L. For a detailed discussion of this decision, see Crane, *After the Deserted Wife's Licence*, 29 Conv. 254 and 464. See also Bailey in [1965] C.L.J. 216.

[2] LORD HODSON (with whom LORD GUEST concurred) at pp. 1223 and 479; LORD UPJOHN ("it may possibly be justified") at pp. 1240 and 489; LORD WILBERFORCE at pp. 1258 and 501, respectively.

[3] [1952] 2 All E.R. 233 (although the *ratio decidendi* is no longer good law). MEGARRY, J., concluded that the case was correctly decided on its facts in *Miles* v. *Bull*, [1969] 1 Q.B. 258; [1968] 3 All E.R. 632, but as he pointed out (at pp. 264 and 636, respectively) the fact that the price is low or not paid in full does not necessarily mean that the transaction is a sham. See further *Miles* v. *Bull* (*No.* 2), [1969] 3 All E.R. 1585.

[4] See *infra*.

[5] See *post*, p. 568. Such an attempt failed in *Ainsworth's* case because the bank was a *bona fide* purchaser for value without notice of the husband's intention.

The real problem is to balance the claims of the deserted wife against those of the husband's purchaser or (as is usually the case) his creditors either acting through his trustee in bankruptcy or seeking to realise their own security as mortgagees of the house in which the wife is living. Looked at from the conveyancing point of view, there are two fatal objections to the "deserted wife's equity". In the first place the wife's rights against the purchaser can clearly be no greater than they are against the husband himself. As against him she would lose her right to remain in the house if, for example, she were to commit adultery or the husband were to offer her suitable alternative accomodation. It is therefore transient and determinable and lacks the qualities of being definable, identifiable, permanent and stable which are essential if it is to be regarded as a right in property capable of binding the land in the hands of subsequent purchasers.[1] In the second place it must be possible for the prospective purchaser to discover precisely what rights exist in the land and these are of such a highly personal nature, known only to the spouses themselves, that he would be in an impossible position when he made enquiries.[2]

One of the main objects of the Matrimonial Homes Act was to overcome these difficulties. For the sake of convenience in the following discussion it will again be assumed that the beneficial interest in the matrimonial home is vested in the husband to the exclusion of the wife, but it must be remembered that exactly the same principles apply if it is vested in the wife to the exclusion of the husband. The way the Act seeks to protect both the wife and the purchaser is by providing that her right to occupy the matrimonial home (whether or not a court order has been made) shall be a charge on the husband's estate or interest in the property. The charge takes effect on the husband's acquisition of the property, the date of the marriage, or the commencement of the Act (1st January 1968) whichever last happens. It terminates on the husband's death or the dissolution or annulment of the marriage unless the court has previously made an order that it shall continue.[3]

The charge is registrable as a Class F Land Charge under the Land Charges Act 1972.[4] As a wife out of occupation may need even greater protection than a wife physically in the house (for example, if she has been constructively deserted), her charge may be registered even though she has not yet been given leave by the court to enter and occupy.[5] The charge will bind any person deriving title under the husband except that it will be void against any subsequent purchaser of the land or any interest in it for value unless it is registered before completion.[6] Whether it has been registered or not, however, it will be void against the husband's trustee in bankruptcy or his creditors' trustees if he assigns the house to them under a deed of arrangement. Even if the court has ordered the right to continue after the husband's

---

[1] *National Provincial Bank, Ltd.* v. *Ainsworth*, [1965] A.C. 1175, at pp. 1224, 1233-1234, and 1248-1250; [1965] 2 All ER. 472, at pp. 479-480, 485-486, and 494-495, H.L.

[2] *Ibid.*, pp. 1234 and 1250, and 486 and 495-496, respectively.

[3] S. 2 (1) and (2).

[4] Land Charges Act 1972, s. 2 (7). In the case of registered land registration is effected by notice or caution: Matrimonial Homes Act 1967, s. 2 (7).

[5] *Watts* v. *Waller*, [1973] Q.B. 153; [1972] 3 All E.R. 257, C.A. If she subsequently makes an unsuccessful application for leave, the registration will be cancelled.

[6] A successor in title to the husband who is bound by the charge has the same right to apply for the termination of the wife's right as the husband would have had.

death, the charge will also be void if the husband's estate is insolvent.[1] One sees here another example of the principle that the claims of the husband's creditors are to be preferred to those of his wife; one can also see the anxiety of the legislature that the creditors should not be defrauded by the registration of a charge intended to defeat their claim to the property.

The wife is entitled to have only one charge registered under the Act. Consequently, if the spouses have two homes (for example, a town flat and a country cottage), she must make up her mind which occupation right she will register. If, after registering one, she registers another, the first registration must be cancelled.[2] Registration must also be cancelled if the court terminates the wife's right of occupation or when the marriage comes to an end unless the court has ordered that her right shall continue.[3] The wife may release her right in whole or in part in writing and may agree in writing that another charge or interest shall take priority over it. If the charge is registered, the normal conveyancing procedure is for the wife to deliver to the purchaser on completion an application for the cancellation of the registration.[4]

Rights against Mortgagees.—The Matrimonial Homes Act will give the non-owning spouse (who will usually be the wife) no rights against anyone taking a mortgage of the matrimonial home before the statutory right of occupation is registered. This will happen frequently, because the mortgage will be taken when the house is bought and therefore before the spouses take possession. If the husband wishes to use the house as security for a loan at a later date and the wife has registered her right, the mortgagee will presumably insist on her agreeing that the charge shall take priority over it because otherwise he might not be able to realise his security. This raises a further problem: can the wife claim any right to occupy the house if the husband defaults and a mortgagee with priority over her wishes to obtain possession with a view to exercising his statutory power of sale?

She is given a degree of protection by the Matrimonial Homes Act, which provides that, if a spouse entitled under the Act to occupy the whole or part of the matrimonial home makes any payment or tender in respect of rent, rates, mortgage payments or other outgoings affecting the home, this shall be as effective as though it were made by the owner.[5] The difficulty is that the mortgagee is not bound to give the wife any notice of the husband's default or of the proceedings;[6] consequently by the time she gets to hear of them, considerable arrears may have accumulated. This may deprive her of any effective remedy because the court has a power to stay or suspend execution of an order giving possession only if the mortgagor is likely to be able to pay all sums due within a reasonable time.[7] Assuming (as seems likely) that the

---

[1] Matrimonial Homes Act 1967, s. 2 (3)-(5); Land Charges Act 1972, ss. 4 (8) and 17 (1). For the power to tack mortgages, see the Matrimonial Homes Act 1967, s. 2 (8).

[2] S. 3.

[3] S. 5. If the wife has an order continuing her right of occupation after the termination of the marriage, she must renew her registration (or register her charge if it was not registered before).

[4] Ss. 4 and 6.

[5] S.1 (5).

[6] *Hastings and Thanet Building Society* v. *Goddard*, [1970] 3 All E.R. 954, C.A. See further Law Com. No. 86, paras. 2.18-2.33. For changes proposed in the Matrimonial Homes and Property Bill, see Appendix E, *post.*

[7] Administration of Justice Act 1970, s. 36; Administration of Justice Act 1973, s. 8; *Halifax Building Society* v. *Clark*, [1973] Ch. 307; [1973] 2 All E.R. 33, C.A.

court would exercise these powers if the mortgagor's spouse in occupation could satisfy this condition, it may be impossible for her to find sufficient money to pay off the arrears within a reasonable period even though she might have been able to pay the instalments as they fell due.

As the cases indicate, in practice the wife has more to fear from a mortgagee than from a purchaser of the whole of the husband's estate. If he tries to sell the matrimonial home, she will be put on her guard by potential buyers' coming to view the premises; but if he mortgages the house to secure his overdraft, she may know nothing about the transaction until the bank tries to enforce its security. *Ex hypothesi* a solicitor will be acting for a husband alone when the matrimonial home is bought so there will be no one to advise her to register her right of occupation and in any event, like the wives in the cases concerned with the ownership of the house, she will not contemplate the necessity of protecting her interest. When the marriage does break down, the property may already be mortgaged and her registration will come too late if she cannot pay the mortgage instalments and arrears herself. Clearly the Act will give effective protection to the wife only when an automatic registration of her right of occupation becomes a common practice.[1]

Decided cases have also shown that the Act can operate unfairly on the husband. The wife may not have told him that she has registered a charge and he may know nothing about it.[2] Again, a spiteful wife may refuse to have the registration cancelled even when the husband offers her other accommodation which it is unreasonable for her to refuse. The house may then become a useless asset which he can sell only after litigation between the spouses. In *Wroth* v. *Tyler*,[3] for example, the wife, who was living in the matrimonial home with the husband, stood by whilst he was negotiating its sale and then registered her charge immediately the contract was entered into. As a result he was unable to make title and, because of the sharp increase in the price of houses at the time, the damages awarded against him for breach of contract probably caused him to become bankrupt. (This, ironically, would have the result that the house would be sold by the husband's trustees in bankruptcy free of the wife's right.)

3. THE RENT ACT

In the preceding discussion it has been assumed that the husband owned the matrimonial home in fee simple or for a long term of years. But so many homes are leasehold property (usually on a weekly, monthly or quarterly tenancy) and subject to the Rent Act that we must now consider the position in the light of its provisions.

Rent control is the immediate outcome of the chronic shortage of houses and began in this country in 1915 as the result of the shortage in the First World War. The details of the scheme are extremely complex and are now contained in the Rent Act 1977. Their purpose is twofold: to prevent the

---

[1] In which case the sheer bulk of registrations might make the system unworkable. See further Palley, *Wives, Creditors and the Matrimonial Home*, 20 N.I.L.Q. 132.

[2] As in *Watts* v. *Waller*, (*supra*).

[3] [1974] Ch. 30; [1973] 1 All E.R. 897. See further Cretney, 117 Sol. Jo. 475; Barnsley, *Conveying the Matrimonial Home*, Current Legal Problems, 1974, 76; Hayton, *The Femme Fatale in Conveyancing Practice*, 38 Conv. 110.

charging of exorbitant rents and to protect the tenant from arbitrary eviction. The former is achieved by severely limiting the landlord's power to increase the rent; the second is achieved by limiting the landlord's right to obtain possession. It is with the latter that we are principally concerned.

Regulated Tenancies.—The Act applies only to a house or part of a house let as a separate dwelling: a definition wide enough to include a flat.[1] Certain tenancies are not protected; of these the more important are holiday lettings, lettings which include board or attendance, and tenancies of premises let at no rent or at a rent which is less than two-thirds of their rateable value, agricultural holdings occupied by the farmer, premises let to students by educational institutions, and premises let by the Crown, Government departments, local authorities, development corporations, housing trusts and (in certain circumstances) housing associations. Furnished premises, which were formerly excluded, were brought within the Acts by the Rent Act 1974; but this Act in turn created another important class of unprotected tenancies. Subject to certain exceptions, a tenancy of a dwelling forming part of a larger building (other than a purpose-built block of flats) will not be protected if it was entered into after 13th August 1974 and the landlord for the time being occupies another dwelling in the same building as his own residence. This is primarily designed to give wider powers of recovering possession to the resident owner of a large house which has been converted into small flats.[2]

A further type of unprotected tenancy was introduced by the Housing Act 1980: the "assured tenancy". This "marks an experiment to see whether there is any chance of a revival of building for rent".[3] It arises if a body approved by the Secretary of State is the landlord of a dwelling-house which is, or forms part of, a building erected since 8th August 1980 and which has not been occupied by any person as his residence except under an assured tenancy.[4] It is contemplated that the bodies that will be approved are those like building societies and pension funds which will wish to use residential buildings as a form of investment.

Rent control is designed to protect the poorer tenant and consequently it has always been limited to leases of premises of less than specified rateable values. During the 1950's it was felt that the building of new houses had sufficiently eased the position to enable a progressive scheme of decontrol to be introduced. The Housing Repairs and Rents Act of 1954 excluded from the operation of the Acts premises erected after 29th August 1954, as well as separate and self-contained premises produced by the conversion of other premises after that date. The Rent Act of 1957 went further and provided that the Acts should not apply to premises the rateable value of which in 1956 exceeded £40 in London and £30 elsewhere in England and Wales or which

---

[1] See Megarry, *Rent Acts*, 10th Ed., 72 *et seq.* For accommodation partly separate and partly shared, see the Rent Act 1977, s. 22.

[2] For full list of excepted tenancies, see the Rent Act 1977, ss. 5-16, as amended by the Housing Act 1980, ss. 65, 73 and 74 and Scheds. 8 and 25. Tenants of resident landlords and certain other tenants are given a more limited protection as parties to "restricted contracts": see *ibid.*, ss. 19 and 20 and Part V, as amended by the Housing Act 1980. Tenants of long tenancies at a low rent are given protection by the Landlord and Tenant Act 1954, as amended.

[3] Arden, Commentary on the Act in *Current Law Statutes*.

[4] For details, see the Housing Act 1980, ss. 56-58.

were let for a period of more than 21 years (thus immediately decontrolling
some 800,000 dwellings) and excluded almost all new lettings coming into
operation after 5th July 1957. It will be seen that these provisions contemplated the eventual extinction of rent control as fewer and fewer leases would
be covered by the Rent Acts—a process which could be speeded up by the
Minister of Housing and Local Government, who was empowered by the
1957 Act to release other dwellings from control from time to time. This Act
also introduced the "rent limit" which enabled landlords to charge an economic rent based upon the gross rateable value of the property and thus
remedied an injustice suffered by many who had to meet their liability to keep
in repair premises let at an absurdly low rent.[1]

Within less than a decade, however, it had become apparent that this policy
of decontrol would not work. Large scale immigration from other Commonwealth countries caused a further shortage of property (especially of the
cheaper type) and this, coupled with some scandalous cases of "racketeering"
by property speculators, produced continuing inflation of rents. The result
was the passing of the Rent Act of 1965, which extended protection by introducing a slightly different concept, that of the regulated tenancy. This covered
all tenancies excluded by the Acts of 1954 and 1957 and all new tenancies. The
Act of 1965 also introduced machinery whereby either the landlord or the
tenant can have a fair rent fixed by a local rent officer from whom an appeal
lies to an area assessment committee.[2] The Housing Finance Act 1972
provided for the gradual conversion of all controlled tenancies (except those
of unfit premises) into regulated tenancies by 1975, but economic conditions
led the Government to slow down and eventually halt this process until 1980,
when the Housing Act converted all remaining controlled tenancies into
regulated tenancies. The result is that, except for those already mentioned, a
tenancy will, generally speaking, be a regulated tenancy if the rateable value
of the premises did not exceed £1,500 in Greater London or £750 elsewhere on
1st April 1973 (or when the rateable value was first shown if this was later).[3]

Statutory Tenants.—So long as a tenant is in occupation under a contractual lease, he is clearly protected from arbitrary eviction by the terms of
his contract. The Act goes much further by giving him a wide measure of protection after his lease ends. A contractual lease to which the Act applies is
known as a *protected tenancy*; if a tenant under a protected tenancy remains
in possession after his contractual lease has been determined—for example, if
his term has expired or he has been given notice to quit in accordance with
the provisions of the lease—his tenancy becomes a *statutory tenancy*.[4]

---

[1] See now Part II of the Rent Act 1977.

[2] See now *ibid.*, Parts III and IV.

[3] For full details, see *ibid.*, ss. 4, 18 and 25; Housing Act 1980, s. 64.

[4] Rent Act 1977, ss. 1 and 2; Megarry, *op. cit.*, 178 *et seq.* If there were two or more joint
contractual tenants but not all are in possession at the end of the contractual tenancy, those
remaining become statutory tenants: *Lloyd* v. *Sadler*, [1978] Q.B. 774; [1978] 2 All E.R. 529,
C.A. A husband's permitting his wife to remain in possession of the matrimonial home as a
condition of paying a reduced sum under a maintenance order does not create the relationship of
landlord and tenant so as to give the wife the protection of the Rent Act: *Bramwell* v. *Bramwell*,
[1942] 1 K.B. 370; [1942] 1 All E.R. 137, C.A. *Cf. Marcroft Wagons, Ltd.* v. *Smith*, [1951]
2 K.B. 496; [1951] 2 All E.R. 271, C.A. (daughter permitted to remain in possession after her
mother's death for a short time not protected by the Act).

more in certain circumstances a member of a deceased statutory or protected tenant's family also becomes a statutory tenant.[1] A statutory tenant is generally speaking bound by all the terms and conditions in the original lease and entitled to the benefit of them.[2]

In order to claim the protection given by the Act against eviction, the statutory tenant must continue in personal occupation of the premises as his home, for the policy of the Act is to protect the home and not to give the tenant any wider privileges. A person may be in occupation of more than one home for this purpose simultaneously, as where he works in two places and has a home in each of them which he occupies when he is at that particular place;[3] and a temporary absence will not suffice to bring his statutory tenancy to an end.[4] But he must retain both the *corpus* of possession and an *animus revertendi*. Thus it has been held that a wife who had gone away because of illness leaving her furniture in the house, in which her husband occasionally slept and to which she hoped to return as soon as her health improved, was still in occupation and was entitled to the protection of the Act.[5] But a mere *animus* without the *corpus* will not be sufficient, and consequently it has been held that a man who left his house deserted whilst serving a sentence of imprisonment ceased to be a statutory tenant.[6] He could have averted this result only "by coupling and clothing his inward intention with some formal, outward, and visible sign of it", for example by installing a caretaker or relative to preserve the premises for his homecoming.[7] Conversely, if the tenant leaves the premises with no intention of ever returning there at all, he loses the status of a statutory tenant even though he leaves his furniture there with a caretaker or relative.[8]

But to this rule that the occupation must be personal is one important statutory exception designed to protect the tenant's spouse—particularly the deserted wife. If one spouse is a protected or statutory tenant but the other is in actual occupation of the premises, this is deemed to be the occupation of the tenant himself even though the spouse in occupation has been deserted by the tenant and is there against his will.[9]

It will be recalled that the provisions of the Matrimonial Homes Act will continue to apply notwithstanding that one spouse holds the premises on a protected or statutory tenancy. Consequently the court can make an order

---

[1] See *post*, pp. 638 *et seq.*

[2] Rent Act 1977, s. 3.

[3] See Megarry, *op. cit.*, 186-188 and the cases there cited.

[4] Megarry, *op. cit.*, 191-195.

[5] *Wigley* v. *Leigh*, [1950] 2 K.B. 305; [1950] 1 All E.R. 73, C.A.

[6] *Brown* v. *Brash*, [1948] 2 K.B. 247; [1948] 1 All E.R. 922, C.A.

[7] *Per* ASQUITH, L.J., *ibid.*, at pp. 254-255 and 926, respectively.

[8] *Skinner* v. *Geary*, [1931] 2 K.B. 546, C.A. (sister); *Robson* v. *Headland* (1948), 64 T.L.R. 596, C.A. (divorced wife and son); *Beck* v. *Scholz*, [1953] 1 Q.B. 570; [1953] 1 All E.R. 814, C.A. (caretakers); *Colin Smith Music, Ltd.* v. *Ridge*, [1975] 1 All E.R. 290, C.A. (deserted mistress and illegitimate children).

[9] Matrimonial Homes Act 1967, s. 1 (5). No order need have been made under the Act. As in the case of the tenant, a spouse who is temporarily absent will remain in occupation for the purpose of the Act if he retains the *corpus* of possession and the *animus revertendi*: *Hoggett* v. *Hoggett* (1979), 39 P. & C.R. 121, C.A. Before the passing of this Act the wife's occupation was attributed to the husband but not *vice versa*.

permitting the tenant's spouse to enter the home and regulating both parties' right to occupy it.[1]

Recovery of Possession.—If the statutory tenant and his or her spouse both leave the premises, this automatically brings the statutory tenancy to an end, and the landlord may retake possession or, if necessary, recover it by suing any trespasser on the property.[2] But if a protected or statutory tenant or his or her spouse is still in occupation, the landlord may obtain an order for possession only if the conditions laid down by the Rent Act are fulfilled. These are of two kinds.[3]

Into the first group come those cases in which the court may not make an order for possession unless it is satisfied that, having regard to all the circumstances, it is reasonable to do so. In addition, the landlord must prove the existence of one of the following statutory grounds on which the court can make an order:

(a) that rent has not been paid or any other of the tenant's covenants has not been performed or observed;

(b) that the tenant, any person residing with him, or his sub-tenant has been guilty of conduct which is a nuisance or annoyance to adjoining occupiers, or has been convicted of using the premises for an immoral or illegal purpose or permitting such use;

(c) that the tenant, his lodger or sub-tenant has caused or permitted the premises to deteriorate by waste, neglect or default;

(d) that, in the case of furnished premises, the furniture has deteriorated because of ill-treatment by the tenant, his lodger or sub-tenant;

(e) that the tenant has given notice to quit and as a consequence the landlord has contracted to sell or let the premises or taken some other step as a result of which he would be seriously prejudiced if he could not obtain possession;

(f) that the tenant has assigned or sub-let the whole of the premises[4] without the landlord's consent;

(g) that, if the premises were let to the tenant in consequence of his being employed by the landlord, that employment has now ceased and the landlord reasonably requires the premises for a person in the whole-time employment of the landlord or one of his tenants;

---

[1] See *ante*, pp. 458-460. Once the landlord has obtained an order for possession and this has taken effect, the tenant is no longer entitled to remain in possession by virtue of the Rent Act and consequently the spouse loses the right of occupation under the Matrimonial Homes Act and becomes a trespasser but she (or he) can still apply for the order to be stayed or suspended: Rent Act 1977, s. 100, as amended by the Housing Act 1980, s. 75 (3).

[2] *Brown* v. *Draper*, [1944] K.B. 309; [1944] 1 All E.R. 246, C.A.; *Middleton* v. *Baldock*, [1950] 1 K.B. 657, 661-662; [1950] 1 All E.R. 708, 710, C.A.

[3] Rent Act 1977, s. 98 and Sched. 15; Housing Act 1980, ss. 66 and 67 and Sched. 7. See further Megarry, *op. cit.,* c. 7. See also the Rent Act 1977, s. 101 (overcrowded premises) and the Landlord and Tenant Act 1954, s. 12 (1). In the case of a protected tenancy the landlord must also be able to show that he would be able to claim possession quite apart from the Acts, *e.g.* by virtue of a forfeiture clause in the lease. For the recovery of premises occupied by agricultural workers, see *post*, p. 476.

[4] Or has sub-let part of the premises, the remainder being already sub-let.

(h) that the landlord reasonably requires the premises for occupation as a
residence for himself, a child of his over the age of 18, his father or mother, or
his spouse's father or mother, provided that greater hardship would not be
caused by granting the order than refusing it;[1]

(i) that the tenant has charged his sub-tenant a rent in excess of that
permitted by the Act;

(j) that suitable alternative accommodation is available to the tenant.

In the second category of cases the court does not have to be satisfied that
it is reasonable to make an order for possession. All that is necessary is for the
landlord to prove that one of the following conditions is satisfied.

(a) If a person who has let premises which he occupied as his residence
(called in the Act an "owner-occupier") requires them as a residence for himself or for any member of his family[2] who was residing with him when he last
occupied them as a residence, the court must make an order for possession in
his favour if he would have been entitled to possession but for the operation
of the Rent Act. Before the commencement of the tenancy[3] the landlord must
give the tenant notice in writing that possession might be recovered under this
provision, but if he omits to do so, the court has a discretion to make an order
for possession if this is just and equitable. It is also possible to recover possession if the owner has died or wishes to sell the premises in order to purchase
another dwelling-house more suitable for his needs. These provisions are
designed to protect the owner-occupier who wishes to let his home during a
temporary absence.[4]

(b) If a person who intends to occupy a dwelling-house as his residence
when he retires from regular employment, lets it before his retirement, he
may recover possession on his retirement if he requires the premises as his
residence. If the owner dies, possession may be claimed by any member of his
family residing with him at the time of his death or, in certain circumstances,
by the owner's successor in title. This is complementary to case (a) above. The
owner must give similar written notice to the tenant before the commencement of the tenancy, which the court may waive.

(c) The landlord may recover possession of premises which had been
occupied as a holiday home within a period of 12 months before the letting
provided that the lease was for a period of not more than eight months and

---

[1] In *McIntyre* v. *Hardcastle*, [1948] 2 K.B. 82; [1948] 1 All E.R. 696, C.A., it was held that, if
there are joint lessors, the word "landlord" must be consistently interpreted to include both (or
all) of them. Hence if a husband and wife jointly let the premises and then separate so that only
one requires the house as a residence, the application will fail. This principle cannot apply if a
joint lessor dies, because the survivor will be the "landlord". The point was left open in *Tilling* v.
Whiteman, (*infra*).

[2] *I.e.*, genuinely desires and intends to use them as a residence: *Kennealy* v. *Dunne*, [1977]
Q.B. 837; [1977] 2 All E.R. 16, C.A. For the meaning of "member of the family", see *post*,
pp. 639-641.

[3] Or by 7th June 1966 in the case of an unfurnished tenancy created before 8th December
1965, or by 13th February 1975 in the case of a furnished tenancy created before 14th August
1974.

[4] In *Tilling* v. *Whiteman*, [1980] A.C. 1; [1979] 1 All E.R. 737, H.L., it was held that, if there
are joint landlords, it is sufficient that the premises are required as a residence for one of them (or
his family) provided that he occupied them as his residence. Otherwise landlords might refuse to
let and the purpose of the Act would be defeated. Contrast *McIntyre* v. *Hardcastle*, (*supra*).

similar written notice was given. This is designed to enable the owner of a holiday home to let it for short periods.

(d) If the landlord was a member of the regular armed forces when he acquired the premises and also when he let them, he may recover possession if he requires them as his residence. The requirements relating to notice are similar to those in (b) above and there are further provisions enabling possession to be recovered after the landlord's death or if he wishes to sell the premises in order to purchase another dwelling-house more suitable to his needs.

(e) Similar provisions exist to enable educational institutions to recover premises let otherwise than to students (for example, during a university vacation) and to enable landlords to recover possession of a redundant farm house, a dwelling-house let for occupation by a minister of religion as such or one required by the landlord for an agricultural employee.

(f) In an attempt to make more leasehold property available on the market, the Housing Act 1980 has created a new protected shorthold tenancy. This is a tenancy for a term certain of not less than one year nor more than five years which cannot be terminated by the landlord except for non-payment of rent or breach of any other covenant.[1] In order that he may take advantage of the provisions relating to recovery of possession, the landlord must give the tenant a valid notice stating that the tenancy is to be a protected shorthold tenancy before the grant of the lease and the rent must be registered; the court, however, may waive these requirements in any case if it is of the opinion that it would be just and equitable to make an order for possession. The landlord may recover possession of the premises provided that he gives the tenant at least three months' written notice of his intention to do so at any time within a period of three months before the tenancy comes to an end or any anniversary of that date.[2]

The parties may not contract out of the Rent Act. Hence a contract between the landlord and tenant that the latter shall surrender the premises (and *a fortiori* a notice by the tenant terminating the lease) will not give the landlord the right to recover possession unless the facts come within ground (e) on page 473.[3] Similarly the court has no jurisdiction to make an order if the landlord rests his case on none of these statutory grounds, even though the tenant does not defend the action;[4] but if the landlord alleges that a ground exists and the tenant does not contest this, the court may make an order without enquiring into the truth of the allegation.[5]

---

[1] If the tenancy is for a term certain coupled with an option to renew on the part of the tenant or for a term certain and thereafter from year to year or some other period, it is a protected shorthold tenancy during the term certain. The tenant may always bring the tenancy to an end notwithstanding any contrary term in the lease on giving the landlord three months' written notice (or one month's notice if the term is for two years or less): Housing Act 1980, s. 53. No assignment of the tenancy is permitted except under a property adjustment order made under s. 24 of the Matrimonial Causes Act 1973.

[2] Housing Act 1980, ss. 51-55. Proceedings must be begun within three months of the expiry of the notice, and no fresh notice may be served within that period. For the landlord's power to obtain possession against a sub-tenant, see *ibid.*, s. 54.

[3] *Brown* v. *Draper*, (*ante*); *Middleton* v. *Baldock*, (*ante*).

[4] *Middleton* v. *Baldock*, (*ante*).

[5] *Middleton* v. *Baldock*, (*ante*), at pp. 661, 669, and 710, 715, respectively.

It will thus be seen that where the matrimonial home is held on a regulated tenancy, the spouses have a large measure of security. The significance of this will be appreciated when it is realised that the dwelling house will be subject to the Rent Act in many cases where hardship would otherwise result.

Premises occupied by Agricultural Workers.—Many agricultural workers are not protected by the Rent Act because they have merely a licence to occupy the premises (as distinct from a lease), because the letting includes board or attendance or because the premises are let at a low rent or are comprised in an agricultural holding. In such cases a court was bound to make an order in favour of a farmer who brought proceedings to recover possession of "tied accommodation" from a worker whose tenancy or licence had been lawfully terminated. This frequently caused hardship, particularly to retired workers and the members of the family of a deceased worker, and consequently the Rent (Agriculture) Act was passed in 1976 to extend security of tenure to farmworkers.

The provisions of this Act are broadly similar to those of the Rent Act. Essentially they apply whenever a whole-time agricultural worker (or former whole-time agricultural worker) is in occupation of a dwelling-house or part of a dwelling-house owned by his employer (or former employer) by virtue of a licence or of a tenancy which is not protected by the Rent Act.[1] Like the Rent Act, the Rent (Agriculture) Act does not apply if the premises are let (or the licence granted) by the Crown or the public bodies specified in the Rent Act or by a person occupying another dwelling in the same building as his own residence.[2]

The grounds on which the owner can apply for possession are the same as those contained in the Rent Acts with some important differences. If he bases his claim on the fact that suitable alternative accommodation is available, the accommodation must satisfy the stringent conditions set out in the Act. Secondly, he may not seek possession solely on the ground that the employment by virtue of which the premises were let to the tenant (or granted to the licensee) has ceased and that he requires the premises for another employee. In such a case the Act throws a duty on the local housing authority to use its best endeavours to provide suitable alternative accommodation for the existing occupant, and a further ground on which the owner can seek possession is that the tenant has unreasonably failed to accept an offer of such accommodation. It should be noted that these provisions apply not only to those holding tenancies and licences protected by the Rent (Agriculture) Act but also to agricultural workers who are protected or statutory tenants under the Rent Act.[3]

---

[1] For the full details, see the Rent (Agriculture) Act 1976, ss. 1 and 2 and Scheds. 2 and 3, and *Normanton* v. *Giles*, [1980] 1 All E.R. 106, H.L. (for the meaning of "qualifying worker"). The Act also applies if the premises are owned by a person who has made arrangements with the occupant's employer to accommodate persons employed by him in agriculture.

[2] *Ibid.*, Sched. 2, para. 4. See *ante*, p. 470, for the bodies specified.

[3] *Ibid.*, ss. 6 and 7 and Sched. 4; Rent Act 1977, s. 99 and Sched. 16. The owner may also claim possession on the ground that he reasonably requires the premises for occupation by a grandparent or his spouse's grandparent, but he cannot base a claim on the fact that he requires the premises for occupation for himself or any relative if he purchased the dwelling-house after

The Position of the Deserted Spouse.—If the wife (or husband) of a tenant holding on a weekly or other periodical tenancy is deserted and continues to pay the rent herself, a number of legal consequences follow. If the landlord is unaware of the desertion and assumes that the husband is still in personal occupation of the premises, he will regard the wife merely as an agent and the lease will still be vested in the husband. If the landlord is aware that the husband has left but continues to take the rent from the wife, it is a question of fact whether he is continuing to treat the wife as her husband's agent (in which case the husband will remain the legal tenant) or whether he has accepted her as a new tenant (in which case the wife will become a new contractual tenant). The mere fact that the landlord accepts rent from the wife with full knowledge of the facts is not *per se* evidence of his having granted a new lease to her, for, as we shall see, he cannot evict the wife and consequently has no alternative to taking the rent from her.[1] But if no new tenancy is brought into existence, the original tenant, and not the spouse, continues to hold under the old tenancy. Hence the members of the spouse's family could not claim a right to remain in possession after her death.[2]

The position of the deserted spouse is the result of her right to occupy the matrimonial home under the Matrimonial Homes Act 1967 and the attribution of occupation to the tenant. If the landlord serves a notice to quit, this will have no other effect than to convert a contractual tenancy into a statutory one and he still cannot obtain possession unless he can prove the existence of one of the statutory grounds.[3] The tenant presumably remains liable for the rent,[4] but as non-payment of rent is one of the grounds on which the landlord may obtain possession, the wife may clearly have to pay it herself to secure her own occupation, in which case she may recover any sums paid from her husband.[5]

It follows from these principles, as well as from the decisions of the Court of Appeal in *Brown* v. *Draper*[6] and *Middleton* v. *Baldock*,[7] that the wife

---

12th April 1976. For the application of the Act to tenancies and licences granted before it came into force, see Sched. 9 and *Skinner* v. *Cooper*, [1979] 2 All E.R. 836, C.A. For a full discussion of the provisions of the Act, see Clements, *The "Demise" of Tied Cottages*, [1978] Conv. 259.

[1] *Cf. Morrison* v. *Jacobs*, [1945] K.B. 577; [1945] 2 All E.R. 430, C.A. See also the alternative ground for the decision in *Wabe* v. *Taylor*, [1952] 2 Q.B. 735; [1952] 2 All E.R. 420, C.A., as explained in *S.L. Dando, Ltd.* v. *Hitchcock*, [1954] 2 Q.B. 317, 324; [1954] 2 All E.R. 335, 337-338, C.A., and *Cove* v. *Flick*, [1954] 2 Q.B. 326 n., 327; [1954] 2 All E.R. 441, 442, C.A. Payment of rent by the spouse in occupation is as good as if made by the tenant: Matrimonial Homes Act 1967, s. 1 (5).

[2] See *post*, p. 639.

[3] He must join the husband as a party since he is the statutory tenant: *Brown* v. *Draper*, [1944] K.B. 309; [1944] 1 All E.R. 246, C.A. He should also join the wife as the person actually in possession: Megarry, *op. cit.*, 244; Miller, *Expenses of the Matrimonial Home*, 35 Conv. 332, 347-350.

[4] Assumed "for the moment" by LORD GODDARD, C.J., in *R.* v. *Twickenham Rent Tribunal; ex parte Dunn*, [1953] 2 Q.B. 425, 430; [1953] 2 All E.R. 734, 735, even though the husband were to give notice to the landlord.

[5] On the principle that if A discharges a legal obligation vested in B in order to preserve his (A's) own rights, B is under a quasi-contractual obligation to compensate A: see Cheshire and Fifoot, *Contract*, 9th Ed., 637-640.

[6] [1944] K.B. 309; [1944] 1 All E.R. 246, C.A. In this case the action was bound to fail as the landlord had not joined the husband as statutory tenant as a party to the action.

[7] [1950] 1 K.B. 657; [1950] 1 All E.R. 708, C.A. See also *Old Gate Estates, Ltd.* v. *Alexander*, [1950] 1 K.B. 311; [1949] 2 All E.R. 822, C.A.

cannot be evicted (except on one of the statutory grounds) even though her husband wishes to terminate the tenancy too. In the latter case the husband had deserted his wife and left her in the matrimonial home. The landlord then served a notice to quit on the husband who acknowledged the landlord's right to the premises and offered to give him immediate possession. The landlord then brought separate actions against the spouses for possession, which the wife alone defended. Judgment was entered for the plaintiff in both actions, but both orders were reversed on the wife's appeal to the Court of Appeal. Since the landlord's claim was based on none of the statutory grounds for obtaining possession, he could succeed only if the premises were vacated; and as the husband could not lawfully evict his wife, his acknowledgment of the landlord's right to enter could have no legal effect whatever. Only if the husband terminates her authority because she has forfeited her right to remain in the husband's house, can she be evicted, and even then an order would have to be obtained terminating her right of occupation under the Matrimonial Homes Act. Thus it will be seen that the deserted wife of, say, a weekly tenant under a regulated tenancy has greater security than the deserted wife of a husband who holds the matrimonial home in fee simple or for a long term of years, for she can in effect claim the protection of a statutory tenant.[1]

These provisions do not apply in the case of a tenancy (or a licence) protected by the Rent (Agriculture) Act 1976. A spouse's occupation is not attributed to the tenant and if a contractual tenancy is lawfully terminated, a statutory tenancy exists only so long as the protected occupier occupies the dwelling-house as his residence.[2] Hence if an agricultural worker deserts his wife and the landlord gives notice to quit, she has no statutory protection under the Act at all.

Transfer of Tenancies on Divorce and Nullity.—If the marriage is dissolved or annulled, the tenant's spouse will lose the right to stay in occupation of the premises given by the Matrimonial Homes Act and consequently could be evicted.[3] To meet this difficulty, section 7 of that Act provides that the court pronouncing a decree nisi of divorce or nullity may make an order transferring a protected or statutory tenancy to the spouse from the date of the decree absolute. In the case of a protected tenancy this takes effect as a compulsory assignment, and the transferee takes subject to all the benefits and burdens of the covenants and the transferor ceases to be liable on them.

---

[1] In the case of a statutory tenancy the husband presumably remains under a liability to pay the rent even though he has given notice to the landlord to determine the lease: see *ante*, p. 477, n. 4. The possibility of the husband and landlord seeking to defeat the wife's right by collusively agreeing that the landlord shall falsely allege a ground for obtaining possession which the husband will not deny is averted only if the wife is joined as a party, when she can challenge the landlord herself. See also Crane, *After the Deserted Wife's Licence*, 29 Conv. 254, at pp. 264-265.

[2] Rent (Agriculture) Act 1976, s. 4 (1). For the proposal to change this rule contained in the Matrimonial Homes and Property Bill, see Appendix E, *post*.

[3] The court may make an order that the right of occupation shall continue after the termination of the marriage (see *ante*, p. 459). If the tenant then gives notice of his intention to terminate the tenancy, it is arguable that the landlord can accept the notice and evict the wife because she is no longer a *spouse* entitled to occupy the dwelling-house. But could it be said that the tenant has produced a merger of his tenancy with the reversion by surrender so as to give the wife the protection of s. 2 (4) of the Matrimonial Homes Act? For proposed changes in the law, see Appendix E, *post*.

This suggests that no transfer could be ordered if the lease contained an express covenant forbidding assignment; all the wife could do if the landlord refused to consent to the order would be to apply to the court for a continuation of her rights of occupation.[1] In the case of a statutory tenancy the transferee becomes the statutory tenant in place of the transferor. If the spouses are joint tenants, the court has a similar power to extinguish the interest of one of them and vest the tenancy exclusively in the other.[2]

These provisions also apply to a statutory tenancy under the Rent (Agriculture) Act 1976.[3] They do not apply to a contractual tenancy (or licence), which produces some anomalies for whether a tenancy is statutory may depend, for example, on whether the landlord has served a notice of increase in rent. It is not immediately apparent why the wife should be able to claim a transfer of the tenancy if this has occurred but not if it has not. In practice, a court is hardly likely to make an order if the husband is still employed by the landlord as an agricultural worker unless he is able to obtain suitable alternative accommodation.

4. PUBLIC SECTOR TENANTS

Secure Tenancies.—We have already seen that tenancies of premises let by various public authorities are not protected by the Rent Act, with the result that tenants lacked any form of security. This gap has been largely closed by Chapter II of Part I of the Housing Act 1980, which creates a new concept, that of the secure tenancy. This arises whenever the landlord is one of the bodies mentioned earlier (except the Crown or a Government Department)[4] and the tenant is an individual occupying the dwelling-house as his only or principal home (or, in the case of joint tenants, each of them is an individual satisfying this condition).[5] A number of tenancies are excluded: among these are tenancies for a term exceeding 21 years, tenancies granted to employees required to live in the property demised for the better performance of their duties, various temporary lettings, tenancies of agricultural holdings and licensed premises, and (subject to certain conditions) lettings to students.[6] The tenancy will cease to be a secure tenancy if the tenant parts with possession of the dwelling-house or sublets the whole of it, if he assigns it except in pursuance of a property adjustment order made under section 24 of the Matrimonial Causes Act or to a person who could have been a qualified successor had the tenant died immediately before the assignment, or if it is vested or disposed of in the course of the administration of a deceased

---

[1] See *ante*, p. 459. The wife would not be able to obtain a property transfer order under s. 24 of the Matrimonial Causes Act 1973 because the husband could not make the assignment voluntarily: see *post*, p. 534. It has been held in a county court that a transfer of a *statutory* tenancy under the Matrimonial Homes Act does not require the landlord's consent because otherwise he could thwart the operation of the section: see Hickman, 129 New L.J. 52.

[2] For the court's power to make orders with respect to liabilities and obligations arising before the decree absolute, see s. 7 (4).

[3] Matrimonial Homes Act 1967, s. 7, as amended by the Rent (Agriculture) Act 1976, Sched. 8, para. 16.

[4] See *ante*, p. 470.

[5] For details, see ss. 28 and 49.

[6] For the full list, see Sched. 3.

tenant's estate. Unless the tenancy passes to a qualified successor, once it has ceased to be a secure tenancy, it cannot become one again.[1] Unless the tenant surrenders the tenancy or quits the premises, a secure tenancy can be brought to an end only by the landlord obtaining an order for possession.[2] The provisions of the Act apply equally to a person occupying a dwelling-house as a licensee if he would have had a secure tenancy had his licence been a lease.[3]

Periodic Secure Tenancies.—So long as the tenant is in possession of permises by virtue of a lease for a term certain which has not expired, he has of course all the protection which his lease would afford to any other tenant. Such leases are likely to be rare but they can arise. As under the Rent Act the need for protection arises under a short tenancy or when a longer lease expires. This is achieved by vesting in the tenant a periodic tenancy, the period being the same as that for which rent was last payable under the contractual lease. If a lease for a term certain contains a provision for re-entry or forfeiture, the court is not to make a possession order in pursuance of such a provision but must instead make an order terminating the tenancy: when such an order takes effect, the tenancy likewise becomes a periodic tenancy.[4] The terms of the new tenancy are the same as the terms of the original tenancy insofar as they are compatible with a periodic tenancy except that any provision for re-entry or forfeiture is disregarded.[5]

Recovery of Possession.—As in the case of a statutory tenancy under the Rent Act, the court cannot make an order for possession unless certain conditions are fulfilled. This means that, if the landlord wishes to regain possession under a provision for re-entry or forfeiture contained in a lease for a term certain, he will have to establish *both* the breach of condition which produces the forfeiture (and which will enable the court to make an order converting the tenancy into a periodic tenancy) *and* one of the statutory conditions.[6] There are 13 grounds on which possession can be ordered, and these are divided into three groups.[7]

In the case of the first six grounds the court may not make an order for possession unless it is *also* satisfied that it is reasonable to do so. The first four grounds correspond to grounds (a)-(d) under the Rent Act set out on p. 473. The other two grounds are:

> that the landlord was induced to grant the tenancy by a false statement made knowingly or recklessly by the tenant; and
> that the tenant (or his predecessor in title) accepted the tenancy temporarily

---

[1] Ss. 28 (5) and 37. For qualified successors, see *post*, p. 644. If it is known that, when a deceased tenant's estate is disposed of, the tenancy will not be a secure tenancy (because it will not pass to a statutory successor), it ceases to be a secure tenancy at once.

[2] S. 32 (1).

[3] Except for certain licensees of almshouses and persons who entered the dwelling-house or any other land as trespassers and to whom a licence was granted as a temporary expedient: s. 48 and Sched. 3, para. 13.

[4] Ss. 29 and 32 (2).

[5] S. 29 (2).

[6] The same facts may satisfy both conditions, *e.g.* non-payment of rent.

[7] S. 34 and Sched. 4, Part I. The landlord must first serve on the tenant a notice in a specified form, which will lapse 12 months after proceedings could have been commenced: s. 33.

while work was being carried out on another dwelling-house of which he was a secure tenant and that the work is complete and the house available.

In the case of the next three grounds the court must *also* be satisfied that suitable accommodation will be available for the tenant when the order takes effect.[1] The grounds are:

that the dwelling-house is overcrowded so as to render the occupier guilty of an offence;

that the landlord intends within a reasonable time to demolish or reconstruct the whole or part of the dwelling-house or to carry out work on it or on land let with it; and

that the landlord is a charity and the tenant's continued occupation of the dwelling-house would conflict with its objects.

In the case of the last four grounds the court must *also* be satisfied that it is reasonable to make the order and, in addition, that suitable accommodation will be available for the tenant when it takes effect. Three of them have in common the fact that the tenancy is intended for people with special needs: this may be because the premises are designed for physically disabled persons, or because the landlord is a housing association or housing trust which lets premises to people whose circumstances make it especially difficult for them to obtain housing, or because the dwelling-house is one of a group which it is the practice of the landlord to let to persons with special needs and a social service or special facility is provided in close proximity to assist them. In each of these cases the landlord may seek to obtain possession if a person for whom the tenancy is intended no longer resides in the dwelling-house and he requires it for occupation by such a person.[2] The last ground, which is designed to enable the landlord to regain the premises if they are not fully occupied, is that the tenant succeeded to a deceased tenant as a qualified successor and that the accommodation is more extensive than he reasonably requires.

Position of the Deserted Spouse.—If one spouse is a secure tenant and the other has a right to occupy the house by virtue of section 1 of the Matrimonial Homes Act 1967, the latter's occupation is treated as occupation by the tenant.[3] From this it follows that if the tenant (who, we will assume for sake of argument, is the husband) deserts his wife and she continues to occupy the premises as her only or principal home, the tenancy remains a secure tenancy and the wife is entitled to the security which her husband would have been able to claim had he still be in occupation. Hence, as in the case of a protected tenancy under the Rent Act, the landlord cannot claim possession of the premises even though the husband purports to surrender the tenancy unless

---

[1] For the meaning of "suitable accommodation", see Sched. 4, Part II.

[2] In the case of premises let by a housing association or housing trust, the landlord may seek possession even though there resides in the house a person whose circumstances make it especially difficult for him to obtain housing if a local authority has offered him a secure tenancy.

[3] Matrimonial Homes Act 1967, s. 1 (5), as amended by the Housing Act 1980, Sched. 25. This will apply in all cases except where the spouse is a legal joint tenant: see *ante*, p. 458.

he can also make out one of the grounds on which he could obtain possession against the wife. She must, of course, continue to pay the rent which, like the wife of a regulated tenant, she could recover from her husband.[1]

Transfer of Tenancies on Divorce and Nullity.—The court has the same power to order the transfer of a secure tenancy to the tenant's spouse on divorce or nullity as it has in respect of regulated tenancies.[2] Although this must take effect as a statutory assignment, it will presumably not bring the secured tenancy to an end because, as the order takes effect on the date of the decree absolute, the transferee was a person in whom the tenancy would have vested as a qualified successor had the tenant died immediately before the assignment. In any event, as the effect of the order is to give the transferee the whole interest which the tenant had together with the rights (and obligations) attached to it, she must be able to claim the same security that the tenant had as a secure tenant. The court has a similar power to extinguish one of the spouse's interests if they are joint tenants.

---

[1] *Cf. ante*, p. 477.
[2] Matrimonial Homes Act 1967, s. 7, as amended by the Housing Act 1980, Sched. 25.

Chapter 14

Financial Support for the Spouses during Marriage

A. INTRODUCTORY[1]

Maintenance at Common Law.—The common law rules relating to the maintenance of a spouse were the inevitable consequence of the doctrine of unity of legal personality. The wife, lacking the capacity to hold property and to contract, could neither own the bare necessities of life nor enter into a binding contract to buy them. Two principles followed. One of the essential obligations imposed upon a married man was to provide his wife with at least necessaries, and a married woman could in no circumstances be held liable to maintain her husband. The common law rule that neither spouse could sue the other precluded her from enforcing her right by action if her husband failed to fulfil his duty to maintain her; this difficulty was overcome by giving the wife a power to pledge her husband's credit for the purchase of necessaries if he did not supply her with them himself.

Scope of the Husband's Duty.—The husband's common law duty to provide his wife with the necessities of life was *prima facie* complied with if he provided a home for her.[2] She had no right to separate maintenance in a separate home unless she could justify living apart from him. Whilst the parties were cohabiting, the husband obviously had to provide his wife with food, clothing and other necessaries. Conversely, provided that the wife was not in desertion, the husband's obligation remained even though the spouses were living apart, for example owing to the illness of one of them, the husband's own desertion,[3] or his irrational belief that she was going to kill him.[4]

The fact of marriage raised a presumption at common law that the husband was under a duty to maintain his wife. But her right to maintenance,

---

[1] See generally Miller, *Family Property and Financial Provision*.

[2] See *Price* v. *Price*, [1951] P. 413, 420-421, C.A.; *W.* v. *W. (No. 2)*, [1954] P. 486, 515-516; [1954] 2 All E.R. 829, 840, C.A.

[3] *Holborn* v. *Holborn*, [1947] 1 All E.R. 32 (constructive desertion).

[4] *Brannan* v. *Brannan*, [1973] Fam. 120; [1973] 1 All E.R. 38. But a reasonable though mistaken belief *induced by the wife's own conduct* relieved him from the duty of maintaining her just as it relieves him from the duty of cohabiting with her: *Chilton* v. *Chilton*, [1952] P. 196; [1952] 1 All E.R. 1322; *West* v. *West*, [1954] P. 444; [1954] 2 All E.R. 505, C.A. See further, *ante*, pp. 217-218.

generally speaking, was co-extensive with her right to her husband's consortium, and if her conduct released him from the duty to cohabit with her, he automatically ceased to be under a duty to maintain her.[1] Thus a single act of adultery automatically deprived her of her right unless the husband connived at it or condoned it.[2] Similarly, she was not entitled to look to him for maintenance if she was in desertion, but whereas adultery terminated the right entirely (unless the husband condoned it), desertion merely suspended it and the right revived immediately the desertion came to an end.[3]

The Agency of Necessity.—The power to pledge the husband's credit was termed the wife's agency of necessity. It extended to the purchase of necessaries both for herself and for the spouses' minor children, and the term "necessaries" in this context included not only necessary goods such as food and clothing but also necessary services such as lodging, medical attention and education. Although the wife might divest herself of the right to be maintained by her own conduct, the husband could not revoke the authority by his unilateral act.

The agency of necessity was obviously of great importance so long as the wife was generally incompetent to contract and own property at common law. Both these disabilities were removed by the Married Women's Property Act of 1882, and by the end of the nineteenth century she could obtain maintenance from her husband not only in the High Court but also much more speedily in a magistrates' court. Consequently it became rare for a married woman to use her agency of necessity because tradesmen were naturally reluctant to give credit to a man who had deserted his wife and left her penniless. When it became possible for the wife to obtain immediate assistance from the Department of Health and Social Security and to claim the benefits of the National Health Act and the legal aid and advice scheme, the doctrine became an anachronism and was eventually abolished by the Matrimonial Proceedings and Property Act 1970.[4]

Bankrupt and Mentally Ill Spouses.—If a spouse becomes bankrupt or mentally ill, the question of maintenance of himself and his family is largely governed by discretionary powers conferred by statute.

Bankruptcy.—Bankruptcy does not discharge a husband's obligation to maintain his wife even though it may limit his power to fulfil it.[5] The Official

---

[1] *Chilton* v. *Chilton*, (*supra*), at pp. 202 and 1325, respectively.

[2] *Wright and Webb* v. *Annandale*, [1930] 2 K.B. 8, C.A.; *Wilson* v. *Glossop* (1888), 20 Q.B.D. 354, C.A. (connivance); *Harris* v. *Morris* (1801), 4 Esp. 41 (condonation). If the wife had committed adultery, the husband's own conduct was irrelevant; *Govier* v. *Hancock* (1796), 6 Term Rep. 603 (husband guilty of adultery and cruelty to wife); *Stimpson* v. *Wood & Sons* (1888), 57 L.J.Q.B. 484 (husband guilty of adultery).

[3] *Jones* v. *Newtown and Llanidloes Guardians*, [1920] 3 K.B. 381. Hence if the wife was in simple desertion she could restore her right to maintenance by taking steps to effect a reconciliation: *Price* v. *Price*, (*supra*).

[4] S. 41. This followed the recommendations of the Law Commission: see Law Com. No. 25, paras. 108-109 and Appendix II, paras. 41-52 and 108. S. 41 was repealed by the Matrimonial Causes Act 1973, Sched. 3, and not re-enacted. See further Diamond, *Repeal and Desuetude of Statutes*, Current Legal Problems, 1975, 107, at pp. 110-111.

[5] *Hounslow London Borough Council* v. *Peake*, [1974] 1 All E.R. 688. But the mere fact that one spouse has a duty (or potential duty) to maintain the other does not make the latter a "person

Receiver may make an allowance for the support of a bankrupt and his family out of the bankrupt's property which is in his hands, as may a trustee in bankruptcy provided that he has the permission of the committee of inspection.[1] The bankrupt may also keep his personal earnings insofar as they are needed for the same purpose.[2]

Mental Illness.—If a person is incapable of managing and administering his property and affairs as a result of mental disorder, the Court of Protection may make such order with respect to them as is necessary or expedient for the maintenance of the patient or the maintenance or other benefit of any member of his family.[3] The Court may also order a settlement or gift of the patient's property for the same purposes.[4] The Court is expressly required to have regard to the desirability of making provision for the patient's obligations even though these are not legally enforceable[5] and accordingly it has been held that orders may be made for any person whom the patient might have been expected to benefit had he been capable of doing so.[6]

We must now consider the various ways in which the spouses' rights to maintenance and financial provision generally may be enforced.

Maintenance Agreements.—Once it was accepted that separation agreements were not contrary to public policy, it became possible for a husband to enter into an enforceable contract to pay maintenance to his wife, and now of course either spouse may covenant to pay maintenance to the other. Their rights will, of course, be basically governed by the general principles of the law of contract but, as we shall see, some special rules apply to maintenance agreements.

Supplementary Benefits.—Broadly speaking, anyone over the age of 16 whose income falls below the relevant sum laid down by the Supplementary Benefits Act 1976 is entitled to apply to the Department of Health and Social Security for supplementary benefit. As any sum awarded will be payable immediately, a spouse left without support will frequently turn to the

---

interested'' who could apply to have the first spouse's bankruptcy annulled under s. 29 (1) of the Bankruptcy Act 1914: *Re Beesley*, [1975] 1 All E.R. 385. *Quaere* if he or she could apply if the spouses' interests were not identical, *e.g.* if the wife were bringing or enforcing proceedings for maintenance against the husband.

[1] Bankruptcy Rules 1952, r. 313; Bankruptcy Act 1914, s. 58.

[2] *Re Roberts*, [1900] 1 Q.B. 122, C.A.

[3] Mental Health Act 1959, ss. 101 and 102 (1). For the definition of mental disorder, see *ibid.*, s. 4 (1).

[4] *Ibid.*, s. 103 (1) (d). A settlement may be varied if material facts were not disclosed when it was made or if there is a substantial change in the circumstances: s. 103 (4).

[5] *Ibid.*, s. 102 (2).

[6] *Re D.M.L.*, [1965] Ch. 1133; [1965] 2 All E.R. 129. *Cf. Re T.B.*, [1967] Ch. 247; [1966] 3 All E.R. 509 (settlement on patient's illegitimate son to exclusion of other relations who had taken no interest in him).

Department before taking any other action. If assistance is given to a married person, its value may in an appropriate case be recovered from that person's spouse.

Maintenance in Magistrates' Courts.—Until 1878 only the ecclesiastical courts or their successors, the Divorce Court and the High Court, could make orders for maintenance. That year saw an entirely new departure, for section 4 of the Matrimonial Causes Act enabled a criminal court, before which a married man had been convicted of an aggravated assault upon his wife, to make an order that she should no longer be bound to cohabit with him if it felt that her future safety was in peril. The court could also order a husband to pay maintenance to a wife in whose favour such a separation order was made and vest in her the legal custody of any children of the marriage under the age of ten years. In 1886 courts of summary jurisdiction were given a further power to make a maintenance order in favour of a woman whose husband had deserted her and was wilfully refusing or neglecting to maintain her.[1] Their jurisdiction to make orders on the application of married women was considerably increased by the Summary Jurisdiction (Married Women) Act of 1895, which in effect introduced a code of law relating to husband and wife to be administered in magistrates' courts. The success of that Act was reflected in the way in which its provisions were extended during the next half century in a series of Acts which became collectively known as the Summary Jurisdiction (Separation and Maintenance) Acts 1895 to 1949.[2] Magistrates' powers were again overhauled and widened by the Matrimonial Proceedings (Magistrates' Courts) Act 1960.

The main purpose of the Act of 1895 was to afford women of the working and lower middle classes, who could not afford to take proceedings in the High Court, an opportunity to obtain matrimonial orders cheaply and speedily; and these advantages, together with the comparative informality and privacy of the proceedings, eventually brought to the courts many women in higher income groups. A parallel development is seen in the introduction of the power (admittedly somewhat more limited) to give matrimonial relief to married men as well.[3] Under the Act of 1960 magistrates had jurisdiction to make three types of orders: (a) to relieve the complainant from the duty of cohabiting with the defendant, the effect of which was, in almost all respects, the same as that of a judicial separation; (b) for the maintenance of one of the spouses; and (c) for the custody and maintenance of the children of the family. Except for orders relating to children, the court could not grant matrimonial relief unless the complainant established one of nine matrimonial offences, the law relating to some of which was highly technical and rigid. This meant that, after the introduction of the new divorce law in 1971, there was a wide divergence between the law administered in the divorce courts and that administered in magistrates' courts. In particular, there was a much greater emphasis laid on the parties' conduct in magistrates' courts and their powers were much less flexible. The Law Commission,

---

[1] Married Women (Maintenance in Case of Desertion) Act 1886.

[2] These were: the Summary Jurisdiction (Married Women) Act 1895; the Licensing Act 1902, s. 5; the Married Women (Maintenance) Act 1920; the Summary Jurisdiction (Separation and Maintenance) Act 1925; and the Married Women (Maintenance) Act 1949.

[3] This was originally conferred by the Licensing Act 1902, s. 5.

reporting in 1976, considered that the function of magistrates' courts was "to provide first aid in a marital casualty clearing station" and saw the objectives of their matrimonial jurisdiction as being:[1]

(a) to deal with family relations during a period of breakdown, which is not necessarily permanent or irretrievable—
  (i) by relieving the financial need which such a breakdown can bring to the parties,
  (ii) by giving such protection to one or other of the parties as may be necessary,
  (iii) by providing for the welfare and support of the children; and
(b) to preserve the marriage in existence, where possible.

So far as orders for the benefit of the wife or husband are concerned (as distinct from those for the benefit of the children), they first proposed the abolition of the power to make separation orders which, they concluded, served little purpose. They recommended that this jurisdiction should be replaced by a power to make much more effective orders for the physical protection of a spouse and the children of the family.[2] Secondly they proposed that the substantive law relating to maintenance should be brought much more into line with the relief that a spouse can obtain on divorce and, in particular, that it should be simplified and that the grounds for application and the guidelines for the court should be the same whichever spouse applied.[3] These recommendations formed the basis of the provisions of Part I of the Domestic Proceedings and Magistrates' Courts Act 1978, which came into force on 1st February 1981. It has completely replaced the code set out in the Matrimonial Proceedings (Magistrates' Courts) Act 1960, which has been repealed. Under the new Act either spouse may apply for an order on any one of four grounds. In addition, magistrates' courts also have powers to make orders for payments which have been agreed by the parties as well as orders reflecting sums actually paid by one spouse to the other when they are separated by agreement.

Maintenance in Divorce Courts.—The granting of financial relief when a marriage is dissolved or annulled will be considered in the next chapter. In practice a spouse usually seeks a decree of judicial separation only as an alternative to divorce when the marriage has irretrievably broken down: consequently the courts' powers are the same and it will be convenient to deal with them together. One aspect of the jurisdiction of divorce courts, however, must be mentioned here. The ecclesiastical courts were able to give financial protection to a wife by ordering the husband to pay her alimony pending suit (or *pendente lite*) and permanent alimony after granting a decree of divorce *a mensa et thoro*. After 1857 this power was vested in the Divorce Court and subsequently in the High Court. A court granting a decree for restitution of conjugal rights to a wife could make similar orders together

---

[1] Law Com. No. 77, Report on Matrimonial Proceedings in Magistrates' Courts, para. 2.4.
[2] See now the Domestic Proceedings and Magistrates' Courts Act 1978, ss. 16-18, *ante*, pp. 126-128. Separation orders made under the Matrimonial Proceedings (Magistrates' Courts) Act 1960 remain in force: *ibid.*, Sched. 1.
[3] See Law Com. No. 77, paras. 2.1-2.14.

with an order for periodical payments (which could be secured) if the husband failed to comply with the decree.[1]

The significance of these orders is that they provided a married woman with the only means of obtaining support through the courts until magistrates were given a power to grant her maintenance, and for many years after this they gave her the only means of obtaining an order for a substantial sum. Even today a wife must apply to a divorce court if she wants an order for secured periodical payments. Consequently a wife might be compelled to seek some other form of matrimonial relief in order to obtain maintenance. Restitution of conjugal rights was often the only decree immediately available, and most wives who petitioned for it did so, not in the expectation that it would encourage their husbands to return to them, but to enforce their right to financial support. This absurd procedure was made unnecessary in 1949 when a wife was enabled to petition for maintenance alone on the ground that her husband had wilfully neglected to provide reasonable maintenance for her or their children.[2] The court could order a guilty husband to make periodical payments (which could be secured).

Two important modifications have been made to the principle underlying this provision. In 1970 a married man was given the same limited power to apply for maintenance in a divorce court as he already possessed in a magistrates' court.[3] Six years later the Law Commission, when making their report on matrimonial proceedings in magistrates' courts, pointed out the need to bring the divorce courts' powers in this respect into line with the new powers they were proposing for magistrates' courts and in particular recommended that both spouses should be given the same rights and that the courts' powers should be made more flexible.[4] These recommendations have now been implemented in section 63 of the Domestic Proceedings and Magistrates' Courts Act 1978.

Concurrent Orders.—The embarrassment which might result if two courts were seised of the question of maintenance simultaneously has led to the formulation of the rule that two orders should not be in force at the same time. A magistrates' court should normally refuse to deal with an application when proceedings are pending in a divorce court;[5] for the same reason a rule of practice was evolved that normally a divorce court would not make an order for maintenance so long as a magistrates' order was in force. Consequently, if the wife had previously obtained an order in a magistrates' court and then wished to apply for financial provision in a divorce court (as she might do if she later petitioned for divorce or wished to obtain security), she usually had to have the first order discharged and thus leave the way clear for relief in the divorce court.

This meant of course that she must run the risk of obtaining less than she was already getting and also that there might be a period before any order

---

[1] These powers were originally given by the Matrimonial Causes Act 1857, s. 17, and the Matrimonial Causes Act 1884, s. 2.

[2] Law Reform (Miscellaneous Provisions) Act 1949, s. 5, subsequently re-enacted in the Matrimonial Causes Act 1950, s. 23, and the Matrimonial Causes Act 1965, s. 22.

[3] Matrimonial Proceedings and Property Act 1970, s. 6, subsequently re-enacted in s. 27 of the Matrimonial Causes Act 1973.

[4] Law Com. No. 77, Part IX.

[5] See *post*, pp. 500-501.

could be made in the divorce court, when she would be in receipt of nothing at all. The second difficulty has now been removed and in such a case the High Court or a divorce county court may direct that any order made under Part I of the Domestic Proceedings and Magistrates' Courts 1978 (other than for the payment of a lump sum) shall cease to have effect at any time.[1] This means that the court will normally discharge the first order from the date on which its own order is to come into force, but the wife still runs the risk of finishing up financially worse off than she was before, for the Act has not apparently altered the old rule of practice that she is not permitted to apply for a second order and then enforce the more favourable.[2]

Rights of Wives of Serving Members of the Armed Forces.—The rights of wives of men serving in the regular army[3] are peculiar in two respects. First, if an order for maintenance is in force in respect of a soldier's wife or any child of his or his wife's,[4] the Defence Council may authorise deductions to be made from his pay and appropriated towards payments due under the order.[5] Secondly, similar deductions may be authorised, even though no order is in force, if the Defence Council is satisfied that he is neglecting without reasonable cause to maintain his wife or any child of his under the age of 16.[6] There are similar provisions with respect to men serving in the Royal Navy and the Royal Air Force.[7]

Whether wives of men serving in visiting forces (for example from the Commonwealth or the U.S.A.) have similar privileges depends upon the nature of orders made under the Visiting Forces Act of 1952.

As this examination of the ways in which one spouse can obtain maintenance from the other will show, maintenance agreements stand in a class apart. In their case the obligation is purely contractual and we shall consider them first. In all other cases the duty to maintain arises directly out of the parties' status. It is proposed to consider these in the order in which a spouse will normally resort to them: supplementary benefits, maintenance orders made by magistrates, and orders made by the High Court and divorce county courts.

B. MAINTENANCE AGREEMENTS

In order to be legally enforceable, a maintenance agreement must constitute a contract between the parties. Consequently, if it is not under seal,

---

[1] Domestic Proceedings and Magistrates' Courts Act 1978, s. 28.

[2] See *Ross* v. *Ross*, [1950] P. 160; [1950] 1 All E.R. 654.

[3] *I.e.*, military forces other than the army reserve, the Territorial Army, the Home Guard and retired officers: Army Act 1955, s. 225 (1).

[4] Including an illegitimate or adopted child.

[5] Army Act 1955, ss. 150 and 152, as amended by the Army and Air Force Act 1961, s. 29, the Maintenance Orders (Reciprocal Enforcement) Act 1972, Sched., the Armed Forces Act 1971, s. 59(2), and the Defence (Transfer of Functions) (No. 1) Order, S.I. 1969 No. 488, Sched. 1.

[6] Army Act 1955, s. 151. In certain circumstances deductions may be made after the child has reached the age of 16. This provision does not extend to illegitimate children.

[7] Naval Forces (Enforcement of Maintenance Liabilities) Act 1947, s. 1 (as amended) (extended to reserve forces by the Naval and Marine Reserves Pay Act 1957, s. 1 (2) and Sched.); Air Force Act 1955, ss. 150-152 (as amended). In addition wives of serving men are entitled to marriage allowances subject to certain conditions.

the party seeking to enforce a promise to pay maintenance must show that she (or he) has furnished consideration. This will normally not be difficult because the undertaking will be embodied in a separation agreement in which each party gives consideration by releasing the other from the duty to cohabit or will be part of a much more complicated financial transaction involving the division of property and the compromising of other claims. If there is no consideration at all, however, a promise not given under seal will be void.

Basically the parties' rights and duties are determined by the general law of contract. If the agreement is a maintenance agreement for the purpose of section 34 of the Matrimonial Causes Act 1973, however, two peculiar rules apply to it: certain provisions may be void by statute, and in certain circumstances either party may apply to have the agreement altered. The result is that in many cases the wife (who will usually be the party to whom payments are to be made) will have the best of both worlds because she can hold her husband to his covenant and also take other proceedings to obtain maintenance. Whilst the provisions of the Act are doubtless necessary to protect some wives who have been induced to accept unreasonably low terms, they may well have the undesirable effect of leading many legal advisers to dissuade husbands from settling financial provisions out of court.[1]

Definition of Maintenance Agreement.—To come within section 34 of the Matrimonial Causes Act 1973, an agreement must be *in writing* and made between spouses or former spouses. It must also be

(a) an agreement containing financial arrangements, whether made during the continuance or after the dissolution or annulment of the marriage; *or*
(b) a separation agreement which contains no financial arrangements in a case where no other agreement *in writing* between the same parties contains such arrangements.

From this it will be seen that an agreement entered into after a decree absolute of divorce or nullity can come within the statute only if it contains financial arrangements. An agreement containing no such arrangements can come within the statute only if it is a separation agreement made whilst the parties are still married to each other.

Financial arrangements are defined as

"provisions governing the rights and liabilities towards one another when living separately of the parties to a marriage (including a marriage which has been dissolved or annulled) in respect of the making or securing of payments or the disposition or use of any property, including such rights and liabilities with respect to the maintenance or education of any child, whether or not a child of the family".[2]

There is some doubt whether an agreement comes within the section if someone other than the spouses is a party to it. In *Young* v. *Young*[3] the spouses and the husband's brother had entered into an agreement in which

---

[1] See Passingham, *Matrimonial Causes*, 3rd Ed., 162-163.
[2] Matrimonial Causes Act 1973, s. 34 (2). It has been held that this does not include the making of a lump sum payment: *Furneaux* v. *Furneaux* (1973), 118 Sol. Jo. 204. *Sed quaere*? A lump sum is a "payment". The point was left open in *Pace* v. *Doe*, [1977] Fam. 18, 23; [1977] 1 All E.R. 176, 181.
[3] (1973), 117 Sol. Jo. 204.

the husband had covenanted to pay the wife £8 a week and the wife had been given the use of a house (which was the joint property of the husband and his brother) on her undertaking to keep it in reasonable repair. On the husband's application to have the agreement altered, it was held that it was not a maintenance agreement for the purpose of the Act because the brother was a party to it and the Act contemplated only agreements between husband and wife. Taken literally, this statement can scarcely be true: if the husband agrees to settle periodical payments on the wife, the agreement cannot fail to be a maintenance agreement solely because trustees are parties to it. There seems to be no objection to the alteration of the kind of agreement in *Young* v. *Young* provided that the rights and obligations of third parties are not affected, and it is urged that it should not be followed.

Void Provisions.—It was at one time fairly common in separation agreements for the husband to covenant to make periodical payments to the wife in exchange for her giving an undertaking not to take any other steps to obtain maintenance from him. An application for maintenance in other matrimonial proceedings might also be compromised by the wife's promising to withdraw it in consideration of the husband's paying her maintenance or transferring property to her. It was held by the House of Lords in *Hyman* v. *Hyman*,[1] however, that no arrangement of this sort can preclude her from applying for financial relief in divorce proceedings. The reason for this decision is that the court's power to order the husband to maintain his former wife after divorce is intended to protect not only her but also any person dealing with her and, indirectly, the state in view of the possibility of her having to apply for supplementary benefit. Consequently it would be contrary to public policy to permit the parties to oust the court's jurisdiction by agreement.[2] This reasoning is equally applicable in nullity proceedings and, despite earlier authority to the contrary in the Court of Appeal,[3] it is submitted that the same principle must also be applied in the case of judicial separation. This does not mean that the court will ignore the agreement in subsequent proceedings and the wife may well be held to it.[4] It must also be stressed that, unless the wife's undertaking not to claim financial provision is the sole or main consideration, it does not make the whole agreement illegal, so that she may still elect to sue the husband on his covenant rather than to apply for maintenance.[5]

Section 34 of the Matrimonial Causes Act 1973 provides that any term in a "maintenance agreement" purporting to restrict any right to apply to a court

---

[1] [1929] A.C. 601, H.L.

[2] *Ibid.*, at pp. 608 and 629.

[3] *Gandy* v. *Gandy* (1882), 7 P.D. 168, C.A. *Cf. Gaisberg* v. *Storr*, [1950] 1 K.B. 107; [1949] 2 All E.R. 411, C.A. (promise not to sue for alimony pending suit on divorce not binding).

[4] See *post*, pp. 540–541.

[5] *Goodinson* v. *Goodinson*, [1954] 2 Q.B. 118; [1954] 2 All E.R. 255, C.A., followed in *Williams* v. *Williams*, [1957] 1 All E.R. 305, C.A. But if this is the sole or main consideration for the husband's promise to pay her maintenance, the whole agreement is illegal and unenforceable even if it is under seal: *Bennett* v. *Bennett*, [1952] 1 K.B. 249; [1952] 1 All E.R. 413, C.A.; *Combe* v. *Combe*, [1951] 2 K.B. 215; [1951] 1 All E.R. 767, C.A.; following *Gaisberg* v. *Storr*, (*supra*). But an agreement by which the jurisdiction of a foreign divorce court is ousted is not contrary to English public policy and consequently the husband's covenant may be enforced here: *Addison* v. *Brown*, [1954] 2 All E.R. 213.

for an order containing financial arrangements shall be void. It also provides that any other financial arrangements in the agreement shall not *thereby* be rendered void or unenforceable but shall be binding on the parties unless void or unenforceable for any other reason.[1] The precise effect of this section is uncertain. Clearly the inclusion of the offensive term no longer makes the whole agreement illegal: consequently even if the wife's undertaking not to apply for an order is the sole or main consideration, the husband can be sued if his covenant to pay her maintenance is given under seal. If it is not under seal, however, it is submitted that the husband's promise is still not actionable if the sole consideration is the wife's undertaking not to institute other proceedings for the further reason that, as her promise is void, his promise is supported by no valuable consideration at all.[2]

Alteration of Agreements.—Although any sum agreed on by the parties by way of maintenance might well have been reasonable at the time the agreement was made, it is obvious that in some cases an adherence to this in the light of subsequent events could work serious hardship. The husband's earning capacity may be reduced, which will make a reduction in the sum he has undertaken to pay the wife reasonable; alternatively, the wife's illness or the constant increase in the cost of living consequent upon chronic inflation may well make the sum absurdly small, particularly if it was agreed on some years ago. In order to overcome difficulties such as these, sections 35 and 36 of the Matrimonial Causes Act 1973 empower the court in certain circumstances to alter any agreement which is a maintenance agreement for the purpose of section 34.[3]

Alteration during the Lifetime of both Parties.—Either party may apply to a divorce county court to have a subsisting agreement altered if each of them is either domiciled or resident in England.[4] Alternatively, the application may be made to a magistrates' court, in which case both parties must reside in England.[5]

No alteration is possible unless one of two conditions is satisfied: either there must have been a change in the circumstances in the light of which the particular financial arrangements were made (or financial arrangements were omitted) or the agreement must fail to contain proper financial arrangements with respect to any child of the family.[6] It will be observed that in the latter case the party seeking the alteration does not have to prove any change of circumstances; but where such a change has to be shown, the Act places the

---

[1] S. 34 (1), replacing provisions originally contained in the Maintenance Agreement Act 1957, s. 1 (2).

[2] See Dew, 56 Law Soc. Gaz. 365. For the contrary view that the statute has made the husband liable on a promise for which there is no consideration, see Treitel, *Mutuality in Contract*, 77 L.Q.R. 83, at pp. 92-95.

[3] For the definition of a maintenance agreement, see *ante*, p. 490. The power was originally given by the Maintenance Agreement Act 1957.

[4] Matrimonial Causes Act 1973, s. 35 (1) and Sched. 2, para. 6 (1) (a); Matrimonial Causes Act 1967, s. 2; *Pace* v. *Doe*, [1977] Fam. 18; [1977] 1 All E.R. 176. The county court judge may order the application to be transferred to the High Court if this seems desirable: Matrimonial Causes Rules 1977, rr. 80 and 103.

[5] Matrimonial Causes Act 1973, s. 35 (3).

[6] *Ibid.*, s. 35 (2). For the meaning of "child of the family", see *ante*, p. 304.

court and the parties in a dilemma. On the one hand, if they are not held to the terms that they have freely entered into, there is no incentive to settle differences out of court; on the other hand, if the courts are slow to make alterations, legal advisers are bound to recommend their clients not to enter into an agreement but to obtain a court order which can be varied from time to time to take account of changes in their financial circumstances. With this difficulty in mind, the Court of Appeal has established two principles. First, as they held in *Gorman* v. *Gorman*,[1] the circumstances in the light of which the financial arrangements were agreed must *prima facie* be viewed objectively. Although in some cases it might be right to have regard only to those circumstances which the evidence shows did influence the parties, normally the court must look at the circumstances which reasonable people in their position would have taken into account. This at least prevents a party from arguing in most cases that the court cannot make an alteration because he did not have particular circumstances in contemplation even though they would clearly have affected the action of a reasonable person. Secondly, the court must be satisfied that the agreement has become unjust as a result of the change. The Act expressly provides that the court is not to be precluded from making an alteration merely because the change was foreseen;[2] if this were not so, a party could rarely rely on an increase in the cost of living or the covenantor's income or on a deterioration in earning capacity due to advancing age. On the other hand, it is unlikely that he will be able to rely on a change brought about by himself, and in *Ratcliffe* v. *Ratcliffe*[3] the court refused to relieve a husband of his obligations under a covenant to pay his wife £450 a year when he voluntarily threw up a post bringing him in £1,400 a year to become a schoolmaster at £550 a year. Similarly in *Gorman* v. *Gorman* they declined to order the husband to pay anything to his wife in view of the fact that he was voluntarily making her an allowance and permitting her to reside in the matrimonial home, whilst she in turn was receiving weekly payments from national insurance and was living with adult children who could be expected to help her financially.

Powers of the Court.—All courts may alter the agreement by varying or revoking any financial arrangements contained in it or by inserting in it financial arrangements for the benefit of either of the parties or a child of the family. In deciding whether to make an order against a party in favour of a child who is not his biological or adopted child, the court must take into account the same matters as it would on an application for maintenance in a magistrates' court.[4]

The High Court and county courts may alter and insert any provisions so long as they are "financial arrangements" within the meaning of the section. There are, however, two or, perhaps, three restrictions on their powers. If the court inserts a provision for the making or securing of periodical payments by one party to the other or increases the rate of such payments, the period for which they (or the increase) are to be made must not exceed the parties' joint lives if they are unsecured or the payee's life if they are secured and, in either

[1] [1964] 3 All E.R. 739, C.A.
[2] S. 35 (2) (a), reversing the decision in *K.* v. *K.*, [1961] 2 All E.R. 266, C.A.
[3] [1962] 3 All E.R. 993, C.A.
[4] Matrimonial Causes Act 1973, s. 35 (2). See *post*, p. 587. For the meaning of "financial arrangements", see *ante*, p. 490.

case, must cease on the payee's remarriage.[1] Secondly, if it inserts a provision for the making or securing of periodical payments for the maintenance of a child of the family or increases the rate of such payments, they (or the increase) may not last for a period longer than the court could order on divorce.[2] Further, in *Pace* v. *Doe*[3] Baker, P., was of the opinion that it would be contrary to the policy of the Matrimonial Causes Act to enable a spouse to obtain under this section financial relief which she (or he) could not have obtained in divorce proceedings. He therefore held that no alteration at all could be made in favour of a divorced wife (as distinct from a child of the family) after she had remarried. Whilst it may be good sense not to permit her to do indirectly that which she cannot do directly, there is no express provision in the Act depriving the court of jurisdiction in these circumstances, and consequently the decision must be treated with reserve. Even if it is not followed, however, there will be few cases where it would be proper to make an alteration in these circumstances.

The powers of magistrates' courts are much more circumscribed. If the agreement contains no provision for the making of periodical payments at all, the court can insert a provision for the payment of *unsecured* periodical payments for the benefit of the other party or for any child of the family. If it contains a provision that one of the parties shall make *unsecured* periodical payments, the court may increase or reduce their rate or terminate them altogether. The maximum period for which any such payments (or increase) may be ordered is the same as in other courts.[4] This limitation is unfortunately narrow. It means, for example, that if the husband has undertaken to maintain the children but not the wife, a magistrates' court cannot insert a term in her favour: there seems no justification for compelling her to go to a county court in these circumstances.

If any agreement is altered, it has effect thereafter as though the alteration had been made by the parties themselves for valuable consideration, so that any person to whom money is due or property is to be transferred under the amended agreement has the normal remedies for breach of contract.[5] It is apparently not possible to order a retrospective alteration.[6] A further valuable power that the payee has is to apply to have set aside any disposition made by the other party with the intention of defeating a claim for alteration or to restrain him from making such a disposition in the future.[7] The alteration does not affect the powers of any court to make any other order containing financial arrangements or of the parties to apply for such an order.[8]

---

[1] Matrimonial Causes Act 1973, s. 35 (4). Remarriage includes a void or voidable marriage: *ibid.*, s. 52 (3). *Cf.* the duration of orders after divorce, etc., *post*, p. 528.

[2] *Ibid.*, s. 35 (5). See *post*, p. 586.

[3] [1977] Fam. 18; [1977] 1 All E.R. 176. For the court's powers on divorce, see *post*, p.526.

[4] *Ibid.*, s. 35 (3)-(5).

[5] *Ibid.*, s. 35 (2).

[6] So held in *Carr* v. *Carr*, [1974] Fam. 65; [1974] 3 All E.R. 366, on the ground that a retrospective alteration would be inconsistent with the provision that an alteration shall have effect *thereafter* as though made by the parties for valuable consideration. But if the parties themselves made a retrospective alteration, would it not thereafter have effect as altered?

[7] Matrimonial Causes Act 1973, s. 37. See further *post*, pp. 568-569. This presumably does not apply if the alternation is made by a magistrates' court.

[8] *Ibid.*, s. 35 (6).

Alteration after the Death of one of the Parties.—If either party dies domiciled in England and the agreement provides for the continuation of payments, either that party's personal representatives or the survivor may apply for an alteration. In such a case only the High Court or a county court has jurisdiction and the application must not be made more than six months after the date when representation was first taken out except with the permission of the court.[1] The court's powers are the same as they are when an application is made during both parties' lifetime, and any alteration takes effect as though the agreement had been varied by the parties themselves for valuable consideration immediately before the death.[2]

C. SUPPLEMENTARY BENEFITS[3]

The old poor law, which dated from Elizabethan times, was swept away by the National Assistance Act of 1948 which introduced a totally new system.[4] This was modified in turn by the Ministry of Social Security Act of 1966.[5] This Act established a new ministry (later amalgamated with the Ministry of Health into the Department of Health and Social Security) responsible for many aspects of social security; it also transferred the powers of the National Assistance Board, set up under the Act of 1948, to a new Supplementary Benefits Commission. The Commission has in turn been abolished and its functions transferred in part to the Secretary of State and in part to a Social Security Advisory Committee.[6] The relevant statutory provisions are now to be found in the Supplementary Benefits Act 1976, as amended by the Social Security Act 1980.[7] The basic principle underlying them is that, with certain exceptions, everyone over the age of 16 whose resources fall short of his requirements, calculated in accordance with the provisions of the Second Schedule, is entitled to have his resources made up to the minimum by a supplementary pension or a supplementary allowance payable through the

---

[1] Matrimonial Causes Act 1973, s. 36, as amended by the Inheritance (Provision for Family and Dependants) Act 1975, s. 26 (1). A county court has jurisdiction only if the deceased's net estate does not exceed £15,000: County Courts Jurisdiction (Inheritance—Provision for Family and Dependants) Order 1978. If the court permits an application after six months, the personal representatives will not be personally liable but assets may be traced in the hands of beneficiaries. The court also has power to alter an agreement if the surviving party applies for an order against the other's estate under the Inheritance (Provision for Family and Dependants) Act 1975: see *post*, p. 637.

[2] But there is no power to avoid transactions intended to defeat the claim unless the court exercises its power under the Inheritance (Provision for Family and Dependants) Act 1975, s. 18, to deem the survivor to have made an application under that Act: see *post*, pp. 637-638.

[3] See generally Ogus and Barendt, *Law of Social Security*, c. 12, particularly pp. 539-547; the Report of the Committee on One-Parent Families (the Finer Report), Cmnd. 5629, particularly Part 4, Section 10; McGregor, Blom-Cooper and Gibson, *Separated Spouses*, c. 10; Lister and Carson, [1980] J.S.W.L. 341.

[4] See the Finer Report, Appendix 5, paras. *50 et seq.*

[5] This Act was given the alternative short title of the Supplementary Benefit Act by the Social Security Act 1973, s. 99 (18).

[6] Social Security Act 1980, ss. 6 (2) and 9.

[7] These provisions, as amended, are set out in Part II of Sched. 2 of the Social Security Act 1980. References to sections of the 1976 Act "(as amended)" below refer to the sections as there set out.

Post Office. The requirements and resources of a husband and wife who are members of the same household are aggregated and treated as the husband's.[1] With certain exceptions a person cannot claim benefit if he is in remunerative full-time work or if he is under the age of 19 and in receipt of full-time education,[2] but further assistance is given to families on low incomes, where there are one or more children under the age of 16, in the form of family income supplement.[3]

For the purpose of the Supplementary Benefits Act spouses are under a duty to maintain each other,[4] and if either of them claims or receives benefit, the Secretary of State may apply to a magistrates' court to recover contribution from the other. Decisions on the old poor law legislation had laid it down as a rule of law that a husband could not be liable to maintain his wife if he was not under an obligation to do so at common law. This principle was carried forward in early cases under the Act of 1948 and so it was held in *National Assistance Board* v. *Wilkinson*[5] that the Board was not entitled to recover the cost of assistance given to a wife who was in desertion: a principle which was clearly going to raise difficulty when an attempt was made to recover from the wife who was under no common law liability to maintain her husband at all. But this case must now be read in the light of the later decision of the Court of Appeal in *National Assistance Board* v. *Parkes.*[6] In that case the defendant and his wife had entered into a separation agreement under which the latter had expressly covenanted that she would not claim maintenance from her husband. She had later obtained assistance from the National Assistance Board who now sought to recover the cost of it from the husband. It was held that they were entitled to do so. Whilst the court approved of the decision in *Wilkinson's* case on the facts, they approached the problem from a rather different angle. It appears that on the true interpretation of the Act *all* spouses are included and the fact that the wife has committed adultery or is in desertion does not automatically exclude the husband from the operation of its provisions. But this is a highly relevant circumstance—in fact it may be a conclusive circumstance—to be taken into account by the court in determining whether to make an order against him, and whilst there may be some other circumstances which may make him liable in a particular case, it seems as a general rule that no order should be made if he has ceased to be under a common law liability to maintain his wife. On the other hand he clearly cannot shift his responsibility on to the community as a whole by entering into a separation agreement which exonerates him from liability to maintain his wife or by which he agrees to pay her no more than a specified

---

[1] Supplementary Benefits Act 1976, Sched. 1, para. 3 (as amended). There is a similar aggregation if a man and woman are living together as husband and wife or if a person is responsible for any other member of the same household not entitled to claim supplementary benefit on his own behalf.

[2] *Ibid.*, s. 6 (as amended).

[3] See the Family Income Supplements Act 1970, as amended by the Social Security Act 1980, s. 7; Ogus and Barendt, *op. cit.*, c. 13.

[4] Supplementary Benefits Act 1976, s. 17 (1) (as amended). If assistance is given to either spouse as a result of the other's persistent refusal or neglect to maintain him or her, the spouse in default is liable to prosecution: s. 25 (as amended).

[5] [1952] 2 Q.B. 648; [1952] 2 All E.R. 255.

[6] [1955] 2 Q.B. 506; [1955] 3 All E.R. 1, C.A.

sum.[1] The same principles presumably apply *mutatis mutandis* to the wife, so that she will not be under any obligation to pay for benefit received by her husband if his conduct has been such that, had the position been reversed, he would not have been liable.

The court hearing the application may order the defendant to pay such sum, weekly or otherwise, as it considers appropriate having regard to all the circumstances and, in particular, to the resources of the spouse in default. Its powers are not limited to obliging him to pay for the value of benefit already given; the order may last indefinitely and the sums may be made payable to the Secretary of State (in so far as they are attributable to any benefit paid before or after the order is made) or to the spouse or some other person on his or her behalf. The order is enforceable in the same way as any other order for maintenance made by magistrates and may be varied or revoked.[2] Obviously an order made or varied so as to be payable to the spouse is indistinguishable from a maintenance order in his or her favour.

The Finer Committee proposed a compromise between supplementary benefit payments and maintenance orders obtainable by a wife in a magistrates' court. They recommended that the then Supplementary Benefits Commission should have the power, after examining both parties' needs and resources, to make an order on the husband (which they termed an "administrative order") which would be enforceable in a magistrates' court subject only to the husband's right to appeal to a tribunal on the amount of the order and to the court if he alleged that his wife's conduct had been such as to take away his liability to maintain her under the Act altogether.[3] In the case of "one-parent families", where there is a lone parent (whether father or mother) with day to day responsibility for a child, they went further and proposed the introduction of a guaranteed maintenance allowance, which would normally be a substitute for maintenance payments. The allowance, which would consist of a child-care allowance and a separate allowance for each child and which would be determined solely by reference to the size of the family and not by need, would be available to all parents in this situation. The allowance would be paid by an administering authority (which might be the Department of Health and Social Security) which would in turn assess the amount which should be paid by any other person liable to maintain the family (that is, the other spouse or the parent of any child). This might be greater than the amount of the guaranteed maintenance allowance, in which case the authority would remit any balance paid to the parent in question. Like the administrative order, the sum assessed would be recoverable by the authority by proceedings in a magistrates' court, subject to the right of the person assessed to appeal to a tribunal on the amount and to the court on any question of conduct or paternity of any child involved.[4]

---

[1] *Stopher* v. *National Assistance Board*, [1955] 1 Q.B. 486; [1955] 1 All E.R. 700, impliedly accepted as correct in *Parkes's* case at pp. 517, 523 and 4, 8, respectively. *Cf. Hulley* v. *Thompson*, [1981] 1 W.L.R. 159, *post*, p. 593, n. 1. See further Brown, *Separation Agreements and National Assistance*, 19 M.L.R. 623.

[2] Supplementary Benefits Act 1976, s. 18 (as amended).

[3] Report of the Committee on One-parent Families, Cmnd. 5629, Part 4, Section 12. The recommendations apply equally to a husband with a claim on his wife.

[4] See *ibid.*, Part 5, particularly Sections 6 and 7. It will be seen that the proposals relate not only to separated spouses but also to divorced parents and to the fathers of illegitimate children.

D. MAINTENANCE ORDERS MADE BY MAGISTRATES' COURTS[1]

1. JURISDICTION

A magistrates' court may make an order under the Domestic Proceedings and Magistrates' Courts Act 1978 if, at the date of the making of the application, either the applicant or the respondent normally resides within the commission area for which the court is appointed.[2] It normally has no jurisdiction at all if the respondent does not reside in England or Wales;[3] it may, however, make an order against a respondent resident in Scotland or Northern Ireland provided that the applicant resides in England and Wales and the parties last ordinarily resided together as man and wife in this country.[4] It is expressly provided that the court may make an order if the applicant resides in Scotland or Northern Ireland provided that the respondent resides in England and Wales;[5] but so long as the respondent is resident here, the applicant's residence seems to be immaterial. The parties' domicile is completely irrelevant.[6]

2. ORDERS FOR FINANCIAL PROVISION

The Act contemplates that an application for financial provision may be made in one of three different sets of circumstances. First, there is what one might term the "normal" application, when the applicant must establish one of the four grounds set out in section 1 of the Act. Secondly, if one spouse has agreed to make financial provision, the other may apply to have the terms of the agreement embodied in a court order. Thirdly, the court may make an order if the spouses are living apart (otherwise than as a result of desertion) and the respondent has been making periodical payments to the applicant.

Applications under Section 1.—Either party to a marriage may apply to a magistrates' court for an order on the ground that the respondent spouse:

(a) has failed to provide reasonable maintenance for the applicant; or

(b) has failed to provide, or to make a proper contribution towards, reasonable maintenance for any child of the family; or

(c) has behaved in such a way that the applicant cannot reasonably be expected to live with the respondent; or

(d) has deserted the applicant.[7]

In all cases the ground must exist when the summons is issued and also at the time of adjudication. Hence, for example, an order cannot be made on the ground of desertion if the spouses resume cohabitation before the hearing.[8]

---

[1] See generally McGregor, Blom-Cooper and Gibson, *Separated Spouses*; Report of the Committee on One-parent Families, Cmnd. 5629, *passim*; Law Com. No. 77 (Matrimonial Proceedings in Magistrates' Courts), Part II.

[2] Section 30 (1). See Law Com. No. 77, paras. 4.77-4.90. As the jurisdiction is statutory, it cannot be enlarged by agreement or submission: *Forsyth* v. *Forsyth*, [1948] P. 125, 132; [1947] 2 All E.R. 623, 624, C.A.

[3] *Macrae* v. *Macrae*, [1949] P. 397; [1949] 2 All E.R. 34, C.A. Mere presence of the respondent may be sufficient: *Forsyth* v. *Forsyth*, (*supra*), at pp. 136 and 627, respectively.

[4] Domestic Proceedings and Magistrates' Courts Act 1978, s. 30 (3) (a).

[5] *Ibid.*, s. 30 (3) (b).

[6] *Ibid.*, s. 30 (5).

[7] *Ibid.*, s. 1.

[8] *Irvin* v. *Irvin*, [1968] 1 All E.R. 271.

At first sight the last two grounds may appear to be unnecessary for, if the respondent is making reasonable provision for the applicant, there will be no occasion to make an order. It is necessary to include the respondent's behaviour, however, to cover the case of the wife who is anxious to leave her husband on account of his conduct but knows that, if she does so, she will receive no maintenance from him. Desertion is included to enable a deserted wife whose husband is providing her with reasonable maintenance to obtain an order immediately without having to wait for him to stop paying her.[1]

Failure to provide Reasonable Maintenance.—This ground is new: under former Acts the applicant was required to show that the respondent had been guilty of wilful neglect to provide reasonable maintenance. This implied that he had failed to comply with his common law duty, and as a husband was under no duty to maintain his wife if she had committed adultery or was in desertion, there could be no wilful neglect in these circumstances.[2] This meant that a wife might fail to obtain maintenance before magistrates although she might claim financial relief on divorce. This argument is no longer valid, and the applicant's own conduct is now only one of the facts to be taken into account in determining whether this ground has been established.

Whether the respondent has provided reasonable maintenance for the applicant or any child of the family is clearly a question of fact. To answer it, it is submitted that the bench must ask itself a hypothetical question: assuming that a ground for applying for an order existed, what order should we make? If the provision in fact being made by the respondent is lower—or at least significantly lower—than this, then he must be failing to provide reasonable maintenance. The word "failure" implies culpability only in so far as it suggests that the respondent has the means to make the provision; and as his resources must be taken into account in deciding what sum to order, the court must *ex hypothesi* be satisfied that he has the capacity to make the payments.

The Respondent's Behaviour.—The wording of this ground is precisely the same as that of the second fact upon which a petitioner can rely to establish the ground for divorce. It must therefore be interpreted in precisely the same way.[3] It is not necessary, of course, for the applicant to show that the marriage has irretrievably broken down.

In common with other matters of summary jurisdiction, a complaint must be made under the Domestic Proceedings and Magistrates' Courts Act within six months of the occurrence of the act complained of.[4] This means that the applicant must rely on at least one incident that has occurred during this period, although acts committed more than six months before may be relevant in putting the respondent's conduct in the correct setting.[5]

---

[1] Law Com. No. 77, paras. 2.6-2.11. It may also enable the applicant to obtain a determination of whether the respondent is in desertion with a view to future divorce proceedings.

[2] *Chilton* v. *Chilton*, [1952] P. 196; [1952] 1 All E.R. 1322.

[3] See *ante*, pp. 199-207.

[4] Magistrates' Courts Act 1980, s. 127 (1).

[5] *Cf. Buxton* v. *Buxton*, [1967] P. 48; [1965] 3 All E.R. 150.

The Respondent's Desertion.—Again reference should be made to desertion in connection with the law of divorce.[1] Three differences between the law applicable in magistrates' courts and that applicable in divorce proceedings should be noted, however. As a ground for a magistrates' order desertion does not have to run for any minimum period of time: all that is necessary is that it should be running at the time of the summons and the hearing. Further, if the respondent becomes incapable of retaining the *animus deserendi* owing to mental illness, magistrates may not treat desertion as continuing. Finally, the provision relating to the continuation of desertion whilst certain orders are in force does not apply: in such circumstances it may be necessary for the applicant to rely on one of the other grounds.

Reconciliation.—When hearing an application under section 1, the court is required to consider whether there is any possibility of a reconciliation between the parties and if, either then or later, it appears that there is a reasonable possibility, it may adjourn the proceedings and, if it sees fit, request a probation officer or other person to attempt to effect one.[2] Some courts claim to have achieved a measure of success in this regard by holding an "application court" at which the applicant meets the justices' clerk, a magistrate and, perhaps, a probation officer before the summons is issued.[3] As in the case of divorce, it may be more practicable in the future to concentrate on conciliation rather than reconciliation.[4]

Cases more Suitable for the High Court.—As under earlier legislation, a magistrates' court may refuse to deal with an application made under section 1 if it considers that it would be more conveniently dealt with by the High Court.[5] This power may be exercised only if the High Court itself could assume jurisdiction;[6] in other cases justices have an absolute discretion, but they rarely refuse to hear a case, nor indeed should they do so, for otherwise the whole purpose of providing a summary procedure would be lost. But there is one class of case where a magistrates' court should make an order only in exceptional circumstances, *viz.* if the High Court or a county court is already seised of substantially the same matter and there is an actual or potential conflict of jurisdiction. If a husband is petitioning for divorce or other matrimonial relief and a magistrates' court entertains an application from his wife, there is a danger that the two courts might well find themselves embarrassed by diametrically opposed orders relating to substantially the

---

[1] See *ante*, pp. 207-225.

[2] Domestic Proceedings and Magistrates' Courts Act 1978, s. 26.

[3] See Law Com. No. 77, paras. 4.9-4.17.

[4] See *ante*, p. 228.

[5] Domestic Proceedings and Magistrates' Courts Act 1978, s. 27. No appeal lies from the justices' decision but the High Court may remit any subsequent proceedings to a magistrates' court: *ibid.* It seems to have escaped the notice of both the Law Commission and the draftsman that all other matrimonial proceedings must now be commenced in a divorce county court. This presumably does not affect the practice established when they were commenced in the High Court, although a county court is given no statutory power to remit the case.

[6] Consequently, a magistrates' court should not refuse to deal with an application to vary or discharge an existing order, for the High Court has no jurisdiction to do so: *Smyth* v. *Smyth*, [1956] P. 247; [1956] 2 All E.R. 476. See also *Davies* v. *Davies*, [1957] P. 357; [1957] 2 All E.R. 444.

same issue.[1] For the same reason a magistrates' court normally ought not to make an order if one of the spouses is about to commence proceedings in a divorce county court.[2] There is, of course, a danger that an unscrupulous husband might try to frustrate the wife's attempts to obtain a magistrates' order by the simple expedient of commencing proceedings in a county court. This led the Divisional Court to hold in *Lanitis* v. *Lanitis*[3] that the wife's need to obtain an order quickly and her anxiety about her children (whom the husband had taken away) could—and on the particular facts did—amount to exceptional circumstances entitling the magistrates to make maintenance and custody orders in her favour. Even if they make no order in favour of the applicant, they should at least consider whether they should make an order for the custody (and, where appropriate, the maintenance) of the children, as failure to do so may lead to intolerable and harmful delay.[4]

Orders that may be made.—On proof of any of the grounds set out above, the court may order the respondent to do one or more of the following:

(a) to make periodical payments to the applicant;
(b) to pay a lump sum not exceeding £500 for the applicant;
(c) to make periodical payments to or for a child of the family to whom the application relates;
(d) to pay a lump sum not exceeding £500 for such a child.[5]
      It may allow him time to pay a lump sum or may order him to pay it by instalments.[6]

The questions of assessment of periodical payments and lump sum orders and of orders with respect to children will be considered later.[7] It should be noted that all orders for periodical payments may run from the date of the application and may be made for a limited period of time.[8] In the case of an order for a wife, this may be very useful if she is likely to need money for only a comparatively short period whilst she adjusts herself to living alone, because the husband will not have to go back to the court at a later date to seek a variation or discharge. Similarly magistrates may deliberately use this device as a means of getting the wife to obtain paid employment if they consider this to be the proper course. If she will continue to need maintenance after the end of the period stipulated, she should take care to have the order

---

[1] *Kaye* v. *Kaye*, [1965] P. 100; [1964] 1 All E.R. 620. But there is no reason why magistrates should not make an order if the wife has made it clear that she does not propose to apply for maintenance in the divorce court: *Cooper* v. *Cooper*, [1953] P. 26; [1952] 2 All E.R. 857.

[2] See *Sanders* v. *Sanders*, [1952] 2 All E.R. 767, at pp. 770, 771.

[3] [1970] 1 All E.R. 466. An alternative way of dealing with the situation would be to make an interim order and then give the husband the choice of letting the court go into the merits: *ibid.*, p. 472.

[4] *Jones* v. *Jones*, [1974] 3 All E.R. 702, 703, C.A. (where, as a consequence of the magistrates' adjourning the case, it was 12 months before a custody order was made).

[5] Domestic Proceedings and Magistrates' Courts Act 1978, s. 2 (1), (3). The Home Secretary may increase the maximum amount that may be awarded by way of a lump sum by statutory instrument. The court may also make an order for costs: Magistrates' Courts Act 1980, s. 64.

[6] Magistrates' Courts Act 1980, s. 75.

[7] See *post*, pp. 505-508 (assessment) and pp. 584-589 (orders with respect to children).

[8] Domestic Proceedings and Magistrates' Courts Act 1978, ss. 2 (1) (a) and (c), 4 (1) and 5 (2).

varied before it runs out, because otherwise it will automatically lapse and she will have to start fresh proceedings.[1] The court may also order that the payments should begin from a future date and it may wish to use this power if, for example, the husband is unemployed but is to start work in a short time.

Consent Orders.—Consent orders were not uncommon under the Matrimonial Proceedings (Magistrates' Courts) Act 1960, but as the court had no jurisdiction unless a ground for complaint was established, it was necessary for the applicant to parade the parties' matrimonial difficulties in court. Consequently the Law Commission recommended that magistrates should be able to make a consent order without the applicant's having to establish any other ground.[2] This proposal has been implemented by section 6 of the Domestic Proceedings and Magistrates' Courts Act. If the court is satisfied that the respondent has agreed to make the financial provision specified in the application, it may make an order giving effect to the agreement.[3] The order may contain precisely the same terms as an order made following an application under section 1 except that, as the respondent has agreed to it, a lump sum may be for any amount and is not limited to £500.

The court may not make the order proposed if it considers that it would be contrary to the interests of justice to do so.[4] This is probably most likely to occur if the amount specified in the application looks far too low: there is always the danger of collusion between the parties in an attempt to swing the liability to maintain the wife on to public funds. Obviously other facts may be taken into account as well. Thus the court should refuse to make the order if it appears that undue pressure has been put on either party. In particular, the court must not implement the proposals if they do not provide for or make a proper contribution towards, the financial needs of any child of the marriage.[5] In such cases, however, it is open to the parties to come forward with a fresh agreement. Alternatively the court itself might take the initiative and suggest what order would be appropriate: if the parties both agree, this may be embodied in an order.[6]

Orders following Separation.—It has already been pointed out that the reason that desertion has been retained as a ground for applying for an order under section 1 of the Act is to enable a wife, who has been deserted but whose husband is in fact providing her with reasonable maintenance, to secure her position. She will not have this advantage, however, if, for

---

[1] It is very doubtful whether a court can revive such an order after it has lapsed.

[2] See Law Com. No. 77, paras. 4.1-4.8.

[3] The Act requires that the respondent should have agreed to make the provision, not that he should have agreed to its being embodied in a court order: see s. 6 (1). This suggests that the applicant could seek to have the terms of a separation agreement implemented without the respondent's consent. On the other hand, s. 6 (8) implies consent to the making of the order, and this construction is more in line with the obvious intention of the section. If proceedings are begun under s. 1 and the respondent then agrees to an order, the applicant may apply for an order under s. 6: s. 6 (4).

[4] Section 6 (1) (b).

[5] Section 6 (3).

[6] Section 6 (5).

example, she has agreed to the separation; if her husband has not agreed to make financial provision she cannot apply under section 6 either. This gap has been partly closed by the provisions of section 7. In order to bring these into play, the parties must have lived apart for a continuous period exceeding three months, neither must be in desertion, and the respondent must have been making periodical payments for the benefit of the applicant or a child of the family.[1] "Living apart" is not defined: it presumably bears the same meaning as it does for the purposes of the law of divorce.[2] It should be noted that there are no provisions akin to those in the Matrimonial Causes Act enabling two or more periods to be added together. Although applications under this section will normally be made when the spouses are living apart by agreement, they could be made exceptionally in other circumstances too, for example if one of the spouses was incapable of forming an *animus deserendi* because of mental illness.[3] The requirement that neither spouse must be in desertion leaves one situation covered by no section at all, for if the applicant has deserted the respondent and the latter has continued to make provision for her or a child of the family, she cannot apply for an order under section 1 or section 7.

If the conditions set out above are satisfied, the court may make an order for periodical payments for the benefit of the applicant or any child of the family for such term as may be specified. The purpose of section 7 is to enable legal effect to be given to the *de facto* situation. Consequently, no order may be made for a lump sum payment and the court may not require the respondent to make payments which exceed in aggregate during any period of three months the amount actually paid by him for the benefit of the applicant or a child of the family during the three months immediately preceding the making of the application. If this is greater than the sum which the court would have ordered on an application under section 1, the respondent is protected by the further provision that the order must not be for more than this smaller sum.[4] Conversely, if the court considers that the sums paid fail to provide reasonable maintenance for the applicant or a child of the family, the first ground for complaint under section 1 must necessarily be made out; the court may therefore treat the application as though made under that section and will then have full powers to make such orders for periodical payments and lump sum payments as it thinks fit.[5]

Interim Orders.—The court may make an interim order at any time before making a final order or dismissing the application. It has a similar power if it refuses to make an order on the ground that the case would be more conveniently dealt with by the High Court. If in the latter case or on appeal

---

[1] Section 7 (1). The payments need not have been made *to* the applicant. Hence, for example, the payment of rent could amount to periodical payments for this purpose.

[2] See *ante*, p. 225.

[3] Although the side note to the section refers to "powers of court where parties are living apart by agreement", this cannot limit its unambiguous wording: see *Chandler* v. *D.P.P.*, [1964] A.C. 763; [1962] 3 All E.R. 142, H.L.

[4] Section 7 (3). Nor may the court require payments to be made for the benefit of a child who is not the child of the respondent if it would not have made an order in its favour on an application under s. 1: see further *post*, p. 587.

[5] Section 7 (4).

the High Court remits the case to a magistrates' court, the High Court may make an interim order, in which case it is deemed to have been made by a magistrates' court for the purpose of enforcement, revocation, suspension, revival and variation.[1]

An interim order may require the respondent to make periodical payments to the applicant or for the benefit of any child of the family under the age of 18. These may be backdated to the making of the application. The court may also make an interim order for the custody of, and access to, any such child if there are special circumstances making this desirable.[2]

The court may put a limit on the time for which the order is to remain in force, and it will cease to have effect when a final order is made (or, alternatively, the application is dismissed) or, in any case, after three months. If a final adjudication has not been made, the court may extend the order for any period or periods not exceeding in total three months from the first extension.[3]

Income Tax.—If the order is for a sum not exceeding £33 a week or £143 a month for the applicant or £18 a week or £78 a month for any child under the age of 21, it will be a "small maintenance order" for the purpose of the Income and Corporation Taxes Act 1970.[4]

Payment of Maintenance.—In order to ensure that payments will be made as promptly as possible (and also to prevent embarrassment) the court must order them to be made to the clerk of a magistrates' court on behalf of the recipient unless the latter shows that for some reason this would be undesirable.[5] Alternatively, the court may order the payments to be made to some other person to the recipient's use.[6] To avoid unnecessary waste of time on the payee's part (perhaps involving loss of working time and therefore of wages), the clerk is obliged to forward by post all payments received unless the payee asks for other arrangements to be made.[7] If the recipient is also in receipt of supplementary benefit, she (or he) may ask that the payments be "diverted" to the Department of Health and Social Security; the Department then keeps the payments received and pays her benefit in full. This has the advantage that the recipient receives full benefit each week whether or not the maintenance order is paid in full and on time.[8]

Maintenance payable under a magistrates' order is inalienable like unsecured periodical payments made under the Matrimonial Causes Act.[9] As

---

[1] Domestic Proceedings and Magistrates' Courts Act 1978, s. 19 (1), (9).

[2] *Ibid.*, s. 19 (1), (3). Normally interim maintenance for a child will be paid to the applicant or to the child himself, but if he has his home with a parent who is not one of the parties to the marriage, it may be made payable to the parent: s. 19 (2). For orders for children, see further pp. 307 (custody) and 585 (maintenance).

[3] Section 19 (5), (6). No appeal lies from the making of or refusal to make an interim *maintenance* order or from the variation, revocation, etc. of such an order: s. 19 (8).

[4] See *post*, p. 531.

[5] Magistrates' Courts Act 1980, s. 59 (1), (2).

[6] Domestic Proceedings and Magistrates' Courts Act 1978, s. 32 (2).

[7] Magistrates' Courts Rules 1968, r. 32, as amended by the Magistrates' Courts (Amendment) Rules 1973.

[8] See the Finer Report, Cmnd. 5629, paras. 4.206-4.209.

[9] *Paquine* v. *Snary*, [1909] 1 K.B. 688, C.A. See further *post*, p. 531.

a lump sum is more in the nature of a debt owed by the respondent, it is possible that it may be assigned.

3. ASSESSMENT

The Domestic Proceedings and Magistrates' Courts Act breaks new ground in that, for the first time, it sets out a comprehensive list of the matters which the court is to take into account when making an order. In determining whether the respondent is to be required to make periodical payments or to pay a lump sum to the applicant and, if so, how much he is to pay, the court must have regard to:[1]

(a) the income, earning capacity, property and other financial resources which each of the parties to the marriage has or is likely to have in the foreseeable future;

(b) the financial needs, obligations and responsibilities which each of the parties to the marriage has or is likely to have in the foreseeable future;

(c) the standard of living enjoyed by the parties to the marriage before the occurrence of the conduct which is alleged as the ground of the application;

(d) the age of each party to the marriage and the duration of the marriage;

(e) any physical or mental disability of either of the parties to the marriage;

(f) the contributions made by each of the parties to the welfare of the family, including any contribution made by looking after the home or caring for the family;

(g) any other matter which in the circumstances of the case the court may consider relevant, including, so far as it is just to take it into account, the conduct of each of the parties in relation to the marriage.

Comparison with the matters which the court must take into account in making an order for financial relief after divorce shows that, with one minor exception,[2] the first six paragraphs are identical. The requirement that conduct should be taken into account is differently worded, but insofar as each statute links conduct with the justice of the order, the effect is the same. This follows the recommendation of the Law Commission who took the view that, as far as possible, the same principles should govern both sets of proceedings.[3] As the law has been much more fully worked out in connection with divorce, the detailed examination of these matters will be deferred until the next chapter,[4] but some general principles and certain points of dissimilarity should be mentioned here.

Absence of Power to adjust Property Rights.—The main difference between the powers of magistrates' courts and those of divorce courts is that magistrates cannot make property adjustment orders. Furthermore, they should resist any suggestion that they should do so indirectly by using their

---

[1] Section 3 (1). In the case of applications made under s. 7, para. (c) is amended to read: "the standard of living enjoyed by the parties to the marriage before they lived apart" (s. 7 (5)).

[2] Paragraph (c) of s. 25 (1) of the Matrimonial Causes Act 1973 refers to "the standard of living enjoyed by the family before the breakdown of the marriage". *gone 1984*

[3] Law Com. No. 77, paras. 2.12-2.29.

[4] See *post*, pp. 547-558.

power to order lump sum payments. It would be wholly improper, for example, to compel a husband to buy his wife's half share in household goods by ordering him to pay her half their value. In the first place, magistrates have no power to make the necessary consequential orders extinguishing and transferring rights in property. More fundamentally, the making of property adjustment orders is inconsistent with the principle that magistrates should regulate the parties' financial position during a period of marital breakdown which is not necessarily permanent or irretrievable.[1] It is to be assumed that whichever spouse is in the matrimonial home will stay there for the time being: if either of them wishes to bring about a change, he or she must invoke the jurisdiction of the High Court or a county court in some other way.[2]

The "One-third Rule".—Following the re-introduction of this principle in the divorce courts, the Divisional Court held in *Gengler* v. *Gengler*[3] that the "one-third rule" should be applied by magistrates. This lays down that, as a starting point and no more, the husband should be ordered to pay such sum as will bring the wife's income (if any) up to one-third of the spouses' joint income.[4] The application of this principle in magistrates' courts has been questioned on the ground that it is based on the supposition that the wife will also receive a third of their capital assets and it is unjust to her to limit the amount she can claim by way of periodical payments when the husband cannot be compelled to transfer any capital assets to her.[5] In practice, the rule is likely to be less relevant in magistrates' courts because comparatively few respondents will be in a position to comply with it; but when they can augment their wives' income to this extent, it may be useful to give a "ranging shot" notwithstanding the criticisms that have been levelled against it.

The Parties' Conduct.—The parties' conduct was of little relevance to assessment under the old law because a spouse who had committed adultery was completely barred from obtaining an order and a husband was under no duty to maintain a wife who was in desertion (including constructive desertion). Now that these two statements are no longer true, it remains to be seen whether magistrates will be directed to apply the same principle as divorce courts and to take conduct into account only if it is so obvious and gross that it would be offensive to one's sense of justice to ignore it.[6] The practice of the divorce courts flows from the recognition of two facts, that divorce is a misfortune that afflicts both parties alike and is rarely due to the conduct of one of them alone and that spouses are to be discouraged from parading their matrimonial grievances in the hope of persuading the court to make a more generous (or less onerous) order. Magistrates, on the other hand, are more likely to have to deal with the consequences of separation

---

[1] See *ante*, p. 487.

[2] Except that magistrates may exclude the respondent from the matrimonial home if he has used or threatened to use violence against the applicant or a child of the family. See *ante*, p. 127.

[3] [1976] 2 All E.R. 81.

[4] The court uses the parties' gross earnings in making the computation: *Rodewald* v. *Rodewald*, [1977] Fam. 192; [1977] 2 All E.R. 609, C.A. (overruling in this respect *Gengler* v. *Gengler*). See further *post*, pp. 543-545.

[5] See Cretney, 127 New L.J. 555; Ellis, 92 L.Q.R. 487; Hall, [1976] C.L.J. 233.

[6] See *post*, pp. 554-558.

manifestly due to one spouse's behaviour and at the same time may be less inclined to view it with the clinical detachment of the professional lawyer. Nevertheless it is to be hoped that they will follow the approach of the divorce courts. They have the same object: to give financial protection to a spouse (usually the wife) and the children when the marriage breaks down. Consequently, the same facts should be taken into account. Furthermore, it is even more in the parties' interest to prevent them from exacerbating the situation by airing their grievances in the magistrates' court than it is in the divorce court when the marriage has irretrievably broken down.

Remarriage and Cohabitation.—The respondent's remarriage will not normally be relevant in magistrates' proceedings, but it may become so if the order continues in force after a later divorce.[1] In this case it may be proper to reduce the order because of his increased financial responsibilities; the same result will follow if he lives with another woman, particularly if they have children whom he has to support. Likewise the wife's living with another man may lead the court to make a much smaller order or no order at all, not because she is committing adultery but because the man will be supporting her himself or, alternatively, because she should look to him for maintenance rather than to her husband.

The Parties' Needs.—In many, if not most, cases coming before magistrates the parties' means will be so slight that all the court can do is to concentrate on their needs. Priority must be given to trying to secure the children's position; what is left will frequently have to be divided in the best way possible to ensure that each spouse will at least have enough to cover his or her essential expenses. The need to support two families will often mean that the husband will not be able to keep both above subsistence level; in that case any order made must not reduce his resources to such an extent that, were he unemployed, he would be entitled to supplementary benefit. Given that he can be ordered to pay something, however, magistrates should make a full assessment of the sum notwithstanding that it will be so small that the wife will still have to look to the Supplementary Benefits Commission to make up the balance.[2] To this extent the court must know what the benefits payable to both parties would be;[3] similarly it must be told what other social security benefits they can claim, such as child benefit and family income supplement. If the parties are legally represented, their advisers should also be able to tell the court what effect the incidence of income tax will have on any order proposed.

Lump Sum Payments.—The power conferred on magistrates to order lump sum payments is entirely new. In the divorce court it is normally used as an alternative or a supplement to the power to make property adjustment orders, and it is likely to be used much less in magistrates' courts. It is, of course, of no practical value unless the respondent has the necessary capital;

---

[1] The applicant's remarriage will automatically discharge the order: see *post*, p. 510.

[2] *Ashley* v. *Ashley*, [1968] P. 582; [1965] 3 All E.R. 554; *Barnes* v. *Barnes*, [1972] 3 All E.R. 872, C.A.; Bissett-Johnson and Pollard, 38 M.L.R. 449.

[3] *Cf. Williams* v. *Williams*, [1974] Fam. 55; [1974] 3 All E.R. 377.

if he has it available, however, there are a number of situations in which relatively small orders may be made. The Act itself provides that a lump sum may be ordered to meet any liability or expenses already incurred in maintaining the applicant or any child of the family:[1] in other words in appropriate cases it will be an alternative to backdating the order. It might also be used to enable a wife to take a course of training, for example to pay the fees of a secretarial course, or even to help provide the capital to set her up in business. If the spouses have low incomes but the respondent has some savings, a just solution might be to order part of the savings to be paid to the applicant.[2] Most applications, however, are likely to be made to pay for children's expenses, for example to buy a uniform or other clothes for a new school or to pay for fees and other incidental expenses on starting a course of training or going to a university.

4. VARIATION, SUSPENSION, REVIVAL, REVOCATION AND CESSATION OF ORDERS

Cohabitation.—Earlier Acts permitted the court to make an order even though the spouses were still cohabiting on the ground that, however anxious the applicant was to leave the respondent, she might have nowhere else to go and might lack the means of paying for food and accommodation. But orders made in such circumstances would not take effect so long as the parties continued to cohabit and would cease to have effect altogether if cohabitation continued for three months. All orders automatically ceased to have effect if the parties subsequently *resumed* cohabitation.

The Domestic Proceedings and Magistrates' Courts Act permits the court to make an order whilst the spouses are living together, but it has introduced two changes in the law, one of which is radical.[3] Both apply to interim and final orders made on an application under section 1 or section 6 requiring either party to the marriage to make periodical payments to the other (whether for her own benefit or for the benefit of a child of the marriage). If the parties are living with each other in the same household when the order is made, it will cease to have effect only if they continue to live with each other for a continuous period exceeding six months. Similarly, if they *resume* living with each other in the same household at a later date (whether or not they were cohabiting when the order was made), it will cease to have effect only if the same condition is fulfilled. "Living with each other in the same household" must have the same meaning as it has in the law of divorce: consequently the parties may not be living with each other even though they are physically resident under the same roof.[4] It will also be observed that the period must be continuous: the spouses may live with each other for any

---

[1] Domestic Proceedings and Magistrates' Courts Act 1978, s. 2 (2).

[2] *Cf.* the facts of *Cann* v. *Cann*, [1977] 3 All E.R. 957, where the parties (who were aged 70 and 67) were both living on small pensions and the husband had some savings. The case was decided before magistrates had the power to order the payment of a lump sum, and it was suggested that one solution might be to find out what annuity could be purchased and to take that into account. Alternatively, the husband could be notionally attributed with whatever income the capital would bring in if wisely invested.

[3] Sections 25 (1) and 88 (2).

[4] See *ante*, p. 225. Under earlier Acts orders ceased to have effect if the parties *resumed cohabitation*; it was therefore held that, if the order remained in force after a divorce and the former spouses lived together, it would not cease to have effect because only spouses can

length of time in the aggregate provided that no single period lasts for more than six months.[1] The reason for this is that cohabitation should bring an order to an end only if it indicates a permanent reconciliation and this could not be inferred if the period were shorter.[2]

The second, and more radical, change provides that, until an order ceases to have effect under the provisions just considered, it shall be enforceable notwithstanding that the parties are living together. The justification for this is that the basic cause of many marital difficulties is the husband's carelessness in financial matters and that it is wrong that a wife who is compelled to obtain an order should be in a worse position if she stays with her husband than if she leaves him.[3] While this is doubtless true, her obtaining an order at all may well exacerbate the position, particularly when it is realized that normally all payments will have to be made through a magistrates' clerk.[4] It is open to the wife to ask the court to waive this requirement, but if she does so, the husband may pay her nothing and any proceedings for enforcement could result in endless argument about the amount actually paid. Another possibility is that a wife who claims that her husband is giving her too little housekeeping money but who has no intention of leaving him might use this procedure to ask the court to "fix the housekeeping". It is open to debate whether this is a proper use of magistrates' time.

As the parties must be living apart before an order can be made under section 7, the provisions relating to cohabitation when the order is made cannot apply. If the parties resume living with each other in the same household, any interim or final order for periodical payments will cease to have effect immediately.[5]

Divorce, Nullity and Remarriage.—A decree of divorce does not automatically terminate an order made under the Domestic Proceedings and Magistrates' Courts Act. In some cases the recipient will prefer to have the order discharged and replaced by an order made by the divorce court.[6] In other cases (or if the marriage is dissolved by a foreign court) it will be open to either party to apply for the order to be varied or revoked if the decree has changed their financial position.[7]

---

cohabit: *Prest* v. *Prest*, [1950] P. 63; [1949] 2 All E.R. 790. But unmarried persons may live together and consequently this case is presumably no longer applicable.

[1] But if the wife were to leave the husband for a short period solely for the purpose of keeping the order alive, this might be a ground for him to apply to have it revoked.

[2] See Law Com. No. 77, para. 2.55. If there is doubt whether an order has ceased to have effect as a result of the parties' living together, the court may determine the matter: Domestic Proceedings and Magistrates' Courts Act 1978, s. 25 (4).

[3] See Law Com. No. 77, paras. 2.58-2.65.

[4] See *ante*, p. 504.

[5] Domestic Proceedings and Magistrates' Courts Act 1978, s. 25 (3).

[6] See further *ante*, pp. 488-489.

[7] *Wood* v. *Wood* [1957] P. 254; [1957] 2 All E.R. 14, C.A., where the court increased an order made in the wife's favour because of the husband's improved financial position even though he had obtained a divorce in Nevada. Contrast *Sternberg* v. *Sternberg*, [1963] 3 All E.R. 319, where, after the wife had obtained a maintenance order on the ground of the husband's desertion, he obtained a divorce on the ground of her desertion. The Divisional Court held that, as the findings of the High Court in the divorce proceedings bound the magistrate's court, it must be conclusively presumed that the latter had no jurisdiction to make the order which must therefore be discharged.

If the marriage is void, the whole order must be inoperative as it rests on the false assumption that the parties were in fact married. If the marriage is voidable, the decree will have the same effect as a decree of divorce.[1]

The remarriage of the party required to make periodical payments will not affect the order although it may give him a ground to have it varied in the light of his new financial position. If the other party remarries, she (or he) can make financial claims against her new spouse; consequently the magistrates' order for periodical payments in her favour will automatically cease to have effect even though the second marriage proves to be void or voidable.[2] If the person liable to make payments continues to do so in the mistaken belief that the order is still subsisting, he (or his personal representatives if he has died) may recover them from the payee (or the payee's personal representatives) in an action in a county court.[3] In some cases an order for the repayment of the whole sum might be unjust, for example if the payee had received the sums paid in good faith and had already spent them; accordingly the court has power to order the repayment of such smaller sum as it thinks fit or to dismiss the application altogether. Magistrates' clerks and collecting officers under attachment of earnings orders are given statutory protection unless they receive written notice of the remarriage from one of the former spouses (or their personal representatives).[4]

Party's Death.—The death of either party will automatically bring the order to an end.[5]

Variation, Revival and Revocation of Orders.—In addition to the cases already considered, the court has a general power to vary or revoke an order for periodical payments (including an interim order) on the application of either spouse.[6] Its powers depend on the section under which the original order was made. In all cases it may increase or reduce the amount of the payments or extinguish them entirely. It may also suspend any order temporarily and revive any order which has been suspended, a power which it might wish to use, for example, if the husband is temporarily unemployed.[7] If the order was made following an application under section 1, the court may also make an order for the payment of a lump sum not exceeding £500 for the benefit of the applicant or any child of the family, whether or not it has previously made such an order.[8] The applicant may therefore bring proceedings for variation purely in order to obtain a lump sum. In the case of an order made under section 6 the court can order the respondent to pay a lump sum only if the original order provided for a lump sum payment; if it did contain such a provision, however, the lump sum ordered in proceedings for variation need not be for the benefit of the same person. Thus, if under the original order the

---

[1] See *ante*, pp. 97-98.

[2] Domestic Proceedings and Magistrates' Courts Act 1978, ss. 4 (2), 6 (6), 7 (6) and 88 (3).

[3] Or in the High Court if the order is registered there and proceedings are being brought there for its enforcement.

[4] Domestic Proceedings and Magistrates' Courts Act 1978, s. 35.

[5] *Ibid.*, ss. 4 (1), 6 (6) and 7 (6).

[6] *Ibid.*, s. 20 (5), (12) (a), (13). An application may be made by or against a party residing outside England and Wales: s. 24.

[7] *Ibid.*, s. 20 (1), (2), (3), (6). The variation may be backdated to the application: s. 20 (9).

[8] *Ibid.*, s. 20 (1), (7).

husband paid a lump sum to the wife, he may be ordered on variation to pay a lump sum to her or to a child of the family. Whatever the amount of the original payment, in proceedings for variation the court may order him to pay up to £500 or, if he consents, any larger sum.[1] As the court has no power to include a lump sum payment in an order made under section 7, it has no power to order such a provision in proceedings for variation.

In considering how to exercise its powers on an application for a variation or revocation, the court must give effect to any agreement reached between the parties if it appears just to do so. If there is no such agreement or if the court declines to give effect to it, the court should start with the existing order and decide how far it should be varied as a result of any change in the relevant circumstances, taking into account the same matters as it does when making a fresh order.[2] It could therefore properly reduce or revoke an order if the party to whom payments were being made had been guilty of "obvious and gross" conduct. Although "fresh evidence" is not required before any alteration can be made to the original order, neither party will probably be permitted to adduce any evidence which he could have adduced in earlier proceedings.[3]

Lump Sums.—A lump sum payment is made once and for all and consequently there is no express power to vary it (except on appeal). The court has, however, a general power to remit arrears in proceedings for enforcement,[4] and this must effectively give it the power to reduce or extinguish a lump sum order although it clearly cannot increase it. In any case, if the sum is payable in instalments, either party may apply for a variation of the number of instalments, the amount of any instalment and the date on which any instalment is to be paid.[5]

5. ENFORCEMENT OF ORDERS[6]

The Domestic Proceedings and Magistrates' Courts Act provides that orders for periodical payments and for lump sum payments shall be enforceable in the same way as affiliation orders.[7] The procedure is now laid down by the Magistrates' Courts Act 1980. If payments are being made to a magistrates' clerk, the clerk himself may take proceedings provided that he has the written consent of the person to whom the money is to be paid.[8] For the purpose of simplicity, it will be assumed in the rest of this section that the wife is seeking to enforce an order made against the husband, but the procedure is precisely the same *mutatis mutandis* if the husband seeks to enforce an order for maintenance against his wife.

---

[1] Domestic Proceedings and Magistrates' Courts Act 1978, s. 20 (2), (7), (8).

[2] *Ibid.*, s. 20 (11). See also *McEwan* v. *McEwan*, [1972] 2 All E.R. 708.

[3] *Cf.* variation, etc. in the divorce court, *post*, p. 564.

[4] This is the combined effect of s. 32 (1) of the Domestic Proceedings and Magistrates' Courts Act 1978 and s. 95 of the Magistrates' Courts Act 1980. See further *post*, p. 512.

[5] Domestic Proceedings and Magistrates' Courts Act 1978, s. 22.

[6] See the Finer Report, Cmnd. 5629, Part 4, Section 9.

[7] S. 32 (1).

[8] Magistrates' Courts Act 1980, s. 59 (3).

The first step in the process is for the wife to apply for a summons in a magistrates' court.[1] The court must first decide whether to enforce the arrears *in toto* or to remit the whole or any part of them;[2] the answer to this question must obviously depend upon the spouses' financial position, their conduct and all the circumstances of the case. The court may then issue a warrant of distress, make an attachment of earnings order or issue a warrant committing the husband to prison.[3]

Distress.—Distress is little used in practice. The warrant directs the police to distrain on the husband's goods and to sell them to raise the sum adjudged to be paid.[4]

Attachment of Earnings.—The Maintenance Orders Act 1958 introduced a wholly new means of enforcing an order for maintenance—that of attaching the husband's earnings. The relevant part of that Act has now been replaced by the Attachment of Earnings Act 1971, which has extended the power to apply for such an order to judgment debtors generally. The payment of any order for maintenance made under the Domestic Proceedings and Magistrates' Courts Act may be secured in this way.[5]

An attachment of earnings order may be applied for by the person to whom payments are due under the related maintenance order, by a magistrates' clerk if an order is in force directing payments to be made through him, or by the debtor himself.[6] Unless the debtor makes the application, the court may make an order only if it appears that he has failed to make one or more payments owing to his wilful refusal or culpable neglect.[7]

The order must specify two rates: the *normal deduction rate*, which is the amount which the court thinks is reasonable to secure the payment of sums falling due under the order in the future together with the arrears already accrued, and the *protected earnings rate*, that is the rate below which the husband's earnings shall not in any event be reduced by payments deducted under the order.[8] The purpose of the latter is to keep the husband's remaining income above subsistence level; consequently only in exceptional circumstances would it be reasonable to fix it below the figure which, if it represented the husband's total resources, would entitle him to apply for

---

[1] Magistrates' Courts Act 1980, s. 93 (1), (2).

[2] *Ibid.*, s. 95. The court may also remit arrears on hearing an application to vary, discharge or revive the order provided that the wife has been given notice: Magistrates' Courts Rules 1968, r. 37. The six months' limitation period does not apply so that arrears up to any amount may be recovered, but normally they should not be enforced if they have been due for more than a year: *Ross* v. *Pearson*, [1976] 1 All E.R. 790. Because arrears can be remitted, they are not provable in the husband's bankruptcy but continue to be enforceable in the same way as before: *James* v. *James*, [1964] P. 303; [1963] 2 All E.R. 465. *Cf post*, p. 566, n. 4.

[3] Magistrates' Courts Act 1980, s. 76 (1); Attachment of Earnings Act 1971, s. 1 (3) (a).

[4] Magistrates' Courts Rules 1968, r. 44. Clothing and bedding are exempt from distress as are tools of the husband's trade up to the value of £50. The court may also order the husband to be searched and any money belonging to him and found on him to be applied towards payment of the arrears: Magistrates' Courts Act 1980, s. 80.

[5] Attachment of Earnings Act 1971, Sched. 1, para. 4, as amended by the Domestic Proceedings and Magistrates' Courts Act 1978, Sched. 2.

[6] *Ibid.*, ss. 3 (1) and 17-21.

[7] *Ibid.*, s. 3 (3), (5). Unless the debtor makes the application, 15 days must have elapsed since the related order was made: s. 3 (2).

[8] *Ibid.*, s. 6 (5), (6).

supplementary benefit.[1] In assessing the protected earnings rate, the court must take into account the husband's resources and needs and the needs of others for whom he is bound to provide or may reasonably be expected to provide[2] but may consider only his actual earnings from his particular employer at the time and not his potential earnings in some other occupation.[3]

The order is directed to the husband's employer, and when it has been served on him, he is bound to deduct certain sums from the husband's earnings[4] and to pay them over to the collecting officer of the court.[5] In the normal way he will on each "pay day" (which may, of course, be weekly, monthly or quarterly) pay over the normal deduction, but if the husband's "attachable" earnings[6] are less than the aggregate of his protected earnings and the normal deduction, then the employer must pay over only the amount by which the attachable earnings exceed the protected earnings, so that the husband takes the latter intact. If on any pay day it is impossible for the employer to pay over the normal deduction, then on any subsequent pay day on which the attachable earnings exceed the sum of the protected earnings and the normal deduction, the employer must deduct and pay over such part of the excess as is necessary to cover the unpaid part of the normal deduction.[7] The collecting officer of the court must then pay the money

---

[1] *Billington* v. *Billington*, [1974] Fam. 24; [1974] 1 All E.R. 546. But this is not a rigid rule of law. There might be exceptional circumstances, *e.g.*, if the husband was living with his parents at no personal expense.

[2] Domestic Proceedings and Magistrates' Courts Act 1978, s. 25 (3).

[3] *Pepper* v. *Pepper*, [1960] 1 All E.R. 529, 534-535.

[4] "Earnings" means any salary, wage or pension and includes sums payable by the Crown or out of public revenue in the United Kingdom (except Northern Ireland); it does not include sums payable by any other government, pay or allowances payable to members of H.M. forces, wages payable to seamen (other than seamen of fishing boats), or pensions, allowances or benefit payable under enactments relating to social security or in respect of the debtor's disablement or disability: Attachment of Earnings Act 1971, ss. 22 and 24 and Sched. 4, as subsequently amended. It also includes payments made at irregular intervals or under discretionary powers: *Edmonds* v. *Edmonds*, [1965] 1 All E.R. 379.

[5] *I.e.*, the clerk of that or another magistrates' court: Attachment of Earnings Act 1971, s. 6 (7).

[6] *I.e.*, his earnings less income tax, social security contributions, and superannuation contributions deductible by the employer: *ibid.*, Sched. 3, para. 3, as amended by the Social Security (Consequential Provisions) Act 1975, Sched. 2.

[7] Attachment of Earnings Act 1971, s. 6 and Sched. 3, Part I. Suppose the normal deduction rate is £20 a week and the protected earnings rate is £50 a week; the following table shows how the husband's earnings will be dealt with:

	ATTACHABLE EARNINGS £	PAID TO HUSBAND £	PAID TO COLLECTING OFFICER £	NORMAL DEDUCTIONS UNPAID £
Week 1	75	55	20	—
Week 2	66	50	16	4
Week 3	60	50	10	14
Week 4	78	50	28	6
Week 5	80	54	26	—
Total	359	259	100	—

If more than one attachment of earnings order is in force, the employer must deal with them in the order laid down in Sched. 3, Part II. For details of the employer's duties generally and penalties for failing to comply with the Act, see ss. 7, 9, 12 and 23; for the powers of the court to obtain statements of earnings and to determine whether particular payments are earnings, see ss. 14 and 16.

received to the wife or other person to whom the money due under the order is payable.[1]

Once an attachment of earnings order has been made, no committal order may be made as a consequence of proceedings begun beforehand; similarly if a committal order is made or a warrant is issued after an attachment of earnings order has been made, the latter will automatically be discharged.[2] A court before which proceedings for committal or distress are brought may always make an attachment of earnings order instead if it thinks that that would be a more efficacious means of securing payment.[3]

Variation and Discharge.—The court has a general power to order the variation or discharge of an attachment of earnings order and must vary or discharge it when the debtor has paid off the arrears and the sum attachable is greater than that payable under the related maintenance order.[4] If the debtor ceases to be employed by the person to whom the order has been directed, it lapses until the court directs it to a fresh employer,[5] and it ceases to have effect if the related maintenance order is discharged unless arrears are still unpaid and the court directs that the attachment order shall remain alive.[6]

Effectiveness of Orders.—In many cases it may be questioned whether the value of an order to the wife is worth the administrative trouble that it causes. In the words of the Finer Report, "the early promise of attachment of earnings orders was not sustained, and ... they have not become established as a major mode of enforcing maintenance orders in magistrates' courts".[7] The procedure will be most effective when the husband is in steady employment, but when he is in casual employment, he may be able to escape the order by the simple expedient of changing jobs frequently if they are available to him.

Committal.—A warrant of committal (which may also be issued if distress is insufficient to satisfy the debt) commits the husband to prison for a period varying from five days to six weeks, the maximum period being graduated according to the sum owed.[8] But since committal proceedings are in effect designed to punish the husband for failing to carry out the order, he may be imprisoned only if the default was due to his wilful refusal or culpable neglect

---

[1] *Ibid.*, s. 13 (1). The sums paid must go first in payment of arrears and then in payment of costs: s. 13 (2).

[2] *Ibid.*, s. 8 (1), (3).

[3] *Ibid.*, s. 3 (4).

[4] *Ibid.*, ss. 9 and 10. To cope with emergencies a single justice (or a justices' clerk) may increase the protected earnings rate for a period of not more than four weeks: s. 9 (3) and the Magistrates' Courts (Attachment of Earnings) Rules 1971, rr. 14 and 22.

[5] *Ibid.*, s. 9 (4). For the duties of the debtor, the old employer and a new employer who knows that the order is in force, see *ibid.*, ss. 7 (2) and 15.

[6] *Ibid.*, s. 11 (1) (c), (3). For the effect of registration of the maintenance order in another court on attachment of earnings orders, see *post*, p. 570.

[7] Cmnd. 5629, para. 4.146. See also Brown, *Attachment of Earnings Orders in Practice*, 24 M.L.R. 486.

[8] Magistrates' Courts Act 1980, ss. 76 (2), (3), 93 (7) and 132 and Sched. 4.

and the court feels that it is inappropriate to make an attachment of earnings order.[1]

Two further powers that the court possesses are those of ordering the payment of arrears by instalments and of postponing the issue of a warrant of committal upon conditions.[2] Used together these powers constitute a valuable weapon, particularly when it is financially impossible for the husband to pay off all the arrears at once. For example, suppose that £200 is due under the order: the court may order the husband to be imprisoned for 30 days but the issue of the warrant of committal to be postponed on condition, say, that he pays off the arrears at the rate of £10 a week.

If the husband pays the arrears, the order of committal immediately ceases to have effect, and if he pays a part of the sum due, the period of imprisonment is proportionately reduced.[3] But serving the sentence does not wipe off the arrears[4] although no further arrears accrue whilst the husband is in custody unless the court orders otherwise.[5] A husband who is in prison may apply to have the warrant of committal cancelled, in which case the court has power to release him either absolutely or with a postponed warrant of committal for a period not exceeding the balance of the term to be served and may at the same time remit the whole or any part of the sum still unpaid.[6]

E. ORDERS FOR FINANCIAL PROVISION UNDER SECTION 27 OF THE MATRIMONIAL CAUSES ACT 1973

Section 27 of the Matrimonial Causes Act 1973 (as amended by section 63 of the Domestic Proceedings and Magistrates' Courts Act 1978) provides that either party to a marriage may apply to a divorce court for an order on the ground that the other party to the marriage has failed to provide reasonable maintenance for the applicant or has failed to provide, or to make a proper contribution towards, reasonable maintenance for any child of the family. The court has jurisdiction if either party is domiciled in England and Wales, if the applicant has been habitually resident here for one year, or if the respondent is resident here.[7] The proceedings must be commenced in a divorce county court. If the respondent contests the application on the ground that he (or she) is not bound to maintain the applicant at all or if he contests the court's jurisdiction, the application *must* be transferred to the

---

[1] Magistrates' Courts Act 1980, s. 93 (6). No order for committal may be made unless the husband has appeared in court; he may be arrested if he fails to answer the summons.

[2] *Ibid.*, ss. 75 and 77; Maintenance Orders Act 1958, s. 18.

[3] Magistrates' Courts Act 1980, s. 79.

[4] *Ibid.*, s. 93 (8). But a husband cannot be imprisoned more than once for failure to pay the same sum: Maintenance Orders Act 1958, s. 17.

[5] Magistrates' Courts Act 1980, s. 94, for the committal will probably deprive the husband of the power of earning his living in the meantime.

[6] Maintenance Orders Act 1958, s. 18 (4), (5), (6). The order cannot be enforced against the husband's personal representatives after his death: *Re Bidie*, [1948] Ch. 697; [1948] 1 All E.R. 885; affirmed, [1949] Ch. 121; [1948] 2 All E.R. 995, C.A. It is doubtful whether an order can ever be enforced after it has been discharged: *per* AVORY, J., in *Outerbridge* v. *Outerbridge*, [1927] 1 K.B. 368; consequently the wife should resist an order for discharge until all arrears have been paid or remitted.

[7] Domicile and Matrimonial Proceedings Act 1973, s. 6 (1).

High Court; in other cases the county court *may* order it to be transferred if this seems desirable.[1]

It will be seen that the grounds for application are identical with the first two grounds on which a spouse may apply to a magistrates' court for an order under section 1 of the Domestic Proceedings and Magistrates' Courts Act, and the court is specifically enjoined to take the same matters into account in determining whether the respondent has failed to provide reasonable maintenance and, if so, what order to make.[2] On these points, therefore, the reader should refer to the discussion of applications in magistrates' courts.[3]

The court may make an interim order for periodical payments to the applicant if it appears that the latter or any child to whom the application relates is in immediate need of financial assistance.[4] If one of the grounds mentioned above is made out, the court may order the respondent to make any one or more of the following payments:[5]

(1) Unsecured periodical payments to the applicant;
(2) Secured periodical payments to the applicant;
(3) A lump sum payment to the applicant;
(4) Unsecured periodical payments for any child to whom the application relates;
(5) Secured periodical payments for such a child;
(6) A lump sum payment for such a child.

The question of the assessment of orders is essentially the same as that of orders made in magistrates' courts with the obvious exception that periodical payments may be secured and there is an unlimited power to order lump sum payments. Both these questions will be dealt with more fully when we consider financial provision after divorce;[6] in the case of lump sum payments, however, it should be borne in mind that the court has no power to make property adjustment orders under section 27 and consequently a lump sum order should not be used as a means of circumventing this restriction. The Act specifically provides that a lump sum may be ordered to enable the applicant to meet any liabilities or expenses already incurred in maintaining herself (or himself) or any child of the family to whom the application relates;[7] in addition, it may properly be ordered (as on divorce) whenever a capital sum is more valuable to the applicant than periodical payments.[8] A

---

[1] Matrimonial Causes Act 1967, s. 2; Matrimonial Causes Act 1973, Sched. 2, para. 6 (1) (a); Matrimonial Causes Rules 1977, r. 99 (1), (2). In *Newmarch* v. *Newmarch*, [1978] Fam. 79; [1978] 1 All E.R. 1, it was held that an interim order could be confirmed notwithstanding that the parties had been divorced abroad in the meantime. There seems to be no reason why the same principle should not be applied even if an interim order has not been made provided that the proceedings were begun while the parties were still married. This is contrary to the earlier decision in *Turczak* v. *Turczak*, [1970] P. 198; [1969] 2 All E.R. 317 (which was not cited in *Newmarch* v. *Newmarch*) but is to be preferred because otherwise the wife might be left with no effective right to support at all. See Karsten, 33 M.L.R. 205; Law Com. Working Paper No. 77 (Financial Relief after Foreign Divorce), para. 18.

[2] Matrimonial Causes Act 1973, s. 27 (3), (3A), (3B) (as amended).

[3] See *ante*, pp. 499 (grounds) and 505 (matters to be taken into account) and *post*, p. 590 (reasonable maintenance for children).

[4] S. 27 (5).

[5] S. 27 (6).

[6] See *post*, pp. 529 (secured payments) and 531 (lump sum payments). See also p. 590 (orders for children).

[7] S. 27 (7) (a). *Cf. post*, p. 532.

[8] See *post*, p. 533.

lump sum may be made payable in instalments and the instalments may be secured.[1]

Interim orders and orders for periodical payments may be varied, discharged, suspended and revived. In the case of a lump sum payable by instalments, the provisions relating to the instalments may be varied but not the total sum payable.[2]

Orders are enforceable in the same way as orders for periodical payments on divorce.[3]

Few applications are made for orders under section 27.[4] Most spouses prefer to take the cheaper and speedier proceedings available in magistrates' courts unless they are also petitioning for divorce or other matrimonial relief in the divorce court. The advantage of proceedings under section 27 is that the court may order periodical payments to be secured and has an unlimited power to order a lump sum payment. Now that magistrates' courts may make orders for lump sums, applications under this section may well become even rarer.

F. REGISTRATION OF ORDERS IN OTHER COURTS

Orders made by a magistrates' courts may be registered in the High Court and orders made by the High Court or a divorce county court under section 27 of the Matrimonial Causes Act may be registered in a magistrates' court. The order must then be paid and can be enforced as though it had been made by the court in which it is registered. The purpose and details of this procedure will be considered in the next chapter.[5]

G. FINANCIAL RELIEF WHEN ONE PARTY IS OUT OF THE JURISDICTION

The powers of an English court to make or enforce an order for financial relief when one of the parties is out of the jurisdiction have become increasingly more important with the greater mobility of population—a mobility that is likely to become more marked with our entry into the European Economic Community. Two questions have to be answered:

(1) In what circumstances can financial relief be obtained by or against the party in England?

(2) In what circumstances can an order, already in existence, be enforced by or against this party?

The jurisdiction of English courts to make an order for financial relief is discussed in connection with each type of order. Whether an order obtained here can be enforced in the country in which the other party is resident and whether an order can be obtained there must of course be determined by the law of the country in question. An order obtained abroad may be enforced here in the same way as any other judgment *in personam* provided that it is "final and conclusive". If, however, the foreign court retains the same power as an English court to vary the order, it will lack this quality of finality and

---

[1] S. 27 (7) (b).

[2] Matrimonial Causes Act 1973, s. 31. See further *post*, pp. 563-565.

[3] *Ibid.*, ss. 31-33 and 37. See *post*, pp. 566-570.

[4] The average number of applications in the years 1975-1979 was 266 a year.

[5] See *post*, pp. 570-571 *et seq.*

consequently will not be enforceable under the general law.[1] Because of this difficulty two statutes have been passed to help dependants who might otherwise find themselves unable to obtain effective relief. The first, the Maintenance Orders Act 1950, provides machinery for the reciprocal enforcement of orders within the three jurisdictions of the United Kingdom; the second, the Maintenance Orders (Reciprocal Enforcement) Act 1972, applies when one party is outside the United Kingdom.

Maintenance Orders Act 1950.—Under Part II of this Act if a person entitled to payments under a maintenance order[2] obtained in one part of the United Kingdom wishes to enforce it in another part, she (or he) must apply to the court that made the order. If that court is satisfied that the person liable to make the payments resides in another part of the United Kingdom and that it is convenient that the order should be enforceable there, a copy of the order is sent to the relevant court in that jurisdiction, which must then register it.[3] The order is then enforceable as though it had been made by the court in which it is registered.[4]

Variation and discharge of orders for periodical payments remain within the jurisdiction of the court that made the order except that, if the order is registered in a magistrate's court, only the latter has power to vary the rate of payments.[5] In order to prevent parties to an order registered in a magistrates' court having to travel from one jurisdiction to another to give evidence in proceedings for variation or discharge, the so-called "shuttlecock procedure" applies:[6] that is, the payee's evidence may be given in the court which made the order and the payer's evidence may be given in the court in which it is registered; in each case a transcript or summary of the evidence is then sent to the other court.[7]

The payee may apply to have the registration cancelled at any time.[8]

Maintenance Orders (Reciprocal Enforcement) Act 1972.—This Act replaces the Maintenance Orders (Facilities for Enforcement) Act 1920 which

---

[1] *Harrop* v. *Harrop*, [1920] 3 K.B. 386. But if the court has no power to remit arrears, these may be enforced as a final and conclusive judgment: *Beatty* v. *Beatty*, [1924] 1 K.B. 807, C.A. An order may also be enforceable under the Colonial and Other Territories (Divorce Jurisdiction) Acts 1926-1950. See Dicey and Morris, *Conflict of Laws*, 10th Ed., 409-416, 1092 *et seq.*

[2] These are defined in s. 16 (as amended). They are all orders for periodical payments and lump sum payments.

[3] S. 17. If the order is to be registered in England, the relevant court is the High Court if the order was made by a superior court and in other cases the magistrates' court in whose jurisdiction the payer appears to be: s. 17 (3).

[4] Ss. 18-20. This includes the enforcement of arrears accrued before registration: s. 20. The order may be further registered under the Maintenance Orders Act 1958: Administration of Justice Act 1977, s. 3 and Sched. 3 (see *post*, pp. 570-571).

[5] S. 22. But the sum as varied must not exceed the maximum which could have been ordered by the original court: s. 22 (4).

[6] So described in *Pilcher* v. *Pilcher*, [1955] P. 318, 330; [1955] 2 All E.R. 644, 651.

[7] S. 22 (5). This also applies to orders registered in sheriff courts in Scotland and courts of summary jurisdiction in Northern Ireland but not to orders registered in superior courts. There is no reason why it should not be extended to them.

[8] S. 24. The registration must be cancelled unless proceedings for variation are pending in the court of registration. The payer may apply for cancellation of an order registered in a magistrates' court (or sheriff court in Scotland) if he has ceased to reside in the country in which the order is registered: s. 24 (2).

introduced machinery for the reciprocal enforcement of maintenance orders between this country and other Commonwealth countries with which we had reached an agreement.[1] It is much wider in its scope than the 1920 Act and deals with two entirely different types of proceeding. Part I enables a party to obtain an order in country X and to enforce it in country Y or to enforce in country Y an order already obtained in country X. Part II enables a party in country X to obtain an order in country Y, which will then be enforceable there.

Part I of the Act.—Any country or territory outside the United Kingdom may be designated a "reciprocating country" by Order in Council if reciprocal facilities will be accorded there for British maintenance orders.[2] For the purpose of this Part of the Act a maintenance order is an order (including an affiliation order) providing for periodical payments towards the maintenance of any person whom the payer is liable to maintain under the law of the place where the order was made.[3] If an order has already been made by an English court, the payee may apply to the court to have it transmitted to a reciprocating country for enforcement there.[4] If a copy of an order made in a reciprocating country is received here, it will be sent for registration in the magistrates' court acting for the petty sessions area in which the payer resides.[5]

Part I also provides additional machinery whereby an applicant may obtain in the country in which she (or he) resides an order against a person resident in a reciprocating country. To prevent either party from having to go to the other country, the proceedings are split between the two countries involved. The applicant starts the proceedings in a court in her own country, and if that court is satisfied that she has made out a *prima facie case*, it may make a provisional order. This is then transmitted to the appropriate court of the reciprocating country in which the other party resides; after hearing the defendant and any evidence he wishes to adduce, that court may confirm the order. The "shuttlecock procedure" for the taking of evidence applies.[6] In each case the appropriate court in England is the magistrates' court, and consequently any proceedings started here must be brought under one of the Acts conferring jurisdiction on magistrates' courts.[7] As the cause of complaint

---

[1] The 1920 Act still applies with respect to certain countries but will ultimately be entirely superseded and repealed. For details, see Dicey and Morris, *op. cit.*, 413-414.

[2] S. 1. The order may limit the operation of the Act to certain types of maintenance orders in any given case. For the countries already designated as reciprocating countries, see S.I. 1974 No. 556, S.I. 1975 No. 2187 and S.I. 1979 No. 115. Except for the Republic of South Africa, they are all within the Commonwealth.

[3] S. 21 (1). It also includes an order made against a putative father for payments incidental to an illegitimate child's birth or funeral expenses.

[4] S. 2.

[5] Ss. 6 and 21 (1).

[6] See ss. 3 (5) (b) and 7 (2) (a). For the "shuttlecock procedure" see *supra*. For evidence generally, see ss. 13-15. The court may not direct blood tests to determine paternity in any proceedings brought under this Act: s. 44 (1).

[7] See s. 3. The Acts are the Domestic Proceedings and Magistrates' Courts Act 1978 (*ante*), the Guardianship of Minors Act 1971 (*post*, p. 593), and the Affiliation Proceedings Act 1957 (*post*, p. 595). The court may make an order for the maintenance of a child even though no order for custody is in force: s. 3 (3). The court may not refuse to make an order on the ground that the case would be more conveniently dealt with by the High Court: s. 3 (4).

does not have to arise within the jurisdiction,[1] a woman newly arrived in this country may bring proceedings alleging, for example, her husband's behaviour or desertion notwithstanding that he has never set foot in the United Kingdom. Whether it is desirable to give the wife a remedy when she might have none under the law of the country in which the spouses have been living is debatable.[2] A provisional order made in a reciprocating country must be sent to the magistrates' court acting for the area in which the defendant resides. The court must refuse to confirm the order if the defendant establishes that he has a defence to the proceedings under the law of the country that made it; in other cases it must confirm the order but may make any alterations that it thinks reasonable. A confirmed order is then registered in the court that confirmed it.[3]

Any order registered in this country, whether already made in a reciprocating country or after confirmation, can be enforced as though it had been made by the registering court.[4] Both that court and the court that made the order (or provisional order) may vary or revoke it; to protect the other party, however, this can be done in most cases only by a provisional order which will not take effect until it is confirmed by the other court, in which case the "shuttlecock procedure" again operates.[5]

No appeal lies from a provisional order made by a magistrates' court or, apparently, from the refusal to make one. But either party may appeal if a magistrates' court confirms a provisional order made in a reciprocating country (including provisional orders for variation or revocation), or varies or revokes any order (otherwise than by a provisional order), or refuses to confirm, vary or revoke it.[6]

Part II *of the Act.*—The provisions of Part I are based on the assumption that the United Kingdom and reciprocating countries have broadly similar laws relating to maintenance and the enforcement of orders, for the registering court must be able to understand the foreign law with which it is dealing and must have a similar procedure. It is therefore unlikely that an Order in Council will be made under section 1 if its effect would be to involve a court in the United Kingdom having to interpret a wholly unfamiliar foreign law, nor will the British Government wish to negotiate a detailed

---

[1] *Collister* v. *Collister*, [1972] 1 All E.R. 334.

[2] It must be remembered that the court potentially has power to deal with *de facto* polygamous marriages: see *ante*, p. 62.

[3] S. 7.

[4] This includes the payee's power to apply for an order to be registered in the High Court under Part I of the Maintenance Orders Act 1958 and the court's power to remit arrears—a matter of importance because there may be a long delay between the application to have the order revoked and its confirmation. See s. 8 (as amended by the Domestic Proceedings and Magistrates' Courts Act 1978, s. 54) and Sched., para. 4. For payment of orders registered in this country and the conversion of foreign currency, see s. 16.

[5] For details, see ss. 5 and 9, as amended by the Domestic Proceedings and Magistrates' Courts Act 1978, s. 54. A provisional order made by a magistrates' court requiring the payer to make periodical payments for his or her spouse will cease to have effect if the payee remarries: s. 42, as amended by *ibid.*, Sched. 2. For the cancellation of registration following revocation and the transfer of registered orders if the payee ceases to reside within the court's jurisdiction, see ss. 10 and 11.

[6] S. 12.

agreement with every country with which we might make arrangements for the reciprocal enforcement of maintenance. This might leave many dependants unprotected and Part II has been passed for their benefit.

This Part gives effect to the United Nations Convention on the Recovery Abroad of Maintenance of 1956. Any country to which this Convention extends may be designated a "convention country" for the purpose of Part II by Order in Council.[1] Once this had been done, an applicant may start proceedings in this country to obtain maintenance from a person subject to the jurisdiction of a convention country, and an applicant in a convention country may start proceedings there to obtain maintenance from a person residing in any part of the United Kingdom. At first sight this looks similar to the procedure laid down in Part I but there is an important difference between them. Under Part I the order is made by the court in which the applicant starts the proceedings (even though it does not take effect until it is confirmed in the reciprocating country) and that court must apply its own law; under Part II, however, the order is made by the court of the country in which the defendant resides and the law of that country applies. The relevant authority in the applicant's country is no more than an agent for transmitting the application to the other country.

An application in England is made through the clerk of a magistrates' court and is then transmitted to the convention country.[2] An application received from a convention country is sent to the magistrates' court acting for the area in which the defendant resides and is then treated as though it were a complaint made under the relevant Act conferring jurisdiction on the court.[3] It will be seen that this might leave a woman divorced abroad wholly unprotected for, no longer being a wife, she could not bring proceedings under the Domestic Proceedings and Magistrates' Courts Act. Consequently a person whose marriage has been dissolved or annulled in a convention country may now apply for an order against her (or his) former spouse resident here if an order for maintenance for the benefit of the applicant or a child of the family has been made in the convention country by reason of the divorce or nullity. Failure to comply with the order is itself a ground for complaint under the Domestic Proceedings and Magistrates' Courts Act. The court has the same powers as it has on an application made under section 1 of that Act except that it may make an order for periodical payments or a lump sum payment for the applicant or a child of the family only if the order made in the convention country contained a similar provision for the applicant or that child, as the case may be.[4]

In all cases the application should be accompanied by a transcript or summary of evidence; if the court requires further evidence, it may ask the Secretary of State to request the appropriate body or court in the convention

---

[1] S. 25. For the countries already designated as convention countries, see S.I. 1975 No. 423 and S.I. 1978 No. 279. They include all the countries of Western Europe.

[2] S. 26.

[3] S. 27, as amended by the Domestic Proceedings and Magistrates' Courts Act 1978, s. 56 and Sched. 2. For the relevant Acts, see p. 519, n. 7, *ante*.

[4] S. 28A (added by the Domestic Proceedings and Magistrates' Courts Act 1978, s. 58). For the powers of the court, see *ante*, p. 501. The court may also make an interim maintenance order. "Child of the family" has the same meaning as it has in that Act. The decree of divorce or nullity must be recognised here but its validity will be presumed and it is for the defendant to prove that an English court will not recognise it.

country to take it.[1] The only orders that may be made are for the payment of money (including lump sum payments and interim orders), and the court may not make any provision for the custody, access, care or supervision of any child.[2] The order may be enforced in the same way as other orders made in magistrates' courts.[3]

An order registered in this country may be varied or revoked by the registering court on the application of either party, and the court may hear a complaint for variation or revocation notwithstanding that either party is outside England and Wales provided that the other has been given notice of the proceedings.[4] An application for variation by a payee in England may be transmitted to a convention country and *vice versa* in the same way as an initial application for an order.[5] Either party may appeal against an order or the refusal to make one (including an order for variation or revocation) in the usual way.

Modified Schemes for Reciprocal Enforcement. —The scheme laid down in Parts I and II of the Act may not be apposite in all cases. Some countries may be unwilling or unable to become parties to the Convention (for example, federal countries like the U.S.A., where maintenance orders come within the jurisdiction of individual states and not of the federal government). To overcome this and similar difficulties, section 40 of the Act enables arrangements to be made with such countries on a reciprocal basis. The provisions of the Act may be extended to any country or territory by Order in Council subject to such exceptions, adaptations and modifications as are specified in the Order. The modifications most likely to be made are to the method by which applications are to be transmitted.[6]

---

[1] Ss. 36 and 37. There is a complementary power enabling the Secretary of State to request a court in this country to take evidence to be sent to a court in a convention country dealing with an application originally made in this country: s. 38.

[2] S. 28, as substituted by the Domestic Proceedings and Magistrates' Courts Act 1978, s. 57. An order may be made even though no order for custody is in force: s. 30 (1).

[3] S. 33. Arrears may be remitted and the order may be registered in the High Court under the Maintenance Orders Act 1958.

[4] Ss. 34 and 35. For the transfer of an order after the payer has ceased to reside within the jurisdiction of the magistrates' court, see s. 32.

[5] Ss. 26 (2), 34 (3) and 35 (2).

[6] For details of arrangements made with the Republic of Ireland, six other European countries and 33 states in the U.S.A., see S.I. 1974 No. 2140 and S.I. 1979 Nos. 1314 and 1317.

Chapter 15

Financial Relief for the Spouses on Divorce, Nullity and Judicial Separation

A. INTRODUCTORY

Development of the Court's Powers.—The ecclesiastical courts were able to give financial protection to a wife by ordering the husband to pay her alimony pending suit (or *pendente lite*) and permanent alimony after granting a decree of divorce *a mensa et thoro*. After 1857 this power was vested in the Divorce Court and subsequently in the High Court and divorce county courts. The Divorce Court set up in 1857 was also empowered on granting a decree of divorce to order the husband to secure maintenance for the wife's life.[1] If the husband had no capital which could be secured, hardship was likely to be caused to the wife; this was cured in 1866, when the court was given the power to order the husband to pay unsecured maintenance to the wife. As this would have to come out of his income, however, the maximum term for which it could be ordered was the spouses' joint lives.[2] In 1907 these powers were extended to nullity.[3] After 1937 a wife petitioning for divorce or judicial separation on the ground of her husband's insanity could be ordered to pay him alimony pending suit and, if the decree was granted, maintenance (secured or unsecured) or permanent alimony.[4] Finally in 1963 the courts were given a power, long overdue, to order the payment of a lump sum in addition to or instead of maintenance or alimony on divorce, nullity and judicial separation.[5] Ancillary orders could also be made by a court granting a decree of restitution of conjugal rights to a wife.[6]

Except when the husband was incurably of unsound mind, orders for alimony and maintenance could be made only against him. This of course reflected the fact that in the middle of the nineteenth century it was very

---

[1] Matrimonial Causes Act 1857, s. 32.
[2] Matrimonial Causes Act 1866, s. 1.
[3] Matrimonial Causes Act 1907, s. 1.
[4] Matrimonial Causes Act 1937, s. 10 (2).
[5] Matrimonial Causes Act 1963, s. 5.
[6] Alimony pending suit, alimony on making the decree on the wife's application, and periodical payments (which could be secured) if the husband failed to comply with the decree: Matrimonial Causes Act 1857, s. 17; Matrimonial Causes Act 1884, s. 2.

523

unlikely that a wife would have an income. She might have property settled to her own use, however, and as early as 1857 the court was empowered to order this to be settled for the benefit of the husband or children if he obtained a divorce or judicial separation on the ground of her adultery. This power was later extended to the property of wives who were divorced for cruelty or desertion or whose husbands obtained a decree for restitution of conjugal rights.[1] On divorce or nullity, either party could benefit from the exercise of the court's jurisdiction, going back to 1859,[2] to vary ante-nuptial and post-nuptial settlements.

We have already seen that the need to bring matrimonial proceedings purely in order to obtain maintenance was made unnecessary by the Law Reform (Miscellaneous Provisions) Act of 1949.[3]

The Matrimonial Proceedings and Property Act 1970.—As often happens, piecemeal modifications of the law spread over more than a century produced confusing anomalies. Whatever reasons there might originally have been for giving the courts different powers according to the nature of the decree, they had largely become obscure by the middle of the present century. Why, for example, could a wife obtain secured maintenance if she petitioned for restitution of conjugal rights but not if she petitioned for judicial separation? Why could the court order maintenance to be secured for the wife's life on divorce or nullity but only for the spouses' joint lives in proceedings for restitution of conjugal rights? It was as difficult for the layman to grasp these subtleties in a branch of the law that was more likely to affect him than most as it was for the lawyer to justify them.

Pressure for immediate reform increased after the passing of the Divorce Reform Act 1969, when the fear was expressed that many innocent wives, divorced against their will, would be left with inadequate provision. The result was the passing of the Matrimonial Proceedings and Property Act 1970, which was based upon the recommendations of the Law Commission.[4] Most of its provisions have been repealed and re-enacted in Part II of the Matrimonial Causes Act 1973, which now governs the award of financial relief in the High Court and divorce county courts. Four basic principles, which are radically different from those underlying the old law, should be noted.

(1) The old confusing terminology (alimony, maintenance and periodical payments) is abolished. All are now described as financial provision and may take the form of periodical payments or a lump sum payment.

(2) The court is no longer virtually restricted to ordering maintenance in favour of the wife. It now has equal powers to order either spouse to make financial provision for the other.

---

[1] Matrimonial Causes Act 1857, s. 45; Matrimonial Causes Act 1884, s. 3; Matrimonial Causes Act 1937, s. 10 (3).

[2] Matrimonial Causes Act 1859, s. 5.

[3] *Ante*, p. 488.

[4] Law Com. No. 25, Report on Financial Provision in Matrimonial Proceedings, 1969. For critical reviews of the provisions of the Act, see Cretney, *The Maintenance Quagmire*, 33 M.L.R. 662; Kahn-Freund, *Recent Legislation on Matrimonial Property*, *ibid.*, 601, particularly at pp. 615 *et seq.*

(3) There is no distinction between the court's powers to order financial provision for the petitioner and its powers to order financial provision for the respondent. This is an essential consequence of the passing of the Divorce Reform Act, because the fact that the petitioner has obtained a decree does not necessarily indicate that the respondent has been responsible for the breakdown of the marriage.

(4) The court's powers to order financial provision, the transfer and settlement of property, and the variation of ante-nuptial and post-nuptial settlements are the same in divorce, nullity and judicial separation.[1]

Powers of the Court.—A court hearing a petition for divorce, nullity or judicial separation can make an order against *either spouse* with respect to any one or more of the following matters:

(1) Maintenance pending suit;
(2) Unsecured periodical payments to the other spouse;
(3) Secured periodical payments to the other spouse;
(4) Lump sum payments to the other spouse;
(5) Unsecured periodical payments for any child of the family;
(6) Secured periodical payments for any child of the family;
(7) A lump sum payment for any child of the family;
(8) Transfer of property to the other spouse or for the benefit of any child of the family;
(9) Settlement of property for the benefit of the other spouse or any child of the family;
(10) Variation of any ante-nuptial or post-nuptial settlement.

Orders coming within (2)-(7) are collectively known as financial provision orders and those coming within (8), (9) and (10) as property adjustment orders.[2]

The court has similar powers in those rare cases where a marriage has been dissolved on the ground that one spouse is presumed to be dead and he or she is later found to be still alive.[3] Orders in favour of children only (that is, (5), (6) and (7) above) will be dealt with in the next chapter when we consider financial provision for children generally. The rest will be dealt with in this chapter.

Application for Relief and Hearing.—A petitioner seeking financial relief should apply for it in the petition. A respondent claiming relief who files an answer should similarly apply for financial relief in the answer. If the party in question fails to make the application in this way, he must obtain the leave of

---

[1] The Act abolished decrees for restitution of conjugal rights: see *ante*, p. 121. For a highly stimulating criticism of the principles underlying the present law and proposals for reform, see Gray, *Reallocation of Property on Divorce*. See also Eekelaar, *Family Law and Social Policy*, c. 9; Deech, 7 Fam. Law 229 (in turn criticised by O'Donovan, 8 Fam. Law 180). The Law Commission have now themselves produced a discussion paper questioning whether the basic policy is still sound: see Law Com. No. 103, The Financial Consequences of Divorce: the Basic Policy.

[2] Matrimonial Causes Act 1973, s. 21.

[3] *Deacock* v. *Deacock*, [1958] P. 230; [1958] 2 All E.R. 633, C.A.

the court unless the parties are agreed on the proposed order.[1] There is no limit on the time in which leave may be sought, but as failure to apply really amounts to no more than a technical omission, the courts tend to look sympathetically at a request for leave if the applicant has a reasonable prospect of success or a seriously arguable case. On the other hand, delay would be fatal if the other party had ordered his affairs in the belief that no application would be made, or was being harassed or would be prejudiced in some other way.[2]

If a respondent does not file an answer claiming relief (as will be the case in all undefended suits), he may apply for financial relief at any time without leave.[3]

It is a general principle of the Matrimonial Causes Act that, if a former spouse remarries, she (or he) must look to her new partner for financial provision for herself, and not to the old one. Consequently, whether leave is required or not, a party who has remarried cannot apply for any order at all except for periodical payments or a lump sum payment for a child of the family,[4] although an application already made can be entertained notwithstanding the remarriage.[5] This rule applies even though the second marriage is void or voidable:[6] the party's remedy lies in seeking financial provision in nullity proceedings.

An application for financial relief is not a cause of action which survives against the other party's estate, so that no order can be made after the death of either of them.[7] The effect of this is now mitigated by the extensive powers given to the court by the Inheritance (Provision for Family and Dependants) Act 1975.[8]

Except for maintenance pending suit and orders with respect to children, no order may be made unless a decree nisi of divorce or nullity or a decree of judicial separation has been granted and, in the case of divorce or nullity, it may not take effect until the decree is made absolute.[9] Unless the parties are agreed on the order to be made, each of them is required to file an affidavit of means setting out full particulars of their property and income.[10] The hearing will normally be before a registrar who may, however, refer the application to

---

[1] Matrimonial Causes Rules 1977, r. 68 (1), (2).

[2] *Chaterjee* v. *Chaterjee*, [1976] Fam. 199; [1976] 1 All E.R. 719, C.A.

[3] Matrimonial Causes Rules 1977, r. 68 (3).

[4] Matrimonial Causes Act 1973, s. 28 (3). The Law Commission, who assumed that this proposal would be highly controversial, found that it received almost unanimous support: Law Com. No. 25, para. 14. It may, however, act as a trap and what is no more than a pleading slip may prevent a property adjustment order from being made when this would be proper: see generally *Hargood* v. *Jenkins*, [1978] Fam. 148; [1978] 3 All E.R. 1001.

[5] *Jackson* v. *Jackson*, [1973] Fam. 99; [1973] 2 All E.R. 395. This does not apply to an application for periodical payments for the spouse which will in any case cease on remarriage: see *post*, p. 528.

[6] Matrimonial Causes Act 1973, s. 52 (3). This means that, if the second husband is a person of no substance, the taxpayer may have to support the wife even though the first husband is capable of doing so.

[7] *Dipple* v. *Dipple*, [1942] P. 65; [1942] 1 All E.R. 234.

[8] See *post*, pp. 623-638.

[9] Matrimonial Causes Act 1973, ss. 23 and 24.

[10] Matrimonial Causes Rules 1977, r. 73; *Practice Direction*, [1973] 1 All E.R. 192. Copies of the *pro forma* affidavit that may be used are to be found in Passingham, *Matrimonial Causes*, 3rd Ed., 498-506.

a judge.[1] As an experiment in the Divorce Registry in London, the registrar conducts a pre-trial review of all applications for property adjustment and lump sum payment in the hope of being able to bring about a settlement or at least a clarification of the issues involved.[2] Even though the suit is undefended, an application for financial relief may be transferred to the High Court, in particular if it gives rise to a contested issue of conduct or if this is desirable to expedite the hearing.[3]

B. ORDERS THAT MAY BE MADE

1. MAINTENANCE PENDING SUIT

On any petition for divorce, nullity or judicial separation, the court may order either spouse to make such periodical payments to the other pending suit as it thinks reasonable.[4]

The power to order the husband to pay maintenance pending suit (or alimony *pendente lite*, as it was formerly called) goes back to the ecclesiastical courts. It was based on the fact that the wife as such was entitled to be maintained by her husband so long as the marriage was still in existence, and the purpose of interim orders of this sort was to ensure that she and any children of the marriage living with her obtained a sufficient allowance until the outcome of the proceedings. Consequently she was entitled to an order even though she was alleged to have been guilty of adultery or desertion or the marriage was alleged to be void, so long as the issue was *sub judice*.

The new powers are of course considerably wider and can no longer be related to the obligation to maintain at common law. No guidelines are laid down to indicate the circumstances in which an order should be made or the facts to be taken into account in assessing the amount to be paid, but even under the old law the courts had a wide and largely unfettered discretion.[5] As in the case of an application under section 27 of the Matrimonial Causes Act,[6] the court should obviously make an order whenever a spouse or child of the family is in immediate need which the other spouse has the means to alleviate. All the circumstances must be taken into account, but it will be appreciated that at this stage there will have been no investigation of the parties' means or conduct and the court must obviously pay most attention to their immediate financial position and the needs of the children of the family.[7]

---

[1] *Ibid.*, r. 79. An invaluable detailed description of the work of registrars in this field is to be found in Barrington Baker *et al.*, *Matrimonial Jurisdiction of Registrars.*

[2] For the details, see *Practice Direction*, [1980] 1 All E.R. 592.

[3] Matrimonial Causes Rules 1977, rr. 80 and 81. For payment of money and transfer of property for the benefit of a party suffering from mental disorder, see Matrimonial Causes Act 1972, s. 40.

[4] Matrimonial Causes Act 1973, s. 22.

[5] *Waller* v. *Waller*, [1956] P. 300; [1956] 2 All E.R. 234, C.A.; *Slater* v. *Slater*, [1962] P. 94; [1960] 3 All E.R. 217, C.A.

[6] See *ante*, p. 516.

[7] The old practice (long since discontinued) was to bring the wife's income (if any) up to one-fifth of the spouses' joint income. At one time the courts were reluctant to give a wife who had entered into a maintenance agreement more than the husband had covenanted to pay her (see *Birch* v. *Birch*, [1908] W.N. 81, C.A.) but it is highly doubtful whether they would feel themselves so bound today. If a magistrates' order is in force, it will be unusual to make an order for maintenance pending suit.

Maintenance pending suit may be ordered to be paid retrospectively from the presentation of the petition. Unless the court orders otherwise, it remains payable until the determination of the suit, that is until decree absolute in the case of divorce and nullity or the decree in the case of judicial separation, or alternatively until the petition or application is dismissed or the suit abates by reason of the death of either party.[1] If no other order has been made when the decree is made absolute (as will often be the case because the necessary investigations will still be incomplete), a former spouse may be given temporary relief by means of an interim order.[2] In the event of an appeal, the court may order the payment of maintenance pending suit to be continued if it is fair and reasonable to do so in the circumstances.[3]

2. PERIODICAL PAYMENTS

On granting a decree of divorce, nullity or judicial separation, the court may order either spouse to make unsecured periodical payments to the other and to secure periodical payments to the other.[4] Any order for periodical payments may be backdated to the making of the application for the order, and a party may properly ask for this to be done if no order was made for maintenance pending suit or if the sum ordered proves to have been disproportionately low.

As periodical payments are intended for the payee's maintenance, they must in any event terminate on her (or his) death. Unsecured periodical payments will normally come out of the payer's income which will presumably come to an end on his death; consequently an order for their payment cannot extend beyond the joint lives of the parties.[5] There is, however, no reason why secured payments should not continue after the payer's death, as the capital will already have been charged; consequently in this case the order can last for the payee's life. Furthermore, on divorce or nullity (whether the payments are secured or not) the order must also provide for their termination on the payee's marriage; if an order made on judicial separation remains in force notwithstanding the subsequent dissolution or annulment of the marriage, it will automatically come to an end on the payee's remarriage.[6] She (or he) must thereafter look to her new partner for support.

There is some doubt whether a claim for periodical payments can be finally dismissed without the applicant's consent so as to preclude the latter from making any further application. When the situation warrants it, the courts try to encourage the spouses to make a clean break, and in his speech in *Minton* v. *Minton*[7] (with which all the other members of the House of Lords agreed) LORD SCARMAN certainly used words suggesting that the court has a power to order a dismissal. This principle was subsequently applied by the

---

[1] Matrimonial Causes Act 1973, s. 22; *Scott* v. *Scott*, [1952] 2 All E.R. 890 (husband's death).

[2] Matrimonial Causes Rules 1977, r. 78 (2).

[3] *Corbett* v. *Corbett* (*No. 2*), [1971] P. 110, 113; [1970] 2 All E.R. 654, 656.

[4] Matrimonial Causes Act 1973, s. 23 (1) (a), (b).

[5] The survivor can then apply for an order under the Inheritance (Provision for Family and Dependants) Act 1975: see *post*, pp. 623-638.

[6] Matrimonial Causes Act 1973, s. 28 (1), (2). It is immaterial that the second marriage is void or voidable: *ibid.*, s. 52 (3).

[7] [1979] A.C. 593, 608; [1979] 1 All E.R. 79, 87, H.L. See further *post*, p. 539.

Court of Appeal in *Dunford* v. *Dunford*,[1] but in the still later case of *Dipper* v. *Dipper*[2] that court declined to follow *Dunford* v. *Dunford* on the ground that it was inconsistent with an earlier decision of the Court of Appeal[3] which LORD SCARMAN mentioned without disapproval in *Minton* v. *Minton*. As the members of the court pointed out in *Dipper* v. *Dipper*, *Minton* v. *Minton* was a case where the wife had consented to her application being dismissed and LORD SCARMAN's statement that the court can order a dismissal must be limited to that situation. If the applicant does not consent, it was held that the court cannot dismiss her claim of its own motion; to do so would be inconsistent with the wording of the Matrimonial Causes Act and with the principle that the court must retain the power to make an order in the future if a change in the applicant's circumstances makes this necessary. Although the position is not entirely clear, it seems that *Dipper* v. *Dipper* must now be followed unless and until it is overruled by the House of Lords. If the facts do not justify making a substantial order in the applicant's favour, the court may either adjourn the application generally or make a nominal order which may be varied at a later date. (It should be stressed that this does not apply to an application for an order for periodical payments for a child of the family. The power to make such orders is exercisable "from time to time" and consequently an application cannot be finally dismissed even with the applicant's consent.)[4]

Secured Payments.—The very fact of security obviously makes secured payments more attractive to the payee, for there is no problem of enforcement. By tying up the payer's capital, it also prevents him from trying to frustrate the order by disposing of his assets, and the payee will be protected even though the payer becomes bankrupt.[5] We have also seen that the payee can continue to benefit from a secured order after the other's death; moreover, although the survivor cannot apply for an order after the other party's death, an order made before his death may be implemented by his personal representatives who may therefore be called upon to carry it out.[6] Because of these advantages, the court may order a smaller sum to be secured than it would have ordered by way of unsecured provision.[7]

Payments are normally secured by ordering the spouse against whom the order is made to transfer specified assets to trustees. They hold them on trust to pay the sum ordered to the payee and the balance to the payer or, alternatively, to pay the income to the payer so long as he complies with the order but to use the income and, if necessary, the capital if he defaults. The court may instead order specific property to be charged with the payment of the sum in

---

[1] [1980] 1 All E.R. 122, C.A.

[2] [1980] 2 All E.R. 722, C.A.

[3] *Carpenter* v. *Carpenter* (1976), C.A., unreported. This case was not cited to the court in *Dunford* v. *Dunford*. In *Carter* v. *Carter*, [1980] 1 All E.R. 827, C.A. (which came after *Dunford* v. *Dunford* but where the decision was not brought to the court's notice) the Court of Appeal also reached the same decision as it did in *Carpenter* v. *Carpenter* and *Dipper* v. *Dipper*.

[4] See *Minton* v. *Minton*, (*supra*), at pp. 608 and 87, respectively.

[5] Passingham, *Matrimonial Causes*, 3rd Ed., 160.

[6] *Hyde* v. *Hyde*, [1948] P. 198; [1948] 1 All E.R. 362; *Mosey* v. *Mosey*, [1956] P. 26; [1955] 2 All E.R. 391.

[7] *Chichester* v. *Chichester*, [1936] P. 129; [1936] 1 All E.R. 271.

question.[1] When the order comes to an end, the capital must be returned to the payer (or his estate, if he has already died) and any charge must be cancelled.

The court is naturally anxious to give the maximum protection, particuarly to a wife whom the husband has maltreated and is likely to leave penniless.[2] Whether periodical payments can be secured, however, must depend on the capital or secured income which the other has available, and the number of spouses against whom such an order can be made is obviously small. A party cannot normally be expected to use all his property for this purpose, for example to sell up all his furniture.[3] The court may order both secured and unsecured periodical payments, and under the old law it was unusual for more than a third or a half of the total sum to be secured.

If a party is not in need of immediate provision but may require it in the future, a nominal order may be made secured on assets yielding a substantial income. She (or he) can then apply for a suitable variation if necessary; in the meantime the income can be paid over to the other party.[4]

Income Tax.—It is of course essential to know whether the sum ordered is to be paid before or after the payer has deducted tax. If the order is "free of tax", he must pay the net sum ordered; if it is "less tax" or no mention is made of tax,[5] he is bound to pay only the balance after he has deducted income tax. An illustration will make this clearer. Suppose that an order for £2,000 a year is made against a husband who is paying income tax at the basic rate of 30%. If it is free of tax, £2,857 of his income must be allocated to pay it, of which £857 will go to Inland Revenue and £2,000 to the wife. On the other hand, if it is less tax, he first deducts from the £2,000 the sum of £600 which will go to Inland Revenue and then pays his wife the balance of £1,400. As the gross amount of the payment is regarded as part of *her* income, she may become liable to tax at higher rates[6] whilst the husband is relieved from tax at higher and additional rates. Conversely, she may be entitled to a "repayment" from Inland Revenue of the whole or part of the £600 depending on her own liability to tax and entitlement to relief. In view of the frequent fluctuations in the rate of income tax, orders free of tax should not be made.[7]

---

[1] The court may refer the matter to one of the conveyancing counsel of the court to settle a proper instrument to be executed by all necessary parties and has power to defer the grant of the decree in question until the instrument has been duly executed: Matrimonial Causes Act 1973, s. 30.

[2] See *Aggett* v. *Aggett*, [1962] 1 All E.R. 190, C.A.

[3] *Barker* v. *Barker*, [1952] P. 184, 194-195; [1952] 1 All E.R. 1128, 1134, C.A. The security must be on specific assets and not a general charge on all the party's property: *Barker* v. *Barker*. It is doubtful whether reversionary interests should be charged because they cannot be used to secure present payments: *Allison* v. *Allison*, [1927] P. 308; but see *Harrison* v. *Harrison* (1887), 12 P.D. 130. The applicant could apply for a variation of the order when the interest fell in. Capital held on protective trusts should not be secured for the order when the interest fell in. *cf. Re Richardson's Will Trusts*, [1958] Ch. 504; [1958] 1 All E.R. 538. For a case where the court ordered payments to be secured on a party's sole asset (the former matrimonial home), see *Aggett* v. *Aggett*, (*supra*).

[4] *Foarde* v. *Foarde*, [1967] 2 All E.R. 660.

[5] *Smith* v. *Smith*, [1923] P. 191, C.A.

[6] But maintenance payments are not investment income so as to attract additional rates: Finance Act 1974, s. 15, as amended by the Finance Act 1978, s. 21.

[7] *Wallis* v. *Wallis*, [1941] P. 69, 74-76; [1941] 2 All E.R. 291, 295-298. Contrast *J.* v. *J.*, [1955] P. 215; [1955] 2 All E.R. 85. See further Adams, *Taxation Problems arising on Marriage Breakdown*, Current Legal Problems 1974, 122, particularly at pp. 134-135. The parties'

This procedure is highly complicated. If the sum is relatively small, the payee will usually be entitled to repayment of the whole of the tax paid from Inland Revenue but may well be a person unused to making official claims and frightened by the idea. Consequently a simplified procedure has been introduced with respect to "small maintenance orders", that is orders in favour of a spouse (or former spouse) not exceeding £33 a week or £143 a month or for the benefit of a person under the age of 21 not exceeding £18 or £78 respectively. The payer pays the gross sum ordered and then deducts it in computing his total income for the purpose of the assessment of his own income tax; the money then becomes a part of the recipient's total income on which her (or his) tax (if any) will be assessed.[1]

Assignment of Periodical Payments.—Unsecured periodical payments have always been regarded as inalienable.[2] Two reasons are given for this rule: they are intended as personal provision for the payee and, as they can be varied at any time, no absolute transfer is possible. Consequently any purported assignment of future payments or charge upon them will be completely void and, for the same reason, the payee may not release them by agreement with the other party.[3] Whilst this restriction fetters the fund in the hands of the payee, it also protects her, for a judgment creditor has no power to seize it in satisfaction of his debts.[4]

Secured payments are regarded more in the nature of the payee's property and consequently it has been held that she can assign them and release the other party from further liability in respect of them.[5] One of the reasons formerly advanced for distinguishing secured from unsecured payments in this respect was that the court had no power to vary the former;[6] it is therefore arguable that the power, introduced in 1949, to vary orders for secured maintenance has had the incidental effect of making them inalienable.

3. LUMP SUM PAYMENTS

On divorce, nullity and judicial separation the court may order either party to pay a lump sum or lump sums to the other.[7]

The power to order the payment of a lump sum was first given to the courts in 1963 and was initially little used. The reason is perhaps to be found in a dictum of WILLMER, L.J., in the Court of Appeal in *Davis* v. *Davis*,[8] where he

---

advocates should always be able to advise the court on the effects of tax on any order proposed: see *Lewis* v. *Lewis*, [1977] 3 All E.R. 992, 995, C.A.

[1] Income and Corporation Taxes Act 1970, s. 65; Income Tax (Small Maintenance Payments) Order, S.I. 1980 No. 951.

[2] *Re Robinson* (1884), 27 Ch.D. 160, C.A.; *Watkins* v. *Watkins*, [1896] P. 222, C.A.

[3] *Campbell* v. *Campbell*, [1922] P. 187. But an agreement to release payments will be taken into consideration in deciding what arrears are to be enforced against the other party.

[4] *J. Walls, Ltd.* v. *Legge*, [1923] 2 K.B. 240, C.A.

[5] *Harrison* v. *Harrison* (1888), 13 P.D. 180, C.A.; *Maclurcan* v. *Maclurcan* (1897), 77 L.T. 474, C.A.

[6] *Watkins* v. *Watkins*, (*supra*); *Harrison* v. *Harrison*, (*supra*).

[7] Matrimonial Causes Act 1973, s. 23 (1) (c). The court may *in the same order* direct the payment of more than one lump sum. These may be payable at different dates (*e.g.*, one payable immediately to enable the wife to put down the deposit on a house and another payable when the husband sells the former matrimonial home); one may be payable by instalments and the other not. But there is no power to make a second or subsequent order for a lump sum: *Coleman* v. *Coleman*, [1973] Fam. 10; [1972] 3 All E.R. 886.

[8] [1967] P. 185, 192; [1967] 1 All E.R. 123, 126, C.A.

said that it was likely to be used only in relatively rare cases where the party
had sufficient assets to justify it. Since the passing of the Matrimonial
Proceedings and Property Act, however, the hope of the Law Commission
that wider use might be made of lump sums has been in part fulfilled although
even now the number of orders is comparatively small.[1] The Matrimonial
Causes Act itself provides that a lump sum may be ordered to enable the
payee to meet any liabilities or expenses already incurred in maintaining
herself (or himself) or any child of the family.[2] By this means the court can
compensate a party (who will, of course, usually be the wife) if the other
spouse failed to provide proper maintenance before the proceedings were
launched or if there was no order for adequate maintenance pending suit. But
the most important use of the power today is to adjust the parties' capital
assets. If, for example, the husband owns shares worth £3,000, the court may
wish the benefit of a third of these to be given to the wife. As we shall see, it
may do this directly by ordering a third of them to be transferred to her *in
specie*; it will be much more common, however, to order him to make a lump
sum payment to her of £1,000. It makes no financial difference to the wife
and it will leave the husband free to sell some of his shares or raise the money
in some other way if he prefers to do so.[3] When dealing with the matrimonial
home, the court will frequently order a transfer of the property because it will
be necessary to give one party the right to occupy it; in other cases, however,
it will rarely make any order other than for the payment of a sum representing
the value of that part of the assets of which the other party is to be given the
benefit.

The award of a lump sum is not confined to these two situations, however.
It is, of course, still true that an order will not be made if the consequence
would be to deprive the payer of his livelihood, for example, if a partner
would have to realize his share of the partnership.[4] But given this restriction,
a lump sum will be ordered whenever it is more valuable to the payee than
periodical payments, and it is impossible to lay down any hard and fast rules.[5]

[1] Law Com. No. 25, para. 9; Barrington Baker *et al.*, *Matrimonial Jurisdiction of Registrars*,
paras. 3.7-3.10. Initially WILLMER, L.J.'s dictum was applied under the new law: see *Millward*
v. *Millward*, [1971] 3 All E.R. 526, C.A. See further Miller, *Maintenance and Property*, 87
L.Q.R. 66; Cretney, 121 New L.J. 218.
[2] Matrimonial Causes Act 1973, s. 23 (3) (a).
[3] But the tax implications should not be ignored. If the husband has to sell property to raise
the money to satisfy a lump sum order, he will have to pay capital gains tax on the disposal of the
property. The Law Commission are of the view that, if the court orders the transfer of property,
it is "reallocating the property so as to give effect to the existing equitable rights of the marital
unit" and consequently no capital gains tax will be payable: Law Com. No. 25, para. 76. *Sed
quaere*? The wife is acquiring something to which she was formerly not entitled and consequently
there appears to be a disposal for the purpose of the Capital Gains Tax Act 1979. There will
normally be no chargeable gain on the transfer of the matrimonial home: *ibid.*, ss. 101-105, and
Inland Revenue Concession No. D6 (reprinted in 117 Sol. Jo. 800). Capital transfer tax will not
be chargeable if money or property is transferred between spouses before decree absolute
(Finance Act 1975, Sched. 6, para. 1) or if the transfer is made in a transaction at arm's length
after decree absolute (*ibid.*, s. 20 (4)). This will include any transfer made in pursuance of a *bona
fide* settlement or of a court order in so far as this is not intended to confer a gratuitous benefit:
Practice Direction (1975), 119 Sol. Jo. 596. If there is an intention to confer such a benefit, it may
be financially advantageous to delay the decree absolute until the transfer has been made.
[4] *P.* v. *P.*, [1978] 3 All E.R. 70, C.A. Similarly an order should not be made if there is no
prospect that the party will be able to comply with it: *Martin* v. *Martin*; [1976] Fam. 335; [1976]
3 All E.R. 625, C.A.
[5] *Per* DAVIES, L.J., in *Jones* v. *Jones*, [1971] 3 All E.R. 1201, 1206, C.A.

Normally a lump sum payment should not be regarded as the capitalisation of periodical payments[1] but occasionally this will be desirable, for example if the husband has large capital assets and an uncertain income[2] or if he is living on capital so that his income does not fairly represent his standard of living.[3] Conversely, the award of a lump sum may be the best solution if the husband has a little capital (for example, the proceeds of sale of the matrimonial home) but little or no income: the capital may be of real value to the wife, because it will give her some financial base, whilst the husband will be relieved of the obligation of finding continuing support for her out of meagre earnings.[4] A lump sum payment with consequent reduction in periodical payments may also be ordered if the wife (or husband) has particular need of capital, for example to enable her to purchase a house, furniture[5] or the goodwill of a business[6] or to clear off a mortgage with which she is buying a new house so that she can make a fresh start.[7] A further use is to protect the payee against probable default on the other's part, for example if it appears that the party against whom financial provision is being sought is likely to remove his assets out of the jurisdiction,[8] or to enable the payee to take bankruptcy proceedings against a contumacious party.[9] Further advantages of a lump sum are that, as the payment is final, there are no continuing problems of enforcement and the wife is left completely free of her former husband—a consideration that may be of particular importance if the parties' relationship is unusually bitter.[10]

The court can order the sum to be paid in instalments and may also require the payment of instalments to be secured.[11] This differs from periodical payments because the total sum will be fixed and cannot be varied, and the balance will still be payable even if one of the parties dies before the whole sum has been paid.

---

[1] *Trippas* v. *Trippas*, [1973] Fam. 134; [1973] 2 All E.R. 1, C.A.

[2] *Griffiths* v. *Griffiths*, [1974] 1 All E.R. 932, C.A. See also *Hakluytt* v. *Hakluytt*, [1968] 2 All E.R. 868, C.A., and *O'Donnell* v. *O'Donnell*, [1976] Fam. 83; [1975] 2 All E.R. 993, C.A., and *cf. Davis* v. *Davis*, [1967] P. 185; [1967] 1 All E.R. 123, C.A. (wife of rich husband given lump sum to use for amenities or in an emergency).

[3] *Brett* v. *Brett*, [1969] 1 All E.R. 1007, C.A.

[4] Their total income will also be increased if the wife can claim supplementary benefit. *Cf. Hunter* v. *Hunter*, [1973] 3 All E.R. 362, C.A. See also *Chamberlain* v. *Chamberlain*, [1974] 1 All E.R. 33, C.A., and *Hector* v. *Hector*, [1973] 3 All E.R. 1070, C.A., in each of which the husband's interest in the proceeds of sale of the matrimonial home was reduced to compensate the wife for loss of other financial provision.

[5] *S.* v. *S.*, [1977] Fam. 127; [1977] 1 All E.R. 56, C.A.

[6] *Von Mehren* v. *Von Mehren*, [1970] 1 All E.R. 153, C.A. (husband ordered to pay £4,000 to his former wife to enable her to purchase a house which she intended to run as a boarding house).

[7] *Harnett* v. *Harnett*, [1974] 1 All E.R. 764, C.A. *Cf. Calderbank* v. *Calderbank*, [1976] Fam. 93; [1975] 3 All E.R. 333, C.A. (husband given lump sum to enable him to buy house in which to live and see children to whom he had been granted access).

[8] *Brett* v. *Brett*, (*supra*).

[9] *Curtis* v. *Curtis*, [1969] 2 All E.R. 207, C.A. (husband, who had considerable means and was taking delaying tactics, ordered to pay wife £33,600, capitalising an annual sum of £2,400). *Cf. Bryant* v. *Bryant* (1976), 120 Sol. Jo. 165, C.A. It will also be the only effective order that can be made if the husband has disappeared so that there is no hope of obtaining periodical payments from him: *Ally* v. *Ally* (1971), *Times*, 24th August.

[10] *Cf. Griffiths* v. *Griffiths*, (*supra*), at p. 942; Cretney, 117 Sol. Jo. 347.

[11] Matrimonial Causes Act 1973, s. 23 (3) (c).

4. TRANSFER AND SETTLEMENT OF PROPERTY

On granting a decree of divorce, nullity or judicial separation, the court may order either party to the marriage to transfer such property as may be specified to the other party or to or for the benefit of a child of the family. The court may also order either of them to settle any property for the benefit of the other party or any child of the family.[1] These orders represent a final adjustment of rights in property when the marriage has broken down: the reason that the court is empowered to make them on judicial separation is that this may be the final severance of the matrimonial bond if the parties have a conscientious objection to divorce.[2]

These provisions are new. The only comparable power that the court had before 1971 was to order a settlement of the wife's property in certain circumstances when she had been responsible for the breakdown of the marriage: in other words it enabled the court to make appropriate provisions notwithstanding that the wife could not be ordered to pay maintenance to the husband. Consequently decisions on the way in which that power was to be exercised appear to be no longer relevant at all. The new power will probably be of importance in three situations: first, as an alternative to the payment of a lump sum when it is more sensible to order one spouse to transfer investments than to compel him to sell them to raise the necessary capital; secondly, to supplement or replace periodical payments when the party in question has a limited interest (for example, a life interest under a family settlement) which can conveniently be used for this purpose; thirdly, to enable the court to make appropriate orders with respect to the matrimonial home and similar assets, for example furniture or the family car.[3]

Property that may be the Subject of an Order.—The Act empowers the court to make an order with respect to any property to which the spouse in question is entitled either in possession or in reversion. This form of words follows that of earlier Acts dealing with settlements of the wife's property, under which it was held that "property" included income as well as capital[4] and "reversionary interests" embraced those to which the wife was contingently entitled as well as those already vested in interest.[5] Apparently there is no power to order a transfer or settlement that the party could not make voluntarily, for example of a protected life interest (which is determinable on the occurrence of any event which will deprive the beneficiary of the right to receive any part of the income) or of a lease containing a covenant against assignment.[6] The latter limitation may be of particular importance when the court is dealing with rights in the matrimonial home. Similarly it seems that the party must be able to claim the property *as of right*; hence, if he is a beneficiary under a discretionary trust, the court apparently has no power

---

[1] Matrimonial Causes Act 1973, s. 24 (1) (a), (b). For limitations on the power to transfer (but not to settle) property on a child over the age of 18, see *post*, pp. 586 and 591.

[2] Law Com. No. 25, para. 65.

[3] See *post*, pp. 558-563.

[4] See *Savary* v. *Savary* (1898), 79 L.T. 607, 610, C.A.; *Style* v. *Style*, [1954] P. 209; [1954] 1 All E.R. 442, C.A.

[5] *Stedall* v. *Stedall* (1902), 86 L.T. 124; *Savary* v. *Savary*, (*supra*).

[6] See *Hale* v. *Hale*, [1975] 2 All E.R. 1090, C.A. The question was left open by LORD PENZANCE in *Milne* v. *Milne* (1871), L.R. 2 P. & D. 295, but *cf. Loraine* v. *Loraine*, [1912] P. 222, C.A.

to order the settlement of any income which the trustees *may* in their discretion pay him,[1] nor presumably could it order the settlement of any property which *might* come to him as the result of the exercise of a power of appointment vested in another.

No transfer or settlement will be ordered if the property is outside the jurisdiction and effective control of the court.[2] But the fact that the property is situated abroad will not prevent the order from being made provided that it can be effectively enforced; and so the court might order the settlement of income receivable in this country from capital invested elsewhere. But if such an order might prove to be difficult to enforce, the court will prefer to make an order with respect to property in England.[3]

Orders that can be made.—The court can apparently order an absolute transfer of the whole of the party's interest in the property specified or any part of it. It has equally wide powers when ordering a settlement and may either divest the spouse of his whole interest[4] or grant a limited interest to the other spouse or children, leaving the beneficial owner with the reversion.[5] The facts which the court should take into account when deciding what order (if any) to make will be considered later.[6]

5. VARIATION OF ANTE-NUPTIAL AND POST-NUPTIAL SETTLEMENTS

On granting a decree of divorce, nullity or judicial separation the court may make

"an order varying for the benefit of the parties to the marriage and of the children of the family or either or any of them any ante-nuptial or post-nuptial settlement (including such a settlement made by will or codicil) made on the parties to the marriage; *and*

an order extinguishing or reducing the interest of either of the parties to the marriage under any such settlement;

and the court may make an order ... notwithstanding that there are no children of the family[7]."

The court's powers are wider than they were before 1971 in two respects: they can be exercised on judicial separation, and the court can now extinguish or reduce a party's interest even though neither the other party nor the children are benefited as a result. These powers are complementary to those already discussed and will now be used less in view of the wider powers to order transfers and settlements of property. For example, a conveyance of a house to the husband and wife jointly clearly constitutes a post-nuptial settlement because it will be held on trust for sale.[8] If it was desired to

---

[1] *Milne* v. *Milne* (1871), L.R. 2 P. & D. 295.

[2] *Tallack* v. *Tallack*, [1927] P. 211 (property situated in Holland and Dutch court would disregard any order made by an English court).

[3] See *Style* v. *Style*, (*supra*).

[4] As in *Compton* v. *Compton*, [1960] P. 201; [1960] 2 All E.R. 70, where property was settled on children for life with remainder to grandchildren. *Quaere* whether the remainder to the grandchildren was not *ultra vires* as this does not benefit *children of the family*.

[5] *Style* v. *Style*, [1954] P. 209; [1954] 1 All E.R. 442, C.A. (settlement on husband for life).

[6] See pp. 541-563 (spouse) and 586-588 and 590-591 (children).

[7] Matrimonial Causes Act 1973, s. 24 (1) (c), (d), (2).

[8] *Ulrich* v. *Ulrich*, [1968] 1 All E.R. 67, C.A. Similarly if the legal estate were in the husband alone but the wife could claim an interest because she had contributed to the purchase (see *ante*, pp. 442-450): *Cook* v. *Cook*, [1962] P. 235; [1962] 2 All E.R. 811, C.A.

extinguish the husband's interest on divorce before 1971, this could be done by varying the settlement; now he should be ordered to transfer his interest to his wife.[1] But there are still cases where the only power that can be exercised is that of varying a settlement, for example if one party has an interest that cannot be transferred (such as a protected life interest) or if it is desired to vary or destroy limitations in favour of children or other beneficiaries.

The parties cannot oust the court's jurisdiction by agreement, nor apparently is this jurisdiction in any way fettered by express provisions in the settlement as to how the property is to be held if the marriage is terminated.[2] In nullity proceedings a settlement may be varied even though the marriage is void,[3] but if it is not to take effect until the celebration of the marriage, it would appear not yet to be in existence and therefore to be incapable of variation.

The court has power to vary any settlement in existence at the time of the decree absolute.[4] Although a party who remarries cannot apply for an order against the other,[5] an application already made can be entertained and an order made notwithstanding the remarriage.[6] The court's jurisdiction is in no way fettered by the remarriage of the other party or by the death of either of them[7] although in the latter case no order will be made if its sole effect would be to benefit someone other than the surviving party or a child of the marriage.[8]

Transactions to which the Act applies.—The terms "ante-nuptial and post-nuptial settlements" are used in a sense much wider than that usually given to them by conveyancers. The courts' desire to do justice between the parties has led them to extend the section to a very large number of transactions indeed.[9] One of the best known definitions is that of HILL, J., in *Prinsep* v. *Prinsep*:[10]

"Is it [*i.e.*, the settlement] upon the husband in the character of husband or in (*sic*) the wife in the character of wife, or upon both in the character of husband and wife? If it is, it is a settlement on the parties within the meaning of the section. The particular form of it does not matter. It may be a settlement in the strictest sense of

---

[1] *Per* ORMROD, L.J., in *Guerrera* v. *Guerrera*, [1974] 1 W.L.R. 1542, 1547, C.A.

[2] *Cf. Prinsep* v. *Prinsep*, [1930] P. 35, 49, C.A.; *Woodcock* v. *Woodcock* (1914), 111 L.T. 924, C.A.; DENNING, L.J., in *Egerton* v. *Egerton*, [1949] 2 All E.R. 238, 242, C.A. The decision to the contrary in the early case of *Stone* v. *Stone* (1864), 3 Sw. & Tr. 372, cannot now be regarded as good law.

[3] *Cf. Radziej* v. *Radziej*, [1967] 1 All E.R. 944; affirmed, [1968] 3 All E.R. 624, C.A.

[4] *Dormer* v. *Ward*, [1901] P. 20, C.A.

[5] Matrimonial Causes Act 1973, s. 28 (3). See *ante*, p. 526.

[6] *Jackson* v. *Jackson*, [1973] Fam. 99; [1973] 2 All E.R. 395. See also *H.* v. *H.*, [1975] Fam. 9; [1975] 1 All E.R. 367.

[7] *Churchward* v. *Churchward*, [1910] P. 195 (remarriage); *Jacobs* v. *Jacobs*, [1943] P. 7; [1942] 2 All E.R. 471, C.A. (death). The latter case was not cited in *D. (J.)* v. *D. (S.)*, [1973] Fam. 55; [1973] 1 All E.R. 349, where it was said that both parties must still be alive unless the application is made on behalf of the children. It is submitted that this is wrong.

[8] *Thomson* v. *Thomson*, [1896] P. 263, C.A.; followed in *D. (J.)* v. *D. (S.)*, (*supra*) (where variation could benefit only the deceased party's estate). In the latter case ORMROD, J., did not consider whether the express power to extinguish a party's interest first conferred in 1970 now gives the court jurisdiction to make an order in such circumstances. It is submitted that it could do so.

[9] See *Melvill* v. *Melvill*, [1930] P. 159, at pp. 173, 175, C.A.

[10] [1929] P. 225, 232. See also *Smith* v. *Smith*, [1945] 1 All E.R. 584, 586.

the term, it may be a covenant to pay by one spouse to the other, or by a third person to a spouse. What does matter is that it should provide for the financial benefit of one or other or both of the spouses as spouses and with reference to the married state.''

The essential therefore is that the benefit must be conferred on either or both of the spouses *in the character of spouse or spouses*.[1] It is immaterial whether it comes from one of the spouses or from a third person, provided that this condition is satisfied.[2] Although this point has never been directly decided, it is possible that a transaction may be a settlement for this purpose if it confers a benefit upon the children of the marriage, even though it confers none upon either spouse, provided that the beneficiaries take *in the character of children of the family*.[3] Conversely, a transaction which would otherwise be a settlement will not cease to be one merely because it makes provision for any after taken spouse of either of the parties or the children of such a marriage.[4]

The most obvious types of transaction coming within this provision are ante-nuptial and post-nuptial settlements in the ordinarily accepted conveyancing sense of the word. As in *Prinsep* v. *Prinsep* itself, provided that the condition stated above is fulfilled, it is immaterial that one or both of the spouses are merely the objects of a discretionary trust and can therefore claim nothing as of right.[5] Further, it is not difficult to see from the definitions of settlements cited above that a separation agreement comes within the section even if it is not in writing.[6] Similarly a bond by which a wife undertakes to pay an annuity to her husband[7] and a policy of life assurance taken out by a husband for the benefit of his wife[8] have been held to be post-nuptial settlements. But there cannot be a settlement for this purpose if there has been an absolute and unqualified transfer of property unless payments of some sort still have to be made at the time that the court has to enquire into the existence of the settlement.[9]

---

[1] See also *Bosworthick* v. *Bosworthick*, [1927] P. 64, 69, C.A.; *Worsley* v. *Worsley* (1869), L.R. 1 P. & D. 648, 651.

[2] *Prinsep* v. *Prinsep*, (*supra*).

[3] Apparently so held in *Compton* v. *Compton*, [1960] P. 201; [1960] 2 All E.R. 70 (where, however, wife was trustee and had a power of appointment in favour of children). *Cf.* GREER, L.J., in *Melvill* v. *Melvill*, (*supra*), at pp. 176, 177. But it is difficult to see how this could be a "settlement *made on the parties to the marriage*".

[4] As in *Prinsep* v. *Prinsep*, (*supra*).

[5] See also *Janion* v. *Janion*, [1929] P. 237 n. A protected life interest can also be varied without producing a forfeiture: *General Accident, Fire and Life Assurance Corporation, Ltd.* v. *Inland Revenue Commissioners*, [1963] 3 All E.R. 259, C.A. In *Howard* v. *Howard*, [1945] P. 1; [1945] 1 All E.R. 91, C.A., MACKINNON, L.J., left open the question whether a discretionary trust can be a post-nuptial settlement merely because one of the spouses comes within the class of possible beneficiaries. The court may vary such a settlement even though it is in a foreign form because the parties were domiciled elsewhere at the time of the marriage: *Forsyth* v. *Forsyth*, [1891] P. 363.

[6] *Tomkins* v. *Tomkins*, [1948] P. 170; [1948] 1 All E.R. 237, C.A. *Jeffrey* v. *Jeffrey* (*No. 2*), [1952] P. 122; [1952] 1 All E.R. 790, C.A. If it were in writing it could also be varied under s. 35 of the Matrimonial Causes Act (*ante*, p. 492).

[7] *Bosworthick* v. *Bosworthick*, [1927] P. 64, C.A. *Cf. Parrington* v. *Parrington*, [1951] 2 All E.R. 916.

[8] *Gunner* v. *Gunner*, [1949] P. 77; [1948] 2 All E.R. 771, followed in *Bown* v. *Bown*, [1949] P. 91; [1948] 2 All E.R. 778.

[9] *Prescott* v. *Fellowes*, [1958] P. 260; [1958] 3 All E.R. 55, C.A.

The Meaning of "Ante-nuptial" and "Post-nuptial".—The court may vary a settlement only if it was made on the footing that the marriage *which is the subject of the decree* should continue.[1] Thus, if a husband marries successively W[1] and W[2], a settlement made by him on the eve of his marriage to W[1] cannot be varied in divorce proceedings brought by W[2].[2] But if a particular transaction appears on the face of it to satisfy this condition, then in accordance with the usual rules of construction other evidence may not be adduced to show that this was not the parties' intention.[3] Conversely, if an agreement was ostensibly entered into on the footing that the marriage would be dissolved, it cannot be a post-nuptial settlement.[4]

Powers of the Court.—As will be seen from the wording of the Act, the court may exercise its powers so as to benefit the spouses or the children of the family or to reduce or extinguish the interest of either spouse. This raises the question whether the court may make a variation which may adversely affect a child or any other beneficiary.

A child is most likely to have his interest potentially cut down by the insertion of a power of appointment in favour of a future spouse or the children of a subsequent marriage. There has been no reported case in which the court has had to consider its powers in this respect since the new law relating to property adjustment orders came into force, but there seems to be no reason for departing from the principles previously laid down. Whilst the court is bound to look after the interests of existing children of the family, it must also be borne in mind that to refuse a request to insert such a power of appointment may well cause the applicant and any future spouse and children to feel that they have been unjustly treated and thus cause friction and ill feeling in the family.[5]

The problem and the leading cases were discussed by CAIRNS, J., in *Purnell* v. *Purnell*.[6] It is now clearly established that whatever intangible advantage the children of the first marriage may get out of permitting their parent to exercise a power to appoint among children of a second marriage, nothing must be done which on the whole would be for the disadvantage of the former; consequently the settlement will not be varied to enable a benefit to be conferred upon a stranger to it unless at the same time some approximately equivalent financial benefit is also conferred upon the child or children of the first marriage as a *quid pro quo*. Whilst the extinction of one spouse's life interest in remainder gives some advantage to the child insofar as it may accelerate the vesting of his own remainder, this is so slight that it cannot now

---

[1] *Young* v. *Young (No. 1)*, [1962] P. 27; [1961] 3 All E.R. 695, C.A.

[2] *Burnett* v. *Burnett*, [1936] P. 1. See also *Hargreaves* v. *Hargreaves*, [1926] P. 42.

[3] *Melvill* v. *Melvill*, [1930] P. 159, C.A.

[4] *Young* v. *Young (No. 1)*, *(supra)*. Surrounding circumstances may be taken into consideration if they do not contradict the written agreement, although the settlor's motive is *per se* immaterial: *Joss* v. *Joss*, [1943] P. 18; [1943] 1 All E.R. 102; *Parrington* v. *Parrington*, [1951] 2 All E.R. 916, 919; *Prinsep* v. *Prinsep*, [1929] P. 225, 236.

[5] *Garforth-Bles* v. *Garforth-Bles*, [1951] P. 218, 222; [1951] 1 All E.R. 308, 310; *Best* v. *Best*, [1956] P. 76, 84; [1955] 2 All E.R. 839, 843.

[6] [1961] P. 141; [1961] 1 All E.R. 369. In this case, as in *Best* v. *Best*, [1956] P. 76; [1955] 2 All E.R. 839, the situation was unusual because the wife wished to have the settlement varied so as to be able to exercise the power in favour of a child whom she and her first husband had adopted.

be regarded as sufficient in itself.[1] But the following, either singly or in combination, have been held to be enough to support such a variation: giving the child an additional vested annuity,[2] giving the child a vested interest instead of a contingent interest under the settlement,[3] increasing the child's share by reducing the portion which the parent is permitted to settle on the children of a subsequent marriage,[4] and by making a consent order under which a spouse settles another fund on the children[5] or a third person covenants to make payments towards the child's maintenance or education.[6]

Third parties' rights are most likely to be affected if there is an ultimate gift to them in the absence of any children of the marriage. May the court strike out this remainder and thus destroy their interest? The answer is apparently "yes", provided that all the persons now alive who have an interest in the fund consent, even though this may have the effect of extinguishing contingent interests of persons as yet unborn.[7] This has even been done where the remainder was in favour of the children of any subsequent marriage of the applicant on the ground that he could be expected to make provision for them himself in any case.[8] But the court will not accede to the proposal if this would extinguish the interest of a living person who does not consent to the order.[9]

Retrospective Variations.—The court apparently has no power to order a retrospective variation. But if a spouse is prejudiced by the delay, the court can compensate for this by giving him or her a temporary or permanent increased benefit.[10]

6. CONSENT ORDERS

There is nothing to prevent the parties themselves from agreeing to the financial provision to be made: indeed the whole trend during recent years has been to encourage them to do so. In *Minton* v. *Minton*[11] LORD SCARMAN, in a speech with which three of the other four members of the House of Lords agreed, stressed the desirability of the parties' making a clean break if this is

---

[1] *Best* v. *Best*, (*supra*); *Tagart* v. *Tagart* (1934), 50 T.L.R. 399.

[2] *Newson* v. *Newson* (1934), 50 T.L.R. 399; *Wadham* v. *Wadham*, [1938] 1 All E.R. 206; *Maxwell* v. *Maxwell*, [1951] P. 212; [1950] 2 All E.R. 979.

[3] *Scollick* v. *Scollick*, [1927] P. 205; *Garforth-Bles* v. *Garforth-Bles*, (*supra*); *Purnell* v. *Purnell*, (*supra*).

[4] *Wadham* v. *Wadham*, (*supra*); *Hodgson Roberts* v. *Hodgson Roberts*, [1906] P. 142; *Colclough* v. *Colclough*, [1933] P. 143. In *Newson* v. *Newson*, (*supra*), as a *quid pro quo* the mother's power to limit the sum which the child should take under his grandmother's settlement was extinguished.

[5] *Purnell* v. *Purnell*, (*supra*).

[6] *Newson* v. *Newson*, (*supra*) (covenant by the wife's mother); *Scollick* v. *Scollick*, (*supra*) (covenant by the wife's second husband).

[7] *Morrissey* v. *Morrissey*, [1905] P. 90; *Bowles* v. *Bowles*, [1937] P. 127; [1937] 2 All E.R. 263.

[8] *Meredyth* v. *Meredyth*, [1895] P. 92.

[9] *Webb* v. *Webb*, [1929] P. 159, distinguishing *Wynne* v. *Wynne* (1898), 78 L.T. 796, where the wife could have defeated the remaindermen in any case by exercising a power of appointment by will.

[10] See *Constantinidi* v. *Constantinidi*, [1905] P. 253, 276, C.A.

[11] [1979] A.C. 593, 608; [1979] 1 All E.R. 79, 87-88, H.L.; LORD FRASER alone felt that any order should enable the wife to seek variation in the event of a totally unforeseeable change of circumstances (at pp. 601-602 and 81, respectively).

what they want and a proper order can be made. The husband would obviously have to be able to settle the wife's whole claim by a lump sum payment or a transfer or settlement of property and consequently this is unlikely to be possible in many cases. The wife in turn would have to consent to her claim for periodical payments being dismissed. She clearly runs the risk of there being some unforeseen turn of events which would otherwise entitle her to apply for a variation: if she wishes to keep alive the power to apply for further provision later, she must stipulate for a nominal order which could be varied if necessary. A clean break is also impossible if there are children for whom continuing provision will have to be made because there is no power to dismiss an application for an order for their benefit.[1]

Any agreement between the parties will be carefully scrutinized by the court which must still take into account the matters set out in section 25 of the Matrimonial Causes Act. In the absence of any change of circumstances or of any allegation of mistake or undue influence, however, the fact that the parties have arrived at a settlement will itself be *prima facie* evidence that it is reasonable, at least if they were at arm's length and were both legally advised. Consequently the court will normally approve such an agreement, provided that it is not contrary to public policy, and will incorporate it in an order.[2]

Difficulty arises, however, if the parties come to an agreement which is perfectly proper in itself but which is in terms outside the powers conferred by the Matrimonial Causes Act—for example, to make periodical payments to the wife for her life even though the husband should predecease her or she should remarry. The inference to be drawn from the judgments of GREENE, M.R., in *Mills* v. *Mills*[3] and of MORRIS, L.J., in *Hinde* v. *Hinde*[4] is that *ultra vires* agreements of this sort should not be embodied in an order and that, even if they are, they are not orders for periodical payments *stricto sensu* and cannot be enforced as such. They could be included in an undertaking to the court (which could be enforced by committal in the event of non-compliance) or the court could dismiss the application conditionally upon the parties' entering into the agreement in question.[5] The payee's remedy would then be an action for breach of contract.[6]

A further problem arises if one of the parties wishes to go back on an agreement before the court approves it and embodies it in an order. We have already seen that the agreement cannot preclude an application to the court,[7]

---

[1] For dismissal of applications, see *ante*, pp. 528-529. It should also be borne in mind that the wife's undertaking not to claim periodical payments for the children of the family will not preclude a court from making an order against the husband under the Supplementary Benefits Act: see *post*, p. 593, n. 1.

[2] *Dean* v. *Dean*, [1978] Fam. 161; [1978] 3 All E.R. 758, following *Brockwell* v. *Brockwell* (1975), 6 Fam. Law 46, C.A. See Miller, 10 Fam. Law 196, 232.

[3] [1940] P. 124; [1940] 2 All E.R. 254, C.A.

[4] [1953] 1 All E.R. 171, C.A.

[5] In *Russell* v. *Russell*, [1956] P. 283; [1956] 1 All E.R. 466, C.A., the Court of Appeal upheld the validity of an undertaking given by the husband and incorporated in the decree that he would not apply for a reduction in an existing maintenance order unless he was out of work.

[6] But an undertaking given neither under seal nor for valuable consideration (and therefore not a contract) creates an obligation only towards the court. Consequently it can be enforced, *e.g.*, by committal but not by an action for arrears by the payee: *Re Hudson*, [1966] Ch. 209; [1966] 1 All E.R. 110. This may leave the payee completely unprotected on the other party's death, as in *Re Hudson*.

[7] *Ante*, p. 491.

but as the Court of Appeal held in *Edgar* v. *Edgar*,[1] considerable attention will be paid to it if it was entered into with full knowledge of all the relevant facts and on legal advice. Obviously a party will not be bound if the agreement was made under duress or undue influence, but the fact that one of the parties was in a superior bargaining position will not justify the other in going back on it unless the former took an unfair advantage by exploiting the position. In *Edgar* v. *Edgar* a multi-millionaire and his wife entered into a separation deed in which the husband made capital provision for her amounting to some £100,000 and undertook to make periodical payments to her of £16,000 a year together with periodical payments for the children. In return she covenanted not to seek financial relief in any divorce proceedings that might take place in the future. She executed the deed after being warned by her legal advisers that she would probably obtain a much better order from the court. When divorce proceedings were launched, she attempted to resile from the agreement and claimed a lump sum payment. Dismissing her application, the Court of Appeal held that, although the husband's financial position put him in a much stronger bargaining position, there was no evidence that he had exploited it, and consequently the wife must be held to her agreement. The court might be justified in ignoring an agreement if the wife found it impossible to maintain herself owing to unforeseen circumstances[2] or, possibly, if injustice would be done for some other reason, but the facts of *Edgar* v. *Edgar* make it clear that a large disparity between the sum that a wife stipulated for and that which the court might have awarded her will not itself be a ground for releasing her from the contract she made.

C. ASSESSMENT OF FINANCIAL PROVISION

1. GENERAL PRINCIPLES

The general principles to be applied when the court is making an order for financial provision or the adjustment of property rights on divorce, nullity or judicial separation are now contained in section 25 of the Matrimonial Causes Act 1973, which re-enacts provisions introduced by the Matrimonial Proceedings and Property Act in 1970.[3] This is a reforming statute which has introduced a new code, and cases decided before 1971 should now be applied only in so far as they laid down common sense principles.[4] Even cases decided since the Act came into force should not be followed slavishly; in the words of SCARMAN, L.J.:[5]

"It would be unfortunate if the very flexible and wide-ranging powers conferred upon the court ... should be cut down or forced into this or that line of decisions by the courts."

Nevertheless several principles have emerged which are being applied in all cases.

---

[1] [1980] 3 All E.R. 887, C.A.

[2] *Wright* v. *Wright*, [1970] 3 All E.R. 209, 214, C.A.

[3] It should be noted that these principles do not apply expressly to maintenance pending suit.

[4] *Wachtel* v. *Wachtel*, [1973] Fam. 72, 91; [1973] 1 All E.R. 829, 836, C.A. *Cf. Trippas* v. *Trippas*, [1973] Fam. 134, 144; [1973] 2 All E.R. 1, 7, C.A.

[5] *Chamberlain* v. *Chamberlain*, [1974] 1 All E.R. 33, 38, C.A.

The basic object of the court when exercising its powers in relation to the spouses is succinctly stated in section 25 (1).[1] In addition to specifying certain matters which must be taken into account (and which will be considered in greater detail shortly), it enacts that the court shall have regard to all the circumstances of the case and so exercise its powers "as to place the parties, so far as it is practicable and, having regard to their conduct, just to do so, in the financial position in which they would have been if the marriage had not broken down and each had properly discharged his or her financial obligations and responsibilities towards the other". Frequently, however, it will not be able to do this, and in most cases the standard of living of one or both of the parties will have to suffer because there will be two families to support instead of one. When this occurs, the court clearly has to decide what the priorities are to be and where the inevitable loss should fall.

It is obvious that in this situation the court's first concern must be for the needs of all the members of the family:[2] it must try to ensure that these do not fall below subsistence level and, if possible, not too far below the standard of living they previously enjoyed. Amongst these the needs of the children of the family rank highest and it is essential above all to seek to give them adequate accommodation and support. This will frequently determine what is to be done with the former matrimonial home, for it will usually be necessary to permit the spouse with actual custody of the children to remain in it to provide a roof over their head. Next must be considered the needs of any other children for whom either spouse is responsible, for example the husband's children by a second wife or a woman with whom he is living, and this may involve considering the needs of their mother as well. Whilst this may at first sight appear unjust to the wife, it must not be forgotten that these children are innocent parties caught up in the consequences of the breakdown of the marriage. Finally come the needs of the spouses themselves. Generally speaking the wife is potentially likely to suffer greater financial loss from the breakdown of the marriage than the husband. In many cases he will have been the sole breadwinner and, in any event, her earning capacity is usually less than his and may be diminished even further (if not entirely extinguished) if she has a young family to look after. Even if she later returns to full-time employment, her prospects of promotion and advancement will often have been greatly reduced. For convenience in the following discussion, therefore, it will be assumed that the wife is the financially dependent spouse. It must be remembered, however, that when the normal position is reversed and the husband has been supported by the wife, the court will apply the same principles in assessing what periodical payments or lump sum payment she should make for him as it will when making an order in favour of a wife. "I rejoice," said SCARMAN, L.J., "that it should be made abundantly plain that husbands and wives come to the judgment seat in matters of money and property upon a basis of complete equality."[3]

In very many cases, of course, it will be possible to keep both spouses and the children above subsistence level but it will not be possible for them all to

---

[1] For the exercise of the powers in relation to the children of the family, see *post*, p. 590.
[2] *Cf. Browne* v. *Pritchard*, [1975] 3 All E.R. 721, 725, C.A.; *Scott* v. *Scott*, [1978] 3 All E.R. 65, 68, C.A. See generally Eekelaar, *Some Principles of Financial and Property Adjustment on Divorce*, 95 L.Q.R. 253.
[3] *Calderbank* v. *Calderbank*, [1976] Fam. 93, 103; [1975] 3 All E.R. 333, 340, C.A.

live at the same standard as they did before the breakdown of the marriage. In the absence of any overriding factor, what the court then tries to do is to spread the loss equally by making an order which will reduce the standard of living of both spouses (and thus of the children as well) to the same extent.[1]

If the wife has the actual custody of the children of the family and the court orders the husband to make financial provision for them all, the practical solution is to assess the total sum that the wife needs to keep herself and the children and then to divide this very roughly when deciding how much should be paid for each. Many husbands who are loth to pay mainten- ance for their wives will willingly pay it for their children. It may therefore sometimes be wise to allocate a disproportionately large fraction for the children and leave the wife to apply for a variation in the amount payable to herself when the orders with respect to the children terminate.[2]

Once the court can satisfy itself that the members of the family are adequately provided for in the future, it must make a final division or settlement of the spouses' capital assets, either by a lump sum order or a property adjustment order. In most cases the only asset of any value will be the matrimonial home: as this generally involves the need of one of the spouses to occupy it as his or her home in the future, as well as raising questions of the division of its value, orders relating to it will be considered separately at the end of this section.

It must also be stressed that it is quite wrong for the court to make an order with some ulterior purpose in view, and cases laying down this principle decided before 1971 must still be good law. An award to a wife will not be reduced merely because she chooses to petition for judicial separation rather than divorce and thus prevents the other party from remarrying until he is in a position to petition for divorce himself. She may have a number of reasons for her action apart from spite: the Act has given her the right to pursue either remedy and her motive is no concern of the court.[3] Similarly periodical payments should not be kept low in order to starve the wife into a reconciliation.[4]

The "One-third Rule".—Somewhat to the surprise of the profession, PHILLIMORE, L.J., re-introduced in *Ackerman* v. *Ackerman*[5] the so-called "one-third rule" which, though widely used in practice, had been judicially discredited. When applied to periodical payments, the principle is that the husband will be ordered to pay such sum as will bring the wife's income (if any) up to one-third of the spouses' joint income. Thus, if the husband is earning £6,000 a year and the wife is earning £1,500 a year (giving a joint income of £7,500), he will be ordered to pay her £1,000 a year so as to bring

---

[1] *Scott* v. *Scott*, [1978] 3 All E.R. 65, C.A.

[2] See Barrington Baker *et al.*, *op. cit.*, para. 3.6.

[3] *Lombardi* v. *Lombardi*, [1973] 3 All E.R. 625, 630, C.A., following *Sansom* v. *Sansom*, [1966] P. 52, 55-56; [1966] 2 All E.R. 396, 399.

[4] *Wharton* v. *Wharton*, [1952] 2 All E.R. 939. But see *Brett* v. *Brett*, [1969] 1 All E.R. 1007, C.A., where the husband was ordered to pay his former wife £5,000 if he did not obtain a Jewish gett within three months, which would enable her to remarry in accordance with her religious beliefs. Could it be argued that, if she remarried, her financial position would be improved so that in effect the court was compensating her for this loss?

[5] [1972] Fam. 225, 234; [1972] 2 All E.R. 420, 426, C.A. See Hall, [1973] C.L.J. 230; Maidment, 4 Fam. Law 172.

her income up to £2,500. The reason for starting with a third rather than, say, a half was defended by LORD DENNING, M.R., in *Wachtel* v. *Wachtel*[1] on the ground that the husband was likely to have greater expenses than the wife (for example, in having to maintain the children and to pay a housekeeper) and that both might remarry (thus increasing the husband's liabilities and the wife's financial resources). This argument is frankly unconvincing: the reference to paying a housekeeper is unrealistic in most cases and, if it is relevant, the wife should be allowed the value of her services in kind; the husband could apply for a variation in the order if he later remarried and the wife's marriage would automatically terminate it. It is clear, however, that this is the approach that is now being generally adopted.

In calculating the spouses' income for the purpose of applying the one-third rule one starts with the gross earnings of each. From this may be deducted national insurance contributions and the expenses incurred in earning their living (including travelling expenses). To this is then added the value of any benefits received in kind. The Court of Appeal has held that income tax may not be deducted because the amount payable will depend on the size of the order made; but in order that the court may see what net sum each will finish up with, the parties' counsel should work out what tax will be paid on the basis of one or two hypothetical orders.[2] It appears, however, that some registrars are still basing their computations on the parties' net income after deduction of tax, particularly when they are dealing with spouses in the lower income brackets.[3]

It cannot be too strongly emphasized that the one-third rule is merely a starting point and the facts which the court is specifically required to take into consideration together with other circumstances may lead it to award a greater or smaller sum in a given case. In particular the rule cannot be rigidly applied when dealing with spouses in the lowest income bracket. If, for example, the wife is not working and the husband is earning £75 a week, to give her one-third of his income would probably leave her below subsistence level but leave him substantially above it. If, on the other hand, he is earning only £45 a week, to deprive him of one-third of this would probably leave him below subsistence level himself. In circumstances like these, it is important to appreciate that the wife will be able to claim supplementary benefit but the husband, being engaged in remunerative full-time work, cannot do so. The practice to be followed in such cases has been laid down by the Court of Appeal as follows.[4] The fact that the wife is receiving (or could claim) supplementary benefit should *prima facie* be ignored in assessing the amount the husband should pay her: otherwise he would be able to shift his duty to provide for her on to the community as a whole. This will apply even though the maximum sum that could possibly be ordered will still be less than the benefit she is receiving, so that there will be no personal advantage to her at all. But if the parties' total resources are so small that it is impossible to keep them both above subsistence level (that is, with an income greater than the

---

[1] [1973] Fam. 72, 94; [1973] 1 All E.R. 829, 839, C.A.
[2] *Rodewald* v. *Rodewald*, [1977] Fam. 192; [1977] 2 All E.R. 609, C.A.
[3] Barrington Baker *et al.*, *op. cit.*, paras. 2.12-2.15.
[4] *Barnes* v. *Barnes*, [1972] 3 All E.R. 872, C.A., approving *Ashley* v. *Ashley*, [1968] P. 582; [1965] 3 All E.R. 554; *Shallow* v. *Shallow*, [1979] Fam. 1; [1978] 2 All E.R. 483, C.A. See further Cretney, 127 New L.J. 555; Bissett-Johnson and Pollard, 38 M.L.R. 449.

amount which would be paid to each of them if they were solely dependent on supplementary benefit), the maximum sum the husband should be ordered to pay should still leave him with as much as he would get by way of supplementary benefit, for if he were ordered to pay more, he would be financially worse off than the wife.[1] In practice, however, many registrars do take into account the fact that the wife is in receipt of supplementary benefit and deliberately make an order which will leave her below "subsistence level" and thus still able to claim benefit even though the husband could afford to pay her a little more.[2] This means that, if he defaults in his payments, she will be able to fall back on supplementary benefit immediately; what is perhaps more important is that she can still claim other benefits that go with supplementary benefit, for example free school meals, medical prescriptions and dental treatment.

Capital Assets.—In *Wachtel* v. *Wachtel*[3] the Court of Appeal extended the one-third rule to capital assets as well as to income, so that it now also gives a flexible starting point for the assessment of a lump sum payment or of the amount of property that should be transferred. Leaving aside any special facts presented by a particular case, the court must try to produce a position of equality. Consequently, as LORD DENNING, M.R., pointed out, if it were possible to close the account between the spouses completely, it would be fair to divide their capital equally between them, but the husband must be given some compensation for the fact that he will usually have to continue to make periodical payments for the wife and children.[4] It follows that, if a lump sum represents not only a division of capital assets but also the capitalisation of income (so that no periodical payments are ordered), the court may award a sum which will equalise their financial position rather than apply the one-third rule.[5] It should also be borne in mind that the court in *Wachtel* v. *Wachtel* was concerned with what LORD DENNING conveniently referred to as "family assets", that is "those things which are acquired by one or other or both of the parties, with the intention that they should be continuing provision for them and their children during their joint lives, and used for the benefit of the family as a whole".[6] As the Court of Appeal pointed out in *O'Donnell* v. *O'Donnell*,[7] the one-third rule will produce a fair result if both

---

[1] In *Shallow* v. *Shallow*, (*supra*), the Court of Appeal rejected an argument that the courts should apply the same principle as that applied by officers administering the supplementary benefits scheme. In negotiating with a husband who is failing to support his wife, they will leave him with a quarter of his net income (or £5, whichever is the greater) over and above the subsistence sum. This would give the husband an incentive to work which he might lack if any increase in his earnings would go straight to his wife and thus merely reduce the burden on the supplementary benefit fund: see Hayes, [1978-79] J.S.W.L. 216.

[2] Barrington Baker *et al.*, *op. cit.*, paras. 2.3-2.7.

[3] [1973] Fam. 72; [1973] 1 All E.R. 829, C.A.

[4] At pp. 95 and 839-840, respectively. Hence if for some reason the husband is not required to make periodical payments, the proper approach is an equal division of capital: *Eshak* v. *Nowojewski* (1980), 125 Sol. Jo. 98, C.A.

[5] *Trippas* v. *Trippas*, [1973] Fam. 134; [1973] 2 All E.R. 1, C.A.; *Griffiths* v. *Griffiths*, [1974] 1 All E.R. 932, C.A.

[6] At pp. 90 and 836, respectively, The wife obtained a third of the value of the matrimonial home (their sole capital asset). The relevant value is that at the time of the hearing, not of the separation: *Wallhead* v. *Wallhead* (1978), 9 Fam. Law 85, C.A.

[7] [1976] Fam. 83; [1975] 2 All E.R. 993, C.A.

spouses have built up their assets by their joint efforts, but it may be unjust to the husband to give so much to the wife if he alone has brought in considerable capital at the time of the marriage or has acquired it later by gifts or inheritance. The courts also seem more reluctant to give the wife as much as a third if the husband's assets are large: this may be because in most cases the wife will have played little part in their acquisition. Conversely, as we shall see later, the wife is frequently given half of the value of the matrimonial home if this represents the spouses' sole asset.

It follows that, despite judicial dicta to the contrary,[2] it may still be necessary in many cases to determine the spouses' beneficial interests in property before an order can be made under the Matrimonial Causes Act. If, for example, the wife can claim a half share in the matrimonial home by virtue of her contribution to the purchase, she will be able to claim this share on divorce, whereas she might be able to claim only a third if she had no beneficial interest at all.[3]

One of the major changes brought about by the new legislation is the great flexibility that the courts now have to deal with the parties' financial position. It is essential for them to retain this[4] and to consider all their powers and to use them together. In particular it should be borne in mind that a larger share of capital may be compensated for by smaller periodical payments and *vice versa*. For example, if the husband is the beneficial owner of the matrimonial home and transfers the whole of his interest to the wife, she will not need a lump sum to buy other accommodation or periodical payments to pay rent or mortgage instalments. In many cases it will be most convenient for the court to indicate the type of order that should be made and the amount that should be transferred and leave the husband to put forward detailed plans for complying with it.[5]

Financial Relief after a Decree of Nullity.—There is clearly power to order financial relief after a decree of nullity even though the marriage is void. But it must be appreciated that a claim must be weaker because neither of the parties is losing a right to be maintained either at common law or by statute. Obviously the parties' knowledge and belief at the time of the ceremony will be of particular importance. There is every difference between, say, a woman who unwittingly contracts a marriage which, as the man knows, is bigamous

---

[1] *O'Donnell* v. *O'Donnell*, (*supra*), at pp. 91 and 997, respectively. *Cf.* Cretney, 36 M.L.R. 653, 655. In *O'Donnell* v. *O'Donnell* the husband's assets (which were worth £215,000) derived largely from the backing he received from his father, but the wife had helped to build up his hotel in its early days by acting as a receptionist, chambermaid, etc. She was awarded £70,000 "which ... may seem to be too high, but inflation has already ... [brought] many cases into the class in which the one-third rule would not have been accepted in the past" (at pp. 91 and 997, respectively). See also *S.* v. *S.* (1980), *Times*, 10th May (husband's assets worth £2,100,000; wife given lump sum of £375,000).

[2] *Kowalczuk* v. *Kowalczuk*, [1973] 2 All E.R. 1042, 1045, C.A., *per* LORD DENNING, M.R.

[3] *Cf. G.* v. *G.*, [1973] 2 All E.R. 1187. For the difficulties produced by the two jurisdictions under s. 17 of the Married Women's Property Act 1882 and s. 24 of the Matrimonial Causes Act 1973 and a comparison with the position in Australia, see Turner, *Confusion in English Family Law*, 38 M.L.R. 397.

[4] *Trippas* v. *Trippas*, [1973] Fam. 134, 144; [1973] 2 All E.R. 1, 7, C.A.; *Smith* v. *Smith*, [1976] Fam. 18, 23; [1975] 2 All E.R. 19, 22; *Doherty* v. *Doherty*, [1976] Fam. 71, 81; [1975] 2 All E.R. 635, 642, C.A.

[5] *O'Donnell* v. *O'Donnell*, (*supra*), at pp. 92 and 998, respectively.

and therefore void, and a woman who takes a risk because she does not know what has happend to her former husband.[1] Consequently the court may be reluctant to make an order in favour of a party who has contracted a marriage knowing it to be void; on the other hand, it must be remembered that if she (or he) has been previously married and divorced, any periodical payments ordered on the divorce will automatically come to an end and her sole source of support for the future will be the other party to the void marriage.

2. FACTS TO BE TAKEN INTO ACCOUNT

Reference has already been made to the fact that, whilst the court must have regard to all the circumstances of the case, it must also take into account certain specific facts. Some of these are relevant to calculating the parties' resources and needs; others will lead the court to make a greater or smaller award than it otherwise would have done. Although the list is not intended to be exhaustive, it covers almost all the matters to which the courts had always had regard in the past. It is proposed to consider the facts in the order in which they are set out in section 25 (1) of the Matrimonial Causes Act.

The Parties' Income, Earning Capacity, Property and other Financial Resources.—The court must have regard not only to the resources which each party has at the time of the hearing[2] but also to those which they are likely to have in the foreseeable future. If the benefit is one to which a party may be contingently entitled in the future, the court may take it into account by ordering him to pay an appropriate lump sum if and when he acquires the interest.[3] In appropriate cases regard must be had to the husband's ability to earn higher wages by working overtime,[4] to raise money by overdrafts,[5] or, if he is unemployed, to obtain work if he wishes.[6] Increases in the husband's income since the parties separated will be relevant because the wife would have reaped the benefit of them had they still been living together:[7] likewise a

---

[1] *Cf.* applications under the Inheritance (Provision for Family and Dependants) Act by persons who have *in good faith* entered into a void marriage: *post*, p. 624.

[2] If a party's income is liable to fluctuate, it is customary to take an average to assess future earnings: *Sherwood* v. *Sherwood*, [1929] P.120, C.A.; and the fact that these fluctuations make it precarious may be a reason for reducing the amount of periodical payments ordered: *Dean* v. *Dean*, [1923] P. 172. On the question of allowances of men serving in the armed forces, see *Powell* v. *Powell*, [1951] P. 257, C.A.; *Collins* v. *Collins*, [1943] 2 All E.R. 474; *Buttle* v. *Buttle*, [1953] 2 All E.R. 646.

[3] *Calder* v. *Calder* (1976), 6 Fam. Law 242, C.A. (interest contingent on husband's surviving his mother); *Priest* v. *Priest* (1979), 9 Fam. Law 252, C.A. (gratuity payable to husband on completion of service in the Royal Marines).

[4] *Klucinski* v. *Klucinski*, [1953] 1 All E.R. 683. It is not unknown for husbands deliberately to refuse overtime before the hearing so as to give a false picture of their normal earnings.

[5] *J.* v. *J.*, [1955] P. 215; [1955] 2 All E.R. 617, C.A.

[6] *McEwan* v. *McEwan*, [1972] 2 All E.R. 708. *Cf. Bromilow* v. *Bromilow* (1976), 7 Fam. Law 16. If the husband is in receipt of supplementary benefit and the payments made to him have not been reduced or stopped, this indicates that the Commission's officers are satisfied after extensive enquiries that he is genuinely unable to find work and, whilst this does not bind any court, is a valuable piece of evidence which should be taken into account: *Williams* v. *Williams*, [1974] Fam. 55; [1974] 3 All E.R. 377.

[7] *Le Roy-Lewis* v. *Le Roy-Lewis*, [1955] P. 1; [1954] 3 All E.R. 57. Where the assets are small and consist partly of savings, it was suggested in *Cann* v. *Cann*, [1977] 3 All E.R. 957, 960, that the party might be notionally credited with the income from an annuity which the savings could buy.

party who has dissipated assets since their separation will be notionally credited with their value if both spouses would have had the enjoyment of them if the marriage had not broken down.[1] In the case of a very rich man, who may well live largely on capital and capital profits, his capital assets will be of particular importance,[2] and such a person's standard of living may be the best guide to the level of his real income.[3]

The court must also take into account any payment made by one party of which the other is enjoying the benefit, for example the husband's repayment of a mortgage on the matrimonial home or hire-purchase instalments in respect of the furniture if the wife still lives in the house and has the use of the furniture.[4] The value of benefits in kind must be similarly assessed.

Damages recovered for loss of earnings or damage to property must form part of the recipient's assets because they represent a resource that has been lost. Insofar as damages for personal injuries represent compensation for pain and suffering and loss of amenity, the position is not so clear. Earlier decisions indicated that they should be left out of account,[5] but after a detailed consideration of the authorities the Court of Appeal concluded in *Daubney* v. *Daubney*[6] that the views expressed in those cases had not been necessary to the decisions and that such damages were assets which should be brought into account. Their reason for reaching this view was that, had the marriage not broken down, the damages would have been invested or used for the benefit of the family as a whole; it would seem, therefore, that it is open to the court in any given case to find as a fact that the damages would not have been used in this way and consequently should not be credited to the party concerned. In any case SCARMAN, L.J., was careful to point out that it would not be a correct exercise of the court's discretion to make an order which would in effect deprive the spouse of all benefit of the compensation:[7] the court apparently must now decide in each case what would be a fair sum to bring into account.

Another area of uncertainty is that of resources which would not have been available had the marriage not broken down. In general, account should be taken of voluntary allowances which are likely to be made to either party because they will swell his or her gross income.[8] The reason that benefits of the type mentioned might be excluded is that the other party would not have had the enjoyment of them if the spouses were still living together, and there have been judicial suggestions that, for example, a husband should not have to account for gifts made to him by his mistress or second wife.[9] To ignore all such payments, however, would be totally unrealistic. It has always been accepted that the court must have regard to the fact that a wife is being supported by the man with whom she is living, and in two reported cases at

[1] *Martin* v. *Martin*, [1976] Fam. 335; [1976] 3 All E.R. 625, C.A.
[2] *Brett* v. *Brett*, [1969] 1 All E.R. 1007, C.A.
[3] *Cf. W.* v. *W.* (*No.* 3), [1962] P. 124; [1962] 1 All E.R. 736.
[4] *Roberts* v. *Roberts*, [1970] P. 1, 10; [1968] 3 All E.R. 479, 487.
[5] *E.g. Jones* v. *Jones*, [1976] Fam. 8; [1975] 2 All E.R. 12, C.A.
[6] [1976] Fam. 267; [1976] 2 All E.R. 453, C.A.
[7] At pp. 277 and 459, respectively.
[8] *Martin* v. *Martin*, [1919] P. 283, C.A. (allowance to husband); *Nott* v. *Nott*, [1901] P. 241 (allowance to wife).
[9] See the judgment of SIMON, P., in *Sansom* v. *Sansom*, [1966] P. 52, 58; [1966] 2 All E.R. 396, 400; and *cf. Lombardi* v. *Lombardi*, [1973] 3 All E.R. 625, C.A.

least the court has refused to disregard the value of free board and lodging together with other profits and allowances that the husband received from the woman with whom he cohabited and who was also his business partner.[1] Where the relationship is less stable and the benefits less certain, however, the court might properly feel that proportionately less credit should be given to the recipient.

In the past the courts were reluctant to force a wife to go out to work if she had not been responsible for the breakdown of the marriage and would not have worked had the marriage continued. This was due partly to their anxiety to retain the economic *status quo ante* and partly to their unwillingness to put the wife in the position where she would feel that her exertions were merely going to relieve her husband of a financial liability which he had himself created.[2] But in many cases today, particularly if the wife is young and childless and the marriage has not lasted for long, it cannot be unreasonable to expect her to work—and this might well prove to be therapeutic. Judges are certainly moving away from the view that marriage necessarily gives the wife a bread-ticket for life. But even today, if the wife would not have worked had the marriage not broken down, the onus is still on the husband to show that it is reasonable to take her earning capacity into account in view of the change in the family's financial cirumstances.[3] If she is actually working, the court need not bring the whole of her earnings into account but may leave her free to enjoy at least a part of the fruits of her own labours.[4]

The fact that the wife has remarried or is about to remarry or is living with another man who is supporting her clearly affects her financial position. Remarriage automatically terminates periodical payments[5] and cohabitation outside marriage may lead the court to conclude that the wife no longer needs the husband's support; but leaving aside the question of the matrimonial home, all these facts should generally be disregarded in dividing capital assets unless a lump sum award represents the capitalisation of periodical payments. The wife is withdrawing her part of the capital from the former family partnership, and the amount she receives should not depend on what she proposes to do with it.[6] The courts' attitude is less clear, however, if she marries the man with whom she has been committing adultery, and two decisions of BAKER, P., are not easy to reconcile. In *Marsden* v. *Marsden*[7] he pointed out that reducing the amount received by an adulterous wife would be tantamount to re-introducing damages for adultery, but in *H.* v. *H.*[8] he refused to award a lump sum to a wife when "most people would find it

---

[1] *Donaldson* v. *Donaldson*, [1958] 2 All E.R. 660; *Ette* v. *Ette*, [1965] 1 All E.R. 341. Both these cases involved claims for support *during* the marriage, but the principle applies equally after divorce.

[2] *Rose* v. *Rose*, [1951] P. 29; [1950] 2 All E.R. 311 C.A.; *Le Roy-Lewis* v. *Le Roy-Lewis*, (*supra*).

[3] *Adams* v. *Adams* (1978), 122 Sol. Jo. 348.

[4] *Attwood* v. *Attwood*, [1968] P. 591; [1968] 3 All E.R. 385. See also *Gengler* v. *Gengler*, [1976] 2 All E.R. 81 (overruled on another point by *Rodewald* v. *Rodewald*, [1977] Fam. 192; [1977] 2 All E.R. 609, C.A.).

[5] See *ante*, p. 528.

[6] *Wachtel* v. *Wachtel*, [1973] Fam. 72, 96; [1973] 1 All E.R. 829, 841, C.A.; *Trippas* v. *Trippas*, [1973] Fam. 134; [1973] 2 All E.R. 1, C.A. But see Ingram, 7 Fam. Law 11.

[7] [1973] 2 All E.R. 851, 855.

[8] [1975] Fam. 9, 16; [1975] 1 All E.R. 367, 373.

distasteful and unjust that a lump sum should be given to a wife for the probable benefit of the new family''. It is submitted that remarriage is *per se* irrelevant but it might be proper to take the wife's adultery into account in those rare cases where it has been "so obvious and gross" as to lead the court to make a smaller award because of her conduct. *A fortiori* the mere chance that the wife may remarry at some time in the future should be ignored when dividing capital assets.[1]

In all cases the parties are entitled to offset their business and other liabilities.[2] A further relevant fact on an application to vary a settlement is the sum which each party (or his or her family) contributed in the first place.[3]

The Parties' Financial Needs, Obligations and Responsibilities.—The most obvious examples of facts to be considered under this head are the parties' need to maintain themselves and their responsibility to provide for their dependants. The maintenance of children must come first; in addition one must take into account the needs of a second spouse,[4] infirm parents, brothers and sisters unable to work, and any other person whom it is reasonable to expect either party to look after in the circumstances. It will be seen that not all these obligations are legally enforceable: in this context a moral obligation and the voluntary assumption of a responsibility (provided that it is reasonable) may be as relevant as a legal obligation. For example, a father's moral duty to make voluntary payments for the upkeep of his illegitimate child is indistinguishable for this purpose from his legal liability to comply with an affiliation order.[5] But if the liability has been assumed in a purely voluntary way, the court can obviously take it into account only if it is reasonable. Thus repayment of a mortgage entered into after the parties separated in order to enable one of them to buy an expensive house may be disregarded if their financial position does not justify the purchase.[6]

As in the case of the parties' resources, the court must have regard to the needs, obligations and liabilities that they are likely to have in the foreseeable future as well as those already incurred at the time of the order.

Two matters require special comment. It may be possible to meet the needs of a wife who is unable to work—either because of her own physical condition or the necessity of looking after a child or other dependant who requires constant care—only by transferring the former matrimonial home to

---

[1] *Smith* v. *Smith*, [1976] Fam. 18, 23; [1975] 2 All E.R. 19, 22. *Cf.* the assessment of damages under the Fatal Accident Act, *ante*, p. 142.

[2] *E.g.*, the husband's insurance and superannuation contributions if the wife may reap the benefits of these on his retirement and (possibly) death: *Sansom* v. *Sansom*, [1966] P. 52, 60; [1966] 2 All E.R. 396, 402. *Cf. Schlesinger* v. *Schlesinger*, [1960] P. 191; [1960] 1 All E.R. 721 (liability for tax abroad).

[3] *March* v. *March* (1867), L.R. 1 P. & D. 440, 443.

[4] *Barnes* v. *Barnes*, [1972] 2 All E.R. 872, C.A. But earlier cases suggest that the rights of a first wife and children must usually take priority over those of a second wife or mistress, at least if the husband has brought about the breakdown of the marriage: *Roberts* v. *Roberts*, [1970] P. 1; [1968] 3 All E.R. 479. Thus it may be reasonable to take the latter's potential earnings into account. Her actual earnings are relevant to determine the size of the husband's liabilities: *Wilkinson* v. *Wilkinson* (1979), 10 Fam. Law 48, C.A.

[5] *Roberts* v. *Roberts*, [1970] P. 1, 7; [1968] 3 All E.R. 479, 484. See also *Williams* v. *Williams*, [1965] P. 125; [1964] 3 All E.R. 526, C.A., and *P. (J.R.)* v. *P.(G.L.)*, [1966] 1 All E.R. 439 (liability to educate children of a previous marriage).

[6] *Cf. G.* v. *P.*, [1978] 1 All E.R. 1099, C.A.

her so that she has at least the security of a roof over her head.[1] Secondly, in its anxiety to protect the wife and children, the court should not lose sight of the difficulties likely to be faced by the husband, particularly if he has remarried. He should never be left in a position where the effect of the order will have a crippling effect on him. In *Backhouse* v. *Backhouse*,[2] for example, BALCOMBE, J., said that it would be repugnant to the court's sense of justice to make an order which would have necessitated the husband's selling the former matrimonial home in which he was living with his second wife and two children, and he limited the husband's liability to paying a lump sum which he could reasonably be expected to raise by a mortgage.

The Standard of Living enjoyed by the Family before the Breakdown of the Marriage.—To this might be added the standard of living which the claimant could have expected to enjoy had the marriage not broken down. This is particularly important when substantial assets are available and one of the spouses has been living at a much higher level than he or she did before the marriage. In *Calderbank* v. *Calderbank*[3] the wife, a relatively rich woman, was ordered to pay a lump sum of £10,000 to the husband (who had no capital and had remarried) so that he might buy a house suitable to the former spouses' way of life in which he might see his children. But neither party's standard of living should be raised above what it otherwise would have been, for this would in effect mean that the order was being used as a means of punishing the other.[4]

The Age of each Party and the Duration of the Marriage.—This must be looked at in conjuction with the contribution made by each of them to the welfare of the family (considered below). Even before 1971 it was clear that a young wife, whose marriage had lasted for only a short time, would generally get much less favourable terms than one who had been deserted after years of married life. Today the courts are not likely to make more than a nominal order if the marriage is childless and has lasted only a matter of months and the wife has made virtually no contribution to the home and is young, fit and capable of earning her own living.[5] They are, however, much more sympathetic to such a wife if the breakdown has been brought about by the husband and has caused her financial loss, in which case she can expect a substantial order in her favour.[6] In the case of an older woman who may find

[1] *Jones* v. *Jones*, [1976] Fam. 8; [1975] 2 All E.R. 12, C.A.; *Smith* v. *Smith*, [1976] Fam. 18; [1975] 2 All E.R. 19.

[2] [1978] 1 All E.R. 1158. See also *Wachtel* v. *Wachtel*, [1973] Fam. 72, 96; [1973] 1 All E.R. 829, 841, C.A.; *H.* v. *H.*, [1975] Fam. 9, 14; [1975] 1 All E.R. 367, 371.

[3] [1976] Fam. 93; [1975] 3 All E.R. 333, C.A.

[4] *Cf. Attwood* v. *Attwood*, [1968] P. 591, 595; [1968] 3 All E.R. 385, 388.

[5] See *Khan* v. *Khan*, [1980] 1 All E.R. 497; *Taylor* v. *Taylor* (1974), 119 Sol. Jo. 30; *Warder* v. *Warder* (1978), 122 Sol. Jo. 713; *West* v. *West*, [1978] Fam. 1; [1977] 2 All E.R. 705, C.A. In *Browne* v. *Pritchard*, [1975] 3 All E.R. 721, C.A., the wife's half share in the matrimonial home (to the purchase of which she had contributed nothing) was reduced to a third after a marriage which lasted only three years.

[6] *Whyte-Smith* v. *Whyte-Smith* (1974), 119 Sol. Jo. 46 (separation after three months; breakdown caused wife illness and loss of job); *Abdureman* v. *Abdureman* (1978), 122 Sol. Jo. 663 (separation after 12 weeks; wife had given up job and lost pension on marriage). In *Brett* v. *Brett*, [1969] 1 All E.R. 1007, C.A., where the wife left the husband 5½ months after the marriage because of his cruelty, it was held that she was entitled to a substantial order based on the loss of her position as the wife of a very rich man. *Quaere* if this principle would still be applied.

it difficult to return to work, it was said in *S.* v. *S.*[1] that the court should concentrate on the parties' needs and try at least to restore them to the position they were in before the marriage. In that case both parties were over 50 when they married and the marriage lasted only two years. The court ordered the husband to settle on the wife a sum which would enable her to buy a house similar to that which she had sold on her marriage and which would revert to the husband or his estate on her death, to pay her a lump sum to enable her to furnish it, and to make periodical payments (which would bring her income up to something less than a fifth of their joint incomes) to compensate her for loss of pension rights and the comfortable old age she could have looked forward to had the marriage continued.

It is tempting to say that what is important is the length of cohabitation rather than the length of the marriage. In *Krystman* v. *Krystman*[2] no order was made at all when the parties had cohabited for only a fortnight at the beginning of a marriage which had taken place 26 years earlier. It should be noted, however, that the wife had made no claim on the husband during the intervening period, and a number of cases have laid down the principle that, if the wife delays making a claim for financial provision without reason so as to lull the husband into assuming that she will not do so, he is entitled to arrange his financial affairs accordingly and the court is unlikely to make any order in her favour.[3] A more difficult problem arises if the parties cohabited before the marriage. Obviously this cannot be taken into account under this heading, but it may be relevant under the general requirement that the court should have regard to all the circumstances of the case. Two different situations have to be considered. If the spouses lived together from choice simply because they could not be bothered "to get round to the paper work" of going through a ceremony of marriage, their cohabitation will generally be disregarded in determining financial provision. Marital rights and duties do not begin before the celebration and it would cheapen marriage to permit such a wife to take advantage of the earlier relationship.[4] This must be distinguished from the case where the parties could not get married because one of them was unable to obtain a divorce, particularly if they lived together for a long time before marriage and there were children of the union. This occurred in *Kokosinski* v. *Kokosinski.*[5] The husband was a Polish refugee who had lived in this country since the Second World War. He started to live with the petitioner in 1947 and a son was born in 1950. He could not marry her until his first wife (who was still living in Poland) divorced him, which she did not do until 1969. In the meantime the petitioner had been loving, faithful and hardworking, had brought up their child and had played a substantial part in building up the husband's business. The parties married in 1971 but separated in the following year. WOOD, J., was of the opinion that in these

[1] [1977] Fam. 127; [1977] 1 All E.R. 56, C.A.

[2] [1973] 3 All E.R. 247, C.A.

[3] *Potts* v. *Potts* (1976), 6 Fam. Law 217, C.A. (delay of five years); *Foster* v. *Foster* (1977), 7 Fam. Law 112, C.A. (divorce 23 years after separation); *Chambers* v. *Chambers* (1979), 123 Sol. Jo. 689 (divorce 21 years after separation).

[4] *Campbell* v. *Campbell*, [1976] Fam. 347; [1977] 1 All E.R. 1.

[5] [1980] 1 All E.R. 1106. The facts are not dissimilar from those which would entitle a mistress to an order under the Inheritance (Provision for Family and Dependants) Act 1975 after the man's death. (See *post*, p. 626.)

circumstances it would offend a reasonable person's sense of justice to ignore this long period of cohabitation and took it into account in deciding what order to make. A similar problem arose in *Chaterjee* v. *Chaterjee*,[1] where the parties lived together for 12 or 13 years *after* being divorced. Following their final separation the wife pursued a claim for financial relief. It was held that this cohabitation was akin to marriage for this purpose and consequently that the court could deal with property acquired since the divorce. It must be emphasised, however, that it is only in the somewhat unusual circumstances of cases like these that cohabitation outside marriage (whether before or after) is likely to affect the order made.

The Physical or Mental Disability of either Party.

The Contribution made by each of the Parties to the Welfare of the Family.—It is expressly provided that this is to include any contribution made by looking after the home or caring for the family,[2] but it could no doubt include a financial contribution as well.[3] This principle, which primarily seeks to give the wife credit for her contribution in kind as a housekeeper, wife and mother, is new. Before 1971 the courts were taking this into account to a limited extent, but their hands were partly tied by their restricted powers to make adjustments to rights in property. The result was that a wife who continued to work and hired domestic help was usually in a better position than the wife who stayed at home and did the job herself because her indirect contribution to the acquisition of the matrimonial home might well give her an equitable interest in it. There seem to be few cases where the court has expressly given the wife a larger award because of her contribution to the welfare of the family,[4] but there can be little doubt that this fact is taken into account when, for example, she is given more than a one-third interest in the matrimonial home. Conversely in *H.* v. *H.*[5] a wife who had left her husband for another man after 15 years of married life and bringing up four children was given a smaller award on the ground that she had "left the job unfinished".

In the Case of Divorce and Nullity, the Value of any Benefit which either Party will lose the Chance of acquiring.—The obvious example of such a benefit (which the Act in fact names) is a pension which can no longer enure for the benefit of the wife as the husband's widow. Another right which the divorced wife loses is that of claiming social security benefits by virtue of her husband's contributions. These problems were made more acute by the passing of the Divorce Reform Act which permits a husband to divorce his

---

1 [1976] Fam. 199; [1976] 1 All E.R. 719, C.A.

2 In *Kokosinski* v. *Kokosinski*, (*supra*), WOOD, J., was of the opinion (at p. 1115) that this referred only to contributions made after the marriage had taken place. The point is of little importance as any premarital contribution will be taken into account (if at all) under the heading of "all the circumstances of the case": see *supra*.

3 So held by ORMROD, L.J., in *P.* v. *P.*, [1978] 3 All E.R. 70, 74, C.A. Normally this would form part of the parties' property, but this would not be the case if for some reason the capital had disappeared.

4 But see *Brisdion* v. *Brisdion* (1974), 119 Sol. Jo. 234, C.A.

5 [1975] Fam. 9; [1975] 1 All E.R. 367. *Cf. West* v. *West*, [1978] Fam. 1; [1977] 2 All E.R. 705, C.A.

wife even though he has been wholly to blame for the breakdown of the marriage; before 1971 an innocent wife could take these potential losses into account before deciding whether to take proceedings for divorce. It is clearly going to be difficult to assess the value of the benefit lost. Not only are there many imponderables (some of which, like the expectation of life of each spouse, can be actuarially assessed) but in many pension schemes the benefits are held on discretionary trusts ,which the widow could not claim as of right. In days of inflation the purchase of an annuity for the wife will not give her protection (even if the husband has sufficient assets to make the necessary payment) when his pension will depend upon his final salary, particularly if it is also linked to the cost of living. If the husband has capital, the best solution may be to make an order for secured periodical payments which can be varied from time to time and will also continue if he predeceases his former wife. The truth is that it is virtually impossible to give adequate compensation to a woman who would have depended largely on a widow's pension or retirement pension for her support on her husband's death.[1]

Another example of a lost benefit is to be seen in *Trippas* v. *Trippas*.[2] After the parties had separated, the husband received a considerable sum from the sale of a family business. The court awarded the wife a lump sum of £10,000 on the ground that, had the marriage still been on foot, she would have received such a benefit either directly in cash or indirectly in kind; furthermore, the husband could have been expected to leave her a large sum if he had predeceased her, so that she had lost something analogous to a pension.

The Parties' Conduct.—Even under the old law the increasing tendency for petitions not to be defended when the marriage had irretrievably broken down had resulted in the court's laying much less stress on the technical finding of innocence or guilt in the decree. The correctness of this approach became much more obvious when irretrievable breakdown became the sole ground for divorce, even when the petitioner relied on one of the facts imputing fault to the respondent, because in many cases the latter might well have been able to bring successful cross-proceedings, a practice which the courts were anxious to discourage. Consequently it looked for a time as though the real investigation for the responsibility of the breakdown of the marriage was going to take place before the registrar hearing an application for financial provision, and the bitterness and recriminations formerly witnessed in open court would now be seen in chambers. In a series of decisions, however, the Court of Appeal has attempted to limit this as far as possible. In doing so they have recognised the fact that in most cases the conduct of neither party is wholly blameless and that both will have

---

[1] *Cf. ante*, pp. 231-233 (grave financial hardship caused by divorce). A wife aged 60 or over when the decree is made absolute will be able to claim a state retirement benefit by virtue of her husband's contributions: see *ibid*.

[2] [1973] Fam. 134; [1973] 2 All E.R. 1, C.A. See also *Kokosinski* v. *Kokosinski,* [1980] 1 All E.R. 1106. This approach is open to criticism on the ground that the express limitation of the operation of this paragraph to cases of divorce and nullity implies that the chance of acquiring the benefit must be lost as a result of the dissolution or annulment and not as the result of the breakdown of the marriage: see *O'Donnell* v. *O'Donnell*, [1976] Fam. 83, 89-90; [1975] 2 All E.R. 993, 996, C.A. If this is correct, the husband's increased capital could still have been taken into account as part of his resources.

contributed to the breakdown. In these circumstances the airing of grievances does nothing but waste time, add to costs and—what is most important—further embitter the parties.

In the first case, *Ackerman* v. *Ackerman*,[1] the Court of Appeal scotched an attempt to introduce a procedure by which the court would assess once for all the amount by which an award should be discounted by reason of the applicant's conduct. This was followed by the leading case of *Wachtel* v. *Wachtel*[2] in which they laid down the basic principle to be followed in all cases. LORD DENNING, M.R., delivering the judgment of the court, said:[3]

> "It has been suggested that there should be a 'discount' or 'reduction' in what the wife is to receive because of her supposed misconduct, guilt or blame (whatever word is used). We cannot accept this argument. In the vast majority of cases it is repugnant to the principles underlying the new legislation. . . . There will be many cases in which a wife (though once considered guilty or blameworthy) will have cared for the home and looked after the family for many years. Is she to be deprived of the benefit otherwise to be accorded to her by section [25 (1) (f)] because she may share responsibility for the breakdown with her husband? There will no doubt be a residue of cases where the conduct of one of the parties is . . . 'both obvious and gross', so much so that to order one party to support another whose conduct falls into this category is repugnant to anyone's sense of justice. In such a case the court remains free to decline to afford financial support or to reduce the support which it would otherwise have ordered. But, short of cases falling into this category, the court should not reduce its order for financial provision merely because of what was formerly regarded as guilt or blame. To do so would be to impose a fine for supposed misbehaviour in the course of an unhappy married life. . . . In the financial adjustments consequent upon the dissolution of a marriage which has irretrievably broken down, the imposition of financial penalties ought seldom to find a place."

In *Harnett* v. *Harnett* BAGNALL, J., commented:[4]

> "In my view to satisfy the test the conduct must be obvious and gross in the sense that the party concerned must be plainly seen to have wilfully persisted in conduct, or a course of conduct, calculated to destroy the marriage in circumstances in which the other party is substantially blameless."

In the Court of Appeal in the same case CAIRNS, L.J., said:[5]

> "Conduct should be taken into account only in a very broad way—that is to say, only where there is something in the conduct of one party which would make it quite inequitable to leave that out of account having regard to the conduct of the other party as well in the course of the marriage."

In brief, conduct will not affect the order made unless it would be offensive to one's sense of justice to ignore it.[6]

---

[1] [1972] Fam. 225; [1972] 2 All E.R. 420, C.A. Hence normally there should be no investigation of conduct at all if only a nominal order will be made: *O'Brien* v. *O'Brien*, [1972] Fam. 20; [1971] 3 All E.R. 254.

[2] [1973] Fam. 72; [1973] 1 All E.R. 829, C.A.

[3] At pp. 90 and 835-836, respectively.

[4] [1973] Fam. 156, 165; [1973] 2 All E.R. 593, 601.

[5] [1974] 1 All E.R. 764, 767-768, C.A.

[6] *Per* ORR, L.J., in *Jones* v. *Jones*, [1976] Fam. 8, 15; [1975] 2 All E.R. 12, 17, C.A. See also *Armstrong* v. *Armstrong* (1974), 118 Sol. Jo. 579, C.A.

As BAKER, P., put it in *W.* v. *W.*:[1]

> "Is the conduct of the kind that would cause the ordinary mortal to throw up his hands and say, 'Surely, that woman is not going to be given any money' or 'is not going to be given a full award'?"

Whether the conduct complained of will be "obvious and gross" will depend upon its seriousness, the length of time over which it occurred, and the parties' circumstances.[2] In view of the judges' approach it is hardly surprising that it has rarely been taken into account.[3] Amongst reported cases the wife's share has been reduced where she had accepted a half share of the matrimonial home whilst carrying on an adulterous affair,[4] where she had fired a shotgun at her husband,[5] and where she had twice wounded her husband and damaged his career by her behaviour.[6] In all these cases the conduct was morally blameworthy, but it is not to be supposed that this is an essential quality. To say that conduct is "obvious and gross" may mean no more than that it was of the utmost importance, at least if this brought about the breakdown of the marriage and affected the parties' financial position.[7] In *West* v. *West*[8] the wife refused to live in the house which the husband had purchased with her agreement and returned to her parents' home immediately after the marriage. The parties cohabited for only seven weeks in the five years which elapsed before the husband petitioned for divorce. The reason for the wife's conduct was that she was unable to break away from her own family and "to cross the threshold into marriage in any effective sense". Although it might be difficult to stigmatise her conduct as morally blameworthy, the Court of Appeal was unanimously of the opinion that it was "obvious and gross" and upheld the judge's award of periodical payments to bring her income up to one-eighth rather than one-third of their joint incomes. Similarly, conduct may be taken into account even though it is due to the party's mental illness if, as in "unreasonable behaviour", it is of sufficient gravity to affect the issue after making all allowances for the cause.[9]

These two cases may in fact indicate a shift in judicial attitudes, and it is possible that conduct may be taken into account rather more readily in the future than it has been during the past few years. This could well reflect the views of the majority of laymen. It may not be wholly coincidental that LAWTON, L.J., has recently said that it would be gross conduct on the husband's part if he went off with another woman and that in these circumstances the wife's standard of living should not fall as far as the husband's if he has brought about a situation where both will have to be

---

[1] [1976] Fam. 107, 110; [1975] 3 All E.R. 970, 972.

[2] *Griffiths* v. *Griffiths*, [1973] 3 All E.R. 1115, 1163.

[3] See also Barrington Baker *et al.*, *op. cit.*, paras. 2.19-2.23.

[4] *Cuzner* v. *Underdown*, [1974] 2 All E.R. 351, C.A. (wife ordered to transfer the half share to husband).

[5] *Armstrong* v. *Armstrong* (1974), 118 Sol. Jo. 579, C.A. (wife's share reduced to a quarter). A comparison of this case with the last suggests that the courts look more leniently on a wife who intends to inflict serious injury on a husband than on one who is unfaithful!

[6] *Bateman* v. *Bateman*, [1979] Fam. 25.

[7] See Schofield, 121 Sol. Jo. 720, 739, 754, 769.

[8] [1978] Fam. 1; [1977] 2 All E.R. 705, C.A.

[9] *J. (H.D.)* v. *J. (A.M.)*, [1980] 1 All E.R. 156 (repeated molestation of husband by schizophrenic wife taken into account).

reduced.[1] If this dictum is followed, much of the old law relating to the "guilty spouse" could well be re-introduced. In any event, there can be little doubt that in some other cases, where the conduct has been less heinous, the court has refused to stretch a point in the spouse's favour.[2]

Whilst the court may take into account events occurring after the breakdown of the marriage, conduct after decree absolute at least is irrelevant unless it immediately affects the other party or changes their financial position.[3] Furthermore, if the court may reduce an award made to the wife because of her conduct, it must be able to increase it in the light of the husband's. These points are illustrated by the decision in *Jones* v. *Jones*.[4] After the wife had obtained a decree absolute of divorce based on the fact that the husband's behaviour was such that she could not reasonably be expected to live with him, he attacked her with a razor and inflicted on her a number of wounds one of which severed the tendons of her right hand. The Court of Appeal held that the whole of the beneficial interest in the matrimonial home (which was vested in both spouses jointly) should be transferred to her. Whilst they were largely influenced by the fact that the marriage had lasted for more than 14 years, that the wife needed a home for the five children of the family, and that she was unlikely to obtain further work as a nurse as a consequence of the injury to her hand, they expressly took into account the husband's conduct.

Even though the real contest (when there is one) is now likely to take place in ancillary proceedings, it must be remembered that the parties are still estopped *per rem judicatam* from contradicting any express findings at the trial (even if the suit is uncontested). So, for example, if the court grants a decree of divorce based on the fact that the wife has deserted the husband, she is not permitted in proceedings for financial provision to deny that she was in desertion by setting up a just cause for leaving him.[5] But in order to prevent a party having to defend a suit unnecessarily, this rule is construed very narrowly and will not extend to matters which were never in issue at the trial and could not have affected the outcome of the proceedings.[6] Hence in the example given above, the wife may still produce evidence of the husband's conduct to mitigate whatever inference the court might draw from the finding of desertion and so leave it free to reach its own conclusions about the responsibility for the breakdown of the marriage.[7] It remains to be seen whether the courts will take an even less rigid attitude towards estoppels now that the introduction of the special procedure means that neither party may have been legally advised when drafting the petition or deciding not to defend it. There is a growing feeling amongst judges that the doctrine should be resorted to sparingly in matrimonial cases,[8] and justice demands that, for

---

[1] *Blezard* v. *Blezard* (1979), 9 Fam. Law 249, C.A. See Berkovits, 10 Fam. Law 164.

[2] *Cf. Griffiths* v. *Griffiths*, [1974] 1 All E.R. 932, 938, C.A.

[3] *W.* v. *W.*, [1975] 3 All E.R. 970, where the court ignored the wife's commission of adultery after decree absolute.

[4] [1976] Fam. 8; [1975] 2 All E.R. 12, C.A.; Ellis, 39 M.L.R. 97. See also *J. (H.D.)* v. *J. (A.M.)*, (*supra*).

[5] *Porter* v. *Porter*, [1971] P. 282; [1971] 2 All E.R. 1037.

[6] *Tumath* v. *Tumath*, [1970] P. 78; [1970] 1 All E.R. 111, C.A.

[7] *Porter* v. *Porter*, (*supra*).

[8] *Rowe* v. *Rowe*, [1980] Fam. 47, at pp. 53 and 58; [1979] 2 All E.R. 1123, at pp. 1127 and 1132, C.A.

example, a husband, who has conceded that some of the particulars in the wife's petition are correct, should later be permitted to deny others. To refuse him the opportunity of doing so would invite unnecessary litigation at the stage of the petition. Obviously this approach creates problems: there is a danger that the husband could pick and choose which allegations he proposes to deny or, in an extreme case, deny so many as to lead the court to conclude that the decree should not have been pronounced at all. It is clearly going to be difficult for the courts to steer a course between the strict rules of estoppel on the one hand and the demands of justice on the other.

3. THE MATRIMONIAL HOME

We have already noticed that the matrimonial home presents particular problems. In many cases it will be the only asset of any value owned by either spouse. Even though the wife has contributed nothing to its purchase, she is frequently given a half share on divorce if there are children, doubtless as a means of compensating her for her contribution to the welfare of the family in bringing them up.[1] The house may also be the only means of giving one of the spouses (whom, for the sake of argument, we shall assume to be the wife) the security of a home with the children in the future. Consequently the parties' interests will often be in direct conflict: the wife will wish to be given the right to occupy the house, whilst the husband will want an immediate sale so as to realise his capital, without which he may be unable to buy another home for his second family. Faced with this, the court's first concern must be to ensure that the children (and therefore the spouse with actual custody of them) have a home.[2] It should certainly do its utmost to avoid ordering a sale of the matrimonial home if this will merely result in having to rehouse the party in occupation. Once the children's accommodation has been secured, the court must try to make an order which will give the other spouse (or both spouses, if there are no children) a home as well. In many cases this will be impossible because, if the house is sold and the proceeds divided, there will not be sufficient to enable either of them to buy anything else. A temporary solution is to defer the sale of the house until the children have left home so that the parent with whom they have been living can reasonably be expected to move into smaller accommodation. By that time, of course, she (or he) may find it difficult to raise a mortgage, and if it is impossible to find a way of giving them both a home, either immediately or in the future, the court will have no alternative to leaving one of them in occupation indefinitely. This occurred in *Martin* v. *Martin*.[3] The husband had gone to live with another woman in a council house of which the latter was the tenant and which would apparently be transferred to them both jointly. The wife was left alone in the former matrimonial home which belonged to both spouses beneficially in equal shares. The Court of Appeal affirmed the judge's order that the house

---

[1] See *ante*, p. 553. But the courts apply the one-third rule if there are no children, when the house is in the same category as any other asset. See generally Cretney, 118 Sol. Jo. 431.

[2] *Browne* v. *Pritchard*, [1975] 3 All E.R. 721, 724, C.A.; *Scott* v. *Scott*, [1978] 3 All E.R. 65, C.A.

[3] [1978] Fam. 12; [1977] 3 All E.R. 762, C.A. *Cf. Eshak* v. *Nowojewski* (1980), 125 Sol. Jo. 98, C.A. (Sale deferred until death of husband who had custody of children and was unable to work. Wife had remarried and her second husband was catering for her needs.)

should be held on trust for the wife so long as she remained unmarried and continued to live there and thereafter on trust for them both in equal shares. The husband was already provided with another home and consequently had no need of the capital; the wife on the other hand would have been unable to purchase alternative accommodation with her half share of the capital and so an immediate sale would have deprived her of the modest comfortable home that she had before the marriage broke down.[1]

We must now consider the various ways in which the court may use the wide range of powers that it has at its disposal.

(1) It may force the wife to buy out the husband's interest by ordering him to transfer his share to her and ordering her to pay him a lump sum equal to its value. This is the ideal solution because she retains a roof over her head and he gets the immediate use of his money. Obviously, however, such an order can be made only if the wife has sufficient capital or, alternatively, a large enough income to pay the sum in instalments,[2] and consequently it is not likely to be met often in practice. If, however, the husband does not need the capital immediately, the payment can be deferred until the house is sold or the wife ceases to live there as in *Martin v. Martin.*

(2) The court can order the husband to transfer his share of the home to the wife without any compensating payment on her part. There are a number of quite dissimilar situations in which this may offer the best solution. If the house forms only part of the capital assets which have to be apportioned, it may be transferred to the wife in part or complete extinction of her claim for a lump sum or other capital settlement. Again, if the husband is a rich man, the wife might take the house as representing the capitalisation of part of her claim for periodical payments which will be proportionately reduced. It might also be felt desirable to capitalise periodical payments if the husband's past behaviour indicated that any other order might prove to be ineffective.[3] At the other end of the economic scale, if the husband's earnings are so small that it will be impossible for him to make an adequate contribution towards the support of the wife and children of the family, the only possible solution might be to transfer the matrimonial home to her unconditionally and make no order, or only a minimal order against him for periodical payments. This occurred, for example, in *S. v. S.*[4], where the husband was ordered to pay a total of £4 a week for his wife and daughter and to transfer his half share in the matrimonial home to the former. This may prove to be very much more valuable to the wife than a considerably larger order for periodical payments if she can claim supplementary benefit because the value of the house will not be taken into account in assessing the benefit payable. Even if the parties are not at either extreme of the economic spectrum, the particular circumstances

---

[1] One important practical point must not be overlooked. If the successful party is legally aided and no order for costs is made against the other party (which will occur *e.g.* if the latter is legally aided too), the Law Society has a charge on any property the ownership or transfer of which was in dispute. The Law Society's practice is not to enforce the charge until the property is sold, when it may accept a substitute charge on replacement property, but in the end the successful party may be little better off: see *Hanlon* v. *Law Society*, [1981] A.C. 124; [1980] 2 All E.R. 199, H.L. This gives a powerful weapon to a husband trying to negotiate the best possible settlement.

[2] The house itself could be used as security for the instalments.

[3] As in *Bryant* v. *Bryant* (1976), 120 Sol. Jo. 165, C.A.

[4] [1976] Fam. 18; [1975] 2 All E.R. 19.

may make it necessary to order a transfer of the matrimonial home without payment, but with a compensating reduction in periodical payments, as the only way of ensuring that either of them has a home. In *Hanlon* v. *Hanlon*[1] the husband was a police officer who, since separating from his wife, was living rent free in a police house. On his retirement he could expect a lump sum payment of up to £7,000. The wife was living in the matrimonial home with the two sons of the marriage (then both apprentices over the age of 18) and the two daughters, who were still at school. The most that the parties could expect from the sale of the house was £5,000[2] which, if divided equally, would give neither of them enough to buy any other accommodation. In the circumstances the Court of Appeal ordered that the husband's half share should be transferred to the wife in return for which she was prepared to forgo any further periodical payments for the two girls.

A transfer of the husband's interest without compensation might also be appropriate if his conduct justified the extinction of his share.[3] In conjunction with other facts this order has also been made when the wife's earning capacity has been so seriously impaired that she is in greater need of security than usual: in *Jones* v. *Jones*[4] this was the result of the husband's conduct in inflicting an injury on her, and in *S.* v. *S.*[5] of having to nurse a young daughter suffering from kidney trouble.

Two further points should be borne in mind which may be of particular importance when dealing with the property of less affluent spouses. In the first place, it will be recalled that on divorce or nullity (but not on judicial separation) the court may make an order transferring a protected or statutory tenancy from one spouse to the other.[6] Secondly, like any other lease a council tenancy is "property" for the purpose of section 24 of the Matrimonial Causes Act and the court may therefore make an order in relation to it.[7] Even though the Housing Act 1980 contemplates the making of such an order,[8] it is submitted that this should not be done without the agreement of the housing authority: this is to ensure that the order will not conflict with their housing policy and their statutory discretion to allocate housing and to determine priorities.[9] In most cases the problem is probably best resolved administratively by the authority's officers.[10]

(3) The order may provide that both spouses shall keep or acquire an interest in the house as equitable tenants in common, which will involve settling it on them on trust for sale (if it is not already so held), but that the sale should be deferred until some specified time in the future. In the meantime the wife will be given exclusive possession. Such an order (often

---

[1] [1978] 2 All E.R. 889, C.A.
[2] This was the consequence of the Law Society's charge for costs. See the later case of *Hanlon* v. *Law Society, ante,* p. 559 n. 1.
[3] See *Bryant* v. *Bryant, (supra); S.* v. *S., (infra).*
[4] [1976] Fam. 8; [1975] 2 All E.R. 12, C.A. See further *ante,* p. 557; Ellis, 39 M.L.R. 97.
[5] [1976] Fam. 18; [1975] 2 All E.R. 19; followed in *Jones* v. *Jones, (supra).*
[6] Under s. 7 of the Matrimonial Homes Act 1967. See *ante,* pp. 478–479.
[7] *Thompson* v. *Thompson,* [1976] Fam. 25; [1975] 2 All E.R. 208, C.A. *Cf. Hale* v. *Hale,* [1975] 2 All E.R. 1090, C.A.
[8] See *ante,* p. 482.
[9] *Cf. Regan* v. *Regan,* [1977] 1 All E.R. 428 (decided before the Housing Act was passed).
[10] They may in any event be under a duty to secure accommodation for the spouse who leaves the property or to give him assistance under the Housing (Homeless Persons) Act 1977.

referred to as a *Mesher* order)[1] enables both spouses to keep their interest in the capital but also resolves the immediate problem of accommodation for the wife and children, and for some years it was probably the commonest type of order made. It is normal to order that the sale should not take place until the youngest child reaches the age of 18 (or, perhaps, until all the children have completed their full-time education), until the wife dies or until further order.[2] A *Mesher* order has two defects. In the first place, the husband and wife will have to act together to effect the sale, perhaps many years after the divorce, and this may cause difficulties, particularly if their relationship was exceptionally bitter. Secondly, children often do not leave home until long after they have completed their education and may therefore still need the house as their home. In many cases, however, this will be the fairest compromise that can be made.[3]

(4) As an alternative to (3), the court may order the husband to transfer his interest to the wife and give him a charge on the house equal to the value of his share. As in (3), the charge should not be realised until the wife no longer needs to live in the house and it can be sold. This solution is to be preferred because the husband will not have to concur in the sale and the spouses can make a clean break. His charge should represent a given fraction of the value of the house at the time of the sale;[4] if it is fixed by reference to its present value, the sum which the husband will eventually receive will not have increased to take account of inflation.[5]

(5) The possibility of settling the house for the benefit of the wife and children[6] appears to be little used in practice. It would usually involve giving the wife a life interest with remainder to the children and consequently will rarely provide the best solution because neither spouse will ever have the use of the capital and, save in exceptional circumstances, the court does not make an order providing for children after they have completed their education or training.[7]

(6) The court could leave the whole beneficial interest in the house with the husband and give the wife exclusive occupation until she no longer needs the security of the house to bring up the children (for example, until all the children have completed their full-time education) or until further order. This will of course in the end leave her homeless and consequently should be

---

[1] From the name of the case in which such an order was made, *Mesher* v. *Mesher* (1973), reported [1980] 1 All E.R. 126, C.A.

[2] It is important that the court should retain the power of ordering an earlier sale in case the wife remarries or some unforeseen event occurs. The power of sale should not be automatically exercisable on the wife's remarriage because it may still be necessary to give her protection until the children have ceased to be dependants.

[3] For examples of *Mesher* orders see *Chamberlain* v. *Chamberlain*, [1974] 1 All E.R. 33, C.A., and *Allen* v. *Allen*, [1974] 3 All E.R. 385, C.A. If the existing matrimonial home is bigger than the wife needs, the court could order it to be sold and a part of the proceeds of sale to be used for the purchase of a new house to be settled on similar trusts. In this way the husband would get part of his capital immediately.

[4] As in *Browne* v. *Pritchard*, [1975] 3 All E.R. 721, C.A. See also *H.* v. *H.*, [1975] Fam. 9; [1975] 1 All E.R. 367.

[5] Such an order was made in *Hector* v. *Hector*, [1973] 3 All E.R. 1070, C.A. but was regarded as out of line by LATEY, J., in *Smith* v. *Smith*, [1976] Fam. 18, 21; [1975] 2 All E.R. 19, 21.

[6] *Cf. Wachtel* v. *Wachtel*, [1973] Fam. 72, 96; [1973] 1 All E.R. 829, 840, C.A., where LORD DENNING, M.R., referred to settling a lump sum.

[7] See *Chamberlain* v. *Chamberlain*, (*supra*), allowing an appeal against such an order.

used only if she will be able to make provision for her own accommodation when her right to occupation comes to an end or the circumstances are such that she should be given no part of the capital value. It may also be necessary to make such an order if the husband has no power to assign the matrimonial home so that the court cannot order it to be transferred or settled.[1] There is apparently no power to make an order relating to occupation alone under the Matrimonial Causes Act, and a wife seeking such an order would have to apply for it under section 17 of the Married Women's Property Act 1882 or ask the court to continue her right of occupation under the Matrimonial Homes Act after the dissolution or annulment of the marriage.[2]

(7) The court could order the house to be sold and the proceeds to be divided in such proportions as it thought fit. This might be the best way of dealing with the situation if there were no children living at home and the house was too big for either spouse to live in alone. The money should be sufficient to give at least one of them (and preferably both) enough to put down as a deposit on the purchase of a new house or flat and this solution is not possible if its effect would be to deprive both of them of a home. The Matrimonial Causes Act does not expressly confer a power to order a sale, but as the object could be achieved by issuing a summons under section 17 of the Married Women's Property Act 1882 or section 30 of the Law of Property Act, the Court of Appeal has boldly said that a court seised of the matter under the Matrimonial Causes Act should exercise its powers under either of these sections without compelling the parties to take unnecessary formal steps.[3] Proceedings under section 17 are available, however, only if there is a question between the spouses as to the title to or possession of property, and section 30 only enables the court to order the execution of an existing trust for sale. If, therefore, the house is vested beneficially in the husband alone, these powers do not exist at all and the only way in which a sale could be ordered would be by first settling it on them both on trust for sale. To obviate the need for this procedure, the Law Commission has recommended that the court's powers under the Matrimonial Causes Act should be extended to ordering a sale and a proposal to implement this is contained in the Matrimonial Homes and Property Bill introduced in 1981.[4]

If there is any danger that the husband will try to dispose of the home before an order is made, the wife's simplest remedy before decree absolute is to register her right of occupation as a Class F land charge; alternatively she could apply to have the husband restrained from selling it on the ground that the disposition would defeat her claim for financial relief.[5] A further problem arises if the house is subject to a mortgage (as will often be the case). If the husband is to continue to pay the instalments, in theory any periodical

---

[1] See *ante*, p. 534.

[2] See *ante*, pp. 460 (Married Women's Property Act) and 459 (Matrimonial Homes Act). An application under the former may be made for three years after dissolution or annulment but an order under the latter must be made before decree absolute. Neither remedy is available if the marriage is void.

[3] *Ward* v. *Ward*, [1980] 1 All E.R. 176, C.A. For s. 17 of the Married Women's Property Act 1882, see *ante*, p. 424.

[4] See Appendix E, *post*, and Law Com. No. 99 (Orders for Sale of Property under the Matrimonial Causes Act 1973).

[5] See *ante*, p. 467 (right to occupation) and *post*, pp. 568-569 (restraining dispositions). But registration of a Class F land charge will be set aside as an abuse of process if the wife has no intention of occupying the house: *Barnett* v. *Hassett* (1981), *Times*, 4th March.

payments should be reduced by the amount of interest repaid (which can be regarded as equivalent to rent)[1] whilst he ought to be given an enlarged share of the proceeds of sale representing the capital repaid. This would involve highly complex calculations and constant variations of periodical payments as a progressively larger fraction of the instalments represented the repayment of capital; in practice, therefore, the husband will be compensated by being ordered to make smaller periodical payments or given a larger share of the capital on sale.

D. VARIATION, DISCHARGE, SUSPENSION AND REVIVAL OF ORDERS

Orders that may be varied.—The court has power to vary, discharge or suspend any of the following orders and to revive any term suspended:[2]

Maintenance pending suit;
Periodical payments (secured and unsecured);
An order relating to instalments in the case of a lump sum payment;
The settlement (but not the transfer) of property on judicial separation;
The variation of ante-nuptial and post-nuptial settlements on judicial separation.

Periodical payments must always be variable because they are intended as maintenance for the payee and, if either party's needs or resources change, justice may demand a corresponding change in the amount payable. On the other hand, once a lump sum has been paid, it cannot be cancelled or varied; it would, therefore, be unfair to the payee if her right to a sum not yet paid could be prejudiced on the ground that the court had softened the blow to the payer by providing that he could pay the sum in question over a period of time. The same objection cannot be raised, however, to a change in the period or manner in which the instalments are paid, and consequently these can be varied by an alteration of their size or frequency. In *Tilley* v. *Tilley*[3] the Court of Appeal held that this power enables the court to remit future instalments entirely; although this seems questionable, it was pointed out in that case that this object could be achieved in any event by ordering the payee to make periodical payments of equal value to the payer. The reason that, generally speaking, orders relating to property cannot be varied is that they are designed to make a final adjustment of the spouses' rights at the time of the decree so that any subsequent change in their needs and resources is irrelevant. Settlements of property and variations of ante-nuptial and post-nuptial settlements made on judicial separation come into a different category, however, because a further adjustment may have to be made if the marriage is later dissolved, and the spouses themselves may wish to have the order varied if they become reconciled. Consequently variations of these orders may be made only in proceedings for the rescission of the decree or the dissolution of the marriage.[4]

---

[1] Cretney, *Principles of Family Law,* 3rd Ed., 238.
[2] Matrimonial Causes Act 1973, ss. 21 and 31 (1), (2). The court may also order any instrument to be varied, etc.: s. 31 (3).
[3] (1980), 10 Fam. Law 89, C.A.
[4] Matrimonial Causes Act 1973, s. 31 (4).

For the same reasons, the court cannot order a lump sum payment, the transfer or settlement of property, or the variation of an ante-nuptial or post-nuptial settlement on an application to vary an order for periodical payments.[1]

An order for the variation, etc., of periodical payments may be retrospective.[2] If an order for secured periodical payments continues in force after the death of the party against whom it was made, either his personal representatives or the person entitled to the payments may apply for a variation, etc. Except with the leave of the court this may not be done more than six months after representation was first taken out; if leave is given, the personal representatives will not be liable for having failed to anticipate the possibility of such an application but a claim may be made against beneficiaries to whom any part of the estate has been transferred.[3]

Facts to be taken into Consideration.—The Act expressly provides that, on hearing an application for variation, the court shall have regard to all the circumstances of the case including any change in the matters to which it was required to have regard when making the order in the first place. If the application is made after the death of the party against whom the order was orginally made, the court must also take into account the changed circumstances resulting from the death.[4] Although in most cases the order itself will be taken as the starting point and most emphasis will be laid on any changes in the parties' financial situation, the court's discretion is completely unfettered.[5] Thus the parties' conduct following the original order may be taken into account if it has been so "obvious and gross" that it would have affected the original order had it occurred before it was made.[6]

Two judicial limitations have been placed on the court's power, however. First, the parties are still estopped *per rem judicatam* from raising matters inconsistent with a previous decree or order and neither party may adduce evidence which could have been put before the court when the original order was made.[7] Secondly, a party who has led the other to act to his or her detriment on the assumption that he will continue to honour the order may not later apply to have it reduced or discharged. In *B. (M.A.L.)* v. *B. (N.E.)*[8] the husband and wife had entered into a separation agreement before the wife

---

[1] Matrimonial Causes Act 1973, s. 31 (5). Apparently the court can order a lump sum payment on an application to vary an order relating to property after a judicial separation.

[2] *MacDonald* v. *MacDonald*, [1964] P. 1; [1963] 2 All E.R. 857, C.A.

[3] Matrimonial Causes Act 1973, s. 31 (6), (8) and (9). The court also has power to vary, discharge or revive an order for secured periodical payments if the payee applies for an order under the Inheritance (Provision for Family and Dependants) Act 1975: see *post*, p. 637. For variation generally, see Law Com. No. 25, paras. 85-93.

[4] *Ibid.*, s. 31 (7). See *Jones* v. *Jones*, [1971] 3 All E.R. 1201, 1206-1207. Neither party is under any duty to make a voluntary disclosure of any change in his or her means: *Hayfield* v. *Hayfield*, [1957] 1 All E.R. 598.

[5] *Lewis* v. *Lewis*, [1977] 3 All E.R. 992, C.A.

[6] *J. (H.D.)* v. *J. (A.M.)*, [1980] 1 All E.R. 156. In this case it was also held that the fact that the party seeking a variation is in arrears or in breach of an injunction will not preclude an application unless the non-payment or breach is such as to impede the course of justice and there is no other effective means of securing compliance.

[7] *B. (M.A.L.)* v. *B. (N.E.)*, [1968] 1 W.L.R. 1109; *Hall* v. *Hall* (1914), 111 L.T. 403, C.A.

[8] [1968] 1 W.L.R. 1109. (The wife's adultery would now be irrelevant unless her conduct had been "obvious and gross".)

petitioned for divorce, with the result that she did not immediately seek financial provision. Some years later the husband was adjudicated bankrupt and the wife agreed to consent to his discharge on his undertaking not to oppose an application by her for leave to apply to the court for maintenance. In the maintenance proceedings the husband alleged that the wife had been guilty of adultery but in the event he did not pursue these allegations and submitted to a consent order for periodical payments against himself. He later established that the wife's youngest child was illegitimate and then sought to have the maintenance order discharged on the ground that the wife had obtained it by fraud. It was held that he must fail for two reasons. Having raised the matter of the wife's adultery at a time when he had evidence to prove it and then submitted to judgment by consent, he was estopped from opening the question again: it certainly did not lie in his mouth to say that she had misled the court. Furthermore, having induced the wife to consent to his discharge in bankruptcy by undertaking to maintain her, he could not now argue that he was under no liability to do so.

If the change of circumstances on which the application is based is not likely to be permanent (for example, the husband's temporary unemployment), the order should be suspended rather than discharged, so that it can be revived later if necessary.[1]

Variation of Consent Orders.—The fact that a party has consented to an order being made against him cannot act as an estoppel or give the other party a contractual right to have the order kept in force indefinitely, and a consent order can generally be varied in the same circumstances as any other order.[2] This is so even though the order provides that the parties shall not apply for a variation: it is doubtful whether such a provision is valid and, even if it is, it may itself be suspended along with the other provisions of the order.[3] Usually, however, the court should be slower to accede to an application to vary consent orders because otherwise parties and their solicitors might be deterred from negotiating them altogether. Hence a variation sought on the ground that the applicant's consent was given as the result of a mistake (for example, about the other party's income) should be made only if justice demands it and a substantially different order would be made.[4] The court might also exercise its power if the applicant had not been independently and competently advised[5] or if, for whatever reason, the order was grossly unjust.[6] In any case, it is very doubtful whether the court can vary or discharge an order which it had no power to make in the first place, for example an order for unsecured periodical payments for the payee's life.[7]

---

[1] *Cf. Mills* v. *Mills*, [1940] P. 124; [1940] 2 All E.R. 254, C.A.

[2] *B. (G.C.)* v. *B. (B.A.)*, [1970] 1 All E.R. 913.

[3] *Jessel* v. *Jessel*, [1979] 3 All E.R. 645, C.A. See Douglas, 96 L.Q.R. 196.

[4] *B. (G.C.)* v. *B. (B.A.)*, (*supra*).

[5] *Per* BAKER, P., in *Wilkins* v. *Wilkins*, [1969] 2 All E.R. 463.

[6] As in *Smethurst* v. *Smethurst*, [1978] Fam. 52; [1977] 3 All E.R. 1110, where, for reasons which were not apparent, the sum originally ordered was about twice that which the husband could reasonably afford to pay. See Miller, 10 Fam. Law 196, 252.

[7] *Cf. Mills* v. *Mills* and *Hinde* v. *Hinde*, *ante*, p. 540. But they probably can be varied, etc., by consent, and an undertaking given to the court may be discharged: *Russell* v. *Russell*, [1956] P. 283; [1956] 1 All E.R. 466, C.A.

E. ENFORCEMENT OF ORDERS

1. METHODS OF ENFORCEMENT

Periodical Payments.—If periodical payments are secured, there is of course no question of enforcement. When arrears of unsecured periodical payments accrue, the payee has a number of means of enforcing the order at his or her disposal. But his position is basically different from that of a successful plaintiff in an action for damages for tort or breach of contract for the order is not a final judgment and he does not have the full rights of a judgment creditor.

In the first place, if the party in default applies to have the order varied or discharged, the court in effect has a discretion to remit the arrears in part or even entirely by making a retrospective order.[1] In order to prevent large sums from mounting up, arrears which have been due for twelve months or more may not be enforced without the leave of the court: this gives some protection to a party who has stopped paying the full sum ordered and has been mistakenly led to believe by the other's acquiescence that he will not enforce the rest.[2] The court can also give the debtor time to pay and, in particular, may order payment by instalments. Because of this discretion, the arrears do not constitute a legal debt and cannot be sued for as such;[3] nor may the payee institute bankruptcy proceedings as a means of execution or prove in the other party's bankruptcy for arrears.[4] But with these important exceptions he has available all the usual means of execution open to a judgment creditor in the High Court or a county court, as the case may be.[5]

One of the most useful ways of enforcing the payment of arrears is by issuing a judgment summons under the Debtors Act of 1869, when the court can make an order for the payment by instalments and commit the payer for contempt if he wilfully fails to pay them.[6] Alternatively, the payee may apply for an attachment of earnings order. The detailed provisions are *mutatis mutandis* the same as those relating to attachment orders made in a magistrates' court.[7]

In view of the personal nature of the obligation and the fact that arrears do

---

[1] *MacDonald* v. *MacDonald*, [1964] P. 1; [1963] 2 All E.R. 857, C.A.

[2] Matrimonial Causes Act 1973, s. 32. See further Law Com. No. 25, para. 92.

[3] *Bailey* v. *Bailey* (1884), 13 Q.B.D. 855, C.A.; *Robins* v. *Robins*, [1907] 2 K.B. 13.

[4] Consequently the arrears are not affected by an adjudication in bankruptcy and may be enforced by other methods: *Linton* v. *Linton* (1885), 15 Q.B.D. 239, C.A.; *Re Henderson* (1888), 20 Q.B.D. 509, C.A.

[5] An undertaking to make payments given to the court may be enforced in the same way as an order (at least if the court would have had jurisdiction to make a similar order): *Gandolfo* v. *Gandolfo*, [1980] 1 All E.R. 833, C.A. An order made by a divorce county court can be transferred to the High Court if it cannot be conveniently enforced in the county court. It is then enforceable as though it had been made by the High Court: Matrimonial Causes Rules 1977, r. 91.

[6] This procedure is preserved for the non-payment of a maintenance order by the Administration of Justice Act 1970, s. 11.

[7] See *ante*, pp. 512-514. If the order is a High Court order, the collecting officer is the proper officer of the High Court or the registrar of a county court specified in the order; if it is a county court order, he is the registrar of that court: Attachment of Earnings Act 1971, s. 6 (7).

not constitute a legal debt, there is some doubt whether they can be enforced against the payer's personal representatives after his death.[1]

Recovery of Overpayments.—The court may well feel that, because of some change of circumstances, the payee has been overpaid. To take two examples: the payee may have failed to inform the other party of an unexpected improvement in her financial position, or the payer may not have realised that a decrease in his income entitled him to apply for a variation. In some cases justice may demand that the payee should repay some or all of the money received since the change in circumstances; in others—for example, where the payee was unaware of the change in the payer's circumstances and has already spent the money—justice may demand that the loss should continue to lie where it has fallen. Consequently by section 33 of the Matrimonial Causes Act, where there has been a change in the circumstances of either the person entitled to the payments or the person liable to make them (including a change produced by the death of the latter) so that the amount received by the payee since then has exceeded the amount which the other should have been required to pay, the court may order the repayment of the whole or any part of the excess as it thinks just. Alternatively it may decide that nothing should be repaid at all. Section 38 of the Act gives the court precisely the same powers if the payee has remarried and the other party (or his personal representatives) has continued to make payments in the mistaken belief that the order was still subsisting. Both sections apply to periodical payments (secured and unsecured); section 33 also applies to maintenance pending suit and interim payments under section 27. In both cases the action may be brought by and against personal representatives and the court may order any sum to be repaid by instalments.

The High Court or a county court may make an order for repayment in proceedings for variation or discharge or for the enforcement of arrears.[2] Alternatively the payer or his personal representatives may bring an action for repayment in a county court.[3]

Other Orders.—An order for the payment of a lump sum is more in the nature of a judgment for damages and may be enforced in the same way. This means that, if the party against whom it is made becomes insolvent before he implements it, the other party may prove in his bankruptcy.[4] The payee may also issue a judgment summons or apply for an attachment of earnings order.[5] As in the case of periodical payments, a lump sum payment (or any

---

[1] In *Re Stillwell*, [1916] 1 Ch. 365, it was held that arrears could be recovered against a solvent estate, but the decision of the Court of Appeal in *Sugden* v. *Sugden*, [1957] P. 120; [1957] 1 All E.R. 300, suggests the contrary. By analogy with the law of bankruptcy, the payee presumably could not claim in any event if the estate were insolvent.

[2] But a magistrates' court has no power to make an order for repayment in the case of a High Court or county court order registered there.

[3] *Cf.* the recovery of overpayments under a magistrates' order, *ante*, p. 510. Magistrates' clerks and collecting officers have similar protection.

[4] See *Curtis* v. *Curtis*, [1969] 2 All E.R. 207, C.A., where the court ordered the husband to pay the wife £33,600 capitalising an annual sum of £2,400 to enable her to take bankruptcy proceedings if he remained contumacious.

[5] See the definition of "maintenance order" in the Administration of Justice Act 1970, s. 28 and Sched. 8, and the Attachment of Earnings Act 1971, Sched. 1, para. 3, as amended in each case by the Matrimonial Causes Act 1973, Sched. 2, and the Domestic Proceedings and Magistrates' Courts Act 1978, Sched. 2.

part payable by instalment) cannot be enforced more than twelve months after it falls due without the leave of the court.[1]

Failure to comply with an order to transfer or settle property may be enforced in the same way as any other similar order in the High Court or a county court.

2. ATTEMPTS TO DEFEAT CLAIMS FOR FINANCIAL RELIEF

A spouse might well try to defeat an application for financial relief by disposing of his property or transferring it out of the jurisdiction. He might do this beforehand in anticipation of an application or order or, alternatively, after an order has been made in order to reduce the property available to meet it. To prevent fraudulent dispositions of this kind, a measure of protection is given by section 37 of the Matrimonial Causes Act 1973.[2] This applies to any order for maintenance pending suit, financial provision or property adjustment made in proceedings for divorce, nullity and judicial separation, any order made under section 27 of the Act on the ground of failure to provide reasonable maintenance, the variation of any of these orders during the payer's lifetime, and the alteration of a maintenance agreement during the parties' joint lives. For the sake of convenience, it will be assumed throughout the following discussion that the wife (or former wife) is applying for or has obtained an order against the husband; it must be appreciated, however, that exactly the same principles apply if the husband is seeking financial provision from the wife or if anyone is seeking it for the children of the family.

If the court is satisfied that the husband is about to make any disposition or to transfer out of the jurisdiction or otherwise deal with any property with the intention of defeating the wife's claim, it may make such order as it thinks fit to restrain him from doing so and to protect the claim. If it is satisfied that he has already made a disposition with this intention, the court may make an order setting the disposition aside. In this case, however, a wife who has not yet obtained an order must also show that, if the disposition were set aside, the court would make a different order from that which it would otherwise make. Defeating the wife's claim may take the form of preventing her from obtaining an order at all, reducing the amount that might be ordered, or impeding or frustrating the enforcement of any order that might be made or has been made.

In many cases it obviously might be difficult to establish what the husband's intention was when he made a disposition. Consequently the Act has introduced a compromise designed to protect in part the interests of the wife, the husband and the transferee. If the husband made the disposition three years or more before the application to set it aside, the wife must prove affirmatively that he had the intention to defeat her claim. If he made it less than three years before or is about to make it, this intention will be presumed if the effect of the transaction would be to defeat her claim or, where the disposition has already taken place and an order is in force, if it has had this

---

[1] Matrimonial Causes Act, s. 32.
[2] The power was originally given by the Matrimonial Causes (Property and Maintenance) Act 1958, s. 2. If the disposition was made fraudulently, it might be set aside under the court's equitable jurisdiction or under s. 172 of the Law of Property Act 1925: see *ante*, pp. 433-434.

effect: the burden then shifts on to him to prove that this was not his intention.[1]

Certain transactions may not be upset at all. No order may be made after the husband's death with respect to any disposition made by him by will or codicil. A disposition *inter vivos already* made may not be set aside if it was made for valuable consideration (other than marriage) to a person acting in good faith and without notice of the husband's intention to defeat the wife's claim.[2] Whether the purchaser had notice (or is to be regarded as having notice) is of course a question of fact: it is arguable, however, that if he knew that the wife was applying for an order which was likely to be defeated by the transfer, this should have put him on enquiry and thus would give him constructive notice of the husband's intention.[3] An application for a property adjustment order relating to a *specific* piece of land (for example, the matrimonial home) is registrable as a pending land action;[4] consequently if the wife fails to register it, she cannot attack any *subsequent* transfer to a person taking any interest in the land or any charge on it for valuable consideration unless he had actual notice that she had made the application.[5]

The disposition is voidable, and not void, and consequently, even if it is set aside, this cannot affect any subsequent dealings with the property in good faith. Hence if the husband's immediate transferee is not protected but disposes of the property to a *bona fide* purchaser for value without notice, the latter's title cannot be upset by the order. In *National Provincial Bank, Ltd.* v. *Hastings Car Mart, Ltd.*[6] the husband, who had deserted his wife, conveyed the matrimonial home to the defendant company who immediately charged it to the plaintiff bank. Although the conveyance to the defendants was set aside on the ground that it was made with the intention of defeating the wife's claim to maintenance, it was held by the Court of Appeal that this did not extinguish the plaintiff's mortgage which remained a valid charge.

3. ENFORCEMENT WHEN ONE PARTY IS OUT OF THE JURISDICTION

This problem has already been considered in the last chapter. Particular attention is drawn to the registration of an order for periodical payments or a

---

[1] Presumably the transaction can be set aside or restrained if the husband had an intention both to defeat the claim and to benefit the transferee. Otherwise the wife's application could always be defeated by showing that the husband genuinely wanted to benefit his mistress or second wife at her expense.

[2] A purchaser acts in good faith provided that he acts honestly: *Central Estates (Belgravia), Ltd.* v. *Woolgar*, [1972] 1 Q.B. 48; [1971] 3 All E.R. 647, C.A. No order may be made if the disposition took place before 1st January 1968, as there was an absolute limitation of three years before the Matrimonial Proceedings and Property Act 1970 came into force: Matrimonial Causes Act 1973, s. 37 (7).

[3] *Cf.* the judgment of BALCOMBE, J., in *Whittingham* v. *Whittingham*, [1979] Fam. 9; [1978] 3 All E.R. 805. (It was not necessary for the Court of Appeal to consider this point.) *Quaere* whether the presence of the wife on premises owned by the husband is sufficient to fix the purchaser with notice of any claim that she might have. This seems very doubtful.

[4] Under the Land Charges Act 1972, s. 5 (7). If the land is registered, a pending action is protected by lodging a caution: Land Registration Act 1925, s. 59.

[5] *Whittingham* v. *Whittingham*, [1979] Fam. 9; [1978] 3 All E.R. 805, C.A. See Hoggett, 122 Sol. Jo. 669.

[6] [1964] Ch. 665; [1964] 3 All E.R. 93, C.A. See further the same case in the House of Lords, *National Provincial Bank, Ltd.* v. *Ainsworth, ante,* p. 466. There was no appeal on the point discussed here. Presumably in circumstances such as these the immediate transferee may be ordered to pay over the value of the property.

lump sum payment in another court in the United Kingdom under the Maintenance Orders Act 1950 and the transmission of an order for periodical payments to a reciprocating country under Part I of the Maintenance Orders (Reciprocal Enforcement) Act 1972.[1]

F. REGISTRATION OF ORDERS IN OTHER COURTS

It will readily be seen that if the spouse ordered to pay money duly fulfils his or her obligations, orders made in magistrates' courts have the advantage that payment is made through the clerk of the court; conversely, if he fails to fulfil them, a spouse who has an order made in the High Court or a county court has superior means of enforcing it at his or her disposal. Consequently the Maintenance Orders Act of 1958 introduced the means of registering in one court a "maintenance order"[2] made by another. Under this Act a person entitled to payments under a maintenance order made by the High Court or a county court may apply to the court that made the order to have it registered in a magistrates' court; whether or not the application is granted lies completely in the discretion of the court.[3] A person entitled to payments under a maintenance order made by a magistrates' court may apply to that court to have it registered in the High Court; in this case the court *must* grant the application if it is satisfied that there is due and unpaid an amount equal to not less than four payments in the case of an order for weekly payments and not less than two payments in other cases.[4]

If the application is granted, no proceedings may be begun or continued to enforce the order in the original court and any attachment of earnings order already in force ceases to have effect.[5] Once the order has been registered, it may be enforced only as though it had been made by the court in which it is registered.[6]

---

[1] See *ante*, pp. 518-520.

[2] The following are "maintenance orders" for the purpose of these provisions (s. 1 (1A), added by the Administration of Justice Act 1970, s. 27 (3) and Sched. 8, as subsequently amended):

> Orders for periodical or other payments made under Part II of the Matrimonial Causes Act;
> Orders for the payment of money made under the Domestic Proceedings and Magistrates' Courts Act;
> Affiliation orders;
> Orders made under the following statutory provisions:
>> Guardianship of Minors Act 1971, ss. 9 (2), 10 (1), 11 and 12 (2);
>> Guardianship Act 1973, s. 2 (3) and (4) (a);
>> Family Law Reform Act 1969, s. 6;
>> Supplementary Benefits Act 1976, ss. 18 and 19;
>> Children Act 1975, ss. 34 and 45;
>> Child Care Act 1980, ss. 47, 50 and 51 (contribution orders, affiliation orders and arrears orders payable to local authorities);
> Maintenance Orders made in other parts of the United Kingdom or reciprocating countries and registered in or confirmed by an English court under the Maintenance Orders Act 1950 or the Maintenance Orders (Reciprocal Enforcement) Act 1972.

[3] Ss. 1 (1) (a), 2 (1).

[4] Ss. 1 (1) (b), 2 (3).

[5] S. 2 (2), (4); Attachment of Earnings Act 1971, s. 11 (1) (a), (2). But a warrant of commitment remains in force if the defendant is *already* detained under it: s. 2 (4) (b).

[6] S. 3. This includes the power to remit the whole or any part of arrears due. In the case of an order registered in a magistrates' court, payment must be made through the clerk unless the court

An order may be varied, revoked, suspended and revived only by the original court except that, in the case of orders made by the High Court or a county court and registered in a magistrates' court, variation of rates of payment (as distinct from a variation of other provisions and complete revocation, suspension and revival of the order) may be made only by the magistrates' court in which it is registered[1] if both parties are in England.[2]

The party entitled to payments under a registered order may give notice to have the registration cancelled. This has a similar effect to an application to have the order registered in the sense that no proceedings may be begun or continued to enforce the order in the court of registration[3] and any attachment of earnings order is automatically discharged. The court in which the order is registered must then cancel the registration provided that no process for the enforcement of the order is in force and, in the case of an order registered in a magistrates' court, no proceedings for variation are pending in that court. If the court that originally made an order registered in a magistrates' court varies or discharges it, it may itself direct that the registration be cancelled; if a magistrates' court discharges an order registered in the High Court, it must direct that the registration be cancelled if there are no arrears remaining to be recovered.[4]

---

orders otherwise. In the case of an order made under the Domestic Proceedings and Magistrates' Courts Act and registered in the High Court, the leave of that court must be obtained to enforce arrears which have been due for more than twelve months: see the Domestic Proceedings and Magistrates' Courts Act 1978, s. 32 (4)-(6).

[1] Or any other magistrates' court having jurisdiction in the place where the complainant is for the time being: Magistrates' Courts (Maintenance Orders Act 1958) Rules 1959, r. 9.

[2] S. 4, as amended by the Administration of Justice Act 1970, Sched. 11. Hence an order for maintenance pending suit and an interim order made under s. 27 of the Matrimonial Causes Act 1973 should normally not be registered in a magistrates' court because this removes control from the divorce court: *Armsby* v. *Armsby* (1973), 118 Sol. Jo. 183. *Cf. Practice Direction,* [1980] 1 All E.R. 1007. The magistrates' court has a discretion to remit the application to the orginal court and the original court may vary the rate of payment in proceedings to vary other provisions of the order.

[3] Save that a warrant of commitment remains in force if the defendant is *already* detained under it.

[4] S. 5; Attachment of Earnings Act 1971, s. 11 (1) (b).

Chapter 16

Rights in Property Affected by the Relationship of Parent and Child and Financial Provision for Children

A. RIGHTS IN PROPERTY

1. GENERAL

Rights in property are not greatly affected by the relationship of parent and child. A parent, it seems, has no rights as such in the property of a child of any age; thus in the absence of any agreement he has no claim on a child's wages,[1] and even an arrangement by which the child promises to pay his father or mother a weekly sum for his board and lodging is probably unenforceable on the ground that the parties never intended to create any legally binding obligation.[2] Similarly, property bought by a child out of his income will remain exclusively his own. With respect to gifts to a child the position is not so clear. Obviously in the case of clothes bought for a young child the property and therefore the right of disposal remain in the parent or parents; clothing bought for an older child presumably belongs to the child: at what stage this transition is effected must be a question of fact in each case. In whom the property (and therefore the right of disposal) vests in the case of other types of presents given to a young child is even more doubtful. Normally they will be of such slight value that the question is of no practical importance; if the chattel is of greater value and the child is too young to have the necessary intention of receiving the gift, it is arguable that the legal interest will vest in the parents who will hold it on trust for the donee.

It is because a minor is rarely the legal owner of property of any value that this problem is usually of no more than academic interest. If he has an interest of any value, he will normally derive it under a settlement or will or on an intestacy, and the legal ownership will therefore usually vest in trustees. His

---

[1] *Cf. Williams* v. *Doulton*, [1948] 1 All E.R. 603.

[2] *Cf. ante*, p. 151. But if a child has a sufficient income to keep himself, a parent could not be guilty of failure to provide him with reasonable maintenance. For the liability of a child engaged in remunerative full-time work to contribute towards his own maintenance when he is in the care of a local authority, see *ante*, p. 401.

572

parents may be able to make a claim on the fund for his maintenance and education; the extent of this will depend on the terms of the instrument creating the interest and the provisions of the Trustee Act 1925 and the Administration of Estates Act 1925—matters which belong rather to the general law of property and impinge only indirectly upon family law.[1]

But four subjects require particular attention.

Occupation of Parent's House.—A child of full age has no right to occupy his parent's home merely by virtue of their relationship, and in *Egan* v. *Egan*[2] a mother obtained an injunction restraining her son, aged 19, from entering her house. This was admittedly a grave case of a son assaulting and mal-treating his mother, stealing from her, and threatening to break in if she tried to exclude him, and in less serious cases the court may be slow to grant an injunction for this purpose.[3] It must be even more difficult to justify the exclusion of a minor child. If he is under the age of 17, the correct procedure is for the parent to get the local authority to take care proceedings on the ground that the child is beyond control;[4] if he is over that age, it is submitted that the parent's safety must in the end prevail over any duty to provide the child with board and lodging and consequently in a proper case the child could be excluded.[5]

Presumption of Advancement.—If a father has property conveyed into the name of his legitimate child, this raises a presumption of advancement, so that, unless the presumption is rebutted, the child takes the whole beneficial interest and there will be no resulting trust in favour of the father.[6] The basis of this presumption is the recognition by equity of the father's obligation to provide for his children and to advance them, but it would seem to arise in every case of father and child and has even been applied where a father aged 92 transferred property to his son with whom he was living and who was looking after him.[7]

In other cases a resulting trust in favour of the purchaser will be presumed unless he has put himself *in loco parentis* to the child, that is, unless he has intentionally taken upon himself a father's duty to make provision for the other.[8] Whether or not one person is *in loco parentis* to another is a question of fact. Little evidence will be required to establish the relationship between a mother and her child (particularly if the mother is widowed)[9] or probably

---

[1] See generally works on equity and trusts.

[2] [1975] Ch. 218; [1975] 2 All E.R. 167.

[3] See *Waterhouse* v. *Waterhouse* (1905), 94 L.T. 133 (injunction to exclude idle son aged 35 refused).

[4] See *ante*, p. 391.

[5] Particularly bearing in mind that the duties to maintain under the Supplementary Benefits Act 1976 (*post*, p. 584) and to protect under s. 1 of the Children and Young Persons Act 1933 (*ante*, p. 321) cease when the child reaches the age of 16.

[6] So held in a series of cases from *Dyer* v. *Dyer* (1788), 2 Cox Eq. Cas. 92, to *Shephard* v. *Cartwright*, [1955] A.C. 431; [1954] 3 All E.R. 649, H.L. On the question of the evidence admissible to rebut the presumption, see *Shephard* v. *Cartwright*.

[7] *Hepworth* v. *Hepworth* (1870), L.R. 11 Eq. 10.

[8] *Per* LORD COTTENHAM, L.C., in *Powys* v. *Mansfield* (1837), 3 My. & Cr. 359, 367, and JESSEL, M.R., in *Bennet* v. *Bennet* (1879), 10 Ch.D. 474, 477.

[9] *Bennet* v. *Bennet*, (*supra*), at pp. 479-480. See also *Re Ashton*, [1897] 2 Ch. 574.

between a parent and an illegitimate child, and today a presumption of advancement would probably be raised automatically in such cases. The relationship may also arise, for example, between grandfather and grandchild,[1] uncle and nephew,[2] stepfather and stepchild,[3] and other strangers in blood, but it would have to be specifically established. If the child is living with his father, this may be evidence that another is not *in loco parentis* to him but it is by no means conclusive.[4]

Undue Influence.—If a transaction between parent (whether father or mother) and child or a transaction entered into by the child at the instance of either parent involves a sum so large that it cannot be reasonably accounted for on the ground of affection, there is a presumption that the parent has exercised undue influence over the other. Hence if the child later seeks to have such a contract or gift set aside for this reason, the burden shifts on to the party wishing to uphold it to prove that there was in fact no such influence. The difficulty of discharging a negative burden is obvious: as was stated in *Re Pauling's Settlement Trusts*[5] it must be shown that the child acted spontaneously and with knowledge of his rights; it is desirable, though not essential, that he should have had independent advice given with knowledge of all the relevant circumstances and such as a competent and honest adviser would give if he were acting solely in the child's interest. The advice must be genuinely independent, and hence the burden is not discharged by showing that the child was advised by a solicitor who was acting for the parent or another interested party at the same time.[6]

The presumption of influence does not cease when the child comes of age or is "emancipated" by marriage: there must be many cases when the natural influence which most parents are bound to have over their children continues after this. The question is purely one of fact, although the presumption will normally last for only a short time after the child attains his majority.[7] These points are well illustrated by *Lancashire Loans, Ltd.* v. *Black*.[8] In this case a daughter, who had come of age and who had left her parental home on marriage, was persuaded by her mother to charge a reversionary interest under her grandfather's will in order to pay off the mother's debts. Later at the mother's instigation she signed a promissory note for £775 plus interest at 85% *per annum* and made a second charge on the reversion. The necessary instruments were drawn up by a solicitor who was also acting for the mother and the moneylenders concerned and who did not give the daughter a full

---

[1] *Ebrand* v. *Dancer* (1680), 2 Cas. in Ch. 26.

[2] *Powys* v. *Mansfield*, (*supra*).

[3] *Re Paradise Motor Co., Ltd.*, [1968] 2 All E.R. 625, C.A.

[4] *Powys* v. *Mansfield*, (*supra*), at p. 368.

[5] [1964] Ch. 303, 336; [1963] 3 All E.R. 1, 10, C.A. See also *Lancashire Loans, Ltd.* v. *Black*, [1934] 1 K.B. 380, C.A.; *Powell* v. *Powell*, [1900] 1 Ch. 243; and *cf. Re Brocklehurst*, [1978] Ch. 14; [1978] 1 All E.R. 767, C.A.

[6] *Lancashire Loans, Ltd.* v. *Black*, (*supra*); *Powell* v. *Powell*, (*supra*); *Bullock* v. *Lloyds Bank, Ltd.*, [1955] Ch. 317; [1954] 3 All E.R. 726.

[7] *Re Pauling's Settlement Trusts*, (*supra*), at pp. 337 and 10, respectively. At the time this case was decided the age of majority was 21. Will the courts now accept that the reduction of the age of majority to 18 implies greater maturity and judgment on the part of a person over that age and give correspondingly less weight to the presumption?

[8] [1934] 1 K.B. 380, C.A. See also *Bainbrigge* v. *Browne* (1881), 18 Ch.D. 188, where the three children were all over the age of 21.

explanation of the true nature and effect of the guarantee and the consequences of entering into it. It was held that the transactions must be set aside, as the moneylenders had full knowledge of all the facts from which undue influence could be inferred and could therefore be in no better position than the mother.

As in the case of all other transactions which are voidable in equity, the child will lose his power to have the contract or gift set aside by laches or by affirming the transaction after he has ceased to be under the parental influence. But, subject to this, it may be avoided against anyone save a *bona fide* purchaser for value without notice of the circumstances surrounding it.[1]

Family Arrangements.—Family arrangements are transactions which "tend to the peace or security of the family, to the avoiding of family disputes and litigation, or to the preservation of family property".[2] Common examples are agreements between members of the family to divide the property of a deceased member or to compromise claims under disputed wills. In arrangements of this sort the parents as heads of the family are bound to exercise some influence over the judgment of their children entering into the agreement, and consequently a strict application of the presumption of undue influence would make many such transactions voidable. A special rule has therefore been developed that family arrangements may be set aside on this ground only if a parent derives some benefit from the agreement which he did not formerly possess.[3] In addition it should be borne in mind that family arrangements are contracts *uberrimae fidei* and may therefore be avoided by any party on the ground that another party failed to disclose a material fact of which he was aware but of which the complaining party was ignorant.[4]

Life Assurance Policies in Favour of Children.—As we have already seen, if either parent takes out a policy of assurance on his or her own life expressed to be for the benefit of any or all of his or her children, this will create a trust in favour of the child or children.[5]

2. DISPOSITIONS IN FAVOUR OF CHILDREN

The Position at Common Law.—The common law knew nothing of legitimation or adoption and regarded a bastard as *filius nullius*. Consequently it became settled law that the term "children" in any

---

[1] *Bainbrigge* v. *Browne*, (*supra*). In *Re Pauling's Settlement Trusts*, (*supra*), it was held that children acting under parental influence could compel trustees to return money paid out in breach of trust when the latter knew (or ought to have known) of the undue influence.

[2] *Per* ROMILLY, M.R., in *Hoghton* v. *Hoghton* (1852), 15 Beav. 278, 300.

[3] *Hoghton* v. *Hoghton*, (*supra*); *Hoblyn* v. *Hoblyn* (1889), 41 Ch.D. 200, 206; *Turner* v. *Collins* (1871), 7 Ch. App. 329 (where the son's action to have the deed set aside was in any case defeated by his own laches).

[4] *Gordon* v. *Gordon* (1819), 3 Swan. 400 (failure to disclose an earlier secret marriage between the parents, as a result of which the eldest son, believed to be illegitimate, was in fact legitimate); *Greenwood* v. *Greenwood* (1863), 2 De G. J. & Sm. 28 (failure to disclose the true value of property). *Cf. Re Roberts*, [1905] 1 Ch. 704, C.A. (compromise effected on a false assumption of the party's rights).

[5] See *ante*, pp. 438-439.

instrument (whether testamentary or made *inter vivos*) *prima facie* must be construed as *legitimate* children. The same rule applied to any other relationship, and a bequest, for example, to the testator's nephews would normally confer a benefit only on the legitimate sons of his legitimate brothers and sisters.[1]

This was purely a rule of construction and the presumption could therefore be displaced if the instrument indicated a contrary intention on the part of the person executing it. It was rare for this to happen in the case of a deed, but in a number of reported decisions illegitimate children have succeeded in taking under a will. But in such a case it must be proved that the testator *must* have meant an illegitimate child to take the benefit: it is not sufficient that he probably intended this. Thus, where a testator married a woman by whom he had already had two illegitimate children and by his will made on the day following his marriage he left property to his children by her, it was held that, since the spouses might still have legitimate children, the presumption was not rebutted and the two illegitimate children could not take even though no legitimate children were ever born.[2]

The problem was considered by the House of Lords in *Hill* v. *Crook*,[3] where LORD CAIRNS specified two cases where illegitimate children could take an interest under a gift to the testator's children. This will occur, first, if he names them or expressly states that illegitimate children are to take under a class gift,[4] and secondly if the facts known to the testator are such that it is possible for illegitimate children but not legitimate children to take.[5] Although the will speaks from the death of the testator, the important facts for the purpose of interpretation are those known to him at the time the will was made. Hence it has been held that illegitimate or reputed children must have been intended as the beneficiaries when at the time of the execution of the will the legatees' parent had no legitimate children and was, to the testator's knowledge, dead,[6] or a woman beyond the age of child bearing,[7] or a man incurably impotent.[8]

As gifts tending to encourage or reward sexual immorality are regarded as contrary to public policy, gifts to illegitimate children to be procreated in the future are void at common law.[9] This is a rule of law and not of interpretation and consequently applies only to children conceived after the deed or will *takes effect*: children born after a will was made and even those *en ventre sa mère* at the testator's death may take.[10]

---

[1] See *Sydall* v. *Castings, Ltd.*, [1967] 1 Q.B. 302; [1966] 3 All E.R. 770, C.A. (illegitimate daughter not a "descendant" for the purpose of the trusts of a pension scheme).

[2] *Dorin* v. *Dorin* (1875), L.R. 7 H.L. 568, H.L.

[3] (1873), L.R. 6 H.L. 265, 282-283, H.L.

[4] See *Owen* v. *Bryant* (1852), 2 De G. M. & G. 697.

[5] In *Re Jebb*, [1966] Ch. 666; [1965] 3 All E.R. 358, C.A., it was held that it was sufficient that it was highly improbable that the parent would have legitimate children. But this is inconsistent with the decisions of the House of Lords in *Dorin* v. *Dorin* and *Hill* v. *Crook*, (*supra*), and must be regarded as wrongly decided. See Morris, *Palm-Tree Justice in the Court of Appeal*, 82 L.Q.R. 196.

[6] *Lord Woodehouselee* v. *Dalrymple* (1817), 2 Mer. 419.

[7] *Re Eve*, [1909] 1 Ch. 796. Contrast *Re Dicker*, [1947] Ch. 248; [1947] 1 All E.R. 317.

[8] *Re Herwin*, [1953] Ch. 701; [1953] 2 All E.R. 782, C.A.

[9] *Hill* v. *Crook*, (*supra*), at pp. 278, 285-286; *Re Shaw*, [1894] 2 Ch. 573 (deed).

[10] *Occleston* v. *Fullalove* (1874), 9 Ch. App. 147; *Crook* v. *Hill* (1876), 3 Ch.D. 773. Some relaxation of the rule has been seen in recent years and in *Re Hyde*, [1932] 1 Ch. 95, it was held

Illegitimate Children.—The common law presumption that "children" in any disposition *prima facie* means legitimate children only has been reversed by section 15 of the Family Law Reform Act 1969. This provides that in any disposition *made* on or after 1st January 1970, any reference to a child of any person shall be construed as including an illegitimate child and any reference to a person related to another in some other manner shall include a person who is illegitimate or whose relationship is traced through an illegitimate person. The section also abolishes the rule prohibiting an illegitimate child not in being when a disposition takes effect from claiming under it. Thus if a deed or will executed in 1981 settles a fund on X for life with remainder to his children in equal shares, all X's children can take whether they are legitimate, legitimated or illegitimate, and the date of their birth is irrelevant. Similarly a bequest made in 1981 to X's nephews will include the illegitimate sons of X's brothers and sisters and the legitimate sons of his illegitimate brothers and sisters.[1] Similarly a gift to X's eldest son can now be claimed by that person even though he is illegitimate.

A disposition includes a disposition made *inter vivos* (whether oral or in writing) and a will or codicil. But a codicil executed after the section came into force is not to be treated for this purpose as republishing a will or codicil made before that date. Hence if a testator dies in 1981 but his will was made in 1968, it must still be construed according to the old law and section 15 has no application.

The operation of the section is subject to three limitations. First, it does not apply if a contrary intention is shown in the disposition itself. A gift to X's legitimate children will still pass an interest only to those born legitimate or legitimated (unless the context indicates that legitimated children are also excluded). Secondly, it does not affect the construction of the word "heir" or the devolution of an entailed interest which can still descend only to those born legitimate at common law or legitimated. Thirdly, it does not affect the devolution of property which would (apart from this section) devolve along with a title or dignity of honour. It must also be remembered that the section in no way alters the effect of adoption.

Trustees and personal representatives are not bound to ascertain whether there are any persons who could take an interest by virtue of the operation of this section and they will not be personally liable for distributing property if they have no notice of their existence. But this does not prevent the beneficiary from following the property (or any property representing it) into the hands of any recipient other than a purchaser.[2]

---

that a power to appoint amongst X's children could be exercised in favour of an illegitimate child conceived after the death of the testator by whose will the power was given. This distinction is difficult to justify logically. See further Theobald, *Wills*, 13th Ed., 294 *et seq.*; Jarman, *Wills*, 8th Ed., c. XLV.

[1] It is more doubtful whether the illegitimate sons of illegitimate brothers and sisters can take. The section applies to persons who would be so related if he *or* some other person through whom the relationship is deduced had been born legitimate. If the word "or" is to be given a disjunctive meaning, the section does not apply if both were born illegitimate: see Ryder, *Property Law Aspects of the Family Law Reform Act 1969*, Current Legal Problems 1971, 157 at p. 164. The section operates only if the child or other relation is a beneficiary. Hence a gift to X's estate if he dies leaving children surviving him will still take effect only if X leaves legitimate children.

[2] Family Law Reform Act 1969, s. 17. "Purchaser" presumably means purchaser for value.

Section 15 was passed despite the views of the Russell Committee on the Law of Succession in Relation to Illegitimate Persons[1] who were of the opinion that its introduction might well force a testatrix who wished to exclude her illegitimate children to disclose by implication that she had some, or a father to offer his daughter a gratuitous insult by expressly limiting a gift to her legitimate children. These fears seem a little exaggerated: the testatrix can name the children she wishes to benefit, and the father can exclude the operation of the section in general terms if he wishes to do so. On the other hand, some testators, unaware of the existence of others' illegitimate children, may unwittingly give them an interest which they do not intend them to take.[2] If statutory effect is given to the proposals of the Law Commission's Working Party to abolish the concept of illegitimacy, the common law rules will disappear in their entirety. Consequently, unless the settlor or testator otherwise provides, all persons otherwise satisfying the conditions of the gift will be beneficiaries whether they or others through whom they claim are born in or out of wedlock.[3]

Legitimated Children.—Even though a child born illegitimate cannot take advantage of the provisions just discussed, he may still be able to claim an interest in property if he is subsequently legitimated. The earlier Legitimacy Acts followed the principle that legitimation should have the effect of giving a legitimated child the rights of a legitimate child but should not operate retrospectively. Consequently, unless a contrary intention was expressed in the disposition, he was entitled to take an interest under a disposition only if it came into operation after the date of his legitimation or by descent under an entailed interest created after that date.[4] Thus if A bequeathed property to B's legitimate children and C claimed it as B's legitimated son, he would succeed if A died after C was legitimated even though A executed the will before that event.[5]

The condition that the legitimation must precede the date on which the disposition comes into operation was removed by the Children Act 1975 (in provisions now re-enacted in the Legitimacy Act 1976) if the instrument was made on or after 1st January 1976 or, in the case of a disposition made by

---

[1] 1966, Cmnd. 3051, paras. 57-58.

[2] It should be noted that the powers of trustees in relation to protective trusts under s. 33 of the Trustee Act 1925 have been similarly extended to enable them to hold the income on trust for the illegitimate children or remoter issue of the principal beneficiary: Family Law Reform Act 1969, s. 15 (3). For a discussion of the operation of s. 15 generally, see Morris, *The Family Law Reform Act 1969, sections 14 and 15*, 19 I.C.L.Q. 328; Samuels, *Succession and the Family Law Reform Act 1969*, 34 Conv. 247, at pp. 249 *et seq*; Ryder, *loc. cit.*, at pp. 163 *et seq.*; Law Com. Working Paper No. 74 (Illegitimacy), paras. 5.12 and 5.13.

[3] Law Com. Working Paper No. 74, Part V. See *ante*, pp. 268-270 and 272.

[4] Legitimacy Act 1926, ss. 1 (3) and 3 (1). For legitimation generally, see *ante*, pp. 268-270.

[5] A *general* power of appointment gives the donee the complete power to dispose of the property so that a person could take under such a power if he was legitimated before it was *exercised*. In the case of a *special* power, however, the disposition for this purpose was the instrument under which it was *granted*, for the property is disposed of by the donor of the power who merely leaves the donee the power to select the ultimate beneficiary out of the persons designated by himself. Consequently a power to appoint amongst X's legitimate children could be exercised in favour of X's legitimated child only if he was legitimated before the instrument granting the power came into operation: *Re Wicks' Marriage Settlement*, [1940] Ch. 475; *Re Hoff*, [1942] Ch. 298; [1942] 1 All E.R. 547.

will, if the testator died on or after that date. A legitimated person (and anyone else claiming through him) can now take an interest under any such disposition as though he had been born legitimate.[1] It is of course possible for the maker of the instrument to express a contrary intention and thus exclude legitimated children who would otherwise take an interest under it or include those who would otherwise be left out.[2] A disposition includes the creation of an entailed interest, but a legitimated person may not succeed to any dignity or title of honour or (unless a contrary intention is expressed in the instrument) to any property limited to devolve therewith.[3]

If any right to property depends upon the relative seniority of a person's children, legitimated persons rank as if they had been born on the date of their legitimation, and if more than one child is legitimated at the same time, they rank *inter se* in order of seniority. This provision, however, does not affect the operation of any condition dependent on the child's reaching an actual age, nor will it apply if its effect would be to deprive a legitimated person of an interest which he could have claimed had he remained illegitimate.[4] Suppose, for example, that a testator dying in 1981 makes a gift in favour of the eldest legitimate child of X conditional upon his reaching the age of 18. X has three children: A and B, born illegitimate in 1965 and 1967 respectively, and C, born legitimate in 1970. If A and B were legitimated in 1969, they will be deemed to have been born then for the purpose of determining their seniority, and consequently A will be X's eldest legitimate child and can claim the interest when he actually reaches the age of 18 in 1983. If, on the other hand, they were legitimated after C's birth, C will be regarded as the eldest legitimate child and will be able to claim the interest in 1988. Had the gift been in favour of X's eldest child, so that A could have claimed it even if he had remained illegitimate, he will still be able to do so even if he is legitimated after C's birth.

If a person is not legitimated because he happens to die before his parents' marriage, the rights of his wife, children and remoter issue (together with the rights of anyone claiming in succession to them) are preserved, and they may take such interest as they could have taken had he been legitimated at the date of the marriage.[5] The following example will show how this provision operates. F and M have an illegitimate child, C, born in 1940. C dies in 1970, leaving a legitimate child, G. F and M intermarry in 1972. A testator dying in 1981 bequeaths a sum of money on trust for F's legitimate grandchildren. G can claim, for he is entitled to take such interest as he could have taken if C had been legitimated on his parents' marriage in 1972.

Trustees and personal representatives are not bound to enquire whether an illegitimate person could be legitimated and are not liable for any conveyance

---

[1] Legitimacy Act 1976, s. 5 (3). This applies to persons legitimated by s. 2 of the Act and to persons legitimated by foreign law whose legitimation is recognised under s. 3 or under the common law rules: *ibid.*, s. 10 (1). A disposition includes a power of appointment: *ibid.*

[2] *Ibid.*, s. 5 (1).

[3] Nor may he succeed to the throne: see *ibid.*, s. 10 (4) and Sched. 1, paras. 4 and 5. By implication this provision has abolished the old rule that a person can succeed as heir only if he is legitimate by the common law test (see *Birtwhistle* v. *Vardill* (1826), 5 B. & C. 438, K.B.; *Doe d. Birtwhistle* v. *Vardill* (1835), 2 Cl. & F. 571, H.L.; *Birtwhistle* v. *Vardill* (1840), 7 Cl. & F. 895, H.L.).

[4] *Ibid.*, ss. 5 (4), (5) and 6 (1), (3).

[5] *Ibid.*, s. 5 (6).

or distribution of property made without regard to such a fact if they have not received prior notice of it. But a beneficiary may follow the property (or any property representing it) into the hands of anyone who has received it other than a purchaser.[1]

Adopted Children.—Under the Adoption of Children Act of 1926, an adopted child was not deemed to be the child of the adopters but remained the child of his natural parents for the purposes of the devolution of interests in property. This anomalous rule was altered by the Adoption of Children Act 1949 with respect to dispositions made after 1949 or, in the case of an intestacy, where the intestate died after 1949. Now as regards interests in property, the general principle is the same as that relating to personal rights and duties: *i.e.*, from the date of the adoption order an adopted child is deemed to become the legitimate child of the adopter or adopters and ceases to be regarded as the child of his natural parents or, if he has been previously adopted, of his former adopters, and therefore is no longer considered as related to any other person through his natural or former adoptive parents.

Earlier legislation followed the same principle as originally applied to legitimation and provided that an adopted person could claim as his adoptive parent's child only under a disposition of property made *inter vivos* after he was adopted or under a will or codicil of a person dying after that date.[2] As in the case of legitimation, this limitation was removed by the Children Act 1975 in the case of instruments made on or after 1st January 1976 or wills of testators dying on or after that date and, subject to any contrary indication, an adopted child may claim in such cases whether the disposition takes effect before or after the adoption. A disposition depending on the date of birth of a child of the adoptive parent or parents is to be construed as though the adopted child was born on the date of his adoption and two or more children adopted on the same day rank *inter se* in the order of their actual births. This provision, however, does not affect the operation of any condition depending on the child's reaching an actual age.[3] Thus, if there is a bequest in 1981 to K's eldest child at 18 and K adopts a child A and subsequently has a natural child B, A can claim when he reaches the age of 18 whether his adoption preceded or followed the testator's death.

The effect of an adoption on an interest which the child could have claimed had he not been adopted is not so clear. Suppose, for example, that there is a gift to X with remainder to his eldest son and that X's eldest son is S. If S has been adopted by someone other than X before the instrument creating the settlement takes effect, he can obviously claim nothing because

---

[1] Legitimacy Act 1976, s. 7. The loose wording of this provision is regrettable. So long as both parents of an illegitimate child are alive, he could always be legitimated: presumably the trustee or personal representative must have more concrete evidence than this (*e.g.*, that the parents intend to intermarry in the immediate future). The term "purchaser" is not defined; presumably it means a purchaser for value.

[2] But if a will or codicil was executed before 1st April 1959, this provision applied only if the adoption order was made before its *execution* unless it was confirmed by codicil after that date: Adoption Act 1958, s. 17 (2) and Sched. 5, para. 4 (3).

[3] Children Act 1975, Sched. 1, paras. 5 and 6 (prospectively repealed and re-enacted in the Adoption Act 1976, s. 42). A disposition includes a power of appointment and the creation of an entailed interest: *ibid.*, paras. 2 and 17 (Adoption Act 1976, s. 46 (1), (2), (3), (5)). *Cf.* the similar provisions relating to legitimated children, *supra*.

he is no longer regarded as X's son at all. If X has died before S's adoption, so that S's interest has vested in possession, it is expressly preserved notwithstanding the adoption.[1] But what is the position if he is adopted after the disposition takes effect but before the interest vests in possession? A vested remainder is a present interest,[2] which suggests that on principle S should keep it. On the other hand, if one applies the maxim *expressio unius exclusio alterius*, the express preservation of an interest vested in possession implies that a vested remainder will be lost, and this is the solution the courts are more likely to adopt. If the interest is contingent and has not vested when the adoption takes place, it is presumably lost in any event. If, for example, the gift had been to X's eldest son at 18, S's adoption before that age must deprive him of all right to it because, when the condition is fulfilled, he is no longer regarded as X's son.

Notwithstanding the general rule, there are various provisions designed to ensure that an illegitimate child *adopted by one of his parents as the sole adoptive parent* is not thereby deprived of an interest he could have taken had he remained illegitimate. In the first place, such an adoption does not affect the child's entitlement to any property depending on his relationship to the adoptive parent.[3] Suppose, for example, that a testator, T, dying in 1981, makes a bequest in favour of his grandchildren alive at his death who reach the age of 18. His daughter, D, has an illegitimate child, C, alive at T's death, whom she subsequently adopts as sole adoptive parent. C can still claim under the bequest. Moreover, if a disposition depends on the date of birth of an illegitimate child, neither his adoption by one of his parents as sole adopter nor his legitimation if he has been adopted will affect his entitlement.[4] Thus, if in the above example T had bequeathed a sum of money to his eldest grandchild when that child reached the age of 18 and C was his eldest grandchild, C could still claim even if he was adopted by D (or, having been adopted by D, he was legitimated by D's subsequent marriage to his father) after the birth of another grandchild.[5]

Other provisions resemble those applying to legitimation. Unless the disposition otherwise provides, adoption does not affect the devolution of any property limited to devolve along with any peerage or dignity or title of honour (the descent of which will not be affected).[6] Trustees and personal representatives have the same protection if they distribute property in ignorance of the making or revocation of an adoption order but beneficiaries may trace property into the hands of anyone other than a purchaser.[7]

---

[1] *Ibid.*, para. 6 (4) (Adoption Act 1976, s. 42 (4)).

[2] Megarry and Wade, *Law of Real Property*, 4th Ed., 173, 177.

[3] Children Act 1975, Sched. 1, para. 9 (Adoption Act 1976, s. 39 (3)).

[4] *Ibid.*, para. 14 (Adoption Act 1976, s. 43); Legitimacy Act 1976, s. 6 (2).

[5] Similarly, the revocation of an adoption order following the legitimation of a child will not affect any claim he could have made to property had the order remained in force: Legitimacy Act 1976, s. 4 (2). If he has been adopted and dies before his parents' marriage, he is deemed to be legitimated on that date for the purpose of preserving interests to be taken by or in succession to his spouse, children and remoter issue: Legitimacy Act 1976, s. 5 (6). *Cf.* the position where he has not been adopted, *supra*. For the effect of an adoption by a woman over 55 and the operation of the presumption that she is incapable of bearing children, see Children Act 1975, Sched. 1, para. 6 (5) (Adoption Act 1976, s. 42 (5)).

[6] Children Act 1975, Sched. 1, para. 16 (Adoption Act 1976, s. 44).

[7] *Ibid.*, para. 15 (Adoption Act 1976, s. 45). See *ante*, pp. 579-581.

B. FINANCIAL PROVISION

At common law a father was under a duty to maintain only his legitimate minor children and to provide them with food, clothing, lodging and other necessaries. But the duty was wholly unenforceable. A child has never had an agency of necessity[1] and a father is under no legal obligation to reimburse one who has supplied his child with necessaries. Unless he constituted the child his agent, the only way in which he could be compelled to fulfil his obligation was through the wife's agency of necessity, which extended to the purchase of necessaries for the children of the marriage as well as for herself.[2] With the abolition of the wife's agency of necessity, the common law position is now of purely historical interest.[3]

On the breakdown of a marriage there are a number of ways in which financial provision can be claimed for children. The mother may also claim maintenance for an illegitimate child from the father to whom she has never been married at all. The provisions are now all statutory and it will be convenient to deal with them under three heads: those relating to children of the family, those relating to legitimate, legitimated and adopted children only, and those relating to illegitimate children only. In the first place, however, we must consider the entitlement to benefit under legislation relating to social security.

Concurrent Orders.—As in the case of orders for custody or for financial provision for a spouse, two orders for financial provision for a child should not be in force at the same time. As we shall see, a mother may obtain maintenance for a child in the High Court, a county court or a magistrates' court under the Guardianship of Minors Act or in a magistrates' court under the Domestic Proceedings and Magistrates' Courts Act. If she later petitions for a divorce, she may wish to obtain an order for financial provision in the divorce court. That court itself can discharge an order made under the Domestic Proceedings and Magistrates' Courts Act,[4] but the old rule of practice that the mother should first have the earlier order discharged may still apply if it was made under the Guardianship of Minors Act.[5] The facts that should be borne in mind in deciding which method of obtaining maintenance a party should pursue are the same as in the case of orders for financial provision for a spouse and for custody of the children.[6]

---

[1] *Mortimer* v. *Wright* (1840), 6 M. & W. 482.

[2] *Bazeley* v. *Forder* (1868), L.R. 3 Q.B. 559.

[3] For the abolition of the wife's agency of necessity, see *ante*, p. 484. There is an old authority at nisi prius for the proposition that a father is also liable for necessaries supplied for the use of his children at the request of a servant who has charge of them: *Cooper* v. *Phillips* (1831), 4 C. & P. 581. Today the courts might require proof of an ostensible authority.

[4] See *ante*, p. 489.

[5] Although it would presumably be rare to apply for the discharge of an order made by the High Court.

[6] See *ante*, p. 311. The fact that a woman already has an order for herself under one Act does not prevent her from applying for maintenance for her children under another: *Re Kinseth*, [1947] Ch. 223; [1947] 1 All E.R. 201. For orders against persons abroad and the reciprocal enforcement of maintenance orders, see *ante*, pp. 517-522.

1. BENEFITS UNDER LEGISLATION RELATING TO SOCIAL SECURITY

Child Benefit.[1]—One of the first statutes passed after the end of the Second World War to give effect to the system of social security recommended in the Beveridge Report[2] was the Family Allowances Act of 1945. Its object was to relieve poverty by providing money payments by the state in respect of the children in a family who are not yet earning their own living. From 1977 family allowances were replaced by a new child benefit. In broad outline the two are very similar: one of the most important differences is that child benefit is payable in respect of every qualified child whereas family allowances were not payable in respect of the first.

Under the Child Benefit Act 1975 a person is entitled to child benefit if he is responsible for any child under the age of 16 or, if the child is receiving full-time primary or secondary education, under the age of 19.[3] No benefit may be claimed in respect of certain children, for example those detained in legal custody.[4] A person is regarded as responsible for a child if he has the child living with him or if he is contributing to the cost of providing for him at a weekly rate not less than the relevant rate of child benefit.[5] As between a person with whom the child is living and one contributing to his maintenance, the former is entitled. If a husband and wife are living together, the allowance belongs to the latter because she is generally the member of the family who will need it to maintain the children and there is a danger in some families that, if it were paid to the husband, it would never reach her at all. Similarly, if two unmarried people are living together and both are parents of the child, the mother is entitled; if only one is a parent, he will be entitled as against the non-parent.[6] Normally both the claimant and the child must be in Great Britain.[7]

The rate of child benefit is prescribed by statutory instrument and different rates may be prescribed for different classes of children. At present a higher rate is prescribed for the first child for whom benefit can be claimed.[8]

Social Security Act.—If the beneficiary is responsible for a child, the amount of some benefits payable under the Social Security Act 1975 may be increased and some additional benefits may be claimed. The rate of contributory benefits is substantially greater if the beneficiary is entitled to

---

[1] See generally Ogus and Barendt, *Law of Social Security*, c. 11.

[2] Cmd. 6404, 1942.

[3] Ss. 1, 2 and 24 (1); S.I. 1976 No. 965.

[4] S. 4 (1) and Sched. 1. Benefit may be claimed for a married child only if he (or she) is not residing with his spouse or the latter is also in receipt of full-time education: S.I. 1976 No. 965.

[5] S. 3. Any absence not exceeding 56 days during the past 16 weeks is to be disregarded when determining whether the child is living with the claimant.

[6] If neither is a parent, they should elect which of them is to receive the benefit. See s. 4 (2) and Sched. 2.

[7] Reciprocal arrangements may be made with Northern Ireland (which has its own social security scheme) and with any countries outside the U.K. with whom we have entered into an agreement for this purpose. See ss. 13-15.

[8] S. 5; S.I. 1980 No. 1246. The benefit is inalienable and any assignment of it or charge on it or agreement to assign or charge it is void. On the bankruptcy of the recipient, the allowance does not pass to the trustee in bankruptcy or any other person acting on behalf of the creditors: s. 12 (1).

child benefit in respect of any child or children.[1] If the former husband of a divorced woman dies and she is entitled to child benefit in respect of a child towards whose maintenance the former husband was contributing or in respect of whom she was entitled to payments under a court order, trust or agreement, she may claim a child's special allowance provided that she has not remarried and is not cohabiting with a man as his wife.[2] The reason is that, had she not been divorced, she would have been entitled to a widow's allowance which would have been increased by reason of her responsibility for the child. A person who is not the parent of a child in respect of whom he is entitled to child benefit may also claim a guardian's allowance if the child's parents are both dead or if one is dead and the other is in prison or cannot be found.[3]

Supplementary Benefit.—No person under the age of 16 (or normally, under the age of 19 if he is receiving full-time education) may apply for supplementary benefit himself, but in calculating the requirements of anyone over that age, the Commission must take into account the requirements of any such child who is a member of the same household.[4] Further assistance is given to families on low incomes in the form of family income supplement.[5] For the purpose of the Supplementary Benefits Act 1976, both parents are liable to maintain their legitimate, illegitimate and adopted children under the age of 16,[6] and if benefit is given in respect of such a child, the Commission may take steps to recover it from either or both parents. The question of recovery will be considered later.[7]

2. CHILDREN OF THE FAMILY

Two statutes enable courts to make orders in favour of children of the family. The meaning of this term has already been discussed.[8]

Domestic Proceedings and Magistrates' Courts Act 1978.—As we have already seen, if either party to a marriage establishes one of the grounds set

---

[1] Social Security Act 1975, ss. 41-43 and 64-65 and Scheds. 4 and 20, as amended by the Child Benefit Act 1975, Sched. 4, and the Social Security Act 1980, Sched. 1. The benefits concerned are unemployment benefit, sickness benefit, invalidity pension, maternity allowance, widow's allowance, category A, B and C retirement pensions and industrial injury and disablement benefits.

[2] *Ibid.*, s. 31, as amended by the Child Benefit Act 1975, Sched. 4. A voidable marriage which has been annulled is regarded as though it was a valid marriage terminated by divorce: Social Security (Child's Special Allowance) Regulations, S.I. 1975 No. 497.

[3] *Ibid.*, s. 38, as amended by the Child Benefit Act 1975, Sched. 4. See Ogus and Barendt, *op. cit.*, 256-263.

[4] Supplementary Benefits Act 1976, ss. 1 and 6 (2) and Sched. 1, as amended by the Social Security Act 1980, Sched. 2. The child's income is aggregated with the parent's so that, if it exceeds the sum which the parent can claim with respect to the child, the parent's claim will be reduced *pro tanto*: *Supplementary Benefits Commission* v. *Jull*, [1980] 3 All E.R. 65, H.L. For the Supplementary Benefits Act generally, see *ante*, pp. 495-497.

[5] See the Family Income Supplements Act 1970, as amended by the Pensioners and Family Income Supplement Payments Act 1972, s. 3, and the Social Security Act 1980, s. 7; Ogus and Barendt, *op. cit.*, c. 13.

[6] Ss. 17 and 34 (1).

[7] *Post*, pp. 592 and 602.

[8] See *ante*, pp. 304-305.

out in section 1 of the Act, a magistrates' court may order the respondent to make periodical payments and to pay a lump sum not exceeding £500 for the benefit of any child of the family to whom the application relates. A similar power exists if a consent order is made under section 6, except that the lump sum may be for any amount and is not limited to £500. If the parties have been living apart for more than three months and the respondent has been making periodical payments for the benefit of the applicant or a child of the family, the court may order him to make periodical payments (but not to pay a lump sum) for the benefit of any child of the family under section 7.[1] In proceedings under sections 6 and 7 the child's financial position is protected by the provision that in neither case may the court make an order which would not provide for, or make a proper contribution towards, his needs.[2]

An interim order may contain a provision requiring the respondent to make periodical payments for the benefit of any child of the family under the age of 18. If at the time the child has his home with a parent who is not a party to the marriage, the respondent may be ordered to make the payments to the parent.[3]

In the above cases the court may make an order for financial provision for a child whether or not it makes an order regarding his legal custody. Four further powers must be noted. First, if the court is not satisfied that any ground for an application has been made out under section 1 but nonetheless gives the applicant the actual custody of a child of the family, it has the same powers to make an order against the respondent for periodical payments and a lump sum as it would have had if a ground had been made out. (It may be noted in passing that there is a gap in the provisions of the Act. A court may give actual custody to the applicant if it declines to make any other order under section 6 or 7 but it has no power in these circumstances to order the respondent to make financial provision.) Secondly, if the court gives actual custody of a child to the respondent in proceedings brought under any section, it may make similar orders against the applicant. Thirdly, if legal custody is given to a parent who is not a party to the marriage, either (or presumably both) of the spouses may be ordered to make periodical payments or to pay a lump sum. Finally, if the child is committed to the care of a local authority, either (or, again, presumably both) of the parties to the marriage may be ordered to make periodical payments for his benefit although in this case there is no power to make an order for a lump sum.[4] Similar powers exist if, following an application to vary an order, custody is given to one of the spouses (including the original applicant for an order under section 6) or a parent or the child is committed to the care of a local authority.[5] In all cases the maximum lump sum that may be ordered is £500.[6]

---

[1] See *ante*, pp. 498 (s. 1) and 502 (ss. 6 and 7).

[2] Ss. 6 (3) and 7 (4) (b). If the application was made under s. 6, the applicant would have to bring fresh proceedings under s. 1; if it was made under s. 7, the court may itself treat it as if it had been brought under s. 1: see *ante*, p. 503.

[3] S. 19 (1), (2). For interim orders generally, see *ante*, pp. 503-504.

[4] S. 11 (1)-(4). If an order for custody is not to take effect until the expiration of a specified time or the occurrence of a specified event, periodical payments by the applicant to the respondent or by either spouse to a parent may begin only when the order for custody takes effect: s. 11 (8).

[5] S. 21 (6).

[6] S. 11 (7). The Home Secretary may increase this sum by statutory instrument.

Although reference has been made above to orders for the benefit of a child of the family, the Act in each case specifically enables the court to order that the periodical payments should be made or the lump sum should be paid to the applicant, respondent, parent or local authority (as the case may be) for the benefit of the child, or alternatively, to the child himself. If, for example, the child is over the age of 18, it might obviously be appropriate to order payment to him direct; there may also be financial advantages in making such an order, regardless of his age. If payments are made to a spouse or parent, they are regarded as his or her income for the purpose of income tax; if they are made to the child, they are regarded as the child's income and so will be free of tax if they are less than his personal relief. Furthermore, a child's income is disregarded in determining the family's resources for the purpose of family income supplement; consequently payments made to the child will not affect the claim of the person with whom he is living, whilst payments made to that person obviously will.[1]

Duration of Orders. —As many children will start earning when they reach the upper limit of the compulsory school age, no order for periodical payments is to extend in the first instance beyond the date of the child's birthday next following his attaining that age unless the court thinks it right to specify a later date (as it obviously must if he is already over that age). No order may be made at all, however, if the child is over the age of 18 and an existing order for periodical payments may not continue after his eighteenth birthday. To both limbs of this rule there are two exceptions: there is no age limit on the making or continuation of orders so long as the child is (or, if an order were made, would be) receiving instruction at an educational establishment or undergoing training for a trade, profession or vocation (whether or not he is also gainfully employed) or, in any event, if there are special circumstances justifying this.[2] It will thus be seen that periodical payments could continue indefinitely if, say, the child were incapable of earning his own living owing to some physical or mental handicap. If the court can make an order only if one of the spouses or a parent is given custody, no fresh order can be made in favour of a child over the age of 18 because no custody order can be made, but an existing order can continue after he reaches this age if one of the conditions stated above is fulfilled.[3]

All orders for periodical payments terminate on the death of the child or of the person liable to make the payments.[4]

Assessment. —As in the case of an order in favour of the applicant spouse, the court must take into account all the circumstances of the case including

---

[1] See Law Com. No. 77 (Report on Matrimonial Proceedings in Magistrates' Courts), paras. 5.68-5.74. For further details of family income supplement, see Ogus and Barendt, *Law of Social Security*, 566. The child's income is not disregarded in determining supplementary benefit payable to the person with whom he is living: see *ante*, p. 584, n. 4. The obvious practical difficulties are overcome by enabling the person with whom the child has his home (or, if he is in care, the local authority) to receive all periodical and lump sum payments on his behalf if he is under the age of 18 and to take proceedings in his name to seek a variation or recover arrears: see the Magistrates' Courts Act 1980, s. 62.
[2] Ss. 5 (1)-(3), 6 (7) and 7 (7).
[3] S. 11 (6), (7).
[4] Ss. 5 (4), 6 (7), 7 (7) and 11 (6).

the income, earning capacity, property and other financial resources which each of the spouses has or is likely to have in the foreseeable future together with their present and foreseeable financial needs, obligations and responsibilities. In particular it must also have regard to:[1]

(a) the financial needs of the child;
(b) the income, earning capacity (if any), property and other financial resources of the child;
(c) any physical or mental disability of the child;
(d) the standard of living enjoyed by the family before the occurrence of the conduct which is alleged as the ground of the application (or before the parties to the marriage lived apart); and
(e) the manner in which the child was being and in which the parties to the marriage expected him to be educated or trained.

These provisions really do no more than spell out the principles which the courts have always applied. Their effect is summarised in the words of BAGNALL, J.,[2] approved by the Court of Appeal in *Lilford* v. *Glynn*:[3]

"In the vast majority of cases the financial position of a child of a subsisting marriage is simply to be afforded shelter, food and education, according to the means of his parents."

It will be seen that the very wide definition of the term "child of the family" gives the court power to make an order against a spouse who would be under no other legal obligation to make financial provision for him and who may have assumed no responsibility for his maintenance. Consequently a measure of protection is necessary and, in deciding whether to make an order against a party to the marriage in favour of a child who is not his natural or adopted child and, if so, how much to award, the court must further have regard:[4]

(a) to whether [he] had assumed any responsibility for the child's maintenance and, if he did, to the extent to which, and the basis on which, he assumed that responsibility and to the length of time during which he discharged that responsibility;
(b) to whether in assuming and discharging that responsibility [he] did so knowing that the child was not his own child; and
(c) to the liability of any other person to maintain the child.

Whether a spouse assumed responsibility for a child must be judged objectively, and in the absence of a clear contrary indication the payment of the expenses of a family unit including the child implies an assumption of responsibility even though other resources may be available for his maintenance.[5] In paragraph (a) the word "extent" refers to the amount of his contribution in contradistinction to the length of time during which he made it.[6] The reference in paragraph (c) to the liability of any other person to

---

[1] Ss. 3 (2), 7 (5) and 11 (5).
[2] *Harnett* v. *Harnett*, [1973] Fam. 156, 161; [1973] 2 All E.R. 593, 598.
[3] [1979] 1 All E.R. 441, 447, C.A.
[4] Ss. 3 (3), 7 (5) and 11 (5).
[5] *Snow* v. *Snow*, [1972] Fam. 74, 111-112; [1971] 3 All E.R. 833, 863, C.A.
[6] *Roberts* v. *Roberts*, [1962] P. 212; [1962] 2 All E.R. 967. See Samuels, 26 M.L.R. 92.

maintain the child covers any liability enforceable at law and thus embraces the potential liability of a parent (including the father of an illegitimate child) or of a party to another marriage who has treated the child as a child of the family.[1] It will be seen that the need to take all these matters into account means that the court might well conclude, for example, that no order should be made against a husband who had married the wife in the mistaken belief that he was the father of her child or who had made it clear at the time of the marriage that he was undertaking no financial responsibility for her children by a previous marriage if their own father was quite capable of providing for them.[2]

As in the case of lump sum payments for the benefit of the applicant, it is expressly provided that they may be ordered to meet any liability or reasonable expense already incurred in maintaining the child.[3] It is easy to envisage many situations in which an order for a lump sum would be appropriate: to purchase a school uniform, to pay for a holiday abroad, or to cover the expenses involved on first going to a university, to name but a few. In many cases coming before magistrates it is much more likely that they will make such an order for the benefit of a child than for the benefit of a spouse.

Variation, Revocation and Cessation of Orders.—There is a general power to vary, suspend or revoke any order for periodical payments and to revive any order that has been suspended. On any application for variation or revocation (except for an order originally made under section 6 or section 7) the court may also make an order for the payment of a lump sum. No order for a lump sum may be made at all on an application to vary an order under section 7 (just as no such order may be made on the original application); if the order was made under section 6, the court may make an order for a lump sum in proceedings for variation only if the original order contained such a provision.[4] No lump sum may exceed £500 (or such larger amount as may be fixed by the Secretary of State) unless the original order was made under section 6, when the court may order payment of a larger sum if the respondent agrees.[5]

The child himself may apply for a variation if he is over the age of 16; and if the order ceased to have effect when he reached the age of 16 or 18 or at some time between these dates, he may apply for it to be revived at any time before he reaches the age of 21.[6] He may well wish to take advantage of the last mentioned provision if he decides to undergo further education or

---

[1] *Snow* v. *Snow*, *(supra)*, at pp. 112 and 863, respectively. The court may adjourn the hearing to enable proceedings to be taken against the person liable: *Caller* v. *Caller*, [1968] P. 39; [1966] 2 All E.R. 754; *Snow* v. *Snow*. This may cause difficulty because if, for example, the child in question is the wife's illegitimate child or her child by a previous marriage, her present husband has no power to institute or intervene in the proceedings.

[2] See *Bowlas* v. *Bowlas*, [1965] P. 450; [1965] 3 All E.R. 40, C.A. In the case of an application under s. 7 the court shall not require the respondent to make payments for the benefit of a child of the family who is not his child if it would not have made an order in the child's favour in proceedings brought under s. 1: s. 7 (3) (c).

[3] Ss. 2 (2) and 11 (7).

[4] But the original order need not have been in favour of the child: it could have been in favour of the spouse or another child.

[5] S. 20 (1)-(8), (13). Proceedings may be brought by or against a party residing outside England and Wales: s. 24.

[6] S. 20 (10), (12).

training at some stage after leaving school and beginning to earn his own living.

In determining how to exercise its powers the court must take into account the same matters as on an application to vary an order for periodical payments in favour of a spouse.[1]

Special attention must be drawn to the effect of the spouses' living together. If one of them is required to make periodical payments *to the other* for the benefit of a child of the family following an application under section 1 or section 6, the effect of their continuing to live with each other or subsequently resuming living with each other will be precisely the same as it is in the case of an order requiring him to make periodical payments for the benefit of the other spouse. Similarly, *any* order made under section 7 will automatically cease to have effect if the spouses live together again.[2] But if payments are ordered to be made (except under section 7) *to the child himself* or to a parent who is not one of the spouses, or to a local authority, neither the continuation nor the resumption of cohabitation will have any effect on the order unless the court otherwise directs.[3] The reason for the last two cases is obvious: the spouses' cohabitation is irrelevant to the provision which needs to be made for the child. The position is slightly different, however, with respect to payments to be made to him personally. If the order so provides because he is not living with either of the spouses, their cohabitation will usually be equally irrelevant; if, on the other hand, payments are in effect being made to one of the parties of the marriage but are technically being made to the child for tax or other financial advantages, the order is really indistinguishable for this purpose from one formally requiring payments to be made to the party, and consequently it should normally be discharged in the same circumstances.[4]

Although the court has no power to vary a lump sum order, if the sum is payable by instalments, the court may vary the number and amount of the instalments and the dates on which they are due.[5]

Enforcement of Orders.—Orders in respect of a child are enforceable in the same way as orders for the benefit of a spouse.[6]

Matrimonial Causes Act 1973.—The High Court or a divorce county court has various powers under this Act.

Divorce, Nullity and Judicial Separation.—In proceedings for divorce, nullity and judicial separation, the court may make an order for periodical payments (which may be secured or unsecured) and for a lump sum payment. The order may be made before the decree is granted, when it is granted, or at any time afterwards; alternatively, to avoid a party's having to take fresh

---

[1] S. 20 (11). See further *ante*, pp. 509-511. The variation may be made to run from any date not earlier than the date of the application: s. 20 (9).

[2] S. 25 (1), (3). The court may make an order declaring that the original order has ceased to have effect: s. 25 (4). See further *ante*, pp. 508-509.

[3] S. 25 (2).

[4] See Law Com. No. 77, paras. 5.97-5.113.

[5] S. 22. But the court may remit arrears on proceedings to enforce the order: see *ante*, p. 511.

[6] See *ante*, pp. 511-515. This includes the power to have the order registered and enforced in the High Court.

proceedings for financial provision for the children if the petition is unsuccessful, an order may be made on the dismissal of the petition or within a reasonable time thereafter. Normally, the sums will be payable by one spouse (or former spouse) to the other, but either (or presumably both)[1] of them may be ordered to make payments to a third person, if the child is in that person's custody or care and control, or to the child himself.[2] As in the case of provision for a spouse, a lump sum may cover any liabilities or expenses already incurred by the child or for his benefit; it may also be made payable by instalments, which may be secured.[3]

It will also be recalled that the court has power to order the transfer and settlement of property and the variation of ante-nuptial and post-nuptial settlements to or for the benefit of any child of the family. This can be exercised, however, only if a decree is pronounced.[4]

Failure to maintain.—Under section 27 of the Act (as amended by section 63 of the Domestic Proceedings and Magistrates' Courts Act 1978) either spouse may apply for an order on the ground that the other has failed to provide, or to make a proper contribution towards, reasonable maintenance for any child of the family. In deciding whether the respondent has failed to do so the court must take into account the same matters as it does on assessing what order to make.[5]

If the court is satisfied that the grounds alleged have been made out, it may order the respondent to make secured or unsecured periodical payments and a lump sum payment for the benefit of any child to whom the application relates.[6] As in the case of similar orders made on divorce, the sums may be payable to the applicant, the child or a third person, and a lump sum may be made payable by instalments, which may be secured.[7]

Assessment.—Whether the application is made on divorce, nullity or judicial separation or under section 27, the court must take into account the same matters as a magistrates' court has to take into account on an application under the Domestic Proceedings and Magistrates' Courts Act, including the facts which must be taken into account if the respondent is not

---

[1] The court had power under previous legislation to make an order against both spouses: *Freckleton* v. *Freckleton*, [1966] C.L.Y. 3938.

[2] For the circumstances in which it would be appropriate to make an order in favour of the child himself, see *ante*, p. 586. Presumably sums could be made payable to a local authority if the child were committed to its care. An application for an order may be made by a guardian, anyone with custody or care and control of the child, a local authority and the Official Solicitor as guardian *ad litem*: Matrimonial Causes Rules 1977, r. 69. The child may be given leave to make an application himself if he is over the age of 18: *Downing* v. *Downing*, [1976] Fam. 288; [1976] 3 All E.R. 474.

[3] S. 23 (1) (d), (e), (f), (2), (3) (b), (c) and (4). For payments to the other spouse, see *ante*, pp. 531-533.

[4] S. 24. See *ante*, pp. 534-539.

[5] S. 27 (3A) (as amended). For the jurisdiction of the court, see *ante*, p. 515.

[6] If the court finds that the respondent has failed to provide reasonable maintenance for the applicant but not for the child, it may take into account the cost to her of looking after the child in assessing financial provision for her: *Cf. Ridley* v. *Ridley*, [1953] P. 150; [1953] 1 All E.R. 798.

[7] S. 27 (6) and (7). An interim order for periodical payments may also be made: s. 27 (5).

the child's parent. In the first three cases (but not in an application under section 27) it is also required[1]

"so to exercise [its] powers as to place the child, so far as it is practicable and ... just to do so, in the financial position in which the child would have been if the marriage had not broken down and each of [the parties to the marriage] had properly discharged his or her financial obligations and responsibilities towards him."

The spouses may not oust the jurisdiction of the court by agreeing between themselves what maintenance should be paid. Any agreement between the parties containing provisions relating to the maintenance or education of any child will be a "maintenance agreement" for the purpose of section 34 of the Act provided that it is in writing. This means that any term restricting the parties' power to apply to a court for an order containing financial arrangements will not be binding but the agreement will not thereby be rendered void: the covenantee may prefer to hold the spouse to his contract and may also apply to the court to have the agreement altered.[2] If the agreement is not in writing, any such restrictive term is contrary to public policy at common law on the ground that the right to apply to the court is given for the child's benefit and therefore cannot be surrendered even for valuable consideration.[3] Consequently either spouse may apply for an order and, if the undertaking not to do so is the sole or main consideration for the other party's promise to pay maintenance, the whole contract will be void and cannot be enforced.[4]

Duration of Orders.—The court's powers to make an order for periodical payments (secured or unsecured), a lump sum payment or the transfer of property for the benefit of a child over the age of 18 are limited in exactly the same way as magistrates' powers to make orders for the benefit of such a child The term for which periodical payments may be ordered is similarly limited.[5]

Although this limitation does not apply to the settlement (as distinct from the transfer) of property, in the absence of special circumstances the court is unlikely to make an order which will have the effect of benefiting a child after the conclusion of his full-time education.[6]

Variation and Discharge of Orders.—As in the case of orders for the benefit of a party to the marriage, there is a general power to vary, discharge, suspend and revive orders for periodical payments. The court may also vary an order relating to the terms on which a lump sum is payable by instalments but not the total sum payable. On an application for variation the court has no power to order the transfer or settlement of property or the variation of an ante-nuptial or post-nuptial settlement, but it can order the payment of a

---

[1] Ss. 25 (2), (3) and 27 (3A) (as amended). See further *ante*, pp. 586-588. There are slight differences in the wording of the two sets of provisions.

[2] See *ante*, pp. 489-495.

[3] *Bishop* v. *Bishop*, [1897] P. 138, 165, C.A.; *Bennett* v. *Bennett*, [1951] 2 K.B. 572; [1951] 1 All E.R. 1088 (affirmed on other grounds, [1952] 1 K.B. 249; [1952] 1 All E.R. 413, C.A.).

[4] *Bennett* v. *Bennett*, (*supra*). But this does not apply to an agreement to oust the jurisdiction of a foreign court: *Addison* v. *Brown*, [1954] 2 All E.R. 213. *Cf.* agreements relating to the maintenance of one of the parties to the marriage, *ante*, p. 491.

[5] Ss. 27 (6) and 29. See further *ante*, p. 586.

[6] See *Lilford* v. *Glynn*, [1979] 1 All E.R. 441, C.A.

lump sum—a power that it does not possess on an application to vary an order in favour of a spouse. The reason for the difference is that a lump sum may be valuable to a child long after the marriage has broken down, for example to enable him to pay fees for a professional education.[1] As in the case of a magistrates' order, if an order for unsecured periodical payments made under section 27 has ceased to have effect when the child reached the age of 16 or at any time thereafter not later than his eighteenth birthday, he may himself apply to have it revived so long as he is still under the age of 21.[2] No application to vary an order for secured periodical payments after the payer's death may be made more than six months after representation to his estate was first taken out except with the leave of the court.[3]

In exercising its powers to make a variation, etc., the court must have regard to all the circumstances of the case including any change in the matters which it was expressly directed to take into account while making the order originally. It must also take into account any change in circumstances resulting from the death of the party against whom the order was made.[4]

Enforcement.—An order can be enforced in exactly the same way as a similar order made for the benefit of either party to the marriage. This includes the power to restrain and set aside dispositions made with the intention of defeating the claim, to register the order in a magistrates' court and to recover overpayments after a change of circumstances.[5]

3. LEGITIMATE, LEGITIMATED AND ADOPTED CHILDREN

As we have already seen, an order may be sought against either parent to recover the cost of supplementary benefit given in respect of a legitimate child. Maintenance may also be obtained under the Guardianship of Minors Act and for wards of court. In each of these cases the term "legitimate child" includes a child who has been legitimated and a child who has been adopted.

Supplementary Benefit.—If benefit is given in respect of a child under the age of 16, the Secretary of State may apply to a magistrates' court for an order against either parent. In determining what order to make, the court must have regard to all the circumstances and particularly to the parent's resources. Any payments ordered must be made to the Secretary of State in so far as they represent reimbursement of benefit given and to the person named

---

[1] But the courts are nevertheless reluctant to order the payment of a lump sum when the child could be adequately protected by increasing periodical payments: see *McKay* v. *Chapman*, [1978] 2 All E.R. 548, 556.

[2] S. 27 (6B) (as amended). This does not apply to secured periodical payments because the property on which they were secured may already have been disposed of: see Law Com. No. 77, para. 9.23. A child over the age of 16 may himself apply for the variation of any existing order for periodical payments (secured or unsecured) made under s. 27: s. 27 (6A) (as amended). *Cf. ante*, p. 588.

[3] The court also has power to vary, etc., an order for secured periodical payments if the child applies for financial provision under the Inheritance (Provision for Family and Dependants) Act 1975: see *post*, p. 637.

[4] Matrimonial Causes Act 1973, s. 31. For variation, etc., of an order in favour of a spouse, see *ante*, pp. 563-565.

[5] See *ante*, pp. 566-571. See also *Practice Direction*, [1980] 1 All E.R. 1007 (registration of orders). Similarly arrears of periodical payments and the payment of a lump sum cannot be enforced more than twelve months after they fall due without the leave of the court.

in the order (who may be the Secretary of State or the person with actual custody of the child) in so far as they represent maintenance for the future. All orders may be subsequently varied or revoked, and they are enforceable like other maintenance orders made by a magistrates' court.[1]

Guardianship of Minors Act.—If any court makes an order under this Act giving actual custody of a *legitimate* child to a parent, it may further order the other parent to make periodical payments or a lump sum payment (or both) for the child's benefit. As under the Domestic Proceedings and Magistrates' Courts Act 1978, magistrates' courts may not order the payment of a lump sum exceeding £500. There is also a power to make an interim order for periodical payments. If the child is placed in the care of a local authority, either (or presumably both) of the parents may be ordered to make periodical payments (but not a lump sum payment).[2]

As in the case of orders under other Acts, the court may order payments to be made to the other parent (or the local authority) or to the child himself.[3] As the power is exercisable only if the court makes a custody order or care order, it follows that no order for maintenance can be made under this Act at all if the child is over the age of 18, but an existing order for periodical payments can remain in force after he reaches this age in the same circumstances as an order under the Domestic Proceedings and Magistrates' Courts Act 1978.[4] The effect of the parent's continuing to live together or of their subsequently resuming living together is also the same as it is under that Act.[5]

In assessing the amount (if any) to be ordered, the court must take into account the same matters as on an application for maintenance for a child under the 1978 Act except that it is not specifically enjoined to have regard to the family's standard of living or the manner in which he was being or expected to be educated.[6]

---

[1] Supplementary Benefits Act 1976, ss. 17 and 18, as amended by the Social Security Act 1980, Sched. 2. The fact that a parent has been released from making periodical payments in a consent order on divorce does not preclude a court from ordering him to make payments, for otherwise the parties might effectively contract out of liability: *Hulley* v. *Thompson*, [1981] 1 W.L.R. 159. For enforcement, see *ante*, pp. 511-515. See further *ante*, p. 584.

[2] Guardianship of Minors Act 1971, ss. 9 (2), 12B and 14 (2); Guardianship Act 1973, ss. 2 (3), (3A), (4), (5)-(5E) and 4 (4), as amended and added by the Children Act 1975, Sched. 3, and the Domestic Proceedings and Magistrates' Courts Act 1978, ss. 41 (2), 43, 44 (1) and 45. The court may order the payment of a lump sum by instalments (which may be varied), and the maximum sum a magistrates' court may order may be increased by an order made by the Secretary of State. For payments to the child himself, see *ante*, p. 586; for interim orders, see *ante*, p. 304.

[3] Guardianship of Minors Act 1971, s. 9 (2); Guardianship Act 1973, s. 2 (3) (as amended in each case).

[4] Guardianship of Minors Act 1971, s. 12; Guardianship Act 1973, s. 2 (3B), as amended and added by the Domestic Proceedings and Magistrates' Courts Act 1978, ss. 42 and 44 (1), and the Children Act 1975, Sched. 3. See further *ante*, p. 586.

[5] Guardianship Act 1973, s. 5A (added by the Domestic Proceedings and Magistrates' Courts Act 1978, s. 46). See further *ante*, p. 589.

[6] Guardianship of Minors Act 1971, ss. 12A and 12B (1); Guardianship Act 1973, s. 2 (3A), added by the Domestic Proceedings and Magistrates' Courts Act 1978, ss. 43 and 44 (1), respectively. These provisions follow the recommendations in Law Com. No. 77, para. 6.22, but it is not clear why the last two matters were omitted. In *Re W.*, [1956] Ch. 384; [1956] 1 All E.R. 368, C.A., it was pointed out that the fact that the mother is working will not necessarily go in diminution of her claim if the court is of the opinion that it is not in the child's interest that she should do so.

There is a general power to vary, suspend, revive and revoke orders for periodical payments, and the court may order the payment of a lump sum on an application for a variation. The power of a child over the age of 16 to apply for a variation or to revive an order is the same as under the 1978 Act.[1]

The usual means of enforcement are open if the order is made in the High Court or a county court; an order made in a magistrates' court is enforceable in the same way as an affiliation order.[2] In all cases the order may be registered and enforced in another court and an attachment of earnings order may be made.

Wards of Court.—We have already seen what rights generally a guardian has to claim maintenance for his ward from the surviving parent.[3] If the child is a ward of court, the parents' liability has been considerably extended by the provisions of section 6 of the Family Law Reform Act 1969. The court may now order either parent to pay to the other such periodical sums towards the maintenance and education of the ward as it thinks reasonable having regard to the means of the parent against whom the order is made. If the ward is in the care and control of a third person, either or both parents may be required to make periodical payments to that person.[4] Such an order may remain in force until the child reaches the age of 21 and, if he is over the age of 18, the sums may be made payable to him personally. Furthermore, so long as a former ward of court is between the ages of 18 and 21, either parent or the child himself may apply for an order requiring either parent to pay maintenance to the other parent, a third person or to the child himself. There is, however, no power to extend payments beyond the age of 21 so that he is not in such a favourable position as he would be if the order had been made in other proceedings and he were, say, still undergoing education or training.

Except for an order requiring a parent to pay maintenance for an existing ward of court to a third person, no order can be made if the parents are residing together at the time, and if they subsequently reside together, no liability will accrue so long as they do so, and the order will cease to have effect if they reside together for a period of three months.[5] There is no power to make an order for maintenance if the child is illegitimate (which is a serious defect). All orders can be varied and discharged by the court and may be enforced in the same way as other orders for payment in the High Court.

---

[1] Guardianship of Minors Act 1971, ss. 9 (4), 12B (3), (4) and 12C; Guardianship Act 1973, s. 4 (3A)-(3D), as amended and added by the Domestic Proceedings and Magistrates' Courts Act 1978, ss. 41 (2), 43 and 44 (2). For the child's power to apply for a variation or revival, see *ante*, p. 588. After the death of either parent, any guardian may apply for a variation, etc. For the position where one of the parties is outside the jurisdiction, see the Maintenance Orders (Reciprocal Enforcement) Act 1972, s. 41, as amended by the Domestic Proceedings and Magistrates' Courts Act 1978, Sched. 2.

[2] Guardianship of Minors Act 1971, s. 13 (3). See *ante*, pp. 511-515 and 570-571.

[3] See *ante*, p. 369.

[4] Presumably sums may be made payable to a local authority if the child is committed to its care.

[5] The provisions relating to the parents' cohabitation if a child over 18 is not residing with them and the period of three months (compared with six months under the Domestic Proceedings and Magistrates' Courts Act) are anomalous: see Law Com. Working Paper No. 74 (Illegitimacy), para. 4.66. They reflect provisions formerly contained in the Guardianship of Minors Act 1971, now repealed.

4. ILLEGITIMATE CHILDREN: AFFILIATION ORDERS

At common law neither the father nor the mother is liable to maintain an illegitimate child.[1] Although the Poor Law legislation cast upon the mother the obligation of maintaining her illegitimate child, she could still not recover the expenses of maintenance from the father in the absence of any contract to that effect between them.[2] A statute of 1576 empowered justices to make an order on the putative father' for the maintenance of an illegitimate child charged on the parish,[3] but it was not until the Poor Law Amendment Act of 1844 that the mother was given the power to apply for an order for maintenance to be paid to herself. The law was amended and consolidated in the Bastardy Laws Amendment Act of 1872 and again in the Affiliation Proceedings Act 1957. The principle of the Act of 1957 is that a "single woman" who is with child or who has been delivered of an illegitimate child may apply to a magistrates' court for a summons to be served on the man she alleges to be the father; if the court adjudges him to be the putative father, it may make an order (known as an affiliation order) that he shall pay maintenance in respect of the child.

If a man has been adjudged to be the father of a child in affiliation proceedings, this is *prima facie* evidence (which may be rebutted) of the fact of his paternity in any subsequent *civil* proceedings, whether or not he is a party to them.[4]

Who may apply for an Order.—In order to apply for an order the mother must prove that she was a "single woman".[5] It is obvious that an unmarried woman—whether she is a spinster, widow or divorced—comes within this category. In certain circumstances a married woman may also be a "single woman" for the purpose of the Act: in order to enable her to look to the putative father for the maintenance of her child, "the courts will have regard to the *de facto* position ... rather than to her status in the eyes of the law".[6] She may not bring proceedings, however, if she is still cohabiting with her husband;[7] in such circumstances, of course, he will usually have treated the child as a child of the family and thus be responsible for his maintenance himself. In most cases the birth of the child will mean that the wife has committed adultery which, if uncondoned, will have deprived her of the right to her husband's consortium and, at common law, to the right to be maintained by him.[8] But provided at least that there is no immediate prospect of

---

[1] *Ruttinger* v. *Temple* (1863), 4 B. & S. 491. In *Hesketh* v. *Gowing* (1804), 5 Esp. 131, the father was held liable if he adopted the child as his own, but today it would probably be necessary to establish an authority to incur expenses on the child's behalf by the person seeking reimbursement.

[2] As to agreements to pay maintenance, see *post*, p. 603.

[3] 18 Eliz. 1, c. 3.

[4] Civil Evidence Act 1968, s. 12.

[5] Affiliation Proceedings Act 1957, ss. 1 and 2 (2).

[6] *Per* DEVLIN, J., in *Kruhlak* v. *Kruhlak*, [1958] 2 K.B. 32, 36; [1958] 1 All E.R. 154, 155. See Douglas, 95 L.Q.R. 196.

[7] The test of cohabitation is presumably the same as in the case of desertion (see *ante*, pp. 208-210): *cf. Watson* v. *Tuckwell* (1947), 63 T.L.R. 634, followed in *Whitton* v. *Garner*, [1965] 1 All E.R. 70, and *Giltrow* v. *Day*, [1965] 1 All E.R. 73.

[8] *Cf. Jones* v. *Evans*, [1944] K.B. 582; [1945] 1 All E.R. 19; *Hockaday* v. *Goodenough*, [1945] 2 All E.R. 335.

reconciliation, the separation may be due to any other cause—for example, the husband's desertion or absence on military service[1] or the spouses' living apart under a court order[2] or perhaps a separation agreement. On the other hand, a married woman may not bring affiliation proceedings if the separation is purely colourable in an attempt to give the court jurisdiction[3] or, possibly, if she is in desertion and could bring the separation to an end by the simple expedient of returning to her husband who is anxious to receive her back.[4] In each of these cases she has voluntarily reduced herself to the status of a single woman and may not be permitted to take advantage of her own conduct.

Earlier legislation required the mother to be a "single woman" at the time she made her application. This worked hardship on a woman who was "single" at the time of the child's birth but who had married or become reconciled with her husband before applying for an order. Consequently section 4 of the Legitimacy Act 1959 now provides that such a woman can apply for an order: in other words the complainant must show that she was a "single woman" at the time of the child's birth or at the time of the application (or, of course, on both occasions).[5] But if the husband condoned her adultery before the child's birth and continued to live with her so that she was never a "single woman", she cannot apply for an order at all and the father may escape all liability. It is regrettable that he should be in a better position if the husband tries to keep the marriage together and there is now no justification for requiring the mother to be a "single woman" in any circumstances.

Effect of Adoption.—No application for an affiliation order may be made in respect of an adopted child, even if he is adopted by his mother as sole adoptive parent. He is to be treated in law as though he was the legitimate child of the adopter or adopters and of no other person and consequently can no longer be regarded as the illegitimate child of his putative father.[6]

Jurisdiction.—The jurisdiction to make affiliation orders (like magistrates' jurisdiction generally) is based upon the parties' residence, and as a general rule the court cannot make an order unless both the mother and the defendant are resident in England.[7] The difficulties which occur when one of

---

[1] *Jones* v. *Evans*, (*supra*). In *Mooney* v. *Mooney*, [1953] 1 Q.B. 38; [1952] 2 All E.R. 812, LORD GODDARD, C.J., left open the question whether the wife would be a "single woman" if her husband were serving a long sentence of imprisonment, although he apparently thought that she would be. In *R.* v. *Pilkington* (1853), 2 E. & B. 546, it was held that an affiliation order could be made when the applicant's husband was serving a sentence of transportation in Van Diemen's Land.

[2] *Kruhlak* v. *Kruhlak*, (*supra*); *Boyce* v. *Cox*, [1922] 1 K.B. 149.

[3] *Jones* v. *Davies*, [1901] 1 Q.B. 118.

[4] *Mooney* v. *Mooney*, (*supra*), as explained in *Kruhlak* v. *Kruhlak*, (*supra*). In both these cases the wife was bringing proceedings against her own husband in respect of a child which (as the law then stood) had not been legitimated by their marriage. Although DEVLIN, J., was considering only this exceptional situation, his words are sufficiently wide to cover all married applicants. (See [1958] 2 Q.B. at p. 37. The report in [1958] 1 All E.R. at p. 156 is to the opposite effect and must be wrong.)

[5] *Gaines* v. *W.*, [1968] 1 Q.B. 782; [1968] 1 All E.R. 189.

[6] See *ante*, p. 357.

[7] Affiliation Proceedings Act 1957, s. 3, as amended by the Domestic Proceedings and Magistrates' Courts Act 1978, s. 49; *Berkley* v. *Thompson* (1884), 10 App. Cas. 45, H.L.

them has moved to another country have been partly alleviated by the provisions of section 3 of the Maintenance Orders Act 1950[1] if both of them are still resident in the United Kingdom. If the defendant resides in England, the mother can apply for an order here if she resides in Scotland or Northern Ireland; if she resides in England, she can apply for an order here if the defendant resides in Scotland or Northern Ireland *and* the act of intercourse resulting in the child's birth (or any act of intercourse which might have had this effect) took place in England.[2] If the defendant is living in a "reciprocating country", the mother can now apply for an order under Part I of the Maintenance Orders (Reciprocal Enforcement) Act 1972.[3]

For years the question of jurisdiction was bedevilled by the historical connection between affiliation proceedings and the old Poor Law which turned largely on the settlement of the person seeking relief. The effect of this was that the mother's power to apply for an order was limited if the child was not born in this country. There is no longer any justification for this rule and the Court of Appeal seized the opportunity of overruling a number of old cases in *R*. v. *Bow Road Domestic Proceedings Court; ex parte Adedigba*[4] and laid down the principle that, provided the residence qualification is satisfied, the place of the child's birth is completely irrelevant.

Time Limit upon Application for Summons.—In order to prevent the mother from commencing proceedings some time after the birth of the child, when the defendant might find it difficult to adduce rebutting evidence, the summons must be applied for within one of the following periods:[5]

(1) Before the birth of the child; *or*
(2) Within three years of the child's birth; *or*
(3) At any time if the defendant has paid money for the child's maintenance within three years of its birth;[6] *or*
(4) Within twelve months of the defendant's return to England, if he ceased to reside in England either before the child's birth[7] or within three years after the birth.

---

[1] As amended by the Domestic Proceedings and Magistrates' Courts Act 1978, Sched. 2.
[2] Scottish and Northern Irish courts have a similar jurisdiction.
[3] See *ante*, pp. 519-520.
[4] [1968] 2 Q.B. 572; [1968] 2 All E.R. 89, C.A. The case raises two questions. Is normal residence necessary or is physical presence sufficient? On this point, see von Landauer in 17 I.C.L.Q. 1015. Does the child also have to be present in this country? SALMON, L.J., implied that this was not necessary (at pp. 581 and 94, respectively): the residence of the child seems irrelevant if the mother is remitting money for its maintenance elsewhere.
[5] Affiliation Proceedings Act 1957, ss. 1 and 2, as amended by the Affiliation Proceedings (Amendment) Act 1972, s. 2 (1). There is no time limit if the mother and the defendant were parties to a marriage which would have been valid but for the statutory provisions making it void because one of them had not attained the age of 16, provided that the defendant had access to the mother within the twelve months preceding the birth: Affiliation Proceedings Act 1957, s. 2 (2), as amended.
[6] Payment by the father's agent will bind him if he authorised it: see *G. (A.)* v. *G. (T.)*, [1970] 2 Q.B. 643; [1970] 3 All E.R. 546, C.A. Provision of maintenance in kind paid for out of money coming from the father (*e.g.*, when the child is living in the father's household) is equivalent to the payment of money for this purpose: *Roberts* v. *Roberts*, [1962] P. 212; [1962] 2 All E.R. 967.
[7] *R*. v. *Evans*, [1896] 1 Q.B. 228. Presumably this applies equally if the child was conceived abroad and the defendant has never resided in England.

But even if the applicant relies on period (3) or (4), no order may be made if the child is over the age of 18.[1]

Procedure.—The application is heard before a magistrates' court sitting as a domestic court.[2] The mother is not bound to give evidence, for the defendant may admit paternity, but if she does, it must be corroborated in some material particular.[3] Of more importance now is the court's power to direct blood tests;[4] but it must be remembered that the burden of proving paternity is upon the applicant, so that if there are two or more men, any of whom might be the father, an affiliation order may be made against none of them.

Appeals.—Either party may appeal to the Crown Court. Such an appeal is a rehearing of the case; consequently, if the mother gives evidence, the court must not reach a decision in her favour unless it is corroborated.[5] An appeal will also lie, on a point of law only, to the High Court. This may be brought by either party and is by way of a case stated by the magistrates' court which heard the summons or by the Crown Court which heard the appeal.[6]

Subsequent Applications.—Before the passing of the Criminal Justice Administration Act in 1914 the mother had no power to appeal if the court dismissed her application. This, coupled with the fact that the court may not declare that the defendant is not the putative father of her child in such circumstances, led the Court of Queen's Bench in *R.* v. *Machen*[7] to hold that it could not have been Parliament's intention that a magistrates' court should finally adjudicate against the mother and that consequently a dismissal of the application—even on the merits of the case—did not prevent the mother from making a second application within the statutory time limit. Although it is no longer true that the mother has no right of appeal, the court still cannot finally adjudicate against the mother in the sense that it may not declare that the defendant is not the putative father, and the Queen's Bench Division therefore held in *Robinson* v. *Williams*[8] that a dismissal is in the nature of a non-suit and that consequently a second application may still be made provided that the mother produces some evidence other than that led before, for the court cannot be asked to come to a different conclusion on identical evidence.[9] On the other hand, it has been held that if a magistrates' court

---

[1] Affiliation Proceedings Act 1957, s. 6 (1), as substituted by the Domestic Proceedings and Magistrates' Courts Act 1978, s. 52 (1).

[2] Magistrates' Courts Act 1980, s. 65 (1) (d).

[3] Affiliation Proceedings Act 1957, s. 4 (1), as amended by the Affiliation Proceedings (Amendment) Act 1972, s. 1 (1). For a detailed examination of the cases on affiliation, see Chislett, *Affiliation Proceedings*, 27-32.

[4] See *ante*, pp. 262-265.

[5] Affiliation Proceedings Act 1957, s. 8, as amended by the Courts Act 1971, s. 56 (2) and Sched. 9, and the Affiliation Proceedings (Amendment) Act 1972, s. 1 (3).

[6] Magistrates' Courts Act 1980, s. 111; Courts Act 1971, s. 10. Either party may also apply to the High Court for an order of *certiorari* if the magistrates' court lacked jurisdiction or acted in breach of the rules of natural justice.

[7] (1849), 14 Q.B. 74.

[8] [1965] 1 Q.B. 89; [1964] 3 All E.R. 12, following *R.* v. *Sunderland Justices*, [1945] K.B. 502; [1945] 2 All E.R. 175.

[9] But this need not be "fresh evidence" in the sense of evidence that could not have been obtained with reasonable diligence at the first hearing: *Robinson* v. *Williams*, (*supra*). The

makes an order and the father appeals to the Crown Court which quashes the order *on the merits of the case*, the mother may not then make a second application to a magistrates' court,[1] but if the Crown Court allows the appeal on a technical point and not on the merits, this does not prevent the mother from making a fresh application.[2] As the Crown Court has no more power to make a declaration that the defendant is not the father of the applicant's child than a magistrates' court has, this distinction is quite illogical and indefensible.

Orders that may be made.—If the court adjudges the defendant to be the putative father of the child, it may further order him to make periodical payments for the child's maintenance and education or a lump sum payment not exceeding £500 (or both).[3] In assessing what order to make, the court must take into account the income, earning capacity, property and other financial resources of both parents, their financial needs, obligations and responsibilities, the child's financial needs and resources (if any) and also any physical or mental disability from which he may suffer.[4] Although the mother may claim nothing for her own maintenance, the court may presumably take into account expenses incurred by her over and above those of feeding and clothing the child, for example increased rent due to her having to live in more expensive accommodation and loss of income caused by the child's birth and the necessity of having to look after it.[5] Difficulty arises if the parents' standard of living is very different: should the court be guided by that of the father or that of the mother? Suppose, for example, that the mother is a woman who is never likely to enjoy a high income and the father is a "pop star" earning a very high salary. Although one feels that the child (for whose benefit the order is being made) ought not to be prejudiced by his mother's position, it might be equally unwise to drive a wedge between him and any brothers and sisters he might have later by giving him an undue advantage over them.[6] In such a case it is regrettable that, as only magistrates

---

application of this rule to a paternity issue arising in proceedings under the Guardianship of Minors Act in *Re F. (W.)*, [1969] 2 Ch. 269; [1969] 3 All E.R. 595, seems wholly misconceived. (The second application was in fact dismissed because the evidence was identical.)

[1] *R. v. Howard*, [1938] 2 K.B. 544; [1938] 3 All E.R. 241.

[2] *R. v. May* (1880), 5 Q.B.D. 382. If the Crown Court quashes the order because of insufficiency of corroborative evidence, this is a decision on the merits and the mother may not make a fresh application: *R. v. Howard, (supra)*. Presumably if the *mother* appeals to the Crown Court from a dismissal of the application and her appeal is dismissed on the merits, she may not then make a second application to a magistrates' court.

[3] Affiliation Proceedings Act 1957, s. 4 (2), (5), as amended by the Domestic Proceedings and Magistrates' Courts Act 1978, s. 50. A lump sum may be made payable by instalments (which may be varied), and the maximum sum that may be ordered may be increased by an order made by the Secretary of State: *ibid.*, ss. 4 (5) and 6A (5), as amended and added by ss. 50 and 53 of the 1978 Act. *Cf. ante*, p. 585.

[4] *Ibid.*, s. 4 (3), as amended by s. 50 (2) of the 1978 Act.

[5] *Cf. Northrop v. Northrop*, [1968] P. 74; [1967] 2 All E.R. 961, C.A.

[6] Bevan, *Children*, 492, suggests that the standard is that which the child would be reasonably likely to enjoy if the parents were married. The father's financial position was taken into account in *Haroutunian v. Jennings* (1977), 7 Fam. Law 210. The fact that payments will merely reduce the amount of supplementary benefit that the mother can claim and will not increase her total income is irrelevant: *ibid. (Cf. ante*, p. 507.)

have jurisdiction, it is impossible to order periodical payments to be secured and thus safeguard the child's position should the father become penniless in a few years' time.

A lump sum is likely to be ordered in the same circumstances as a lump sum for a child under the Domestic Proceedings and Magistrates' Courts Act 1978.[1] The Act further provides that, in particular, a lump sum may be ordered to meet liabilities and expenses already incurred in connection with the birth and maintenance of the child and also with the funeral expenses if it has died before the making of the order.[2]

Unless the court otherwise orders, an affiliation order is not to run in the first instance beyond the date of the birthday of the child next following his attaining the upper limit of the compulsory school age, but it may be extended. It may continue in force after his eighteenth birthday, however, only in the same circumstances as an order made for a child's benefit under the 1978 Act.[3]

Payments may be made to the mother for the benefit of the child or to the child himself.[4] The advantages that may accrue from making payments to the child have been explained when dealing with the 1978 Act.[5] Unless the court otherwise orders, they must be made through a magistrates' clerk.[6]

After the mother's death or whilst she is of unsound mind or confined in prison, the court may grant the custody of the child to any other person and order payments to be made to him.[7] In addition, the court may, upon the application of any person for the time being having the custody of the child, make or vary an order so as to provide that the payments shall be made to the applicant.[8] Although the word "make" suggests that a person other than the mother may apply for an order in the first instance, this, it is submitted, is not possible, for all affiliation proceedings must be commenced by her; the hardship of this can be seen in the case where the mother leaves her child to be brought up by someone else and then refuses to apply for an affiliation order so that that other person has no means of getting the father to contribute to the child's maintenance.

There is, however, in certain circumstances a power vested in local authorities to apply for an affiliation order even though the mother has not done so, for if an illegitimate child is in the care of the authority either under a care order (other than an interim order) or under section 2 of the Child Care Act 1980[9] the authority may apply for an order.[10] Apart from the fact that an

---

[1] See *ante*, p. 588.

[2] Affiliation Proceedings Act 1957, s. 4 (4) (added by s. 50 (2) of the 1978 Act). But the child must have been born alive. No order may be made at all if it was still-born: *R.* v. *De Brouquens* (1811), 14 East 277.

[3] *Ibid.*, s. 6, as substituted by s. 52 (1) of the 1978 Act. See *ante*, p. 586. The order can normally be backdated to the making of the application, but if proceedings are brought before the child's birth or within two months after it, the order may run from the date of the birth.

[4] *Ibid.*, s. 5 (1), as amended by s. 51 (1) of the 1978 Act.

[5] See *ante*, p. 586.

[6] Magistrates' Courts Act 1980, s. 59 (1), (2). *Cf. ante*, p. 504.

[7] Affiliation Proceedings Act 1957, s. 5 (4), as amended by s. 51 (3) of the 1978 Act.

[8] *Ibid.*, s. 5 (3), as amended by s. 51 (2) of the 1978 Act. The applicant must have custody either legally or by virtue of an arrangement approved by the court.

[9] See *ante*, pp. 393 and 395. A contribution (see *ante*, p. 401) can also be made against the mother.

[10] Child Care Act 1980, s. 50. See further Bevan, *op. cit.*, 496-497.

application may be made within three years of the making of the care order or of the child's being taken into the authority's care, the procedure is the same as when the mother herself applies.[1] Moreover, if an affiliation order is already in force, it may be varied in similar circumstances so as to make the sums payable to the local authority concerned.[2] In one respect, however, the liability of the putative father is less if the child is in the care of a local authority, for no application can be made to extend the duration of the affiliation order beyond the child's sixteenth birthday unless he is permitted to reside with the mother.[3]

Variation and Discharge of Orders.—The court which made the order has a general power to vary, suspend, revive or revoke periodical payments. On an application for variation it may order the father to pay a lump sum not exceeding £500. The child himself may apply for a variation if he is over the age of 16.[4] Two specific cases of the variation of an order have already been noticed—the extension of it after the child has reached the age of 17 and a direction that payments under it shall be made to someone other than the mother. Changes in the financial circumstances of either the mother or the putative father may well, of course, lead either of them to ask for the amount payable to be increased or decreased.

The death of the child automatically discharges the order as does the death of the putative father, whose liability upon it is purely personal.[5] The order will also be discharged if the child is adopted.[6] On the other hand, as we have already seen, the order is not discharged by the mother's death; nor does liability upon it cease if she subsequently marries[7] or resumes cohabitation with her husband[8] although the fact that the latter is capable of supporting the child might well be relevant if the putative father applied for a variation of the order. Just as the mother cannot deprive herself of the power to apply for an order by entering into an agreement with the putative father,[9] an existing order will not be discharged by any agreement between them.[10]

Enforcement of Affiliation Orders.—The methods by which affiliation orders may be enforced have already been discussed when dealing with

---

[1] Presumably, therefore, if the mother gives evidence, it must be corroborated, but an order may be made even though she was not a "single woman", for the Affiliation Proceedings Act merely requires that the *applicant* shall be a "single woman". *Cf. post*, p. 602 (supplementary benefit).

[2] Child Care Act 1980, s. 49.

[3] Affiliation Proceedings Act 1957, s. 7 (4), (5), (6). The parents of a legitimate child are not required to contribute to his maintenance in such circumstances after he has reached the age of 16: see *ante*, p. 401.

[4] Magistrates' Courts Act 1980, s. 60; Affiliation Proceedings Act 1957, s. 6A (added by s. 53 of the 1978 Act). There is no power to revoke, revive or vary the order in so far as it relates to the adjudication of paternity: *Colchester* v. *Peck*, [1926] 2 K.B. 366; *R.* v. *Copestake*, [1927] 1 K.B. 468, C.A. For the position where one of the parties is outside the jurisdiction, see the Maintenance Orders (Reciprocal Enforcement) Act 1972, s. 41, as amended by Sched. 2 of the 1978 Act.

[5] Affiliation Proceedings Act 1957, s. 6 (5), as substituted by s. 52 (1) of the 1978 Act.

[6] See *ante*, p. 357.

[7] But if she marries the father, the legitimation of the child may be a ground for applying for the order to be discharged.

[8] *Hardy* v. *Atherton* (1881), 7 Q.B.D. 264; *R.* v. *Pilkington* (1835), 2 E. & B. 546.

[9] See *post*, p. 603.

[10] *Griffith* v. *Evans* (1882), 46 L.T. 417.

maintenance orders made under the Domestic Proceedings and Magistrates' Courts Act which are enforceable in the same way.[1] As in the case of other orders, magistrates hearing proceedings for enforcement may remit the whole or any part of the arrears. An affiliation order may also be registered and enforced in the High Court.[2]

Recent research into the whole question of affiliation orders fills one with grave disquiet. Comparatively few orders are made, they are usually for small sums, and many lapse after a few years. Many of the problems are personal and social, for example the mother's reluctance to invoke the law, the poverty of many fathers (who will often be young men earning very little), and the tendency of the parties to lose touch with each other. As a result mothers of illegitimate children frequently have to rely on assistance provided by the state and their plight can be alleviated only by an improvement in the benefit payable to them.[3]

5. ILLEGITIMATE CHILDREN: OTHER FINANCIAL PROVISIONS

Supplementary Benefit.—Under the Supplementary Benefits Act 1976, the mother of an illegitimate child and a man adjudged to be its putative father are liable to maintain it until it reaches the age of 16.[4] If assistance is given by reference to the requirements of an illegitimate child, the Secretary of State may recover the cost from the mother in the same way as he could in the case of a legitimate child; if (as will be more likely) it is desired to recover the cost from the putative father, he must apply to have the affiliation order varied so that the sums under it are made payable direct to him. If no affiliation order is already in existence,[5] the Secretary of State himself may apply for one within three years of giving assistance. This power is quite independent of the mother's, so that the Secretary of State may obtain an order even though the mother could not apply because her application would be out of time or she was not a "single woman", and even though the Crown Court has already dismissed an appeal by her on its merits; but in all other respects the provisions of the Affiliation Proceedings Act must be complied with, as in the case where a local authority applies for an order under the power given to it by the Child Care Act 1980.[6]

An order in favour of the Secretary of State may be varied in favour of the mother or anyone else having custody of the child.[7] It will thus be seen that the mother of an illegitimate child who is out of time to apply for an order

---

[1] See *ante*, pp. 511-515. For the power to deduct sums due under an affiliation order from the pay of a serving member of the armed forces, see *ante*, p. 489.

[2] Maintenance Orders Act 1958, s. 21. See *ante*, pp. 570-571.

[3] See McGregor, Blom-Cooper and Gibson, *Separated Spouses*, c. 11; the Report of the Committee on One-parent Families (the Finer Report), Cmnd. 5629, *passim*.

[4] S. 17, as amended by the Social Security Act 1980, Sched. 2.

[5] *I.e.*, no order requiring payments to be made to the mother. An order adjudging the defendant to be the putative father *simpliciter* does not prevent the Secretary of State from applying: *Oldfield* v. *National Assistance Board*, [1960] 1 Q.B. 635; [1960] 1 All E.R. 524.

[6] Supplementary Benefits Act 1976, s. 19, as amended by the Social Security Act 1980, Sched. 2; *National Assistance Board* v. *Mitchell*, [1956] 1 Q.B. 53; [1955] 3 All E.R. 291; *National Assistance Board* v. *Tugby*, [1957] 1 Q.B. 506; [1957] 1 All E.R. 509; *Clapham* v. *National Assistance Board*, [1961] 2 Q.B. 77; [1961] 2 All E.R. 50. For local authorities' powers under the Child Care Act, see *ante*, pp. 600-601.

[7] Supplementary Benefits Act 1976, s. 19 (6) (as amended); *Payne* v. *Critchley*, [1962] 2 Q.B. 83; [1962] 1 All E.R. 619.

herself may nevertheless obtain the benefit of one if she receives supplementary benefit and the Secretary of State takes proceedings against the father.

Maintenance Agreements.—As early as 1842 it was recognised that an agreement between the mother and father of an illegitimate child that the latter should pay the former maintenance for the child was actionable.[1] The consideration for the father's promise has been variously stated: it is usually recognised as a counter-promise on the mother's part either to maintain the child herself (notwithstanding her liability to do so under the Supplementary Benefits Act)[2] or to refrain from taking affiliation proceedings.[3] If there is no agreement as to the time for which the father is to remain bound, it would seem that either side may terminate the contract by giving the other reasonable notice.[4] The father's liability will automatically terminate on the mother's death unless the parties otherwise agree, for her personal representatives cannot claim the benefit of the agreement without at the same time accepting the burden of maintaining the child—an obligation which will not normally have been contemplated.[5] On the other hand, since the father's obligation is not personal but can be met out of his estate, there seems to be no reason why his personal representatives should not be bound.[6]

In one respect agreements of this type seem singular, for it was held in *Follitt* v. *Koetzow*[7] that although the mother may sue the father on his promise to pay her maintenance made in consideration of her counter-promise not to take affiliation proceedings, this does not prevent her from commencing proceedings to obtain an affiliation order. Like the power to award maintenance in a matrimonial cause, the power to order the putative father to pay maintenance under an affiliation order is not given for the benefit of the mother alone and consequently she cannot by agreement deprive herself of the right to apply for it. Unlike agreements made in consideration of the wife's undertaking not to apply for maintenance in a matrimonial cause, however, these agreements are valid in so far as the mother may sue the father upon them: they therefore present what is probably a unique example of a promise which is valid for one purpose but contrary to public policy for another. But if the mother takes affiliation proceedings, this will obviously entitle the father to treat himself as discharged on his promise to pay maintenance and he could also presumably sue the mother for damages for breach of the contract. Moreover, the existence of the agreement is one of the factors which the court should take into consideration in determining the amount of maintenance to award.[8]

---

[1] *Jennings* v. *Brown* (1842), 9 M. & W. 496. *Cf. Tanner* v. *Tanner*, [1975] 3 All E.R. 776, C.A.

[2] *Ward* v. *Byham*, [1956] 2 All E.R. 318, C.A. Whilst this decision is in accordance with the merits of the case, it can be criticised on the ground that DENNING, L.J., held that the performance of an existing obligation can be valuable consideration (contrary to earlier authorities) and MORRIS and PARKER, L.JJ., did not discuss this point at all.

[3] *Jennings* v. *Brown*, (*supra*); *Linnegar* v. *Hodd* (1848), 5 C.B. 437.

[4] *Knowlman* v. *Bluett* (1873), L.R. 9 Exch. 1, Ex.; *ibid.*, 307, Ex. Ch.

[5] *James* v. *Morgan*, [1909] 1 K.B. 564.

[6] This was apparently accepted in *Jennings* v. *Brown*, (*supra*). In each case, of course, it will be a question of the construction of the particular contract.

[7] (1860), 2 E. & E. 730.

[8] *Follitt* v. *Koetzow*, (*supra*).

Chapter 17

Property and Financial Provision on the Death of a Member of the Family

A. TESTATE SUCCESSION

The law relating to wills and testate succession generally presents few problems peculiar to family law. Until the beginning of this century the most important question was the testamentary capacity of a married woman. At common law she had virtually no power to make a will at all,[1] although she could always devise and bequeath property held to her separate use in equity even if it were subject to a restraint upon anticipation.[2] When the equitable concept of separate property was extended to legal separate property by the Married Women's Property Act 1882, her power to dispose of it by will was likewise extended, so that her testamentary incapacity remained only with respect to property acquired by her before 1883. Now by the Law Reform (Married Women and Tortfeasors) Act 1935 she has full power to dispose of all her property as if she were a feme sole.

There are, however, still one or two matters of particular importance to spouses and children which we must note.

Revocation of Wills by Marriage.—By section 18 of the Wills Act 1837 every will made by a man or woman is revoked by his or her marriage.[3] This

---

[1] She had no power at all to dispose of realty and leaseholds, although she could exercise a power of appointment by will. With the consent of her husband copyholds could be surrendered to the use of her will. Although all her choses in possession vested in her husband, she could bequeath personalty if there were an ante-nuptial contract to that effect or if her husband assented to the bequest and did not revoke his consent before probate was granted. For further details, reference must be made to the editions of standard works on property, wills and married women published in the late nineteenth and early twentieth centuries.

[2] But until the passing of the Married Women's Property Act 1893, s. 3, a will made by a woman during coverture would not pass property acquired after the marriage was terminated unless it was republished after the termination of coverture.

[3] But this will not be a breach of an ante-nuptial contract not to revoke a will already made: *Re Marsland*, [1939] Ch. 820; [1939] 3 All E.R. 148, C.A. For a full review of the problems posed by this section, see the 22nd Report of the Law Reform Committee 1980 (Cmnd. 7902). The Committee felt that no case had been made out for altering the law except in certain detailed respects. A decree of divorce or nullity does not affect a will made during the marriage; this may obviously work an injustice and consequently both the Morton Commission (1956, Cmd. 9678, paras. 1187-1191) and the majority of the Law Reform Committee recommended that in such a

applies only to persons domiciled in England at the time of the marriage; consequently if by the testator's *lex domicilii* his will was not revoked by his marriage, it will not be automatically revoked if he later acquires an English domicile.[1] Nor will the section apply if the marriage is void.[2]

There are two exceptions to the general rule. First, section 18 itself provides that a will shall not be revoked insofar as it is made in exercise of a power of appointment if the property thereby appointed would not pass in default of appointment to the testator's heir, executor, administrator or statutory next-of-kin.[3] The reason for this exception is obvious: the marriage cannot conceivably affect the devolution of the property appointed. Secondly, in order to fulfil the intention of the testator who makes his will on the eve of his wedding, section 177 of the Law of Property Act 1925 now provides that "a will expressed to be made in contemplation of a marriage shall ... not be revoked by the solemnisation of the marriage contemplated". In order to bring this section into operation two conditions must be satisfied: the testator must express the fact that he is contemplating marriage with a particular person and the ensuing marriage must be to that person. Hence the mere fact that the will is expressed to be made in contemplation of marriage will not save it unless there is a reference to the particular marriage by which it is followed.[4] Generally speaking, however, the courts have construed the section liberally and have caught at straws to save wills, the revocation of which would deprive surviving spouses of substantial legacies. This has produced some very fine distinctions, the application of which is likely to cause difficulty in the future. In *In the Estate of Langston*,[5] for example, a will by which the testator devised and bequeathed his whole estate "unto my fiancée M.E.B." was held not to have been revoked by his marriage to that lady two months later. In *Re Coleman*,[6] however, MEGARRY, J., held that a will was not saved when the testator made bequests and a devise "unto my fiancée M.J." but gave the residue of his estate (amounting to more than half of it) to others. MEGARRY, J.'s argument, that the bequests and the devise to the fiancée indicated that the particular clauses were made in contemplation of marriage but that the section could not save a will of which only bits were so made, is unconvincing. Testators do not make parts of a will in

---

case a gift to, or appointment in favour of, a former spouse should lapse unless the testator expressly directs to the contrary.

[1] *In the Goods of Reid* (1886), L.R. 1 P. & D. 74; *In the Goods of Groos*, [1904] P. 269. Contrast *Re Martin*, [1900] P. 211, C.A. (woman's will revoked by her acquisition of English domicile on marriage).

[2] *Mette* v. *Mette* (1859), 1 Sw. & Tr. 416.

[3] Hence the will may be revoked in part but not insofar as the power is exercised: *In the Goods of Russell* (1890), 15 P.D. 111. See also *In the Goods of Gilligan*, [1950] P. 32; [1949] 2 All E.R. 401; Mitchell, *The Revocation of Testamentary Appointments on Marriage*, 67 L.Q.R. 351.

[4] *Sallis* v. *Jones*, [1936] P. 43. In *Pilot* v. *Gainfort*, [1931] P. 103, the testator made a will by which he bequeathed his personalty to "D.F.P. my wife". Although he was living with her at the time, he did not marry her until 18 months later. It was held that the will was made in contemplation of this marriage and was therefore not revoked. *Sed quaere*? On the face of the will it appeared that the testator was *already* married.

[5] [1953] P. 100; [1953] 1 All E.R. 928.

[6] [1976] Ch. 1; [1975] 1 All E.R. 675. See Edwards and Langstaff, *The Will to survive Marriage*, 39 Conv. 121; 22nd Report of the Law Reform Committee, para. 3.18.

contemplation of marriage, and if the clauses in question indicate such an intention, the whole will must be so made. Difficulty arises from the fact that the question is one of construction and extrinsic evidence of the testator's intention is inadmissible;[1] consequently it is frequently impossible to tell whether, by making a gift to his fiancée, he was providing for his future spouse or was merely making a temporary arrangement in case he should die before the proposed marriage took place. If he leaves his whole estate to her, it can be inferred that the former was his intention; in other cases the court may well say that it has insufficient evidence to bring section 177 into operation.[2]

Mutual Wills.—Although mutual wills are rare, they are still occasionally made, and they are of particular interest in family law since mutual testators are almost invariably husband and wife. They usually take the form of a gift to the second testator provided that he survives the first with identical remainders over on the death of the survivor; alternatively (and this will have the same effect) each gives an absolute interest to the other with identical provisions in case the beneficiary predeceases the testator.[3] The peculiarity of mutual wills is that, provided certain conditions are satisfied, the survivor is bound by the provisions of his or her own will after the death of the other testator and cannot revoke it—the property of both, in other words becomes subject to a trust in favour of the remaindermen.

The trust arises out of the agreement between the testators. Hence, in the first place it must be affirmatively proved that the wills were made in pursuance of an agreement: whilst their very execution is some evidence of an agreement to that effect, it is by no means conclusive.[4] Secondly, it is clear that the trust does not take effect until one of the two testators dies, and if either revokes his or her will before then, the other is not bound and is free to make any other disposition before or after the death of the first. But what is not clear is whether the party revoking is bound to give notice of this to the other. The basis of the doctrine is that the survivor, having let the other die in the belief that he will not go back on the bargain, will not be permitted to do so after the will of the first takes effect. Now let us suppose that A and B are the testators and that A secretly revokes his will before B's death. If A dies first, B is bound to know of the revocation and may make a fresh will: hence the mutual wills create no trust.[5] But if B dies first unaware of the revocation, it seems contrary to the whole basis of the rule to permit A to take the benefits under B's will without at the same time being bound by the bargain.[6]

---

[1] *Re Coleman*, (*supra*), at pp. 11 and 683, respectively.

[2] The surviving spouse now needs less protection because of the substantial sums that she (or he) takes on intestacy and the court's wide powers to make financial provision for a dependant under the Inheritance (Provision for Families and Dependants) Act (see *post*, pp. 617 and 623-638). But other beneficiaries, with no alternative claim, may be deprived of their gifts by revocation. See Tiley, [1975] C.L.J. 205; Bates, 129 New L.J. 547.

[3] But since the apparent intention to make an absolute gift is inconsistent with the life interest that will result, it will probably be easier to rebut the presumption of a trust in such a case: see *Re Oldham*, [1925] Ch. 75, 88.

[4] *Re Oldham*, (*supra*); *Gray* v. *Perpetual Trustee Co., Ltd.*, [1928] A.C. 391, P.C.

[5] *Stone* v. *Hoskins*, [1905] P. 194.

[6] See LORD CAMDEN, L.C., in *Dufour* v. *Pereira* (1769), 1 Dick. 419, 420-421; 2 Hargr. Jurid. Arg. 304.

Thirdly, it is still not clear whether the survivor is bound by the agreement if he disclaims the gift to himself. The dicta are conflicting,[1] but since the trust arises from the prior agreement, the better view is that it is automatically impressed on the property on the first party's death and the survivor's accepting the gift is therefore immaterial.[2]

If these conditions are satisfied, the trust takes effect from the moment the first testator dies.[3] Consequently the remaindermen have a vested interest from this time, and the gifts to them will not lapse if they die after this date but before the surviving testator.[4] But even now it is not settled whether any property acquired by the survivor after the first party's death is also subject to the trust or whether this will attach only to the property which he has at that time.[5] Since the beneficiaries may not know that the wills were mutual until the death of the surviving testator, not the least of the practical difficulties is to see how he can effectively be prevented from disposing of the trust property *inter vivos*.[6]

Gifts to the Testator's Wife or Husband.—Provided that this was obviously the testator's intention, a gift to the testator's wife (or husband) will take effect in favour of a woman (or man) with whom he (or she) is living as husband and wife even though they are not legally married.[7] Such a gift will even be valid if it is directed to be held on trust during widowhood; in this case it will be construed as being determinable upon the other's contracting a valid marriage after the testator's death.[8]

It will be observed that, unlike the position on intestacy,[9] the surviving spouse cannot demand that the matrimonial home or personal chattels should be appropriated as part of a gift (for example, a residuary bequest). If they have not been specifically disposed of by the will, the only thing a widow or widower wishing to retain such property can do is to ask the personal representatives to exercise their power of appropriation in this way.[10]

---

[1] See the different interpretations placed on LORD CAMDEN's judgment in *Dufour* v. *Pereira*, (*supra*), by LORD HAILSHAM, L.C., in *Gray* v. *Perpetual Trustee Co., Ltd.,* (*supra*), at p. 399, and by CLAUSON, J., in *Re Hagger*, [1930] 2 Ch. 190, 195. See Mitchell, *Some Aspects of Mutual Wills*, 14 M.L.R. 136.

[2] If this were not so and the survivor were the widow or widower of the other, he or she might disclaim the legacy and take the estate on intestacy, thus obtaining the benefit whilst going back on the agreement: Mitchell, *loc. cit.* See also Burgess, *A Fresh Look at Mutual Wills*, 34 Conv. 230, at p. 240.

[3] *Re Hagger*, (*supra*); *Re Green*, [1951] Ch. 148; [1950] 2 All E.R. 913.

[4] *Re Hagger*, (*supra*).

[5] See Mitchell, *loc. cit.*, for a fuller discussion of this and other difficulties.

[6] Mitchell, *loc. cit.*

[7] *Re Brown* (1910), 26 T.L.R. 257. *A fortiori* if he names her (*e.g.*, "to my wife E.A.S."): *Re Smalley*, [1929] 2 Ch. 112, C.A.

[8] Even though the "wife" is already married to another man: *Re Wagstaff*, [1908] 1 Ch. 162, C.A.; *Re Hammond*, [1911] 2 Ch. 342. The decision to the contrary in *Re Gale*, [1941] Ch. 209; [1941] 1 All E.R. 329, cannot be reconciled with these decisions and must be wrong. Contrast *Re Boddington* (1884), 25 Ch.D. 685, C.A., where it was held that a wife who had obtained a decree of nullity after the will was made but before the testator's death was not entitled to an annuity payable during widowhood. Neither can a divorced husband or wife be regarded as a *surviving* spouse: *Re Allan*, [1954] Ch. 295; [1954] 1 All E.R. 646, C.A. See Theobald, *Wills*, 13th Ed., 281-285.

[9] See *post*, pp. 617-619.

[10] For the personal representatives' powers of appropriation, see the Administration of Estates Act 1925, s. 41.

Gifts to Children.—The only problem that arises here is over the power of illegitimate, legitimated and adopted children to take under a testamentary disposition. This has already been discussed.[1]

Testamentary Gift to a Deceased Child.—In the normal way if a devisee or legatee predeceases the testator, the gift lapses and either it drops into residue or the testator is deemed to die intestate with respect to it. But by section 33 of the Wills Act 1837, if the beneficiary is a child or other issue of the testator, the gift does not lapse but takes effect as if the beneficiary had died immediately after the testator, provided that the interest is not determinable at or before the beneficiary's death and provided also that the beneficiary leaves issue living at the testator's death.[2] Just as the testator may prevent the usual rule from operating, a gift to issue will not be preserved if a contrary intention appears in the will.

It is not essential that the issue surviving the testator should be alive when the devisee or legatee died. Thus, suppose that A by his will made in 1977 bequeathed property to his son, B, and that B died in 1978 leaving a son, C, who in turn had a son, D, born in 1979. If C died in 1980 and A died in 1981, the legacy would not lapse, because D, who is issue of B, would be living on A's death even though he was not born till after B's death.[3] But it has been doubted whether a child *en ventre sa mère* is "issue living" for this purpose,[4] although it is submitted that it would be more in keeping with the spirit of the Act to include him in this class.

But this rule does not apply to class gifts, for it is always presumed that the testator intends the benefit to be taken by those members of the class alive at his death. Hence if the testator has three children, X, Y and Z when he makes his will and X predeceases him, a gift to the testator's children in general terms will pass the whole interest to Y and Z even though X leaves issue.[5] Further, although the testamentary exercise of a *general* power of appointment in favour of a child or other issue will not lapse if the person in whose favour the donee has exercised it predeceases him, the provision does not apply to the exercise of a *special* power which is not technically a devise or bequest for the purpose of the section and which will therefore lapse.[6]

Whilst it might appear that the purpose of the section is to enable the gift to be taken by the issue instead of the beneficiary named in accordance with

---

[1] *Ante*, pp. 575-581.

[2] The section operates even though the beneficiary had died before the will was made: *Wisden* v. *Wisden* (1854), 2 Sm. & G. 396. It always applied if the beneficiary was legitimated: *Re Brodie*, [1967] Ch. 818; [1967] 2 All E.R. 97. If the testator died on or after 1st January 1970, it will apply if the beneficiary or his issue was illegitimate or legitimated or is descended through such a person: Family Law Reform Act 1969, s. 16; Legitimacy Act 1976, s. 5 (3). For the difficulties caused by this provision, see Ryder, *Property Law Aspects of the Family Law Reform Act* 1969, Current Legal Problems 1971, 157, pp. 174-177.

[3] *In the Goods of Parker* (1860), 1 Sw. & Tr. 523.

[4] In *Re Griffiths' Settlement*, [1911] 1 Ch. 246, JOYCE, J., held that such a child was "issue living", but this was doubted by LORD TOMLIN and LORD RUSSELL in *Elliot* v. *Joicey*, [1935] A.C. 209, at pp. 216, 230, H.L.

[5] Even though in the event the class consists of only one member: *Re Harvey's Estate*, [1893] 1 Ch. 567. *Secus* if the gift had been to the children *by name* as tenants in common.

[6] *Eccles* v. *Cheyne* (1856), 2 K. & J. 676 (general power); *Holyland* v. *Lewin* (1883), 26 Ch.D. 266, C.A (special power).

the testator's presumed wish, this in fact is not so, and the gift forms a part of the deceased beneficiary's estate. Hence if the latter died an undischarged bankrupt, the gift passes directly to his trustee in bankruptcy.[1] Furthermore, all the modern cases (admittedly all at first instance) have followed the rule that the fiction that the child or other issue survives the testator is to be applied solely for the purpose of preventing the lapse and that for all other purposes the property must be dealt with on the assumption that the beneficiary in fact died when he did.[2] Hence a gift to the testator's daughter, who had covenanted to settle all property acquired during coverture and who predeceased the testator, was not caught by the covenant for it did not form a part of the daughter's estate until the coverture had been terminated by her death.[3] Again in *Re Basioli*,[4] where the testatrix's daughter died intestate in 1929 and the testatrix died in 1940, it was held that a devise and bequest to the daughter must be distributed on the assumption that she died in 1929 and not in 1940.

The Rule against Double Portions.—This rule is a direct application of the equitable presumption that a father or other person *in loco parentis* intends to favour none of his children at the expense of the others and in particular intends to divide his estate or fortune amongst them all equally. They may obviously take a share of this in two ways: by payments made to the child by the parent during the latter's lifetime, and by a gift to the child in the parent's will.[5] Consequently in certain circumstances, unless the presumption that all the children were to share alike can be rebutted, they must bring into account what they have received during the testator's lifetime before they can take the gift under the will. Hence equity is said "to lean against double portions".

But it is not every gift that the child received from the testator while he was alive that must be brought into account. Like the presumption of advancement, this rule applies only to gifts and payments made by his father or other person *in loco parentis* to him.[6] Further, it would clearly be impractical to make the beneficiary account for every penny received, and consequently he must bring in only such gifts as may fairly be called advancements by way of portion, that is, something given to the child to establish him in life. Whether or not this is the purpose of any particular payment must be a question of fact in each case: payments made to a child on his marriage always come into this category, and the gift of a substantial sum raises a presumption that it was

---

[1] *Re Pearson*, [1920] 1 Ch. 247.

[2] Some of the cases are discussed by UPJOHN, J., in *Re Basioli*, [1953] Ch. 367; [1953] 1 All E.R. 301. In *Re Mason's Will* (1865), 34 Beav. 494, it was questioned whether this was the right construction; *Re Hone's Trusts* (1883), 22 Ch.D. 663, is clearly inconsistent with the rule as stated in the text.

[3] *Pearce* v. *Graham* (1863), 32 L.J.Ch. 359. *Cf. Re Wolson*, [1939] Ch. 780; [1939] 3 All E.R. 852.

[4] [1953] Ch. 367; [1953] 1 All E.R. 301, following *Re Hurd*, [1941] Ch. 196; [1941] 1 All E.R. 238. A curious case of circuity arose in *Re Hensler* (1881), 19 Ch.D. 612, where a father devised realty to his son who predeceased him having devised all his realty to his father. HALL, V.C., held that the son's son took as the son's heir; the only way of breaking the vicious circle is to accept that, in this particular case, if the son is to be regarded as having survived the father, the father cannot also be regarded as surviving the son: see *Re Basioli*, at pp. 375-376 and 304, respectively.

[5] Or, of course, by the child's taking a benefit on the latter's intestacy: see *post*, p. 620.

[6] For the meaning of "person *in loco parentis*", see *ante*, pp. 573-574.

intended as an advancement by way of portion.[1] On the other hand, a mere bounty is not a portion,[2] nor is a payment made to extricate a child from financial embarrassment;[3] and a gift will not *prima facie* amount to an advancement by way of portion unless it is made early in life.[4] An instructive case is *Taylor* v. *Taylor*.[5] A father had two sons, A and B. A originally intended to go to the Bar and his father paid (1) his fees to enter the Middle Temple and (2) his fees to enter the chambers of a special pleader. Later A joined the army and the father then paid for (3) his commission, (4) his uniform, and (5) his outfit and his wife's passage when his regiment went to India. Whilst he was there, he became financially embarrassed and his father paid (6) his debts to the tune of £650. Finally A decided to go into mining in Wales and the father gave him (7) £850 to buy plant and materials. B on the other hand went into the Church and the father made several payments to him (on one occasion of £200) to assist him in his housekeeping. Of these sums it was held that (1), (3), (4) and (7) were all obviously portions. It was held that (2) was not as it "appeared to be rather in the nature of a payment for preliminary education", although it is submitted that a court today might hold otherwise.[6] (5) was not a portion as it clearly did nothing to set A up in any sort of career, nor was (6) as this was a payment made to extricate the son from financial embarrassment. Similarly the payments made to B were not portions, as they came into the category of casual payments intended as temporary assistance.

For brevity, an enforceable obligation to make an advancement by way of portion is known as a "portion debt". Thus, if a father on his daughter's marriage settles £5,000 on her, this will be a portion; if in consideration of her marriage he covenants to do so, his covenant will be a portion debt.

It will be seen that the rule against double portions may arise in three different situations.

(1) *Satisfaction of Portion Debts by Portions.* —This can be illustrated by *Re Lawes*.[7] The putative father of an illegitimate youth executed a bond

---

[1] *Re Hayward*, [1957] Ch. 528; [1957] 2 All E.R. 474, C.A.

[2] *Re Livesey*, [1953] 2 All E.R. 723; *Re Vaux*, [1939] Ch. 465, 481; [1938] 4 All E.R. 703, 709, C.A.

[3] *Taylor* v. *Taylor* (1875), L.R. 20 Eq. 155; *Re Scott*, [1903] 1 Ch. 1, C.A.

[4] *Re Hayward*, (*supra*), at pp. 538 and 479, respectively.

[5] (1875), L.R. 20 Eq. 155. This case reminds one of the parable of the prodigal son who, it will be recalled, asked his father "for his portion". See also *Re George's Will Trusts*, [1949] Ch. 154; [1948] 2 All E.R. 1004 (*post*, p. 614) (gift of live and dead stock with which son was to set up as a farmer held to be a portion); *Hardy* v. *Shaw*, [1976] Ch. 82; [1975] 2 All E.R. 1052 (substantial gift of shares giving children controlling interest in family printing business held to be portions).

[6] If payment for preliminary education is not to be regarded as advancement by way of portion, some anomalous results follow. Why should a son who becomes a barrister have to bring into account money payable before and on call, whilst another, who receives a professional training at a university, may not have to do so? If on the other hand money received for educational purposes is a portion, further anomalies arise. If the student lived away from home and were given, say, £6,000 to see him through the university, he would presumably have to bring it in; but if he lived at home and received pocket money from time to time, he would not have to do so.

[7] (1881), 20 Ch.D. 81, C.A.

whereby he bound himself to pay his son £10,000 on a certain day. A month before this day he took his son into partnership and brought in capital of £37,500, of which £19,000 was to be considered as belonging to the son. The £10,000 was never paid and when the son sought to claim it from the father's personal representatives after the father's death, it was held that the debt had been satisfied by the gift of the capital.

But the debt and the gift must be *ejusdem generis* if the latter is to satisfy the former. In *Re Lawes* all the members of the Court of Appeal were agreed that the father had in effect given his son a gift of the sum of £19,000; but had he given him a share of the partnership property without putting a value on it or, say, given him a gift of land without specifying its value, it seems clear that this would have been essentially different from the sum of £10,000 which the father was bound to pay and therefore would not have satisfied the debt.[1]

It will be seen that the child is not bound to take the gift: it is his voluntarily doing so that extinguishes the contractual obligation. If the portion is of the same value as the debt or of greater value, the latter will be satisfied entirely. If it is of less value, it will presumably be satisfied *pro tanto*.[2]

(2) *Satisfaction of Portion Debts by Legacies.*—Let us suppose that a father, in consideration of his daughter's marriage, covenants to pay her the sum of £5,000. He later makes a will by which he gives her and her brother a legacy of £5,000 each. The rule against double portions comes into play and *prima facie* she is entitled to only one sum of £5,000. She is immediately put to her election. She may decline to take the legacy, in which case she gets only the £5,000 on the covenant; but if she wishes to take the legacy, she may do so only on condition that she will not enforce the covenant. The legacy in short satisfies the portion debt.

Since the father is no longer alive to make the satisfaction of the debt an express condition of the receipt of the gift, satisfaction by a legacy will be more easily presumed than satisfaction by a subsequent portion. It is obvious that the contracting of the debt must precede the *making* of the will or codicil by which the legacy is given, for it is presumed to be the testator's intention at the time he makes the will that the legatee shall take the gift in place of the debt, and he cannot intend the satisfaction of a debt which is not yet in existence. If the legacy is of less value than the debt, it can satisfy it *pro tanto*,[3] and the gift of the residue of the testator's estate (or a part of the residue) may on valuation have the same effect.[4]

But there must be a substantial similarity between the terms of the contract and the provisions of the legacy. A slight difference between the two will not prevent the presumption from arising, but a marked difference will do so. How thin the line between these may be can be shown by contrasting two decisions of the House of Lords in the nineteenth century. In the first, *Thynne* v. *Glengall*,[5] the testator, on his daughter's marriage, agreed to give

---

[1] See *Re Lawes*, at pp. 87-89, and *Re Jaques*, [1903] 1 Ch. 267, C.A.

[2] By analogy with satisfaction by a legacy and ademption (*infra*). But see *Re Lawes*, at pp. 84, 89.

[3] *Thynne* v. *Glengall* (1848), 2 H.L. Cas. 131, 154, H.L.; *Chichester* v. *Coventry* (1867), L.R. 2 H.L. 71, 95, H.L.

[4] *Thynne* v. *Glengall*, (*supra*).

[5] (1848), 2 H.L. Cas. 131, H.L.

her a portion of £100,000. He transferred stock of a third of this value to the four trustees of the settlement and gave them a bond for the transfer of the balance on his death. The stock was to be held on trust for the daughter's separate use for her life, with remainder to such of the children of the marriage as she and her husband should jointly appoint or as the survivor of them should appoint, and in default of appointment in trust for the child or children of the marriage. By his will, which was made after he had entered into this covenant, the father devised and bequeathed the whole of his residue to two of these trustees on trust for sale and investment and as to one half of it to hold it on trust for the daughter for life for her separate use, with remainder to such of her children as *she* should appoint, and in default of appointment in trust for *all* her children in equal shares. The residue was worth about £185,000, and it was held that she was not entitled first to claim the £66,000 odd that was still owed to her on the covenant and then, having depleted the residue by this amount, to claim half the balance, but that she must take her half of the £185,000 as satisfaction of the portion debt.

In the second case, *Chichester* v. *Coventry*,[1] the father on his daughter's marriage covenanted to pay to trustees £10,000 within three months of their demanding it, and in the meantime to pay 3% interest on this sum together with £1,700 a year to make up £2,000 a year. The income and capital (when assigned) were to be held on trust to pay £200 a year to the daughter for her life and to pay the residue to the husband for life. After the death of either, the trustees were to hold the fund on trust for the survivor for life, with remainder on certain trusts for their children, and in default of children for the wife absolutely or, if she predeceased the husband, for such persons as she should by will appoint and in default of appointment on trust for her next-of-kin. By his will made 15 years later, the father gave certain specific devises and bequests to his two daughters (who were his only children) and then directed that his residue should be divided into two equal shares each of which was to be held on trust for one of the daughters for her life, with remainder to such *persons* as she should appoint, and in default of appointment in trust for his nephew, C. He expressly directed that no part of his estate should go to his daughters' husbands, and that, if this should happen either by construction or by operation of law, the interest should immediately go over to C. It was held that this gift did not satisfy the covenant (which was still unfulfilled on the father's death) and that the daughter could consequently claim first her £10,000 and then half the reduced residue.

It will be seen that the difference between the two limitations was much more marked in *Chichester* v. *Coventry* than in *Thynne* v. *Glengall*. In the latter case the chief difference was that under the testamentary disposition the husband was given no power of appointment and the objects of the power and the ultimate beneficiaries in default of appointment were all the daughter's children and not merely those of that particular marriage. In *Chichester* v. *Coventry* not only were the ultimate remainders completely different, but the husband, who was given a life interest under the settlement, was expressly excluded from taking any interest under the residuary gift. Furthermore (although this alone would hardly be enough to rebut the presumption against the double portions) the testator in *Chichester* v.

[1] (1867), L.R. 2 H.L. 71, H.L. See also *Re Tussaud's Estate* (1878), 9 Ch.D. 363, C.A.

Coventry had expressly directed that all his debts should be paid and the portion debt was apparently the only debt that he had. No general rules can be laid down to determine whether or not there is sufficient difference to prevent the presumption from arising: the trial judge must exercise his own discretion in the matter[1] and his task is clearly not an easy one.

Just as there can be satisfaction *pro tanto* if the debt is greater than the legacy, there may be satisfaction of some interests and not others if the beneficiaries under the covenant are different from those under the will. The fact that the latter do not include all the former is strong evidence that there is no intention of satisfaction anyway;[2] but assuming that the court is satisfied that a question of satisfaction is raised, a covenant to settle property on a daughter for life with remainder to her children, followed by a legacy to the daughter absolutely, can be satisfied only with respect to the daughter's life interest. She alone therefore is put to her election; her children may claim only under the covenant and have no interest in the legacy.[3]

(3) *Ademption of Legacies by Portions and Portion Debts.* —Ademption in a sense is the converse of satisfaction, for here the making of the will precedes the giving of the portion or the creation of the portion debt. Thus if a father executes a will in which he gives a legacy of £2,000 to his son and then he gives him £3,000 to set him up in business, he will once more be presumed to have intended that the son should not take both sums and therefore the legacy is *prima facie* adeemed by the portion.

It will be seen that ademption differs from satisfaction in another important respect. As we have already seen, a beneficiary can never be compelled to take a gift or legacy; consequently in satisfaction he is strictly put to his election and he can take the gift only on condition that he does not enforce his debt. But the testator is always free to vary and revoke the provisions of his will, so that if the presumption is raised and not rebutted, it will adeem the legacy automatically: the child may not claim it at all. The revocable nature of the will makes it easier to infer an intention that a legacy should be adeemed than it does to infer an intention that a legacy shall be taken in satisfaction of a portion debt.[4]

Like satisfaction, there may be ademption *pro tanto*[5] or with respect to only one beneficiary's interest.[6] It would also seem to apply even though one or both of the gifts have been made in pursuance of the exercise of a special power of appointment.[7] But the two gifts must still be *ejusdem generis*; thus it has been held that a devise is not adeemed by a portion,[8] nor in the usual way

---

[1] *Chichester* v. *Coventry*, (*supra*), at p. 83.

[2] *Re Tussaud's Estate*, (*supra*), at p. 380. In *Chichester* v. *Coventry* LORD ROMILLY denied that there could ever be a case of satisfaction when the parties were not the same (at p. 91).

[3] See *Re Blundell*, [1906] 2 Ch. 222, and the observations of LORD ROMILLY on *Thynne* v. *Glengall* in *Chichester* v. *Coventry*, at pp. 93-94. Similarly, beneficiaries who acquire a derivative interest are not put to their election: *Re Blundell*.

[4] *Chichester* v. *Coventry*, (*supra*), at pp. 82, 87; *Re Tussaud's Estate*, (*supra*), at p. 380.

[5] *Montefiore* v. *Guedalla* (1859), 1 De G. F. & J. 93.

[6] *Durham* v. *Wharton* (1836), 3 Cl. & F. 146, H.L., as explained in *Chichester* v. *Coventry*, (*supra*).

[7] *Re Peel's Settlement*, [1911] 2 Ch. 165.

[8] *Davys* v. *Boucher* (1839), 3 Y. & C. (Ex.) 397. But *quaere* whether the *ratio decidendi* is still good law.

would a pecuniary legacy probably be adeemed by a gift *in specie*. But if a value is put on the gift, then, as in the case of satisfaction, the legacy may be adeemed. In *Re George's Will Trusts*[1] a farmer devised and bequeathed his residuary estate on trust for sale and conversion as to two-thirds for his son, Ernest, and as to the other third for his son, Robert. Ernest, unlike Robert, was also a farmer and he had worked two farms with his father for some years; consequently the testator directed that Ernest might take his share of the residue *in specie*. A few months later the County War Agricultural Committee threatened to evict the father (who was already over 80 years of age) on account of his inefficient farming, but they eventually withdrew their notice on his virtually handing over the farms to Ernest. Under this arrangement he assigned all his live and dead stock (valued at more than £2,000) to his son together with a share in the tenancy of one of the farms (of which he and Ernest were joint lessees). He also granted to him a lease of his other farm (of which the father was tenant in fee simple) at a rent of £172 *per annum* and made arrangements with his bank to secure adequate financial resources to enable Ernest to run the farms. At the time the father had an overdraft of £151, but, as a result of the son's successful management, within two years this had been converted into a credit balance of over £529. After the father's death the question arose whether Ernest's share of the residue had been adeemed (at any rate *pro tanto*) by this arrangement, and JENKINS, J., held that it was. Since the assignment of the farm amounted to a portion, it was immaterial that it had been carried out on pain of eviction; and the fact that Ernest received the half share of the tenancy in the first farm negatived any inference that this was no more than a business transaction that might be drawn from his taking a lease in the second farm. In view of the fact that under the will Ernest was to be permitted to take the stock *in specie*, the assignment and the testamentary gift were clearly *ejusdem generis*; but even had this not been so, JENKINS, J., would have been prepared to hold that the latter was adeemed because a value had been placed upon the stock at the time of the transfer.[2] Hence the value of the farm (*viz.* the value of the stock transferred less the £151 overdraft which had to be off-set) had to be brought into account in calculating the interest which the two sons took in the residue.

Although the presumption is more difficult to rebut in the case of ademption, it will nevertheless not apply where the circumstances obviously indicate that the testator had no intention that the legacy should be adeemed. Thus in *Re Vaux*[3] the testator gave his residue to trustees on trust to apply it for his children and the issue of his deceased children at their absolute discretion. He subsequently settled £10,000 on each of his four children. It was held by the Court of Appeal that he could not have intended that the trustees' discretion should be fettered by his own act in settling the property and therefore the rule against double portions could not apply. But as it will be seen from *Re George's Will Trusts*, the mere fact that the estate is to be

---

[1] [1949] Ch. 154; [1948] 2 All E.R. 1004.

[2] *Cf. Re Lawes, ante*, p. 610.

[3] [1939] Ch. 465; [1938] 4 All E.R. 703, C.A. See also *Re Lacon*, [1891] 2 Ch. 482, C.A. In *Re Vaux* the Court of Appeal left open the question whether the rule against double portions could apply where there was a partial intestacy. SIMONDS, J., had held that it could in the court below ([1938] Ch. 581; [1938] 2 All E.R. 177); but as he was overruled on the main question in the Court of Appeal, this point did not have to be considered.

divided in unequal shares does not of itself prevent the rule from being applied.

It need hardly be added that, if the portion is larger than the legacy, there is no question of the beneficiary's having to pay a part of this back. Thus suppose that a father has bequeathed his residue (valued at £10,000 on his death) to his two sons, A and B, in equal shares and that he later gives A a portion of £4,000. A must bring this sum into account, so that he will take £3,000 from the residue (giving him £7,000 in all) and B will take £7,000 from the residue. If the father had given A a portion of £12,000, he would keep this and B would take all £10,000 of the residue. Moreover, the purpose of the rule is to secure equality between children and no other person may benefit from its operation. Let us suppose now that the testator has directed that his residue is to be divided equally among his two children, A and B, and his widow, W. He later gives a portion of £2,000 to A, and the residue is worth £12,000. W can take no more than a third of this, that is £4,000; in distributing the other £8,000 between A and B, account must now be taken of the £2,000 already received by A. Hence A takes £3,000 of this (which with his £2,000 will give him £5,000 in all) and B takes the other £5,000.[1]

Extrinsic Evidence to rebut the Presumption.—The rule that the testator did not intend any child to take a double portion is rebuttable by evidence *dehors* the will as well as by intrinsic evidence. But if the construction of the will and contract or gift does not give rise to a presumption of satisfaction or ademption, no extrinsic evidence may be led to raise the presumption.[2]

B. INTESTATE SUCCESSION

Intestate Succession before 1926.—Before the Administration of Estates Act 1925 came into force, there was a considerable difference between the descent of realty and the descent of personalty.

Succession to Realty.—All inheritable estates of freehold still descended to the heir at law subject to the husband's curtesy and the wife's dower.[3]

Succession to Personalty.—Until 1857 the granting of letters of administration with respect to personalty fell within the jurisdiction of the ecclesiastical courts. Although in the Middle Ages the Ordinary would try to ensure that the deceased's dependants were provided for out of the estate, the

---

[1] *Meinertzagen* v. *Walters* (1872), 7 Ch. App. 670. Any person claiming a deceased child's share must bring the advances to the child in as well, for he can obviously claim no more than the child: *Re Scott*, [1903] 1 Ch. 1, 9, C.A. (*per* VAUGHAN WILLIAMS, L.J.).

[2] See Pettit, *Equity*, 4th Ed., 553. There is still some doubt what effect the execution of a codicil has. If a father gives a legacy to his son and then gives him a portion and subsequently republishes the will by executing a codicil, may the son take the legacy? The portion will *prima facie* have adeemed the original legacy, and there is authority for the proposition that a legacy once adeemed cannot be revived by a republication: *per* LORD COTTENHAM, L.C., in *Powys* v. *Mansfield* (1837), 3 My. & Cr. 359, 376; but if the testator republishes the will without *expressly* revoking the legacy, common sense dictates that he intends the son to take it in addition to his portion. See also *Re Scott*, (*supra*).

[3] See *ante*, pp. 410 and 411. See works on real property for a fuller discussion.

law became chaotic. It was put on a less confused and more rational footing by the three Statutes of Distributions passed in 1670, 1677 and 1685, the policy of which was to make provision for the deceased's dependants and to ensure that the property descended in much the same way as a thoughtful testator would have directed. We have already seen that on the death of a married woman her husband took all her personalty at common law.[1] On the death of a married man his widow took one third of his estate if there were issue of the marriage alive; in other cases she took a half. The remainder of the estate was divided amongst the issue *per stirpes* or, in default of issue, amongst the deceased's next-of-kin as defined in the Statutes.[2]

Married Women's Separate Property.—If a married woman predeceased her husband without having disposed of her separate property *inter vivos* or by will, the whole interest vested in her husband as at common law. This rule still applied to statutory separate property after the Married Women's Property Act 1882.

The Intestates' Estates Act 1890.—This Act was passed in order to give an intestate's widow a larger provision than she had had under the old law. Under this Act if a person died wholly intestate leaving a widow but no issue, she was in future to take the whole of the real and personal estate if the total value did not exceed £500. If the value exceeded this sum, the estate was to stand charged with the payment to her of £500.

The Administration of Estates Act 1925.—This Act radically overhauled the law relating to intestate succession in two respects. First, the law relating to realty and personalty has been put on exactly the same footing; and secondly the distribution of estates has been completely changed. The principal effect of this Act has been to give the surviving widow a much greater interest than she had before 1926 and to give the surviving widower the same rights as the surviving widow. The details of this have been modified by the Intestates' Estates Act 1952 and the Family Provision Act 1966, which have given the surviving spouse an even larger share of the estate and, as will be seen, have made him or her in most cases the universal successor.[3]

It must be remembered that the general law of intestate succession does not apply to entailed interests, which still descend according to the old laws of intestate succession applicable to entailed realty.[4] For the rest, the whole of the intestate's estate vests in his personal representatives on trust for sale and conversion, and after the payment of all expenses and debts they must then distribute it in the way about to be described.[5] It must also be borne in mind that the distribution is liable to be upset by claims under the Inheritance (Provision for Family and Dependants) Act.[6]

---

[1] *Ante*, p. 412.

[2] See, further, works on the law of personal property.

[3] Ss. 46-49 of the Administration of Estates Act, as amended by the Intestates' Estates Act, are now set out in the 1st Sched. to the latter Act. References to these sections "(as amended)" are to the sections as set out in that Schedule.

[4] The widower of a deceased female tenant in tail is still entitled to a life interest by the curtesy, see *ante*, p. 417.

[5] Administration of Estates Act 1925, s. 33.

[6] See *post*, section C.

The Rights of the Surviving Spouse.—The surviving widow or widower now takes the following interests.[1]

Personal Chattels.—The surviving spouse is always entitled to the personal chattels (provided that the estate is solvent), and personal representatives may not sell them unless this is necessary to pay debts and expenses.[2] Personal chattels are defined as:[3]

"Carriages, horses, stable furniture and effects (not used for business purposes), motor cars and accessories (not used for business purposes), garden effects, domestic animals, plate, plated articles, linen, china, glass, books, pictures, prints, furniture, jewellery,[4] articles of household or personal use or ornament, musical and scientific instruments and apparatus, wines, liquors and consumable stores, but [they] do not include any chattels used at the death of the intestate for business purposes[5] nor money or securities for money."

Residuary Interests.—The interest which the surviving spouse takes over and above the personal chattels depends upon what other relatives the intestate leaves surviving.

If he leaves any children or remoter issue, the spouse takes £40,000 with interest at £7% *per annum* until it is paid and a *life* interest in half the residue.

If he leaves no issue but a parent or a brother or sister of the whole blood or issue of such a brother or sister, the surviving spouse takes £85,000 with interest at £7% *per annum* until it is paid and an *absolute* interest in half the residue.

If he leaves neither issue nor any of the above relations, the surviving spouse takes the whole of the residue absolutely.

In view of the large interest which the surviving spouse takes in the other's estate, the rule that, where it is uncertain which of two persons died first, the younger shall be deemed to have survived the elder does not apply as between a person dying intestate and his or her spouse.[6] Where there are no issue, it is obviously not desirable that the presumption should operate so as to put £85,000 or more at the disposal of a man's parents-in-law rather than at the disposal of his own parents.

Redemption of Life Interest.—The spouse may, if he wishes to do so, insist on the personal representatives' redeeming his life interest by paying the

---

[1] Administration of Estates Act 1925, s. 46 (as amended); Family Provision Act 1966, s. 1; Administration of Justice Act 1977, s. 28 (1); Family Provision (Intestate Succession) Order, S.I. 1981 No. 255; Intestate Succession (Interest and Capitalisation) Order, S.I. 1977 No. 1491.

[2] Administration of Estates Act 1925, s. 33 (1).

[3] *Ibid.*, s. 55 (1) (x). This section has been widely construed and has been held to include a 60-foot motor yacht (*Re Chaplin*, [1950] Ch. 507; [1950] 2 All E.R. 155) and a collection of clocks and watches (*Re Crispin's Will Trusts*, [1975] Ch. 245; [1974] 3 All E.R. 772, C.A.). The mere fact that the property might be regarded as an investment does not prevent it from being a personal chattel too: *Re Reynold's Will Trusts*, [1965] 3 All E.R. 686 (valuable stamp collection, which was deceased's principal hobby, held to be an article of personal use). See R.E.M. in 82 L.Q.R. 18.

[4] Including cut but unmounted jewels: *Re Whitby*, [1944] Ch. 210; [1944] 1 All E.R. 299, C.A.

[5] See *Re Ogilby*, [1942] Ch. 288; [1942] 1 All E.R. 524.

[6] Administration of Estates Act 1925, s. 46 (3) (as amended).

capital value to him.¹ He must elect to do so within 12 months after representation is taken out, but the court may extend this period if it considers that the limit will operate unfairly because a previous will was revoked or invalid, or because the interest of some person in the estate has not been determined when representation was taken out, or because of any other circumstances affecting the administration or distribution of the estate.²

Rights with respect to the Matrimonial Home.—The Act of 1952 has given the surviving spouse a right within certain limits to retain the matrimonial home *in specie.*³ Where the intestate's estate comprises an interest in a dwelling-house in which the surviving spouse was resident at the time of the intestate's death, the survivor may require the personal representatives to appropriate the house in or towards satisfaction of any absolute interest that the survivor has in the estate,⁴ and if the value of the house exceeds the value of the survivor's interest, he may exercise this option if he pays the excess value to the representatives.⁵ He must exercise this option within 12 months of representation being taken out, but this period may be extended by the court as in the case of an application to have a life interest redeemed.⁶ Consequently the personal representatives are forbidden to sell the house within this period without the written consent of the surviving spouse unless this is necessary for the payment of expenses or debts.⁷

There are two limitations upon this power. First, these provisions normally do not apply if the house is held upon a lease which had less than two years to run from the date of the intestate's death or which could be determined by the landlord within this period.⁸ This means that many houses (for example, those held on weekly tenancies) come outside these provisions, but to off-set this it must be remembered that, if the tenancy is a regulated or secure one, there will usually be an automatic transmission to the surviving spouse under the Rent Act or the Housing Act.⁹ Secondly, the spouse cannot require the personal representatives to appropriate the house in the following cases except on an order of the court which must be satisfied that the appropriation is not likely to diminish the value of assets in the residuary estate (other than the interest in the house) or make these assets more difficult to dispose of.¹⁰ This is where

---

¹ Administration of Estates Act 1925, s. 47A (as amended) and as further amended by the Administration of Justice Act 1977, s. 28 (2), (3), and S.I. 1977 No. 1491.

² *Ibid.*, s. 47A (5) (as amended).

³ Intestates' Estates Act 1952, Sched. 2.

⁴ *Ibid.*, para. 1 (1). "Dwelling-house" includes part of a building occupied as a separate dwelling and an absolute interest includes a redeemed life interest: *ibid.*, para. 1 (4), (5).

⁵ *Ibid.*, para. 5 (2); *Re Phelps*, [1979] 3 All E.R. 373, C.A. The value is to be assessed at the date of appropriation: *Robinson* v. *Collins*, [1975] 1 All E.R. 321.

⁶ *Ibid.*, para. 3. It cannot be exercised after the surviving spouse's death by his or her personal representatives: *ibid.*, para. 3 (1) (b).

⁷ *Ibid.*, para. 4. But if they fail to observe this provision, the spouse has no right to claim the house from the purchaser: *ibid.*, para. 4 (5).

⁸ *Ibid.*, para. 1(2). For exceptional cases (where the surviving spouse would be entitled to acquire the freehold or an extended lease), see the Leasehold Reform Act 1967, s. 7 (8).

⁹ See *post*, section D.

¹⁰ Intestates' Estates Act 1952, Sched. 2, para. 2.

(a) the dwelling-house forms part of a building and an interest in the whole of the building is comprised in the residuary estate;[1] or
(b) the dwelling-house is held with agricultural land and an interest in the agricultural land is comprised in the residuary estate; or
(c) the whole or part of the dwelling-house was at the time of the intestate's death used as a hotel or lodging house; or
(d) a part of the dwelling-house·was at the time of the intestate's death used for purposes other than domestic purposes.

Judicial Separation.—By section 18 (2) of the Matrimonial Causes Act 1973, if either spouse dies wholly or partially intestate whilst a decree of judicial separation is in force and the separation is continuing, his or her property is to devolve as though the other were dead. The reason for this provision is that the rules of intestate succession are intended to reflect the testamentary dispositions the deceased might reasonably be expected to have made, and as judicial separation almost always marks the *de facto* end of the marriage, it is highly unlikely that either would have left anything to the other.[2]

Interests taken by the Intestate's Children and Remoter Issue.—If the intestate leaves a surviving spouse, the personal representatives must hold one half of the residue (after taking out the personal chattels and the spouse's £40,000) on the statutory trusts for the intestate's issue and the other half on the same trusts subject to the surviving spouse's life interest. If the intestate leaves no surviving spouse, the personal representatives must hold the whole of the residue on the statutory trusts for the issue.[3]

The Statutory Trusts.—The property is to be held on trust for all the children alive at the intestate's death who reach the age of 18 or marry under that age in equal shares. But if any of his children has predeceased him, that child's share is held upon the same trusts for his own children or remoter issue.[4]

Thus suppose that the intestate had four children, A, B, C and D. The first three are alive at their parent's death but D is already dead. D had two children, K and L, of whom K is still alive but L is also dead, leaving two children, X and Y. By applying the above rules, we see that A, B and C each take one quarter; K takes half of D's share (*i.e.*, one-eighth) and the other half of D's share goes to X and Y, who thus get one-sixteenth each. If the share of any of the above fails to vest because he dies a minor and unmarried, his share will go over to the others as if he had predeceased the testator.[5] Thus if A were to die in such circumstances, B and C would each take one third of

[1] *E.g.*, if the house is attached to a shop and the owner would normally live in it.
[2] This does not apply to separation orders made by magistrates' courts under earlier statutes (which in other respects had the same effect as decrees of judicial separation) because they might well be followed by a reconciliation: Matrimonial Causes Act 1973, s. 18 (3). See further Law Com. No. 25, pp. 107-109. S. 18 (2) replaces earlier legislation going back to 1857 which applied only to certain property with respect to which the wife died intestate.
[3] Administration of Estates Act 1925, s. 46 (1) (as amended).
[4] *Ibid.*, s. 47 (1) (i) (as amended); Family Law Reform Act 1969, s. 3 (2).
[5] *Re Young*, [1951] Ch. 185; [1950] 2 All E.R. 1040.

his share, K would take a sixth, and X and Y would each take a twelfth. If K were to die, his share would pass to X and Y equally; and if X were to die, his share would go to Y.

Until a beneficiary obtains a vested interest by attaining his majority or marrying, the trustees may use the whole of the income of the part to which he is contingently entitled for his maintenance, education or benefit, and they may use one half of the capital to which he is contingently entitled for his advancement.[1] Subject to this they must accumulate the income at compound interest.[2] They may also at their discretion permit him to have the use of any personal chattels.[3]

Hotchpot.—The Administration of Estates Act expressly brings the rule against double portions into operation by enacting that any portion or portion debt must be brought into account in satisfaction in whole or part of that child's share of the intestacy unless a contrary intention on the part of the intestate can be inferred.[4] This is frequently known as "bringing into hotchpot".

Interests taken by other Members of the Family.—If the intestate dies leaving a surviving spouse but no issue, the other half of the residue (after taking out the personal chattels, the £85,000 and the half interest which has gone to the surviving spouse) is to be held on trust for the intestate's parents in equal shares (or for one parent absolutely if only one parent survives the intestate), and if neither of his parents survives him, on the statutory trusts for his brothers and sisters of the whole blood and their issue.

If the intestate leaves neither a spouse nor issue surviving, his whole estate must be held on trust for the persons coming into the first of the following classes that can be satisfied. In other words, if neither of the parents (who came in class (1)) is alive, then the persons coming into class (2) will take and so forth. If none of these classes is filled, the whole estate will go to the Crown as *bona vacantia.*[5]

(1) For the intestate's parents (if they are both alive) in equal shares, or, if one only is still alive, for that parent absolutely.

(2) On the statutory trusts for the brothers and sisters of the whole blood of the intestate and their issue.

(3) On the statutory trusts for the brothers and sisters of the half blood of the intestate and their issue.

(4) For the surviving grandparents of the intestate in equal shares.

(5) On the statutory trusts for the uncles and aunts of the intestate (being brothers or sisters of the whole blood of one of his parents) and their issue.

(6) On the statutory trusts for the uncles and aunts of the intestate (being brothers or sisters of the half blood of one of his parents) and their issue.

---

[1] Administration of Estates Act 1925, s. 47 (1) (ii) (as amended); Trustee Act 1925, ss. 31 (1), 32 (1).

[2] Trustee Act 1925, s. 31 (2).

[3] Administration of Estates Act 1925, s. 47 (1) (iv) (as amended).

[4] *Ibid.*, s. 47 (1) (iii) (as amended); *Hardy* v. *Shaw*, [1976] Ch. 82; [1975] 2 All E.R. 1052.

[5] Administration of Estates Act 1925, s. 46 (1) (as amended).

The statutory trusts are exactly the same in the above cases as the statutory trusts for the intestate's children and issue except that the hotchpot rule does not apply. Hence the members of each class take *per capita* and the issue of any deceased member of the class take *per stirpes*. All the interests are contingent upon the beneficiary's attaining his majority or marrying, and if no member of any class takes a vested interest, the members of the next class will take.[1]

Illegitimate, Legitimated and Adopted Children.—Originally, in accordance with the general rule at common law, only legitimate persons and those claiming a relationship through legitimate persons could participate in intestate succession. A claim may now be made by or through a legitimated person as though he had been born legitimate as well as by the issue of a person who would have been legitimated had he not died before his parents' marriage.[2] Similarly if a legitimated person or his issue dies intestate, his estate is to be distributed as though he were born legitimate. The same principles now apply to adopted children, and if an adopted child, his adoptive parent or any other person dies intestate, the estate is to be distributed as though he were the legitimate child of his adopters and not the child of any other person.[3] If he was adopted by two spouses jointly, he will be in the position of a brother (or sister) of the whole blood of any other child or adopted child of both the adopters and a brother of the half blood of any child or adopted child of one of them; if he was adopted by one person only, he will be in the position of a brother of the half blood of any child or adopted child of his adopter.

The position of illegitimate persons who have been neither legitimated nor adopted is now governed by section 14 of the Family Law Reform Act 1969.[4] The principle underlying this section is that illegitimate children and their parents should be entitled to succeed to each other. Thus on the death of a person intestate his illegitimate child (or, if the child has predeceased the intestate, his *legitimate* issue) may now participate in the intestacy on exactly the same terms as though he were legitimate, and on the death of an illegitimate child without issue, his parents have the same claims as they would have on the death of a legitimate child. But it should be noted that claims to succeed by, to or through an illegitimate person are limited to these two cases;

---

[1] Administration of Estates Act 1925, s. 46 (4), (5) (as amended). If all the members of a particular class (except (1) and (4)) are dead, but one or more have left issue, the issue will take in preference to the members of a more remote class: *Re Lockwood*, [1958] Ch. 231; [1957] 3 All E.R. 520. Thus, *e.g.*, issue of a brother or sister of the whole blood will take before a brother and sister of the half blood.

[2] Legitimacy Act 1976, s. 5. If the intestate died before 1976, the claimant could succeed only if he was legitimated before the death and, if an entailed interest was created before 1976, he can still claim by descent only if it was *created* after his legitimation: Legitimacy Act 1926, s. 3 (1) (a), (c). See *ante*, pp. 578-580.

[3] Children Act 1975, Sched. 1, paras. 3, 5 and 6 (prospectively repealed and re-enacted in the Adoption Act 1976, ss. 39 (1), (2), (5) and 46 (4)). Hence a child adopted by one parent cannot claim on the death of the other. If the intestate died before 1976, the claimant would succeed only if he had been adopted before the death: Adoption Act 1958, s. 16 (1). *Cf. ante*, p. 580.

[4] This implements the recommendations of the majority of the Committee on the Law of Succession in Relation to Illegitimate Persons 1966, Cmnd. 3051. It applies if the intestate died on or after 1st January, 1970. Any reference to statutory next of kin in an instrument taking effect on or after this date is to be likewise construed: s. 14 (6).

thus he can claim nothing on the intestacy of a grandparent or any collateral relative, nor can they claim on his intestacy.[1]. Furthermore the section does not affect the devolution of an entailed interest and an illegitimate person cannot take as heir.[2]

One difficulty that may well arise is that of establishing the relationship of the claimant to the deceased. A more cogent criticism that has been levelled against the section is that it permits a father to take advantage of the relationship on the child's death even though he did nothing to support him or even recognise him during his lifetime. Because of the difficulty in tracing the fathers of many illegitimate children, whose identity might well not be known, an illegitimate child is to be presumed not to have been survived by his father unless the contrary is shown.[3] Nor are personal representatives bound to ascertain whether there are illegitimate children (or fathers of illegitimate children) who could take on an intestacy and they will not be personally liable for distributing the estate if they have no notice of their existence.[4]

Partial Intestacy.—These rules apply equally to a partial intestacy. But in this case if the deceased devises or bequeaths property to the surviving spouse (other than personal chattels or under the exercise of a special power of appointment), the spouse must take this in partial or whole satisfaction of the £40,000 or £85,000 to which he is entitled under the intestacy. Similarly a child *or any remoter issue* of the deceased must bring into hotchpot any beneficial interests acquired by him under the will (except those acquired by virtue of the exercise of a special power of appointment).[5]

---

[1] Nor can a legitimate person succeed on the death of his legitimate cousin if the relevant parent of either of them is illegitimate.

[2] These limitations would all disappear if the proposals contained in Law Com. Working Paper No. 74 (Illegitimacy) were adopted. See *ante*, pp. 273-274.

[3] Family Law Reform Act 1969, s. 14 (4).

[4] *Ibid.*, s. 17. But the beneficiary may follow the property, or other property representing it, into the hands of a recipient. See further Morris, *The Family Law Reform Act* 1969, *sections* 14 *and* 15, 19 I.C.L.Q. 328. For a comparison with other systems, see Stone, *Illegitimacy and Claims to Money and other Property: a Comparative Study*, 15 I.C.L.Q. 505, at pp. 520-527.

[5] Administration of Estates Act 1925, s. 49 (as amended). In *Re Young*, [1951] Ch. 185; [1950] 2 All E.R. 1040, and *Re Grover's Will Trusts*, [1971] Ch. 169; [1970] 1 All E.R. 1185, it was held that, if the will confers a life interest on the testator's child with remainder over to his children, the capital value of the *whole* fund must be brought into account if the child also claims on a partial intestacy. This is based on the principle that the interest taken by the whole *stirps* must be regarded as a gift to the testator's issue. *Quaere* whether the child should not have to bring into account only the capitalised value of the life interest which is all that *he* takes under the will: *cf. Re Morton*, [1956] Ch. 644; [1956] 3 All E.R. 259. For difficulties presented by these decisions, see Ryder, *Hotchpot on a Partial Intestacy*, Current Legal Problems 1973, 208; Scott, 120 New L.J. 848. If the surviving spouse is given a life interest in the estate and the testator dies intestate with respect to the remainder, the spouse is entitled to £40,000 or £85,000 less the capitalised value of the life interest immediately: *Re Bowen-Buscarlet's Will Trusts*, [1972] Ch. 463; [1971] 3 All E.R. 636. In this case the testator left issue so that his widow's life interest in the rest of the residue merged with her life interest under the bequest. But if there had been no issue, she could presumably also have claimed her absolute half interest in the rest immediately. The trustees will have to sell sufficient of the reversion to raise the sum presently due.

C. PROVISION FOR MEMBERS OF THE FAMILY AND OTHER DEPENDANTS

By permitting a husband to extinguish his wife's right to dower, the Dower Act 1833 abolished the last vestige of family provision in English law.[1] After that there was nothing to stop a man (or a woman with respect to her separate property) from devising and bequeathing his whole estate to a charity or a complete stranger and leaving his widow and children penniless. To prevent this evil, in 1938 Parliament passed the Inheritance (Family Provision) Act. This did not cast upon a testator any positive duty to make reasonable provision for his dependants—indeed it would have been impossible to do so—but enacted that, if he failed to do so, the court might order such reasonable provision as it thought fit to be made out of his estate for the benefit of the surviving spouse and certain classes of children. In 1952 the principle underlying this Act was applied to cases of intestacy.[2] It is easy to see that the law of intestate succession might leave a child without adequate support: the whole estate might go to a widow who refused to make any provision for the children of a previous marriage or might be divided between a daughter married to a rich man and a minor son whose education was incomplete. In 1958 a similar power to apply for provision was given to a former spouse, that is, one whose marriage to the deceased had been dissolved or annulled and who had not remarried.[3] This, of course, was of particular value to a divorced wife who had obtained an order for unsecured periodical payments which would cease on her former husband's death.

Notwithstanding these extensions there were still many gaps and deficiencies in the law. The term "dependant" was so narrowly defined that it excluded many who had been supported by another during his lifetime and who had a moral, if not a legal, claim on his estate. Thus no application could be made, for example, by a parent, brother or sister, another's children who had been treated as members of the deceased's family, or a person with whom he had been cohabiting outside marriage. Provision could be ordered only out of property which the deceased had power to dispose of by will, so that he could defeat the operation of the Act altogether by settling his property during his lifetime or by contracting to leave it to a third person after his death.[4] Furthermore, the court was limited to ordering reasonable provision for the dependant's maintenance and had no power to divide capital assets: the result was that a surviving wife could be in a worse position than a divorced wife who obtained a property adjustment order. When the Law Commission examined the whole question of family property law, they rejected the proposal that a surviving spouse should have a right to inherit a fixed proportion of the deceased's estate in favour of the much more flexible approach of family provision. They added, however, that this would need considerable strengthening, and in particular "the surviving partner of a marriage should have a claim upon the family assets at least equivalent to that

---

[1] See *ante*, p. 411; Unger, *The Inheritance Act and the Family*, 6 M.L.R. 215.

[2] Intestates' Estates Act 1952.

[3] Matrimonial Causes (Property and Maintenance) Act 1958, subsequently re-enacted in the Matrimonial Causes Act 1965, ss. 26-28.

[4] *Schaefer* v. *Schuhmann*, [1972] A.C. 572; [1972] 1 All E.R. 621, P.C. But the disposition might possibly have been set aside had it been fraudulent: see *post*, p. 632, n. 1.

of a divorced person".[1] Their detailed recommendations, overhauling the whole of the law, were published in 1974[2] and effect was given to them by the Inheritance (Provision for Family and Dependants) Act 1975, which came into force on 1st April 1976. This repealed all the existing relevant legislation and replaced it by a new and comprehensive code.[3]

Jurisdiction.—The Act applies only if the person against whose estate the claim is being made died domiciled in England and Wales.[4] An application for an order may be made to the High Court or, if the net estate does not exceed £15,000, a county court.[5]

Who may apply for an Order.—Application for provision may be made only by the following persons:[6]

(1) The deceased's wife or husband. This category includes a person who had in good faith entered into a void marriage with the deceased. The reason is that such a person is *de facto* in the position of a surviving spouse and may not discover that the marriage is void until after the other party's death, when it will be too late to apply for financial relief in nullity proceedings. Consequently the survivor may not make an application under this head if during the deceased's lifetime the marriage has been dissolved or annulled by a decree recognised in England or he has entered into a later marriage and thus in effect treated the first marriage as at an end.[7]

(2) A former wife or husband of the deceased, that is, a person whose marriage with the deceased was dissolved or annulled during his lifetime by a decree of an English court and who has not remarried.[8] This enables the court to make or continue financial provision for those to whom it could award financial relief under the Matrimonial Causes Act.[9]

(3) A child of the deceased. This includes an illegitimate child, an adopted child, and a child *en ventre sa mère* at the time of the death.[10]

---

[1] Law Com. No. 52, First Report on Family Property: a New Approach, paras. 31-45.

[2] Law Com. No. 61, Second Report on Family Property: Family Provision on Death.

[3] Existing orders continue in force as though made under the Inheritance (Provision for Family and Dependants) Act: s. 26 (3), (4).

[4] S. 1 (1). See Law Com. No. 61, paras. 258-262.

[5] S. 22; County Courts Jurisdiction (Inheritance—Provision for Family and Dependants) Order 1978. Applications in the High Court may be made in the Chancery Division or the Family Division: R.S.C. O.99 (as substituted).

[6] S. 1 (1). See Hand, 10 Fam. Law 141.

[7] S. 25 (4). A later marriage includes a void or voidable marriage (because the person in question would have a claim against the other party to it): s. 25 (5). This category was originally added by the Law Reform (Miscellaneous Provisions) Act 1970 which, by abolishing actions for breach of promise of marriage, took away the remedy formerly possessed by the survivor. For the reason for excluding persons whose marriages have been dissolved or annulled by a foreign court, see *infra*, n. 9.

[8] S. 25 (1). Remarriage includes a void or voidable marriage: s. 25 (5).

[9] Hence "former wife or husband" does not include a former spouse whose marriage has been dissolved or annulled by a foreign court because otherwise she would have been in a better position than she was in his lifetime when she had no power to apply for financial relief from an English court.

[10] S. 25 (1); Children Act 1975, Sched. 1, para. 3 (prospectively repealed and re-enacted in the Adoption Act 1976, s. 39).

(4) Any other person whom the deceased had treated as a child of the family in relation to any marriage to which he had at any time been a party. This corresponds to the court's power to award financial relief to a child of the family under the Matrimonial Causes Act, but the category of persons able to apply for provision after death is wider in two respects: only the deceased (and not his or her spouse) need have treated the child as a child of the family[1] and children boarded out are not excluded.

(5) Any other person who was being maintained, either wholly or in part, by the deceased immediately before his death. This provision is entirely new and is likely to give rise to a great deal of litigation before it will be possible to state with certainty the principles that the courts will apply. It is not necessary to establish any family relationship between the applicant and the deceased: what is essential is a *de facto* dependence, and the former must show that the latter had been making a substantial contribution in money or money's worth towards his or her reasonable needs otherwise than for full valuable consideration.[2] These requirements and the difficulties they give rise to were subject to a lengthy and detailed examination by MEGARRY, V.-C., in *Re Beaumont*. He concluded in the first place that a person would have no claim if, immediately before his death, the deceased had been maintaining him on a purely temporary basis or by chance; otherwise the personal representatives could find themselves faced with a claim by someone whom the deceased had taken in for a few days whilst he recovered from an illness. What must be established is "some settled basis or arrangement between the parties as regards maintenance";[4] if there was such an arrangement, it is immaterial that for some reason such as a temporary absence the applicant was not in fact in receipt of maintenance at the moment of the other's death. MEGARRY, V.-C., was also of the opinion that section 3 (4) of the Act goes further and requires the deceased to have assumed responsibility for the applicant's maintenance.[5] Whilst this point is open to some doubt,[6] there can be few cases where a claim would succeed in the absence of such an assumption. It cannot have been Parliament's intention to give a claim to everyone who receives maintenance out of kindness or charity; and whereas in some cases the circumstances surrounding the provision of maintenance might themselves imply an undertaking to continue to do so, this could not apply, for example, if two friends agreed to share accommodation and the deceased made a much greater contribution towards the expenses because he was better off than the other.[7]

---

[1] Although there are likely to be few cases where one spouse only has treated a child as a child of the family.

[2] S. 1 (3); *Re Beaumont*, [1980] Ch. 444, 450-451; [1980] 1 All E.R. 266, 270-271. See also *Re Wilkinson*, [1978] Fam. 22, 23; [1978] 1 All E.R. 221, 222-223.

[3] [1980] Ch. 444; [1980] 1 All E.R. 266. For a detailed and valuable discussion of the implications of this case, see Naresh, *Dependants' Applications under the Inheritance (Provision for Family and Dependants) Act* 1975, 96 L.Q.R. 534.

[4] At pp. 452 and 272, respectively.

[5] At pp. 456 and 274, respectively. For s. 3 (4), see further *post*, p. 629.

[6] MEGARRY, V.-C., laid great stress on the fact that the sub-section requires the court to have regard to the extent to which the deceased assumed this responsibility and therefore implies that he must have assumed it. The point is a very narrow one and another court may well take a different view.

[7] *Re Beaumont*, (*supra*), at pp. 458 and 276, respectively.

Further difficulty is likely to arise from the requirement that the contribution towards the claimant's needs shall not have been for full valuable consideration. This clearly excludes the housekeeper or companion who works for an economic salary, but it is not essential that there should have been a contract between the applicant and the deceased. A claim may well be made by a relative or friend who lived with the deceased and performed personal and domestic services for him in exchange for free board and lodging. In such a case the obvious approach is to assess what the latter would have had to pay for the benefit he received: he will probably rarely be found to have given full valuable consideration because a paid help would have received a substantial salary in addition to free board.[2]

Many other illustrations can be imagined. The court is hardly likely to exclude a person to whose needs the deceased contributed by complying with an order of a foreign court, for example a former spouse who obtained a divorce abroad. But the person most likely to apply under this head is the woman (or man) with whom the deceased had been living but to whom he or she was not married. The critical question is whether the contribution was a substantial one towards the applicant's reasonable needs, and this will obviously depend upon the size of the contributions made, the applicant's other sources of income and her standard of living.[3] Thus the deceased's mistress must have a claim if he set her up in her own home and paid all her domestic bills but not if he did no more than make her casual payments or gifts. The striking aspect of this provision is that the applicant now has a legal claim after the deceased's death whereas she (or he) may have had no claim at all during his lifetime. However anomalous this may be, it can be justified on the ground that the deceased would presumably have continued to provide for the applicant had he survived, and her claim will therefore be stronger if he had assumed a responsibility not to leave her unprovided after his death.[4] In many cases there will be a clear moral claim, and the deceased's failure to provide for her after his death may be due to oversight or accident, for example the failure to make a will in time or the revocation of an earlier will by marriage.[5]

Reasonable Provision.—It is not sufficient that the applicant can bring himself within one of the above categories; he must also show that the provisions of the deceased's will or the law relating to intestacy (or the combination of both if there is a partial intestacy) is not such as to make reasonable financial provision for him.[6] It is not the purpose of the Act to enable the court to provide legacies or rewards for meritorious conduct; nor is it its function to ask whether what has happened is reasonable or to consider how the available assets should be divided.[7] In defining reasonable

---

[1] *Re Wilkinson*, (*supra*); *Re Beaumont*, (*supra*), at pp. 453 and 272, respectively.

[2] Cf. *Re Wilkinson*, (*supra*).

[3] *Malone* v. *Harrison*, [1979] 1 W.L.R. 1353.

[4] *Malone* v. *Harrison*, (*supra*), at pp. 1364-1365.

[5] See Law Com. No. 61, paras. 85-94.

[6] Ss. 1 (1) and 2 (1).

[7] *Re Coventry*, [1980] Ch. 461, at pp. 486 and 495; [1979] 3 All E.R. 815, at pp. 821 and 828, C.A., In *Re Christie*, [1979] Ch. 168; [1979] 1 All E.R. 546, the court appears to have done this. The deceased devised her house to her son and left her interest in another house to her daughter.

financial provision, however, the Act draws a significant distinction between surviving spouses and all other applicants. If the application is made by a surviving husband or wife (except where a decree of judicial separation had been pronounced and the decree was in force and the separation continuing at the deceased's death), reasonable financial provision means such financial provision as it would be reasonable in all the circumstances of the case for a husband or wife to receive, *whether or not that provision is required for his or her maintenance*: in all other cases it means such financial provision as it would be reasonable in all the circumstances of the case for the applicant to receive *for his maintenance*.[1] Thus, whilst most applicants can look for no more than reasonable maintenance, a surviving spouse will generally be entitled to at least a part of the deceased's capital as well (unless he has had the opportunity of seeking a property adjustment order on judicial separation).

Whether reasonable provision has been made for the applicant is of course a question of fact. The term is not limited to the provision of bare necessities; on the other hand it does not cover everything which may be regarded as reasonably desirable for the applicant's benefit or welfare. One must ask whether the applicant will be able to maintain himself in a manner suitable to the circumstances.[2] The Act specifically requires the court to have regard to the following matters.[3]

(a) The financial resources and needs of the applicant, any other applicant for an order, and any beneficiary of the estate;[4] any obligations and responsibilities which the deceased had towards any of these people; and any physical or mental disability from which any of them suffers. In this connection, the court must take into account the individual's earning capacity, any resources and needs which he is likely to have in the foreseeable future, and his financial obligations and responsibilities. It is of course necessary to consider the position of other applicants and beneficiaries because any order made will limit the property available for them. Generally speaking, the court must pay regard to similar matters when considering the question of financial relief on divorce and they have already been considered more fully in the discussion of that problem,[5] but in one or two respects the court's approach may be slightly different. The standard at which the applicant lived whilst the deceased was alive is clearly relevant but cannot be

---

The devise was adeemed because, after making her will, the testatrix sold the house in question and bought another which, under a residuary gift, was held in trust for both children in equal shares. It was held that the son was entitled to this house in a claim under the Inheritance Act because it had been the testatrix's intention that he should take it and it was fair and just to redress the balance in this way. GOFF, L.J., questioned the decision in *Re Coventry* at pp. 490 and 824, respectively: it is submitted that it should not be followed.

[1] S. 1 (2).

[2] *Re Coventry*, (*supra*), at pp. 485 and 819-820 (*per* GOFF, L.J.), and 494 and 827, respectively (*per* BUCKLEY, L.J.) Hence if a rich man's bounty has enabled his parents to live in luxury whilst their own income would keep them in comfort, it might be reasonable to give them such provision as would permit them to maintain their previous standard of living.

[3] S. 3 (1), (6).

[4] Beneficiary includes not only a person claiming under the deceased's will or on his intestacy but also anyone nominated by him to receive money or property after his death and any recipient of a *donatio mortis causa*, because all this property forms part of the net estate: s. 25 (1).

[5] See *ante*, pp. 547-551.

conclusive in the changed circumstances brought about by the death.[1] It will usually be much more reasonable to expect a woman to make provision for her widower, particularly if his earning capacity is reduced, than to support her divorced husband.[2] In the case of a small estate it is particularly important to consider the extent to which an applicant will be supported by supplementary benefit or a supplementary pension or may be expected to make use of free hospital facilities under the National Health Act. If an order for financial provision will merely reduce the amount payable to him out of public funds without giving him any advantage, it may be eminently reasonable to use the whole estate to give a benefit to another applicant or beneficiary.[3]

(b) *The size and nature of the estate.* If, for example, the deceased had a large income but little capital, it might be reasonable for him to leave the whole of his estate to his widow to the total exclusion of others whom he had supported during his lifetime.

(c) *Any other relevant matter, including the conduct of the applicant or any other person.* In the case of a former spouse the test should be the same whether the application is made on divorce or after the other party's death—in other words it should affect the issue only if it was "obvious and gross".[4] It is submitted that this should be applied if the applicant is a widow or widower because he should be in no worse position than he would have been in if the marriage had been dissolved.[5] It is more difficult to see what weight the courts are likely to attach to children's conduct. It is submitted that the test should be this: bearing in mind the deceased's treatment of the applicant, was the latter's conduct towards him such that a reasonable parent would have considered that he had forfeited any further claim to financial provision?

If the applicant is a surviving spouse or a former spouse, the court must also have regard to the duration of the marriage, the applicant's age, and the contribution he or she made to the deceased's family including any contribution by looking after the home or caring for the deceased. Again the similarity with the law of divorce will be seen. In the case of a surviving spouse (except when a judicial separation was in force and the separation was continuing at the deceased's death), the court must also consider what provision the applicant might reasonably be expected to receive had the marriage been terminated by divorce instead of death.[6] Except in the rare case of an eccentric testator, he will have cut such an applicant out of his will only if the marriage had broken down *de facto* and it would be anomalous if the latter could expect less on death than she would have got on divorce. Former spouses and judicially separated spouses are excluded because they will

---

[1] *Cf.* (under the old law) *Re Inns*, [1947] Ch. 576, 581; [1947] 2 All E.R. 308, 311, and contrast *Re Charman*, [1951] 2 T.L.R. 1095, with *Re Borthwick*, [1949] Ch. 395; [1949] 1 All E.R. 472.

[2] *Cf. Re Clayton*, [1966] 2 All E.R. 370 (widower crippled and earning only £10 a week); *Re Wilson* (1969), 113 Sol. Jo. 794 (widower aged 92).

[3] *Cf. Re E.*, [1966] 2 All E.R. 44; *Re Clayton*, (*supra*); *Re Watkins*, [1949] 1 All E.R. 695.

[4] See *ante*, p. 555.

[5] See *infra.*

[6] S. 3 (2).

already have had an opportunity of applying for financial relief in the matrimonial proceedings in question.[1]

If the applicant is a child of the deceased or a person whom he treated as a child of the family, in addition to the general matters set out above the court must also have regard to the manner in which he was being or might expect to be educated or trained. If he is a child of the family but not the deceased's own child, the court must also consider the same matters as it has to take into account when deciding whether to make an order in favour of such a child on divorce.[2]

If the applicant comes within none of these categories but is relying on a *de facto* dependence during the deceased's lifetime, the court must specifically have regard to the extent to which the deceased had assumed responsibility for his maintenance, the basis upon which he had done so, and the length of time for which he had discharged it.[3] These are three of the matters which the court has to take into account when considering applications from persons who have been treated as children of the family and the similarity of their position is obvious. Bearing these points in mind, the court might well decide in a given case that the deceased had acted reasonably in leaving his estate to his wife and children to the exclusion of, say, the woman with whom he had been living.

Under the old law the most important consideration in all cases was the extent to which the deceased was under a moral obligation to make provision for the applicant.[4] So if his estate came largely from a former spouse, the children of that marriage might have a stronger claim than his widow,[5] and it was held that a father was under no obligation to provide for his unmarried daughter who had lived with a married man as his wife for 42 years.[6] OLIVER, J., appeared to apply this principle at first instance in *Re Coventry*[7] but it is doubtful whether it is now generally applicable in view of the insistence of the Court of Appeal that it was relevant only to the facts of the particular case.[8] The plaintiff, who at the time of the application was aged 48 and divorced, had left the Royal Navy and lived with his father for the last 19 years of the latter's life. Shortly after he returned home, his mother left because of the way in which her husband and son treated her. The plaintiff ran the house and looked after his father, and sought an order under the Act on the latter's death intestate. His disposable income was about £40 a week; his mother

---

[1] Hence if the deceased died within twelve months of the decree absolute (or the decree in the case of a judicial separation) and no application for financial relief has been made or, if it has, the proceedings have not been determined, the court on an application for an order under the Inheritance Act may treat the former spouse (or spouse) as though no decree had been made: s. 14. Otherwise the applicant would lose the benefit of both statutes.
[2] S. 3 (3). For the matters to be taken into account on divorce, see *ante*, p. 587.
[3] S. 3 (4). See Law Com. No. 61, paras. 91-93, and *cf. ante*, p. 625.
[4] *Per* WYNN-PARRY, J., in *Re Andrews*, [1955] 3 All E.R. 248, 249. See also *Re Joslin*, [1941] Ch. 200; [1941] 1 All E.R. 302; *Re Bellman*, [1963] P. 239; [1963] 1 All E.R. 513; *Roberts* v. *Roberts*, [1964] 3 All E.R. 503.
[5] *Re Styler*, [1942] Ch. 387; [1942] 2 All E.R. 201; *Re Sivyer*, [1967] 3 All E.R. 429.
[6] *Re Andrews*, (*supra*). But in an appropriate case the court might make an order in favour of an adult child who had chosen to follow an unremunerative career: *Re Ducksbury*, [1966] 2 All E.R. 374.
[7] [1980] Ch. 461, 475; [1979] 2 All E.R. 408, 418.
[8] [1980] Ch. 461, at pp. 488 and 495; [1979] 3 All E.R. 815, at pp. 822 and 827, C.A.

(who was the only other person interested in the estate which was worth about £7,000) lived entirely on social security benefits. The Court of Appeal held that it would be rare for a relatively young and able-bodied man in employment to succeed in a claim under the Act, and even though the plaintiff was a qualified claimant as the deceased's son, he would have to establish some special circumstances over and above his relationship. This he failed to do, and it is not surprising that the court upheld OLIVER, J.'s decision to dismiss his claim. Despite the court's apparent rejection of the principle that it is necessary to prove a moral obligation as a condition precedent to establishing a claim, it is submitted that in many cases it will remain the most important fact in determining its success.

Objective Test.—There was doubt under the old legislation whether it had to be shown that the testator had acted unreasonably in failing to make provision for the applicant, in which case his conduct must be judged by the circumstances known to him at the time of his death, or whether the court could take an objective view and enquire whether the provision was reasonable in the light of the facts as they existed at the time of the hearing.[1] The latter view is to be preferred because it looks at the reality of the applicant's financial position. The doubts have been resolved by the new Act which comes down in favour of the objective test and provides that the court shall take into account the facts as known at the hearing.[2] The injustice that could otherwise be worked can be seen by examining the facts of *Re Goodwin*,[3] which was decided under the old law. A testator provided for his children by making specific bequests in their favour and for his widow, their stepmother, by a legacy and the bequest of the residue of his estate. He expected the residue to be worth over £8,000 whereas it turned out to be worth about £1,500. Had the court applied the subjective test, it would have been bound to conclude that he acted reasonably; MEGARRY, J., however, applying the objective test, concluded that in the event the provision for the widow was not reasonable and made an order in her favour.

Evidence.—Earlier legislation gave the court much greater freedom in family provision cases by enabling evidence of the deceased's reasons for making particular provisions in his will (or for failing to make provision for the applicant) to be put in notwithstanding that it would otherwise have been inadmissible as hearsay. The new Act similarly provides that any oral or written statement made by the deceased may be admitted as evidence of any fact stated therein.[4]

Time in which the Application must be made.—In order to enable the personal representatives to distribute the estate, an application for provision

---

[1] See the fourth edition of this book at pp. 510-511.
[2] S. 3 (5).
[3] [1969] Ch. 283; [1968] 3 All E.R. 12. For other cases, see *Re Franks*, [1948] Ch. 62; [1947] 2 All E.R. 638 (testatrix died two days after the son's birth without altering will in his favour); *Re Clarke*, [1968] 1 All E.R. 451 (death of legatee immediately after testator); *Re Shanahan*, [1973] Fam. 1; [1971] 3 All E.R. 873, and *Lusternik* v. *Lusternik*, [1972] Fam. 125; [1972] 1 All E.R. 592, C.A. (change in value of estate after death).
[4] S. 21.

may not be made more than six months after the date on which representation is first taken out without the permission of the court.[1] Personal representatives will not be personally liable for distribution after this time if no application is then pending, but property may be recovered from the beneficiaries to whom it has been transferred if it is needed to make provision for a dependant to whom the court gives leave to make a late application.[2]

Property available for Financial Provision.—Except for the court's power to order the variation of an ante-nuptial or post-nuptial settlement (which will be considered later), it can only make orders for the payment of money out of the deceased's net estate or affecting property comprised in that estate.[3] Basically, this means such property as the deceased had power to dispose of by will (otherwise than by virtue of a special power of appointment) less the amount of funeral, testamentary and administration expenses and any liabilities.[4] Five other types of property are also comprised within the definition. First, property in respect of which the deceased had a general power of appointment not exercisable by will is included if the power was never exercised, for he could have exercised the power in his own favour and thus brought it within his estate.[5] Secondly, some statutes enable a person to nominate another to take the benefit of a fund after his death. This is equivalent to a testamentary disposition and such property is therefore part of his estate for this purpose notwithstanding any nomination.[6] For a similar reason *donationes mortis causa* made by the deceased are included.[7] Fourthly, the court may order the severance of a joint tenancy (or any part of a joint tenancy) to which the deceased was entitled immediately before his death and which would therefore otherwise pass to the other joint tenants *jure accrescendi*, for the same reason that he could have effected a severance himself and thus brought the property into his estate.[8] The undivided share will then form part of the net estate. Finally, the estate includes any money or property ordered to be restored or provided if a disposition or contract is set aside under the provisions now to be considered.

Transactions intended to defeat Applications.—We have seen that one of the weaknesses of earlier legislation was that the deceased could defeat an application by settling or disposing of his property during his lifetime so that it never formed part of his estate at all or, alternatively, could contract to

---

[1] Ss. 4 and 23. The applicant must establish grounds for taking the case out of the general rule. For the facts which the court will take into account, see *Re Salmon*, [1980] 3 All E.R. 532. In particular, permission is more likely to be given if negotiations were begun before the time limit expired and if the estate has not been distributed.

[2] S. 20 (1). On the question of distribution before the hearing of the application, see *Re Ralphs*, [1968] 3 All E.R. 285.

[3] S. 2 (1). For net estate generally, see Law Com. No. 61, paras. 127-143.

[4] S. 25 (1), (2).

[5] S. 25 (1).

[6] S. 8 (1).

[7] S. 8 (2). In this case and the last any person giving effect to the nomination or gift is protected.

[8] S. 9. This power can be exercised only if an application for an order for financial provision was made within six months from the date on which representation was first taken out. Any person dealing with the property before an order for severance is protected.

leave it to a third person after his death.[1] The new Act contains provisions designed to frustrate such transactions.

Under section 10 the court has a power to set aside a disposition made with the intention of defeating an application for financial provision under the Act which is similar to, but not identical with, the power to set aside transactions made with the intention of defeating an application for financial relief under the Matrimonial Causes Act.[2] There is no presumption of such an intention and the applicant must prove that the deceased intended to prevent an order being made under the Act or to reduce the amount of provision which might otherwise be granted, but this does not have to be his sole intention or, apparently, his principal intention.[3] This will undoubtedly create considerable difficulty in practice: if a man gives a substantial sum to his mistress, his apparent intention is to benefit her; how can it be proved that he also intended to reduce the amount of property available to his wife after his death? In many cases the court will probably have to fall back on the principle that a person may be presumed to have intended the natural and probable consequences of his acts. Because of the difficulty of establishing intention at a remote time in the past, the court has no power to set aside a disposition made more than six years before the deceased's death (or, in any case, before 1st April 1976, when the Act came into force).[4] Nor, whatever his intention was, can any disposition be set aside if the transferee gave full valuable consideration.[5]

If the court is satisfied that the exercise of the powers given by the section would facilitate the making of financial provision for the applicant, it may order the donee of the property in question to provide such sum of money or other property as it shall direct. It is immaterial that the latter no longer holds any interest in the original property, but he may not be ordered to pay or transfer more than the amount paid to him by the deceased (if the disposition took the form of the payment of money) or the value at the date of the deceased's death of any property transferred in other cases.[6] A similar order may be made against the donee's personal representatives, in which case it

---

[1] If the transaction was effected fraudulently with intent to defeat the defendant's claim, it is arguable that it could be set aside under the court's general power to upset fraudulent transactions or perhaps under s. 172 of the Law of Property Act 1925: see *Cadogan* v. *Cadogan*, [1977] 3 All E.R. 831, C.A. This might still be relevant *e.g.* if the transaction was made more than six years before the deceased's death.

[2] See *ante*, pp. 568-569. See further generally Law Com. No. 61, Part V.

[3] Ss. 10 (2) (a) and 12 (1). The court must be satisfied on the balance of probabilities that this was the deceased's intention.

[4] S. 10 (2) (a), (8).

[5] S. 10 (1) (b). Valuable consideration does not include marriage or a promise of marriage: s. 25 (1). A disposition does not include any testamentary gift, nomination or *donatio mortis causa* (all of which form part of the net estate) or any appointment made under a special power, but subject to these exceptions it includes any payment of money (including the payment of a premium under a policy of insurance) and any conveyance, assurance, appointment or gift of property: s. 10 (7).

[6] S. 10 (2)-(4). The value of any capital transfer tax borne by the donee must also be deducted. If the donee has himself disposed of the property he may not be required to restore more than its value when he disposed of it. If the disposition was made to the donee as trustee, the latter is further protected because the amount he is ordered to pay or transfer must not exceed the money or the value of the property in his hands at the time of the order (or the value of any property representing the money or original property): see s. 13.

must be limited to the payment of money or transfer of property out of that part of the donee's estate which has not yet been distributed.[1] Some measure of protection is given to the donee by the further provision that, before exercising its powers, the court must have regard to all the circumstances of the case, including particularly the circumstances in which the disposition to him was made, any valuable consideration given for it, the relationship (if any) of the donee to the deceased, and the donee's conduct and financial resources.[2] Thus, even if the deceased intended to defeat an application for financial provision by, say, the deceased's wife, the court is likely to be slower to set aside a gift to his indigent parents than to his unscrupulous mistress.

An application for an order under section 10 may be made not only by an applicant for financial provision but also by a donee or the personal representatives of a donee against whom the application is being made.[3] The court has wide powers to make consequential directions and to secure the adjustment of the rights of persons affected by its orders.[4]

Section 11 deals with contracts by which the deceased agreed that a sum of money or other property would be left by his will or paid or transferred out of his estate. If an agreement to dispose of property after the death were unimpeachable, it would obviously be more valuable than an actual disposition *inter vivos* which could be set aside. Consequently, if such a contract was made with the intention of defeating an application for financial provision under the Act and full valuable consideration was not given or promised for it, the court may direct the personal representatives not to pay or transfer the whole or any part of the money or property involved. If any payment or transfer has already been made to any person (who, for convenience, is also referred to as the donee), the court may order him to provide such sum of money or other property as may be specified.[5] There is, however, one important qualification to the court's powers under section 11: it may restrain the personal representatives and order restitution only to the extent that the amount of the sum or the value of the property in question exceeds the value of the consideration given or promised under the contract.[6] As in the case of a disposition already made, the deceased's intention to prevent the making of an order or to reduce the amount available need not have been his sole intention, but there is an important difference between contracts and dispositions in that, if no valuable consideration was given or promised for the contract, it will be presumed that he had this intention unless the contrary is shown.[7] A contract may be attacked however long before the deceased's

---

[1] S. 12 (4). A personal representative will not be liable for having distributed any part of the estate before he has notice that an application is being made for an order.

[2] S. 10 (6).

[3] Ss. 10 (1), (5) and 12 (4). The purpose of this is to enable the donee to argue that another transaction should be set aside rather than the one in his favour, or at least that the burden should be shared.

[4] S. 12 (3).

[5] S. 11 (2). The personal representatives may themselves postpone performance for six months without an order: s. 20 (3).

[6] S. 11 (3). Valuable consideration does not include marriage or a promise of marriage: s. 25 (1). If money or property has already been paid or transferred to the other party as trustee, he has the additional protection conferred by s. 13: see *ante*, p. 632, n. 6.

[7] S. 12 (1), (2).

deceased's death it was entered into, except that there is no power at all to upset a contract made before the Act came into force (1st April 1976).[1]

In other respects the provisions relating to the two types of transaction are similar. The court may exercise its powers only if there is an application for financial provision under the Act and it must be satisfied that this would facilitate the making of an order.[2] It may make an order against the donee's personal representatives; it must have regard to the same matters before exercising its powers; and it has the same power to give consequential directions, in particular with respect to the rights of any person to sue for breach of contract.[3]

Orders that may be made.—If a dependant is in immediate need of financial assistance and property forming part of the net estate can be made available to meet his needs but it is not yet possible to make a final order, the court may make an *interim order*. This may take the form of one payment or of periodical payments, and the court may later direct that any sum paid under an interim order shall be treated as having been paid on account of the final order. As far as possible, the same matters should be taken into account in making an interim order as in making a final order.[4]

If the court is satisfied that reasonable financial provision has not been made for the applicant, it may make a *final order* containing one or more of the provisions set out below.[5] In determining what order (if any) to make, the court must have regard to the same matters as it has when deciding whether reasonable provision has been made.[6]

(1) An order for periodical payments.[7] This may be for such a term and subject to such conditions as the court directs. Remarriage of the deceased's widow or widower will not automatically discharge the order (although it may be a ground for an application to have it discharged by the court) because a life interest on intestacy does not come to an end on that event and testators bequeath interests during widowhood much less frequently than they used to do.[8] It would be anomalous, however, to give former spouses and judicially separated spouses greater rights on the deceased's death than they had when the decree was made, and consequently an order for periodical payments made in their favour will terminate automatically on remarriage.[9]

---

[1] S. 11 (6).

[2] S. 11 (1), (2) (d).

[3] Ss. 11 (4), (5) and 12 (3), (4). The donee's personal representatives have the same protection as they have under s. 10. A right to sue for breach of contract survives only so far as is consistent with giving effect to the order restraining performance of the contract or directing restitution.

[4] S. 5. For the protection of personal representatives, see s. 20 (2).

[5] S. 2 (1). See generally Law Com. No. 61, paras. 109-126.

[6] S. 3 (1). See *ante*, pp. 626-630.

[7] This may be for a specified amount or for an amount equal to the whole or any part of the net estate or for an amount equal to the income of such part of the estate as the court directs to be set aside or appropriated for this purpose: s. 2 (2), (3).

[8] Law Com. No. 61, paras. 37-43.

[9] S. 19 (2). This applies to judicially separated spouses only if the decree was in force and the separation continuing at the time of the deceased's death. Treating such a spouse as though no decree had been made (see *ante*, p. 629, n. 1) does not appear to affect the operation of this sub-section and periodical payments would still cease on remarriage. Any other rule would produce a serious anomaly.

In other cases it would be reasonable to direct that payment to a child should terminate on his ceasing to receive education or training or that payment to a parent who is temporarily unable to work owing to illness should terminate on his ceasing to be under a disability.[1]

(2) The payment of a lump sum. This could be of particular importance if the estate is so small that any periodical payments would be valueless or if, say, a widow wishes to purchase the goodwill of a business or a child wants capital to set himself up in life. In *Malone* v. *Harrison*,[2] where it was agreed that the most appropriate form of provision for the deceased's mistress was the payment of a lump sum, HOLLINGS, J., resorted to the practice in claims under the Fatal Accidents Act of assessing her dependency and applying a multiplier to it. Whilst this has the merit of using a recognised principle for the quantification of the award, there are so many imponderables that it is submitted that only in exceptional circumstances should periodical payments be capitalised in this way. As on divorce, the court may order that a lump sum be paid by instalments.[3]

(3) The transfer or settlement of any property comprised in the net estate to or for the benefit of the applicant. The court might well order that the former matrimonial home be transferred or settled for the benefit of a surviving spouse, particularly if he or she has to bring up young children. In other cases it may be more convenient, as on divorce, to order the transfer of property *in specie* than the payment of a lump sum.

(4) The transfer or settlement of property to be acquired out of the estate to or for the benefit of the applicant. This has no counterpart in the Matrimonial Causes Act and is designed particularly to enable a home to be bought for the applicant.[4]

(5) The variation of any ante-nuptial or post-nuptial settlement made on the parties to a marriage of which the deceased was one. This is strictly equivalent to the court's powers on divorce and the variation may be made only for the benefit of the surviving party to the marriage or a child of the family in relation to that marriage.[5]

The similarity with orders that can be made under the Matrimonial Causes Act on divorce will be immediately apparent. It may at first sight appear anomalous that a former spouse can apply for orders for the transfer or settlement of property on the deceased's death when he could not have obtained a property adjustment order if he had sought a variation of an order for periodical payments under the Matrimonial Causes Act. It must be

---

[1] For examples of conditions under the old law see *Re Lidington*, [1940] Ch. 927; [1940] 3 All E.R. 600 (condition that widow should maintain minor children of the marriage); *Re Hills*, [1941] W.N. 123 (condition that applicant should inform trustees of the will if she became entitled to property worth £100 or more).

[2] [1979] 1 W.L.R. 1353. See Bryan, 96 L.Q.R. 165. For claims under the Fatal Accidents Act, see *ante*, pp. 138-143.

[3] S. 7. The court may subsequently vary the number and amount of instalments and the dates on which they are to be paid but not the total sum payable. A lump sum or the transfer of property could also be of particular benefit to an applicant in receipt of supplementary benefit because it would not affect his income and might enable him to make a capital purchase which he might not otherwise be able to afford (for example, a television set): *Millward* v. *Shenton*, [1972] 2 All E.R. 1025, C.A.

[4] See Law Com. No. 61, para. 116.

[5] For the variation of settlements, see *ante*, pp. 535-539.

realised, however, that a completely different situation is brought about by the death, which usually produces a major redistribution of capital. If the deceased had been living on investment income, for example, he will no longer need the securities for his own support.

When an order is made, the will or the law relating to intestacy (or both in the case of a partial intestacy) takes effect retrospectively from the deceased's death subject to its provisions.[1] The court has wide powers to give consequential directions and in particular must try to ensure that the order operates fairly as between the various beneficiaries. To this end it has a general power to vary the dispositions effected by the will and the law of intestacy.[2]

Variation of Orders.—A change in the financial circumstances of a person in whose favour an order has been made, any other person who comes within the category of those who might apply for an order, or a beneficiary of the deceased's estate, whom the order has deprived of the immediate benefit of his interest, may indicate that it is desirable to vary an order that has already been made. One thing is immediately apparent, however: the whole estate will have been distributed except for that part appropriated for the making of periodical payments. There are three consequences of this: an application for variation can be made only if an order for periodical payments is in existence,[3] it may affect only property presently applicable for the making of such payments,[4] and a variation in favour of another person can be made only at the expense of their recipient.

An application for variation may be made by anyone who has already applied for an order or would be entitled to apply for one if he were not time barred. It may also be made by the deceased's personal representatives, the trustees of any property affected, and any beneficiary of the estate.[5] The court may vary, suspend or discharge any existing order for periodical payments and revive any provision suspended.[6] If the payments are due to cease on the happening of a specified event (other than the remarriage of a former wife or husband) or at the expiration of a specified period of time, the court may direct that they shall continue.[7] It may also make an order for periodical payments, the payment of a lump sum, or the transfer of any part of the property available, to anyone eligible for financial provision (whether or not an order has previously been made in his favour).[8] There is no power to make an order for the settlement of property, the acquisition of other

---

[1] Ss. 19 (1) and 24.

[2] S. 2 (4). Although this appears to give the court a huge discretion, it necessarily had to exercise these powers under the old law: see *Re Preston*, [1969] 2 All E.R. 961. For the meaning of "beneficiary", see *ante*, p. 627, n. 4.

[3] Or within six months of the cessation of an order for periodical payments terminable on the happening of a specified event or the expiration of a specified time (other than the remarriage of a former spouse): s. 6 (3), (6) (b).

[4] Or applicable for the making of payments under an order of the type mentioned in the last note: s. 6 (6).

[5] S. 6 (5). For the meaning of beneficiary, see p. 627, n. 4, *ante*. An application may be made notwithstanding that there has been a previous variation: s. 6 (4).

[6] S. 6 (1).

[7] S. 6 (10).

[8] S. 6 (2). This includes power to make an order in favour of a person who would be entitled to apply for provision if he were not time barred.

property or the variation of an ante-nuptial or post-nuptial settlement.¹ In exercising its powers, the court must look at all the circumstances of the case, including any change in the matters to which it was bound to have regard when making the original order, and it may give such consequential directions as necessary.²

Relationship to Existing Agreements and Matrimonial Orders.—It must not be forgotten that other liabilities to support a dependant may survive the deceased's death. An order for secured periodical payments may have been made in his favour during previous matrimonial proceedings or he may be a party to a maintenance agreement under which payments continue. Not only will the existence of the continuing right affect any order that may be made if he applies for financial relief under the Act but also, in the changed circumstances brought about by the death, it may make unfairly generous provision for him compared with the amount left for other applicants. To prevent the unnecessary duplication of proceedings, the court may vary existing orders and agreements in proceedings under the Inheritance (Provision for Family and Dependants) Act.³

If an applicant for financial relief under the Inheritance Act continues to be entitled to secured periodical payments on an order made under the Matrimonial Causes Act, the court may vary or discharge the order or revive the operation of any provision which has been previously suspended.⁴ Similarly, if the applicant is still entitled to payments under a maintenance agreement, the court may vary or revoke the agreement.⁵ The definition of a maintenance agreement is the same as that contained in section 34 of the Matrimonial Causes Act except that it need not be in writing.⁶ These powers are exercisable only on the application of the personal representatives or the payee under the order or agreement and only if the payee brings proceedings under the Inheritance Act. In other cases the court has no power to reduce the sums payable if, in proceedings brought by another applicant under the Act, it comes to the conclusion that they are too large. This can be done only if the personal representatives themselves take proceedings to have the order or agreement varied under the Matrimonial Proceedings Act, which they may be unwilling to do.

Conversely, if the personal representatives, the recipient of secured periodical payments or a party to a maintenance agreement applies for a

---

¹ Nor may the court order the severance of a joint tenancy or set aside dispositions and contracts made with the intention of defeating a claim for financial provision: s. 6 (9). *Cf.* the court's powers on an application to vary an order under the Matrimonial Causes Act, *ante*, pp. 563 and 591.

² S. 6 (7), (8).

³ See further Law Com. No. 61, Part VII.

⁴ S. 16. The court must have regard to the same matters as it has when exercising its powers under the Inheritance Act and to any change in the matters to which it was required to have regard when making the order for secured periodical payments.

⁵ S. 17. The court must have regard to the same matters as it has when exercising its powers under the Inheritance Act and to any change in the circumstances in the light of which the agreement was made.

⁶ S. 17 (4). For the definition of a maintenance agreement under s. 34 of the Matrimonial Causes Act, see *ante*, p. 490.

variation of the order or agreement under the Matrimonial Causes Act,[1] the court may deem the application to have been accompanied by an application for an order under the Inheritance Act and exercise all the powers it has under that Act.[2] This may be of particular importance to a party to an agreement because it will be recalled that under the Matrimonial Causes Act there is no power to set aside a disposition intended to defeat an application for a variation of a maintenance agreement after the payer's death. By invoking this jurisdiction the court can exercise its jurisdiction to set aside dispositions and contracts under sections 10 and 11.

As part of an agreed financial settlement in matrimonial proceedings the parties may wish to exclude the possibility of an application for financial provision under the Inheritance Act. Whatever may be the danger that a party might find herself (or himself) in straitened financial circumstances after the other's death, the advantage lies in giving effect to their own wishes and finalising the proceedings. Accordingly such an agreement will be binding provided that it is embodied in a court order on divorce, nullity or judicial separation. The court must be satisfied that it is just to make the order and it can bar an application only from the parties to the marriage and not from any other person.[3]

D. THE STATUTORY TRANSMISSION OF TENANCIES

1. THE RENT ACT AND THE RENT (AGRICULTURE) ACT

We have already seen that the Rent Act and the Rent (Agriculture) Act prevent a landlord from arbitrarily evicting a tenant under a regulated tenancy.[4] In addition to protecting the tenant and his (or her) spouse, this must necessarily give security to members of the tenant's family so long as they are living with him. This secondary purpose of the Acts would be completely defeated if it were possible for the landlord to evict the members of the tenant's family immediately the tenancy was ended by the tenant's death. Consequently the Acts provide that, subject to certain conditions, security shall be given to members of the deceased tenant's family by vesting a statutory tenancy in them. It is, of course, open to the landlord to grant a fresh contractual tenancy to the person remaining in possession. Whether or not he has done so must be a question of fact in each case, but a contractual tenancy cannot be inferred from the mere receipt of rent as the landlord is bound to accept the new tenant.[5] If he does not do so, the new tenant has all

---

[1] See *ante*, pp. 495 and 564. In this case of course the agreement must be a maintenance agreement within s. 34 of the Matrimonial Causes Act.

[2] S. 18.

[3] S. 15. See Law Com. No. 61, paras. 185-188. On divorce and nullity the order will not take effect until the decree is made absolute; on judicial separation it will be effective only if the decree was in force and the separation was continuing at the time of the other party's death. It will also prevent the court from deeming an application for variation under the Matrimonial Causes Act to be accompanied by an application for an order under the Inheritance Act: s. 18 (3).

[4] *Ante*, pp. 471 *et seq.*

[5] *Dealex Properties, Ltd.* v. *Brooks*, [1966] 1 Q.B. 542; [1965] 1 All E.R. 1080, C.A.

the protection given by the Acts to the person who becomes a statutory tenant by remaining in possession after his contractual tenancy has ended.

To whom the Tenancy may be transmitted.—There are two classes of persons to whom a statutory tenancy may be transmitted.[1]

(1) *The Tenant's Surviving Spouse.*—There is an automatic transfer to the surviving spouse of the tenant provided that she or he was residing in the dwelling-house immediately before the tenant's death. The widow (or widower) remains a statutory tenant so long as she occupies the dwelling-house as her residence even though she subsequently remarries.[2] It will be observed that the residence qualification prevents the wife (or husband), who is in desertion or who has been constructively deserted and, in either case has left the premises from claiming the benefit of the Act.

(2) *Members of the Tenant's Family.*—If the tenant leaves no widow or widower residing in the same dwelling-house, there is a transmission to any member of his or her family who has been residing with the tenant for not less than six months immediately before the death. Such a tenancy can vest in only one person;[3] consequently if there are more members of the family than one, they should decide amongst themselves to whom it is to be transmitted. If they cannot come to an agreement, the question must be determined by the county court.[4]

The words "residing with" must be given their ordinary and popular meaning.[5] As EVERSHED, M.R., said in *Edmunds* v. *Jones*,[6] the successor must have "lived [in] and shared for living purposes the whole of the premises to which he or she claims to have succeeded". Hence, as in that case, there will be no transmission of the tenancy if the successor was in fact the sub-tenant of the deceased tenant.

It is not sufficient that the claimant and the deceased should have been members of the same family: the former must show that he was a member of the latter's family.[7] This expression is not easy to define and has given rise to a spate of litigation. It is not a term of art and must be construed in its ordinary and popular sense.[8] Some judicial limit, however, has been placed upon the term. With one exception either the tenant and the claimant have been related by blood or marriage or, alternatively, the claimant was adopted by the tenant (if not by a legal adoption order at least *de facto*) as a child. Thus

---

[1] Rent Act 1977, s. 2 and Sched. 1, Part I; Rent (Agriculture) Act 1976, s. 4 (2)-(5); Housing Act 1980, s. 76.

[2] *Apsley* v. *Barr*, [1928] N.I. 183.

[3] *Dealex Properties, Ltd.* v. *Brooks*, (*supra*).

[4] The court must take into account the merits of the rival claims, the claimants' needs and perhaps the wishes (or probable wishes) of the deceased tenant: see *Williams* v. *Williams*, [1970] 3 All E.R. 988.

[5] *Morgan* v. *Murch*, [1970] 2 All E.R. 100, C.A.

[6] [1957] 1 W.L.R. 1118, n., 1120, C.A. See further *Foreman* v. *Beagley*, [1969] 3 All E.R. 838, C.A. (son living in mother's flat whilst she was in hospital not "residing with" her); Megarry, *Rent Acts*, 10th Ed., 212-214.

[7] *Langdon* v. *Horton*, [1951] 1 K.B. 666, at pp. 669, 671; [1951] 1 All E.R. 60, at pp. 60, 61, C.A.

[8] *Carega Properties S.A.* v. *Sharratt*, [1979] 2 All E.R. 1084, at pp. 1086, 1088, H.L.

tenancies have been successfully claimed by the tenant's legitimate children (together with their husbands or wives),[1] children adopted *de facto* during minority,[2] and thè tenant's brothers and sisters.[3] It has also been suggested that the class includes illegitimate children and step-children,[4] and there can be no doubt that this is correct.

It does not follow, however, that all persons related to the tenant can be regarded as members of his family. The parties' conduct must be taken into account as well[5] and, the more remote the relationship, the more important this may become. In *Langdon* v. *Horton*,[6] for example, where two sisters had gone to live with their widowed cousin and had stayed with her until she died 29 years later, the Court of Appeal held that they were no more members of her family than would be two strangers to the blood who shared a flat for their convenience. In *Jones* v. *Whitehill*[7] on the other hand, it was held that a niece who had gone to look after her elderly aunt and uncle in their declining years was a member of their family as she had assumed "out of natural love and affection the duties and offices peculiarly attributable to members of a family".[8] Where there is no blood relationship or relationship by marriage at all, however, the House of Lords has held that the tenant cannot possibly turn another adult into a member of his family for this purpose simply by treating him as though he were, and it rejected the claim of a young man who, at the age of 25, went to live with and look after a woman more than 50 years older than himself notwithstanding that she treated him as her nephew.[9]

The one exception that the Court of Appeal has admitted to this principle is the case of a man and woman who were not married to each other but who had been living together outwardly as husband and wife. In 1950 the Court took the view that the survivor was not entitled to be treated as a member of the other's family—at least if they had no children—on the ground that a purely platonic relationship cannot produce this result and consequently it would not be right to give the survivor a stronger claim if the parties had been "living in sin".[10] In *Dyson Holdings, Ltd.* v. *Fox*,[11] however, they held that in 1975 the attitude of society generally towards such unions had now changed to such an extent that they would be popularly regarded as members of the

---

[1] *Standingford* v. *Probert*, [1950] 1 K.B. 377; [1949] 2 All E.R. 861, C.A. In *Perry* v. *Dembowski*, [1951] 2 K.B. 420; [1951] 2 All E.R. 50, C.A., the Court of Appeal left open the interesting question whether a child of four or five years of age could be a member of his deceased parent's family for the purpose of the Rent Act.

[2] *Brock* v. *Wollams*, [1949] 2 K.B. 388; [1949] 1 All E.R. 715, C.A.

[3] *Price* v. *Gould* (1930), 143 L.T. 333.

[4] *Brock* v. *Woollams*, (*supra*), at pp. 394 and 717 (*per* BUCKNILL, L.J.), 396 and 718 (*per* DENNING, L.J.), respectively.

[5] *Ross* v. *Collins*, [1964] 1 All E.R. 861, 865, C.A.

[6] [1951] 1 K.B. 666; [1951] 1 All E.R. 60, C.A.

[7] [1950] 2 K.B. 204; [1950] 1 All E.R. 71, C.A. See further EVERSHED, M.R.'s remarks on this case in *Langdon* v. *Horton*, (*supra*), at pp. 669 and 61, respectively.

[8] At pp. 207 and 72, respectively.

[9] *Carega Properties S.A.* v. *Sharratt*, (*supra*). *Cf. Ross* v. *Collins*, (*supra*). Nor do servants and lodgers come within the definition, for it could not have been the intention of Parliament to protect them: *per* COHEN, L.J., in *Brock* v. *Wollams*, (*supra*), at pp. 394 and 718, respectively.

[10] *Gammans* v. *Ekins*, [1950] 2 K.B. 328; [1950] 2 All E.R. 140, C.A.

[11] [1976] Q.B. 503; [1975] 3 All E.R. 1030, C.A. See Bradley, 39 M.L.R. 222.

same family; consequently a woman was able to claim a statutory tenancy when she and the deceased tenant had lived together as husband and wife for over 20 years. This does not mean that every mistress is entitled to the protection of the Rent Act or that every sexual relationship, however casual, intermittent or impermanent, could create a family unit: this will occur only if it had a sufficient degree of apparent permanence and stability to justify the court's concluding as a question of fact that the survivor could be regarded as a member of the tenant's family.[1] The inference will be stronger if they had children or if they held themselves out as being husband and wife; it will be correspondingly weaker if they continued to use their own surnames and if one (or both) of them was already married and had another family elsewhere.[2] None of these matters, however, is conclusive, and in *Watson* v. *Lucas*[3] the man (who had a wife and child in Ireland) was able to claim a statutory tenancy even though he and the deceased tenant (with whom he had lived for 19 years before her death) had no children and had used their own surnames on most occasions. In *Helby* v. *Rafferty*,[4] on the other hand, the Court of Appeal refused to extend the principle to a case where the parties had lived together for some five years before the woman's death but had never held themselves out as husband and wife because the woman, at least, chose to retain the freedom to withdraw from the relationship. The decision in *Dyson Holdings, Ltd.* v. *Fox* has been heavily criticised on the ground that a change of social habit cannot change the meaning of a word which first appeared in the Rent Acts over 50 years ago:[5] the House of Lords has left the point open[6] and it clearly needs a decision of that House before the law can be stated with certainty.[7]

Limitations on Transmission.—There are two important limitations on transmission. First, the statutory tenancy must still be in existence. Hence, if the tenancy has been terminated by the tenant's vacating the premises or by the landlord's obtaining an order for possession against him before his death, the landlord is entitled to possession against the members of his family remaining on the premises.[8]

---

[1] *Watson* v. *Lucas*, [1980] 3 All E.R. 647, C.A.

[2] *Watson* v. *Lucas*, (*supra*). See also *Hawes* v. *Evenden*, [1953] 2 All E.R. 737, C.A., where *Gammans* v. *Ekins*, (*supra*), was distinguished on the ground that the couple had a child.

[3] [1980] 3 All E.R. 647, C.A.

[4] [1978] 3 All E.R. 1016, C.A.

[5] *Helby* v. *Rafferty*, (*supra*), at pp. 1018, 1024 and 1026.

[6] *Carega Properties S.A.* v. *Sharratt*, (*supra*), at p. 1086.

[7] Zuckermann, *Formality and the Family*, 96 L.Q.R. 248, proposes a novel test (at p. 264): was the relationship between the deceased tenant and the claimant such that it may be inferred that the former assumed such a responsibility for the latter's welfare that lack of security for him would have undermined the tenant's own security? This might effectively prevent transmission in some cases where it has been allowed. See generally Berkovits, [1981] J.S.W.L. 83.

[8] This is so even though the court has suspended the execution of an order for possession and the tenant dies before the order takes effect: *American Economic Laundry, Ltd.* v. *Little*, [1951] 1 K.B. 400; [1950] 2 All E.R. 1186, C.A. The Court of Appeal left open the question what the position would be if a conditional order had been made (at pp. 406 and 1190, respectively), but they have subsequently said that, in order to prevent this difficulty from arising, courts should not make orders suspended indefinitely or for a long period of time: *Mills* v. *Allen*, [1953] 2 Q.B. 341, at pp. 357, 364; [1953] 2 All E.R. 534, at pp. 544, 547, C.A.

Secondly, there must obviously be some limitation upon the number of times that a statutory tenancy can be transmitted, for otherwise it could be tied up in the family in perpetuity and the landlord could never obtain possession. Under the Rent (Agriculture) Act there cannot be more than one transmission; under the Rent Act there cannot be more than two and the second can operate only if the person who became the statutory tenant by the first continues to occupy the premises as his or her residence.[1] The rules and limitations relating to the second transmission are exactly the same as those relating to the first. Thus, if on the death of a statutory tenant there is a transmission to his widow, there may be a second transmission on her death to any member of her family who had been residing with her for not less than six months immediately beforehand. There cannot be any further transmission after the death of that person, however.[2]

To protect a landlord who might inadvertently prejudice his position by granting a fresh tenancy to a statutory successor, it is expressly provided that his doing so shall not affect the number of transmissions.[3]

Nature of a Transmitted Tenancy.—The new tenant takes the tenancy on the same terms as his predecessor, with all the rights and liabilities, advantages and disadvantages unaltered.[4] Thus the burden of paying the same rent, of repairs, or of restrictive covenants will fall on him as it fell on the deceased tenant.[5] Similarly he may exercise any power the statutory tenant had to sub-let a part of the premises, and consequently, as the Court of Appeal held in *Lewis* v. *Reeves*,[6] his sub-tenant is protected by the Acts. Thus if the tenant under a second transmitted tenancy wishes to give further security to a member of his family, his best plan is to grant a sub-tenancy to that person provided that he may lawfully do so.[7]

Contractual Tenants.—Up till now we have been considering the position where the deceased tenant was a statutory tenant. Originally it was held that there could be no transmission if the deceased tenant was a contractual lessee, with the result that the protection given to the widow of a statutory tenant would not be accorded to the widow of a protected tenant if he chose to bequeath his interest to someone else. It was partly because of this anomaly

---

[1] Rent Act 1977, s. 2 and Sched. 1, Part I; Rent (Agriculture) Act 1976, s. 3. Nor can there be more than one transmission of a regulated tenancy which would come within the latter Act if it were not within the former: Rent Act 1977, Sched. 1, para. 11.

[2] If the court vests a statutory tenancy (arising under the Rent Act or the Rent (Agriculture) Act) in the tenant's spouse on divorce or nullity (see *ante*, p. 478), this does not affect the total number of transmissions that can take place: Matrimonial Homes Act 1967, s. 7 (3), (3A), as amended and added by the Rent Act 1977, Sched. 23, and the Rent (Agriculture) Act 1976, Sched. 8.

[3] Rent Act 1977, Sched. 1, para. 10.

[4] *Bolsover Colliery Co., Ltd.* v. *Abbott*, [1946] K.B. 8, 12, C.A.; *Tickner* v. *Clifton*, [1929] 1 K.B. 207, 211.

[5] *Bolsover Colliery Co., Ltd.* v. *Abbott*, (*supra*), followed in *American Economic Laundry, Ltd.* v. *Little*, [1951] 1 K.B. 400; [1950] 2 All E.R. 1186, C.A. But the new tenant is not liable for arrears of rent owed by his predecessor: *Tickner* v. *Clifton*, (*supra*), and therefore could not have a possession order made against him on this ground, since the rent is not due *from the tenant*.

[6] [1952] 1 K.B. 19; [1951] 2 All E.R. 855, C.A.

[7] See the remarks of DENNING, L.J., at pp. 26 and 859, respectively. He could not do so, *e.g.*, if the terms of the tenancy forbade sub-letting.

that the House of Lords held in *Moodie* v. *Hosegood*[1] that the widow or other member of the family is entitled to the same protection whether the deceased was a statutory or protected tenant provided, of course, that the dwelling-house is held on a regulated tenancy. This rule has now been given statutory effect.[2] Suppose that a husband, H, dies leaving a widow, W, and a son, S, to whom he has bequeathed the balance of the lease on which H held the matrimonial home. The contractual lease passes to H's personal representatives who must then vest it in S, whilst at the same time a statutory tenancy vests in W. It seems impossible that there should be two adverse tenancies in existence at the same time; the true position is that the contractual tenancy is in abeyance until the statutory tenancy is determined. The result was thus described by LORD MORTON OF HENRYTON in *Moodie* v. *Hosegood*:[3]

> "If a contractual tenancy is still subsisting at her husband's death and devolves upon someone other than the widow, it is not destroyed, but the rights and obligations which would ordinarily devolve upon the successor in title of the contractual tenant are suspended so long as the widow retains possession of the dwelling-house.
>
> "If the contractual tenancy is determinable by notice, the landlord or the contractual tenant can determine it by giving the appropriate notice, but such notice will not affect the widow's rights and obligations ... and, if no notice is given, the contractual tenancy will come into full operation when the widow gives up possession.... If the contractual tenancy is a lease for years, it will remain in being, but so long as the widow remains in possession she, and not the contractual tenant, is bound to observe the terms and conditions of the lease and has the benefit thereof.... At no time are there two tenants, each one entitled to the benefit and subject to the burden of the contractual tenancy. The so-called statutory tenant is not a tenant in the true sense. He or she is merely a person who is given certain protection by the Acts...."

But whilst this rule removes one anomaly, it creates a number of injustices and difficulties. Thus if H were to devise another house to W with the intention that she should live in that and that S should live in the house bequeathed to him, his intentions can be completely defeated, for W can claim the beneficial interest in the former as devisee and remain in the latter as statutory tenant, and S cannot obtain a possession order against her as he is not the landlord. Moreover, if the lessor determines the contractual tenancy by giving notice to S, S is deprived of the protection of the Rent Act as he is not a contractual tenant in possession. There is little incentive for the landlord to obtain a possession order since this could enure only for the benefit of S whose contractual tenancy will then resume its full force. Nor will the position be eased when the widow dies, for there can be a second transmission to a member of her family residing with her.[4]

---

[1] [1952] A.C. 61; [1951] 2 All E.R. 582, H.L.

[2] See now the Rent Act 1977, s. 2 (1) (b), and the Rent (Agriculture) Act 1976, s. 4 (2).

[3] At pp. 74 and 586, respectively.

[4] For a fuller criticism of *Moodie* v. *Hosegood* and the difficulties which it raises, see Megarry, *Rent Acts*, 10th Ed., 221-224, and *The Rent Acts and the Invention of New Doctrines*, 67 L.Q.R. 505, 512 *et seq.*

2. SECURE TENANCIES

Periodic Tenancies.—In order to prevent housing in the public sector from being tied up for an unduly long period of time, succession to periodic secure tenancies on the death of the tenant is much more limited than transmission under the Rent Act. Three important differences may be noted.

First, there may be only one succession (as under the Rent (Agriculture) Act).[1]

Secondly, there can be no succession at all in the following circumstances:[2]

(a) If the deceased tenant was originally a joint tenant and had become the sole tenant. The reason for this is that the majority of joint tenants will be husbands and wives and consequently the survivor will be in the same position as a widow or widower who has taken by succession.

(b) If the periodic tenancy followed a tenancy for a term certain and the first tenancy had been granted to another person or to another person and the deceased tenant jointly.

(c) If the tenant became tenant by assignment or on the tenancy being vested in him on the death of the previous tenant. Most assignments will, as we have seen, deprive the tenancy of the quality of a secure tenancy: in the case of one, assignment in pursuance of a property adjustment order under section 24 of the Matrimonial Causes Act, it is expressly provided that this is not to affect succession. Hence, in such a case if there could have been a succession on the death of the original tenant, there can still be a succession on the death of the transferee if she is still occupying the same dwelling-house on her death. The position if the court has made an order under section 7 of the Matrimonial Homes Act vesting the tenancy in one of the spouses on divorce or nullity is obscure. This would appear to be an assignment (or alternatively the transferee would be a joint tenant who had become a sole tenant). This implies that there could be no succession to the latter. On the other hand, the Act provides that "where the ... spouse is a successor ..., [the transferee] shall be deemed also to be a successor".[3] The inference is that if the former is not a successor, the latter will not be one either. The provisions are in conflict, and whilst the more obvious conclusion is that there can be a succession so that it is immaterial under which Act the order is made, the matter must remain in doubt until we have an authoritative judicial decision.

Thirdly, there can be a succession only by a *qualified successor*. No person is qualified unless he occupied the dwelling-house as his only or principal home at the time of the tenant's death. In addition he or she must be either the tenant's spouse or a member of his family who, in the latter case, has resided with the tenant throughout the period of twelve months ending with the tenant's death. The term "residing with" presumably has the same meaning as it has in the Rent Act.[4] If there is more than one person qualified to succeed, the surviving spouse is preferred to any other member of his family; if there is no surviving spouse and two or more persons are qualified, they

---

[1] Housing Act 1980, s. 30 (1).

[2] *Ibid.*, ss. 30 (1) and 31 (1).

[3] Matrimonial Homes Act 1967, s. 7 (2), as amended by the Housing Act 1980, Sched. 25, para. 16.

[4] See *ante*, p. 639.

must agree amongst themselves which of them is to succeed and, if they cannot agree, the landlord may select one of them.[1]

Another important difference between the two Acts is that membership of the tenant's family is precisely defined for the purpose of the Housing Act. A person is a member of the tenant's family if

> "he is his spouse, parent, grandparent, child, grandchild, brother, sister, uncle, aunt, nephew or niece; treating—
> (a) any relationship by marriage as a relationship by blood, any relationship of the half blood as a relationship of the whole blood and the stepchild of any person as his child; and
> (b) an illegitimate person as the legitimate child of his mother and reputed father;
> or if they live together as husband and wife."[2]

It will thus be seen that the mass of litigation to which this term has given rise under the Rent Act will not be repeated under the Housing Act.

The landlord who gives a successor a fresh tenancy is given similar protection under the Housing Act to that given to a landlord under the Rent Act. If a tenant under a periodic secure tenancy to which there could be no (or no further) succession is given a further periodic secure tenancy and either the premises or the landlord (or both) is the same under both tenancies, there can be no succession to the second tenancy provided that it was granted within six months of the termination of the first.[3] Consequently, for example, if a widow moves to a smaller house on the death of her husband and both houses are leased to her by the same local authority, there can be no succession to the second tenancy on her death.

The successor will become a periodic secure tenant.

Tenancies for a Term Certain.—The Act refers only to succession to a secure tenancy which is a periodic tenancy. This raises the question whether a person who would be a qualified successor in such a case can claim to be a successor if a secure tenancy is for a term certain. Suppose, for example, that a tenant under a lease for seven years dies intestate; can the woman with whom he has been cohabiting in the house claim a right to stay there? It will be recalled that the rule that there can be a transmission of a protected tenancy under the Rent Act was originally laid down not by statute but by the House of Lords in *Moodie* v. *Hosegood*[4] in order to remove an anomaly. The arguments which led to this decision are equally strong in the case of secure tenancies and it should be applied.

---

[1] Housing Act 1980, s. 30.
[2] *Ibid.*, s. 50 (3). The definition is not free from ambiguity. Can two limbs be run together? *E.g.*, can the child of a stepchild or of an illegitimate child succeed as a grandchild?
[3] *Ibid.*, s. 31 (2).
[4] [1952] A.C. 61; [1951] 2 All E.R. 582, H.L. See further *ante*, p. 643.

Part IV

Extra-Marital Cohabitation

SUMMARY OF CONTENTS

Chapter 18

Extra-Marital Cohabitation

A. INTRODUCTORY

Until about ten years ago extra-marital cohabitation gave neither party any rights over and above those possessed by other persons living together who were not married to each other. Indeed they might find themselves, legally speaking, in a worse position than, say, a brother and sister living together because their relationship, involving, as it did, fornication, might deprive them of rights which they might otherwise have. If, for example, a woman contributed a sum towards the purchase of a house in which she was to live with her brother in consideration of his undertaking to have it conveyed into their joint names, she could have the agreement enforced; if, however, she contributed towards the purchase of a house in which she was to cohabit with a man to whom she was not married, the illicit purpose of the transaction probably precluded her from relying on the agreement.

There were at least three reasons why the courts should take this view. In the first place, extra-marital intercourse was regarded as immoral and therefore contrary to public policy. As a result, the application of the maxim *Ex turpi causa non oritur actio* led the courts to regard as void any agreement entered into with this object in view. In *Upfill* v. *Wright*[1] the plaintiff let a flat to the defendant who was to his knowledge the mistress of a man who intended to visit her there. In holding that the plaintiff could not recover the rent, DARLING, J., said:[1]

> "The flat was let to the defendant for the purpose of enabling her to receive the visits of the man whose mistress she was and to commit fornication with him there. I do not think that it makes any difference whether the defendant is a common prostitute or whether she is merely the mistress of one man ..."

As late as 1959 the Court of Appeal was of the view in *Diwell* v. *Farnes*[2] that any attempt by a woman to claim an interest in a house bought by the man with whom she had been living by spelling out an agreement that they should buy it as a joint venture was doomed to failure because such a contract would be unenforceable as founded on an immoral consideration.

Secondly, it is in the interests of society generally that the relationship that parties enter into should be as stable as possible, particularly if they have

---

[1] [1911] 1 K.B. 506.
[2] At p. 510.
[3] [1959] 2 All E.R. 379, at pp. 384 (*per* ORMEROD, L.J.) and 388 (*per* WILLMER, L.J.), C.A. *Cf. Gammans* v. *Ekins*, [1950] 2 K.B. 328; [1950] 2 All E.R. 140, C.A.

children. If, as it was believed, marital relationships are more stable than extra-marital ones, the law can encourage social stability by giving rights and privileges to married couples which are not shared by those who are not married. This argument can also be put in another form: if the parties choose not to undertake the obligations of marriage, they cannot claim the attendant rights. Looked at in one way, the law is seen to penalise people cohabiting outside marriage; looked at in another, it is giving effect to the independence which they appear to prefer.

A third reason for refusing to accord rights to extra-marital cohabitants is the difficulty of determining precisely what relationship should create them. A spouse claiming a right as a spouse merely has to establish the marriage. Extra-marital relations, on the other hand, can take a number of forms, from the casual act of intercourse through intermittent and temporary affairs to a long lasting cohabitation indistinguishable from marriage except for the absence of a legal ceremony. To say, for example, as does the Domestic Violence and Matrimonial Proceedings Act, that claims can be made by "a man and a woman who are living with each other in the same household as husband and wife" begs the whole question. Unless the parties are actually passing themselves off as husband and wife (which is apparently not what the Act means), it implies a unique and readily identifiable relationship which does not exist in fact. One of the most difficult aspects of the development of the principle that extra-marital relationships can give rise to claims is the definition of the relationships involved.

During the past ten years or so, however, there has been a considerable departure from the traditional view. A series of cases going back to 1972 has established the principle that a cohabitant can claim a contractual licence to remain in occupation of a house owned by her partner and can establish a proprietary interest under a resulting or constructive trust or the doctrine of estoppel. Whether *Upfill* v. *Wright* itself is still to be regarded as good law is doubtful because it appears to be inconsistent with the decision of the Court of Appeal in 1977 in *Heglibiston Establishment* v. *Heyman*.[1] The plaintiff had let a flat to the defendant. One of the covenants in the lease provided that the premises should not be used for an immoral purpose. The plaintiff brought proceedings for possession alleging that the tenant was in breach of this covenant by permitting his son to live in the flat with a woman to whom he was not married. The Court of Appeal held that this did not produce a forfeiture: what the clause was aimed at was preventing the flat from being used as a brothel or for the purposes of prostitution. This seems irreconcilable with the views of DARLING, J., and to reflect a change in judicial attitude. Whilst a contract to promote illicit sexual relations will still be void, it is possible that this rule now applies only to meretricious transactions involving sexual intercourse for a money consideration.

At the same time Parliament has given claims to cohabitants which could scarcely have been imagined in the earlier years of this century. By enabling a *de facto* dependant to apply for an order under the Inheritance (Provision for Family and Dependants) Act 1975, it has given a cohabitant the right to claim

---

[1] (1977), 121 Sol. Jo. 851, C.A. Only MEGAW, L.J., suggested that *Upfill* v. *Wright* should not be regarded as good law; BROWN, L.J., distinguished it on the facts and ROSKILL, L.J., did not find it necessary to decide the point.

provision after her (or his) partner's death which she did not have during his lifetime. The Domestic Violence and Matrimonial Proceedings Act 1976 expressly gives a cohabitant the same right as a spouse to apply for an injunction to restrain the other party from molestation and to exclude him from the house in which they are living. The judges have also interpreted the Rent Act in such a way as to give a cohabitant the right to succeed to a tenancy as a member of the deceased tenant's family.

The judicial and parliamentary attitude towards extra-marital cohabitation does no more than reflect the attitude of society generally towards those who choose to live together outside marriage rather than in it. As we shall see, the rights arising from cohabitation are still very limited indeed, although in one of the fields in which they matter most—that of property—they have advanced quite a long way. What we shall examine in the next section is the extent to which cohabitation as such can give rise to claims; in the final section we will consider how far it is possible for the parties to regulate their relationship by a legally enforceable agreement.[1]

B. RIGHTS ARISING FROM EXTRA-MARITAL COHABITATION

1. PERSONAL RIGHTS

With two, or possibly three, exceptions the legal consequences of marriage examined in chapter 4 will not apply to cohabitants at all. So the man will be guilty of rape if he has sexual intercourse with the woman against her will. The rules relating to a spouse's competence to give evidence and the privilege accorded to matrimonial communications will not apply. The substantive rules of criminal law relating to conspiracy and theft are equally inapplicable. Of greater importance is the fact that a man with no right of abode cannot gain admission to this country or claim to remain here on the ground that he is living with a woman if he is not married to her. Nor will either party have any claim against a tortfeasor for loss of the other's consortium either at common law or under the Fatal Accidents Act.

The first exception to this rule is a relatively trivial one: the presumption of agency arising from cohabitation applies when a woman is living with a man as his wife even though they are not married to each other. The cases suggest that this principle operates only if they hold themselves out as married,[2] and the presumption will not apply, of course, once they have separated.[3] The second, and doubtful, exception relates to the protection of confidences. As we have seen, the courts will restrain one spouse from publishing confidential

---

[1] A number of articles have been written on the rights of cohabitants. The fullest discussion is to be found in Pearl, *The Legal Implications of a Relationship outside Marriage*, [1978] C.L.J. 252; attention is also drawn to Dwyer, *Immoral Contracts*, 93 L.Q.R. 386; Zuckerman, *Formality and the Family*, 96 L.Q.R. 248; Freeman and Lyon, 130 New L.J. 228.

[2] *Munro* v. *De Chemant* (1815), 4 Camp. 215; *Blades* v. *Free* (1829), 9 B. & C. 167. But in *Watson* v. *Threlkeld* (1798), 2 Esp. 637, it was held that the tradesman could recover even though he was aware of all the facts, and in *Debenham* v. *Mellon* (1880), 6 App. Cas. 24, 33, H.L., LORD SELBORNE, L.C., stated *obiter* that the presumption arises if the woman lives with the man whether or not she assumes the name of his wife. For the presumption, see *ante*, pp. 152-154.

[3] *Munro* v. *De Chemant*, (*supra*). *A fortiori* the presumption will not arise if they never cohabited at all even though the man permits the woman to use his name: *Gomme* v. *Franklin* (1859), 1 F. & F. 465.

communications received from the other,[1] and there seems no reason in principle why this should not apply to any other couple whose relationship is such that similar confidences will be exchanged. The third, and most important, exception concerns physical protection.

Physical Protection.—As in the case of married couples, either cohabitant may bring criminal or civil proceedings against the other for assault, but they are likely to be of no greater practical value.[2] Violence, however, is as likely to occur amongst unmarried cohabitants as it is amongst married ones. In order to give them the same degree of protection, the provisions of section 1 of the Domestic Violence and Matrimonial Proceedings Act 1976 apply "to a man and a woman who are living with each other in the same household as husband and wife as they apply to the parties to a marriage and any reference to the matrimonial home shall be construed accordingly".[3] It will be recalled that, in broad terms, that section enables a county court to grant an injunction (i) restraining either partner from molesting the applicant or a child living with the applicant, (ii) excluding him from the matrimonial home, any part of it or a specified area in which it is situated, and (iii) requiring him to permit the applicant to enter the matrimonial home or a part of it.

The first question that arises is the meaning of the phrase "a man and woman living in the same household as husband and wife". In the leading case of *Davis* v. *Johnson*[4] members of the House of Lords referred to "an unmarried housewife",[5] "an unmarried woman commonly but not very appropriately referred to as a 'common law wife' ",[6] and "unmarried partners".[7] It has not been suggested that they should be holding themselves out as married: there is no evidence that the parties had done so in *Davis* v. *Johnson*. The phrase implies, however, that they have been living together on a day to day basis: thus if a man living with his wife visits his mistress daily, he could hardly be said to be living with the latter as her husband. It is arguable, however, that the same person could be living with two partners in this relationship in different households simultaneously: if a man living with his wife in London spends a considerable amount of his time on business in Manchester and, whilst there, regularly lives with another woman, could they not also be said to be living as husband and wife?[8] It is probable that the parties must also intend that the cohabitation should be permanent or at least for an indefinite period of time: a man and woman living together whilst on holiday or, for example, for so long as they are both residing in the same town as students *prima facie* do not appear to be living with each other as husband and wife.

The phrase "living with each other in the same household" is identical with that used in the Matrimonial Causes Act to determine whether or not spouses have lived apart for the requisite period to establish that the marriage

---

[1] *Ante*, p. 116.

[2] See *ante*, p. 122.

[3] S. 1 (2). For details of the Act, see *ante*, pp. 123-125 and 461.

[4] [1979] A.C. 264; [1978] 1 All E.R. 1132, H.L.

[5] *Per* Lord Kilbrandon at pp. 339 and 1148, respectively.

[6] *Per* Lord Salmon at pp. 340 and 1149, respectively.

[7] *Per* Lord Scarman at pp. 347 and 1155, respectively.

[8] *Cf. Watson* v. *Lucas*, [1980] 3 All E.R. 647, at pp. 651 and 658, C.A., where it was said that a man may be a member of two families for the purpose of the Rent Act 1977.

has broken down irretrievably. Consequently the applicant must show that degree of cohabitation which would prevent separation from running if they were married.[1] On the other hand, they clearly do not have to be living together at the time the application is made: the court's power to require the defendant to permit the applicant to enter the matrimonial home, for example, envisages that they may be living apart. In *Davis* v. *Johnson* the applicant had left the defendant more than three weeks before bringing the proceedings; in *McLean* v. *Nugent*[2] the parties had lived together from October to December and the applicant did not obtain her injunction till the following February. It seems that the sub-section must be construed as meaning that the parties lived with each other in the same household as husband and wife until the events which occasioned the bringing of the proceedings.[3] Obviously after a separation of some length it will no longer be possible to regard the parties as coming within the sub-section at all, but this fact would in itself probably indicate that there was no need for an injunction anyway.

The other matter of importance is that this section can confer on one of the partners a right which she (or he) did not previously have. If they are joint tenants of the matrimonial home, each will have a right as legal owner to possession of it; if, however, one of them (say, the man) is the sole beneficial owner, the other has no proprietary right at all and cannot, like the wife, claim a right to occupy the home by virtue of her husband's duty to maintain her and cohabit with her. Nevertheless, as the House of Lords held in *Davis* v. *Johnson*, the purpose of the Act would be defeated if the applicant could succeed in having the defendant excluded only if she could rely on a proprietary right. The Act thus confers on county courts a jurisdiction which the High Court does not have.

It is clear that the court must bear the same facts in mind in deciding whether to grant an injunction as they do when the parties are married.[4] But the fact that she is not married may itself be a reason for not extending the period in which a woman, who has no proprietary interest in the former matrimonial home, may remain in it beyond that necessary to enable her to obtain other accommodation.

The court may attach a power of arrest to an injunction in the same circumstances as it may when the parties are married.[5]

Finally, it must be emphasised that, as the parties are not married to each other, neither of them can apply to a magistrates' court for an order under the Domestic Proceedings and Magistrates' Courts Act 1978.

2. RIGHTS IN PROPERTY

Again, one must start with the principle that in law cohabitants are strangers to each other and consequently the same rules apply to them as

---

[1] In *Adeoso* v. *Adeoso*, [1981] 1 All E.R. 107, C.A., it was held that a couple living behind locked doors in separate rooms in a two-roomed flat were living in the same household, although the position might have been different had the house been larger. For separation, see *ante*, pp. 225-226.

[2] (1979), 123 Sol. Jo. 521, C.A.

[3] *Adeoso* v. *Adeoso*, (*supra*).

[4] *Spindlow* v. *Spindlow*, [1979] Fam. 52; [1979] 1 All E.R. 169, C.A. See *ante*, pp. 462-465.

[5] Domestic Violence and Matrimonial Proceedings Act 1976, s. 2 (2).

apply to other unmarried persons. Obviously the provisions of the Married
Women's Property Acts[1] and the Matrimonial Homes Act can give them
neither rights nor remedies, and neither has any claim to the other's estate if
the latter dies intestate. Nor do the particular rules relating to income tax as
between husband and wife apply to them. This works to their disadvantage if
the woman is not working because the man will not be able to claim a married
man's personal relief. On the other than, they may be better off if the woman
has unearned income because aggregation might bring the husband's income
into a higher band than the unmarried cohabitant's.[2] Furthermore, if the
parties' relationship breaks down, there is no power in the court to make a
property adjustment order as there is on divorce.

The Parties' Home. —During the past few years the courts have gone some
way to ameliorate the position by giving cohabitants rights in their home
analogous to those possessed by spouses. In the first place this has been done
by the application of the doctrine of resulting and constructive trusts. In
Diwell v. *Farnes*[3] in 1959 the defendant had made a significant contribution
towards the purchase of the house which had been bought by the man with
whom she was living as a home for them both. Although the majority of the
Court of Appeal held that the principles applicable to cases between husband
and wife were not relevant when the parties were not married, they none the
less held that the defendant had an equitable interest in the proceeds of sale of
the house proportionate to her contribution to the purchase. Thirteen years
later the same court in *Cooke* v. *Head*[4] held that the property rights of
cohabitants who intended to marry as soon as they were free to do so should
be determined in the same way as the rights of spouses. In that case the parties
had built a bungalow partly by their own labour, and although the plaintiff
contributed nothing to the price, she did a lot of physical work such as
demolishing old buildings and painting the new one: the court held that the
result of contributions in kind was to give her a third interest in the proceeds
of sale. In the later case of *Eves* v. *Eves*[5] where the parties also intended to
marry when they were free to do so, the Court of Appeal seems to have
resorted to the concept of the constructive trust. At the time when the
purchase of the house was contemplated, the plaintiff was a minor and consequently the defendant told her that, although he would have put the house in
their joint names had she been of full age, it would have to be conveyed into
his name alone. He admitted at the trial that he had used her age as an excuse
and had never intended her to take any interest. Nevertheless, acting in the
belief that she was to have some interest, the plaintiff, like the plaintiff in
Cooke v. *Head*, did a great deal of work on the house and it was held that this
entitled her to a quarter interest.

---

[1] Unless they were living together whilst engaged to be married: see *ante*, pp. 18-19.

[2] See *ante*, p. 439. But a transfer of property from one cohabitant to the other *inter vivos* or
on death will attract capital transfer tax and capital gains tax.

[3] [1959] 2 All E.R. 379, C.A. See Dwyer, *loc. cit.*; Zuckerman, *loc. cit.*, 251-271.

[4] [1972] 2 All E.R. 38, C.A. Contrast *Richards* v. *Dove*, [1974] 1 All E.R. 888, where it was
held that the woman's paying for food and fuel could not be regarded as a contribution towards
the purchase of the house and therefore gave her no interest in it.

[5] [1975] 3 All E.R. 768, C.A. The property is to be valued at the date of separation: *Hall* v.
Hall (1981), *Times*, 4th April, C.A.

Although in two of these cases the parties intended to marry when they could, it is submitted that this can no longer be regarded as a relevant fact and that the same principles should apply to the parties' rights in their home whether they are married or not. The point is of less importance since the House of Lords gave a check to the undue application of the principle of the equal division of the proceeds of sale between husband and wife in *Gissing* v. *Gissing*:[1] in a case like *Diwell* v. *Farnes* the court would now come to the same conclusion if the parties were married. In one respect, however, the position of unmarried cohabitants may still be different from that of spouses. As we have seen, it may occasionally be necessary to fall back on the presumption that, if a husband buys property in his wife's name, he intends to make a gift to her.[2] As this rests in theory on his obligation to maintain her, it is very doubtful whether an unmarried woman cohabiting with a man could rely on any presumption of advancement.[3]

Apart from the rights given her by the Domestic Violence and Matrimonial Proceedings Act, an unmarried cohabitant *as such* has no right to occupy premises owned solely by the man with whom she is living for she has no right to his cohabitation or to be maintained by him. She will, of course, have the same rights as a wife if she has a legal or equitable interest in the property, and she may also be able to rely on a contractual licence to remain there. In *Tanner* v. *Tanner*[4] the plaintiff bought a house for the defendant and her twin daughters of whom he was the father, and the defendant surrendered a rent controlled tenancy to move into it. When the plaintiff later claimed possession from her, it was held that, as the defendant had furnished consideration by giving up her flat, the licence was a contractual one to occupy the house so long as the children were of school age and it was needed for their and the defendant's accommodation. It may well be difficult to infer the period for which the parties intended that the woman should be permitted to remain on the premises because, like spouses, cohabitants are apt not to contemplate the breakdown of their relationship. In *Chandler* v. *Kerley*,[5] for example, the defendant and her husband had sold their former matrimonial home to the plaintiff on the understanding that the defendant (who proposed to marry the plaintiff after her divorce) would continue to live there with him and the two children of her marriage. The relationship between the parties broke down very shortly afterwards and the plaintiff sought to gain possession of the house. It was held by the Court of Appeal that the plaintiff could not have intended to assume the burden of housing the defendant and her children indefinitely and that the licence was terminable upon her being given 12 months' notice, which would enable her to find other accommodation.[6]

---

[1] [1971] A.C. 886; [1970] 2 All E.R. 780, H.L. See *ante*, p. 450.

[2] See *ante*, p. 429.

[3] It has been held in an old case that the presumption does not apply if a husband knows the marriage to be void because he knows he is under no obligation to maintain the wife: *Soar* v. *Foster* (1858), 4 K. & J. 152.

[4] [1975] 3 All E.R. 776, C.A. Contrast *Horrocks* v. *Forray*, [1976] 1 All E.R. 737, C.A., where it was held that, in the absence of a contract, the licence was revocable at will.

[5] [1978] 2 All E.R. 942, C.A. It is not clear what the consideration for the licence was: presumably it was the defendant's taking less than half the proceeds of sale because she was to continue to live in the house.

[6] The licence probably binds any transferee of the property except a purchaser for value without notice of it: see *Re Sharpe*, [1980] 1 All E.R. 198, at p. 204.

It must be emphasised that in these cases the licence was being used as a defence against a claim for possession brought by the legal owner. It does not follow that the court would give effect to an executory contract to grant a licence—for example, that the defendant in *Tanner* v. *Tanner* could have successfully sued for damages or specific performance if the plaintiff had refused to let her enter the house he had bought. This will depend on whether such contracts are enforceable, a matter which will be discussed at the end of this chapter.

Trusts for Sale.—If both parties have a beneficial interest in their home, it will be held on trust for sale, and both of them will have to concur if it is to be sold. If their relationship breaks down and they cannot agree on what is to happen to the property, either of them may apply to the court for an order directing the other to give effect to the trust.[1] As in the case of a married couple's home, the court in its discretion may refuse to do so if either of them still needs to occupy the premises as his or her home. This is most likely to occur if one of them (for example, the woman) has children living with her and it is difficult or impossible for her to find other accommodation. In *Re Evers' Trust*[2] the parties bought a cottage in which they lived with their own child and the woman's two children by a previous marriage. It was conveyed into their joint names on trust for sale for themselves as beneficial joint tenants and was intended to be a home for all five of them for the indefinite future. When the parties separated, the man applied for an order for sale of the property. It was held that, as he had a home with his mother and the woman needed the cottage as a home for herself and the children, the application would be dismissed on her undertaking to discharge the liability under the mortgage and to meet all other outgoings.

Succession to Tenancies.—It will be recalled that on the death of a statutory or protected tenant a person who had cohabited with him (or her) for not less than six months before his death may be able to claim a statutory tenancy as a member of his family under the Rent Act. Similarly a cohabitant who had resided with a deceased tenant for not less than twelve months may be qualified to succeed to a secure tenancy under the Housing Act.[3] She (or he) will therefore be in a stronger position than if the couple had been living in freehold premises or in leasehold premises not protected by the Rent Act.

3. SUPPORT RIGHTS

The main difference between the legal position of spouses and that of unmarried cohabitants is that the latter have no claims for maintenance against their partners. There is no obligation to maintain at common law, and, not being married to each other, they cannot take advantage of the provisions of the Domestic Proceedings and Magistrates' Courts Act or the Matrimonial Causes Act.

On the other hand, for the purposes of supplementary benefit "where two persons are cohabiting as man and wife, their requirements and resources

---

[1] Law of Property Act 1925, s. 30.

[2] [1980] 3 All E.R. 399, C.A. See also *Dennis* v. *McDonald* (1981), *Times*, 26th February (sale refused but man in possession ordered to pay woman occupation rent). *Cf. ante*, pp. 464-465.

[3] See *ante*, pp. 639-641 and 644-645.

shall, unless there are exceptional circumstances, be aggregated and treated as the man's".[1] Cohabitants are similarly regarded as constituting one family for the purposes of the Family Income Supplements Act,[2] and a woman will lose other benefits (for example, a widow's benefit) for any period during which she and a man are living together as husband and wife.[3] The reason for this principle is that unmarried couples should not be better off than married ones; its effect is to deprive the woman of the only claim to support that she may have. Her position is made even worse by the rule that she cannot claim any contributory benefits by virtue of the contributions of the man with whom she is (or has been) cohabiting, however long the relationship lasted.

The fact that one cohabitant may apply for provision out of the other's estate after the latter's death under the Inheritance (Provision for Family and Dependants) Act has already been noted.[4]

Provision for Children.—As the parties' children must necessarily be illegitimate, the only way in which one parent may obtain maintenance for them (apart from an agreement between the parties) is by the mother's applying for an affiliation order. A claim may also be made on behalf of the illegitimate children of a person killed as the result of another's tortious act under the Fatal Accidents Act. Attention is drawn to the fact that the court must take the mother's needs into account when deciding what order to make under the Affiliation Proceedings Act and that compensation for a parent's death may also include a sum to cover the surviving parent's expenses for holidays and so forth if these are necessary to enable the children's standard of life to be maintained.[5]

C. COHABITATION CONTRACTS

It has been suggested that those embarking on extra-marital cohabitation may wish to enter into an agreement defining their rights and obligations and, indeed, that it might be desirable for them to do so. The result would be that their relationship would be terminable by consent or at the will of either party (depending on the terms of the agreement) and that they would be completely free to determine what rights each was to have with respect to property, how their household was to be funded, how assets were to be divided on separation, and so forth. This contrasts with the position of the married couple whose union can be dissolved only by the order of a court which can then intervene and control their financial position and the division of their property.

It is far from clear that the courts would give legal effect to such an agreement. The party seeking to enforce it would have to face two possible lines of defence: that the agreement is contrary to public policy and therefore illegal and that it could not have been the parties' intention that it should be legally

---

[1] Supplementary Benefits Act 1976, Sched. 1, para. 3 (1) (b).

[2] Family Income Supplements Act 1970, s. 1 (1) (b).

[3] For the list of benefits involved, see Pearl, *The Legal Implications of a Relationship outside Marriage*, [1978] C.L.J. 252, 255-256; Ogus and Barendt, *Law of Social Security*, 404. See generally *ibid.*, 404-408.

[4] *Ante*, pp. 625-626.

[5] See *ante*, pp. 141 (Fatal Accidents Act) and 599 (affiliation proceedings).

binding. Furthermore, any clause relating to the custody of children would clearly not bind the court in any event. It is proposed to discuss each of these points in turn.

Illegality.—It has already been suggested that the rule that contracts tending to promote illicit sexual intercourse are contrary to public policy and therefore void may now be confined to contracts made with prostitutes and the like. It must not be assumed, however, that English courts will necessarily take this view. There are a number of reasons why cohabitation agreements might be struck down. In the first place, it is impossible to ignore the fact that sexual intercourse will be one of the dominant characteristics of the parties' relationship even though this is not expressly mentioned in the agreement (as it probably would not be): against this, however, it can be argued that the agreement does not tend to promote this, as the parties would probably cohabit (or at least have sexual intercourse) in any event. More cogent reasons for regarding the contract as contrary to public policy are that any provisions for terminating it by agreement contemplate a temporary union, which is likely to be less stable than marriage; that either expressly or by implication it contemplates the conception and birth of illegitimate children; and that the court will have no power to intervene to protect them and, if necessary, a dependent parent on the parties' separation. Each of these could be countered: marriage is now terminable by consent (at least after two years' separation or immediately if one spouse commits adultery and the other is willing to petition for divorce), the stigma attached to illegitimacy is now very slight (and the concept may well be abolished altogether), and the courts encourage the parties to reach an agreed settlement of their financial affairs on divorce. Nor will the agreement prevent the mother from taking affiliation proceedings if she wishes to do so.[1]

On balance, therefore, it is submitted that, although the position is doubtful, such contracts should not be regarded as contrary to public policy in that they are unlikely to encourage persons to cohabit who would not do so anyway and that, if two people intend to cohabit, it is better that they should give some thought to their financial and other arrangements.[2]

Intention to enter into Legal Relations.—We have already noted that in *Balfour* v. *Balfour*[3] the Court of Appeal refused to enforce an agreement by which spouses sought to regularise their domestic affairs during cohabitation because it was presumed that they had no intention to be legally bound. By analogy it could be argued that similar agreements between unmarried cohabitants would be unenforceable, particularly if they were entered into when the parties were already living together. On the other hand, it must be borne in mind that this is the only way in which legal effect can be given to their relationship. It has already been urged that the effect of *Balfour* v. *Balfour* should be limited as far as possible, and it certainly should not be

---

[1] See *ante*, p. 603.

[2] This is the conclusion reached by Dwyer, *Immoral Contracts*, 93 L.Q.R. 386, 388; Poulter, 124 New L.J. 999, 1034. Honoré, *Sex Law*, 45, argues that a contract might be lawful only if the parties had already decided to live together before making it. *Sed quaere*? It would still tend to promote or continue their relationship.

[3] [1919] 2 K.B. 571, C.A. See *ante*, p. 151.

extended to unmarried partners if it is clear that they intended to be bound by their agreement.

Terms of the Agreement.—It is relatively easy for the parties to agree on their respective rights in any property acquired and on their financial obligations towards each other. Difficulty arises when they try to determine their rights and duties with respect to any children they may have. Any term relating to custody will be void and any dispute must be resolved primarily by reference to the children's welfare.[1] Nor is it easy to see how the parties can determine in advance how far each is to be responsible for the children's maintenance when it is not known how many children there will be and what the parties' financial position and earning capacity will be. The application of a formula (for example, that each party shall contribute a given fraction of his or her income for the maintenance of each child)[2] is likely to be unjust when the total sum involved is unknown; an undertaking to pay a flat sum is likely to be unjust for the same reason and because it takes no account of inflation.[3] A provision that the home in which the parties are living shall be sold on separation could also work hardship for it may leave neither party with enough to acquire any other property and the woman with no accommodation for herself and the children of the union. In the latter case she would obviously be better off if the parties were joint tenants of their home because this would give rise to a trust for sale; if she refused to concur in a sale, the court might take the view that this should be postponed at least until the property was no longer needed as a home for the children.[4]

It is obvious that a clear warning must be given to a couple contemplating making a cohabitation contract. Not only do they run the risk of finding that their agreement is legally unenforceable but it is virtually impossible to draft terms which will operate justly in all circumstances, particularly if they have children. The only sound piece of advice is that the maximum protection can be obtained by having their home conveyed into joint names, but even this may have the effect of keeping the man from claiming what may be his only capital asset if the court refuses to order a sale so long as the woman needs to reside in it to bring up their children.

---

[1] See *ante*, p. 288.

[2] As suggested by Poulter, *loc. cit.* 1035.

[3] *Cf.* the need to introduce legislation to enable the courts to alter maintenance agreements entered into by spouses: *ante*, pp. 492 *et. seq.*

[4] *Cf. ante*, p. 464.

Appendices

SUMMARY OF CONTENTS

Appendix A

Business Assigned to the Family Division of the High Court

(The Administration of Justice Act 1970, First Schedule, as amended)

Business at first instance

Proceedings for a decree of divorce, nullity, judicial separation, presumption of death and dissolution of marriage, or jactitation of marriage and for any ancillary relief connected therewith.

The following proceedings under the Matrimonial Causes Act 1973:—
    (a) For an order under section 27 (failure to provide reasonable maintenance);
    (b) For the alteration of a maintenance agreement.

Proceedings for a declaration—
    (a) under section 45 of the Matrimonial Causes Act 1973, as to a person's legitimacy, or the validity of a marriage, or a person's right to be deemed a British subject; or
    (b) with respect to a person's matrimonial status.

Proceedings under section 17 of the Married Women's Property Act 1882 (determination of title to property in dispute between spouses).

Proceedings under sections 1 and 7 of the Matrimonial Homes Act 1967 (means whereby a spouse can continue in occupation of, or obtain entry to, a dwelling-house which is, or has been, the matrimonial home and can obtain the transfer of a protected or statutory tenancy).

Proceedings in relation to the wardship of minors.

Proceedings under the Adoption Acts 1958 and 1968 and, when it comes into force, the Adoption Act 1976.

Proceedings under the Guardianship of Minors Act 1971 or the Guardianship Act 1973 and otherwise in relation to the guardianship of minors, except proceedings for the appointment of a guardian of a minor's estate alone.

Proceedings under section 3 of the Marriage Act 1949 for obtaining the court's consent to the marriage of a minor.

Proceedings in which a parent or guardian of a minor applies for a writ of habeas corpus ad subjiciendum relative to the custody, care or control of the minor.

Proceedings under the following enactments: –
    (a) the Maintenance Orders (Facilities for Enforcement) Act 1920 (enforcement in England and Wales of orders made overseas for periodical payments to a man's wife or dependant);
    (b) Part II of the Maintenance Orders Act 1950 (enforcement in England and Wales of certain maintenance and other orders made in Scotland or Northern Ireland);
    (c) the Maintenance Orders Act 1958 (registration and enforcement of certain maintenance and other orders).

664 *Appendix* A

Appellate business

Proceedings on appeal under section 6 of the Child Care Act 1980 (confirming or terminating resolutions by local authorities assuming parental rights and duties).

Proceedings on appeal under—

    (a) section 16 (3) of the Guardianship of Minors Act 1971 (appeal to High Court from order of a magistrates' court under that Act or the Guardianship Act 1973);

    (b) section 29 of the Domestic Proceedings and Magistrates' Courts Act 1978 (appeal from certain decisions of a magistrates' court under that Act).

Proceedings on appeal from a magistrates' court against the making of, or refusal to make, an adoption order.

Proceedings on appeal from a magistrates' court under section 4 (7) of the Maintenance Orders Act 1958 against the variation of, or refusal to vary, an order registered in accordance with the provisions of that Act.

Proceedings on appeal under section 13 of the Administration of Justice Act 1960 (appeal in cases of contempt of court) from an order or decision of a magistrates' court under section 63 (3) of the Magistrates' Courts Act 1980 where the order or decision was made to enforce an order of such a court under the Guardianship of Minors Act 1971, the Guardianship Act 1973 or Part I of the Domestic Proceedings and Magistrates' Courts Act 1978.

Proceedings on appeal by case stated against an order or determination of the Crown Court, or a magistrates' court, made or given in affiliation proceedings.

Proceedings on appeal by case stated against an order or determination of a magistrates' court with regard to the enforcement of—

    (a) an order for the payment of money made by virtue of Part I of the Domestic Proceedings and Magistrates' Courts Act 1978;

    (b) an order for the payment of money registered in a magistrates' court under the Maintenance Orders Act 1958 or registered in a court in England and Wales under Part II of the Maintenance Orders Act 1950 or the Maintenance Orders (Facilities for Enforcement) Act 1920 or confirmed by a magistrates' court under the last-mentioned Act.

Proceedings on appeal by case stated against an order or determination of a magistrates' court under section 35 of the Matrimonial Causes Act 1973 (alteration of maintenance agreement between spouses).

Proceedings on appeal under the Children Act 1975 and, when it comes into force, Part II or sections 39 or 55 of the Adoption Act 1976.

Appendix B

Prohibited Degrees of Kindred and Affinity

(The Marriage Act 1949, First Schedule, as amended by the
Marriage (Enabling) Act 1960 and the Children Act 1975)

Mother

Adoptive mother or former adoptive
mother

Daughter

Adoptive daughter or former adoptive
daughter

Father's mother

Mother's mother

Son's daughter

Daughter's daughter

Sister

Wife's mother

Wife's daughter

Father's wife

Son's wife

Father's father's wife

Mother's father's wife

Wife's father's mother

Wife's mother's mother

Wife's son's daughter

Wife's daughter's daughter

Son's son's wife

Daughter's son's wife

Father's sister

Mother's sister

Brother's daughter

Sister's daughter

Father

Adoptive father or former adoptive
father

Son

Adoptive son or former adoptive
son

Father's father

Mother's father

Son's son

Daughter's son

Brother

Husband's father

Husband's son

Mother's husband

Daughter's husband

Father's mother's husband

Mother's mother's husband

Husband's father's father

Husband's mother's father

Husband's son's son

Husband's daughter's son

Son's daughter's husband

Daughter's daughter's husband

Father's brother

Mother's brother

Brother's son

Sister's son

Appendix C

Consents Required to the Marriage of a Minor by Common Licence or Superintendent Registrar's Certificate

(The Marriage Act 1949, Section 3 (1) and Second Schedule, as amended by the Children Act 1975)

The consent of the following person or persons is required unless the minor is subject to a custodianship order, when the consent of the custodian and, where the custodian is the husband or wife of a parent of the minor, of that parent is required.

1. WHERE THE MINOR IS LEGITIMATE

Circumstances	*Person or Persons whose consent is required*
1. Where both parents are living:	
(a) if parents are living together;	Both parents.
(b) if parents are divorced or separated by order of any court or by agreement;	The parent to whom the custody of the minor is committed by order of the court or by the agreement, or, if the custody of the minor is so committed to one parent during part of the year and to the other parent during the rest of the year, both parents.
(c) if one parent has been deserted by the other;	The parent who has been deserted.
(d) if both parents have been deprived of custody of minor by order of any court.	The person to whose custody the minor is committed by order of the court.
2. Where one parent is dead:	
(a) if there is no other guardian;	The surviving parent.
(b) if a guardian has been appointed by the deceased parent or by the court under section 3 of the Guardianship of Minors Act 1971.	The surviving parent and the guardian if acting jointly, or the surviving parent or the guardian if the parent or guardian is the sole guardian of the minor.

666

3. Where both parents are dead.   The guardians or guardian appointed by the deceased parents or by the court under section 3 or 5 of the Guardianship of Minors Act 1971.

II. WHERE THE MINOR IS ILLEGITIMATE

Circumstances   *Person whose consent is required*

If the mother of the minor is alive.   The mother, or if she has by order of any court been deprived of the custody of the minor, the person to whom the custody of the minor has been committed by order of the court.

If the mother of the minor is dead.   The guardian appointed by the mother.

Appendix D

Orders Relating to Financial Relief and Children under the Matrimonial Causes Act 1973

Nature of Provision	Proceedings in which it can be ordered	Whether it can be secured	Whether it can be varied	Whether repayment can be ordered	
				(1) after change of circumstances	(2) after remarriage
Maintenance pending suit	Divorce, nullity, judicial separation, s. 27	No	Yes	Yes	No
Periodical payments for spouse	Divorce, nullity, judicial separation, s. 27	Yes	Yes	Yes	Yes
Lump sum payment for spouse	Divorce, nullity, judicial separation, s. 27	Yes, if payable by instalments	Payment by instalments only	No	No
Transfer and settlement of property	Divorce, nullity, judicial separation	—	Only order for settlement made on judicial separation	No	No
Variation of settlements	Divorce, nullity, judicial separation	—	Only if made on judicial separation	No	No
Custody of children of the family	Divorce, nullity, judicial separation, s. 27	—	Yes	—	—
Education of children of the family	Divorce, nullity, judicial separation	—	Yes	—	—
Periodical payments for children of the family	Divorce, nullity, judicial separation, s. 27	Yes	Yes	Yes	—
Lump sum payment for children of the family	Divorce, nullity, judicial separation, s. 27	Yes, if payable by instalments	Payment by instalments only	No	—

Appendix E
Matrimonial Homes and Property Bill

This Bill was introduced in the House of Lords in February 1981. Its purpose is to implement the recommendations of the Law Commission contained in Book Two of their Third Report on Family Property (Law Com. No. 86) and in their Report on Orders for Sale of Property under the Matrimonial Causes Act 1973 (Law Com. No. 99).

Amendments to the Matrimonial Homes Act 1967.—The following are the main amendments which the Bill proposes to make to this Act. (There are also some detailed proposals relating to land registration and mortgages.)

(1) It is to be made clear that a spouse's rights of occupation under the Act shall be a charge solely on the other spouse's *beneficial* estate or interest. Hence if, say, the husband is entitled to occupy the matrimonial home as a beneficiary under a trust of which he is also one of the trustees, the wife's rights could not be a charge on his legal estate. But if no one other than the spouses is or could be a beneficiary, the rights will be a charge on the legal estate as well. This means, for example, that the wife could make mortgage repayments herself if the trustees failed to do so and thus prevent the mortgagee's exercising his statutory power of sale.

(2) If a mortgagee of the matrimonial home brings proceedings to enforce his security, a spouse with rights of occupation will usually be entitled to be made a party to the action if she may be expected to make payments in satisfaction of the debt and so possibly affect the outcome of the proceedings. A mortgagee must give notice of the action to the spouse if she has registered a Class F land charge. This will overcome the practical difficulties exemplified by *Hastings and Thanet Building Society* v. *Goddard, ante,* p. 468.

(3) It is to be made clear that the Act applies if the marriage is *de jure* or *de facto* polygamous.

(4) A spouse's occupation is to be attributed to the tenant for the purposes of the Rent (Agriculture) Act 1976 as it is for the purposes of the Rent Act 1977. This will protect the deserted spouse of an agricultural tenant. (See *ante,* p. 478.)

(5) The court is to be given power to order the transfer of a regulated or secure tenancy on judicial separation (and not only on divorce or nullity as at present). An application for a transfer may be made before or after the decree (including decree absolute) but may not be made by an applicant who has remarried (even though the second marriage is void or voidable). In the case of a transfer on divorce or nullity, the order may not take effect until the decree is made absolute. (See *ante,* p. 478.)

Amendments to the Matrimonial Causes Act.—It is to be made clear that a divorce court has a power to order the sale of property in which either or both spouses have a beneficial interest. This will be exercisable if the court makes an order for secured periodical payments or the payment of a lump sum or a property adjustment order. The court may order the sale to be deferred and may direct how the proceeds are to be used. This might include, for example, their use as security for periodical payments. (See *ante*, p. 562.)

Index

HOTCHPOT, 620

HUSBAND AND WIFE
absence, presumption of death, 185–186
actions between—
  damages, for, 422
  tort, in, 157–158, 422
adoption by, 340
arrest, spouse, of, impeding, 160
assault, 122
  sexual intercourse amounting to, 115
bill of sale, validity of, 433
child benefit payable to, 583
civil proceedings, evidence in, 116–117
communication between—
  breaking of confidence, 116
  privilege, 117
    abolition, 117
conspiracy between, 159, 160
contract—
  spouses, between, 151, 152
  wife, by, 109, 149–152
corporal punishment, right to administer, 110
crime, marital coercion, 159–160
criminal proceedings, evidence in, 118–120
death of spouse, damages for, 135. *See also* FATAL ACCIDENT
  matrimonial home, provisions in case of, 455–456
defamation, communication between, 158
domicile and nullity proceedings, 100
  spouses having different domiciles, 103–104
equality of rights of, 111–112
evidence—
  civil proceedings, in, 116–117
  criminal proceedings, in, 118–120
  incriminating spouse, 117
  sexual intercourse, as to, 259
exclusion from matrimonial home, 459 *et seq.*
extra-marital cohabitation. *See* EXTRA-MARITAL COHABITATION
family provision for, 623 *et seq. And see* FAMILY PROVISION
gifts—
  between, validity of, 430–431, 432
  husband, by, avoidance by creditors, 432
  spouse, to, by will, 607
  third party, by, 430
habitual residence and nullity proceedings, 100
husband's earnings, attachment of, 512 *et seq.*
ill-treatment of spouse, 122
income tax, 439–440. *And see* INCOME TAX
injunction, action for, by wife, 422
  enforcement, 125
  exercise of power to grant, 124–125
  molestation, against, 122–123, 124

HUSBAND AND WIFE—*continued*
insurable interest—
  each other, in, 437–438
  matrimonial home, 438
intestacy, rights on, 615 *et seq. And see* INTESTATE SUCCESSION
loan by one to other, 437
maintenance. *See* MAINTENANCE
marital coercion, 159–160
marital confidences—
  breaking of, 116
  civil proceedings, in, 117
  criminal proceedings, in, 118
  privilege, 117
    abolition, 117
matrimonial home. *See* MATRIMONIAL HOME
mutual wills by, 606–607
nationality after marriage, 161, 162
partnership contract between, 152
physical protection of spouse, 122–128
property rights, 407 *et seq.*
  actions between spouses, 157–158, 408, 421–424
  bankruptcy of one, in case of, 408, 433 *et seq.*, 465
  breakdown of marriage, on, 408
  creditors, protection of, 432, 433 *et seq.*
  death of one, effect of, 408, 426, 428
  deserted wife, of, 415
  disputes between—
    one spouse and stranger, 408, 424
    spouses, 157–158, 408, 421–424
  extra-marital cohabitation. *See* EXTRA-MARITAL COHABITATION
  formulation of, need for, 407
  furniture, as to, 427, 465–466
    bankruptcy, in case of, 432
  gifts to spouses, 430
  history of, 410 *et seq.*
  housekeeping allowance, savings from, 427–428
  improvements to property, 433
  income from spouse, 425
  insolvency of one, on, 408
  investment from joint account, 425–427
  joint savings, 425
  judicial separation, effect of, 415
  law of domicile, effect of, 424*n*–425*n*
  maintenance, relation with, 409
  Married Women's Property Act 1964, under, 427–428
  matrimonial home, 408, 441 *et seq. And see* MATRIMONIAL HOME
  polygamous marriage, 63–64
  property at time of marriage, 424
  purchase by one spouse, 428–430
    in name of other, 429
  separate estate, development of, 415 *et seq.*

MAINTENANCE—*continued*
  child, of—*continued*
    Guardianship of Minors Act, under, 593–594
    local authority, in care of, 401, 585 *et seq.*
    magistrates courts, orders made by, 486–487, 498 *et seq. And see* MAGISTRATES' COURTS
    neglect to provide, custody in case of, 307
    obligation of parents, 409
    order. *See* MAINTENANCE ORDER
    over sixteen, 588
    responsibility of person having control, 362
    separation agreement, in, 175
    share in trust fund, using, 573, 619–620
    wards of court, 594
  cohabitation, order during, 303, 508–509
  common law, at, 483
  concurrent orders, 488–489, 582
  covenant not to sue for, 175, 496
  custodianship order, under, 386–387
  decree of nullity, on, 73, 525 *et seq.*, 541 *et seq.*, 546–547, 589–590
  dependants, of, 584 *et seq.*
  divorce courts, powers of, 487–488
  ecclesiastical courts, powers of, 486, 487
  estate of deceased spouse, out of, 623 *et seq.*
    And see FAMILY RELIEF
  extra-marital cohabitant, 656
  High Court, power of, 486, 487
  husband, of, wife's duty as to, 485, 488
  illegitimate child, of—
    affiliation order, 595 *et seq. And see* AFFILIATION ORDER
    agreement, by, 603
    death or incapacity of mother, 600
    supplementary benefits, 584, 602–603
  income tax on, 441, 504
  judicial separation, after, 525 *et seq.*, 541 *et seq. And see* FINANCIAL RELIEF
  legitimated child, of, 270, 592–594
  lump sum, payment of, 507–508, 511
  magistrates' courts, in, 486–487, 498 *et seq.*
    And see MAINTENANCE ORDER
  mental illness, provision in case of, 484, 485
  nullity of marriage, after decree, 73, 525 *et seq.*, 541 *et seq.*, 546–547, 589–590
    And see FINANCIAL RELIEF
  order. *See* MAINTENANCE ORDER
  polygamous marriage, 62
  property and, interrelation, 409
  right to, contracting out of, 17
  spouse, of, death of other spouse, on, 408
  supplementary benefits, provisions as to, 485–486
  ward of court, of, 381
  wife, of—
    adultery, in case of, 484, 550, 565
    bankruptcy of husband, 484–485
    co-extensive with right to consortium, 484

MAINTENANCE—*continued*
  wife, of—*continued*
    common law, at, 483
    death of husband, 408
    desertion, after, 483
    divorce, nullity or judicial separation, after, 525 *et seq.*, 541 *et seq.*, 589–590. *And see* FINANCIAL RELIEF
    High Court proceedings, 517, 570–571
    husband's duty as to, 483 *et seq.*
    magistrates' court, powers of, 486–487, 498 *et seq.*
    methods of enforcement, 511 *et seq.*
    necessaries, power to purchase, 484
    nullity, in case of, 73, 525 *et seq.*, 541 *et seq.*, 546–547, 589–590
    pledging husband's credit. *See* HUSBAND AND WIFE
    presumption as to right to, 484
    separation agreement, provision in, 172–173
    wilful neglect to provide, 499

MAINTENANCE AGREEMENT
  adoption, effect of, 357
  alteration of, 492
    death of one party, after, 495
    lifetime of both parties, during, 492–493
    powers of court, 493–494
  consideration for, 490
  effect of divorce, 177
  family provision on death, effect, 637
  meaning, 490–491
  void provisions, 491–492

MAINTENANCE ORDER
  adoption, effect on, 357
  adultery, subsequent, not relevant, 565
  British, enforcement abroad, 518 *et seq.*
  county court, made by—
    meaning, 570*n*
    registration in magistrates' court, 517, 570–571
  death of party, 510
  divorce, nullity and remarriage, effect of, 509–510
  enforcement, 511 *et seq.*
    reciprocal, 517 *et seq.*
    one party outside U.K., 518 *et seq.*
    within U.K., 518
  family provision on death, effect on, 637
  Guardianship of Minors Act, under, 593–594
  High Court, made by,
    maintenance, 570*n*
    registration in magistrates' courts, 517, 570–571
  magistrates' court, made by, 486–487, 498 *et seq. And see* MATRIMONIAL ORDERS
    application for, 498 *et seq.*
    grounds for, 498 *et seq. And see* MATRIMONIAL ORDERS

MAINTENANCE ORDER—*continued*
magistrates' court, made by—*continued*
application for—*continued*
 wilful neglect to maintain, 499
assessment, 505–508
cessation of, 508 *et seq.*
child of the family, in favour of, 584 *et seq. And see* MAINTENANCE
divorce, effective after, 509
 remarriage, effect of, 510
enforcement of, 511 *et seq.*
 attachment of earnings, by, 512 *et seq.*
 committal to prison, by, 514–515
 distress, by, 512
 instalments, payment of arrears by, 515
income tax provisions, 504
interim orders, 503–504, 563
jurisdiction, 498
lump sum payment, 511
nullity decree, effect of, 510
payment, provisions as to, 504–505
pending suit, power to make, 525, 527–528
periodical payments, to make, 501
registration in other courts, 517, 570–571
revival of, 510
revocation of, 510
suspension of, 510
variation of, 510
wife, in favour of, 499 *et seq.*
wilful neglect to maintain, in case of, 499
meaning, 570*n*
provisional, 520
reciprocal enforcement, 517 *et seq.*
 one party outside U.K., 518 *et seq.*
 within U.K., 518
reciprocating country, made in, 518–520

MANSLAUGHTER
child, death from neglect, 320

MARRIAGE
absence of witnesses, 79
affiliation proceedings, effect on, 596, 601
authorised person, presence of, 38, 48, 51*n*
breakdown of, 169 *et seq.*
capacity of parties—
 age, 31, 32–33
 change of sex, in case of, 31–32
 domicile, governed by, 22–27
  conflict of laws, 30
  dual domicile test, 22 *et seq.*
  exceptions, 22–27
  intended matrimonial home test, 22 *et seq.*, 60, 78
  nullity proceedings, 102
  polygamous marriage, 55 *et seq.*, 77–78
 lack of, 72, 77–78
 law governing, 22–27
 presumption as to, 65–67

MARRIAGE—*continued*
capacity of parties—*continued*
 relationship, 33–35
certificate authorising, 38. *And see* CERTIFICATE
child, recognition by English courts, 55
common law—
 effect, 108
 recognition of, 28–30
 validity of, 30
conflict of laws, 29–31
conflicting presumptions as to validity, 66–67
consent to, 39–41
 age of majority, reduction of, 39
 conflict of laws, 31
 lack of, 87–92
 minor, of, 280, 281, 282, 666–667
consummation of, 83–87. *And see* CONSUMMATION OF MARRIAGE; SEXUAL INTERCOURSE
contract, as, 16
declaratory judgment as to validity, 68, 274
delay in solemnization of, 79–80
divorce, effect of rescission of decree, 194
divorced person, of, refusal to officiate, 194*n*
domicile, capacity governed by, 22–27
 conflict of laws, 30
 dual domicile test, 22 *et seq.*
 exceptions, 22–27
 intended matrimonial home test, 22 *et seq.*, 60, 78
 nullity proceedings, 102
 polygamous marriage, 55 *et seq.*, 77–78
dying persons, special provisions for, 39, 49, 50
effect at common law, 108
embassy, celebrated in, 28
foreign—
 common law marriages, 30
 duress under, 90
 prohibited degrees, within, 26, 55
 recognition of, 54 *et seq.*
 validity of, test, 54–55
formal validity, jurisdiction as to, 99
formalities of, 21, 35 *et seq.*
 history of, 35–39
 non-observance, 37, 78
 persons under 18 . . . 39–41
 rites of Church of England, 41
gifts made in contemplation of, 19–20
heterosexual, must be, 18
illegitimate child, of, 667
infant, of. *See* CHILDREN
intention of parties, relevance of, 57
interest under intestacy, vesting on, 620
jactitation of, 67–68, 113
legitimation by subsequent. *See under* LEGITIMATION
licence. *See* MARRIAGE LICENCE